Dreamweaver® and Fireworks® Bible

Dreamweaver® and Fireworks® Bible

Joseph W. Lowery

Best-Selling Books • Digital Downloads • e-Books • Answer Networks • e-Newsletters • Branded Web Sites • e-Learning

New York, NY ✦ Cleveland, OH ✦ Indianapolis, IN

Dreamweaver® and Fireworks® Bible

Published by
Hungry Minds, Inc.
909 Third Avenue
New York, NY 10022
www.hungryminds.com

Copyright © 2001 Hungry Minds, Inc. All rights reserved. No part of this book, including interior design, cover design, and icons, may be reproduced or transmitted in any form, by any means (electronic, photocopying, recording, or otherwise) without the prior written permission of the publisher.

Library of Congress Control Number: 2001118277

ISBN: 0-7645-4873-5

Printed in the United States of America

10 9 8 7 6 5 4 3 2 1

1B/SV/QX/QR/IN

Distributed in the United States by Hungry Minds, Inc.

Distributed by CDG Books Canada Inc. for Canada; by Transworld Publishers Limited in the United Kingdom; by IDG Norge Books for Norway; by IDG Sweden Books for Sweden; by IDG Books Australia Publishing Corporation Pty. Ltd. for Australia and New Zealand; by TransQuest Publishers Pte Ltd. for Singapore, Malaysia, Thailand, Indonesia, and Hong Kong; by Gotop Information Inc. for Taiwan; by ICG Muse, Inc. for Japan; by Intersoft for South Africa; by Eyrolles for France; by International Thomson Publishing for Germany, Austria, and Switzerland; by Distribuidora Cuspide for Argentina; by LR International for Brazil; by Galileo Libros for Chile; by Ediciones ZETA S.C.R. Ltda. for Peru; by WS Computer Publishing Corporation, Inc., for the Philippines; by Contemporanea de Ediciones for Venezuela; by Express Computer Distributors for the Caribbean and West Indies; by Micronesia Media Distributor, Inc. for Micronesia; by Chips Computadoras S.A. de C.V. for Mexico; by Editorial Norma de Panama S.A. for Panama; by American Bookshops for Finland.

For general information on Hungry Minds' products and services please contact our Customer Care department within the U.S. at 800-762-2974, outside the U.S. at 317-572-3993 or fax 317-572-4002.

For sales inquiries and reseller information, including discounts, premium and bulk quantity sales, and foreign-language translations, please contact our Customer Care department at 800-434-3422, fax 317-572-4002 or write to Hungry Minds, Inc., Attn: Customer Care Department, 10475 Crosspoint Boulevard, Indianapolis, IN 46256.

For information on licensing foreign or domestic rights, please contact our Sub-Rights Customer Care department at 212-884-5000.

For information on using Hungry Minds' products and services in the classroom or for ordering examination copies, please contact our Educational Sales department at 800-434-2086 or fax 317-572-4005.

For press review copies, author interviews, or other publicity information, please contact our Public Relations department at 317-572-3168 or fax 317-572-4168.

For authorization to photocopy items for corporate, personal, or educational use, please contact Copyright Clearance Center, 222 Rosewood Drive, Danvers, MA 01923, or fax 978-750-4470.

LIMIT OF LIABILITY/DISCLAIMER OF WARRANTY: THE PUBLISHER AND AUTHOR HAVE USED THEIR BEST EFFORTS IN PREPARING THIS BOOK. THE PUBLISHER AND AUTHOR MAKE NO REPRESENTATIONS OR WARRANTIES WITH RESPECT TO THE ACCURACY OR COMPLETENESS OF THE CONTENTS OF THIS BOOK AND SPECIFICALLY DISCLAIM ANY IMPLIED WARRANTIES OF MERCHANTABILITY OR FITNESS FOR A PARTICULAR PURPOSE. THERE ARE NO WARRANTIES WHICH EXTEND BEYOND THE DESCRIPTIONS CONTAINED IN THIS PARAGRAPH. NO WARRANTY MAY BE CREATED OR EXTENDED BY SALES REPRESENTATIVES OR WRITTEN SALES MATERIALS. THE ACCURACY AND COMPLETENESS OF THE INFORMATION PROVIDED HEREIN AND THE OPINIONS STATED HEREIN ARE NOT GUARANTEED OR WARRANTED TO PRODUCE ANY PARTICULAR RESULTS, AND THE ADVICE AND STRATEGIES CONTAINED HEREIN MAY NOT BE SUITABLE FOR EVERY INDIVIDUAL. NEITHER THE PUBLISHER NOR AUTHOR SHALL BE LIABLE FOR ANY LOSS OF PROFIT OR ANY OTHER COMMERCIAL DAMAGES, INCLUDING BUT NOT LIMITED TO SPECIAL, INCIDENTAL, CONSEQUENTIAL, OR OTHER DAMAGES.

Macromedia Software, Copyright © 1998-2000 Macromedia, Inc. 600 Townsend Street, San Francisco, CA 94103 USA. All Rights Reserved. Macromedia, Fireworks, Dreamweaver, Flash, UltraDev, and Freehand are trademarks or registered trademarks of Macromedia, Inc. in the United States and/or other countries.

Trademarks: All trademarks are the property of their respective owners. Hungry Minds, Inc. is not associated with any product or vendor mentioned in this book.

 is a trademark of Hungry Minds, Inc

About the Author

Joseph Lowery has been writing about computers and new technology since 1981. He is the author of the previous editions of *Dreamweaver Bible* and *Fireworks Bible* as well as *Buying Online For Dummies* (all from Hungry Minds, formerly IDG Books Worldwide). He recently co-wrote a book on Flash with designer Hillman Curtis and has also written books on HTML and using the Internet for business. In addition to developing commerical extensions for Dreamweaver with Deva Associates, LLC, Joseph is a Webmaster for a variety of sites and a Web design trainer and consultant. Joseph and his wife, dancer/choreographer Debra Wanner, have a daughter, Margot.

Credits

Acquisitions Manager
Chris Webb

Senior Acquisitions Editor
Michael L. Roney

Project Editors
Laura Brown
Jodi Jensen
Julie M. Smith

Technical Editor
Derren Whiteman

Copy Editors
Kelly Campbell Hogue
Roxane Marini
Nancy Rapoport
Jeremy Zucker

Editorial Manager
Colleen Totz

Project Coordinators
Jennifer Bingham
Dale White
Emily Wichlinski

Graphics and Production Specialists
Sean Decker
John Greenough
Joyce Haughey
Stephanie Jumper
Gabriele McCann
Kristen Pickett
Kendra Span
Brian Torwelle
Erin Zeltner

Quality Control Technicians
Laura Albert
John Bitter
Valery Bourke
Joel Draper
David Faust
Angel Perez
Nancy Price
Linda Quigley
Marianne Santy

Senior Permissions Editor
Carmen Krikorian

Media Development Specialists
Megan Decraene
Angela Denny

Media Development Coordinator
Marisa E. Pearman

Proofreading and Indexing
TECHBOOKS Production Services

For the Dreamweaver and Fireworks communities — from the program creators to the program users — this book would not exist without your enthusiasm, support, and vision.

Foreword

Professionally speaking, I grew up in the world of traditional photography — a very process-driven world. While the ingredients may vary, developing a photograph follows a strict sequence: First the film goes in the developer solution, then the stop bath, followed by the fixer, and finally the rinse. In my career at Macromedia, I'm still developing — but my new goal is working with customers to create products like Fireworks and Dreamweaver, not photographs. Best of all, people rather than chemicals, are the primary ingredients in my development process now.

I consider myself very lucky. I get to spend a good portion of my time with our customers, talking with them about how they work, what problems they face and what solutions they need. Members of the development team often join me on our customer visits. Our goal is to seek ways to make our tools more focused and better fitting to our customers, the people who use them day-in and day-out to build the world's Web sites.

The Dreamweaver Fireworks Studio grew out of such visits. We found that regardless of whether the Web site was created by one person or many, it was the workflow between page layout and graphic design that cried out for attention. Throughout the entire Web site development process, we saw our customers constantly shifting from one tool to the other. We began to look for ways to streamline the workflow progression into a more organic process of moving back and forth between toolsets. The tight product integration between Dreamweaver and Fireworks is the result. Now you can effortlessly insert your graphics from Fireworks — complete with HTML structures and JavaScript behaviors — into a Dreamweaver layout. When those images have to be modified (and they always have to be modified), Dreamweaver sends a command to Fireworks to edit the graphic source and reoptimize the results. The ebb and flow from image editor to authoring tool has become much more fluid.

The Studio series has been very successful, and we owe so much of that success to the support of our customers. But we know our job isn't finished yet. Processes on the Web are constantly evolving as new technologies and tools emerge. Our customers continue to look for new ways to be even more creative and productive. While I can't be specific about future product features, you can be sure that we'll continue to watch, listen, and learn. With the combined chemistry of our sophisticated customers and talented engineers, the results are sure to be explosive.

I'd like to thank Joe for his wonderful, resourceful books. With the volume you hold in your hands, Joe has created the perfect complement to the Dreamweaver Fireworks Studio. Enjoy.

Diana Smedley
Director of Product Management
Dream Products Division
Macromedia, Inc.

Preface

Web designers are relentless explorers in the ever-expanding frontier that is the World Wide Web. Boundary-pushing is not only the norm, it's practically a job requirement — which is one of the reasons Dreamweaver is the leading Web design program today. Among other accolades, Macromedia's Dreamweaver has one of the most appropriate product names in recent memory. Web page design is a blend of art and craft; whether you're a deadline-driven professional or a vision-filled amateur, Dreamweaver is the perfect tool for many Web designers. Dreamweaver is not only the first Web authoring tool to bring the ease of visual editing to an HTML code–oriented world, it also brings a point-and-click interface to complex JavaScript coding.

And then there's a little graphics program called Fireworks. Remember that burst of pleasure when you first realized how exciting the Web could be? I'll let you in on a little secret: Macromedia Fireworks makes creating graphics for the Web fun again. Images produced with Fireworks are as sophisticated and rich as those created with any other combination of programs, plus they're Web-ready — as optimized as possible and bundled with HTML and JavaScript code for amazing interactive effects.

It seems only natural to combine Macromedia's exciting Web-graphics solution with its premier Web-authoring tool . . . in fact, Macromedia encourages you to do just that with its Dreamweaver Fireworks Studio. And that's the path I followed in putting together this book. Whether you're a Dreamweaver user interested in employing the power of Fireworks to create and manipulate your graphics, or you've been working with Fireworks for a while, and now you're ready to get into full-scale Web development with Dreamweaver, *Dreamweaver and Fireworks Bible* brings you the best of both worlds! By combining the most important information from my *Dreamweaver 4 Bible* with the best of my *Fireworks 4 Bible,* you have one handy volume that can answer just about any Dreamweaver or Fireworks question you may have. It's the perfect companion for all your Web-development needs.

To use this book, you need only three items: the Dreamweaver and Fireworks software and a desire to make cutting-edge Web pages. (Actually, you don't even need the software to begin; the CD-ROM that accompanies this book contains fully functional trial versions of both programs.)

Underneath their simple, intuitive interfaces, Dreamweaver and Fireworks are complex programs that make high-end Web concepts accessible for the first time. *Dreamweaver and Fireworks Bible* is designed to help you master every nuance of the program. Are you creating a straightforward layout with the visual editor? Do you need to extend Dreamweaver's and/or Fireworks' capabilities by building your own custom objects? With the Dreamweaver/Fireworks combination and this book, you can weave your dreams into reality for the entire world to experience.

Who Should Read This Book?

Dreamweaver attracts a wide range of Web developers. Because it's the first Web authoring tool that doesn't rewrite original code, veteran designers are drawn to using Dreamweaver as their first visual editor. Because it also automates complicated effects, beginning Web designers are interested in Dreamweaver's power and performance. *Dreamweaver and Fireworks Bible* addresses the full spectrum of Web professionals, providing basic information on HTML if you're just starting as well as advanced tips and tricks for seasoned pros. Moreover, this book is a complete reference for everyone working with Dreamweaver and Fireworks on a daily basis.

The Web is, without a doubt, one of the key phenomena of our time, and it has attracted an enormous amount of talent, both artistic and technical. After all, how often does a new mass medium appear? The range of Web designers extends from first-generation artists drawn to the exciting Internet possibilities to print professionals who need to expand their creative horizons. *Dreamweaver and Fireworks Bible* talks to all those groups, offering solutions to everyday graphics problems, as well as providing a complete reference for the program.

What Hardware and Software Do You Need?

Dreamweaver and Fireworks Bible includes coverage of Dreamweaver 4 and Fireworks 4. If you don't own a copy of the programs, you can use the trial versions on this book's CD-ROM. Written to be platform-independent, this book covers both Macintosh and Windows versions of Dreamweaver 4 and Fireworks 4.

Macintosh

Macromedia recommends the following minimum requirements for running Dreamweaver and Fireworks on a Macintosh:

- ✦ Power Macintosh PowerPC (G3 or higher recommended)
- ✦ MacOS 8.6 or 9.*x*

- ✦ 64MB of available RAM
- ✦ 190MB of available disk space
- ✦ Color monitor capable of 800 × 600 resolution
- ✦ CD-ROM drive

Windows

Macromedia recommends the following minimum requirements for running Dreamweaver and Fireworks on a Windows system:

- ✦ Intel Pentium processor, 166MHz or equivalent (Pentium II or higher recommended)
- ✦ Windows 9x/ME, NT 4.0 (with Service Pack 5), or Windows 2000
- ✦ 64MB of available RAM
- ✦ 215MB of available disk space
- ✦ 256-color monitor capable of 800 × 600 resolution
- ✦ CD-ROM drive

Note: These are the minimum requirements. As with all graphics-based design tools, more capability is definitely better for using Dreamweaver or Fireworks, especially in terms of memory and processor speed.

How This Book Is Organized

Dreamweaver and Fireworks Bible can take you from raw beginner to full-fledged professional if read cover to cover. You're more likely, however, to read each section as needed, taking the necessary information and coming back later. *Dreamweaver and Fireworks Bible* is divided into two major parts, one for Dreamweaver and the other for Fireworks. Once you're familiar with the programs, feel free to skip around the book, using it as a reference guide as you build up your own knowledge base.

The early chapters in each section present the basics, and all chapters contain clearly written steps for the tasks you need to perform. In later chapters, you encounter sections labeled "Dreamweaver Techniques" or "Fireworks Techniques." These techniques are step-by-step instructions for accomplishing specific Web designer tasks — for example, building an image map that uses rollovers or eliminating underlines from hyperlinks through Cascading Style Sheets. Naturally, you can also use the Dreamweaver and Fireworks Techniques as stepping stones for your own explorations into Web page creation.

If you're running Dreamweaver and/or Fireworks while reading this book, don't forget to use the CD-ROM. An integral element of the book, the one accompanying CD-ROM offers a vast number of additional Dreamweaver behaviors, objects, commands, and browser profiles, as well as Fireworks commands, extensions, and relevant code from the book.

Part I: Working with Dreamweaver

Part I begins with an overview of Dreamweaver's philosophy and design. To get the most out of the program, you need to understand the key advantages it offers over other authoring and their deficiencies it addresses. In Chapter 1, you'll get an overview of the Web development process as a quick start to Dreamweaver.

The other opening chapters give you a full reference to the Dreamweaver interface and all its customizable features. You also learn how you can access Dreamweaver's full-bodied online Help and find additional resources on the Web. Chapter 2 takes you from the consideration of various Web site design models to publishing your finished site on the Internet while Chapter 3 shows you how to make the most of Dreamweaver's FTP Site window.

Using basic HTML in Dreamweaver

Although Dreamweaver is partly a visual design tool, its roots derive from the language of the Web: HTML. The next chapters give you a solid foundation in the basics of HTML, even if you've never seen code. Chapter 4 covers HTML theory, describing how a Web page is constructed and alerting you to some potential pitfalls to look out for. The three fundamentals of Web pages are text, images, and links. You explore how to incorporate these elements to their fullest extent in Chapters 5, 6, and 7, respectively.

Incorporating advanced HTML

The following chapters begin to investigate some of the more advanced structural elements of HTML as implemented in Dreamweaver. Chapter 8 examines the various uses of tables — from a clear presentation of data to organizing entire Web pages. Here you learn how to use Dreamweaver 4's greatly enhanced visual table editing capabilities to resize and reshape your HTML tables quickly.

Forms are the focus of Chapter 9, where you find out all you need to know about gathering information from your Web page visitors. Chapter 10 investigates the somewhat complex world of frames — and shows how Dreamweaver has greatly simplified the task of building and managing these multifile creations, particularly with the new Frame objects. You also learn how to handle more advanced design tasks such as updating multiple frames with just one click.

Extending HTML through Dreamweaver

HTML is a language with extensive capabilities for expanding its own power. With its own set of objects and behaviors, Dreamweaver complements HTML's extensibility. Chapter 11 offers an in-depth look at the capabilities of Dreamweaver behaviors. Each standard behavior is covered in detail with step-by-step instructions.

Adding multimedia elements

In recent years, the Web has moved from a relatively static display of text and simple images to a full-blown multimedia circus with streaming video, background music, and interactive animations. The next chapters contain the power tools for incorporating various media files into your Web site.

Graphics remain the key medium on the Web today, and Macromedia's Fireworks is a top-notch graphics generator. Chapter 12 delves into methods for incorporating Fireworks graphics — with all the requisite rollover and other code intact. Special focus is given to the Dreamweaver-to-Fireworks communication link and how your Web production efforts can benefit from it.

In addition to Dreamweaver, Macromedia is perhaps best known for one other contribution to Web multimedia: Flash. Chapter 13 explores the possibilities offered by incorporating Flash and Shockwave movies into Dreamweaver-designed Web pages and includes everything you need to know about configuring MIME types. You also find step-by-step instructions for building Shockwave inline controls and playing Shockwave movies in frame-based Web pages, as well as how to add Flash buttons, Flash text, and Generator objects.

Dynamic HTML and Dreamweaver

Dynamic HTML brought a new world of promises to Web designers — promises that went largely unfulfilled until Dreamweaver was released. The next chapters of *Dreamweaver and Fireworks Bible* examine this brave new world of pixel-perfect positioning, layers that fly in and then disappear as if by magic, and Web sites that can change their look and feel at the click of a mouse.

Chapter 14 takes a detailed look at the elegance of Cascading Style Sheets and offers techniques for accomplishing the most frequently requested tasks, such as creating an external style sheet. Many of the advantages of Dynamic HTML come from the use of layers, which enable absolute positioning of page elements, visibility control, and a sense of depth. You discover how to handle all these layer capabilities and more in Chapter 15. Chapter 16 focuses on timelines, which have the potential to take your Web page into the fourth dimension. The chapter concludes with a blow-by-blow description of how to create a multiscreen slide show, complete with layers that fly in and out on command.

Enhancing Web site management and workflow in Dreamweaver

Although Web page design gets all the glory, Web site management pays the bills. In Chapters 17 and 18, you see how Dreamweaver makes this essential part of any Webmaster's day easier to handle. Chapter 17 starts off the section with a look at the use of Dreamweaver templates and how they can speed up production while ensuring a unified look and feel across your Web site. Chapter 18 covers the Library, which can significantly reduce any Webmaster's workload by providing reusable — and updateable — page elements.

Part II: Working with Fireworks

Part II begins with an overview of the Fireworks philosophy and design. To get the most out of the program, you need to understand the key advantages it offers and the deficiencies it addresses. Part I takes you all the way from setting up documents to getting the most out of Fireworks.

The opening chapter in this section, Chapter 19, gives you a full reference to the Fireworks interface and all of its customizable features. In Chapter 20, you'll see how to set up your documents to work best in your environment.

Mastering the tools

The Fireworks approach to graphics is fundamentally different from any other tool on the market. Consequently, you'll need to travel the short learning curve before you can get the most out of Fireworks. The next chapters in Part II cover all the essentials, from basic object creation to full-blown photo manipulation.

Color is a key component of any graphic designer's tool kit, and color on the Web requires special attention, as you'll see in Chapter 23. The object-oriented nature of Fireworks is explored in chapters on creating simple strokes and combining paths in a variety of ways to help you make more sophisticated graphics. Fireworks excels at creating graphical text for the Web — you'll see how in Chapter 26.

Achieving effects

Fireworks graphics really begin to gain depth in the next chapters. The variety of fills and textures available — as well as the ability to add your own — are critical for the wide range of image production for which a Web designer is responsible. Chapter 28 explores the exciting world of Fireworks Live Effects and Xtras, which are exciting not just because they're easy to use and they look great, but also because of the positive impact that their always-editable nature will have on your workflow.

Most of the time, a graphic will actually contain a number of images. Chapter 29 explains the Fireworks methods for arranging and compositing multiple objects in order to achieve stunning results. Fireworks' mask-group feature in particular is an especially creative and powerful tool that takes the hard work out of alpha channels. Although Fireworks is a great drawing tool, it's also adept at handling bitmap imagery.

Coordinating workflow

Web design is an ongoing process, not a single event. The next chapters are dedicated to helping you streamline your workflow efficiently as you acquire images via scanning or importing, manipulate them in Fireworks, and then optimize them on export, either for the Web or for import into other creative tools, such as Macromedia Director or Flash.

While it's true that Web graphic design is an art form, it's also a business — and one element of that business is applying a consistent look and feel to each element of a particular Web site. Fireworks Styles enable you to save formatting instructions from one object and apply them to other objects again and again. The Library panel (new in Fireworks 4) is a place to store *Symbols*, objects you use again and again, such as logos and navigation buttons. Fireworks Symbols further minimize repetitive work by linking similar objects so that changes need only be made once.

Entering the Web

Fireworks broke new ground as the first image editor to output HTML and JavaScript code. With its full-featured hotspots, image maps, and sliced images embedded in HTML tables, Fireworks is incredibly Web savvy. The next chapters explain the basics of Web interactivity for those designers unfamiliar with the territory and also offer specific step-by-step instructions for linking JavaScript behaviors to graphics.

Animation

Animations have become important to the Web. Not only do they offer an alternative to static displays, but GIF animations are used extensively in the creation of banner ads. Animation in Fireworks 4 is surprisingly full-featured and easy to use. You'll walk step-by-step through the creation of a banner ad and discover tweening, onion skinning, and other basic animation techniques.

Appendix

An appendix describes the contents of the CD-ROM that accompanies this book. Throughout this book, whenever you encounter a reference to files or programs on the CD-ROM, please check this appendix for more information.

Conventions Used in This Book

I use the following conventions throughout this book.

Windows and Macintosh conventions

Because *Dreamweaver and Fireworks Bible* is a cross-platform book, it gives instructions for both Windows and Macintosh users when keystrokes for a particular task differ. Throughout this book, the Windows keystrokes are given first; the Macintosh are given second in parentheses, as follows:

> To undo an action, press Ctrl+Z (Command+Z).

The first action instructs Windows users to press the Ctrl and Z keys in combination, and the second action (in parentheses) instructs Macintosh users to press the Command and Z keys together.

Key combinations

When you are instructed to press two or more keys simultaneously, each key in the combination is separated by a plus sign. For example:

> Ctrl+Alt+T (Command+Option+T)

The preceding tells you to press the three listed keys for your system at the same time. You can also hold down one or more keys and then press the final key. Release all the keys at the same time.

Mouse instructions

When instructed to *click* an item, move the mouse pointer to the specified item and click the mouse button once. Windows users use the left mouse button unless otherwise instructed. *Double-click* means clicking the mouse button twice in rapid succession.

When instructed to select an item, you may click it once as previously described. If you are selecting text or multiple objects, click the mouse button once, press Shift, and then move the mouse to a new location and click again. The color of the selected item or items inverts to indicate the selection. To clear the selection, click once anywhere on the Web page.

Menu commands

When instructed to select a command from a menu, you see the menu and the command separated by an arrow symbol. For example, when instructed to execute the Open command from the File menu, you see the notation File ⇨ Open. Some menus use submenus, in which case you see an arrow for each submenu, as follows: Insert ⇨ Form Object ⇨ Text Field.

Typographical conventions

I use *italic* type for new terms and for emphasis, and **boldface** type for text that you need to type directly from the computer keyboard.

Code

A special typeface indicates HTML or other code, as demonstrated in the following example:

```
<html>
<head>
<title>Untitled Document</title>
</head>
<body bgcolor="#FFFFFF">
</body>
</html>
```

This code font is also used within paragraphs to designate HTML tags, attributes, and values such as `<body>`, `bgcolor`, and `#FFFFFF`. All HTML tags are presented in lowercase, as written by Dreamweaver, although browsers are not generally case-sensitive in terms of HTML.

The ¬ character at the end of a code line means you should type the next line of code before pressing the Enter (Return) key.

Navigating Through This Book

Various signposts and icons are located throughout *Dreamweaver and Fireworks Bible* for your assistance. Each chapter begins with an overview of its information and ends with a quick summary.

Icons appear in the text to indicate important or especially helpful items. Here's a list of the icons and their functions:

 Tips provide you with extra knowledge that separates the novice from the pro.

 Notes provide additional or critical information and technical data on the current topic.

 Sections marked with a New Feature icon detail an innovation introduced in Dreamweaver 4 or Fireworks 4.

 Cross-Reference icons indicate places where you can find more information on a particular topic.

 The Caution icon is your warning of a potential problem or pitfall.

 The On the CD-ROM icon indicates that the accompanying CD-ROM contains a related file in the given folder. See the appendix for more information about where to locate specific items.

Further Information

You can find more help for specific problems and questions by investigating several Web sites. Macromedia's own Web site is the best place to start:

    www.macromedia.com

I heartily recommend that you visit and participate in the official Dreamweaver and Fireworks newsgroups:

    news://forums.macromedia.com/macromedia.dreamweaver
    news://forums.macromedia.com/macromedia.fireworks

You're also invited to visit my Web sites for book updates and new developments:

    www.idest.com/dreamweaver
    www.idest.com/fireworks

You can also e-mail me:

    jlowery@idest.com

I can't promise an instantaneous response, but I answer all my mail to the best of my abilities.

Acknowledgments

Whoever said "writing is a lonely business" never wrote a computer book. Sometimes I feel like the point man of a large swing band filled with seasoned pros. All the folks in this group can both play their parts exceedingly well, supporting the main theme, and are ready to solo at the drop of a hat. And now it's time to introduce, and applaud, the band.

First and foremost among these folks is Simon White. Simon White, and his company MediaFear, is known among the Fireworks and Dreamweaver newsgroup regulars as one of the most knowledgeable and generous experts around. I'd especially like to thank Simon for his major contributions, not to mention his availability as a sounding board for some of my more off-the-wall concepts. It's always refreshing to find someone whose artistic vision is so well-formed and energized, and with whom I can laugh about the bizarre world that is book authoring. You'll find numerous examples of Simon's work throughout the book.

A great deal of credit goes to my technical editor, Derren Whiteman. Derren has been absolutely top notch in providing insightful background comments, on-the-money tips, and real-world work experience. It also doesn't hurt that Derren is, as my Grandma used to say, persnickety about the details.

You can always identify people who have only read about the Internet when they despair about how the Internet increases our isolation. Baloney. I've got more colleagues and friends around the world now than I ever did. The Dreamweaver community has been especially gracious and giving of their time and expertise to further the goals of this book. I'd like to express my gratitude to the growing pool of developers who have taken their valuable time to create Dreamweaver extensions and offer them freely to the public. While the group has literally become too numerous to mention, I would like to highlight a few luminaries: Andrew Wooldridge, Massimo Foti, Jaro von Flocken, Brendan Dawes, Taylor and Al Sparber. I'm particularly grateful because all of these authors (and many others) have kindly permitted their work to be included in this book's CD-ROM. I now owe a good 40 percent of the user base a drink.

The Fireworks community has grown considerably over the past year and its generosity even more so. Special thanks to those designers who graciously allowed me to include their work on the CD-ROM: Kleanthis Economou, Massimo Foti, Linda Rathgeber, Eddie Traversa, Simon White, and the others. Several other top designers contributed work to demonstrate the power of Fireworks, including Lisa Lopuck, Donna Casey, and Ruth Peyser — warm hugs and great thanks all 'round. I owe a debt of gratitude — and probably a drink or two — to another Fireworks community member, author Sandee Cohen. Sandee's work continues to inspire, and I wish her continued success.

Macromedia has been wonderfully supportive of my efforts to bring out the most detailed *Bible* possible. I can only imagine the collective groan that goes up when yet another e-mailed question from me — with a deadline, no less — arrives. Warm thanks and heartfelt appreciation to Dave George, Sho Kuwamoto, Hava Edelstein, Heidi Bauer, Darrick Brown, and all the other Dreamweaver engineers and techs who opened up their brains for me to pick. A special "Gawd, what would I have done without you?" award goes to Lori Hylan for help above and beyond the call of duty. I'd also like to single out the Dreamweaver Technical Support staff, whose answers to users' queries have been tremendous sources of information. And who's that in the back of the room? Macromedia management — in the form of David Mendels, Beth Davis, Eric Ott, Matt Brown, and others — has opened many, many doors to me and should stand up and take a bow. And finally, the entire Dreamweaver community is beholden to Kevin Lynch and Paul Madar for their vision and hard work in bringing this dream home.

On the Fireworks side of the equation, a hearty thank you and a round of applause to Dennis Griffin, Doug Benson, John Ahlquist, Jeff Ahlquist, Matt Bendicksen, Steven Johnson, Jeff Doar, and Eric Wolff. I'd also like to single out Mark Haynes for not only the specific questions he helped me with, but for all the users he's helped aboard the Fireworks team with his tireless answers in the newsgroup. Finally, let me offer a special thanks to David Morris, Fireworks Product Manager, for his early support and encouragement, as well as the openness and access he has granted me.

To me, there's no higher compliment than to be told that I know my business. Well, the folks I work with at Hungry Minds (known as IDG Books Worldwide when I started this effort) sure know their business: acquisitions editors Mike Roney and Chris Webb; project editors Julie Smith, Laura Brown, and Jodi Jensen; copy editors Kelly Campbell Hogue, Roxane Marini, Nancy Rapoport, and Jeremy Zucker; and all the additional support staff. And to someone whose business is to know my business, a double thank you with a cherry on top for my agent, Laura Belt, of Morris Belt Literary Management.

One last note of appreciation — for all the people who took a chance with some of their hard-earned money and bought a copy of one of my books. That small sound you hear in the background is me applauding you as thanks for your support. I hope my efforts continue to be worthy.

Contents at a Glance

Foreword ix
Preface xi
Acknowledgments xxi

Part I: Working with Dreamweaver 1
Chapter 1: QuickStart for Beginners 3
Chapter 2: Setting Up Your First Site 19
Chapter 3: Publishing with the Site Window 39
Chapter 4: Understanding How HTML Works 71
Chapter 5: Adding Text to Your Web Page 103
Chapter 6: Inserting Images 159
Chapter 7: Establishing Web Links 193
Chapter 8: Setting Up Tables 209
Chapter 9: Interactive Forms 253
Chapter 10: Using Frames and Framesets 277
Chapter 11: Using Behaviors 305
Chapter 12: Fireworks Integration 351
Chapter 13: Inserting Flash and Shockwave Elements 375
Chapter 14: Building Style Sheet Web Pages 421
Chapter 15: Working with Layers 453
Chapter 16: Working with Timelines 493
Chapter 17: Using Dreamweaver Templates 521
Chapter 18: Using the Repeating Elements Library 539

Part II: Working with Fireworks 557
Chapter 19: Understanding the Interface 559
Chapter 20: Setting Up Documents 629
Chapter 21: Creating Vector Objects 651
Chapter 22: Working with Bitmaps 677
Chapter 23: Managing Color 705
Chapter 24: Choosing Strokes 729
Chapter 25: Structuring Paths 765
Chapter 26: Composing with Text 795
Chapter 27: Using Fills and Textures 821
Chapter 28: Creating Live Effects and Xtras 851

Chapter 29: Arranging and Compositing Objects 903
Chapter 30: Exporting and Optimizing 953
Chapter 31: Working with Fireworks Styles 1007
Chapter 32: Using Symbols and Libraries 1019
Chapter 33: Mastering Image Maps and Slices 1043
Chapter 34: Activating Fireworks with Behaviors 1077
Chapter 35: Applying Animation Techniques 1111

Appendix: What's on the CD-ROM? 1151

Index 1161
Hungry Minds, Inc. End-User License Agreement 1204
CD-ROM Installation Instructions 1207

Contents

Foreword ix

Preface. xi

Acknowledgments xxi

Part I: Working with Dreamweaver — 1

Chapter 1: QuickStart for Beginners 3
Setting up a Site 3
Creating Your Home Page Layout 6
    Starting with the <head> 6
    Specifying page colors 8
    Initial graphic layout 9
Including Client Text 11
Activating the Page 13
Previewing and Posting the Page 15

Chapter 2: Setting Up Your First Site 19
Planning Your Site 19
    Primary considerations 20
    Design options 21
Defining a Site 24
    Establishing local connections 25
    Specifying the remote site 27
Managing Site Info 30
Creating and Saving New Pages 31
    Starting Dreamweaver 31
    Opening an existing file 32
    Opening a new window 33
    Opening a new page 33
    Saving your page 34
    Closing the page 34
    Quitting the program 34
Previewing Your Web Pages 35
Putting Your Pages Online 36

Chapter 3: Publishing with the Site Window 39
Site Management with Dreamweaver 39
Setting Up a New Site 41
    Local directory information 42
    Remote Info 43

Integrating Design Notes 45
Modifying the Site Map 47
File View Columns 48
Using the Site Window 50
Remote Site and Local Root windows 51
Connect/Disconnect button 51
Get and Put buttons 51
Refresh button 53
Stop Current Task button 53
Check Out/Check In buttons 53
Checking a File In and Out 53
Synchronizing Local and Remote Sites 55
Checking Links 57
Launching External Editors 59
Working with the Site Map 59
Storyboarding with the Site Map 61
Modifying pages through the Site Map 66
Viewing the Site Map 67

Chapter 4: Understanding How HTML Works 71

The Structure of an HTML Page 71
Defining <head> Elements 73
Establishing page properties 73
Choosing a Page palette 75
Understanding <meta> and other <head> tags 77
Adding to the <body> 85
Logical styles 85
Physical styles 86
Working with the Code View and Code Inspector 87
Rapid Tag Modification with the Quick Tag Editor 91
Insert HTML mode 92
Wrap Tag mode 95
Edit HTML mode 96
Inserting Symbols and Special Characters 98
Named characters 98
Decimal characters 99
Using the Character objects 99

Chapter 5: Adding Text to Your Web Page 103

Starting with Headings 103
Working with Paragraphs 105
Editing paragraphs 107
Using Find and Replace 113
The <br> tag 128
Other whitespace tags 129
Importing Word HTML 130
Styling Your Text 134
Working with preformatted text 134
Depicting various styles 135
Using the <address> tag 137

Using HTML Styles 138
    Applying HTML Styles 139
    Removing HTML Styles 140
    Defining HTML Styles 141
Modifying Text Format 144
    Adjusting font size 144
    Absolute size 144
    Relative size 146
    Adding font color 147
    Assigning a specific font 150
    Aligning text 152
    Indenting entire paragraphs 153
Incorporating Dates 154
Commenting Your Code 156

Chapter 6: Inserting Images 159

Web Graphic Formats 159
    GIF 160
    JPEG 161
    PNG 162
Using Inline Images 163
    Inserting inline images 163
    Dragging images from the Assets panel 166
    Modifying images 168
    Working with alignment options 173
Putting Pictures in the Background 177
Dividing the Web Page with Horizontal Rules 178
Applying Simple Web Animation 181
Dreamweaver Technique: Including Banner Ads 182
Inserting Rollover Images 184
Adding a Navigation Bar 186

Chapter 7: Establishing Web Links 193

Understanding URLs 193
Surfing the Web with Hypertext 195
    Inserting URLs from the Assets panel 197
    Pointing to a file 199
    Addressing types 200
Adding an E-Mail Link 201
Navigating with Anchors 202
    Moving within the same document 204
    Using named anchors in a different page 204
Targeting Your Links 205

Chapter 8: Setting Up Tables 209

HTML Table Fundamentals 210
    Rows 211
    Cells 211
    Column/row headings 211

Inserting Tables in Dreamweaver 211
Setting Table Preferences 214
Modifying Tables 214
    Selecting table elements 214
    Editing a table's contents 218
    Working with table properties 222
    Setting cell, column, and row properties 231
Working with Table Formats 235
Sorting Tables 237
Importing Tabular Data 239
Designing with Layout Mode 241
    Drawing cells and tables 242
    Modifying layouts 246

Chapter 9: Interactive Forms 253

How HTML Forms Work 253
Inserting a Form in Dreamweaver 255
Using Text Boxes 257
    Text fields 257
    Password fields 260
    Multiline text areas 260
Providing Checkboxes and Radio Buttons 261
    Checkboxes 262
    Radio buttons 263
Creating Form Lists and Menus 264
    Drop-down menus 264
    Scrolling lists 266
Navigating with a Jump Menu 268
    Modifying a jump menu 270
    Activating Go buttons 271
Activating Your Form with Buttons 272
    Submit, Reset, and Command buttons 272
    Graphical buttons 274
Using the Hidden Field and the File Field 275
    The hidden input type 275
    The file input type 275

Chapter 10: Using Frames and Framesets 277

Frames and Framesets: The Basics 278
    Columns and rows 278
    Sizing frames 278
Creating a Frameset and Frames 279
    Adding more frames 280
    Using the menus 281
    Using the mouse 282
Quick Framesets with the Frames Objects 283
Working with the Frameset Property Inspector 286
    Resizing frames in a frameset 286
    Manipulating frameset borders 287

Saving a frameset and frames 288
Closing a frameset 289
Modifying a Frame 289
Page properties 289
Working with the Frame Property Inspector 291
Modifying content 295
Deleting frames 295
Targeting Frame Content 296
Targeting sections of your frameset 296
Targeting specific frames in your frameset 297
Updating two frames or more at once 298
Handling Frameless Browsers 299
Investigating Iframes 301

Chapter 11: Using Behaviors 305

Understanding Behaviors, Events, and Actions 305
Attaching a Behavior 306
Using the Behaviors panel 307
Adding a behavior 308
Managing events 310
Standard actions 313
Managing and Modifying Your Behaviors 347
Altering the parameters of a behavior 348
Sequencing your behaviors 349
Deleting behaviors 349

Chapter 12: Fireworks Integration 351

Easy Graphics Modification 352
Optimizing an image in Fireworks 353
Editing an image in Fireworks 356
Inserting Rollovers 358
Using Dreamweaver's behaviors 358
Using Fireworks' code 361
Modifying sliced images 364
Controlling Fireworks with Dreamweaver 366
Web photo album 366
Building Dreamweaver/Fireworks extensions 370

Chapter 13: Inserting Flash and Shockwave Elements 375

Shockwave and Flash: What's the Difference? 376
Including Flash and Shockwave Movies in Dreamweaver Projects 378
Specifying Shockwave Properties 381
Additional parameters for Shockwave 383
Automatic settings for Shockwave files 384
Designating Flash Attributes 384
Setting the scale in Flash movies 385
Additional parameters for Flash 386
Creating Flash Buttons and Crafting Templates 387
Working with Flash Text 392
Configuring MIME Types 394

Adding Generator Objects 394
Managing Links in Flash Movies with Dreamweaver 396
Providing User Interaction with Shockwave Movies 397
    Dreamweaver technique: Creating inline Shockwave controls 398
    Dreamweaver technique: Playing Shockwave movies in frames . . . 399
    Dreamweaver technique: Triggering behaviors from Flash movies . 402
Dreamweaver Technique: Using the JavaScript
  Integration Kit for Flash 5 405
    Macromedia Flash Player Controls 406
    Advanced Form Validations 410
    Browser Scripts for Flash 415
    Flash Dispatcher Behavior 417

Chapter 14: Building Style Sheet Web Pages 421

Understanding Cascading Style Sheets 422
    Grouping properties 422
    Inheritance of properties 423
    Cascading characteristics 423
    Defining new classes for extended design control 424
    How styles are applied 424
Creating and Applying a Style Sheet in Dreamweaver 426
    Dreamweaver technique: Eliminating underlines from links 427
    Using the CSS Styles panel to apply styles 428
    Attaching an external style sheet 429
    Applying, changing, and removing a style 429
    Defining new styles 432
    Editing and managing style sheets 434
    Importing an external style sheet 435
Styles and Their Attributes 436
    Type options 437
    Background options 439
    Block options 440
    Box options 442
    Border options 443
    List options 444
    Positioning options 445
    Extensions options 446

Chapter 15: Working with Layers 453

Layers 101 454
Creating Layers with Dreamweaver 455
    Inserting a layer object 456
    Using the Insert ⇨ Layer command 458
    Setting default characteristics of a layer 458
    Embedding a layer with style sheets 460
    Choosing relative instead of absolute positioning 461
Modifying a Layer 463
    Selecting a layer 464
    Resizing a layer 465
    Moving a layer 465

Contents

      The Layers panel 473
      Aligning layers with the ruler and grid 475
      Adding elements to a layer 477
      Forms and layers 478
   Creating Your Page Design with Layers 479
      Using the Tracing Image 480
      Preventing overlaps 481
      Designing precision layouts and converting content to layers 482
      Converting layers to tables 484
   Activating Layers with Behaviors 485
      Drag Layer 486
      Set Text of Layer 488
      Show-Hide Layers 490
   Dreamweaver Technique: Creating a Loading Layer 491

Chapter 16: Working with Timelines 493

   Entering the Fourth Dimension with Timelines 494
      Timeline capabilities 494
      A few ground rules 495
   Creating Animations with Timelines 496
   Adding Layers to the Timelines Panel 497
   Modifying a Timeline 499
      Altering the animation bars 499
      Using the Timeline controls 500
      Adding keyframes 503
      Removing timeline elements 505
      Changing animation speed 506
      Recording a layer's path 506
   Triggering Behaviors in Timelines 508
   Dreamweaver Technique: Creating a Multiscreen Slideshow 510
      Step 1: Preparing the graphic elements 511
      Step 2: Creating the slideshow timeline 513
      Step 3: Creating the moving layers timeline 515
      Step 4: Adding the behaviors 517

Chapter 17: Using Dreamweaver Templates 521

   Understanding Templates 521
   Creating Your Own Templates 522
   Using Editable Regions 524
      Marking existing content as editable 524
      Inserting a new editable region 525
      Locking an editable region 526
   Adding Content to Template Documents 528
      Adding behaviors to template-derived documents 530
      Inserting meta tags in documents based on templates 530
   Working with Templates in the Assets Panel 531
      Creating a blank template 533
      Deleting and opening templates 533
      Applying templates 534

Updating Templates 535
Changing the Default Document 536

Chapter 18: Using the Repeating Elements Library 539

Dreamweaver Libraries 539
Using the Library Assets Panel 540
    Adding a Library item 542
    Moving Library items to a new site 542
    Inserting a Library item in your Web page 543
    Deleting an item from the Library 545
    Renaming a Library item 546
Editing a Library Item 546
Updating Your Web Sites with Libraries 548
Applying Server-Side Includes 550
    Adding server-side includes 551
    Editing server-side includes 553

Part II: Working with Fireworks   557

Chapter 19: Understanding the Interface 559

Examining the Fireworks Environment 559
Understanding the Document Window 561
    Document window controls 564
    Display options 568
Exploring the Tools Panel 570
Accessing Toolbars (Windows Only) 574
    Main toolbar 574
    Modify toolbar 575
    Status bar 577
Managing the Floating Panels 578
    Grouping and moving panels 578
    Panel Layout Sets 579
    Hiding and revealing panels 579
    Windowshade 580
    Examining common features 580
    Optimize panel 582
    Object panel 583
    Stroke panel 585
    Fill panel 587
    Effect panel 588
    Color Table panel 590
    Swatches panel 591
    Color Mixer panel 592
    Tool Options panel 593
    Layers panel 594
    Frames panel 596
    History panel 597
    Info panel 598

　　　　Behaviors panel 599
　　　　URL panel 600
　　　　Styles panel 601
　　　　Library panel 603
　　　　Find and Replace panel 604
　　　　Project Log panel 605
　　Using the Menus 606
　　　　File menu 606
　　　　Edit menu 608
　　　　View menu 610
　　　　Insert menu 613
　　　　Modify menu 614
　　　　Text menu 620
　　　　Commands menu 622
　　　　Xtras 623
　　　　Window menu 625
　　　　Help menu 627

Chapter 20: Setting Up Documents 629

　　Creating New Documents 629
　　　　Exploring two approaches 629
　　　　Understanding the canvas options 631
　　　　Discovering the steps to create a new document 634
　　Opening Existing Images 635
　　　　Examining file formats 636
　　　　Opening multiple images 639
　　Storing Files 640
　　　　Closing a file 641
　　　　Reverting to a saved file 642
　　Modifying Canvases 642
　　　　Altering the canvas size 643
　　　　Trimming the canvas 648
　　　　Picking a new canvas color 649
　　　　Rotating the canvas 649

Chapter 21: Creating Vector Objects 651

　　Understanding Vector Objects in Fireworks 651
　　Examining Paths 652
　　　　Applying a stroke 652
　　　　Looking at open and closed paths 653
　　　　Grasping the center point 654
　　　　Examining direction 654
　　Starting from Shapes 655
　　　　Examining rectangles and squares 656
　　　　Using ellipses and circles 659
　　　　Exploring polygons and stars 660
　　Drawing Lines and Freeform Paths 665
　　　　Making straight lines 665
　　　　Drawing with the Freeform Pencil and Brush 666

Constructing Bézier Curves 668
　　　　　Drawing lines with the Pen 669
　　　　　Creating smooth curves with the Pen 670
　　　　　Mixing lines and curves 672
　　　　　Adjusting curves 673
　　　　　Using the keyboard modifiers 675

Chapter 22: Working with Bitmaps 677

　　　Understanding Bitmaps in Fireworks 678
　　　　　Examining bitmap mode 678
　　　　　Opening existing bitmaps 681
　　　　　Scaling bitmaps 682
　　　　　Inserting a bitmap into a document 683
　　　　　Inserting an empty bitmap 684
　　　　　Using bitmap mode tools 684
　　　Fireworks Technique: Limiting Your Drawing Area 697
　　　Making Pixel Selections 698
　　　　　Selecting all 698
　　　　　Selecting similar 698
　　　　　Selecting none 699
　　　　　Selecting inverse 699
　　　　　Feathering an existing selection 700
　　　　　Expanding or contracting a marquee 701
　　　　　Adding a border 701
　　　　　Using the Smooth command 701
　　　　　Saving and restoring selections 701
　　　Applying Vector Tools to Bitmaps 701
　　　Converting a Vector into a Bitmap 702

Chapter 23: Managing Color 705

　　　Working with Color on the Web 705
　　　　　Examining bit depth 706
　　　　　Understanding hexadecimal colors 707
　　　　　Exploring Web-safe colors 708
　　　　　Looking at platform differences 709
　　　　　Working with color management 710
　　　Mixing Colors 711
　　　　　Using the Color Mixer 711
　　　　　Choosing a color 712
　　　　　Accessing the color models 713
　　　Selecting Swatches of Color 716
　　　　　Choosing from the color wells 716
　　　　　Using the Eyedropper 718
　　　　　Accessing the system color picker(s) 718
　　　　　Opting for no color 720
　　　　　Using the Swatches panel 721
　　　　　Accessing the Color Table 724
　　　Fireworks Technique: Converting Pantone Colors to Web-Safe Colors . . 725
　　　　　Using ColorWeb Pro for Windows 726
　　　　　Using ColorWeb Pro for Macintosh 727

Chapter 24: Choosing Strokes 729

Using the Stroke Panel 729
    Stroke categories and types 731
    Stroke edge and size 732
    Stroke texture 732
Working with the Built-in Strokes 734
    Pencil 735
    Basic 736
    Air Brush 737
    Calligraphy 738
    Charcoal 739
    Crayon 740
    Felt Tip 741
    Oil 742
    Watercolor 743
    Random 744
    Unnatural 745
Creating New Strokes 746
    Managing your strokes 747
    Editing the stroke 749
Fireworks Technique: Making Dotted Lines 758
Orienting the Stroke 761

Chapter 25: Structuring Paths 765

Transforming Objects Visually 766
    Using scaling 766
    Examining skewing 768
    Discovering distorting 769
    Understanding rotating 770
Transforming Objects Numerically 771
Fireworks Technique: Creating Perspective 773
Managing Points and Paths 774
    Moving points with the Subselection tool ... 775
    Adding and removing points 776
    Closing an open path 777
    Working with multiple paths 778
Editing Paths 779
    Redrawing a path 779
    Examining the Freeform and Reshape Area 780
    Discovering the Path Scrubber 785
    Discerning Path Operations 787

Chapter 26: Composing with Text 795

Using the Text Editor 795
    Previewing on the fly 797
    Choosing basic font characteristics 798
    Adjusting text spacing 800
    Enabling Text Editor options 806
Re-Editing Text 806

Importing Text 807
Transforming Text 808
    Adding strokes 808
    Enhancing fills 810
    Using the transform tools 811
    Converting text to paths 812
    Converting text to an image 812
Fireworks Technique: Cookie-Cutter Text 813
Fireworks Technique: A Font Safety Net 813
Using the Text on a Path Command 815
Fireworks Technique: Masking Images with Text 818

Chapter 27: Using Fills and Textures 821

Using Built-in Fills 821
    Turning off an object's fill 822
    Using a Solid fill 823
    Using the Web Dither fill 824
Managing Gradients 827
    Applying a Gradient fill 827
    Altering gradients 828
    Using the Styles feature 833
Fireworks Technique: Making Transparent Gradients 833
Using Patterns 834
    Adding new Patterns 836
    Adding Patterns to a document 837
    Altering Patterns 838
Fireworks Technique: Creating Seamless Patterns 839
Adding Texture to Your Fills 844
    Adding new textures 846
    Converting a color image to grayscale 847
    Assigning an additional textures folder 847
    Adding textures to a document 847
Filling with the Paint Bucket Tool 848

Chapter 28: Creating Live Effects and Xtras 851

Understanding Fireworks Effects 851
    Using the Effect panel 852
    Applying Live Effects 852
    Examining the Xtras menu 855
Working with Included Live Effects 857
    Adjusting color 858
    Adjusting tonal range 859
    Using three dimensions with Bevel and Emboss 866
    Adding depth with blurring 871
    Learning holdover effects 872
    Examining Shadow and Glow 872
    Sharpening to bring out detail 876
Fireworks Technique: Making Perspective Shadows 878

Managing Live Effects 880
   Storing a customized effect 881
   Grasping missing effects 882
   Saving effects in Styles 883
Reading All About Xtras 884
   Using vector objects 884
   Examining bitmap objects 885
   Identifying pixel selections in a bitmap object 885
   Checking out false pixel selections 885
   Evaluating multiple objects 886
Using Third-Party, Photoshop-Compatible Filters 887
   Installing third-party filter packages 887
   Using filters with multiple applications 888
   Using shortcuts (aliases) to plug-in folders 889
   Exploring Alien Skin Eye Candy 890
   Investigating Kai's Power Tools 5 896

Chapter 29: Arranging and Compositing Objects 903

Using Layers 903
   Adding a layer 905
   Naming a layer 905
   Duplicating a layer 905
   Deleting a layer 906
   Changing stacking order 906
   Editing layer by layer 906
   Using the Selection column 907
   Opening layers 908
   Examining the Web Layer 910
Aligning and Distributing Objects 911
   Using a theoretical rectangle 911
   Aligning to the canvas 915
Looking at Layout Assistance 916
   Using rulers 917
   Working with guides 918
   Exploring the grid 921
Grouping Objects 923
Working with Alpha Masks 924
   Creating vector masks 926
   Applying bitmap masks 929
   Editing masks 932
   Masking suggestions 936
   Fireworks technique: Quick photo edges 936
Examining Opacity and Blending 938
   Controlling opacity 939
   Using blending modes 940
   Investigating blending modes 941
   Fireworks technique: Simulating a light source
      with blending modes 943
Fireworks Technique: Feathering Selections 945
Fireworks Technique: Applied Compositing 946

Chapter 30: Exporting and Optimizing 953

Exploring Optimization Features 953
    Optimize panel 955
    Color Table panel 956
    Workspace preview 957
    Frame controls 963
Exporting Indexed Color 964
    Color palette 966
    Number of colors 967
    Matte 970
    Lossy GIF compression 970
    Dither 971
    Transparency 972
    Remove unused colors 976
    Interlaced 976
    Saved settings 977
    Fireworks technique: Creating GIF-friendly images 977
Exporting Photographic Images 980
    JPEG 981
    PNG 32 and 24 987
    Other formats 988
Working in the Export Preview 988
    Cropping 990
    Scaling exported images 991
Using the Export Wizards 992
Examining Additional Export Options 995
    Exporting as CSS layers 995
    Exporting for Director 998
    Exporting files 999
    Exporting as Image Wells 999
    Exporting vectors 1000
    Exporting Photoshop documents 1003

Chapter 31: Working with Fireworks Styles 1007

Understanding Styles 1008
Applying Styles 1009
Creating New Styles 1010
Managing Styles 1013
Fireworks Technique: Isolating Patterns and Textures from Styles 1015

Chapter 32: Using Symbols and Libraries 1019

Understanding Symbols and Instances 1019
Introducing the Library Panel 1023
Making and Modifying Symbols 1025
    Creating a symbol 1025
    Modifying symbols 1028
    Creating Instances 1030
    Modifying Instances 1031

Working with Buttons 1032
    Making and modifying Button Symbols 1032
    Using Button Instances 1035
    Examining the Link Wizard 1036
Managing Libraries 1037
    Importing a Library 1037
    Exporting and sharing Libraries 1039

Chapter 33: Mastering Image Maps and Slices 1043

Understanding Image Maps and Hotspots 1043
Using the Hotspot Tools 1045
    Examining the rectangle hotspot 1045
    Examining the circle hotspot 1047
    Examining the polygon hotspot 1047
    Assigning links to hotspots 1048
    Converting an object to a hotspot 1049
Exporting Image Map Code 1050
    Choosing an HTML style 1050
    Inserting image map code in a Web page 1053
Understanding Slices 1057
Slicing Images in Fireworks 1058
    Looking at rectangle slices 1059
    Looking at polygon slices 1060
    Working with slice guides 1061
    Copying an image to a slice 1062
    Setting URLs in slices 1063
Exporting Slices 1065
    Exporting slices as different image types 1065
    Setting the Export options 1066
    Inserting slices in a Web page 1067
    Exporting single slices 1069
Fireworks Technique: Exporting Dreamweaver Library Items 1070
Fireworks Technique: Animating a Slice 1073

Chapter 34: Activating Fireworks with Behaviors 1077

Understanding Behaviors 1077
Using the Behaviors Panel 1078
    Attaching Behaviors 1079
    Modifying a Behavior 1080
    Deleting a Behavior 1081
Creating Rollovers 1081
    Examining how rollovers work 1082
    Learning rollover states 1082
    Creating rollover images 1083
    Applying the Simple Rollover Behavior 1085
Exporting Rollovers for the Web 1086
    Exporting the code from Fireworks 1088
    Inserting rollover code in your Web page 1089

Looking at Nav Bar Behavior 1091
    Creating a Nav Bar 1092
    Building buttons in the Button Editor 1094
Examining Advanced Rollover Techniques 1096
    Making disjointed rollovers 1097
    Creating external rollovers 1098
    Working with hotspot rollovers 1099
    Displaying a status bar message 1101
Working with Pop-Up Menus 1102
Using Drag-and-Drop Behaviors 1106
    Creating a simple rollover with drag and drop 1107
    Creating disjoint rollovers with drag and drop 1108
    Removing drag-and-drop Behaviors 1109

Chapter 35: Applying Animation Techniques 1111

Understanding Web Animation 1111
    Getting a handle on bandwidth 1112
    Making a statement 1112
    Examining why to animate a GIF 1113
Using the Fireworks Animation Toolkit 1115
    Managing frames 1115
    Animating objects 1120
    Using the VCR controls 1123
    Setting frame delay timing 1124
    Using Onion Skinning 1125
    Examining export settings and options 1127
Examining Web Design with Animated GIF Images 1131
    Animating background images 1132
    Reusing animations 1132
    Scaling an animation 1132
    Using the browser's background image 1132
    Preloading an animation 1132
    Using animated rollovers 1133
    Slicing animations 1134
Tweening Graphic Symbols 1135
    Fireworks technique: Tweening Xtras 1138
    Fireworks technique: Tweening depth 1140
    Fireworks technique: Fading in and out 1142
Using Animation Symbols 1144
    Creating animation symbols 1144
    Editing an animation symbol 1146

Appendix: What's on the CD-ROM? 1151

Index 1161

Hungry Minds, Inc. End-User License Agreement 1204

CD-ROM Installation Instructions 1207

Working with Dreamweaver

PART

1

In This Part

Chapter 1
QuickStart for Beginners

Chapter 2
Setting Up Your First Site

Chapter 3
Publishing with the Site Window

Chapter 4
Understanding How HTML Works

Chapter 5
Adding Text to Your Web Page

Chapter 6
Inserting Images

Chapter 7
Establishing Web Links

Chapter 8
Setting Up Tables

Chapter 9
Interactive Forms

Chapter 10
Using Frames and Framesets

Chapter 11
Using Behaviors

Chapter 12
Fireworks Integration

Chapter 13
Inserting Flash and Shockwave Elements

Chapter 14
Building Style Sheet Web Pages

Chapter 15
Working with Layers

Chapter 16
Working with Timelines

Chapter 17
Using Dreamweaver Templates

Chapter 18
Using the Repeating Elements Library

QuickStart for Beginners

Designing a Web site is a big job, and Dreamweaver is a big program; both can be overwhelming when you first approach them. If you're new to Web design in general or to Dreamweaver in particular, the best way to learn about either of them is to build several sample sites. I've found that working on a project helps most people absorb all the little nuances of a program needed to be productive.

This chapter presents an overview of how I use Dreamweaver to begin building a Web site. A hallmark of any world-class software program such as Dreamweaver, is its capability to be used in many ways by many different people. Don't get the idea that what follows is the only way to construct a site; it is, however, the basic methodology that I've used successfully over the years.

If you are totally new to Web-site creation or to Dreamweaver, I recommend reading through the chapter in one sitting. Doing so will give you an overview of both the process and the program. Throughout this chapter, you can find many cross-references to other sections of the book where step-by-step instructions are detailed. As you begin to build your sites, use this chapter as a jumping-off place to delve deeper into each topic.

Setting up a Site

The first phase of designing a Web site involves pure input. You need to gather as much information from your client as possible. Some of this information relates to the overall message of the Web site along with its purpose, intended audience, and goals. Other elements, such as logos, textual content, and prior marketing materials are more tangible. I've found it best to get up front as much information — in both categories — as possible.

C H A P T E R
1

♦ ♦ ♦ ♦

In This Chapter

Establishing a local site

Mapping out the home page

Creating linked pages

Laying out the graphics

Adding content

Going live

♦ ♦ ♦ ♦

Part I ✦ Working with Dreamweaver

Tip Whenever possible, get your data in digital format; the images ideally should be in a format that your graphics program can read and the content should be in a standard word processing file. Your workflow will be greatly enhanced if you don't have to spend time recreating logos or keying in faxed text.

As you are sketching out design ideas for the look of the site (on paper and in your head), you can begin to set up the structure of the site on your computer. Dreamweaver uses a folder on your hard drive as the local site root; when the site goes live on the Internet, the local site is mirrored on the Web server, also known as the *remote site*. So the very first physical step is to create a folder with the site or client name. All you need is a single folder to define a site in Dreamweaver and to begin building your Web site. Here's one way to start:

1. Using the system file manager, create a folder on your local hard drive and give it a unique name, reflective of the client or site.

2. In Dreamweaver, open the Site window, as shown in Figure 1-1, by choosing the Show Site button from the Launcher. Alternatively, you could select Window ⇨ Site Files or use the keyboard shortcut F8.

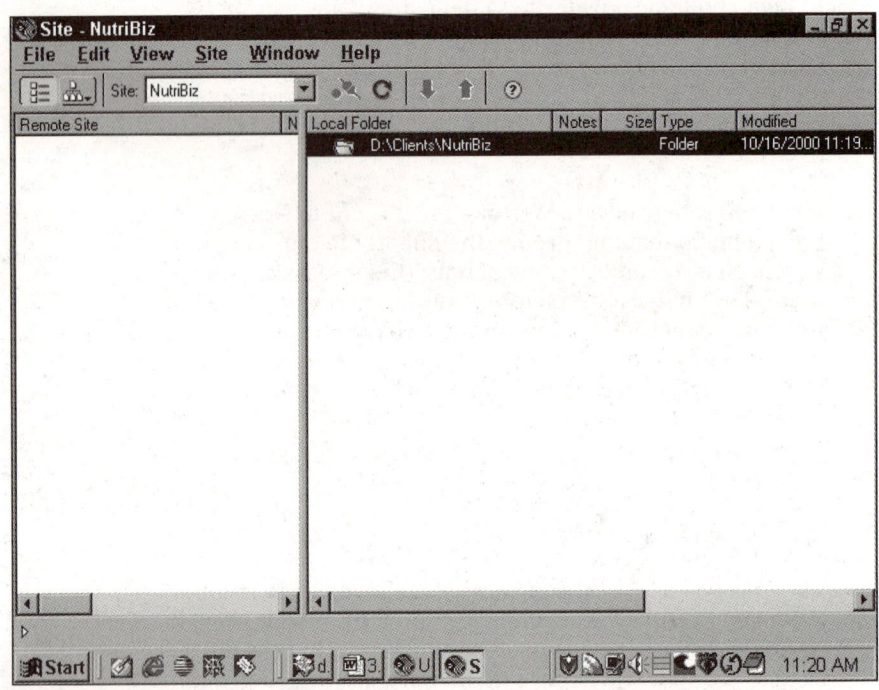

Figure 1-1: Use Dreamweaver's Site window to lay out the structure of your Web site.

3. From the site list, choose Define Sites. The Define Sites dialog box opens, displaying a list of your currently available sites, if any.

Chapter 1 ✦ **QuickStart for Beginners**   5

4. Select the New button to set the parameters of your new site.

5. In the Site Definition dialog box, enter the name of the new site, its local root folder, its HTTP address, and the name of the home page.

Cross-Reference   A detailed breakdown of the process of defining a site can be found in Chapter 2.

After the site is initially defined, you have a folder and a single file set up as the home page, as shown in the Site Map view displayed in Figure 1-2. Dreamweaver's Site Map is not just a useful tool for maintaining a Web site; it is also useful when developing the site structure. I recommend that you use it to develop the entire structure of your Web site before you begin adding content.

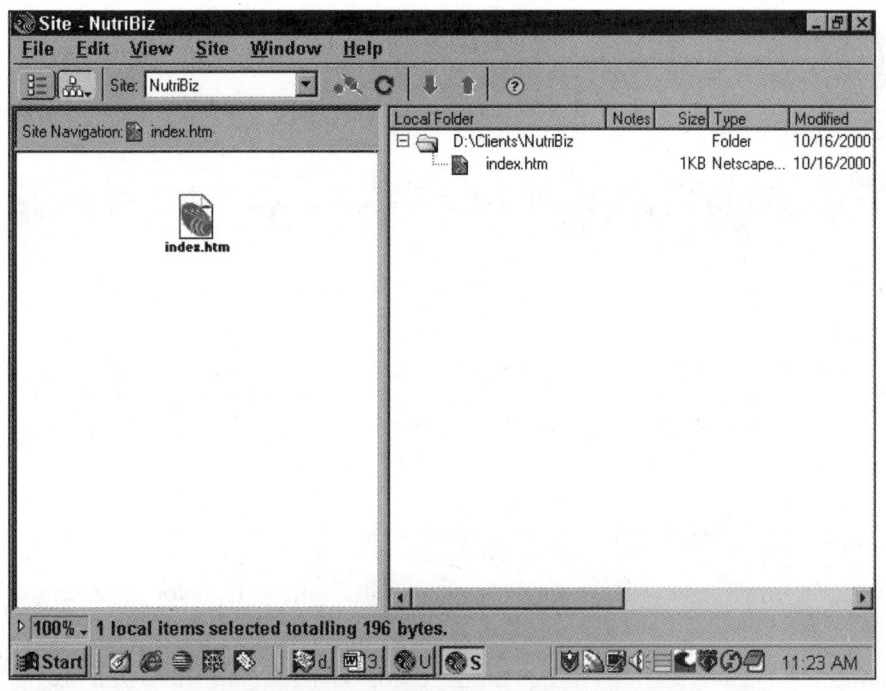

Figure 1-2: The Web site is defined and the home page is created.

Using the techniques outlined in Chapter 2, you can then create new blank files, already linked to your home page. These new pages act as placeholders for content to come. They also help to ease the building of the site by providing existing pages to link to and to preview the navigation of your site. To function properly, many of Dreamweaver's commands depend on a file being saved. So, by prebuilding your site pages, you avoid unnecessary delays and warning dialog boxes. By the time you're finished, your Web site is beginning to take form, as shown in Figure 1-3.

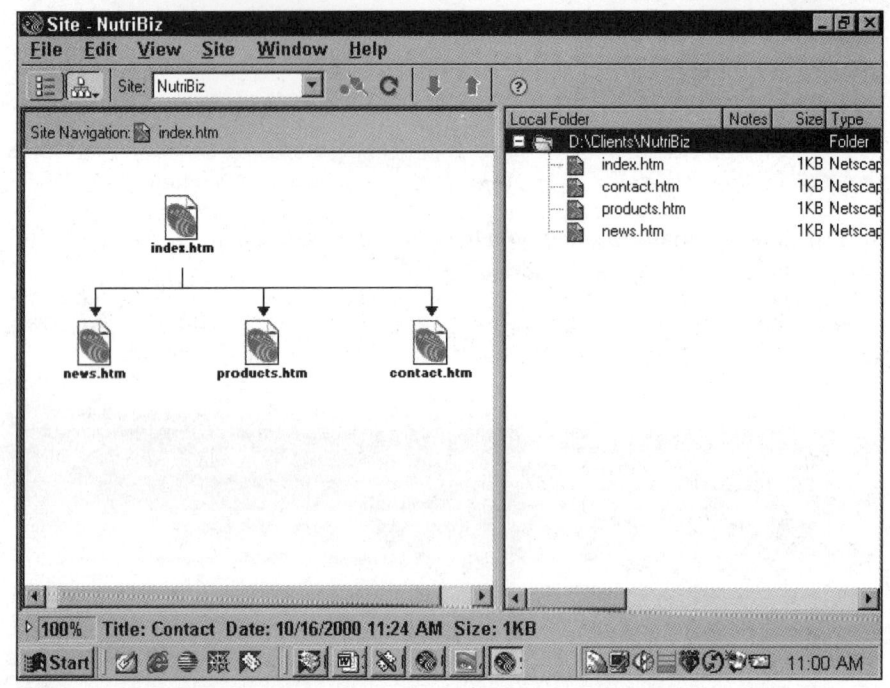

Figure 1-3: Dreamweaver's Site window is a valuable Web-site prototyping tool.

> **Note** While it's not necessary to create all the pages a site might use, I find it helpful to make the primary ones linked to the home page. Then, when I work on each section, such as Products, I use the Site window to create the pages in that division.

Creating Your Home Page Layout

With the site's structure beginning to emerge, it's time to turn your attention to the page that most visitors' first see at the Web site: the home page. Although any page can act as a doorway to your site, the home page is by far the most commonly used entrance. I like to start my design on the home page for another reason also — I frequently reuse core elements from the home page, such as the logo and navigation system, throughout the site. By setting these designs early — and getting approval for them — I can save myself a fair amount of work down the road while maintaining a consistent look-and-feel to the site.

Starting with the <head>

One of the most important sections of a Web page is also one of those most frequently — and wrongly — ignored: the <head> section. Under normal circumstances, the <head> area (as opposed to the <body>) is not seen, but its effect is enormous. The <head> section contains vital information about the page and the site itself, including the page's title, its description, and the keywords used to describe the page for search engines. Much of this information is contained in a page's <meta> tags. I like to add this information at the beginning of my Web site development, partly to get the chore out of the way, but primarily so that I don't forget to do it! Dreamweaver offers an easy way to input <head> information:

1. Change the Title field in the Toolbar from Unnamed Document to whatever you'd like to appear in the browser title bar. Remember that a page's title is a primary criterion that search engines use to rank a site.

2. Choose View ⇨ Head Content from the main menu or choose Head Content under the View Options button on the Toolbar. The <head> section appears at the top of the Document window as shown in Figure 1-4.

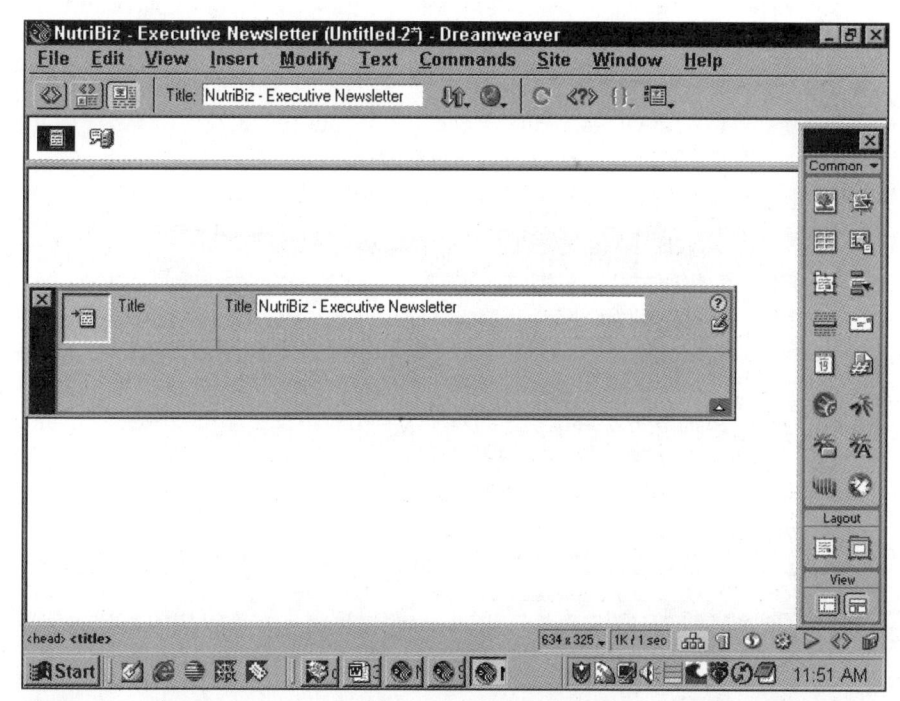

Figure 1-4: The <head> area holds important information for search engines.

3. From the Head category of the Objects panel insert both a Keywords and a Description object, and fill them out appropriately. I prefer that my clients supply both the keywords and the description whenever possible. They know their business best and how best to market it.

Cross-Reference

For a detailed description of the <head> section and its various tags, turn to Chapter 4.

4. Close the Head Content view by deselecting that option under the View Options button of the Toolbar.

Specifying page colors

After the first *Dreamweaver Bible* was published, I received an irate e-mail from a beginning Web designer who was infuriated by one of Macromedia's practices. By default, Dreamweaver pages all specify a white background color—and nothing else. The gentleman who was complaining set his browser colors to have a black background with white lettering—an austere look, but it was his preference. Whenever he previewed default Dreamweaver pages with his browser, his text seemed to disappear. His text was still there, of course, but because it was white text on a white background, it was invisible. The moral of this story is to always specify your background, text, and link colors if you want your Web pages to maintain your designed look.

After entering the `<head>` content, I next define the page's colors and margins through Dreamweaver's Page Properties dialog box, shown in Figure 1-5. Choose Modify ⇨ Page Properties to set these parameters. This is also the location for setting up a background image, if you're using one. I often alter these settings several times in the home page design stage as I try out different looks, so I've memorized the keyboard shortcut Ctrl+J (Command+J).

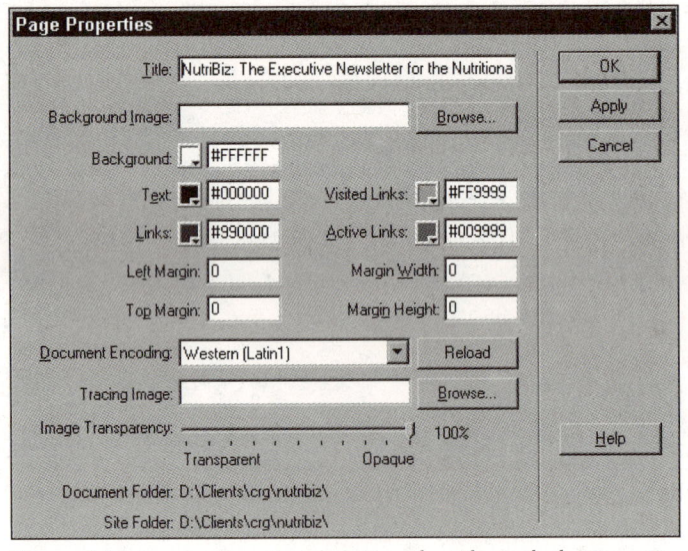

Figure 1-5: Be sure to set your page colors through the Page Properties dialog box.

> **Tip** Not sure about your color combinations? Dreamweaver has a useful command, Set Color Scheme, which contains background, text, and link color selections that are designed to work together.

Initial graphic layout

Like many small-shop Web designers, I create the majority of the graphics to use on my pages myself, and the Dreamweaver/Fireworks Studio has been a major boon to my productivity. Typically, I create or modify the logo for the home page in Fireworks while Dreamweaver is open, for instant placement and integration. Although the use of layers is always a possibility for placement, I prefer to lay out my pages with tables for most situations. Many designers new to the Web — especially those from a print background — prefer the exact positioning of layers and can use Dreamweaver's excellent layers-to-tables conversion features. The approach that is used is up to you, but remember that many clients still balk at using layers for fear of excluding visitors with older browsers.

Dreamweaver 4 includes a new feature that makes composing the basic layout of a page very straightforward: the Layout View. Here's how a typical home page is developed using this new tool:

1. Start by creating a logo for the Web in your favorite graphics editor. Remember that Web graphics are of a particular format, usually GIF or JPEG with a screen resolution of 72 dpi. Although most Web page visitors' monitors display thousands of colors, it's still good practice to use Web-safe colors wherever possible.

> **Cross-Reference**
> You can find an explanation of Web graphic formats and Web-safe colors in Chapter 6.

2. In Dreamweaver, choose the Layout View from the bottom of the Objects panel. With Layout View enabled, both the Draw Layout Cell and Draw Layout Table tools, also on the Objects panel, become available.

3. Select Draw Layout Cell and drag out the initial cell for holding the logo. Dreamweaver automatically creates a layout table — a borderless table that is the full width of your window — around the layout cell.

4. Press the Ctrl (Command) key to continue drawing out other layout cells for your navigational elements and any other upfront information such as company name.

   Although your layout is likely to be different from mine, in the example shown in Figure 1-6, I start with a two-row by two-column configuration and modify it as needed.

> **Cross-Reference**
> Tables are an important layout tool for Web designers. Chapter 8 shows you how to create and modify tables in Dreamweaver.

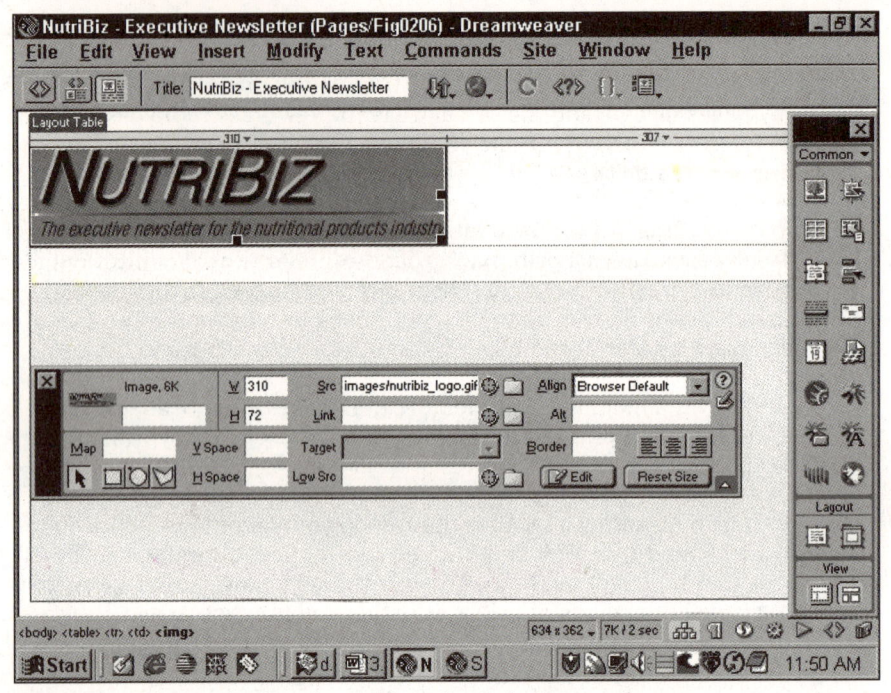

Figure 1-6: Placing the logo in a table to begin laying out the page.

5. Place your logo in the layout cell by choosing Insert Image from the Objects panel or dragging the graphic into place from the Assets panel.

6. Add background color to the table or rows, if desired, by picking a color from the Property Inspector.

    Using a table's background color features is a good, no overhead way to add color to your page. Dreamweaver enables me to sample colors directly from the logo to begin to tie the page together graphically.

7. If desired, adjust the positioning of the logo by using the Align option on the Property Inspector.

I continue to add and modify elements to the logo area until I'm satisfied. In the case of the example site, I added right-justified contact information on one side of the table and then added navigation elements below the logo, as shown in Figure 1-7. I used a contrasting background color for the second smaller row to set off the navigation bar. Initially, the navigation bar is just text and not graphics; this enables me to prototype the page quickly, and I can always replace the text with images at a later date. Cascading Style Sheets or Dreamweaver's HTML Styles control the look of the text.

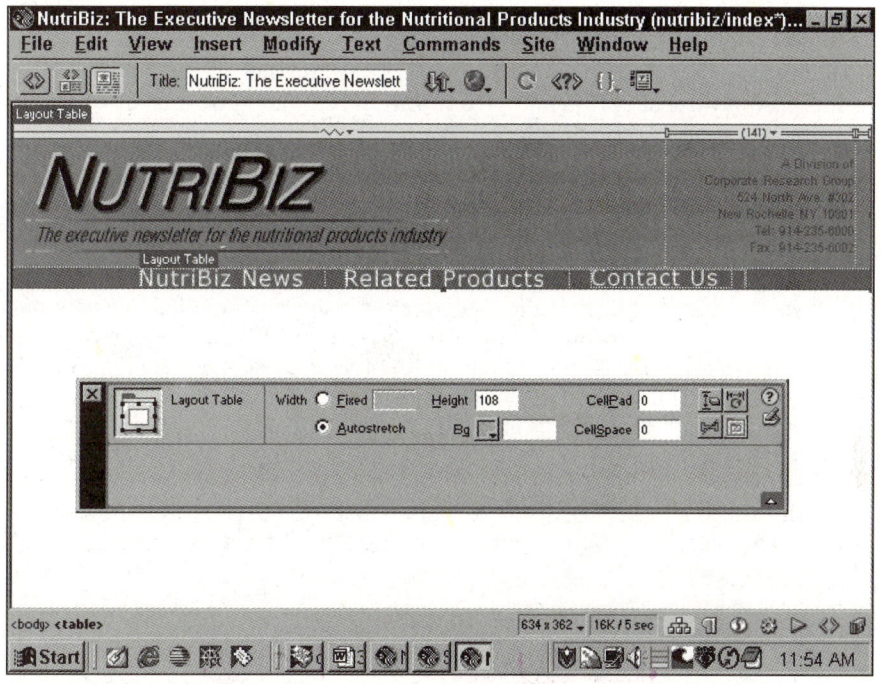

Figure 1-7: All the graphic elements are now in place in the logo area.

> **Note** One advantage of using tables instead of layers is that tables can adjust in width more consistently across browsers than layers can. Dreamweaver's layout tables are set to 100 percent width. If I use the Page Properties dialog to change the margins to zero, I can be sure the background color will stretch across the page, regardless of the user's browser window size.

Including Client Text

Now that your home page is beginning to attract some eyeballs with its graphic look, it is time to throw in some content to get the message across. Text from a client comes in many forms: from the headings and paragraphs of a marketing brochure to bulleted copy points written especially for the Web, and everything in between. Your job as a Web designer is to make it all flow together in a logical, attractive, understandable fashion.

Many print designers coming to the Internet are appalled at the lack of typographic control on the Web. Particular fonts are, for the most part, suggested rather than specified, with alternatives always available. Sizes are often relative and line spacing — outside of Cascading Style Sheets — is nonexistent. A typical first response is to render blocks of text into graphics to achieve exactly the look desired. In a word, don't. Graphics, unlike text, aren't searchable, and displaying text as graphics defeats much of the purpose of the Web. Moreover, large blocks of graphics can take a long time to download. It's far better to learn the ins and outs of HTML text and take advantage of its universality. Besides, Cascading Style Sheets are increasingly a real option and give the Web designer almost as much control as the print designer.

To facilitate including client-generated text in my Web page designs, I often work with my word processing program and Dreamweaver open simultaneously. This arrangement enables me to quickly cut and paste text from one to the other.

Note If you have a great deal of already-formatted client text to include on your page — and a copy of Microsoft Word — take advantage of Dreamweaver's new Import Word HTML feature. When you run the command, Dreamweaver brings the Word-generated HTML document into a new page, and you can copy the needed sections (or all of it, if you like) and paste them directly into the home page. Dreamweaver preserves all the coding during the copy-and-paste operation.

I generally adopt a top-down approach when inserting text: I place the headings followed by the body copy. Then I can try different heading sizes, independently of the main paragraphs.

Tip If you're copying multiple paragraphs from your word processing document, make sure that your paragraphs are separated by two returns. When pasted into Dreamweaver, the paragraph breaks will be preserved. If you just have a single return between paragraphs, Dreamweaver converts the paragraphs to line breaks.

Although it depends on the design, I rarely let the text flow all the way across the page. If my page margins are set at zero — which they often are for the graphics I use — the text then bumps right up against the edge of the browser windows. I frequently use two techniques in combination. First, I place the text in a table that is set at 95 percent width or less and that is centered on the page. This assures me that some "air" or gutter-space is on either side of my text, no matter how the browser window is sized. I'm also fond of the `<blockquote>` tag, which indents text by a browser-defined amount. You can access the `<blockquote>` tag by selecting your text and choosing the Indent button on the Property Inspector. The text blocks on the example page shown in Figure 1-8 use both techniques.

I feel that it's important to style your text in some fashion to maintain the desired look. Unless you specify the font, size, and color, you're at the mercy of your visitors' browser preferences — which can totally wreck your layout. You have two methods for defining text formatting: standard HTML tags and Cascading Style Sheets (CSS). Whenever possible, I use CSS because of its greater degree of control and flexibility. With CSS, if a client doesn't like the color of body text I've chosen or its size, I can modify it sitewide with one alteration. HTML tags, on the other hand, offer backward compatibility with 3.0 browsers. However, for most clients, the relatively small percentage of visitors still using the earlier browser versions is a fair trade-off for the power of CSS.

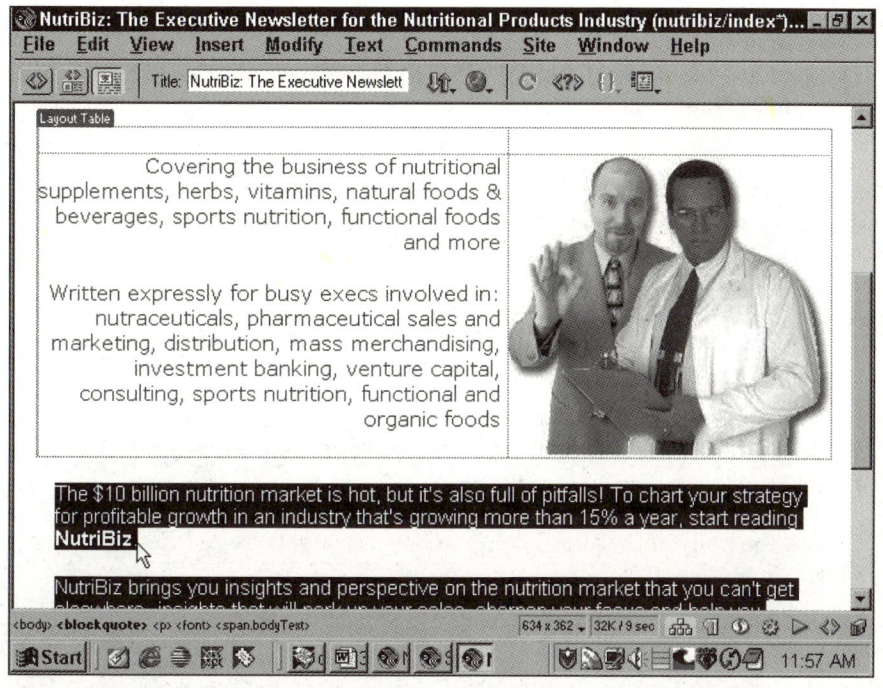

Figure 1-8: The text in the top paragraph (next to the image) is set within a centered table, whereas the text below is indented with the `<blockquote>` tag.

> **Cross-Reference:** To get the full scope of what CSS can do for you and your Web sites, see Chapter 14.

Activating the Page

Study after study has proven that an engaged viewer remembers your message better than a passive viewer. One method of grabbing people's attention is to activate your Web page in some fashion, so that some element of the page reacts to the visitor's mouse movements. This reaction could be anything from a simple rollover to the complete rewriting of a frame. Activating a page typically requires a combination of HTML and JavaScript, frequently beyond the programming skill level — or interest — of the Web designer. Luckily, Dreamweaver makes such effects possible through behaviors.

After I have the basic layout of a page done, I go back and activate the page in a fitting manner. As with any effect, too many behaviors can be more distracting than attractive; it's best to use them only when called for. At the very least, I typically use some form of rollover for the navigation bar; this is especially feasible now with Dreamweaver's tighter integration with Fireworks. But even without Fireworks, Dreamweaver enables you to construct a complete multistate navigation bar, or you can just use the Swap Image behavior to create your own.

Here's one method of activating your page:

1. In Fireworks, or another graphics program, create a series of rollover buttons with one image for each state.

   You need at least two states (Up and Over) and as many as four (Up, Over, Down, and Over While Down).

2. In Dreamweaver, remove the temporary text links for the navigation bar.

3. If you've created your rollover buttons in Fireworks, you can just choose Insert Fireworks HTML from the Objects panel.

   Dreamweaver inserts a table of sliced images, such as those in Figure 1-9, complete with all the necessary code.

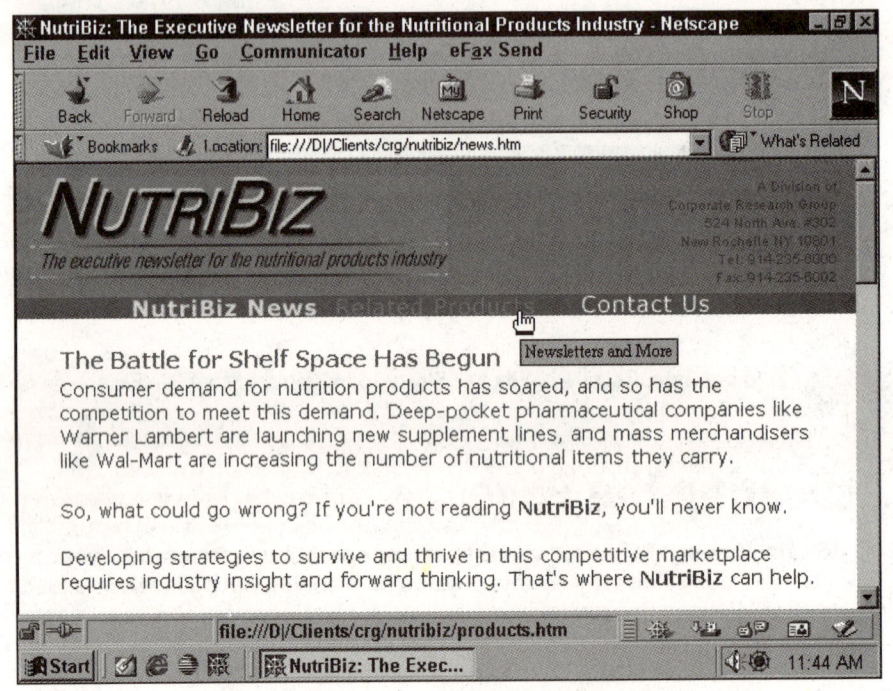

Figure 1-9: These rollover buttons were imported directly from Fireworks-generated HTML.

4. If you're working with separate images for the various rollover states, either use the Swap Image behavior or insert a Navigation Bar object. Either method enables you to select the separate images for your rollover states.

Cross-Reference

All of Dreamweaver's standard behaviors are covered in Chapter 11; information on the Navigation Bar object can be found in Chapter 6.

If I'm using tables for my layouts, I tend to nest the table containing the Navigation Bar inside the cell of another table. This technique gives me a fluid design that resizes and realigns well to match the user's browser window. For instance, in the NutriBiz example site, I merged all the columns in the row beneath the logo and then centered the table containing the navigation buttons.

New Feature

Another alternative, sure to give your page some pizzazz, are the new Flash Button objects. A *Flash Button* is a predesigned graphic template with animation and possibly sound that uses your specified text. Flash Buttons are great for quickly turning out a professional quality navigation system. Because the are actually Flash animations, they depend on the user having the Flash Player plugin installed — which, as of this writing, is the case in over 92 percent of the systems running.

After I've completed the initial elements of my page, I take advantage of one of Dreamweaver's key features: Library items. By turning my Navigation Bar into a Library item, I can easily reuse it on the same page (as I do in the example page at the bottom), and on every other page of the site. Not only does this keep consistent elements on every page — an important consideration for design — but if I ever need to update the navigation system by changing a link or adding more buttons, I can do it in one step. Moreover, Dreamweaver's Library items, if activated with behaviors, retain all the necessary code.

Cross-Reference

Library items are extremely useful for cutting your production time. Learn more about them in Chapter 18.

Previewing and Posting the Page

No matter how beautiful or spectacular your home page design, it's not a Web page until it's viewed through a Web browser and posted on the Web. Now, "the Web" could just as easily be a company intranet or the Internet. But chances are that if the page is intended to be viewed by numerous people, it will be seen under a number of different circumstances. Different operating systems, browsers, screen sizes, and resolutions are just some of the variables you have to take as a given — which is why previewing and testing your Web page is vitally important.

Here are a few pointers for initially testing your pages in development:

✦ At the very least, you should look at your Web page through versions of both major browsers. Dreamweaver enables you to specify up to 13 browsers with its Preview in Browser feature; I currently have 5 available on my system.

✦ During the initial building phase, my routine is to preview my page with both my primary browser (as of this writing, Netscape 4.7) and secondary browser (Internet Explorer 5.5) whenever I add a major component to the page.

- ✦ I make it a point to resize the page several times to see how my layout is affected by different screen sizes. If the client has specified maximum browser compatibility as a site requirement, I also look at the page under various screen resolutions.

- ✦ When a page is largely completed, I run Dreamweaver's Check Target Browsers command to make sure I'm not committing some grievous error. If incompatibilities do appear — as they do especially when checking the earliest browsers as shown in Figure 1-10 — I have to decide whether to keep the offending tag or risk the page being visited by users with those browsers.

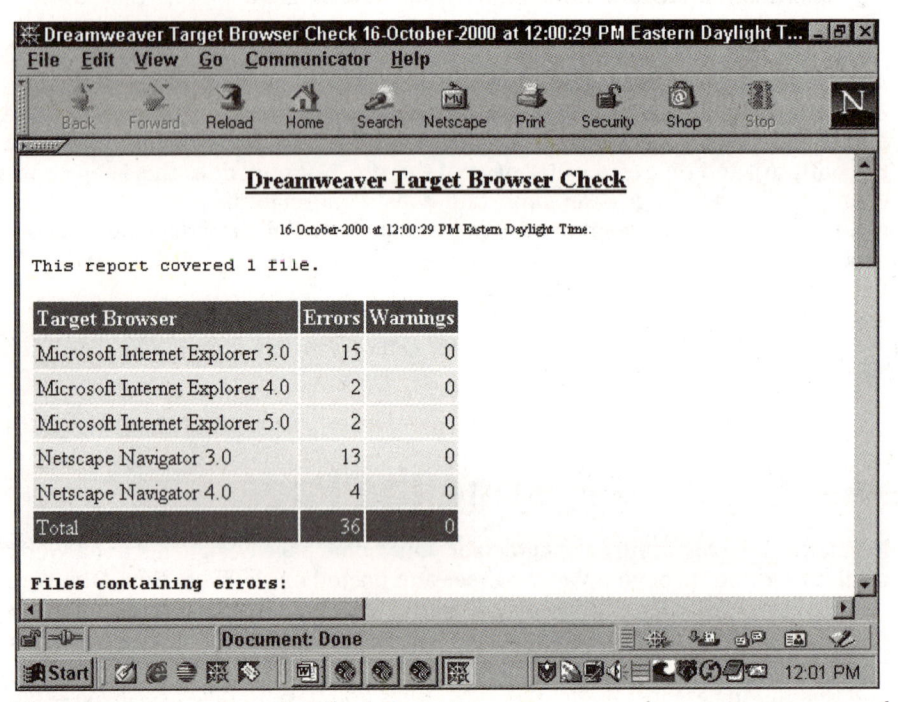

Figure 1-10: Errors from the Check Target Browser command are not uncommon when checking early browser versions.

I also make it a habit to routinely check the Download Stats found in Dreamweaver's status bar. The Download Stats show the "weight" of a page — its file size and the download time at a set speed. By default, the speed is set for a 28.8 Kbps modem, but you can alter that in the Status Bar category of Preferences. Remember that the Download Stats include all the dependent files (images and other media) as well as the size of the page itself.

Chapter 1 ✦ **QuickStart for Beginners** 17

To be sure that all my ducks are in a row and that all my links are valid, I run Dreamweaver's Check Links Sitewide command. Not only does this give me a report of broken links, but it also displays orphaned files and offers a list of external links that I can verify from its report.

My final testing phase is always conducted online. Here's a procedure that you can use for uploading your site and testing it:

1. Choose Window ⇨ Site Files to open the Site window. By this time you've already established a domain with an Internet host and edited your site definition to include the necessary FTP information.

2. Select the Connect button on the Site window. Dreamweaver logs in to the remote system and displays the remote files in the category opposite the local files.

3. Select the HTML files for the completed Web pages.

4. Choose the Put button.

5. By default, Dreamweaver asks if you'd like to include the dependent files; click Yes.

    Dreamweaver begins to transfer the HTML files and all the dependent files. All necessary subfolders (images, media) are created to replicate the local site structure on the remote site.

Note

If the Include Dependent Files dialog box does not appear, then open Preferences and, on the Site FTP category, select the Dependent Files: Prompt on Put/Check In option.

6. After the file transfer is complete, open a browser and connect to the URL for the site.

7. Navigate to every page and try all links and user actions, including rollovers. Note any "files not found" or other errors.

8. If errors occurred, return to Dreamweaver and verify the links for the problem files.

9. If necessary, repair the links and re-upload the HTML file. In most cases, you will not need to resend the dependent files.

10. Repeat Steps 6 through 9 with all available browsers and systems.

Tip

If the site is publicly viewable on the Internet, be sure to view the pages through an America Online (AOL) browser. Although AOL uses an Internet Explorer-derived browser, it also compresses graphics with its own algorithm and tends to open with smaller-than-normal windows. If you find problems, consult AOL's Webmaster Site at `http://webmaster.info.aol.com`.

Summary

When people ask me what I like about designing Web sites, I tell them that it appeals to me because it engages both my left and right brain. Web site design is, at turns, both creative and pragmatic, and Dreamweaver balances that equation with grace. Although everyone works differently, these are some of the points I try to keep in mind as I'm working:

✦ The more time spent in planning, the less time spent in revision. Get as much information as possible from the client before you begin designing.

✦ Use Dreamweaver's Site Map to prototype the site; the existing structure saves time as you begin to fill in the content.

✦ Work from the home page out. The home page is primarily used to succinctly express the client's message, and it often sets the tone for the entire site.

✦ Include some interactivity in your Web page. A static page may be beautiful to behold, but an active page enables the visitor to interact and leaves a more lasting impression.

✦ Preview your pages early and often during the development phase. It's far better to discover an incompatibility with the page half done than when you're demoing for the client.

✦ ✦ ✦

Setting Up Your First Site

CHAPTER 2

In This Chapter

Web site design and structure

Making a local site

Generating and saving pages

Previewing your Web site

Publishing online

Web sites — especially those integrating Web applications — are far more than collections of HTML documents. Every image — from the smallest navigational button to the largest image map — is a separate file that must be uploaded with your HTML page. And if you use any additional elements, such as an included script, background sound, digital video, or Java applet, their files must be transferred as well. To preview the Web site locally and view it properly on the Internet, you have to organize your material in a specific manner.

In Dreamweaver, the process of creating a site also involves developing Web applications in a particular server model. Dreamweaver is unique in its ability to author sites for a variety of application servers. While it is feasible to mix pages developed for different server models, it's not really practical. Dreamweaver enables you to select one server model for each site.

Each time you begin developing a new site, you must define several initial parameters, including the chosen server model, as described in this chapter. These steps lay the groundwork for Dreamweaver to properly link your local development site with your remote online site as well as linking properly to your data sources. For those who are just starting to create Web sites, this chapter begins with a brief discussion of approaches to online design. The remainder of the chapter is devoted to the mechanics of setting up your site and basic file manipulation.

Planning Your Site

Planning in Web design, just as in any other design process, is essential. Not only will careful planning cut your development time considerably, but it also makes it far easier to achieve a uniform look and feel for your Web site — and thus make it friendlier and easier to use. This first section briefly covers some of the basics of Web site design: what to focus on, what options to consider, and what pitfalls to avoid. If you are an established Web site developer who has covered this ground before, feel free to skip this section.

Primary considerations

Even before you choose from various models to design your site, you'll need to address the all-important issues of message, audience, and budget.

What do you want to say?

If I had to pick one overriding concern for Web site design, it would be to answer the following question: "What are you trying to say?" The clearer your idea of your message, the more focused your Web site will be. To this end, I find it useful to try to state the purpose of a Web site in one sentence. "I want to create the coolest Web site on the planet" doesn't count. Although it could be regarded as a goal, it's so open-ended that it's almost no concept at all.

Here are some examples of clearly stated Web site concepts:

- "To provide the best small-business resource center focused on Microsoft's Office software."
- "To chronicle the world's first voyage around the world by hot air balloon."
- "To advertise music lessons offered by a collective of keyboard teachers in New York City."

Who is your audience?

Right behind a site's concept — some would say neck-and-neck with it — is the site's audience. Who are you trying to reach? Quite often a site's style is heavily influenced by a clear vision of the site's intended audience. Take, for example, Macromedia's Dynamic HTML Zone (www.dhtmlzone.com). This is an excellent example of a site that is perfectly pitched toward its target; in this case, the intended audience is composed of professional developers and designers. Hence, you'll find the site snazzy but informative and filled with exciting examples of cutting-edge programming techniques.

In contrast, a site that is devoted to mass-market e-commerce must work with a very different group in mind: shoppers. Everyone at one time or another falls into this category, so we're really talking about a state of mind, rather than a profession. Many shopping sites use a very straightforward page design — one that is easily maneuverable and comforting in its repetition, and one that enables visitors to quickly find what they are looking for and, with as few impediments as possible, buy it.

What are your resources?

Unfortunately, Web sites aren't created in a vacuum. Virtually all development work happens under real-world constraints of some kind. A professional Web designer is accustomed to working within a budget. In fact, the term *budget* can apply to several concepts.

First, you have a monetary budget — how much is the client willing to spend? This translates into a combination of development time (for designers and programmers), materials (custom graphics, stock photos, and the like), and ongoing maintenance. You can build a large site with many pages that pulls dynamically from an internal database and requires very little hands-on upkeep. Or you can construct a small, graphics-intensive site that must be updated by hand weekly. Yet it's entirely possible that both sites will end up costing the same.

Second, budget also applies to the amount of time you can afford to spend on any given project. The professional Web designer is quick to realize that time is an essential commodity. The resources needed when undertaking a showcase for yourself with no deadline are very different from contracting on June 30th for a job that must be ready to launch on July 4th.

The third real-world budgetary item to consider is bandwidth. The Web, with faster modems and an improved infrastructure, is slowly shedding its image as the "World Wide Wait." That means today's Webmaster must keep a steady eye on a page's weight — how long it takes to download under typical modem rates. Of course, you can always decide to include that animated video masterpiece that takes 33 minutes to download on a 28.8 modem — you just can't expect anyone to wait to see it.

In conclusion, when you are trying to define your Web page, filter it through these three ideas: message, audience, and the various faces of the budget. The time spent visualizing your Web page in these terms will be time decidedly well spent.

Design options

Many Web professionals borrow a technique used extensively in developing other mass-marketing forms: *storyboarding*. Storyboarding for the Web entails first diagramming the various pages in your site — much like the more traditional storyboarding in videos or filmmaking — and then detailing connections for the separate pages to form the overall site. How you connect the disparate pages determines how your visitors will navigate the completed Web site.

There are several basic navigational models; the modern Web designer should be familiar with them all because each one serves a different purpose and they can be mixed and matched as needed.

The linear approach

Prior to the World Wide Web, most media formats were linear — that is, one image or page followed another in an unalterable sequence. In contrast, the Web and its interactive personality enable the user to jump from topic to topic. Nevertheless, you can still use a linear approach to a Web site and have one page appear after another, like a multimedia book.

The linear navigational model, shown in Figure 2-1, works well for computer-based training applications and other expository scenarios in which you want to tightly control the viewer's experience. Some Web designers use a linear-style entrance or exit from their main site, connected to a multilevel navigational model. One advantage that Dynamic HTML brings is that you can achieve the effects of moving through several pages in a single page through layering.

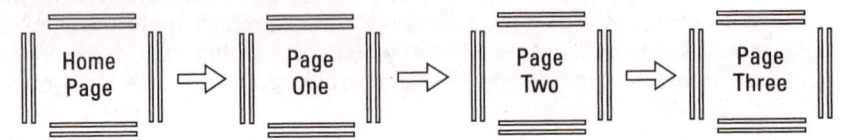

Home Page ⇒ Page One ⇒ Page Two ⇒ Page Three

Figure 2-1: The linear navigational model takes the visitor through a series of Web pages.

Caution: Keep in mind that Web search engines can index the content of every page of your site separately. Each page of your site — not just your home page — then becomes a potential independent entrance point. So be sure to include, on every page, navigation buttons back to your home page, especially if you use a linear navigational model.

The hierarchical model

Hierarchical navigational models emerge from top-down designs. These start with one key concept that becomes your home page. From the home page, users branch off to several main pages; if needed, these main pages can, in turn, branch off into many separate pages. Everything flows from the home page; it's very much like a company's organization chart, with the CEO on top followed by the various company divisions.

The hierarchical Web site, shown in Figure 2-2, is best known for maintaining a visitor's sense of place in the site. Some Web designers even depict the treelike structure as a navigation device and include each branch traveled as a link. This enables visitors to quickly retrace their steps, branch by branch, to investigate different routes.

The spoke-and-hub model

Given the Web's flexible hyperlink structure, the spoke-and-hub navigational model works extremely well. The hub is, naturally, the site's home page. The spokes projecting out from the center connect to all the major pages in the site. This layout permits fairly immediate access to any key page in just two jumps — one jump always leading back to the hub/home page and one jump leading off to a new direction. Figure 2-3 shows a typical spoke-and-hub structure for a Web site.

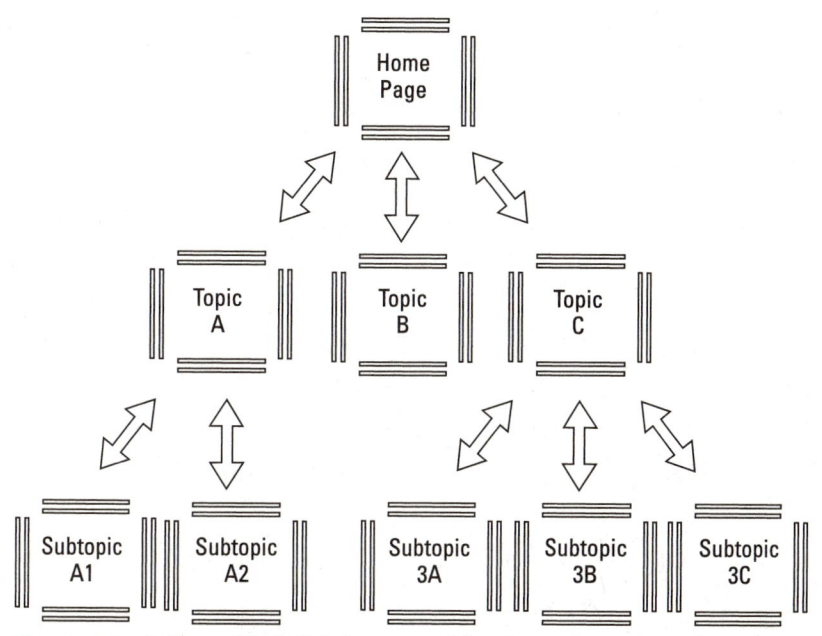

Figure 2-2: A hierarchical Web layout enables the main topics to branch into their own subtopics.

The main drawback to the spoke-and-hub structure is the constant return to the home page. Many Web designers get around this limitation by making the first jump off the hub into a Web page using frames, in which the navigation bars are always available. This design also enables visitors using nonframes-capable browsers to take a different path.

The full Web design

The approach that seems the least structured for a Web site — fullWeb — takes the most advantage of the Web's hyperlink capabilities. This design enables virtually every page to connect to every other page. The full Web design, shown in Figure 2-4, works well for sites that are explorations of a particular topic because the approach encourages visitors to experience the site according to their own needs, not based on the notions of any single designer. The danger in using full Web for your site design is that the visitor can literally get lost. As an escape hatch, many Web designers include a link to a clickable site map, especially for large-scale sites of this design.

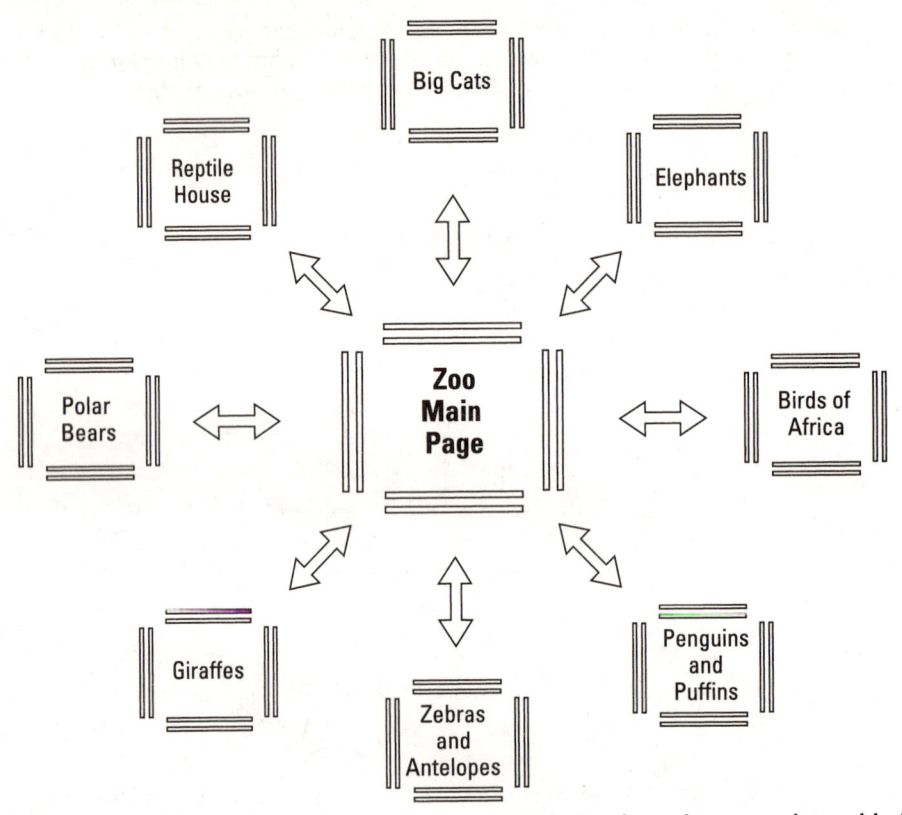

Figure 2-3: This storyboard diagram for a zoo's Web site shows how a spoke-and-hub model might work.

Defining a Site

Now that you've decided on a design and mapped your site, you're ready to set it up in Dreamweaver. When you define a site, you are telling Dreamweaver where to store your Web pages locally, where to transfer them to remotely, as well as the style of code in which to write them. Defining a site is an essential first step.

The Site Definitions dialog box is comprised of five categories of information. Only the first two — Local Info and Remote Info — are essential for site definition and are detailed in the remainder of this section.

Cross-Reference: The other categories in the Site Definition dialog box (File View Columns, Site Map Layout, and Design Notes) are helpful for working in a team environment and working visually with Dreamweaver's Site Map. You can find more information on these features in Chapter 3.

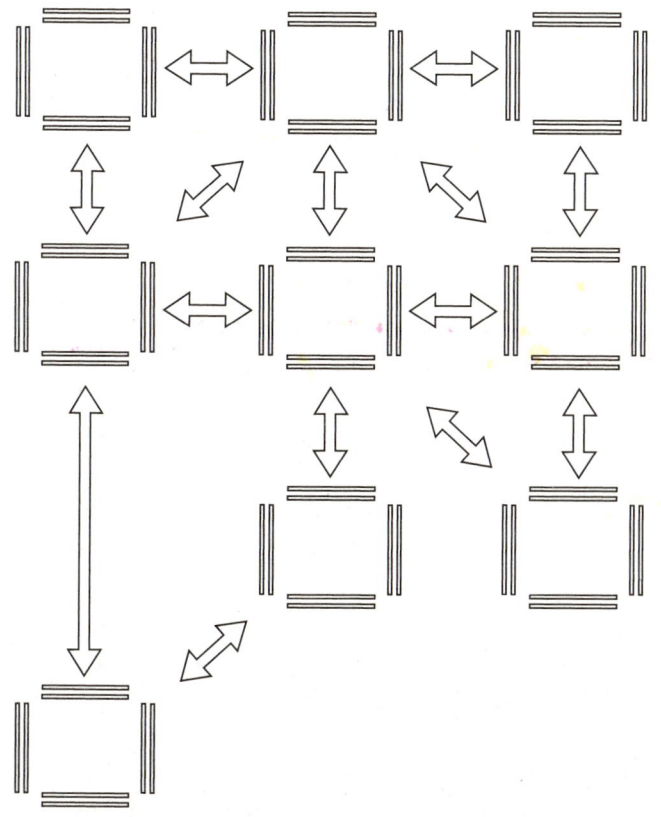

Figure 2-4: In a full Web design, each page can have multiple links to other pages.

There are three main steps to defining a site in Dreamweaver:

1. Locate the folder to be used for the local, development site.
2. Enter the remote site information.
3. Specify the application server model to be used for the site.

Establishing local connections

Once your site is on your Web server and fully operational, the site consists of many files — plain HTML, graphics and other media files — that make up the individual Web pages. All of these associated files are kept on the server in one folder, which may use one or more subfolders. This main folder is called the *remote site root*. In order for Dreamweaver to properly display your linked pages and embedded images — just as they are displayed online — the program creates a mirror of your remote site on your local development system. This primary mirror folder on your system is known as the *local site root*.

It's necessary for you to establish the local site root at the beginning of a project. This ensures that Dreamweaver duplicates the complete structure of the Web development site when it comes time to publish your pages to the Web. One of Dreamweaver's key site-management features enables you to select just the HTML pages for publication; Dreamweaver then automatically transfers all the associated files, creating any needed folders in the process. The mirror images of your local and remote site roots are critical to Dreamweaver's ability to expedite your workload in this way.

Tip If you do decide to transfer an existing Web site to a new Dreamweaver local site root, run Dreamweaver's Link Checker after you've consolidated all your files. Choose File ⇨ Check Links or press the keyboard shortcut, Shift+F8. The Link Checker tells you of broken links and orphan files as well. For more information on the Link Checker, see Chapter 3.

To set up a local site root folder in Dreamweaver, follow these steps:

1. Select Site ⇨ New Site from the main Dreamweaver menu.

   The Site window opens, followed shortly by the Site Definition dialog box, as shown in Figure 2-5.

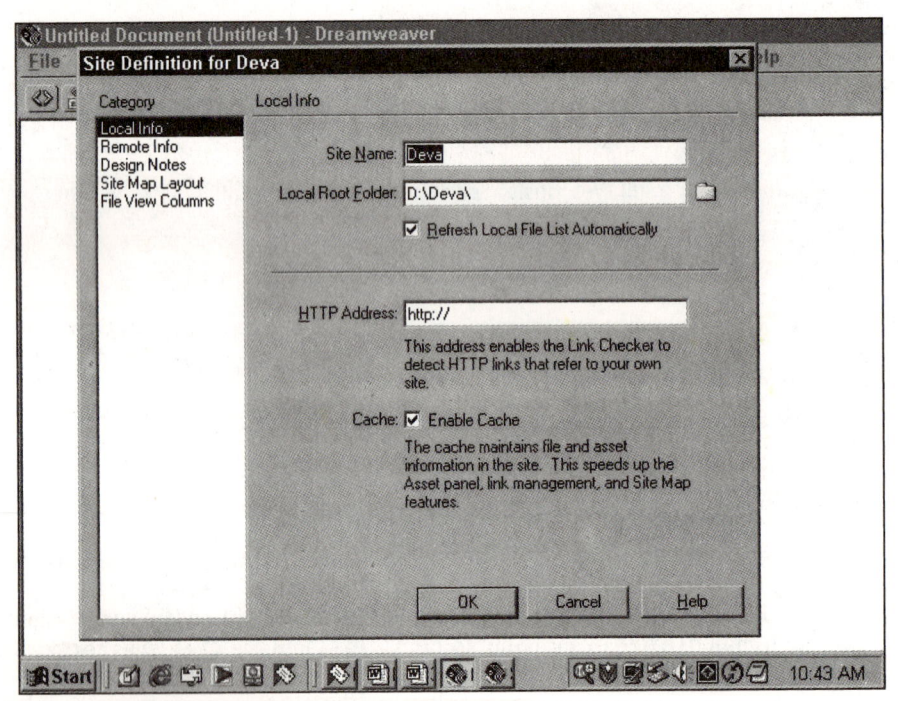

Figure 2-5: Set up your local site root through the Site Definition dialog box.

2. From the Local Info category, type a name for your site in the Site Name text box.

   This name appears in the user-defined site list displayed when you select File ➪ Open Site.

3. Specify the folder to serve as the local site root, by either typing the path name directly into the Local Root Folder text box or clicking the folder button. The Browse button opens the Choose Local Directory dialog box. When you've made your choice there, click the Select button.

4. Leave the Refresh Local File List Automatically option selected. This option ensures that new files are automatically included in the list and relieves you from having to select the Refresh command.

5. Enter the full URL for your site in the HTTP Address text box.

   When checking links for your Web site, Dreamweaver uses the HTTP address to determine whether absolute links, such as `http://www.idest/Dreamweaver/index.htm`, reference external files or files on your site.

6. For fastest performance, select the Cache option. Typically, the use of the cache speeds up link updates.

Specifying the remote site

In addition to defining the local site root, you also need to detail information pertaining to the remote site. The remote site may either be a folder accessed through the local network or via FTP (File Transfer Protocol). If your remote site is located on the local network — in this arrangement the remote site is often said to be on a *staging server* — all you need do is select or create the particular folder to house the remote site. At the appropriate time, the network administrator or other designated person from the Information Technology department, will migrate the files from the staging server to the Web or intranet server.

> **Note**
> Many Dreamweaver developers have a Web server located on their development system making it possible to have both the local and remote site on the same machine.

If, on the other hand, you post your material to a remote site via FTP, you'll need various bits of information to complete the connection. In addition to the FTP host's name — used by Dreamweaver to find the server on the Internet — you'll also need, at a minimum, the user name and password to log into the server. The host's technical support staff will provide you with this and any other necessary info.

> **Caution**
> Although it's entirely possible to develop your site locally without establishing a remote site root, it's not a recommended practice. Web sites require extensive testing in real-world settings — something that's just not possible with a local development setup. If you don't have the necessary information to establish a remote site root initially, you can still begin development locally; just be sure to transfer your files to your remote site and begin testing as soon as possible.

To enter the remote site information, follow these steps:

1. Continuing in the Site Definition dialog box, select the Remote Info category.
2. From the Remote Info category, as shown in Figure 2-6, choose the type of remote connection that applies to your site:

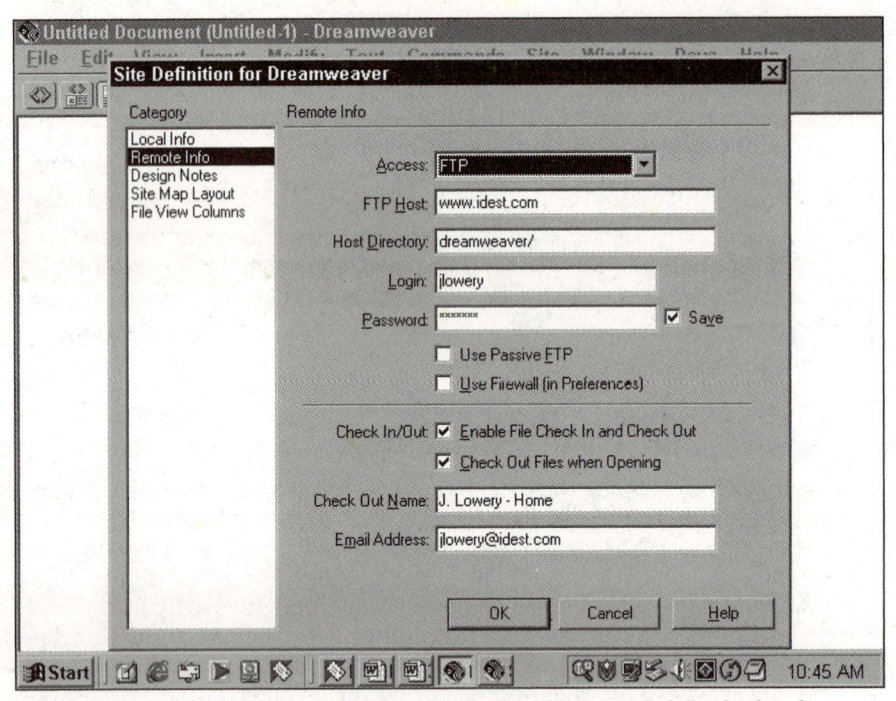

Figure 2-6: Choose whether your remote site is to be accessed via the local network or by FTP in the Web Server Info panel.

- **None:** Choose this option if your site is being developed locally and will not be uploaded to a Web server at this time.

  If you selected None for Server Access, proceed to entering the App Server Info as described in the next section.

- **Local/Network:** Select this option if you are running a local Web server and wish to store your remote site on your local drive or if your Web server is mounted as a network drive.

  If you selected Local/Network for Server Access, enter the name of the remote folder in the Remote Folder text box or click the Browse button to locate the folder. If you wish to automatically update the remote file list (recommended), leave the Refresh Remote File List Automatically option selected. Then proceed to entering the App Server Info as described in the following section.

- **FTP:** Select this option if you connect to your Web server via File Transfer Protocol (FTP).

- **SourceSafe Database:** Choose this option if your site is maintained within a SourceSafe database compatible with Microsoft Visual SourceSafe Client, version 6 on Windows or MetroWerks SourceSave version 1.10 on Macintosh.

- **WebDAV:** Select WebDAV (short for Web-based Distributed Authoring and Versioning) if your site is managed by a collaborative authoring system using WebDAV standards.

3. If FTP is selected, complete the following options:

   - **FTP Host:** The host name of the FTP connection for your Web server, usually in the form `www.sitename.com`. Do not include the full URL, such as `ftp://www.sitename.com/index.html`.

   - **Host Directory:** The directory in which publicly accessible documents are stored on the server. Typical Host Directory names are `www/public/docs/` and `public_html/htdoc/`. Your remote site root folder will be a subfolder of the Host Directory. If you are unsure of the exact name of the Host Directory, check with your Web server administrator for the proper directory path. Oftentimes the FTP Host connects to the correct directory automatically and this field is left blank.

   - **Login:** The login name you have been assigned for access to the Web server.

   - **Password:** The password necessary for you to gain access to the Web server. Many servers are case-sensitive when it comes to logins and passwords.

   - **Save:** Dreamweaver automatically selects this option after you enter a password. Deselect this box only if you and others access the server from the current system.

   - **Use Passive FTP:** Passive FTP establishes the FTP connection through the local software rather than the server. Certain firewall configurations use passive FTP; check with your network administrator to see if you need it.

   - **Use Firewall:** This option will be selected for you if you've set the Preferences with the correct host and port information.

4. If SourceSafe Database is selected, choose Settings to display the Open SourceSafe Database dialog box. In the dialog box, complete the following:

   - **Database Path:** Enter the path to the SourceSafe database; choose Browse to locate the database in a dialog box.

   - **Project:** Enter the name of the project within the SourceSafe database; this will serve as the remote site's root directory.

- **Username:** Enter your login name.
- **Password:** Enter your password.
- **Save:** Keep the Save option enabled, unless you are sharing your system and want to log in into the database each time you access it.

5. If you're building your site with a team and using a WebDAV server, complete the following information:

- **URL:** Enter the absolute URL to the directory of your site on the WebDAV server.
- **Username:** Enter your login name.
- **Password:** Enter your password.
- **Email:** Enter your e-mail address. Unlike with Dreamweaver's own Check In/Check Out feature, an e-mail address is required with WebDAV.
- **Save:** Keep the Save option enabled, unless you are sharing your system and want to log in to the database each time you access it.

> **Note:** Dreamweaver doesn't save the Site Definition information until the program exits. If Dreamweaver should "unexpectedly quit" — the politically correct term for "crash" — any changes made to the Site Definition dialog box in the session will be lost.

Managing Site Info

You can change any of the information associated with your local site roots by selecting File ➪ Open Site ➪ Define Sites (Site ➪ Open Site ➪ Define Sites) from either the main Dreamweaver menu or from the Site Window menu. Choose the site you want to modify from the Site list box at the top of the Site Information dialog box; you'll see the corresponding information for you to edit.

After your participation in a project has ended, you can remove the site from your list. Select File ➪ Open Site ➪ Define Sites (Site ➪ Open Site ➪ Define Sites) to open the Site Information dialog box, choose the site you want to remove in the Site list box, and click the Delete Site button. Note that this action removes the site only from Dreamweaver's internal list; it does not delete any files or folders from your hard drive.

With the local site root folder established, Dreamweaver can properly manage links no matter which address format is used. The various address formats are explained in the following section.

Chapter 2 ✦ Setting Up Your First Site   31

Creating and Saving New Pages

You've considered message, audience, and budget issues. You've chosen a design. You've set up your site and its address. All the preliminary planning is completed, and now you're ready to really rev up Dreamweaver and begin creating pages. This section covers the basic mechanics of opening and saving Web pages in development.

Starting Dreamweaver

Start Dreamweaver as you would any other program. Double-click the Dreamweaver program icon, or single-click if you are using Internet Explorer's Desktop Integration feature in Windows.

Building Placeholder Pages

One technique that I've found helpful over the years — and especially so with the use of document relative addressing in Dreamweaver Web projects — is what I call *placeholder pages*. These placeholder pages can fill the need to include links as you create each Web page in as effortless a manner as possible.

Let's say, for example, you've just finished laying out most of the text and graphics for your home page and you want to put in some navigational buttons. You drop in your button images and align them just so. All that's missing is the link. If you're using document relative addressing, the best way to handle assigning the link would be to click the Browse for File button in the Property Inspector and select your file. But what do you do if you haven't created any other pages yet and there aren't any files to select? That's when you can put placeholder pages to work.

After you've designed the basics of your site and created your local site root, as described elsewhere in this chapter, start with a blank Dreamweaver page. Type a single identifying word on the page and save it in the local site root. Do this for all the Web pages in your plan. When it comes time to make your links, all you have to do is point and click to the appropriate placeholder page. This arrangement also gives you an immediate framework for link testing. When it comes time to work on the next page, just open up the correct placeholder page and start to work.

Another style of working involves using the Site window as your base of operations, rather than the Document window. It's very easy in Dreamweaver to choose File ➪ New File from the Site Window menu several times and create the basic files of your site. You can even create a file and immediately link to it by choosing File ➪ Link to New File; a dialog box opens, allowing you to specify the file name, title of the new document and text for the link. Moreover, any needed subfolders, such as ones for images or other media, can be created by selecting File ➪ New Folder.

Opening Other Types of Files

Dreamweaver defaults to searching for HTML files with an extension of either .html or .htm. To look for other types of files, select the Files of Type arrow button. Dreamweaver allows several other file types, including server-side includes (.shtml, .shtm, or .stm), Active server pages (.asp), and Cold Fusion (.cfm or .cfml). If you need to load a valid HTML file with a different extension, select the All Files option.

If you are working consistently with a different file format, you can add your own extensions and file types to the Dreamweaver Open File dialog box. In the Configuration folder, there is an editable text file called Extensions.txt. Open this file in your favorite text editor to make any additions. If you use Dreamweaver, be sure to edit the file in the HTML Inspector to see the correct format.

The syntax must follow the format of the standard Extensions.txt file:

```
HTM,HTML,ASP,JSP,CFM,CFML,TXT,SHTM,SHTML,STM,LASSO,XML:
All Documents
HTM,HTML:HTML Documents
SHTM,SHTML,STM:Server-Side Includes
XML:XML Files
LBI:Library Files
DWT:Template Files
CSS:Style Sheets
ASP:Active Server Pages
CFM,CFML:Cold Fusion Templates
TXT:Text Files
PHP:PHP Files
LASSO:Lasso Files
JSP:Java Server Pages
```

After the splash screen, Dreamweaver opens with a new blank page. This page is created from the Default.html file found in the Dreamweaver/Configuration/Templates folder. Of course, it's possible that you'll want to replace the original Default.html file with one of your own — perhaps with your copyright information. All of your blank pages will then be created from a template that you've created.

> **Tip** If you do decide to create your own Default template, it's probably a good idea to rename the Dreamweaver Default template — as Original-Default.html or something similar — prior to creating your new, personalized Default template.

Opening an existing file

If you're looking to work on a Web page in Dreamweaver that was created in another application, choose File ➪ Open, or the keyboard shortcut Ctrl+O (Command+O). From the standard Open File dialog box, you can browse to your file's location and select it.

If you have just started Dreamweaver or if your current document is blank, your selected file will load into the current window. If, however, you have another Web page open or have begun creating a new one, Dreamweaver opens your file in a new window.

When you first open an existing Web page, Dreamweaver checks the HTML syntax. If it finds any errors, Dreamweaver corrects them and then informs you of the corrections through the HTML Parser Results dialog box. You can turn off this HTML syntax-checking feature. Select Edit ⇨ Preferences and then, from the Code Rewriting category of the Preferences dialog box, deselect one or more of the checkbox options for HTML syntax-checking.

To add an entry, place your cursor at the end of the line above where you want your new file format to be placed, and press Enter (Return). Type in your file extension(s) in capital letters, followed by a colon and then the text description. Save the Extensions.txt file and restart Dreamweaver to see your modifications.

Opening a new window

You can work on as many Dreamweaver documents as your system memory can sustain. When you choose File ⇨ New or one of the keyboard shortcuts (Ctrl+N or Command+N), Dreamweaver opens a new blank page in a separate window. Once the window is open, you can switch among the various windows. To do this in Windows, you select the appropriate icon in the taskbar or use the Alt+Tab method. To switch between Dreamweaver windows on a Macintosh, click on the individual window or use the Window menu.

Opening a new page

After working for a while on a design, you sometimes need to start over or switch entirely to a new project. In either case, choose File ⇨ New or, in Windows, one of the keyboard shortcuts, Ctrl+Shift+N (Command+Shift+N). This closes the current document and opens a new blank page in the same window.

Tip You can also drag and drop an HTML file onto the Dreamweaver Document window or — if you're just starting a session — onto the Dreamweaver icon on your desktop.

If you've made any modifications to your page, Dreamweaver asks if you would like to save the page. Click the Yes button to save the file or the No button to continue without saving it. To abort the new page opening, click Cancel.

Note You can easily tell a page has been altered since the last save by looking at the title bar. Dreamweaver places an asterisk after the filename in the title bar for modified pages. Dreamweaver is even smart enough to properly remove the asterisk should you reverse your changes with the Undo command or the History palette.

Each time you open a new page, whether in the existing window or in a new window, Dreamweaver temporarily names the file "Untitled-n," where *n* is the next number in sequence. This prevents you from accidentally overwriting a new file opened in the same session.

Saving your page

Saving your work is very important in any computer-related task, and Dreamweaver is no exception. To initially save the current page, choose File ➪ Save or the keyboard shortcut Ctrl+S (Command+S). The Save dialog box opens; you can enter a filename and, if desired, a different path.

By default, all files are saved with a .htm filename extension for Windows and .html for Macintosh. To save your file with another extension, such as .shtml, change the Files of Type option to the specific file type and then enter your full filename, without the extension.

> **Caution**
> It seems kind of backward in this day and age of long filenames, but it's still a good idea to choose names for your files without spaces or punctuation other than an underscore or hyphen. Otherwise, not all servers will read the filename correctly and you'll have problems linking your pages.

Closing the page

When you're finished with a page you can close a file without quitting Dreamweaver. To close a page, select File ➪ Close or the keyboard shortcuts, Ctrl+W (Command+W). If you made any changes to the page since you saved it last, Dreamweaver prompts you to save it.

Windows users will note that if you only have one Dreamweaver window open and you close the current page, Dreamweaver asks you if you'd like to quit the program.

Quitting the program

Once you're done for the day—or, more often, the late, late night—you can close Dreamweaver by choosing File ➪ Exit (File ➪ Quit) or one of the standard keyboard shortcuts, Ctrl+Q (Command+Q).

In Windows systems, to make sure you're really ready to shut down the program, Dreamweaver asks you to confirm your desire to quit. If you're confident that you won't quit the program accidentally, select the Don't Warn Me Again option to stop this dialog box from reappearing.

> **Caution**
> You won't receive an opportunity to confirm your choice if you quit from the Site window in Windows or in Macintosh systems. That's because, on Windows, Dreamweaver's Site window and Document window are really separate applications.

Previewing Your Web Pages

When using Dreamweaver or any other Web authoring tool, it's important to constantly check your progress in one or more browsers. Dreamweaver's Document window offers a near-browser view of your Web page, but because of the variations among the different browsers, it's imperative that you preview your page early and often. Dreamweaver offers you easy access to a maximum of 20 browsers — and they're just a function key away.

> **Note:** Don't confuse Dreamweaver's Design view with the Preview in Browser feature. In Design view, Dreamweaver can only show you an approximation of how your page will look on the Web but not all aspects — such as links and rollovers — are active. You need to preview and test your page in a variety of browsers to truly see how your page looks and behaves on the Web.

You add a browser to your preview list by selecting File ⇨ Preview in Browser ⇨ Edit Browser List or by choosing the Preview in Browser category from the Preferences dialog box. Both actions open the Preview in Browser Preferences panel. Here's a brief description of the steps for editing your browser list:

1. Select File ⇨ Preview in Browser ⇨ Edit Browser List.

2. To add a browser (up to 20), click the Add button and fill out the following fields:

    - **Name:** How you want the browser listed.

    - **Application:** Type in the path to the browser program or click the Browse button to locate the browser executable (.EXE) file.

    - **Primary Browser/Secondary Browser:** If desired, select one of these checkboxes to designate the current browser as such.

3. After you've added a browser to your list, you can easily edit or delete it. Choose File ⇨ Preview in Browser ⇨ Edit Browser List as before, and highlight the browser you want to modify or delete.

4. To alter your selection, click the Edit button. To delete your selection, click the Remove button.

5. After you've completed your modifications, click OK to close the dialog box.

Once you've added one or more browsers to your list, you can preview the current page in these browsers. Select File ⇨ Preview in Browser ⇨ BrowserName, where BrowserName indicates the particular program. Dreamweaver saves the page to a temporary file, starts the browser, and loads the page.

Note that in order to view any changes you've made to your Web page under construction, you must select the Preview in Browser menu option again (or press one of the function keys for primary/secondary browser previewing, described in the following paragraph). Clicking the Refresh/Reload button in your browser will not load in any modifications. The temporary preview files are deleted when you quit Dreamweaver.

> **Tip** Dreamweaver saves preview files with a file namelike this: TMP5c34jymi4q.htm; a unique name is generated with each preview to ensure that the browser does not load the page from the cache. If Dreamweaver unexpectedly quits, these TMP files are not deleted. Feel free to delete any TMP files you find in your site.

You can also use keyboard shortcuts to preview two different browsers, by pressing a function key: Press F12 to preview the current Dreamweaver page in your primary browser, and Ctrl+F12 (Command+F12) to preview the same page in your secondary browser. These are the Primary and Secondary Browser settings you establish in the Preferences/Preview in Browser dialog box.

In fact, with Dreamweaver's Preview in Browser Preferences you can so easily switch the designations of Primary and Secondary browser that you can use that setup for "debugging" a Web page in any browser, simply by changing the preferences. Go to the Preview in Browser Preferences pane, select the browser you want to use for debugging, and check the appropriate checkbox to designate the browser as Primary or Secondary. In the list of browsers in this Preferences pane, you'll see the indicator of F12 or Ctrl+F12 (Command+F12) appear next to the browser's name.

> **Tip** In addition to checking your Web page output on a variety of browsers on your system, it's also a good idea to preview the page on other platforms. If you're designing on a Macintosh, try to view your pages on a Windows system, and vice versa. Watch out for some not-so-subtle differences between the two environments, in terms of color rendering (colors in Macs tend to be brighter than in PCs) and screen resolution.

Putting Your Pages Online

The final phase of setting up your Dreamweaver site is publishing your pages to the Web. When you begin this publishing process is up to you. Some Web designers wait until everything is absolutely perfect on the local development site and then upload everything at once. Others like to establish an early connection to the remote site and extend the transfer of files over a longer period of time.

I fall into the latter camp. When I start transferring files at the beginning of the process, I find that I catch my mistakes earlier and avoid having to effect massive changes to the site after everything is up. For example, in developing one large site, I started out using filenames with mixed case, as in ELFhome.html. After publishing some early drafts of a few Web pages, however, I discovered that the host had switched servers; on the new server, filenames had to be all lowercase. Had I waited until the last moment to upload everything, I would have been faced with an unexpected and gigantic search-and-replace job.

Once you've established your local site root — and you've included your remote site's FTP information in the setup — the actual publishing of your files to the Web is a very straightforward process. To transfer your local Web pages to an online site, follow these steps:

1. Choose File ⇨ Open Site ⇨ Site Name (Site ⇨ Open Site ⇨ Site Name), where Site Name is the current site.

   The Site window opens, displaying the current site.

2. From the Site window, click the Connect button. (You may need to complete your connection to the Internet prior to choosing the Connect button.)

   Dreamweaver displays a message box showing the progress of the connection.

3. If you didn't enter a password in the Site Information dialog box, or if you entered a password but didn't opt to save it, Dreamweaver asks you to type in your password.

   Once the connection is complete, the directory listing of the remote site appears in the Remote (left-hand by default) pane of the Site window.

4. In the Local (right-hand by default) pane, highlight the HTML files you would like to transfer.

5. Click the Put button at the top of the Site window.

6. Dreamweaver asks if you would like to move the dependent files as well. Select Yes to transfer all embedded graphics and other objects, or No if you'd prefer to move these yourself. You can also select the Don't Ask Me Again box to make transfers of dependent files automatic in the future.

   Dreamweaver displays the progress of the file transfer in the Site window's status bar.

7. When each file transfer is finished, Dreamweaver places a green checkmark next to each file (if File Check In/Out has been enabled in the Site FTP Preferences pane).

8. When you've finished transferring your files, click the Disconnect button.

> **Cross-Reference**
> Some files, especially CGI programs, require that you set the file permissions before they can be used.

Remember, the only files you have to highlight for transfer to the remote site are the HTML files. As noted previously, Dreamweaver automatically transfers any dependent files (if you allow it), which means that you'll never forget to move a GIF again! (Nor will you ever move an unnecessary file, such as an earlier version of an image, by mistake.) Moreover, Dreamweaver automatically creates any subfolders necessary to maintain the site's integrity. These two features combined will save you substantial time and worry.

So now your site has been prepped from the planning stages, through the local site root, and onto the Web. Congratulations — all that's left is to fill those pages with insightful content, amazing graphics, and wondrous code. Let's get to it!

Summary

In this chapter, you studied some options for planning your Web site and what you need to do in Dreamweaver to initialize the site. This planning and initialization process is not a detailed one, but there are particular steps to take that can greatly smooth your development path down the road.

- ✦ Put as much time into planning your site as possible. The more clearly conceived the site, the cleaner the execution.
- ✦ Set up your local site root in Dreamweaver right away. The local site root is essential for Dreamweaver to properly publish your files to the remote site later.
- ✦ Preview early, often, and with various browsers. Dreamweaver gives you quick function-key access to a primary and secondary browser. Check your pages frequently in these browsers, and then spend some time checking your pages against other available browsers and browser versions.
- ✦ Establish an early connection to the Web and use it frequently. You can begin publishing your local site through Dreamweaver's Site window almost immediately.

In the next chapter, you'll learn how to publish your site to the Internet in Dreamweaver.

✦ ✦ ✦

CHAPTER 3

Publishing with the Site Window

In This Chapter

Site management principles

Working with the Site window

Managing Web site files

Using the Site window's file Check In/Check Out

Running the Link Checker

Exploring the Site Map

Site management is an essential part of a Webmaster's job description. Far from static designs, the Web site is not like a magazine advertisement that you're finished with as soon as you send the file to the printer. Publishing your Web site pages on the Internet is really just the first step in an ongoing — often day-to-day — management task.

Dreamweaver includes an integrated but separate window known as the Site window to handle all your Web management needs. With the Site window, you can do the following:

- ✦ Transfer files to your remote site from your local development site and back again
- ✦ Issue system commands to enable CGI programs on the server
- ✦ Monitor your Web site for broken links and orphaned files
- ✦ Check a file in or out during team Web development

This chapter covers these site management functions and more. However, before you begin exploring the Site window features, it's helpful to know a little more about site management in Dreamweaver.

Site Management with Dreamweaver

At the simplest level, *site management* means transferring your files from the local drive to a publishing server. This is standard File Transfer Protocol (FTP), and many designers are accustomed to working with tools such as WS_FTP and Fetch. These utilities, however, only help you to move files back and forth. In a medium-to-large Web site, other issues must be addressed. For instance, consider the following:

- What happens when a large group is working on a single Web site? What prevents the graphics designer from altering the same file the JavaScript programmer is modifying?
- How can you tell which version of your logo is the final one among the 15 working versions in your local site root folder?
- Do you have to update all your files every time some change is made to a few? Or can you only update those that have changed? How can you tell which ones have changed?

To help the Dreamweaver developer cope with these issues and avoid the type of frustration they can produce, a useful site management tool is included within Dreamweaver: the Site window. Its key features include the following:

- A quick, visual view of the elements of your site on your local and remote directories
- Fast drag-and-drop functionality for transferring files with dependent file support
- Site management check-in and check-out tools for groups working on files within the same Web site
- A Link Checker that helps you identify broken or unused objects being posted to your site
- A Site Map that enables you to both visualize your Web site structure and alter it

On Windows systems, the Site window runs as a connected but independent process, so that you can close your document window when you're finished designing and then publish your files to the Web through the Site window.

Note: The Dreamweaver commands related to the Site window features are in different places on the Windows and Macintosh systems. In Windows, the Site window has its own menu bar; all the Windows-oriented references in this chapter refer to this menu. In addition, Dreamweaver includes a Site menu in the Document window that repeats many commands for easy access. Because Macintosh systems don't have a separate menu for a program's individual windows, Dreamweaver organizes the Site functions in a Site category of the main menu bar.

Setting Up a New Site

The first step in developing an effective site — one that links to other Web pages, uses images and library files, and offers other site root–relative links — is, of course, to establish a site. Dreamweaver has made this very easy to do.

> **Cross-Reference**: For complete, detailed information on establishing your initial site, see Chapter 2.

You need to create a folder on your development system that contains the entire HTML, as well as graphics, media, and other files, needed by the site. To create a new site, choose Site ⇨ New Site. The Site Definition dialog box opens with the Local Info category selected, as shown in Figure 3-1. Here you find the information and settings for the current site you are developing. Once you've entered this information, you seldom need to modify it.

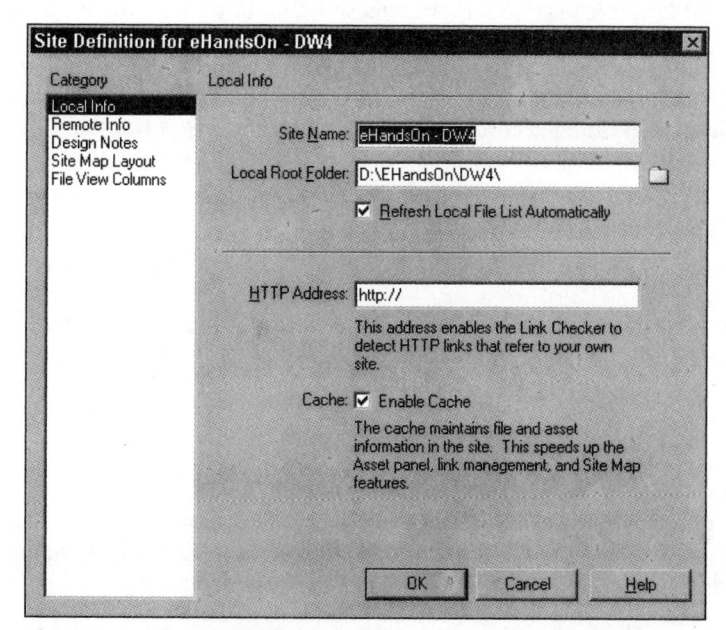

Figure 3-1: The Site Definition dialog box contains settings for the current site you are developing.

The data in the Site Definition dialog box is divided into five categories: Local Info, Remote Info, Design Notes, Site Map Layout, and File View Columns.

Local directory information

The local directory is in a folder on your development system, either on your own hard drive or on a network server.

Site Name

The site name is the name that appears in the Site ➪ Open Site list. The site name is a reference only you need to know, and it can be as fancy as you want. No hard-and-fast rules exist for creating a site name, except you should keep the name simple so you can easily reference it later. In a large Web design firm, you may need to develop more structured methods for naming various clients' Web sites.

Local Root Folder

The Local Root Folder is the location on your hard drive, or in a network folder, where you place your HTML pages, images, plug-in files, and Library items. Remember, the root folder is essential to an effective Dreamweaver site. As you add links to other Web pages and images, Dreamweaver needs to maintain the relative links between files. The benefit of this becomes apparent when you upload your files to a Web server. By maintaining a root-relative relationship, you ensure that all of the files and associated images can transfer seamlessly together onto any Web site. You won't have to go back and replace the code for any broken images.

Refresh Local File List Automatically

When the Refresh Local File List Automatically option is selected, Dreamweaver updates the list every time Dreamweaver or any other program adds a new file. Although it takes a bit more processing power to constantly watch and update the folder, it's a helpful option and I recommend always selecting it. Without the option checked, you need to choose View ➪ Refresh Local (Site ➪ Site Map View ➪ Refresh Local) or use the keyboard shortcut, Shift+F5, to see the latest files.

HTTP Address

The information entered in the HTTP Address field is used when you access the Link Checker. In this field, you enter the remote URL that corresponds to the local root folder, as if it were a regular Web address.

For example, say you are developing a Web site for My Frozen Custard, Inc. In the HTTP Address field, you would enter the URL for the Web site, as follows:

```
http://www.myfrozencustard.com/
```

With this information, the Link Checker can compare absolute addresses embedded in your Web page to see whether those addresses refer to internal or external files.

Cache

Put a checkmark in the Cache checkbox to speed up Dreamweaver's links and site management tasks.

Remote Info

The Remote Info category contains all of the information required for you to post your files to a remote server. The setup allows for any type of host directory. Typically, though, you upload your files to either a Unix or an NT Web server.

From the Remote Info category (see Figure 3-2), choose Local/Network from the Access drop-down menu to enter or select a folder on your hard drive or on the network from which your files will be served. If you're working on a big site in development with a team of Web-builders, you'll find Dreamweaver 4's new connectivity to SourceSafe databases and WebDAV servers extremely helpful. Should you choose either of these options for remote site access, you'll need to select the Settings button that appears and fill out the required information in the displayed dialog box.

Select FTP from the Access drop-down menu to be presented with a dialog box requesting information needed to access your remote site.

Tip: If you don't know the name of your FTP host server or any of the other required host site information (directory, login, password, and firewall preferences), contact your ISP or system administrator. If a hosting server is not yet established, keep Server Access set to None.

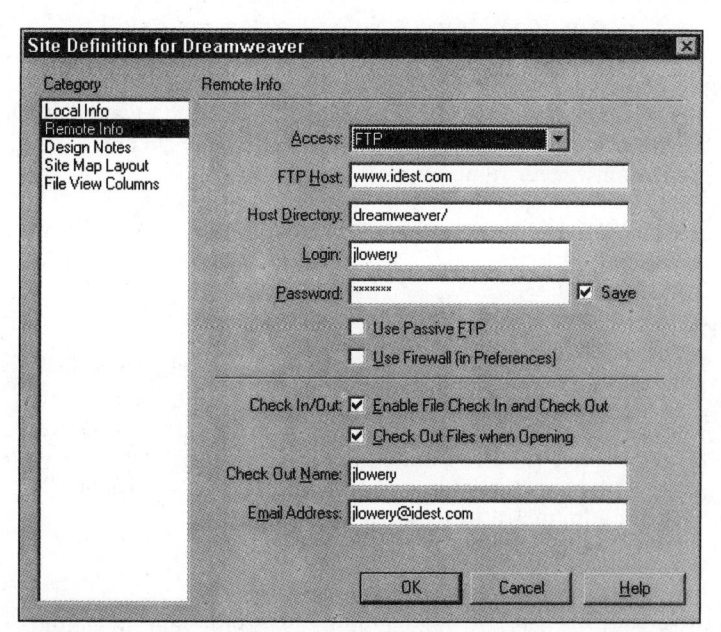

Figure 3-2: Information entered in the Remote Info category is essential for Dreamweaver to connect with your remote site.

FTP Host

The FTP Host is the name of the server on which you will be placing your files. The names for the host will be something like the following:

```
www.yourdomain.com
ftp.yourdomain.com
```

Do not include the protocol information, such as `http://` or `ftp://`, in the FTP host name.

Host Directory

The host directory is the one in which publicly accessible documents are stored on the server. Your remote site root folder will be a subfolder of the host directory. Here's an example of the host directory information:

```
/usr/www/htdocs/jlowery
```

If you don't know the proper directory path, check with your Web server administrator or ISP.

Login and Password

A login and password are required to transfer your files from your local root folder to the host. Your login is a unique name that tells the host who you are. Only you and the host should know your password. Every time you upload or download a file from the host server, you are asked for your password. If you don't want to have to retype your password each time you log on, just select the Save checkbox next to your password, and Dreamweaver remembers it.

Caution For security reasons, it is highly recommended that you do not allow anyone to know your password.

Use Passive FTP

During a normal FTP process, one computer (the client) establishes a connection with another (the server) and then requests data to be sent. Firewall-protected servers do not allow the initial connection to be made, so no data can be transferred. Passive FTP establishes the FTP connection through the local software rather than the server. The majority of firewall configurations use passive FTP; check with your network administrator to see if you need it.

Use Firewall

Firewalls are security features used by many companies to prevent unwanted access to internal documents. Many different types of firewalls exist, and all have a multitude of security settings. For instance, some firewalls enable people within a company to move documents back and forth through the firewall without any problems. Other companies will not allow Java or ActiveX controls to be moved through the firewall.

If you have a firewall that requires additional security to upload and download files, you should enable the Use Firewall checkbox in the Site Definition window. Selecting this checkbox requires that you go to Dreamweaver Preferences and fill out additional information on proxy servers. A proxy server enables you to navigate files through a firewall.

To make the appropriate proxy server changes, go to Edit ⇨ Preferences and choose the Site category from the Preferences dialog box. This category of settings contains selections for firewall information. Enter the firewall host name and port number, which can be provided to you by your ISP or system administrator. By default, most firewalls use port 21.

Check In/Out

You can enable or disable Dreamweaver's file management features by choosing the Check In/Out option. When you select Enable File Check In and Check Out, additional fields become available. You then can select the Check Out Files While Opening option, which automates the check-out process to some degree.

The name you enter in the Check Out Name field is used to inform others in your group when you have downloaded a file from the host server. Because the Check Out Name is one of several columns of information in the Local and Remote panes of the Site window, it's a good idea to keep the name relatively short. (Your initials are an ideal choice for Check Out Name, if that is appropriate.)

New Feature: If you enter your e-mail address in the aptly named field, Dreamweaver presents the check out name as a clickable link that invokes your system's e-mail editor to send a message. The E-mail Address feature enables team members to communicate directly with other team members who may have checked out a particular file.

Integrating Design Notes

Web sites can be complex creations, particularly when worked on by a team of designers, coders, and content providers. Dreamweaver offers a feature aimed at enhancing the communication between various team members: Design Notes. A Design Note can be attached to any Dreamweaver-created page, or any media inserted into a Dreamweaver page, and easily read from within Dreamweaver. Design Notes are also used extensively to facilitate the integration of Flash and Fireworks with Dreamweaver.

To be truly useful, the entire team needs to gain access to the Design Notes. Dreamweaver enables you to maintain the Design Notes on the remote server, as if another dependent file. The preferences in the Define Sites dialog box, shown in Figure 3-3, set up this option, and also give you a simple way to remove all unused Design Notes.

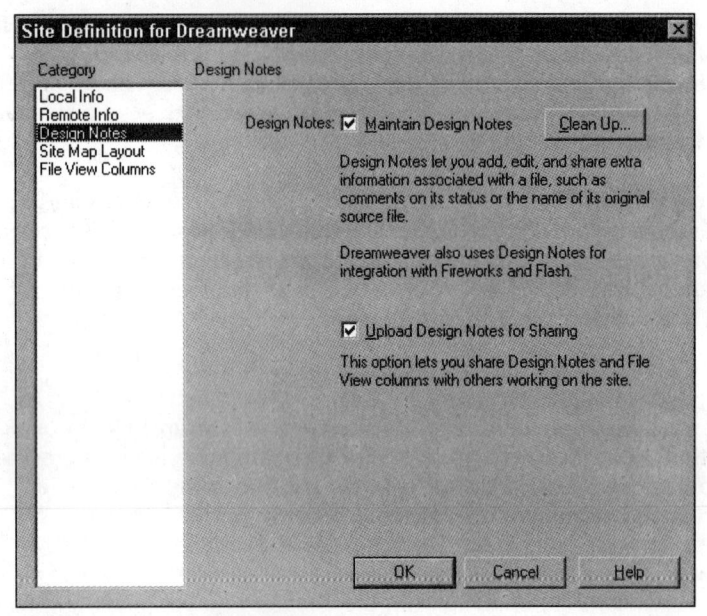

Figure 3-3: Use Design Notes to store information about HTML pages, graphics, or any other Web elements.

Options

Design Notes have only two options. The first option, Maintain Design Notes, enables Design Notes functionality for the site. It must be enabled to add or modify a Design Note for any page within the site. When a file is moved, this option also causes a Design Note to follow its associated file. The second option, Upload Design Notes for Sharing, "gets" or "puts" the Design Note when its associated file is transferred.

> **Tip** Design note files have an extension of .mno and are stored in a _notes folder. While they physically take up little room, typically under 1K, they greatly enhance your workflow, especially if you're using Fireworks and Flash. I strongly recommend that you keep Maintain Design Notes enabled.

Clean Up

If the Maintain Design Notes option is enabled and a Dreamweaver file is deleted from within Dreamweaver, the associated Design Note is removed also. However, if you delete, move, or rename your HTML files in any other way — with a file manager or other program — the Design Note remains. Select the Clean Up button to remove any Design Notes that no longer have associated HTML files.

Modifying the Site Map

You can control the way that Dreamweaver displays a Site Map in the Site Map Layout category (see Figure 3-4). In the Site Definition dialog box, select Site Map Layout from the Category list to access the Site Map options.

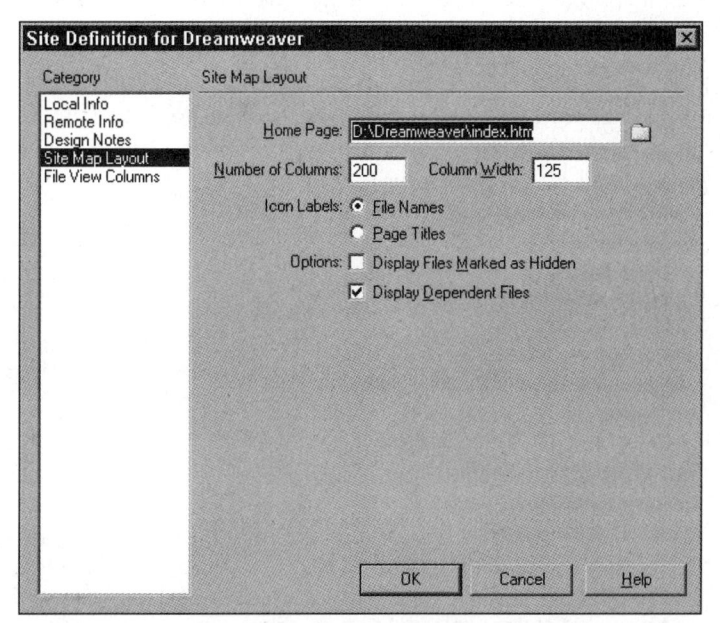

Figure 3-4: You can control what the Site Map shows as well as its overall appearance through the Site Map Layout category.

Home Page

By default, Dreamweaver looks for a file called index.html, index.htm, or default.htm (in that order) in your Local root folder from which to begin creating a Site Map. You can choose another page to appear at the top level of your Site Map by selecting a different file to serve as your home page.

> **Tip** It's best to include a home page if you plan on using the Site Map feature at all when defining the site. If one is not available, you can just enter the name for the file, like index.htm, in the Home Page field and press Tab; Dreamweaver will create the file for you.

Number of Columns/Column Width

These options (Number of Columns/Column Width) control the way your Site Map is displayed on your screen. You can modify these values in order to make the Site Map fit more easily onto a single page for printing.

Tip: By default, the Site Map displays horizontally. You can switch the layout to vertical by changing the Number of Columns field to 1.

Icon Labels

The Icon Labels option enables you to select whether the icons in your Site Map should be displayed using their filenames or their page titles. Page titles are derived from the `<title>` tag in the `<head>` section of an HTML document. While this method can be more descriptive, you have to remember to insert the title, either through the Page Properties dialog box — by revealing the Head Content, selecting the Title icon, and entering the desired text in the Title Property Inspector — or entering it into the Title field of the Document window's toolbar. If you don't assign each page a title, Dreamweaver uses "Untitled Document" as the title.

Options

Checking Display Files Marked as Hidden includes hidden HTML files in your Site Map Layout; checking Display Dependent Files includes non-HTML files, such as graphics image files or external JavaScript files, in your Site Map Layout.

File View Columns

Building a major Web site can be an organizational nightmare. Different teams — consisting of graphic artists, coders, and layout designers — are often working on different sections of the site at the same time. While certain pages are finished, others are in process, or have yet to be drafted. Even relatively small Web-design shops need to track the progress of their various clients' sites in order to be productive.

New Feature: For Web developers, a major organizational advantage, now available in Dreamweaver 4, is the ability to create custom informational columns in the Site window's file view. The File View Columns feature works by storing information in an HTML or other file's Design Note; in essence, with a custom file view column, you can see what's in the Design Note at a glance. File view columns may also be re-ordered to put your project's most important details up front and less necessary built-in columns may be hidden.

Why are custom file view columns important? Let's say your team is working on a large site with a tight deadline. You need to keep track of which pages are completed and which need work. Create a custom file view column called Status, and then list for each file the percentage of completed work, such as 0%, 50%, or 100%. With one click of the Status column header, you can sort all the files, grouping them by the completed percentages, and instantly identifying which files need immediate attention. Add another custom column to include the name of the team member assigned to each page and you've got an instant contact list.

To add a new column in the file view, follow these steps:

1. Choose View ⇨ File View Columns from the Site window on a Windows system or Site ⇨ Site Files View ⇨ File View Columns on a Mac.

    The File View Columns category of the Site Definition dialog box appears.

2. Select the Add button.

    A new entry, initially called untitled, is added to the bottom of the column list.

3. In the Column Name field, enter a unique name to identify your column.

    There are no real restrictions for a column name, but it's best from a practical standpoint to keep them short.

4. In the Associate with Design Note field, enter a custom design note field or choose one of the existing fields from the drop-down list.

5. From the Align option, choose how the information is to be aligned in the column: Left, Center, or Right.

6. Make sure the Show option is selected.

7. To change the order in which your column is displayed on the screen — initially it's the final column, all the way on the right — use the Up and Down buttons to reposition the new column in the list.

    All of the built-in columns, except for Name, can also be moved to a new position. You can also hide a column by selecting it and deselecting the Show option.

8. Click OK when you're done.

With the custom column showing in the file view, enter information for that column in one of the following two ways:

✦ Right-click (control-click) on the filename and choose Design Notes. Then select the All Info tab of the Design Notes dialog box and enter the data in the Value field.

✦ In the file view pane of the Site window, click twice on the custom column for the file in question. The current information in the custom column, if any, will highlight and can be modified directly. Press Enter (Return) when you're done.

Using the Site Window

In Dreamweaver, some site commands, such as Put (which transfers a file from your local to remote site), can be called without using the Site window, but the Site window is "home base" for almost all of Dreamweaver's sitewide functions. You can open the Site window by any of the following methods:

- Choose Site ⇨ Open Site ⇨ Your Site.
- Select the Site button from the Launcher or Show Site from the Mini Launcher.
- Choose Window ⇨ Site Files.
- Press the keyboard shortcut F8.

The Site window is your vehicle for moving files back and forth between your local and remote folders. Figure 3-5 illustrates the various parts of the Site window.

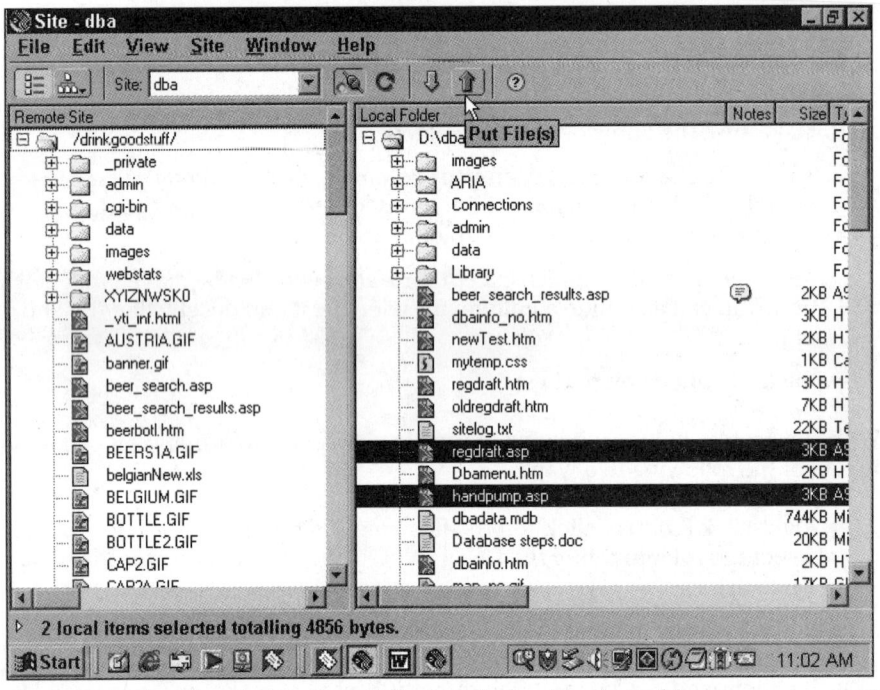

Figure 3-5: The Site window is used for transferring files to and from your remote Web server.

Remote Site and Local Root windows

The Site window is arranged in two main windows: By default, the remote site is on the left and the local root directory is on the right. These two windows enable you to view all the files contained within the two directories.

Another helpful view enables you to see which files have been most recently added or modified since the last FTP transfer. Choose either Select Newer Local or Select Newer Remote in the Edit menu (or on a Macintosh, Site ⇨ Site Files View ⇨ Select Newer Local or Site Files View ⇨ Select Newer Remote). Dreamweaver compares the files within the two folders to see which ones have been saved since the last FTP session. The newer files are highlighted and can be easily transferred by selecting the Get or Put button (described in a later section).

Tip

In large sites, the Select Newer Remote operation can take a fairly long time to complete. If possible, selecting individual folders to be checked, while leaving the others unscanned, can speed up the process.

Connect/Disconnect button

The Connect/Disconnect button to the right of the Site drop-down list enables you to begin or end a live session with a remote host server. By clicking the Connect button, you start a new FTP session. You must have a way to connect to the Internet, and you must have a Remote server defined, when you select Connect. You won't see any information in the Remote Site pane until you connect to it.

After Dreamweaver has made the connection to your remote site — as identified in the Site Information dialog box — the Connect button becomes the Disconnect button. To end your FTP session with the host server, click the Disconnect button.

Tip

You can monitor all of your site management transactions by looking at the FTP Log. Select Window ⇨ Site FTP Log (Windows) or Site ⇨ FTP Log (Macintosh) from within the Site window. A new window pops up and shows you all your transactions as you perform them.

Get and Put buttons

Two of the most useful controls on the Site window are the Get and Put buttons. The Get button retrieves selected files and folders from the host server. The Put button transfers selected files from your local root directory to the host server. Dreamweaver offers several ways to transfer files in the Site window during an active FTP session.

To transfer one or more files from the local directory to the host server, use one of the following methods:

- Select the files from the Local Folder pane and drag them over to the Remote Folder pane.
- Use the keyboard shortcut — select the files and press Ctrl+Shift+U (Command+Shift+U).
- Highlight the files and choose Site ⇨ Put.
- Select the files in the Local Folder pane and click the Put button.

If the file you are transferring has any dependent files, such as inserted images or Java applets, the Dependent Files dialog box (see Figure 3-6) asks if you want to include dependent files. If you select Yes, all such files are transferred. Select No to move only the file you selected.

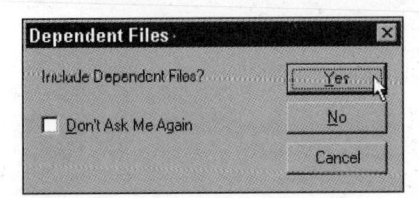

Figure 3-6: After selecting the HTML files, say Yes to the Dependent Files dialog box to transfer all the needed files.

Tip: The Dependent Files dialog box includes a checkbox that asks if you want to be reminded of this feature again. If you choose this option, but later want the reminder to reappear, you can select either of the Dependent Files options from the Site category of Preferences. To bring up the Dependent Files dialog box on a case-by-case basis, press Alt (Option) when selecting the Get, Put, Check In, or Check Out buttons.

To transfer one or more files from the host server to the local folder, use one of these techniques:

- Select the files you want from the Remote Site pane and drag them over to the Local Folder pane.
- Use the keyboard shortcut — select the files and press Ctrl+Shift+D (Command+Shift+D).
- Highlight the files and select Site ⇨ Get.
- Select the files in the remote directory and click the Get button.

Caution: If you select either Site ⇨ Get or the Get button without having selected any files in the Remote Site pane, all the files from your host server are moved. Dreamweaver does warn you, however.

Refresh button

As the name implies, the Refresh button re-reads the currently selected directory, whether locally or remotely. This can be useful when other people are working on the same site at the same time — refreshing your screen enables you to see if any additional files have been added or removed during your FTP session. You also need to refresh the Site window if you have modified a file during the FTP session. If you have enabled the Refresh Local Files Automatically option in the Define Site preferences, you only have to use this button to refresh the remote files. The Refresh button is found to the right of the Connect button.

The View (Windows) or Site ⇨ Site Files View (Macintosh) menu options also enable you to refresh the two windows. You can choose from two refresh commands: Refresh Local and Refresh Remote.

Stop Current Task button

Use the Stop Current Task button to halt the current transfer of files in an active FTP session. The Stop Current Task button is the octagonal red X button located in the lower-right corner of the Site window; it appears only while you are actually moving files.

Check Out/Check In buttons

The Check In/Check Out buttons, which are visible to the right of the Get and Put buttons only if you've selected the Check In/Out category in the Site Definition window (as previously shown in Figure 3-2), enable a user to officially check out an item from either the local or host server. The Check Out button provides a visual cue to everyone with access to the server that a file is currently in use. Details on how to use this feature are covered in the next section.

Checking a File In and Out

Your control over the files used for your Web site is very important if you are developing a site with a team. On larger sites, the various Webmaster chores — design, programming, and management — are distributed among several people. Without proper check-in and check-out procedures, it's easy for the same HTML page to get updated by more than one person, and you can wind up with incompatible versions.

Dreamweaver's Check In/Check Out facility solves this file-control problem by permitting only one person at a time to modify a Web page or graphic. Once a file has been checked out — accessed by someone — the file must be checked in again before another person using the Site window can download it and work on it.

Dreamweaver handles the functionality of Check In/Check Out very efficiently. Whenever you establish an active FTP session between your local root folder and the remote server, any files you get or put are displayed with a green checkmark. If other people in your group are also moving files back and forth, their transferred files are marked with a red checkmark. This method provides a quickly recognized, visual representation of the status of files you and your teammates are handling. Files that do not have either a red or green checkmark are not currently checked out by anyone and are available to work on.

If you want to see who is working on what, you can view user names in the Remote Site window. (You may have to scroll the window horizontally to see the column.) The name shown is the Check Out name that they use for logging on to the remote server. The Check Out name is entered through the Site Information dialog box.

Knowing who is working on what, and when, is a good control mechanism, but to really prevent duplication, site file control has to go one step further. Under Dreamweaver's Check In/Check Out system, when you transfer a file from your local root folder to the host server, the file on your local folder becomes read-only. Making the file read-only enables others to see the Web page but prevents anyone else from overwriting the file. The file must be checked in again before others can modify it.

Dreamweaver accomplishes Check In/Check Out by using a set of special files. When a file is checked out, a text file of the same filename but with the extension .lck is placed on the server. The .lck file contains the name of the user who checked out the file, as well as the date and the time that the file was checked out. The .lck files cannot be viewed in the Site window display but can be seen when a third-party FTP program is used.

Caution Unfortunately, Dreamweaver is not able to make checked-out files in the host server read-only. This means someone in your group using an FTP program other than the Site window could easily overwrite the checked-out file on the server.

To check out one or more files, use any of the following methods:

✦ Select the files you want to transfer and then click the Check Out button at the top of the Site window. All the files are downloaded into your local folder and checked out in your name (denoted by a green checkmark).

✦ Select the files and choose Site ⇨ Check Out.

✦ Select the files and use the keyboard shortcut Ctrl+Alt+Shift+D (Command+Option+Shift+D).

To check one or more files back in, do either of the following:

✦ Select the files you want to transfer and then click the Check In button at the top of the Site window. All of the selected files will be uploaded from your local folder to the remote site, and the green checkmark will be removed from their names.

- Select the checked-out files and choose Site ➪ Check In.
- Select the files and use the keyboard shortcut Ctrl+Alt+Shift+U (Command+Option+Shift+U).

To change the checked-out status of a file, use one of these methods:

- Select the file that's checked out and then click the Check In button at the top of the Site window.
- Select the file and choose Site ➪ Undo Check Out.

Synchronizing Local and Remote Sites

The necessity of having sets of files stored both locally and remotely often leads to confusion over which file is the most current. The problem is far more likely to occur if you're working in a team situation where numerous people are maintaining the same site.

Dreamweaver includes a one-step command to solve this local-remote dilemma: Synchronize. Found under the Site menu in Windows and on the menu bar in Macintosh systems, the Synchronize command ensures that the most current version of the same files is on both systems. Synchronize can also delete files on one site that do not appear on another. You can apply the Synchronize command sitewide or to selected files or folders.

To synchronize your files, follow these steps:

1. If you want to synchronize only selected files or folders, select those in the local pane of the Site window.
2. Choose Site ➪ Synchronize.

   The Synchronize Files dialog box opens, as shown in Figure 3-7.

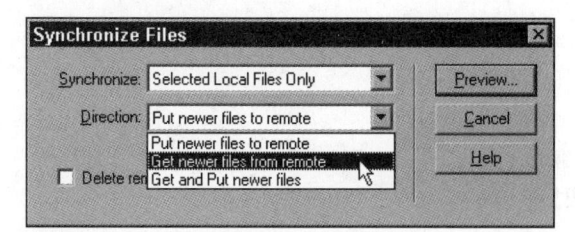

Figure 3-7: The Synchronize command makes sure that both the local and remote sites contain the same files.

3. To synchronize the full site, select Entire *Site Name* Site from the Synchronize list, where *Site Name* is the current site. Otherwise, choose Selected Local Files Only.

4. Set the direction of the synchronization:

   - **Put Newer Files to Remote:** Examines local files and transfers those with more recent modification dates to the remote server.

   - **Get Newer Files from Remote:** Examines remote files and transfers those with more recent modification dates to the local server.

   - **Get and Put Newer Files:** Transfers the most current versions of all files to and from both sites.

5. By selecting the Delete Remote Files Not on Local Drive option, you can remove any local files without a corresponding file on the server side when using the Get Newer Files from Remote direction. If the Put Newer Files to Remote direction is chosen with the Delete option, files on the remote site without a local equivalent are removed.

> **Caution:** As with all file deletions, these operations cannot be undone. Use this feature with extreme care.

6. When you're ready, click Preview to begin the process.

   Dreamweaver compares the local and remote sites and begins displaying files in a new Site dialog box for confirmation, as shown in Figure 3-8. If no files are mismatched, Dreamweaver tells you that no synchronization is necessary.

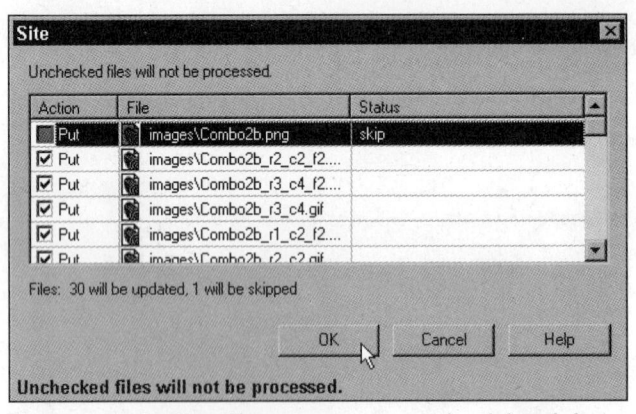

Figure 3-8: Confirm files to get, put, or to be deleted during the Synchronization process in the Site dialog box.

7. Deselect any file for action by removing its checkmark from the Action column.

8. Click OK when you're ready.

   Dreamweaver displays the process of the synchronization in the dialog box and the status bar of the Site window.

9. When the synchronization is complete, you can keep a record of the changes by selecting the Save Log button; if you do, Dreamweaver asks for a file location. When you're done, select the Close button.

Caution
On Windows, if you have Dreamweaver windows open other than just the Site window, the Site dialog box may not appear on top of the Site window. Select the other Dreamweaver windows to find the Site dialog box.

Synchronization is a powerful tool in Dreamweaver's site management arsenal. However, care needs to be taken when first using the feature to make sure that team members' system clocks are in sync.

Checking Links

During a Web site's development, hundreds of different files and links are often referenced from within the HTML code. Unfortunately, it's not uncommon for a user to enthusiastically follow a link only to encounter the dreaded Web server error 404: File Not Found. Broken links are one of a Webmaster's most persistent headaches, because a Web page may have not only internal links pointing to other pages on the Web site, but external links as well—over which the Webmaster has no control.

Orphaned files constitute a parallel nightmare for the working Web developer. An orphaned file is one that is included in the local or remote site but is no longer actively referenced by any Web page. Orphaned files take up valuable disk space and can erroneously be transferred from an old site to a new one.

Dreamweaver includes, for the Web designer, a useful feature to ease the labor in solving both of these problems: the Link Checker. The Link Checker command can be used to check a single page, selected pages, a subfolder, or an entire site. Once the Link Checker has completed its survey, you can view broken links, external files (links outside the site, such as absolute references and mailto: links), and orphaned files. You can also repair broken links immediately or save the Link Checker results in a file for later viewing.

To check for links, follow these steps:

1. Make sure that the most current versions of the files have been saved.

2. To check a single document from within Dreamweaver, open the file and then choose File ⇨ Check Links, or use the keyboard shortcut Shift+F8.

3. To check for links on an entire site from within Dreamweaver, choose Site ⇨ Check Links Sitewide or use the keyboard shortcut Ctrl+F8 (Command+F8).

After Dreamweaver checks all the links on your page or site, it opens the Link Checker dialog box. The Link Checker dialog box, shown in Figure 3-9, provides a summary report of the broken links, external links, and when an entire site is reviewed, orphaned files. You can also use the Save button to store for future reference, in a tab-delimited text file, a report of the problems that the Link Checker has found.

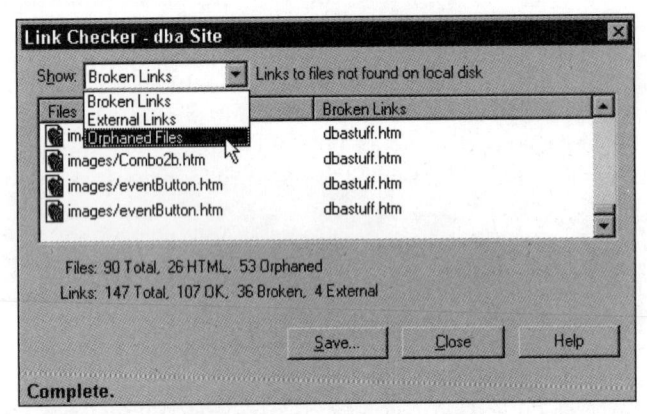

Figure 3-9: The Link Checker dialog box helps you determine which files have broken links and then fix the links directly.

When you list broken links, you can observe any file that is included as a link, inserted as an image, or embedded in the page, but which cannot be located. If you want to fix the broken link, you can do so by double-clicking the highlighted broken-link file. This brings up the file in Dreamweaver, where you can fix any problems using the Property Inspector. You can use the Property Inspector to locate the Src attribute. To open the page from the Link Checker, double-click the Dreamweaver icon next to the broken link.

You can also fix the link directly in the Link Checker window by following these steps:

1. Run the Link Checker command, either for the entire site or a single Web page.
2. In the Link Checker window, select the path and filename of the broken link you want to repair.
3. Enter the correct path for the missing file.

You can also access the Link Checker for both your local and remote folders. After you've selected your files or folders, choose File ⇨ Check Links, from the main Dreamweaver menu, to check either the selected files or the entire Web site. Or, you can right-click (Control+click) any of the selected files to display the shortcut menu and choose the Check Link options from there.

Launching External Editors

As Web pages grow in complexity, many different types of media are involved in the creation of a page. Graphic editors, audio editors, word processors, spreadsheet programs, and database systems are all used in the creation and modification of files that can be included on a Web page — and the list grows daily. With Dreamweaver 4's capability to invoke editors for any file type, the workflow has been greatly simplified.

In Dreamweaver, you can assign an editor to any file type — actually you can assign multiple editors to the same file type for maximum flexibility. Because the editors are assigned according to file extension rather than kind of file, you can associate different editors for every different graphic format, if you so choose.

To launch a file's primary editor from the Site window, just double-click the filename. If you have multiple editors assigned to a file type, you can open the file with an alternative editor by right-clicking (Control+clicking) the filename and choosing the editor from the Open With menu option. There's even a Browse option under the Open With menu to enable you to select an unassigned editor.

You may note that certain editors are preassigned on Windows systems. For example, on my system, if I double-click any .zip file, WinZip loads the archive. Dreamweaver recognizes file extension associations registered on your system. If a file extension has a particular association, it's listed under the Type category in the Site window. My file chap03.zip, for instance, is shown to be a WinZip file.

> **Tip** Macintosh users should check to see if the desired editor opens when the file is double-clicked before assigning new editors in Dreamweaver. On Macintosh, Dreamweaver uses system assignments through creator codes, if available.

Working with the Site Map

A Web site consists primarily of pages linked to other pages, which in turn can be linked to more pages. The more complex the site, the more difficult it becomes to comprehend — or remember — the entire structure when looking at just a directory listing.

With Dreamweaver, you can easily view your entire Web site and its links as a hierarchical tree using the Site Map feature. Not only do problems such as broken links jump out at you — after all, they're depicted in red — but also the Site Map can give you a much needed overview of the entire site. Poor site design can lead to visitors getting "lost" or frustrated with the number of links it takes to get to an important page. Dreamweaver's Site Map gives you a visual reference and enables you to create the structure for entire sites in a point-and-click environment.

The Site Map is a graphical representation of your site, with all its Web pages symbolized by icons, as shown in Figure 3-10. The Site Map resembles both an organizational chart and a flow chart. The Web site's home page is shown at the top of the chart. A link from one page to another is represented by a connecting line with an arrowhead. Any document, other than the home page, that is linked to additional pages indicates these pages with a plus or minus symbol in Windows systems and a right or down arrow in Macintosh systems. By default, Dreamweaver displays your Site Map only two levels deep. Selecting the plus/minus (arrow) symbols shows and hides the view of the linked pages on deeper levels.

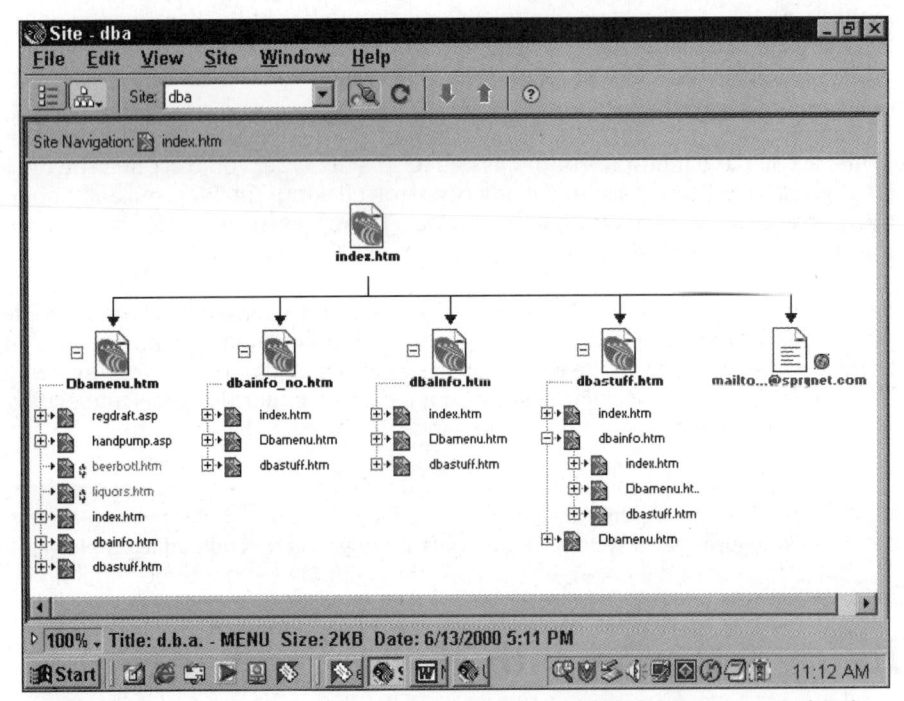

Figure 3-10: Clicking the Site Map icon in the Site window brings up a graphical representation of your site.

To open the Site Map from the Document window, choose Window ⇨ Site Map or use the keyboard shortcut Alt+F8 (Option+F8). If the Site window is open, you can select the Site Map button to bring up the Site Map. The Site Map button has two settings, which you can activate by clicking and holding down the corresponding button. The Map Only setting displays just the Site Map. The Map and Files setting shows the Site Map in one pane of the Site window and the Local Files pane in the other.

The Site Map represents internal HTML pages with Dreamweaver page icons. If the link is good, the name is in blue type; if the link is broken, it's red. External files — files on another site — and special links, such as a `mailto:` or `javascript:` link, are indicated with globes. Initially, the Site Map displays only the HTML files, and not any hidden or dependent files, in a site. (Hidden and dependent files are covered later in this section.)

If your site has enabled Dreamweaver's Check In/Check Out features, you see additional symbols on the Site Map. A file checked out by you is indicated by a green checkmark. If someone else has checked out the file, the checkmark is red. It's not uncommon for teams to prevent an important Web page from being altered by making it read-only (Windows) or locking it (Macintosh). Such files are noted with a lock symbol.

> **Note:** To view a Site Map of your site, it must be in a local folder. To view a Site Map of a remote site, you must first download it to a local folder.

Storyboarding with the Site Map

Increasingly, Web designers lay out the structure of their sites in a process called storyboarding before filling in the details with text, image, and media content. This approach is all but essential on larger sites where development is divided among many people. In many ways, laying out the site's structure ahead of the content makes the content phase go much faster. You can, for example, pick an existing page (even if it is empty of content) from the Select File dialog box when building your links, rather than entering a nonexistent page's filename in the Link text box — and then trying to remember to create it later.

All you need to begin building your site with the Site Map is a single file, typically the site's home page. This home page is then defined as such in the Site Map Layout category of the Site Definition dialog box.

To create a Web site structure from the Site Map, follow these steps:

1. Open the Site Map by choosing Window ⇨ Site Map or one of the other methods previously described.
2. Select the icon of the site's home page.
3. Choose Site ⇨ Link to a New File (Site ⇨ Site Map View ⇨ Link to a New File). You can also right-click (Ctrl+click) the page's icon and choose Link to New File from the shortcut menu. Or use the key shortcut: Ctrl+Shift+N (Command+Shift+N).

   The Link to New File dialog box appears, as shown in Figure 3-11.

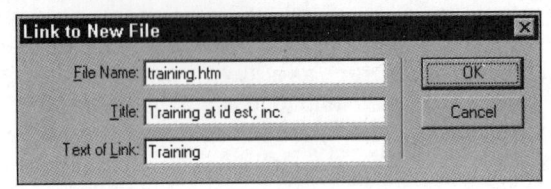

Figure 3-11: Use the Site Map to build the Web site's structure by creating new linked pages in one operation.

4. In the Link to New File dialog box, enter the correct filename, with an extension such as .htm or .html, in the File Name text box. Press Tab to move to the next text box.

5. Enter a title for the new page in the Title text box. Press Tab.

6. Enter the descriptive word or phrase to appear as a link on the original page in the Text of Link text box. Select OK or press Enter (Return) when you're done.

   The HTML page is created, and an icon for the new page appears, with a line connecting it to the original page.

7. To add another link to the home page, select the home page icon again and repeat Steps 3 through 6.

8. To add a new link to the newly created page, select its icon and repeat Steps 3 through 6.

When text links are added to a page, they are placed at the bottom of an existing page, one after another in the same line, like a text-only navigation bar. If the page is new, the text links are naturally the only items on the page.

Connecting to existing pages

Adding existing files to the Site Map is even easier than adding a new file, especially if the file to which you're linking is already in the same site. Part of building a Web-like structure is connecting from one page to another. With the Site Map, this is literally a drag-and-drop affair.

When an HTML icon is selected in the Site Map, a Point to File icon appears. The Point to File feature on the Site Map is basically used the same way it is on the Property Inspectors — just click the symbol and drag your pointer to another file. You can point and link to files in the current site whether or not they're already in the Site Map.

To link to a file that's in the current site but not on the Site Map (in other words, a file that's not linked to the home page or any connected pages), it's best to have both the Site Map and the Local Files panes displayed. To show both panes, select and hold down the Site Map button and then choose Map and Files from the drop-down list. Next, in the Site Map pane, select the file you want to link from—and a Point to File icon appears. Click and drag the Point to File icon from the Site Map to the Local Files pane to select the linking page. A line is drawn from the Point to File icon to the selected file, as shown in Figure 3-12. When your pointer is over the desired file, release the mouse button. The link is added, with a new icon appearing on the Site Map, and a text link is added to the originating page.

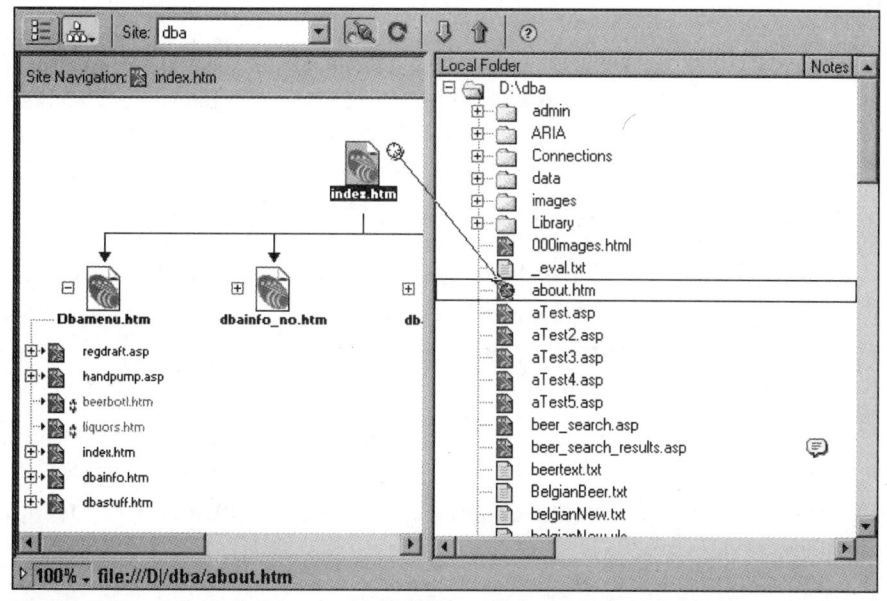

Figure 3-12: Quickly link to an existing file with Dreamweaver's Point to File feature.

If you're linking from one Site Map page to another, the Point to File icon is handy. Just select the originating page's icon and drag its Point to File symbol to the page you want to link to. Rather than draw another line across the screen—which would quickly render the Site Map screen indecipherable with crisscrossing lines—links to existing Site Map files are shown in italics.

Several other methods exist for linking to an existing file. First, you can open a Select File dialog box by selecting the originating file and then choosing Site ⇨ Link to Existing File (Site ⇨ Site Map View ⇨ Link to an Existing File). The keyboard short-cut for this command is Ctrl+Shift+K (Command+Shift+K). You can also invoke the command by choosing Link to an Existing File from the shortcut menu, brought up by right-clicking (Control+clicking) the originating file's Site Map icon. Any of these techniques opens the Select File dialog box to enable you to browse for your file, which is useful for selecting files not in the current site.

If you want to drag and drop external files to create a link, you can use the Site Map in combination with the Windows Explorer or Finder, depending on your operating system. Instead of pointing from the originating file to the linked file, you drag the name or icon representing the external file from Windows Explorer (Finder) and drop it on the Site Map icon of the originating page. To accomplish this, it's best to either have the Site Map and Windows Explorer (Finder) windows side by side or, if they are overlapping, have the Windows Explorer (Finder) window in front.

Modifying links

If you have spent any time in Web site design and management, you know nothing is written in stone. Luckily, Dreamweaver 4 makes changing a link from one page to another a breeze and handles the tedious task of updating changes in all linked pages. Moreover, if you have multiple pages linking to a single page, you can make all the pages in the Web site link to a different page.

To change a link from one page to another, follow these steps:

1. Select the icon of the linked page you want to alter in the Site Map.

2. Choose Site ⇨ Change Link (Site ⇨ Site Map View ⇨ Change Link) or use the keyboard shortcut Ctrl+L (Command+L).

   The Select File dialog box opens.

3. Enter the path and filename in the File Name text box or select the Browse (Choose) button to locate the file. Click OK when you've selected your file.

   Dreamweaver displays the Update Files dialog box with all the connecting pages, as shown in Figure 3-13.

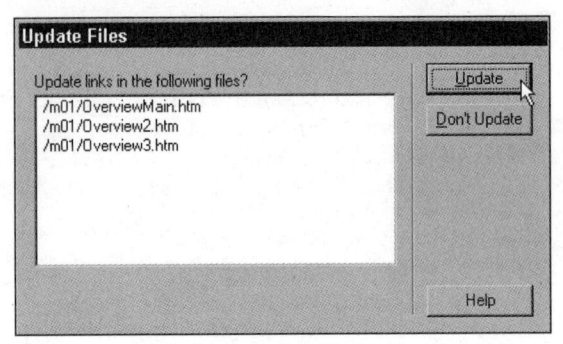

Figure 3-13: Changing a link in the Site Map brings up the Update Files dialog box.

4. To change the link in all the files, choose the Update button.

5. To change the link in some of the files, select the files first, using either the Shift+click or Ctrl+click (Command+click) method, and then choose the Update button.

   6. To cancel the link change, choose the Don't Update button.

If you have multiple pages linking to a single page that you want to alter, you can change a link sitewide. Simply select the icon for the linked page you want to modify and choose Site ⇨ Change Link Sitewide. As with the Change Link command, the Update Files dialog box opens; the balance of the procedure remains the same.

> **Tip**
> I recommend that you enable the Refresh Local File List Automatically option found in the Define Sites dialog box. Dreamweaver picks up changes made inside of its own program and outside of it — even the Site Map view is updated when a change is made on a page.

Deleting links

You can delete a link from one page in several ways. First, select the icon and then do any of the following:

- Press the Delete key (Windows only).
- Choose Site ⇨ Remove Link (Site ⇨ Site Map View ⇨ Remove Link).
- Press Ctrl+Shift+L (Command+Shift+L).
- Right-click (Control+click) the icon and, from the shortcut menu, choose Remove Link.

In all cases, the link is deleted without confirmation, and the deletion cannot be undone.

> **Note**
> Deleting a link does not delete the file itself, just the link. For the text link, the href attribute is eliminated, but the actual text remains.

Changing titles

Dreamweaver 4 gives you an easy way to change a Web page's title right in the Site Map. Before you can use this feature, however, you must be sure the titles are used to identify the icons, rather than the filenames. Choose View ⇨ Show Page Titles (Site ⇨ Site Map View ⇨ Show Page Titles) or use the keyboard shortcut, Ctrl+Shift+T (Command+Shift+T), to switch to a title view.

To retitle a Web page, click the title twice, slowly — make sure you don't double-click the title, which will open the file. Alternatively, you can select the icon and then click the title. You can also select the icon and then choose File ⇨ Rename (Site ⇨ Rename) from the menu. In Windows, F2 is the key shortcut. All of these methods make the title an editable field that you can then modify.

Modifying pages through the Site Map

Once you've created and refined your site structure, you're ready to begin adding the content. The Site Map enables you to open a single page or a collection of pages. You can even quickly locate the text or graphic that serves as the source for the link in the connecting page.

Open a page in Dreamweaver's Document window for editing by double-clicking the page's icon in the Site Map. To open more than one page, you must first select all icons. Multiple files can be selected by selecting one file and then Shift+clicking the additional files. Another method of multiple selection is to click into an empty area in the Site Map and then drag a rectangle around the desired files. After all the needed files are selected, choose File ➪ Open Selection (Site ➪ Open), and the key shortcut is Ctrl+Alt+Shift+O (Command+Option+Shift+O). Every file opens in a separate Dreamweaver Document window.

Occasionally, you need to go right to the source of a link. Dreamweaver 4 enables you to open the connecting page and instantly select the actual link used to make the connection. To view the actual text or graphic used to make a link, first select the file's icon in the Site Map. Then, choose Site ➪ Open Source of Link (Site ➪ Site Map View ➪ Open Source of Link). Dreamweaver loads the page containing the link, opens the Property Inspector, and selects the link.

Altering the home page

As noted earlier, the Site Map assigns a home page to use as the base for its organization. As with most items in Dreamweaver, this assignment can be changed. But why would you want to change a Web site's home page? One of the primary purposes for the Site Map is to provide a visual representation of a site's structure — one that can easily be presented to a client for discussion. You can set up multiple views of a site, each with its own structure, by just switching the home page.

You can replace the home page with an existing page or a new one. To create a new page and make it the home page, select Site ➪ New Home Page (Site ➪ Site Map View ➪ New Home Page). The New Home Page dialog box opens with two fields to fill out: File Name and Title. After you enter the needed information, the file is created, and the icon appears by itself in the Site Map. Now you can use the Link to Existing File and Link to New features to build your new site organization.

To change the home page to an existing file, choose Site ➪ Set as Home Page (Site ➪ Site Map View ➪ Set as Home Page). The Select File dialog box opens and enables you to choose a new file. Once you've selected a file, the Site Map is recreated using the new file as a base and displaying any existing links.

Viewing the Site Map

The more complex the site, the more important it is to be able to view the Site Map in different ways. To cut down on the number of pages showing, Dreamweaver 4 enables you to hide any pages you choose. For maximum detail, you can also display all the dependent files (such as a page's graphics) in the Site Map. You even have the option of temporarily limiting the view to a particular "branch" of the Site Map. Dreamweaver also enables you to zoom out to get the big picture of a particularly large site or save the Site Map as a graphic.

> **Tip**
>
> If the Site Map columns are too narrow to see the full title or filename, use the ToolTips feature. Enabling View ⇨ Tool Tips (Site ⇨ Tool Tips) causes Dreamweaver to display the full text of the title or filename in a ToolTip box when your pointer passes over the name.

Working with hidden and dependent files

Web sites are capable of containing several hundred, if not several thousand, pages. In these situations, the Site Map can become overcrowded. Dreamweaver can mark any file (and its associated linked files) as hidden with a single command, View ⇨ Show/Hide Link (Site ⇨ Site Map View ⇨ Show/Hide Link). The key shortcut is Ctrl+Shift+Y (Command+Shift+Y). The Show/Hide Link command is a toggle — applying it a second time to a file removes the "hidden" designation.

To see previously hidden files, choose View ⇨ Show Files Marked as Hidden (Site ⇨ Site Map View ⇨ Show Files Marked as Hidden). Hidden files made visible are displayed in italics.

Dependent files include any image, external style sheet, or media file (such as a Flash movie). By default, dependent files are not displayed in the Site Map; however, you can opt to view them by choosing View ⇨ Show Dependent Files (Site ⇨ Site Map View ⇨ Show Dependent Files). Once visible on the Site Map, you can send any image to its designated image editor by double-clicking its icon. You can also open the Styles panel by double-clicking any external CSS file.

Focusing on part of a Site Map

Most of the time, the overall view, centered on the Web site's home page, is most useful. Sometimes, though, you want to examine a section of the site in greater detail. Dreamweaver enables you to set any page to be treated like a temporary home page or root, ignoring all linking pages above it.

To view just a portion of your Web site, first select the page you wish to choose as the new root. Next, choose View ⇨ View As Root (Site ⇨ Site Map View ⇨ View As Root) or use the keyboard shortcut Ctrl+Shift+R (Command+Shift+R). The Site Map now depicts your selected file as if it were the home page. Notice also that the Site Navigation bar has changed, as shown in Figure 3-14. The Site Navigation bar shows the actual home page and any pages that have been chosen as roots, separated by right-pointing arrows. You can switch from one root to another, or to the actual home page, by clicking its icon in the Site Navigation bar.

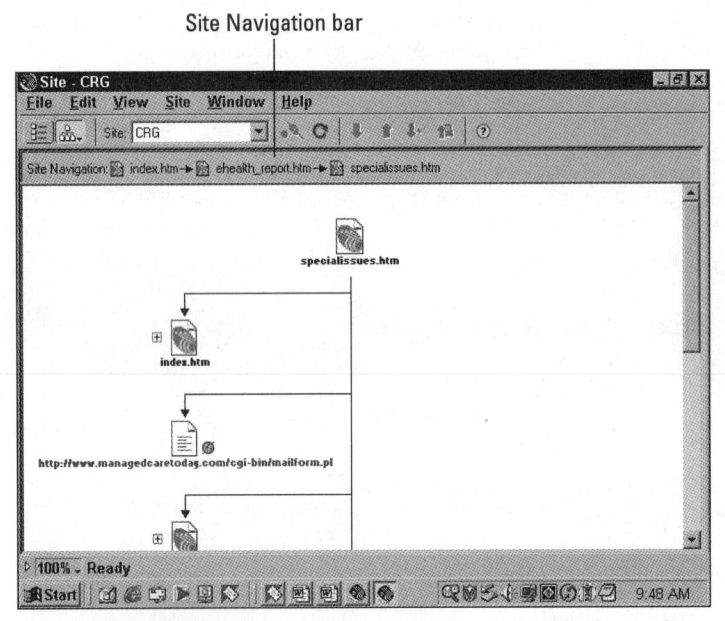

Figure 3-14: To view a section of your Site Map in detail, use the View As Root command.

Zooming out of your Site Map

What do you do when your site is so big that you can't see it all in one screen? Dreamweaver provides a Zoom feature that enables you to pull back for a more encompassing view. The Site Map Zoom button is located on the far left of the Site Window's status bar. Selecting the Zoom button reveals the magnification options to choose from: 100%, 75%, 50%, 25%, and 12%.

Tip If you find that Dreamweaver is displaying page icons only, with no filenames or titles, you can expand the column width in the layout. Choose View ⇨ Layout (Site ⇨ Site Map View ⇨ Layout) and change the value in the Column Width text box to a higher number. The default column width is 125 pixels.

Converting the Site Map into a graphic

Web designers like to believe that the whole world is wired and on the Web, but in truth, we're not there yet. Sometimes it's necessary to present a client or other interested party with a printout of a site design. Dreamweaver makes it possible to take a snapshot of the current Site Map and save it as a graphic file that can then be inserted into another program for printing — or attached to an e-mail for easy transmission.

To convert the Site Map into a graphic in Windows, choose File ➪ Save Site Map and then choose either BMP or PNG from the drop-down box in the Save box. On the Macintosh, choose Site ➪ Site Map View ➪ Save Site Map, and then the menu flies out to give you two file type options: Save Site Map as PICT or Save Site Map as JPEG.

When you save a Site Map as a graphic, the image is saved at the size necessary to contain all the displayed icons. Figure 3-15 shows a 352×1,118 pixel-sized graphic, saved from a Site Map, in Fireworks.

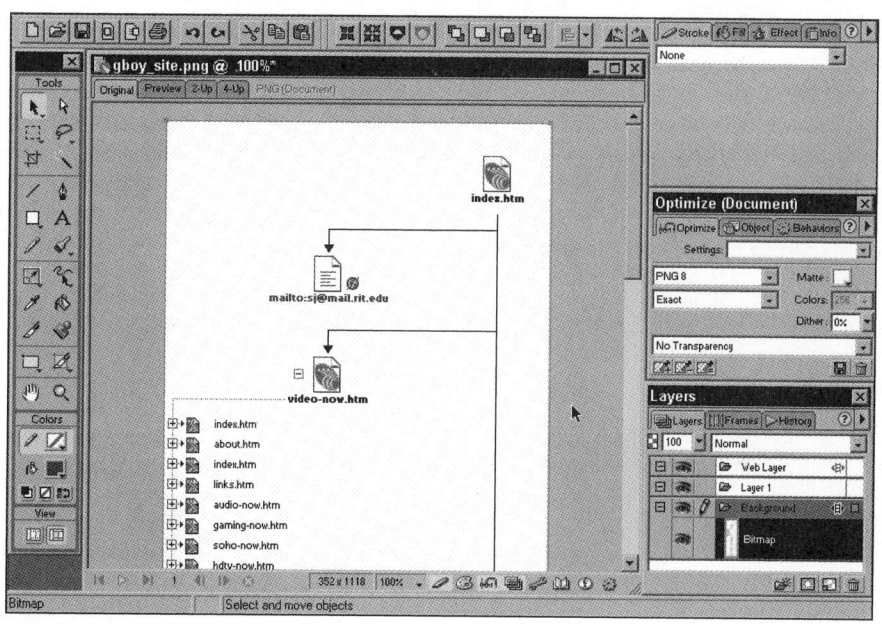

Figure 3-15: This Site Map image, ready for editing in Fireworks, was created in Dreamweaver.

Summary

With the Site window and Dreamweaver's site management tools, a group or an individual Web designer can manage even large and diverse sites.

- ✦ Setting up a new site is an essential element in managing a Dreamweaver Web site. Without the root directory for the local files, Dreamweaver cannot properly manage the Web pages and associated links.

- ✦ The Site window enables you to drag and drop files from the host server to the local root folder.

- ✦ All file check-in and check-out functions for teams can be handled through the Site window.
- ✦ Broken links can be quickly found and fixed with the Link Checker. You can also find orphaned files and identify external links.
- ✦ With Dreamweaver's Synchronize command, keeping your local and remote sites in sync is easier than ever.
- ✦ Dreamweaver's Site Map enables you to quickly visualize your overall site structure.
- ✦ The Site Map is also useful for creating new pages and their associated links. You can storyboard the entire site structure — links and all — before adding any content.

In the next chapter, you'll see how to use Dreamweaver to begin coding your Web pages.

✦ ✦ ✦

Understanding How HTML Works

CHAPTER 4

In This Chapter

Laying the HTML foundation

Working with the `<head>` section

Developing the `<body>` section

Adding special characters

In a perfect world, you could lay out the most complex Web site with a visual authoring tool and never have to see the HTML, much less code in it. Dreamweaver takes you a long way toward this goal—in fact, you can create many types of Web pages using only Dreamweaver's Document window. As your pages become more complex, however, you will probably need to tweak your HTML just a tad.

This chapter gives you a basic understanding of how HTML works and gives you the specific building blocks you need to begin creating Web pages. Also in this chapter, you get your first look at a Dreamweaver 4 innovation: the new Code view for altering the code, side-by-side with the visual environment. The other Dreamweaver-specific material in this chapter—which primarily describes how Dreamweaver sets and modifies a page's properties—is suitable for even the most accomplished Web designers. Armed with these fundamentals, you are ready to begin your exploration of Web page creation.

The Structure of an HTML Page

The simplest explanation of how HTML works derives from the full expansion of its acronym: HyperText Markup Language. *HyperText* refers to one of the World Wide Web's main properties—the capability to jump from one page to another, no matter where the pages are located on the Web. *Markup Language* means that a Web page is really just a heavily annotated text file. The basic building blocks of HTML, such as `<strong>` and `<p>`, are known as markup elements, or tags. The terms *element* and *tag* are used interchangeably.

An HTML page, then, is a set of instructions (the tags) suggesting to your browser how to display the enclosed text and images. The browser knows what kind of page it is handling based on the tag that opens the page, `<html>`, and the tag that closes the page, `</html>`. The great majority of HTML tags come in such pairs, in which the closing tag always has a forward slash before the keyword. Two examples of tag pairs are: `<p>`...`</p>` and `<title>`...`</title>`. A few important tags are represented by a single element: the image tag `<img>`, for example.

The HTML page is divided into two primary sections: the `<head>` and the `<body>`. Information relating to the entire document goes in the `<head>` section: the title, description, keywords, and any language subroutines that may be called from within the `<body>`. The content of the Web page is found in the `<body>` section. All the text, graphics, embedded animations, Java applets, and other elements of the page are found between the opening `<body>` and the closing `</body>` tags.

When you start a new document in Dreamweaver, the basic format is already laid out for you. Listing 4-1 shows the code from a Dreamweaver blank Web page.

Listing 4-1: The HTML for a New Dreamweaver Page

```
<html>
<head>
<title>Untitled Document</title>
<meta http-equiv="Content-Type" content="text/html; charset=iso-8859-1">
</head>

<body bgcolor="#FFFFFF" text="#000000">

</body>
</html>
```

Notice how the `<head>`...`</head>` pair is separate from the `<body>`...`</body>` pair, and that both are contained within the `<html>`...`</html>` tags.

Also notice that the `<body>` tag has two additional elements:

```
bgcolor="#FFFFFF"
```

and

```
text="#000000"
```

These types of elements are known as *attributes*. Attributes modify the basic tag and either can be equal to a value or can stand alone; in this example, the first attribute, `bgcolor`, is set to a hexadecimal number that represents the color white and the second, `text`, is set to the hexadecimal value for black. Thus, this attribute sets the background color of the body—the page—to white and the default text color to black. Not every tag has attributes, but when they do, the attributes are specific.

One last note about an HTML page: You are free to use carriage returns, spaces, and tabs as needed to make your code more readable. The interpreting browser ignores all but the included tags and text to create your page. Some minor, browser-specific differences in interpretation of these elements are pointed out throughout the book, but by and large, you can indent or space your code as you desire.

Defining <head> Elements

Information pertaining to the Web page overall is contained in the <head> section of an HTML page. Browsers read the <head> to find out how to render the page—for example, is the page to be displayed using the Western, the Chinese, or some other character set? Search engine spiders also read this section to quickly glean a summary of the page.

When you begin inserting JavaScript (or code from another scripting language such as VBScript) into your Web page, all the subroutines and document-wide declarations go into the <head> area. Dreamweaver uses this format by default when you insert a JavaScript behavior.

Dreamweaver enables you to insert, view, and modify <head> content without opening an HTML editor. Dreamweaver's View Head Content capability enables you to work with <meta> tags and other <head> HTML code as you do with the regular content in the visual editor.

Establishing page properties

When you first start Dreamweaver, your default Web page is untitled, with no background image but a plain white background. You can change all these properties and more through Dreamweaver's Page Properties dialog box.

New Feature You can also change the document title in the Toolbar in Dreamweaver 4. Just enter the information in the Title field and press Enter (Return) to confirm the modification. You'll see the new title appear in the program's title bar and whenever you preview the page in a browser.

As usual, Dreamweaver gives you more than one method for accessing the Page Properties dialog box. You can select Modify ⇨ Page Properties, or you can use the keyboard shortcut Ctrl+J (Command+J).

Tip Here's the other way to open the Page Properties dialog box. Right-click (Control+click) any open area in the Document window—that is, any part of the screen not occupied by an image, table, or other object (text outside of tables is okay to click, however). From the bottom of the Shortcut menu, select Page Properties.

The Page Properties dialog box, shown in Figure 4-1, gives you easy control of your HTML page's overall look and feel.

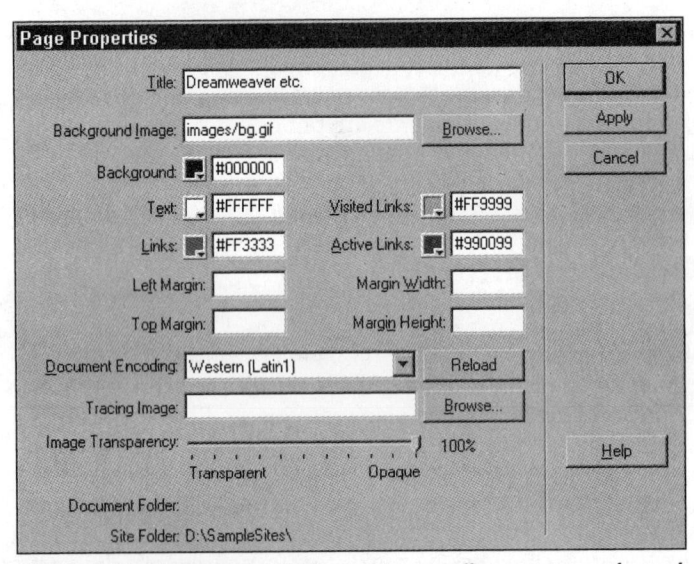

Figure 4-1: Change your Web page's overall appearance through the Page Properties dialog box.

Note: Technically, some of the values you assign through the Page Properties dialog box are applied to the `<body>` tag; because they affect the overall appearance of a page, however, they are covered in this `<head>` section.

The key areas of the Page Properties dialog box are as follows:

Page Property	Description
Title	The title of your Web page. The name you enter here appears in the browser's title bar when your page is viewed. Search engine spiders also read the title as one of the important indexing clues.
Background Image	The file name of the graphic you want in the page background. Either type in the path directly or pick a file by clicking the Browse (Choose) button. You can embed the graphic of your choice in the background of your page; if the image is smaller than your content requires, the browser tiles the image to fill out the page. Specifying a background image overrides any selection in the Background color field.

Page Property	Description
Background	Click this color swatch to change the background color of the Web page. Select one of the browser-safe colors from the pop-up menu, or enter its name or hexadecimal representation (for example, "#FFFFFF") directly into the text box.
Text	Click this color swatch to control the color of default text.
Links	Click this color swatch to modify the color of any text designated as a link, or the border around an image link.
Visited Links	Click this color swatch to select the color that linked text changes to after a visitor to your Web page has selected that link and then returned to your page.
Active Links	Click this color swatch to choose the color to which linked text changes briefly when a user selects the link.
Left Margin, Top Margin, Margin Width, Margin Height	Enter values here to change the default margin settings used by browsers. The Left and Top Margin settings are used by Microsoft, whereas Margin Width and Margin Height are used by Netscape.
Document Encoding	The character set in which you want your Web page to be displayed. Choose one from the drop-down list. The default is Western (Latin 1).
Tracing Image	Selects an image to use as a layout guide.
Image Transparency	Sets the degree of transparency for the tracing image.

The Page Properties dialog box also displays the document folder if the page has been saved, and the current site root folder if one has been selected.

Cross-Reference: The Tracing Image option is a powerful feature for quickly building a Web page based on design comps. For details about this feature and how to use it, see the section "Tracing Your Design with Layers" in Chapter 15.

Choosing a Page palette

Getting the right text and link colors to match your background color has been largely a trial-and-error process. Generally, you'd set the background color, add a contrasting text color, and then add some variations of different colors for the three different link colors — all the while clicking the Apply button and checking your results until you found a satisfactory combination. This is a time-intensive chore, to say the least.

Choosing Colors from an Onscreen Image

One of the features found throughout Dreamweaver, the Eyedropper tool, is especially useful in the Page Properties options. The Eyedropper tool appears whenever you open any of Dreamweaver's color swatches, such as those attached to the Background, Text, and Links colors. You can not only pick a color from the Web-safe palette that appears, but also use the Eyedropper to select any color on any page — including system colors such as those found in dialog boxes and menu strips.

To use the Eyedropper tool to choose a color for the background (or any of the other options) from an onscreen image, follow these steps:

1. Insert your image on the page and, using the vertical scroll bar, position the Document window so that the image and the Page Properties dialog box can be viewed simultaneously.

   If your image is too big to fit both it and the Page Properties dialog box on the same screen, temporarily resize your image by dragging its sizing handles. You can restore the original image size when you're done by selecting the Refresh button on the Image Property Inspector.

2. Open the Page Properties dialog box by choosing Modify ⇨ Page Properties or using the keyboard shortcut Ctrl+J (Command+J).

3. Drag the Page Properties dialog box to a place where the image can be seen.

4. Select the Background color swatch (or whichever one you wish to change).

   The Dreamweaver color picker opens and the pointer becomes an eyedropper.

5. Move the Eyedropper tool over the image until you find the correct color. (On Windows, you must hold the mouse button down as you drag the Eyedropper off the Dreamweaver dialog box to the image.) As you move the Eyedropper over an image, its colors are reflected in the color well and its hex value is shown on the color picker. Click once when you've found the appropriate color.

   The color picker closes.

6. Repeat Steps 4 and 5 to grab other colors from the screen for other color swatches. Click OK when you've finished modifying the page properties.

You don't have to keep the image on your page to get its color. Just insert it temporarily and then delete it after you've used the Eyedropper to grab the shade you want.

However, Dreamweaver ships with a command that enables you to quickly pick an entire palette for your page in one fell swoop. The Set Color Scheme command, shown in Figure 4-2, features palette combinations from noted Web designers Lynda Weinman and Bruce Heavin. The colors available in the command are all Web safe — which means that they will appear the same in the major browsers on all Macintosh and Windows systems without dithering.

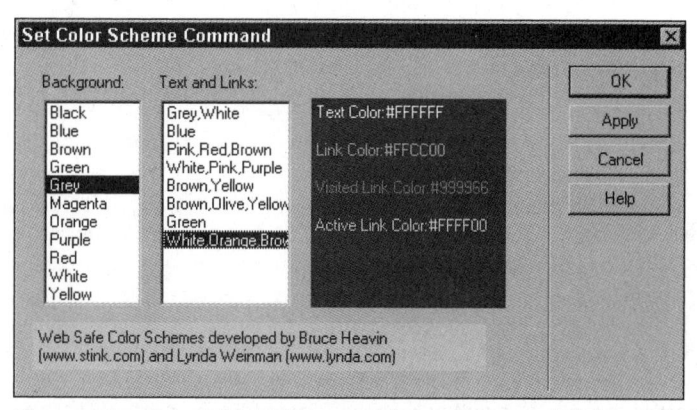

Figure 4-2: Get a Web-safe page palette with one click by using the Set Color Scheme command.

To use the Set Color Scheme command, follow these steps:

1. Choose Commands ⇨ Set Color Scheme.

   The Set Color Scheme dialog box opens.

2. Select the background color from the Background column on the left.

   The Text and Links column is updated to show available combinations for the selected background color.

3. Select a color set from the Text and Links column to see various combinations in the Preview pane.

   The color names — such as White, Pink, Brown — refer to the Text, Link, and Visited Link colors, generally. If only one color name is offered, the entire color scheme uses shades of that color. Note that the background color changes slightly for various color combinations to work better with the foreground color choices.

4. Click Apply to see the effect on your current page. Click OK when you finish.

Understanding <meta> and other <head> tags

Summary information about the content of a page — and a lot more — is conveyed through `<meta>` tags used within the `<head>` section. The `<meta>` tag can be read by the server to create a header file, which makes it easier for indexing software used by search engines to catalog sites. Numerous different types of `<meta>` tags exist, and you can insert them in your document just like other objects.

One `<meta>` tag is included by default in every Dreamweaver page. The Document Encoding option of the Page Properties dialog box determines the character set used by the current Web page and is displayed in the `<head>` section as follows:

```
<meta http-equiv="Content-Type" content="text/html; charset=iso-8859-1">
```

The preceding `<meta>` tag tells the browser that this page is, in fact, an HTML page and that the page should be rendered using the specified character set (the `charset` attribute). The key attribute here is `http-equiv`, which is responsible for generating a server response header.

Tip: Once you've determined your `<meta>` tags for a Web site, the same basic `<meta>` information can go on every Web page. Dreamweaver gives you a way to avoid having to insert the same lines again and again: templates. Once you've set up the `<head>` elements the way you'd like them, choose File ⇨ Save As Template. If you want to add `<meta>` or any other `<head>` tags to an existing template, you can edit the template and then update the affected pages. For more on templates, turn to Chapter 17.

In Dreamweaver, you can insert a `<meta>` tag or any other tag using the `<head>` tag objects, which you access via the Head category in the Objects panel or the Insert ⇨ Head Tags menu option. The `<head>` tag objects are described in Table 4-1 and subsequent subsections.

Table 4-1
Head Tag Objects

Head Tag Object	Description
Meta	Inserts information that describes or affects the entire document.
Keywords	Includes a series of words used by the search engine to index the current Web page and/or site.
Description	Includes a text description of the current Web page and/or site.
Refresh	Reloads the current document or loads a new URL within a specified number of seconds.
Base	Establishes a reference for all other URLs in the current Web page.
Link	Inserts a link to an external document, such as a style sheet.

Inserting tags with the Meta object

The Meta object is used to insert tags that provide information for the Web server, through the HTTP-equiv attribute, and other overall data that you want to include in your Web page but not make visible to the casual browser. Some Web pages, for example, have built-in expiration dates after which the content is to be considered outmoded. In Dreamweaver, you can use the Meta object to insert a wide range of descriptive data.

You can access the Meta object in the Head category of the Objects panel or via the Insert menu by choosing Insert ⇨ Head Tags ⇨ Meta. Like all the Head objects, you don't have to have the Head Content visible to insert the Meta object; although you do have to choose View ⇨ Head Content if you wish to edit the object. To insert a Meta object, follow these steps:

1. Select Insert ⇨ Head Tags ⇨ Meta or select the Meta object from the Head category of the Objects panel. Your current cursor position is irrelevant.

   The Insert Meta dialog box opens, as shown in Figure 4-3.

Figure 4-3: The Meta object enables you to enter a full range of `<meta>` tags in the `<head>` section of your Web page.

2. Choose the desired attribute: Name or an HTTP-equivalent from the Attribute list box. Press Tab.

3. Enter the value for the selected attribute in the Value text box. Press Tab.

4. Enter the value for the content attribute in the Content text box.

5. Click OK when you're done.

> ## Built-in Meta Commands
>
> Although Dreamweaver presents six different Head objects, `<meta>` tags form the basis of four of them: Meta, Keywords, Description, and Refresh. By specifying different `name` attributes, the purpose of the `<meta>` tags changes. For example, a Keywords object uses this format:
>
> ```
> <meta name="keywords" content="dreamweaver, web, authoring, ¬
> HTML, DHTML, CSS, Macromedia">
> ```
>
> whereas a Description object inserts this type of code:
>
> ```
> <meta name="description" content="This site is devoted to ¬
> extensions made possible by Macromedia's Dreamweaver, the ¬
> premier Web authoring tool.">
> ```
>
> It is possible to create all your `<meta>` tags with the Meta object by specifying the name attribute and giving it the pertinent value, but it's easier to just use the standard Dreamweaver Head objects.

You can add as many Meta objects as you need to by repeating Steps 1 through 4. To edit an existing Meta object, you must first choose View ➪ Head Content to reveal the `<head>` code, indicated by the various icons. Select the Meta tag icon and make your changes in the Property Inspector.

Aiding search engines with the Keywords and Description objects

Let's take a closer look at the tags that convey indexing and descriptive information to search engine spiders. These chores are handled by the Keywords and Description objects. As noted in the sidebar, "Built-in Meta Commands," the Keywords and Description objects output specialized `<meta>` tags.

Both objects are straightforward to use. Choose Insert ➪ Head Tags ➪ Keywords or Insert ➪ Head Tags ➪ Description. You can also choose the corresponding objects from the Head category of the Objects panel. Once selected, these objects open similar dialog boxes with a single entry area, a large text box, as shown in Figure 4-4. Enter the values — whether keywords or a description — in the text box and click OK when you're done. You can edit the Keywords and Description objects, like the Meta object, by selecting their icons in the Head area of the Document window, revealed by choosing View ➪ Head Contents.

Caution Although you can enter paragraph returns in your Keywords and Description objects, there's no reason to. Browsers ignore all such formatting when processing your code.

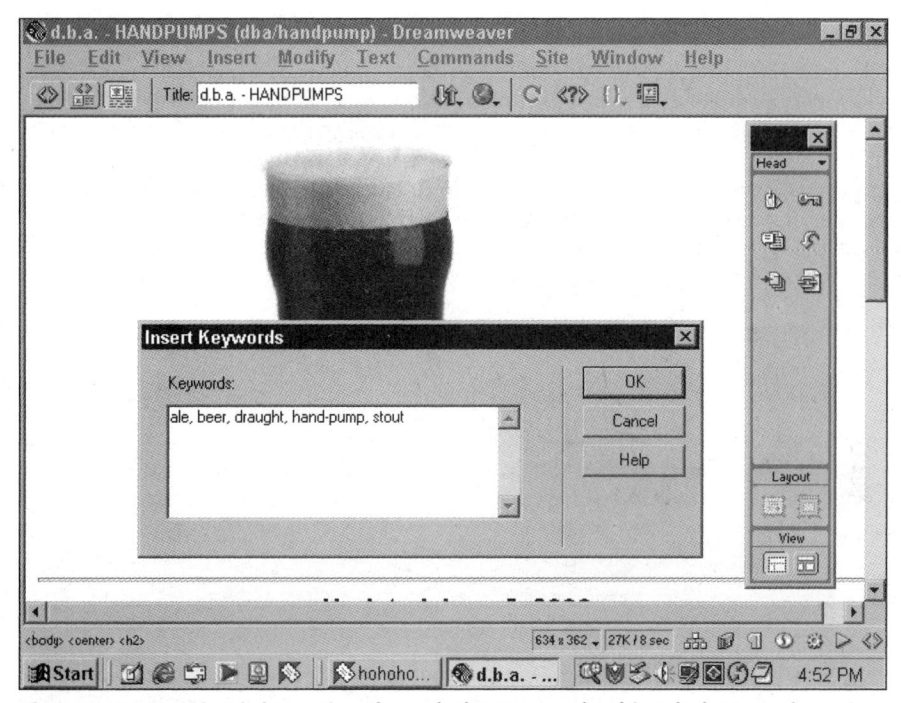

Figure 4-4: Entering information through the Keywords object helps search engines correctly index your Web page.

What you place in the Keywords and Description objects can have a big impact on your Web page's accessibility. If, for example, you want to categorize your Web page as an homage to the music of the early seventies, you could enter the following in the Content area of the Keywords object:

```
music, 70s, 70's, eagles, ronstadt, bee gees, pop, rock
```

In the preceding case, the content list is composed of words or phrases, separated by commas. Use sentences in the Description object, like this:

```
The definitive look back to the power pop rock stylings of early 1970s music, ¬
with special sections devoted to the Eagles, Linda Ronstadt, and the Bee Gees.
```

Keep in mind that the content in the Description should complement and extend both the Keywords and the Web page title. You have more room in both the Description and Keywords objects — really, an unlimited amount — than in the page title, which should be on the short side in order to fit into the browser's title bar.

> **Caution** When using `<meta>` tags with the Keywords or Description objects, don't stuff the `<meta>` tags with the same word repeated over and over again. The search engines are engineered to reject multiple words, and your description will not get the attention it deserves.

Refreshing the page and redirecting users

The Refresh object forces a browser to reload the current page or to load a new page after a user-set interval. The Web page visitor usually controls refreshing a page; if, for some reason, the display has become garbled, the user can choose Reload from the menu to redraw the screen. Impatient Web surfer that I am, I often stop a page from loading to see what text links are available and then — if I don't see what I need — hit Reload to bring in the full page. The code inserted by the Refresh object tells the server, not the browser, to reload the page. This can be a powerful tool but leads to trouble if used improperly.

To insert a Refresh object, follow these steps:

1. Choose Insert ⇨ Head Tags ⇨ Refresh or select the Insert Refresh object from the Head category of the Objects panel.

   The Insert Refresh dialog box, shown in Figure 4-5, opens.

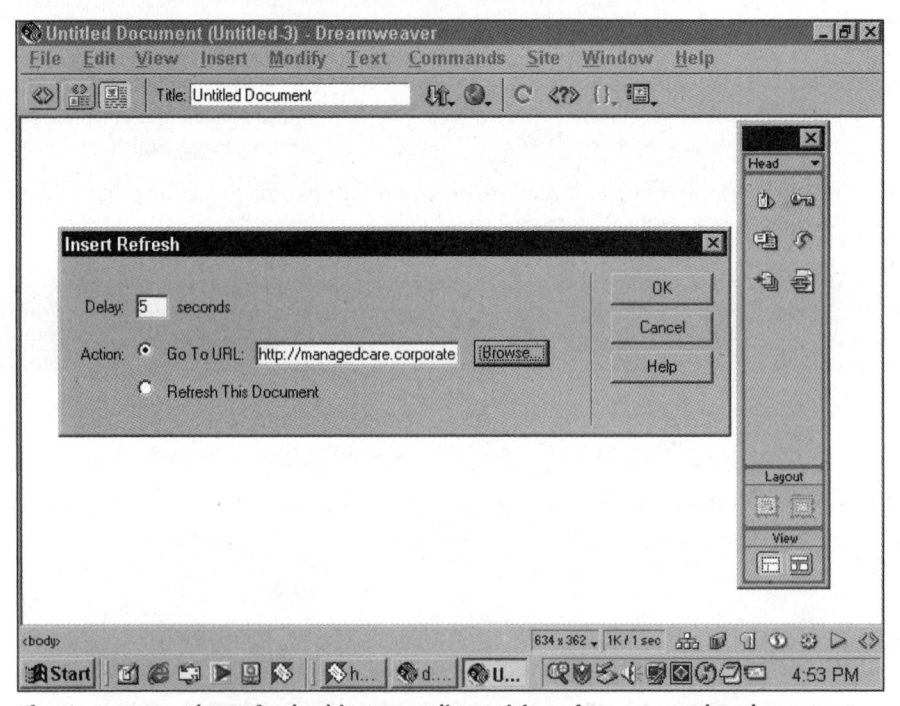

Figure 4-5: Use the Refresh object to redirect visitors from an outdated page.

2. Enter the number of seconds you want to wait before the Refresh command takes effect in the Delay text box.

   The Delay value is calculated from the time the page finishes loading.

3. Select the desired Action:
   - Go to URL
   - Refresh This Document
4. If you selected Go to URL, enter a path to another page in the text box or select the Browse button to select a file.
5. Click OK when you're done.

The Refresh object is most often used to redirect a visitor to another Web page. The Web is a fluid place, and sites often move from one address to another. Typically, a page at the old address contains the Refresh code that automatically takes the user to the new address. It's good practice to include a link to your new URL on the "change-of-address" page because not all browsers support the Refresh option. One other tip: Keep the number of seconds to a minimum — there's no point in waiting for something to happen automatically when you could click a link.

Caution

If you elect to choose the Refresh This Document option, use extreme caution for several reasons. First, you can easily set up an endless loop for your visitors in which the same page is constantly being refreshed. If you are working with a page that updates often, enter a longer Refresh value, such as 300 or 500. You should be sure to include a link to another page to enable users to exit from the continually refreshed page. You should also be aware that many search engines will not index pages using the meta refresh tag because of wide-spread abuse by certain industries on the Web.

Changing bases

Through the Base object, the `<head>` section enables you to exert fundamental control over the basic HTML element: the link. The code inserted by this object specifies the base URL for the current page. If you use relative addressing (covered in Chapter 2), you can switch all your links to another directory — even another Web site — with one command. The Base object takes two attributes: `Href`, which redirects all the other relative links on your page; and `target`, which specifies where the links will be rendered.

To insert a Base object in your page, follow these steps:

1. Choose Insert ⇨ Head Tags ⇨ Refresh or select the Insert Base object from the Head category of the Objects panel.

   The Insert Base dialog box opens.

2. Input the path that you want all other relative links to be based on in the Href text box or choose the Browse button to pick the path.

3. If desired, enter a default target for all links without a specific target to be rendered in the Target text box.

4. Click OK when you're done.

How does a `<base>` tag affect your page? Let's say you define one link as follows:

```
images/backgnd.gif
```

Normally, the browser looks in the same folder as the current page for a subfolder named images. A different sequence occurs, however, if you set the `<base>` tag to another URL in the following way:

```
<base href="http://www.testsite.com/client-demo01/">
```

With this `<base>` tag, when the same `images/backgnd.gif` link is activated, the browser looks for its file in the following location:

```
http://www.testsite.com/client-demo01/images/backgnd.gif
```

> **Caution:** Because of the all-or-nothing capability of `<base>` tags, many Webmasters use them cautiously, if at all.

Linking to other files

The Link object is used to indicate a relationship between the current page and another page or file. Although many other intended uses exist, the `<link>` tag is most commonly used to apply an external Cascading Style Sheet (CSS) to the current page. This code is entered automatically in Dreamweaver when you create a new linked style sheet (as described in Chapter 14), but to apply an existing style sheet, you need to use the Link object. The Link tag is also used to include TrueDoc dynamic fonts.

To insert a Link object, first choose Insert ⇨ Head Tags ⇨ Link or select the Insert Link object from the Head category of the Objects panel. This opens the Insert Link dialog box, shown in Figure 4-6.

Figure 4-6: The Link object is primarily used to include external style sheets.

Next, enter the necessary attributes:

Attribute	Description
Href	The path to the file being linked. Use the Browse button to open the Select File dialog box.
ID	The ID attribute can be used by scripts to identify this particular object and affect it if need be.
Title	The Title attribute is displayed as a ToolTip by Internet Explorer browsers.
Rel	A keyword that describes the relationship of the linked document to the current page. For example, an external style sheet uses the keyword `stylesheet`.
Rev	Rev, like Rel, also describes a relationship but in the reverse. For example, if home.html contained a link tag with a Rel attribute set to intro.html, intro.html could contain a link tag with a Rev attribute set to home.html.

Note: Aside from the style sheet use, there's little browser support for the other link functions. However, the World Wide Web Consortium (W3C) supports an initiative to use the `<link>` tag to address other media, such as speech synthesis and Braille devices, and it's entirely possible that the Link object will be used for this purpose in the future.

Adding to the `<body>`

The content of a Web page — the text, images, links, and plug-ins — is all contained in the `<body>` section of an HTML document. The great majority of `<body>` tags can be inserted through Dreamweaver's visual layout interface.

To use the `<body>` tags efficiently, you need to understand the distinction between logical styles and physical styles used in HTML. An underlying philosophy of HTML is to keep the Web as universally accessible as possible. Web content is intended to be platform- and resolution-independent, but the content itself can be styled by its intent as well. This philosophy is supported by the existence of logical `<body>` tags (such as `<code>` and `<cite>`), with which a block of text can be rendered according to its meaning, and physical style tags for directly italicizing or underlining text. HTML enables you to choose between logical styles, which are relative to the text, or physical styles, which can be regarded as absolute.

Logical styles

Logical styles are contextual rather than explicit. Choose a logical style when you want to ensure that the meaning, rather than a specific look, is conveyed. Table 4-2 shows a listing of logical style tags and their most common usage. Tags not supported through Dreamweaver's visual interface are noted.

Table 4-2
HTML Logical Style Tags

Tag	Usage
`<big>`	Increases the size of the selected text relative to the surrounding text. Not currently supported by Dreamweaver.
`<cite>`	Citations, titles, and references; usually shown in italic.
`<code>`	Code; for showing programming code, usually displayed in a monospaced font.
`<dfn>`	Defining instance; used to mark the introduction of a new term.
`<em>`	Emphasis; usually depicted as underlined or italicized text.
`<kbd>`	Keyboard; used to render text to be entered exactly.
`<s>`	Strikethrough text; used for showing text that has been deleted.
`<samp>`	Sample; a sequence of literal characters.
`<small>`	Decreases the size of the selected text relative to the surrounding text. Not currently supported by Dreamweaver.
`<strong>`	Strong emphasis; usually rendered as bold text.
`<sub>`	Subscript; the text is shown slightly lowered below the baseline. Not currently supported by Dreamweaver.
`<sup>`	Superscript; the text is shown slightly raised above the baseline. Not currently supported by Dreamweaver.
`<tt>`	Teletype; displayed with a monospaced font such as Courier.
`<var>`	Variable; used to distinguish variables from other programming code.

Logical styles are becoming increasingly important now that more browsers accept Cascading Style Sheets. Style sheets make it possible to combine the best elements of both logical and physical styles. With CSS, you can easily make the text within your `<code>` tags blue, and the variables, denoted with the `<var>` tag, green.

Caution If a tag is not currently supported by Dreamweaver, you must enter the tag by hand — either through the Code Inspector, the Quick Tag Editor, or another text editor — and preview the result in a browser. For example, you can use the `<sub>` tag to create a formula for water (H2O), but you don't see the subscripted 2 in the formula until you view the page through a browser.

Physical styles

HTML picked up the use of physical styles from modern typography and word processing programs. Use a physical style when you want something to be absolutely bold, italic, or underlined (or, as we say in HTML, `<b>`, `<i>`, and `<u>`, respectively).

You can apply the bold and the italic tags to selected text through the Property Inspector or by selecting Text ⇨ Style; the underline style is available only through the Text menu.

With HTML version 3.2, a fourth physical style tag was added: `<font>`. Most browsers recognize the size attribute, which enables you to make the selected text larger or smaller, relatively or directly. To change a font size absolutely, select your text and then select Text ⇨ Size; Dreamweaver inserts the following tag, where *n* is a number from 1 to 7:

```
<font size=n>
```

To make text larger than the default text, select Text ⇨ Size Increase and then choose the value you want. Dreamweaver inserts the following tag:

```
<font size=+n>
```

The plus sign (+) indicates the relative nature of the font. Make text smaller than the default text by selecting Text ⇨ Size Decrease; Dreamweaver inserts this tag:

```
<font size=-n>
```

You can also expressly change the type of font used and its color through the face and color attributes. Because you can't be sure what fonts will be on a user's system, common practice and good form dictate that you should list alternatives for a selected font. For instance, rather than just specifying Palatino — a sans serif font common on PCs but relatively unknown on the Mac — you could insert a tag such as the following:

```
<font face=" Palatino, Times New Roman, Times, sans-serif">
```

Caution: In the preceding case, if the browser doesn't find the first font, it looks for the second one (and so forth, as specified). Dreamweaver handles the font face attribute through its Font List dialog box, which is explained fully in Chapter 5.

Working with the Code View and Code Inspector

Although Dreamweaver offers many options for using the visual interface of the Document window, sometimes you just have to tweak the code by hand. Dreamweaver's acceptance by professional coders is due in large part to the easy access of the underlying code. Dreamweaver includes several methods for directly viewing, inputting, and modifying code for your Web page. For large-scale additions and changes, you might consider using an external HTML editor such as BBEdit or Homesite, but for many situations, the built-in Code view and Code Inspector are perfectly suited and much faster to work with.

New Feature: The Code view is the latest addition to Dreamweaver's code-savvy toolbox. With the addition of the Code view, you can either view your code full-screen in the Document Window, split-screen with the Design view, or in a separate panel, the Code Inspector. The underlying engine for all code views is the same—and, for Dreamweaver 4, the code editor has been rewritten from the ground up with significant enhancements to the feature set and performance.

To display the full-screen Code view:

✦ Select View ➪ Code.

✦ Choose the Show Code View button from the Toolbar.

The split-screen Code and Design view is revealed by:

✦ Choose View ➪ Code and Design.

✦ Select the Show Code and Design Views button on the Toolbar.

✦ Press Ctrl+Tab (Option+Tab) when in Design view and the Code Inspector is closed.

To change the relative size of the Code and Design views, drag the splitter bar up or down. In the split-screen Code and Design view, the Code view is shown on top of the Design view. You can reverse that order by choosing View ➪ Design View on Top or selecting Design View on Top from the View Options button on the Toolbar.

You have several ways to open the Code Inspector:

✦ Choose Window ➪ Code Inspector.

✦ Select the Show Code Inspector button in either Launcher.

✦ Use the keyboard shortcut F10.

Tip: To move between Design view and a code view, press Ctrl+Tab (Option+Tab). By default, this shortcut switches to Code view from Design view. However, if you are in the split-screen Code and Design view, this keyboard combination alternates focus between the two windows. If the Code Inspector is open, pressing Ctrl+Tab (Option+Tab) toggles the focus between Design view and the Code Inspector.

Once opened, the Code Inspector (Figure 4-7) behaves like any other floating panel in Dreamweaver: the window can be resized, moved, or hidden, and the inspector can be grouped with any other panel or dragged out onto its own. When the Code Inspector is opened initially, it is automatically selected. If you click in the Document window with the Code Inspector open, the inspector dims but still reflects changes made in the document.

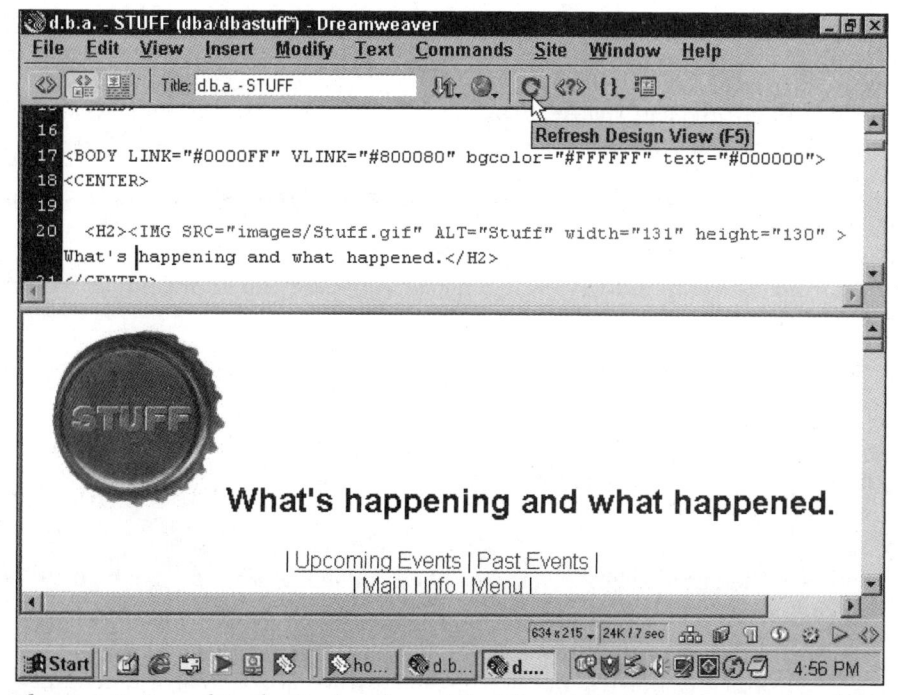

Figure 4-7: To update the Design view while still working in Code view select the handy Refresh button on the Toolbar or choose F5.

In all code views, Dreamweaver does not update the Design view of the document immediately—whereas changes in the Design view are instantly reflected in any open code view. This delay is enforced to enable the code to be completed before being applied. To apply modifications made in the code, switch to the Design view; if the Design view is open, click anywhere in it to give it focus. Should Dreamweaver detect any invalid HTML, such as an improperly closed tag, the offending code is flagged with a yellow highlight in both Design and Code views. Select the marked tag to see an explanation and suggestions for correcting the problem in the Property Inspector.

You can also apply code changes to the Design view by saving the document or by choosing the Refresh button on the Toolbar. The Refresh button becomes active only when modifications are made in any code view. You also have a keyboard and menu alternative: pressing F5 has the same effect as choosing View ⇨ Refresh Design View.

By and large, the Code View and Code Inspector acts like a regular text editor. Simply click anywhere in the inspector to add or modify code. Double-click a word to select it. Select an entire line by moving your pointer to the left edge of the code—where the pointer becomes a right-pointing arrow—and clicking once.

Multiple lines can be selected in this same fashion by dragging the right-pointing arrow. Once a section of code is selected, you can drag and drop it into a new location; pressing the Ctrl (Option) key while dragging makes a copy of the selection. Moving from word to word is accomplished by pressing Ctrl (Command) in combination with any of the arrow keys.

There are, however, some special features in Dreamweaver's code editor to simplify the task of writing HTML and other types of code. When in Code or Code and Design view, some of these features can be toggled on and off by choosing the command from the View ➪ Code View Options list or under the View Options button on the Toolbar:

- **Word Wrap** — Wraps lines within the boundaries of the Code View window or Code Inspector to eliminate the need for horizontal scrolling.

- **Line Numbers** — Displays a number for every line in the code; this feature is extremely helpful when used in combination with the JavaScript Debugger, which reports the line number of an error in the code.

- **Highlight Invalid HTML** — Toggles the highlighting of invalid tags in the Code view when the Design view is refreshed. Invalid tags are always highlighted in the Design view.

- **Syntax Coloring** — Syntax coloring makes code easier to read. Basic tags and keywords are shown in one color while text in another. Three different types of code are given different colors: Reserved Keywords, Other Keywords, and Strings. These colors are set in the Code Color category of Preferences. You can also set a color for an individual tag to further distinguish it if you like.

Caution: Disabling coloring in the code has a rather unexpected repercussion. With Syntax Coloring disabled, the Reference panel is no longer context-sensitive. In other words, you cannot select a tag, attribute, or CSS style rule in the Code view and then select the Reference button to find that particular entry in the Reference panel.

- **Auto Indent** — Auto Indent is another feature intended to improve code readability. With Auto Indent enabled, pressing Enter (Return) at the end of a line causes the new line to start at the same indentation as the preceding line. Press Backspace (Delete) to move the indented line closer to left margin. The number of characters for each indentation is set in the Code Format category of Preferences.

You can also change the indentation — in or out — for selected blocks of code with one command. To further indent a block of code, select it and then choose Edit ➪ Indent Code or use the keyboard shortcut Ctrl+] (Command+]). To decrease the level of indentation for a selected code block, choose Edit ➪ Outdent Code or the keyboard shortcut Ctrl+[(Command+[).

New Feature: As a further aid to help you find your way through a maze of code, Dreamweaver 4 includes the Balance Braces command. JavaScript is notorious for using parentheses, brackets, and curly braces to structure its code — and it's easy to lose sight of where one enclosing brace begins and it's closing mate ends. Dreamweaver highlights the content found within the closest pair of braces to the cursor when you select Edit ⇨ Balance Braces or use the keyboard shortcut Ctrl-' (Command-'). If you select the command again, the selection expands to the set of surrounding braces. When the selection is not enclosed by parentheses, brackets, or curly braces, Dreamweaver sounds an alert.

Although most Web designers prone to using the code editor in Dreamweaver prefer to handwrite their code, the power of the Objects panel is still at your disposal for rapid code development. Any element available from the Objects panel can be inserted directly into the Code view or inspector. To use the Objects panel, you must first position your cursor where you would like the code for the object to appear and then select the element. You cannot, however, drag-and-drop an element from the Objects panel to the Code view or inspector.

Cross-Reference: Keep in mind that the Dreamweaver's code editor is highly customizable. You can change the way the lines wrap, by using indents for certain tag pairs; you can even control the amount of indentation. All the options are outlined for you in Chapter 4.

Rapid Tag Modification with the Quick Tag Editor

I tend to build Web pages in two phases: First, I generally lay out my text and images to create the overall design, and then I go back, adding details and alterations to get the page just right. The second phase of Web page design often requires that I make a small adjustment to the HTML code, typically through the Property Inspector, but occasionally I need to go right to the source — code, that is.

Dreamweaver offers a feature for making minor but essential alterations to the code: the Quick Tag Editor. The Quick Tag Editor is a small pop-up window that appears in the Document window and enables you to edit an existing tag, add a new tag, or wrap the current selection in a tag. One other feature makes the Quick Tag Editor even quicker to use: A handy list of tags or attributes appears to cut down on your typing.

To call up the Quick Tag Editor, use any of the following methods:

- Choose Modify ⇨ Quick Tag Editor.
- Press the keyboard shortcut Ctrl+T (Command+T).
- Select the Quick Tag Editor icon on the Property Inspector.

The Quick Tag Editor has three modes: Insert HTML, Wrap Tag, and Edit HTML. Although you can get to all three modes from any situation, which mode appears initially depends on the current selection. The Quick Tag Editor's window (Figure 4-8) appears above the current selection when you use either the menu or keyboard method of opening it, or next to the Property Inspector when you select the icon. In either case, you can move the Quick Tag Editor window to a new location onscreen by dragging its Title bar.

Tip Regardless of which mode the Quick Tag Editor opens in, you can toggle to the other modes by pressing the keyboard shortcut Ctrl+T (Command+T).

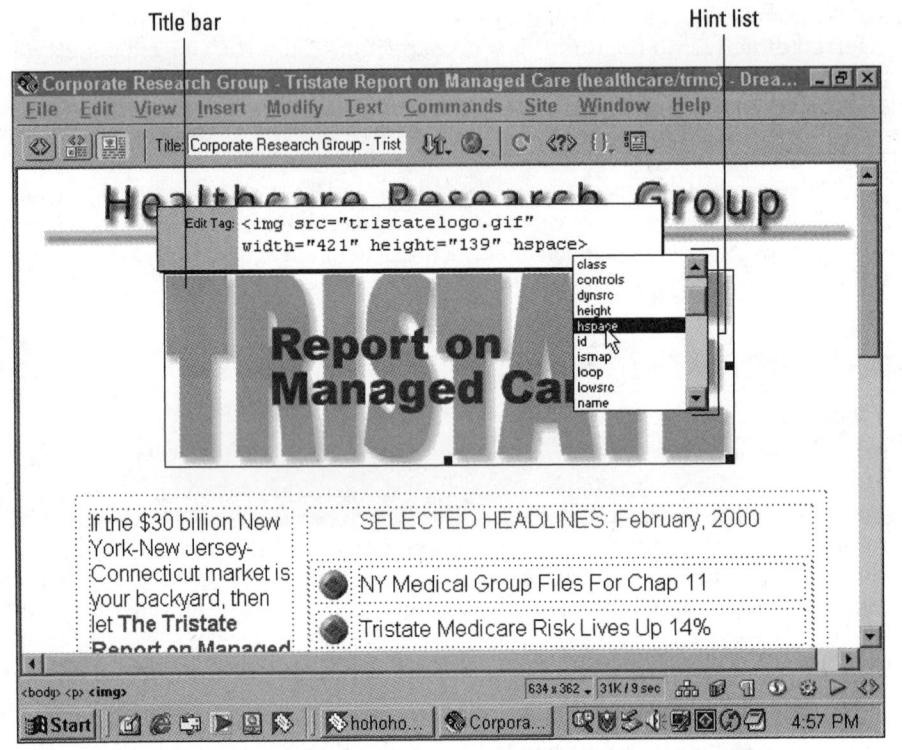

Figure 4-8: The Quick Tag Editor is great for quickly tweaking your code.

See the "Working with the Hint List" sidebar later in this chapter for details about this feature.

Insert HTML mode

The Insert HTML mode of the Quick Tag Editor is used for adding new tags and code at the current cursor position; it is the initial mode when nothing is selected. The Insert HTML mode starts with a pair of angle brackets enclosing a blinking cursor.

You can enter any desired tag—whether standard HTML or custom XML—and any attribute or content within the new tag. When you're done, just press Enter (Return) to confirm your addition.

To add new tags to your page using the Quick Tag Editor Insert HTML mode, follow these steps:

1. Position your cursor where you would like the new code to be inserted.
2. Choose Modify ⇨ Quick Tag Editor or use the keyboard shortcut, Ctrl+T (Command+T), to open the Quick Tag Editor.

   The Quick Tag Editor opens in Insert HTML mode, as shown in Figure 4-9.

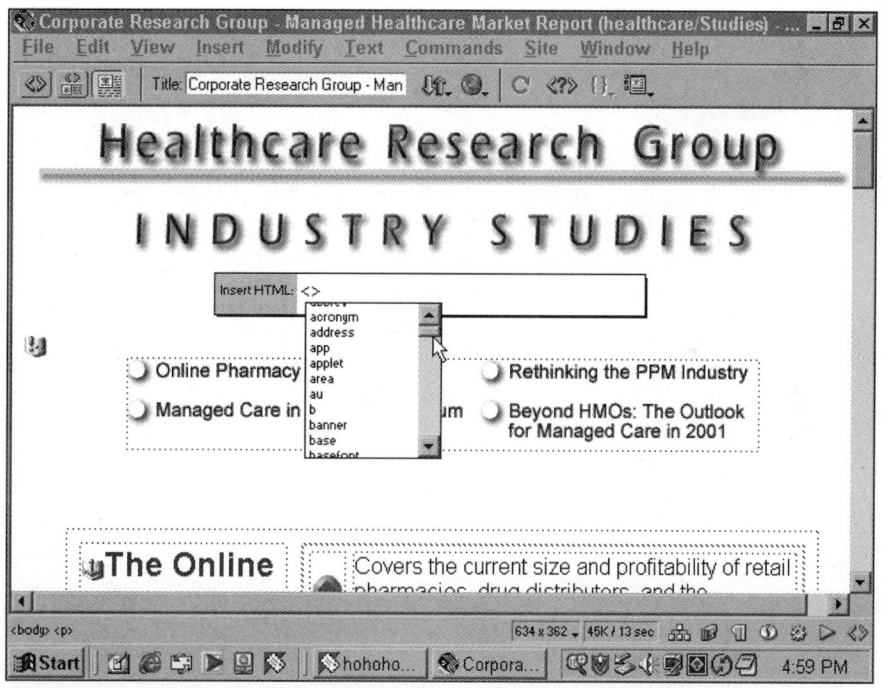

Figure 4-9: Use the Quick Tag Editor's Insert HTML mode to add tags not available through Dreamweaver's visual interface.

3. Enter your HTML or XML code.

Tip Use the right-arrow key to move quickly past the closing angle bracket and add text after your tag.

4. If you pause while typing, the hint list appears, selecting the first tag that matches what you've typed so far. Use the arrow keys to select another tag in the list and press Enter (Return) to select a tag.

Working with the Hint List

The Quick Tag Editor has a rather nifty feature referred to as the *hint list*. To make it even quicker to use the Quick Tag Editor, a list of tags pops up when you pause in your typing. When you're entering attributes within a tag, a list of appropriate parameters pops up instead of tags. These lists are tied to what, if anything, you've already typed. Say, for instance, you've begun to enter **blockquote** and have only gotten as far typing **b** and **l**. When the hint list appears, it scrolls to "blink"—the first tag in the list starting with those two letters. If you continue typing "o," "blockquote" is selected. All you have to do to insert it into your code is to press Enter (Return).

Here's a few other hint list hints:

- Scroll to a tag by using the up- or down-arrow keys.
- Double-clicking the selected hint list item also inserts it into the code.
- Once the hint list is open, press Esc if you decide not to enter the selected tag or attribute.
- If an attribute has a set series of values that can be applied (for example, the <div> tag align attribute can only be set to left, right, or center), those values are accessible via the hint list.
- Control how quickly the hint list appears—or even if it appears at all—by altering the Quick Tag Editor preferences.

The tags and attributes that appear in the hint list are contained in the TagAttributeList.text file found in the Dreamweaver Configuration folder. The list is in a format known as Data Type Declaration (DTD), where each tag is listed as a separate element and any corresponding attributes are displayed under each of those elements. Here, for example, is the DTD listing for the background sound tag, <bgsound>:

```
<!ELEMENT BGSOUND Name="Background sound" >
<!ATTLIST BGSOUND
    Balance
    Loop
    Src
    Volume
>
```

As with almost all other Dreamweaver aspects, the TagAttribute.txt list can be modified to include any special tags and their attributes you might need to include on a regular basis. Just relaunch Dreamweaver after making your changes in a standard text editor and your modifications are included the next time you use the Quick Tag Editor.

5. Press Enter (Return) when you're done.

The Quick Tag Editor is fairly intelligent and tries to help you write valid HTML. If, for example, you leave off a closing tag, such as </b>, the Quick Tag Editor automatically adds it for you.

Wrap Tag mode

Part of the power and flexibility of HTML is the capability to wrap one tag around one or more other tags and content. To make a phrase appear bold and italic, the code is written this way:

```
<b><i>On Sale Now!</i></b>
```

Note how the inner `<i>...</i>` tag pair is enclosed by the `<b>...</b>` pair. The Wrap Tag mode of the Quick Tag Editor surrounds any selection with your entered tag in one easy operation.

The Wrap Tag mode appears initially when you have selected just text (with no surrounding tags) or an incomplete tag (the opening tag and contents but no closing tag). The Wrap Tag mode is visually similar to the Insert HTML mode, as can be seen in Figure 4-10. However, rather than just include exactly what you've entered into the Quick Tag Editor, Wrap Tag mode also inserts a closing tag that corresponds to your entry. For example, let's say I want to apply a tag not available in Dreamweaver's Document window, the subscript or `<sub>` tag. After highlighting the text I want to mark up as subscript (a "2" in the formula, H_2O, for example), I open the Quick Tag Editor and enter **sub**. The resulting code looks like this:

```
H<sub>2</sub>O
```

Caution You can only enter one tag in Wrap Tag mode; if more than one tag is entered, Dreamweaver displays an alert informing you that the tag you've entered appears to be invalid HTML. The Quick Tag Editor is then closed, and the selection is cleared.

To wrap a tag with the Quick Tag Editor, follow these steps:

1. Select the text or tags you want to enclose in another tag.
2. Choose Modify ⇨ Quick Tag Editor or use the keyboard shortcut, Ctrl+T (Command+T), to open the Quick Tag Editor.

   The Quick Tag Editor opens in Wrap Tag mode.
3. If you select a complete tag, the Quick Tag Editor opens in Edit HTML mode; press the keyboard shortcut, Ctrl+T (Command+T), to toggle to Wrap Tag mode.
4. Enter the desired tag.
5. If you pause while typing, the hint list appears, selecting the first tag that matches what you've typed so far. Use the arrow keys to select another tag in the list and press Enter (Return) to select a tag from the hint list.
6. Press Enter (Return) to confirm your tag.

   The Quick Tag Editor closes and Dreamweaver adds your tag before your selection and a corresponding closing tag after it.

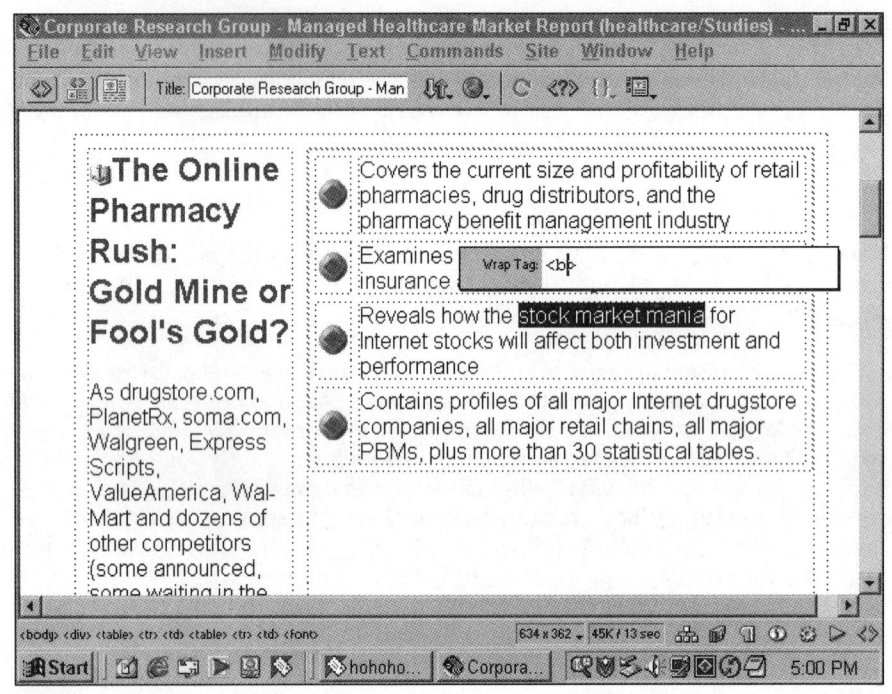

Figure 4-10: Enclose any selection with a tag by using the Quick Tag Editor's Wrap Tag mode.

Edit HTML mode

If a complete tag—either a single tag, such as `<img>`, or a tag pair, such as `<h1>...</h1>`—is selected, the Quick Tag Editor opens in Edit HTML mode. Unlike the other two modes where you are presented with just open and closing angle brackets and a flashing cursor, the Edit HTML mode displays the entire selected tag with all the attributes, if any. The Edit HTML mode is always invoked when you start the Quick Tag Editor by clicking its icon in the Property Inspector.

The Edit HTML mode has many uses. I've found it to be terrific for adding a parameter not found on Dreamweaver's Property Inspector. For example, when building a form that returns the information formatted, you need to declare the enctype attribute to be equal to "text/plain." However, the enctype attribute cannot be assigned from the Property Inspector for the `<form>` tag. So, I just select the tag from the Tag Selector and then click the Quick Tag Editor icon to open the Quick Tag Editor. The `<form>` tag appears with my current parameters, as shown in Figure 4-11.

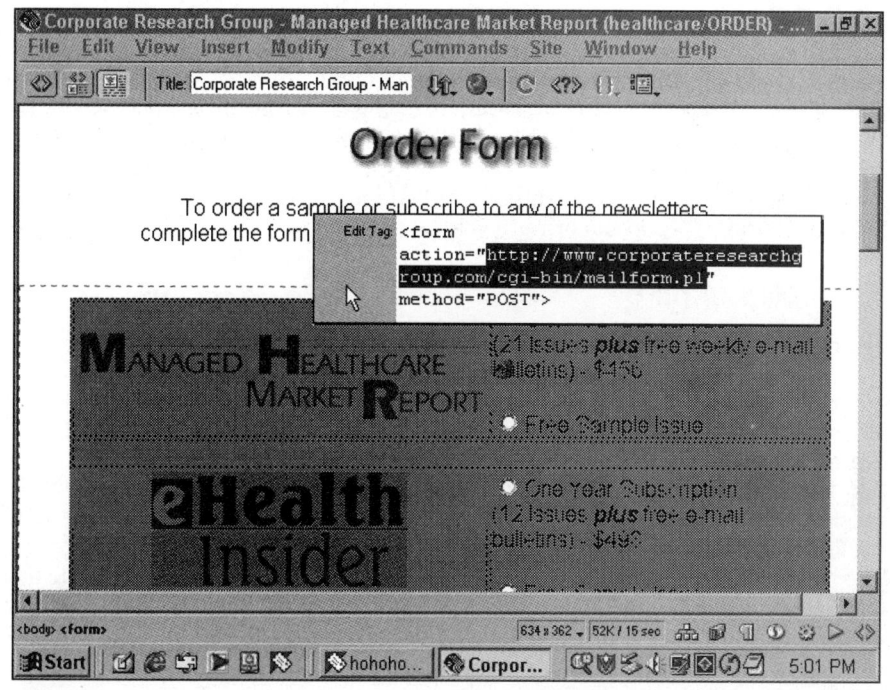

Figure 4-11: In Edit HTML mode, the Quick Tag Editor shows the entire tag with attributes and their values.

To use the Quick Tag Editor in Insert HTML mode, follow these steps:

1. Select an entire tag by clicking its name in the Tag Selector.
2. Choose Modify ➪ Quick Tag Editor.
3. To change an existing attribute, tab to the current value and enter a new one.
4. To add a new attribute, tab and/or use the arrow keys to position the cursor after an existing attribute or after the tag and enter the new parameter and value.

> **Tip:** If you don't close the quotation marks for a parameter's value, Dreamweaver does it for you.

5. If you pause briefly while entering a new attribute, the hint list appears with attributes appropriate for the current tag. If you select an attribute from the hint list, press Enter (Return) to accept the parameter.
6. When you're done editing the tag, press Enter (Return).

In addition to this capability to edit complete tags, Dreamweaver has a couple of navigational commands to help select just the right tag. The Select Parent Tag command—keyboard shortcut Ctrl+Shift+< (Command+Shift+<)—highlights the tag immediately surrounding the present tag. Going the other direction, Select Child Tag—keyboard shortcut Ctrl+Shift+> (Command+Shift+>)—chooses the next tag, if any, contained within the current tag. Both commands are available under the Edit menu. Exercising these commands is equivalent to selecting the next tag in the Tag Selector to the left (parent) or right (child).

Inserting Symbols and Special Characters

When working with Dreamweaver, you're usually entering text directly from your keyboard, one keystroke at a time, with each keystroke representing a letter, number, or other keyboard character. Some situations, however, require special letters that have diacritics or common symbols, such as the copyright mark, which are outside of the regular, standard character set represented on your keyboard. HTML enables you to insert a full range of such character entities through two systems. The more familiar special characters have been assigned a mnemonic code name to make them easy to remember; these are called *named characters*. Less typical characters must be inserted by entering a numeric code; these are known as *decimal characters*. For the sake of completeness, named characters also have a corresponding decimal character code.

Both named and decimal character codes begin with an ampersand (&) symbol and end with a semicolon (;). For example, the HTML code for an ampersand symbol follows:

    &

Its decimal character equivalent follows:

    &

Caution If, during the browser-testing phase of creating your Web page, you suddenly see an HTML code onscreen rather than a symbol, double-check your HTML. The code could be just a typo; you may have left off the closing semicolon, for instance. If the code is correct and you're using a named character, however, switch to its decimal equivalent. Some of the earlier browser versions are not perfect in rendering named characters.

Named characters

HTML coding conventions require that certain characters, including the angle brackets that surround tags, be entered as character entities. Table 4-3 lists the most common named characters.

Table 4-3
Common Named Characters

Named Entity	Symbol	Description
&lt;	<	A left angle bracket or the less-than symbol
&gt;	>	A right angle bracket or the greater-than symbol
&amp;	&	An ampersand
&quot;	"	A double quotation mark
	°	A nonbreaking space
&copy;	©	A copyright symbol
&reg;	®	A registered mark
&trade;	™	A trademark symbol, which cannot be previewed in Dreamweaver but is supported in Internet Explorer

Tip Those characters that you can type directly into Dreamweaver's Document window, including the brackets and the ampersand, are automatically translated into the correct named characters in HTML. Try this with the Code Inspector open. Also, you can enter a nonbreaking space in Dreamweaver by typing Ctrl+Shift+spacebar (Command+Shift+spacebar) or by choosing the Non-breaking Space object.

Decimal characters

To enter almost any character that has a diacritic—such as á, ñ, or â—in Dreamweaver, you must explicitly enter the corresponding decimal character into your HTML page. As mentioned in the preceding section, decimal characters take the form of &#number;, where the number can range from 00 to 255. Not all numbers have matching symbols; the sequence from 14 through 31 is currently unused and the upper range (127 through 159) is only partially supported by Internet Explorer and Netscape Navigator. Also, not all fonts have characters for every entity.

Using the Character objects

Not only is it difficult to remember the various name or number codes for the specific character entity you need, it's also a bit of a process to enter the code by hand. The Dreamweaver engineers recognized this need and created a series of Character objects on their own category of the Objects panel.

Ease-of-use is the guiding principal for the new Character objects. Nine of the most commonly used symbols, such as © and ™ are instantly available as separate objects. And a single object exists offering access to 99 different character entities. Inserting the single Character objects is a straightforward point-and-click affair. Either drag the desired symbol to a place in the Document window or position your cursor and select the object.

The nine individual Character objects are detailed in Table 4-4.

Table 4-4
Character Objects

Icon	Name	HTML Code Inserted
©	Insert Copyright	&copy;
®	Insert Registered Trademark	&reg;
™	Insert Trademark	&#153;
£	Insert Pound	&pound;
¥	Insert Yen	&yen;
€	Insert Euro	&euro;
—	Insert Em-Dash	&#151;
"	Insert Left Quote	&#147;
"	Insert Right Quote	&#148;

Note You may notice that the Character objects insert a mix of named and number character entities. Not all browsers recognize the easier-to-identify named entities, so for the widest compatibility, Dreamweaver uses the number codes for a few objects.

The final object on the Characters category is used for inserting these or any other character entity. The Other Characters object displays a large table with symbols for 99 different characters, as shown in Figure 4-12. Simply select the desired symbol and Dreamweaver inserts the appropriate HTML code into the current cursor position. By the way, the very first character — which appears to be blank — actually inserts the code for a nonbreaking space, also accessible via a keyboard shortcut, Ctrl+Shift+spacebar (Command+Shift+spacebar). The nonbreaking space is also available on the Characters category of the Objects panel.

Note Keep in mind that the user's browser must support the character entity for it to be visible to the user. In the case of the Euro symbol, that support is still very haphazard.

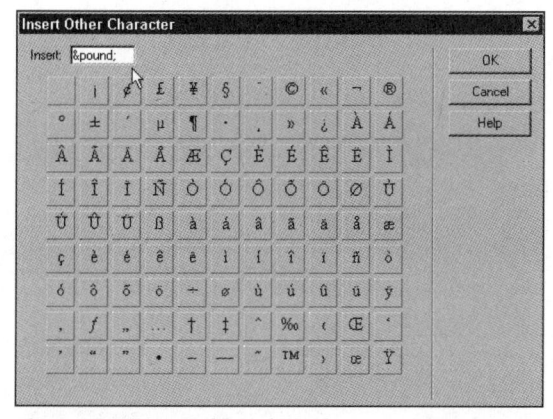

Figure 4-12: Use the Other Character objects to insert the character entity code for any of 99 different symbols.

Summary

Creating Web pages with Dreamweaver is a special blend of using visual layout tools and HTML coding. Regardless, you need to understand the basics of HTML so that you have the knowledge and the tools to modify your code when necessary. This chapter covered these key areas:

✦ An HTML page is divided into two main sections: the <head> and the <body>. Information pertaining to the entire page is kept in the <head> section; all the actual content of the Web page goes in the <body> section.

✦ You can change the color and background of your entire page, as well as set its title, through the Page Properties dialog box.

♦ Use `<meta>` tags to summarize your Web page so that search engines can properly catalog it. In Dreamweaver, you can use the View Head Contents feature to easily alter these and other `<head>` tags.

♦ When possible, use logical style tags, such as `<strong>` and `<cite>`, rather than hard-coding your page with physical style tags. Style sheets bring a great deal of control and flexibility to logical style tags.

♦ Special extended characters such as symbols and accented letters require the use of HTML character entities, which can either be named (as in `&quot;`) or in decimal format (as in `&#34;`).

In the next chapter, you learn how to insert and format text in Dreamweaver.

♦ ♦ ♦

Adding Text to Your Web Page

If content is king on the Web, then certainly style is queen—together they rule hand in hand. Entering, editing, and formatting text on a Web page is a major part of a Webmaster's job. Dreamweaver gives you the tools to make the task as clear-cut as possible. From headlines to comments, this chapter covers the essentials of working with basic text.

At first, Web designers didn't have many options for manipulating text. However, now the majority of browsers understand a number of text-related commands, and the designer can specify the font as well as its color and size. Dreamweaver includes a range of text manipulation tools. These topics are covered in this chapter, along with an important discussion of manipulating whitespace on the Web page.

Starting with Headings

Text in Hypertext Markup Language (HTML) is primarily composed of headings and paragraphs. Headings separate and introduce major sections of the document, just as a newspaper uses headlines to announce a story and subheads to provide essential details. HTML has six levels of headings; the syntax for the heading tags is `<hn>`, where *n* is a number from 1 to 6. The largest heading is `<h1>` and the smallest is `<h6>`.

Remember that HTML headings are not linked to any specific point size, unlike type produced in a page layout or word processing program. Headings in an HTML document are sized relative to one another, and their final, exact size depends on the browser used. The sample headlines in Figure 5-1 depict the basic headings as rendered through Dreamweaver and as compared to the default paragraph font size. As you can see, some headings are rendered in type smaller than that used for the default paragraph. Headings are usually displayed with a boldface attribute.

CHAPTER

5

✦ ✦ ✦ ✦

In This Chapter

Creating headings in Dreamweaver

Styling paragraphs

Importing Word HTML

Using special text formats

Changing fonts, font size, and font color

Running the Spell Checker

Automating your work with Find and Replace

Handling whitespace

Inserting HTML comments

✦ ✦ ✦ ✦

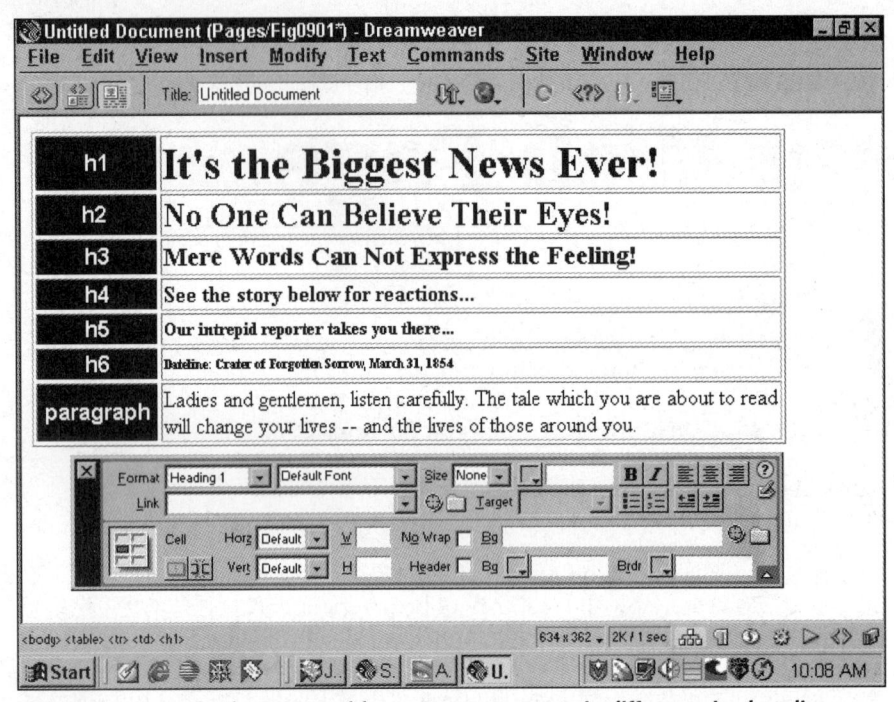

Figure 5-1: Standard HTML enables you to use up to six different size headings.

Two methods set text as a particular heading size in Dreamweaver. In both cases, you first need to select the text you want to affect. If you are styling a single line or paragraph as a heading, just position the cursor anywhere in the paragraph to select it. If you want to convert more than one paragraph, click and drag out your selection.

> **Tip**
>
> You can't mix heading levels in a single paragraph. That is, you can't have in the same line a word with an `<h1>` heading next to a word styled with an `<h4>` heading. Furthermore, headings belong to a group of HTML text tags called *block elements*. All block elements are rendered with a paragraph return both above and below, which isolates ("blocks") the text. To work around both of these restrictions, you can use `<font size=n>` tags to achieve the effect of varying sizes for words within the same line or for lines of different sizes close to one another. The `<font size=n>` tag is covered later in this chapter, in the section "Styling Your Text."

Once the text for the heading is selected, you can choose your heading level by selecting Text ⇨ Paragraph Format and then one of the Headings 1 through 6 from the submenu. Alternatively, you can make your selection from the Text Property Inspector. (If it's not already open, display the Property Inspector by selecting Window ⇨ Properties.) In the Text Property Inspector, open the Format drop-down list (see Figure 5-2) and choose one of the six headings.

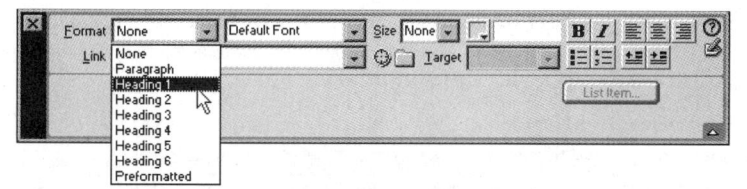

Figure 5-2: You can convert any paragraph or line into a heading by using the Format options in the Text Property Inspector.

Headings are often used in a hierarchical fashion, largest to smallest — but you don't have to do it that way. You can have an `<h3>` line followed by an `<h1>` paragraph, if that's what your design needs. Be careful using the smallest headings, `<h4>`–`<h6>`; they are likely to be difficult to read on any resolution higher than 800×600.

Working with Paragraphs

Usually the bulk of text on any Web page is composed of paragraphs. Paragraphs in HTML are denoted by the `<p>` and `</p>` pair of tags. When your Web page is processed, the browser formats everything between those two tags as one paragraph and renders it to fit the user's screen, word wrapping as needed at the margins. Any additional line breaks and unnecessary whitespace (beyond one space between words and between sentences) in the HTML code are ignored.

> **Tip** In the early version of HTML, paragraphs used just the opening `<p>` tag, and browsers rendered everything between `<p>` tags as one paragraph; the closing tag was optional. As of HTML 3.2, however, an optional closing `</p>` tag was added. Because so many Web pages have been created with just the opening paragraph tag, most browsers still recognize the single-tag format. To be on the safe side in terms of future compatibility, enclose your paragraphs within both opening and closing tags when you do any hand-coding.

Dreamweaver starts a new paragraph every time you press Enter (Return) when composing text in the Document window. If you have the Code view or the Code Inspector open when you work, you can see that Dreamweaver inserts the following code with each new paragraph:

```
<p> </p>
```

The code between the tags creates a nonbreaking space that enables the new line to be visible. You won't see the new line if you have just the paragraph tags with nothing (neither a character nor a character entity, such as) in between:

```
<p></p>
```

When you continue typing, Dreamweaver replaces the nonbreaking space with your input, unless you press Enter (Return) again. Figure 5-3 illustrates two paragraphs with text and a third paragraph with the nonbreaking space still in place.

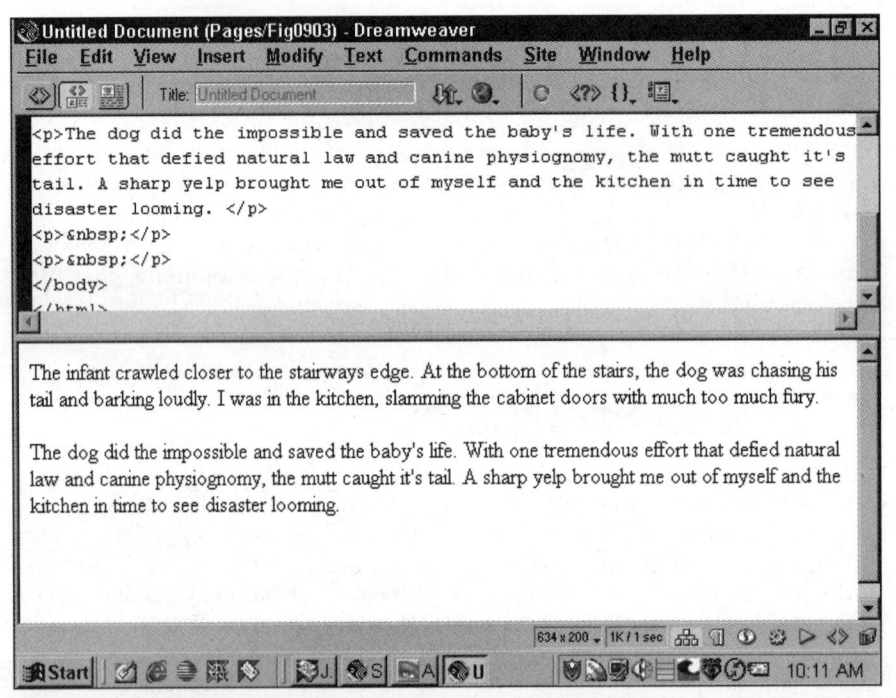

Figure 5-3: Dreamweaver automatically wraps any text inserted into the Document window. If you press Enter (Return) without entering text, Dreamweaver enters paragraph tags surrounding a nonbreaking space.

You can easily change text from most other formats, such as a heading, to paragraph format. First, select the text you want to alter. Then, in the Property Inspector, open the Format options drop-down list and choose Paragraph. You can also choose Text ⇨ Paragraph Format ⇨ Paragraph from the menu or use the keyboard shortcut Ctrl+Shift+P (Command+Shift+P).

All paragraphs are initially rendered on the page in the default font at the default size. The user can designate these defaults through the browser preferences, although most people don't bother to alter them. If you want to change the font name or the font size for selected paragraphs explicitly, use the techniques described in the upcoming section, "Styling Your Text."

Tip: Remember, you can always use the Tag Selector on the status bar to select and highlight any tag surrounding your current cursor position. This method makes it easy to see exactly what a particular tag is affecting.

Editing paragraphs

By and large, the editing features of Dreamweaver are similar to other modern word processing programs — with one or two Web-oriented twists. Dreamweaver has Cut, Copy, and Paste options, as well as Undo and Redo commands. You can search for and replace any text on your Web page under construction and even check its spelling.

The "twists" come from the relationship between the Design and Code views of the Document window, which give Dreamweaver special functionality for copying and pasting text and code. Let's see how that works.

Inserting text

You've already seen how you can position the cursor on the page and directly enter text. In this sense, Dreamweaver acts like a word processing program, rather than a page layout program. On a blank page, the cursor starts at the top-left corner of the page. Words automatically wrap to the next line when the text exceeds the right margin. Press Enter (Return) to end the current paragraph and start the next one.

Indenting text

In Dreamweaver, you cannot indent text as you can with a word processor. Tabs normally have no effect in HTML. To indent a paragraph's first line, one method uses nonbreaking spaces, which can be inserted with the keyboard shortcut Ctrl+Shift+spacebar (Command+Shift+spacebar). Nonbreaking spaces are an essential part of any Web designer's palette because they provide single-character spacing — often necessary to nudge an image or other object into alignment. You've already seen the code for a nonbreaking space —   — that Dreamweaver inserts between the <p>...</p> tag pair to make the line visible.

Aside from the keyboard shortcut, two other methods involve inserting a nonbreaking space. You can enter its character code —   — directly into the HTML code. You can also style your text as *preformatted*; this technique is discussed later in this chapter.

Tip: Another method exists for indenting the first line of a paragraph: Cascading Style Sheets. You can set an existing HTML tag, such as <p>, to any indent amount using the Text Indent option found on the Block panel of the Style Sheet dialog box. Be aware, however, that the various browsers support style sheets differently and to a different extent. A full discussion of text indent and other style sheet controls is in Chapter 14.

Inserting Text from Other Applications

The Paste command can also insert text from another program into Dreamweaver. If you cut or copy text from a file in any other program — whether it is a word processor, spreadsheet, or database program — Dreamweaver inserts it at the cursor position. The results of this Paste operation vary, however.

Dreamweaver can paste only plain, unformatted text — any bold, italic, or other styling in the original document are not retained in Dreamweaver. Paragraph breaks, however, are retained and reproduced in two different ways. A single paragraph return becomes a line break (a <br> tag) in Dreamweaver, whereas text separated by two returns is formatted into two HTML paragraphs, using the <p>... </p> tag pair.

If you need to import a great deal of text and want to retain as much formatting as possible, you can use another application, such as Microsoft Word, to save your text as an HTML file. Then open that file in Dreamweaver with the Import Word HTML command.

Cutting, copying, and pasting

Text can be moved from one place to another — or from one Web document to another — using the standard cut-and-paste techniques. No surprises here: Before you can cut or copy anything, you must select it. Select by clicking the mouse at the beginning of the text you want to cut or copy, drag the highlight to the end of your selection, and then release the mouse button.

Here are some other selection methods:

✦ Double-click a word to select it.

✦ Move the pointer to the left margin of the text until the pointer changes to a right-facing arrow. Click once to highlight a single line. Click and drag down the margin to select a group of lines.

✦ Position the cursor at the beginning of your selection. Hold down the Shift key and then click once at the end of the selection.

✦ You can select everything in the body of your document by using Edit ➪ Select All or the keyboard shortcut Ctrl+A (Command+A).

✦ Use the Tag Selector to select text or other objects contained within specific tags.

✦ You can also select text by holding down Shift and using the right- or left-arrow key to select one character at a time. If you hold down Ctrl+Shift (Command+Shift), you can press the right- or left-arrow key to select a word at a time.

When you want to move a block of text, first select it and then use Edit ⇨ Cut or the keyboard shortcut Ctrl+X (Command+X). This sequence removes the text from the document and places it on your system's clipboard. To paste the text, move the pointer to the new location and click once to place the cursor. Then select Edit ⇨ Paste or the keyboard shortcut Ctrl+V (Command+V). The text is copied from the clipboard to its new location. You can continue pasting this same text from the clipboard until another block of text is copied or cut.

To copy text, the procedure is much the same. Select the text using one of the preceding methods and then use Edit ⇨ Copy or Ctrl+C (Command+C). The selected text is copied to the clipboard, and the original text is left in place. Then position the cursor in a new location and select Edit ⇨ Paste (or use the keyboard shortcut).

Using drag-and-drop

The other, quicker method for moving or copying text is the drag-and-drop technique. Once you've selected your text, release the mouse button and move the cursor over the highlighted area. The cursor changes from an I-beam to an arrow. To move the text, click the selected area with the arrow cursor and drag your mouse to a new location. The arrow cursor now has a box attached to it, indicating that it is carrying something. As you move your cursor, a bar (the insertion point) moves with you, indicating where the text will be positioned. Release the mouse button to drop the text. You can copy text in the same manner by holding down the Ctrl (Option) key as you drag and drop your selected text. When copying this way, the box attached to the cursor is marked with a plus sign (on Macintosh computers the box is the same size as the text selection and no plus sign appears).

To remove text completely, select it and then choose Edit ⇨ Clear or press Delete. The only way to recover deleted text is to use the Undo feature described in the following section.

Copying and Pasting Code

The "Editing paragraphs," section earlier in this chapter mentioned that Dreamweaver includes a couple of "twists" to the standard Cut, Copy, and Paste options. The combination of Dreamweaver's Design and Code views enables you to copy and paste both text and code. Previous versions of Dreamweaver used a couple of additional commands — Copy Text Only and Paste As Text — to accomplish what Dreamweaver 4 now does with the dual page views.

Put simply, to copy just text from Dreamweaver to another application, use the Design view; to copy both text and code, use the Code view. To understand how two views interact, let's examine how they are used. Table 5-1 explains the variations.

Table 5-1
Results of Copy/Paste from Design and Code views

Selected Text	Copy From	Paste To	Result
Example Text	Design view	Other program	Example Text
Example Text	Design view	Design view	**Example Text**
<b>Example Text</b>	Code view or other program	Code view	**Example Text** (Design view) <b>Example Text</b> (Code view)
<b>Example Text</b>	Code view or other program	Design view	<b>Example Text</b> (Design view) &lt;b&gt;Example Text&lt;/b&gt; (Code view)

Notice that in the final row of Table 5-1, if you copy formatted text such as the boldface "Example Text" sample and insert it in the Design view, you get the following:

```
&lt;b&gt;Example Text&lt;/b&gt;
```

If you remember the section on named character entities in Chapter 4, you may recognize `&lt;` as the code for the less-than symbol (<) and `&gt;` as the code for the greater-than symbol (>). These symbols are used to represent tags such as `<b>` and `</b>` to prevent a browser from interpreting them as tag delimiters.

So what possible real-life uses could there be for Dreamweaver's implementation of the regular Copy and Paste commands in the different views? First, these options are a major benefit for programmers, teachers, and writers who constantly have to communicate in both HTML code and regular text. If an instructor is attempting to demonstrate a coding technique on a Web page, for example, she can just copy the code in the Code view and Paste it into the Design view — instantly transforming the code into something readable online.

Undo, Redo, and the History panel

The Undo command has to be one of the greatest inventions of the twentieth century. Make a mistake? Undo! Want to experiment with two different options? Undo! Change your mind again? Redo! The Undo command reverses your last action, whether you changed a link, added a graphic, or deleted the entire page. The Redo command enables you to reverse your Undo actions.

Dreamweaver displays all of your previous actions on the History panel, so you can easily see what steps you took. To use the Undo command, you can either choose Edit ⇨ Undo or press the keyboard shortcut Ctrl+Z (Command+Z); either command undoes a single action at a time. To undo multiple actions, drag the slider in the History panel to the last action you want to keep or just click the slider track at that action.

The complement to Undo is the Redo command. To reverse an Undo command, choose Edit ⇨ Redo or Ctrl+Y (Command+Y). To reverse several Undo commands, drag the slider in the History panel back over the grayed-out steps; alternately, you can click the slider track once at the step up to which you'd like to redo.

> **Tip**
>
> The best use I've found for the Redo command is in concert with Undo. When I'm trying to decide between two alternatives, such as two different images, I'll replace one choice with another and then use the Undo/Redo combination to go back and forth between them. Because Dreamweaver replaces any selected object with the current object from the clipboard — even if one is a block of text and the other is a layer — you can easily view two separate options with this trick. The History panel enables you to apply this procedure over any number of steps.

Dreamweaver's implementation of the Undo command enables you to back up as many steps as set in the Maximum Number of History Steps found in Preferences. The History steps can even undo actions that had taken place before a document was saved. Note that the History panel has additional features besides multiple undos.

> **On the CD-ROM**
>
> Although the History panel lets you replay any series of selected steps at the press of a button, you have to press that button every time you want to replay the steps. I developed a custom extension called Repeat History with which you can repeat any selected steps any number of times. You'll find Repeat History in the Additional Extensions folder on the CD-ROM.

Checking your spelling

A typo can make a significant impression. Not many things are more embarrassing than showing a new Web site to a client and having that client point out a spelling error. Dreamweaver includes an easy-to-use Spell Checker to help you avoid such awkward moments. I make it a practice to spell-check every Web page before it's posted online.

You start the process by choosing Text ⇨ Check Spelling or you can press the keyboard shortcut Shift+F7. This sequence opens the Check Spelling dialog box, as seen in Figure 5-4.

Spell-Checking in Non-English Languages

Macromedia has made additional language dictionaries available. As of this writing, dictionaries in these other languages are also available: German, Spanish, French, Italian, Brazilian-Portuguese, Catalan, and Swedish. You can download these dictionaries from Macromedia's Dreamweaver Object Exchange at `www.macromedia.com/support/dreamweaver/dictionary.html`.

To use the dictionaries, download the compressed file to your system. After uncompressing them, store the file with the .dat extension in the Configuration\Dictionaries folder and restart Dreamweaver. Finally, open Preferences (Edit ⇨ Preferences) and, from the General panel, select the Dictionary option button. Choose the new language from the drop-down list, and you're ready to spell correctly in another tongue.

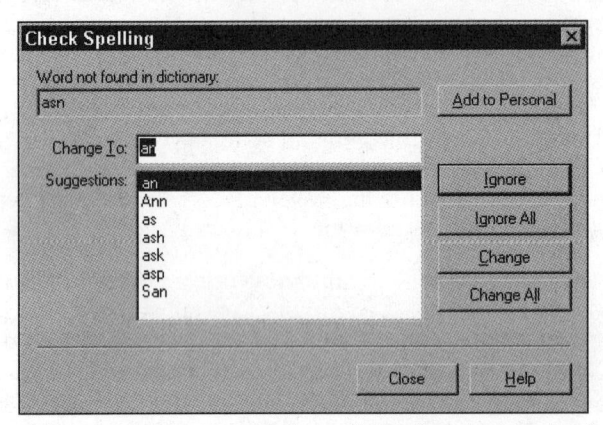

Figure 5-4: Dreamweaver's Spell Checker double-checks your spelling and can find the typos on any Web page.

Once you've opened the Check Spelling dialog box, Dreamweaver begins searching your text for errors. Unless you have selected a portion of your document, Dreamweaver checks the full document regardless of where your cursor is placed. When text is selected, Dreamweaver checks the selection first and then asks if you'd like to do the entire document.

Dreamweaver checks your Web page text against two dictionaries: a standard English (or your chosen language) dictionary and a personal dictionary, to which you can add words. If the Spell Checker finds any text not in either of the program's dictionaries, the text is highlighted in the Document window and appears in the Word not found in dictionary field of the dialog box. A list of suggested corrections appears in the Suggestions list box, with the topmost one highlighted and also displayed in the Change To box. If Dreamweaver cannot find any suggestions, the Change To box is left blank. At this point, you have the following options:

- **Add to Personal:** Select this button to include the highlighted word in your personal dictionary and prevent Dreamweaver from tagging it as an error in the future.
- **Ignore:** Select this button when you want Dreamweaver to leave the currently highlighted word alone and continue searching the text.
- **Ignore All:** Select this button when you want Dreamweaver to disregard all occurrences of this word in the current document.
- **Change:** If you see the correct replacement among the list of suggestions, highlight it and select the Change button. If no suggestion is appropriate, you can type the correct word into the Change To text box and then select this button.
- **Change All:** Choosing this button causes all instances of the current word to be replaced with the word in the Change To text box.

> **Tip** Have you ever accidentally added a misspelled word to your personal dictionary and then been stuck with the error for all eternity? Dreamweaver enables you to recover from your mistake by giving you access to the dictionary itself. The personal dictionary, stored in the Dreamweaver\Configuration\Dictionaries\personal.dat file, can be opened and modified in any text editor.

Using Find and Replace

Dreamweaver's Find and Replace features are both timesaving and lifesaving (well, almost). You can use Find and Replace to cut your input time substantially by searching for abbreviations and expanding them to their full state. You can also find a client's incorrectly spelled name and replace it with the correctly spelled version—that's a lifesaver! However, that's just the tip of the iceberg when it comes to what Find and Replace can really do. The Find and Replace engine should be considered a key power tool for any Web developer. You can not only search multiple files but also easily check the code separately from the content.

Here's a short list of what the Find and Replace feature makes possible:

- Search the Document window to find any type of text.
- Search the underlying HTML to find tags, attributes, or text within tags.
- Look for text within specific tags with specific attributes—or look for text that's outside of a specific tag with specific attributes.
- Find and replace patterns of text, using wildcard characters called *regular expressions*.
- Apply any of the preceding Find and Replace operations to the current document, the current site, any folder, or any group of selected files.

The basic command, Find and Replace is found, with it's companion, Find Next (Find Again, on the Macintosh), under the Edit menu. You can use both commands in either Dreamweaver's Design or Code view, and —in Windows systems —the Site window. Although invoked by a single command, you can use the Find feature independently or in conjunction with Replace.

Find and Replace operations can be applied to one or a series of documents. In addition to searching the current document, you can also apply Find and Replace to all of the files in a folder or a site. Furthermore, individual files selected in the Site window are also searchable.

Finding and replacing text on the visual page

The most basic method of using Find and Replace takes place in the Document window. Whenever you need to search for any text that can be seen by the public on your Web page—whether it's to correct a spelling or change a name— Dreamweaver makes it fast and simple.

Tip The Find and Replace dialog box, unlike most of Dreamweaver's dialog boxes, is actually a *nonmodal window.* This technical term just means that you can easily move back and forth between your Document window and the Find and Replace dialog box without having to close the dialog box first, as you do with the other Dreamweaver windows.

To find some text on your Web page, follow these steps:

1. From the Document window, choose Edit ⇨ Find and Replace or use the keyboard shortcut Ctrl+F (Command+F).

2. In the Find and Replace dialog box, shown in Figure 5-5, make sure that Text is the selected Search For option.

3. In the text box next to the Search For option, type the word or phrase you're looking for.

Tip If you select your text *before* launching the Find dialog box, it automatically appears in the Search For text box.

4. Select the appropriate search options, if any:

    - If you want to find an exact replica of the word as you entered it, select the Match Case checkbox; otherwise, Dreamweaver searches for all variations of your text, regardless of case.

    - To force Dreamweaver to disregard any whitespace variations, such as additional spaces, hard spaces or tabs, select the Ignore Whitespace Differences option. For most situations, it's a good idea to leave this default option enabled.

    - Selecting Use Regular Expressions enables you to work with Dreamweaver's wildcard characters (discussed later in this section). Use Regular Expressions and Ignore Whitespace Differences are mutually exclusive options.

Chapter 5 ✦ Adding Text to Your Web Page   **115**

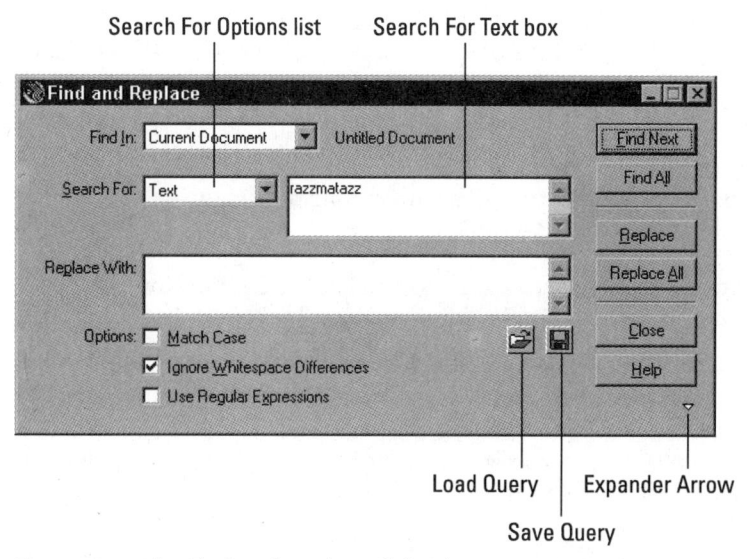

Figure 5-5: The Find and Replace dialog box.

Callouts: Search For Options list; Search For Text box; Load Query; Save Query; Expander Arrow.

5. Select the Find Next button to begin the search from the cursor's current position.

   • If Dreamweaver finds the desired text, it highlights the text in the Document window.

   • If Dreamweaver doesn't find the text in the remaining portion of the document, it asks if you want to continue searching from the beginning. Select Yes to continue or No to exit.

6. If you want to look for the next occurrence of your selected text, click the Find Next button again.

7. To look for all occurrences of your text, choose Find All.

   The Find dialog box expands to display the List window. Dreamweaver lists each found occurrence on a separate line in the List window.

> **Tip**
>
> You can quickly move from one found selection to another by double-clicking the line in the List window. Dreamweaver highlights the selection, scrolling the Document window, if necessary.

   After searching the page, Dreamweaver tells you how many occurrences of your selection, if any, were found.

8. You can enter other text to search or exit the Find dialog box by clicking the Close button.

The text you enter in the Find dialog box is kept in memory until it's replaced by your next use of the Find feature. After you have executed the Find command once, you can continue to search for your text without redisplaying the Find dialog box, by selecting Edit ⇨ Find Next (Find Again) or the keyboard shortcut F3 (Command+G). If Dreamweaver finds your text, it is highlighted — in fact, Dreamweaver acts exactly the same as when the Find dialog box is open. The Find Next (Find Again) command gives you a quick way to search through a long document — especially when you put the F3 (Command+G) key to work.

When you add the Replace command to a Find operation, you can search your text for a word or phrase and, if it's found, replace it with another word or phrase of your choice. As mentioned earlier, the Replace feature is a handy way to correct mistakes and expand abbreviations. Figure 5-6 shows an example of the latter operation. This example intentionally uses the abbreviation DW throughout the input text of a Web page article. Then the example uses the Replace All function to expand all the DWs to Dreamweaver — in one fell swoop. This technique is much faster than typing "Dreamweaver" nine times.

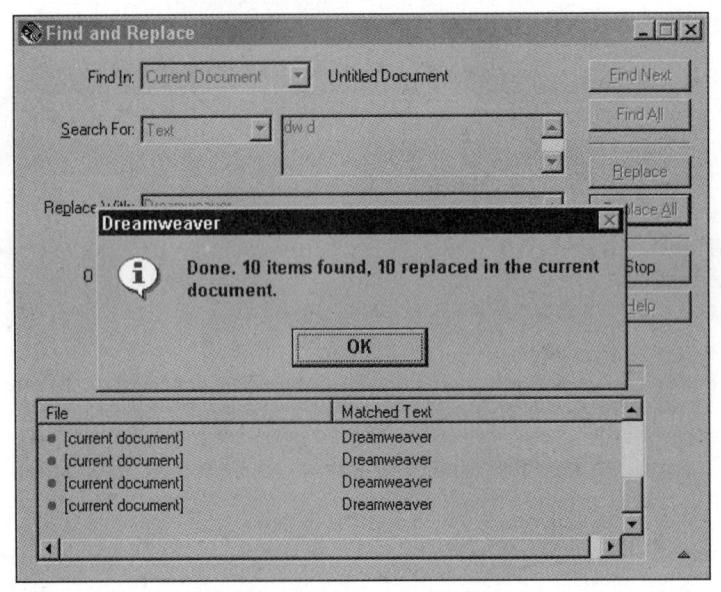

Figure 5-6: Use the Edit ⇨ Replace command to correct your text one item at a time or all at once.

When you replace text in the Document window, it is replaced regardless of its formatting. For example, suppose you had the following paragraph:

Mary's accusation reminded Jon of studying synchrones in high school. *Synchrones*, he recalled, were graphs in which the lines constantly approached zero, but never made it. "Yeah," he thought, "That's me, all right. I'm one big **synchrone**."

Upon discovering that "synchrone" should actually be "asymptote," you could use the Find and Replace feature to replace all the plain, italic, and bold versions of the "synchrone" text simultaneously.

> **Tip:** It's possible to alter formatting as well — to change all the formatting to just underlining for example — but for that, you need to perform your Find and Replace operations in the Code Inspector, as discussed in the following section.

Follow these steps to use Dreamweaver's Replace feature in the Document window:

1. Choose Edit ⇨ Find and Replace, or the keyboard shortcut Ctrl+F (Command+F).

2. In the Find and Replace dialog box, make sure that Text is the selected Search For option and then, in the text box next to the Search For option, type the word or phrase you're looking for.

3. In the Replace With text box, type the substitute word.

4. Click the Find Next button. Dreamweaver begins searching from the current cursor position. If Dreamweaver finds the text, it is highlighted.

   If the text is not found, Dreamweaver asks if you want to continue searching from the top of the document. Select Yes to continue or No to exit.

5. To replace the highlighted occurrence of your text, select the Replace button. Dreamweaver replaces the found text with the substitute text and then automatically searches for the next occurrence.

6. If you want to replace all instances of the Find text, select the Replace All button.

   When Dreamweaver has found all the occurrences of your Find text, it displays the number of replacement operations and a line for each in the List window.

   Double-clicking a line in the List window highlights the changed text in the Document window.

7. When you've finished using the Replace dialog box, click the Close button to exit.

> **Tip:** You can also rerun Find and Replace operations by highlighting the appropriate step in the History panel and choosing the Replay button.

Searching the code

The power curve ramps up significantly when you start to explore Dreamweaver's HTML Find and Replace capabilities. Should your client decide that he wants the company's name to appear in blue, bold, 18-point type throughout the 300-page site, you can accommodate him with a few keystrokes — instead of hours of mind-numbing grunt work.

Storing and Retrieving Queries

Dreamweaver enables you to develop extremely complex queries. Rather than forcing you to reenter queries over and over again, Dreamweaver enables you to save and load them when needed. You can store and retrieve Find and Replace queries; Dreamweaver saves them with .dwr file extensions, respectively.

To save a query, select the diskette icon on the Find and Replace dialog box. The standard Save Query (Save Query to file) dialog box appears for you to enter a file name; the appropriate file extension is appended automatically. To load a previously saved query, select the folder icon on the Find and Replace dialog box to open the Load Query dialog box. Although only queries with a .dwr extension are being saved in the current version, you can still load both .dwq and .dwr files saved from previous Dreamweaver versions.

Although saving and opening queries is an obvious advantage when working with complex wildcard operations, you can also make it work for you in an every day situation. If, for example, you have a set series of acronyms or abbreviations that you must convert repeatedly, you can save your simple text queries and use them as needed without having to remember all the details.

You can perform three different types of searches that use the HTML in your Web page:

- You can search for text anywhere in the HTML code. With this capability, you can look for text within Alt or any other attribute — and change it.
- You can search for text relative to specific tags. Sometimes you need to change just the text contained within the `<b>` tag and leave all other matching text alone.
- You can search for specific HTML tags and/or their attributes. Dreamweaver's Find and Replace feature gives you the capability to insert, delete, or modify tags and attributes.

Looking for text in the Code

Text that appears onscreen is often replicated in various sections of your off-screen HTML code. It's not uncommon, for example, to use the Alt attribute in an `<img>` tag that repeats the caption under the picture. What do you think would happen under those circumstances if you replaced the wording with the standard Find and Replace features in the Design view of the Document window? You're still left with the task of tracking down the Alt attribute and making that change as well. Dreamweaver enables you to act on both content and programming text in one operation — a major savings in time and effort, not to mention aggravation.

To find and replace text in both the content and the code, follow these steps:

1. Choose Edit ⇨ Find and Replace to open the dialog box.

2. Select the parameters of your search from the Find In option: Current Document, Current Site, or Folder.

   Remember, you can also search specific files if you launch the Find and Replace dialog box from the Site window.

3. Choose the Search For option button and select the Source Code option from the drop-down list.

4. Enter the text you're searching for in the text box next to the Search For option.

5. If you are replacing, enter the new text in the Replace With text box.

6. Select any options desired: Match Case, Ignore Whitespace Differences, or Use Regular Expressions.

7. Choose your Find/Replace option: Find Next, Find All, Replace, or Replace All.

8. Select Close when finished.

Caution As with all Find and Replace operations — especially those in which you decide to Replace All — you need to exercise extreme caution when replacing text throughout your code. If you're unsure about what's going to be affected, choose Find All first and, with your Code view or Inspector open, step through all the selections to be positive no unwanted surprises exist. Should you replace some code in error, you can always undo the operation — but only if the document is open. Replacing text or code in a closed file, as is done when the operation is performed on a folder, the current site, or selected files in the Site window, is not undoable.

Using advanced text options in Find and Replace

In Find and Replace operations, the global Replace All isn't appropriate for every situation; sometimes you need a more precise approach. Dreamweaver enables you to fine-tune your searches to pinpoint accuracy. You can look for text within particular tags — and even within particular tags with specific attributes. Moreover, you can find (and replace) text that is outside of particular tags with specific attributes.

Dreamweaver assists you by providing a drop-down list of every standard HTML tag, as well as numerous special function tags such as those used for Cold Fusion applications. You can also search for your own custom tags. You don't have to try to remember which attributes go with which tag either. Dreamweaver also supplies you with a context-sensitive list of attributes that changes according to the tag selected.

In addition to using the tag's attributes as a search filter, Dreamweaver can also search within the tag for text or another tag. Most HTML tags are so-called container tags that consist of an opening tag and a closing tag, such as <b> and </b>. You can set up a filter to look for text within a specific tag — or text outside of a specific tag. For example, if you were searching for the word *big*:

```
The big, red boat was a <b>big</b> waste of money.
```

you could build a Find and Replace operation that changed one instance of the one word (big, red) but not the other (big) — or vice versa.

To look for text in or out of specific tags and attributes, follow these steps:

1. Choose Edit ⇨ Find and Replace to open the Find and Replace dialog box.
2. Select the parameters of your search from the Find In option: Current Document, Current Site, or Folder.
3. Choose the Search For option button and select the Text (Advanced) option from the drop-down list.

    The Add and Remove (+ and –) tag options are made available, as shown in Figure 5-7.

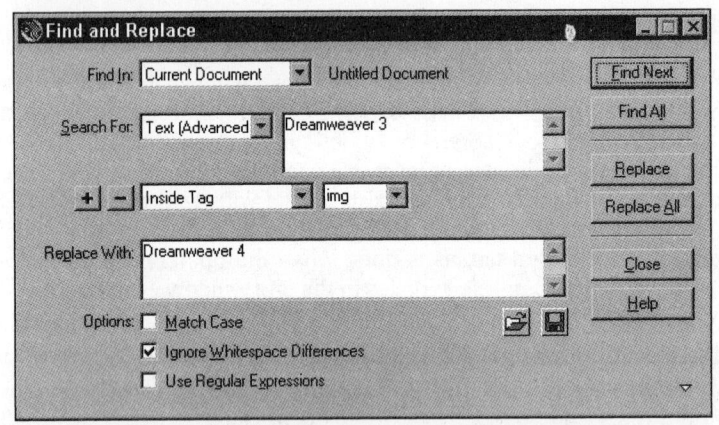

Figure 5-7: The advanced text features of Find and Replace enable you to manipulate text and code simultaneously.

4. Enter the text you're searching for in the text box next to the Search For option.
5. Select either Inside Tag or Not Inside Tag from the option list.
6. Select the tag to include or exclude from the adjacent option list.
7. To add a further restriction on the search, click the Add button (the plus sign).

    Another line of search options is added to the dialog box.

8. Select the additional search filter. The available options include the following:

Filter	Description
With Attribute	Enables you to select any attribute from the adjacent option list. You can set this attribute to be equal to, less than, greater than, or not equal to any given value by choosing from the available drop-down lists.
Without Attribute	Finds text within a particular tag that does not include a specific attribute. Choose the attribute to be equal to, less than, greater than, or not equal to any given value by choosing from the available drop-down lists.
Containing	Searches the tag for either specified text or another user-selectable tag found within the initial tag pair.
Not Containing	Searches the tag for either text or a tag not found within the initial tag pair.
Inside Tag	Enables you to look for text that is within two (or more) sets of specific tags.
Not Inside Tag	Enables you to look for text that is in one tag, but not in another tag, or vice versa.

9. To continue adding filter conditions, select the Add button (the plus sign) and repeat Steps 7 and 8.
10. To remove a filter condition, select the Remove button (the minus sign).
11. If you are replacing, enter the new text in the Replace With text box.
12. Select any options desired: Match Case, Ignore Whitespace Differences, or Use Regular Expressions.
13. Choose your Find/Replace option: Find Next, Find All, Replace, or Replace All.
14. Select Close when finished.

Tip: You can continue to add conditions by clicking the Add (+) button. In fact, I was able to add so many conditions, the Find/Replace dialog box began to disappear off the screen! To erase all conditions, change the Search For option to Text or Source Code and then change it back to Text (Advanced).

Replacing HTML tags and attributes

Let's say a new edict has come down from the HTML gurus of your company: No longer is the `<strong>` tag to be used to indicate emphasis; from now on; use only the `<b>` tag. Oh, and by the way, change all the existing pages — all 3,000+ Web and intranet pages — so that they're compliant. Dreamweaver makes short work out of nightmare situations such as these by giving you the power to search and replace HTML tags and their attributes.

But Dreamweaver doesn't stop there. Not only can you replace one tag with another, you can also perform the following:

- Change or delete the tag (with or without its contents)
- Set an attribute in the tag to another value
- Remove any or all attributes
- Add text and/or code before or after the starting or the ending tag

To alter your code using Dreamweaver's Find and Replace feature, follow these steps:

1. As with other Find and Replace operations, choose Edit ⇨ Find and Replace to open the dialog box.
2. Select the parameters of your search from the Find In option: Current Page, Current Site, or Folder.
3. Choose the Search For option button and select the tag option from the drop-down list.

   The dialog box changes to include the tag functions.
4. Select the desired tag from the option list next to the Search For option.

Tip

You can either scroll down the list box to find the tag or you can type the first letter of the tag in the box. Dreamweaver scrolls to the group of tags that begin with that letter when the list is visible (Windows only).

5. If desired, you can limit the search by specifying an attribute and value, or with other conditions, as discussed in detail in the previous section.

Note

If you want to search for just a tag, select the Remove button (the minus key) to eliminate the additional condition.

6. Make a selection from the Action list, shown in Figure 5-8. The options are as follows:

Action	Description
Replace Tag & Contents	Substitutes the selected tag and all included content with a text string. The text string can include HTML code.
Replace Contents Only	Changes the content between the specified tag to a given text string, which can also include HTML code.
Remove Tag & Contents	Deletes the tag and all contents.
Strip Tag	Removes the tag but leaves the previously enclosed content.

Action	Description
Change Tag	Substitutes one tag for another.
Set Attribute	Sets an existing attribute to a new value or inserts a new attribute set to a specific value.
Remove Attribute	Deletes a specified attribute.
Add Before Start Tag	Inserts a text string (with or without HTML) before the opening tag.
Add After End Tag	Inserts a text string (with or without HTML) after the end tag.
Add After Start Tag	Inserts a text string (with or without HTML) after the opening tag.
Add Before End Tag	Inserts a text string (with or without HTML) before the end tag.

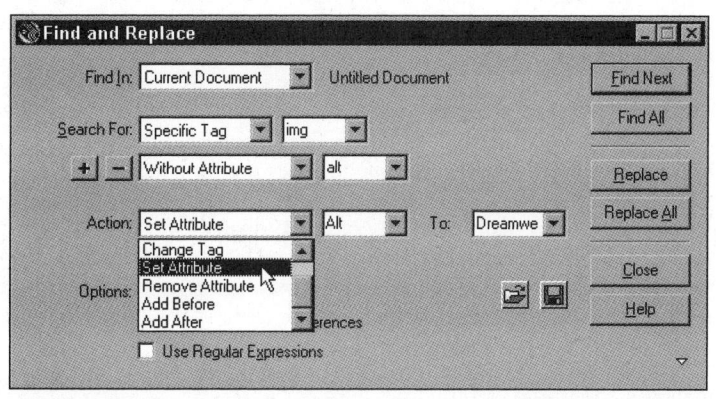

Figure 5-8: The Action list enables you to replace tags or modify them by setting the existing attributes or adding new ones.

Note Not all the options listed in the preceding table are available for all tags. Some so-called empty tags, such as <img>, consist of a single tag and not tag pairs. Empty tags have only Add Before and Add After options instead of Add Before Start Tag, Add After Start Tag, Add Before End Tag, and Add After End Tag.

7. Select any options desired: Match Case, Ignore Whitespace Differences, or Use Regular Expressions.
8. Choose your Find/Replace option: Find Next, Find All, Replace, or Replace All.
9. Select Close when finished.

Tip: You don't have to apply a single action to all the instances Dreamweaver locates if you choose Find All. In the list of found expressions, select a single item and then choose Replace. Dreamweaver makes the revision and places a green dot next to the item so you can tell it has been altered. If you want, you can then select another item from the list, choose a different action, and then select Replace.

Concentrating your search with regular expressions

As powerful as all the other Find and Replace features are, they are boosted to a higher level of flexibility with the addition of regular expressions. I've referred to regular expressions as being similar to wildcards in other programs, but their capabilities are really far more extensive.

Regular expressions are best described as a *text pattern matching system*. If you can identify any pattern in your text, you can manipulate it with regular expressions. What kind of pattern? Let's say you have a spreadsheet-like table with lots of numbers, showing both dollars and cents, mixed with explanatory text. With regular expressions, you can match the pattern formed by the dollar sign and the decimal point and reformat the entire table, turning all the figures deep blue with a new font — all in one Find and Replace operation.

Note: If you're into Unix, you recognize regular expressions as being very close to the grep utility — *grep*, by the way, stands for Get Regular Expressions and Print. The Find and Replace feature in BBEdit also features a grep-like syntax.

You can apply regular expressions to any of the types of Find and Replace operations previously discussed, with just a click of the Use Regular Expressions checkbox. Note that when you select Use Regular Expressions, the Ignore Unnecessary Whitespace option is deselected. This is because the two options are mutually exclusive and cannot be used together.

The most basic regular expression is the text itself. If you enable the feature and then enter **th** in the Search For text box, Dreamweaver locates every example of "th" in the text and/or source. Although this capability by itself has little use beyond what you can also achieve with standard Find and Replace operations, it's important to remember this functionality as you begin to build your patterns.

Using wildcard characters

Initially, it's helpful to be able to use what traditionally are know as *wildcards* — characters that match different types of characters. The wildcards in regular expressions represent single characters and are described in Table 5-2. In other words, no single regular expression represents all the characters, as the asterisk does when used in PC file searches (such as *.*). However, such a condition can be represented with a slightly more complex regular expression (described later in the "Matching character positions and repeating characters" section).

Table 5-2
Regular Expression Wildcard Characters

Character	Matches	Example
.	Any single character	**w.d** matches **wid**e but not world.
\w	Any alphanumeric character, including the underscore	**w\wd** matches **wid**e and **w**or**d**.
\W	Any nonalphanumeric character	**jboy\Widest.com** matches **jboy@idest.com**.
\d	Any numeric character 0–9	**y\dk** matches **Y2K**.
\D	Any nonnumeric character	**\D2\D** matches **Y2K** and **H2O**.
\s	Any whitespace character, including space, tab, form feed, or line feed	**\smedia** matches **media** but not Macromedia.
\S	Any nonwhitespace character	**\Smedia** matches Macro**media** but not media.
\t	A tab	Matches any single tab character in the HTML source.
\f	Form feed	Matches any single form-feed character in the HTML source.
\n	Line feed	Matches any single line-feed character in the HTML source.
\r	Carriage return	Matches any single carriage-return character in the HTML source.

Tip The backslash character (\) is used to escape special characters so that they can be included in a search. For example, if you want to look for an asterisk, you need to specify it in this way: *. Likewise, when trying to find the backslash character, precede it with another backslash character, as follows: \\.

Matching character positions and repeating characters

With regular expressions, not only can you match the type of character, but you can also match its position in the text. This feature enables you to perform operations on characters at the beginning, end, or middle of the word or line. Regular expressions also enable you to find instances in which a character is repeated an unspecified number of times or a specific number of times. Combined, these features broaden the scope of the patterns that can be found.

Table 5-3 details the options available for matching by text placement and character repetition.

Table 5-3
Regular Expression Character Positions and Repeating Characters

Character	Matches	Example
^	Beginning of a line	**^C** matches the first c in "**C**all me Ishmael."
$	End of a line	**d$** matches the final "d" in "Be afraid. Be very afrai**d**."
\b	A word boundary, such as a space or carriage return	**\btext** matches **text**book but not SimpleText.
\B	A nonword boundary inside a word	**\Btext** matches Simple**Text** but not textbook.
*	The preceding character zero or more times	**b*c** matches **BB**C and **c**old.
+	The preceding character one or more times	**b+c** matches **BB**C but not cold.
?	The preceding character zero or one time	**st?un** matches **stun** and **sun** but not strung.
{n}	Exactly *n* instances of the preceding character	**e{2}** matches reed and each pair of two e's in "Ai**ee**eeeee!" but nothing in Dreamweaver.
{n,m}	At least *n* and *m* instances of the preceding character	**C{2,4}** matches #**CC**00FF and #**CCCC**00 but not the full string #CCCCCC.

Matching character ranges

Beyond single characters, or repetitions of single characters, regular expressions incorporate the capability of finding or excluding ranges of characters. This feature is particularly useful when you're working with groups of names or titles. Ranges are specified in set brackets. A match is made when any one of the characters, not necessarily all of the characters, within the set brackets is found.

Descriptions of how to match character ranges with regular expressions can be found in Table 5-4.

Table 5-4
Regular Expression Character Ranges

Character	Matches	Example
[abc]	Any one of the characters a, b, or c	**[lmrt]** matches the l and m's in **lemm**ings and the r and t in **r**oad**t**rip.
[^abc]	Any character except a, b, or c	**[^etc]** matches **GIFs** but not etc in the phrase "GIFs etc."
[a-z]	Any character in the range from a to z	**[l-p]** matches l and o in **lo**wery and m, n, o an p in **p**oint**m**a**n**.
x|y	Either x or y	**boy|girl** matches both **boy** and **girl**.

Grouping with regular expressions

Grouping is perhaps the single most powerful concept in regular expressions. With it, any matched text pattern is easily manipulated — for example, the following list of names:

- John Jacob Jingleheimer Schmidt
- James T. Kirk
- Cara Fishman

could be rearranged so that the last name is first, separated by a comma, like this:

- Schmidt, John Jacob Jingleheimer
- Kirk, James T.
- Fishman, Cara

Grouping is handled primarily with parentheses. To indicate a group, enclose it in parentheses in the Find text field. Regular expressions can manage up to nine grouped patterns. Each grouped patterned is designated by a dollar sign ($) in front of a number (1–9), in the Replace text field, like this: **$3**.

Caution   Remember that the dollar sign is also used after a character or pattern to indicate the last character in a line.

Table 5-5 shows how regular expressions use grouping.

Table 5-5
Regular Expressions Grouping

Character	Matches	Example
(p)	Any pattern p	**(\b\w*)\.(\w*\b)** matches two patterns, the first before a period and the second, after — such as in a file name with an extension. The backslash before the period escapes it so that it is not interpreted as a regular expression.
$1, $2 . . . $9	The *n*th pattern noted with parentheses	The replacement pattern **$1's extension is ".$2"** would manipulate the pattern **(\b\w*)\.(\w*\b)** so that Chapter09.txt and Image12.gif would become **Chapter09's extension is ".txt"** and **Image12's extension is ".gif."**

The <br> tag

As with headings, the paragraph tag falls among the class of HTML objects called *block elements*. As such, any text marked with the <p>...</p> tag pair is always rendered with an extra line above and below the text, often called whitespace. To have a series of blank lines appear one after the other, use the break tag <br>. Multiple break tags may also be used to provide whitespace between elements.

Break tags are used within block elements, such as headings and paragraphs, to provide a line break where the <br> is inserted. Dreamweaver provides two ways to insert a <br> tag: You can choose the Enter Line Break button from the Characters panel of the Objects panel or you can use the keyboard shortcut Shift+Enter (Shift+Return).

Figure 5-9 demonstrates the effect of the <br> tag. The menu items in Column A on the left are the result of using the <br> tag within a paragraph. In Column B on the right, paragraph tags alone are used. The <h1> heading is also split at the top (modified through style sheet selections) with a break tag to avoid the insertion of an unwanted line.

By default, Dreamweaver marks <br> tags with a symbol: A gold shield with the letters BR and the standard Enter/Return symbol. You can turn off this display feature by choosing Preferences ⇨ Invisible Elements and deselecting the Line Breaks checkbox.

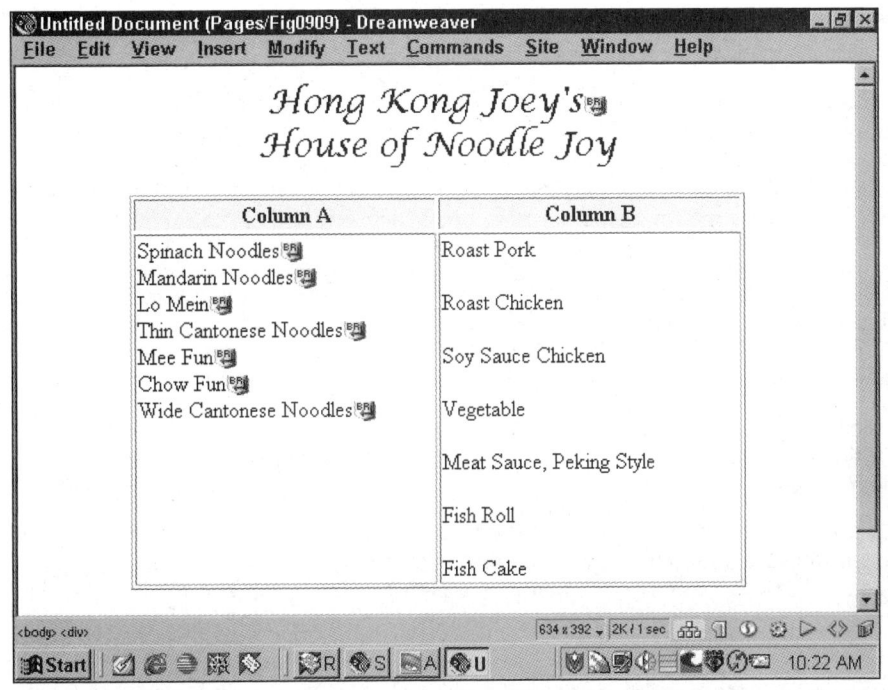

Figure 5-9: Use break tags to wrap your lines without the additional line spacing brought about by <p> tags.

Other whitespace tags

If you can't get the alignment effect you want through the regular text options available in Dreamweaver, two other HTML tags can affect whitespace: <nobr> and <wbr>. Although a tad on the obscure side, these tags can be just the ticket in certain circumstances. Let's see how they work.

The <nobr> tag

Most of the time, you want the user's browser to handle word-wrapping chores automatically. Occasionally, however, you may need to make sure that a particular string of text is rendered in one piece. For these situations, you can use the no break tag <nobr>. Any text that comes in between the opening and closing tag pair—<nobr>...</nobr>—is displayed in one continuous line. If the line of text is wider than the current browser window, a horizontal scroll bar automatically appears along the bottom of the browser.

The <nobr> tag is supported only through the Netscape and Microsoft browsers and must be entered by hand into your HTML code. Use the <nobr> tag under very special circumstances.

> ### Overcoming Line-Spacing Difficulties
>
> Line spacing is a major issue and a common problem for Web designers. A design often calls for lines to be tightly spaced, and also of various sizes. If you use the break tag to separate your lines, you get the tight spacing required, but you won't be able to make each line a different heading size. As far as HTML and your browser are concerned, the text is still one block element, no matter how many line breaks are inserted. If, on the other hand, you make each line a separate paragraph or heading, the line spacing will be unattractively "open."
>
> You can use one of several workarounds for this problem. First, if you're using line breaks, you can alter the size of each line by selecting it and choosing a different font size, either from the Property Inspector or the Text ⇨ Size menu.
>
> A second option renders all the text as a graphics object and inserts it as an image. This gives you total control over the font's appearance and line spacing, at the cost of added download time.
>
> For a third possible solution, take a look at the section on preformatted text later in this chapter. Because you can apply styles to a preformatted text block (which can include line breaks and extra whitespace), you can alter the size, color, and font of each line, if necessary.
>
> Ultimately the best solution is to use Cascading Style Sheets (CSS). The majority of browsers now in use support line spacing through CSS; however, if 3.0 browser compatability is a site requirement, you'll have to use one of the other methods outlined here.

The <wbr> tag

The companion to the <nobr> tag is the word break tag <wbr>. Similar to a soft hyphen in a word processing program, the <wbr> tag tells the browser where to break a word, if necessary. When used within <nobr> tags, <wbr> is the equivalent of telling a browser, "Keep all this text in one line, but if you have to break it, break it here."

As with the <nobr> tag, <wbr> is supported only by Netscape and Microsoft browsers and must be entered by hand via the Quick Tag Editor, Code view, Code Inspector, or your external editor.

Importing Word HTML

Microsoft Word has offered an option to save its documents as HTML since the release of Word 97. Unfortunately, Microsoft's version of HTML output is, at best, highly idiosyncratic. Although you could always open a Word HTML file in

Dreamweaver, if you ever had to modify the page — which you almost always do — it took so long to find your way through the convoluted code that you were almost better off building the page from scratch. Fortunately, that's no longer the case with Dreamweaver.

The capability to Import Word HTML is a key workflow enhancement for Dreamweaver. Dreamweaver can successfully import and automatically clean up files from Microsoft Word 97, Word 98, or Word 2000. The cleanup takes place automatically upon import, but you can also finely tune the modifications that Dreamweaver makes to the file. Moreover, you can even apply the current Source Format profile so that the HTML is styled to look like native Dreamweaver code.

Naturally, before you can import a Word HTML file, you have to have created one. To export a document in HTML format in Word 97/98, choose File ➪ Save as HTML; in Word 2000, the command has changed to File ➪ Save as Web Page. Although the wording change may seem to be a move toward less jargon, what Word actually exports is significant. With Word 2000 (and all the Office 2000 products), Microsoft heartily embraced the XML standard and uses a combination of standard HTML and custom XML code throughout their exported Web pages. For example, here's the opening tag from a Word 2000 document, saved as a Web page:

```
<html xmlns:o="urn:schemas-microsoft-com:office:office"
xmlns:w="urn:schemas-microsoft-com:office:word"
xmlns:dt="uuid:C2F41010-65B3-11d1-A29F-00AA00C14882"
xmlns="http://www.w3.org/TR/REC-html40">
```

which Dreamweaver alters to:

```
<html>
```

If you accept the defaults, importing a Word HTML file is a two-step affair:

1. Choose File ➪ Import ➪ Import Word HTML.

    The Import Word HTML dialog box opens and Dreamweaver detects whether the HTML file was exported from Word 97/98 or 2000. The interface options change accordingly.

    Caution: If Dreamweaver can't determine what version of Word generated the file, an alert appears. Although Dreamweaver will still try to clean up the code, it may not function correctly. The same alert appears if you inadvertently select a standard nonHTML Word document.

2. Click OK to confirm the import operation.

    Dreamweaver creates a new HTML document, imports the file, and cleans up the code. If the Show Log on Completion option is selected, Dreamweaver informs you of the modifications made.

For most purposes, accepting the defaults is the best way to quickly bring in your Word HTML files. However, because Web designers have a wide range of code requirements, Dreamweaver provides a full set of options so you can tailor the Word-to-Dreamweaver transformation to your liking. Two different sets of options exist — one for documents saved from Word 97/98 and one for those saved from Word 2000. The different sets of options can be seen on the Detailed tab of the Import Word HTML dialog box; the Basic tab is the same for both file types. Table 5-6 details the Basic tab options, the Word 97/98 options, and the Word 2000 options.

Table 5-6
Import Word HTML Options

Option	Description
Basic	
Remove all Word-specific markup	Deletes all Word-specific tags, including Word XML, conditional tags, empty paragraphs, and margins in `<style>` tags.
Clean up CSS	Deletes all Word-specific CSS code, including inline CSS styles where styles are nested, "mso" designated styles, non-CSS style declarations, CSS style attributes from tables and orphaned (unused) style definitions.
Clean up `<font>` tags	Deletes `<font>` tags that set the default body text to an absolute font size 2.
Fix invalidly nested tags	Deletes tags surrounding paragraph and block-level tags.
Set background color	Adds a background color to the page. Word does not supply one. The default added color is white (#ffffff). Colors can be entered as hexadecimal triplets with a leading hash mark or as a valid color name — that is, red.
Apply source formatting	Formats the imported code according to the guidelines of the current Source Format profile used by Dreamweaver.
Show log on completion	Displays a dialog box that lists all alterations when the process is complete.
Detailed Options for Word 97/98	
Remove Word specific markup	Enables the general clean up of Word-inserted tags.
Word meta and link tags from `<head>`	Specifically enables Dreamweaver to remove Word-specific `<meta>` and `<link>` tags from the `<head>` section of a document.
Clean up `<font>` tags	Enables the general clean up of `<font>` tags.

Option	Description
Convert size [7-1] to	Specifies which tag, if any, is substituted for a <font size=n> tag. Options are: * `<h1>` through `<h6>` * `<font size=1>` through `<font size=7>` * Default size * Don't change
Detailed Options for Word 2000	
Remove Word specific markup	Enables the general clean up of Word-inserted tags.
XML from `<html>` tag	Deletes the Word-generated XML from the `<html>` tag.
Word meta and link tags from `<head>`	Specifically enables Dreamweaver to remove Word-specific `<meta>` and `<link>` tags from the `<head>` section of a document.
Word XML markup	Enables the general clean up of Word-inserted XML tags.
`<![if...]>` `<![endif]>` conditional tags and their contents	Removes all conditional statements.
Remove empty paragraphs and margins from styles	Deletes `<p>` tags without a closing `</p>` and styles tags including margin attributes — for example, `style='margin-top:0in'`.
Clean up CSS	Enables the general clean up of Word inserted CSS tags.
Remove inline CSS styles when possible	Deletes redundant information in nested styles.
Remove any style attribute that starts with "mso"	Eliminates all Microsoft Office (mso) specific attributes.
Remove any non-CSS style declaration	Deletes nonstandard style declarations.
Remove all CSS styles from table rows and cells	Eliminates style information from `<table>`, `<tr>`, and `<td>` tags.
Remove all unused style definitions	Deletes any declared styles that are not referenced in the page.

You don't have to remember to run the Import Word HTML command to take advantage of Dreamweaver's cleanup features. If you've already opened a document saved as Word HTML, you can choose Commands ⇨ Clean Up Word HTML and gain access to the exact same dialog box for the existing page.

Styling Your Text

When the Internet was founded, its intended focus was to make scientific data widely accessible. Soon it became apparent that even raw data could benefit from being styled contextually, without detracting from the Internet's openness and universality. Over the short history of HTML, text styles have become increasingly important, and the World Wide Web Consortium (W3C) has sought to keep a balance between substance and style.

Dreamweaver enables the Web designer to apply the most popular HTML styles directly through the program's menus and Property Inspector. Less prevalent styles can be inserted through the integrated text editors or by hand.

Working with preformatted text

Browsers ignore formatting niceties considered irrelevant to page content: tabs, extra line feeds, indents, and added whitespace. However, you can force browsers to read all the text, including whitespace, exactly as you have entered it. By applying the preformatted tag, `<pre>`, you tell the browser that it should keep any additional whitespace encountered within the text. By default, the `<pre>` tag also renders its content with a monospace font such as Courier. For these reasons, the `<pre>` tag was used to lay out text in columns in the early days of HTML, before tables were widely available.

You can apply the preformatted tag either through the Property Inspector or the menus. Before you use either technique, however, be sure to select the text or position the cursor where you want the preformatted text to begin. To use the Property Inspector, open the Format list box and choose Preformatted. To use the menus, choose Text ⇨ Paragraph Format ⇨ Preformatted.

The `<pre>` tag is a block element format, like the paragraph or the headings tags, rather than a style. This designation as a block element format has two important implications. First, you can't apply the `<pre>` tag to part of a line; when you use this tag, the entire paragraph is altered. Second, you can apply styles to preformatted text — this enables you to increase the size or alter the font, but at the same time maintain the whitespace feature made possible with the `<pre>` tag. All text in Figure 5-10 uses the `<pre>` tag; the column on the left is the standard output with monospaced font; the column on the right uses a different font in a larger size.

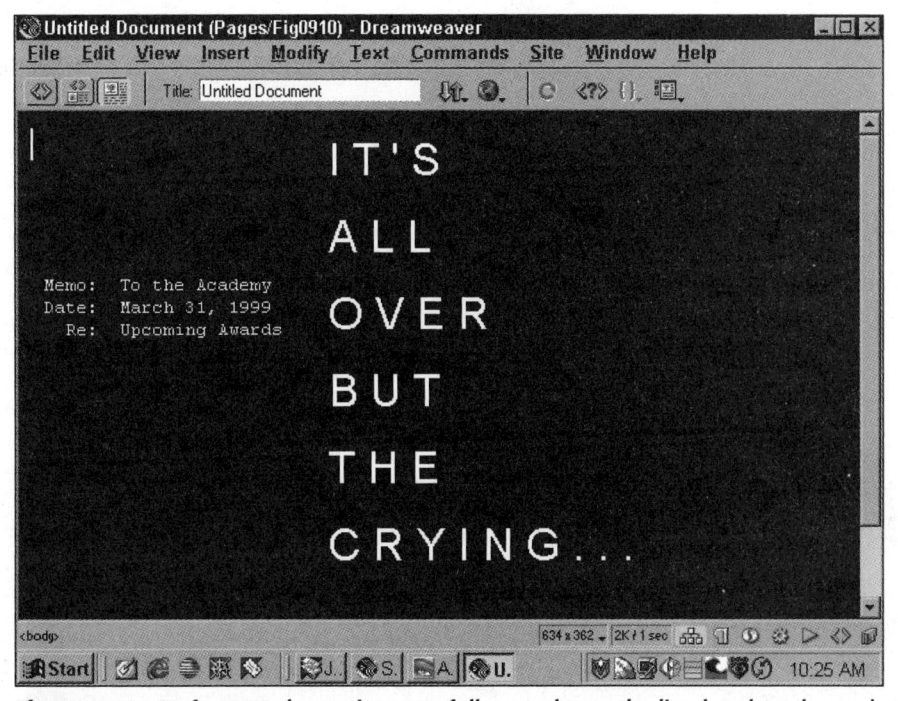

Figure 5-10: Preformatted text gives you full control over the line breaks, tabs, and other whitespace in your Web page.

Depicting various styles

As explained in Chapter 4, HTML's logical styles are used to mark text relatively or within a particular context, rather than with a specific look. The eventual displayed appearance of logical styles is completely up to the viewer's browser. This is useful when you are working with documents from different sources — reports from different research laboratories around the country, for instance — and you want certain conformity of style. Logical styles are utilitarian; physical styles such as boldface and italic are decorative. Both types of styles have their uses in material published on today's Web.

All of Dreamweaver's styles are accessed by choosing Text ⇨ Style and selecting from the 13 available style name options. A checkmark appears next to the selected tags. Style tags can be nested (put inside one another), and you can mix logical and physical tags within a word, line, or document. You can have a bold, strikethrough, variable style; or you can have an underlined, cited style. (Both variable and cite are particular logical styles covered later in this section.) If, however, you are trying to achieve a particular look using logical styles, you should probably use the Cascading Style Sheets feature.

Cross-Reference: The styles that can be applied through regular HTML are just the tip of the iceberg compared to the possibilities with Cascading Style Sheets. For details on using this feature, see Chapter 14.

Take a look at Figure 5-11 for a comparison of how the styles are rendered in Dreamweaver, Internet Explorer 5.0, and Netscape Communicator 4.7. While the various renderings are mostly the same, notice the browser differences in the Definition styles and the difference in how the Keyboard style is rendered in Dreamweaver and either browser.

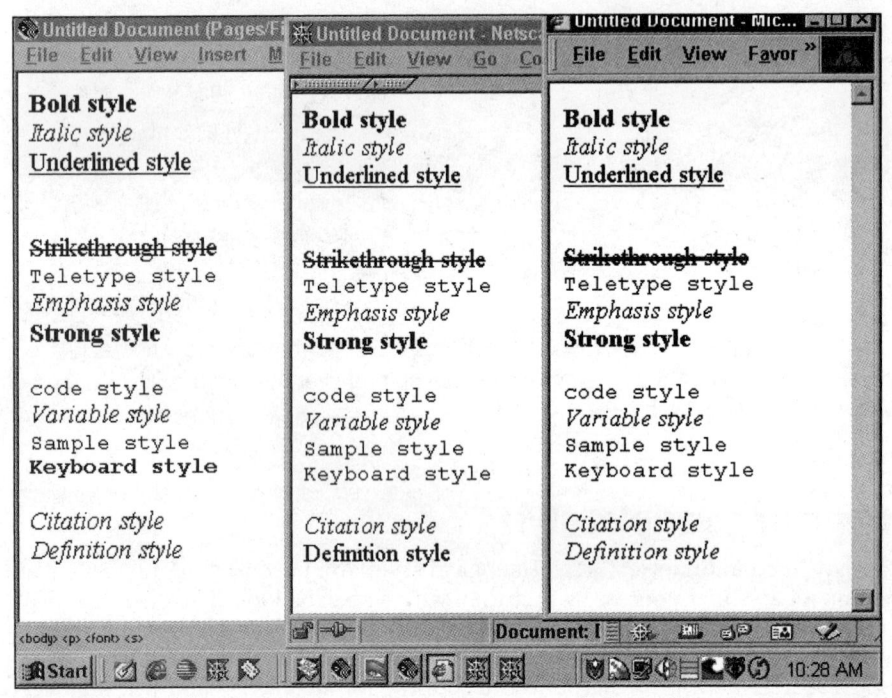

Figure 5-11: In this comparison chart, the various renderings of Dreamweaver style tags are from Dreamweaver, Netscape Communicator 4.7, and Internet Explorer 5.0 (from left to right).

Two of the three physical style tags — bold and italic — are both available from the Text Property Inspector and through keyboard shortcuts (Ctrl+B or Command+B, and Ctrl+I or Command+I, respectively). The Underline tag, <u>, is available only through the Text ⇨ Style menu. Underlining text on a Web page is generally discouraged in order to avoid confusion with links, which are typically displayed underlined.

Both physical and logical style tags are described, with examples, in Table 5-7.

Table 5-7
Dreamweaver Style Tags

Style	Tag	Description
Bold	`<b>`	Text is rendered with a bold style.
Italic	`<i>`	Text is rendered with an italic style.
Underline	`<u>`	Text is rendered underlined.
Strikethrough	`<s>`	Used primarily in edited documents to depict edited text. Usually rendered with a line through the text.
Teletype	`<tt>`	Used to represent an old-style typewriter. Rendered in a monospace font such as Courier.
Emphasis	`<em>`	Used to accentuate certain words relative to the surrounding text. Most often rendered in italic.
Strong Emphasis	`<strong>`	Used to strongly accentuate certain words relative to the surrounding text. Most often rendered in boldface.
Code	`<code>`	Used to depict programming code, usually in a monospaced font.
Sample	`<samp>`	Used to display characters in a literal sequence, usually in a monospaced font.
Variables	`<var>`	Used to mark variables in programming code. Most often displayed in italics.
Keyboard	`<kbd>`	Used to indicate what should be user input. Often shown in a monospaced font, sometimes in boldface.
Citation	`<cite>`	Used to mark citations, references, and titles. Most often displayed in italic.
Definition	`<dfn>`	Used to denote the first, defining instance of a term. Usually displayed in italic.

Using the `<address>` tag

Currently, Dreamweaver does not support one useful style tag: the `<address>` tag. Rendered as italic text by browsers, the `<address>`...`</address>` tag pair often marks the signature and e-mail address of a Web page's creator. The `<address>` tags should go around a paragraph tag pair; otherwise, Dreamweaver flags the closing `</p>` as invalid.

The easiest way to do this in Dreamweaver is to use the Quick Tag Editor. Select your text and press Ctrl+T (Command T) to automatically enter Wrap Tag mode. If Tag Hints is enabled, all you'll have to type is **ad** and press Enter (Return) twice to accept the hint and confirm the tag.

If you're applying the `<address>` tag to multiple lines, use `<br>` tags to form line breaks. The following example shows the proper use of the `<address>` tags:

```
<address><p>The President<br>
  1600 Pennsylvania Avenue<br>
  Washington, DC 20001</p></address>
```

This preceding code is shown on a Web browser as follows:

The President
1600 Pennsylvania Avenue
Washington, DC 20001

Tip To remove a standard style, highlight the styled text, choose Text ⇨ Style, and select the name of the style you want to remove. The checkmark disappears from the style name. To remove a nonstandard tag such as `<address>`, choose the tag in the Tag Selector and right-click (Control+click) to open the shortcut menu and select Remove Tag.

Using HTML Styles

In the world of Web design, consistency is a good thing. A site where headings, subheads, and body text are consistent from page to page is far easier for the visitor to quickly grasp than one where each page has its own style. Although the best approach for a consistently designed site may be the use of Cascading Style Sheets, that approach requires 4.0 and later browsers, and many clients are not willing to write off those potential Web visitors using older software.

To bridge the gap between old and new — and to make it easier to apply the same set of tags over and over again — Dreamweaver includes HTML Styles. HTML Styles are similar to CSS in that you define a custom style for text and give it any attributes you want: font name, size, color, format, and so on. Then you apply that style to either a selection or an entire block of text. The primary difference is that, with HTML Styles, Dreamweaver adds the necessary standard HTML tags, instead of CSS style declarations, to recreate your style. In other words, if you always set your legal disclaimers in Verdana at a –1 size in a deep red color, you can define your "legal" style once and apply it over and over again with one step, anywhere on the site.

HTML Styles, however, are not a replacement for CSS styles, and you should keep in mind some important differences:

- ✦ Modifying a HTML Style definition affects only subsequent applications of the style. When a CSS style is altered, the change is immediately seen wherever the style has been applied on the current page as well as in all future applications.
- ✦ HTML Styles use standard text tags and cannot, therefore, create some of the special effects possible in CSS. For example, you could not create a HTML Style that eliminates the underline from a link or changes the leading of a paragraph.
- ✦ Although defined HTML Styles are accessible from anywhere within a site, they are applied on a document-to-document basis, whereas with CSS, an external style sheet could be defined and linked to pages anywhere on your site.

Even with these differences, however, HTML Styles are an enhancement to a designer's workflow and extremely easy to use.

Note In the remainder of this section, when I refer to a style or styles, I'm referring to HTML Styles. CSS Style references are designated as such.

Applying HTML Styles

The HTML Styles panel, shown in Figure 5-12, displays all currently available styles as well as options for removing style formatting, editing existing styles, adding new styles, or removing styles from the panel.

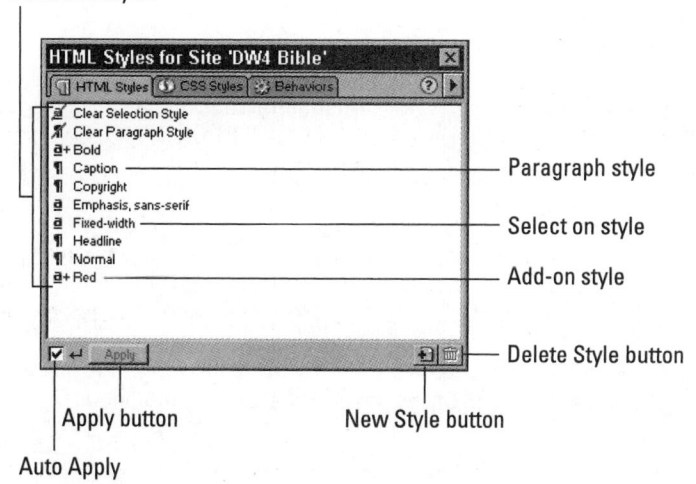

Figure 5-12: Manage your standard formatting through the HTML Styles panel.

HTML Styles are divided into two distinct types: paragraph and selection styles. A paragraph style affects an entire block element, whether it is a single heading, a paragraph, or another block element such as a block quote. Paragraph styles are designated with a ¶ symbol in the HTML Styles panel. A paragraph style is applied to the entire current block element, whether the cursor has selected the text or is just within the block. A selection style, on the other hand, applies formatting only to selected text. Selection styles are marked in the HTML Styles panel with an underlined lowercased a, like this (a).

It's possible for both paragraph and selection styles to either clear the existing style before adding the new formatting or add the new formatting to the existing style. The default behavior is for existing formatting to be removed; if the style is to be added, a small plus sign (+) is shown in front of the style name.

To apply an HTML Style, follow these steps:

1. Open the HTML Styles panel in one of the following ways:
    - Select Window ⇨ HTML Styles.
    - Choose the HTML Styles button from either Launcher.
    - Press the keyboard shortcut, Ctrl+F11 (Command+F11).
2. To apply a style to the currently selected text, choose any designated (a) HTML Style.

Tip: It's easiest to always have the Auto Apply option selected, so that your choices immediately are applied; if this option is not selected, click the Apply button.

3. To apply a style to the current block element, choose any so-designated (¶) HTML Style.

Removing HTML Styles

As useful as applying new HTML Styles is, I find that the capability to remove all such formatting even more beneficial. It's not unusual for me to style a paragraph and then want to try a completely different approach — with the HTML Styles panel, I can wipe out all the formatting in one click and start fresh.

As with applying styles, you can remove either a paragraph or a selection style. Both are available as the first items in the HTML Styles panel. Clear Selection Style removes all `<font>` and other text formatting tags surrounding the current selection. Clear Paragraph Style eliminates all such tags from the current block element.

Caution: Removing a paragraph style removes all styles to the paragraph, not just ones you may have added via the HTML Styles panel. For example, if a line is styled in this way:

```
<h1><font color="#FFFF00">Welcome</font></h2>
```

> ### Moving HTML Styles from Site to Site
>
> Custom HTML styles are available from any page in your site. But what happens if you start a new site? Do you have to recreate your custom styles again? Every new site starts with the same set of default styles standard in Dreamweaver. (The next section describes how to alter even those defaults.) But you can easily transfer styles you've created for one site to another, just by copying the right file.
>
> The information describing the custom HTML styles is stored in each site's Library folder in a file named styles.xml. To transfer the HTML styles, just copy the styles.xml file from one site's Library folder to the Library folder for another site. Library folders are created within a site when they are first needed, so if you've just defined your site, the Library folder may not exist yet. You can, however, safely create it within the local site root and move your styles.xml file into the folder.

Selecting Clear Paragraph Style converts the line to this:

```
<p>Welcome</p>
```

The Clear Selection Style command does not require that the formatting tags be adjacent to the selection. If you select some text in the middle of a paragraph styled in a particular color and font, choosing Clear Selection Style inserts appropriate tags before and after the selection so that the selection has no style whatsoever, but the surrounding text remains styled. A before and after view of the process is shown in Figure 5-13.

If you no longer wish to have a defined style displayed in the HTML Styles panel, select that style and choose the Delete Style button. Alternatively, you could select the style and choose Delete Style from the context-sensitive menu on the panel.

Defining HTML Styles

Naturally, the standard list of styles is just a jumping-off place for the HTML Styles panel. To get the most out the feature, you should design your own custom styles. Dreamweaver gives you a number of methods to define a style:

✦ **Style by Example** — Create a new style from formatted text onscreen.

✦ **Modify an Existing Style** — Edit a standard or custom style to your liking. You can even duplicate the style first, so both old and new versions are available.

✦ **Build a New Style** — Select all the desired attributes for your selection or paragraph style and try it out right away on selected text.

Part I ✦ Working with Dreamweaver

Clear Paragraph style   Clear Selection style

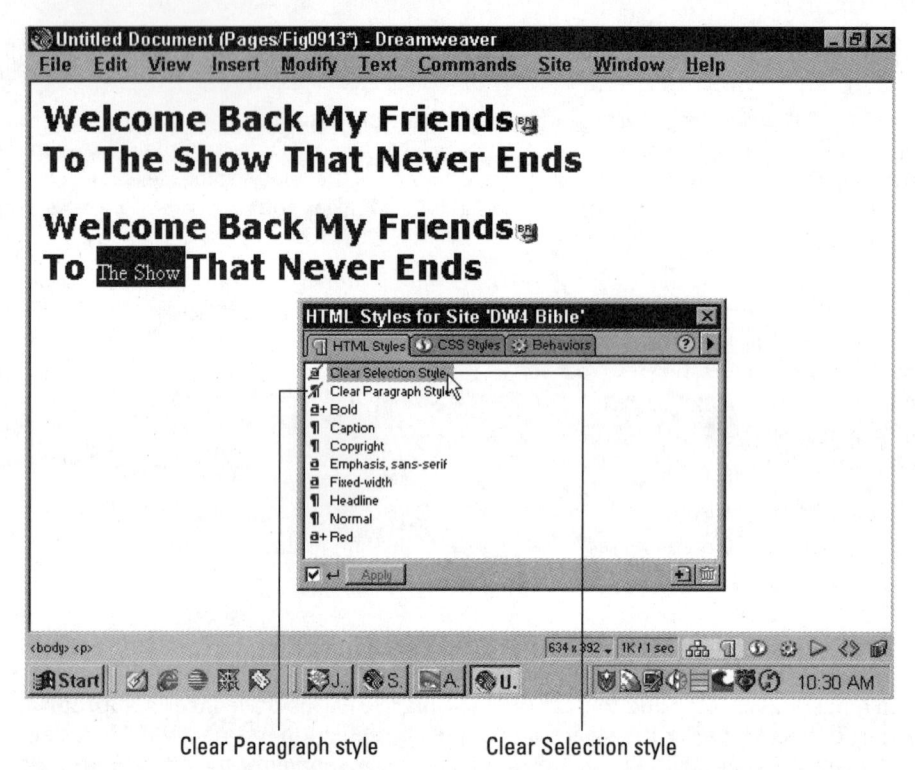

Figure 5-13: You can remove all styling from a bit of text and keep the surrounding styling with the Clear Selection Style command.

All style definitions are managed in the Define HTML Style dialog box, shown in Figure 5-14. How the dialog box is opened depends on which method you're using to create or modify your style.

✦ To create a style from example, select tags you want to include in the style from the Document window or the Tag Selector and then choose the New Style button from the HTML Styles panel.

✦ To modify an existing style, double-click its name in the HTML Styles panel list.

✦ To create a new style built on an existing one, select the style and then, from the context-sensitive menu of the HTML Styles panel, select Duplicate.

✦ To create a style from the ground up, choose the New Style button on the HTML Styles panel.

To define an HTML Style, follow these steps:

1. Open the Define HTML Style dialog box using one of the previously described methods.

2. Enter a unique name for your style, if creating a new one.
3. Choose whether your style is to apply to a selection or a paragraph.
4. Select whether your style will add to the existing style or clear existing style.
5. Choose the desired font attributes:
    - Font
    - Size
    - Color
    - Style: Bold, Italic, or Bold-Italic
    - Other . . . (Additional Optional Styles): Underline, Strikethrough, Teletype, Emphasis, Strong, Code, Variable, Sample, Keyboard, Citation, Definition

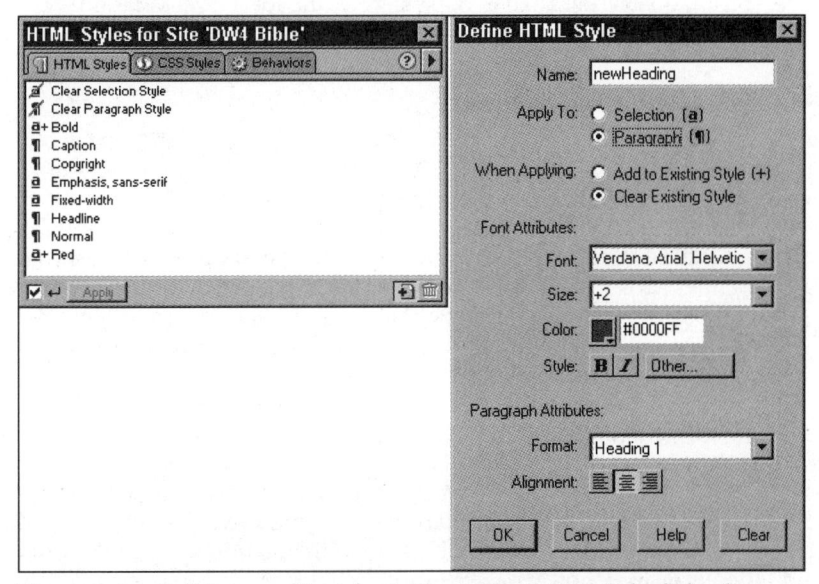

Figure 5-14: Build or modify styles in the Define HTML Style dialog box.

6. If defining a paragraph style, select from the following attribute options:
    - Format: None, Heading 1 through Heading 6, or Preformatted
    - Alignment: Right, Center, Left.
7. Click OK when you're done.

Tip To start over at any time, select the Clear button.

Modifying Text Format

As a Web designer, you easily spend at least as much time adjusting your text as you do getting it into your Web pages. Luckily, Dreamweaver puts most of the tools you need for this task right at your fingertips. All the text-formatting options are available through the Text Property Inspector. Instead of hand-coding `<font>`, `<blockquote>`, and alignment tags, just select your text and click a button.

> **Note**
> In HTML text formatting today, programmers are moving toward using Cascading Style Sheets and away from hard-coding text with `<font>` and other tags. Both 4.0+ versions of the major Web browsers support Cascading Style Sheets to some extent, and Internet Explorer has had some support since the 3.0 version. The current realities of browser competition, however, dictate that to take advantage of the widest support range, Web designers must continue to use the character-specific tags. Even after Cascading Style Sheets gain widespread acceptance, you'll probably still need to apply tags on the local level occasionally.

Adjusting font size

The six HTML heading types (H1 to H6) enable you to assign relative sizes to a line or to an entire paragraph. In addition, HTML gives you a finer degree of control through the size attribute of the font tag. In contrast to publishing environments, both traditional and desktop, font size is not specified in HTML with points. Rather, the `<font>` tag enables you to choose one of seven different explicit sizes that the browser can render (absolute sizing), or you can select one relative to the page's basic font. Figure 5-15 shows the default absolute and relative sizes, compared to a more page designer–friendly point chart (accomplished with Dreamweaver's Cascading Style Sheets features).

Which way should you go — absolute or relative? Some designers think that relative sizing gives them more options. As you can see by the chart in Figure 5-15, browsers are limited to displaying seven different sizes no matter what — unless you're using Cascading Style Sheets. Relative sizing does give you additional flexibility, though, because you can resize all the fonts in an entire Web page with one command. Absolute sizes, however, are more straightforward to use and can be coded in Dreamweaver without any additional HTML programming. Once again, it's the designer's choice.

Absolute size

You can assign an absolute font size through either the Property Inspector or the menus. In both cases, you choose a value, 1 (smallest) through 7 (largest), to which you want to resize your text; you might note that this order is the reverse of the heading sizes, which range from H1 to H6, largest to smallest.

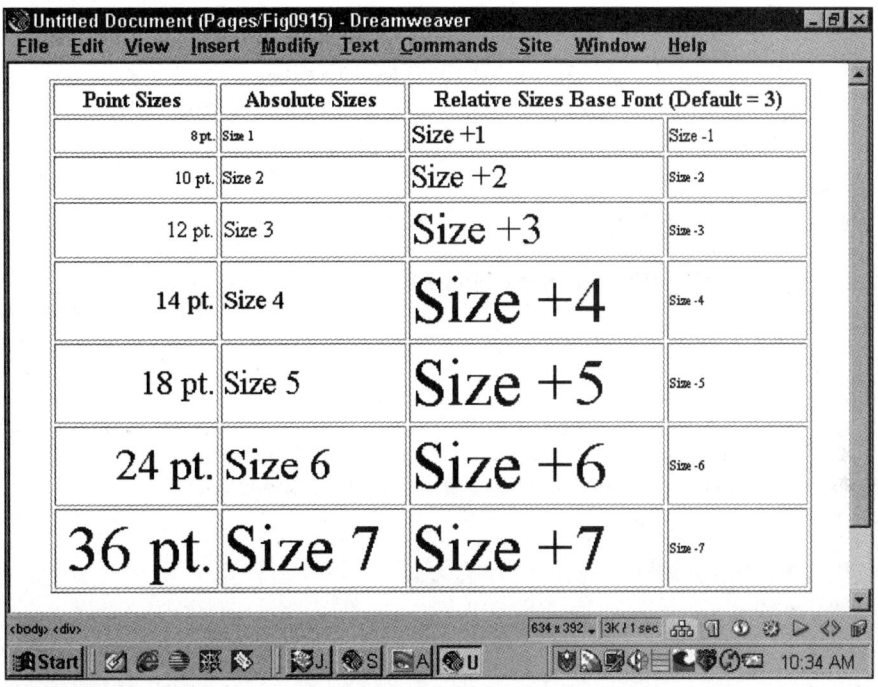

Figure 5-15: In this chart, you can see the relationships between the various font sizes in an HTML browser and as compared to "real-world" point sizes.

To use the Property Inspector to pick an absolute font size, follow these steps:

1. Select your text.
2. In the Property Inspector, open the Font Size drop-down list of options.
3. Choose a value from 1 to 7.

To pick an absolute font size from the menu, follow these steps:

1. Select your text.
2. Choose Text ⇨ Size and pick a value from 1 to 7, or Default (which is 3).

Tip You can also use the keyboard shortcuts for changing absolute font sizes. Headings 1 through 6 correspond to Ctrl+1 through Ctrl+6 (Command+1 through Command+6). The Paragraph option is rendered with a Ctrl+Shift+P (Command+Shift+P); you can remove all formatting with Ctrl+0 (Command+0).

Relative size

To what exactly are relative font sizes relative? The default font size, of course. The advantage of relative font sizes is that you can alter a Web page's default font size with one command, the `<basefont>` tag. The tag takes the following form:

```
<basefont size=value>
```

where value is a number from 1 to 7. The `<basefont>` tag is usually placed immediately following the opening `<body>` tag. Dreamweaver does not support previewing the results of altering the `<basefont>` tag and the tag has to be entered by hand or through the external editor.

You can distinguish a relative font size from an absolute font size by the plus or minus sign that precedes the value. The relative sizes are plus or minus the current `<basefont>` size. Thus, a `<font size=+1>` is normally rendered with a size 4 font because the default `<basefont>` is 3. If you include the following line in your Web page:

```
<basefont size=5>
```

text marked with a `<font size=+1>` is displayed with a size 6 font. Because browsers display only seven different size fonts with a `<basefont size=5>` setting — unless you're using Cascading Style Sheets — any relative size over `<font size=+2>` won't display differently when previewed in a browser.

Relative font sizes can also be selected from either the Property Inspector or the menus. To use the Property Inspector to pick a relative font size, follow these steps:

1. Select your text or position the cursor where you want the new text size to begin.
2. In the Property Inspector, open the Font Size drop-down list of options.
3. To increase the size of your text, choose a value from +1 through +7.

   To decrease the size of your text, choose a value from –1 to –7.

To pick a relative font size from the menus, follow these steps:

1. Select your text or position the cursor where you want the new text size to begin.
2. To increase the size of your text, choose Text ⇨ Size Increase and pick a value from +1 to +7.

   To reduce the size of your text, choose Text ⇨ Size Decrease and pick a value from –1 to –7.

> ### Dreamweaver's Color Pickers
>
> Dreamweaver includes a color picker for selecting colors for all manner of HTML elements: text, table cells, and page background. Dreamweaver's color picker — in keeping with the Macromedia common user interface — offers a number of palettes from the context menu to choose your colors: Color Cubes, Continuous Tone, Windows OS, Mac OS, and Grayscale. The most common choices for Web designers are Color Cubes and Continuous Tone, both of which display the 216 Web safe colors common to the Macintosh and Windows palettes. By default, the Snap to Web Safe option, also found in the context menu, is chosen.
>
> Once you've opened the text color picker by selecting the color swatch on the Property Inspector, the cursor changes shape into an eye-dropper. This eye-dropper can sample colors from any of the displayed swatches or from any color on-screen. Simply click the color swatch and drag the eye-dropper over any graphic to choose a color.
>
> If you choose a color outside of the "safe" range, you have no assurances of how the color is rendered on a viewer's browser. Some systems select the closest color in RGB values; some use dithering (positioning two or more colors next to each other to simulate another color) to try to overcome the limitations of the current screen color depth. So be forewarned: If at all possible, stick with the browser-safe colors, especially when coloring text.
>
> **Mac Users:** The system color picker — brought up when the Palette icon on the color picker menu is selected — for Macintosh is far more elaborate than the one available for Windows. The Mac version has several color schemes to use: CMYK (for print-related colors), RGB (for screen-based colors), HTML (for Web-based colors), and Crayon (for kid-like colors). The CMYK, HTML, and RGB systems offer you color swatches and three or four sliders with text entry boxes, and accept percentage values for RGB and CMYK, and hex values for HTML. Both RGB and HTML also have a snap-to-Web color option for matching your chosen color to the closest browser-safe color. The Hue, Saturation, and Value (or Lightness) sliders also have color wheels.

Adding font color

Unless you assign a color to text on your Web page, the browser uses its own default, typically black. As noted in "Establishing Page Properties" in Chapter 4, you can change the font color for the entire page by choosing Modify ⇨ Page Properties and selecting a new color from the Text Color swatch. You can also color any specific headings, words, or paragraphs that you have selected in Dreamweaver.

> **Tip**
>
> When adding a new font color, size, or name to text that already has one `<font>` tag applied to it, it's best to use the Tag Selector to highlight the text by selecting that `<font>` tag. If you select your text by clicking and dragging, you're likely to not select the entire contents of the tag, which results in multiple `<font>` tags being applied.

The `<font>` tag goes to work again when you add color to selected elements of the page — this time, with the color attribute set to a particular value. HTML color is expressed in either a hexadecimal color number or a color name. The hexadecimal color number is based on the color's red-green-blue value and is written as follows:

```
#FFFFFF
```

The preceding represents the color white. You can also use standard color names instead of the hexadecimal color numbers. A sample color code line follows:

```
I'm <font color="green">GREEN</font> with envy.
```

Dreamweaver understands both color names and hexadecimal color numbers, but its HTML code output is in hexadecimal color numbers only.

Again, you have two ways to add color to your text in Dreamweaver. The Property Inspector displays a drop-down list of the browser-safe colors and also gives you an option to choose from a full-spectrum Color dialog box. If you approach your coloring task via the menus, the Text ⇨ Color command takes you immediately to the Color dialog box.

To use the Property Inspector to color a range of text in Dreamweaver, follow these steps:

1. Select the text you want to color or position the cursor where you want the new text color to begin.

2. From the Property Inspector, you can

    - Type a hexadecimal color number directly into the Font Color text box.
    - Type a color name directly into the Font Color text box.
    - Select the Font Color swatch to open the browser-safe color picker.

3. If you chose to type a color name or number directly into the Font Color text box, press Tab or click the Document window to see the color applied.

4. If you clicked the Font Color swatch, select your color from the browser-safe colors available. As you move your pointer over the color swatches, Dreamweaver displays the color in the corner and the color's hexadecimal number below.

5. For a wider color selection from the Color dialog box, select the Palette icon in the lower-right corner of the color swatch.

To access the full-spectrum color picker in Windows, follow these steps:

1. Select your text or position your cursor where you want the new text color to begin.

2. Choose Text ⇨ Color to open the Color dialog box, as shown in Figure 5-16.

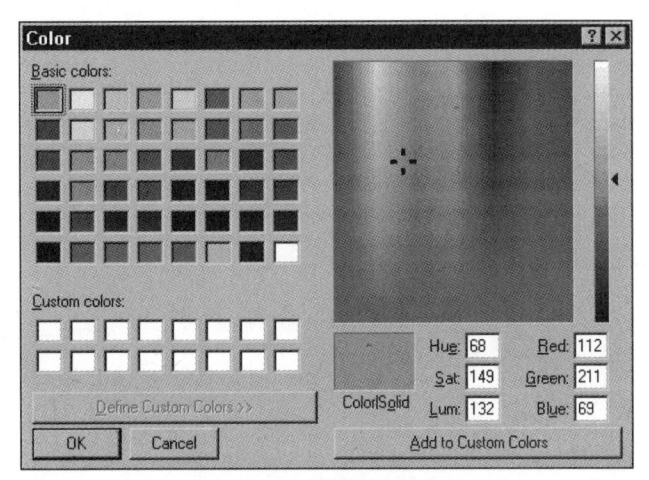

Figure 5-16: Use the Color dialog box in Windows to choose a color for your font outside of the browser-safe palette.

3. Select one of the 48 preset standard colors from the color swatches on the left of the Color dialog box, or use either of the following methods:

   - Select a color by moving the Hue/Saturation pointer and the Luminance pointer.
   - Enter decimal values directly into either the Red, Green, and Blue boxes or the Hue, Saturation, and Luminance boxes.

4. If you create a custom color, you can add it to your palette by selecting Add to Custom Colors. You can add up to 16 custom colors.

5. Click OK when you are finished.

Caution

When you add a custom color to your palette in Windows, the new color swatch goes into the currently selected swatch or, if no swatch is selected, the next available swatch. Make sure you have selected an empty or replaceable swatch before selecting the Add to Custom Color button. To clear the custom colors, first set the palette to white by bringing the Luminance slider all the way to the top. Then, select the Add to Custom Color button until all the color swatch text boxes are empty.

To access the full-spectrum color picker in Macintosh systems, follow these steps:

1. Select the text or position your cursor where you want the new text color to begin.

2. Choose Text ⇨ Color to open the Color dialog box.

3. From the Color dialog box, select the Color Palette icon.

   The Macintosh color picker opens.

4. In the Macintosh color picker, the list of available pickers is displayed in the left pane, and each particular interface is shown in the right. Choose the specific color picker icon from the left pane and create the color desired in the right.

   The number and type of color pickers vary from system to system, depending on the version of the operating system and whether you've added any third-party color pickers.

5. When you've found the desired color, click OK.

Assigning a specific font

Along with size and color, you can also specify the typeface in which you want particular text to be rendered. Dreamweaver uses a special method for choosing font names for a range of selected text, due to HTML's unique way of handling fonts. Before you learn how to change a typeface in Dreamweaver, let's further examine how fonts in HTML work.

About HTML fonts

Page layout designers can incorporate as many different fonts as available to their own systems. Web layout designers, on the other hand, can use only those fonts on their viewers' systems. If you designate a paragraph to be in Bodoni Bold Condensed, for instance, and put it on the Web, the paragraph is displayed with that font only if that exact font name is on the user's system. Otherwise, the browser uses the default system font, which is often Times or Times New Roman.

Fonts are specified with the `<font>` tag, aided by the `name` attribute. Because a designer can never be certain of which fonts are on visitors' computers, HTML enables you to offer a number of options to the browser, as follows:

```
<font name="Arial, Helvetica, sans-serif">Swiss Maid Foundry</font>
```

The browser encountering the preceding tag first looks for the Arial font to render the enclosed text. If Arial isn't there, the browser looks for the next font in the list, which in this case is Helvetica. Failing to find any of the specified fonts listed, the browser uses whichever font has been assigned to the category for the font — sans-serif in this case.

The W3C and some Web browsers recognize five main categories of fonts: serif, sans-serif, monospace, cursive, and fantasy. Internet Explorer has a higher compliance rating on this issue than Netscape Communicator.

Selecting a font

The process for assigning a font name to a range of text is similar to that of assigning a font size or color. Instead of selecting one font name, however, you're usually selecting one font series. That series could contain three or more fonts, as previously explained. Font series are chosen from the Property Inspector or through a menu item. Dreamweaver enables you to assign any font on your system — or even any font you can name — to a font series, as covered in the section "Editing the Font List," later in this chapter.

To assign a specific font series to your text, follow these steps:

1. Select the text or position your cursor where you want the new text font to begin.

2. From the Property Inspector, open the drop-down list of font names. You can also choose Text ⇨ Font from the menu bar. Your font list is displayed.

3. Select a font from the Font List. To return to the system font, choose Default Font from the list.

It's also possible to enter the font name or font series directly in the Property Inspector's Font drop-down list.

Tip

Font peculiarities are one of the key reasons to always test your Web pages on several platforms. Macintosh and Windows have different names for the same basic fonts (Arial in Windows is almost identical to Helvetica in Macintosh, for instance), and even the standard font sizes vary between the platforms. On the plus side, standard Microsoft fonts (Arial, Verdana for example) are more common on the Macintosh since Mac OS 8.1, but differences still exist. Overall, PC fonts are larger than fonts on a Macintosh. Be sure to check out your page on as many systems as possible before finalizing your design.

Editing the Font List

With the Edit Font List dialog box, Dreamweaver gives you a point-and-click interface for building your font lists. Once the Edit Font List dialog box is open, you can delete an existing font series, add a new one, or change the order of the list so your favorite ones are on top. Take a look at Figure 5-17 to see the sections of the Edit Font List dialog box: the current Font List, the Available Fonts on your system, and the Chosen Fonts. The Chosen Fonts are the individual fonts that you've selected to be incorporated into a font series.

Let's step through the process of constructing a new font series and adding it to the Font List:

1. To open the Edit Font List dialog box, either choose Edit Font List through the Font Name option arrow in the Property Inspector, or select Text ⇨ Font ⇨ Edit Font List.

2. If the Chosen Fonts box is not empty, clear the Chosen Fonts box by selecting the plus (+) button at the top of the dialog box. You can also scroll down to the bottom of the current Font List and select "(Add fonts in list below)."

3. Select a font from the Available Fonts list.

4. Click the << button to transfer the selected font to the Chosen Fonts list.

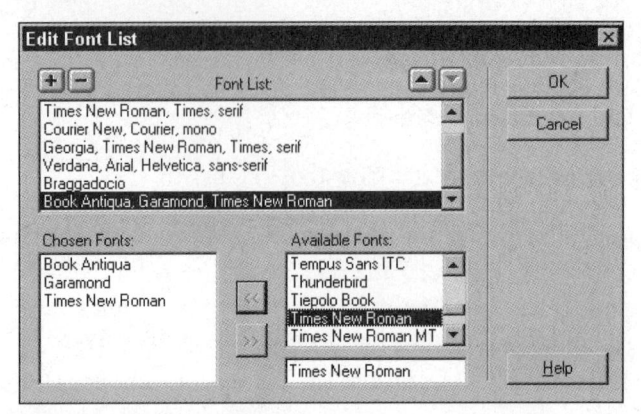

Figure 5-17: Dreamweaver's Edit Font List dialog box gives you considerable control over the fonts that you can add to your Web page.

   5. To remove a font you no longer want or have chosen in error, highlight it in the Chosen Fonts list and select the >> button.

   6. Repeat Steps 3 through 5 until the Chosen Fonts list contains the alternative fonts desired.

   7. If you want to add another, separate font series, repeat Steps 2 through 5.

   8. Click OK when you are finished adding fonts.

To change the order in which font series are listed in the Font List, follow these steps:

   1. In the Font List dialog box, select the font series that you want to move.

   2. If you want to move the series higher up the list, select the up-arrow button at the top-right of the Font List. If you want to move the series lower down the list, select the down-arrow button.

To remove a font series from the current Font List, highlight it and select the minus (–) button at the top-left of the list.

Remember, you need to have the fonts on your system to make them a part of your Font List. To add a font that's unavailable on your computer, type the name of the font into the text box below the Available Fonts list and press Enter (Return).

Aligning text

You can easily align text in Dreamweaver, just like in a traditional word processing program. HTML supports the alignment of text to the left or right margin, or in the center of the browser window. Like a word processing program, Dreamweaver aligns text one paragraph at a time. You can't left-align one word, center the next, and then right-align the third word in the same paragraph.

To align text, you can use one of three methods: a menu command, the Property Inspector, or a keyboard shortcut. To use the menus, choose Text ⇨ Alignment and then pick the alignment you prefer (Left, Right, or Center). Table 5-8 explains the Text Property Inspector's Alignment buttons and the associated keyboard shortcuts.

Table 5-8
Text Alignment Options in the Property Inspector

Button	Alignment	Keyboard Shortcut
	Left	Ctrl+Alt+L (Command+Option+L)
	Center	Ctrl+Alt+C (Command+Option+C)
	Right	Ctrl+Alt+R (Command+Option+R)

Note: A fourth way to align text is through the Cascading Style Sheets. Any style can be set to align your text. Moreover, not only are Left, Right, and Center supported—so is Justify, which causes text to be flush against both left and right margins, creating a block-like appearance. The Justify value is supported in browsers 4.0 and later.

Cross-Reference: Traditional HTML alignment options are limited. For a finer degree of control, be sure to investigate precise positioning with layers in Chapter 15.

Indenting entire paragraphs

HTML offers a tag that enables you to indent whole paragraphs, such as inset quotations or name-and-address blocks. Not too surprisingly, the tag used is called the `<blockquote>` tag. Dreamweaver gives you instant access to the `<blockquote>` tag through the Indent and Outdent buttons located on the Text Property Inspector, as shown in Figure 5-18.

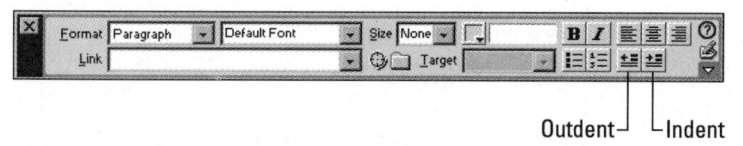

Figure 5-18: Indent paragraphs and blocks of text with the Indent and the Outdent buttons.

To indent one or more paragraphs, select them and click the Indent button in the Property Inspector. Paragraphs can be indented multiple times; each time you click the Indent button, another `<blockquote>...</blockquote>` tag pair is added.

Note You can't control how much space a single `<blockquote>` indents a paragraph — that characteristic is determined by the browser.

If you find that you have over-indented, you can use the Outdent button, which is also located on the Property Inspector. The Outdent button has no effect if your text is already at the left edge.

You also have the option of indenting your paragraphs through the menus; choose Text ➪ Indent or Text ➪ Outdent.

Tip You can tell how many `<blockquote>` tags are being used to create a particular look by placing your cursor in the text and looking at the Tag Selector.

Incorporating Dates

With the Web constantly changing, keeping track of when information is updated is important. Dreamweaver includes a new command that enables you to insert today's date in your page, in almost any format imaginable. Moreover, you can set the inserted date to be automatically updated every time the page is saved. This means every time you make a modification to a page and save it, the current date is added.

The Insert Date command uses your system clock to get the current date. In addition, you can elect to add a day name (for example, Thursday) and time to the basic date information. Once the date text is inserted, it can be formatted in the same way as any other text — adding color or a specific font type or changing the date's size.

To insert the current date, follow these steps:

1. Choose Insert ➪ Date or select the Insert Date object from the Common panel of the Objects panel.

    The Insert Date dialog box, shown in Figure 5-19, is displayed.

2. If desired, select a Day Format to include in the date from the drop-down list. The options are:

[No Day]	Thu
Thursday,	thu,
Thursday	thu
Thu,	

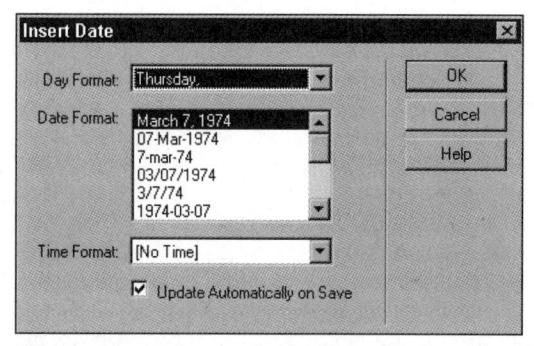

Figure 5-19: Keep track of when a file is updated by using the Insert Date command.

3. Select the desired date format from the drop-down list. The example formats are:

March 7, 1974	7./03/7.4
07.-Mar-1974	07.03.1974
7.-mar-7.4	07.03.74
03./07/1994	7.-03-197.4
3./7/747.	March, 197.4
1974.-03-07	74.-03-07
7./3/7.4	

> **Tip**
> If you are creating Web pages for the global market, consider using the format designated by the 1974-03-07 example. This year-month-day format is an ISO (International Organization for Standardization) standard and is computer sortable.

4. Select the desired time format, if any, from the drop-down list. The two example time formats are:

   [No Time]

   10.:18 PM

   22.:18

5. If you want the date modified to include the current date every time the file is saved, select the Update Automatically on Save option.

6. Click OK when you're done.

Tip: It's no problem at all to format an inserted date when the Update Automatically on Save option is *not* selected — then it's just plain text and the formatting can be added easily through the Text Property Inspector. However, if the date is to be automatically updated, it's inserted as a special Macromedia datatype with its own Property Inspector. You can style it, however, by selecting options from the Text menu or applying an HTML or CSS style.

If your date object includes the Automatic Update option, you can modify the format. Select the date and, in the Property Inspector, choose the Edit Date Format button. The Edit Date Format dialog box opens and is identical to the Insert Date dialog box, except the Update Automatically on Save option is not available.

Commenting Your Code

When will you know to start inserting comments into your HTML code? The first time you go back to an earlier Web page, look at the code and say, "What on earth was I thinking?" You should plan ahead and develop the habit of commenting your code now.

Browsers run fine without your comments, but for any continued development — of the Web page or of yourself as a Webmaster — commenting your code is extremely beneficial. Sometimes, as in a corporate setting, Web pages are codeveloped by teams of designers and programmers. In this situation, commenting your code may not just be a good idea; it may be required.

An HTML comment looks like the following:

```
<!-- Created by Hummer Associates, Inc. -->
```

You're not restricted to any particular line length or number of lines for comments. The text included between the opening of the comment, <!--, and the closing, -->, can span regular paragraphs or HTML code. In fact, one of the most common uses for comments during the testing and debugging phase of page design is to "comment out" sections of code as a means of tracking down an elusive bug.

To insert a comment in Dreamweaver, first place your cursor in Code View, Design View, or in the Code Inspector where you want the comment to appear. Then select the Insert Comment button from the Invisibles panel of the Objects panel. This sequence opens the Insert Comment dialog box, where you can insert the desired text; click OK when you've finished. Figure 5-20 shows the Insert Comment dialog box, with the corresponding completed comment in the split Design/Code View.

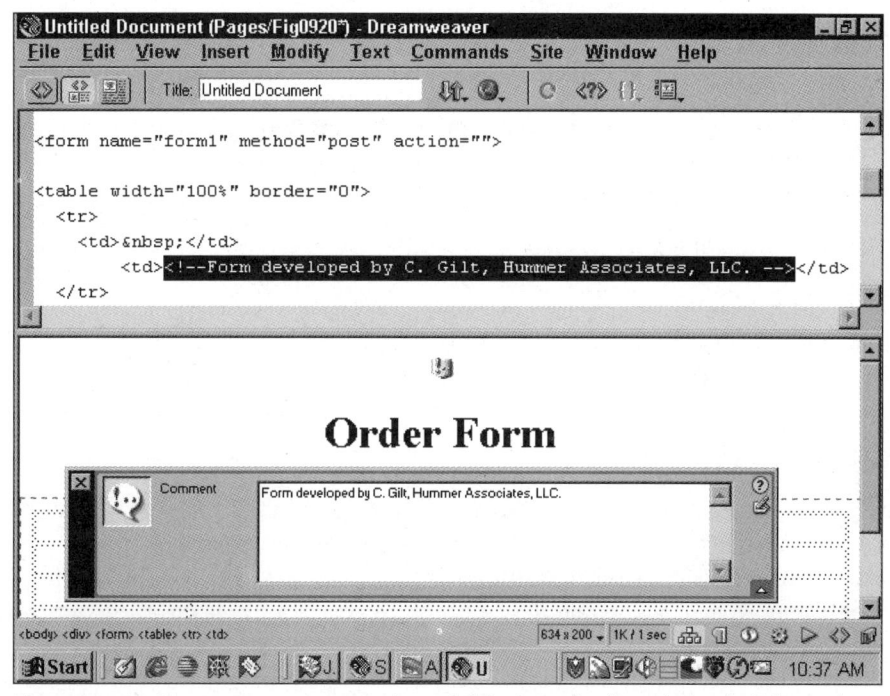

Figure 5-20: Comments are extremely useful for inserting into the code information not visible on the rendered Web page.

By default, Dreamweaver inserts a Comment symbol in the Document window. As with the other Invisibles, you can hide the Comment symbol by choosing Edit ⇨ Preferences and then deselecting the Comments checkbox in the Invisible Elements panel. You can also hide any displayed Invisibles by selecting View ⇨ Invisible Elements or using the keyboard shortcut, Ctrl+Shift+I (Command+Shift+I).

When you need to edit a comment, double-click the Comment symbol to display the current comment in an editable window. After you've finished making your changes to the comment, select the Close button of the Comment window. A comment can be moved or duplicated by selecting its symbol and using the Cut, Copy, and Paste commands under the Edit menu. You can also right-click (Command+click) the Comment symbol to bring up the shortcut menu. Finally, you can click and drag Comment symbols to move the corresponding comment to a new location.

Summary

Learning to manipulate text is an essential design skill for creating Web pages. Dreamweaver gives you all the tools you need to insert and modify the full range of HTML text quickly and easily. This chapter covered the following topics related to adding text to your Web page:

- HTML headings are available in six different sizes: `<h1>` through `<h6>`. Headings are used primarily as headlines and subheads to separate divisions of the Web page.

- Blocks of text are formatted with the paragraph tag `<p>`. Each paragraph is separated from the other paragraphs by a line of whitespace above and below. Use the line break tag, `<br>`, to make lines appear directly above or below one another.

- Dreamweaver offers a full complement of text-editing tools — everything from Cut and Paste to Find and Replace. Two commands, Copy Text Only and Paste As Text, are unique to Dreamweaver and make short work of switching between text and code.

- Dreamweaver's Find and Replace feature goes a long way toward automating your work on the current page as well as throughout the Web site. Both content and code can be searched in a basic or very advanced fashion.

- Where possible, text in HTML is formatted according to its meaning. Dreamweaver applies the styles selected through the Text ⇨ Style menu. For most styles, the browser determines what the user views.

- You can format Web page text much as you can text in a word processing program. Within certain limitations, you can select a font's size and color, as well as the font itself.

- Dreamweaver's HTML Styles feature enables you to consistently and quickly format your text.

- HTML comments are a useful (and often requisite) vehicle for embedding information into a Web page that remains unseen by the casual viewer. Comments can annotate program code or insert copyright information.

In the next chapter, you learn how to insert and work with graphics.

✦ ✦ ✦

Inserting Images

CHAPTER 6

The Internet started as a text-based medium primarily used for sharing data among research scientists and among U.S. military commanders. Today, the Web is as visually appealing as any mass medium. Dreamweaver's power becomes even more apparent as you use its visual layout tools to incorporate background and foreground images into your Web page designs.

Completely baffled by all the various image formats out there? This chapter opens with an overview of the key Web-oriented graphics formats, including PNG. Also, this chapter covers techniques for incorporating both background and foreground images — and modifying them using new methods available in Dreamweaver 4. Animation graphics and how you can use them in your Web pages are also covered here, as are techniques for creating rollover buttons. Finally, this chapter introduces integration with Fireworks, Macromedia's award-winning Web graphics tool; Dreamweaver and Fireworks make a potent team for creating and publishing Web graphics.

Web Graphic Formats

If you've worked in the computer graphics field, you know that virtually every platform — as well as every paint and graphics program — has its own proprietary file format for images. One of the critical factors in the Web's rapid, expansive growth is the use of cross-platform graphics. Regardless of the system you use to create your images, these versatile files ensure that the graphics can be viewed by all platforms.

The trade-off for universal acceptance of image files is a restricted field: just two file formats, with a possible third just coming into view. Currently, only GIF and JPEG formats are fully supported by browsers. A third alternative, the PNG graphics format, is experiencing a limited but growing acceptance.

✦ ✦ ✦ ✦

In This Chapter

Image file formats

Inserting images from the Assets panel

Modifying image height, width, and margins

Using the `lowsrc` attribute

Aligning and wrapping text and images

Working with background and foreground images

Dividing your page with HTML lines

Graphics in motion

Adding rollovers

Inserting navigational buttons

✦ ✦ ✦ ✦

You need to understand the uses and limitations of each of the formats so you can apply them successfully in Dreamweaver. Let's look at the fundamentals.

GIF

GIF, the Graphics Interchange Format, was developed by CompuServe in the late 1980s to address the problem of cross-platform compatibility. With GIF viewers available for every system from PC and Macintosh to Amiga and NeXT, the format became a natural choice for an inline (adjacent to text) image graphic. GIFs are bitmapped images, which means that each pixel is given or mapped to a specific color. You can have up to 256 colors for a GIF graphic. These images are generally used for illustrations, logos, or cartoons — anything that doesn't require thousands of colors for a smooth color blend, such as a photograph. With a proper graphics tool, you can reduce the number of colors in a GIF image to a minimum, thereby compressing the file and reducing download time.

The GIF87a and GIF89a varieties

The GIF format has two varieties: "regular" (technically, GIF87a) and an enhanced version known as GIF89a. This improved GIF file brings three important attributes to the format. First, GIF89a supports transparency, in which one or more of the colors can become invisible. This property is necessary for creating nonrectangular-appearing images. Whenever you see a round or irregularly shaped logo or illustration on the Web, a rectangular frame is displayed as the image is loading — this is the actual size and shape of the graphic. The colors surrounding the irregularly shaped central image are set to transparent in a graphics-editing program (such as Fireworks or Adobe Photoshop) before the image is saved in GIF89a format.

Note Most of the latest versions of the popular graphic tools default to using GIF89a, so unless you're working with older, legacy images, you're not too likely to encounter the less flexible GIF87a format.

Although the outer area of a graphic seems to disappear with GIF89a, you won't be able to overlap your Web images using this format without using layers. Figure 6-1 demonstrates this situation. In this figure, the same image is presented twice — one lacks transparency, and one has transparency applied. The image on the left is saved as a standard GIF without transparency, and you can plainly see the shape of the full image. The image on the right was saved with the white background color made transparent, so the central figure seems to float on the background.

Interlacing capabilities of GIF89a

The second valuable attribute contributed by GIF89a format is *interlacing*. One of the most common complaints about graphics on the Web is lengthy download times. Interlacing won't speed up your GIF downloads, but it gives your Web page visitors something to view other than a blank screen. A graphic saved with the interlace feature turned on gives the appearance of "developing," like an instant picture, as the file is downloading. Use of this design option is up to you and your clients. Some folks swear by it; others can't abide it.

Figure 6-1: The same image, saved without GIF transparency (left) and with GIF transparency (right)

Animation capabilities of GIF89a

Animation is the final advantage offered by the GIF89a format. Certain software programs enable you to group your GIF files together into one large page-flipping file. With this capability, you can bring simple animation to your page without additional plug-ins or helper applications. Unfortunately, the trade-off is that the files get very big, very fast. For more on animated GIFs in Dreamweaver, see the section "Applying Simple Web Animation" later in this chapter.

JPEG

The JPEG format was developed by the Joint Photographic Experts Group specifically to handle photographic images. JPEGs offer millions of colors at 24 bits of color information available per pixel, as opposed to the GIF format's 8-bit and 256 colors. To make JPEGs usable, the large amount of color information must be compressed, which is accomplished by removing what the algorithm considers redundant information. This is often referred to as *lossy* compression — in which pixels are lost — as opposed to *lossless* compression, a characteristic of GIF images.

The more compressed your JPEG file, the more degraded the image. When you first save a JPEG image, your graphics program asks you for the desired level of compression. As an example, take a look at the three pictures in Figure 6-2. Here you can compare the effects of JPEG compression ratios and resulting file sizes to the original image itself. As you can probably tell, JPEG does an excellent job of compression, with even the highest degree of compression having only a little visible impact. Keep in mind that each picture has its own reaction to compression.

Figure 6-2: JPEG compression can save your Web visitors substantial download time, with little loss of image quality.

Tip   With the JPEG image-compression algorithm, the initial elements of an image "compressed away" are least noticeable. Subtle variations in brightness and hue are the first to disappear. When possible, preview your image in your graphics program while adjusting the compression level to observe the changes. With additional compression, the image grows darker and less varied in its color range.

With JPEGs, what is compressed for storage must be uncompressed for viewing. When a JPEG picture on your Web page is accessed by a visitor's browser, the image must first be downloaded to the browser and then uncompressed before it can be viewed. This dual process adds additional time to the Web-browsing process, but it is time well spent for photographic images.

JPEGs, unlike GIFs, have neither transparency nor animation features. A newer strand of JPEG called Progressive JPEG gives you the interlace option of the GIF format, however. Although not all browsers support the interlace feature of Progressive JPEG, they render the image regardless.

PNG

The latest entry into the Web graphics arena is the Portable Network Graphics format, or PNG. Combining the best of both worlds, PNG has lossless compression, like GIF, and is capable of millions of colors, like JPEG. Moreover, PNG offers an interlace scheme that appears much more quickly than either GIF or JPEG, as well as transparency support that is far superior to both the other formats.

One valuable aspect of the PNG format enables the display of PNG pictures to appear more uniform across various computer platforms. Generally, graphics made on a PC look brighter on a Macintosh, and Mac-made images seem darker on a PC. PNG includes gamma correction capabilities that alter the image depending on the computer used by the viewer.

Before the 4.0 versions, the various browsers supported PNG only through plug-ins. After PNG was endorsed as a new Web graphic format by the W3C, both 4.0 versions of Netscape and Microsoft browsers added native, inline support of the new format. Perhaps most important, however, Dreamweaver was among the first Web authoring tools to offer native PNG support. Inserted PNG images preview in the Document window just like GIFs and JPEGs. Browser support is currently not widespread enough to warrant a total switch to the PNG format (it's still lacking in Internet Explorer for Macintosh, for example), but its growing acceptance certainly bears watching.

> **Tip** If you're really excited about the potential of PNG, check out Macromedia's Fireworks, the first Web graphics tool to use PNG as its native format. Fireworks takes full advantage of PNG's alpha transparency features and enhanced palette.

Two excellent resources for more on the PNG format is the PNG home page at `www.freesoftware.com/pub/png/` and the W3C's PNG page at `www.w3.org/Graphics/PNG`.

Using Inline Images

An *inline image* can appear directly next to text — literally in the same line. The capability to render inline images is one of the major innovations of the World Wide Web's transition from the Internet. This section covers all the basics of inserting inline images into Dreamweaver and modifying their attributes.

Inserting inline images

Dreamweaver can open and preview any graphic in a GIF, JPEG, or PNG format. With Dreamweaver, you have six methods for placing a graphic on your Web page:

- From the Objects panel, select the Insert Image button.
- From the menu bar, choose Insert ⇨ Image.
- From the keyboard, press Ctrl+Alt+I (Command+Option+I).
- Point to an image file in the Site window using Dreamweaver's Point to File feature.
- Drag either the Insert Image button or an icon from your file manager (Explorer or Finder) to your page.

✦ Drag a *thumbnail* (a small version of an image) or filename from the Images category of the Assets panel onto your page. This capability is new in Dreamweaver 4 and is covered in detail in a following section.

The first four methods require that you first position the cursor at the point where you want the image to appear on the page; the drag-and-drop method enables you to place the image inline with any existing element.

For all but the method using the Assets panel, Dreamweaver opens the Select Image Source dialog box (shown in Figure 6-3) and asks you for the path or address to your image file. Remember that in HTML, all graphics are stored in separate files linked from your Web page. The image's address can be just a filename, a directory path and filename on your system, a directory path and filename on your remote system, or a full URL to a graphic on a completely separate Web server. You don't have to have the file immediately available to insert the code into your HTML.

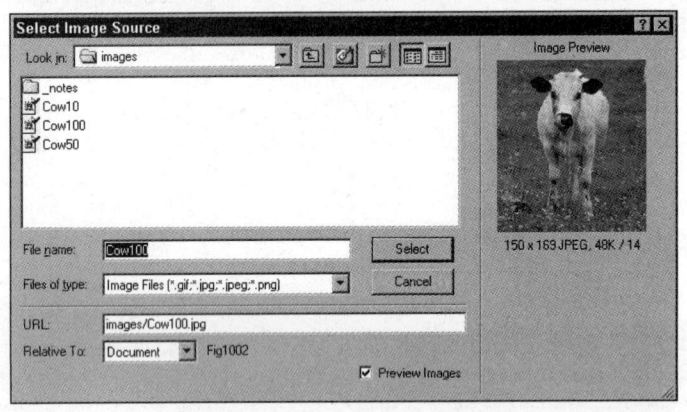

Figure 6-3: In this Select Image Source dialog box, you can keep track of your image's location relative to your current Web page.

From the Select Image Source dialog box, you can browse to your image folder, and preview images before you load them. To enable this feature, make sure the Preview Images option is selected. Dreamweaver can preview GIF, JPEG, or PNG files.

In the lower portion of the dialog box, the URL text box displays the format of the address Dreamweaver inserts into your code. Below the URL text box is the Relative To list box. Here you can choose to declare an image to be relative to the document you're working on (the default) or relative to the site root. (After you've saved your document, you see its name displayed beside the Relative To box.)

Cross-Reference: To take full advantage of Dreamweaver's site management features, you must open a site, establish a local site root, and save the current Web page before beginning to insert images. For more on how to begin a Dreamweaver project, and about document-relative and site root–relative addressing, see Chapter 2.

Relative to Document

Once you've saved your Web page and chosen Relative to Document, Dreamweaver displays the address in the URL text box. If the image is located in a folder on the same level as, or within, your current site root folder, the address is formatted with just a path and filename. For instance, if you're inserting a graphic from the subfolder named images, Dreamweaver inserts an address like the following:

```
images/men10.jpg
```

If you try to insert an image currently stored outside of the local site root folder, Dreamweaver temporarily appends a prefix that tells the browser to look on your local system for the file. For instance, the file listing would look like the following in Windows:

```
file:///C|/Dreamweaver/Figs/men10.jpg
```

while on the Macintosh, the same file is listed as follows:

```
file:///Macintosh HD/Dreamweaver/Figs/men10.jpg
```

Caution: Dreamweaver also appends the `file:///C|` prefix (or just `file:///Macintosh HD` in Macintosh) if you haven't yet saved your document. It is strongly recommended that you save your file before you begin developing the Web page. You can easily upload Web pages with this `file:///C|` (`file:///Macintosh HD`) prefix in place—and miss the error completely. Because your local browser can find the referenced image on your system, even when you are browsing the remote site, the Web page appears perfect. However, anyone else browsing your Web site only sees placeholders for broken links. Saving your page before you begin enables Dreamweaver to help you avoid these errors. To this end, do not check the Don't show me this message again checkbox that appears when you're reminded to save your file the first time. This message can save you an enormous amount of grief!

After you select your image file, you see the prompt window shown in Figure 6-4. Dreamweaver asks if you want to copy this image to your local site root folder. Whenever possible, keep all of your images within the local site root folder so that Dreamweaver can handle site management efficiently. Click Yes, and you next see the Save Copy As dialog box, which points to the local site root folder. If you select No, the file is inserted with the `src` attribute pointing to the path of the file.

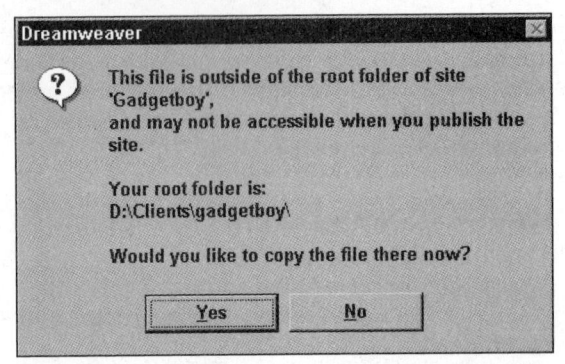

Figure 6-4: Dreamweaver reminds you to keep all your graphics in the local site root folder for easy site management.

Relative to Site Root

Should you select Site Root in the Relative To field of the Select Image Source dialog box, and you are within your site root folder, Dreamweaver appends a leading forward slash to the directory in the path so the browser can correctly read the address. Thus, the same men10.jpg file appears in both the URL box and the HTML code as follows:

```
/images/men10.jpg
```

When you use site root–relative addressing and you select a file outside of the site root, you get the same reminder from Dreamweaver about copying the file into your local site root folder — just as with document-relative addressing.

Dragging images from the Assets panel

Quite often, a Web designer works from a collection of images, much like a painter uses a palette of colors. Reusing images builds consistency in the site look and feel and makes it easier for a visitor to navigate through the site. However, trying to remember the differences between two versions of a logo — one named logo03.gif and another named logo03b.gif — often required inserting them both to find the correct image. Dreamweaver 4 eliminates the visual guesswork and simplifies the reuse of graphics with the new Assets panel.

New Feature The Images category is key to the Assets panel. Not only does the Assets panel list all the GIF, JPEG, and PNG files found in your site — whether or not they are embedded in a Web page — selecting any graphic from the list instantly displays a thumbnail. Previewing the images makes it easy to select the proper one. Moreover, once you've found the correct image, all you need do it drag it from the Assets panel to the page.

Chapter 6 ✦ **Inserting Images** 167

Before you can use graphics from the Assets panel, you must catalog the site by choosing the Refresh Site List button, as shown in Figure 6-5. When you click the Refresh button (or choose Refresh Site List from the context menu on the Assets panel), Dreamweaver examines the current site and creates a list of the graphics, their sizes, file types, and full paths. To see an image, just click its name and a thumbnail appears in the preview area of the panel.

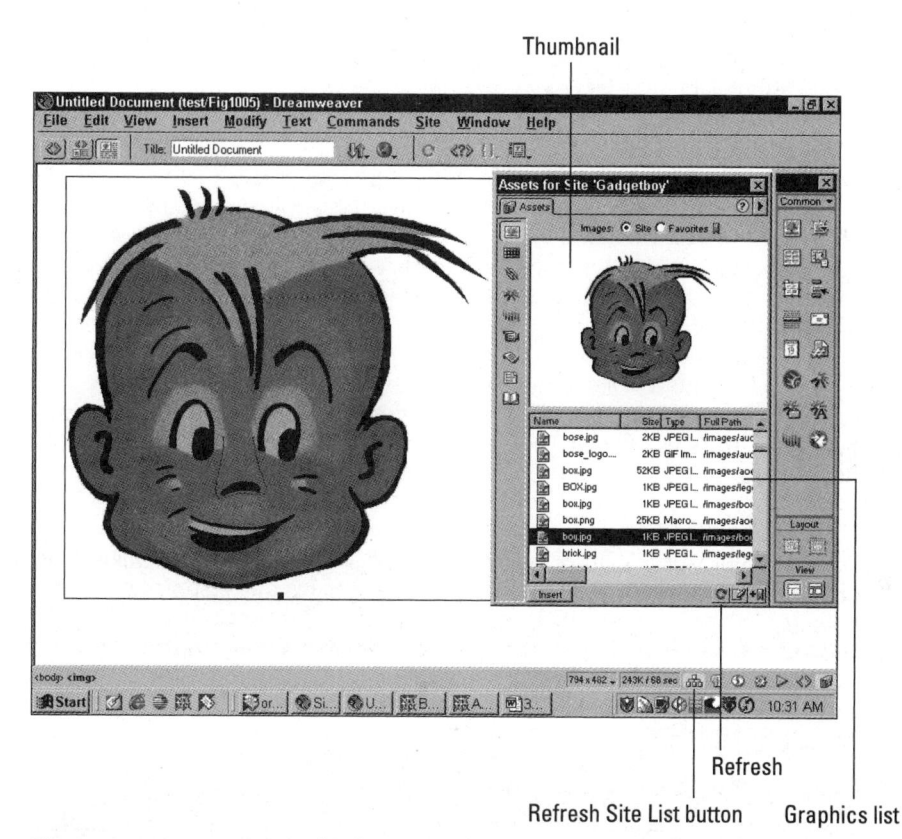

Figure 6-5: Reuse any graphic in your site or from your Favorites collection by dragging it out from the Assets panel.

Tip To increase the size of the thumbnail, make the preview area larger by dragging open the border between the preview and list areas. You can also expand the size of the entire panel by dragging its corner. Dreamweaver increases the size of the thumbnail while maintaining the width:height ratio so if you just move the border or resize the panel a little bit you may not see a significant change. Thumbnails are never displayed larger than their actual size.

You can insert an image from the Assets panel onto your Web page in two ways:

- Drag the image or the file listing onto the page.
- Place your cursor where you'd like the image to appear, and — once the listing of the desired image is highlighted in the Assets panel — select the Insert button.

The image you desire does not have to be in the current site, if you've added it to the Favorites collection. To retrieve an image from Favorites, first select the Favorites option at the top of the Assets panel. To switch back to the current site, choose the Site option.

Tip In sites with many images, it's often difficult to scroll through all the names looking for a particular image. To aid your search, Dreamweaver enables you to sort the Images category by any of the columns displayed in the Assets panel: Name, Size, Type, or Full Path. Clicking once on the column heading sorts the assets in an ascending order by that criteria; click the column again to sort by that same criteria, but in a descending order.

If one or more objects are selected on the page, the inserted image is placed after the selection; Dreamweaver does not permit you to replace a selected image with another from the Assets panel. To change one image into another, double-click the graphic on the page to display the Select Image Source dialog box.

Caution Do not double-click the image or listing in the Assets panel to insert it onto the page. Double-clicking invokes the designated graphics editor, whether it be Fireworks, Photoshop, or another program, and opens that graphic for editing.

One final note on adding images from the Assets panel: If you bring in a graphic from a location outside of the site, Dreamweaver asks that you copy the file to the current site. You must select the Refresh button to display this new image in the Assets panel.

Tip When you select the Refresh button, Dreamweaver adds new images (and other assets) to the cache of current assets. If you add assets from outside of Dreamweaver, using, for example, a file manager, you might need to completely re-create the Assets panel by Ctrl-clicking (Command-clicking) the Refresh button.

Modifying images

When you insert an image in Dreamweaver, the image tag, `<img>`, is inserted into your HTML code. The `<img>` tag takes several attributes, all of which can be entered through the Property Inspector. Code for a basic image looks like the following:

```
<img src="images/Collection01.gif" width="172" height="180">
```

Dreamweaver centralizes all of its image functions in the Property Inspector. The Image Property Inspector, shown in Figure 6-6, displays a small thumbnail of the image as well as its file size. Dreamweaver automatically inserts the image filename in the Src text box (as the `src` attribute). To replace a currently selected image with another, click the folder icon next to the Src text box, or double-click the image itself. This sequence opens the Select Image Source dialog box. When you've selected the desired file, Dreamweaver automatically refreshes the page and corrects the code.

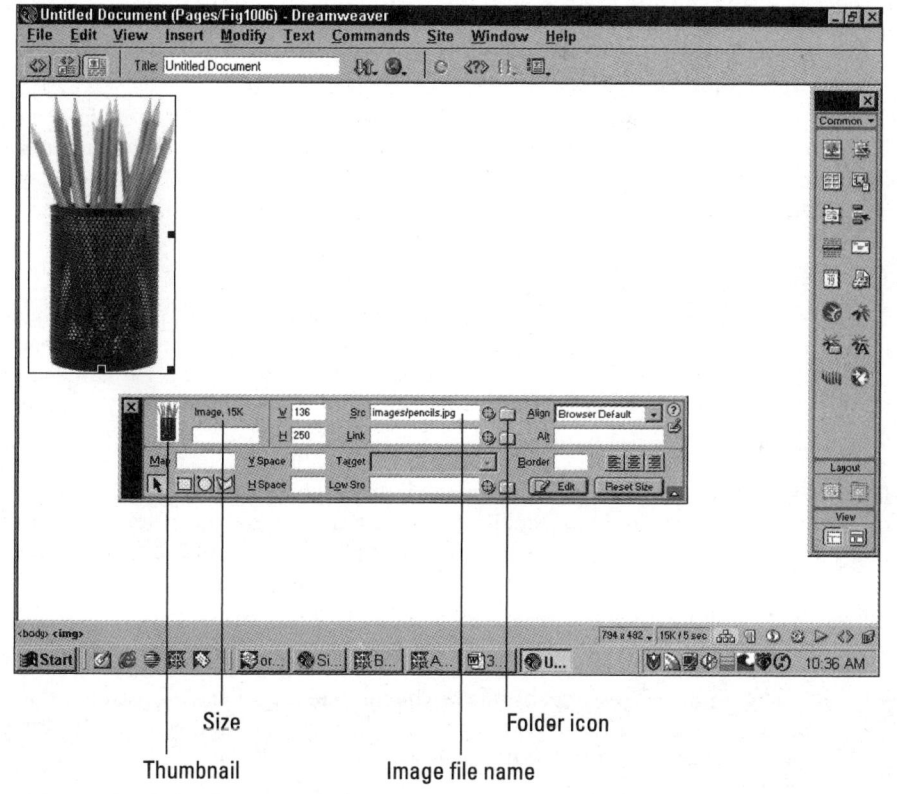

Figure 6-6: The Image Property Inspector gives you total control over the HTML code for every image.

With the Property Inspector open when you insert your image, you can begin to modify it immediately.

Editing the image

Dreamweaver is a terrific Web authoring tool, but it's not a graphics editor. Quite often, after you've inserted an image into your Web page, you find that the picture needs to be altered in some way. Perhaps you need to crop part of the image or make the background transparent. Dreamweaver enables you to specify your primary graphics editor for each type of graphic in the File Types/Editors category of the Preferences.

Once you've picked an image editor, clicking the Edit button in the Property Inspector opens the application with the current image. After you've made the modifications, just save the file in your image editor and switch back to Dreamweaver. The new, modified graphic has already been included in the Web page.

Note Dreamweaver seamlessly refreshed the images being edited in all the image editors I tested. However, there have been reports of images not reappearing in their modified form. If this happens, click the Refresh button in the Property Inspector after you select your image.

Adjusting height and width

The `width` and `height` attributes are important: Browsers build Web pages faster when they know the size and shape of the included images. Dreamweaver reads these attributes when the image is first loaded. The width and height values are initially expressed in pixels and are automatically inserted as attributes in the HTML code.

Browsers can dynamically resize an image if its height and width on the page are different from the original image's dimensions. For example, you can load your primary logo on the home page and then use a smaller version of it on subsequent pages by inserting the same image with reduced height and width values. Because you're only loading the image once and the browser is resizing it, download time for your Web page can be significantly reduced.

Note Resizing an image just means you're changing its appearance onscreen; the file size stays exactly the same. To reduce a file size for an image, you need to scale it down in a graphics program such as Fireworks.

You don't have to use pixels to enter your resizing measurements into Dreamweaver's Property Inspector. You can also use inches (in), picas (pc), points (pt), millimeters (mm), or centimeters (cm). The values must be entered without spaces between the number and the measurement abbreviation, as follows:

```
72pt
```

You can also combine measurement systems. Suppose, for example, you want to resize a picture's height to 2 inches and 5 centimeters. In the Property Inspector, you enter the following value in the H text box:

```
2in+5cm
```

Dreamweaver translates both inches and centimeters to their equivalent in pixels and then adds them together. The measurements are system-dependent; on the Macintosh, an inch equals 72 pixels and on Windows, an inch is 96 pixels.

When you use values with a combined measurement system, you can only add values — you can't subtract them. When you press the Tab key or click outside of the height and width boxes, Dreamweaver converts your value to pixels.

Tip With Dreamweaver, you can visually resize your graphics by using the click-and-drag method. A selected image has three sizing handles located on the right, bottom, and lower-right corners of its bounding box. Click any of these handles and drag it out to a new location — when you release the mouse, Dreamweaver resizes the image. Hold down the Shift key after dragging the corner sizing handle, and Dreamweaver maintains the current height/width aspect ratio.

If you alter either the height or the width of an image in the Property Inspector, Dreamweaver displays the values in bold in their respective fields. You can restore an image's default measurements by selecting the H or the W independently — or you can choose the Refresh button to restore both values.

Caution If you elect to enable your viewer's browser to resize your image on the fly using the height/width values you specify, keep in mind that the browser is not a graphics-editing program and that its resizing algorithms are not sophisticated. View your resized images through several browsers to make sure that the results are acceptable.

Using margins

You can offset images with surrounding whitespace by using the margin attributes. The amount of whitespace around your image can be designated both vertically and horizontally through the vspace and hspace attributes, respectively. These margin values are entered, in pixels, into the V Space and H Space text boxes in the Image Property Inspector.

The V Space value adds the same amount of whitespace along the top and bottom of your image; the H Space value increases the whitespace along the left and right sides of the image. These values must be positive; HTML doesn't allow images to overlap text or other images (outside of layers). Unlike in page layout, "negative whitespace" does not exist.

Titling your image

When you first insert a graphic into the page, the Image Property Inspector displays a blank text box next to the thumbnail and file size. Fill in this box with a unique name for the image, to be used in JavaScript and other applications.

As a page is loading over the Web, the image is first displayed as an empty rectangle if the `<img>` tag contains the width and height information. Sometimes these rectangles include a brief title to describe the coming image. You can enter this alternative text in the Alt text box of the Image Property Inspector.

> **Tip** Good coding practice associates an Alt title with all of your graphics. Aside from giving the user some clue as to what's coming, these mini-titles are also used to display the screen tips that pop up in some browsers when the user's pointer passes over the graphic. The real benefit of mini-titles, however, is providing input for browsers not displaying graphics. Text-only browsers are still in use, and some users, interested only in content, turn off the graphics to speed up the text display. Moreover, the W3C is working toward standards for browsers for the visually impaired, and the Alt text can be used to describe the page.

Bordering a graphic

When you're working with thumbnails (a series of small versions of images) on your Web page, you may need a quick way to distinguish one from another. (Refer to Figure 6-5 for an example of a thumbnail.) The `border` attribute enables you to place a one-color rectangular border around any graphic. The width of the border is measured in pixels, and the color is the same as the default for the page's text color as specified in the Page Properties dialog box. To turn on the border, enter a value in the Border text box located on the lower half of the Image Property Inspector. Entering a value of zero explicitly turns off the border.

One of the most frequent cries for help among beginning Web designers (using Dreamweaver or another program) results from the sudden appearance of a bright blue border around their image. Whenever you assign a link to an image, HTML automatically places a border around that image; the color is determined by the Page Properties' Link color, where the default is bright blue. Dreamweaver intelligently assigns a zero to the `border` attribute whenever you enter a URL in the Link text box. If you've already declared a border value and enter a link, Dreamweaver won't zero-out the border. You can, of course, override the no-border option by entering a value in the Border text box.

Specifying a lowsrc

Another option for loading Web page images, the `lowsrc` attribute, displays a smaller version of a large graphic file while the larger file is loading. The `lowsrc` file can be a grayscale version of the original, or a version that is physically smaller or reduced in color or resolution. This option is designed to reduce the file size significantly for quick loading.

Select your `lowsrc` file by choosing the File icon next to the Low text box in the Image Property Inspector. The same criteria that applies to inserting your original image also applies to the `lowsrc` picture.

Tip One handy `lowsrc` technique first proportionately scales down a large file in a graphics-processing program. This file becomes your `lowsrc` file. Because browsers use the final image's height and width information for both the `lowsrc` and the final image, your visitors immediately see a "blocky" version of your graphic, which is replaced by the final version when the picture is fully loaded.

Working with alignment options

Just like text, images can be aligned to the left, right, or center. In fact, images have much more flexibility than text in terms of alignment. In addition to the same horizontal alignment options, you can align your images vertically in nine different ways. You can even turn a picture into a floating image type, enabling text to wrap around it.

Horizontal alignment

When you change the horizontal alignment of a line — from left to center or from center to right — the entire paragraph moves. Any inline images that are part of that paragraph also move. Likewise, selecting one of a series of inline images in a row and realigning it horizontally causes all the images in the row to shift.

In Dreamweaver, the horizontal alignment of an inline image is changed in exactly the same way you realign text, with alignment buttons found on the Property Inspector. As with text, buttons exist for Left, Center, and Right. Although these are very conveniently placed on the lower portion of the Graphics Property Inspector, the alignment attribute is actually written to the `<p>` or other block element enclosing the image.

Vertical alignment

Because you can place text next to an image — and images vary so greatly in size — HTML includes a variety of options for specifying just how image and text line up. As you can see from the chart in Figure 6-7, a wide range of possibilities is available.

To change the vertical alignment of any graphic in Dreamweaver, open the Align drop-down list in the Image Property Inspector and choose one of the options. Dreamweaver writes your choice into the `align` attribute of the `<img>` tag.

The various vertical alignment options are listed in the following table, and you can see examples of each type of alignment in Figure 6-7.

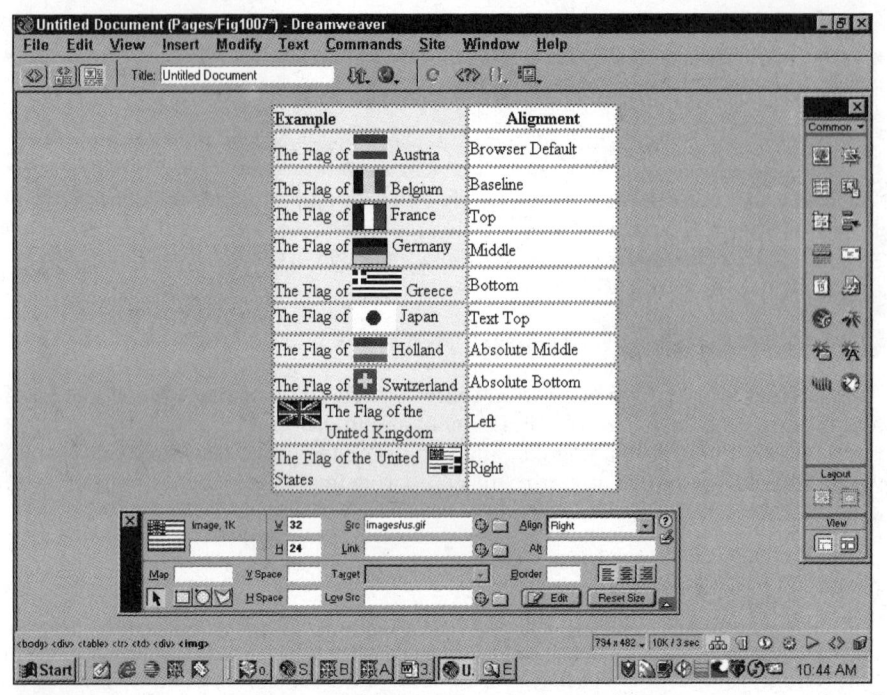

Figure 6-7: You can align text and images in one of nine different ways using the Align option box on the Image Property Inspector.

Vertical Alignment Option	Result
Browser Default	No alignment attribute is included in the `<img>` tag. Most browsers use the baseline as the alignment default.
Baseline	The bottom of the image is aligned with the baseline of the surrounding text.
Top	The top of the image is aligned with the top of the tallest object in the current line.
Middle	The middle of the image is aligned with the baseline of the current line.
Bottom	The bottom of the image is aligned with the baseline of the surrounding text.
Text Top	The top of the image is aligned with the tallest letter in the current line.
Absolute Middle	The middle of the image is aligned with the middle of the text or object in the current line.

Vertical Alignment Option	Result
Absolute Bottom	The bottom of the image is aligned with the descenders (as in y, g, p, and so forth) that fall below the current line.
Left	The image is aligned to the left edge of the browser or table cell, and all text in the current line flows around the right side of the image.
Right	The image is aligned to the right edge of the browser or table cell, and all text in the current line flows around the left side of the image.

The final two alignment options, Left and Right, are special cases; details about how to use their features are covered in the following section.

Wrapping text

Long a popular design option in conventional publishing, wrapping text around an image on a Web page is also supported by most, but not all, browsers. As noted in the preceding section, the Left and Right alignment options turn a picture into a floating image type, so called because the image can move depending on the amount of text and the size of the browser window.

Tip Using both floating image types (Left and Right) in combination, you can actually position images flush-left and flush-right, with text in the middle. Insert both images side by side and then set the leftmost image to align left and the rightmost one to align right. Insert your text immediately following the second image. Unless you place a `<p>` or `<br>` at the top, this arrangement does not render correctly in Dreamweaver (the first line overlaps the left image), but it does display as expected in most browsers.

Your text wraps around the image depending on where the floating image is placed (or anchored). If you have the feature enabled in the Invisibles pane of Preferences, Dreamweaver inserts a Floating Image Anchor symbol to mark the floating image's place. Figure 6-8 shows two examples of text wrapping. In the top case, the Floating Image Anchor symbol is placed in the midst of the first paragraph, which causes the three paragraphs to flow around the right-aligned image. In the bottom case, the image is left-aligned.

The Floating Image Anchor is not just a static symbol. You can click and drag the anchor to a new location and cause the paragraph to wrap in a different fashion. Be careful though — if you delete the anchor, you also delete the image it represents.

You can also wrap a portion of the text around your left- or right-aligned picture and then force the remaining text to appear below the floating image. However, the HTML necessary to do this task cannot currently be inserted by Dreamweaver and must be coded by hand. You have to force an opening to appear by inserting a break tag, with a special `clear` attribute, where you want the text to break. This special `<br>` tag has three forms:

Floating image anchor

Figure 6-8: Aligning an image left or right enables text to wrap around your images.

`<br clear=left>`	Causes the line to break, and the following text moves down vertically until no floating images are on the left.
`<br clear=right>`	Causes the line to break, and the following text moves down vertically until no floating images are on the right.
`<br clear=all>`	Moves the text following the image down until no floating images are on either the left or the right.

On the CD-ROM

One of the Dreamweaver objects included on CD-ROM that accompanies this book is an enhanced break tag that enables you to include any version of the `clear` attribute. To access these objects, copy the new_break.htm and new_break.gif files from the Additional Extensions\Dreamweaver Extensions\Configuration\Objects\Invisibles folder into the same folder on your system, and then restart Dreamweaver.

Putting Pictures in the Background

In this chapter, you've learned about working with the surface graphics on a Web page. As seen in Chapter 4, you can also have an image in the background of an HTML page. This section covers some of the basic techniques for incorporating a background image in your Dreamweaver page.

Note: Remember, you add an image to your background in Dreamweaver by modifying the Page Properties. Either choose Modify ⇨ Page Properties or select Page Properties from the contextual menu that pops up when you right-click (Command+click) any open area on the Web page. In the Page Properties dialog box, select a graphic by choosing the Browse (Choose) button next to the Background Image text box. You can use any file format supported by Dreamweaver — GIF, JPEG, or PNG.

Two key differences exist between background images and the foreground inline images discussed in the preceding sections of this chapter. First and most obvious, all other text and graphics on the Web page are superimposed over your chosen background image. This capability can bring extra depth and texture to your work; unfortunately, you have to make sure the foreground text and images work well with the background.

Cross-Reference: You can quickly try out a number of professionally designed background and foreground color combinations with the Set Color Scheme command. For more information on how to use this Dreamweaver command, see Chapter 4.

Basically, you want to ascertain that enough contrast exists between foreground and background. You can set the default text and the various link colors through the Page Properties dialog box. When trying out a new background pattern, you should set up some dummy text and links. Then use the Apply button on the Page Properties dialog box to test different color combinations. See Figure 6-9 for an example of this test at work.

The second distinguishing feature of background images is that the viewing browser completely fills either the browser window or the area behind the content of your Web page, whichever is larger. So, if you've created a splash page with only a 200×200 foreground logo, and you've incorporated an amazing 1,024×768 background that took you weeks to compose, no one can see the fruits of your labor in the background — unless they resize their browser window to 1,024×768. On the other hand, if your background image is smaller than either the browser window or what the Web page content needs to display, the browser and Dreamweaver repeat (or tile) your image to make up the difference.

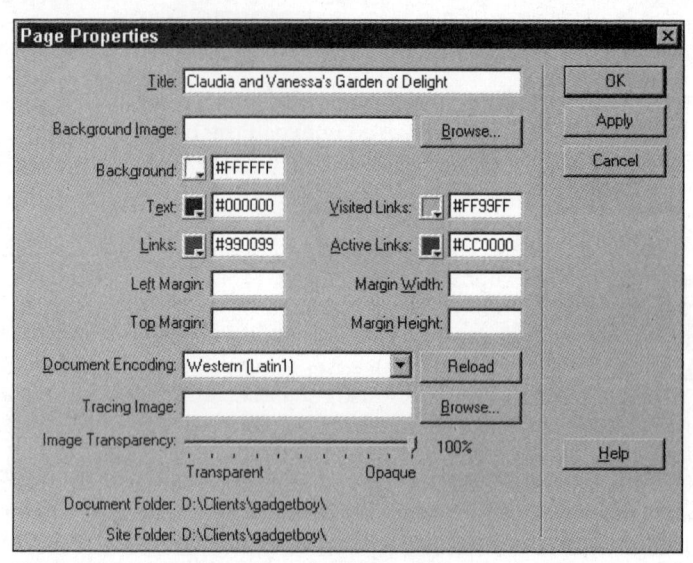

Figure 6-9: If you're using a background image, be sure to check the default colors for text and links to make sure enough contrast exists between background and foreground.

Dividing the Web Page with Horizontal Rules

HTML includes a standard horizontal line that can divide your Web page into specific sections. The horizontal rule tag, <hr>, is a good tool for adding a little diversion to your page without adding download time. You can control the width (either absolutely or relative to the browser window), the height, the alignment, and the shading property of the rule. These horizontal rules appear on a line by themselves; you cannot place text or images on the same line as a horizontal rule.

To insert a horizontal rule in your Web page in Dreamweaver, follow these steps:

1. Place your cursor where you want the horizontal rule to appear.

2. From the Common pane of the Objects panel, select the Insert Horizontal Rule button or choose the Insert ⇨ Horizontal Rule command.

    Dreamweaver inserts the horizontal rule and opens the Horizontal Rule Property Inspector, as shown in Figure 6-10.

3. To change the width of the line, enter a value in the width (W) text box. You can insert either an absolute width in pixels or a relative value as a percentage of the screen.

    • To set a horizontal rule to an exact width, enter the measurement in pixels in the width (W) text box and press the Tab key. Then select pixels in the drop-down list.

Chapter 6 ✦ **Inserting Images** 179

Tiling Images

Web designers use the tiling property of background images to create a variety of effects with very low file-size overhead. The columns typically found on one side of Web pages are a good example of tiling. Columns are popular because they enable the designer to place navigational buttons in a visual context. An easy way to create a column that runs the full length of your Web page uses a long, narrow background image.

Take a look at the following figure:

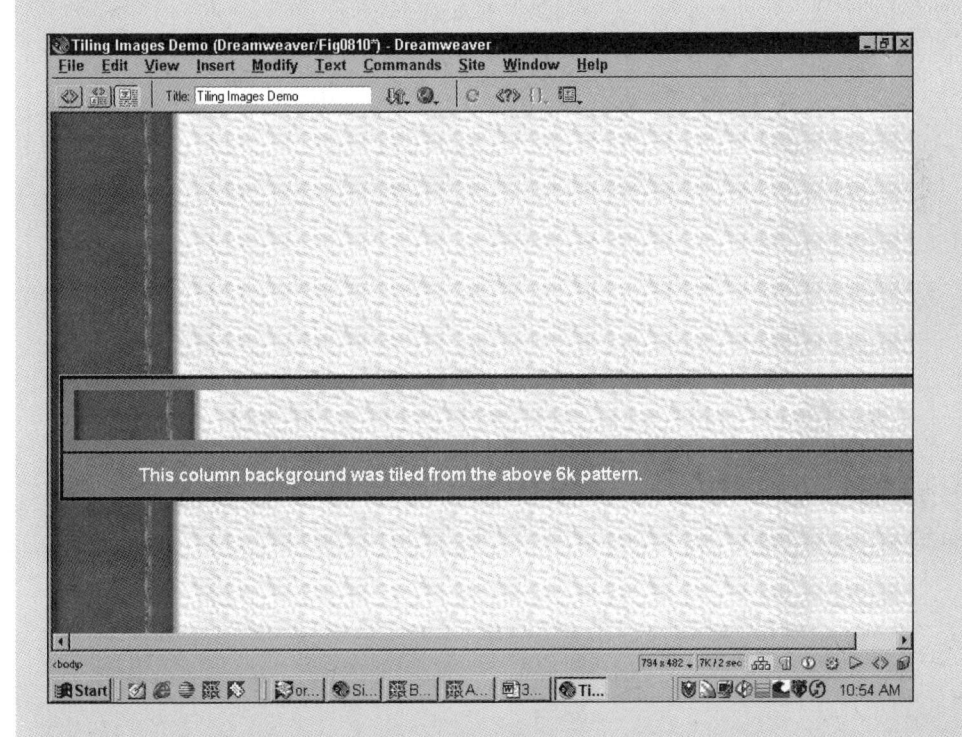

The background image is 45 pixels high, 800 pixels wide, and only 6K in size. When the browser window is set at 640×480 or 800×600, the image is tiled down the page to create the vertical column effect. You could just as easily create an image 1,000 pixels high by 40 pixels wide to create a horizontal column.

- To set a horizontal rule to a width relative to the browser window, enter the percentage amount in the width (W) text box and press Tab. Then select the percent sign (%) in the drop-down list.

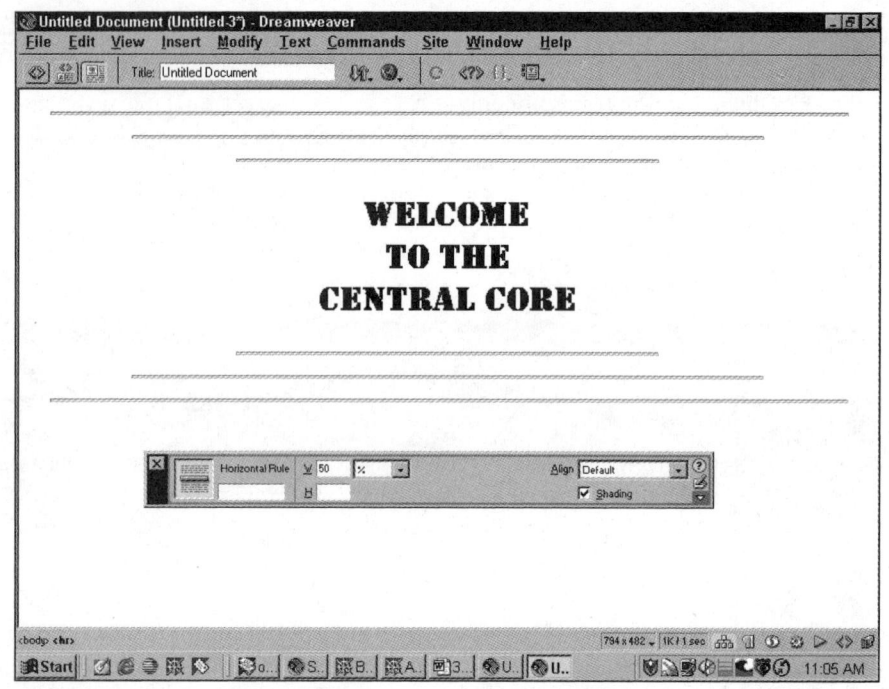

Figure 6-10: The Horizontal Rule Property Inspector controls the width, height, and alignment for these HTML lines.

4. To change the height of the horizontal rule, type a pixel measurement in the height (H) text box.

    For both the width and height values, you can also enter a value in inches (in), picas (pc), points (pt), millimeters (mm), or centimeters (cm), just as with images. When you press Tab to leave the text box, Dreamweaver converts your entry to pixels.

5. To change the alignment from the default (centered), open the Align drop-down list and choose another alignment.

6. To disable the default "embossed" look for the rule, deselect the Shading checkbox.

7. If you intend to address (call) your horizontal rule in JavaScript or another application, you can give it a unique name. Type it into the unlabeled name text box located directly to the left of the H text box.

To modify any inserted horizontal rule, simply click it. (If the Property Inspector is not already open, you have to double-click the rule.) As a general practice, size your horizontal rules using the percentage option if you are using them to separate items on a full screen. If the horizontal rules are being used to divide items in a specifically sized table column or cell, use the pixel method.

Tip To use the Shading property of the horizontal rule properly, your background should be a shade of gray. The default shading is black along the top and left, and white along the bottom and right. The center line is generally transparent (although Internet Explorer enables you to assign a color attribute). If you use a different background color or image, be sure to check the appearance of your horizontal rules in that context.

Many designers prefer to create more elaborate horizontal rules; in fact, these rules are an active area of clip art design. These types of horizontal rules are regular graphics and are inserted and modified as such.

Applying Simple Web Animation

Why include a section on animation in a chapter on inline images? On the Web, animations are, for the most part, inline images that move. Outside of the possibilities offered by Dynamic HTML, Web animations typically either are animated GIF files or are created with a program such as Flash that requires a plug-in. This section takes a brief look at the capabilities and uses of GIF animations.

A GIF *animation* is a series of still GIF images flipped rapidly to create the illusion of motion. Because animation-creation programs compress all the frames of your animation into one file, a GIF animation is placed on a Web page in the same manner as a still graphic.

In Dreamweaver, click the Insert Image button in the Objects panel or choose Insert ⇨ Image and then select the file. Dreamweaver shows the first frame of your animation in the Document window. To play the animation, preview your Web page in any graphics-capable browser.

As you can imagine, GIF animations can quickly grow to be very large. The key to controlling file size is to think small: Keep your images as small as possible with a low bit-depth (number of colors) and use as few frames as possible.

To create your animation, use any graphics program to produce the separate frames. One excellent technique uses an image-processing program such as Adobe Photoshop and progressively applies a filter to the same image over a series of frames. Figure 6-11 shows the individual frames created with Photoshop's Lighting Effects filter. When animated, a spotlight appears to move across the word.

You need an animation program to compress the separate frames and build your animated GIF file. Many commercial programs, including Macromedia's Fireworks, can handle GIF animation. QuickTime Pro can turn individual files or any other kind of movie into an animated GIF, too. Most animation programs enable you to control the number of times an animation loops, the delay between frames, and how transparency is handled within each frame.

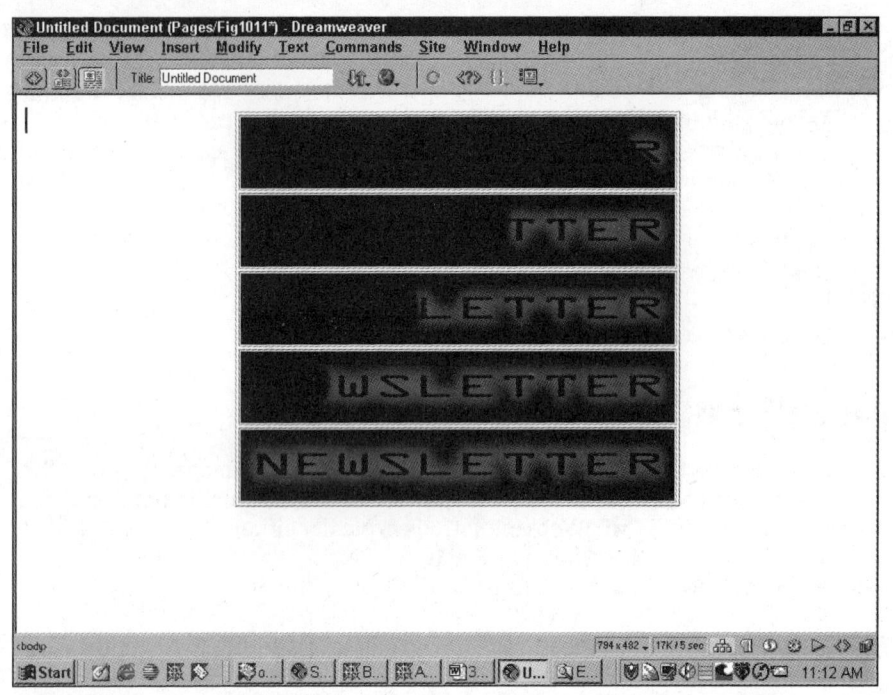

Figure 6-11: Five of twelve frames are compressed into one animated file.

> **Tip** If you want to use an advanced animation tool but still have full backward compatibility, check out Flash, from Macromedia. Flash is best known for outputting small vector-based animations that require a plug-in to view, but it can also save animations as GIFs or AVIs.

Dreamweaver Technique: Including Banner Ads

Banner ads have become an essential aspect of the World Wide Web; for the Web to remain, for the most part, freely accessible, advertising is needed to support the costs. Banner ads have evolved into the de facto standard. Although numerous variations exist, a banner ad is typically an animated GIF of a particular width and height and under a specified file size.

Two organizations, the Standards and Practices Committee of the Internet Advertising Bureau (IAB) and the Coalition for Advertising Supported Information and Entertainment (CASIE), established a series of standard sizes for banner ads. Although no law dictates that their guidelines have to be followed, the vast majority of commercial sites adhere to the suggested dimensions. The most common banner sizes (in pixels) and their official names are listed in Table 6-1.

Table 6-1
IAB/CASIE Advertising Banner Sizes

Dimensions	Name
468×60	Full Banner
392×72	Full Banner with Vertical Navigation Bar
234×60	Half Banner
125×125	Square Button
88×31	Micro Button
120×90	Button 1
120×60	Button 2
120×240	Vertical Banner

File size for a banner ad is not as clearly determined, but it's just as important. The last thing a hosting site wants is for a large, too heavy banner to slow down the loading of its page. Usually a commercial site has an established maximum file size for a particular banner ad size. Generally banner ads are around 10K and no more than 12K. The lighter your banner ad, the faster it loads and — as a direct result — the more likely Web page visitors stick around to see it.

Inserting a banner ad on a Web page is very straightforward. As with any other GIF file, animated or not, all you have to do is insert the image and assign the link. As any advertiser can tell you, the link is as important as the image itself, and you should take special care to ensure that it is correct when inserted. Advertising links are often quite complex as they not only link to a specific page, but may also carry information about the referring site. Several companies monitor how many times an ad is selected — the *clickthru rate* — and often a CGI program is used to communicate with these companies and handle the link. Here's a sample URL from CNet's News.com site:

```
http://home.cnet.com/cgi-acc/clickthru.acc?¬
clickid=00001e145ea7d80f00000000&adt=003:10:100&edt=cnet&cat=1:1002:&site=CN
```

Obviously, copying and pasting such URLs is highly preferable to entering them by hand.

It's not unusual for an advertisement to come from an outside source, so a Web page designer often has to allow space for the ad without incorporating the actual ad. Some Web designers use special placeholder images. In Dreamweaver, placeholder ads can easily be maintained as a Library item and placed as needed from the Assets panel, as shown in Figure 6-12. If you'd prefer not to use placeholder graphics such as these, you could also just insert a plain `<img>` tag — with no `src` parameter — using the Quick Tag Editor. When an `<img>` tag without a `src` is in the code, Dreamweaver displays a broken image icon that could then be resized to the proper banner ad dimensions in the Property Inspector.

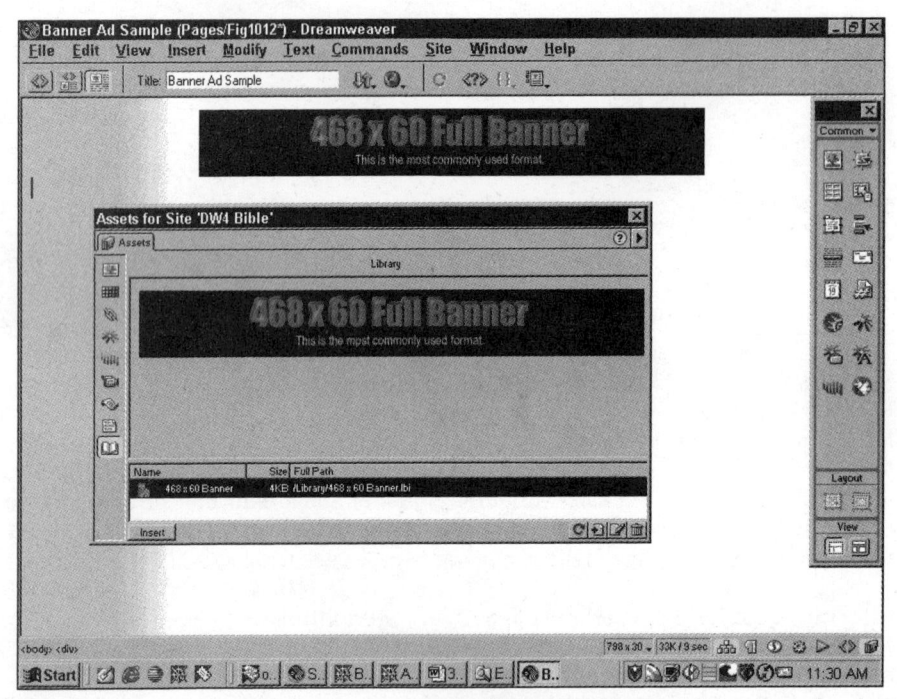

Figure 6-12: Use the Library to store standard banner ad images for use as placeholders.

Inserting Rollover Images

Rollovers are among the most popular of all Web page effects. A *rollover* (also known as a *mouseover*) occurs when the user's pointer passes over an image and the image changes in some way. It may appear to glow or change color and/or shape; when the pointer moves away from the graphic, the image returns to its original form. The rollover indicates interactivity and attempts to engage the user with a little bit of flare.

Rollovers are usually accomplished with a combination of HTML and JavaScript. Dreamweaver was among the first Web authoring tools to automate the production of rollovers through its Swap Image and Swap Image Restore behaviors. Later versions of Dreamweaver make rollovers even easier with the Rollover Image object. With the Rollover Image object, if you can pick two images, you can make a rollover.

Technically speaking, a rollover is accomplished by manipulating an `<img>` tag's `src` attribute. You'll recall that the `src` attribute is responsible for providing the actual file name of the graphic to be displayed; it is, quite literally, the source of the image. A rollover changes the value of `src` from one image file to another. Swapping the `src` value is analogous to having a picture within a frame and changing the picture while keeping the frame.

> **Caution** The picture frame analogy is appropriate on one other level: It serves as a reminder of the size barrier inherent in rollovers. A rollover changes only one property of an `<img>` tag, the source — it cannot change any other property such as the height or width. For this reason, both your original image and the image that is displayed during the rollover should be the same size. If they are not, the alternate image is resized to match the dimensions of the original image.

Dreamweaver's Rollover Image object automatically changes the image back to its original source when the user moves the pointer off the image. Optionally, you can elect to preload the images with the selection of a checkbox. Preloading is a Web page technique that reads the intended file or files into the browser's memory before they are displayed. With preloading, the images appear on demand, without any download delay.

Rollovers are typically used for buttons that, when clicked, open another Web page. In fact, JavaScript requires that an image include a link before it can detect when a user's pointer moves over it. Dreamweaver automatically includes the minimum link necessary: the #target link. Although JavaScript recognizes this symbol as indicating a link, no action is taken if the image is clicked by the user; the #, by itself, is an empty link. You can, naturally, supply whatever link you want in the Rollover Image object.

To include a Rollover Image object in your Web page, follow these steps:

1. Place your cursor where you want the rollover image to appear and choose Insert ⇨ Rollover Image or select Insert Rollover Image from the Common panel of the Objects panel. You can also drag the Insert Rollover Image button to any existing location on the Web page.

    Dreamweaver opens the Insert Rollover Image dialog box shown in Figure 6-13.

2. If desired, you can enter a unique name for the image in the Image Name text box, or you can leave the name automatically generated by Dreamweaver.

3. In the Original Image text box, enter the path and name of the graphic you want displayed when the user's mouse is not over the graphic. You can also choose the Browse (Choose) button to select the file. Press Tab when you're done.

4. In the Rollover Image text box, enter the path and name of the graphic you want displayed when the user's pointer is over the graphic. You can also choose the Browse (Choose) button to select the file.

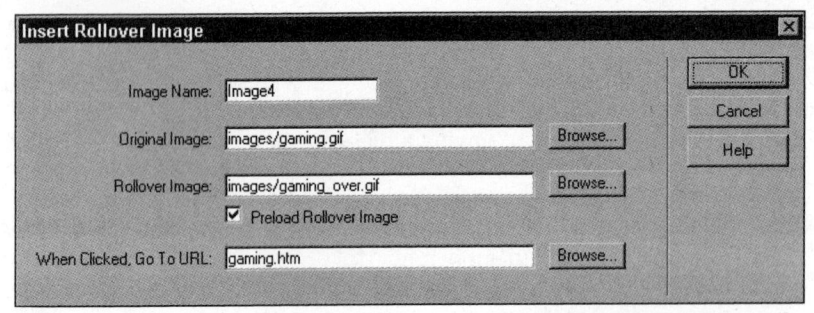

Figure 6-13: The Rollover Image object makes rollover graphics quick and easy.

5. If desired, specify a link for the image by entering it in the When Clicked, Go To URL text box. If you are entering a path and file by hand, be sure to delete the initial target link, #. If you use the Browse (Choose) button to select your file, the target link is deleted for you.

6. To enable images to load only when they are required, deselect the Preload Images option. Generally, it is best to leave this option selected (the default) so that no delay occurs in the rollover appearing.

7. Click OK when you're finished.

> **Tip:** Keep in mind that the Rollover Image object inserts both the original image and its alternate, whereas the Swap Image technique is applied to an existing image in the Web page. If you prefer to use the Rollover Image object rather than the Swap Image behavior, nothing prevents you from deleting an existing image from the Web page and inserting it again through the Rollover Image object. Just make sure that you note the path and name of the image before you delete it so you can find it again.

Adding a Navigation Bar

Rollovers are nice effects, but a single button does not make a navigation system for a Web site. Typically, several buttons with a similar look and feel are placed next to each other to form a *navigation bar*. To make touring a site as intuitive as possible, the same navigation bar is usually repeated on each page or used once, as a frame element. Consistency of design and repetitive use of the navigation bar simplifies getting around a site — even for a first-time user.

Some designers build their navigation bars in a separate graphics program and then import them into Dreamweaver. Fireworks, with its capability to export both images and code, makes this a strong option. Other Web designers, however, prefer to build separate rollover images in a graphics program and then assemble all the pieces at the HTML layout stage. Dreamweaver now automates such a process with its Navigation Bar object.

The Navigation Bar object incorporates rollovers — and more. A Navigation Bar element can use up to four different images, each reflecting a different user action:

+ Up — The user's pointer is away from the image.
+ Over — The pointer is over the image.
+ Down — The user has clicked the image.
+ Over While Down — The user's pointer is over the image after it has been clicked.

You don't have to use all four states — it's up to you whether you use just the first two, like a standard rollover, or add the third and possibly the fourth. You can even skip the Over state and just use Up and Down. While it's possible to display an Over While Down state without a Down state, it doesn't make much sense to do so.

One key difference separates a fully functioning navigation bar from a group of unrelated rollovers. When the Down state is available, if the user clicks one of the buttons, any other Down button is changed to the Up state. The effect is like a series of mutually exclusive radio buttons: You can show only one selected in a group. The Down state is often used to indicate the current selection.

> **Tip**
>
> While you can use the Navigation Bar object on any type of Web design, it works best in a frameset situation with a frame for navigation and one for content. If you insert a navigation bar with Up, Over, Down, and Over While Down states for each button in the navigation frame, you can target the content frame and gain the full effect of the mutually exclusive Down states.

Before you can use Dreamweaver's Navigation Bar object, you have to create a series of images for each button — one for each state you plan to use. It's completely up to the designer how the buttons appear, but it's important that a consistent look and feel be applied for all the buttons. For example, if rolling over Button A reveals a green glow, rolling over Buttons B, C, and D should also cause the same green glow, as demonstrated in Figure 6-14.

To insert a navigation bar, follow these steps:

1. From the Objects panel, select the Insert Navigation Bar object.

   The Insert Navigation Bar dialog box appears, as shown in Figure 6-15.

2. Enter a unique name for the first button in the Element Name field and press Tab.

> **Caution**
>
> Be sure to use Tab rather than Enter (Return) when moving from field to field. When Enter (Return) is pressed, Dreamweaver attempts to build the navigation bar. If you have not completed the initial two steps (providing an Element Name and a source for the Up Image), an alert is displayed; otherwise, the navigation bar is built.

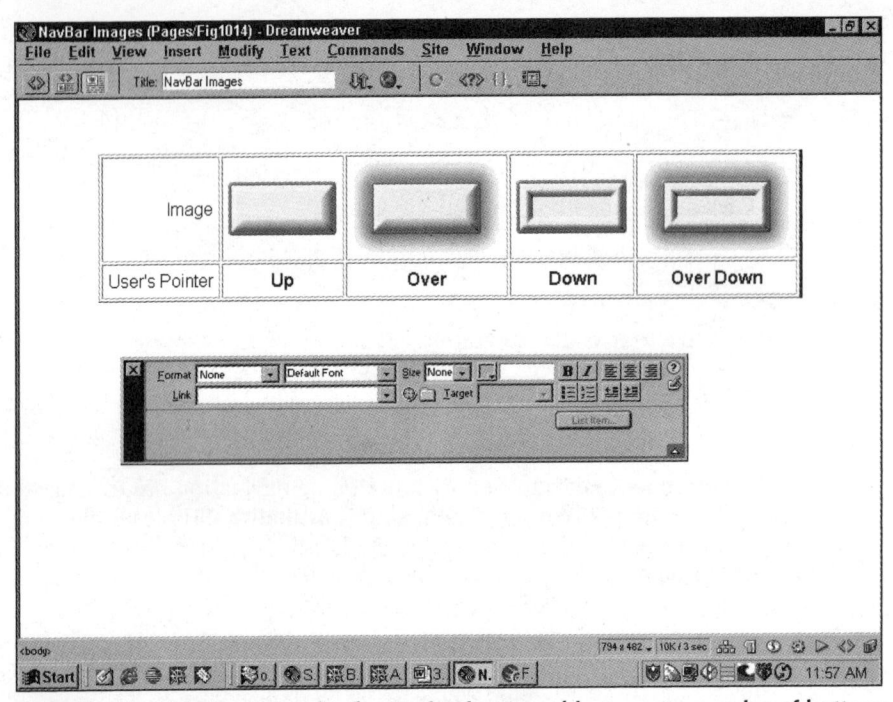

Figure 6-14: Before you invoke the Navigation Bar object, create a series of buttons with a separate image for each state to be used.

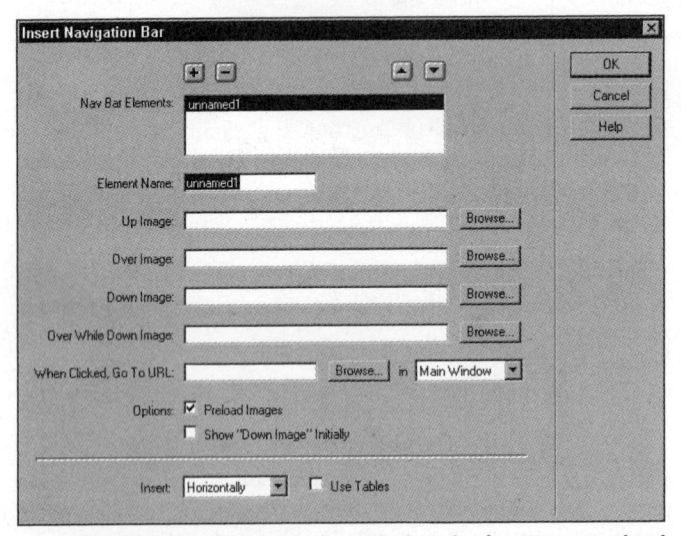

Figure 6-15: Add elements one at a time in the Insert Navigation Bar dialog box.

3. In the Up Image field, enter a path and filename or browse to a graphic file to use.

4. Select files for each of the remaining states you wish to use: Over, Down, and Over While Down.

5. Enter a URL or browse to a file in the When Clicked, Go To URL field.

6. If you're using a frameset, select a target for the URL from the drop-down list.

7. Enable or disable the Preload Images option as desired.

   For a multistate button to be effective, the reaction has to be immediate, and the images must be preloaded. It is highly recommended that the Preload Images option be enabled.

8. If you want the current button to display the Down state first, select the Show "Down Image" Initially option.

   When this option is chosen, an asterisk appears next to the current button in the Nav Bar Element list. Generally, you don't want more than one Down state showing at a time.

9. To set the orientation of the navigation bar, select either Horizontally or Vertically from the Insert drop-down list.

10. If you want to contain your images in a table, keep the Use Table option selected.

    If you decide not to use tables in a horizontal configuration, images are presented side by side; when a vertical navigation bar is built without tables, Dreamweaver inserts a line break (`<br>` tag) between each element.

11. Select the add (plus) button and repeat Steps 2 through 8 to add the next element.

12. To reorder the elements in the navigation bar, select an element in the Nav Bar Elements list and use the up and down buttons to reposition it in the Element list.

13. To remove an element, select it and click the delete (minus) button.

Each page can have only one Dreamweaver-built navigation bar. If you try to insert a second, Dreamweaver asks if you'd like to modify the existing series. Clicking OK opens the Modify Navigation Bar dialog box, shown in Figure 6-16, which is identical to the Insert Navigation Bar dialog box, except you can no longer change the orientation or table settings. You can also alter the inserted navigation bar by choosing Modify ⇨ Navigation Bar.

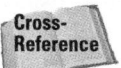

Cross-Reference If you're looking for even more control over your navigation bar, Dreamweaver also includes the Set Navigation Bar behavior, which is fully covered in Chapter 11.

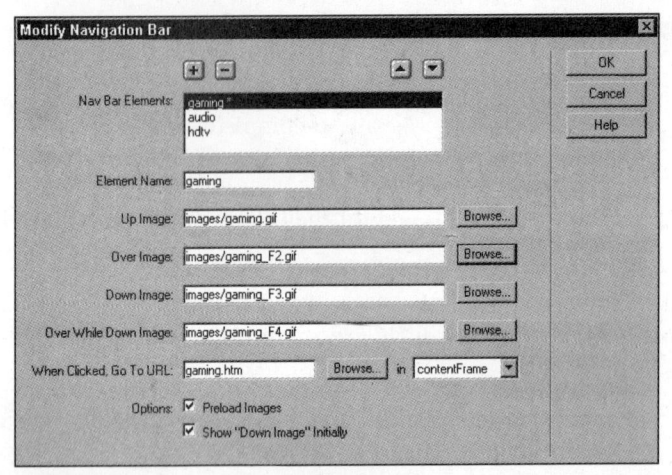

Figure 6-16: Once you've inserted your navigation bar, you can adjust it through the Modify Navigation Bar dialog box.

Summary

In this chapter, you learned how to include both foreground and background images in Dreamweaver. Understanding how images are handled in HTML is an absolute necessity for the Web designer. Some of the key points follow:

✦ Web pages are restricted to using specific graphic formats. Virtually all browsers support GIF and JPEG files. PNG is also gaining acceptance. Dreamweaver can preview all three image types.

✦ Images are inserted in the foreground in Dreamweaver through the Insert Image command of the Objects panel or from the Assets panel. Once the graphic is inserted, almost all modifications can be handled through the Property Inspector.

✦ You can use HTML's background image function to lay a full-frame image or a tiled series of the same image underneath your text and graphics. Tiled images can be employed to create columns and other designs with small files.

✦ The simplest HTML graphic is the built-in horizontal rule. Useful for dividing your Web page into separate sections, the horizontal rule can be sized either absolutely or relatively.

✦ With the Rollover Image object, you can easily insert simple rollovers that use two different images. To build a rollover that uses more than two images, you have to use the Swap Image behavior.

✦ Animated images can be inserted alongside, and in the same manner as, still graphics. The individual frames of a GIF animation must be created in a graphics program and then combined in an animation program.

✦ When used in conjunction with Fireworks, images can now be optimized from within Dreamweaver. Moreover, it's easier to integrate code generated from Fireworks — and you can even specify Dreamweaver-style HTML.

✦ You can add a series of interrelated buttons — complete with four-state rollovers — by using the Navigation Bar object.

In the next chapter, you learn how to use hyperlinks in Dreamweaver.

✦   ✦   ✦

Establishing Web Links

CHAPTER 7

In This Chapter

All about Internet addresses

Linking Web pages

Pointing to a file

Creating anchors within Web pages

URL targeting

To me, links are the Web. Everything else about the medium can be replicated in another form, but without links, there would be no World Wide Web. As your Web design work becomes more sophisticated, you'll find more enhanced uses for links: sending mail, connecting to an FTP site — even downloading software. In this chapter, you learn how Dreamweaver helps you manage the various types of links, set anchors within documents to get smooth and accurate navigation, and establish targets for your URLs. But first, let's begin with an overview on Internet addresses to give you the full picture of the possibilities.

Understanding URLs

URL stands for Uniform Resource Locator. An awkward phrase, it nonetheless describes itself well — the URL's function is to provide a standard method for finding anything on the Internet. From Web pages to newsgroups to the smallest graphic on the most esoteric of pages, everything can be referenced through the URL system.

The URL can use up to six different parts, although all parts are not necessary for the URL to be read. Each part is separated by some combination of a slash, colon, and hash mark delimiter. When entered as an attribute's value, the entire URL is generally enclosed within quotes to ensure that the address is read as one unit. A generic URL using all the parts looks like the following:

```
method://server:port/path/file#anchor
```

Here's a real-world example that also uses every section:

```
http://www.idest.com:80/dreamweaver/index.htm#bible
```

In order of appearance in the body of an Internet address, left to right, the parts denote the following:

- **The method used to access the resource.** The method to address Web servers is the HyperText Transport Protocol (HTTP). Other methods are discussed later in this section.

- **The name of the server providing the resource.** The server can either be a domain name (with or without the "www" prefix) or an Internet Protocol (IP) address, such as 199.227.52.143.

- **The port number to be used on the server.** Most URLs do not include a port number, which is analogous to a telephone extension number on the server, because most servers use the defaults.

- **The directory path to the resource.** Depending on where the resource (for example, the Web page) is located on the server, the following paths can be specified: no path (indicating that the resource is in the public root of the server), a single folder name, or a number of folders and subfolders.

- **The filename of the resource.** If the filename is omitted, the Web browser looks for a default page, often named index.html or index.htm. The browser reacts differently depending on the type of file. For example, GIFs and JPEGs are displayed by themselves; executable files and archives (Zip, StuffIt, and so on) are downloaded.

- **The named anchor in the HTML document.** This part is another optional section. The named anchor enables the Web designer to send the viewer to a particular section of an HTML page.

Because it is used to communicate with servers, the HTTP access method is far and away the most prevalent method on today's World Wide Web. In addition to the HTTP access method, other methods connect with other types of servers. Table 7-1 discusses some of these options.

Table 7-1
Various Internet Access Methods and Protocols

Name	Syntax	Usage
File Transfer Protocol	ftp://	Links to an FTP server that is generally used for uploading and downloading files. The server can be accessed anonymously, or it may require a user name and password.
Gopher	gopher://as	Connects to a directory tree structure primarily used for disseminating all-text documents.
HyperText Transfer Protocol	http://	Used for connecting to a document available on a World Wide Web server.

Name	Syntax	Usage
JavaScript	javascript://	Executes a JavaScript function.
Mailto	mailto:	Opens an e-mail form with the recipient's address already filled in. These links are useful when embedded in your Web pages to provide visitors with an easy feedback method.
News	news://	Connects to the specified Usenet newsgroup. Newsgroups are public, theme-oriented message boards where anyone can post or reply to a message.
Telnet	telnet://	Enables users to log directly onto remote host computers and interact directly with the operating system software.

Part of the richness of today's Web browsers stems from their capability to connect with all the preceding (and additional) services.

Tip The mailto: access method enables you not only to open up a preaddressed e-mail form but also to specify the topic, with a little extra work. For example, if Joe Lowery wants to include a link to his e-mail address with the subject heading "Dreamweaver Bible," he can insert a link such as the following:

```
mailto:jlowery@idest.com?subject=Dreamweaver Bible
```

The question mark acts as a delimiter that enables a variable and a value to be passed to the browser. When you're trying to encourage feedback from your Web page visitors, every little bit helps. A note of caution: This method is not standardized HTML, and while it works with most browsers and mail programs, you could get unexpected results with some systems.

Surfing the Web with Hypertext

Most often, you assign a link to a word or phrase on your page, an image such as a navigational button, or a section of graphic for an image map (a large graphic in which various parts are links). Once you have created the link, you have to preview it in a browser; links are not active in Dreamweaver's Document window.

Designate links in HTML through the anchor tag pair: <a> and </a>. The anchor tag generally takes one main attribute — the hypertext reference, which is written as follows:

```
href="link name"
```

When you create a link in Dreamweaver, the anchor pair surrounds the text or object that is being linked. For example, if you link the phrase "Back to Home Page," it may look like the following:

```
<a href="index.html">Back to Home Page</a>
```

When you attach a link to an image, logo.gif, your code looks as follows:

```
<a href="home.html"><img src="images/logo.gif"></a>
```

Creating a basic link in Dreamweaver is easy. Simply follow these steps:

1. Select the text, image, or object you want to establish as a link.
2. In the Property Inspector, enter the URL in the Link text box as shown in Figure 7-1. You can use one of the following methods to do so:
   - Type the URL directly into the Link text box.
   - Select the folder icon to the right of the Link text box to open the Select File dialog box, where you can browse for the file.
   - Select the Point to File icon and drag your mouse to an existing page or link. This feature is explained later in this section.
   - Drag a link from the Assets panel onto a text or image selection.

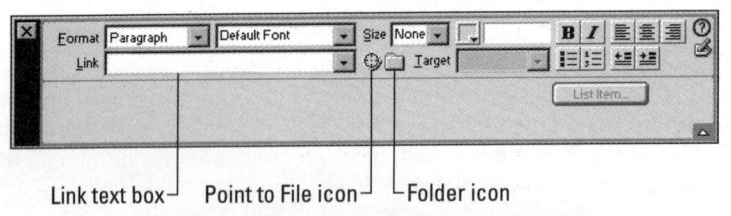

Figure 7-1: You can enter your link directly into the Link text box, point to it directly with the Point to File icon, or select the folder icon to browse for a file.

Only a few restrictions exist for specifying linked URLs. Dreamweaver does not support any letters from the extended character set (also known as High ASCII), such as ¡, à, or ñ. Complete URLs must have fewer than a total of 255 characters. You should be cautious about using spaces in path names and, thus, URLs. Although most browsers can interpret the address, spaces are changed to a %20 symbol for proper Unix usage, which can make your URLs difficult to read.

Note: Whitespace in your HTML usually doesn't have an adverse effect. However, Netscape browsers are sensitive to whitespace when assigning a link to an image. If you isolate your image tag from the anchor tags as in the following example:

> ### Links Without Underscores
>
> To remove the underlined aspect of a link, you can use one of two methods. The classic method—which works for all graphics-capable browsers—uses an image rather than text as the link. You must make sure the `border` attribute of your image is set to 0 because a linked image usually displays a blue border if a `border` attribute exists. Dreamweaver adds border="0" to all image links now, as a default.
>
> The second, newer method uses Cascading Style Sheets. While this is an excellent one-stop solution for 4.0 and later browsers, the links will still be seen with underlines on the earlier browser versions. Refer to the Dreamweaver Technique for eliminating the underlines in links in Chapter 14.

```
<a href="index.htm">
<img src="images/Austria.gif" width="34" height="24">
</a>
```

Netscape browsers attach a small blue underscore—a tail, really—to your image. Because Dreamweaver codes the anchor tag properly, without any additional whitespace, this odd case applies only to hand-coded or previously coded HTML.

Text links are most often rendered with a blue color and underlined. You can specify the document link color by choosing Modify ⇨ Page Properties and selecting the Link Color swatch. In Page Properties, you can also alter the color to which the links change after being selected (the Visited Link Color) and the color flashed when the link is clicked (the Active Link Color).

Tip Want to add a little variety to your text links? You can actually change the color of the link on an individual basis. To do this, you have to enter the link in the Property Inspector before you apply the color. Be sure to exercise a little discretion though—you don't want to use so many different colors that your Web page visitors can't figure out the navigation.

Inserting URLs from the Assets panel

Internet addresses get more complicated every day. Trying to remember them all correctly and avoid typos makes the Web designer's job unnecessarily difficult. At least, it's unnecessary if you make use of the URLs category of Dreamweaver 4's new Assets panel. With the Assets panel, you can drag-and-drop the trickiest URLs with a flick of the mouse tail.

New Feature As with other Assets panel categories, you'll need to select the Refresh Site List button to make available all the possible URLs in a site. Alternatively, you could choose Refresh Site List from the context menu on the panel. Either action causes

Dreamweaver to scan all the Web pages within the site and extract all the complete Internet addresses found. Only full Internet addresses — whether to files (such as `www.idest.com/dreamweaver`) or to e-mail addresses (for example, mailto:jlowery@idest.com) — are visible in the Assets panel. Document or site relative links are not listed as an Asset. To assign a link to a document or site relative page, use one of the other methods, such as pointing to a file, discussed in this chapter.

To assign a URL from the Assets panel, follow these steps:

1. If it's not already visible, select Window ➪ Assets or click the Assets icon on the Launcher to display the Assets panel. Alternatively, you show the Assets panel by pressing the keyboard shortcut, F11.
2. Select the URLs icon on the side of the Assets panel to show that category, as seen in Figure 7-2.

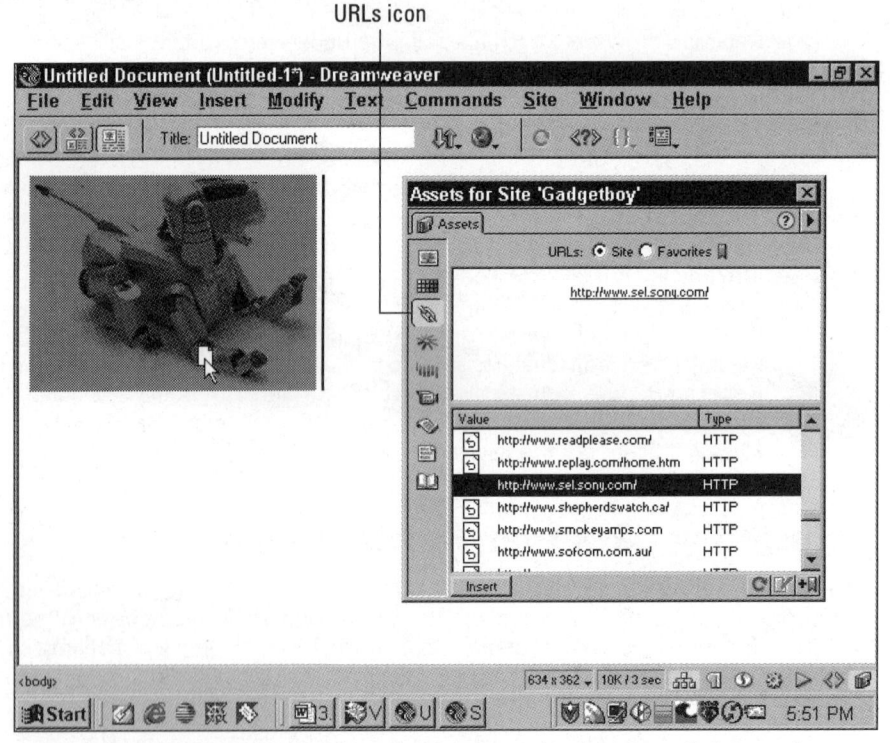

Figure 7-2: Banish typos from your absolute URLs by dragging a link from the Assets panel to any selected text or graphic.

3. If necessary, select the Refresh button on the Assets panel to list the most current links found in the site.

   4. In the Document window, select the text or image you want the link assigned to.

   5. Drag the desired link from the Assets panel onto the selected text or image; alternatively, highlight the link in the panel and then choose the Apply button.

You'll notice that the Edit button on the Assets panel is unavailable for the URLs category. Links cannot be edited; they can only be applied as shown in the preview area.

Pointing to a file

Dreamweaver has an alternative method of identifying a link — pointing to it. By using the Point to File icon on the Property Inspector, you can quickly fill in the Link text box by dragging your mouse to any existing named anchor or file visible in the Dreamweaver environment. The Point to File feature saves you from having to browse through folder after folder as you search for a file you can clearly see onscreen.

You can point to a file in another open Dreamweaver window or one in another frame in the same window. If your desired link is a named anchor located further down the page, Dreamweaver automatically scrolls to find it. You can even point to a named anchor in another page, and Dreamweaver enters the full syntax correctly. Named anchors are covered in detail later in this chapter.

Perhaps one of the slickest applications of the Point to File icon is when it is used in tandem with the Site window. The Site window lists all the existing files in any given Web site, and when both it and the Document window are onscreen, you can quickly point to any file.

Cross-Reference For more details about using the Site window in this fashion, see Chapter 3.

Pointing to a file uses what could be called a "drag-and-release" mouse technique, as opposed to the more ordinary point-and-click or drag-and-drop method. To select a new link using the Point to File icon, follow these steps:

   1. Select the text or the graphic that you'd want to make into a link.

   2. In the Property Inspector, click and hold the Point to File icon located to the right of the Link text box.

   3. Holding down the mouse button, drag the mouse until it is over an existing link or named anchor in the Document window or a file in the Site window.

      As you drag the mouse, a line extends from the Point to File icon, and the reminder "Point to a file to make a link" appears in the Link text box.

4. When you locate the file you want to link to, release the mouse button. The filename with the accompanying path information is written into the Link text box as shown in Figure 7-3.

Link   Point to File icon

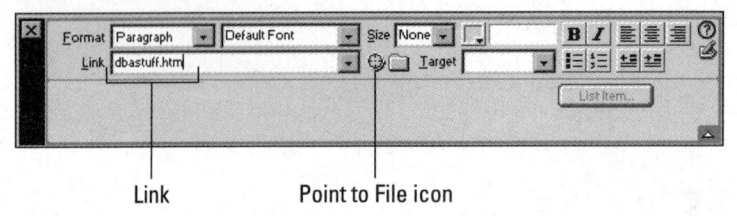

Figure 7-3: The Point to File capability enables you to quickly insert a link to any onscreen page.

Addressing types

As you learned in Chapter 2, three types of URLs are used as links: absolute addresses, document-relative addresses, and site root–relative addresses. Let's briefly recap these address types.

- **Absolute addresses** require the full URL, as follows:

  http://www.macromedia.com/software/dreamweaver/

  This type is most often used for referencing links on another Web server.

- **Document-relative addresses** know the method, server, and path aspects of the URL. You need to include only additional path information if the link is outside of the current Web page's folder. Links in the current document's folder can be addressed with their filename only. To reference an item in a subfolder, just name the folder, enter a forward slash, and then enter the item's filename, as follows:

  images/background.gif

- **Site root–relative addresses** are indicated with a leading forward slash. For example:

  /navigation/upndown.html

  The preceding address links to a file named upndown.html stored in the navigation directory at the current site root. Dreamweaver translates site-relative to document-relative links when the Preview in Browser feature is used.

A Webmaster often must perform the tedious but necessary task of verifying the links on all the Web pages in a site. Because of the Web's fluid nature, links can work one day and then be broken the next. Dreamweaver has enhanced its powerful link-checking capabilities with link-updating features.

Cross-Reference: To find out how to keep your site up to date with a minimum of effort, see Chapter 3.

Adding an E-Mail Link

E-mail links are very common on the Web. Rather than opening a new Web page like a regular link, when an e-mail link is clicked, a window for sending a new e-mail message is displayed. The message window is already preaddressed to the recipient, making it convenient to use. All the user has to do is add a subject, enter a message, and select Send.

E-mail links no longer need be added by hand. Dreamweaver includes an object that streamlines the process. Just enter the text of the line, and the e-mail address and the link is ready. E-mail links, like other links, do not work in Dreamweaver when clicked and must be previewed in the browser.

To enter an e-mail link with the new object, follow these steps:

1. Position your cursor where you want the e-mail link to appear.
2. From the Common category of the Objects panel, select the Insert E-Mail Link button.

   The Insert E-Mail Link dialog box, shown in Figure 7-4, appears.

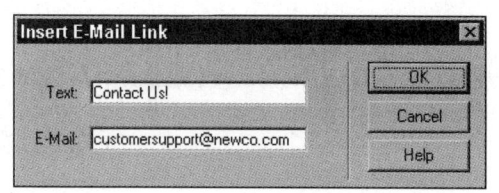

Figure 7-4: The Insert E-Mail Link object creates links that make it simple for your Web page visitors to send an e-mail.

3. In the Insert E-Mail Link dialog box, enter the visible text for the link in the Text field.
4. Enter the e-mail address in the E-Mail field.

Caution: The e-mail address must be in the format name@company.com. Dreamweaver does not check to make sure you've entered the proper format.

5. Click OK when you're done.

> **Note:** If you already have the text for the e-mail link in the document, you can also use the Property Inspector to insert an e-mail link. Just highlight the text and in the Link field of the Property Inspector, enter the URL in this format:
>
> ```
> mailto:name@company.com
> ```
>
> Make sure that the URL is a valid e-mail address with the @ sign properly placed.

Here's a bit of the frustration that Web designers sometimes face: On some browsers, notably Internet Explorer, the user may see a dialog box when the e-mail link is first selected. The dialog box informs them that they are about to send an e-mail over the Internet. The user has an option to not see these warnings, but there's no way for the Web designer to prevent them from appearing.

Navigating with Anchors

Whenever you normally link to an HTML page, through absolute or relative addressing, the browser displays the page from the top. Your Web visitors must scroll to any information rendered below the current screen. One HTML technique, however, links to a specific point anywhere on your page regardless of the display window's contents. This technique uses *named anchors*.

Using named anchors is a two-step process. First you place a named anchor somewhere on your Web page. This placement is coded in HTML as an anchor tag using the `name` attribute, with nothing in between the opening and closing tags. In HTML, named anchors look like the following:

```
<a name="bible"></a>
```

The second step includes a link to that named anchor from somewhere else on your Web page. If used, a named anchor is referenced in the final possible portion of an Internet address, designated by the hash mark (#), as follows:

```
<a href="http://www.idest.com/dreamweaver/index.htm#bible>
```

You can include any number of named anchors on the current page or another page. Named anchors are commonly used with a table of contents or index.

To insert a named anchor in Dreamweaver, follow these steps:

1. Place the cursor where you want the named anchor to appear.
2. Choose Insert ⇨ Named Anchor. You can also select the Insert Named Anchor button from the Invisibles category of the Objects panel. Or use the key shortcut Ctrl+Alt+A (Command+Option+A).
3. The Named Anchor dialog box opens. Type the anchor name into the text box.

Caution: Named anchors are case-sensitive and must be unique within the page.

When you press Enter (Return), Dreamweaver places a named anchor symbol in the current cursor location and opens the Named Anchor Property Inspector (shown in Figure 7-5).

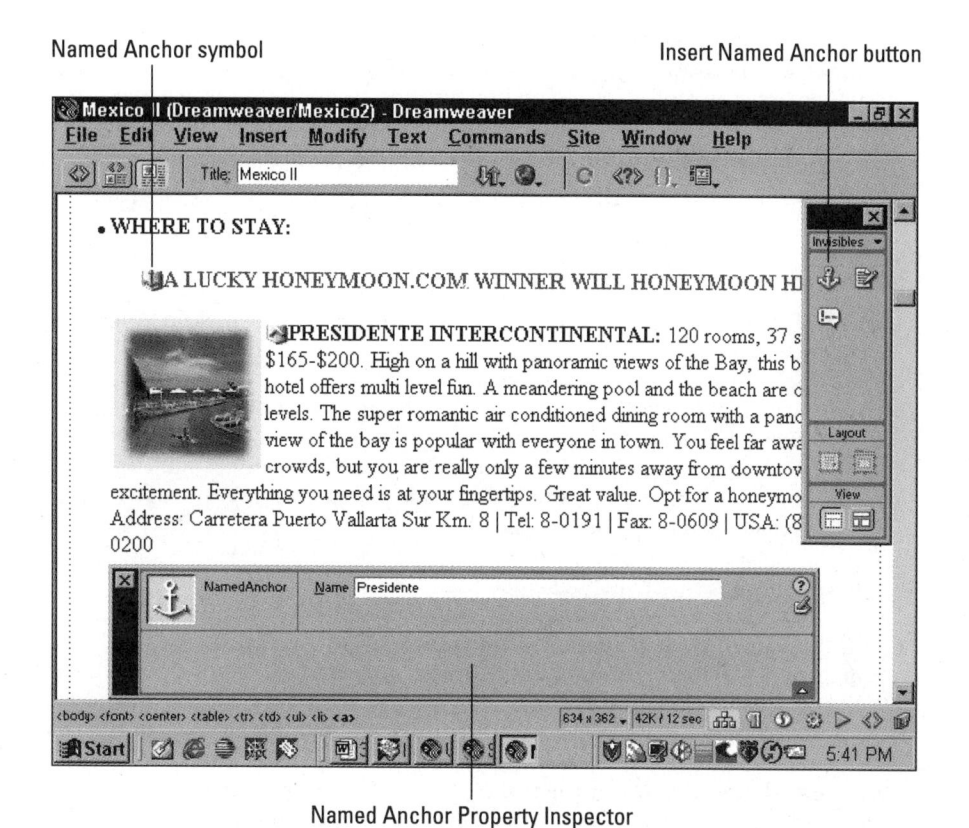

Figure 7-5: The Named Anchor tag enables you to link to specific areas of a Web page.

4. To change an anchor's name, click the named anchor symbol within the page and alter the text in the Property Inspector.

As with other invisible symbols, the named anchor symbol can be cut and pasted or moved using the drag-and-drop method.

Moving within the same document

One of the major advantages of using named anchors is the almost instantaneous response the viewer receives when they click them. The browser only needs to scroll to the particular place in the document because the entire page is loaded. For long text documents, this capability is an invaluable time-saver.

Once you have placed a named anchor — or all of them at once — in your document, you can link to these anchors. Follow these steps to create a link to a named anchor in the same document:

1. Select the text or image that you want to designate as a link.
2. In the Link text box of the Property Inspector, type a hash mark, #, followed by the exact anchor name. For example:

   `#top`

   Remember, anchor names are case-sensitive and must be unique in each document.

Tip: You should place the named anchor one line above the heading or image to which you want to link the viewer. Browsers tend to be quite literal. If you place the named anchor on the same line, the browser renders it up against the top of the window. Placing your named anchor up one line gives your topic a bit of breathing room in the display.

In Dreamweaver, you can also use the Point to File icon to choose a named anchor link. If your named anchor is in the same document, just drag the Point to File icon to the named anchor symbol. When you release the mouse, the proper named anchor is inserted into the Link text box. If the named anchor is on the same page but offscreen, Dreamweaver automatically scrolls the Document window as you approach the edge. In Windows, the closer you move to the edge, the faster Dreamweaver scrolls. Dreamweaver even returns the screen to your original location, with the new link at the top of the screen, after you release the mouse button.

In long documents with a table of contents or index linking to a number of named anchors, it's common practice — and a good idea — to place a link back to the top of the page after every screen or every topic. This technique enables your users to return to the menu quickly and pick another topic without having to manually scroll all the way back.

Using named anchors in a different page

If your table of contents is on a separate page from the topics of your site, you can use named anchors to send the viewer anywhere on a new page. The technique is exactly the same as already explained for placing named anchors, but one minor difference exists when it comes to linking. Instead of placing a hash mark and name to denote the named anchor, you must first include the URL of the linked page.

Let's say you want to call the disclaimer section of a legal page from your table of contents. You could insert something like the following in the Link text box of the Property Inspector:

```
legal.htm#disclaimer
```

This link, when activated, first loads the referenced Web page (legal.htm) and then goes directly to the named anchor place (#disclaimer). Figure 7-6 shows how you would enter this in the Property Inspector. Keep in mind, you can use any form of addressing prior to the hash mark and named anchor.

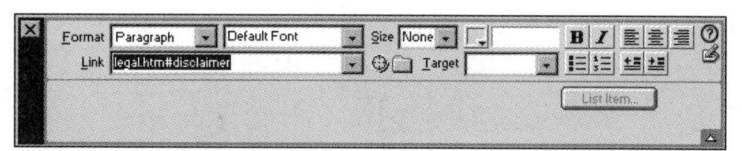

Figure 7-6: You can also link to any part of a separate Web page using named anchors.

> **Tip** One of the more obscure uses for named anchors comes into play when you are trying to use Dreamweaver's JavaScript Behavior feature. Because JavaScript needs to work with a particular type of tag to perform `onMouseOver` and other events, one trick marks some text or image with a link to #nowhere. You can use any name for the nonexistent named anchor. In fact, you don't even have to use a name — you can just use a hash mark by itself (#). One problem area: Netscape browsers have a tendency to send the page to the top if a link of this type is used. Many programmers have begun to substitute a JavaScript function instead, such as `javascript:;`. Dreamweaver itself now uses `javascript:;` instead of # when a new behavior is attached to an image.

Targeting Your Links

Thus far, all of this chapter's links have had a similar effect: They open another Web page or section in your browser's window. What if you want to force the browser to open another window and load that new URL in the new window? HTML enables you to specify the target for your links.

Targets are most often used in conjunction with frames — that is, you can make a link in one frame open a file in another. (Chapter 10 covers the subject of frames in depth.) Here, though, let's take a look at one of the HTML predefined targets useful in a situation where you want to load another URL into a new window.

To specify a new browser window as the target for a link in Dreamweaver, follow these steps:

1. Select the text or image you want to designate as your new link.
2. In the Property Inspector, enter the URL into the Link text box.

   After you've entered a link, the target option becomes active.

3. Choose the option button next to the Target list box and select _blank from the drop-down list. You can also type it in the list box.

   Dreamweaver inserts a _blank option in the Target list box, as shown in Figure 7-7. Now, when your link is activated, the browser spawns a new window and loads the referenced link into it. The user has both windows available.

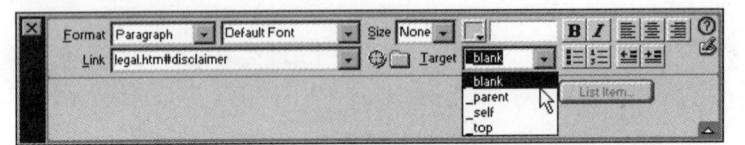

Figure 7-7: You can force a user's browser to open a separate window to display a specific link with the Target command.

The _blank target is most often used when the originating Web page is acting as a jump station and has numerous links available. By keeping the original Web page open, the user can check out one site without losing the origin point.

> **Note** Three other system-wide targets exist: _top, _parent, and _self. Both _top and _parent are primarily used with framesets: _top target replaces the outermost frameset and _parent replaces the frameset containing the current page. These two have the same effect, except in the case of nested framesets. The _self target is the default behavior and only the current page is replaced.

You can even use the _blank target technique on named anchors in the same document, thereby emulating frames to some degree.

> **Caution** Some key online services, such as America Online and WebTV, don't enable their built-in browsers to open new windows. Every link that is accessed is displayed in the same browser window.

Summary

Whether they are links for Web site navigation or jumps to other related sites, hypertext links are an essential part of any Web page. Dreamweaver gives you full control over your inserted anchors.

- ✦ Through a unique URL, you can access virtually any Web page, graphic, or other item available on the Internet.
- ✦ The HyperText Transfer Protocol (HTTP) is the most common method of Web connection, but Web pages can link to other formats, including FTP, e-mail, and newsgroups.
- ✦ Any of the three basic address formats — absolute, document relative, or site root relative — can be inserted in the Link text box of Dreamweaver's Property Inspector to create a link.
- ✦ Dreamweaver has a quick linking capability through its Point to File feature.
- ✦ The Assets panel tracks all of your absolute and mailto: URLs and makes it easy to apply any of them to your pages. Document or site relative URLs are not displayed in the Assets panel, however.
- ✦ Named anchors give you the power to jump to specific parts of any Web page, whether the page is the current one or located on another server.
- ✦ With the `_blank target` attribute, you can force a link to open in a new browser window, leaving your original window available to the user.

In the next chapter, you learn how to set up tables in Dreamweaver.

✦ ✦ ✦

CHAPTER 8

Setting Up Tables

In This Chapter

All about tables in HTML

Setting up a Dreamweaver table

Customizing tables

Importing tabular data

Formatting tables

Using tables as a design tool

Tables bring structure to a Web page. Whether used to align numbers in a spreadsheet or to arrange columns of text on a page, an HTML table brings a bit of order to otherwise free-flowing content. Initially, tables were implemented to present raw data in a more readable format. But it didn't take long for Web designers to take up tables as the most capable tool to control page layout.

Dreamweaver's implementation of tables reflects this current trend in Web page design. Drag-and-drop table sizing, easy organization of rows and columns, and instant table reformatting all help get the job done in the shortest time possible. Table editing features enable you to select and modify anything in a table from a single cell to multiple columns. Moreover, using Dreamweaver commands, you can sort your table in a variety of ways or completely reformat it.

Dreamweaver 4 introduces a new feature that takes table layout to the next level of ease-of-use and power. With the Layout view, designers are able to draw individual cells with a stroke of the mouse and Dreamweaver automatically creates a borderless, content-ready table. You can even add nested tables to maintain design integrity. While you still need to know the basics of table functionality to make the most out of this new tool, Layout view offers a fully backward-compatible technique for visually structuring your Web page.

Although the absolute positioning capabilities offered by Dynamic HTML give Web designers another route to precise layout control, many Web designers use a combination of tools to get desired effects and maintain wide browser compatibility. In other words, HTML tables are going to be around for a long time.

HTML Table Fundamentals

A table is basically a grid that expands as you add text or images. Tables consist of three main components: rows, columns, and cells. *Rows* go across a table from left to right, and *columns* go up and down. A *cell* is the intersection of a row and a column; it's where you enter your information. Cells expand to fit whatever they hold. If you have enabled the table border, your browser shows the outline of the table and all its cells.

In HTML, all the structure and all the data of a table are contained between the table tag pair, `<table>` and `</table>`. The `<table>` tag can take numerous attributes, determining a table's width and height (which can be given in absolute measurement or as a percentage of the screen) as well as the border, alignment on the page, and background color. You can also control the size of the spacing between cells and the amount of padding within cells.

HTML uses a strict hierarchy when describing a table. You can see this clearly in Listing 8-1, which shows the HTML generated from a default table in Dreamweaver.

Listing 8-1: Code for an HTML Table

```
<table border="1" width="75%">
  <tr>
    <td> </td>
    <td> </td>
    <td> </td>
  </tr>
  <tr>
    <td> </td>
    <td> </td>
    <td> </td>
  </tr>
  <tr>
    <td> </td>
    <td> </td>
    <td> </td>
  </tr>
</table>
```

Note The ` ` seen in the table code is HTML for a nonbreaking space. Dreamweaver inserts the code in each empty table cell because some browsers collapse the cell without it. Enter any text or image in the cell, and Dreamweaver automatically removes the ` ` code.

Rows

After the opening `<table>` tag comes the first row tag `<tr>`. Within the current row, you can specify attributes for horizontal alignment or vertical alignment. In addition, browsers recognize row color as an added option.

Cells

Cells are marked in HTML with the `<td>`...`</td>` tag pair. No specific code exists for a column; rather, columns are seen as the number of cells within a row. For example, in Listing 8-1, notice the three sets of `<td>` tags between each `<tr>` pair. This means the table has three columns. A cell can span more than one row or column — in these cases, you see a `rowspan=value` or `colspan=value` attribute in the `<td>` tag.

Cells can also be given horizontal or vertical alignment attributes; these attributes override any similar attributes specified by the table row. When you give a cell a particular width, all the cells in that column are affected. Width can be specified in either an absolute pixel measurement or as a percentage of the overall table.

Tip
After the initial `<table>` tag, you can place an optional caption for the table. In Dreamweaver, you have to enter the `<caption>` tag by hand in the Code view or inspector. Here's an example to show how the tag works:

```
<caption align="center" valign="bottom">Table of
Periodic Elements</caption>
```

Column/row headings

A special type of cell called a *table header* is used for column and row headings. Information in these cells is marked with a `<th>` tag and is generally rendered in boldface, centered within the cell.

Inserting Tables in Dreamweaver

You can control almost all of a table's HTML features through Dreamweaver's point-and-click interface. To insert a Dreamweaver table in the current cursor position, use one of the following three methods:

- Select the Insert Table button on the Objects panel.
- Choose Insert ⇨ Table from the menus.
- Use the keyboard shortcut: Ctrl+Alt+T (Command+Option+T).

The Insert Table dialog box, shown in Figure 8-1, contains the following default values when it is first displayed:

Attribute	Default	Description
Rows	3	The number of horizontal rows.
Columns	3	The number of vertical columns.
Width	75%	Sets the preset width of the table. Available in a percentage of the containing element (screen, layer, or another table) or an absolute pixel size.
Border	1 pixel	The width of the border around each cell and the entire table.
Cell Padding	(Empty)	The space between a cell's border and its contents. Although not shown, Dreamweaver displays 1 pixel of cell padding unless a different value is entered.
Cell Spacing	(Empty)	The number of pixels between each cell. Although not shown, Dreamweaver displays 2 pixels of cell spacing unless a different value is entered.

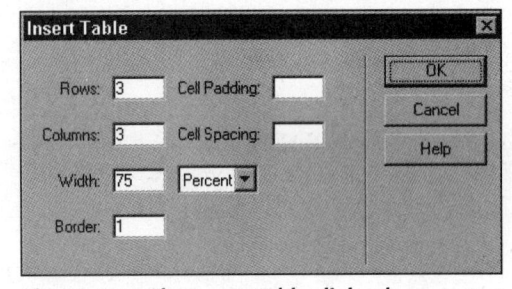

Figure 8-1: The Insert Table dialog box starts out with a default of three columns and three rows; you can adjust as needed.

If you aren't sure of the number of rows and/or columns you need, put in your best guess — you can add or delete rows or columns as necessary.

The default table is sized to take up 75 percent of the browser window. You can alter this percentage by changing the value in the Width text box. The table maintains this proportion as you add text or images, except in two situations:

✦ When an image is larger than the specified percentage

✦ When the nowrap attribute is used for the cell or table row and there is too much text to fit

In either case, the percentage set for the table is ignored, and the cell and table expand to accommodate the text or image. (For further information on the `nowrap` attribute, see the section "Cell wrap," later in this chapter.)

Note The Insert Table dialog box uses what are called *sticky* settings and displays your previously used settings the next time you open the dialog box. This handy feature enables you to set the border width to zero and forget about resetting it each time.

If you prefer to enter the table width as an absolute pixel value, as opposed to the relative percentage, type the number of pixels in the Width text box and select pixels in the drop-down list of width options.

Figure 8-2 shows three tables: At the top is the default table with the width set to 75 percent. The middle table, set to 100 percent, will take up the full width of the browser window. The third table is fixed at 300 pixels — approximately half of a 640×480 window.

Tip You don't have to declare a width for your table at all. If you delete the value in the Width text box of the Insert Table dialog box, your table starts out as small as possible and only expands to accommodate inserted text or images. However, this can make it difficult to position your cursor inside a cell to enter content. You can always delete any set size — pixel or percentage — later.

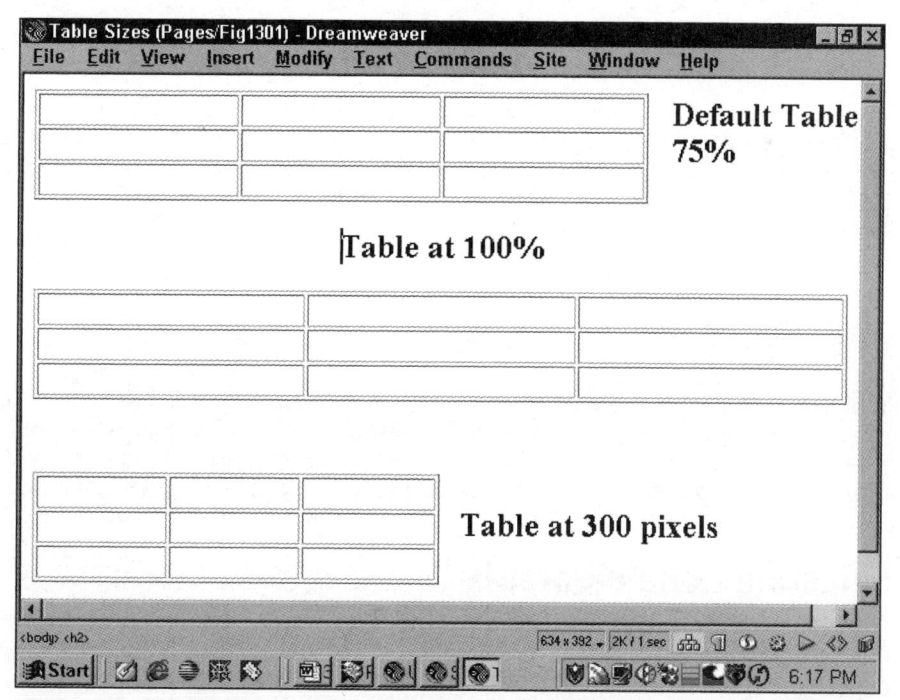

Figure 8-2: The width of a table can be relative to the browser window or set to an absolute width in pixels.

Setting Table Preferences

Two preferences directly affect tables. Both can be set by choosing Edit ⇨ Preferences and looking in the General category.

The first pertinent option is the Show Dialog when Inserting Objects checkbox. If this option is turned off, Dreamweaver always inserts a default table (3 rows by 3 columns at 75 percent width of the screen with a 1-pixel border), without displaying a dialog box and asking for your input. Should you wish to change these values, you can adjust them from the Table Property Inspector once the table has been inserted.

The second notable preference is labeled Faster Table Editing (Deferred Update). Because tables expand and contract dynamically depending on their contents, Dreamweaver gives you the option of turning off the continual updating. (Depending on the speed of your system, the updating can slow down your table input.) If the Faster Table Editing option is enabled, the table is updated whenever you click outside of it or when you press the keyboard shortcut, Ctrl+Space (Command+Spacebar).

> **Note** If you have enabled Faster Table Editing and begin typing in one cell of your table, notice that the text wraps within the cell, and the table expands vertically. However, when you click outside of the table or press Ctrl+Space (Command+Spacebar), the table cells adjust horizontally as well, completing the redrawing of the table.

You should decide whether to leave the Faster Table Editing option on or turn it off, depending on your system and the complexity of your tables. Nested tables tend to update more slowly, and you may need to take advantage of the Faster Table Editing option if tables aren't getting redrawn quickly enough. I recommend turning off Faster Table Editing until it seems that you need it.

Modifying Tables

Most modifications to tables start in the Property Inspector. Dreamweaver helps you manage the basic table parameters — width, border, and alignment — and provides attributes for the other useful but more arcane features of a table, such as converting table width from pixels to percentage of the screen, and vice versa.

Selecting table elements

As with text or images, the first step in altering a table (or any of its elements) is selection. Dreamweaver simplifies the selection process, making it easy to change both the properties and the contents of entire tables, selected rows or columns, and even nonadjacent cells. You can change the font size and color of a row with a click or two of the mouse — instead of highlighting and modifying each individual cell.

Note: All of the following discussions about table selections pertain only to the Standard view and are not applicable in Layout view.

In Dreamweaver, you can select the following elements of a table:

- The entire table
- A single row
- Multiple rows, either adjacent or separate
- A single column
- Multiple columns, either adjacent or separate
- A single cell
- Multiple cells, either adjacent or separate

Once a table element is selected, you can modify its contents.

Selecting an entire table

Several methods are available for selecting the entire table, whether you're a menu- or mouse-oriented designer. To select the table via a menu, do one of the following:

- Choose Modify ⇨ Table ⇨ Select Table.
- With the cursor positioned in the table, choose Edit ⇨ Select All or use the keyboard shortcut, Ctrl+A (Command+A).
- Right-click (Control+click) inside a table to display the shortcut menu and choose Table ⇨ Select Table.

To select an entire table with the mouse, use one of these techniques:

- Click the bottom or right border of the table. You can also click anywhere along the table border when the pointer becomes a four-sided arrow.
- Select the `<table>` tag in the Tag Selector.
- Click immediately to one side of the table and drag the mouse over the table.

However you select the table, the selected table is surrounded by a black border with sizing handles on the right, bottom, and bottom-right corner (as shown in Figure 8-3), just as a selected graphic.

Selecting a row or column

Altering rows or columns of table text without Dreamweaver is a major time-consuming chore. Each cell has to be individually selected, and the changes applied. Dreamweaver has an intuitive method for selecting single or multiple columns and rows, comparable — and in some ways, superior — to major word processing programs.

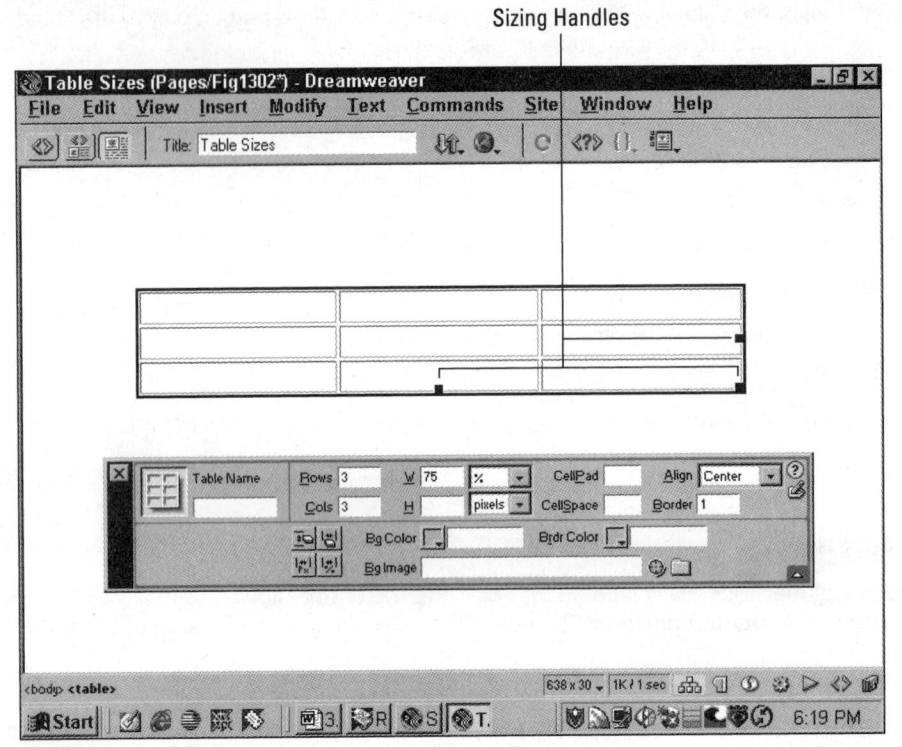

Figure 8-3: A selected table can be identified by the black border outlining the table and the three sizing handles.

As with entire tables, you have several methods for selecting columns or rows. None of the techniques, however, use the menus; row and column selection is handled primarily with the mouse. In fact, you can select an entire row or column with one click.

The one-click method for selecting a single column or row requires that you position your pointer directly over the column or to the left of the row you want to choose. Move the pointer slowly toward the table — when the pointer becomes a single arrow, with the arrowhead pointing down for columns and to the right for rows, click the mouse. All the cells in the selected column or row are bounded with a black border. Any changes now made in the Property Inspector, such as a change in font size or color, affect the selected column or row.

You can select multiple, contiguous columns or rows by dragging the single arrow pointer across several columns or rows. To select a number of columns or rows that are not next to one another, use the Ctrl (Command) key. Press the Ctrl (Command) key while selecting each individual column, using the one-click method. (Not even Word 2000 can handle this degree of complex table selection.)

Tip: If you have trouble positioning the mouse so that the single arrow pointer appears, you can use two other methods for selecting columns or rows. With the first method, you can click and drag across all the cells in a column or row. The second method uses another keyboard modifier, the Shift key. With this technique, click once in the first cell of the column or row. Then, hold down the Shift key while you click in the final cell of the column or row. You can also use this technique to select multiple adjacent columns or rows; just click in another column's or row's last cell.

Selecting cells

Sometimes you need to change the background color of just a few cells in a table, but not the entire row — or you might need to merge several cells to form one wide column span. In these situations, and many others, you can use Dreamweaver's cell selection capabilities. As with columns and rows, you can select multiple cells, whether they are adjacent to one another or separate.

Individual cells are generally selected by dragging the mouse across one or more cell boundaries. To select a single cell, click anywhere in the cell and drag the mouse into another cell. As you pass the border between the two cells, the initial cell is highlighted. If you continue dragging the mouse across another cell boundary, the second cell is selected, and so on. Note that you have to drag the mouse into another cell and not cross the table border onto the page; for example, to highlight the lower-right cell of a table, you need to drag the mouse up or to the left.

Tip: You can also select a single cell by pressing the Ctrl (Command) key and clicking once in the cell, or you can select the rightmost <td> tag in the Tag Selector.

Extended cell selection in Dreamweaver is handled identically to extended text selection in most word processing programs. To select adjacent cells, click in the first desired cell, press and hold the Shift key, and click in the final desired cell. Dreamweaver selects all in a rectangular area, using the first cell as the upper-left corner of the rectangle and the last cell as the lower-right corner. You could, for instance, select an entire table by clicking in the upper-left cell and then Shift+clicking the lower-right cell.

Just as the Shift key is used to make adjacent cell selections, the Ctrl (Command) key is used for all nonadjacent cell selections. You can highlight any number of individual cells — whether or not they are next to one another — by pressing the Ctrl (Command) key while you click in the cell.

Tip: If you Ctrl+click (Command+click) a cell that is already selected, that cell is deselected — regardless of the method you used to select the cell initially.

Editing a table's contents

Before you learn how to change a table's attributes, let's look at basic editing techniques. Editing text in Dreamweaver tables is slightly different from editing text outside of tables. When you begin to enter text into a table cell, the table borders expand to accommodate your new data, assuming no width has been set. The other cells appear to shrink, but they, too, expand once you start typing in text or inserting an image. Unless a cell's width is specified, the cell currently being edited expands or contracts, and the other cells are forced to adjust their width. Figure 8-4 shows the same table (with one row and three columns) in three different states. In the top table, only the first cell contains text; notice how the other cells have contracted. In the middle table, text has been entered into the second cell as well, and you can see how the first cell is now smaller. Finally, in the bottom table, all three cells contain text, and the other two cells have adjusted their width to compensate for the expanding third cell.

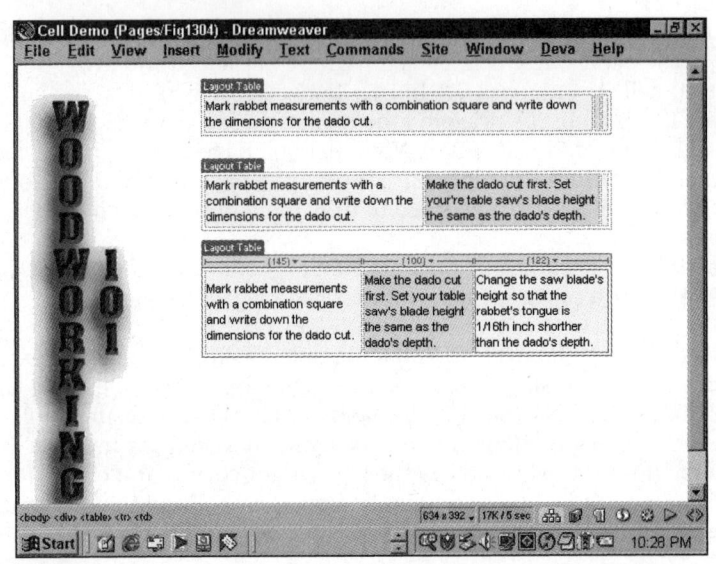

Figure 8-4: As text is entered into a cell, the cell expands; other cells contract, even if they already contain text.

If you look closely at the bottom table in Figure 8-4, you can also see that the text doesn't line up vertically. That's because the default vertical alignment in Dreamweaver, as in most browsers, provides for entries to be positioned in the middle of the cell. (Later in this section, you learn how to adjust the vertical alignment.)

Moving through a table

When you've finished entering your text in the first cell, you can move to the next cell in the row by pressing the Tab key. When you reach the end of a row, pressing Tab takes your cursor to the first cell of the next row. To go backward, cell to cell, press Shift+Tab.

> **Tip** Pressing Tab has a special function when you're in the last cell of a row — it adds a new row, with the same column configuration as the current one.

The Home and End keys take you to the beginning and end, respectively, of the cursor's current line. If a cell's contents are large enough for the text to wrap in the cell, move to the top of the current cell by pressing Ctrl+Home (Command+up arrow or Command+Home). To get the bottom of the current cell in such a circumstance, press Ctrl+End (Command+down arrow).

When you're at the beginning or end of the contents in a cell, the arrow keys can also be used to navigate from cell to cell. Use the left and right arrows to move from cell to cell in a row, and the up and down arrows to move down a column. When you come to the end of a row or column, the arrow keys move to the first cell in the next row or column. If you're moving left to right horizontally, the cursor goes from the end of one row to the beginning of the next row — and vice-versa, if you move from right to left. When moving from top to bottom vertically, the cursor goes from the end of one column to the start of the next, and vice-versa when moving bottom to top.

Cutting, copying, and pasting in tables

In the early days of Web design (about four years ago), woe if you should accidentally leave out a cell of information. It was often almost faster to redo the entire table than to make room by meticulously cutting and pasting everything, one cell at a time. Dreamweaver ends that painstaking work forever with its advanced cutting and pasting features. You can copy a range of cells from one table to another and maintain all the attributes, such as color and alignment as well as the content — text or images — or you can copy just the contents and ignore the attributes.

Dreamweaver has one basic restriction to table cut-and-paste operations: Your selected cells must form a rectangle. In other words, although you can select non-adjacent cells, columns, or rows and modify their properties, you can't cut or copy them. Should you try, you get a message from Dreamweaver such as the one shown in Figure 8-5; the table above the notification in the figure illustrates an incorrect cell selection.

Copying attributes and contents

When you copy or cut a cell using the regular commands, Dreamweaver automatically copies everything — content, formatting, and cell format — in the selected cell. Then, pasting the cell reproduces it all — however, you can get different results depending on where the cell (or column or row) is pasted.

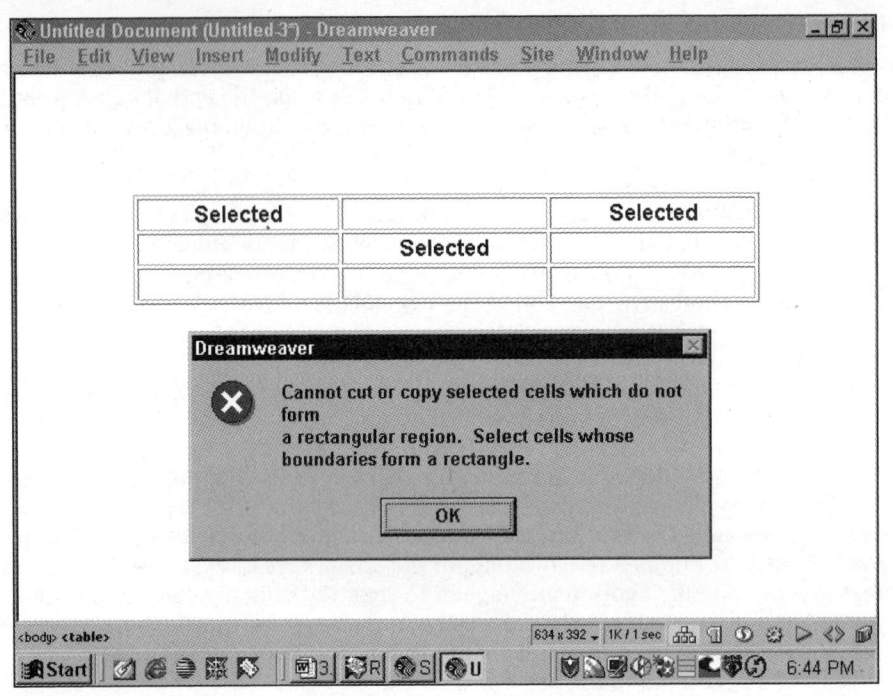

Figure 8-5: Dreamweaver enables you to cut or copy selected cells only when they form a rectangle, unlike the cells in the table depicted here.

To cut or copy both the contents and the attributes of any cell, row, or column, follow these steps:

1. Select the cells you wish to cut or copy.

   Remember that to cut or copy a range of cells in Dreamweaver, they must form a solid rectangular region.

2. To copy cells, choose Edit ⇨ Copy or use the keyboard shortcut, Ctrl+C (Command+C).

3. To cut cells, choose Edit ⇨ Cut or use the keyboard shortcut, Ctrl+X (Command+X).

   If you cut an individual cell, the contents are removed, but the cell remains. If, however, you cut an entire row or column, the cells are removed.

4. Position your cursor to paste the cells in the desired location:

   - To replace a cell with a cell on the clipboard, click anywhere in the cell to be replaced. If you cut or copied multiple cells that do not make up a full column or row, click in the upper-left corner of the cells you wish to replace. For example, a range of six cells in a 2×3 configuration replaces the same configuration when pasted.

Dreamweaver alerts you to the differences if you try to paste one configuration of cells into a different cell configuration.

- To insert a new row with the row on the clipboard, click anywhere in the row below where you'd like the new row to appear.
- To insert a new column with the column on the clipboard, click anywhere in the column to the right of where you'd like the new column to appear.
- To replace an existing row or column in a table, select the row or column. If you've cut or copied multiple rows or columns, you must select an equivalent size and shape of cells to replace.
- To insert a new table based on the copied or cut cells, click anywhere outside of the table.

5. Paste the copied or cut cells by choosing Edit ⇨ Paste or pressing Ctrl+V (Command+V).

Tip: To move a row or column that you've cut from the interior of a table to the exterior (the right or bottom), you have to first expand the number of cells in the table. To do this, first select the table by choosing Modify ⇨ Table ⇨ Select Table or using one of the other techniques previously described. Next, in the Table Property Inspector, increase the number of rows or columns by altering the values in the Rows or Cols text boxes. Finally, select the newly added rows or columns and choose Edit ⇨ Paste.

Copying contents only

It's not uncommon to need to move data from one cell to another, while keeping the destination cell's attributes, such as its background color or border, intact. For this, you need to use Dreamweaver's facility for copying just the contents of a cell.

To copy only the contents, select a cell as previously described and then choose Edit ⇨ Copy or use the keyboard shortcut, Ctrl+C (Command+C). Then put your cursor in the destination cell and, instead of choosing Edit ⇨ Paste, choose Edit ⇨ Paste HTML, or use the keyboard shortcut, Ctrl+Shift+V (Command+Shift+V). Instead of selecting the entire cell to copy, you can also just select the text, or a portion of the text, and use the standard Edit ⇨ Copy and Edit ⇨ Paste commands to avoid pasting in the format of the copied text.

Unlike the copying of both contents and attributes described in the previous section, content-only copying has a couple of limitations:

✦ First, you can copy only the contents of one cell at a time. You can't copy contents only across multiple cells.

✦ Second, you can't replace the entire contents of one cell with another and maintain all the text attributes (font, color, and size) of the destination cell. If you select all the text to be replaced, Dreamweaver also selects the `<font>` tag that holds the attributes and replaces those as well. The workaround is to select all but one letter or word, paste the contents, and then delete the unwanted text.

Working with table properties

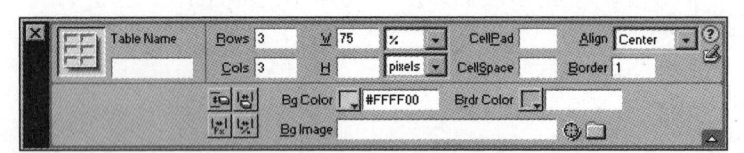

The `<table>` tag has a large number of attributes, and most of them can be modified through Dreamweaver's Property Inspector. As with all objects, the table must be selected before it can be altered. Choose Modify ⇨ Table ⇨ Select Table or use one of the other selection techniques previously described.

Once you've selected the table, if the Property Inspector is open, it presents the table properties as shown in Figure 8-6. Otherwise, you can open the Table Property Inspector by choosing Window ⇨ Properties Inspector.

Figure 8-6: The expanded Table Property Inspector gives you control over all the tablewide attributes.

Setting alignment

Aligning a table in Dreamweaver goes beyond the expected left, right, and center options — you can also make a table into a free-floating object around which text can wrap to the left or right.

With HTML, you can align a table using two different methods, and each gives you a different effect. Using the text alignment method (Text ⇨ Align) results in the conventional positioning (left, right, and center), and using the Table Property Inspector method enables you to wrap text around your realigned table. Figure 8-7 compares some of the different results you get from aligning your table with the two methods.

To align your table without text wrapping, follow these steps:

1. Select your table using one of the methods described earlier.
2. In the Property Inspector, make sure the Align option is set to Default.
3. Select the Text ⇨ Align command and then choose one of the three options: Left, Center, or Right.

    Dreamweaver surrounds your table code with a division tag pair, `<div>...</div>`, with an `align` attribute set to your chosen value.

To align your table with text wrapping, making your table into a floating object, follow these steps:

1. Select the table.

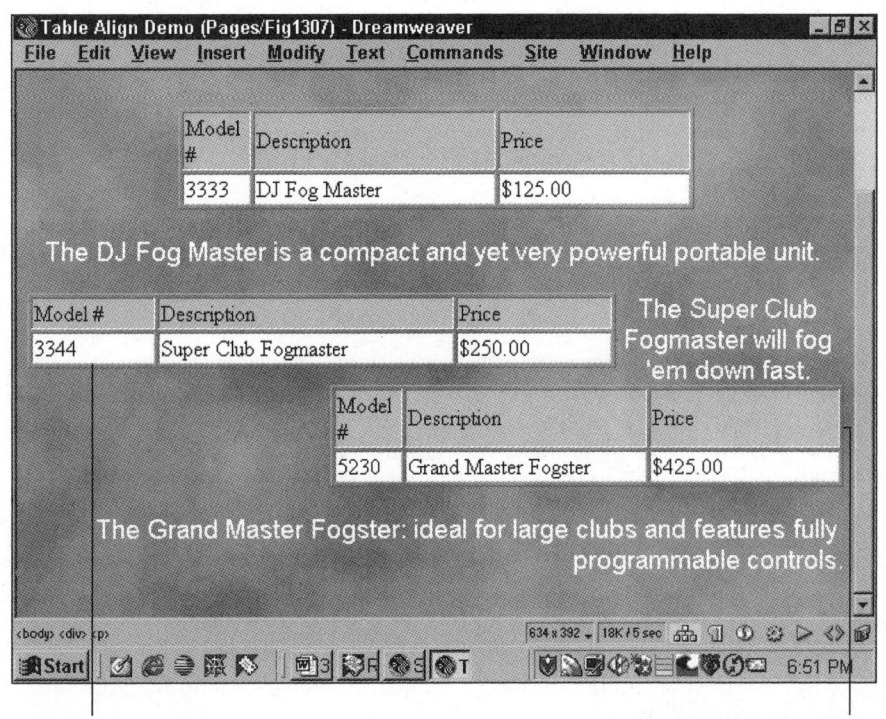

Left-aligned with the
Table Property Inspector

Right-aligned with the
Text Alignment command

Figure 8-7: Tables can be centered, as well as aligned left or right — with or without text wrapping.

2. In the Table Property Inspector, open the Align drop-down list and choose one of the four options:

Alignment Option	Result
Default	No alignment is written. Table aligns to the browser's default, usually left, with no text wrapping.
Left	Aligns the table to the left side of the browser window and wraps text around the right side.
Right	Aligns the table to the right side of the browser window and wraps text around the left side.
Center	The table aligns to the center of the browser window. Text does not wrap around either side. Note: This alignment option works only with 4.0 and above browsers.

Dreamweaver codes these alignment attributes in the `<table>` tag. As with floating images, Dreamweaver places an anchor point for floating elements on the Web page. However, you cannot drag-and-drop or cut-and-paste the anchor point, unlike most other Invisible symbols, for a floating table.

Resizing a table

The primary sizing control on the Table Property Inspector is the Width text box. You can enter a new width value for the entire table in either a screen percentage or pixels. Just enter your value in the Width text box and then select % or pixels in the drop-down list of options.

Dreamweaver also provides a quick and intuitive way to resize the overall table width, column widths, or row height. Pass your pointer over any of the table's borders, and the pointer becomes a two-headed arrow; this is the resizing pointer. When you see the resizing pointer, you can click and drag any border to new dimensions.

As noted earlier, tables are initially sized according to their contents. Once you move a table border in Dreamweaver, however, the new sizes are written directly into the HTML code, and the column width or row height is fixed — unless the contents cannot fit. If, for example, an inserted image is 115 pixels wide and the cell has a width of only 90 pixels, the cell expands to fit the image. The same is true if you try to fit an extremely long, unbroken text string, such as a complex URL, in a cell that's too narrow to hold it.

Dreamweaver enables you to set the height of a table using the Height text box in much the same way as the Width box. However, the height of a table — whether in pixels or a percentage — is maintained only as long as the contents do not require a larger size. A table's width, though, takes precedence over its height, and a table expands vertically before it expands horizontally.

Changes to a cell or column's width are shown in the `<td>` tags, as are changes to a row's height and width, using the `width` and `height` attribute, respectively. You can see these changes by selecting the table, cell, column, or row affected and looking at the W (Width) and H (Height) text box values.

For an overall view of what happens when you resize a cell, row, or column, it's best to look at the HTML. Here's the HTML for an empty table, resized:

```
<table border="1" width="70%">
  <tr>
    <td width="21%"> </td>
    <td width="34%"> </td>
    <td width="45%"> </td>
  </tr>
  <tr>
    <td width="21%" height="42"> </td>
```

```
        <td width="34%" height="42"> </td>
        <td width="45%" height="42"> </td>
    </tr>
    <tr>
        <td width="21%" height="42"> </td>
        <td width="34%" height="42"> </td>
        <td width="45%" height="42"> </td>
    </tr>
</table>
```

Notice how the width for each cell and the entire table is expressed as percentages. If the table width were initially set at a pixel value, the cell widths would have been, too. The row height values, on the other hand, are shown as an absolute measurement in pixels.

You can switch from percentages to pixels in all the table measurements, and even clear all the values at once—with the click of the right button. Four measurement controls appear in the lower-left portion of the expanded Table Property Inspector, as shown in Figure 8-8.

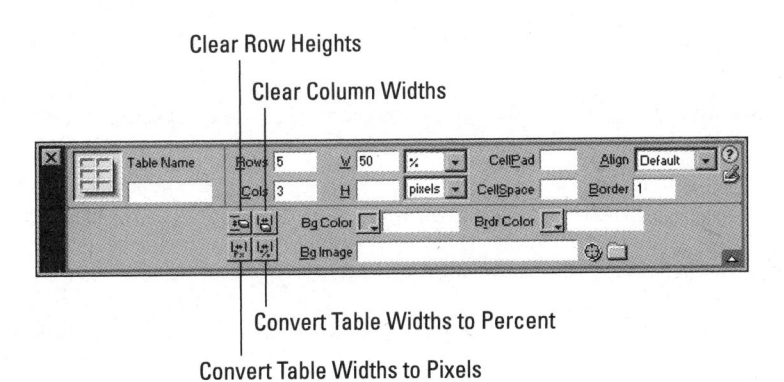

Figure 8-8: You can make tablewide changes with the four control buttons in the Table Property Inspector.

From left to right, the measurement controls are as follows:

Measurement Control Button	Description
Clear Row Heights	Erases all the `height` attributes in the current table
Clear Column Widths	Deletes all the `width` attributes found in the `<td>` tags
Convert Table Widths to Pixels	Translates the current widths of all cells and for the entire table from percentages to pixels
Convert Table Widths to Percent	Translates the current widths of all cells and for the entire table from pixels to percentages

Note: Selecting Clear Row Heights doesn't affect the table height value.

If you clear both row heights and column widths, the table goes back to its "grow as needed" format and, if empty, shrinks to its smallest possible size.

Caution: When converting width percentages to pixels, and vice versa, keep in mind that the percentages are relative to the size of the browser window — and in the development phase that browser window is Dreamweaver. Use the Window Size option on the status bar to expand Dreamweaver's Document window to the same sizes as what you expect to be seen in various browser settings.

Inserting rows and columns

The default Dreamweaver table configuration of three columns and three rows can be changed at any time. You can add rows or columns almost anywhere in a table, using various methods.

You have three methods for adding a single row:

- Position the cursor in the last cell of the last row and press Tab to add a new row below the present one.
- Choose Modify ⇨ Table ⇨ Insert Row to insert a new row above the current row.
- Right-click (Control+click) to open the shortcut menu and select Table ⇨ Insert Row. Rows added in this way are inserted above the current row.

You have two ways to add a new column to your table:

- Choose Modify ⇨ Table ⇨ Insert Column to insert a new column to the left of the current column.
- Right-click (Control+click) to open the shortcut menu and select Table ⇨ Insert Column from the shortcut menu. The column is inserted to the left of the current column.

You can add multiple rows and columns in one of two different ways:

- Increase the number of rows indicated in the Rows text box of the Table Property Inspector. All new rows added in this manner appear below the last table row. Similarly, you can increase the number of columns indicated in the Cols text box of the Table Property Inspector. Columns added in this way appear to the right of the last column.
- Use the Insert Rows or Columns dialog box.

The Insert Rows or Columns feature enables you to include any number of rows or columns anywhere relative to your current cursor position.

To add multiple columns using the Insert Rows or Columns dialog box, follow these steps:

1. Open the Insert Rows or Columns dialog box (shown in Figure 8-9) by selecting Modify ⇨ Table ⇨ Insert Rows or Columns or by choosing Table ⇨ Insert Rows or Columns from the shortcut menu.

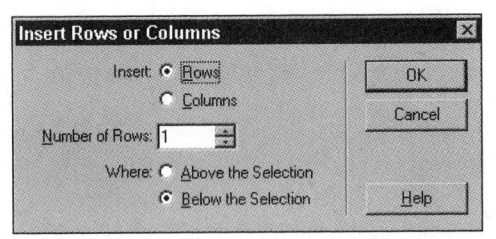

Figure 8-9: Use the Insert Rows or Columns feature to add several columns or rows simultaneously.

2. Select either Rows or Columns.

3. Enter the number of rows or columns you wish to insert — you can either type in a value or use the arrows to increase or decrease the number.

4. Select where you want the rows or columns to be inserted.

   - If you have selected the Rows option, you can insert the rows either Above or Below the Selection (the current row).
   - If you have selected the Columns options, you can insert the columns either Before or After the Current Column.

5. Click OK when you're finished.

Deleting rows and columns

When you want to delete a column or row, you can use either the shortcut menu or the Table Property Inspector. On the shortcut menu, you can remove the current column or row by choosing Delete Column or Delete Row, respectively. Using the Table Property Inspector, you can delete multiple columns and rows by reducing the numbers in the Cols or Rows text boxes. Columns are deleted from the right side of the table, and rows are removed from the bottom.

Caution Watch out — exercise extreme caution when deleting columns or rows. Dreamweaver does not ask for confirmation and removes these columns and/or rows whether or not data exists in them. You can, of course, undo the operation, if necessary.

Setting table borders and backgrounds

Borders are the solid outlines of the table itself. A border's width is measured in pixels; the default width is one pixel. This width can be altered in the Border field of the Table Property Inspector.

You can make the border invisible by specifying a border of 0 width. You can still resize your table by clicking and dragging the borders, even when the border is set to 0. When the View ⇨ Table Borders option is selected, Dreamweaver displays a thin dashed line to represent the border.

When the border is visible, you can also see each cell outlined. The width of the outline around the cells stays constant, regardless of the width of the border. However, you can control the amount of space between each cell with the CellSpace value in the Table Property Inspector, covered later in this chapter.

To change the width of a border in Dreamweaver, select your table and enter a new value in the Border text box. With a wider border, you can see the default shading: The top and left side are a lighter shade, and the bottom and right sides are darker. This gives the table border a pseudo-3D appearance. Figure 8-10 shows single-cell tables with borders of various widths.

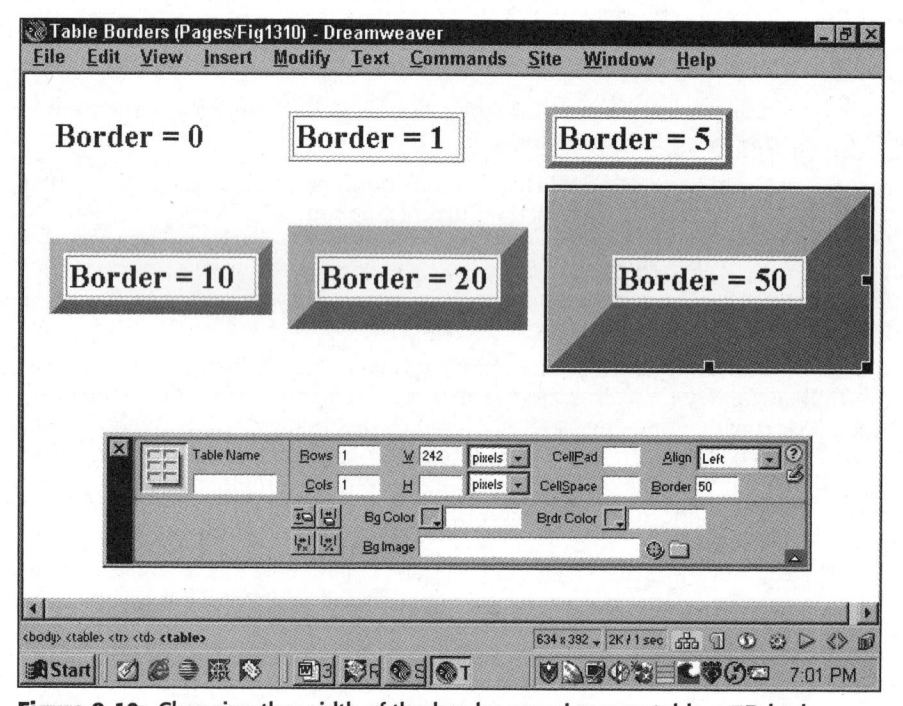

Figure 8-10: Changing the width of the border can give your table a 3D look.

In Dreamweaver, you can directly assign colors to the border. To choose a color for the border, select the Border color swatch or enter a color name in the adjacent text box.

In addition to colored borders, a table can also have a colored background. (By default, the table is initially transparent.) Choose the background color in the Table Property Inspector by selecting a color in the Bg Color swatch or entering a color name in the adjacent text box. As you see later in the chapter, you can also assign background colors to rows, columns, and individual cells — if used, these specific colors all override the background color of the overall entire table.

Working with cell spacing and cell padding

HTML gives you two methods to add white space in tables. *Cell spacing* controls the width between each cell, and *cell padding* controls the margins within each cell. These values can be set independently through the Table Property Inspector.

> **Tip** Although not indicated in the Table Property Inspector, the default value is 2 pixels for cell spacing and 1 pixel for cell padding. Some Web page designs call for a close arrangement of cells and are better served by changing either (or both) the CellSpace or CellPad values to 1 or 0.

To change the amount of white space between each cell in a table, enter a new value in the CellSpace text box of the Table Property Inspector. If you want to adjust the amount of white space between the borders of the cell and the actual cell data, alter the value in the CellPad text box of the Table Property Inspector. Figure 8-11 shows an example of a table with wide (10 pixels) cell spacing and cell padding values.

Merging and splitting cells

You have seen how cells in HTML tables can extend across (span) multiple columns or rows. By default, a cell spans one column or one row. Increasing a cell's span enables you to group any number of topics under one heading. You are effectively merging one cell with another to create a larger cell. Likewise, a cell can be split into multiple rows or columns.

Dreamweaver enables you to combine and divide cells in two different ways. If you're more comfortable with the concept of merging and splitting cells, you can use two handy buttons on the Property Inspector. If, on the other hand, you prefer the older method of increasing and decreasing row or column span, you can still access these commands through the main and shortcut menus.

To combine two or more cells, first select the cells you want to merge. Then, from the Property Inspector, select the Merge Cells button or press the keyboard shortcut Ctrl+Alt+M (Command+Option+M); Windows users also have the option of just pressing M. If the Merge button is not available, multiple cells have not been selected.

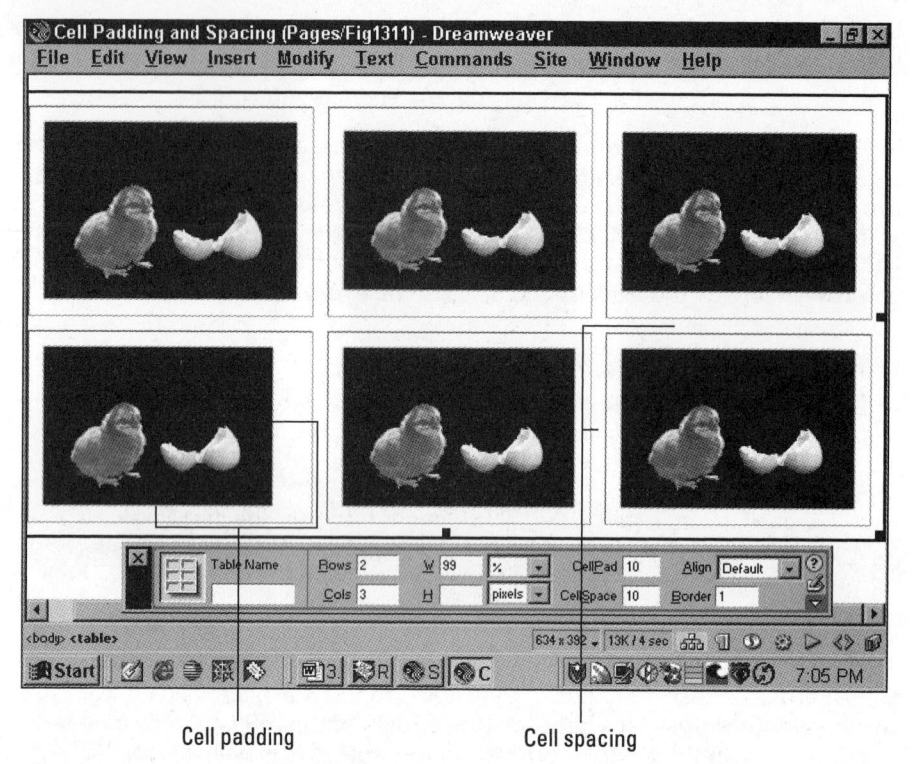

Figure 8-11: You can add additional white space between each cell (cell spacing) or within each cell (cell padding).

To divide a cell, follow these steps:

1. Position your cursor in the cell to split.
2. From the Property Inspector, select the Split Cell button or press the keyboard shortcut, Ctrl+Alt+S (Command+Option+S).

   The Split Cell dialog box (shown in Figure 8-12) appears.

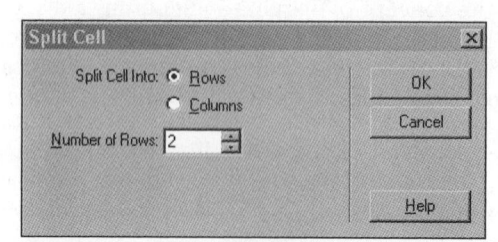

Figure 8-12: Use the Split Cell dialog box to divide cells horizontally or vertically.

3. Select either the Rows or Columns option to decide whether the cell will be split horizontally or vertically.

4. Enter the Number of Rows or Columns in the text box or use the arrows to change the value.

5. Select OK when you're done.

The same effect can be achieved by using the menus. To do so, first position the cursor in the cell to be affected and then choose one of the following commands from the Modify ⇨ Table menu:

Command	Description
Increase Row Span	Joins the current cell with the cell below it
Decrease Row Span	Separates two or more previously spanned cells from the bottom cell
Increase Column Span	Joins the current cell with the cell immediately to its right
Decrease Column Span	Separates two or more previously spanned cells from the right edge

Existing text or images are put in the same cell if the cells containing them are joined to span rows or columns. Figure 8-13 shows a table containing both row and column spanning.

Tip When you need to build a complex table such as this one, it's best to map out your table before you begin constructing it, and complete it prior to entering your data.

Setting cell, column, and row properties

In addition to the overall table controls, Dreamweaver helps you set numerous properties for individual cells one at a time, by the column or by the row. When attributes overlap or conflict, such as different background colors for a cell in the same row and column, the more specific target wins out. The hierarchy, from most general to most specific, is as follows: tables, rows, columns, and cells.

You can call up the specific Property Inspector by selecting the cell, row, or column you want to modify. The Cell, Row, and Column Property Inspectors each affect similar attributes. The following sections explain how the attributes work in general and — if any differences exist — specifically in regard to the cell, column, or row.

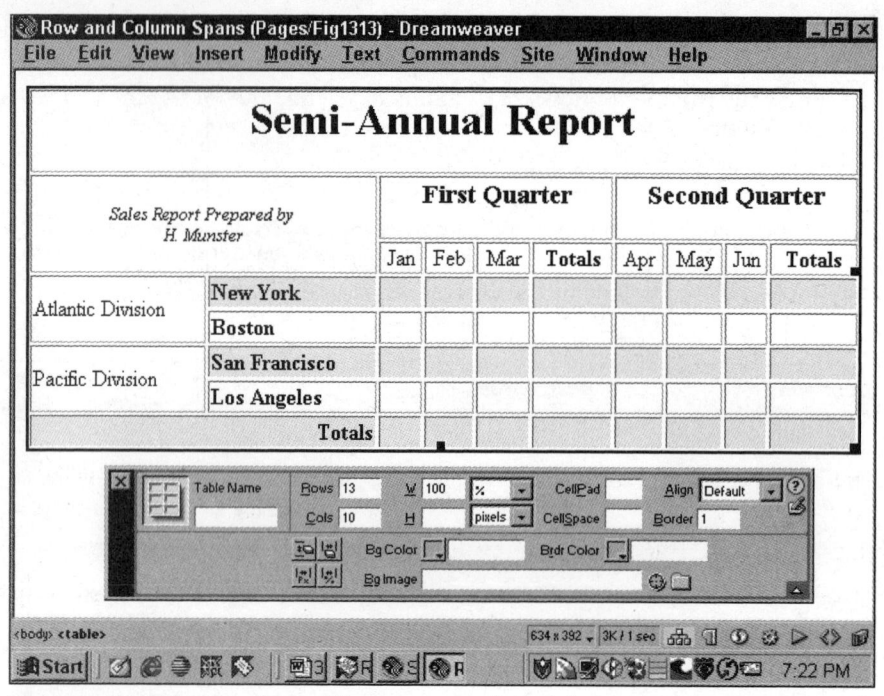

Figure 8-13: This spreadsheet-like report was built using Dreamweaver's row- and column-spanning features.

Horizontal alignment

You can set the Horizontal Alignment attribute, `align`, to specify the default alignment, or Left, Right, or Center alignment, for the element in the cell, column, or row. This attribute can be overridden by setting the alignment for the individual line or image. Generally, Left is the default horizontal alignment for cells.

Vertical alignment

The HTML `valign` attribute determines whether the cell's contents are vertically aligned to the cell's top, middle, bottom, or along the baseline. Typically, browsers align cells vertically in the middle by default. Select the Vertical Alignment option arrow in the Cell, Column, or Row Properties dialog box to specify a different alignment.

Top, Middle, and Bottom vertical alignments work pretty much as you would expect. A Baseline vertical alignment displays text near the top of the cell and positions the text—regardless of font size—so that the baselines of all the text in the affected row, column, or cell are the same. You can see how images and text of various sizes are displayed under the various vertical alignment options in Figure 8-14.

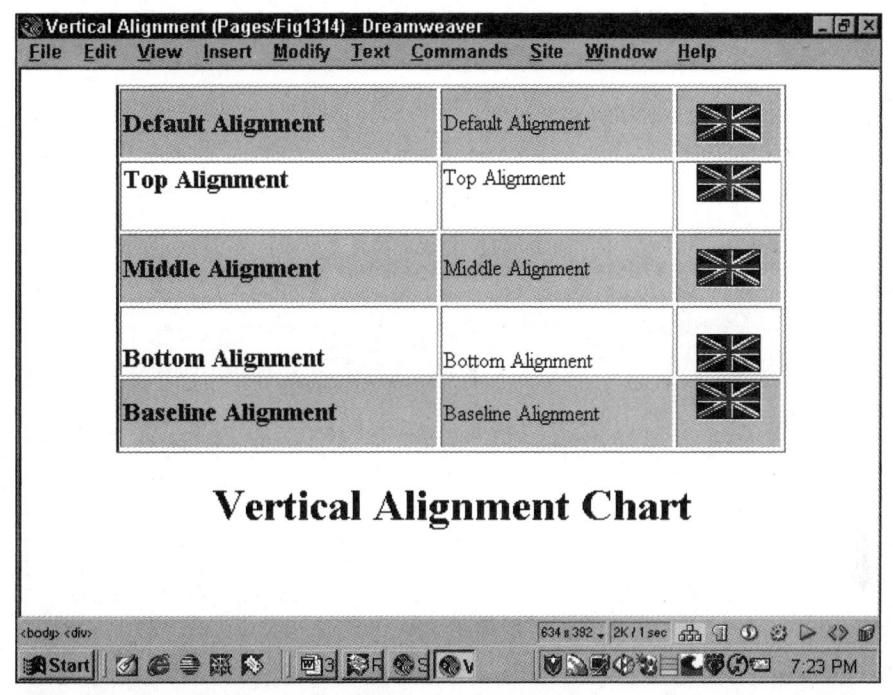

Figure 8-14: You can vertically align text and images in several arrangements in a table cell, row, or column.

Cell wrap

Normal behavior for any cell is to automatically wrap text or a series of images within the cell's borders. You can turn off this automatic feature by selecting the No Wrap option in the Property Inspector for cell, column, or row.

> **Note** I've had occasion to use this option when I absolutely needed three images to appear side by side in one cell. In analyzing the results, I found that on some lower-resolution browsers, the last image wrapped to the next line.

Table header cells

Quite often in tables, a column or a row functions as the heading for that section of the table, labeling all the information in that particular section. Dreamweaver has an option for designating these cells: the Header option. Table header cells are usually rendered in boldface and centered in each cell. Figure 8-15 shows an example of a table in which both the first row and first column are marked as table header cells.

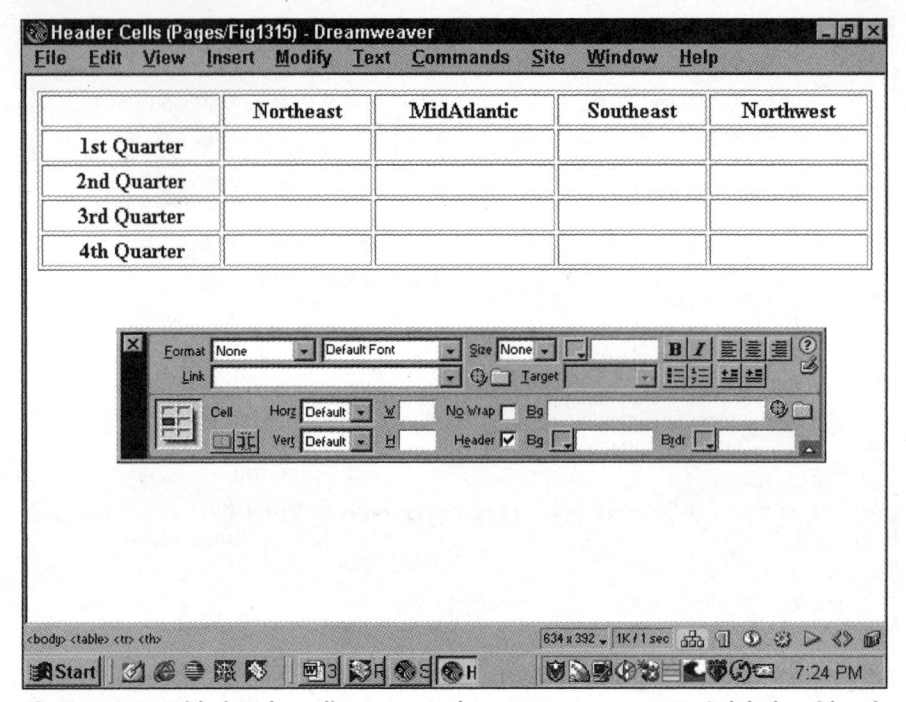

Figure 8-15: Table header cells are a good way to note a category's label — either for a row or a column, or both.

Width and height

The gridlike structure of a table makes it impossible to resize only one cell in a multicolumn table. Therefore, the only way you can enter exact values for a cell's width is through the Width section available only in the Column Properties dialog box. In this section of the dialog box, you can enter values in pixels or as a percentage of the table. The default enables cells to automatically resize with no restrictions outside of the overall dimensions of the table.

Similarly, whenever you change a cell's height, the entire row is altered. If you drag the row to a new height, the value is written into the H (Height) text box for all cells in the row. On the other hand, if you specify a single cell's height, the row resizes, but you can see the value only in the cell you've changed.

Color elements

Just as you can specify color backgrounds and borders for the overall table, you can do the same for columns, rows, or individual cells. Corresponding color swatches and text boxes are available in all dialog boxes for the following categories:

- **Background Color:** Specifies the color for the selected cell, row, or column. Selecting the color swatch opens the standard color picker.
- **Border Color:** Controls the color of the single-pixel border surrounding each cell.

As with all Dreamweaver color pickers, you can use the Eyedropper tool to select a color from the Web-safe palette or from any item on a page. You can also select the Eraser tool to delete any previously selected color. Finally, choose the Palette tool to open the Color dialog box and select any available color.

Working with Table Formats

Tables keep data organized and generally make it easier to find information quickly. Large tables with many rows, however, tend to become difficult to read unless they are formatted with alternating rows of color or some other device. Formatting a large table is often an afterthought as well as a time-consuming affair. Unless, of course, you're using Dreamweaver's Format Table command.

The Format Table command enables you to choose from 17 preset formats or customize your own. This versatile command can style the top row, alternating rows in the body of the table, the left column, and the border. It's best to completely build the structure of your table — although you don't have to fill it with data — before formatting it; otherwise, you might have to reformat it when new rows or columns are added.

To apply one of the preset table formats, follow these steps:

1. Select your table by choosing Modify ⇨ Table ⇨ Select Table or by using one of the other techniques.
2. Choose Commands ⇨ Format Table.

   The Format Table dialog box (shown in Figure 8-16) opens.
3. Select any of the options from the scrolling list box on the left side of the Format Table dialog box.

   As you select an option, a representation of the table appears to the right, and the attribute values used are displayed below.
4. When you've found a table format that's appropriate, select OK to close the dialog box, and the format is applied.

The preset formats are divided into three groups: Simple, AltRows, and DblRows. The Simple formats maintain the same background color for all rows in the body of the table but change the top row and the left column. The AltRows formats alternate the background color of each row in the body of the table; you have eight different color combinations from which to choose. The final category, DblRows, alternates the background color of every two rows in the body of the table.

[Screenshot of the Format Table dialog box]

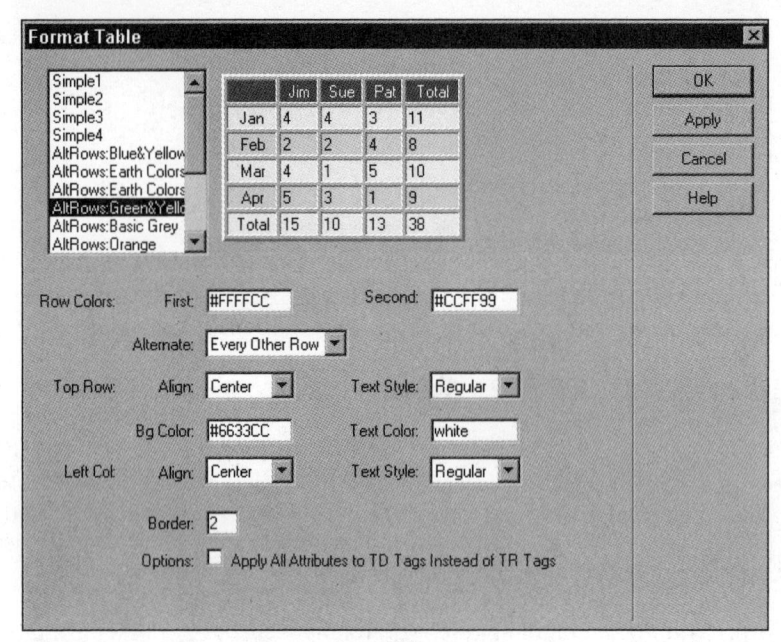

Figure 8-16: Select any one of 17 different preset formats from the Format Table dialog box or customize your own.

Although 17 different formats may seem as if there are plenty of choices, it's really just the jumping-off place for what's possible with the Format Table command. Each variable applied to create the preset formats can be customized. Moreover, you don't have to apply the changes to your selected table to see the effect — you can preview the results directly in the Table Format dialog box. Following are the variable attributes in the Table Format dialog box:

Attribute	Description
Row Colors: First	Enter a color (in color name or hexadecimal format) for the background colors of the first row in the body of a table. The Row Colors do not affect the top row of a table.
Row Colors: Second	Enter a color (in color name or hexadecimal format) for the background colors of the second row in the body of a table. The Row Colors do not affect the top row of a table.
Row Colors: Alternate	Establishes the pattern for using the specified Row Colors. Options are `<do not alternate>`, Every Other Row, Every Two Rows, Every Three Rows, and Every Four Rows.
Top Row: Align	Sets the alignment of the text in the top row of the table to left, right, or center.

Attribute	Description
Top Row: Text Style	Sets the style of the text in the top row of the table to Regular, Bold, Italic, or Bold Italic.
Top Row: Bg Color	Sets the background color of the top row of the selected table. Use either color names or hexadecimal values.
Top Row: Text Color	Sets the color of the text in the top row of the selected table. Use either color names or hexadecimal values.
Left Col: Align	Sets the alignment of the text in the left column of the table to Left, Right, or Center.
Left Col: Text Style	Sets the style of the text in the left column of the table to Regular, Bold, Italic, or Bold Italic.
Border	Determines the width of the table's border in pixels.
Options: Apply All Attributes to TD Tags Instead of TR Tags	Writes attribute changes at the cell level, <td>, rather than the default, the row level, <tr>.

The final option in the Format Table dialog box, Apply All Attributes to TD Tags Instead of TR Tags, should be used in only one of two situations: One, the selected table is nested inside another table and you want to override the outer table's <tr> format; or two, you anticipate moving cells from one table to another and want to maintain the formatting. Generally, the code produced by selecting this option is bulkier and could impact a page's overall download size, if the table is sufficiently large.

Caution Currently, there's no way to save your custom format without editing the tableFormats.js JavaScript file in the Commands folder. Otherwise, you need to reenter the selections each time you apply them.

Sorting Tables

Have you ever painstakingly built a table, alphabetizing every last entry by last name and first name, only to have the client call up with a list of 13 additional names that just have to go in? "Oh, and could you sort them by zip code instead of last name?" Dreamweaver contains a Table Sort command designed to make short work of such requests. All you need to do is select your table, and you're ready to do a two-level-deep sort, either alphabetically or numerically.

The Table Sort command can rearrange any size table; more important, it's HTML savvy and gives you the option of keeping the formatting of your table rows. This capability enables you to maintain a table with alternating row colors and still sort the data — something not even the most powerful word processors can handle. The Table Sort command is useful for generating different views of the same data, without having to use a database.

The Table Sort command is straightforward to use; just follow these steps:

1. Select your table by choosing Modify ➪ Table ➪ Select Table or by using one of the other techniques.
2. Choose Commands ➪ Sort Table.

   The Sort Table dialog box (shown in Figure 8-17) opens.

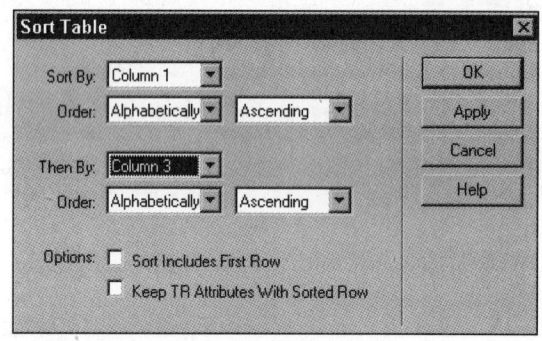

Figure 8-17: Sort your tables numerically or alphabetically with the Sort Table command.

3. Choose the primary sort column from the Sort By option list.

   Dreamweaver automatically lists the number of columns in the selected table in the option list.

4. Set the type of the primary sort by choosing either Alphabetically or Numerically from the first Order option list.
5. Choose the direction of the sort by selecting either Ascending or Descending from the second Order option list.
6. If you wish to add a second level of sorting, repeat Steps 3 through 5 in the Then By section.
7. If your selected table does not include a header row, select the Sort Includes First Row option.
8. If you have formatted your table with alternating row colors, choose the Keep TR Attributes with Sorted Row option.
9. Click OK when you're finished.

> **Tip** As with any sorting program, if you leave blank cells in the column you're basing the sort on, those rows appear as a group on top of the table for an ascending sort and at the end for a descending sort. Be sure that all the cells in your sort criteria column are filled correctly.

Importing Tabular Data

In the computer age, there's nothing much more frustrating than having information in a digital format and still having to enter it manually — either typing it in or cutting and pasting — to get on the Web. This frustration is multiplied when it comes to table data, whether created in a spreadsheet or database program. You have to transfer lots of small pieces of data, and it all has to be properly related and positioned.

Dreamweaver's Import Tabular Data goes a long way toward alleviating the tedium — not to mention the frustration — of dealing with tabular information. The Import Tabular Data command reads any delimited text file and inserts the information in a series of rows and columns. You can even set most characteristics for the table to be created, including the width, cell padding, cell spacing, and border.

Quite often, the first step in the process of importing table data into Dreamweaver is to export it from your other program. Most spreadsheet and database programs have some capability of outputting information in a text file; each bit of data (whether it's from a cell of a spreadsheet or field of a database) is separated — or *delimited* — from every other data by a special character, typically a tab or comma. In Dreamweaver, you can choose which delimiter is used in the Import Tabular Data dialog box to ensure a clean transfer with no loss of data.

> **Tip** Although you have many types of delimiters to choose from, I generally default to exporting tab-delimited files. With a tab-delimited file, you usually don't have to worry if any of your data contains the delimiter — which would throw off the import. However, testing shows that Dreamweaver correctly handles comma-delimited files with and without quotes, so you could also use that format safely.

To import a tabular data file, follow these steps:

1. Be sure the data you wish to import has been saved or exported in the proper format: a delimited text file.
2. Choose File ⇨ Import ⇨ Import Tabular Data.

The Import Table Data dialog box, shown in Figure 8-18, is displayed.

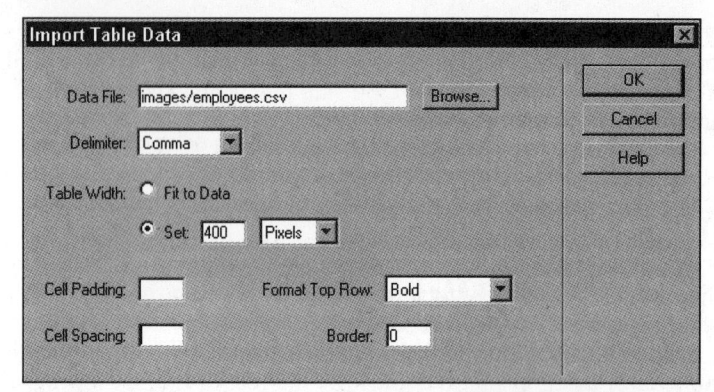

Figure 8-18: Any external data, saved in a delimited text file, can be brought into Dreamweaver through the Import Tabular Data command.

3. Select the Data File Browse button to find the desired file.
4. Choose the delimiter used to separate the fields or cells of data from the Delimiter option list. The choices are Tab, Comma, Semicolon, Colon, and Other.

> **Tip** If you select a file with a .csv extension, the Comma delimiter is automatically chosen. CSV is short for Comma Separated Values.

5. If you choose Other from the Delimiter list, a blank field appears to the right of the list. Enter the special character, such as a pipe (|), used as the delimiter in the exported file.

    Now that the imported file characteristics are set, you can predefine the table the information will be imported into, if desired.

6. If you want to set a particular table width, enter a value in the Set field and choose either Pixels or % from the option list. If you want the imported file to determine the size of the table, keep the Fit to Data option selected.
7. Enter any Cell Padding or Cell Spacing values desired, in their respective fields.

    As with standard tables, by default Cell Padding is set to 2 pixels and Cell Spacing to 1 if no specific values are entered.

8. If you'd like to style the first row, choose Bold, Italic, or Bold Italic from the Format Top Row option list.

    This option is typically used when the imported file contains a header row.

9. Set the Border field to the desired width, if any. If you don't want a border displayed at all, set the Border field to 0.
10. Click OK when you're done.

Even though the Import Tabular Data option is under the File menu, it doesn't open a new file — the new table is created at the current cursor position.

> **Caution** If your data comes in wrong, double-check the delimiter used by opening the file in a text editor. If Dreamweaver is expecting a comma delimiter and your file uses tabs, data is not separated properly.

Designing with Layout Mode

As discussed earlier in this chapter, experienced Web designers regard tables as one of their primary layout tools because, outside of Dynamic HTML's layers, tables are the only way for you to get close to positioning your page elements the way you want them to appear. It's a lot of work to do this with raw tables, but designers are a persistent group — and for good reason: Persistence has a big payoff.

> **New Feature** Thanks to the introduction of the Layout view in Dreamweaver 4, structuring your page with tables just got a whole lot easier. When you're in Layout view, you simply draw out separate areas to hold your content and Dreamweaver automatically converts these areas to cells and tables. The layout cells are very pliable and can be moved easily about the page, resized, and reshaped. Moreover, Layout view gives you professional design power with options such as tables that stretch to fit the browser window and transparent spacer images that maintain the structural integrity of tables across all browsers.

Although they share the same underlying HTML structure, tables and cells created in Layout view differ from those created in Standard view in the following ways:

- ✦ Borders are set to zero and, thus, turned off.
- ✦ Cell padding and cell spacing are also set to zero to enable content to appear directly next to each other.
- ✦ Layout tables optionally include a row for each column that holds a one pixel high transparent GIF image called a spacer.
- ✦ Columns in a layout table are set to either a fixed pixel width or designed to automatically stretch to the full width of the page.

In addition to these physical differences, Layout view has a different appearance. Each layout table is marked with a tab and the column width is identified at the top of each column as shown in Figure 8-19.

Dreamweaver puts the entrance to Layout view right up front on the Objects panel. At the bottom of the panel, two new areas have been added for Dreamweaver 4. To switch modes, click the Layout View button; to return to the traditional mode, select the Standard View button. If the Objects panel is not open, use the menu by choosing View ➪ Table View ➪ Layout View or the keyboard shortcut Ctrl+F6 (Command+F6). Once Layout view has been enabled, two buttons above the view modes become active: Draw Cell and Draw Table.

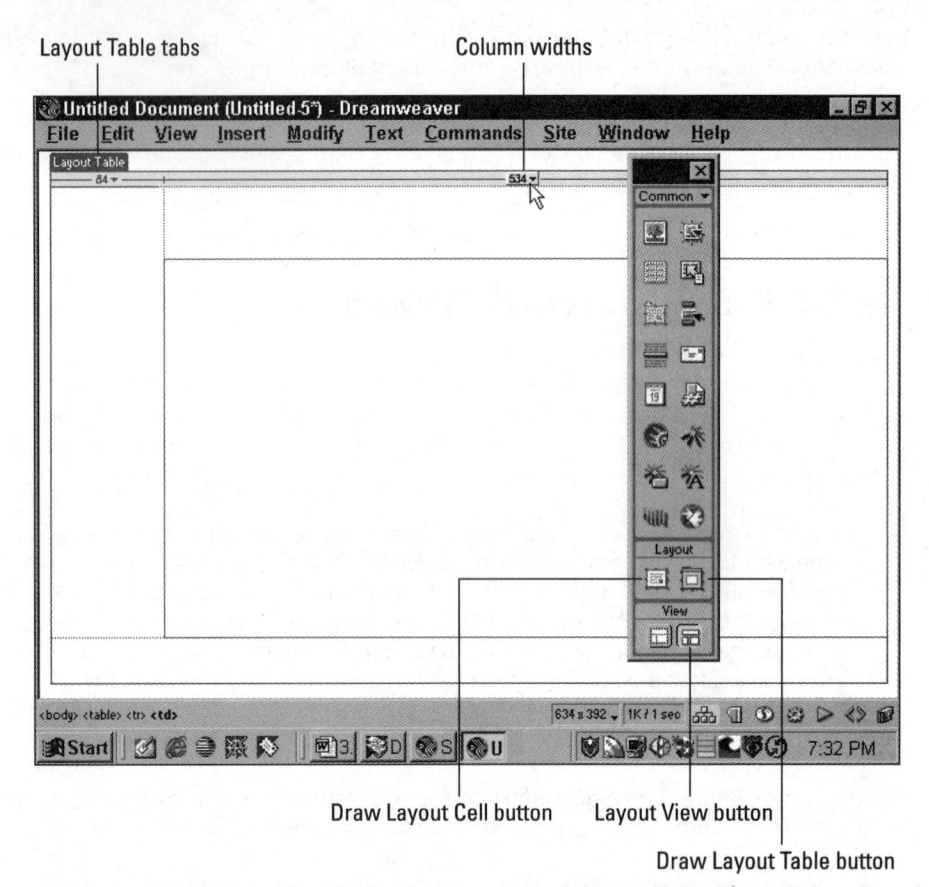

[Screenshot of Dreamweaver Layout view with labels: Layout Table tabs, Column widths, Draw Layout Cell button, Layout View button, Draw Layout Table button]

Figure 8-19: In Layout view, tables and columns are immediately identifiable and extremely flexible.

> **Note:** By the way, don't fret about your existing pages: they'll show up just fine in Layout view. In fact, looking at a well-designed legacy page in Layout view is very helpful to understanding how the pages of a professional Web designer are built.

Drawing cells and tables

Although you can use the Layout view to modify the structure of existing pages, this mode is best when designing Web pages from the ground-up. The Draw Cell and Draw Table commands enable you to quickly layout the basic structure of your page by defining the key document areas. For example, with just four mouse moves in Layout view, I could design a page with sections for a logo, a navigation bar, a copyright notice, and a primary content area. Now I'm ready to fill out the design with graphics, text, and other assets.

Here's how it works:

1. On a blank page, choose the Layout View button from the bottom of the Objects panel.

   When you first enter Layout view, Dreamweaver displays a help screen to explain how the new feature works. After you get the hang of working in Layout view, feel free to select the Don't Show Me This Message Again option to prevent further appearances of the dialog box.

2. Select the Draw Cell button, directly above the View modes. The cursor changes to a plus (+) sign.

   Although it may seem backwards, it's best to initially use the Draw Cells rather than Draw Table. Dreamweaver automatically creates the HTML table necessary to hold any cells you draw, resulting in less tables and tighter code. The Draw Table command is best used to make a nested table.

3. Move your cursor anywhere on the page and drag out a layout cell, as shown in Figure 8-20.

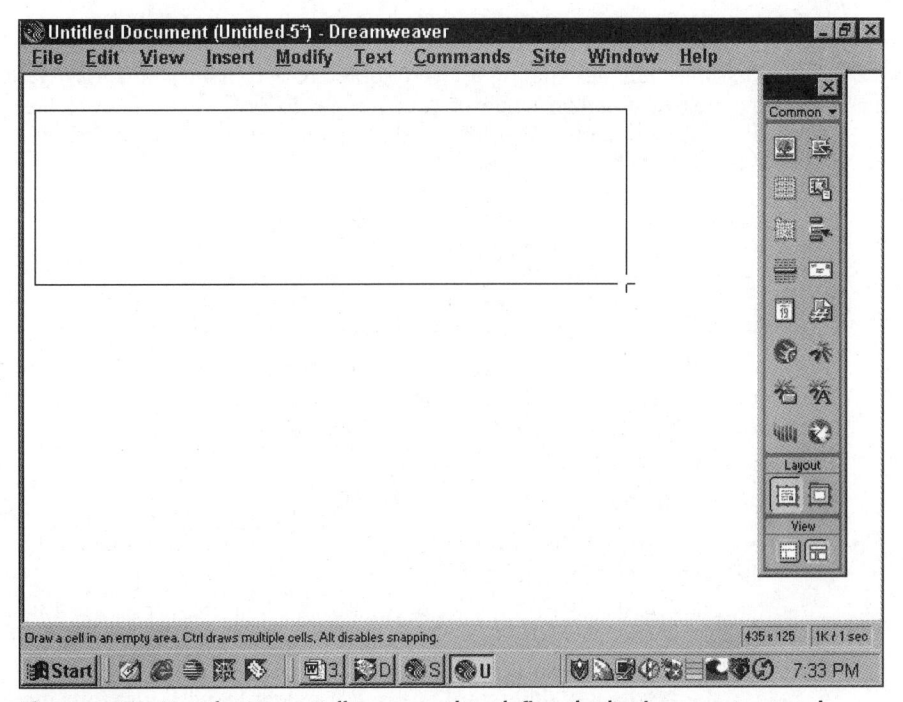

Figure 8-20: Use the Draw Cell command to define the basic page structure in Layout view.

Dreamweaver creates a table around the cell; the cell is drawn in the current background color with the surrounding table shown in white. When the mouse moves over it, the outline of a layout cell highlights in red, and turns blue when selected; likewise a Layout table's outline is green. These colors can be user-defined in Preferences.

> **Tip** If you're within eight pixels of the edge of the Document window or another layout cell, the border of the new layout cell snaps to that edge. Press the Alt (Option) key when drawing a layout cell to temporarily disable snapping.

4. Repeat Step 3 until your layout is complete.

   Dreamweaver drops out of Draw Cell mode after your first cell is created to prevent unintentional cells. To create several layout cells in a row, hold down Ctrl (Command) while dragging.

As indicated earlier, the Draw Table command is best suited for creating nested tables. A table is said to be nested when it is placed within an existing table. Nested tables are useful when a design requires that a number of elements, for example, a picture and a related caption, remain stationary in relation to one another while text on the page flows according to the size of the browser window.

> **Tip** While the tabs designating a layout table are very handy, you may want to turn them off at a certain stage of your design. To hide them, choose View ➪ Table View ➪ Show Layout Table Tabs to disable the option. Select the command again to bring them back into view.

To create a nested table in Layout view, follow these steps:

1. Choose the Layout View button on the Objects panel.
2. Select the Draw Layout Table button, also from the Objects panel.
3. When the cursor is over an area of the table unoccupied by a layout cell, the cursor changes to a plus (+) sign and a layout table can be dragged out. When not over a valid area, the cursor is shown as a slashed circle — the universal sign for "not allowed."

   The new layout table is inserted as shown in Figure 8-21.

4. To divide the nested layout table into multiple areas, choose the Draw Cell button to drag out new cells.
5. As with the Draw Cell command, the Draw Table command defaults to dragging one table at a time. To draw several tables in a row, select Ctrl (Command) while dragging out a layout table.

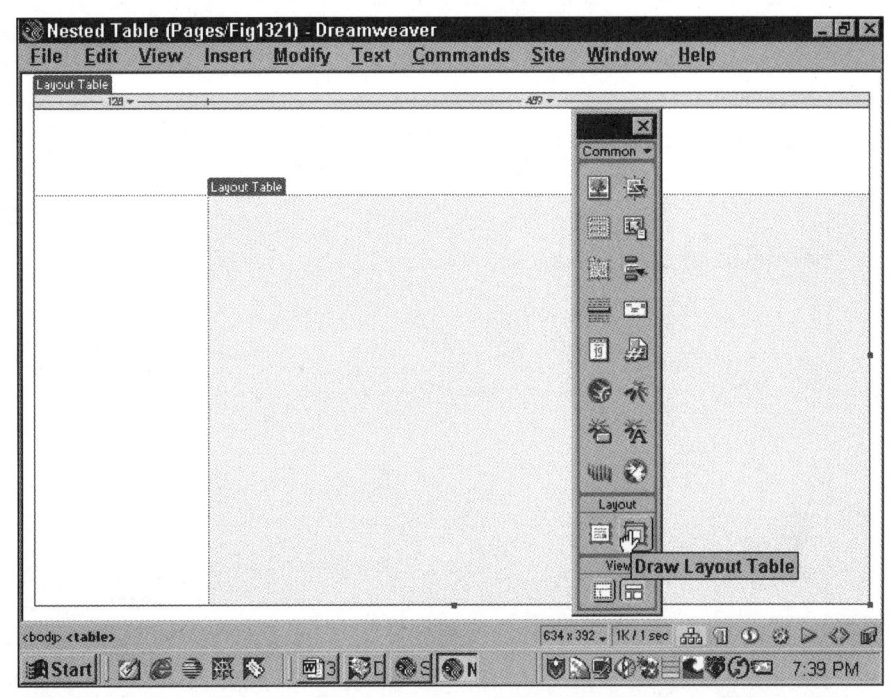

Figure 8-21: Nested tables are easily added with the Draw Layout Table command.

While the Layout view is an excellent method for quickly structuring a page, there are some limitations you should be aware of:

✦ Layout tables and cells can only be drawn in the area of the Document window that does not have any code associated with it. In other words, you need to draw cells and tables below the apparent end of the document. The result is that the new table code is placed right before the closing body tag.

✦ Two objects are disabled in Layout view: the Standard Table and the Layer objects. To add either of these objects to the page, you need to return to Standard view.

✦ Layout cells and tables cannot be copied, cut, or pasted. These operations are available from the Standard view, however.

It's worthwhile to note that the Layout view works exceedingly well with Dreamweaver's Grid feature. With the Grid showing (View ⇨ Grid ⇨ Show Grid) and Snap to Grid enabled (View ⇨ Grid ⇨ Snap to Grid), precisely laying out cells and tables is quite literally a snap. With Dreamweaver's Layout view, complex but useful designs, such as the one shown in Figure 8-22, are within reach.

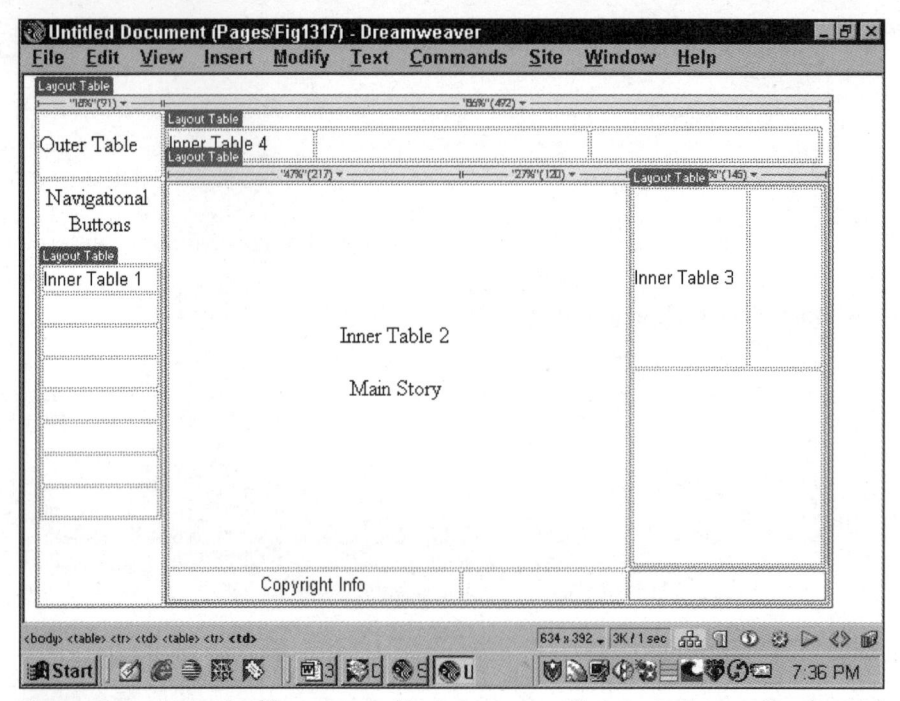

Figure 8-22: Nested tables — created in Dreamweaver's Layout view — offer the Web designer tighter command of Web page elements.

Modifying layouts

Layout view is not only a boon for creating the initial page design, but it also makes the inevitable modifications more straightforward. Cells are positionable within a layout table much the same as layers on a page. However, one difference exists; cells, unlike layers, cannot overlap. Resizing layout cells and tables is also easier. Unlike in Standard view where any table or cell border is draggable, in Layout view cells and tables have sizing handles — much the same as a selected image.

To easily manipulate layout and cells, they have to be easily selectable. Dreamweaver handles that chore with colorful flair. Pass your cursor over any layout cell, when you pass the border of a cell it changes from blue to red. Click once on the red highlight and the cell is selected. A selected cell is notable by the eight sizing handles placed on its perimeter. Once a cell is selected, the Property Inspector displays the available attributes.

Tip To select a cell without moving the cursor over the border, Ctrl+click (Command+click) anywhere in the cell.

The Layout Cell Property Inspector (see Figure 8-23) offers six key attributes:

- **Width:** Enter a pixel value for a Fixed cell width or select the Autostretch option to enable the cell to grow as needed. (Autostretch is covered in the next section.) The width of each cell is shown on top of each column in Layout view. The column width property is an important one and is explained in greater detail later in this section.

- **Height:** Enter a pixel value for cell height. Percentages cannot be entered in Layout view.

- **Horz:** Select a horizontal alignment for the cell's content; the options are Default, Left, Center, and Right.

- **No Wrap:** When enabled, this option keeps content — text and images — from wrapping to the next line, which, if the column is in Autostretch mode, may alter the width of the cell.

- **Bg:** Choose a background color for the cell.

- **Vert:** Choose a vertical alignment for the cell's content; the options are Default, Top, Middle, Bottom, and Baseline.

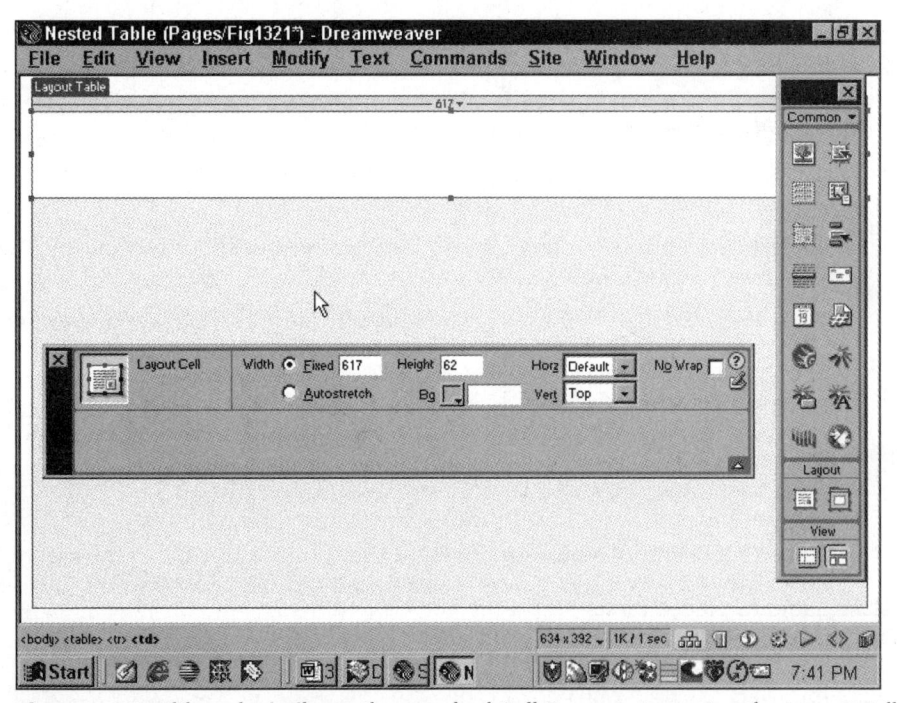

Figure 8-23: Although similar to the standard Cell Property Inspector, the Layout Cell Property Inspector offers a different set of options.

Note Not all the attributes of a table cell are available through the Layout cell Property Inspector. To add a background image, specify a border color, designate it as a header cell or split the cell, you need to switch to Standard view.

To reshape or resize a layout cell, drag any one of the sizing handles on the cell's border into the unused area of a table. Likewise, you can drag a cell into any open table area, for example, any area of the table unoccupied by another cell.

Tip To maintain the width-height ratio of a cell, press Shift when resizing.

Tables may be similarly selected and resized. Layout tables are selected by clicking the title bar marking the table, or by clicking inside an open, gray-colored area within the table or on the table border. If the layout table is nested within another table, it can be dragged to a new location within the outer table. Non-nested tables cannot be dragged to a new location on the page, however.

Once a layout table is selected, the attributes in the Property Inspector become available as shown in Figure 8-24. These attributes include:

+ **Width:** Enter a pixel value for a Fixed table width or select the Autostretch option to enable the table to grow as needed. (Autostretch is discussed in the next section.)
+ **Height:** Enter a pixel value for table height. Percentages cannot be entered in Layout view.
+ **CellPad:** Controls the amount of space between the content and the cell border throughout the table. The default value is zero.
+ **CellSpace:** Controls the amount of space between cells throughout the table. The default value is zero.
+ **Clear Row Heights:** Removes any set height values for all rows and reduces the table to existing content.

Caution When the Clear Row Heights option is used with nested tables, Dreamweaver doesn't redraw the cell border to match the table border — in other words, the cell height is not cleared. To correct, drag the bottom cell border to match that of the table.

+ **Make Cell Widths Consistent:** Reduces the width of all cells to the size of their respective content. If a cell is stretched beyond its original fixed size by an image or some text, the column header of the layout cell shows the fixed size next to the actual size in parenthesis. Choosing Make Cell Widths Consistent adjusts the fixed size to match the actual size.
+ **Remove All Spacers:** Choosing this option deletes all single pixel images used to ensure browser compatibility for layout tables and their corresponding rows. Spacers are discussed in detail in a later section.
+ **Remove Nesting:** Converts a nested table to rows and cells of the outer table.

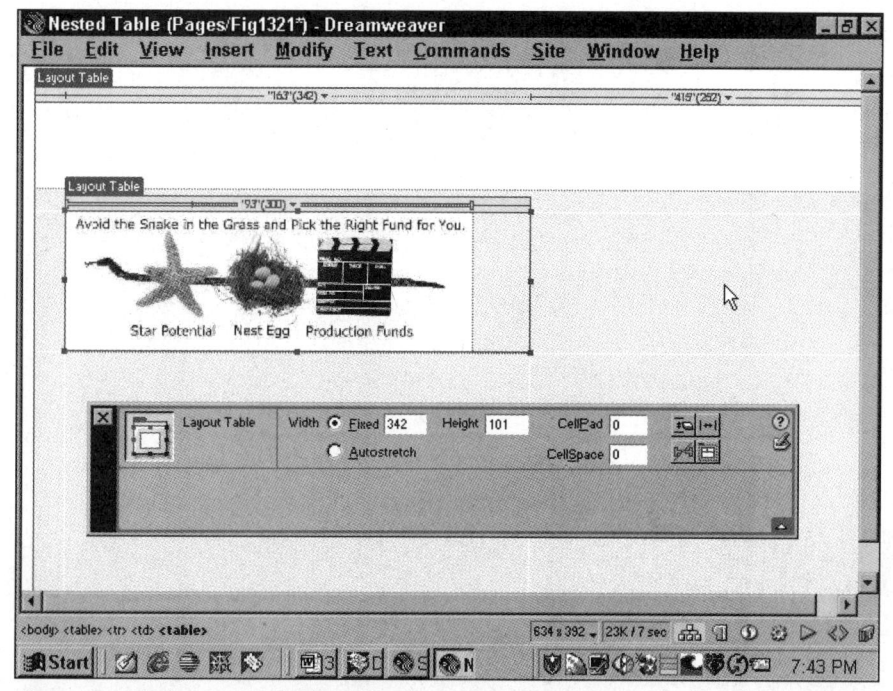

Figure 8-24: The Layout Table Property Inspector includes important options for converting nested tables and sizing cells to fit existing content.

Altering column widths

The table elements in Layout view borrow a couple of pages from the professional Web designer's playbook. First, any column can easily be converted from a fixed width to a flexible width — in Dreamweaver this is known as *autostretch*. Second, when the autostretch option is chosen for a layout table, Dreamweaver inserts a spacer (a single-pixel high transparent GIF) in a new row along the bottom of the table. The spacer is sized to match the fixed width of each of the columns except for one — which is designated as an autostretch column. For a table to use the Autostretch option, one column must be flexible.

You can alter the width of a column in a number of ways:

+ Visually, select the cell and then drag a sizing handle to a new position.

+ For pixel precise width, use the Layout Cell Property Inspector and enter the desired size in the Width field. If the cell is currently in Autostretch mode, select the Fixed Width option to enable the value field.

+ To convert an Autostretch column to its current on-screen pixel width, choose Make Column Fixed Width from the column header menu as shown in Figure 8-25.

- To make a fixed width column automatically stretch, choose Make Column Autostretch from the column header menu.
- Insert content wider than the set width and then choose Make Column Width Consistent from the Layout Table Property Inspector.

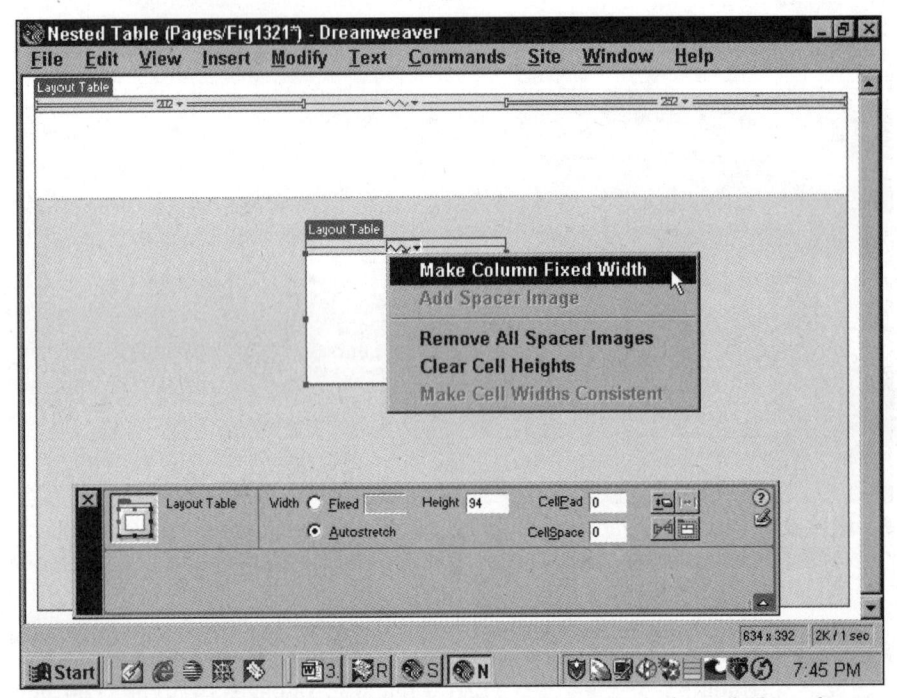

Figure 8-25: The switch between fixed width and autostretch through the column header menu.

Working with the spacer image

If you've ever painstakingly created a complex table only to find that it looks great in one browser but collapses into an unidentifiable mess in another, you're going to love spacer images. Long used by Web site designers as a method of ensuring a table's stability, a spacer image is simply an image — usually a single-pixel transparent GIF — that is resized to match the width of a column. Because no browser collapses a column smaller than the size of the largest image it contains, spacer images retain a table's design under any circumstance.

Dreamweaver gives you several options when working with spacer images:

- You can have Dreamweaver create a spacer image for you.
- You can use an existing image as a spacer image.
- You can opt to never include spacer images.

The first time Autostretch is applied as an option in a table, Dreamweaver displays a dialog box (see Figure 8-26) that enables you to create or locate a spacer image. If you choose to create a new spacer image, you are then asked to select a location in the current site to store it. Generally you would save such a file in an images, assets, or media folder.

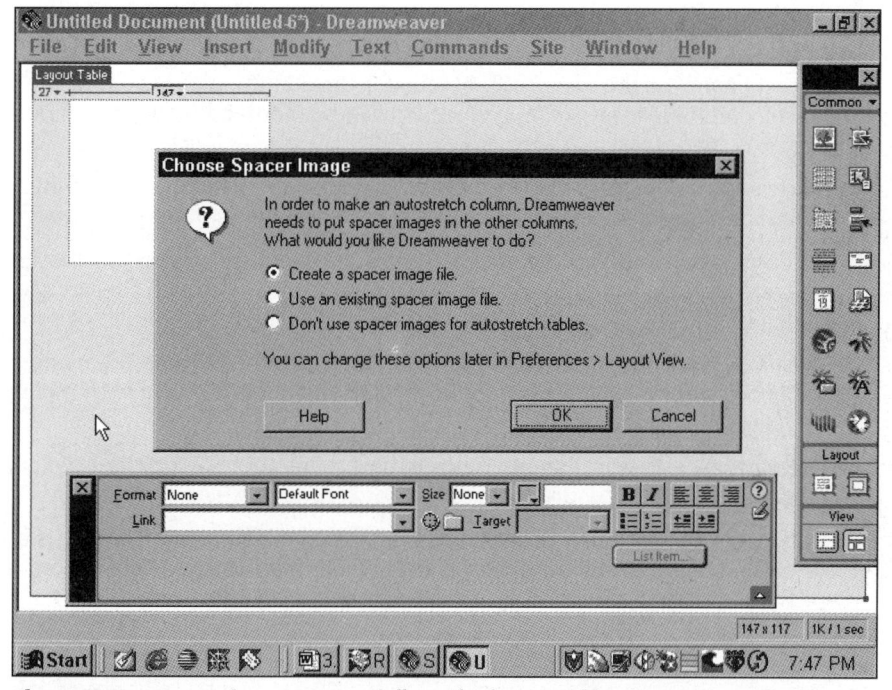

Figure 8-26: Spacer images essentially make layout tables browser-proof and Dreamweaver can either create one for you or enable you to use an existing image.

This image is then automatically inserted whenever an autostretch table or cell is created. One reason to use an existing image rather than a new one is if you work with sliced tables from Fireworks. Fireworks creates a single-pixel GIF image titled spacer.gif. The choice of a spacer image is a sitewide preference that can be viewed or changed by selecting the Layout View category of Preferences. Although it's not a commonly recommended practice, the Layout View category is also where you can disable spacer images.

Summary

Tables are an extremely powerful Web page design tool. Dreamweaver enables you to modify both the appearance and the structure of your HTML tables through a combination of Property Inspectors, dialog boxes, and click-and-drag mouse movements. Mastering tables is an essential task for any modern Web designer and worth the somewhat challenging learning curve. The key elements to keep in mind are as follows:

- ✦ An HTML table consists of a series of rows and columns presented in a grid-like arrangement. Tables can be sized absolutely, in pixels, or relative to the width of the browser's window, in a percentage.

- ✦ Dreamweaver inserts a table whose dimensions can be altered through the Objects panel or the Insert ⇨ Table menu. Once in the page, the table needs to be selected before any of its properties can be modified through the Table Property Inspector.

- ✦ Table editing is greatly simplified in Dreamweaver. You can select multiple cells, columns, or rows — and modify all their contents in one fell swoop.

- ✦ You can assign certain properties — such as background color, border color, and alignment — for a table's columns, rows, or cells through their respective dialog boxes. A cell's properties override those set for its column or row.

- ✦ Dreamweaver brings power to table building with the Format Table and Sort Table commands as well as a connection to the outside world with its Import Tabular Data option.

- ✦ Dreamweaver 4's new Layout view enables you to quickly prepare the basic structure of a page by drawing out layout cells and tables.

- ✦ Putting a table within another table — also known as *nesting tables* — is a powerful (and legal) design option in HTML. Nested tables are easily accomplished in Dreamweaver's Layout view by inserting a layout table.

✦ ✦ ✦

Interactive Forms

CHAPTER 9

In This Chapter

Forms overview

Including forms in your Web page

Using text fields and text areas

Enabling options with radio buttons, checkboxes, and drop-down lists

Building a jump menu

Incorporating buttons in your form

Adding hidden fields and password fields

A form, in the everyday world as well as on the Web, is a type of structured communication. When you apply for a driver's license, you're not told to just write down all your personal information, you're asked to fill out a form that asks for specific parts of that information, one at a time, in a specific manner. Web-based forms are just as precise, if not more so.

Dreamweaver has a robust and superior implementation of HTML forms — from the dedicated Forms category in the Objects panel to various form-specific Property Inspectors. In addition to their importance as a tool for communication between the browsing public and Web site administrators, forms are integral to building some of Dreamweaver's own objects.

In this chapter, you learn how forms are structured and then created within Dreamweaver. Each form object is explored in detail — text fields, radio buttons, checkboxes, menus, list boxes, command buttons, hidden fields, and password fields.

How HTML Forms Work

Forms have a special function in HTML: They support interaction. Virtually all HTML elements apart from forms are concerned with design and presentation — delivering the content to the user, if you will. Forms, on the other hand, give the user the ability to pass information back to Web site creators and administrators. Without forms, the Web would be a one-way street.

Forms have many, many uses on the Web, such as for surveys, electronic commerce, guest books, polls, and even real-time custom graphics creation. For such feedback to be possible, forms require an additional component to what's seen onscreen so that each form can complete its function. Every form needs some type of connection to a Web server, and usually this connection uses a *common gateway interface (CGI)* script, although JavaScript and Java can also be used. This means that, in addition to designing your forms onscreen, you or someone who works with you must implement a program that collects and manages the information from the form.

Forms, like HTML tables, can be thought of as self-contained units within a Web page. All the elements of a form are contained within the form tag pair `<form>` and `</form>`. Unlike tables, you cannot nest forms, although there's nothing to stop you from having multiple forms on a page.

The `<form>` tag has three attributes, only two of which (method and action) are commonly used:

- The `method` attribute tells the server how the contents of the form should be presented to the CGI program. The two possible `method` values are `get` and `post`. `Get` passes the attached information to a URL; it is rarely used these days because it places limitations on the amount of data that can be passed to the gateway program. `Post` causes the server to present the information as standard input and imposes no limits on the amount of passed data.

- The second `<form>` attribute is `action`. The `action` attribute determines what should be done with the form content. Most commonly, `action` is set to a URL for running a specific CGI program or for sending e-mail.

- The third attribute for `<form>` is `enctype`, which specifies the MIME media type. It is used infrequently.

Typical HTML for a `<form>` tag looks something like this:

```
<form method="post" action="http://www.idest.com/_cgi-bin/mailcall.pl">
```

Tip The .pl extension in the preceding example form tag stands for *Perl* — a scripting language often used to create CGI programs. Perl can be edited in any regular text editor.

Within each form is a series of input devices — text boxes, radio buttons, checkboxes, and so on. Each type handles a particular sort of input; in fact, the main tag for these elements is the `<input>` tag. With one exception, the `<textarea>` tag, all form input types are called by specifying the `type` attribute. The text box tag, for example, is written as follows:

```
<input type=text value="lastname">
```

All form input tags have `value` attributes. Information input by the user is assigned to the given value. Thus, if I were to fill out a form with a text box asking for my last name, such as the one produced by the foregoing tag, part of the message sent would include the following string:

```
lastname=Lowery
```

Web servers send all the information from a form in one long text string to whatever program or address is specified in the `action` attribute. It's up to the program or the recipient of the form message to parse the string. For instance, if I were to fill out a small form with my name, e-mail address, and a quick comment such as "Good work!" the server would send a text string similar to the following:

name=Joseph+Lowery&address=jlowery@idest.com&comment=Good+work%21

As you can see, the various fields are separated by ampersands, and the individual words within the responses are separated by plus signs. Characters outside of the lower end of the ASCII set — like the exclamation mark in the example — are represented by their hexadecimal values. Decoding this text string is called *parsing the response.*

> **Tip** If you're not using the mailto method for getting your Web feedback, don't despair. Most CGI programs parse the text string as part of their basic functionality before sending it on its way.

Inserting a Form in Dreamweaver

A form is inserted just like any other object in Dreamweaver. Place the cursor where you want your form to start and then either select the Insert Form button from the Forms category of the Objects panel or choose Insert ⇨ Form from the menus. Dreamweaver inserts a red dashed outline stretching across the Document window to indicate the form.

If you have the Property Inspector open, the Form Property Inspector appears when you insert a form. As you can see from Figure 9-1, you can specify only three values regarding forms: the Form Name, the Action, and the Method.

Specifying a form name enables the form to be directly referenced by JavaScript or other languages. Because of the interactive nature of forms, Web programmers often use this feature to gather information from the user.

In the Action text box, you can directly enter a URL or mailto address, or you can select the folder icon and browse for a file.

> **Note** Sending your form data via a mailto address is not without its problems. Some browsers, most notably Internet Explorer, are set to warn the user whenever a form button using mailto is selected. While many users let the mail go through, they do have the option to stop it from being sent.

The Method defaults to POST, the most commonly used option. You can also choose GET or DEFAULT, which leaves the method up to the browser. In most cases, you should leave the method set to POST.

Part I ✦ Working with Dreamweaver

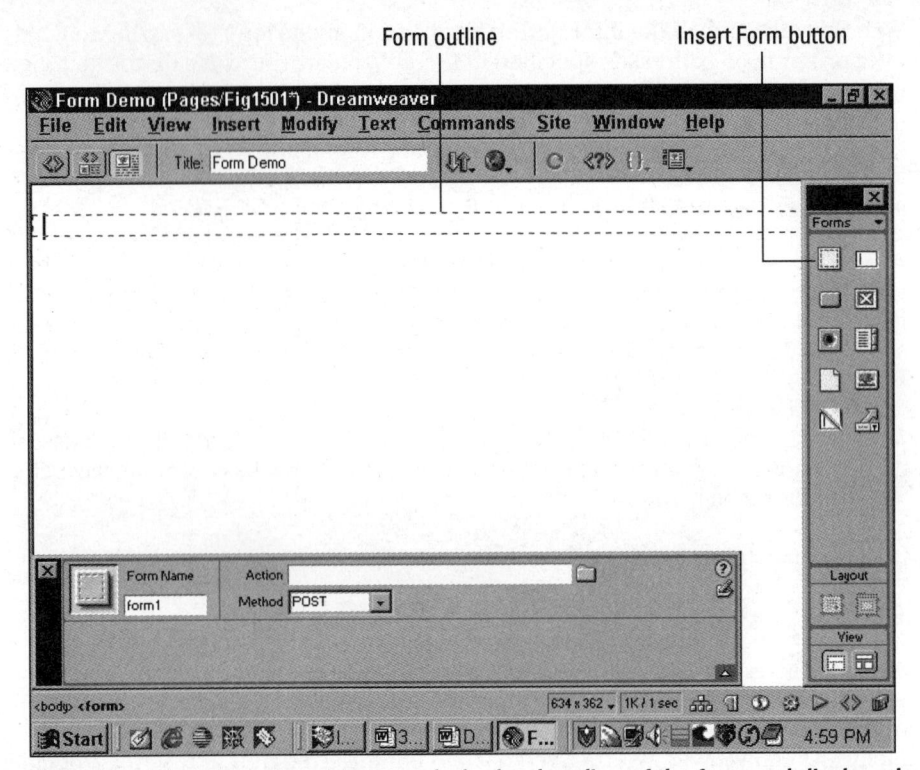

Figure 9-1: Inserting a form creates a dashed red outline of the form and displays the Form Property Inspector, if available.

> **Note:** Forms cannot be placed inline with any other element such as text or graphics.

Keep in mind a few considerations when it comes to mixing forms and other Web page elements:

✦ Forms expand as objects are inserted into them; you can't resize a form by dragging its boundaries.

✦ The outline of a form is invisible; there is no border to turn on or off.

✦ Forms and tables can be used together only if the form either completely encloses or is completely enclosed inside the table. In other words, you can't have a form spanning part of a table.

✦ Forms can be inserted within layers, and multiple forms can be in multiple layers. However, the layer must completely enclose the form. As with forms spanning tables, you can't have a form spanning two or more layers. (A workaround for this limitation is discussed in Chapter 15.)

> **Declaring the Enctype**
>
> The `<form>` attribute `enctype` is helpful in formatting material returned via a form. Enctype can have three possible values. By default `enctype` is set to `application/x-www-form-urlencoded`, which is responsible for encoding the form response with ampersands between entries, equal signs linking form element names to their values, spaces as plus signs, and all nonalphanumeric characters in hexadecimal, such as `%3F` (a question mark).
>
> The second `enctype` value, `text/plain`, is useful for e-mail replies. Instead of one long string, your form data is transmitted in a more readable format with each form element and its value on a separate line as in this example:
>
> ```
> fname=Joseph
> lname=Lowery
> email=jlowery@idest.com
> comment=Please send me the information on your new products!
> ```
>
> The final `enctype` value, `multipart/form-data`, is used only when a file is being uploaded as part of the form. There's a further restriction: The Method should be set to POST, instead of GET.
>
> Dreamweaver doesn't include a space on the Form Property Inspector for the `enctype` attribute, so you have to add it manually either through the HTML Source Inspector or the Quick Tag Editor. To use the Quick Tag Editor, select the `<form>` tag in the Tag Selector and press Ctrl+T (Command+T). Tab to the end of the tag and enter `enctype="value"`, substituting one of the three possible values.

Tip You can turn off the red dashed form outline in Dreamweaver's preview, if you like. Choose Edit ⇨ Preferences and, in the Invisible Elements category, deselect the Form Delimiter option.

Using Text Boxes

Anytime you use a form to gather text information typed in by a user, you use a form object called a *text field*. Text fields can hold any number of alphanumeric characters. The Web designer can decide whether the text field is displayed in one line or several. When the HTML is written, a multiple-line text field uses a `<textarea>` tag, and a single-line text field is coded with `<input type=text>`.

Text fields

To insert a single-line text field in Dreamweaver, you can use any of the following methods:

- From the Forms category of the Objects panel, select the Insert Text Field button to place a text field at your current cursor position.
- Choose Insert ⇨ Form Objects ⇨ Text Field from the menu, which inserts a text field at the current cursor position.
- Drag the Insert Text Field button from the Objects panel to any existing location in the Document window and release the mouse button to position the text field.

When you insert a text field, the Property Inspector, when displayed, shows you the attributes that can be changed (see Figure 9-2). The size of a text field is measured by the number of characters it can display at one time. You can change the length of a text field by inserting a value in the Char Width text box. By default, Dreamweaver inserts a text field approximately 20 characters wide. The *approximately* is important here because the *final* size of the text field is ultimately controlled by the browser used to view the page. Unless you limit the number of possible characters by entering a value in the Max Chars text box, the user can enter as many characters as desired, and the text box scrolls to display them.

Note that the value in Char Width determines the visible width of the field, whereas the value in Max Chars actually determines the number of characters that can be entered.

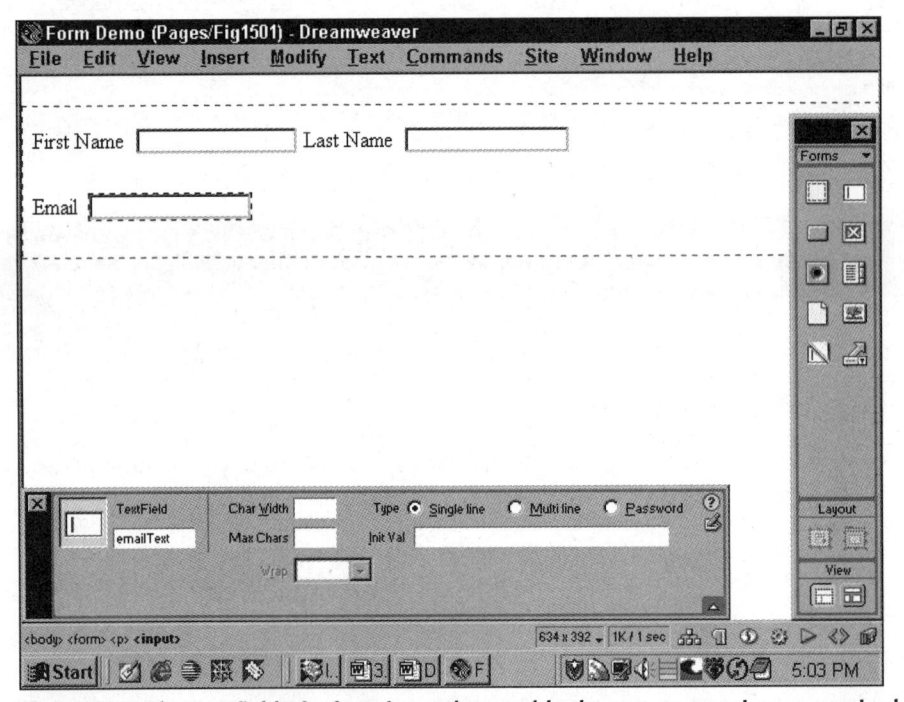

Figure 9-2: The text field of a form is used to enable the user to type in any required information.

Neat Forms

Text field width is measured in a monospaced character width. Because regular fonts are not monospaced, however, lining up text fields and other form objects can be problematic at best. The two general workarounds are preformatted text and tables.

Switching the labels on the form to preformatted text enables you to insert any amount of white space to properly space (or *kern*) your text and other input fields. Previously, Web designers were stuck with the default preformatted text format — the rather plain-looking Courier monospaced font. Now, however, newer browsers (3.0 and later) can read the `face=fontname` attribute. So you can combine a regular font with the preformatted text option and get the best of both worlds.

Going the preformatted text route requires you to insert a lot of spaces. So when you are working on a larger, complex form, using tables is probably a better way to go. Besides the speed of layout, the other advantage that tables offer is the capability to right-align text labels next to your text fields. The top form in the following figure gives an example of using preformatted text to get different-sized form fields to line up properly, while the bottom form in the figure uses a table.

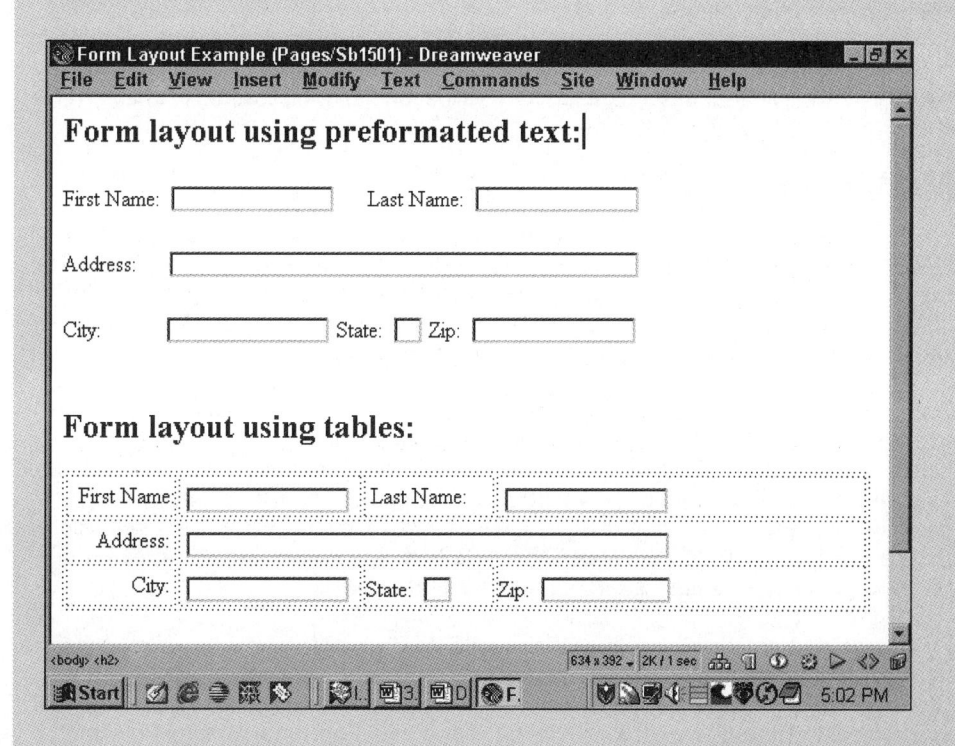

Combining differently sized text fields on a single row — for example, when you're asking for a city, state, and zip code combination — can make the task of lining up your form even more difficult. Most often, you'll spend a fair amount of time in a trial-and-error effort to make the text fields match. Be sure to check your results in the various browsers as you build your form.

The Init Value text box on the Text Field Property Inspector is used to insert a default text string. The user can overwrite this value, if desired.

Password fields

Generally, all text entered into text fields displays as you expect — programmers refer to this process as *echoing*. You can turn off the echoing by selecting the Password option in the Text Field Property Inspector. When a text field is designated as a password field, all text entered by the user shows up as asterisks in Windows systems or as dots on Macintoshes.

Use the password field when you want to protect the user's input from prying eyes (as your PIN number is hidden when you enter it at an ATM, for instance). The information entered in a password field is not encrypted or scrambled in any way, and when sent to the Web administrator, it displays as regular text.

Only single-line text fields can be set as password fields. You cannot make a multiline `<textarea>` tag act as a password field without employing JavaScript or some other programming language.

> **Cross-Reference:** Making sure that your user fills out the form properly is called validating the input. Dreamweaver includes a standard form validation behavior, covered in Chapter 11.

Multiline text areas

When you want to give your users a generous amount of room to write, set the text field to the Multiline option on the Text Field Property Inspector. This converts the default 20-character width for single-line text fields to a text area approximately 18 characters wide and 3 lines high, with a horizontal and vertical scroll bar. Figure 9-3 shows a typical multiline text field embedded in a form.

You control the width of a multiline text area by entering a value in the Char Width text box of the Text Field Property Inspector, just as you do for single-line text fields. The height of the text area is set equal to the value in the Num Lines text box. As with the default single-line text field, the user can enter any amount of text desired. Unlike the single-line text field, which can restrict the number of characters that can be input through the Max Chars text box, you cannot restrict the number of characters the user enters into a multiline text area.

By default, text entered into a multiline text field does not wrap when it reaches the right edge of the text area; rather, it keeps scrolling until the user presses Enter (Return). Dreamweaver 4 enables you to force the text to wrap by selecting Virtual or Physical from the Wrap drop-down list. The Virtual option wraps text on the screen but not when the response is submitted. To wrap text in both situations, use the Physical wrap option.

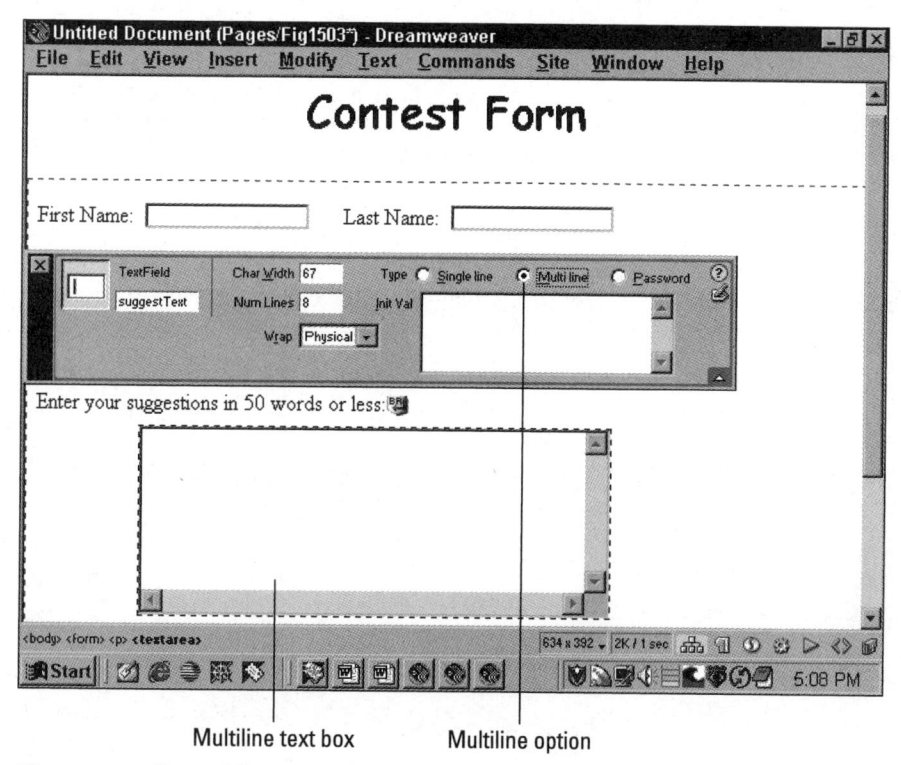

Figure 9-3: The Multiline option of the Text Field Property Inspector opens up a text box for more user information.

One other option is to preload the text area with any default text you like. Enter this text in the Init Val text box of the Text Field Property Inspector. When Dreamweaver writes the HTML code, this text is not entered as a value, as for the single-line text field, but rather goes in between the `<textarea>...</textarea>` tag pair.

Providing Checkboxes and Radio Buttons

When you want your Web page reader to choose between a specific set of options in your form, you can use either checkboxes or radio buttons. Checkboxes enable you to offer a series of options from which the user can pick as many as desired. Radio buttons, on the other hand, enable your user to choose only one selection from a number of options.

> **Tip**
> You can achieve the same functionality as checkboxes and radio buttons with a different look by using the drop-down list and menu boxes. These options for presenting choices to the user are described shortly.

Checkboxes

Checkboxes are often used in a "Select All That Apply" type of section, when you want to enable the user to choose as many of the listed options as desired. You insert a checkbox in much the same way you do a text box: Select or drag the Insert Check Box object from the Objects panel or choose Insert ➪ Form Objects ➪ Check Box.

Like other form objects, checkboxes can be given a unique name in the text box provided in the Check Box Property Inspector (see Figure 9-4). If you don't provide one, Dreamweaver inserts a generic one, such as checkbox4.

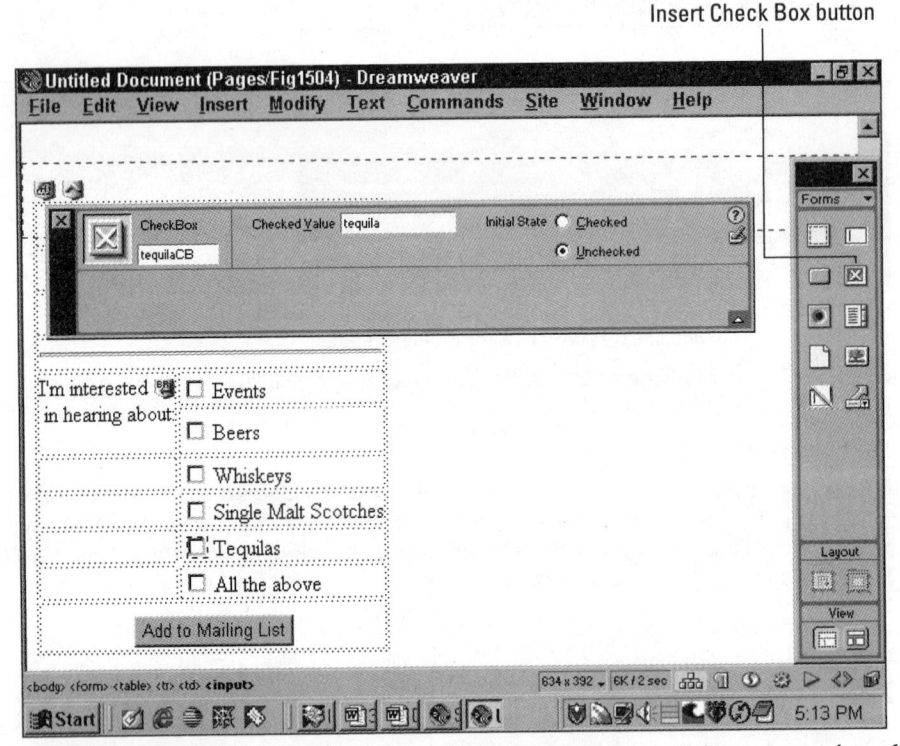

Figure 9-4: Checkboxes are one way of offering the Web page visitor any number of options to choose.

In the Checked Value text box, fill in the information you want passed to a program when the user selects the checkbox. By default, a checkbox starts out unchecked, but you can change that by changing the Initial State option to Checked.

Radio buttons

Radio buttons on a form provide a set of options from which the user can choose only one. If users change their minds after choosing one radio button, selecting another one automatically deselects the first choice. You insert radio buttons in the same manner as checkboxes. Choose or drag Insert Radio Button from the Forms category of the Objects panel, or choose Insert ⇨ Form Objects ⇨ Radio Button.

Unlike checkboxes and text fields, each radio button in the set does not have a unique name — instead, each *group* of radio buttons does. Giving the entire set of radio buttons the same name enables browsers to assign one value to the radio button set. That value is determined by the contents of the Checked Value text box. Figure 9-5 shows two different sets of radio buttons. One is named computersRadio and the other, osRadio.

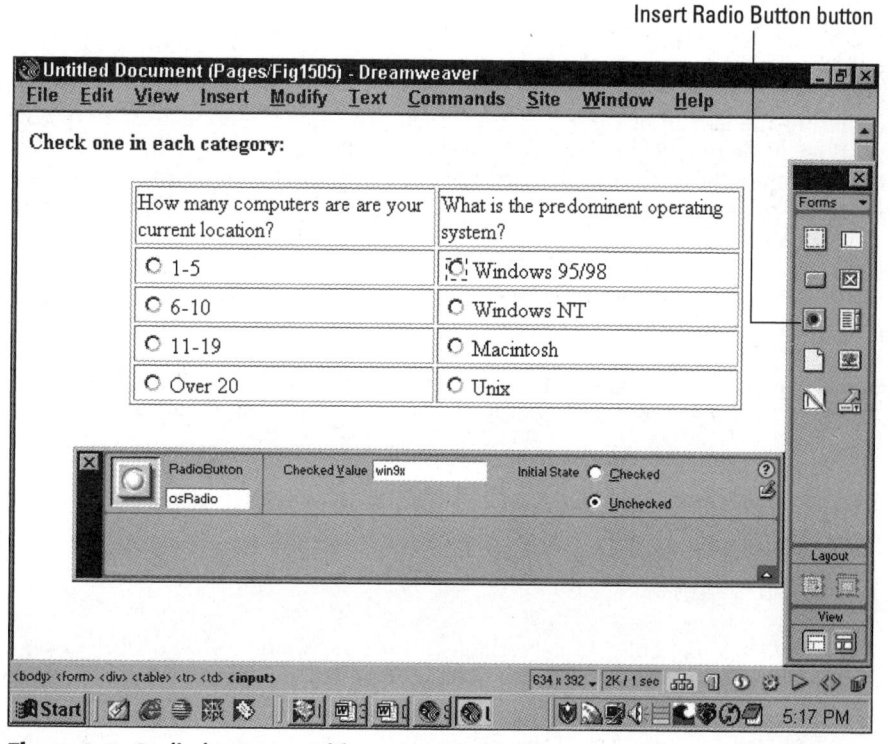

Figure 9-5: Radio buttons enable a user to make just one selection from a group of options.

To designate the default selection for each radio button group, you select the particular radio button and make the Initial State option Checked instead of Unchecked.

Tip: Because you must give radio buttons in the same set the same name, you can speed up your work a bit by creating one button, copying it, and then pasting the others. Don't forget to change the Checked Value for each button, though.

Creating Form Lists and Menus

Another way to offer your user options, in a more compact form than radio buttons and checkboxes, is with form lists and menus. Both objects can create single-line entries in your form that expand or scroll to reveal all the available options. You can also determine how deep you want the scrolling list to be; that is, how many options you want displayed at a time.

Drop-down menus

A drop-down menu should be familiar to everyday users of computers: The menu is initially displayed as a single-line text box with an option arrow button at the right end; when the button is clicked, the other options are revealed in a list or menu. (Whether the list "pops up" or "drops down" depends on its position in the browser window at the time it is selected. Generally, the list drops down, unless it is close to the bottom of the screen.) The user selects one of the listed options, and when the mouse is released, the list closes up and the selected value remains displayed in the text box.

Insert a drop-down menu in Dreamweaver as you would any other form object, with one of these actions:

+ From the Forms category of the Objects panel, select the Insert List/Menu button to place a drop-down menu at the current cursor position.

+ Choose Insert ⇨ Form Objects ⇨ List/Menu from the menu to insert a drop-down menu at the current cursor position.

+ Drag the Insert List/Menu button from the Property Inspector to any location in the Document window and release the mouse button to position the drop-down menu.

With the List/Menu object inserted, make sure the Menu option (not the List option) is selected in the Property Inspector, as shown in Figure 9-6. You can also name the drop-down menu by typing a name in the Name text box; if you don't, Dreamweaver supplies a generic "select" name.

The HTML code for a drop-down menu uses the `<select>...</select>` tag pair surrounding a number of `<option>...</option>` tag pairs. Dreamweaver gives you a straightforward user interface for entering labels and values for the options on your menu. The menu item's *label* is what is displayed on the drop-down list; its *value* is what is sent to the server-side processor when this particular option is selected.

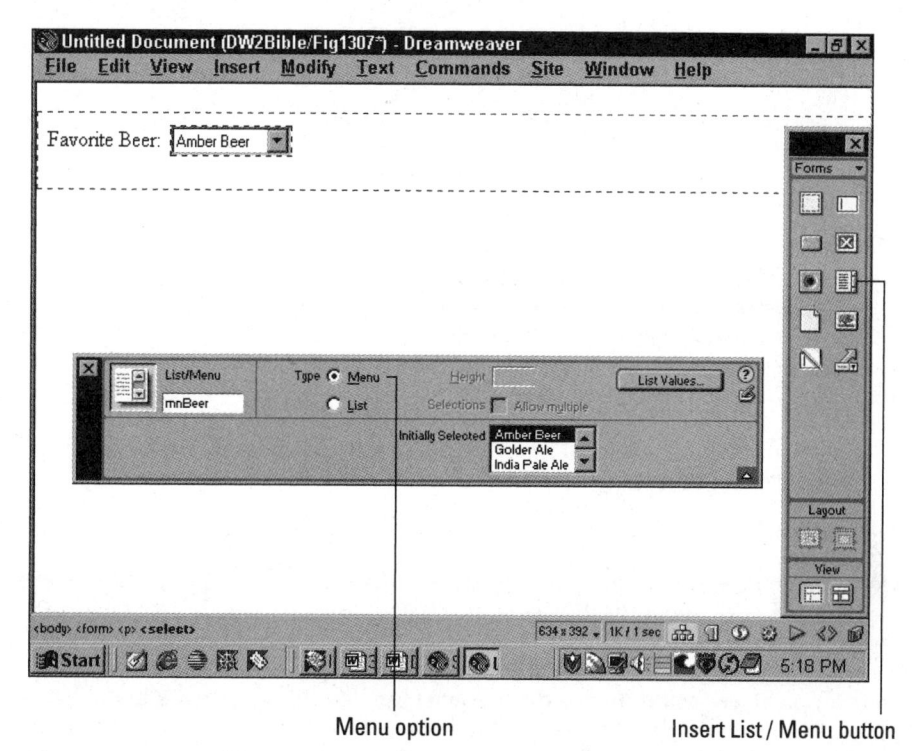

Figure 9-6: Drop-down menus are created by inserting a List/Menu object and then selecting the Menu option in the List/Menu Property Inspector.

To enter the labels and values for a drop-down menu — or for a scrolling list — follow these steps:

1. Select the menu for which you want to enter values.
2. From the List/Menu Property Inspector, select the List Values button. The List Values dialog box appears (see Figure 9-7).
3. In the Item Label column, enter the label for the first item. Press the Tab key to move to the Value column.
4. Enter the value to be associated with this item. Press the Tab key.
5. Continue entering items and values by repeating Steps 3 and 4.
6. To delete an item's label *and* value in the List Values dialog box, highlight it and select the Remove button at the top of the list. To delete either the item's label or value, but not both, highlight either the label or the value and press the Delete or Backspace key.
7. To continue adding items, select the Add button or continue using the Tab key.

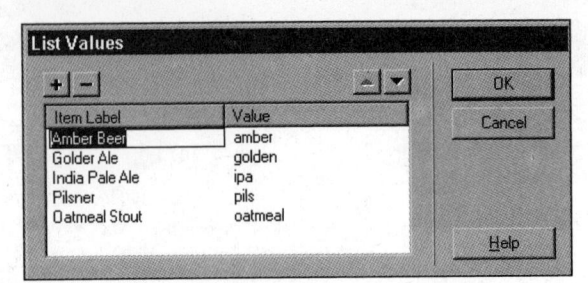

Figure 9-7: Use the List Values dialog box to enter and modify the items in a drop-down menu or scrolling list.

8. To rearrange the order of items in the list, select an item and then press the up- or down-arrow keys to reposition it.

9. Click OK when you've finished.

If you haven't entered a value for every item, the server-side application receives the label instead. Generally, however, it is a good idea to specify a value for all items.

You can preselect any item in a drop-down menu so that it appears in the list box initially and is highlighted when the full list is displayed. Dreamweaver enables you to pick your selection from the Initially Selected menu in the Property Inspector. The Initially Selected menu is empty until you enter items through the List Values dialog box. You can preselect only one item for a drop-down menu.

Scrolling lists

A scrolling list differs from a drop-down menu in three respects. First, and most obviously, the scrolling list field has up- and down-arrow buttons, rather than an option arrow button, and the user can scroll the list, showing as little as one item at a time, instead of the entire list. Second, you can control the height of the scrolling list, enabling it to display more than one item — or all available items — simultaneously. Third, you can enable the user to select more than one item at a time, as with checkboxes.

A scrolling list is inserted in the same manner as a drop-down menu — through the Objects panel or the Insert ⇨ Form Objects menu. Once the object is inserted, select the List option in the List/Menu Property Inspector.

You enter items for your scrolling list just as you do with a drop-down menu, by starting with the List Values button and filling in the List Values dialog box.

As it does for drop-down menus, Dreamweaver automatically shows the first list item in the scrolling list's single-line text box. However, all the list items are displayed in the Document window, as shown in Figure 9-8.

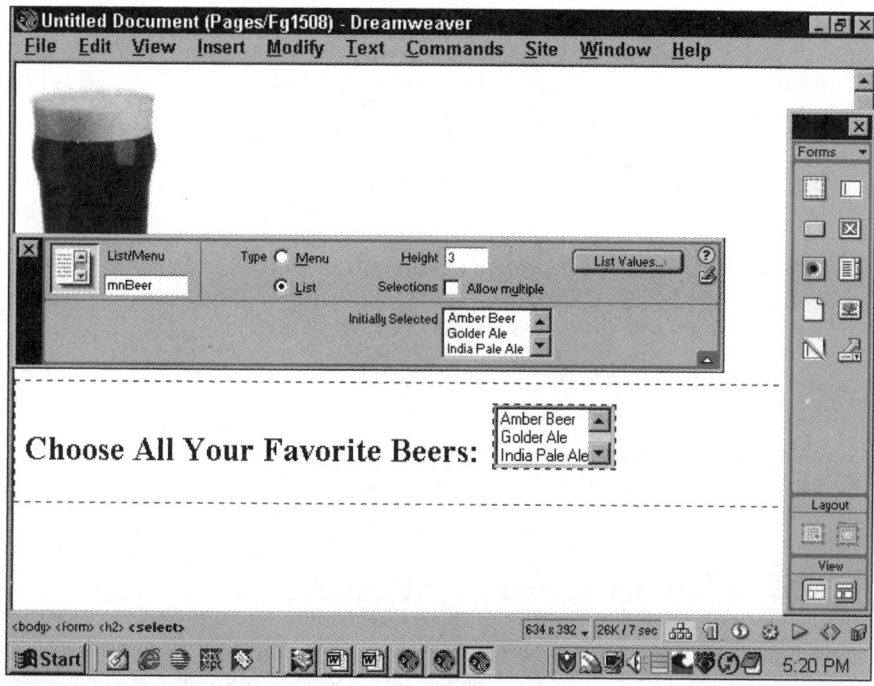

Figure 9-8: Scrolling lists enable multiple selections.

By default, the Selections checkbox for Allow multiple selections is enabled in the List/Menu Property Inspector, and the Height box (which controls the number of items visible at one time) is empty.

When multiple selections are enabled (by selecting the Allow multiple selections checkbox), the user can then make multiple selections by using two keyboard modifiers, the Shift and Control keys:

✦ To select several adjacent items in the list, the user must click the first item in the list, press the Shift key, and select the last item in the list.

✦ To select several nonadjacent items, the user must hold down the Control (Command) key while selecting the items.

Other than the highlighted text, no other acknowledgment (such as a checkmark) appears in the list. As with drop-down menus, the Web designer can preselect options by highlighting them in the Initially Selected menu. Use the same techniques with the Shift and Control (Command) keys as a user would.

Keep in mind several factors as you are working with scrolling lists:

✦ If you disable the Allow multiple selections box and do not set a Height value greater than 1, the list appears as a drop-down menu.

- ✦ If you do not set a Height value at all, the number of items that appear onscreen is left up to the browser. Internet Explorer, by default, shows four items at a time, and Navigator displays all the items in your list. To exercise control over your scrolling list, it is best to insert a Height value.

- ✦ The widths of both the scrolling list and the drop-down menu are determined by the number of characters in the longest label. To widen the List/Menu object, you must directly enter additional spaces ( ) in the HTML code; Dreamweaver does not recognize additional spaces entered through the List Values dialog box. For example, to expand the Favorite Beer List/Menu object in our example, you'd need to switch to Code view, or use the Code Inspector or an external text editor, to change the following code:

```
<option value="oatmeal">Oatmeal Stout</option>
```

to this:

```
<option value="oatmeal">Oatmeal Stout ¬
   </option>
```

Navigating with a Jump Menu

It's not always practical to use a series of buttons as the primary navigation tool on a Web site. For sites that want to offer access to a great number of pages, a *jump menu* can be a better way to go. A jump menu uses the menu form element to list the various options; when one of the options is chosen, the browser loads — or jumps to — a new page. In addition to providing a single mechanism for navigation, a jump menu is easy to update because it doesn't require relaying out the page. Because they are JavaScript-driven, jump menus can even be updated dynamically.

Dreamweaver includes a jump menu object that handles all the JavaScript coding for you — all you have to provide is a list of item names and associated URLs. Dreamweaver even drops in a Go button for you, if you choose. The Jump Menu object is easily used in a frame-based layout for targeting specific frames. Once inserted, the Jump Menu object is modified like any other list object, through the List/Menu Property Inspector.

To insert a jump menu, follow these steps:

1. Position your cursor in the current form, if one exists, where you'd like the jump menu to appear.

    If you haven't already inserted a form, don't worry. Dreamweaver automatically inserts one for you.

2. From the Forms category of the Objects panel, choose the Insert Jump Menu button.

    The Insert Jump Menu dialog box, shown in Figure 9-9, is displayed.

3. In the Insert Jump Menu dialog box, enter the label for the first item in the Text field.

When you confirm your entry by tabbing out of the field, Dreamweaver updates the Menu Items list.

4. Enter the path and filename of the page you want opened for the current item in the When Selected, Go To URL field; alternatively, you can select the Browse (Choose) button to select your file.

5. To add additional jump menu items, select the add (+) button and repeat Steps 3 and 4.

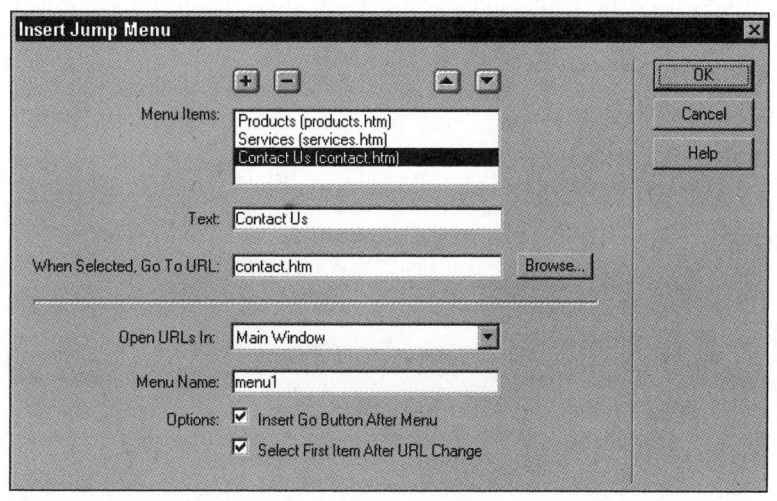

Figure 9-9: Consolidate your Web site navigation through a jump menu.

6. You can adjust the positioning of the items in the jump menu by selecting an item in the Menu List and using the up and down arrows to move it higher or lower.

7. Pick the destination target for the page from the Open URLs In list.

   Unless you're working in a frameset, you have only one option — Main Window. When a Jump Menu object is added in a frameset, Dreamweaver displays all frame names as well as Main Window as options.

Tip The Main Window option always replaces your current page with the new page. If you want to have your new page open in a separate window, and keep your current page active, you'll have to edit the HTML. Select the jump menu object on the page and open the Quick Tag Editor. In the code, locate the onChange event and change "parent" to "_blank." If you're working with a Go button, you need to follow the same procedure with the onClick event of the tag.

8. If desired, enter a unique name for the jump menu in the Menu Name field.

9. To add a button that activates the jump menu choice, select the Insert Go Button After Menu option.

10. To reset the menu selection to the top item after every jump, choose the Select First Item After URL Change.

11. Click OK when you're done.

Dreamweaver inserts the new jump menu with the appropriate linking code.

Modifying a jump menu

Once you've inserted your Jump Menu object, you can modify it in one of two ways: through the standard List/Menu Property Inspector or through the Jump Menu behavior. While the List Property Inspector uses a List Value dialog box, editing the Jump Menu behavior opens a dialog box similar to the one used to insert the jump menu object.

To alter the items in an existing jump menu via the List/Menu Property Inspector, select the jump menu and click the List Values button. In the List Values dialog box, you see the jump menu labels on the left and the URLs on the right. You can add, move, or delete items as you would with any other list.

Wrapping Graphics Around a Jump Menu

Jump menus are useful in many circumstances, but as a raw form element, they often stick out of a Web page design like a sore thumb. Some designers solve this dilemma by including their jump menu within a specially constructed graphic. The easiest way to create such a graphic is to use a program like Fireworks, which enables a single image to be sliced up into separate parts. The slices are then exported to an HTML file and reassembled in a table.

When you create your graphic, you need to leave room for the jump menu to be inserted in Dreamweaver. This usually entails designating one slice as a nongraphic or text-only slice in your graphics program. Fireworks uses a transparent GIF—called a *spacer image*—as a placeholder. Once you bring the HTML into Dreamweaver, delete the spacer image and insert the Jump Menu object in its place. The figure below shows a jump menu wrapped in a graphic.

Here are a few pointers for wrapping a graphic around a jump menu:

✦ Use a flat color—not a gradient—as the background for the menu.

✦ Select the background color of the graphic to be the background color of the cell of the table holding your jump menu.

✦ Make sure you leave enough height in your graphic to accommodate the jump menu in all browsers. Netscape displays a standard list/menu form element approximately 24 pixels high on a PC; I typically leave about 30 pixels in my graphic.

✦ Form elements are drawn by the user's operating system and are vastly different on each platform. Test your designs extensively.

✦ Integrate your Go button, if you're using one, right in the graphic. Be sure to set it as its own slice, so it comes in as a separate image and can be activated with a Jump Menu Go behavior.

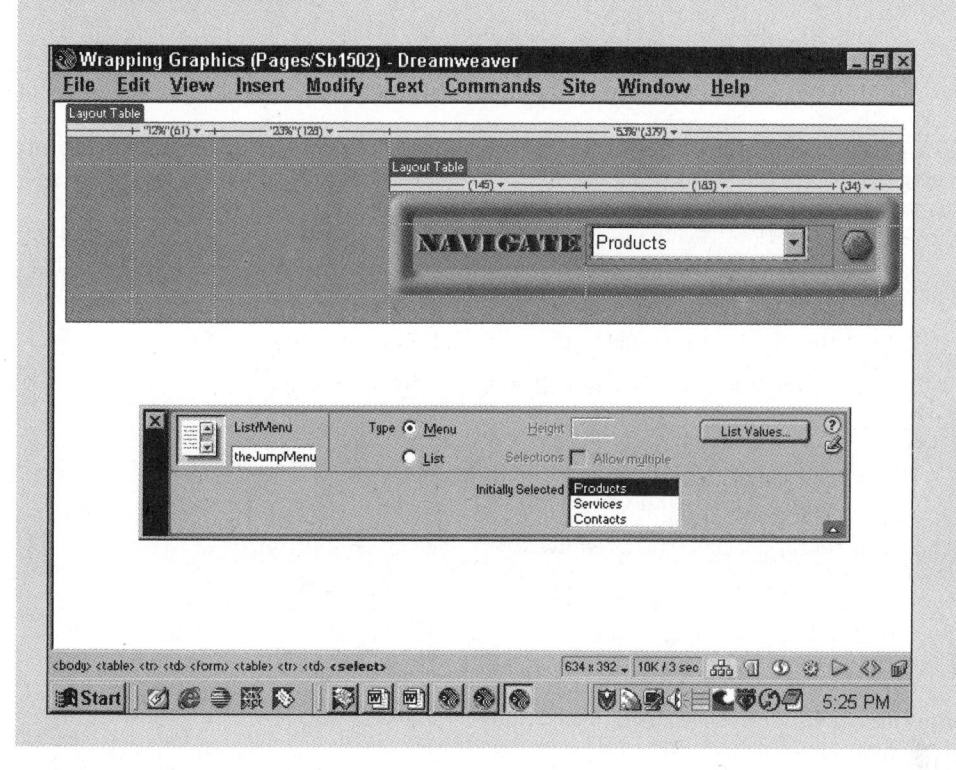

Caution: Note one caveat for adding new URLs to the jump menu through the Property Inspector: Any filenames with spaces or special characters should be URL-encoded. In other words, if one of your filenames is `about us.htm`, it should be entered using the hexadecimal equivalent for a space (%20): `about%20us.htm`.

If you'd prefer to work in the same environment as you did when creating the Jump Menu object, go the Behaviors panel route. Select the jump menu and from the Behaviors panel double-click the Jump Menu event. The Jump Menu dialog box opens — it is identical to the Insert Jump Menu dialog box except the Go button option is not available.

Activating Go buttons

The Dreamweaver jump menu is activated immediately whenever a user makes a choice from the list. So why would you want a Go button? The Go button, as implemented in Dreamweaver, is useful for selecting the first item in a jump menu list. To ensure that the Go button is the sole means for activating a jump selection, you need to remove an attached behavior. Select the jump menu item and then open the Behaviors panel. From the Behaviors panel, delete the Jump Menu event.

> **Tip** Some Web designers prefer to use a non-URL choice for the first item, such as "Please Select A Department." When entering such a non-URL option, set the Go to URL (or the Value in the List Value Properties) to #.

The generic Go button is a nice convenience, but it's a little, well, generic. To switch from a standard Go button to a graphical Go button of your choosing, follow these steps:

1. Insert the image that you want to use as your new Go button next to the jump menu.
2. With the new graphic selected, open the Behaviors panel.
3. Select Jump Menu Go from the Add Event drop-down list.

   Dreamweaver displays a dialog box showing all available jump menus.
4. Choose the name of the current jump menu from the Jump Menu Go dialog box list; click OK when you're done.
5. If necessary, delete the Dreamweaver-inserted Go button.

Activating Your Form with Buttons

Buttons are essential to HTML forms. You can place all the form objects you want on a page, but until your user presses that Submit button, there's no interaction between the client and the server. HTML provides three basic types of buttons: Submit, Reset, and Command buttons.

Submit, Reset, and Command buttons

A Submit button sends the form to the specified Action (generally the URL of a server-side program or a mailto address) using the noted Method (generally `post`). A Reset button clears all the fields in the form. Submit and Reset are both reserved HTML terms used to invoke specific actions.

A Command button permits the execution of functions defined by the Web designer, as programmed in JavaScript or other languages.

To insert a button in Dreamweaver, follow these steps:

1. Position the cursor where you want the button to appear. Then either select the Insert Button icon from the Form category of the Objects panel, or choose Insert ⇨ Form Objects ⇨ Button from the menu. Or you can simply drag the

Insert Button icon from the Objects panel and drop it into place on an existing form.

2. Choose the button Action type. As shown in Figure 9-10, the Button Property Inspector indicates that the Submit form button action is selected. (This is the default.) To make a Reset button, select the Reset form option. To make a Command button, select the None option.

3. To change the name of any button as you want it to appear on the Web page, enter the new name in the Label text box.

Tip When working with Command buttons, it's not enough to just insert the button and give it a name. You have to link the button to a specific function. A common technique is to use JavaScript's `onClick` event to call a function detailed in the `<script>` section of the document:

```
<input type="BUTTON" name="submit2" value="yes" ¬
onClick="doFunction()">
```

Figure 9-10: You can choose a function and a label for a button through the Button Property Inspector.

Graphical buttons

HTML doesn't limit you to the browser-style default buttons. You can also use an image as a Submit, Reset, or Command button. Dreamweaver has the capability to add an image field just like other form elements: Place the cursor in the desired position and choose Insert ⇨ Form Objects ⇨ Image Field, or select the Image Field icon from the Forms category of the Objects panel. You can use multiple image fields in a form to give the user a graphical choice, as shown in Figure 9-11.

When the user clicks the picture that you've designated as an image field for a Submit button, the form is submitted. Any other functionality, such as resetting the fields, must be coded in JavaScript or another language and triggered by attaching an `onClick` event to the button. This can be handled through the Dreamweaver behaviors, covered in Chapter 11 or by hand-coding the script and inserting the `onClick` code.

In fact, when the user clicks a graphical button, not only does it submit your form, but also it passes along the x, y coordinates of the image. The x coordinate is submitted using the name of the field and an `.x` attached; likewise, the y coordinate is submitted with the name of the field and a `.y` attached. Although this latter feature isn't often used, it's always good to know all the capabilities of your HTML tools.

Figure 9-11: Each flag in this page is not just an image; it's an image field that also acts as a Submit button.

Using the Hidden Field and the File Field

You should also be aware of a couple of other special-purpose form fields. The *hidden field* and the *file field* are supported through all major browsers. The hidden field is extremely useful for passing variables to your gateway programs, and the file field enables the user to attach a file to the form being submitted.

The hidden input type

When passing information from a form to a CGI program, the programmer often needs to send data that should not be made visible to the user. The data could be a variable needed by the CGI program to set information on the recipient of the form, or it could be a URL to which the CGI program will redirect the user after the form is submitted. To send this sort of information unseen by the form user, you must use a hidden form object.

The hidden field is inserted in a form much like the other form elements. To insert a hidden field, place your cursor in the desired position and choose Insert ⇨ Form Objects ⇨ Hidden Field or choose the Insert Hidden Field icon from the Forms category of the Objects panel.

The hidden object is another input type, just like the text, radio button, and checkbox types. A hidden variable looks like this in HTML:

```
<input type="hidden" name="recipient" value="jlowery@idest.com">
```

As you would expect, this tag has no representation when it's viewed though a browser. However, Dreamweaver does display a Hidden Form Element Invisible symbol in the Document window. You can turn off the display of this symbol by deselecting the Hidden Form Element option from the Invisible Elements category of Preferences.

The file input type

Much more rarely used is the file input type, which enables any stored computer file to be attached to the form and sent with the other data. Used primarily to enable the easy sharing of data, the file input type has been largely supplanted by modern e-mail methods, which also enable files to be attached to messages.

The file field is inserted in a form much like the other form elements. To insert a file field, place your cursor in the desired position and choose Insert ⇨ Form Objects ⇨ File Field or choose the Insert File Field icon from the Forms category of the Objects panel. Dreamweaver automatically inserts a text box for the filename to be input, with a Browse (Choose) button on the right. In a browser, the user's selection of the Browse (Choose) button displays a standard Open File dialog box from which a file can be selected to go with the form.

Summary

HTML forms provide a basic line of communication from Web page visitor to Web page administrator. With Dreamweaver, you can enter and modify most varieties of form inputs, including text fields and checkboxes. This chapter covered the following important points:

- For the most part, a complete form requires two working parts: the form object inserted in your Web page and a CGI program stored on your Web server.
- To avoid using a server-side script, you can use a mailto address rather than a URL pointing to a program in a form's `action` attribute. However, you still have to parse the form reply to convert it to a usable format.
- The basic types of form input are text fields, text areas, radio buttons, checkboxes, drop-down menus, and scrolling lists.
- Dreamweaver includes a Jump Menu object, which uses a drop-down list as a navigational system.
- Once a form is completed, it must be sent to the server-side application. This is usually done through a Submit button on the form. Dreamweaver also supports Reset and user-definable Command buttons.

In the next chapter, you learn how to use Dreamweaver to develop frames and framesets.

✦ ✦ ✦

Using Frames and Framesets

CHAPTER 10

Frames constitute one of the Webmaster's major design tools. A *frame* is a Web page that is subdivided into both static and changing HTML pages. Not too long ago, the evolution of frames was right where Dynamic HTML is today in terms of general acceptance. The use of frames and framesets has become even more widespread over the last year or so, and the technology is now supported through every major browser version. It's safe to say that every Web designer today needs a working knowledge of frames to stay competitive.

The first time I fully appreciated the power of frames, I was visiting a site that displayed examples of what the Webmaster considered "bad" Web pages. The site was essentially a jumpstation with a series of links. The author used a frameset with three frames: one that ran all the way across the top of the page, displaying a logo and other basic information; one narrow panel on the left with a scrolling set of links to the sites themselves; and the main viewing area, which took up two-thirds of the center screen. Selecting any of the links caused the site to appear in the main viewing frame.

I was astounded when I finally realized that each frame was truly an independent Web page and that you didn't have to use only Web pages on your own site—you could link to any page on the Internet. That was when I also realized the amount of work involved in establishing a frame Web site: Every page displayed on that site used multiple HTML pages.

Dreamweaver takes the head-pounding complexity out of coding and managing frames with a point-and-click interface. You get easy access to the commands for modifying the properties of the overall frame structure as well as each individual frame. This chapter gives you an overview of frames, as well as all the specifics you need for inserting and modifying frames and framesets. Special attention is given to defining the unique look of frames through borders, scroll bars, and margins.

In This Chapter

Fundamentals of HTML frames and framesets

Creating frames visually

Fast framesets with Frame objects

Altering frames and framesets

Opening links in specific frames

Working with borders, scroll bars, and margins

Inserting frameless content

Understanding iframes

Frames and Framesets: The Basics

It's best to think of frames in two major parts: the frameset, and the frames themselves. The frameset is the HTML document that defines the framing structure — the number of individual frames that make up a page, their initial size, and the shared attributes among all the frames. A frameset by itself is never displayed. Frames, on the other hand, are complete HTML documents that can be viewed and edited separately or together in the organization described by the frameset.

A frameset takes the place of the <body> tags in an HTML document, where the content of a Web page is found. Here's what the HTML for a basic frameset looks like:

```
<frameset rows="50%,50%">
  <frame src="top.html">
  <frame src="bottom.html">
</frameset>
```

Notice that the content of a <frameset> tag consists entirely of <frame> tags, each one referring to a different Web page. The only other element that can be used inside of a <frameset> tag is another <frameset> tag.

Columns and rows

Framesets, much like tables, are made up of columns and rows. The columns and rows attributes (cols and rows) are lists of comma-separated values. The number of values indicates the number of either columns or rows, and the values themselves establish the size of the columns or rows. Thus, a <frameset> tag that looks like this:

```
<frameset cols="67,355,68">
```

denotes three columns of widths, 67, 355, and 68, respectively. And this frameset tag:

```
<frameset cols="270,232" rows="384,400">
```

declares that two columns exist with the specified widths (270 and 232) and two rows with the specified heights (384 and 400).

Sizing frames

Column widths and row heights can be set as absolute measurements in pixels, or expressed as a percentage of the entire screen. HTML frames also support an attribute that assigns the size relative to the other columns or rows. In other words, the relative attribute (designated with an asterisk) assigns the balance of the remaining available screen space to a column or row. For example, the following frameset:

```
<frameset cols="80,*">
```

sets up two frames, one 80 pixels wide and the other as large as the browser window allows. This ensures that the first column will always be a constant size — making it perfect for a set of navigational buttons — while the second is as wide as possible.

The relative attribute can also be used proportionally. When preceded by an integer, as in n*, this attribute specifies that the frame is allocated *n* times the space it would have received otherwise. So frameset code like this:

```
<frameset rows="4*,*">
```

ensures that one row is proportionately four times the size of the other.

Creating a Frameset and Frames

Dreamweaver offers several ways to divide your Web page into frames and make your frameset. The first method uses the menus. Choose Modify ⇨ Frameset and, from the submenu, select the direction in which you would like to split the frame: left, right, up, or down. Left or right splits the frame in half vertically; up or down splits it horizontally in half.

You can also create a frameset visually, using the mouse. To create frames with this method, follow these steps:

1. Turn on the frame borders in your Dreamweaver Document window by selecting View ⇨ Visual Aids ⇨ Frame Borders.

   A 3-pixel-wide inner border appears along the edges of your Document window.

2. Position the cursor over any of the frame borders.

3. Press Alt (Option).

   If your pointer is over a frame border, the pointer changes into a two-headed arrow when over an edge and a four-headed arrow (or a drag-hand on the Mac) when over a corner.

4. Drag the frame border into the Document window. Figure 10-1 shows a four-frame frameset being created.

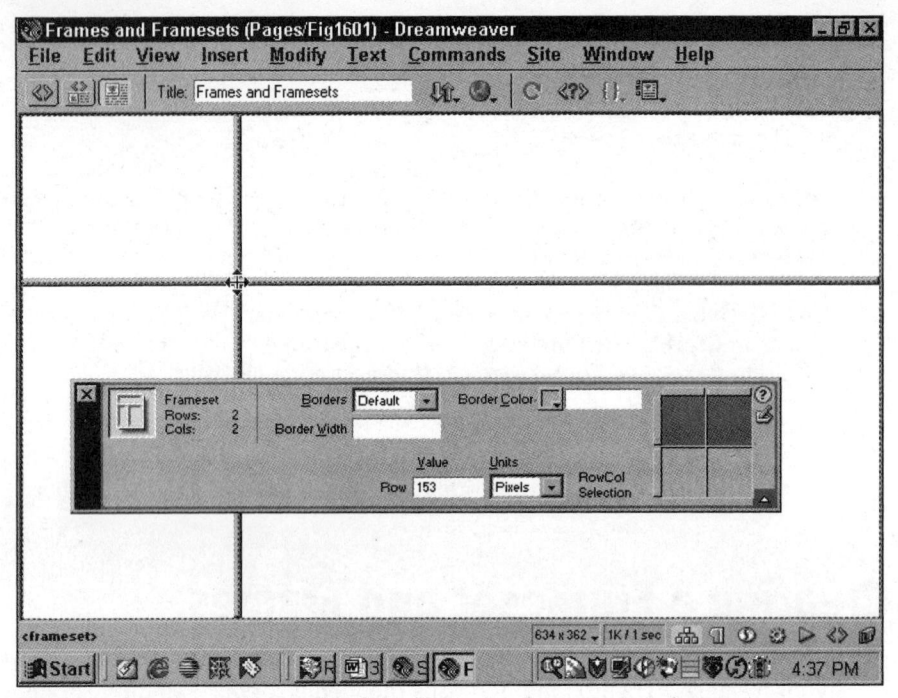

Figure 10-1: After you've enabled the frame borders, you can drag out your frameset structure with the mouse.

Dreamweaver initially assigns a temporary filename and an absolute pixel value to your HTML frameset code. Both can be modified later, if you wish.

> **Tip** With the menu method of frameset creation, you can initially create only a two-way frame split. To further split the frame using the menu commands, you must first select each frame. However, by Alt+dragging (Option+dragging) the corner of the frame border, you can quickly create a four-frame frameset.

When the frameset is selected, Dreamweaver displays a black, dotted line along all the frame borders and within every frame. You can easily reposition any frameset border by clicking and dragging it. If you just want to move the border, make sure you don't press the Alt or Option key while dragging the border; this action creates additional frames.

Adding more frames

You're not at all limited to your initial frame choices. In addition to being able to move them visually, you can also set the size through the Frameset Property Inspector, as described in the next section. Furthermore, you can continue to split either the entire frame or each column or row as needed. When you divide a column or row into one or more frames, you are actually nesting one frameset inside another.

> **Tip**
>
> Once you've created the basic frame structure, you can select View ⇨ Frame Borders again (it's a toggle) to turn the borders off and create a more accurate preview of your page.

Using the menus

To split an existing frame using the menus, position the cursor in the frame you want to alter and choose Modify ⇨ Frameset ⇨ Split Frame Left, Right, Up, or Down. Figure 10-2 shows a two-row frameset in which the bottom row was split into two columns and then repositioned. The Frameset Property Inspector indicates that the inner frameset (2 columns, 1 row) is selected. The direction in the command (Left, Right, Up, and Down) indicates the frame the existing page will be placed in. For example, I selected Split Frame Right for Figure 10-2, and the current page is placed in the right frame.

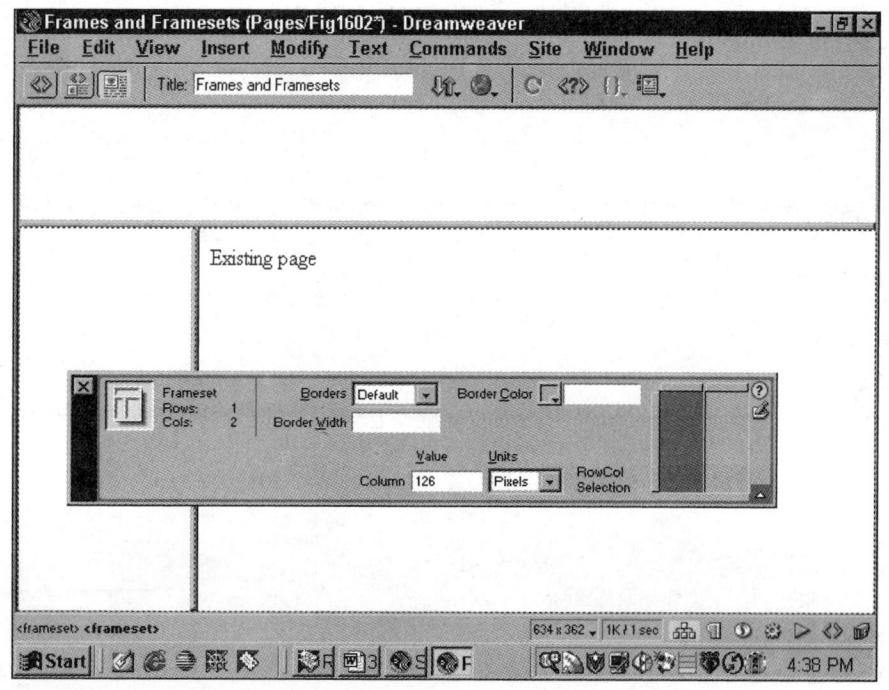

Figure 10-2: Use the Modify ⇨ Frameset menu option to split an existing frame into additional columns or rows and create a nested frameset.

You can clearly see the "nested" nature of the code in this HTML fragment describing the frameset in Figure 10-2:

```
<frameset rows="163,333" cols="784">
  <frame src="file://Dev/UntitledFrame-34">
  <frameset cols="115,663" rows="*">
    <frame src="file://Dev/UntitledFrame-57">
    <frame src="file://Dev/UntitledFrame-35">
  </frameset>
</frameset>
```

Tip You can also split an existing frame by Alt+dragging (Option+dragging) the current frame's border, but you have to choose an inner border that does not extend across the page.

Using the mouse

When you need to create additional columns or rows that span the entire Web page, use the mouse method instead of the menus. Alt+drag (Option+drag) any of the current frame's borders that go across the entire page, such as one of the outer borders. Figure 10-3 shows a new row added along the bottom of our previous frame structure.

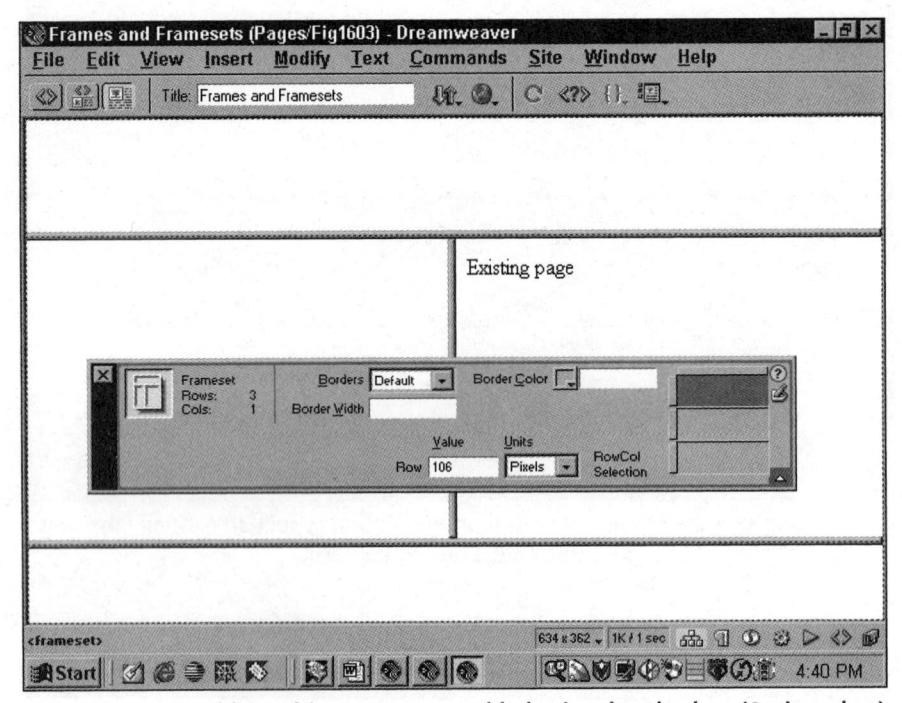

Figure 10-3: An additional frame row was added using the Alt+drag (Option+drag) method.

Tip: You can also split a smaller frame by first selecting it and then Alt+dragging or Option+dragging one of its borders. As you can see in this chapter, you select a frame by Alt+clicking (Windows) or Option+Shift+clicking (Macintosh) inside the frame.

Quick Framesets with the Frames Objects

Dragging out your frameset in Dreamweaver is a clear-cut method of setting up the various frames. However, now matter how easy it is, it can still be a bit of a chore to create even simple framesets by clicking and dragging. To hasten the development workflow, Dreamweaver uses Frame objects, which can build a frameset with a single click.

Although a frame-based Web design could potentially be quite complex with numerous nested framesets, most of the sites using frames follow a more simple, general pattern. Dreamweaver offers eight of the most common frameset configurations in the Frames category of the Objects panel, shown in Figure 10-4. Choose one of the basic designs, and you're ready to tweak the frame sizes and begin filling in the content. It's a great combination of ease-of-use mixed with design flexibility.

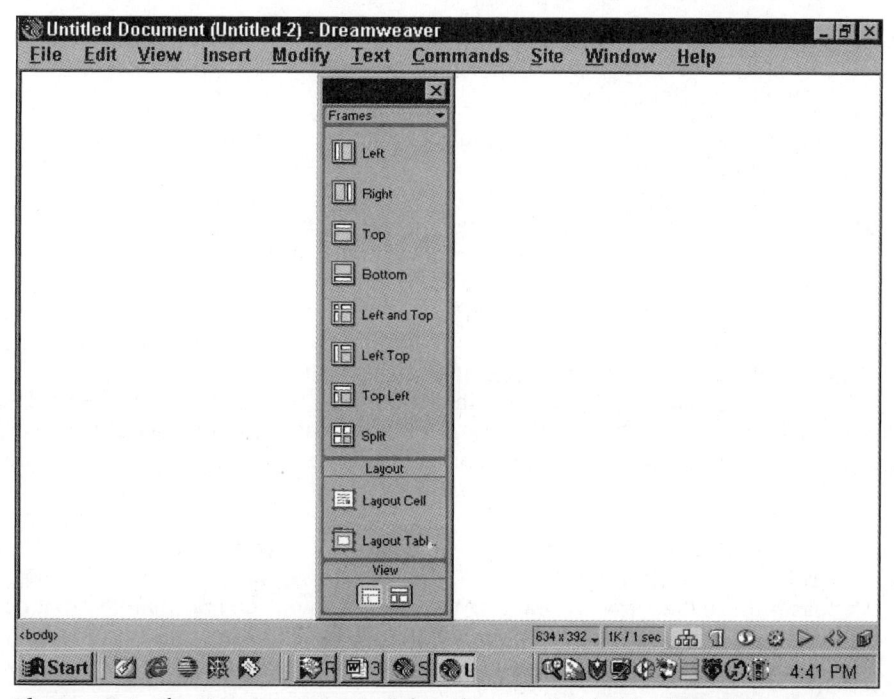

Figure 10-4: The Frames category of the Objects panel holds eight of the most commonly used frameset configurations.

The Frames category is roughly organized from simplest framesets to most complex. You might notice that each of the icons on the panel shows an example frameset with one blue section. The placement of the color is quite significant. The blue indicates in which frame the current page will appear when the frameset is constructed. For example, if I had begun to construct my main content page, and then decided to turn it into a frameset with a separate navigation strip frame beneath it, I would choose the Bottom Frames object. Figure 10-5 provides a before-and-after example with the preframe content on the left and the same content after a Bottom Frame object has been applied.

The eight different framesets available from the Frames category are:

- **Left:** Inserts a blank frame to the left of the current page.
- **Right:** Inserts a blank frame to the right of the current page.
- **Top:** Inserts a blank frame above the current page.
- **Bottom:** Inserts a blank frame below the current page.
- **Left and Top:** Makes a frameset with four frames where the current page is in the lower right.
- **Left Top:** Makes a frameset where the left spans the two rightmost frames; a nested frameset is used to create the right frames. The existing page is placed in the lower-right frame.
- **Top Left:** Makes a frameset where the top spans the lower two frames; the lower frames are created using a nested frameset. The existing page is placed in the lower-right frame.
- **Split:** Creates a frameset with four equal frames and moves the existing page to the lower right.

Using the Frames objects is quite literally a one-click operation. Just select the desired frameset, and Dreamweaver automatically turns on Frame Borders, if necessary, and creates and names the required frames. For all Frames objects, the existing page is moved to a frame where the scrolling option is set at Default, and the size is relative to the rest of the frameset. In other words, the existing page can be scrolled and expands to fill the content. For this reason, it's best to apply a Frames object to an existing page only if it is intended to be the primary content frame. Otherwise, it's better to select the Frames object while a blank page is open and then use the File ⇨ Open in Frame command to load any existing pages into the individual frames.

Note: For almost all of the Frames objects, Dreamweaver creates one or more frames with a set size. Although by default, the set width or height is 80 pixels, you can easily resize the frame by dragging the frame border. The only frameset that does not have at least one set frame is the Split object where the four frames are divided equally. Dreamweaver also sets the Scroll option to No for frames with absolute sizes.

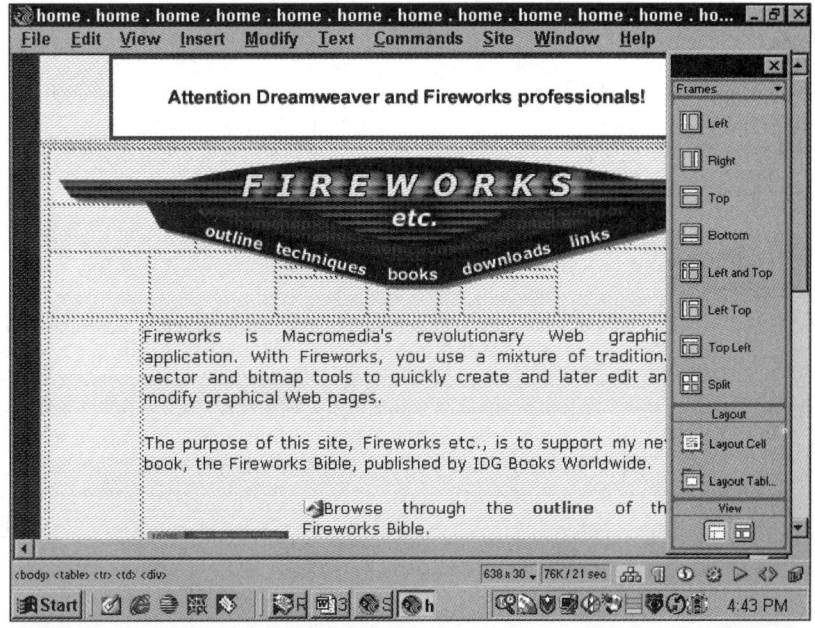

Before Bottom Frame object has been applied.

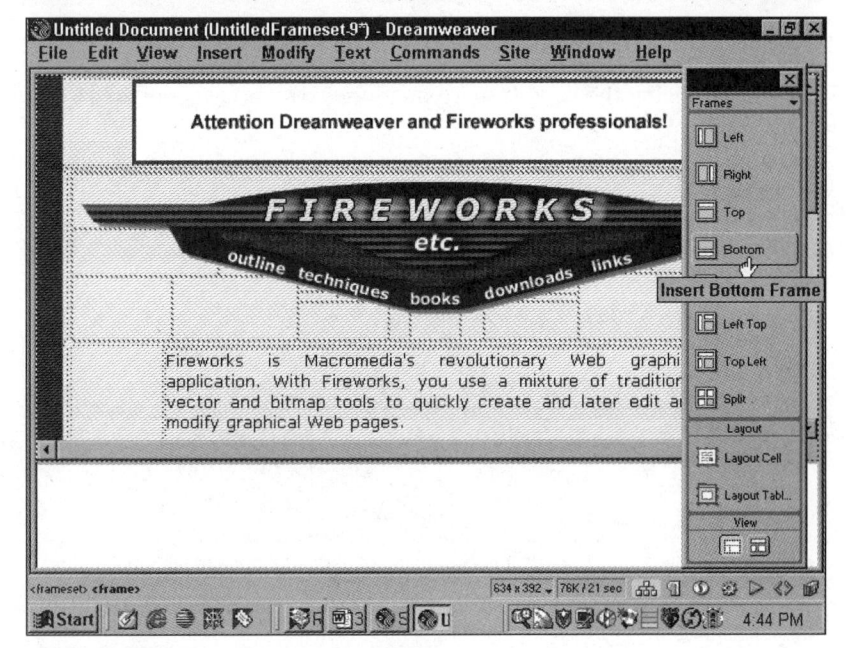

After Bottom Frame Object has been applied.

Figure 10-5: Existing content is incorporated in a new frameset when a Frames object is chosen.

Working with the Frameset Property Inspector

The Frameset Property Inspector manages those elements, such as the borders, that are common to all the frames within a frameset; it also offers more precise sizing control over individual rows and columns than you can do visually. To access the Frameset Property Inspector, choose Window ⇨ Properties, if the Property Inspector is not already open, and then select any of the frame borders.

Tip
When a browser visits a Web page that uses frames, it displays the title found in the frameset HTML document for the entire frame. The easiest method to set that title is to select the frameset and then enter the name directly in the Title field of the toolbar, if visible. You can also set the title by selecting the frameset and then choosing Modify ⇨ Page Properties. In the Page Properties dialog box, enter your choice of title in the Title text box, as you would for any other Web page. All the other options in the Page Properties dialog box—including background color and text color—apply to the <noframes> content, covered in the section "Handling Frameless Browsers," later in this chapter.

Resizing frames in a frameset

With HTML, when you want to specify the size of a frame, you work with the row or column in which the frame resides. Dreamweaver gives you two ways to alter a frame's size: by dragging the border or, to be more precise, by specifying a value in the Frameset Property Inspector.

As shown in Figure 10-6, Dreamweaver's Frameset Property Inspector contains a Row/Column selector to display the structure of the selected frameset. For each frameset, you select the tab along the top or left side of the Row/Column selector to choose the column or row you want to modify.

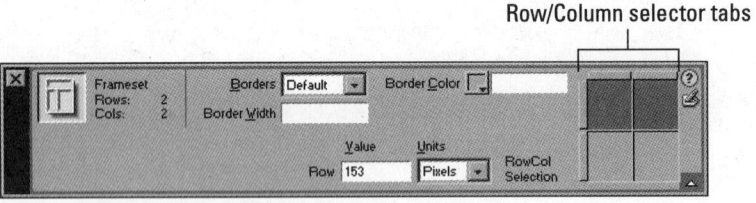

Figure 10-6: In the Frameset Property Inspector, you use the Row/Column Selector tabs to choose which frame you are going to resize.

Tip
The Row/Column Selector shows only one frameset at a time. So if your design uses nested framesets, you won't see an exact duplicate of your entire Web page in the Row/Column Selector.

Whether you need to modify just a row, a column, or both a row and a column depends on the location of the frame.

- If your frame spans the width of an entire page, like the top or bottom row in Figure 10-3, select the corresponding tab on the left side of the Row/Column Selector.
- If your frame spans the height of an entire page, select the equivalent tab along the top of the Row/Column Selector.
- If your frame does not span either height or width, like the middle row in Figure 10-3, you need to select both its column and its row and modify the size of each in turn.

Once you have selected the row or column, follow these steps to specify its size:

1. To specify the size in pixels, enter a number in the Frameset Property Inspector's Value text box and select Pixels as the Units option.
2. To specify the size as a percentage of the screen, enter a number from 1 to 100 in the Value text box and select Percent as the Units option.
3. To specify a size relative to the other columns or rows, first select Relative as the Units option. Now you have two options:
   - To set the size to occupy the remainder of the screen, delete any number that may be entered in the Value text box; optionally, you can enter 1.
   - To scale the frame relative to the other rows or columns, type the scale factor in the Value text box. For example, if you want the frame to be twice the size of another relative frame, put a 2 in the Value text box.

Tip The Relative size operator is generally used to indicate that you want the current frame to take up the balance of the frameset column or row. This makes it easy to specify a size without having to calculate pixel widths and ensures that the frame has the largest possible size.

Manipulating frameset borders

By default, Dreamweaver sets up your framesets so all the frames have gray borders that are 6 pixels wide. You can alter the border color, change the width, or eliminate the borders altogether. All of the border controls are handled through the Frameset Property Inspector.

Tip Border controls for individual frames also exist. Just as table cell settings can override options set for the entire table, the individual frame options override those determined for the entire frameset, as described in the section "Working with the Frame Property Inspector," later in this chapter. Use the frameset border controls when you want to make a global change to the borders, such as turning them all off.

If you are working with nested framesets, it's important that you select the outermost frameset before you begin making any modifications to the borders. You can tell that you've selected the outermost frameset by looking at the Dreamweaver Tag Selector; it shows only one `<frameset>` in bold. If you select an inner nested frameset, you see more than one `<frameset>` in the Tag Selector.

Eliminating borders

When a frameset is first created, Dreamweaver leaves the borders display up to the browser's discretion. You can expressly turn the frameset borders on or off through the Frameset Property Inspector.

To eliminate borders completely, enter a zero in the Border Width text box. Even if no width value is displayed, the default is a border 6 pixels wide. If you turn off the borders for your frameset, you can still work in Dreamweaver with View ⇨ Visual Aids ⇨ Frame Borders enabled, which gives you quick access to modifying the frameset. The borders are not displayed, however, when your Web page is previewed in a browser.

Border appearance options

You can control the appearance of your borders to a limited degree. In the Borders drop-down list of options, choosing Yes causes browsers to draw the borders with a 3D appearance. Select No, and the frameset borders are drawn as a single color. Browsers generally interpret the three-dimensional look as the default option.

Border color options

To change the frameset border color, select the Border Color text box and then enter either a color name or a hexadecimal color value. You can also select the color swatch and choose a new border color from the browser-safe color picker. Clicking the Palette icon on the color picker opens the extended color selector, just as for other color swatches in Dreamweaver.

Caution If you have nested framesets on your Web page, make sure you've selected the correct frameset before you make any modifications through the Frameset Property Inspector. You can move from a nested frameset to its "parent" by using the keyboard shortcut Alt+up arrow (Command+up arrow). Likewise, you can move from a parent frameset to its "child" by pressing Alt+down arrow (Command+down arrow).

Saving a frameset and frames

As mentioned earlier, when you're working with frames, you're working with multiple HTML files. You must be careful to save not only all the individual frames that make up your Web page but also the frameset itself.

Dreamweaver makes it easy to save framesets and included frames by providing several special commands. To save a frameset, choose File ⇨ Save Frameset to open the standard Save File dialog box. You can also save a copy of the current frameset by choosing File ⇨ Save Frameset As. You don't have to select the frameset border or position your cursor in any special place to activate these functions.

Saving each frame in the frameset can be a chore unless you choose File ⇨ Save All Frames. The first time this command is invoked, Dreamweaver cycles through each of the open frames and displays the Save File dialog box. Each subsequent time you choose File ⇨ Save All Frames, Dreamweaver automatically saves every updated file in the frameset.

To copy an individual frame, you must use the regular File ⇨ Save As command.

Closing a frameset

There's no real trick to closing a Dreamweaver frameset: just choose File ⇨ Close. If the frameset is your last open file, Dreamweaver asks if you'd like to quit the program (unless you've previously selected the Don't Ask Me Again option).

Modifying a Frame

What makes the whole concept of a Web page frameset work so well is the flexibility of each frame.

- ✦ You can design your page so that some frames are fixed in size while others are expandable.
- ✦ You can attach scroll bars to some frames and not others.
- ✦ Any frame can have its own background image, and yet all frames can appear as one seamless picture.
- ✦ Borders can be enabled — and colored — for one set of frames but left off for another set.

Dreamweaver uses a Frame Property Inspector to specify most of a frame's attributes. Others are handled through devices already familiar to you, such as the Page Properties dialog box.

Page properties

Each frame is its own HTML document, and as such, each frame can have independent page properties. To alter the page properties of a frame, position the cursor in the frame and then choose Modify ⇨ Page Properties. You can also use the keyboard shortcuts, Ctrl+J or Command+J. Or you can select Page Properties from the shortcut menu by right-clicking (Control+clicking) any open space on the frame's page.

Joining Background Images in Frames

One popular technique is to insert background images into separate frames so they blend into a seamless single image. This takes careful planning and coordination between the author of the graphic and the designer of the Web page.

To accomplish this image consolidation operation, you must first "slice" the image in an image-processing program, such as Fireworks or Adobe Photoshop. Then save each part as a separate graphic, making sure that no border is around these image sections — each cut-up piece becomes the background image for a particular frame. Next, set the background image of each frame to the matching graphic. Be sure to turn off the borders for the frameset and set the Border Width to zero.

You can find a command on the CD-ROM that accompanies this book to help you eliminate your borders. Look for the Zero Page Borders Command in Andrew Wooldridge's folder.

Correct sizing of each piece is important to ensure that no gaps appear in your joined background. A good technique is to use absolute pixel measurements for images that fill the frame and, where the background images tile, set the frame to Relative spacing. In the following figure, the corner frame has the same measurement as the background image (107×126 pixels), and all the other frames are set to Relative.

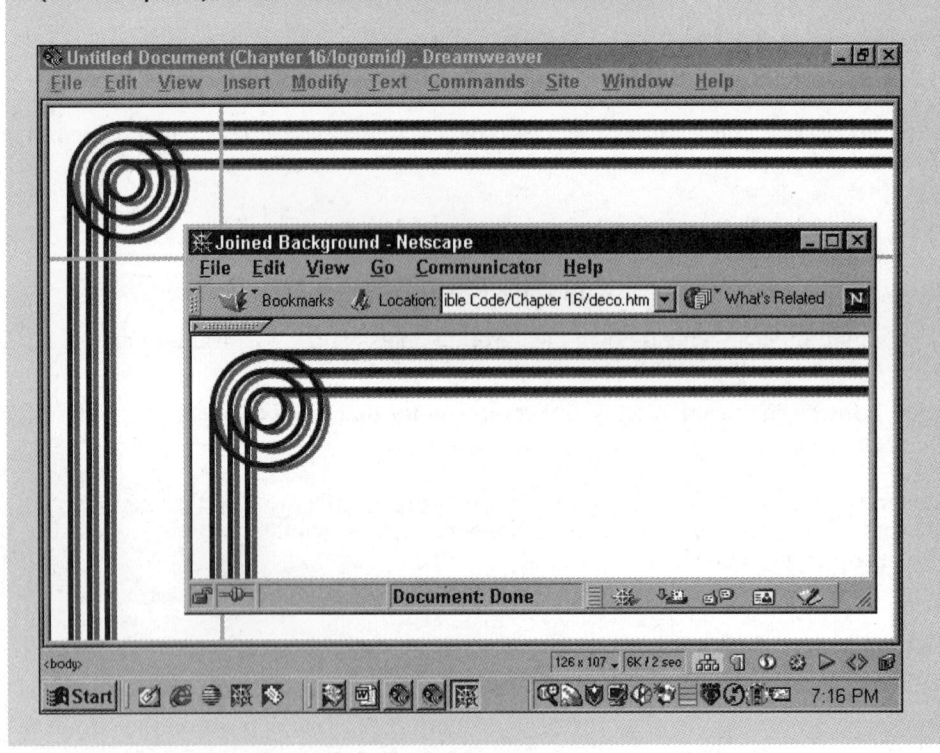

From the Page Properties dialog box, you can assign a title, although it is not visible to the user unless the frame is viewed as a separate page. If you plan on using the individual frames as separate pages in your <noframes> content (see "Handling Frameless Browsers" at the end of this chapter), it's good practice to title every page. You can also assign a background and the various link colors by selecting the appropriate color swatch or entering a color name into the correct text box.

Working with the Frame Property Inspector

To access the Frame Property Inspector, you must first select a frame. Selecting a frame is different from just positioning the cursor in the frame. You have two ways to properly select a frame: using the Frames panel or using the mouse in the Document window.

The Frames panel shows an accurate representation of all the frames in your Web page. Open the Frames panel by choosing Window ⇨ Frames. As you can see in Figure 10-7, the Frames panel displays names, if assigned, in the individual frames, and (no name) if not. Nested framesets are shown with a heavier border.

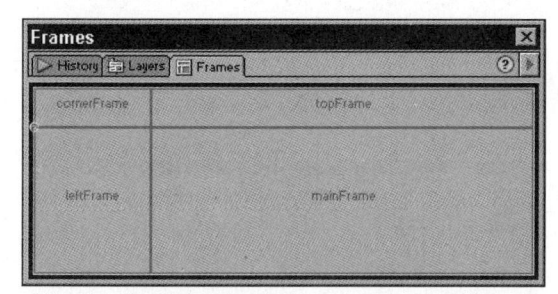

Figure 10-7: Use the Frames panel to visually select a frame to modify.

To select a frame, click directly on its represented image in the Frames panel. If the Frame Property Inspector is open, it reflects the selected frame's options. For more complex Web pages, you can resize the Frames panel to get a better sense of the page layout. To close the Frames panel, select the Close button or choose Window ⇨ Frames again.

Tip When you are working with multiple framesets, use the Tag Selector together with the Frames panel to identify the correct nested frameset. Selecting a frameset in the Tag Selector causes it to be identified in the Frames panel with a heavy black border.

To select a frame with the mouse, press Alt (Option+Shift) and click in the desired frame. Once the frame is selected, you can move from one frame to another by pressing Alt (Command) and then using the arrow keys.

Naming your frames

Naming each frame is essential to getting the most power from a frame-structured Web page. The frame's name is used to make the content inserted from a hyperlink appear in that particular frame. For more information about targeting a link, see the section "Targeting Frame Content," later in this chapter.

Frame names must follow specific guidelines, as explained in the following steps:

1. Select the frame you want to name. You can either use the Frames panel or Alt+click (Option+Shift+click) inside the frame.
2. If necessary, open the Property Inspector by choosing Window ⇨ Properties.
3. In the Frame Property Inspector, shown in Figure 10-8, add the frame's name in the text box next to the frame logo. Frame names have the following restrictions:
   - You must use one word, with no spaces.
   - You may not use special characters such as quotation marks, question marks, and hyphens.
   - You may use the underscore character.
   - You may not use certain frame names: `_blank`, `_parent`, `_self`, and `_top`.

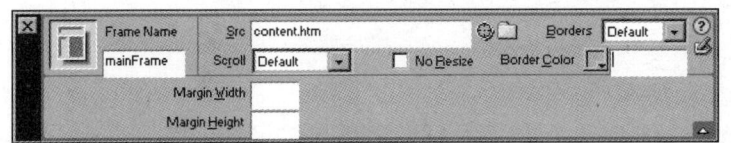

Figure 10-8: The Frame Property Inspector enables you to name your frame and control all of a frame's attributes.

Opening a Web page into a frame

You don't have to build all Web pages in frames from scratch. You can load an existing Web page into any frame. If you've selected a frame and the Frame Property Inspector is open, just type the link directly into the Src text box or choose the folder icon to browse for your file. Or you can position your cursor in a frame (without selecting the frame) and choose File ⇨ Open in Frame.

Setting borders

You can generally set most border options adequately in the Frameset Property Inspector; you can also override some of those options, such as color, for each frame. These possibilities have practical limitations, however.

To set borders from the Frame Property Inspector for a selected frame, you can make the borders three-dimensional by choosing Yes in the Borders drop-down option list, or use the monochrome setting by choosing No. Leaving the Borders option at Default gives control to the frameset settings. You can also change a frame's border color by choosing the Border Color swatch in a selected frame's Property Inspector.

Now, about those limitations: They come into play when you try to implement one of your border modifications. Because frames share common borders, it is difficult to isolate an individual frame and have the change affect just the selected frame. As an example, Figure 10-9 shows a frameset in which the borders are set to No for all frames except the one on the lower right. Notice how the left border of the lower-right frame extends to the top, all the way over the upper frame. You have two possible workarounds for this problem. First, you can design your frames so that their borders do not touch, as in a multi-row frameset. Second, you can create a background image for a frame that includes a border design.

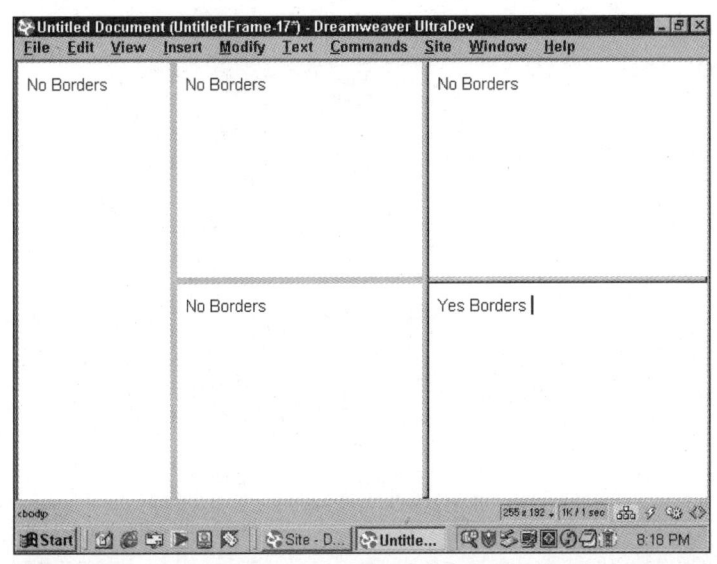

Figure 10-9: If you want to use isolated frame borders, you have to carefully plan your Web page frameset to avoid overlapping borders.

Adding scroll bars

One of the features that has given frames the wide use they enjoy is the capability to enable or disable scroll bars for each frame. Scroll bars are used when the browser window is too small to display all the information in the Web page frame. The browser window size is completely user controlled, so the Web designer must apply the various scroll bar options on a frame-by-frame basis, depending on the look desired and the frame's content.

Four options are selectable from the Scroll drop-down list on the Frame Property Inspector:

- **Default:** Leaves the use of scroll bars up to the browser.
- **Yes:** Forces scroll bars to appear regardless of the amount of content.
- **No:** Disables scroll bars.
- **Auto:** Turns scroll bars on if the content of the frame extends horizontally or vertically beyond what the browser window can display.

Figure 10-10 uses an automatic vertical scroll bar in the lower frame; you can see it on the far right.

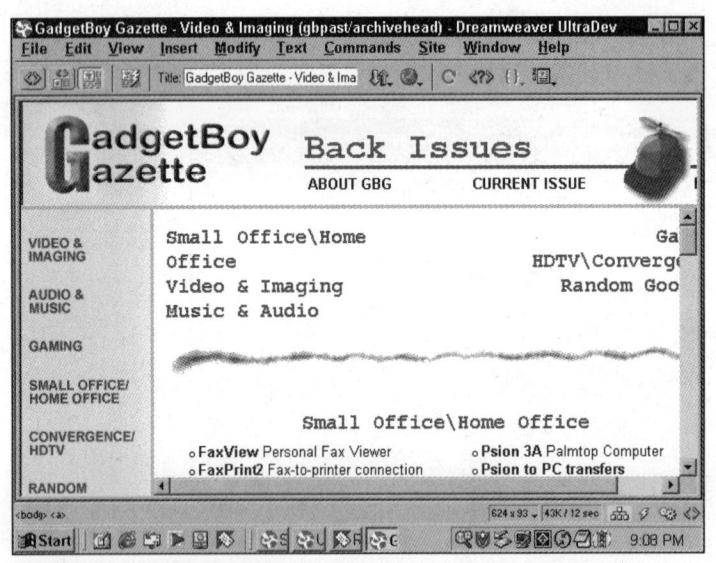

Figure 10-10: The top frame of the Web page has the scroll bars turned off, and the bottom-right frame has scroll bars enabled.

Resizing

By default, all frames are resizable by the user; that is, a visitor to your Web site can widen, narrow, lengthen, or shorten a frame by dragging the border to a new position. You can disable this resizing capability, however, on a frame-by-frame basis. In the Frame Property Inspector, select the No Resize option to turn off the resizing feature.

Tip

Although it might be tempting to select No Resize for every frame, it's best to enable resizing, except in frames that require a set size to maintain their functionality (for instance, a frame containing navigational controls).

Setting margins

Just as you can pad table cells with additional space to separate text and graphics, you can offset content in frames. Dreamweaver enables you to control the left/right margins and the top/bottom margins independently. By default, about 6 pixels of space are between the content and the left or right frame borders, and about 15 pixels of space are between the content and the top or bottom frame borders. You can increase or decrease these margins, but even if you set the values to zero, some room still exists between the borders and the content.

To alter the left and right margins, change the value in the Frame Property Inspector's Margin Width text box; to change the top and bottom margins, enter a new value in the Margin Height text box. If you don't see the Margin Width and Height text boxes, select the Property Inspector expander arrow.

Modifying content

You can update a frame's content in any way you see fit. Sometimes, it's necessary to keep an eye on how altering a single frame's content affects the entire frameset. Other times, it is easier — and faster — to work on each frame individually and later load them into the frameset to see the final result.

With Dreamweaver's multiwindow structure, you can have it both ways. Work on the individual frames in one or more windows and the frameset in yet another.

Although switching back to the frameset window won't automatically update it to show your changed frames, you can use one shortcut. After saving changes in the full frame windows, go to the frameset window. In any window you've altered elsewhere, make another small change, such as inserting a space. Then, choose File ⇨ Revert. This command is normally used to revert to the previously saved version, but in this case, you're using it to update your frames.

> **Caution** To preview changes made to a Web page using frames, you must first save the changed files. Currently, Dreamweaver creates a temporary file of the frameset, but not any of the included frames.

Deleting frames

As you're building your Web page frameset, you inevitably try a frame design that does not work. How do you delete a frame once you've created it? Click the frame border and drag it into the border of the enclosing, or parent, frame. When no parent frame is present, drag the frame border to the edge of the page. If the frame being deleted contains any unsaved content, Dreamweaver asks if you'd like to save the file before closing it.

Tip: Because the enclosing frameset and each individual frame are all discrete HTML pages, each keeps track of its own edits and other changes — and therefore each has its own Undo memory. If you are in a particular frame and try to undo a frameset alteration, such as adding a new frame to the set, it won't work. To reverse an edit to the frameset, you have to select the frameset and then choose File ⇨ Undo, or use one of the keyboard shortcuts (Ctrl+Z or Command+Z). To reverse the creation of a frameset, you must select Undo twice.

Targeting Frame Content

One of the major uses of frames is for navigational control. One frame acts as the navigation center, offering links to various Web pages in a site. When the user selects one of the links, the Web page appears in another frame on the page; and that frame, if necessary, can scroll independently of the navigation frame. This technique keeps the navigation links always visible and accessible.

When you assign a link to appear in a particular frame of your Web page, you are said to be assigning a target for the link. You can target specific frames in your Web page, and you can target structural parts of a frameset. In Dreamweaver, targets are assigned through the Text and Image Property Inspectors.

Targeting sections of your frameset

In the earlier section on naming frames, you learned that certain names are reserved. These are the four special names HTML reserves for the parts of a frameset that are used in targeting: `_blank`, `_parent`, `_self`, and `_top`. With them, you can cause content from a link to overwrite the current frame or to appear in an entirely new browser window.

To target a link to a section of your frameset, follow these steps:

1. Select the text or image you want to use as your link.
2. In the Text (or Image) Property Inspector, enter the URL and/or named anchor in the Link text box. Alternatively, you can select the folder icon to browse for the file.
3. Select the Target text box. You may need to expand the Image Property Inspector to see the Target text box.
4. Select one of the following reserved target names from the drop-down list of Target options (see Figure 10-11) or type an entry into the text box:

    - **_blank:** Opens the link into a new browser window and keeps the current window available.
    - **_parent:** Opens the link into the parent frameset of the current frame, if any.

- **_self:** Opens the link into the current frame, replacing its contents (the default).

- **_top:** Opens the link into the outermost frameset of the current Web page, replacing all frames.

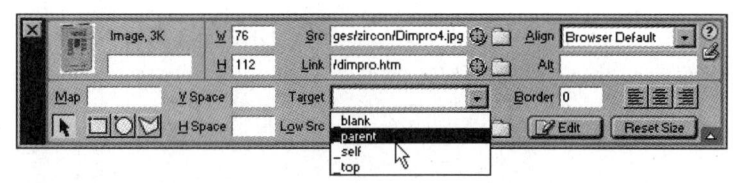

Figure 10-11: Choose your frame target from the Property Inspector's Target drop-down list.

The generic nature of these reserved target names enables them to be used repeatedly on different Web pages, without your having to code a particular reference each time.

For an example of structural targeting, look at the code for the Dreamweaver Help system. The Index frame, for example, uses the implied `_self` target whenever a major Help topic is selected to open an HTML document that shows all the subtopics.

Caution A phenomenon known as *recursive frames* can be dangerous to your site setup. Let's say you have a frameset named index_frame.html. If you include in any frame on your current page a link to index_frame.html and set the target as _self, when the user selects that link, the entire frameset loads into the current frame — including another link to index_frame.html. Browsers can handle about three or four iterations of this recursion before they crash. To avoid the problem, set your frameset target to _top.

Targeting specific frames in your frameset

Earlier I stressed the importance of naming each frame in your frameset. Once you have entered a name in the Name text box of the Frame Property Inspector, Dreamweaver dynamically updates the Target list to include that name. This feature enables you to target specific frames in your frameset in the same manner that you target the reserved names noted previously.

Although you can always type the frame name directly in the Name text box, the drop-down option list comes in handy for this task. You avoid not only having to keep track of the various frame names in your Web page, but you avoid typing errors as well. Targets are case-sensitive, and names must match exactly or the browser won't be able to find the target.

Updating two frames or more at once

Sooner or later, most Web designers using frames have the need to update more than one frame with a single click. The problem is, you can't group two or more URLs together in an anchor tag. Here is an easy-to-implement solution, thanks to Dreamweaver's behaviors.

> **Cross-Reference:** If you're not familiar with Dreamweaver's JavaScript behaviors, you might want to look over Chapter 11 before continuing.

To update more than one frame target from a single link, follow these steps:

1. Select your link in the frame.
2. Open the Behaviors panel from the Launcher or by choosing Window ⇨ Behaviors.
3. Make sure that 4.0 Browsers is selected in the Show Events For category of the add behavior button on the Behaviors panel.
4. Select the + (add behavior) button to display the list of available behaviors.
5. Choose Go To URL from the drop-down option list.
6. Dreamweaver displays the Go To URL dialog box (Figure 10-12) and scans your document for all named frames. Select a target frame from the list of windows or frames.

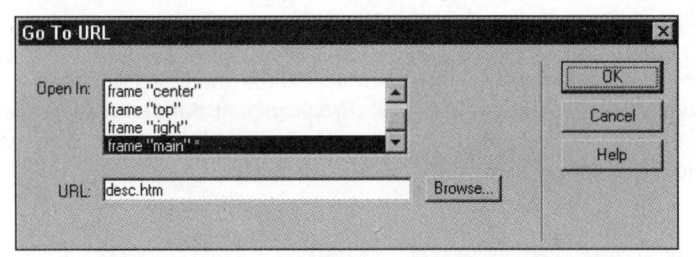

Figure 10-12: You can cause two or more frames to update from a single link by using Dreamweaver's Go To URL behavior.

> **Caution:** You won't be able to use this behavior until you name your frames as detailed in the section "Naming your frames" earlier in this chapter.

7. Enter a URL or choose the Browse (Choose) button to select one.

   Dreamweaver places an asterisk after the targeted frame to indicate that a URL has been selected for it. You can see this in Figure 10-12.

8. Repeat Steps 6 and 7 for any additional frames you want to target.

9. Click OK when you're finished.

   Dreamweaver automatically selects the `onClick` event for the Go To URL behavior.

Now, whenever you click your one link, the browser opens the URLs in the targeted frames in the order specified.

Handling Frameless Browsers

Not all of today's browsers support frames. Netscape began supporting frames in Navigator version 2.0; Microsoft didn't start until IE version 3.0 — and a few of the earlier versions for both browsers are still in use, particularly among AOL users. Some less prevalent browsers also don't support frames. HTML has a built-in mechanism for working with browsers that are not frame-enabled: the `<noframes>...</noframes>` tag pair.

When you begin to construct any frameset, Dreamweaver automatically inserts a `<noframes>` area just below the closing `</frameset>` tag. If a browser is not frames-capable, it ignores the frameset and frame information and renders what is found in the `<noframes>` section.

What should you put into the `<noframes>` section? To ensure the widest possible audience, Webmasters typically insert links to a nonframe version of the site. The links can be as obvious or as discreet as you care to make them. Perhaps a more vital reason is that most of the search engine indexing systems (called *spiders*) don't work with frames. If your frameset is index.html and you want the spider to find the rest of your site, you need to have a descriptive text from your home page as well as a link to each page in the noframes content. Many Webmasters also include links to current versions of Netscape or Internet Explorer, to encourage their nonframe-capable visitors to upgrade.

Dreamweaver includes a facility for easily adding and modifying the `<noframes>` content. Choose Modify ⇨ Frameset ⇨ Edit NoFrames Content to open the NoFrames Content window. As you can see in Figure 10-13, this window is identical to the regular Dreamweaver Document window, with the exception of the "NoFrames Content" in the title bar. In this window, you have access to all the same objects and panels that you normally do. When you have finished editing your `<noframe>` content, choose Modify ⇨ Frameset ⇨ Edit NoFrames Content again to deselect the option and return to the frameset.

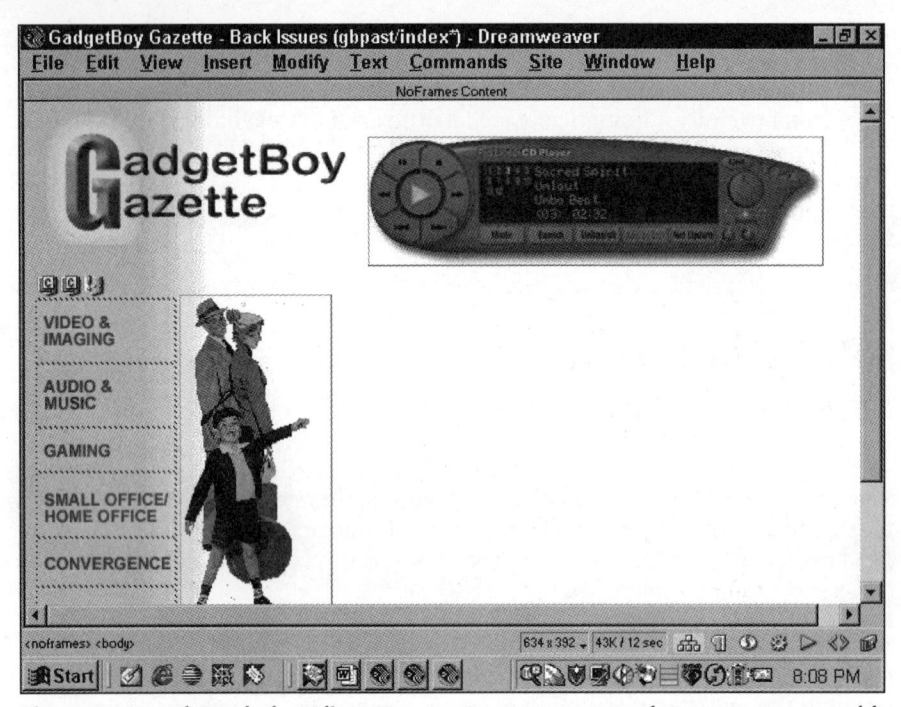

Figure 10-13: Through the Edit NoFrames Content command, Dreamweaver enables you to specify what's seen by visitors whose browsers are not frame-capable.

Here are some pointers to keep in mind when working in the NoFrames Content window:

- The page properties of the `<noframes>` content are the same as the page properties of the frameset. You can select the frameset and then choose Modify ⇨ Page Properties to open the Page Properties dialog box. While in the NoFrames Content window, you can also right-click (Control+click) in any open space to access the Page Properties command.

- Dreamweaver disables the File ⇨ Open commands when the NoFrames Content window is onscreen. To move existing content into the `<noframes>` section, use Dreamweaver's Copy and Paste features.

- The `<noframes>` section is located in the frameset page, which is the primary page examined by search engine spiders. It's a good idea to enter `<meta>` tag information detailing the site, as described in Chapter 4, in the frameset page. While you're in the NoFrames Content window, you can switch to Code view, or open the Code Inspector, and add the `<meta>` tags.

Investigating Iframes

Iframes (short for inline frames) are an HTML 4.0 specification worth noting. An iframe is used to include one HTML document inside another — without building a frameset. What makes iframes visually arresting and extremely useful is their ability to display scroll bars automatically, as shown in Figure 10-14. While iframes are supported by Internet Explorer 4 and above and Netscape 6, you'll have to hand-code or use an extension to insert the tags into Dreamweaver; currently, no menu or object option exists within the standard configuration of Dreamweaver.

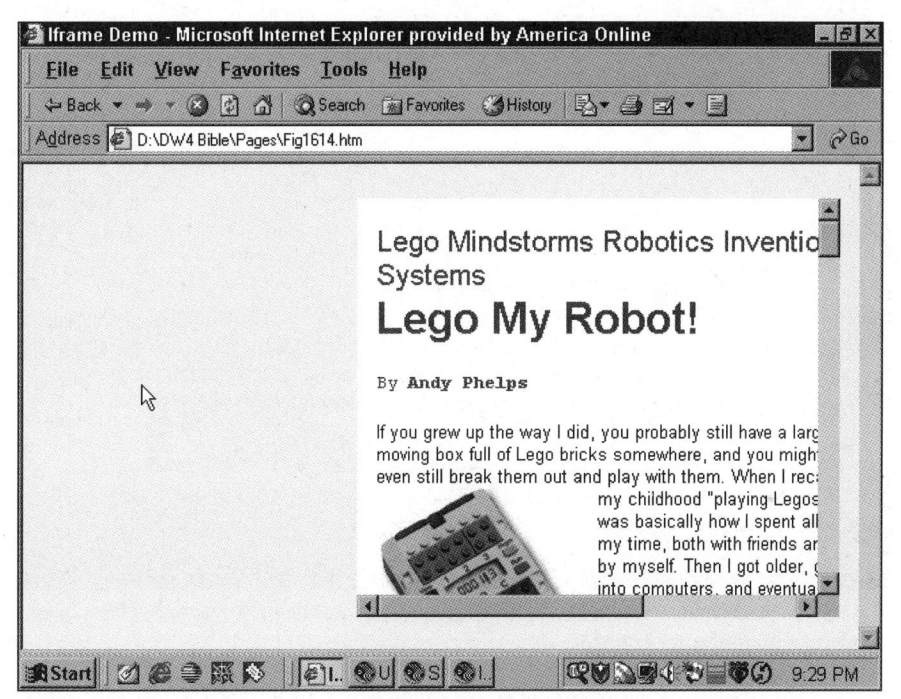

Figure 10-14: The iframe — also known as an inline frame — is a cutting-edge technique for including one HTML page within another.

The `iframe` tag uses the `src` attribute to specify which HTML file is to be included. Any content — whether text, images or whatever — found between the opening and closing `iframe` tags is displayed only if the browser does *not* support iframes. In other words, it's the no-iframe content. Here's an iframe code example:

```
<iframe src="/includes/salespromo.htm" name="promoFrame"
style="position:absolute; width:200px; height:300px; top:139px;
left:530px">Iframes are not supported by this browser.</iframe>
```

If you're familiar with Cascading Style Sheet layers, you'll notice that the style attribute is identical in iframes. This has an interesting effect in Dreamweaver: iframe code is displayed like a layer with the "no-iframe content" visible as shown in Figure 10-15. This makes positioning and resizing the iframe very straightforward. To see the actual iframe content, you'll need to preview the page in a compatible browser.

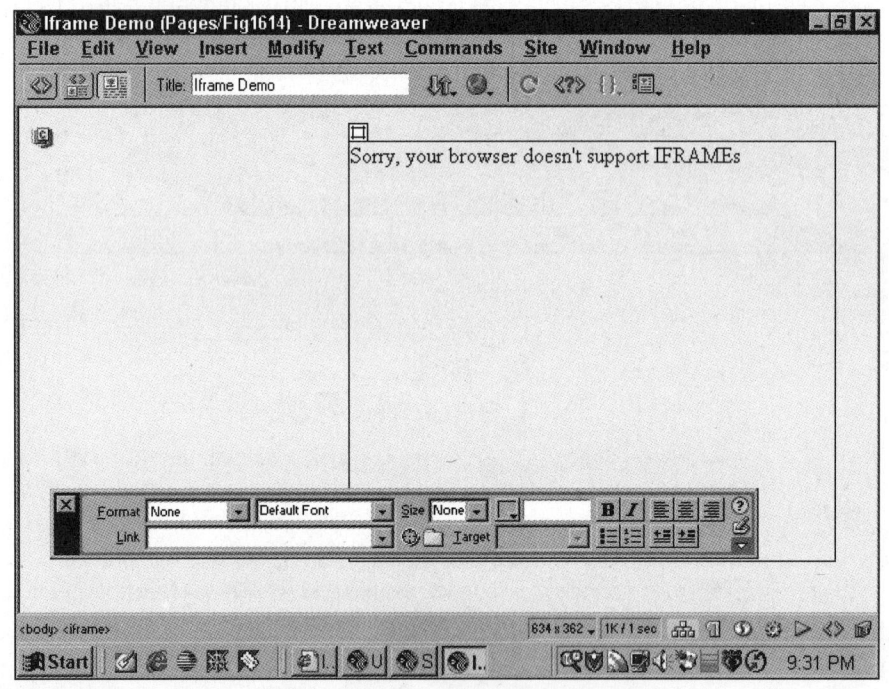

Figure 10-15: When you view an iframe tag in Dreamweaver, it appears like a layer showing the no-iframe content.

Can't wait to start using iframes but don't want to hand-code? Be sure to check out Massimo Foti's Iframe object, which takes advantage of Dreamweaver's interpretation of iframes as a layer. You'll find it under his name on the CD-ROM under Additional Extensions.

Summary

Frames are a significant Webmaster design tool. With frames and framesets, you can divide a single Web page into multiple, independent areas. Dreamweaver gives Web designers quick and easy access to frame design through the program's drag-and-drop interface.

✦ A framed Web page consists of a separate HTML document for each frame and one additional file that describes the frame structure, called the *frameset*.

✦ A frameset comprises columns and rows, which can be sized absolutely in pixels, as a percentage of the browser window, or relative to the other columns or rows.

✦ Dreamweaver enables you to reposition the frame borders by dragging them to a new location. You can also add new frames by Alt+dragging (Option+dragging) any existing frame border.

✦ Framesets can be nested to create more complex column and row arrangements. Selecting the frame border displays the Frameset Property Inspector.

✦ Select any individual frame through the Frames panel or by Alt+clicking (Option+Shift+clicking) within any frame. Once the frame is selected, the Frame Property Inspector can be displayed.

✦ You make your links appear in a specific frame by assigning targets to the links. Dreamweaver supports both structured and named targets. You can update two or more frames with one link by using a Dreamweaver JavaScript behavior.

✦ You should include information and/or links for browsers that are not frame-capable, through Dreamweaver's Edit NoFrames Content feature.

✦ ✦ ✦

CHAPTER 11

Using Behaviors

Behaviors are truly the power tools of Dreamweaver. With Dreamweaver behaviors, any Web designer can make layers appear and disappear, execute any number of rollovers, or control a Shockwave movie — all without knowing even a snippet of JavaScript. In the hands of an accomplished JavaScript programmer, Dreamweaver behaviors can be customized or created from scratch to automate the most difficult Web effect.

Creating behaviors is one of the more challenging Dreamweaver features to master. Implementing these gems, however, is a piece of cake. This chapter examines the concepts behind and the reality of using behaviors — detailing the use of all the behaviors included with Dreamweaver and some from other notable third-party sources. This chapter also contains tips on managing your ever-increasing library of behaviors.

Here's a guarantee for you: Once you get the hang of using Dreamweaver behaviors, your Web pages will never be the same.

Understanding Behaviors, Events, and Actions

A *behavior*, in Macromedia parlance, is the combination of an event and an action. In the electronic age, one pushes a button (the event), and something (the action) occurs — such as changing the channel on the TV. In Dreamweaver, events can be anything as interactive as a user's click of a link or something as automatic as the loading of a Web page. Behaviors are said to be *attached* to a specific element on your page, whether it's a text link, an image, or even the `<body>` tag.

Dreamweaver has simplified the process of working with behaviors by including default events in every possible object on the Web page. Instead of having to think about both *how* you want to do something and *what* you want to do, you only have to focus on the *what* — the action.

In This Chapter

Behavior basics

Adding a behavior's event and action

Looking at the standard behaviors

Managing behaviors

To help you understand conceptually how behaviors are structured, let's examine the four essential steps for adding a behavior to your Web page:

- **Step 1: Pick a tag.** All behaviors are connected to a specific HTML element. You can attach a behavior to everything from the `<body>` to the `<textarea>` of a form. If a certain behavior is unavailable, it's because the necessary element isn't present on the page.

- **Step 2: Choose your target browser.** Different browsers — and the various browser versions — support different events. Dreamweaver enables you to choose either a specific browser, such as Internet Explorer 4, or a browser range, such as version 3 and 4 browsers.

- **Step 3: Select an action.** Dreamweaver makes active only those actions available to your specific page. You can't, for instance, choose the Show-Hide Layer action until you insert one or more layers. Behaviors guide you to the workable options.

- **Step 4: Enter the parameters.** Behaviors get their power from their flexibility. Each action comes with a specific parameter form (which represents the dialog box that the user sees) designed to customize the JavaScript code output. Depending on the action, you can choose source files, set attributes, and enable features. The parameter form can even dynamically update to reflect your current Web page.

Dreamweaver 4 comes with 25 cross browser–compatible actions, and both Macromedia and third-party developers have made many additional actions available, with even more in the works. Behaviors greatly extend the range of possibilities for the modern Web designer — without learning to program JavaScript. All you need to know about attaching behaviors is presented in the following section.

Attaching a Behavior

When you see the code generated by Dreamweaver, you understand why setting up a behavior is also referred to as *attaching* a behavior. As previously noted, Dreamweaver needs a specific HTML tag in order to assign the behavior (Step 1). The link tag `<a>` is often used because, in JavaScript, links can respond to several different events, including `onClick`. Here's an example:

```
<a href="#" onClick="MM_popupMsg('Thanks for coming!')">Exit Here</a>
```

You're not restricted to one event per tag or even one action per event. Multiple events can be attached to a tag to handle various user actions. For example, you may have an image that does all of the following things:

- Highlights when the user's pointer moves over the image
- Reveals a hidden layer in another area of the page when the user clicks the mouse button on the image

♦ Makes a sound when the user releases the mouse button over the image

♦ Starts a Flash movie when the user's pointer moves away from the image

Likewise, a single event can trigger several actions. Updating multiple frames through a single link used to be difficult — but no more. Dreamweaver makes it easy by enabling you to attach several Go to URL actions to the same event, `onMouseClick`. In addition, you are not restricted to attaching multiple instances of the same action to a single event. For example, in a site that uses a lot of multimedia, you could tie all of the following actions to a single `onClick` event:

♦ Begin playing an audio file (with the Play Sound action).

♦ Move a layer across the screen (with the Play Timeline action).

♦ Display a second graphic in place of the first (with the Swap Image action).

♦ Show the copyright information for the audio piece in the status bar (with the Set Text of Status Bar action).

You can even determine the order in which the actions connected to a single event are executed.

With Dreamweaver behaviors, hours of complex JavaScript coding is reduced to a handful of mouse clicks and a minimum of data entry. All behavior assigning and modification is handled through the Behaviors panel.

Using the Behaviors panel

The Behaviors panel is a two-columned window (see Figure 11-1) that neatly sums up the behaviors concept in general. After attaching a behavior, the triggering event (onClick, onMouseOver, and so on) is shown on the left and its associated action — what exactly is triggered — is on the right. A down arrow between the event and action, when clicked, displays other available events for the current browser model. Double-click the action to open the associated parameter window, where you can modify the action's attributes.

As typical in Dreamweaver, you have your choice of methods for opening the Behaviors panel:

♦ Choose Window ⇨ Behaviors.

♦ Select the Show Behaviors button from either Launcher.

♦ Use the keyboard shortcut Shift+F3 (an on/off toggle).

Expert Tip The Behaviors panel can be closed by toggling it off with Shift+F3 or hidden with the other floating panels by pressing F4.

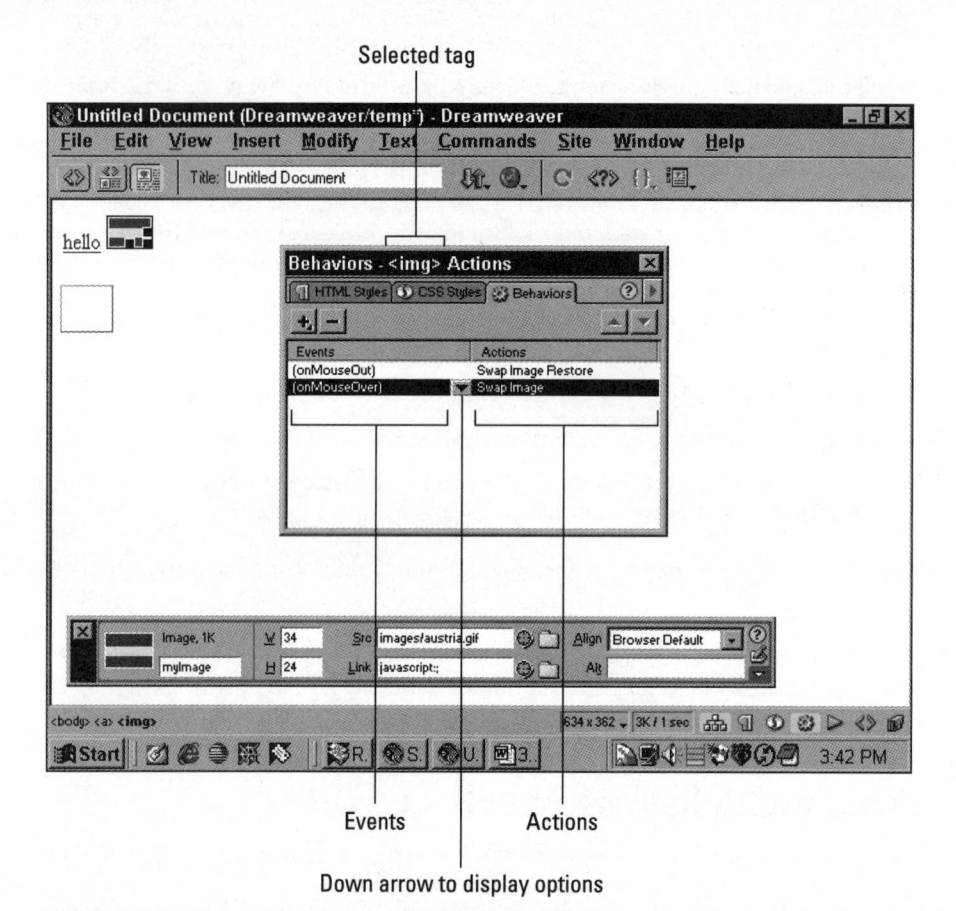

Figure 11-1: You can handle everything about a behavior through the Behaviors panel.

After you have attached a behavior to a tag and closed the associated action's parameter form, Dreamweaver writes the necessary HTML and JavaScript code into your document. Because it involves functions that can be called from anywhere in the document, the JavaScript code is placed in the `<head>` section of the page, and the code that links the selected tag to the functions is written in the `<body>` section. A few actions, including Play Sound, place additional HTML code at the bottom of the `<body>`, but most of the code — there can be a lot of code to handle all the cross-browser contingencies — is placed in the `<head>` HTML section.

Adding a behavior

Now let's look more closely at the procedure for adding (or attaching) a behavior. As noted earlier, you can assign only certain events to particular tags, and those options are further defined by the type of selected browser.

Note: Even in the latest browsers, key events such as `onMouseDown`, `onMouseOver`, and `onMouseOut` work only with anchor tags. To circumvent this limitation, Dreamweaver can enclose an element, such as `<img>`, with an anchor tag that links to nowhere — `src="javascript:;"`. Events that use the anchor tag in this fashion are seen in parentheses in the pop-up menu of events.

To add a behavior to your Web page, follow these steps:

1. Select an object in the Document window.

Expert Tip: If you want to assign a behavior to the entire page, select the `<body>` tag from the Tag Selector.

2. Open the Behaviors panel by choosing Window ➪ Behaviors or selecting the Show Behaviors button from either Launcher. You can see the selected tag at the top of the Behaviors panel.

3. Select the + (add action) button to reveal the available options, as shown in Figure 11-2. Choose one from the pop-up menu.

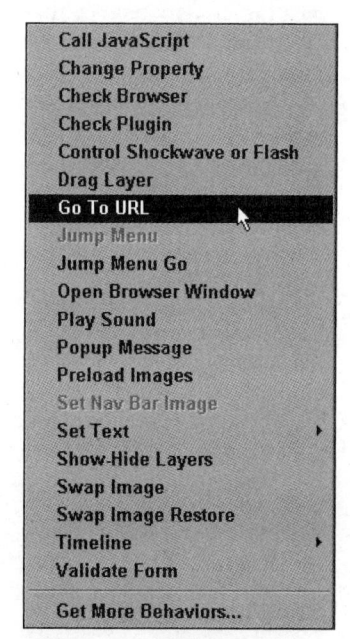

```
Call JavaScript
Change Property
Check Browser
Check Plugin
Control Shockwave or Flash
Drag Layer
Go To URL
Jump Menu
Jump Menu Go
Open Browser Window
Play Sound
Popup Message
Preload Images
Set Nav Bar Image
Set Text                    ▶
Show-Hide Layers
Swap Image
Swap Image Restore
Timeline                    ▶
Validate Form

Get More Behaviors...
```

Figure 11-2: The Add Action pop-up menu dynamically changes according to what's on the current page and which tag is selected.

4. Enter the necessary parameters in the Action's dialog box.

5. Click OK when you're finished to close the dialog box.

    Dreamweaver adds a line to the Behaviors panel displaying the added action and its default action.

A trigger — whether it's an image or a text link — may have multiple behaviors attached to it. One graphical navigation element could, for instance, perform a Swap Image when the user's mouse moves over it, a Swap Image Restore when the mouse moves away and, when clicked, show another Web page in an additional smaller window with the Open Browser Window behavior.

Expert Tip Dreamweaver includes a menu item at the bottom of the Add Action list: Get More Behaviors. To use this feature, go online and then choose the option. You will be connected with the Dreamweaver Exchange, a service from Macromedia with a huge selection of extensions of all flavors, including behaviors.

Managing events

Every time Dreamweaver attaches a behavior to a tag, it also inserts an event for you. The default event that is chosen is based on two selections: the browser type and the tag selected. The different browsers in use have widely different capabilities, notably when it comes to understanding the various event handlers and associated tags.

For every browser and browser combination shown in the Browser drop-down list, Dreamweaver has a corresponding file in the Configuration\Behaviors\Events folder. Each of the tags listed in each file, such as I.E. 4.0.htm, has at least one event associated with it. The entries look like this:

```
<INPUT TYPE="Text" onBlur="*" onChange="" onFocus="" onSelect="">
```

The default event for each tag is marked with an asterisk; in the example, `onBlur` is the default event. After you've selected an action and completed the dialog box, the default event appears in the Events column alongside the action in the Actions column.

Expert Tip If you find yourself changing a particular default event over and over again to some other event, you might want to modify the Event file to pick your alternative as the default. To do this, open the relevant browser file found in the Configuration\Behaviors\Events folder in a regular text editor (not Dreamweaver) and move the asterisk to a different event for that particular tag. Resave the file and restart Dreamweaver to try out your new default behavior.

Should the default event not be the one you prefer to use, you can easily choose another. Choose a different event by selecting the down arrow next to the displayed default event in the Behaviors panel and select any event in the drop-down list (see Figure 11-3).

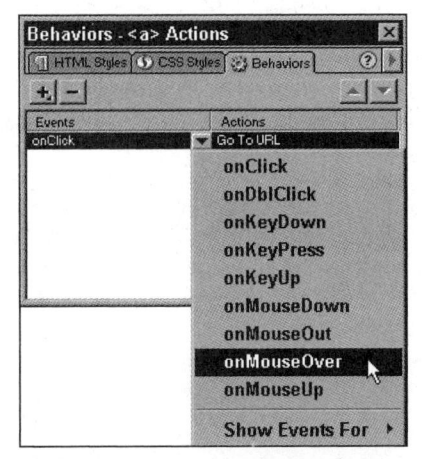

Figure 11-3: You can change the event by selecting the Events arrow button.

Which events are available depends on the browser model selected. By default, 3.0 and Later Browsers is chosen. To change browser models, choose Show Events For from the Events list and select one of the following:

- 3.0 and Later Browsers
- 4.0 and Later Browsers
- IE 3.0
- IE 4.0
- IE 5.0
- Netscape 3.0
- Netscape 4.0

The Dreamweaver\Configuration\Behaviors\Events folder contains HTML files corresponding to the six browsers offered in the Show Events For submenu. You can open these files in Dreamweaver, but Macromedia asks that you not edit them — with one exception. Each file contains the list of tags that have supported *event handlers* (the JavaScript term for events) in that browser.

The older the browser, the fewer event handlers are included—unfortunately, this also means that if you want to reach the broadest Internet audience, your event options are limited. In the broadest category, 3.0 and Later Browsers, only 13 different tags can receive any sort of event handler. This is one of the reasons why, for example, Internet Explorer 3 can't handle rollovers: the browser doesn't understand what an `onMouseOut` event is, and so the image can't revert to its original state.

If you do open and examine an event file in Dreamweaver, notice a group of yellow tags and a few form objects (see Figure 11-4). The yellow tags identify what Dreamweaver sees as invalid HTML. Those form objects — the buttons, checkbox, radio button, and text — render normally but aren't active.

> **Caution:** It's far better to use a standard text editor such as HomeSite or BBEdit to open and modify an event file than to use Dreamweaver. By default, Dreamweaver attempts to correct the invalid HTML it finds in the file, and if you save the file with these unwanted corrections in place, your file will be corrupted, and you'll lose access to certain events.

In this case, viewing the HTML is far more instructive than the Document window, as you can see by looking at Listing 11-1. This example gives the event handler definitions for the 3.0 and Later Browsers category.

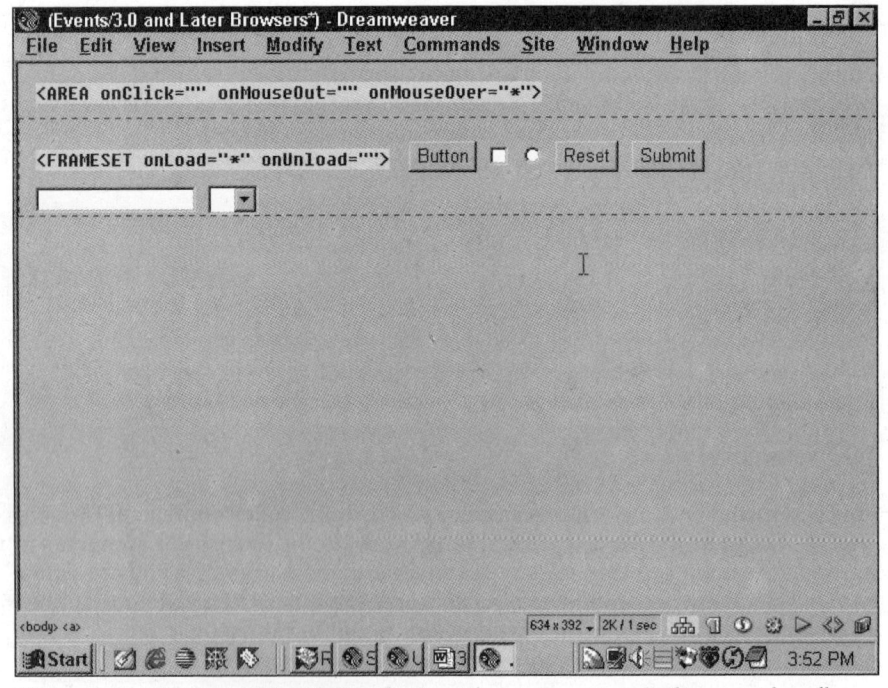

Figure 11-4: The event files define the tags that support particular event handlers in a selected browser.

Listing 11-1: **The Events File for 3.0 and Later Browsers**

```
<A onMouseOver="*">
<AREA onClick="" onMouseOut="" onMouseOver="*">
<BODY onLoad="*" onUnload="">
<FORM onReset="" onSubmit="*">
<FRAMESET onLoad="*" onUnload="">
<INPUT TYPE="Button" onClick="*">
<INPUT TYPE="Checkbox" onClick="*">
<INPUT TYPE="Radio" onClick="*">
<INPUT TYPE="Reset" onClick="*">
<INPUT TYPE="Submit" onClick="*">
<INPUT TYPE="Text" onBlur="*" onChange="" onFocus=""
onSelect="">
<SELECT onBlur="" onChange="*" onFocus="">
<TEXTAREA onBlur="" onChange="*" onFocus="" onSelect="">
```

By contrast, the events file for Internet Explorer 5.0 shows support for every tag under the HTML sun — 92 in all — with almost every tag able to handle any type of event.

> **Expert Tip** Although any HTML tag could potentially be used to attach a behavior, the most commonly used by far are the `<body>` tag (for entire-page events such as onLoad), the `<img>` tag when used as a button, and the link tag, `<a>`.

To locate the default events for any tag as used by a particular browser, consult Table 11-1. The table also shows, at a glance, which browsers support which tags to receive events.

Standard actions

The following 25 standard actions ship with Dreamweaver 4:

Call JavaScript	Open Browser Window	Show-Hide Layers
Change Property	Play Sound	Swap Image
Check Browser	Popup Message	Swap Image Restore
Check Plugin	Preload Images	Play Timeline
Control Shockwave or Flash	Set Nav Bar Image	Stop Timeline
Drag Layer	Set Text of Frame	Go to Timeline Frame
Go to URL	Set Text of Layer	Validate Form
Jump Menu	Set Text of Status Bar	
Jump Menu Go	Set Text of Text Field	

Table 11-1
Default Events by Browser

Tag	3.0 and Later Browsers	4.0 and Later Browsers	IE 3.0	IE 4.0	IE 5.0	Netscape 3.0	Netscape 4.0
<a>	onMouseOver	onClick	OnMouseOver	onClick	onClick	onClick	onClick
<acronym>					onClick		
<address>				onLoad	onLoad		
<applet>				onClick	onClick		
<area>	onMouseOver	onMouseOver		onMouseOver	onMouseOver	onMouseOver	onMouseOver
<b>					onClick		
<bdo>				onMouseOver	onMouseOver		
<big>				onMouseOver	onMouseOver		
<blink>							
<body>	onLoad	onLoad	OnLoad	onLoad	onLoad	onLoad	onLoad
<button>				onClick	onClick		
<caption>				onMouseOver	onMouseOver		
<center>				onMouseOver	onMouseOver		
<cite>				onMouseOver	onMouseOver		
<code>				onMouseOver	onMouseOver		
<col>					onLoseCapture		
<colgroup>					onLoseCapture		
<dd>				onMouseOver	onMouseOver		
<del>					onMouseOver		
<dfn>				onMouseOver	onMouseOver		
<dir>				onMouseOver	onMouseOver		
<div>				onClick	onClick		
<dl>				onMouseOver	onMouseOver		
<dt>				onMouseOver	onMouseOver		
<em>				onMouseOver	onMouseOver		
<embed>				onLoad	onLoad		
<fieldset>				onClick	onClick		
<font>				onMouseOver	onMouseOver		
<form>	onSubmit	onSubmit	OnSubmit	onSubmit	onSubmit	onSubmit	onSubmit
<frame>				onLoad	onLoad		
<frameset>	onLoad	onLoad	OnLoad	onLoad	onLoad	onLoad	onLoad
<h1>...<h6>				onMouseOver	onMouseOver		
<hr>				onMouseOver	onMouseOver		
<i>				onMouseOver	onMouseOver		
<iframe>				onMouseOver	onMouseOver		
<ilayer>				onFocus	onFocus		
<img>	onClick	onMouseDown	OnClick	onClick	onClick	(None selected)	onLoad onMouseDown
<input type=button | checkbox | image | radio | reset | submit>		onClick		onClick	onClick	onClick	onClick

Tag	3.0 and Later Browsers	4.0 and Later Browsers	IE 3.0	IE 4.0	IE 5.0	Netscape 3.0	Netscape 4.0
`<input type=file | password>`		onChange		onChange	onChange	onChange	onChange
`<input type=text>`	onBlur	onBlur	OnBlur	onBlur	onBlur	onBlur	onBlur
`<ins>`				onMouseOver onClick onClick	onMouseOver onClick onClick		
`<kbd>`							
`<label>`							onMouseOver
`<layer>`							
`<legend>`				onMouseOver onMouseOver onClick	onClick onMouseOver onClick		
`<li>`							
`<listing>`							
`<map>`				onMouseOver	onMouseOver		
`<marquee>`				onMouseOver	onMouseOver		
`<menu>`				onMouseOver	onMouseOver		
`<nobr>`				onLoad	onLoad		
`<object>`				onMouseOver	onMouseOver		
`<ol>`				onMouseOver	onMouseOver		
`<p>`				onMouseOver	onMouseOver		
`<plaintext>`				onMouseOver	onMouseOver		
`<pre>`				onMouseOver	onMouseOver		
`<q>`					onClick		
`<rt>`				onMouseOver	onMouseOver		
`<s>`				onMouseOver	onMouseOver		
`<samp>`				onChange	onChange		
`<select>`	onChange	onChange	OnChange	onMouseOver	onMouseOver	onChange	
`<small>`				onMouseOver	onMouseOver		
`<span>`				onMouseOver	onMouseOver		
`<strike>`				onMouseOver	onMouseOver		
`<strong>`				onMouseOver	onMouseOver		
`<sub>`				onMouseOver	onMouseOver		
`<sup>`				onMouseOver	onMouseOver		
`<table>`				onMouseOver	onMouseOver		
`<tbody>`				onMouseOver	onMouseOver		
`<td>`				onChange	onChange		
`<textarea>`	onChange	onChange	onChange	onMouseOver	onMouseOver	onChange	onChange
`<tfoot>`				onMouseOver	onMouseOver		
`<th>`				onMouseOver	onMouseOver		
`<thead>`				onMouseOver	onMouseOver		
`<tr>`				onMouseOver	onMouseOver		
`<tt>`				onMouseOver	onMouseOver		
`<u>`				onMouseOver	onMouseOver		
`<ul>`				onMouseOver	onMouseOver		
`<var>`				onMouseOver	onMouseOver		
`<xmp>`				onMouseOver	onMouseOver		

Each action operates independently and differently from the others, although many share common functions. Each action is associated with a different dialog box or parameter form to enable easy attribute entry.

The following sections describe each of the standard actions: what the action does, what requirements must be met for it to be activated, what options are available, and most important of all, how to use it. Each action is written to work with all browser versions 4 and above; however, some actions do not work as designed in the older browsers. The charts included with every action show the action's compatibility with older browsers. (The information in these charts was adapted from the Dreamweaver Help pages and is used with permission.)

> **Note** The following descriptions assume that you understand the basics of assigning behaviors and that you know how to open the Behaviors panel.

Call JavaScript

With Call JavaScript, you can execute any JavaScript function — standard or custom — with a single mouse click or other event. As your JavaScript savvy grows, you'll find yourself using this behavior again and again.

Call JavaScript is straightforward to use; simply type in the JavaScript code or the name of the function you want to trigger into the dialog box. If, for example, you wanted to get some input from a visitor, you could use JavaScript's built-in `prompt()` method, like this:

```
result=prompt("Whom shall I say is calling?","")
```

When this code is triggered, a small dialog box appears with your query (here, "Whom shall I say is calling?") and a space for an input string. The second argument in the `prompt()` method enables you to include a default answer — to leave it blank, just use two quotes.

> **Note** You can use either single or double quotes in your Call JavaScript behavior; Dreamweaver automatically adjusts for whichever you choose. However, I find it easier to use single quotes because Dreamweaver translates double quotes into character entities; that is, " becomes `&quot;`.

Naturally, you could use Call JavaScript to handle much more complex chores as well. To call a specific custom function that is already in the `<head>` section of your page, just enter its name — along with any necessary arguments — in the Call JavaScript dialog box, shown in Figure 11-5.

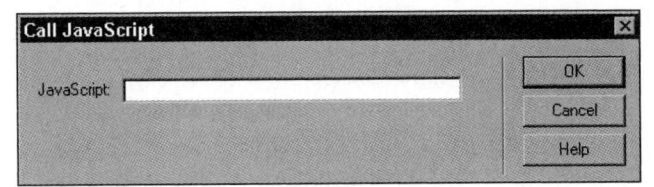

Figure 11-5: Trigger any JavaScript function by attaching a Call JavaScript behavior to an image or text.

To use the Call JavaScript behavior, follow these steps:

1. Select the object to trigger the action.
2. From the Behaviors panel, select the add action button and choose Call JavaScript.
3. In the Call JavaScript dialog box, enter your code in the text box.
4. Click OK when you're done.

> **Note:** In the following charts that detail action behaviors for both newer and older browsers, the phrase "Fails without error" means that the action won't work in the older browser, but that it doesn't generate an error message for the user to see. Where the table indicates "error," it means the user receives a JavaScript alert message.

Here's the browser compatibility chart for the Call JavaScript behavior:

Call JavaScript	Netscape 3.x	Internet Explorer 3.0	Internet Explorer 3.01
Macintosh	Okay	Fails without error	
Windows	Okay		Okay

Change Property

The Change Property action enables you to dynamically alter a property of one of the following tags:

```
<layer>      <div>      <form>      <textarea>
<span>       <img>      <select>
```

You can also alter the following `<input>` types:

```
radio        checkbox        text        password
```

Exactly which properties can be altered depends on the tag as well as on the browser being targeted. For example, the `<div>` tag and Internet Explorer 4.0 combination enables you to change virtually every style sheet option on the fly. The Change Property dialog box (see Figure 11-6) offers a list of the selected tags in the current page.

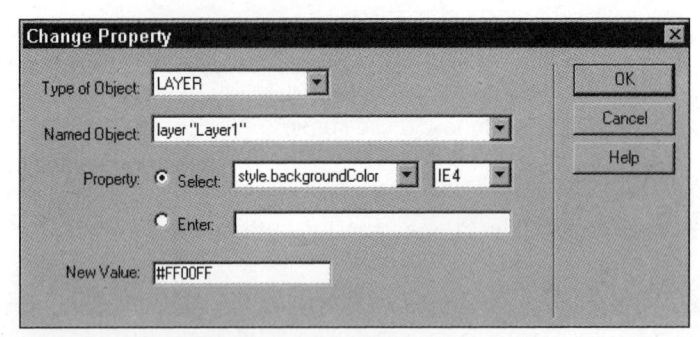

Figure 11-6: The Change Property action enables you to alter attributes of certain tags dynamically.

Caution It's important that you name the objects you want to alter so that Dreamweaver can properly identify them. Remember to use unique names that begin with a letter and contain no spaces or special characters.

This behavior is especially useful for changing the properties of forms and form elements. Be sure to name the form if you wish to use Change Property in this manner.

To use the Change Property action, follow these steps:

1. Select the object to trigger the action.
2. From the Behaviors panel, select the add action button and choose Change Property.
3. In the Change Property dialog box, choose an object type, such as FORM or SELECT, from the Type of Object drop-down list.
4. In the dynamic Named Object drop-down list, choose the object on your page you wish to affect.
5. Click the Select radio button. Select the target browser in the small list box on the far right and then choose the property to change. If you don't find the property in the drop-down list box, you can type it yourself into the Enter text box.

Note Many properties in the various browsers are read-only and cannot be dynamically altered. Those properties listed in the option list are always dynamic.

6. In the New Value text box, type the property's new value to be inserted when the event is fired.

7. Click OK when you're done.

Here's the browser compatibility chart for the Change Property behavior:

Change Property	Netscape 3.x	Internet Explorer 3.0	Internet Explorer 3.01
Macintosh	Okay	Fails without error	
Windows	Okay		Okay

Check Browser

Some Web sites are increasingly split into multilevel versions of themselves to gracefully handle the variety of browsers in operation. The Check Browser action acts as a type of browser "router" capable of sending browsers to appropriate URLs, or just letting them stay on the current page. The Check Browser action is generally assigned to the `<body>` tag and uses the `onLoad` event. If used in this fashion, it's a good idea to keep the basic page accessible to all browsers, even those with JavaScript disabled.

The Check Browser parameter form (see Figure 11-7) is quite flexible and enables you to specify decimal version numbers for the two main browsers. For instance, you may want to let all users of Navigator 4.04 or later stay on the current page and send everyone else to an alternative URL. The URLs can be either relative, such as `alt/index.html`, or absolute, such as `www.idest.com/alt/index.html`.

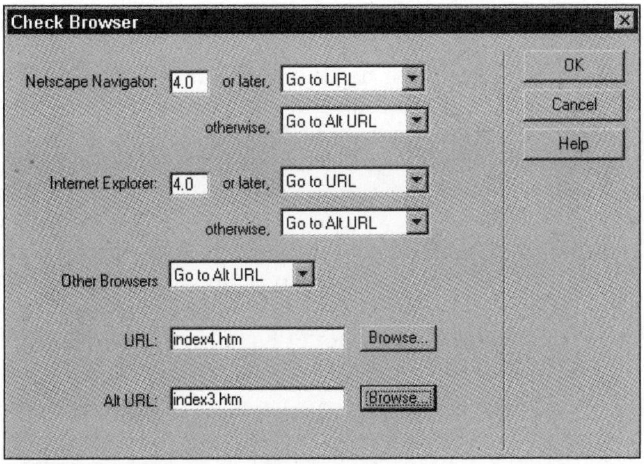

Figure 11-7: The Check Browser action is a great tool for segregating old and new browsers.

To use the Check Browser action, follow these steps:

1. Select the object to trigger the action.
2. From the Behaviors panel, select the add action button and choose Check Browser.
3. Specify the Netscape Navigator and Internet Explorer versions and whether you want the browser to stay on the current page, go to another URL, or proceed to a third alternative URL.

Note: With both major browsers, you can specify the URL that the lower version numbers should visit.

4. Set the same options for all other browsers, such as Opera or OMNIWeb.
5. Enter the URL and alternative URL options in their respective text boxes or select the Browse (Choose) button to locate the files.

Cross-Reference: The Check Browser action works well with another Dreamweaver feature: Convert to 3.0 Compatible.

Here's the browser compatibility chart for the Check Browser behavior:

Check Browser	Netscape 3.x	Internet Explorer 3.0	Internet Explorer 3.01
Macintosh	Okay	Fails without error	
Windows	Okay		Okay

Check Plugin

If certain pages on your Web site require the use of one or more plug-ins, you can use the Check Plugin action to see if a visitor has the necessary plug-in installed. Once this has been examined, Check Plugin can route users with the appropriate plug-in to one URL, and users without it to another URL. You can look for only one plug-in at a time, but you can use multiple instances of the Check Plugin action, if needed.

By default, the parameter form for Check Plugin (see Figure 11-8) offers five plug-ins: Flash, Shockwave, LiveAudio, Netscape Media Player, and QuickTime Plug-in. You can check for any other plug-in by entering its name in the Enter text box; use the name that appears when choosing Help ➪ About Plugins in the Navigator menus.

[Screenshot of "Check Plugin" dialog box showing Plugin Select: Flash, If Found Go To URL: index_flash.htm, Otherwise Go To URL: index_nonflash.htm, with OK, Cancel, Help buttons and "Always go to first URL if detection is not possible" checkbox.]

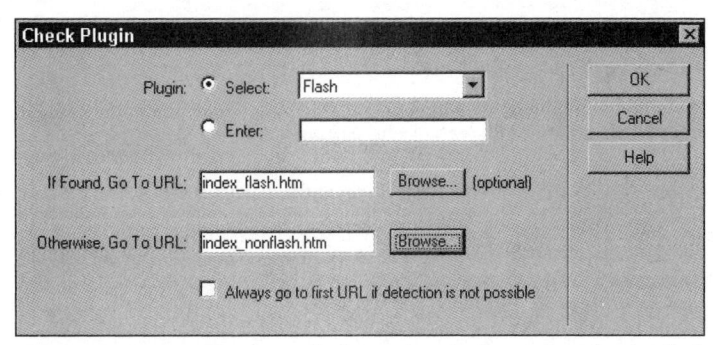

Figure 11-8: Running a media-intensive site? Use the Check Plugin action to divert visitors without plug-ins to alternate pages.

Expert Tip If you use a particular plug-in regularly, you may want to also modify the Check Plugin.js file found in your Actions folder. Add your new plug-in name to the PLUGIN_NAMES array and the corresponding PLUGIN_VALUES array in the initGlobal function.

Although Check Plugin cannot check for specific ActiveX controls, this action can route the Internet Explorer user to the same page as users who have plug-ins. The best way to handle both browsers is to use both ActiveX controls and plug-ins, through the <object> and <embed> methods.

On the CD-ROM Another method for determining whether a plug-in or other player is available is to use the Check MIME action included on the CD-ROM that accompanies this book. This action works in the same way as the Check Plugin action, except you enter the MIME type.

To use the Check Plugin action, follow these steps:

1. Select the object to trigger the action.
2. From the Behaviors panel, select the add action button and choose Check Browser.
3. Select a plug-in from the drop-down list. You can also type another plug-in name in the Enter text box.

Note The names presented in the drop-down list are abbreviated, more recognizable names, and not the formal names inserted into the code. For example, when the option Shockwave is selected, the phrase Shockwave for Director is actually input into the code. On the other hand, any plug-in name you enter manually into the Enter field is inserted verbatim.

4. If you want to send users who are confirmed to have the plug-in to a different page, enter that URL (absolute or relative) in the If Found, Go To URL text box or use the Browse (Choose) button to locate the file. If you want them to stay on the current page, leave the text box empty.

5. In the Otherwise, Go To URL text box, enter the URL for users who do not have the required plug-in.

6. Should the browser detection method fail — as with certain browsers, such as some versions of Internet Explorer on the Macintosh — you can keep the user on the initial page by enabling the "Always go to first URL if detection is not possible" option. Otherwise, if the detection fails, for any reason, the users are sent to the URL listed in the Otherwise field.

Here's the browser compatibility chart for the Check Plugin behavior:

Check Browser	Netscape 3.x	Internet Explorer 3.0	Internet Explorer 3.01
Macintosh	Okay	Fails without error	
Windows	Okay		Okay

Control Shockwave or Flash

The Control Shockwave or Flash action enables you to command your Shockwave and Flash movies through external controls. With Control Shockwave or Flash, you can build your own interface for your Shockwave or Flash material. This action can be used in conjunction with the `autostart=true` attribute (entered through the Property Inspector's Parameter dialog box for the Shockwave or Flash file) to enable a replaying of the movie.

You must have a Shockwave or Flash movie inserted in your Web page in order for the Control Shockwave or Flash action to be available. The parameter form for this action (see Figure 11-9) lists all the Shockwave or Flash movies by name that are found in either an `<embed>` or `<object>` tag. You can set the action to control the movie in one of four ways: Play, Stop, Rewind, or Go to Frame. You can choose only one option each time you attach an action to an event. If you choose the last option, you need to specify the frame number in the text box. Note that specifying a Go to Frame number does not start the movie there; you need to attach a second Control Shockwave or Flash action to the same event to play the file.

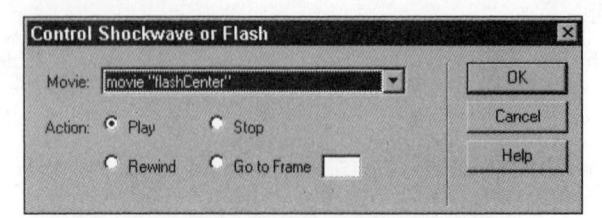

Figure 11-9: Build your own interface and then control a Shockwave and Flash movie externally with the Control Shockwave or Flash action.

Expert Tip: Be sure to name your Shockwave or Flash movie. Otherwise, the Control Shockwave or Flash action lists both unnamed <embed> and unnamed <object> for each file, and you cannot write to both tags as you can with a named movie.

To use the Control Shockwave or Flash action, follow these steps:

1. Select the object to trigger the action.
2. From the Behaviors panel, select the add action button and choose Control Shockwave or Flash.
3. In the Control Shockwave or Flash dialog box, select a movie from the Named Shockwave Object drop-down list.
4. Select a control by choosing its radio button:
    - **Play:** Begins playing the movie at the current frame location.
    - **Stop:** Stops playing the movie.
    - **Rewind:** Returns the movie to its first frame.
    - **Go to Frame:** Displays a specific frame in the movie. Note: For this option, you must enter a frame number in the text box.
5. Click OK when you're done.

Here's the browser compatibility chart for the Control Shockwave or Flash behavior:

Control Shockwave or Flash	Netscape 3.x	Internet Explorer 3.0	Internet Explorer 3.01
Macintosh	Okay	Fails without error	
Windows	Okay		Fails without error

Drag Layer

The Drag Layer action provides some spectacular — and interactive — effects with little effort on the part of the designer. Drag Layer enables your Web page visitors to move layers — and all that they contain — around the screen with the drag-and-drop technique. With the Drag Layer action, you can easily set up the following capabilities for the user:

✦ Enable layers to be dragged anywhere on the screen.

✦ Restrict the dragging to a particular direction or combination of directions — a horizontal sliding layer can be restricted to left and right movement, for instance.

- Limit the drag handle to a portion of the layer such as the upper bar or enable the whole layer to be used.
- Provide an alternative clipping method by enabling only a portion of the layer to be dragged.
- Enable changing of the layers' stacking order while dragging or on mouse release.
- Set a snap-to target area on your Web page for layers that the user releases within a defined radius.
- Program a JavaScript command to be executed when the snap-to target is hit or every time the layer is released.

Cross-Reference

Layers are one of the more powerful features of Dreamweaver. To get the most out of the layer-oriented behaviors, familiarize yourself with layers by examining Chapter 15.

Layers must be inserted in your Web page before the Drag Layer action becomes available for selection from the Add Action pop-up menu. You must attach the action to the `<body>` — you can, however, attach separate versions of Drag Layer to different layers for different effects.

Drag Layer's parameter form (see Figure 11-10) includes a Get Current Position button that puts the left and top coordinates of a selected layer into the appropriate boxes for the Drop Target parameters. If you plan on using targeting, place your layer at the target location before attaching the behavior.

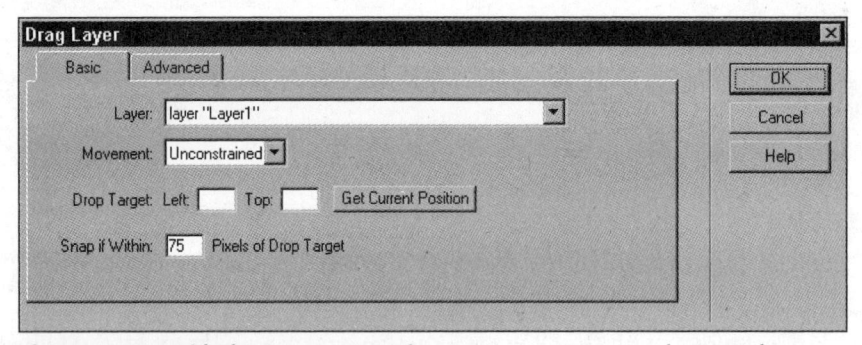

Figure 11-10: With the Drag Layer action, you can set up your layers to be repositioned by the user.

To use the Drag Layer action, follow these steps:

1. Select the `<body>` tag.
2. From the Behaviors panel, select the add action button and choose Drag Layer.

3. In the Layer drop-down list of the parameter form in the Basic tabbed panel, select the layer you want to make draggable.

4. To limit the movement of the layer, change the Movement option from Unconstrained to Constrained. Text boxes for Up, Down, Left, and Right appear. Enter pixel values in the text boxes to control the range of motion:
   - To constrain movement vertically, enter positive numbers in the Up and Down text boxes and zeros in the Left and Right text boxes.
   - To constrain movement horizontally, enter positive numbers in the Left and Right text boxes and zeros in the Up and Down text boxes.
   - To enable movement in a rectangular region, enter positive values in all four text boxes.

5. To establish a location for a target for the dragged layer, enter coordinates in the Drop Target: Left and Top text boxes. Select the Get Current Position button to fill these text boxes with the layer's present location.

6. To set a snap-to area around the target coordinates where the layer falls, if released in the target location, enter a pixel value in the Snap if Within text box.

7. For additional options, select the Advanced tab.

8. If you want to limit the area to be used as a drag handle, select the radio button for Drag Handle: Area Within Layer. Left, Top, Width, and Height text boxes appear. In the appropriate text boxes, enter the Left and Top coordinates of the drag handle in pixels, as well as the Width and Height dimensions.

Note If you want to enable the whole layer to act as a drag handle, make sure the Drag Handle: Entire Layer radio button is selected.

9. To control the positioning of the dragged layer, set the following While Dragging options:
   - To keep the layer in its current depth and not bring it to the front when it is dragged, deselect the checkbox for While Dragging: Bring Layer to the Front.
   - To change the stacking order of the layer when it is released, select either Leave on Top or Restore z-order from the drop-down list.

10. To execute a JavaScript command while the layer is being dragged, enter the command or function in the Call JavaScript text box.

11. To execute a JavaScript command when the layer is dropped on the target, enter the code in the When Dropped: Call JavaScript text box. If you want the JavaScript to execute only when the layer is snapped to its target, select the Only if snapped option — this option requires that a value be entered in the Snap if Within text box.

12. Click OK when you're done.

Note: If you — or someone on your team — has the JavaScript programming skills, you can gather information output from the Drag Layer behavior to enhance your pages. Dreamweaver declares three variables for each draggable layer: MM_UPDOWN (the *y* coordinate), MM_LEFTRIGHT (the *x* coordinate), and MM_SNAPPED (true, if the layer has reached the specified target). Before you can get any of these properties, you must get an object reference for the proper layer. Another function, MM_findObj (layername), handles this chore.

Here's the browser compatibility chart for the Drag Layer behavior:

Drag Layer	*Netscape 3.x*	*Internet Explorer 3.0*	*Internet Explorer 3.01*
Macintosh	Fails without error	Fails without error	
Windows	Fails without error		Fails without error

Go to URL

Dreamweaver brings the same power of links — with a lot more flexibility — to any event with the Go to URL action. One of the trickier tasks in using frames on a Web page is updating two or more frames simultaneously with a single button click. The Go to URL action handily streamlines this process for the Web designer. Go to URL can also be used as a preload router that sends the user to another Web page once the `onLoad` event has finished.

The dialog box for Go to URL (see Figure 11-11) displays any existing anchors or frames in the current page or frameset. To load multiple URLs at the same time, open the drop-down list and select the first frame that you want to alter; then enter the desired page or location in the URL text box. Select the second frame from the list and enter the next URL (or Browse/Choose to find it). If you select a frame to which you have previously assigned a URL, that address appears in the URL text box.

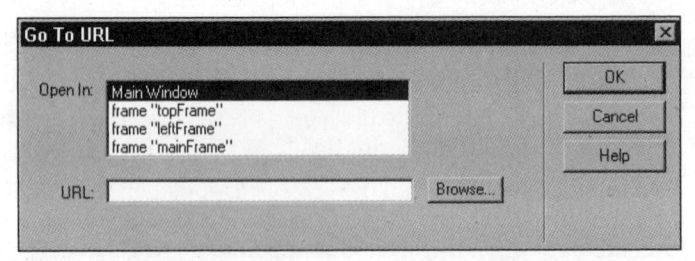

Figure 11-11: Update two or more frames at the same time with the Go to URL action.

To use the Go to URL action, follow these steps:

1. Select the object to trigger the action.
2. From the Behaviors panel, select the add action button and choose Go to URL.
3. From the Go to URL dialog box, select the target for your link from the list in the Open In window.
4. Enter the path of the file to open in the URL text box or click the Browse (Choose) button to locate a file.

   An asterisk appears next to the frame name to indicate that a URL has been chosen.
5. To select another target to load a different URL, repeat Steps 3 and 4.
6. Click OK when you're done.

Here's the browser compatibility chart for the Go to URL behavior:

Go to URL	Netscape 3.x	Internet Explorer 3.0	Internet Explorer 3.01
Macintosh	Okay	Fails without error	
Windows	Okay		Okay

Jump Menu and Jump Menu Go

Although most behaviors insert original code to activate an element of the Web page, several behaviors are included to edit code inserted by a Dreamweaver object. The Jump Menu and Jump Menu Go behaviors both require a previously inserted Jump Menu object before they become active. The Jump Menu behavior is used to edit an existing Jump Menu object, while the Jump Menu Go behavior adds a graphic image as a "Go" button.

To use the Jump Menu behavior to edit an existing Jump Menu object, follow these steps:

1. Select the Jump Menu object previously inserted into the page.
2. In the Behaviors panel, double-click the listed Jump Menu behavior.
3. Make your modifications in the Jump Menu dialog box, as shown in Figure 11-12.

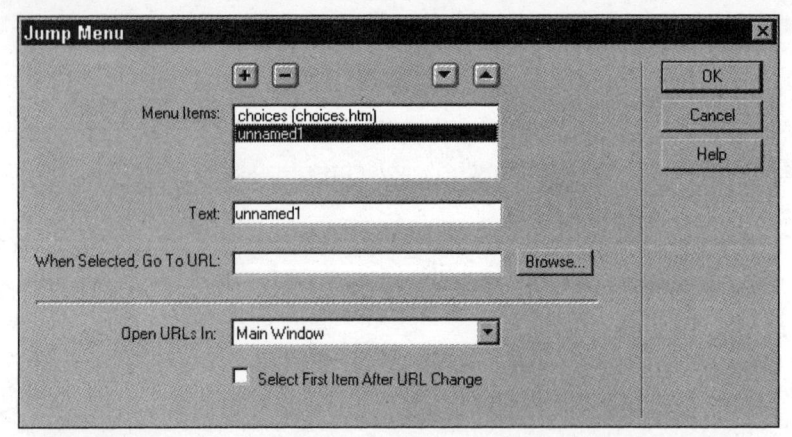

Figure 11-12: The Jump Menu behavior is used to modify a previously inserted Jump Menu object.

You can alter the existing menu item names or their associated URLs, add new menu items, or reorder the list through the Jump Menu dialog box.

4. Click OK when you're done.

To add a button to activate the Jump Menu object, follow these steps:

1. Select the image or form button you'd like to make into a Go button.

   A Jump Menu object must be on the current page for the Jump Menu Go behavior to be available.

2. From the Behaviors panel, select Jump Menu Go from the Add behavior list.

   The Jump Menu Go dialog box, shown in Figure 11-13, is displayed.

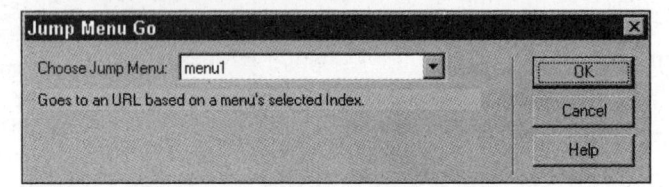

Figure 11-13: Add a graphic or standard button as a Go button with the Jump Menu Go behavior.

3. Select the name of the Jump Menu object you want to activate from the option list.

4. Click OK when you're done.

Here's the browser compatibility chart for both Jump Menu behavior:

Jump Menu	Netscape 3.x	Internet Explorer 3.0	Internet Explorer 3.01
Macintosh	Okay	Fails without error	
Windows	Okay		Fails without error

Open Browser Window

Want to display your latest design in a borderless, nonresizable browser window that's exactly the size of your image? With the Open Browser Window action, you can open a new browser window and specify its exact size and attributes. You can even set it up to receive JavaScript events.

You can also open a new browser window with a regular link by specifying `target="_blank"`, but you can't control any of the window's attributes with that method. You do get this control with the parameter form of the Open Browser Window action (see Figure 11-14); here you can set the window width and height, and whether or not to display the Navigation Toolbar, Location Toolbar, Status Bar, Menu Bar, Scrollbars, and Resize Handles. You can also name your new window, a necessary step for advanced JavaScript control.

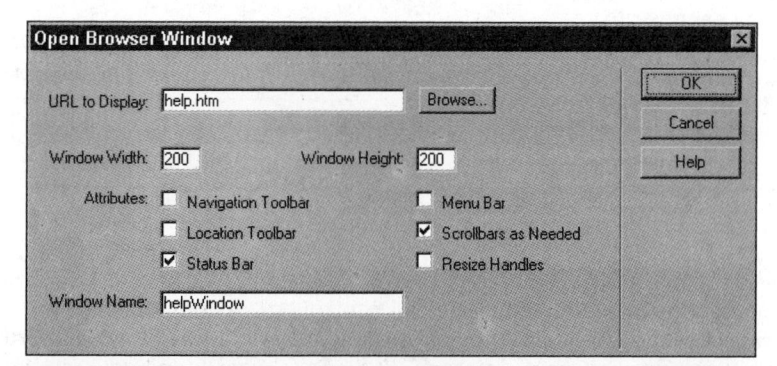

Figure 11-14: Use the Open Browser Window action to program in a pop-up advertisement or remote control.

You have to explicitly select any of the attributes you want to appear in your new window. Your new browser window contains only the attributes you've checked, plus basic window elements such as a title bar and a Close button.

To use the Open Browser Window action, follow these steps:

1. Select the object to trigger the action.
2. From the Behaviors panel, select the add action button and choose Open Browser Window.
3. In the URL to Display text box, enter the address of the Web page you want to display in the new window. You can also select the Browse (Choose) button to locate the file.
4. To specify the window's size and shape, enter the width and height values in the appropriate text boxes.

   You must enter both a width and height measurement, or the new browser window opens to its default size.
5. Check the appropriate Attributes checkboxes to enable the parameters you want.
6. If you plan on using JavaScript to address or control the window, type a unique name in the Window Name text box. This name cannot contain spaces or special characters. Dreamweaver alerts you if the name you've entered is unacceptable.
7. Click OK when you're done.

Here's the browser compatibility chart for the Open Browser Window behavior:

Open Browser Window	Netscape 3.x	Internet Explorer 3.0	Internet Explorer 3.01
Macintosh	Okay	Fails without error	
Windows	Okay		Okay

Play Sound

The Play Sound action is used to add external controls to an audio file that normally uses the Netscape LiveAudio plug-in or the Windows Media Player. Supported audio file types include .wav, .mid, .au, and .aiff files — generally to add background music with a hidden sound file. The Play Sound action inserts an `<embed>` tag with the following attributes set:

- loop=false
- autostart=false
- mastersound
- hidden=true
- width=0
- height=0

Instead of automatically detecting which sound files have been inserted in the current Web page, Play Sound looks for the sound file to be inserted though the action's dialog box (see Figure 11-15).

Figure 11-15: Give your Web page background music and control it with the Play Sound action.

> **Note:** Dreamweaver can detect if a visitor's browser has the Windows Media Player installed and, if so, issue the appropriate commands.

To use the Play Sound action, follow these steps:

1. Select the object to trigger the action.
2. From the Behaviors panel, select the add action button and choose Play Sound.
3. To play a sound, enter the path to the audio file in the Play Sound text box or select the Browse (Choose) button to locate the file.
4. Click OK when you're done.

Here's the browser compatibility chart for the Play Sound behavior:

Play Sound	Netscape 3.x	Internet Explorer 3.0	Internet Explorer 3.01
Macintosh	Okay	Fails without error	
Windows	Okay		Fails without error

Popup Message

You can send a quick message to your users with the Popup Message action. When triggered, this action opens a JavaScript Application Alert with your message. You enter your message in the Message text box on the action's parameter form (see Figure 11-16).

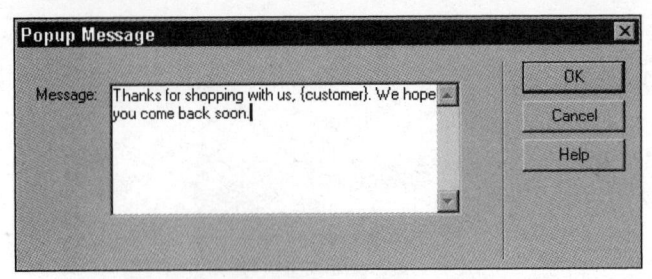

Figure 11-16: Send a message to your users with the Popup Message action.

To use the Popup Message action, follow these steps:

1. Select the object to trigger the action.
2. From the Behaviors panel, select the add action button and choose Popup Message.
3. Enter your text in the Message text box.
4. Click OK when you're done.

Expert Tip You can include JavaScript functions or references in your text messages by surrounding the JavaScript with curly braces. For example, today's date could be incorporated in a message like this:

```
Welcome to our site on {new Date()}!
```

You could also pull data entered into a form to incorporate into a message, as in this example:

```
Thanks for filling out our form, ¬
{document.theForm.firstname.value}.
```

If you need to display a curly brace in a message, you must precede it with a backslash character, \.

Here's the browser compatibility chart for the Popup Message behavior:

Popup Message	Netscape 3.x	Internet Explorer 3.0	Internet Explorer 3.01
Macintosh	Okay	Fails without error	
Windows	Okay		Okay

Preload Images

Designs commonly require a particular image or images to be displayed immediately when called by an action or a timeline. Because of the nature of HTML, all graphics are separate files that normally are downloaded when needed. To get the snappy response required for certain designs, graphics need to be preloaded or cached so that they will be available. The Preload Images action performs this important service. You designate the images you want to cache for later use through the Preload Images parameter form (see Figure 11-17).

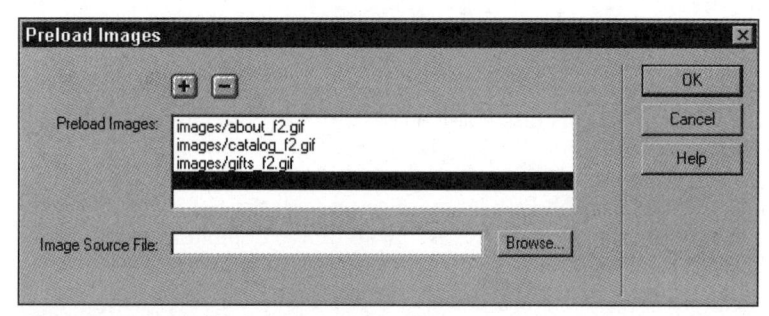

Figure 11-17: Media-rich Web sites respond much faster when images have been cached with the Preload Images action.

Note You don't need to use the Preload Images action if you're creating rollovers. Both the Rollover object and the Swap Image action enable you to preload images from their dialog boxes.

To use the Preload Images action, follow these steps:

1. Select the object to trigger the action.
2. From the Behaviors panel, select the add action button and Preload Images.
3. In the action's parameter form, enter the path to the image file in the Image Source File text box or select the Browse (Choose) button to locate the file.
4. To add another file, click the + (add) button and repeat Step 2.

Caution After you've specified your first file to be preloaded, be sure to press the + (add) button for each successive file you want to add to the list. Otherwise, the highlighted file is replaced by the next entry.

5. To remove a file from the Preload Images list, select it and click the – (delete) button.
6. Click OK when you're done.

Here's the browser compatibility chart for the Preload Images behavior:

Preload Image	Netscape 3.x	Internet Explorer 3.0	Internet Explorer 3.01
Macintosh	Okay	Fails without error	
Windows	Okay		Fails without error

Set Nav Bar Image

The Set Nav Bar Image action, like the Jump Menu actions, enables you to edit an existing Dreamweaver object. The Nav Bar object, inserted from the Common category of the Objects panel, consists of a series of user-specified images acting as a group of navigational buttons. The Set Nav Bar Image action enables you to modify the current Nav Bar object, adding, reordering, or deleting images as buttons as well as setting up advanced rollover techniques. In fact, the Set Nav Bar Image action could be thought of as a superduper Swap Image behavior.

> **Cross-Reference**
> To refresh your memory about the capabilities of the Nav Bar Image, see Chapter 6.

The main aspect that sets a nav bar apart from any other similar series of rollover images is that the nav bar elements relate to one another. When you select one element of a nav bar, by default, all the other elements are swapped to their up state. The Set Nav Bar Image action enables you to modify that default behavior to a rollover in another area or any other image swap desired. You can also use the Set Nav Bar Image to include another image button in the nav bar.

To modify an existing Nav Bar object, follow these steps:

1. Choose any image in a Nav Bar object.
2. From the Behaviors panel, double-click any of the Set Nav Bar Image actions displayed for the image.

   The same Set Nav Bar Image dialog box (see Figure 11-18) opens regardless of whether you select an action associated with the `onClick`, `onMouseOver`, or `onMouseOut` event.

3. Make any desired edits — changing the Up, Over, Down, or Over While Down state images or their respective URLs or targets — from the Basic tab of the dialog box.
4. To change any other images when the current image is interacted with, select the Advanced tab.
5. On the Advanced tab of the dialog box, choose which state you want to trigger any changes from the drop-down list:
   - Over Image or Over While Down
   - Down State

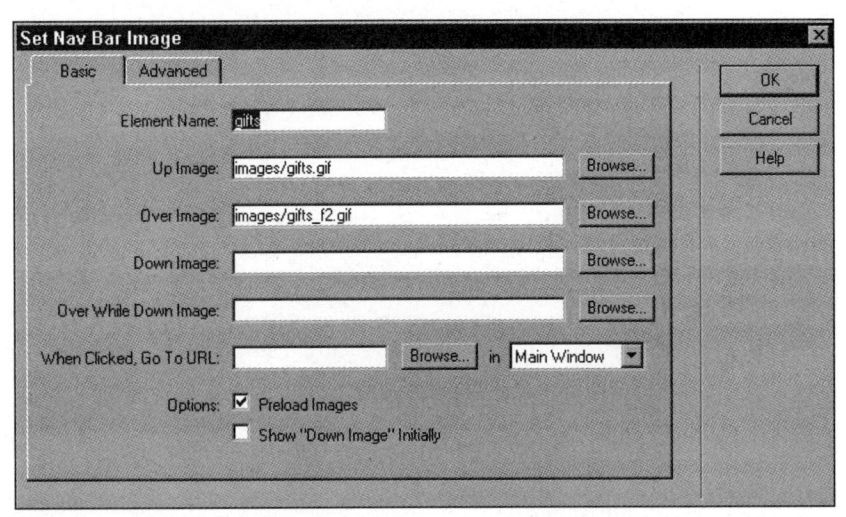

Figure 11-18: Modify an existing Nav Bar element through the Set Nav Bar Image action.

6. Select the image you wish to change from the Also Set Image list.

   Dreamweaver lists all the named images on the current page, not just those in the nav bar.

7. Select the path of the new image to be displayed in the To Image Field text field.

   An asterisk appears after the current image in the list box, signifying that a swap image has been chosen.

8. If you chose Over Image or Over While Down as the triggering event, an optional field, If Down, enables you to specify another graphic to swap the image of the down state image as well.

9. To alter other images with the same triggering event, repeat Steps 6 through 8.

Here's the browser compatibility chart for the Set Nav Bar Image behavior:

Set Nav Bar Image	Netscape 3.x	Internet Explorer 3.0	Internet Explorer 3.01
Macintosh	Okay	Fails without error	
Windows	Okay		Fails without error

Set Text of Frame

Dreamweaver has grouped together four similar behaviors under the Set Text heading:

- Set Text of Frame
- Set Text of Layer
- Set Text of Status Bar
- Set Text of Text Field

Set Text of Frame enables you to do much more than change a word or two — you can dynamically rewrite the entire code for any frame. You can even incorporate JavaScript functions or interactive information into the new frame content.

The Set Text of Frame action replaces all the contents of the `<body>` tag of a frame. Dreamweaver supplies a handy "Get Current HTML" button that enables you to easily keep everything you want to retain and change only a heading or other element. Naturally, you must be within a frameset to use this behavior, and the frames must be named correctly — that is, uniquely without special characters or spaces.

To change the content of a frame dynamically, follow these steps:

1. Select the triggering object.
2. In the Behaviors panel, choose Set Text ⇨ Set Text of Frame from the Add Behavior list.

   The Set Text of Frame dialog box opens as shown in Figure 11-19.

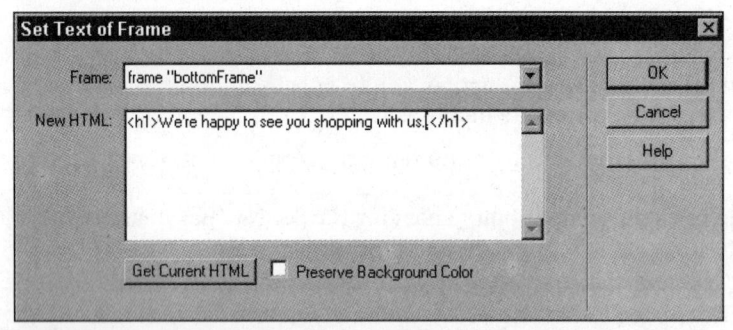

Figure 11-19: The Set Text of Frame behavior enables you to interactively update the contents of any frame in the current frameset.

3. Choose the frame you wish to alter from the Frame option list.
4. Enter the code for the changing frame in the New HTML text area.

   Keep in mind that you're changing not just a word or phrase, but all the HTML contained in the `<body>` section of the frame.

5. If you want to keep the majority of the code, select the Get Current HTML button and change only those portions necessary.

Expert Tip The same JavaScript capabilities outlined in the Popup Message section are available in the Set Text of Frame behavior.

6. To maintain the frames `<body>` attributes, such as the background and text colors, select the Preserve Background Color option.

   If this option is not selected, the frames background and text colors are replaced by the default values (a white background and black text).

7. Click OK when you're done.

Here's the browser compatibility chart for the Set Text of Frame behavior:

Set Text of Frame	Netscape 3.x	Internet Explorer 3.0	Internet Explorer 3.01
Macintosh	Okay	Fails without error	
Windows	Okay		Okay

Set Text of Layer

The Set Text of Layer behavior is similar to the previously described Set Text of Frame behavior in that it replaces the entire HTML contents of the target. The major difference, of course, is that with one you're replacing the code of a layer and with the other, the `<body>` tag of a frame. You're also able to include any valid JavaScript functions within a pair of curly braces, { }, in the HTML code as with other Set Text behaviors. You should also note that, unlike Set Text of Frame, no button exists for getting the current HTML in Set Text of Layer.

To set the text of a layer dynamically, follow these steps:

1. Make sure that the layer you want to change has been created and named properly.
2. Select the tag, link, or image you want to trigger the behavior.
3. From the Behaviors panel, select the add action button and choose Set Text ⇨ Set Text of Layer from the option list.

   The Set Text of Layer dialog box opens, as shown in Figure 11-20.

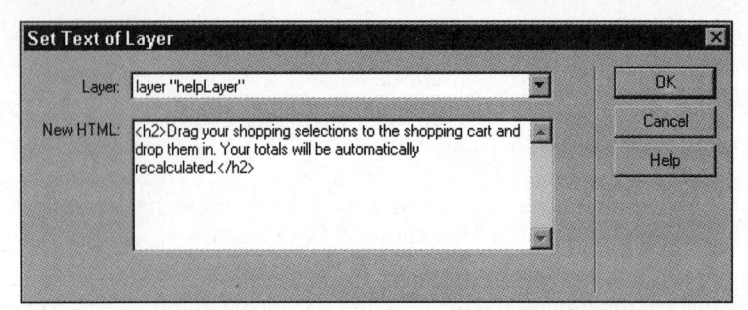

Figure 11-20: Replace all the HTML in a layer with the Set Text of Layer behavior.

4. Select the layer to modify from the Layer option list.
5. Enter the replacement code in the New HTML text area.

> **Expert Tip**
> Although no "Get Current HTML" button exists here as with the Set Text of Frame behavior, a workaround does exist. Before invoking the behavior, select and copy all the elements inside the layer. Because Dreamweaver copies tags as well as text in the Document window, you can then just paste the clipboard into the New HTML text area. Be careful not to select the layer tag, `<div>`, or the layer's contents — if you do, you are pasting a layer in a layer.

6. Click OK when you're done.

Here's the browser compatibility chart for the Set Text of Layer behavior:

Set Text of Layer	Netscape 3.x	Internet Explorer 3.0	Internet Explorer 3.01
Macintosh	Fails without error	Fails without error	
Windows	Fails without error		Fails without error

Set Text of Status Bar

Use the Set Text of Status Bar action to show your choice of text in a browser's status bar, based on a user's action such as moving the pointer over an image. The message stays displayed in the status bar until another message replaces it. System messages, such as URLs, tend to be temporary and visible only when the user's mouse is over a link.

The only limit to the length of the message is the size of the browser's status bar; you should test your message in various browsers to make sure that it is completely visible.

Expert Tip

To display a message only when a user's pointer is over an image, use one Set Text of Status Bar action, attached to an `onMouseOver` event, with your associated text. Use another Set Text of Status Bar action, attached to an `onMouseOut` event, that has a null string (a couple of spaces) as the text.

All text is entered in the Set Text of Status Bar parameter form (see Figure 11-21) in the Message text box.

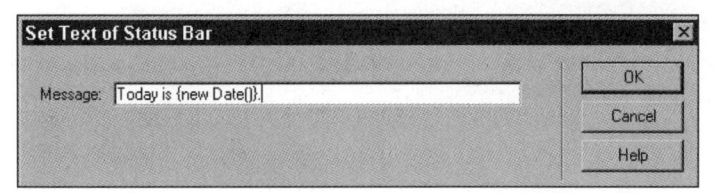

Figure 11-21: Use the Set Text of Status Bar action to guide your users with instructions in the browser window's status bar.

To use the Set Text of Status Bar action, follow these steps:

1. Select the object to trigger the action.
2. From the Behaviors panel, select the add action button and choose Set Text of Status Bar.

Expert Tip

As with the other Set Text behaviors, you can include valid JavaScript functions and variables in the Set Text of Status Bar behavior by offsetting them with curly braces.

3. Enter your text in the Message text box.
4. Click OK when you're done.

Here's the browser compatibility chart for the Set Text of Status Bar behavior:

Set Text of Status Bar	Netscape 3.x	Internet Explorer 3.0	Internet Explorer 3.01
Macintosh	Okay	Fails without error	
Windows	Okay		Okay

Set Text of Text Field

The final Set Text behavior enables you to update any text or textarea field, dynamically. The Set Text of Text Field behavior accepts any text or JavaScript input. (JavaScript functions and variables must be enclosed in a set of curly braces.) A text field must be present on the page for the behavior to be available.

To change the displayed text of a text field, follow these steps:

1. From the Behaviors panel, choose Set Text ⇨ Set Text of Text Field from the Add Action list.

    The Set Text of Text Field dialog box is displayed, as shown in Figure 11-22.

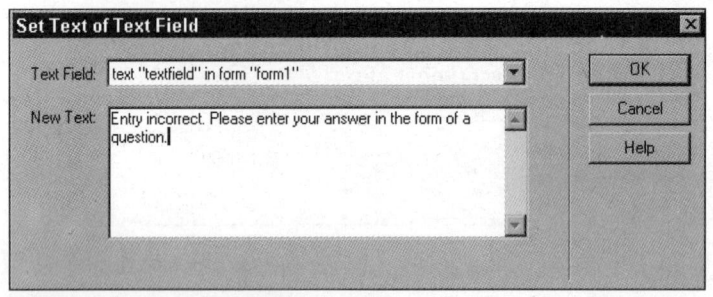

Figure 11-22: Dynamically update text form elements with the Set Text of Text Field behavior.

2. Choose the desired text field from the drop-down list.
3. Enter the new text and/or JavaScript in the New Text area.
4. Click OK when you're done.

Here's the browser compatibility chart for the Set Text of Text Field behavior:

Set Text of Text Field	Netscape 3.x	Internet Explorer 3.0	Internet Explorer 3.01
Macintosh	Okay	Fails without error	
Windows	Okay		Okay

Show-Hide Layers

One of the key features of Dynamic HTML layers is their capability to appear and disappear on command. The Show-Hide Layer action gives you easy control over the visibility attribute for all layers in the current Web page. In addition to explicitly showing or hiding layers, this action can also restore layers to the default visibility setting.

The Show-Hide Layers action typically reveals one layer while concealing another; however, you are not restricted to hiding or showing just one layer at a time. The action's parameter form (see Figure 11-23) shows you a list of all the layers in the current Web page, from which you can choose as many as you want to show or hide.

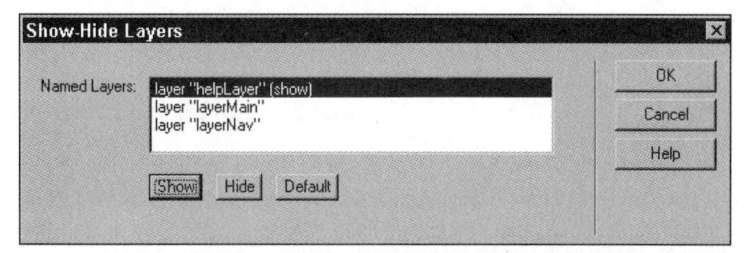

Figure 11-23: The Show-Hide Layers action can make any number of hidden layers visible, hide any number of visible layers, or both.

To use the Show-Hide Layers action, follow these steps:

1. Select the object to trigger the action.
2. From the Behaviors panel, select the add action button and choose Show-Hide Layer.

   When the dialog box opens, the parameter form shows a list of the available layers in the open Web page.
3. To reveal a hidden layer, from the Show-Hide Layer dialog box, select the layer from the Named Layers list and click the Show button.
4. To hide a visible layer, select its name from the list and click the Hide button.
5. To restore a layer's default visibility value, select the layer in the list and click the Default button.

Here's the browser compatibility chart for the Show-Hide Layers behavior:

Show-Hide Layer	Netscape 3.x	Internet Explorer 3.0	Internet Explorer 3.01
Macintosh	Fails without error	Fails without error	
Windows	Fails without error		Fails without error

Swap Image and Swap Image Restore

Button rollovers are one of the most commonly used techniques in Web design today. In a typical button rollover, a user's pointer moves over one image, and the graphic appears to change in some way, seeming to glow or change color. Actually, the onMouseOver event triggers the almost instantaneous swapping of one image for another. Dreamweaver automates this difficult coding task with the Swap Image action and its companion, the Swap Image Restore action.

In recognition of how rollovers most commonly work in the real world, Dreamweaver makes it possible to combine Swap Image and Swap Image Restore in one easy operation — as well as to preload all the images. Moreover, you can use a link in one frame to trigger a rollover in another frame without having to tweak the code as you did in early versions.

When the parameters form for the Swap Image action opens, it automatically loads all the images it finds in the current Web page (see Figure 11-24). You select the image you want to change — which could be the same image to which you are attaching the behavior — and enter the address for the file you want to replace the rolled-over image. You can swap more than one image with each Swap Image action. For example, if you want an entire submenu to change when a user rolls over a particular option, you can use a single Swap Image action to switch all of the sub-menu button images.

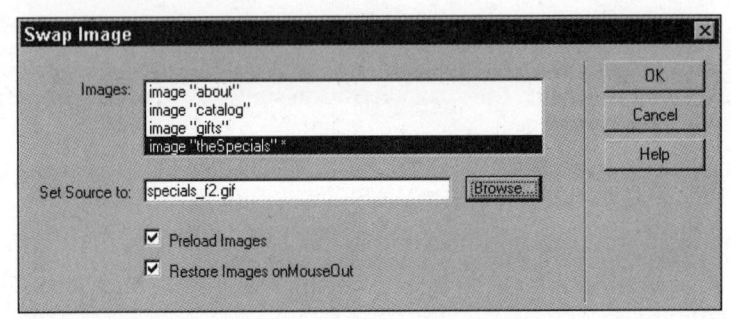

Figure 11-24: The Swap Image action is used primarily for handling button rollovers.

If you choose not to enable the Restore Images `onMouseOut` option, which changes the image back to the original, you need to attach the Swap Image Restore action to another event. The Swap Image Restore action can be used only after a Swap Image action. No parameter form exists for the Swap Image Restore action — just a dialog box confirming your selection.

> **Note** If the swapped-in image has different dimensions than the image it replaces, the swapped-in image is resized to the height and width of the first image.

To use the Swap Image action, follow these steps:

1. Select the object to trigger the action.
2. From the Behaviors panel, select the add action button and choose Swap Image.
3. In the parameter form, choose an available image from the Named Images list of graphics on the current page.

4. In the Set Source To text box, enter the path to the image that you want to swap in. You can also select the Browse (Choose) button to locate the file.

   An asterisk appears at the end of the selected image name to indicate an alternate image has been selected.

5. To swap additional images using the same event, repeat Steps 3 and 4.

6. To preload all images involved in the Swap Image action when the page loads, make sure the Preload Images option is checked.

7. To cause the selected images to revert to their original source, make sure that the Restore Images `onMouseOut` option is selected.

8. Click OK when you're done.

Here's the browser compatibility chart for the Swap Image and Swap Image Restore behaviors:

Swap Image and Swap Image Restore	Netscape 3.x	Internet Explorer 3.0	Internet Explorer 3.01
Macintosh	Okay	Fails without error	
Windows	Okay		Fails without error

Timelines: Play Timeline, Stop Timeline, and Go to Timeline Frame

Any Dynamic HTML animation in Dreamweaver happens with timelines, but a timeline can't do anything without the actions written to control it. The three actions in the timeline set — Play Timeline, Stop Timeline, and Go to Timeline Frame — are all you need to set your Web page in motion.

Before the Timeline actions become available, at least one timeline must be on the current page. All three of these related actions are located in the Timeline pop-up menu. Generally, when you are establishing controls for playing a timeline, you first attach the Go to Timeline Frame action to an event and then attach the Play Timeline action to the same event. By setting a specific frame before you enable the timeline to start, you ensure that the timeline always begins at the same point.

Cross-Reference: For more detailed information on using timelines, see Chapter 16.

The Play Timeline and Stop Timeline actions have only one element on their parameter form: a drop-down list box offering all timelines in the current page.

The Go to Timeline Frame action's parameter form (see Figure 11-25), aside from enabling you to pick a timeline and enter a specific go-to frame, also gives you the option to loop the timeline a set number of times.

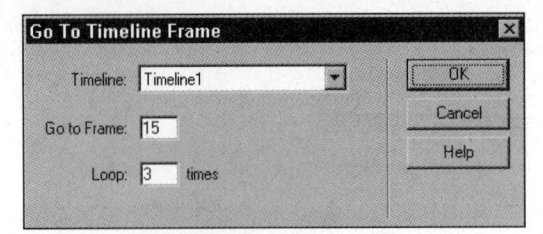

Figure 11-25: Control your timelines through the three Timeline actions. The Go to Timeline Frame parameter form enables you to choose a go-to frame and designate the number of loops for the timeline.

Expert Tip If you want the timeline to loop an infinite number of times, leave the Loop text box empty and turn on the Loop option in the Timelines panel.

To use the Go to Timeline Frame action, follow these steps:

1. Select the object to trigger the action.
2. From the Behaviors panel, select the add action button and choose Go to Frame.
3. In the dialog box Timeline list, choose the timeline for which you want to set the start frame.
4. Enter the frame number in the Go to Frame text box.
5. If you want the timeline to loop a set number of times, enter a value in the Loop text box.
6. Click OK when you're done.

To use the Play Timeline action, follow these steps:

1. Select an object to trigger the action and then choose Timeline ⇨ Play Timeline from the Add Action pop-up menu in the Behaviors panel.
2. In the parameter form's Timeline list, choose the timeline that you want to play.

To use the Stop Timeline action, follow these steps:

1. Select an object to trigger the action and then choose Timeline ⇨ Stop Timeline from the Add Action pop-up menu in the Behaviors panel.
2. In the parameter form's Timeline list, choose the timeline that you want to stop.

Note You can also choose All Timelines to stop every timeline on the current Web page from playing.

Here's the browser compatibility chart for the Timeline behaviors:

Timelines: Play Timeline, Stop Timeline, and Go to Timeline Frame	Netscape 3.x	Internet Explorer 3.0	Internet Explorer 3.01
Macintosh	Image source animation and invoking behaviors work, but layer animation fails without error.	Fails without error	
Windows	Image source animation and invoking behaviors work, but layer animation fails without error.		Fails without error

Validate Form

When you set up a form for user input, each field is established with a purpose. The name field, the e-mail address field, the zip code field — each has its own requirements for input. Unless the CGI program is specifically written to check the user's input, forms usually take input of any type. Even if the CGI program can handle it, this server-side method ties up server time and is relatively slow. The Validate Form action checks any text field's input and returns the form to the user if any of the entries are unacceptable. You can also use this action to designate any text field as a required field.

The Validate Form action can be used to check either individual fields or multiple fields for the entire form. Attaching a Validate Form action to an individual text box alerts the user to any errors as the form is being filled out. To check the entire form, the Validate Form action must be linked to the form's Submit button.

The Validate Form dialog box (see Figure 11-26) enables you to designate any text field as required, and you can evaluate its contents. You can require the input of a text field to be a number, an e-mail address (for instance, jdoe@anywhere.com), or a number within a range. The number range you specify can include positive whole numbers, negative numbers, or decimals.

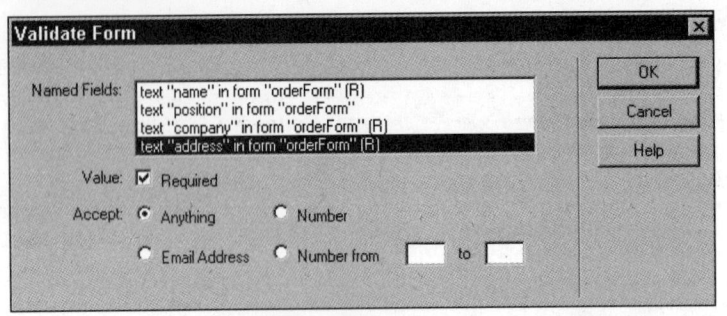

Figure 11-26: The Validate Form action can check your form's entries without CGI programming.

To use the Validate Form action, follow these steps:

1. Select the form object, such as a Submit button or text field, to trigger the action.

   Expert Tip: You can also attach the Validate Form to a checkbox or radio button, but it's really useful only if you want to require the field.

2. From the Behaviors panel, select the add action button and choose Validate Form.

3. If validating an entire form, select a text field from the Named Fields list.

   If you are validating a single field, the selected form object is chosen for you and appears in the Named Fields list.

4. To make the field required, select the Value: Required checkbox.

5. To set the kind of input expected, choose from one of the following Accept options:

   - **Anything:** Accepts any input.
   - **Number:** Enables any sort of numeric input. You cannot mix text and numbers, however, as in a telephone number such as (212) 555-1212.
   - **Email Address:** Looks for an e-mail address with the @ sign.
   - **Number from:** Enables you to enter two numbers, one in each text box, to define the number range.

6. Click OK when you're done.

On the CD-ROM: Date validation is currently problematic when attempted with Dreamweaver's Validate Form action—you can't enter a date such as "011200" and have it recognize the entry as a number because of the leading zero. For easy date validation, use the Validate Form Plus action included on this book's CD-ROM.

Here's the browser compatibility chart for the Validate Form behavior:

Validate Form	Netscape 3.x	Internet Explorer 3.0	Internet Explorer 3.01
Macintosh	Okay	Fails without error	
Windows	Okay		Okay

Managing and Modifying Your Behaviors

The standard behaviors that come with Dreamweaver are indeed impressive, but they're really just the beginning. Because existing behaviors can be modified and new ones created from scratch, you can continue to add behaviors as you need them.

The process of adding a behavior is simplicity itself. Just copy the HTML file to the Configuration\Behaviors\Actions folder and restart Dreamweaver.

If you find that your Add Action pop-up list is starting to get a little unwieldy, you can create subfolders to organize the actions better. When you create a folder within the Actions folder, that subfolder appears on the Add Action pop-up menu as a submenu, as you saw when you worked with the Timelines actions in the preceding section. Figure 11-27 shows a sample arrangement. This example has a subfolder called Beatnik - Advanced and another called Tracks to organize these diverse behaviors from Beatnik. You can even create sub-subfolders to maintain several levels of nested menus.

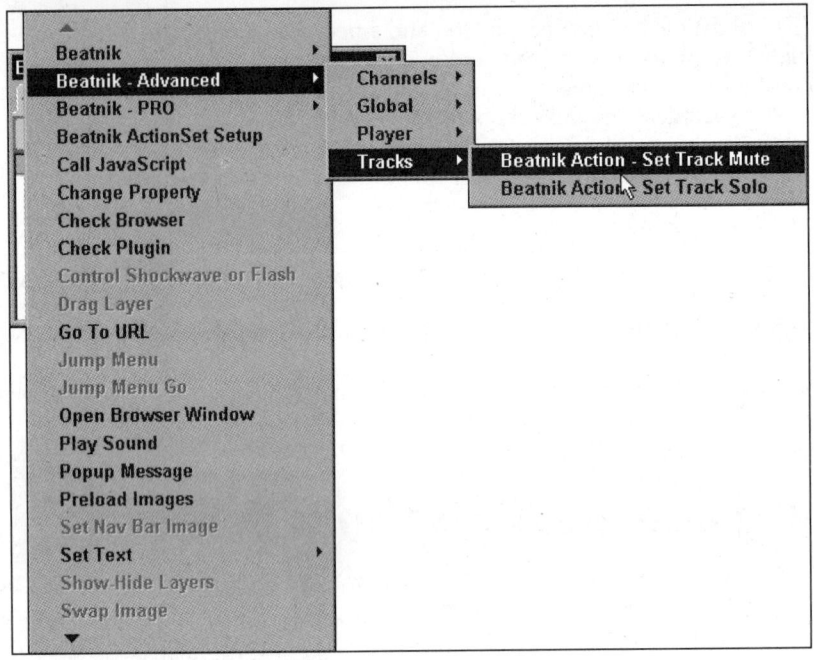

```
Beatnik                    ▶
Beatnik - Advanced         ▶   Channels  ▶
Beatnik - PRO              ▶   Global    ▶
Beatnik ActionSet Setup        Player    ▶
Call JavaScript                Tracks    ▶   Beatnik Action - Set Track Mute
Change Property                                Beatnik Action - Set Track Solo
Check Browser
Check Plugin
Control Shockwave or Flash
Drag Layer
Go To URL
Jump Menu
Jump Menu Go
Open Browser Window
Play Sound
Popup Message
Preload Images
Set Nav Bar Image
Set Text                   ▶
Show-Hide Layers
Swap Image
```

Figure 11-27: To create a new submenu in the Actions pop-up menu, just create a folder in the Actions directory.

Altering the parameters of a behavior

You can alter any of the attributes for your inserted behaviors at any time. To modify a behavior you have already attached, follow these steps:

1. Open the Behaviors panel (go to Window ⇨ Behaviors or click the Show Behaviors button in either Launcher, or press Shift+F3).
2. Select the object in the Document window or the tag in the Tag Selector to which your behavior is attached.
3. Double-click the action that you want to alter. The appropriate dialog box opens, with the previously selected parameters.
4. Make any modifications to the existing settings for the action.
5. Click OK when you are finished.

Sequencing your behaviors

When you have more than one action attached to a particular event, the order of the actions is often important. For example, you should generally implement the Go to Timeline Frame action ahead of the Play Timeline action. To specify the sequence in which Dreamweaver triggers the actions, reposition as necessary in the Actions page by highlighting one and using the up and down arrow buttons to reposition it in the list.

Deleting behaviors

To remove a behavior from your list of actions attached to a particular event, simply highlight the behavior and select the – (delete) button. If the removed behavior is the last action added, the event is also removed from the list; this process occurs after you select any other tag or click anywhere in the Document window.

Summary

Dreamweaver behaviors can greatly extend the Web designer's palette of possibilities — even a Web designer who is an accomplished JavaScript programmer. Behaviors simplify and automate the process of incorporating common, and not so common, JavaScript functions. The versatility of the behavior format enables anyone proficient in JavaScript to create custom actions that can be attached to any event. When considering behaviors, keep the following points in mind:

- ✦ Behaviors are a combination of events and actions.
- ✦ Behaviors are written in HTML and are completely customizable from within Dreamweaver.
- ✦ Different browsers support different events. Dreamweaver enables you to select a specific browser or a browser range, such as all 4.0 browsers, on which to base your event choice.
- ✦ Dreamweaver includes 25 standard actions. Some actions are not available unless a particular object is included on the current page.

✦ ✦ ✦

Fireworks Integration

CHAPTER 12

✦ ✦ ✦ ✦

In This Chapter

Exploring the Fireworks/Dreamweaver connection

Using Fireworks from within Dreamweaver

Sending a graphic to Fireworks

Embedding Fireworks code

Driving the Fireworks graphics engine

✦ ✦ ✦ ✦

Imagine demonstrating a newly completed Web site to a client who *didn't* ask for an image to be a little bigger, or the text on a button to be reworded, or the colors for the background to be revised. In the real world, Web sites — particularly the images — are constantly being tweaked and modified. This fact of Web life explains why Fireworks, Macromedia's premier Web graphics tool, is so popular. One of Fireworks' main claims to fame is that everything is editable all the time. If that were all that Fireworks did, the program would have already earned a place on every Web designer's shelf just for its sheer expediency. But Fireworks is far more capable a tool — and now, that power can be tapped directly in Dreamweaver.

With the release of Dreamweaver 4 and Fireworks 4, an even greater level of integration between the two Macromedia products has been achieved. You can optimize your images — reduce the file size, crop the graphic, and make colors transparent — within Dreamweaver using the Fireworks interface. Moreover, you can edit your image in any fashion in Fireworks and, with one click of the Update command, automatically export the graphic with its original export settings. Perhaps most importantly, now Dreamweaver can control Fireworks — creating graphics on the fly — and then insert the results in Dreamweaver.

A key Fireworks feature is its capability to output HTML and JavaScript for easy creation of rollovers, sliced images, and image maps with behaviors. With Fireworks, you can specify Dreamweaver-style code, so that all your Web pages are consistent. Once HTML is generated within Fireworks, Dreamweaver's Insert Fireworks HTML object makes code insertion effortless. Dreamweaver now recognizes images — whether whole or sliced — as coming from Fireworks and displays a special Property Inspector.

Web pages and Web graphics are closely tied to one another. With the tight integration between Dreamweaver and Fireworks, the Web designer's world is moving toward a single design environment.

Easy Graphics Modification

It's not uncommon for graphics to need some alteration before they fully integrate into a Web design. In fact, I'd say it's far more the rule than the exception. The traditional workflow generally goes like this:

1. Create the image in one or more graphics-editing programs.
2. Place the new graphic on a Web page via your Web authoring tool.
3. Note where the problems lie — perhaps the image is too big or too small, maybe the drop shadow doesn't blend into the background properly, or maybe the whole image needs to be flipped.
4. Reopen the graphics program, make the modifications, and save the file again.
5. Return to the Web page layout to view the results.
6. Repeat Steps 3 through 5 ad infinitum until you get it right.

Although you're still using two different programs even with Dreamweaver and Fireworks integration, there is a feature that enables you to open a Fireworks window on the Dreamweaver screen: Optimize Image in Fireworks. Now you can make your alterations with the Web page noticeable in the background. I've found that this small advantage cuts my trial-and-error to a bare minimum and streamlines my workflow.

If you're not familiar with Fireworks, you're missing an extremely powerful graphics program made for the Web. Fireworks combines the best of both vector and bitmap technologies and was one of the first graphics programs to use PNG as its native format. Exceptional export capabilities are available in Fireworks with which images can be optimized for file size, color, and scale. Moreover, Fireworks is terrific at generating GIF animations, rollovers, image maps, and sliced images.

With the latest versions of Dreamweaver and Fireworks, you have two ways to alter your inserted graphics: the Optimize Image in Fireworks command and the Edit button in the Image Property Inspector.

Note: The full integration described in this chapter requires that Fireworks 4 be installed after Dreamweaver 4. Certain features, such as the Optimize Image in Fireworks command, work with Dreamweaver 4 and Fireworks 2 and above, but any others requiring direct communication between the two programs work only with Fireworks 4.

Optimizing an image in Fireworks

Although you can design the most beautiful, compelling image possible in your graphics program, if it's intended for the Internet, you need to view it in a Web page. Not only must the graphic work in the context of the entire page, but the file size of the Web graphic must also be taken into account. All these factors mean that most, if not all, images need to undergo some degree of modification once they're included in a Web page. Fireworks makes these alterations as straightforward as possible by including a command for Dreamweaver during its installation.

The Optimize Image in Fireworks command opens the Export module of Fireworks, as shown in Figure 12-1, right in Dreamweaver's Document window.

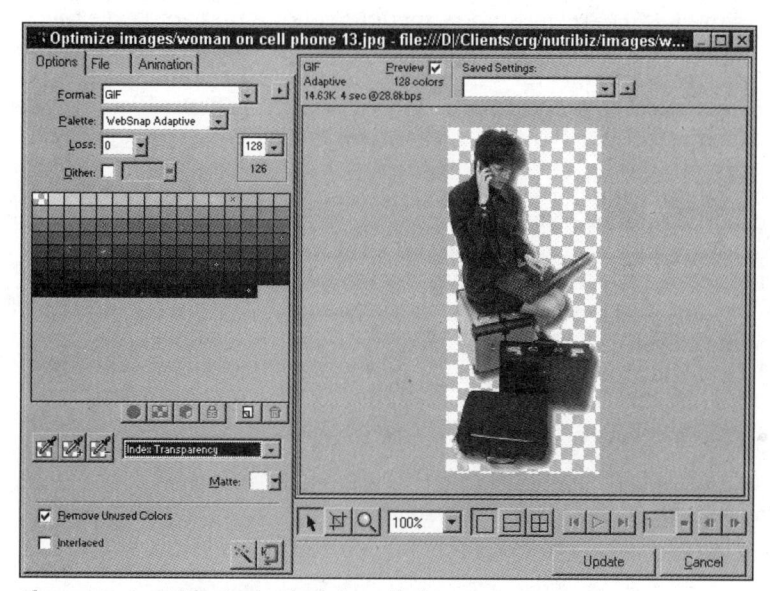

Figure 12-1: With Fireworks 4 installed, you can optimize your images from within Dreamweaver.

The Export module consists of three tabbed panels: Options, File, and Animation. Although a complete description of all of its features is beyond the scope of this book, here's a breakdown of the major uses of each area:

- ✦ **Options:** The Options panel is primarily used to try different export options and preview them. You can switch file formats from GIF to JPEG (or Animated GIF or PNG) as well as alter the palette, color depth, and dithering. Transparency for GIF and PNG images is set in the Options panel. Fireworks also has an Export to Size wizard that enables you to target a particular file size for your graphic.

- ✦ **File:** An image's dimensions are defined in the File panel. Images can be rescaled by a selected percentage or pixel size. Moreover, you can crop your image either numerically—by defining the export area—or visually with the Cropping tool.

✦ **Animation:** Frame-by-frame control for animated GIFs is available on the Animation panel. Each frame's *delay* (how long it is onscreen) is capable of being defined independently, and the entire animation can be set to either play once or loop a user-determined number of times.

> **Note**   If you crop or rescale an inserted image in Fireworks, you need to update the height and width in Dreamweaver. The easiest way to accomplish this is to select the Refresh button in the image's Property Inspector.

Fireworks saves its source files in an expanded PNG format to maintain full editability of the images. Graphics for the Web must be exported from Fireworks in GIF, JPEG, or standard PNG format. Dreamweaver's Optimize Image in Fireworks command can modify either the source or exported file. In most situations, better results are achieved from using the source file, especially when optimizing includes rescaling or resampling. However, some situations require that you leave the source file as is and modify only the exported files. Let's say, for example, that one source file is used to generate several different export files, each with different backgrounds (or *canvases*, as they are called in Fireworks). In that case, you'd be better off modifying the specific exported file rather than the general source image.

Dreamweaver enables you to choose which type of image you'd like to modify. When you first execute the Optimize Image in Fireworks or the Edit Image command, a Find Source dialog box (Figure 12-2) appears. If you want to locate and use the source file, choose Yes; to use the exported image that is inserted in Dreamweaver, select No. If you opt for the source file — and the image was created in Fireworks — Dreamweaver reads the Design Note associated with the image to find the location of the source file and open it. If the image was created with an earlier version of Fireworks or the image has been moved, Dreamweaver asks you to locate the file with a standard Open File dialog box. By setting the Fireworks Source Files option, you can always open the same type of file: source or exported. Should you change your mind about how you'd like to work, open Fireworks and select Edit ⇨ Preferences, and then choose the desired option from the Launch and Edit category.

> **Note**   There's one exception to Fireworks always following your Launch and Edit preferences. If the image chosen is a sliced image, Fireworks always optimizes the exported file rather than the source, regardless of your settings.

Figure 12-2: Set the Find Source dialog box to always use the source graphics image or the exported image, or to choose from a popup menu for each optimization.

Exploring Fireworks Source and Export Files

The separate source file is an important concept in Fireworks, and its use is strongly advised. Generally, when working in Fireworks, there is a minimum of two files for every image output to the Web: your source file and your exported Web image. Whenever major alterations are made, it's best to make them to the source file and then update the export files. Not only is this an easier method of working, but also you get a better image this way.

Source files are always Fireworks-style PNG files. Fireworks-style PNG files differ slightly from regular PNG format because they include additional information, such as paths and effects used that can be read only by Fireworks. The exported file is usually in GIF or JPEG format, although it could be in standard PNG format. Many Web designers keep their source files in a separate folder from their exported Web images so the two don't get confused. This source-and-export file combination also prevents you from inadvertently re-editing a lossy compressed file such as a JPEG image and reapplying the compression.

To use the Optimize Image in Fireworks command, follow these steps:

1. In Dreamweaver, select the image that you'd like to modify.

Note You must save the current page at least once before running the Optimize Image in Fireworks command. The current state of the page doesn't have to have been saved, but a valid file must exist for the command to work properly. If you haven't saved the file, Dreamweaver alerts you to this fact when you call the command.

2. Choose Commands ⇨ Optimize Image in Fireworks.

Tip You can also invoke the Optimize Image in Fireworks command from the context menu — just right-click (Control+click) on the image.

3. If your Fireworks Preferences are set to ask whether a source file should be used in editing, the Find Source dialog box opens. Choose Yes to use the PNG format source file and No to work with the exported file.

   The Optimize Images dialog box appears.

4. Make whatever modifications are desired from the Options, File, or Animation tabs of the Optimize Images dialog box.

5. When you're finished, select the Update button.

Note If you're working with a Fireworks source file, the changes are saved to both your source file and exported file; otherwise, only the exported file is altered.

Editing an image in Fireworks

Optimizing an image is great when all you need to do is tweak the file size or to rescale the image. Other images require more detailed modification — as when a client requests that the wording or order of a series of navigational buttons be changed. Dreamweaver enables you to specify Fireworks as your graphics editor; and if you've done so, you can take advantage of Fireworks' capability to keep every element of your graphic always editable. And believe me, this is a major advantage.

In Dreamweaver, external editors can be set for any file format; you can even assign more than one editor to a file type. When installing the Dreamweaver/Fireworks Studio, Fireworks is preset as the primary external editor for GIF, JPEG, and PNG files. If Fireworks is installed outside of the Studio setup, the external editor assignment is handled through Dreamweaver Preferences.

To assign Fireworks to an existing file type, follow these steps:

1. Choose Edit ⇨ Preferences.
2. Select the External Editors category.
3. Select the file type (GIF, JPEG, or PNG) from the Extensions list as shown in Figure 12-3.

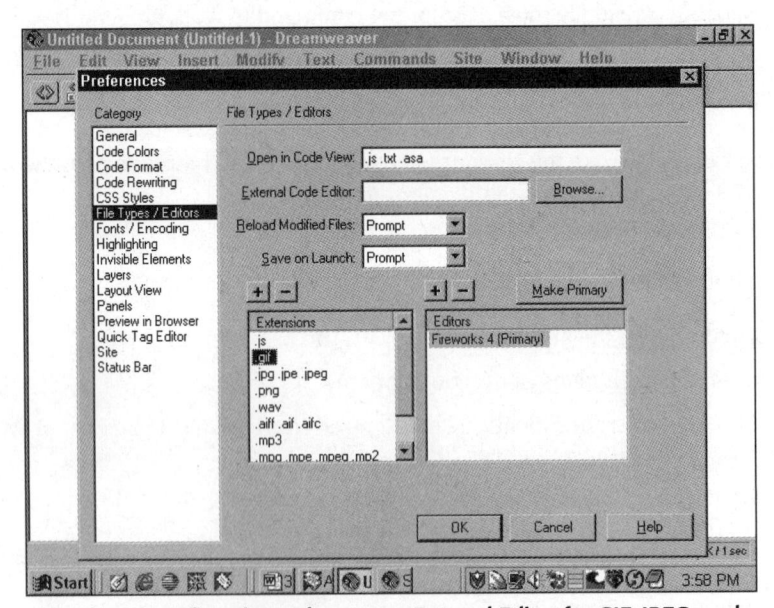

Figure 12-3: Define Fireworks as your External Editor for GIF, JPEG, and PNG files to enable the back-and-forth interaction between Dreamweaver and Fireworks.

4. Click the Add (+) button above the Editors list. The Add External Editor dialog box opens.

5. Locate the editor application and click Open when you're ready.

> **Note** The default location in Windows systems is in C:\Program Files\Macromedia\Fireworks 4\Fireworks 4.exe; on the Macintosh it's Macintosh HD:Applications: Fireworks 4:Fireworks 4. (The .exe extension may or may not be visible in your Windows system.)

6. Click Make Primary while the editor is highlighted.

Now, whenever you want to edit a graphic, select the image and click the Edit button in the Property Inspector. You can also right-click (Control+click) the image and select Edit Image to start editing it. Fireworks starts up, if it's not already open. As with the Optimize Image in Fireworks command, if the inserted image is a GIF or a JPEG and not a PNG format, Fireworks asks if you'd like to work with a separate source file, if that option in Fireworks Preferences is set. If so, Fireworks automatically loads the source file.

When the image opens in Fireworks, the graphic's window indicates that this particular graphic is being edited from Dreamweaver in Fireworks as shown in Figure 12-4. In the same title bar, a Done button is available for completing the operation after you've made your alterations to your file in Fireworks. Alternatively, you can choose File ⇨ Update or use the keyboard shortcut Ctrl+S (Command+S). If you're working with a Fireworks source file, both the source file and the exported file are updated and saved.

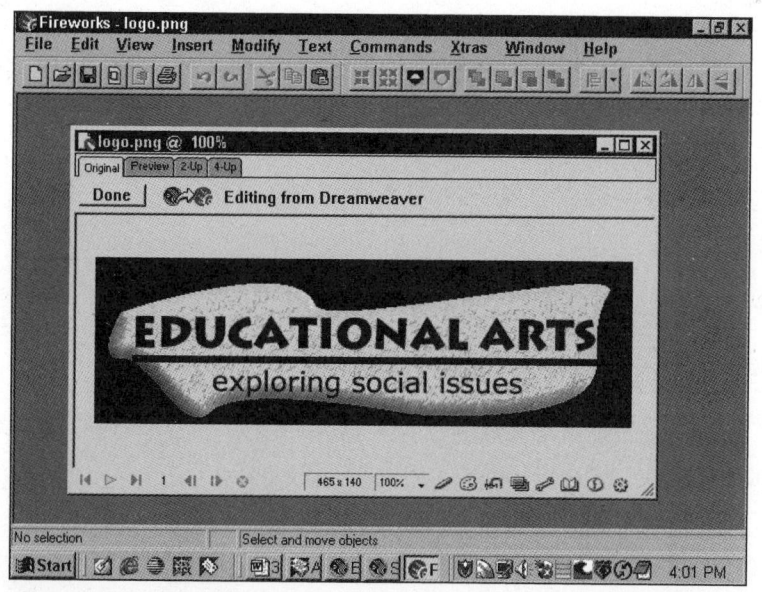

Figure 12-4: Fireworks now graphically depicts where the current image being edited is from.

Inserting Rollovers

The rollover is a fairly common, but effective, Web technique that you can use to indicate interactivity. Named after the user action of "rolling the mouse pointer over" the graphic, this technique uses from two to four different images per button. With Fireworks, you can both create the graphics and output the necessary HTML and JavaScript code from the same program. Moreover, Fireworks has some sophisticated twists to the standard "on/off" rollovers to further easily enhance your Web page.

Rollovers created in Fireworks can be inserted into Dreamweaver through several methods. First, you can use Fireworks to just build the images and then export them and attach the behaviors in Dreamweaver. This technique works well for graphics going into layers or images with other attached behaviors. The second method of integrating Fireworks-created rollovers involves transferring the actual code generated by Fireworks into Dreamweaver — a procedure that can be handled with one command: Insert Fireworks HTML.

Using Dreamweaver's behaviors

With its full-spectrum editability, Fireworks excels at building consistent rollover graphics simply. The different possible states of an image in a rollover — Up, Over, Down, and Over While Down — are handled in Fireworks as separate frames. As with an animated GIF, each frame has the same dimensions as the document, but the content is slightly altered to indicate the separate user actions. For example, Figure 12-5 shows the different frame states of a rollover button, side by side.

> **Note** Many Web designers use just the initial two states — Up and Over — in their rollover buttons. The third state, Down, takes place when the user clicks the button, and it is useful if you want to indicate that moment to the user. The Down state also indicates which button has been selected (which is "down") when a new page appears, but the same navigation bar is used, notably with frames. The fourth state, Over While Down, is called when the previously selected button is rolled over by the user's pointer.

Chapter 12 ✦ **Fireworks Integration** 359

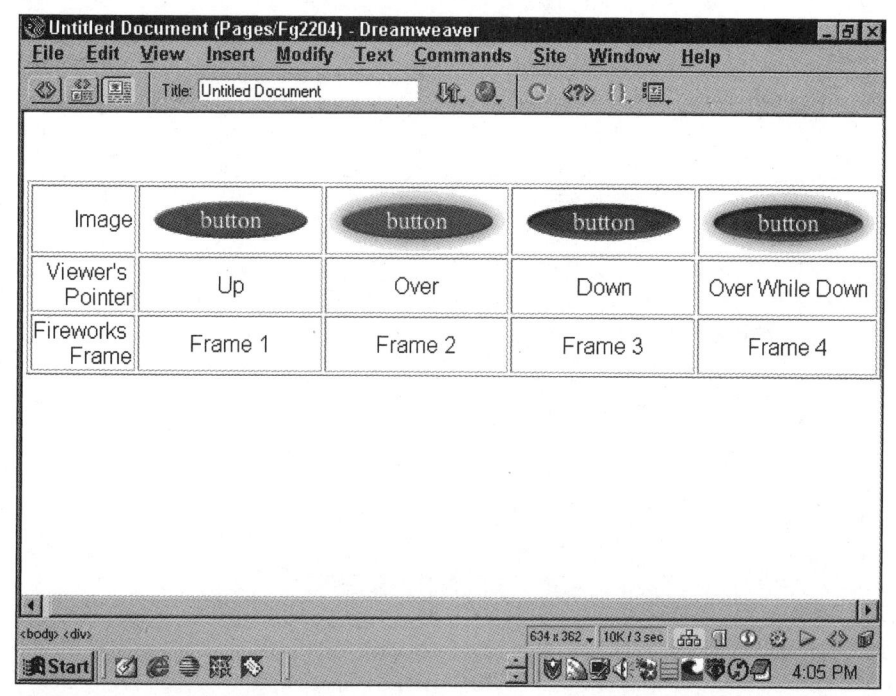

Figure 12-5: A Fireworks-created rollover can be made of four separate frames.

To insert Fireworks-created graphics using Dreamweaver behaviors, follow these steps:

1. Create your graphics in Fireworks, using a different frame for each rollover state.

   Caution

   You cannot use Fireworks's Insert ⇨ New Button command to build your button for this technique because the separate states are now stored as frames.

2. In Fireworks, choose File ⇨ Export. The Export dialog box opens (see Figure 12-6).

3. Enter a new filename in the Base Name text box, if desired.

   In this operation, Fireworks uses the filename as a base name to identify multiple images exported from a single file. When exporting frames, the default settings append "_fn", where n is the number of the frame. Frame numbers 1 to 9 are listed with a leading zero (for example, MainButton_f01).

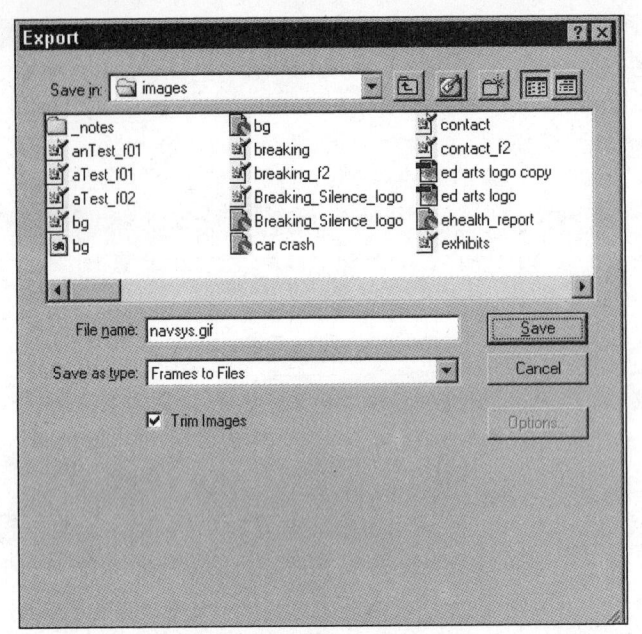

Figure 12-6: From Fireworks, you can export each frame as a separate file to be used in Dreamweaver rollovers.

4. In the Save As Type list box, select Frames to Files.
5. If desired, select the Trim Images option. I recommend that the default practice be to trim your images when exporting frames as files. This option results in smaller, more flexible files.
6. Select the Save button to store your frames as separate files.

Note: You can attach the rollover behaviors to your images in several ways in Dreamweaver. The following technique uses Dreamweaver's Rollover object.

7. From the Common panel of the Objects palette, choose the Insert Rollover Image object.
8. In the Insert Rollover Image dialog box, choose the Original Image Browse (Choose) button to locate the image stored with the first frame designation, _f01.
9. If desired, give your image a different unique name than the one automatically assigned in the Image Name text box.
10. Choose the Rollover Image Browse button to locate the image stored with the second frame designation, _f02.
11. Click OK when you're done.

12. If you'd like to use the Down (_F03) and Over While Down (_F04) images, attach additional swap image behaviors by opening the Swap Image behavior and following the steps outlined in Chapter 11.

> **Note** Many Web designers build their entire navigation bar — complete with rollovers — in Fireworks. Rather than create and export one button at a time, all the navigation buttons are created as one graphic, and slices or hotspots are used to make the different objects or areas interact differently. You learn more about slices and hotspots later in this chapter under "Using Fireworks' Code."

Using Fireworks' code

In some ways, Fireworks is a hybrid program, capable of simultaneously outputting terrific graphics and sophisticated code. You can even select the type of code you want generated in Fireworks 4: Dreamweaver; Dreamweaver Library compatible; or code compatible with other programs such as GoLive and FrontPage. You'll also find a Generic code option. You can choose these options during the Export procedure.

For rollovers, Fireworks generally outputs to two different sections of the HTML document, the `<head>` and the `<body>`; only the FrontPage style keeps all the code together. The `<head>` section contains the JavaScript code for activating the rollovers and preloading the images; `<body>` contains the HTML references to the images themselves, their links, and the event triggers (`onClick` or `onMouseOver`) used.

The general procedure is to first create your graphics in Fireworks and then export them, simultaneously generating a page of code. Now, the just-generated Fireworks HTML page can be incorporated in Dreamweaver. Dreamweaver includes two slick methods for including your Fireworks-output code and images. The Insert Fireworks HTML object places the code — and the linked images — right at your current cursor position. You also have the option of exporting your Fireworks HTML directly to the clipboard and pasting it, verbatim, into Dreamweaver. Just as an image requires a link to create a rollover in Dreamweaver, Fireworks images need to be designated as either a *slice* or a *hotspot*. Slices are rectangular areas that permit different areas of the same graphic to be saved as separate formats — the entire graphic is formatted as an HTML table. Each slice can also be given its own URL; Fireworks requires either slices or hotspots to attach behaviors.

A Fireworks *hotspot* is a region defined for an image map. Hotspots can be rectangular, elliptical, or polygonal — just like those created by Dreamweaver by using the Image Map tools. Because Fireworks is an object-oriented graphics program, any selected image (or part of an image) can be automatically converted to a hotspot. Like slices, hotspots can have both URLs and behaviors assigned to them.

The Fireworks program describes slices and hotspots as being part of the graphic's Web layer. The Web layer can be hidden or locked, but not deleted. Figure 12-7 shows the same button with both a slice and a hotspot attached.

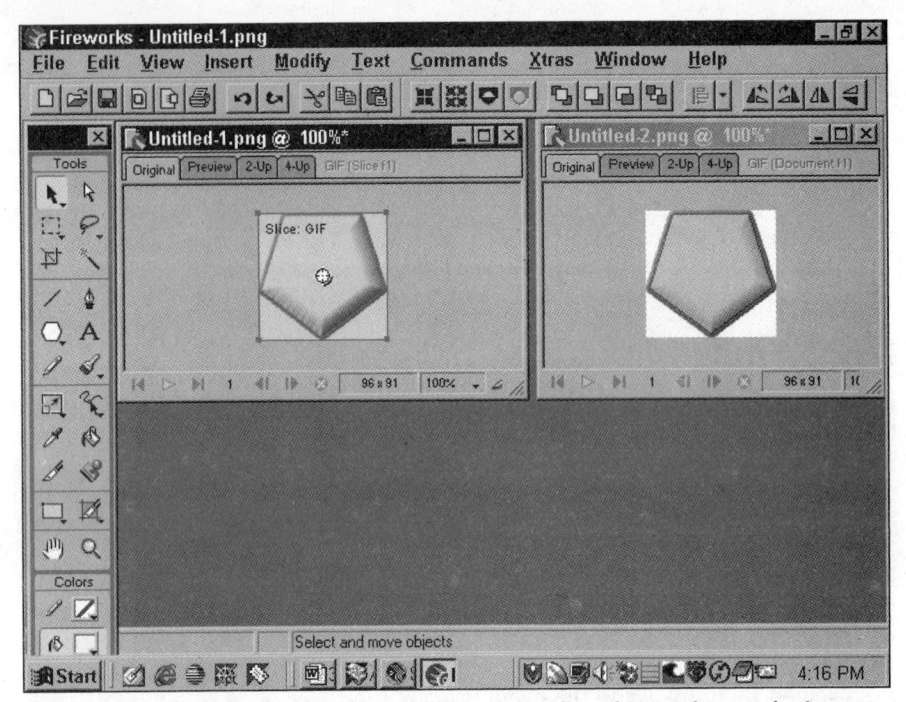

Figure 12-7: The Fireworks image on the left uses a slice object, whereas the image on the right uses a polygon hotspot.

> **Note:** In addition to the technique outlined in the text that follows, you could also use Fireworks's Button Editor (available by choosing Insert ⇨ New Button) to create your rollover images and behaviors.

To include Fireworks-generated code in your Dreamweaver document, first follow these steps in Fireworks:

1. Create your graphics in Fireworks, placing the image for each interactive state on its own frame.

2. When the object is selected, choose Insert ⇨ Hotspot or Insert ⇨ Slice to add the item to your Web layer for attaching behaviors. Alternatively, you can use any of the Hotspot or Slice tools found in the Fireworks toolbox.

3. Select the hotspot or slice and use Fireworks' Object Inspector to assign an Internet address to the selected graphic.

4. Click the target symbol displayed in the center of the hotspot or hotspot to display a menu of available behaviors. Alternatively, you could open Fireworks' Behavior Inspector and choose the Add Behavior button (the + sign).

5. Select Simple Rollover.

Tip: The Simple Rollover behavior is used to create single-button or multiple-button rollovers in which one image is replaced by another image in the same location; only two frames are used for a Simple Rollover. Use Swap Image to create more complex rollovers such as those in which the rollover triggers an image change in another location. A third alternative, Nav Bar, should be used in situations where the navigation system is to be placed in a frameset; Nav Bar can hold all four states (Up, Over, Down, and Over While Down).

6. Export the object by choosing File ➪ Export.

7. From the Export dialog box, enter a name in the filename text box and make sure HTML and Images is displayed in the Save as Type drop-down list.

   If you intend to use the graphics in several places on your site, choose Dreamweaver Library (*.lbi) from the Save as Type list.

8. To change the type of HTML code generated, choose the Options button and make a choice from the Style drop-down list.

   Dreamweaver code is the default Style; other options include GoLive, FrontPage, and Generic.

9. Choose the location to store your HTML code by navigating to the desired folder. Note that Dreamweaver 4 Library code must be saved in a site's Library folder.

   If you'd prefer to not save your HTML, choose Copy to Clipboard from the HTML drop-down list.

10. To save your graphics in a separate folder, select the Put Images in Subfolder option.

Caution: Fireworks defaults to placing the graphics in the images subfolder, even if one does not exist. Select a folder by choosing Browse.

11. Click Export when you're done.

When Fireworks completes the exporting, you have one HTML file (unless you've chosen the Copy to Clipboard option) and one object file for each slice and frame. Now you're ready to integrate these images and the code into your Dreamweaver page. Which method you use depends on the HTML style selected when the graphics were exported from Fireworks:

- ✦ If you chose Dreamweaver, use the Insert Fireworks HTML object.
- ✦ If you chose Dreamweaver Library, open the Library palette in Dreamweaver and insert the corresponding Library item.
- ✦ If you chose Copy to Clipboard, position your cursor where you'd like the graphics to appear and select Edit ➪ Paste or press Ctrl+V (Command+V).

Both the Library and Clipboard methods are one-step, self-explanatory techniques — and the Insert Fireworks HTML is hardly more complex. To insert the

Fireworks code and images into your Dreamweaver page using the Insert Fireworks HTML object, follow these steps:

1. Make sure that you've exported your graphics and HTML from Fireworks with Dreamweaver HTML Style selected.

2. Select the Insert Fireworks HTML object from the Common panel of the Objects palette or choose Insert ⇨ Interactive Media ⇨ Fireworks HTML.

   The Insert Fireworks HTML dialog box, shown in Figure 12-8, appears.

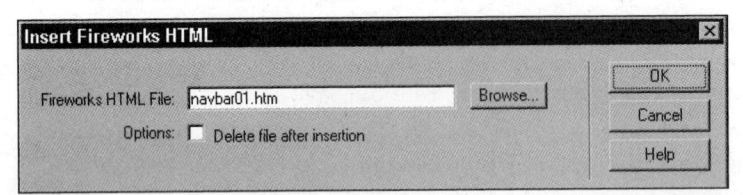

Figure 12-8: Import Fireworks code directly into Dreamweaver with the Insert Fireworks HTML object.

3. If you want to remove the Fireworks-generated HTML file after the code is inserted, select the Delete file after insertion option.

4. Enter the path to the Fireworks HTML file or select the Browse button to locate the file.

5. Click OK when you're done. Dreamweaver inserts the Fireworks HTML and graphics at the current cursor location.

Note If you're a hands-on kind of Web designer, you can also use the HTML Inspector to copy and paste the JavaScript and HTML code. If you do, you can find helpful comments in the Fireworks file such as "Begin copying here" and "Stop copying here."

All the methods for inserting Fireworks HTML work with images with either hotspots or sliced objects (or both), with or without behaviors attached.

Modifying sliced images

Placing sliced images on your Web page couldn't be simpler, thanks to the Insert Fireworks HTML command. But, like standard nonsliced graphics, sliced images often need to be modified. One technique that many designers use is to create a framing graphic that encompasses HTML text; in Fireworks, a sliced area designated as a text slice can hold any HTML content. Text is often modified, and if it's in a framing graphic, that could mean that the images need to be changed or the table will separate making the separate slices apparent.

New Feature: In Dreamweaver 4, sliced images from Fireworks are recognized as a Fireworks Table and may be modified through a dedicated Property Inspector.

The Fireworks Table Property Inspector shown in Figure 12-9 displays the PNG source file and an Edit button for sending the entire table back to Fireworks for alterations. As with nonsliced graphics, select Done from the document title bar in Fireworks when your modifications are complete to update the source and exported files. The newly exported images are then reloaded into Dreamweaver.

Caution: While Fireworks attempts to honor any changes that you make to the HTML table, certain alterations may result in Fireworks overwriting your table. If, for example, you add or remove one or more cells from the table in Dreamweaver, Fireworks recognizes that the tables no longer match. An alert is displayed indicating that Fireworks will replace the table in Dreamweaver. To keep your table the same in Dreamweaver, make no changes in Fireworks and select Done.

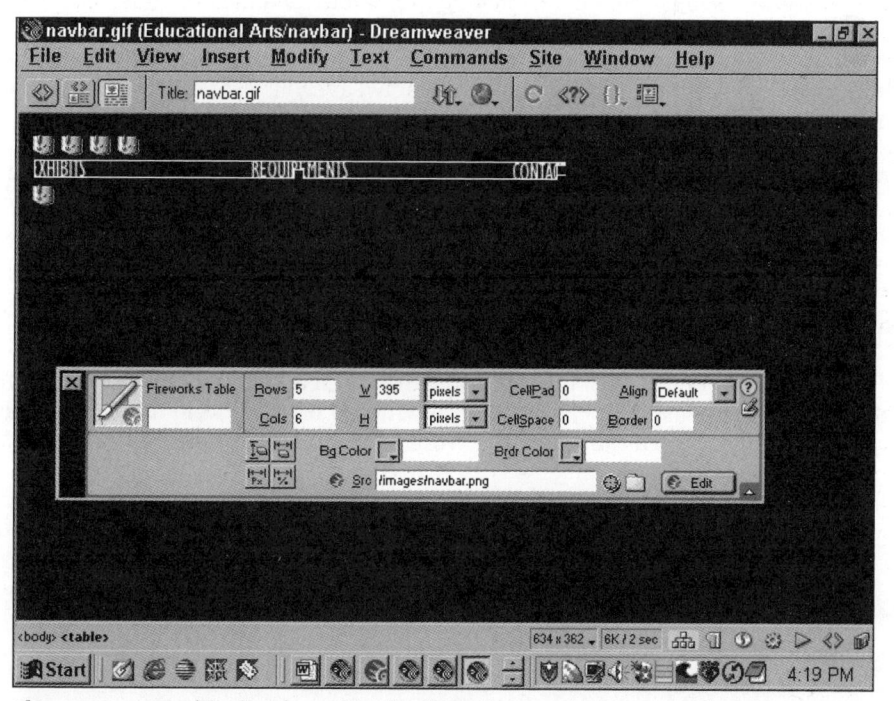

Figure 12-9: Modify sliced graphics by first selecting the surrounding table and then choosing Edit from the Fireworks Table Property Inspector.

Controlling Fireworks with Dreamweaver

Dreamweaver and Fireworks integration extends deeper than just the simplified insertion of code and graphics. Dreamweaver can communicate directly with Fireworks, driving it to execute commands and return custom-generated graphics. This facility enables Web designers to build their Web page images based on the existing content. This interprogram communication promises to streamline the work of the Webmaster — and that promise is already beginning to come through with existing Dreamweaver commands.

Web photo album

Online catalogs and other sites often depend on imagery to sell their products. Full-scale product shots can be large and time-consuming to download, so it's not uncommon for Web designers to display a thumbnail of the images instead. If the viewer wants to see more detail, clicking the thumbnail loads the full-size image. Although it's not difficult to save a scaled-down version of an image in a graphics program and link the two in a Web layout program, creating page after page of such images is an overwhelming chore. The Dreamweaver/Fireworks interoperability offers a way to automate this tedious task.

A new Dreamweaver command, Create Web Photo Album, examines any user-specified folder of images and then uses Fireworks to scale the graphics to a set size. When the scaling is completed, the thumbnail graphics are brought into a Dreamweaver table, complete with links to a series of pages with the full-size image. Create Web Photo Album is an excellent example of the potential that Dreamweaver and Fireworks intercommunication offers.

The Create Web Photo Album command works with a folder of images in any format that Fireworks reads: GIF, JPEG, TIFF, Photoshop, PICT, BMP, and more. The images can be scaled to fit in a range of sizes, from 36×36 to 200×200. These thumbnails are exported in one of four formats:

- **GIF WebSnap 128:** Uses the WebSnap Adaptive palette, which is limited to 128 colors or fewer
- **GIF WebSnap 256:** Same as preceding format but with as many as 256 colors available
- **JPEG Better Quality:** Sets the JPEG quality setting at 80 percent with no smoothing
- **JPEG Smaller File:** Sets the JPEG quality setting at 60 percent with a smoothing value of 2

The images are also exported in one of the same four settings, at a user-selected scale; the default scale is 100 percent.

To create a thumbnail gallery using Create Web Photo Album, follow these steps:

1. Choose Commands ⇨ Create Web Photo Album.

    The Create Web Photo Album dialog box appears, as shown in Figure 12-10.

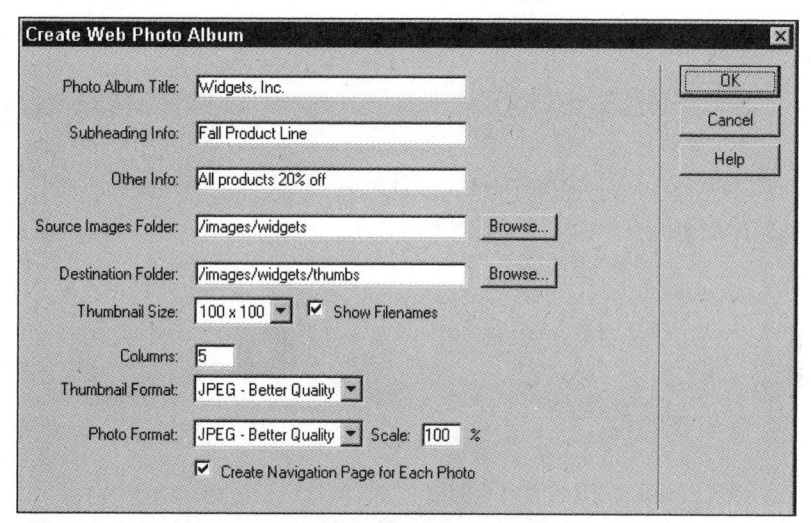

Figure 12-10: Use the Creat Web Photo Album dialog box to build a thumbnail gallery page, linked to full-size orignals.

2. Enter the Photo Album Title, Subheading Info, and Other Info into their respective text fields, if desired.

3. Enter the path to the folder of source images or select the Browse (Choose) button to locate the folder in the Source Images Folder field.

4. Enter the path to the Destination Folder or select the Browse (Choose) button to locate the folder in its field.

    Dreamweaver creates up to three subfolders in the Destination Folder: one for the original, rescaled images, another for the thumbnail images, and a third for the HTML pages created.

5. Select the desired thumbnail size from the drop-down list with the following options: 36×36, 72×72, 100×100, 144×144, and 200×200.

6. Select the Show Filenames option if you want the file name to appear below the image.

7. Choose the number of Columns for the table.

8. Select the export settings for the thumbnail images from the Thumbnail Format option list.

9. Select the export settings for the linked large-sized images from the Photo Format option list.//
10. Choose the size of the linked large-sized images in the Scale field.
11. Select the Create Navigation Page for Each Photo option, if desired. Each photo's navigation page includes links to the Next and Previous images as well as the Home (main thumbnail) page, as shown in Figure 12-11.

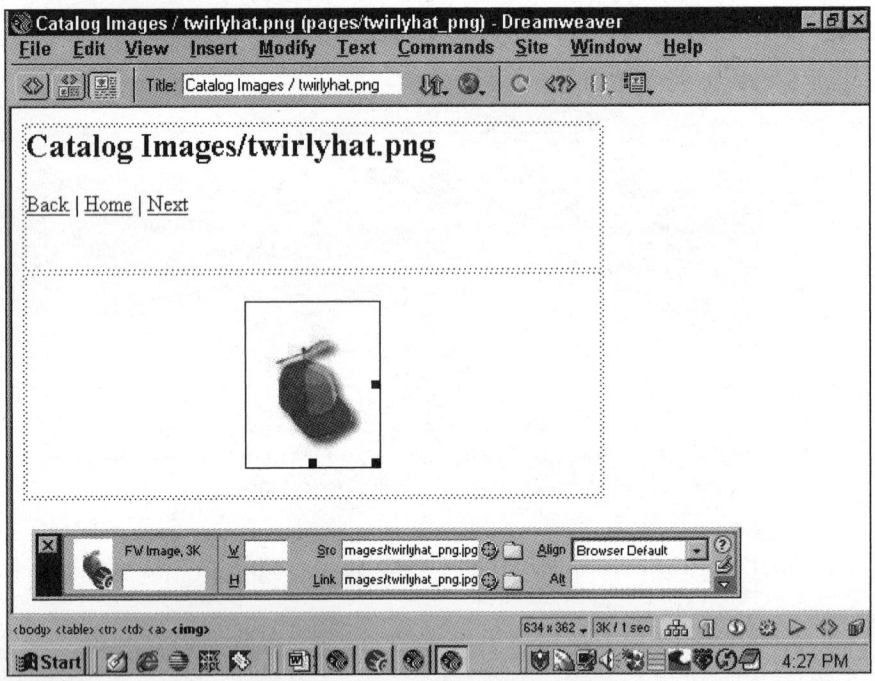

Figure 12-11: You can add simple, clear navigation options to your Web Photo Album.

12. Click OK when you're done.

If Fireworks is not open, the program launches and begins processing the images. When all the images are created and exported, Fireworks returns control to Dreamweaver. Dreamweaver then creates a single HTML page with the title, subheading, and other information at the top, followed by a borderless table. As shown in Figure 12-12, each image is rescaled proportionately to fit within the limits set in the dialog box.

Custom Graphic Makers: Convert Text to Graphics and Convert Bullets to Graphics

Excited by the potential of Dreamweaver and Fireworks communication, I built two custom extensions that I originally called StyleBuilder and BulletBuilder. Macromedia took these extensions, enhanced them, and then released them as two-thirds of the InstaGraphics Extensions. StyleBuilder — now called Convert Text to Graphics — enables you to convert any standard text in your Dreamweaver Web page to a graphic. The command converts all text in a standard HTML tag, such as `<h1>` or `<b>`, any custom XML tag, or any selection. The graphics are based on Fireworks styles, displayed in a small swatch in the dialog box; you can specify a font on your system as well as a text size to be used. Fireworks styles can be updated at any time, and the swatch set recreated on the fly in Fireworks.

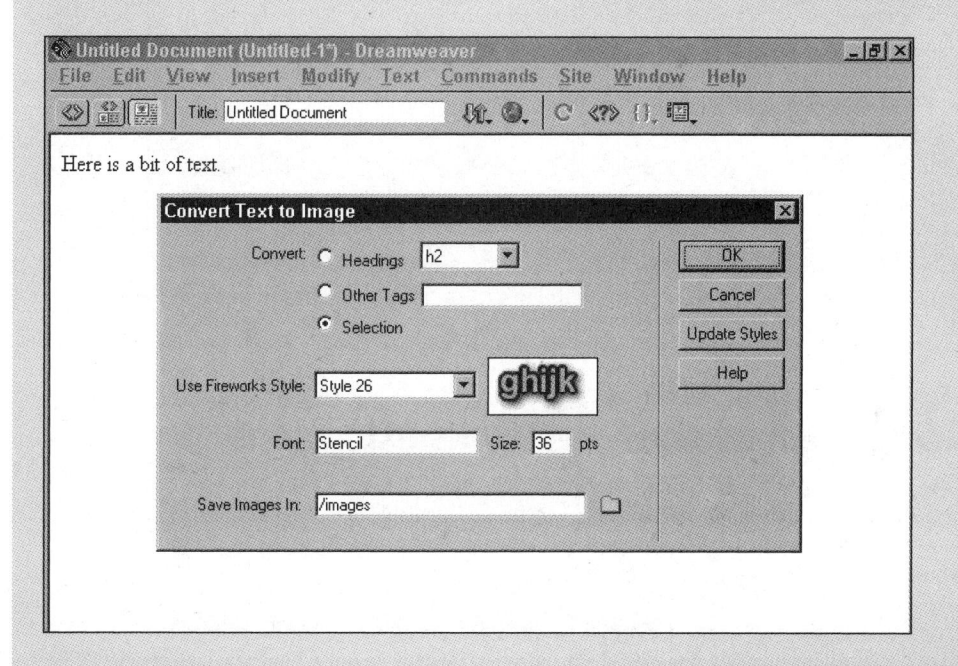

Convert Bullets to Graphics (nee BulletBuilder) is similar to Convert Text to Graphics, but instead of changing text to graphics, this command converts the bullets of an unordered list to different graphic shapes. Choose from 10 different shapes, including diamonds, stars, starbursts, and 4 different triangles. The chosen shape is rendered in any available Fireworks style at a user-selected size. You have the option to convert the current bullet list or all such lists on the page.

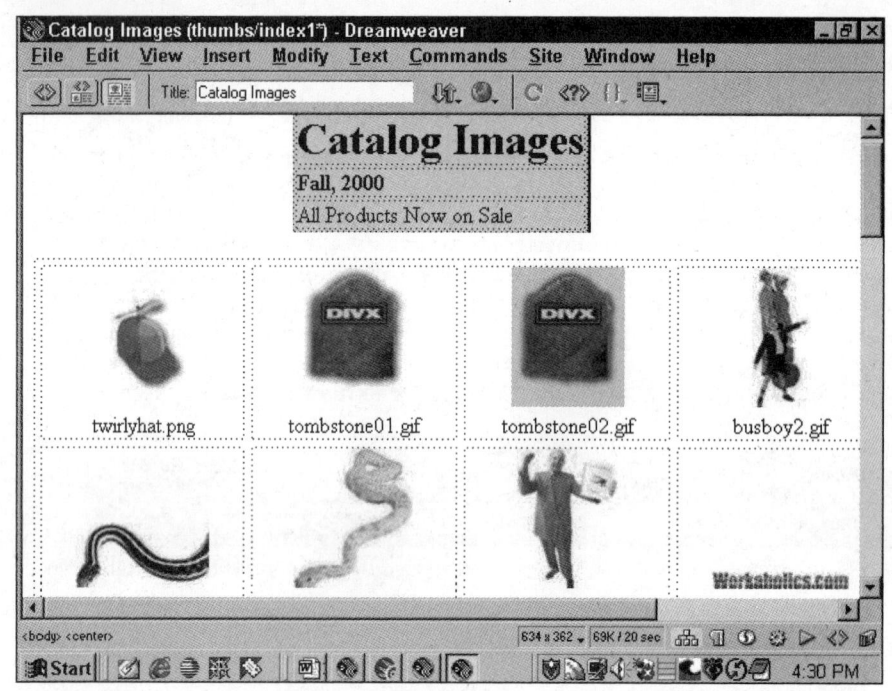

Figure 12-12: Build a thumbnail gallery with Fireworks right from Dreamweaver with the Create Web Photo Album command.

Building Dreamweaver/Fireworks extensions

To make communication between Dreamweaver and Fireworks viable, two conditions had to be met. First, Fireworks had to be scriptable. Second, a link between the two programs needed to be forged. The Dreamweaver 4/Fireworks 4 combination meets both criteria — and then some.

As with Dreamweaver 4, almost every operation is under command control in Fireworks 4. This is most apparent when using either program's History palette. If your action appears as a repeatable item in the History palette, a corresponding JavaScript function controls it. Fireworks' wealth of JavaScript functions also serves to expose its control to Dreamweaver — and the first condition for interoperability is handled. To create a strong link between programs, Dreamweaver engineers expanded on the Fireworks API used in the Optimize Image in Fireworks command, where Dreamweaver actually launches a streamlined version of Fireworks. This operation is controlled by a C-level extension called FWLaunch.

Here's a step-by-step description of how Dreamweaver is typically used to communicate with Fireworks:

1. The user selects a command in Dreamweaver.
2. Dreamweaver opens a dialog box, as with other extensions.
3. After the user has filled in the dialog box and clicked OK, the command begins to execute.
4. All user-supplied parameters are read and used to create a JavaScript scriptlet or function, which serve as instructions for Fireworks.
5. If used, the scriptlet is stored on the disk.
6. Fireworks is launched with a command to run the Dreamweaver-created scriptlet or function.
7. Fireworks processes the scriptlet or function, while Dreamweaver tracks its progress via a cookie on the user's machine.
8. Once Fireworks is finished, a positive result is returned. The Fireworks API includes several error codes if problems such as a full disk are encountered.
9. While tracking the Fireworks progress, Dreamweaver sees the positive result and integrates the graphics by rewriting the DOM of the current page.
10. The dialog box is closed, and the current page is refreshed to correctly present the finished product.

To successfully control Fireworks, you need a complete understanding of the Fireworks DOM and its extension capabilities. Macromedia provides documentation for extending Fireworks at its support site: www.macromedia.com/support/fireworks.

> **Tip** I've also found the History palette in Fireworks to be useful — especially the Copy Command to Clipboard function. To see the underlying JavaScript used to create an object in Fireworks, first make the object. Then highlight the History palette steps and select the Copy to Clipboard button. Paste the clipboard contents in a text editor to see the exact steps Fireworks used; you can then begin to generalize the statements with variables and other functions.

On the Dreamweaver side, six useful methods are in the FWLaunch C Library. Table 12-1 details the methods.

Table 12-1
FWLaunch Methods

Method	Returns	Use
`bringDWToFront()`	N/A	Brings the Dreamweaver window in front of any other application running.
`bringFWToFront()`	N/A	Brings the Fireworks window in front of any other application running.
`execJsInFireworks(javascriptOrFileURL)`	Result from running the scriptlet in Fireworks. If the operation fails, returns an error code: 1: The argument proves invalid 2: File I/O error 3: Improper version of Dreamweaver 4: Improper version of Fireworks 5: User canceled operation	Executes the supplied JavaScript function or scriptlet.
`mayLaunchFireworks()`	Boolean	Determines whether Fireworks may be launched.
`optimizeInFireworks(fileURL, docURL, {targetWidth}, {targetHeight})`	Result from running the scriptlet in Fireworks. If the operation fails, returns an error code: 1: The argument proves invalid 2: File I/O error 3: Improper version of Dreamweaver 4: Improper version of Fireworks 5: User canceled operation	Performs an Optimize in Fireworks operation, opening the Fireworks Export Preview dialog box.
`validateFireworks(versionNumber)`	Boolean	Determines if the user has a specific version of Fireworks.

Summary

Creating Web pages is almost never done with a single application: In addition to a Web layout program, you need a program capable of outputting Web graphics — and Fireworks is a world-class Web graphics generator and optimizer. Macromedia has integrated several functions with Dreamweaver and Fireworks to streamline production and ease modification. Here are some of the key features of the integration:

- ✦ You can update images placed in Dreamweaver with Fireworks in two ways: Optimize or Edit. With the Optimize Image in Fireworks command, just the Export Preview portion of Fireworks opens; with the Edit Image command, the full version of Fireworks is run.

- ✦ Graphics and HTML exported from Fireworks can be incorporated into a Dreamweaver page in numerous ways: as a Library item, an HTML file (complete with behavior code), or just pasted from the clipboard.

- ✦ New interapplication communication between Dreamweaver and Fireworks makes commands such as Create Web Photo Album possible.

- ✦ Dreamweaver includes a special C-level extension called FWLaunch, which provides the primary link to Fireworks.

In the next chapter, you see how you can add downloaded or streaming video to your Dreamweaver-created Web pages.

✦ ✦ ✦

Inserting Flash and Shockwave Elements

CHAPTER 13

In This Chapter

Getting to know Shockwave and Flash

Using Shockwave and Flash in Dreamweaver

Managing Flash links

Dreamweaver technique: Custom controls for Shockwave movies

Dreamweaver technique: Playing Shockwave movies in frames

Dreamweaver technique: Triggering behaviors from Flash movies

Dreamweaver technique: Cross-application control with Flash and Dreamweaver

---

Animated splash screens, sound-enabled banners, button bars with special fonts, and other exciting Web elements are often built with Macromedia's Flash. Flash combines vector graphics and streaming audio into great-looking, super–low bandwidth files that can be viewed in a browser using the Flash player plug-in. Flash's vector graphics have also turned out to be just the thing for Web-based cartoons. Beginning with version 4, Flash gained its own scripting language, ActionScript, and added MP3 compression to its streaming audio. With a huge base of installed players — as of this writing, well over 90 percent of browsers can view basic Flash content — Flash is an excellent way to liven up a Web page.

But Flash is not Macromedia's only solution for building interactive presentations for the Web. To many Web designers, Shockwave has represented the state of the art in Web interactivity since Macromedia first created the format in 1995. With Shockwave, multimedia files created in Macromedia's flagship authoring package, Director, can be compiled to run in a browser window. This gives Web designers the capability to build just about anything — from interactive Web interfaces with buttons that look indented when pushed, to arcade-style games, multimedia Web front-ends, and complete Web sites built entirely in Director — bringing a CD-ROM "look and feel" to the Web. Today, Shockwave continues to be an important force on the Web, as the enormous success of Macromedia's Shockwave.com amply demonstrates.

The final component in Macromedia's vector-graphic tool chest is a server-side technology called Generator. Generator works with templates built in Flash to display customized graphics, built on-demand. In its initial release, Generator was available only to designers working on big-budget, high-end sites and did not gain a sizeable foothold in the market.

However, Macromedia has recently changed its pricing policy on Generator and made the technology much more accessible to developers.

As you might expect, Macromedia makes it easy to incorporate Shockwave, Flash and Generator files into your Dreamweaver projects. All of these formats have special objects that provide control over virtually all of their parameters through the Property Inspector — and each format is cross-browser compatible by default. In Dreamweaver 4, Macromedia has moved to capitalize on the popularity of Flash and the flexibility of Generator with the introduction of two new tools: Flash Buttons and Flash Text. Now, it's easier than ever to incorporate customized, well-crafted Flash elements in your Web page without knowing a bit of Flash.

To take full advantage of the enhanced graphics potential of Flash and Shockwave's multimedia capabilities, you need to understand the differences between Director and Flash, as well as the various parameters available to each format. In addition to covering this material, this chapter also shows you how to use independent controls — both inline and with frames — for your Shockwave and Flash movies.

Shockwave and Flash: What's the Difference?

Director and Flash share many features: interactivity, streaming audio, support for both bitmaps and vector graphics, and "shocked fonts." Both can save their movies in formats suitable for viewing on the Web. So how do you choose which program to use? Each has its own special functions, and each excels at producing particular types of effects. Director is more full featured, with a complete programming language called Lingo that enables incredible interactivity. And Director movies can include Flash animations. Director also has a much steeper learning curve than does Flash. Flash is terrific for short, low-bandwidth animations with or without a synchronized audio track; however, the interactive capabilities in Flash are limited compared to Director.

Director is really a multimedia production program used for combining various elements: backgrounds, foreground elements called *sprites*, and various media such as digital audio and video (see Figure 13-1). With Director's Lingo programming language, you can build extraordinarily elaborate demos and games, with Internet-specific commands. When you need to include a high degree of interactivity, build your movie with Shockwave.

One of the primary differences between Director and Flash is the supported graphic formats. Director is generally better for bitmap graphics, in which each pixel is mapped to a specific color; both GIF and JPEG formats use bitmap graphics. Flash, on the other hand, uses primarily vector graphics, which are drawing elements described mathematically. Because vector graphics use a description of a drawing — a blue circle with a radius of 2.5 centimeters, for instance — rather than a bitmap, the resulting files are much smaller. A fairly complex animation produced with Flash might be only 10K or 20K, whereas a comparable digital video clip could easily be 10 times that size.

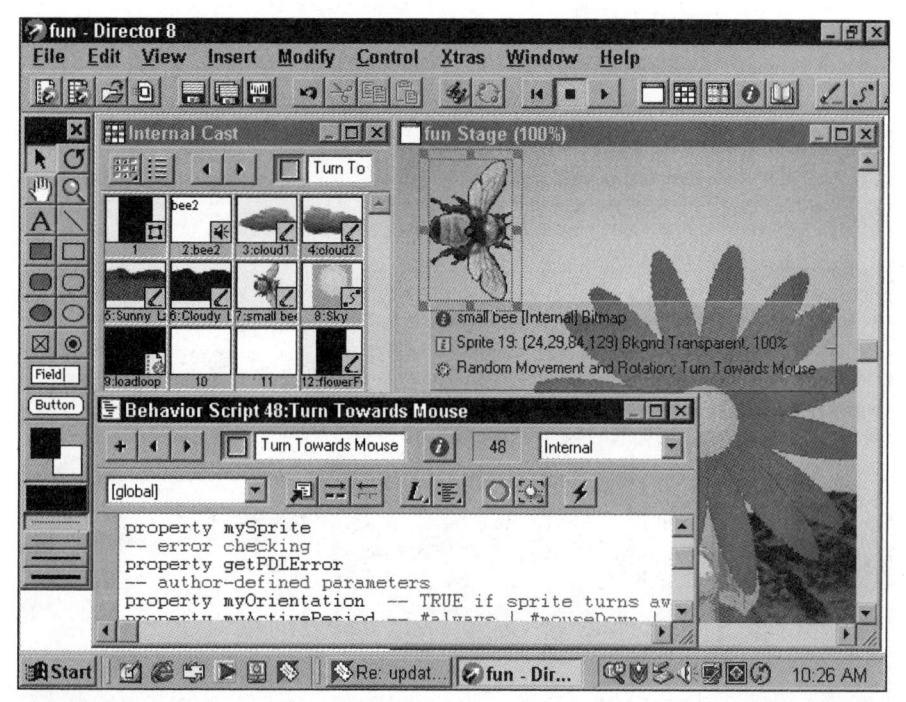

Figure 13-1: Director works mainly with bitmaps and video, and enables "multimedia programming" using Lingo.

Aside from file size, the other feature that distinguishes vector graphics from bitmap graphics is the smoothness of the line. When viewed with sufficient magnification, bitmap graphics always display telltale "stair-steps" or "jaggies," especially around curves. Vector graphics, on the other hand, are almost smooth. In fact, Flash takes special advantage of this characteristic and enables users to zoom into any movie — an important effect that saves a lot of bandwidth when used correctly.

However, these differences were significantly blurred with the release of Director 7, which incorporates its own native vector graphics and introduces the capability to include Flash movies within Director movies. Flash 4 blurred the line the other way by incorporating streaming MP3-encoded audio and QuickTime integration, both things that were traditionally the province of Director. In Flash 5, Flash's scripting capabilities have been significantly beefed up with the expansion of ActionScript into a JavaScript-based programming language.

Flash animations can be used as special effects, cartoons, and navigation bars within (or without) frames (see Figure 13-2). Although Flash isn't the best choice for games and other complex interactive elements, you can use Flash to animate your navigation system — complete with sound effects for button-pushing feedback.

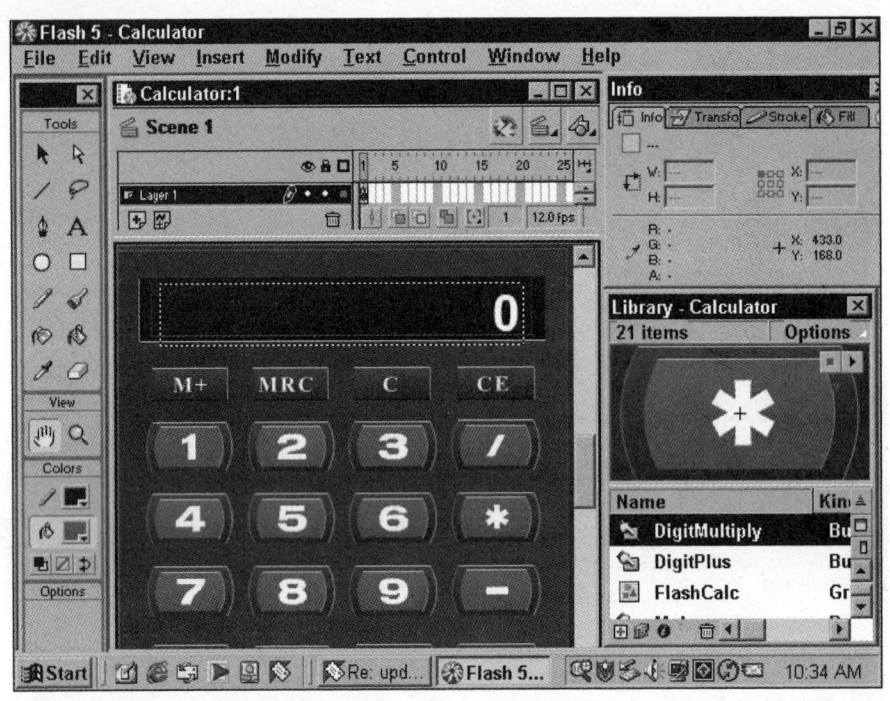

Figure 13-2: Flash movies tend to look more cartoon-like, thanks to Flash's lightweight vector graphics.

If Flash is a power tool, Director is a bulldozer. Director has been significantly expanded to handle a wide variety of file types, such as QuickTime and MP3, with advanced streaming capabilities. Supporting multimedia interactivity is Director's own programming language, Lingo, which has also been enhanced. Furthermore, Director now includes multiplayer support for network game play and chat rooms, XML parsing, embedded compressed fonts, up to 1,000 sprite channels, and a potential frame rate of 999 frames per second. Luckily, Dreamweaver enables you to pack all that power into a Web page with its Shockwave object.

Including Flash and Shockwave Movies in Dreamweaver Projects

Dreamweaver makes it easy to bring Shockwave and Flash files into your Web pages. The Objects panel provides an object for each type of movie, both located in the Common category.

Because Shockwave and Flash objects insert both an ActiveX control and a plug-in, Dreamweaver enables you to play the movie in the Document window. First it displays a plug-in placeholder icon (see Figure 13-3).

Chapter 13 ✦ **Inserting Flash and Shockwave Elements** 379

Flash placeholder

Insert Shockwave object

Insert Flash object

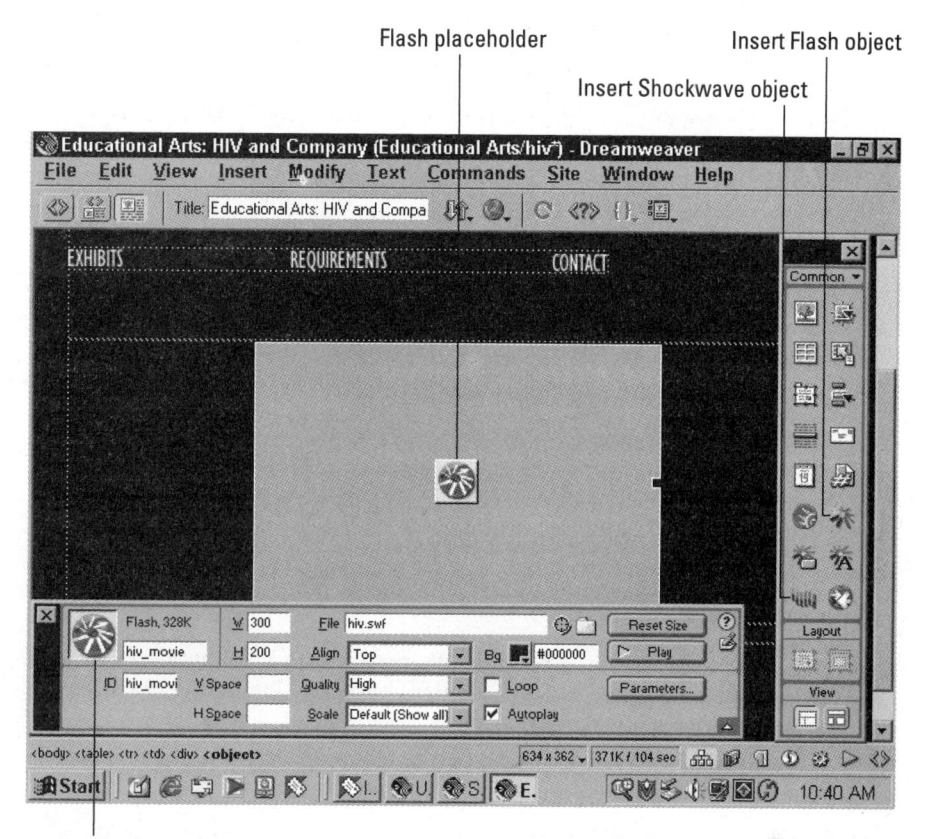

Flash property inspector

Figure 13-3: Dreamweaver includes many interface elements for working with Shockwave and Flash.

Before you can successfully include a Shockwave file, you need to know one small bit of information—the dimensions of your movie. Dreamweaver automatically reads the dimensions of your Flash file when you use the Insert Flash Movie object. Unfortunately, if you're incorporating a Shockwave movie, you still need to enter the dimensions by hand in the Shockwave Property Inspector.

To check the width and height of your movie in Director, load your file and then choose Modify ➪ Movie ➪ Properties to open the Movie Properties dialog box.

Note
It is essential to know the movie's height and width before you can include it successfully in Dreamweaver-built Web pages. During the development phase of a Dreamweaver project, I often include the movie dimensions in a file name, as an instant reminder to take care of this detail. For example, if I'm working with two different Shockwave movies, I can give them names such as navbar125x241.dcr and navbar400x50.dcr. (The .dcr extension is automatically appended by Director when you save a movie as a Shockwave file.) Because I consistently put width

before height in the filename, this trick saves me the time it would take to reopen Director, load the movie, and choose Modify ⇨ Movie to check the measurements in the Movie Properties dialog box. The alternative to keeping track of the Director movie's dimensions is to choose File ⇨ Save as Shockwave Movie in Director; this creates an HTML file with all the necessary parameters—including width and height—that can be inserted into Dreamweaver. You'll find a detailed description of this process later in this chapter.

To include either a Shockwave or Flash file in your Web page, follow these steps:

1. Position the cursor in the Document window at the point where you'd like the movie to appear.

2. Insert the movie using any of these methods:
   - Choose Insert ⇨ Media ⇨ Shockwave or Insert ⇨ Media ⇨ Flash from the menus.
   - In the Common category of the Objects panel, select either the Insert Shockwave or Insert Flash button.
   - Drag the movie object from the Objects panel to any location in the Document window.

3. In the Select File dialog box, enter the path and the filename in the File Name text box or select the Browse (Choose) button to locate the file. Click OK.

   Dreamweaver inserts a small plug-in placeholder in the current cursor position, and the Property Inspector displays the appropriate information for Shockwave or Flash.

4. Preview the Flash or Shockwave movie in the Document window by selecting the Play button found in the Property Inspector. You can also choose View ⇨ Plugins ⇨ Play.

5. End the preview of your file by selecting the Stop button in the Property Inspector or selecting View ⇨ Plugins ⇨ Stop.

Tip If you have more than one Flash or Shockwave movie on your page, you can control them all by choosing View ⇨ Plugins ⇨ Play All and View ⇨ Plugins ⇨ Stop All. If your files appear in different pages in a frameset, you have to repeat the Play All command for each page.

As noted earlier, you must specify the dimensions of your file in the Property Inspector before you can preview the movie in a browser; again, Dreamweaver supplies this information automatically for Flash files, but you have to enter it yourself for Shockwave movies. Shockwave and Flash have some different features in the Dreamweaver Property Inspector. These differences are covered separately in the following sections.

Specifying Shockwave Properties

Once you've inserted your Shockwave file, you're ready to begin entering the specific parameters in the Property Inspector. The Property Inspector takes care of all but one Shockwave attribute, the palette parameter. Some of the information, including the ActiveX Class ID, is automatically set in the Property Inspector when you insert the movie.

On the CD-ROM

You can find a custom command called Insert Shockwave HTML that automates the process of inserting a Shockwave movie and its Director-generated HTML. Look in the Configuration\Commands folder on the CD-ROM that accompanies this book. If you'd prefer a version developed by Macromedia that does the same job, visit the Dreamweaver Exchange to download the Insert Shockwave extension.

To set or modify the parameters for a Shockwave file, follow these steps:

1. Select the Shockwave placeholder icon.
2. In the Shockwave Property Inspector, enter the width and the height values in the W and H text boxes, respectively, as shown in Figure 13-4. Alternatively, you can click and drag any of the three resizing handles on the placeholder icon.

Generating HTML Within Director

In Director, you can generate a file with all the appropriate HTML code at the same time that you save your Shockwave movie, with just the selection of a checkbox. When you choose File ⇨ Save as Shockwave Movie in Director, the dialog box contains a Generate HTML option. Selecting this option causes Director to save an HTML file with the same name as your Shockwave movie but with an appropriate file extension (.html for Macintosh and .htm for Windows). You can easily copy and paste this HTML code directly into Dreamweaver.

When you open the Director-generated HTML file, you see the name of your file and the Shockwave placeholder, correctly sized and ready to preview. To move this object into another Web page in progress, just select the Shockwave object and choose Edit ⇨ Copy. Then switch to your other page and choose Edit ⇨ Paste. Naturally, you can also use the keyboard shortcuts or, if both pages are accessible, just drag and drop the object from one page to another.

Figure 13-4: Modify parameters for a Shockwave property through the Shockwave Property Inspector.

> **Tip** Pressing the Shift key while dragging the corner resizing handle maintains the current aspect ratio.

3. To designate how the Shockwave HTML code is written, select one of these three options from the Tag drop-down list:

   - **Object and Embed:** This is the default option and ensures that code is written for both Internet Explorer and Netscape. Use this option unless your page is on an intranet where only one browser is used.
   - **Object only:** Select this option to enable your movie to be viewed by Internet Explorer–compatible browsers.
   - **Embed only:** Select this option to enable your movie to be viewed by Netscape-compatible browsers.

4. Set and modify other object attributes as needed; see Table 13-1 for a list.

Table 13-1
Property Inspector Options for Shockwave Objects

Shockwave Property	Description
Align	Choose an option to alter the alignment of the movie. In addition to the browser default, your options include Baseline, Top, Middle, Bottom, Texttop, Absolute Middle, Absolute Bottom, Left, and Right.
Alt Image	The Alt Image file is displayed in browsers that do not support the `<embed>` tag and is available if you select Embed Only. This image does not display in Dreamweaver. Enter the path to the alternative image, or select the Folder icon to open a Select Image Source dialog box.
BgColor	The background color is visible only if the width and height of the plug-in are larger than the movie. To alter the background color of your plug-in, choose the color swatch and select a new color from the pop-up menu; or enter a valid color name in the BgColor text box.
Border	To place a border around your movie, enter a number in the Border text box. The number determines the width of the border in pixels. The default is zero or no border.
H Space	You can increase the space to the left and right of the movie by entering a value in the H (Horizontal) Space text box. The default is zero.
ID	The ID field is used to define the optional ActiveX ID parameter, most often used to pass data between ActiveX controls.
(Name)	If desired, you can enter a unique name in this unlabeled field on the far left of the Property Inspector. The name is used by JavaScript and other languages to identify the movie.
V Space	To increase the amount of space between other elements on the page and the top and bottom of the movie plug-in, enter a pixel value in the V (Vertical) Space text box. Again, the default is zero.

Additional parameters for Shockwave

As you can with other plug-ins, you can pass other attributes to the Shockwave movie via the Parameters dialog box — available by clicking the Parameters button on the Property Inspector. Press the add (+) button to begin inserting additional parameters. Enter the attributes in the left column and their respective values in the right. To remove an attribute, highlight it and select the delete (–) button.

Automatic settings for Shockwave files

When you insert a Shockwave or Flash file, Dreamweaver writes a number of parameters that are constant and necessary. In the `<object>` portion of the code, Dreamweaver includes the ActiveX Class ID number as well as the `codebase` number; the former calls the specific ActiveX control, and the latter enables users who don't have the control installed to receive it automatically. Likewise, in the `<embed>` section, Dreamweaver fills in the `pluginspage` attribute, designating the location where Navigator users can find the necessary plug-in. Be sure you don't accidentally remove any of this information — however, if you should, all you have to do is delete and reinsert the object.

Only one other general attribute is usually assigned to a Shockwave file, the `palette` parameter. This parameter takes a value of either foreground or background.

- If `palette` is set to background, the movie's color scheme does not override that of the system; this is the default.
- When `palette` is set to foreground, the colors of the selected movie are applied to the user's system, which includes the desktop and scroll bars.

Note that `palette` is not supported by Internet Explorer.

Caution Web designers should take care when specifying the `palette=foreground` parameter. This effect is likely to prove startling to the user; moreover, if your color scheme is sufficiently different, the change may render the user's system unusable. If you do use the `palette` parameter, be sure to include a Director command to restore the original system color scheme in the final frame of the movie.

Designating Flash Attributes

Flash movies require the same basic parameters as their Shockwave counterparts — and Flash movies have a few additional optional ones as well. As it does for Shockwave files, Dreamweaver sets almost all the attributes for Flash movies through the Property Inspector. The major difference is that several more parameters are available.

To set or modify the attributes for a Flash file, follow these steps:

1. After your Flash movie has been inserted in the Document window, make sure it's selected. Dreamweaver automatically inserts the correct dimensions for your Flash movie.
2. Set any attributes in the Property Inspector as needed for your Flash movie. (Refer to the previous descriptions of these attributes in the section "Specifying Shockwave Properties.") In addition, you can also set the parameters described in Table 13-2.

Table 13-2
Property Inspector Options for Flash Objects

Flash Parameter	Possible Values	Description
Autoplay	Checked (default)	Enables the Flash movie to begin playing as soon as possible.
Loop	Checked (default)	If Loop is checked, the movie plays continuously; otherwise, it plays once.
Quality		Controls antialiasing during playback.
	High	Antialiasing is turned on. This can slow the playback frame rate considerably on slower computers.
	Low	No antialiasing is used; this setting is best for animations that must be played quickly.
	AutoHigh (default)	The animation begins in High (with antialiasing) and switches to Low if the host computer is too slow.
	AutoLow	Starts the animation in Low (no antialiasing) and then switches to High if the host machine is fast enough.
Scale		Scale determines how the movie fits into the dimensions as specified in the width and height text boxes.
	ShowAll (default)	Displays the entire movie in the given dimensions while maintaining the file's original aspect ratio. Some of the background may be visible with this setting.
	ExactFit	Scales the movie precisely into the dimensions without regard for the aspect ratio. It is possible that the image could be distorted with this setting.
	NoBorder	Fits the movie into the given dimensions so that no borders are showing and maintains the original aspect ratio. Some of the movie may be cut off with this setting.

Setting the scale in Flash movies

Be careful with your setting for the Scale parameter, in order to avoid unexpected results. If you have to size a Flash movie out of its aspect ratio, the Flash player needs to know what to do with any extra room it has to fill. Figure 13-5 demonstrates the different results that the Scale attribute can provide. Only the figure in the lower right is at its proper dimensions. The gray box is the actual size of the authoring canvas.

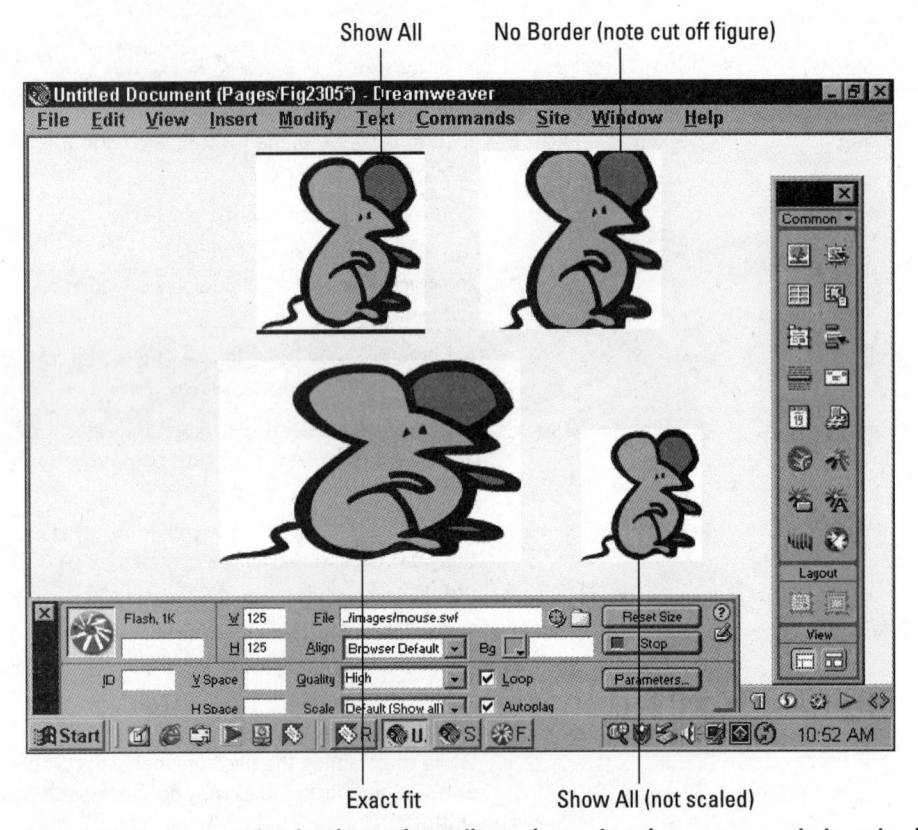

Figure 13-5: Your setting for the Scale attribute determines how your movie is resized within the plug-in width and height measurements.

Tip

Dreamweaver makes it easy to rescale a Flash movie. First, from the Property Inspector, enter the precise width and height of your file in the W and H text boxes. Then, while holding down the Shift key, click and drag the corner resizing handle of the Flash placeholder icon to the new size for the movie. By Shift+dragging, you retain the aspect ratio set in the Property Inspector. This enables you to quickly enlarge or reduce your movie without distortion.

Additional parameters for Flash

Flash has two additional attributes that can be entered through the Parameters dialog box (click the Parameters button on the Property Inspector): salign and swliveconnect. The salign attribute determines how the movie aligns itself to the surrounding frame when the Scale attribute is set to ShowAll. In addition, `salign` determines which portion of the image gets cut off when the Scale attribute is set to NoBorder. The alignment can be set to L (left), R (right), T (top), or B (bottom). You can also use these values in combination. For example, if you set `salign=RB`, the movie aligns with the right-bottom edge or the lower-right corner of the frame.

The `swliveconnect` attribute comes into play when you're using FSCommands or JavaScripting in your Flash movies. FSCommands are interactive commands, such as Go to URL, issued from inside the Flash movie. The latest versions of the Netscape browser initialize Java when first called — and if your Flash movie uses FSCommands or JavaScript, it uses Java to communicate with the Netscape plug-in interface, LiveConnect. Because not all Flash movies need the LiveConnect connection, you can prevent Java from being initialized by entering the `swliveconnect` attribute in the Parameters dialog box and setting its value to false. When the `swliveconnect=false` parameter is found by the browser, the Java is not initialized as part of the loading process — and your movie loads more quickly.

Creating Flash Buttons and Crafting Templates

The primary argument against using Flash has always been, "Not everyone has the Flash plug-in, so not everyone can see Flash movies." When Macromedia began promoting the 96.4 percent and above market penetration of the Flash Player, that argument started to fade. True, this almost universally installed base applies to the Flash 2 player — as of this writing, over 88 percent of browsers have Flash 4 players and almost 40 percent, Flash 5 — but the basic ability to play back .swf files is all that's necessary to display simple animations and enable sounds.

While Flash is often used to create standalone movies, cartoons, and interactive games, it is also capable of making excellent navigation aids. One feature of traditional user interfaces — audio feedback, the "click" that one hears when a button has been chosen onscreen — has been long missing on the Web because of the lack of a universally available sound engine. With navigation buttons created in Flash, sound is very easy to incorporate, as are animation effects and smooth blends. Best of all, these effects are extremely low bandwidth and often weigh less on a page than a comparable animated GIF file, even without the sound.

New Feature
Dreamweaver designers may now add the power and beauty of Flash objects to their Web page design palette. Both animated Flash Buttons and static Flash Text (covered later in this chapter) may now be created directly within Dreamweaver. Flash Buttons are based on template designs created in Flash and customized in Dreamweaver. This separation of design and implementation allows Flash graphic designers to create the overall look for a navigational button or button series and

Dreamweaver layout artists to incorporate them into the proper page design, adding the appropriate button text, links, and background color where needed. Flash Buttons, like any Flash movie, may be previewed in Dreamweaver and resized as needed.

Dreamweaver comes with 44 different Flash Button templates with additional styles available at the Macromedia Exchange. The buttons are primarily intended to be used as links to other Web pages although some are designed as VCR-like player controls. To insert a Flash Button, follow these steps:

1. Make sure that the current document has been previously saved.

   If you're working on a new document, Dreamweaver requires that you save it before adding a Flash Button.

2. Choose Insert Flash Button from the Common category of the Objects panel or select Insert ⇨ Interactive Images ⇨ Flash Button.

   The Insert Flash Button dialog box, shown in Figure 13-6, is displayed.

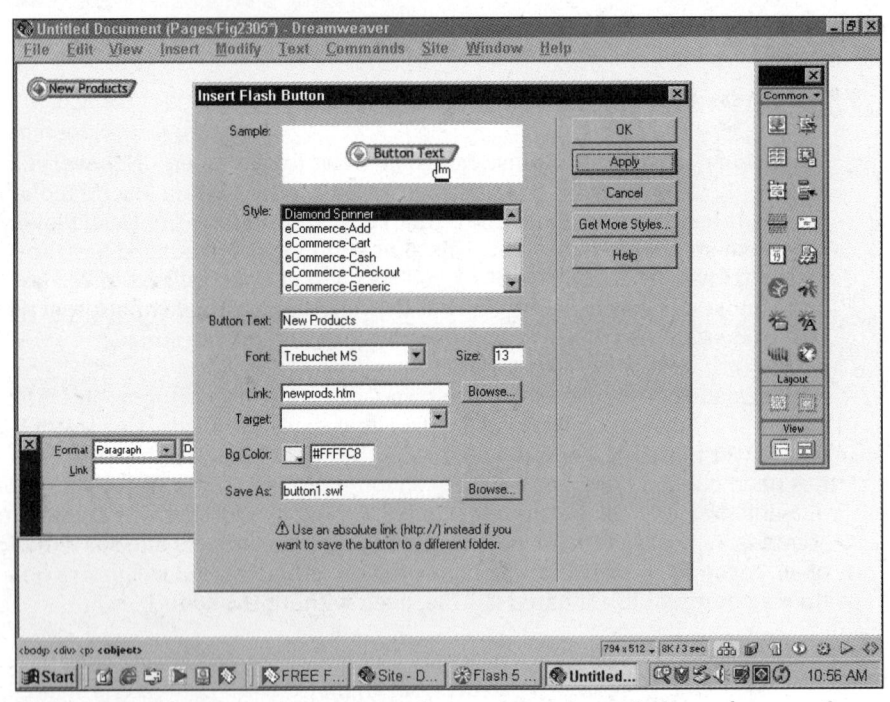

Figure 13-6: Choose Apply to test typeface and text size variations when creating your Flash Button.

3. Select a button type from the Style list.

   The previews shown in the Sample area are live demonstrations and will play as designed when moused-over and/or clicked. There is, however, one exception: no sound is heard in preview; you'll have to preview the Flash Button in the browser to get the full effect.

4. If it's a navigation button, enter the custom text desired in the Button Text field.

   The Button Text field is physically limited to 50 characters, although for most practical purposes, your text will be shorter. Certain symbols, such as those in the Control group, ignore the text and font settings.

5. Select a typeface from the Font drop-down list.

   The fonts listed are TrueType fonts found on your system. Most of the button templates have a preselected font and text size. If the preselected font is not found on your system, a small alert appears at the bottom of the dialog box.

6. Enter the desired font size, in points, in the Size field.

7. If the button is to link to another page, enter the absolute or document relative URL in the Link field. Alternatively, you can choose the Browse button to locate the file.

   Flash movies don't handle site root–relative links correctly, so your link needs to either be absolute, such as www.idest.com/contact.htm, or document relative. Use document relative links only if the Flash Button is to be stored in the same folder as the page referenced.

8. If working in a frame-based site or you want the link to open in another page, select an option from the Target drop-down list.

   The standard system targets — _blank, _self, _parent, and _top — are always available. Additional frame names appear if the Flash Button is inserted in an existing frameset.

9. If the Flash Button is to be placed on a page or in a table with a background color other than white, select the Bg Color swatch to choose an appropriate background. Alternatively, the hexadecimal color number or standard color name may be entered directly into the Bg Color text field.

10. Enter a path and filename for the Flash Button file. If you like, you can use the suggested default name in the site root or select the Browse button to choose a different location.

11. Choose Apply to insert the button in the cursor location on the page.

12. Click OK when you're done.

> **Tip**: If you'd like to see what other styles are available, open the Insert Flash Button dialog box and choose Get More Styles. Your primary browser will launch and go to the Dreamweaver Exchange where you can search for new styles. Once you've installed the additional extensions using the Extension Manager, you'll need to relaunch Dreamweaver to see the new styles. One word of caution: selecting Get More Styles immediately closes the dialog box without creating a button.

Once your Flash Button is inserted, it can be modified on the page. Choose the Flash Button to activate the specific Property Inspector that, along with standard Flash object parameters, offers a couple of new controls: Edit and Reset Size. Selecting Edit reopens the Insert Flash Button dialog box and allows you to modify any of the settings. Use Reset Size if you have altered the dimensions of the Flash Button — by dragging one of the sizing handles or entering new values in the Width and/or Height fields — and want to return to the preset size.

> **Tip**
> If you've moved an existing Flash Button to a frame-based design, select the button and choose Edit from the Property Inspector. Under Target, you'll find names for all the frames in your new frameset to make it easy to position your content.

The Flash Button samples that ship with Dreamweaver are nice, but to be truly useful, you — or someone on your team — must be able to create your own templates that fit the design of your site. The Flash Button templates you see previewed in Dreamweaver are actually Generator templates, created in Flash.

To create the Generator templates, you'll need Flash, of course, and the free Generator authoring extensions from Macromedia. The authoring extensions are included in Flash 5 or can be downloaded from the Macromedia site at `www.macromedia.com/software/generator/trial`. Additionally, you'll need to copy two Generator object files from the Dreamweaver CD-ROM to their proper place in the Flash and Generator installations. From the Dreamweaver 4/More Extensions/Flash Objects/Generator Text Object folder, copy these files:

- InsertText.def to Flash 5/generator/template folder
- InsertText.class to Generator 2/extras

If you don't have the Dreamweaver CD-ROM, you can download these files from the same Macromedia site listed previously.

Once you have the Generator Text object files in place, the next step is to create your button in Flash. As with other Flash Buttons, your graphic should be converted to a button-type symbol and it may use all four keyframes: Up, Over, Down, and Hit. Once you've built the button, follow these steps to add the Generator functionality:

1. In Flash, choose Window ➪ Generator Objects.
2. From the Generator Objects panel, drag the Insert Text object over the previously built button.

    Position the Insert Text object so that its center is over where you'd like your button text to appear.

3. When the Insert Text object is in place and selected, the Generator Insert Text panel displaying the appropriate properties appears. Double-click the Insert Text object to bring the panel to the front if necessary.

    Within the panel, you'll need to set several parameters to placeholder values so that the Insert Flash Button dialog box in Dreamweaver can function properly. In each case, enter the value in the right column.

4. Enter the following values in the Generator Insert Text panel:
   - **Text:** Enter {Button Text}
   - **Font:** Enter {Button Font}
   - **Font Size:** Enter {Button Size}
   - **Alignment:** Enter either left, right, center or justified.
   - **Vertical Alignment:** Enter either top, center or bottom.
   - **URL:** Enter {Button URL}
   - **Window:** Enter {Button Target}
5. Shrink the movie to the size of your button by dragging the button to the upper-left corner of the stage and choosing Modify ⇨ Movie. In the Movie Properties dialog box, select the Match Contents option.
6. Save the movie as a .fla file so that you may adjust it later.
7. Choose File ⇨ Export Movie and select Generator Template as the file type. Save the template in the Dreamweaver/Configuration/Flash Objects/Flash Buttons folder.

Now your Flash Button is almost ready to use. If you like, you can choose the Insert Flash Button object in Dreamweaver and see your button; however, no sample text will be displayed. There's one last procedure that's required if you want to preview your Flash Button with example text. Interestingly enough, you use the Insert Flash Button object to create the preview:

1. Open Dreamweaver and save a blank page.
2. Choose the Insert Flash Button object.
3. Select your newly inserted button from the Style list.

   New buttons are found at the end of the list.

4. Enter desired default values in the Text, Font, and Size fields.

   These values will be preset whenever this particular Flash Button is chosen.

5. In the Save As field, store the file under the same name as your style in the Dreamweaver/Configuration/Flash Objects/Flash Buttons Preview folder.
6. Click OK when you're done.

The next time you access the Flash Button object, your custom template will display a full preview, with text.

Working with Flash Text

The addition of Flash Text to Dreamweaver goes a long way toward solving one of the Web designer's most perplexing problems: how to achieve good-looking text that uses non-standard fonts. While standard HTML text allows font families — a series of fonts offered in hopes that one of them is installed on the user's system — few designers stray outside of tried and true options such as Arial, Helvetica, and Times New Roman for the majority of their content. This is especially grating to print designers coming to the Web who rely on typography as a primary design tool. The advent of Dynamic HTML promised to bring a wider selection of typefaces with so-called dynamic font technology, but lack of built-in cross-browser support for any one system dashed those hopes.

New Feature

The new Flash Text feature allows the designer to use any TrueType font to create low-weight, jaggie-free headings, right from within Dreamweaver itself. The ubiquitous nature of the Flash Player ensures cross-browser support without resorting to GIF images, which are often not as crisp as required. Moreover, with Flash Text, you can easily declare a second color for automatically enabled rollovers — you don't even have to attach a Dreamweaver behavior.

The Flash Text feature is especially useful for creating headings in a corporate-approved typeface. Because it doesn't involve downloading a font resource as dynamic font technologies do, there is no concern about the misuse of copyrighted fonts. The only downside to Flash Text over a dynamic font technology is that unlike dynamically created fonts, Flash Text cannot be searched on a page. To overcome this limitation, Web designers can include key phrases in `<meta>` tags.

To use the Flash Text object, follow these steps:

1. Make sure your page has been saved before proceeding.
2. Choose Insert Flash Text from the Common category of the Objects panel or select Insert ➪ Interactive Images ➪ Flash Text.

   The Insert Flash Text dialog box appears, as shown in Figure 13-7.
3. Select the desired typeface from the Font drop-down list.
4. Enter the font size desired in the Size field.
5. Choose Bold and/or Italic styles for your text.
6. Select the alignment on the page: left, center, or right.
7. Select a basic color from the color swatch or enter a hexadecimal value or valid color name in the Color field.
8. If desired, choose a secondary color for the text to change to when the user moves his or her mouse over the Flash Text from the Rollover Color swatch.

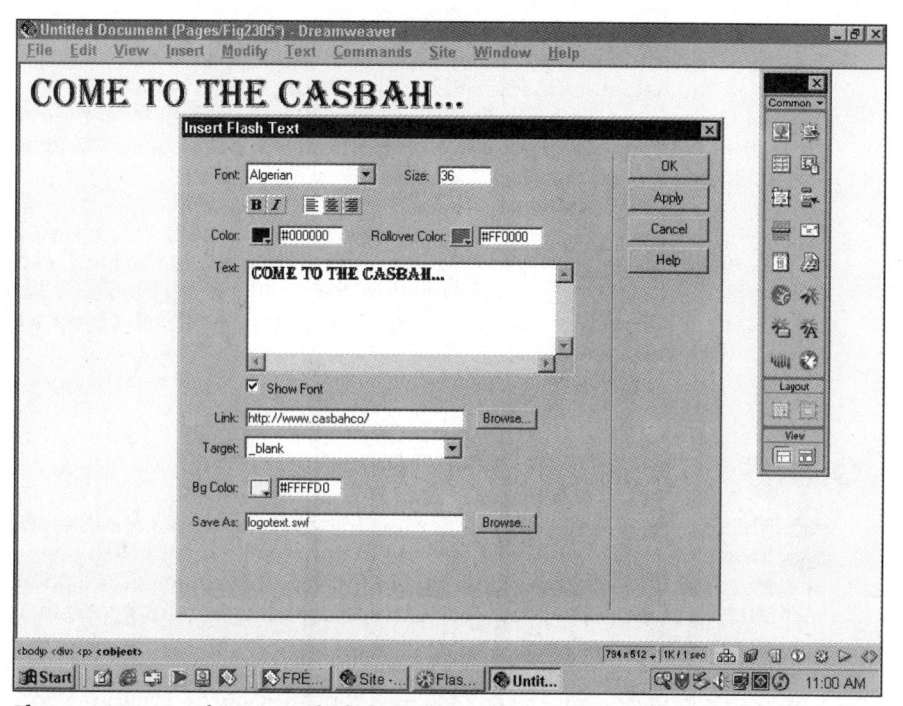

Chapter 13 ✦ Inserting Flash and Shockwave Elements 393

Figure 13-7: Use the Insert Flash Text object to create headlines with a non-standard or custom font.

9. Enter the desired text in the Text field.

   There's no real limit to the amount of text that can be entered other than practical considerations, and line returns are acceptable.

10. If you want to see the text in the default font in the Text field, disable the Show Font option.

11. If desired, enter an absolute or document relative URL in the Link field.

    As with Flash Buttons, site relative links are not available in Flash Text objects.

12. If you're working in a frame-based site or want the link to open in a new browser window, choose the appropriate Target from the drop-down list.

13. Optionally, choose a background color from the Bg Color swatch.

14. Enter a filename and path to store the object in the Save As field. Alternatively, select the Browse button to locate a folder.

    If you're using document relative links in the Flash Text object, be sure to store the object in the same folder as the current document.

15. Click Apply to preview what your button will look like in your document and then click OK when you're done.

As with Flash Buttons, you can resize a Flash Text object by dragging the resizing handles; press the Shift key while dragging to constrain the dimensions to their initial width and height ratio. Click Reset Size on the Property Inspector to restore the original dimensions. To edit a Flash Text object, choose Edit from the Property Inspector; alternatively, you can double-click the object to open the Insert Flash Text dialog box again.

When you create a Flash Text object, Dreamweaver makes a GIF representation for display during layout — you may notice some roughness in the lines, especially if you resize the object. You can, at any time, select Play from the Flash Text Property Inspector (or choose Preview in Browser) to see the true Flash object with its smooth vector shape.

Configuring MIME Types

As with any plug-in, your Web server has to have the correct MIME types set before Shockwave files can be properly served to your users. If your Web page plays Shockwave and Flash movies locally, but not remotely, chances are good the correct MIME types need to be added. The system administrator generally handles configuring MIME types.

The system administrator needs to know the following information in order to correctly configure the MIME types:

- **Shockwave:** application/x-director (.dcr, .dir, .dxr)
- **Flash:** application/x-shockwave-flash (.swf)

Both Shockwave and Flash are popular plug-ins, and it's likely that the Web server is already configured to recognize the appropriate file types.

> **Tip** Movies made by an earlier version of Flash, called FutureSplash, can also be played by the Flash plug-in — but only if the correct MIME type is added: `application/futuresplash` with the file extension .spl.

Adding Generator Objects

Generator is Macromedia's tool for personalizing and delivering Flash content. While developers create Flash movies on their own systems, Generator graphics are built on-demand, by the server. Generator works with a series of variables in each template, which is filled in when the page containing the Generator object is requested by the browser. Think of Generator as a graphic mail-merge system in which the basic letter is the animation and the form fields can be anything from a user's name to data returned from a database. Although Generator is largely used to customize Flash content on the fly, it can also output other formats including GIF, JPEG, PNG, and QuickTime.

Inserting a Generator template into a Web page is very straightforward in Dreamweaver. Most of the work comes from providing values for the variables through a name/value pair interface. To add a Generator template, follow these steps:

1. Position your cursor where you'd like the Generator object to appear and choose Insert Generator from the Common category of the Objects panel or select Insert ⇨ Media ⇨ Generator.

   The Insert Generator dialog box, shown in Figure 13-8, appears.

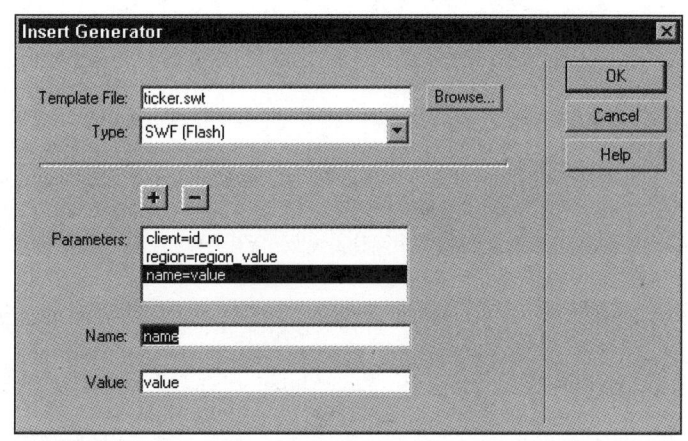

Figure 13-8: Generator templates allow Flash movies and other graphics to be personalized by the server.

2. Enter the path to the Generator template file or choose the Browse button to locate the file.

   Generator templates have a .swt file extension.

3. Choose the kind of media to be created by Generator from the Type drop-down list: SWF (Flash), GIF, JPEG, MOV (QuickTime), or PNG.

4. To enter parameters for the object, first select the Add button.

   In the Parameters list, the temporary name=value listing appears.

5. Enter the name for your parameter in the Name field.

6. Enter the value of your parameter in the Value field.

7. Repeat Steps 4 through 6 for each parameter.

8. To remove a parameter, highlight it in the Parameters list and choose the Remove button.

9. Click OK when you're done.

Managing Links in Flash Movies with Dreamweaver

Many Web sites rely heavily on Flash movies, substituting movies for entire pages that would otherwise be created with HTML. Others take advantage of Flash's interactivity in their main navigation buttons. Adding links to buttons in Flash is easy, but embedding multiple URLs into multiple SWF files can make modifying a site's structure a nightmare, forcing you to re-create every SWF file in your site. Luckily, Dreamweaver comes to the rescue, with link management features that are SWF-savvy.

Dreamweaver extends its link management to include the links contained in Flash SWF movies. Edit links within a SWF file manually in the Site Map, or move SWF files in the Site Files view and let Dreamweaver clean up behind you.

Within the Site window, you can drag SWF files to new folders just as you would an HTML file. Unless your Update Links preference is set to Never, Dreamweaver will either modify the links in the SWF file accordingly or prompt you for permission to do so.

Caution Be careful with the type of links you use — Flash (or, more accurately, browser playback of Flash) can't handle them all. Absolute URLs are very common in Flash movies because they can be used in every situation. Document relative links may be used successfully in all cases if the Web page and the Flash file are stored in the same folder. Site root relative links, such as `/products/widgets.htm`, should not be used in Flash movies.

To modify the links in a SWF file manually, follow these steps:

1. Choose Window ⇨ Site Map to view the Site Map.
2. Choose View ⇨ Show Dependent Files (Site ⇨ Site Map View ⇨ Show Dependent Files) to include dependent files such as Flash movies in the Site Map.
3. Locate the SWF file that you want to modify. If it contains any links, a plus sign is shown next to its icon. Click the plus sign to expand a branch of links from the SWF file, as shown in Figure 13-9.
4. To change a link, select it and choose Site ⇨ Change Link (Site ⇨ Site Map View ⇨ Change Link) or use the key shortcut Ctrl+L (Command+L). Alternatively, you can right-click (Control+click) the link and choose Change Link from the contextual menu. Dreamweaver displays a Select HTML File dialog box.
5. Select a new file by navigating to an HTML file or entering an URL. Click OK when you're done.

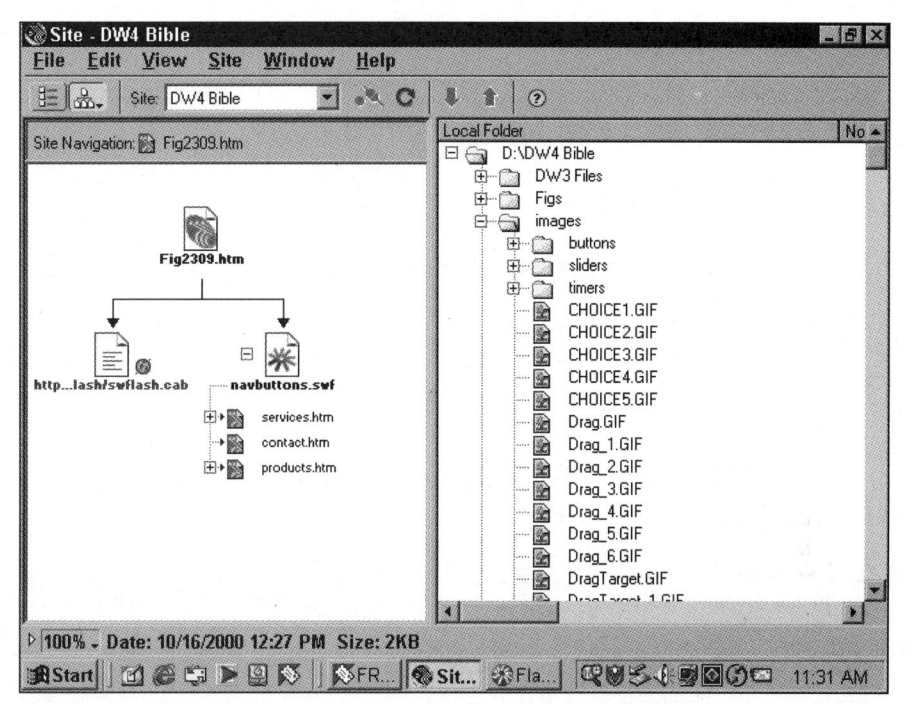

Figure 13-9: Dreamweaver's Site Map displays links contained in Flash SWF movies.

Note If your preferences call for Dreamweaver to prompt you before updating links, Dreamweaver will ask you to confirm that you want this link changed.

The link in your SWF file is changed.

Just as with HTML files, you can also remove links from a SWF file by selecting the link and choosing Site ⇨ Remove Link (Site ⇨ Site Map View ⇨ Remove Link) or use the keyboard shortcut Ctrl+Shift+L (Command+Shift+L).

Caution Dreamweaver changes links within SWF files, but the links in the original Flash document that you edit in Flash itself will remain unchanged. Make sure to update your Flash document before exporting a revised SWF file.

Providing User Interaction with Shockwave Movies

What happens once you've installed your Director or Flash Shockwave files? Many movies are set to play automatically or upon some action from the user, such as a mouse click of a particular hotspot within the page. The Show Me movies used in

Dreamweaver are good examples of the kind of interactivity you can program within a Director Shockwave movie. But what if you want the user to be able to start or stop a movie in one part of the page, using controls in another part? How can controls in one frame affect a movie in a different frame?

Dreamweaver includes a Control Shockwave or Flash behavior that makes inline controls — controls on the same Web page as the movie — very easy to set up. However, establishing frame-to-frame control is slightly more complex in Dreamweaver and requires a minor modification to the program-generated code.

Cross-Reference: Both of the following step-by-step techniques rely on Dreamweaver behaviors. If you're unfamiliar with using behaviors, you should review Chapter 11 before proceeding.

Dreamweaver technique: Creating inline Shockwave controls

Certainly it's perfectly acceptable to make your Director or Flash movies with built-in controls for interactivity, but sometimes you want to separate the controls from the movie. Dreamweaver includes a JavaScript behavior called Control Shockwave or Flash. With this behavior, you can set up external controls to start, stop, and rewind Shockwave and Flash movies.

To create inline Shockwave or Flash controls:

1. Insert your Shockwave or Flash file by choosing either the Insert Shockwave or Insert Flash button from the Objects panel.
2. From the Select File dialog box, enter the path to your file in the File Name text box or select the Browse (Choose) button to locate your file.
3. For Shockwave, enter the width and height of your movie in the W and H text boxes, respectively, in the Property Inspector. The dimensions for Flash movies are entered automatically.
4. Enter a unique name for your movie in the text box provided.
5. If you are inserting a Flash movie, deselect the Autoplay and Loop options.
6. To insert the first control, position the cursor where you'd like the control to appear on the page.
7. Select Insert Image from the Objects panel or select some text.
8. In the Link box of the Property Inspector, enter a dummy link or just a hash symbol, #, to create an empty target.
9. Open the Behaviors panel by selecting the Show Behaviors button from the Launcher or by pressing Shift+F3.

10. If necessary, change the selected browser to 4.0 Browsers; you can do this by selecting an option from the Show Events For submenu of the Add Behavior menu.

11. Select the + (Add Action) button and choose Control Shockwave or Flash from the drop-down list.

12. In the Control Shockwave or Flash dialog box (see Figure 13-10), select the movie you want to affect from the Movie drop-down list.

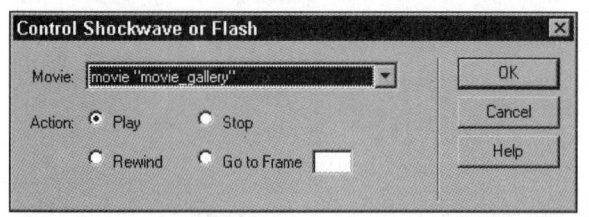

Figure 13-10: In the Control Shockwave or Flash dialog box, you assign a control action to an image button or link.

13. Now select the desired action for your control. Choose from the four options: Play, Stop, Rewind, and Go to Frame. If you choose the Go to Frame option, enter a frame number in the text box.

14. Click OK to close the Control Shockwave or Flash dialog box.

15. Repeat Steps 6 through 14 for each movie control you'd like to add. Figure 13-11 shows a sample Web page with Play and Stop controls.

Dreamweaver technique: Playing Shockwave movies in frames

Framesets and frames are great for Web sites in which you want your navigation and other controls kept in one frame and the freedom to vary the content in another frame. It's entirely possible to set up your movie's playback buttons in one frame and the Shockwave movie in another. The method and the tools used are similar to those used in the preceding technique for adding same-page controls to a Shockwave movie. For this technique using frames, some HTML hand-coding is necessary, but it is relatively minor — only one additional line per control!

As you saw in the previous section, Dreamweaver's Control Shockwave or Flash behavior lists all the Shockwave and Flash movies in the page and enables you to choose the one you want to affect (as previously shown in Figure 13-11). Unfortunately, the behavior looks on only one page and not through an entire frameset. However, with a little sleight-of-hand and a bit of JavaScript, you can get the effect you want.

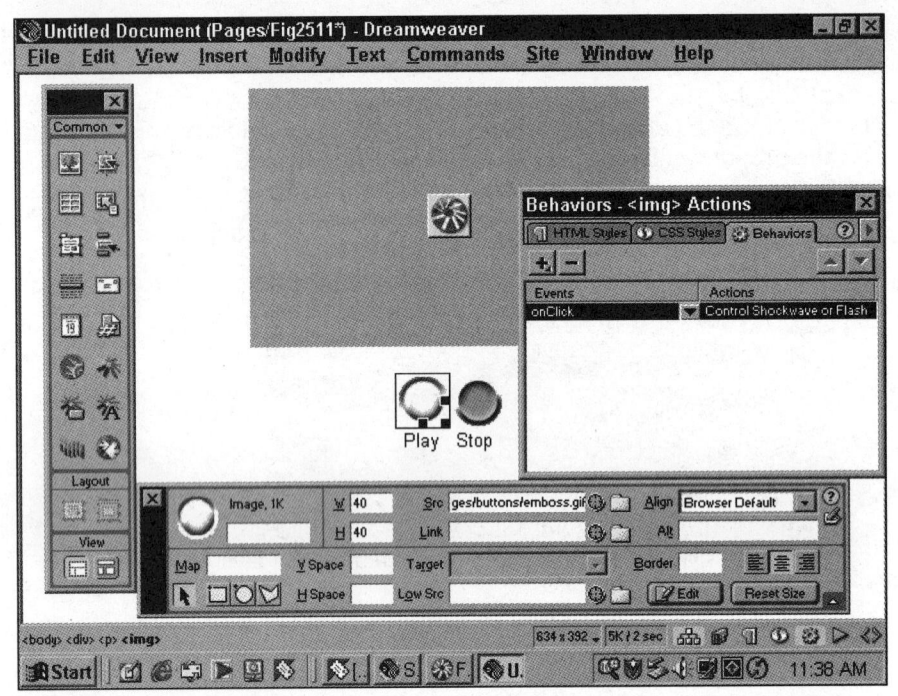

Figure 13-11: This Web page contains Play and Stop controls using the Control Shockwave or Flash behavior.

> **Note:** Before you begin applying this technique, you should construct (and save) your frameset and individual frames. Be sure to name each frame uniquely, because you have to provide the names in order to address the correct frames.

To place Shockwave controls in frames:

1. In one frame, insert the images or links that are going to act as the Shockwave controls. (For this demonstration, the control frame is named `frControl`.)

2. In another frame, insert the Shockwave file (either Shockwave or Flash) by choosing the appropriate object from the Objects panel. (For this demonstration, the movie frame is named `frMovie`.)

3. Be sure to modify the Shockwave Property Inspector with the necessary parameters: name, width, height, and source; and, if you're inserting a Flash file, deselect the Autoplay and Loop checkboxes.

4. Copy the Shockwave placeholder by selecting it and choosing Edit ⇨ Copy.

5. Position the cursor in the `frControl` frame and paste the placeholder in a temporary position by choosing Edit ⇨ Paste. At this point, the placement for the placeholder is not critical, as long as it is in the same frame as the images or links you are going to use as controls. The placeholder will be deleted shortly.

Instead of using the Copy and Paste commands, you can hold down Ctrl (Command) and click and drag the placeholder to its new temporary position.

6. Now select the first image or link you want to use as a control. As described in the preceding technique, attach the Control Shockwave or Flash behavior to the selected object. As you learned in the preceding exercise, this entails the following actions:

    - With the image or link selected, open the Behaviors panel.
    - Add the Control Shockwave or Flash action.
    - In the Control Shockwave or Flash dialog box, specify the movie and select the required action (Play, Rewind, Stop, or Go to Frame).

7. The major work is finished now. All you still need to do is add a little HTML. Switch to Code view, open the Code Inspector, or use your favorite external editor to edit the file.

8. Locate the image or link controls in the code. Each JavaScript routine is called from within an `<a>` tag and reads something like the following, where fMovie is the name of the Flash movie:

    ```
    <a href="#" onClick="MM_controlShockwave ¬
    ('document.fMovie','document.fMovie','Play')">
    ```

9. Wherever you see the JavaScript reference to document, change it to

    ```
    parent.frameName.document
    ```

    where frameName is the unique name you gave to the frame in which your movie appears. In our example, frameName is frMovie, so after the replacement is made, the tag reads as follows:

    ```
    <a href="#" onClick="MM_controlShockwave('parent.ù
    frMovie.document.fMovie','document.fMovie','Play')">
    ```

    By making this substitution, you've pointed the JavaScript function first to the "parent" of the current document — and the parent of a frame is the entire frameset. Now that we're looking at the entire frameset, the next word (which is the unique frame name) points the JavaScript function directly to the desired frame within the frameset.

    Tip If you have a number of controls, you might want to use Dreamweaver's Find and Replace features to ensure that you've updated all the code.

10. Finally, delete the temporary Shockwave movie that was inserted into the frame containing the controls.

Test the frameset by pressing F12 (primary browser) or Shift+F12 (secondary browser). If you haven't changed the Property Inspector's default Tag attribute (the default is Object and Embed), the Shockwave movie should work in both Netscape and Internet Explorer.

Dreamweaver technique: Triggering behaviors from Flash movies

Flash includes a number of its own behaviors for creating interactivity, but Flash behaviors don't do JavaScript as Dreamweaver behaviors do. A Flash-heavy project might benefit from Dreamweaver's Open Browser Window or Pop-up Message behaviors as much as the next site. The technique in this section shows you how to trigger Dreamweaver behaviors from buttons in a Flash movie.

What Flash buttons do is specified in the Flash authoring environment, not in Dreamweaver. Dreamweaver can attach behaviors to HTML elements such as anchor tags and body tags but not to plug-ins. The solution lies in creating dummy "buttons" in Dreamweaver and copying the JavaScript code from those links into the actions attached to Flash buttons, within Flash itself.

Note The following technique can be used for any Dreamweaver behavior. The JavaScript Integration Kit for Flash 5 (JIK) extension, covered later in this chapter, has several built-in functions including Open Browser Window and Swap Image. Use the following procedure if you don't want to use the JIK extension or need to incorporate a behavior not included in that extension.

To trigger Dreamweaver behaviors from Flash buttons, follow these steps:

1. Create a new Dreamweaver document or open an existing one.

2. Create a dummy link that represents a button in your Flash movie. If you want a Flash button to open a new browser window, attach the Open Browser Window behavior to your dummy link, as in Figure 13-12.

3. Place your cursor within the dummy link and choose the `<a>` tag from the Tag Chooser in Dreamweaver's status bar to completely select the link.

4. Click the Show Code and Design views button on the toolbar or choose View ⇨ Code and Design from the menus. Note that the dummy link is selected in both the Code and Design portions of the document window and looks something like this:

   ```
   <a href="#"
   onClick="MM_openBrWindow('myBuddy.htm','','scrollbars=yes','w
   idth=250,height=200')">popup copywrite message</a>
   ```

5. Select everything between the quotes in the `onClick` attribute — including the parentheses — as shown in Figure 13-13, and copy it to the clipboard. This is the actual JavaScript that we want the Flash button to execute.

6. In Flash, double-click the button you want to add the Dreamweaver behavior to. The Instance Properties dialog box opens. Select the Object Actions tab, as shown in Figure 13-14.

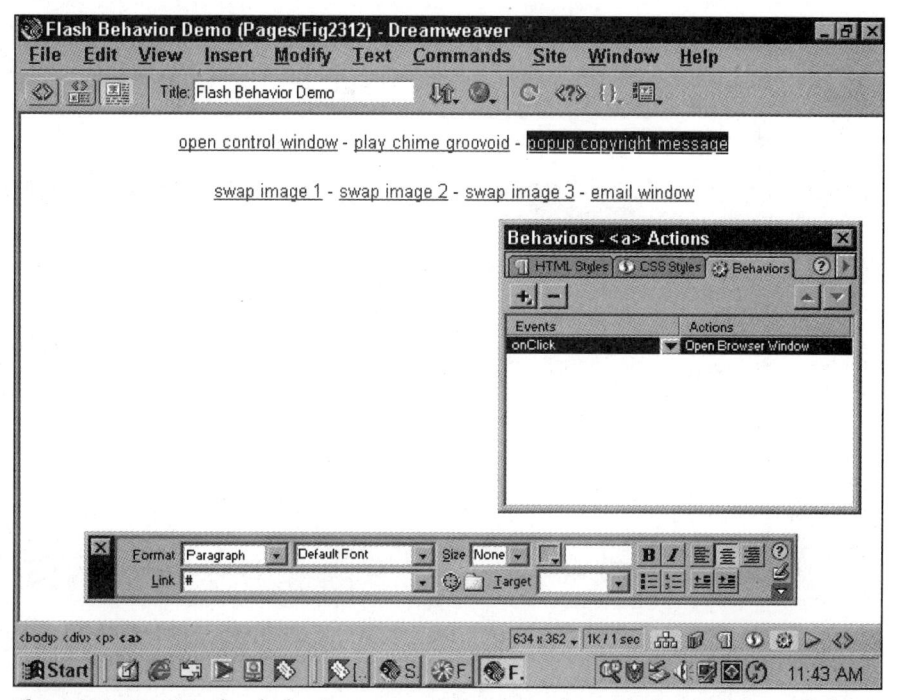

Chapter 13 ✦ **Inserting Flash and Shockwave Elements** 403

Figure 13-12: Attach a behavior you want to trigger from Flash to a dummy link in Dreamweaver.

7. Click the + (add) button and choose Get URL from the Basic Actions category to add a Flash Get URL behavior to your Flash button. In the URL box, type:

   ```
   javascript:
   ```

   and then paste the contents of the clipboard — your JavaScript code — so that you have something like this (refer back to Figure 13-14):

   ```
   javascript:MM_openBrWindow('myBuddy.htm','','scrollbars=yes',
   'width=250,height=200')
   ```

   Click OK when you're done.

8. Repeat Steps 2 through 7 for each additional button or behavior you'd like to use.

9. Export your Flash movie as a SWF file and place it into the same page in Dreamweaver where you built your dummy links. Note that the <head> tag of this page contains JavaScript functions that match your dummy links and the JavaScript inside your Flash movie, as shown in Figure 13-15.

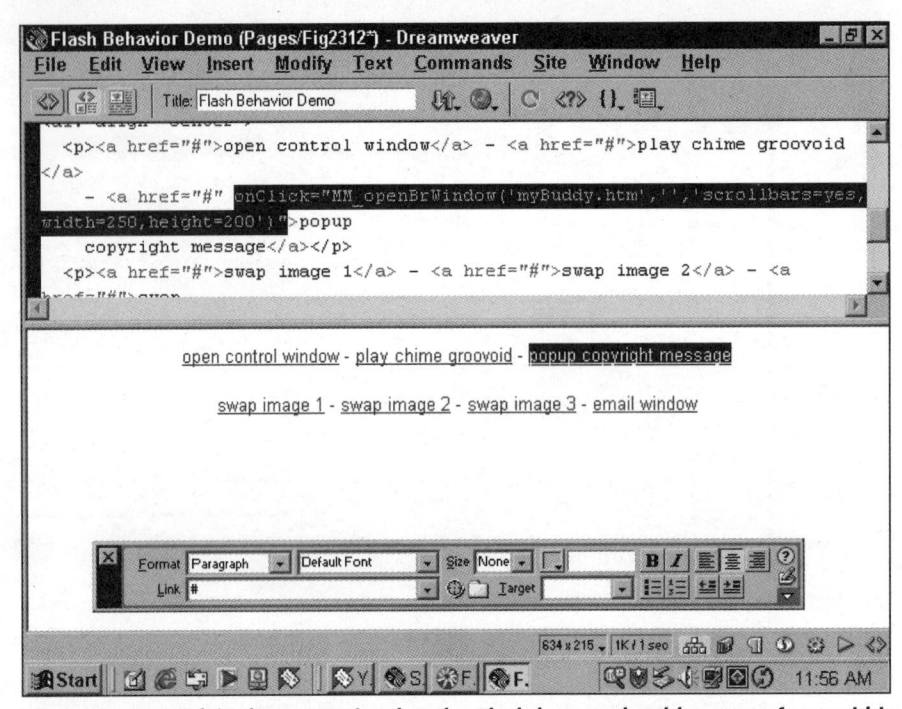

Figure 13-13: Select the JavaScript that the Flash button should execute from within the `onClick` attribute of your anchor tag.

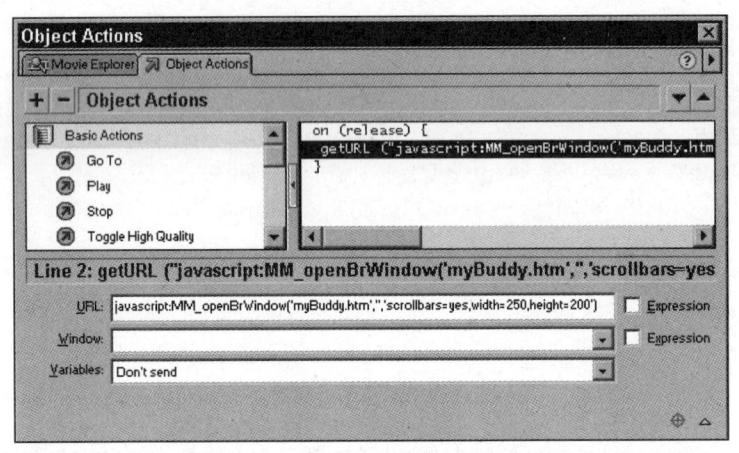

Figure 13-14: Add your JavaScript code to a Flash button Get URL behavior in the Instance Properties dialog box in Flash.

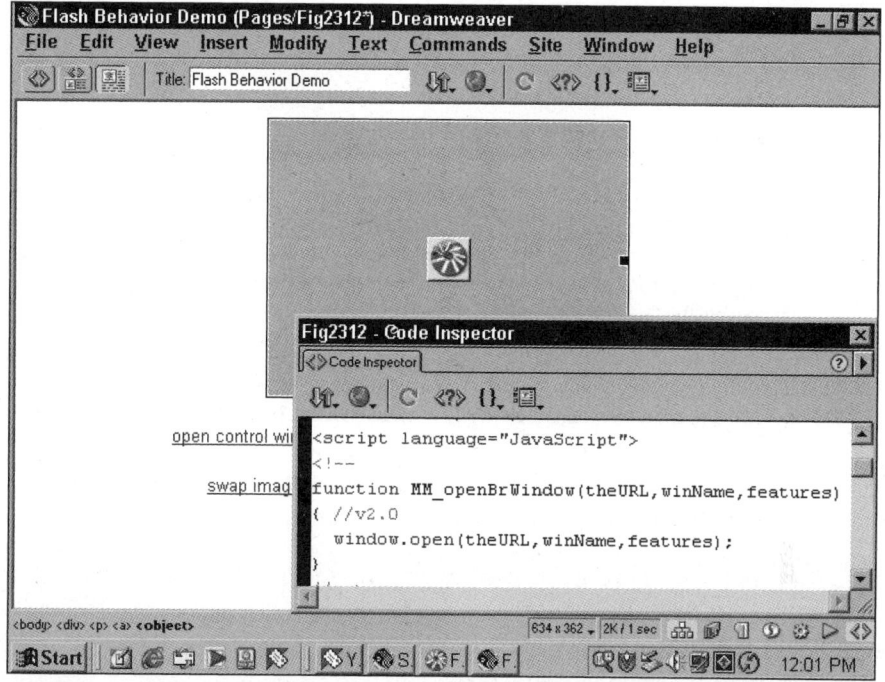

Figure 13-15: The JavaScript in your Flash movie relies on the same JavaScript functions that Dreamweaver inserted in the `<head>` tag as you built your dummy links.

10. Delete your dummy links — but not the JavaScript functions in the `<head>` tag — and publish your page.

When users click the buttons in your Flash movie, `javascript: URL` sends the commands to the browser, executing the JavaScript functions in your Web page. Flash buttons open new browser windows, pop-up messages, and so on. This works in Netscape and in Internet Explorer.

> **Tip** Shockwave authors can also use JavaScript URLs from Lingo to trigger Dreamweaver behaviors in a manner similar to the preceding. The JavaScript-savvy can also reference their own JavaScript functions using this method.

Dreamweaver Technique: Using the JavaScript Integration Kit for Flash 5

With an eye toward smoothing the integration between Flash and Dreamweaver, Macromedia released the JavaScript Integration Kit for Flash 5 (JIK). The JIK is a suite of commands and behaviors installable in Dreamweaver — versions 3 and above—via the Extension Manager. You can download the current version from the Macromedia Exchange; choose Commands ➪ Get More Commands to go directly online.

The JavaScript Integration Kit for Flash 5 consists of four main components:

- **Macromedia Flash Player Controls:** Allows the designer to include interactive control over Flash movies in a Web page. New Dreamweaver behaviors assign play, stop, rewind, fast-forward, pan, and zoom actions to any graphic element. In addition, an HTML drop-down menu can be turned into a Flash movie selector.

- **Advanced Form Validations:** Ensures that your visitors are entering the proper type of information in your Flash form. You can apply any of 18 client-side form validations—everything from a required, non-blank to an International Phone Validation.

- **Browser Scripts for Flash:** Embeds up to 10 different JavaScript functions in the Dreamweaver page, callable from any Flash 5 movie. With these functions, your Flash movie can control form elements such as text fields and select lists, open remote browser windows, set cookies, and swap images on the Web page.

- **Flash Dispatcher Behavior:** Detects the visitor's Flash Player version and redirects to a suitable Web page.

The beauty of the JIK is that its various components can be mixed and matched to achieve a wide range of effects and control. The resulting Web page offers a greater degree of interactivity for the visitor as well as for the Flash designer.

Macromedia Flash Player Controls

One method of engaging your Web page visitors is to give them more control over their viewing experience. Rather than just displaying a movie from beginning to end, allow the viewer to pause, rewind, and play the animation at will. Flash's vector-based nature even allows you to zoom in and out, without loss of image clarity. While all of this functionality is available through Flash ActionScripting, not all designs require the controls to be maintained within a Flash movie. The Flash Player Controls allow all of the common VCR-like functionality—and then some—to be assigned to HTML elements such as images or hotspots.

When the JavaScript Integration Kit is installed, 10 different behaviors are grouped under the MM Flash Player Controls:

- Fast Forward Flash
- Go To Flash Frame
- Go To Flash Frame Based on Cookie

- Load Flash Movie
- Pan Flash
- Play Flash
- Rewind Flash
- Set Flash by List
- Stop Flash
- Zoom Flash

As with any other Dreamweaver behavior, the player controls must be assigned to a target: a text link, an image map hotspot, or a graphic with a link attached. Typically, such a graphic button would use a false link, such as # or `javascript:;` so that it may act as a trigger but not actually open a URL.

You must have at least one Flash movie in the page before the Flash Player Controls become available, as shown in Figure 13-16. Once activated, the user interfaces for the Flash Player Controls vary according to their function as detailed below. With the Play, Stop, Rewind Flash behaviors, you just pick the Flash movie you want to control from the drop-down list. All the other behaviors include this option as well so you can affect any movie on the page.

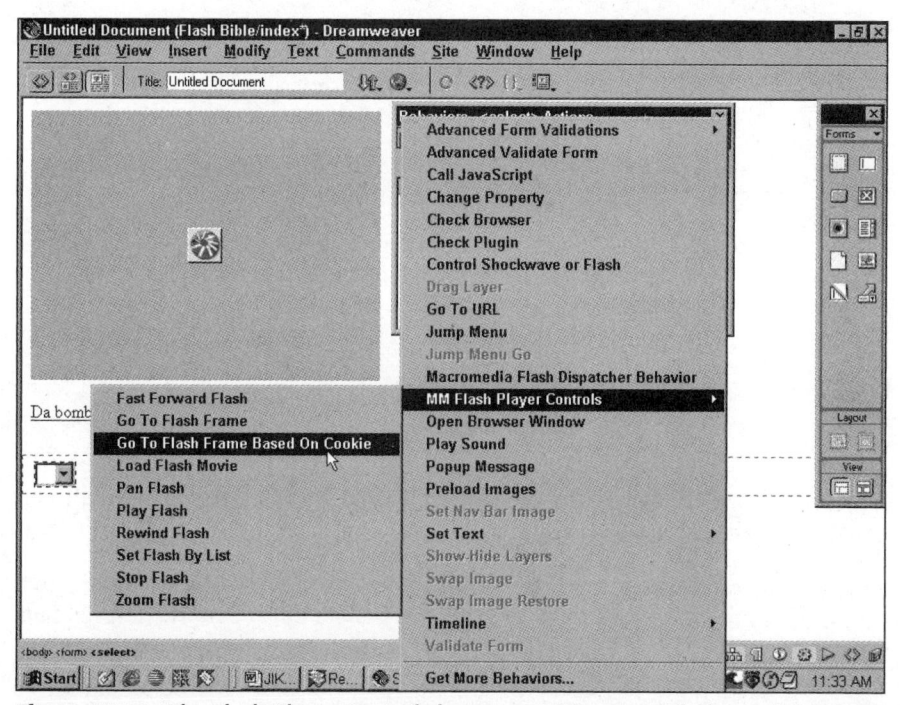

Figure 13-16: The Flash Player Controls become active once a Flash movie is present in the current Dreamweaver document.

To use the Flash Player Controls, follow these steps:

1. Insert at least one Flash movie by choosing an animation from the Assets panel or applying the Insert Flash object.
2. Enter a unique name in the ID field of the Flash Property Inspector for each movie. A distinct ID avoids browser compatibility problems; if one is not initially supplied, Dreamweaver offers to make one for you when any of the behaviors are applied.
3. Select the text link, hotspot, or image to trigger the behavior.

   If you'd like to apply the Set Flash by List behavior, select a form list object.
4. Choose Window ⇨ Behaviors to open the Behaviors panel, if necessary. Alternatively, you can select the Show Behavior icon from the Launcher or use the keyboard shortcut, Shift+F3.
5. Choose the Add button from the Behaviors panel and select the desired behavior under the MM Flash Player Controls heading.

   The chosen behavior's dialog box appears, similar to the one shown in Figure 13-17.

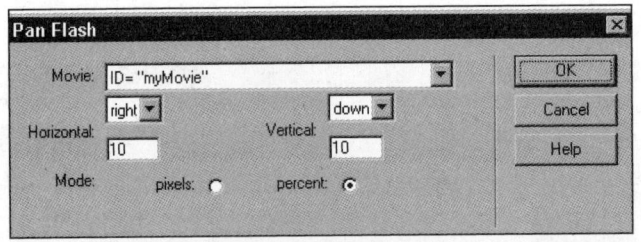

Figure 13-17: With the Pan Flash behavior, your viewer can move around a Flash movie in any direction. As shown, this behavior pans in a diagonal direction, down and to the right, every time it is triggered.

6. Select the parameters for your behavior.
   - For the Play Flash, Rewind Flash, and Stop Flash behaviors, select the desired animation to affect from the Movie drop-down list.
   - For the Fast Forward Flash behavior, select the desired animation to affect from the Movie drop-down list. In the first blank field, enter the desired value you want the movie to advance by. Select either Frames or Percent from the drop-down list. For example, to advance the movie by 5 percent each time the behavior is called, enter 5 in the first field and choose Percent from the list.
   - For the Go To Flash Frame behavior, select the desired animation to affect from the Movie drop-down list and then enter the frame number to move to in the Go To Frame field.

- For the Go To Flash Frame Based on Cookie behavior, select the desired animation to affect from the Movie drop-down list, enter the name of the cookie to read in the Cookie Name field, enter the value to look for in the Cookie Value field, and then enter the frame number to advance to when the cookie name and value are read in the Go To Frame field.

- For the Load Flash Movie behavior, select the desired animation to you want to replace from the Replace Movie drop-down list. Enter the filename for the movie to load in the With Movie field or locate the movie by selecting the Browse button. Input the level to load the movie into in the Level field.

To replace an existing movie with the loaded movie, enter a level number that is currently occupied by another movie. To replace the original movie and unload every level, choose 0 for the Level. To begin playing the movie immediately, set the Play option to Yes; otherwise, set Play to No.

Caution: As Dreamweaver warns you, the Load Flash Movie behavior is not supported for Netscape browsers.

- For the Pan Flash behavior, select the desired animation to affect from the Movie drop-down list, choose the Horizontal and/or Vertical direction — up, down, right, or left — to pan to from the drop-down lists, and then select the degree of the pan by entering a value in the fields below each direction. You can pan diagonally by entering non-zero values for both the Horizontal and Vertical direction. Choose whether you'd like the pan values to operate in either Pixel or Percent mode.

- For the Set Flash by List behavior, select the desired animation to affect from the Movie drop-down list, choose the list object from the Select Box drop-down list, and input the level to load the movie into in the Level field. To replace an existing movie with the loaded movie, enter a level number that is currently occupied by another movie. To replace the original movie and unload every level, choose 0 for the Level.

To begin playing the movie immediately, set the Play option to Yes; otherwise, set Play to No. For the Set Flash by List behavior to work properly, you'll also need to set the values of each of the list items to a relative or absolute file URL pointing to a .swf file. Click the Parameters button on the List/Menu Property Inspector to enter new labels and their corresponding values.

Caution: As Dreamweaver warns you, the Set Flash by List behavior is not supported for Netscape browsers.

- For the Zoom Flash behavior, select the desired animation to affect from the Movie drop-down list. Enter the value desired in the Zoom field. To zoom in, enter a number greater than 100; to zoom out, enter a number below 100. To reset the movie to the original zoom level, enter 0.

7. After you've chosen all the desired parameters from the dialog box, select OK to close it.

   The Behaviors panel displays the event and action for the behavior just applied.

8. By default, `onClick` is the selected event. To change the triggering event to `onMouseOver` or `onMouseOut`, select the down arrow between the event and the action and choose the desired event from the list.

Advanced Form Validations

HTML forms can be tricky: The more you use forms to gather information from your visitors, the greater the possibility for user error. In a sense, forms are a classic double-edged sword and a few people taking advantage of Flash's increased interactivity are getting nicked by them. If, for example, your online form includes two fields for a telephone number, one for the U.S. and one for international visitors, you'll want to be sure that the proper data is entered in the correct field. To ensure that a user enters the type of information you're expecting in your Flash form, that information needs to be validated. The JavaScript Integration Kit includes methods for validating 18 different types of data.

For the Advanced Form Validations to work, you'll need to work both with your Flash movie and with the Dreamweaver page the movie is embedded in. Here's an overview of the process:

On the Dreamweaver side:

1. Create a form with hidden fields — one for each of the Flash fields you want to validate.
2. Attach the Advanced Validate Form behavior to the form itself.
3. Add one of the Browser Scripts for Flash functions, `FDK_setFormText`, to the page.
4. Attach the desired validation behavior to the `<body>` tag of the current document.

On the Flash side:

1. Make sure every form field has a unique variable name assigned to it.
2. Add a `getURL` action to the `on (press)` event of the submit button, calling the `FDK_setFormText` function inserted into the Dreamweaver page.
3. Add another `getURL` action to the `on (release)` event of the submit button, which invokes the `FDK_Validate` function — which was put on the Dreamweaver document by the Advanced Validate Form behavior.

You'll need to keep track of the names of the Hidden field inputs inserted in Dreamweaver, as well as the name of the form itself; they both are referenced when the functions are added in Flash.

Now that you have an overview, let's go through the process with a little more detail. Again, we'll start with the Dreamweaver page:

1. Choose Insert ⇨ Form to add a form to your document.

   In Dreamweaver, the form is automatically named.

2. Within the form, add a Hidden form field for every Flash field you'd like to validate. Give each Hidden field a unique name and leave the Value blank.

3. Select the `<form>` tag in the Tag Selector and, from the Behaviors panel, choose the Advanced Validate Form behavior.

   The Advanced Validate Form dialog box appears, as shown in Figure 13-18.

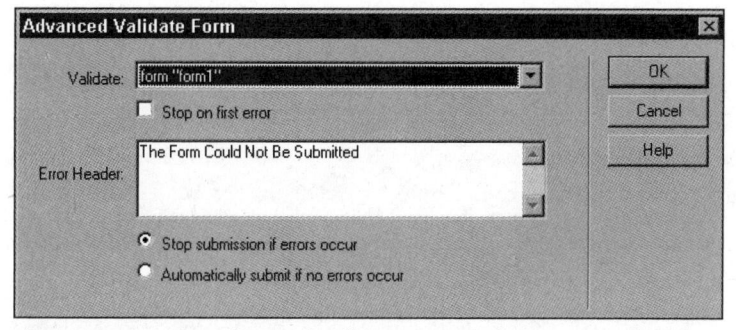

Figure 13-18: The Advanced Validate Form behavior controls how validations overall are applied.

4. In the Advanced Validate Form dialog box:

   - Select the form containing the Hidden elements you want to use from the Validate drop-down list.

   - To stop validating when an incorrect entry is encountered, check the Stop on First Error option.

   - Enter any desired message in the Error Header text area. The Error Header is displayed in addition to any validation-specific error messages.

   - If your behavior is assigned to an `onSubmit` event (the default) choose the Stop Submission If Errors Occur option; otherwise, select the Automatically Submit If No Errors Occur option.

   - Select OK to close the dialog box when you're done.

5. Choose Commands ⇨ Browser Scripts for Flash.

   The Browser Scripts for Flash command, discussed in more detail later in this section, embeds functions in the Dreamweaver page for communicating with Flash.

6. When the Browser Scripts for Flash dialog box opens, select the `FDK_setFormText` option; close the dialog box when you're done.

   Our final preparation in Dreamweaver is to add the individual validation behaviors required.

7. Select the `<body>` tag from the Tag Selector and choose the Add (+) button in the Behaviors panel. From the drop-down list, select a validation behavior from the Advanced Form Validations category.

   Most of the Advanced Form Validation behaviors have similar dialog boxes in which you can choose the particular form element (the Hidden field relating to the Flash form field) affected, make the field required, and set the error message. The differences between the various behaviors are detailed in Table 13-3.

8. Repeat Step 7 for every validation you'd like to apply in the form.

Table 13-3
Advanced Form Validation Behaviors

Behavior	Description
Alphanumeric Validation	Displays an error if non-alphanumeric characters are entered.
Credit Card Validation	Removes any spaces or hyphens and then displays an error message if the card number is not valid. This behavior does not authorize credit card purchases.
Date Validation	Optionally allows dates in the future, past, or in a particular range and specific format.
E-mail Validation	Makes sure that the entry contains an @ and a period.
Entry Length Validation	Accepts a defined number range of characters — for example, from 5 to 10.
Floating Point Validation	Displays an error if a non-number is entered; floating point numbers can contain decimals.
Integer Validation	Displays the message if a non-number or a number with decimals is entered. You can also set an acceptable number range.
International Phone Validation	Removes parentheses, spaces, and hyphens and then makes sure at least six digits are entered.
Like Entry Validation	Checks one form field entry against another; typically used for password verification.

Behavior	Description
Mask Validation	Allows the designer to require a specific pattern of text, and numbers to be entered. Use A to indicate a letter, # for numbers and ? if the entry could be either a letter or a number. For example, the mask A###?? would require a letter followed by three numbers, followed by two other alphanumeric characters.
Nonblank Validation	Displays a message if the field is left empty.
Radio Button Validation	Ensures that at least one option in a specified radio button group is selected. Note: This behavior is only used with HTML form elements.
Selection Made in List Validation	Displays an error if the user does not make a selection from a specific drop-down list. Note: This behavior is only used with HTML form elements.
Social Security Validation	Removes any hyphens, checks for a proper length and then reformats the number into a 3-2-4 configuration, as in 113-45-6789.
Time Validation	Displays an error if a valid time with minutes within a certain range is not entered. Military time and most variations of a.m. and p.m. are accepted.
URL Validation	Looks for valid URL protocols and displays an error message if one is not found at the start of the entry. Accepted URLs include: `ftp://`, `http://`, `javascript:`, `file://`, `gopher://`, `https://`, `mailto:`, `rlogin://`, `shttp://`, `snews://`, `telnet://`, `tn3270://`, `swais://`
US Phone Validation	Verifies that the entered information is either 7 or 10 digits after removing any parentheses and hyphens.
Zip Code Validation	Requires the entry to be either 5 or 9 digits.

Now that the Dreamweaver page is prepped, you're ready to prepare the Flash movie:

1. In Flash, add the required form fields as text input fields.
2. In the Text Options panel, enter a unique name in the Variable field.
3. Make sure your form has a graphic that acts as a submit button.
4. Select the submit button graphic and open the Object Actions panel.
5. Add an `on (press)` event and attach a `getURL` function to the event.
6. In the `getURL` function, call the `FDK_setFormText` function that was embedded into the Dreamweaver page. The `FDK_setForm Text` function takes three arguments: the name of the form, the name of the field to be validated, and the variable name assigned to the corresponding field in Flash.

   For example, let's say the form is named `theForm` and you've created a field for gathering an e-mail address and given it a name in Dreamweaver such as emailHidden. In Flash, the variable assigned to the corresponding text field might be called emailField. In this case, the getURL function would read:

```
getURL("javascript:FDK_setFormText('theForm','emailHidden','"
add emailField add "')";)
```

Note the addition of the word add on either side of the variable name, as shown in the code and Figure 13-19. This syntax is required for the parameters to be passed correctly.

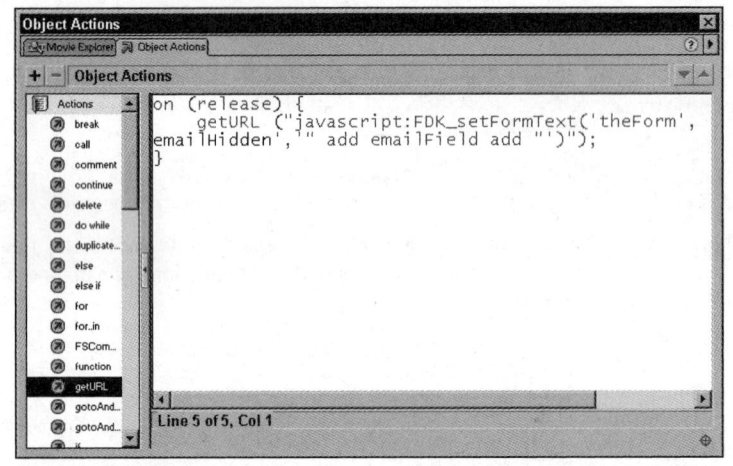

Figure 13-19: Enter a FDK_setFormText function for every Flash field you need to qualify.

7. Continue adding as many FDK_setFormText functions as you have fields to validate to the same getURL action. Separate each function with a semicolon.

   After you've entered all the required FDK_setFormText functions, you'll need to add one last event and function.

8. In the Object Actions panel for the submit button graphic, add an on (release) event and attach a getURL action to it.

9. In the getURL action, insert the FDK_Validate function. This function takes four arguments, which correspond to the options available in Dreamweaver's Advanced Validate Form dialog box: FormName, stopOnFailure, AutoSubmit, and ErrorHeader. Both stopOnFailure and AutoSubmit are Booleans and accept either true or false.

   As an example, suppose the form is again called theForm, that you'd like the form to stop processing when an error is encountered as well as automatically be submitted, and that your general error message reads, "Attention!! I found an error on the form!" Here, the getURL function would look like this:

```
getURL("javascript:FDK_Validate('theForm',true,true,'Attentio
n!! I found an error on the form!\\n\\n');");
```

The \n\n after the function call acts as a hard return in the alert box to separate the generic message header and the specific validation error.

The final step is to cross the bridge again from Flash to Dreamweaver, bringing your exported Flash movie into the Dreamweaver page. Be sure to give it both a name and ID (both of which can be the same) in the Property Inspector.

Browser Scripts for Flash

With the JavaScript Integration Kit, integration is a two-way street: not only is it easier to control Flash movies, the Flash movies can also affect the HTML page. The JIK includes one overall command called Browser Scripts for Flash, which offers over 5 different types of control:

- Setting a form element's value
- Setting a cookie
- Opening a remote browser window
- Swapping images for rollovers
- Setting list menu items

Implementing these functions in Dreamweaver is simplicity itself: Just choose Commands ⇨ Browser Scripts for Flash and check off the desired options you see in Figure 13-20. The various functions are grouped into five different categories. If you open a page with these functions already in place, you'll find the option already selected; deselecting the checkbox removes the function from the page when the dialog box is closed.

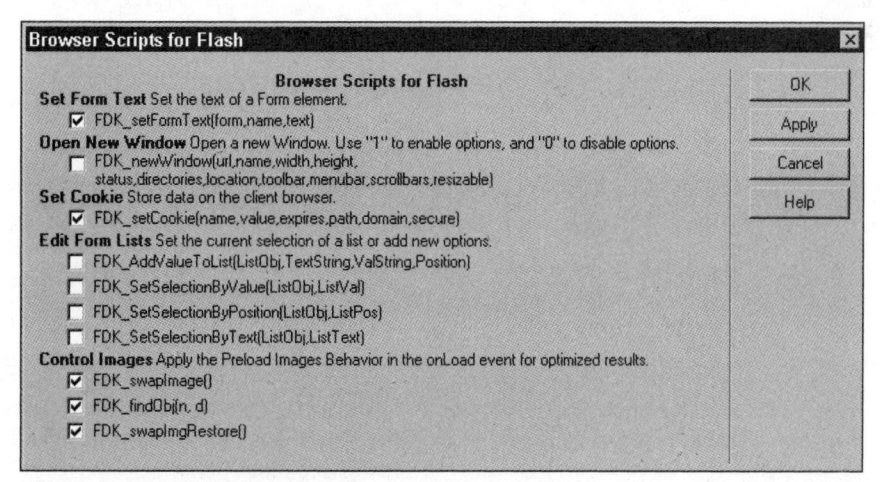

Figure 13-20: The Browser Scripts for Flash dialog box enables you to easily insert or remove functions that you can call from Flash.

Like the form validations, using the Browser Scripts is a two-program process. Once you've installed them in Dreamweaver you need call the function in a Flash action. Each of the functions takes its own series of parameters and typically, each one is invoked using an action such as `getURL`. The functions and their arguments are explained in Table 13-4.

Table 13-4
Browser Scripts for Flash Functions

Function	Arguments	Description

`FDK_setFormText`
`elementName`
`variableName`
	FormName	Sets the value of a form element.

`FDK_newWindow`
`windowName`
`width`
`height`
`status`
`directories`
`location`
`toolbar`
`menubar`
`scrollbars`
`resizable`
	URL	Opens a remote browser window. The width and height values are entered in pixels; for all other parameters (except URL and windowName) enter a 0 to disallow the element and a 1 to include it.

`FDK_setCookie`
`cookieValue`
`expiresWhen`
`path`
`domain`
`secureBoolean`
	CookieName	Sets a cookie from within a Flash movie and can be used in conjunction with the Go To Flash Frame Based on Cookie behavior.

`FDK_swapImage`
`[blank]`
`replacementPath`
`1`
	ImageName	Performs an image swap in the HTML document. The second parameter is intentionally left blank.

`FDK_swapImgRestore`	n/a	Restores a previously executed image swap. For complex pages using multiple image swaps, it's best to explicitly swap the image from its replacement to its original source rather than use the FDK_SwapImgRestore behavior.
`FDK_findObj`	n/a	Used in conjunction with the FDK_SwapImage behavior.

Function	Arguments	Description
FDK_AddValueToList TextString ValString Position	ListObj	Inserts a new value into a form list element.
FDK_SetSelectionByValue ListValue	ListObj	Determines the selection of a list item with a given value.
FDK_SetSelectionByPosition ListPos	ListObj	Determines the selection of a list item in a particular list position.
FDK_SetSelectionByText ListText	ListObj	Determines the selection of a list item with a given label.

Flash Dispatcher Behavior

The final component of the JavaScript Integration Kit, the Flash Dispatcher Behavior, is designed to smooth visitor access to your Web-based Flash content. The Flash Dispatcher checks to see if the visitor to your site already has the Flash player and, if so, what version. If the proper version — or no player at all — is found, this behavior gives you several options. The visitor's browser can be redirected to a Flash-less page or to a site for downloading an appropriate version, if an automatically downloaded version is not possible.

To apply this behavior, select the `<body>` tag from the Tag Selector and, from the Behaviors panel, choose Macromedia Flash Dispatcher Behavior. In the dialog box (see Figure 13-21), you have the following options:

+ **Macromedia Flash Content URL:** Enter or locate the path to the page containing the Flash movie.

+ **Alternate URL:** Enter or locate the path to a Web page the visitor should go to if the proper Flash player is not found.

+ **Macromedia Flash Version:** Choose the lowest permissible version from 2.0, 3.0, 4.0, or 5.0.

+ **Require Latest Plugin:** Select this option to require the latest version of the Flash Player.

+ **No Player Options:** Any visitors who do not have the Flash Player installed are sent to a selectable download page or are directed to use the Alternate URL.

+ **Improper Version Options:** Any visitors who do not have the required version of the Flash Player installed will be sent to a selectable upgrade page or are directed to use the Alternate URL.

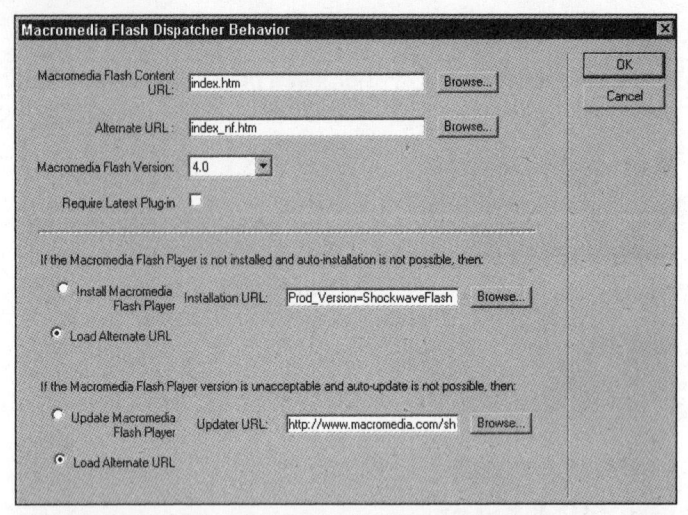

Figure 13-21: Make sure that only visitors with the proper Flash player can see your movies with the Flash Dispatcher Behavior.

The Flash Content URL can be the same page that the behavior is applied to or, in the case of what is referred to as a gateway script, another page.

Summary

Together, the interactive power of Shockwave and the speedy glitz of Flash can enliven Web content like nothing else. Dreamweaver is extremely well-suited for integrating and displaying Shockwave and Flash movies. Here are some key pointers to keep in mind:

- ✦ Saving your Director movies as Shockwave enables them to be played on the Web with the help of a plug-in or ActiveX control.

- ✦ Flash movies are a way to enhance your Web pages with vector animations, interactivity, and streaming audio. Flash movies require the Flash player plug-in or ActiveX Control.

- ✦ Dreamweaver has built-in objects for both Director and Flash movies. All the important parameters are accessible directly through the Property Inspector.

- ✦ You need only three parameters to incorporate a Shockwave movie: the file's location, height, and width. Dreamweaver automatically imports a Flash movie's dimensions. You can get the exact measurements of a Shockwave movie from within Director.

✦ Dreamweaver comes with a JavaScript behavior for controlling Shockwave and Flash movies. This Control Shockwave or Flash behavior can be used as-is for adding external controls to the same Web page or — with a minor modification — for adding the controls to another frame in the same frameset.

✦ Dreamweaver behaviors can be triggered from a Shockwave or Flash movie.

✦ The JavaScript Integration Kit for Flash 5 is a powerful set of extensions that enable Flash movies to control Dreamweaver behaviors and for HTML elements to activate Flash movies.

✦ ✦ ✦

Building Style Sheet Web Pages

CHAPTER 14

In This Chapter

Cascading Style Sheets basics

Defining and inserting styles

Dreamweaver technique: Clearing underlines in links

Style sheet options: Eight categories of attributes

Using external style sheets

All publications, whether on paper or the Web, need a balance of style and content to be effective. Style without content is all flash with no real information. Content with no style is flat and uninteresting, thus losing the substance. Traditionally, HTML has tied style to content wherever possible, preferring logical tags such as `<strong>` to indicate emphasis to physical tags such as `<b>` for bold. Although this emphasis on the logical worked for many single documents, its imprecision made it unrealistic, if not impossible, to achieve style consistency across a broad range of Web pages.

The Cascading Style Sheets specification has changed this situation — and much more. As support for Cascading Style Sheets (CSS) grows, more Web designers can alter font faces, type size and spacing, and many other page elements with a single command — and have the effect ripple not only throughout the page, but also throughout a Web site. Moreover, an enhancement of CSS called CSS-P (for positioning) is the foundation for what has become commonly known as *layers*.

Dreamweaver was one of the first Web authoring tools to make the application of Cascading Style Sheets user friendly. Through Dreamweaver's intuitive interface, the Web designer can access over 70 different CSS settings, affecting everything from type specs to multimedia-like transitions. Dreamweaver enables you to work the way you want: Create your style sheet all at once and then link it when you're ready, or make up your styles one-by-one as you build your Web page.

In this chapter, you find out how CSS works and why you need it. A Dreamweaver Technique for removing underlines from links walks you through a typical style sheet session. With that experience under your belt, you're ready for the sections with detailed information on the current CSS commands and how to apply them to your Web page and site. Also, the section on defining styles helps you understand what's what in the Style Definition dialog box. Finally, you learn how you can create external style sheets to create — and maintain — the look and feel of an entire Web site with a single document.

Understanding Cascading Style Sheets

The Cascading Style Sheets system significantly increases the design capabilities for a Web site. If you are a designer used to working with desktop publishing tools, you will recognize many familiar features in CSS, including the following:

- Commands for specifying and applying font characteristics
- Traditional layout measurement systems and terminology
- Pinpoint precision for page layout

Cascading Style Sheets are able to apply many features with a simple syntax that is easy to understand. If you're familiar with the concept of using styles in a word processing program, you'll have no trouble grasping style sheets.

Here's how the process works: CSS instructions are given in rules; a style sheet is a collection of these rules. A rule is a statement made up of an HTML or custom tag, called a *selector*, and its defined properties, referred to as a *declaration*. For example, a CSS rule that makes the contents of all <h1> tags (the selector) red in color (the declaration) looks like the following:

```
h1 {color:red}
```

In the following sections, you see the various characteristics of CSS — grouping, inheritance, and cascading — working together to give style sheets their flexibility and power.

Grouping properties

A Web designer often needs to change several style properties at once. CSS enables declarations to be grouped by separating them with semicolons. For example:

```
h1 {color:red; font-family:Arial,Helvetica,sans-serif; font-size:18pt}
```

The Dreamweaver interface provides a wide range of options for styles. Should you ever need to look at the code, you'll find that Dreamweaver groups your selections exactly as shown in the preceding example. Although Dreamweaver keeps each selector in its own rule, when you are hand-coding your style sheets, you can group selectors as well as declarations. Separate grouped selectors with commas, rather than semicolons. For example:

```
h1, h2, p, em {color:green; text-align:left}
```

Inheritance of properties

CSS rules can also be applied to more than one tag through inheritance: the ability of a parent or outer tag to pass on characteristics to the child or inner tags. Most, but not all, CSS declarations can be inherited by the HTML tags enclosed within the CSS selector. Suppose you set all `<p>` tags to the color red. Any tags included within a `<p>...</p>` tag pair then inherit that property and are also colored red.

Inheritance is also at work within HTML tags that involve a parent-child relationship, as with a list. Whether numbered (ordered, `<ol>`) or bulleted (unordered, `<ul>`), a list comprises any number of list items, designated by `<li>` tags. Each list item is considered a child of the parent tag, `<ol>` or `<ul>`. Take a look at the following example:

```
ol {color:red}
ul {color:blue}
```

With the preceding example, all ordered list items appear in red, whereas all unordered list items appear in blue. One major benefit to this parent-child relationship is that you can change the font for an entire page with one CSS rule. The following statement accomplishes this change:

```
body {font-family: Arial}
```

The change is possible in the previous example because the `<body>` tag is considered the parent of every HTML element on a page.

> **Tip** There's one exception to the preceding rule: tables. Netscape browsers (through version 4.75) treat tables differently than the rest of the HTML `<body>` when it comes to style sheets. To change the font of a table, you'd have to specify something such as the following:
>
> ```
> td {font-family: Arial}
> ```
>
> Because every cell in a table uses the `<td>` tag, this style sheet declaration affects the entire table. Dreamweaver is uneven in its application of this treatment. Setting the entire `<body>` to a particular font family is displayed correctly in the Document window, with even tables being affected. However, changing the color of a font in the `<body>` style sheet declaration does not alter the font color of text in a table in the Document window.

Cascading characteristics

The term *cascading* describes the capability of a local style to override a general style. Think of a stream flowing down a mountain; each ledge encountered by the stream has the potential to change its direction. The last ledge determines the final direction of the stream. In the same manner, one CSS rule applying generally to a block of text can be overridden by another rule applied to a more specific part of the same text.

For example, let's say you've defined, using style sheets, all normal paragraphs — `<p>` tags — as a particular font in a standard color, but you mark one section of the text using a little-used tag such as `<samp>`. If you make a CSS rule altering both the font and color of the `<samp>` tag, the section takes on the characteristics of that rule.

The cascading aspect of style sheets also works on a larger scale. One of the key features of CSS is the capability to define external style sheets that can be linked to individual Web pages, acting on their overall look and feel. Indeed, you can use the cascading behavior to fine-tune the overall Web site style based on a particular page or range of pages. Your company may, for instance, define an external style sheet for the entire company intranet, and each division could then build upon that overall model for its individual Web pages. For example, let's say that the company style sheet dictates that all `<h2>` headings are in Arial and black. One department could output their Web pages with `<h2>` tags in Arial, but colored red rather than black, while another department could make them blue.

Defining new classes for extended design control

Redefining existing HTML tags is a step in the right direction toward consistent design, but the real power of CSS comes into play when you define custom tags. In CSS-speak, a custom tag is called a *class*, and the selector name always begins with a period. Here's a simple example: To style all copyright notices at the bottom of all pages of a Web site to display in 8-point Helvetica all caps, you could define a tag as follows:

```
.cnote {font-family:Helvetica; font-size:8pt; font-transform:uppercase}
```

If you define this style in an external style sheet and apply it to all 999 pages of your Web site, you have to alter only one line of code (instead of all 999 pages) when the edict comes down from management to make all the copyright notices a touch larger. Once a new class has been defined, you can apply it to any range of text, from one word to an entire page.

How styles are applied

CSS applies style formatting to your page in one of three ways:

✦ Via an external, linked style sheet
✦ Via an internal style sheet
✦ Via embedded style rules

External style sheets

An *external* style sheet is a file containing the CSS rules; it links one or more Web pages. One benefit of linking to an external style sheet is that you can customize and change the appearance of a Web site quickly and easily from one file.

Two different methods exist for working with an external style sheet: the `link` method and the `import` method. Dreamweaver defaults to the link method, but you can also choose import if you prefer.

For the `link` method, a line of code is added outside of the `<style>` tags, as follows:

```
<link rel="stylesheet" href="mainstyle.css">
```

The `import` method writes code within the style tags, as follows:

```
<style type="text/css">
@import "newstyles.css";
</style>
```

Between the `link` and the `import` methods, the `link` method is better supported among browsers.

Internal style sheets

An *internal* style sheet is a list of all the CSS styles for a page.

Dreamweaver inserts all the style sheets at the top of a Web page within a `<style>...</style>` tag pair. Placing style sheets within the header tags has become a convention that many designers use, although you can also apply a style sheet anywhere on a page.

The `<style>` tag for a Cascading Style Sheet identifies the type attribute as `text/css`. The following is a sample internal style sheet:

```
<style type="text/css">
<!--
p { font-family: "Arial, Helvetica, sans-serif"; color: #000000}
.cnote { font: 8pt "Arial, Helvetica, sans-serif"; text-transform: uppercase}
h1 { font: bold 18pt Arial, Helvetica, sans-serif; color: #FF0000}
-->
</style>
```

The HTML comment tags `<!--` and `-->` prevent older browsers that can't read style sheets from displaying the CSS rules.

Embedded style rules

The final method of applying a style inserts it within HTML tags using the `style` attribute. This method is the most "local" of all the techniques; that is, it is closest to the tag it is affecting and therefore has the ultimate control—because of the cascading nature of style sheets as previously discussed.

When you create a layer within Dreamweaver, you notice that the positioning attribute is a Cascading Style Sheet embedded within a `<div>` tag such as the following:

```
<div id="Layer1" style="position:absolute; visibility:inherit; left:314px; ¬
top:62px; width:194px; height:128px; z-index:1">
</div>
```

For all its apparent complexity, the Cascading Style Sheets system becomes straightforward in Dreamweaver. You often won't have to write a single line of code. But even if you don't have to write code, you should understand the CSS fundamentals of grouping, inheritance, and cascading.

Creating and Applying a Style Sheet in Dreamweaver

Dreamweaver uses three primary tools to implement Cascading Style Sheets: the CSS Styles panel, the Edit Style Sheet dialog box, and the Style Definition dialog box. Specifically, the CSS Styles panel is used to apply styles created in the Edit Style Sheet dialog box and specified with the Style Definition dialog box. With these three interfaces, you can accomplish the following:

- Link or import all your styles from an external style sheet
- View and edit most of the attributes included in the official release of CSS Level 1
- Modify any styles you have created
- Apply styles to selected text or to a particular tag surrounding that text

Caution The fourth-generation browsers (and above) support many of the attributes from the first draft of the Cascading Style Sheets standard. Neither Netscape Navigator 4.0 nor Microsoft Internet Explorer 4.0 fully supports CSS Level 1, however. Of the earlier browsers, only Internet Explorer 3.0 supports a limited set of the CSS Level 1 features: font attributes, indents, and color. However, this support is rendered differently in Internet Explorer 3.0 and 4.0. Netscape Navigator 3.0 does not support any of the features of CSS Level 1. On the brighter side, Netscape Navigator 6.0 offers virtually complete compliance of CSS 1 and quite a lot of CSS 2. The current version of Internet Explorer for Windows (5.5 for Windows and 5.0 for Macintosh) is not as complete, but better than the 4.x versions.

Dreamweaver technique: Eliminating underlines from links

Because Dreamweaver's interface for CSS has so many controls, initially creating and applying a style can be a little confusing. Before delving into the details of the various panels, dialog boxes, and floating windows, let's quickly step through a typical style sheet session. Then, you can have an overall understanding of how all the pieces fit together.

Note Don't panic if you encounter unfamiliar elements of Dreamweaver's interface in this introductory technique. You see them at work again and again as you work through the chapter.

Disabling the underline for the anchor tag, <a>, which is normally associated with hyperlinked text, is one modification commonly included in style sheets. To accomplish this task, follow these steps:

1. Open the CSS Styles panel by choosing Windows ⇨ CSS Styles or selecting the Show CSS Styles button from either Launcher.

2. In the CSS Styles panel, select the New Style button. This sequence opens the New Styles dialog box.

3. In the New Styles dialog box, select Redefine HTML Tag and choose the anchor tag, a, from the drop-down list. Finally select Define In This Document Only to create an internal CSS style sheet. Click OK, and the Style Definition window opens.

Tip You can also select the Use CSS Selector option and choose a:link from the drop-down list. You can even employ the a:hover style, which enables text to change color or style on rollover. You must, however, define the four CSS Selector styles in a particular order for them to work correctly. Start by defining the a:link class and then proceed to define a:visited, a:hover, and a:active, in that order. Note that these altered styles do not preview in Dreamweaver.

4. In the Style Definition window, select Type from the list of categories.

5. In the Decoration section of the Type category, select the option none. You can also make any other modifications to the anchor tag style, such as color or font size. Click OK when you're done.

Tip Many designers, myself included, like to make the link apparent by styling it bold and in a different color.

The Style Definition window closes, and any style changes instantly take effect on your page. If you have any previously defined links, the underline disappears from them.

Now, any links that you insert on your page still function as links — the user's pointer still changes into a pointing hand, and the links are active — but no underline appears.

> **Tip** This technique works for any text used as a link. To eliminate the border around an image designated as a link, the image's border must be set to zero in the Image Property Inspector. Dreamweaver handles this automatically when a graphic is made into a link.

Using the CSS Styles panel to apply styles

The CSS Styles panel, shown in Figure 14-1, is a flexible and easy-to-use interface with straightforward command buttons listing all available style items. As with all of Dreamweaver's primary panels, you can open the CSS Styles panel in several ways:

✦ Choose Windows ➪ CSS Styles.

✦ Select the New Style button from either Launcher.

✦ Press Shift+F11.

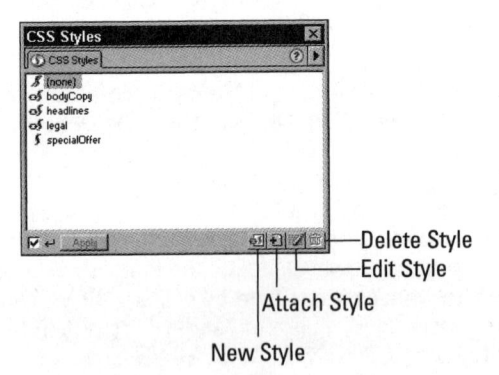

Figure 14-1: The Dreamweaver CSS Styles panel helps you apply consistent styles to a Web page.

The main part of the CSS Styles panel is the list of defined custom styles or classes. Every custom tag you create is listed alphabetically in this window. Once you've chosen the portion of your HTML document that you're stylizing, you can choose one of the custom styles listed here by simply selecting it, if the Apply option is selected. If the option is not checked, select the desired style and choose the Apply button.

At the bottom right-hand corner of the CSS Styles panel are four buttons. The first of these, Attach Style Sheet is a new addition in Dreamweaver 4 and is used for quickly linking the current Web page to an existing style sheet. Clicking the second — the New Style button — begins the process of defining a new CSS style, either in an external or internal style sheet. The third button, Edit Style Sheet, opens the multifaceted Edit Style Sheet dialog box, in which you can create a new style, link a style sheet, edit or remove an existing style, or duplicate a style that you can then alter. Before you can begin applying styles to a Web page or site, the styles must be defined, and using the Edit Style Sheet dialog box is the pain-free method of accomplishing this task. You can, of course, switch to Code view or open the Code Inspector and add the style by hand, but you can avoid this process with the Edit Style Sheet dialog box. You get a close look at this tool in the upcoming section "Editing and managing style sheets." The final button is for deleting styles once they are defined.

Attaching an external style sheet

As CSS-enabled browsers begin to become predominant, more Web designers are encountering clients with existing external style sheets. To apply the site's design specifications to a new page, all the designer need do is link the current page to the CSS document. Dreamweaver 4 provides a streamlined method for doing just that.

New Feature
The Attach Style Sheet button, found on the CSS Styles panel, is a one-step solution for linking external style sheets to the current document. When Attach Style Sheet is selected, a standard Select File dialog box appears with the *.css filter set. Simply locate the desired style sheet and select it: Dreamweaver inserts the necessary code into the <head> of your document. If any HTML tags — such as <p> or any of the heading tags — on your page are defined in the style sheet, you'll see an immediate change in your document.

When the Attach Style Sheet feature is applied, Dreamweaver uses the link attribute to connect style sheet to Web page. The link attribute is much more widely used by professional designers than the import attribute; however, if you'd prefer to use import instead, you can still attach a style sheet with this method as described in a section later in this chapter, "Importing an External Style Sheet."

Applying, changing, and removing a style

As noted above, any HTML tags redefined as CSS styles in an attached style sheet will automatically be applied to your document. However, any custom CSS styles must be applied on a case-by-case basis. Most Web designers use a combination of HTML and custom CSS styles. Only custom CSS styles appear in the CSS Styles panel.

New Feature
Dreamweaver 4 enables you to tell where a custom style is from — whether it's from a linked external style sheet or included in the current document — at a glance. The CSS Styles panel now displays a small chain-link symbol next to the listing if the style can be found on a separate style sheet. In larger sites, it's often important to differentiate between two similarly named custom styles.

To apply an existing custom style, follow these steps:

1. Choose Windows ➪ CSS Styles or select the Show CSS Styles button from either Launcher to open the CSS Styles panel.
2. To apply the style to a section of the page enclosed by an HTML tag, select the tag from the Tag Selector.

   To apply the style to a section that is not enclosed by a single HTML tag, use your mouse to select that section in the Document window.
3. Select the desired custom style from the CSS Styles panel.

   Dreamweaver applies the custom style either by setting the `class` attribute of the selected tag to the custom style or — if just text is selected, not an enclosing tag — to a `<span>` tag which wraps around the text.

As you might expect, Dreamweaver offers a second way of applying a style to your pages. The following method, using the menus, does not employ the CSS Styles panel:

1. Highlight the text to which you're applying the style, either through the Tag Selector or by using the mouse.
2. Select Text ➪ CSS Styles ➪ Your Style.

   The same dynamic CSS Styles list is maintained in the context menu, accessible through a right-click (Ctrl+click) on the selected text.

Changing styles

In prior versions of Dreamweaver, multiple `<span>` tags were a common phenomenon as designers tried out different styles without properly selecting the `<span>` tag. It was not unusual to see this type of code:

```
<span class="head1"><span class="head2"><span
class="head3">News of the Moment</span></span></span>
```

In situations such as these, the CSS style in the span tag closest to the text, in this example head3, is rendered. The other span tags are just so much cluttered code. Dreamweaver 4 now strives to prevent nested `<span>` tags, automatically.

New Feature Changing from applied custom style to another is extremely straightforward in Dreamweaver4. No longer do you have to be sure to select the enclosing tag — whether it's a `<span>` or other tag — to replace the style. In fact, you don't have to select anything: just place your cursor anywhere within the styled text and select a different custom style from the CSS Styles panel. Dreamweaver changes the old style to the new without adding additional `<span>` tags.

But what if you want to apply a new style to a text range within an existing `<span>` tag? Again, Dreamweaver's default is to avoid nested span tags. Here's how it works. Let's say you're working with the following code:

```
<span class="bodyCopy">Developing strategies to survive
requires industry insight and forward thinking in this
competitive marketplace.</span>
```

If you apply a custom style called hype to the phrases industry insight and forward thinking by first selecting those phrases and then choosing hype from the CSS Styles panel, the code looks like this:

```
<span class="bodyCopy">Developing strategies to survive
requires </span><span class="hype">industry insight</span> and
<span class="hype">forward thinking</span><span
class="bodyCopy"> in this competitive marketplace.</span>
```

Dreamweaver wraps each phrase in a distinct `<span>` tag so that nesting is entirely avoided. This behavior enables the style of each phrase to be altered more easily.

Tip If you positively, absolutely would prefer to nest your `<span>` tags, you can do so by Shift+clicking on the desired style in the CSS Styles panel.

If your cursor is positioned within a tag without an existing style, you can still quickly apply the custom CSS style. Dreamweaver now automatically applies the chosen style to the following tags:

- `<p>`
- `<h1>`-`<h6>`
- `<td>`
- `<th>`
- `<caption>`
- `<li>`
- `<ul>`
- `<ol>`
- `<pre>`
- `<blockquote>` or `<bq>`

Caution In most cases, this new functionality means that it's far easier to apply—and change—CSS styles than ever before. However, should your cursor be in a tag other than those listed above, such as an `<address>` tag, Dreamweaver wraps the text in a paragraph tag and assigns the style to the `<p>` tag. If your text is not within a span or one of the tags listed above, be sure to select the tag you want to apply the style to from the Tag Selector.

Removing applied styles

Getting rid of an applied style also gets a whole lot simpler in Dreamweaver 4. Now, just position your cursor anywhere in the stylized text and select (none) from the

CSS Styles panel. Dreamweaver removes the class attribute if the style was attached to a tag other than `<span>` while surrounding `<span>` tags are completely deleted. Naturally, if you choose the tag containing the style through the Tag Selector, selecting (none) also eliminates the style from the tag.

> **Note:** Be sure your cursor is just positioned within styled text and not selecting any. Selecting (none) from the CSS Styles panel when text alone — no tags — is highlighted, has no effect.

Defining new styles

Selecting the New Style button in the CSS Styles panel brings up a new dialog box (see Figure 14-2) where you specify the type of style you're defining. You can opt to create the new styles in an external style sheet or in the current document. After you've chosen the type of style desired, select the Define In This Document Only option to create an internal style sheet. Any style sheets already linked to (or imported into) the current document appear in the drop-down list along with the New Style Sheet File option. If you choose Define In New Style Sheet File, a standard file dialog box opens for you to name and store your new .css file.

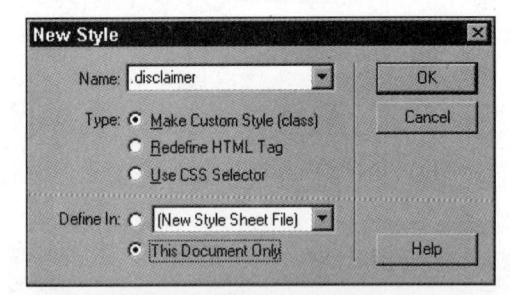

Figure 14-2: The first step in defining a new style is to select a style type and enter a name for the style, if it's a custom one.

The following sections explain the three style types in depth:

✦ Make Custom Style (class)

✦ Redefine HTML Tag

✦ Use CSS Selector

Make Custom Style (class)

Making a custom style is the most flexible way to define a style on a page. The first step in creating a custom style is to give it a name; this name is used in the `class` attribute. The name for your class must start with a period and must be alphanumeric without punctuation or special characters. If you do not begin the name of your custom style with a period, Dreamweaver inserts one for you.

Following are typical names you can use:

```
.master
.pagetitle
.bodytext
```

Caution: Although you can use names such as body, title, or any other HTML tag, this approach is not a good idea. Dreamweaver warns you of the conflict if you try this method.

Redefine HTML Tags

The second radio button in the New Style dialog box is Redefine HTML Tag. This type of style is an excellent tool for making quick, global changes to existing Web pages. Essentially, the Redefine HTML Tag style enables you to modify the features of your existing HTML tags. When you select this option, the drop-down list displays over 40 HTML tags in alphabetical order. Select a tag from the drop-down list and click OK.

Use CSS Selector

When you use the third style type, Use CSS Selector, you define what are known as *pseudo-classes* and *pseudo-elements*. A pseudo-class represents dynamic states of a tag that may change under user action or over time. Several standard pseudo-classes associated with the `<a>` tag are used to style hypertext links.

When you choose Use CSS Selector, the drop-down list box contains four customization options, which can all be categorized as pseudo-classes:

- `a:active` customizes the style of a link when the user selects it.
- `a:hover` customizes the style of a link while the user's mouse is over it.

Note: The `a:hover` pseudo-class is a CSS Level 2 specification and is currently supported only by Internet Explorer 4.0 and above as well as Netscape 6.

- `a:link` customizes the style of a link that has not been visited recently.
- `a:visited` customizes the style of a link to a page that has been recently visited.

Tip: Dreamweaver does not preview pseudo-class styles, although they can be previewed through a supported browser.

A pseudo-element, on the other hand, enables control over contextually defined page elements: for example, pseudo-elements enable you to style paragraphs within a table differently than paragraphs outside of a table. Similarly, text that is nested within two blockquotes (giving the appearance of being indented two levels) can be given a different color, font, and so on than text in a single blockquote.

Because of their specific nature, Dreamweaver does not display any pseudo-elements in the Use CSS Selector list. You can, however, enter your own. For example, to style text within nested blockquotes, enter the following in the Use CSS Selector field of the New Style dialog box:

```
blockquote blockquote
```

Basically, you are creating a custom style for a set of HTML tags used in your document. This type of CSS selector acts like an HTML tag that has a CSS style applied to it; that is, all page elements fitting the criteria are automatically styled.

Editing and managing style sheets

The Edit Style Sheet dialog box, shown in Figure 14-3, displays all your current styles — including HTML tags and custom styles — and provides various controls to link a style sheet and edit, create, duplicate, or remove a style. To access the Edit Style Sheet dialog box, choose the Edit Style Sheet button on the CSS Styles panel.

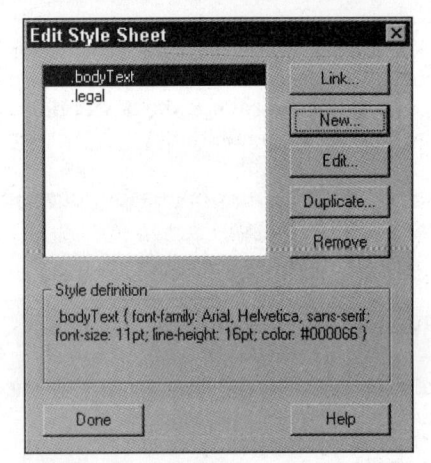

Figure 14-3: The Edit Style Sheet dialog box lists and defines any given style, in addition to presenting several command buttons for creating and managing styles.

Tip   To start editing one of your styles immediately, double-click the style in the list window of the Edit Style Sheet dialog box. This sequence takes you to the Style Definition dialog box, in which you redefine your selected style.

Use the following five command buttons along the right side of the Edit Style Sheet dialog box to create new external sheets or manage your existing style sheets:

- **Link:** Enables you to create an external style sheet or link to (or import) an existing external style sheet.
- **New:** Begins the creation of a new style by first opening the New Style dialog box, described in the following section.
- **Edit:** Modifies any existing style.
- **Duplicate:** Makes a copy of the selected style as a basis for creating a new style.
- **Remove:** Deletes an existing style.

Importing an external style sheet

As noted earlier, most Web designers prefer the link method of including an external style sheet to the import method. However, Dreamweaver offers both options, albeit in a slightly more difficult to get to place.

To import a separate style sheet, follow these steps:

1. Open the CSS Styles panel by choosing Windows ⇨ CSS Styles or selecting the Show CSS Styles button from either Launcher.
2. Select the Edit Style Sheet button.
3. In the Edit Style dialog box, select the Link command button.

    The Link External Style Sheet dialog box pops up, where you can access all your style sheets, by browsing and linking.

4. Either type in the File/URL path or select the Browse button to locate a style sheet; the Cascading Style Sheet file has the .css file name extension on your hard drive. If you have not already created a style sheet, you can do so by locating the place you want the style sheet and then creating a name for it. Useful names for style sheets can be master.css, contents.css, or body.css.
5. Choose the Import option.

    Naturally, you could also, at this point, choose the Link option.

When you go back to the Edit Style Sheet dialog box, you see a link file referenced in the listing above all the styles, followed by (link) or (import). You can double-click the file listing to open a new Edit Style Sheet dialog box for your external style sheet file. The defined styles within the style sheet then appear in the CSS Styles panel.

Tip Once you've defined your external style sheet, a couple of shortcuts exist for the Edit Style Sheet dialog box. First, you can press the Ctrl (Option) key and click the Edit Style Sheet button in the CSS Styles panel. Rather than displaying the Edit Style Sheet dialog box with a link to your external style sheet (which you'd have to double-click or highlight and select Edit to modify), you'll see the dialog box for the external style sheet immediately.

The second method is useful if you have the Site window open. Just double-click any .css file, and the Edit Style Sheet dialog box for that file opens instantly.

If you've already defined styles in the current document and you want to convert them to an external style sheet, Dreamweaver has you covered. Just choose File ➪ Export ➪ Export CSS Styles and enter a file name in the Export Styles as CSS File dialog box. Follow the directions in this section for linking this newly created file to your other Web pages as a style sheet.

Tip You can also export internal styles to an external style sheet by pressing Ctrl (Option) while clicking the Done button in the Edit Style Sheet dialog box.

Styles and Their Attributes

After you've selected a type and name for a new style or chosen to edit an existing style, the Style Definition dialog box opens. A Category list from which you select a style category (just as you select a category in Dreamweaver's Preferences dialog box) is located on the left side of this dialog box.

Dreamweaver offers you eight categories of CSS Level 1 styles to help you define your style sheet:

- Type
- Background
- Block
- Box
- Border
- List
- Positioning
- Extensions

You can apply styles from one or all categories. The following sections describe each style category and its available settings.

> **Note:** Dreamweaver doesn't preview all the possible CSS attributes. Those attributes that can't be seen in the Document window are marked with an asterisk in the Style Definition dialog box.

Type options

The Type category (see Figure 14-4) specifies the appearance and layout of the typeface for the page in the browser window. The Type category is one of the most widely used and supported categories — it can be rendered in Internet Explorer 3.0 and above and Netscape Navigator 4.0 and above. Table 14-1 explains the settings available in this category.

Table 14-1
CSS Type Attributes

Type Setting	Description
Font	Specifies the font or a collection of fonts, known as a *font family*. You can edit the font list by selecting Edit Font List from the drop-down list. (This sequence opens the Edit Font List dialog box, as described in Chapter 5.)
Size	Selects a size for the selected font. If you enter a value, you can then select the measurement system in the adjacent text box (the default is points). The relative sizes, such as small, medium, and large, are set relative to the parent element.
Style	Specifies a normal, oblique, or italic attribute for the font. An oblique font may have been generated in the browser by electronically slanting a normal font.
Line Height	Sets the line height of the line (known as *leading* in traditional layout). Typically, line height is a point or two more than the font size, although you can set the line height to be the same as or smaller than the font size, for an overlapping effect.
Decoration	Changes the decoration for text. Options include underline, overline, line-through, blink, and none. The blink decoration is displayed only in Netscape browsers.
Weight	Sets the boldness of the text. You can use the relative settings (light, bold, bolder, and boldest) or apply a numeric value. Normal is around 400; bold is 700.
Variant	Switches between normal and small caps. Small caps is a font style that displays text as uppercase, but the capital letters are a slightly larger size. The Variant option is not currently fully supported by either primary browser.
Case	Forces a browser to render the text as uppercase, lowercase, or capitalized.
Color	Sets a color for the selected font. Enter a color name or select the color swatch to choose a browser-safe color from the pop-up menu.

Figure 14-4: Type settings for your style.

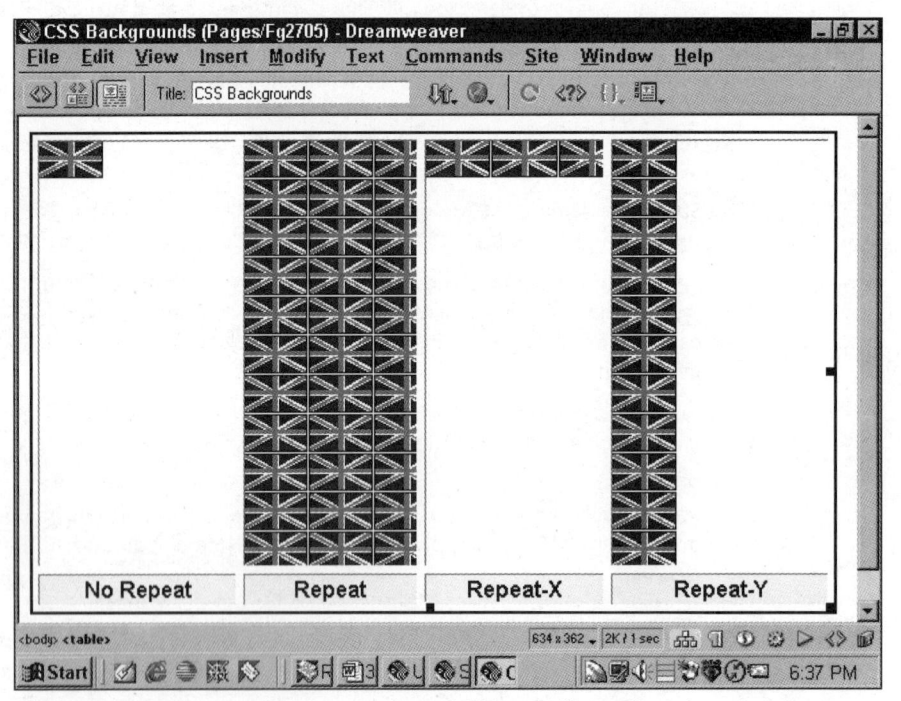

Figure 14-5: You can achieve a number of different tiling effects by using the Repeat attribute of the CSS Background category.

Background options

Since Netscape Navigator 2.0, Web designers have been able to use background images and color. Thanks to CSS Background attributes, designers can now use background images and color with increased control. Whereas traditional HTML background images are restricted to a single image for the entire browser window, CSS backgrounds can be specified for a single paragraph or any other CSS selector. (To set a background for the entire page, apply the style to the `<body>` tag.) Moreover, instead of an image automatically tiling to fill the browser window, CSS backgrounds can be made to tile horizontally, vertically, or not at all (see Figure 14-5). You can even position the image relative to the selected element.

Currently only Netscape 6 fully supports the CSS Background attributes shown in Figure 14-6 and listed in Table 14-2. The Repeat attribute enjoys full support across 4.*x* browsers and above, but Positioning and Attachment are rendered only in Internet Explorer 4.0 and above and Netscape 6.

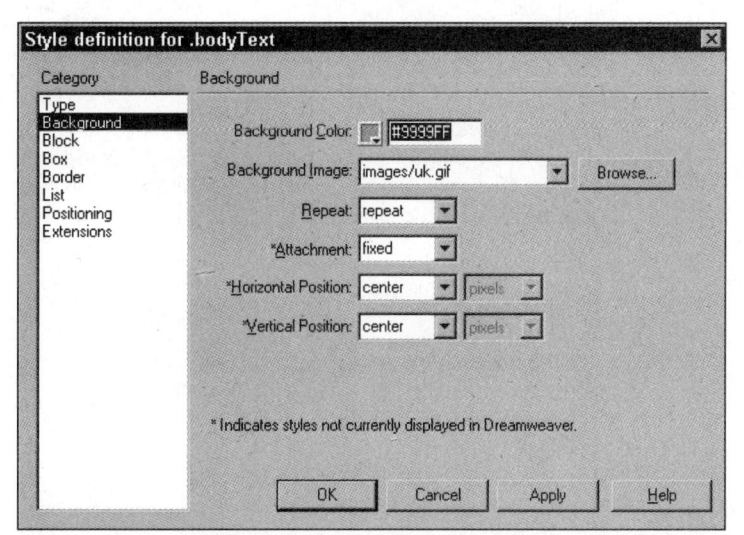

Figure 14-6: The CSS Background options enable a much wider range of control over background images and color.

Table 14-2
CSS Background Attributes

Background Setting	Description
Background Color	Sets the background color for a particular style. Note that this setting enables you to set background colors for individual paragraphs or other elements.
Background Image	Specifies a background image.
Repeat	Determines the tiling options for a graphic:
	no repeat displays the image in the upper-left corner of the applied style
	repeat tiles the background image horizontally and vertically across the applied style
	repeat-x tiles the background image horizontally across the applied style
	repeat-y tiles the background image vertically down the applied style
Attachment	Determines whether the background image remains fixed in its original position or scrolls with the page. This setting is useful for positioned elements. If you use the overflow attribute, you often want the background image to scroll in order to maintain layout control.
Horizontal Position	Controls the positioning of the background image in relation to the style sheet elements (text or graphics) along the horizontal axis.
Vertical Position	Controls the positioning of the background image in relation to the style sheet elements (text or graphics) along the vertical axis.

Block options

One of the most common formatting effects in traditional publishing long absent from Web publishing is justified text — text that appears as a solid block. Justified text is possible with the Text Align attribute, one of the six options available in the CSS Block category, as shown in Figure 14-7. Indented paragraphs are also a possibility. Table 14-3 lists the CSS Block options.

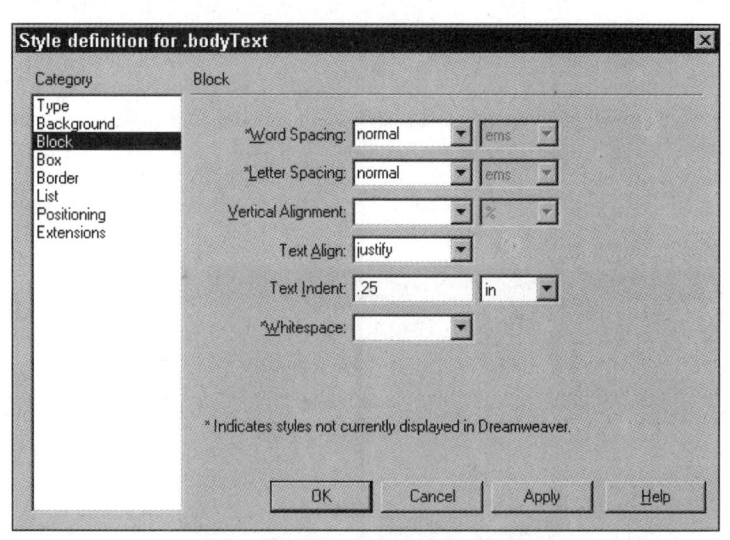

Figure 14-7: The Block options give the Web designer enhanced text control.

Table 14-3
CSS Block Attributes

Block Setting	Description
Word Spacing	Defines the spacing between words. You can increase or decrease the spacing with positive and negative values, set in ems.
Letter Spacing	Defines the spacing between the letters of a word. You can increase or decrease the spacing with positive and negative values, set in ems.
Vertical Alignment	Sets the vertical alignment of the style. Choose from baseline, sub, super, top, text-top, middle, bottom, or text-bottom, or add your own value.
Text Align	Sets text alignment (left, right, center, and justified).
Text Indent	Indents the first line of text on a style by the amount specified.
Whitespace	Controls display of spaces and tabs. The normal option causes all whitespace to collapse. The pre option behaves similarly to the `<pre>` tag; all white space is preserved. The nowrap option enables text to wrap if a ` ` tag is detected.

Box options

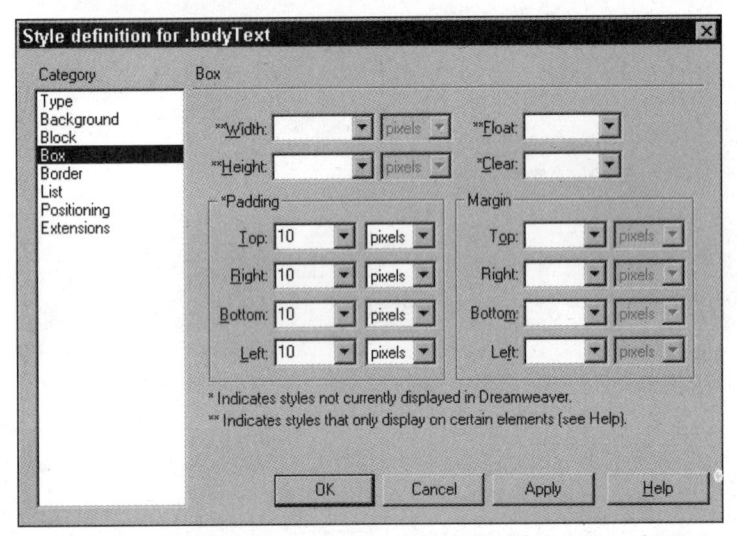

The Box attribute defines the placement and settings for elements (primarily images) on a page. Many of the controls (shown in Figure 14-8) emulate spacing behavior similar to that found in `<table>` attributes. If you are already comfortable using HTML tables with cell padding, border colors, and width/height controls, you can quickly learn how to use these Box features, which are described in Table 14-4.

Figure 14-8: The CSS Box attributes define the placement of HTML elements on the Web page.

Table 14-4
CSS Box Attributes

Box Setting	Description
Width	Sets the width of the element.
Height	Defines the height of the element.
Float	Places the element at the left or right page margin. Any text that encounters the element wraps around it.
Clear	Sets the side on which layers cannot be displayed next to the element. If a layer is encountered, the element with the Clear attribute places itself beneath the layer.
Padding	Sets the amount of space between the element and the border or margin, if no border is specified. You can control the padding for the left, right, top, and bottom independently.
Margin	Defines the amount of space between the borders of the element and other elements in the page.

Dreamweaver imposes some specific restrictions on which Box attributes can and cannot be previewed in the Document window. For example, the Float and Clear attributes can be previewed only when applied to an image. The Margin attributes can be previewed when applied to block-level elements, such as any of the `<h1>` through `<h6>` tags or the `<p>` tag. Padding is not displayed within Dreamweaver.

Border options

With Cascading Style Sheets, you can specify many parameters for borders surrounding text, images, and other elements such as Java applets. In addition to specifying separate colors for any of the four box sides, you can also choose the width of each side's border, as shown in the CSS Border category (see Figure 14-9). You can use eight different types of border lines, including solid, dashed, inset, and ridge. Table 14-5 lists the Border options.

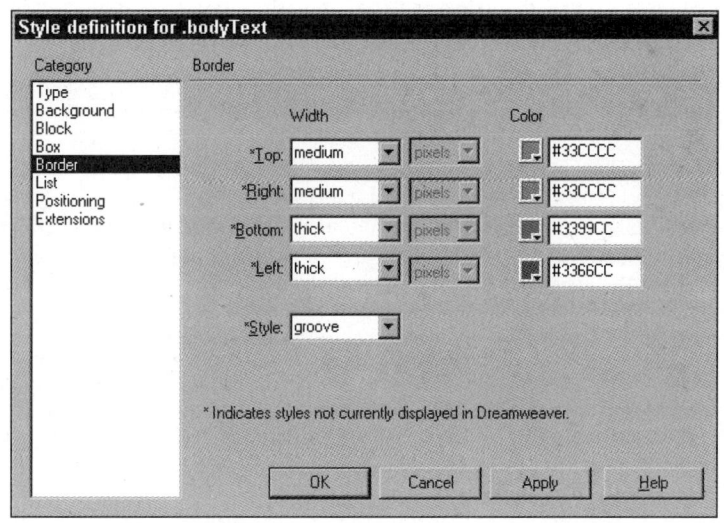

Figure 14-9: Borders are useful when you need to highlight a section of text or a graphic.

Table 14-5
CSS Border Attributes

Border Setting	Description
Top	Sets the color and settings for a border along the top of an element.
Right	Sets the color and settings for a border along the right side of an element.
Bottom	Sets the color and settings for a border along the bottom of an element.
Left	Sets the color and settings for a border along the left side of an element.
Style	Sets the style of the border. You can use any of the following as a border: Dotted, Dashed, Solid, Double, Groove, Ridge, Inset, and Outset.

> **Tip** CSS Border attributes are especially useful for highlighting paragraphs of text with a surrounding box. Use the Box category's Padding attributes to inset the text from the border.

List options

CSS gives you greater control over bulleted points. With Cascading Style Sheets, you can now display a specific bulleted point based on a graphic image, or you can choose from the standard built-in bullets, including disc, circle, and square. The List category also enables you to specify the type of ordered list, including decimal, Roman numerals, or A-B-C order.

Figure 14-10 shows, and Table 14-6 describes, the settings for lists.

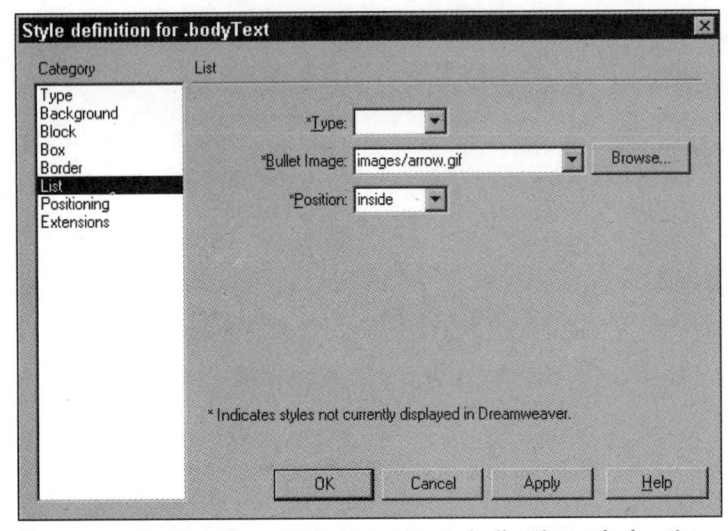

Figure 14-10: Specify a graphic to use as a bullet through the List category.

Table 14-6
List Category for Styles

List Setting	Description
Type	Selects a built-in bullet type. The options include disc, circle, square, decimal, lowercase roman, uppercase roman, lowercase alpha, and uppercase alpha.
Bullet Image	Sets an image to be used as a custom bullet. Enter the path to the image in the text box.
Position	Determines if the list item wraps to an indent (the default) or to the margin.

Positioning options

For many designers, positioning has increased creativity in page layout design. With positioning, you have exact control over where an element is placed on a page. Figure 14-11 shows the various attributes that provide this pinpoint control of your page elements. The options are described in Table 14-7.

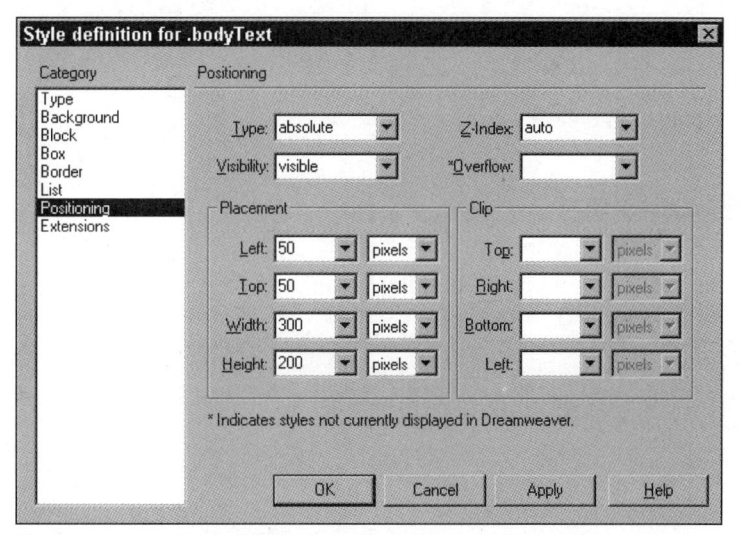

Figure 14-11: Control over the placement of elements on a page frees the Web designer from the restrictions imposed with HTML tables and other old-style formats.

Table 14-7
CSS Positioning Attributes

Positioning Setting	Description
Type	Determines whether an element can be positioned absolutely or relatively on a page. The third option, static, does not enable positioning.
Visibility	Determines whether the element is visible or hidden, or inherits the property from its parent.
Z-Index	Sets the apparent depth of a positioned element. Higher values are closer to the top.
Overflow	Specifies how the element is displayed when it's larger than the dimensions of the element. Options include the following: Clip, where the element is partially hidden; none, where the element is displayed and the dimensions are disregarded; and Scroll, which inserts scroll bars to display the overflowing portion of the element.
Placement	Sets the styled element's placement with the left and top attributes, and the dimensions with the width and height attributes.
Clip	Sets the visible portion of the element through the top, right, bottom, and left attributes.

Cross-Reference: Dreamweaver layers are built upon the foundation of CSS positioning. For a complete explanation of layers and their attributes, see Chapter 15.

Extensions options

The specifications for Cascading Style Sheets are rapidly evolving, and Dreamweaver has grouped some cutting-edge features in the Extensions category. As of this writing, the majority of the Extensions attributes (see Table 14-8) are supported only by Internet Explorer 4.0 and above; Netscape 6 supports only the cursor property. The Extensions settings shown in Figure 14-12 affect three different areas: page breaks for printing, the user's cursor, and special effects called *filters*.

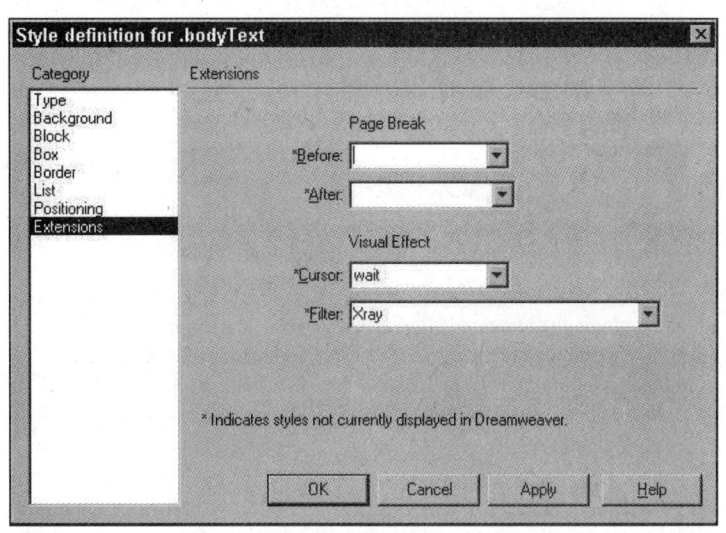

Figure 14-12: The Extensions category is currently supported only by Internet Explorer 4 and above, as well as Netscape 6.

Table 14-8
CSS Extensions Attributes

Extensions Setting	Description
Pagebreak	Inserts a point on a page where a printer sees a page break. Not supported by any current browser.
Cursor	Defines the type of cursor that appears when the user moves the cursor over an element. Currently supported only by Internet Explorer 4.0 and above, as well as Netscape 6.
Filter	Filters enable you to customize the look and transition of an element without having to use graphic or animation files. Currently supported only by Internet Explorer 4.0 and above.

Note One of the problems with the Web's never-ending evolution of page design is evident when you begin to print the page. The Pagebreak attribute alleviates this problem by enabling the designer to designate a style that forces a page break when printing; the break can occur either before or after the element is attached to the style. Although no browser currently supports this feature, it's a good candidate for support by future browsers.

The Filter attribute offers 16 different special effects that can be applied to an element. Many of these effects, such as wave and xray, are quite stunning. Several effects involve transitions, as well. Table 14-9 details all these effects.

Table 14-9
CSS Filters

Filter	Syntax	Description
Alpha	alpha(Opacity=*opacity*, FinishOpacity=*finishopacity*, Style=*style*, StartX=*startX*, StartY=*startY*, FinishX=*finishX*, FinishY=*finishY*)	Sets the opacity of a specified gradient region. This can have the effect of creating a burst of light in an image.
	Opacity is a value from 0 to 100, where 0 is transparent and 100 is fully opaque.	
	Style can be 0 (uniform), 1 (linear), 2 (radial), or 3 (rectangular).	
BlendTrans*	blendtrans(duration=*duration*)	Causes an image to fade in or out over a specified time.
	Duration is a time value for the length of the transition, in the format of *seconds.milliseconds*.	
Blur	blur(Add=*add*, Direction=*direction*, Strength=*strength*)	Emulates motion blur for images.
	Add is any integer other than 0.	
	Direction is any value from 0 to 315 in increments of 45.	
	Strength is any positive integer representing the number of pixels affected.	
Chroma	chroma(Color=*color*)	Makes a specific color in an image transparent.
	Color must be given in hexadecimal form, for example, #rrggbb.	
DropShadow	dropshadow(Color=*color*, OffX=*offX*, OffY=*offY*, Positive=*positive*)	Creates a drop shadow of the applied element, either image or text, in the specified color.
	Color is a hexadecimal triplet.	

Filter	Syntax	Description
	OffX and *OffY* are pixel offsets for the shadow.	
	Positive is a Boolean switch; use 1 to create shadow for nontransparent pixels and 0 to create shadow for transparent pixels.	
FlipH	FlipH	Flips an image or text horizontally.
FlipV	FlipV	Flips an image or text vertically.
Glow	Glow(Color=*color*, Strength=*strength*)	Adds radiance to an image in the specified color.
	Color is a hexadecimal triplet.	
	Strength is a value from 0 to 100.	
Gray	Gray	Converts an image in grayscale.
Invert	Invert	Reverses the hue, saturation, and luminance of an image.
Light*	Light	Creates the illusion that an object is illuminated by one or more light sources.
Mask	Mask(Color=*color*)	Sets all the transparent pixels to the specified color and converts the nontransparent pixels to the background color.
	Color is a hexadecimal triplet.	
RevealTrans*	RevealTrans(duration=*duration*, transition=*style*)	Reveals an image using a specified type of transition over a set period of time.
	Duration is a time value that the transition takes, in the format of *seconds.milliseconds*.	
	Style is one of 23 different transitions.	
Shadow	Shadow(Color=*color*, Direction=*direction*)	Creates a gradient shadow in the specified color and direction for images or text.
	Color is a hexadecimal triplet.	

Continued

Table 14-9 *(continued)*

Filter	Syntax	Description
	Direction is any value from 0 to 315 in increments of 45.	
Wave	Wave(Add=*add*, Freq=*freq*, LightStrength=*lightstrength*, Phase=*phase*, Strength=*strength*)	Adds sine wave distortion to the selected image or text.
	Add is a Boolean value, where 1 adds the original object to the filtered object and 0 does not.	
	Freq is an integer specifying the number of waves.	
	LightStrength is a percentage value.	
	Phase specifies the angular offset of the wave, in percentage (for example, 0% or 100% = 360 degrees, 25% = 90 degrees).	
	Strength is an integer value specifying the intensity of the wave effect.	
Xray	Xray	Converts an image to inverse grayscale for an X-rayed appearance.

* These three filters require extensive documentation beyond the scope of this book.

Note: Although only Internet Explorer uses the filters described here, Netscape 6 does have the capability to control opacity. The MozOpacity property of the style command may be set programmatically to a percentage value as in this code:

```
document.myImage.style.MozOpacity = '50%';
```

You can also declare the MozOpacity property as part of a CSS style. The following code example shows a CSS style that changes the opacity to 77% to whatever it's applied for both Internet Explorer 4 (and above) and Netscape 6.

```
.myOpacity { filter: alpha(opacity=77); -moz-opacity: 77% }
```

Summary

In this chapter, you discovered how you can easily and effectively add and modify Cascading Style Sheets. You can now accomplish all of the following:

- ✦ Update and change styles easily with the CSS Styles panel.
- ✦ Easily apply generated styles to an element on a page.
- ✦ Apply a consistent look and feel with linked style sheets.
- ✦ Position fonts and elements, such as images, with pinpoint accuracy.
- ✦ Exercise control over the layout, size, and display of fonts on a page.
- ✦ Define external style sheets to control the look and feel of an entire site.

In the next chapter, you learn how to position elements on a page in Dreamweaver using layers.

✦ ✦ ✦

Working with Layers

For many years, page designers have taken for granted the capability to place text and graphics anywhere on a printed page — even enabling graphics, type, and other elements to "bleed" off a page. This flexibility in design has eluded Web designers until recently. Lack of absolute control over layout has been a high price to pay for the universality of HTML, which makes any Web page viewable by any system, regardless of the computer or the screen resolution.

Lately, however, the integration of positioned layers within the Cascading Style Sheets specification has brought true absolute positioning to the Web. Page designers with a yen for more control can move to the precision offered with Cascading Style Sheets-Positioning (CSS-P).

Dreamweaver's implementation of layers turns the promise of CSS-P into an intuitive, designer-friendly, layout-compatible reality. As the name implies, layers offer more than pixel-perfect positioning. You can stack one layer on another, hide some layers while showing others, move a layer across the screen — and even move several layers around the screen simultaneously. Layers add an entirely new dimension to the Web designer's palette. Dreamweaver enables you to create page layouts using layers and then convert those layers to tables that are viewable by earlier browsers.

This chapter explores every aspect of how layers work in HTML — except for animation with timelines, which is saved for Chapter 16. With the fundamentals under your belt, you learn how to create, modify, populate, and activate layers on your Web page.

CHAPTER 15

In This Chapter

How layers work in Dreamweaver

Three ways to make layers in Dreamweaver

Modifying layers: Resizing, moving, and altering properties

Using alignment tools

Nesting layers

Forms in layers

Creating page layouts with layers

Converting layers to tables for viewing with earlier browsers

Making interactive layers with Dreamweaver behaviors

Dreamweaver technique: Creating a loading layer

Layers 101

When the World Wide Web first made its debut in 1989, few people were concerned about the aesthetic layout of a page. In fact, because the Web was a descendant of SGML — a multiplatform text document and information markup specification — layout was trivialized. Content and the capability to use hypertext to jump from one page to another were emphasized. After the first graphical Web browser software (Mosaic) was released, it quickly became clear that a page's graphics and layout could enhance a Web site's accessibility and marketability. Content was still king, but design was moving up quickly.

The first attempt at Web page layout was the server-side image map. This item was a typically large graphic (usually too hefty to be downloaded comfortably) with hotspots. Clicking a hotspot sent a message to the server, which returned a link to the browser. The download time for these files was horrendous, and the performance varied from acceptable to awful, based on the server's load.

The widespread adoption of tables, released with HTML 2.0 and enhanced for versions 3.2 and 4.0, radically changed layout control. Designers gained the capability to align objects and text — but a lot of graphical eye candy was still left to graphic files strategically located within the tables. The harder designers worked at precisely laying out their Web pages, the more they had to resort to workarounds such as nested tables and 1-pixel-wide GIFs used as spacers. To relieve the woes of Web designers everywhere, the W3C included a feature within the new Cascading Styles Sheet specifications that allows for absolute positioning of an element upon a page. Absolute positioning enables an element, such as an image or block of text, to be placed anywhere on the Web page. Both Microsoft Internet Explorer 4.0 (and above) and Netscape Navigator 4.0 (and above) support layers under the Cascading Style Sheets-Positioning specification.

The addition of the third dimension, depth, truly turned the positioning specs into layers. Now objects can be positioned side-by-side, and they have a *z-index* property as well. The z-index gets its name from the practice in geometry of describing three-dimensional space with x, y, and z coordinates; z-index is also called the *stacking order* because objects can be stacked upon one another.

A single layer in HTML looks like the following:

```
<div id="Layer1" style="position:absolute; visibility:inherit; width:200px; ¬
height:115px; z-index:1"></div>
```

Positioned layers are most commonly placed within the `<div>` tag. Another popular location is the `<span>` tag. These tags were chosen because they are seldom used in the HTML 3.2 specification (Dreamweaver supports both tags). Both Microsoft and Netscape encourage users to employ either of these tags, because the two primary browsers are designed to credit full CSS-P features to either the `<div>` or `<span>` tag. You should generally use these tags when anything but specific Navigator 4.*x* compatibility is desired.

Positioning Measurement

The positioning of layers is determined by aligning elements on an x-axis and a y-axis. In CSS, the x-axis (defined as "Left" in CSS syntax) begins at the left side of the page, and the y-axis (defined as "Top" in CSS syntax) is measured from the top of the page down. As with many of the other CSS features, you have your choice of measurement systems for Left and Top positioning. All measurements are given in Dreamweaver as a number followed by the abbreviation of the measurement system (without any intervening spaces). The measurement system options follow:

Unit	Abbreviation	Measurement
Pixels	px	Relative to the screen
Points	pt	1 pt = 1/72 in
Inches	in	1 in = 2.54 cm
Centimeters	cm	1 cm = 0.3937 in
Millimeters	mm	1 mm = 0.03937 in
Picas	pc	1 pc = 12 pt
EMS	em	The height of the element's font
Percentage	%	Relative to the browser window

If you don't define a unit of measurement for layer positioning, Dreamweaver defaults to pixels. If you decide to edit out the unit of measurement, the Web browser defaults to pixels.

Note: Netscape has developed two additional proprietary tags for using layers in its 4.x browser: `<layer>` and `<ilayer>`. The primary difference between the two tags has to do with positioning: the `<layer>` tag is used for absolute positioning, and the `<ilayer>` tag for relative positioning. Unfortunately, layers created by the `<div>` tag and the `<layer>` tag have different feature sets. These tags are no longer supported in Navigator 6.0; instead Netscape's latest browser fully supports the CSS standard tags, `<div>` and `<span>`.

Creating Layers with Dreamweaver

Dreamweaver enables you to create layers creatively and precisely. You can drag out a layer, placing and sizing it by eye, or choose to do it by the numbers — it's up to you. Moreover, you can combine the methods, quickly eyeballing and roughing out a layer layout and then aligning the edges precisely. For Web design that approaches conventional page layout, Dreamweaver even includes rulers and a grid to which you can snap your layers.

You can handle the creation of layers in Dreamweaver in one of three ways:

- You can drag out a layer, after selecting the Draw Layer button from the Objects panel.
- You can put a layer in a predetermined size by choosing Insert ⇨ Layer.
- You can create a layer with mathematical precision through the CSS Styles panel.

The first two methods are quite intuitive and are explained in the following section. The CSS Styles panel method is examined later in this chapter in the section "Embedding a Layer with Style Sheets."

Inserting a layer object

When you want to draw out your layer quickly, use the object approach. If you come from a traditional page-designer background and are accustomed to using a program such as QuarkXPress or PageMaker, you're already familiar with drawing out frames or text boxes with the click-and-drag technique. Dreamweaver uses the same method for placing and sizing new layer objects.

To draw out a layer as an object, follow these steps:

1. From the Common category of the Objects panel, select the Draw Layer button. Your pointer becomes a crosshair cursor. (If you decide not to draw out a layer, you can press Shift+Esc at this point or just click once without dragging to abort the process.)

2. Click anywhere in your document to position the layer and drag out a rectangle. Release the mouse button when you have an approximate size and shape with which you're satisfied (see Figure 15-1).

After you've dragged out your layer, notice several changes to the screen. First, the layer now has a small box on the outside of the upper-left corner. This box, shown in Figure 15-2, is the selection handle, which you can use to move an existing layer around the Web page. When you click the selection handle, eight sizing handles appear around the perimeter of the layer.

Chapter 15 ✦ **Working with Layers** 457

Layer icon · Selected layer · Draw Layer button

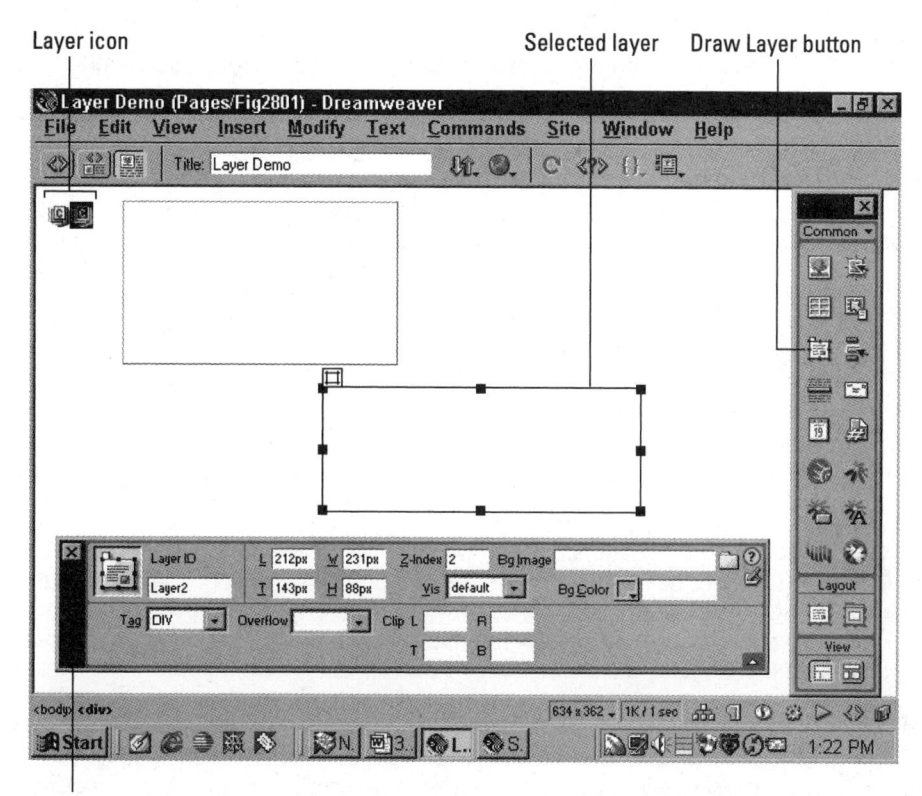

Layer Property Inspector

Figure 15-1: After selecting the Drag Layer object in the Objects panel (Common), the pointer becomes crosshairs when you are working on the page. Click and drag to create the layer.

Selection handle

Sizing handles

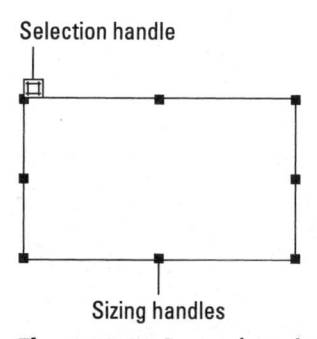

Figure 15-2: Once a layer is created, you can move it by dragging the selection handle and size it with the sizing handles.

Another subtle but important addition to the screen is the Layer icon. Like the other Invisibles icons — so named because they represent the unseen code — the Layer icon can be cut, copied, pasted, and repositioned. When you move the Layer icon, however, its corresponding layer does not move — you are actually only moving the code for the layer to a different place in the HTML source. Generally, the layer code's position in the HTML is immaterial — however, you may want to locate your layer source in a specific area to be backwards compatible with 3.0 browsers. Dragging and positioning Layer icons one after another is a quick way to achieve this task.

Using the Insert ⇨ Layer command

The second method to create a layer is through the menus. Instead of selecting an object from the Objects panel, choose Insert ⇨ Layer. Unlike the click-and-drag method, inserting a layer through the menu automatically creates a layer in the upper-left corner; the default size is 200 pixels wide and 115 pixels high.

Although the layer is by default positioned in the upper-left corner of the Document window, it does not have any coordinates listed in the Property Inspector. The position coordinates are added when you drag the layer into a new position. If you repeatedly add new layers through the menus without moving them to new positions, each layer stacks directly on top of one another, with no offset.

Caution It's important for every layer to have a specific position (left and top) assigned to it. Otherwise, the browser displays all layers directly on top of one another. To give a layer measurements, after you've inserted it through the menu, be sure to drag the layer, even slightly.

Setting default characteristics of a layer

You can designate the default size — as well as other features — of the layer that is inserted with Insert ⇨ Layer. Choose Edit ⇨ Preferences or use the keyboard shortcut Ctrl+U (Command+U) to open the Preferences dialog box. Select the Layers category. The Layers Preferences category (see Figure 15-3) helps you to set the layer attributes listed in Table 15-1.

Table 15-1
Layer Preferences

Layer Preference	Description
Tag	Sets the HTML code to use when creating layers. The options are `<div>` (the default), `<span>`, `<layer>`, and `<ilayer>`.
Visibility	Determines the initial state of visibility for a layer. The options are default, inherit, visible, and hidden.

Layer Preference	Description
Width	Sets the width of the layer in the measurement system of your choice. The default is 200 pixels.
Height	Sets the height of the layer in the measurement system of your choice. The default is 115 pixels.
Background Color	Sets a color for the layer background. Select the color from the pop-up menu of Web-safe colors.
Background Image	Sets an image for the layer background. In the text box, enter the path to the graphics file or click the Browse (Choose) button to locate the file.
Nesting Option	If you want to nest layers when one layer is placed in the other automatically, check the Nest when Created Within a Layer checkbox.
Netscape 4 Compatibility	To add code for a workaround to a known problem in Navigator 4.x browsers, which causes layers to lose their positioning coordinates when the user resizes the browser window, select this option.

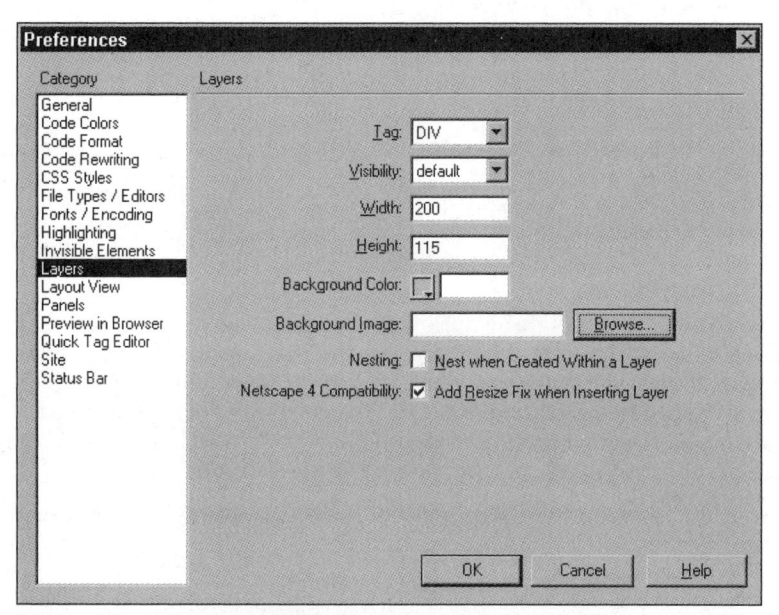

Figure 15-3: If you're building layers to a certain specification, use the Layers Preferences category to designate your options.

Embedding a layer with style sheets

In addition to laying out your layer by eye, or inserting a default layer with Insert ⇨ Layer, you can also specify your layers precisely through style sheets. Although this method is not as intuitive as either of the preceding methods, creating layers through style sheets has notable advantages:

- You can enter precise dimensions and other positioning attributes.
- The placement and shape of a layer can be combined with other style factors such as font family, font size, color, and line spacing.
- Layer styles can be saved in an external style sheet, which enables similar elements on every Web page in a site to be controlled from one source.

Cross-Reference: If you haven't yet read Chapter 14, which discusses building style sheet Web pages, you may want to look it over before continuing here.

To create a layer with style sheets, follow these steps:

1. Choose Window ⇨ CSS Styles or select the Show CSS Styles button from the Launcher. This selection opens the CSS Styles panel.

2. From the CSS Styles panel, select the New Style button. This selection opens the New Style dialog box.

3. From the New Style dialog box, set the Type option set to Make Custom Style (class). Enter a name for your new style and then choose Define In This Document Only. Click OK.

4. This opens the Style Definition dialog box. Select the Positioning category.

5. From the Positioning category (see Figure 15-4), enter desired values for these attributes: Type, Visibility, Z-Index, Overflow, Placement (Left, Top, Width, and Height), and Clip settings (Top, Right, Bottom, Left). Overflow and Clip settings are optional.

    The Type attribute offers three options: Absolute, Relative, and Static. While you are familiar with the first two options, the third option, Static, is probably new to you. Use Static when you don't want to add content to a layer, but you still want to specify a rectangular block. Static `<div>` types ignore the Left and Top attributes. Dreamweaver does not display a static `<div>` type, so you'll have to preview your page in a browser to see the results.

6. If appropriate, select other categories and enter any additional style sheet attributes desired. Click OK when you're done.

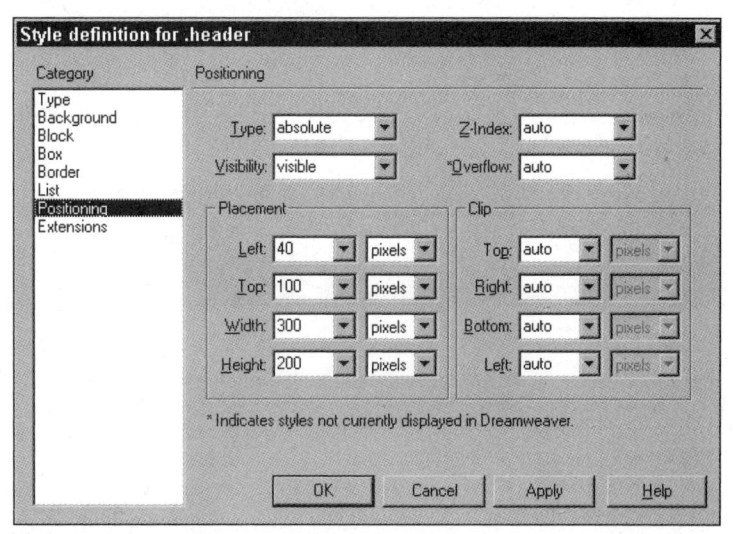

Figure 15-4: Use the Positioning category of the Style Definition dialog box to set layer attributes in an internal or external style sheet.

Keep in mind that layers are part of the overall Cascading Style Sheet specification and can benefit from all of the features of style sheets. You may decide that a specific area of text — a header, for instance — must always be rendered in a bold, red, 18-point Arial font with a green background, and that it should always be placed 35 pixels from the left margin and 25 pixels from the top of the page. You can place the style sheet within a .css file, link your Web pages to this file, and receive a result similar to what's shown (in black and white) in Figure 15-5. Within one component — the Cascading Style Sheet file — you can contain all of your positioning features for a page's headers, titles, and other text, graphics, or objects. This capability gives you the benefit of controlling the position and look of every title linked to one style sheet.

Choosing relative instead of absolute positioning

In most cases, absolute positioning uses the top-left corner of the Web page or the position where the <body> tag begins as the point of origin from which the Web browser determines the position of the text, image, or object. You can also specify measurements relative to objects. Dreamweaver offers two methods to accomplish relative positioning: the relative attribute and nested layers.

Using the relative attribute

In the first method, you select Relative as the Type attribute in the Style Sheet Positioning category. Relative positioning does not force a fixed position; instead, the HTML tags around it guide the positioning. For example, you may place a list of some items within a table and set the positioning relative to the table. You can see the effect of this sequence in Figure 15-6. In this illustration's Positioning category, the Type attribute is set to Relative and the Placement/Left value is set to 0.5 inch for a style applied to the listed items.

Figure 15-5: You can apply the layer style to any element on any Web page linked to the style sheet.

> **Note** Dreamweaver 4 doesn't preview relative positioning unless you're working with a nested layer, so you should check your placement by previewing the page in a browser, as shown in Figure 15-6.

Relative attributes can be useful, particularly if you want to place the positioned objects within free-flowing HTML. Free-flowing HTML repositions itself if the browser window is larger or smaller than the designer is aware. When you're using this technique, remember to place your relative layers within absolutely positioned layers. Otherwise, when the end user resizes the browser, the relative layers position themselves relative to the browser and not to the absolutely positioned layers. This situation can produce messy results — use relative positioning with caution when mixed with absolute layers.

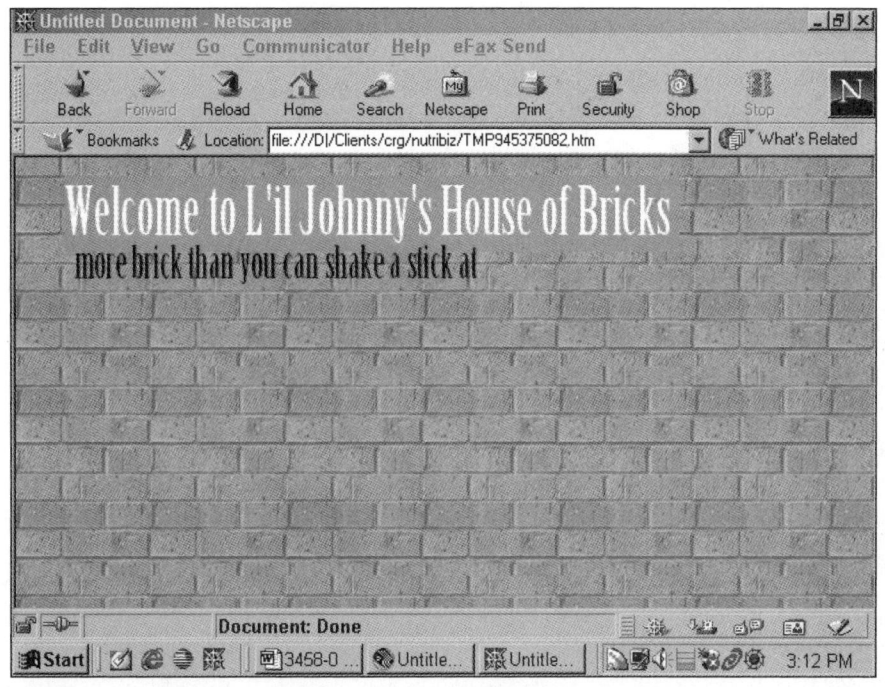

Figure 15-6: Relative positioning through styles can give your document a clean look, although the effect is not previewed in Dreamweaver.

Using nested layers

The second technique for positioning layers relatively uses nested layers. Once you nest one layer inside another, the inner layer uses the upper-left corner of the outer layer as its orientation point. For more details about nesting layers, refer to the section "Nesting with the Layers panel," later in this chapter.

Modifying a Layer

Dreamweaver helps you deftly alter layers once you have created them. Because of the complexity of managing layers, Dreamweaver offers an additional tool to the usual Property Inspector: the Layers panel. This tool enables you to select any of the layers on the current page quickly, change layer relationships, modify their visibility, and adjust their stacking order. You can also alter the visibility and stacking order of a selected layer in the Property Inspector, along with many other attributes. Before any modifications can be accomplished, however, you have to select the layer.

Selecting a layer

You can choose from several methods to select a layer for alteration (see Figure 15-7).

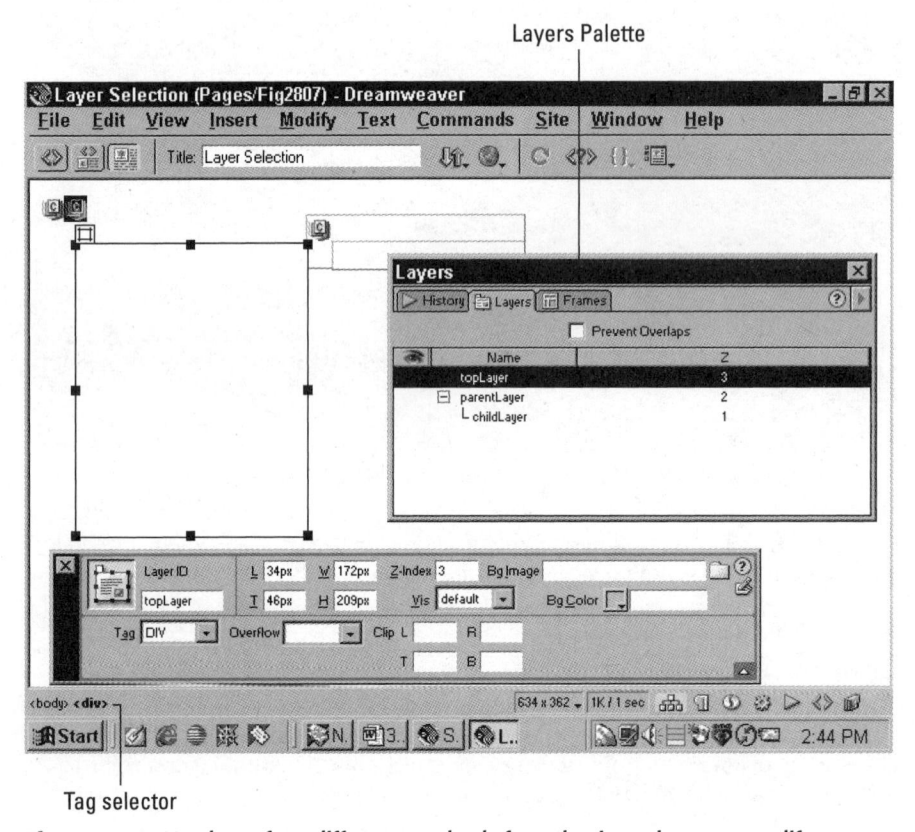

Figure 15-7: You have four different methods for selecting a layer to modify.

Your method of choosing a layer most likely depends on the complexity of your page layout:

- ✦ When you have only a few layers that are not overlapping, just click the selection handle of the layer with which you want to work.

- ✦ When you have layers placed in specific places in the HTML code (for example, a layer embedded in a table using relative positioning), choose the Layer icon.

- ✦ When you have many overlapping layers that are being addressed by one or more JavaScript functions, use the Layers panel to choose the desired layer by name.

♦ When you're working with invisible layers, click the `<div>` (or `<span>`) tag in the Tag Selector to reveal the outline of the layer.

Resizing a layer

To resize a layer, position the pointer over one of the eight sizing handles surrounding the selected layer. When over the handles, the pointer changes shape to a two- or four-headed arrow. Now click and drag the layer to a new size and shape.

You can also use the arrow keys to resize your layer with more precision. The following keyboard shortcuts change the width and height dimensions while the layer remains anchored by the upper-left corner:

♦ When the layer is selected, press Ctrl+arrow (Command+arrow) to expand or contract the layer by one pixel.

♦ Press Shift+Ctrl+arrow (Shift+Command+arrow) to increase or decrease the selected layer by the current grid increment. The default grid increment is five pixels.

Tip   You can quickly preview the position of a layer on a Web page without leaving Dreamweaver. Deselecting the View ⇨ Visual Aids ⇨ Layer Borders option leaves the layer outline displayed only when the layer is selected, but otherwise it is not shown.

Moving a layer

The easiest way to reposition a layer is to drag the selection handle. If you don't see the handle on a layer, click anywhere in the layer. You can drag the layer anywhere on the screen — or off the bottom or right side of the screen. To move the layer off the left side or top of the screen, enter a negative value in the left and top (L and T) text boxes of the Layer Property Inspector.

Tip   To hide the layer completely, match the negative value with the width or height of the layer. For example, if your layer is 220 pixels wide and you want to position it offscreen to the left (so that the layer can slide on at the click of a mouse), set the Left position at –220 pixels.

As with resizing layers, you can also use the arrow keys to move the layer more precisely:

♦ Press any arrow key to move the selected layer one pixel in any direction.

♦ Use Shift+arrow to move the selected layer by the current grid increment.

Using the Layer Property Inspector

You can modify almost all the CSS-P attributes for your layer right from the Layer Property Inspector (see Figure 15-8). Certain attributes, such as width, height, and background image and color are self-explanatory or recognizable from other objects. Other layers-only attributes such as visibility and inheritance require further explanation. Table 15-2 describes all the Layer properties, and the following sections discuss the features unique to layers.

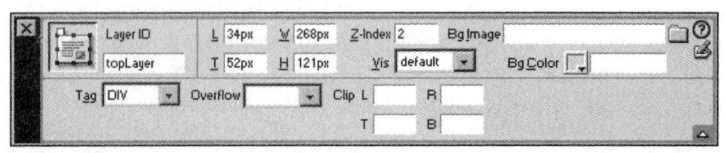

Figure 15-8: The Layer Property Inspector makes it easy to move, resize, hide, and manipulate all of the visual elements of a layer.

Table 15-2
Layer Property Inspector Options

Layer Attribute	Possible Values	Description
BgColor	Any hexadecimal or valid color name	Background color for the layer.
BgImage	Any valid graphic file	Background image for the layer.
Clip (Top, Bottom, Left, Right)	Any positive integer region of the layer. If the values are not specified, the entire layer is visible.	Measurements for the displayable.
H (Height)	Any integer measurement in pixels, centimeters, millimeters, inches, points, percentage, ems, or picas	Vertical measurement of the layer.
L (Left)	Any integer measurement in pixels, centimeters, millimeters, inches, points, percentage, ems, or picas	Distance measured from the origin point on the left.
Name	Any unique name without spaces or special characters	Labels the layer so that it can be addressed by style sheets or JavaScript functions.
Overflow	visible, scroll, hidden, or auto	Determines how text or images larger than the layer should be handled.
T (Top)	Any integer measurement in pixels, centimeters, millimeters, inches, points, percentage, ems, or picas	The distance measured from the origin point on the top.

Layer Attribute	Possible Values	Description
Tag	span, div, layer, or ilayer	Type of HTML tag to use for the layer.
Vis (Visibility)	default, inherit, visible, or hidden	Determines whether a layer is displayed. If visibility is set to inherit, then the layer takes on the characteristic of the parent layer.
W (Width)	Any integer measurement in pixels, centimeters, millimeters, inches, points, percentage, ems, or picas	The horizontal measurement of the layer.
Z-Index	Any integer	Stacking order of the layer in relation to other layers on the Web page. Higher numbers are closer to the top.

Name

Names are important when working with layers. To refer to them properly for both CSS and JavaScript purposes, each layer must have a unique name: unique among the layers and unique among every other object on the Web page. Dreamweaver automatically names each layer as it is created in sequence: Layer1, Layer2, and so forth. You can enter a name that is easier for you to remember by replacing the provided name in the text box on the far left of the Property Inspector.

Caution   Netscape Note: Netscape Navigator 4.x is strict with its use of the ID attribute. You must ensure that you call the layer with an alphanumeric name that does not use spacing or special characters such as the underscore or percentage sign. Moreover, make sure your layer name begins with a letter and not a number—in other words, layer9 works but 9layer can cause problems.

Tag attribute

The Tag drop-down list contains the HTML tags that can be associated with the layer. By default, the positioned layer has <div> as the tag, but you can also choose <span>, <layer>, or <ilayer>. As previously noted, the <div> and <span> tags are endorsed by the World Wide Web Consortium group as part of their CSS standards. The <layer> and <ilayer> tags are Netscape Navigator 4.x proprietary tags, although Netscape also supports the CSS tags.

Indeed, if you are working on a Navigator 4.x-based intranet, you may want to change the default layer tag. Choose Edit ⇨ Preferences and then, from the Layers category, select either <layer> or <ilayer> from the Tag drop-down list.

Visibility

Visibility (`Vis` in the Property Inspector) defines whether or not you can see a layer on a Web page. The following four values are available:

- **Default:** Enables the browser to set the visibility attribute. Most browsers use the `inherit` value as their default.
- **Inherit:** Sets the visibility to the same value as that of the parent layer, which enables a series of layers to be hidden or made visible by changing only one layer.
- **Visible:** Causes the layer and all of its contents to be displayed.
- **Hidden:** Makes the current layer and all of its contents invisible.

Remember the following when you're specifying visibility:

- Whether or not you can see a layer, you must remember that the layer still occupies space on the page and demands some of the page loading time. Hiding a layer does not affect the layout of the page, and invisible graphics take just as long to download as visible graphics.
- When you are defining the visibility of a positioned object or layer, you should not use `default` as the visibility value. A designer does not necessarily know whether the site's end user has set the default visibility to `visible` or `hidden`. Designing an effective Web page can be difficult without this knowledge. The common browser default is for visibility to be inherited, if not specifically shown or hidden.

Overflow

Normally, a layer expands to fit the text or graphics inserted into it. You can, however, restrict the size of a layer by changing the height and width values in the Property Inspector. What happens when you define a layer to be too small for an image, or when an amount of text depends on the setting of the layer's overflow attribute? CSS layers (the `<div>` and `<span>` tags) support four different overflow settings:

- **Visible (Default):** All of the overflowing text or image is displayed, and the height and width settings established for the layer are ignored.
- **Hidden:** The portion of the text or graphic that overflows the dimensions is not visible.
- **Scroll:** Horizontal and vertical scroll bars are added to the layer regardless of the content size or amount, and regardless of the layer measurements.
- **Auto:** When the content of the layer exceeds the width and/or height values, horizontal and vertical scroll bars appear.

Currently, support for the overflow attribute is spotty at best. Dreamweaver doesn't display the result in the Document window; it must be previewed in a browser to be seen. Navigator offers limited support: Only the attribute's hidden value works correctly and, even then, just for text. Only Internet Explorer 4.0 or above and Netscape 6 render the overflow attribute correctly, as shown in Figure 15-9.

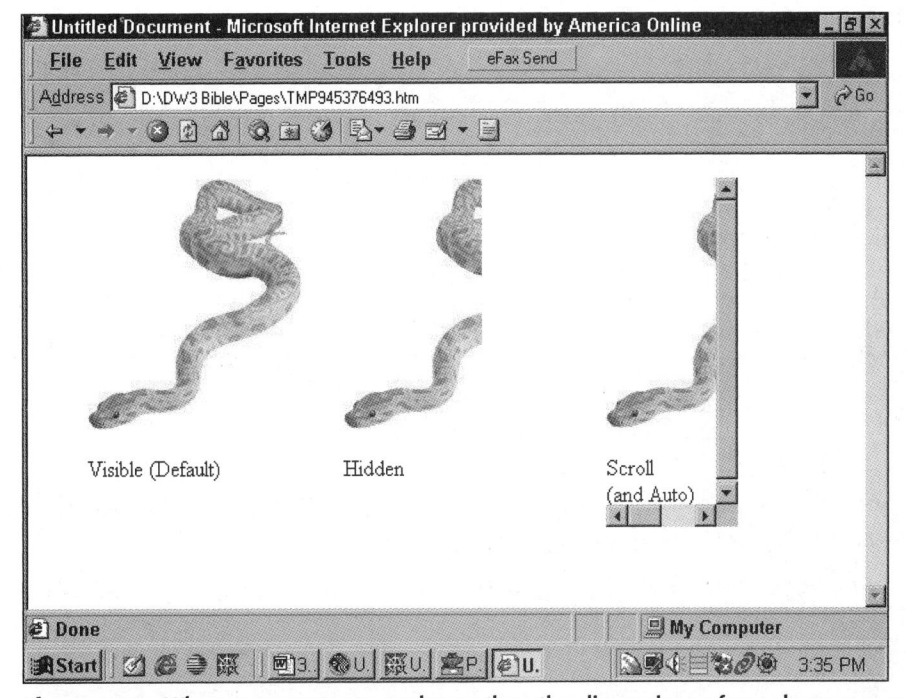

Figure 15-9: When your contents are larger than the dimensions of your layer, you can regulate the results with the overflow attribute.

> **Caution**
> Netscape Note: The Overflow property is not recognized by the Netscape Navigator 4.x proprietary layer tags, <layer> and <ilayer>.

Clipping

If you're familiar with the process of cropping an image, you'll quickly grasp the concept of clipping layers. Just as desktop publishing software hides but doesn't delete the portion of the picture outside of the crop marks, layers can mask the area outside the clipping region defined by the Left, Top, Right, and Bottom values in the Clip section of the Layer Property Inspector.

All clipping values are measured from the upper-left corner of the layer. You can use any CSS standard measurement system: pixels (the default), inches, centimeters, millimeters, ems, or picas.

The current implementation of CSS only supports rectangular clipping. When you look at the code for a clipped layer, you see the values you inserted in the Layer Property Inspector in parentheses following the clip attribute, with the `rect` (for rectangular) keyword, as follows:

```
<div id="Layer1" style="position:absolute; left:54px; top:24px; ¬
width:400px; height:115px; z-index:1; visibility:inherit; ¬
clip:rect(10 100 100 10)">
```

Generally, you specify values for all four criteria: Left, Top, Right, and Bottom. You can also leave the Left and Top values empty or use the keyword `auto`—which causes the Left and Top values to be set at the origin point: 0,0.

Z-index

One of a layer's most powerful features is its capability to appear above or below other layers. You can change this order, known as the *z-index*, dynamically. Whenever a new layer is added, Dreamweaver automatically increments the z-index—layers with higher z-index values are positioned above layers with lower z-index values. The z-index can be adjusted manually in either the Layer Property Inspector or the Layers panel. The z-index must be an integer, either negative or positive.

A Visual Clipping Technique

In Dreamweaver, you cannot draw the clipping region visually—the values have to be explicitly input in the Clip section of the Layer Property Inspector. That said, a trick using a second temporary layer makes it easier to position your clipping. Follow these steps to get accurate clipping values:

1. Insert your original layer and image.

2. Nest a second, temporary layer inside the first, original layer (select the Draw Layer button in the Objects panel and draw out the second layer inside the first).

    If you have your Layer Preferences set so that a layer does not automatically nest when created inside another layer, press the Ctrl (Command) key while you draw your layer, to override the preference.

3. Position the second layer over the area you want to clip. Use the layer's sizing handles to alter the size and shape, if necessary.

4. Note the position and dimensions of the second layer (the Left, Top, Width, and Height values).

5. Delete the second layer.

6. In the Property Inspector for the original layer, enter the Clip values as follows:

- **L:** Enter the Left value for the second layer.
- **T:** Enter the Top value for the second layer.
- **R:** Add the second layer's Left value to its Width value.
- **B:** Add the second layer's Top value to its Height value.

Dreamweaver displays the clipped layer after you enter the final value. The following figure shows the original layer and the temporary layer on the left, and the final clipped version of the original layer on the right.

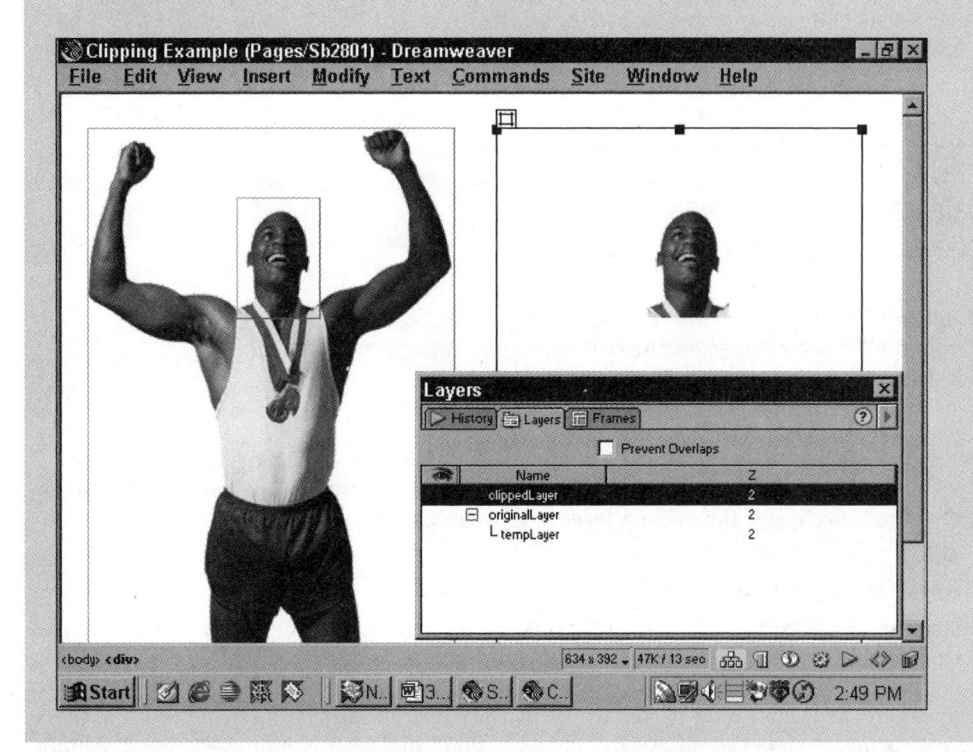

Tip Although some Web designers use high values for the z-index, such as 3,000, the z-index is completely relative. The only reason to increase a z-index to an extremely high number is to ensure that that particular layer remains on top.

The z-index is valid for the CSS layer tags as well as the Netscape 4.*x* proprietary layer tags. Netscape 4.*x* also has two additional attributes that can affect the apparent depth of either the `<layer>`- or `<ilayer>`-based content: above and below. With above and below, you can specify which existing layer is to appear directly on top of or beneath the current layer. You can only set one of the depth attributes, the z-index, or above or below.

Caution: Certain types of objects—including Java applets, plug-ins, and ActiveX controls—ignore the z-index setting when included in a layer and appear as the uppermost layer. However, certain ActiveX Controls—most notably Flash—can be made to respect the z-index.

When you designate the layer's tag attribute to be either <layer> or <ilayer>, the Property Inspector displays an additional field: the A/B attribute for setting the above or below value, as shown in Figure 15-10. Choose either attribute from the A/B drop-down list and then select the layer from the adjacent list. The layer you choose must be set up in the code before the current layer. You can achieve this condition in the Document window by moving the icon for the current layer to a position after the other layers. Although you must use either <layer> or <ilayer> to specify the above or below attribute, the layer specified can be either a CSS or Netscape type.

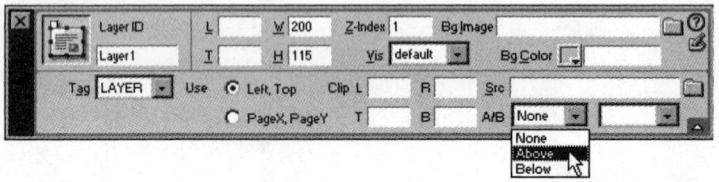

Figure 15-10: Choosing the Netscape-specific tags LAYER or ILAYER from the Property Inspector causes several new options to appear, including the A/B switch for the above/below depth position.

Caution: Working with the above and below attributes can be confusing. Notice that they determine which layer is to appear on top of or underneath the current layer, and not which layer the present layer is above or below.

Background image or color

Inserting a background image or color with the Layer Property Inspector works in a similar manner to changing the background image or color for a table (as explained in Chapter 8). To insert an image, enter the path to the file in the Bg Image text box or select the Folder icon to locate the image file on your system or network. If the layer is larger than the image, the image is tiled, just as it would in the background of a Web page or table.

To give a layer a background color, enter the color name (either in its hexadecimal or nominal form) in the Bg Color text box. You can also select the color swatch to pick your color from the color picker.

Additional Netscape 4.x properties

In addition to the above and below values for the z-index attribute, two other Netscape 4.x variations must be noted for the sake of completeness — both of which appear as options in the Property Inspector when either <layer> or <ilayer> is selected as the layer tag.

When either <layer> or <ilayer> is selected, the Page X, Page Y option becomes available as a radio button in the Property Inspector in addition to Left, Top. With Netscape 4.x layers, Left, Top places the layer relative to the top-left corner of its parent (whether that's the page or another layer if the layer is nested). Page X, Page Y positions the layer based on the top-left corner of the page, regardless of whether the layer is nested.

The other additional Netscape 4.x layer attribute is the source property. You can specify another HTML document to appear within a <layer> or <ilayer> — much like placing other Web pages in frames. To specify a source for a Netscape 4.x layer, enter the path to the file in the Src text box or select the Folder icon to locate the file.

> **Caution** Although these properties are available in Dreamweaver, they should really only be used if your Web site is used as a Netscape 4.x intranet. Neither of these properties is supported by Internet Explorer or Netscape 6.

The Layers panel

Dreamweaver offers another tool to help manage the layers in your Web page: the Layers panel. Although this tool doesn't display as many properties about each element as the Property Inspector, the Layers panel gives you a good overview of all the layers on your page. It also provides a quick method of selecting a layer — even when it's offscreen — as well as enabling you to change the z-index and the nesting order.

The Layers panel, shown in Figure 15-11, can be opened either through the Window menu (Window ⇨ Layers) or by pressing the keyboard shortcut F2.

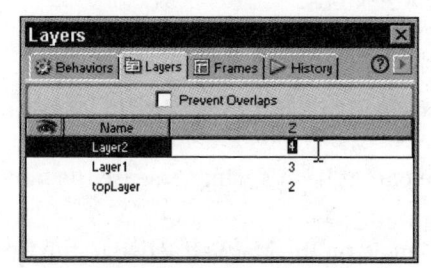

Figure 15-11: Use the Layers panel to select quickly or alter the visibility or relationships of all the layers on your page.

Modifying properties with the Layers panel

The Layers panel lists the visibility, name, and z-index settings for each layer. All of these properties can be modified directly through the Layers panel.

The visibility of a particular layer is noted by the eye symbol in column one of the Layers panel. Selecting the eye symbol cycles you through three different visibility states as follows:

+ **Eye closed:** Indicates that the layer is hidden.

+ **Eye open:** Indicates that the layer is visible.

+ **No eye:** Indicates that the visibility attribute is set to the default (which, for both Navigator and Internet Explorer, means inherit).

Tip To change all of your layers to a single state simultaneously, select the eye symbol in the column header. Unlike the individual eyes in front of each layer name, the overall eye toggles between open and shut.

You can also change a layer's name (in the second column of the Layers panel). Just double-click the current layer name in the Layers Property Inspector; the name is highlighted. Type in the new name and press Enter (Return) to complete the change.

The z-index (stacking order) in the third column can be altered in the same manner. Double-click the z-index value; then type in the new value and press Enter (Return). You can enter any positive or negative integer. If you're working with the Netscape proprietary layer tags, you can also alter the above or below values previously set for the z-index through the Property Inspector. Use A for above and B for below.

Tip To change a layer's z-index interactively, you can drag one layer above or below another in the Layers panel.

Nesting with the Layers panel

Another task managed by the Layers panel is nesting or unnesting layers. This process is also referred to as *creating parent-child layers*. To nest one layer inside another through the Layers panel, follow these steps:

1. Choose Window ⇨ Layers or press F2 to open the Layers panel.

2. Press the Ctrl (Command) key, then click the name of the layer to be nested (the child), and drag it on top of the other layer (the parent).

3. When you see a rectangle around the parent layer's name, release the mouse.

   The child layer is indented underneath the parent layer, and the parent layer has a minus sign (a down-pointing triangle on the Mac) attached to the front of its name.

4. To hide the child layer from view, select the minus sign (down-pointing triangle) in front of the parent layer's name. Once the child layer is hidden, the minus sign turns into a plus sign (a right-pointing triangle on the Mac).

5. To reveal the child layer, select the plus sign (right-pointing triangle on the Mac).

6. To undo a nested layer, select the child layer and drag it to a new position in the Layers panel.

Caution When it comes to nested layers, Netscape 4.x does not "play well with others." In fact, the expected results are so rarely achieved that it's best to avoid nested layers in cross-browser sites for the time being.

You can use the nesting features of the Layers panel to hide many layers quickly. If the visibility of all child layers is set to default — with no eye displayed — then by hiding the parent layer, you cause all the child layers to inherit that visibility setting and also disappear from view.

Tip You can also delete a layer from the Layers panel. Just highlight the layer to be removed and press Delete. Dreamweaver does not enable you to delete nested layers as a group, however — you have to remove each one individually.

Aligning layers with the ruler and grid

With the capability to position layers anywhere on a page comes additional responsibility and potential problems. In anything that involves animation, correct alignment of moving parts is crucial. As you begin to set up your layers, their exact placement and alignment becomes critical. Dreamweaver includes two tools to simplify layered Web page design: the ruler and the grid.

Rulers and grids are familiar concepts in traditional desktop publishing. Dreamweaver's ruler shows the x-axis and y-axis in pixels, inches, or centimeters along the outer edge of the Document window. The grid crisscrosses the page with lines to support a visual guideline when you're placing objects. You can even enable a snap-to-grid feature to ensure easy, absolute alignment.

Using the ruler

With traditional Web design, "eyeballing it" was the only option available for Web page layout. The absolute positioning capability of layers filled this deficiency. Now online designers have a more precise and familiar system of alignment: the ruler. Dreamweaver's ruler can be displayed in several different measurement units and with your choice of origin point.

To enable the ruler in Dreamweaver, choose View ➪ Rulers ➪ Show or use the keyboard shortcut Ctrl+Alt+R (Command+Option+R). Horizontal and vertical rulers appear along the top and the left sides of the Document window, as shown in Figure 15-12. As you move the pointer, a light-gray line indicates the position on both rulers.

Figure 15-12: Use the horizontal and vertical rulers to assist your layer placement and overall Web page layout.

By default, the ruler uses pixels as its measurement system. You can change the default by selecting View ⇨ Rulers and choosing either inches or centimeters.

Dreamweaver also enables you to move the ruler origin to a new position. Normally, the upper-left corner of the page acts as the origin point for the ruler. On some occasions, it's helpful to start the measurement at a different location — at the bottom-right edge of an advertisement, for example. To move the origin point, select the intersection of the horizontal and the vertical rulers and drag the crosshairs to a new location. When you release the mouse button, both rulers are adjusted to show negative values above and to the right of the new origin point. To return the origin point to its default setting, choose View ⇨ Rulers ⇨ Reset Origin, or you can simply double-click the intersection of the rulers.

Tip You can access a ruler shortcut menu by right-clicking (Command+clicking) the ruler itself. The shortcut menu enables you to change the system of measurement, reset the origin point, or hide the rulers.

Lining up with the grid

Rulers are generally good for positioning single objects, but a grid is extremely helpful when aligning one object to another. With Dreamweaver's grid facility, you can align elements visually or snap them to the grid. You can set many of the grid's other features, including grid spacing, color, and type.

To turn on the grid, choose View ⇨ Grid ⇨ Show Grid or press Ctrl+Alt+G (Command+Option+G). By default, the grid is displayed with mustard-yellow (#CCCC99) lines set at 50-pixel increments.

The snap-to-grid feature is enabled by choosing View ⇨ Grid ⇨ Snap To Grid or with the keyboard shortcut Ctrl+Alt+Shift+G (Command+Option+Shift+G). When activated, Snap to Grid causes the upper-left corner of a layer to be placed at the nearest grid intersection when the layer is moved.

Like most of Dreamweaver's tools, the grid can be customized. To alter the grid settings, choose View ⇨ Grid ⇨ Edit Grid. In the Grid Settings dialog box, shown in Figure 15-13, you can change any of the following settings (just click OK when you're done):

Grid Setting	Description
Color	Change the default color by selecting the color swatch to open the Dreamweaver color picker where you can click on a new swatch, or type a new value in the text box.
Show Grid	Show or hide the grid with this checkbox toggle.
Snap to Grid	Checkbox toggle to enable or disable the Snap to Grid feature.
Spacing	Adjust the distance between grid points by entering a numeric value in the text box.
Spacing Unit of Measure	Select Pixels, Inches, or Centimeters from the Spacing drop-down list.
Display	Choose either solid lines or dots for the gridlines.

Adding elements to a layer

Once you have created and initially positioned your layers, you can begin to fill them with content. Inserting objects in a layer is just like inserting objects in a Web page. The same insertion methods are available to you:

- ✦ Position the cursor inside a layer, choose Insert in the menu bar, and select an object to insert.

- With the cursor inside a layer, select any object from the Objects panel. Note: you cannot select the Draw Layer object.
- Drag an object from the Objects panel and drop it inside the layer.

A known problem exists with Netscape Navigator 4.*x* browsers and nested layers — and layers in general — using the `<div>` tag. Whenever the browser window is resized, the layers lose their left and top position and are displayed along the left edge of the browser window or parent layer. Dreamweaver includes the capability to insert code that serves as a workaround for this problem. With this code in place, if the browser is resized, the page reloads, repositioning the layers. If you want the code to be automatically inserted the first time you add a layer to your page, select the Add Resize Fix When Inserting Layers option found on the Layers category of Preferences. You can also insert it on a case-by-case basis by choosing Commands ⇨ Add/Remove Netscape Resize Fix. As the name implies, this command also deletes the Netscape Resize Fix code.

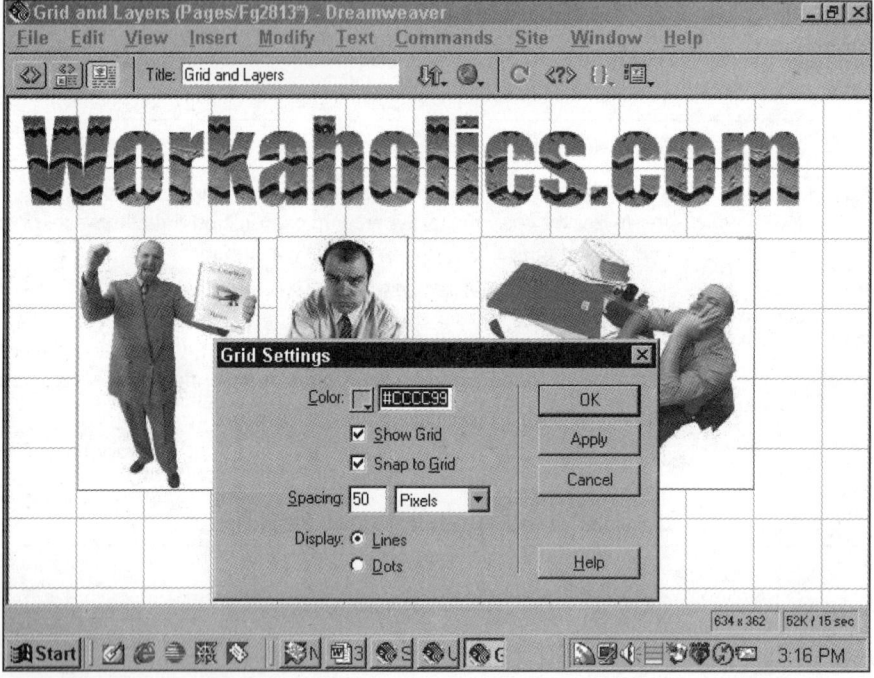

Figure 15-13: Dreamweaver's grid feature is extremely handy for aligning a series of objects.

Forms and layers

When you're mixing forms and layers, follow only one rule: Always put the form completely inside the layer. If you place the layer within the form, all form elements after the layer tags are ignored. With the form completely enclosed in the layer, the form can safely be positioned anywhere on the page and all form elements still remain completely active.

Although this rule means you can't split one form onto separate layers, you can set up multiple forms on multiple layers — and still have them all communicate to one final CGI or other program. This technique uses JavaScript to send the user-input values in the separate forms to hidden fields in the form with the Submit button. Let's say, for example, that you have three separate forms gathering information in three separate layers on a Web page. Call them formA, formB, and formC on layer1, layer2, and layer3, respectively. When the Submit button in formC on layer3 is selected, a JavaScript function is first called by means of an onClick event in the button's <input> tag. The function, in part, looks like the following:

```
function gatherData() {
  document.formC.hidden1.value = document.formA.text1.value
  document.formC.hidden2.value = document.formB.text2.value
}
```

Notice how every value from the various forms gets sent to a hidden field in formC, the form with the Submit button. Now, when the form is submitted, all the hidden information gathered from the various forms is submitted along with formC's own information.

> **Note** Netscape Note: The code for this separate-forms approach, as written in the preceding listing, works in Internet Explorer. Netscape 4.x, however, uses a different syntax to address forms in layers. To work properly in Netscape 4.x, the code must look like the following:
>
> ```
> document.layers["layer3"].document.formC.hidden1.value=¬
> document.layers["layer1"].document.formA.text1.value
> ```
>
> To make the code cross-browser compatible, you can use an initialization function that allows for the differences, or you can build it into the onClick function.

Creating Your Page Design with Layers

While the advantage to designing with layers is the greater flexibility it affords, one of the greatest disadvantages of using layers is that they are viewable in only the most recent generation of browsers. Dreamweaver enables you to get the best of both worlds by making it possible for you to use layers to design complex page layouts, and then to transform those layers into tables that can be viewed in earlier browsers. Designing this way has some limitations — you can't, for example, actually layer items on top of each other. Nevertheless, Dreamweaver's capability to convert layers to tables (and tables to layers) enables you to create complex layouts with ease.

Using the Tracing Image

Page-layout artists are often confronted with Web-page designs that have been mocked up in a graphics program. Dreamweaver's Tracing Image function enables you to use such images to guide the precise placement of graphics, text, tables, and forms in your Web page, enabling you to match the original design as closely as possible.

In order to use a Tracing Image, the graphic must be saved in either JPG, GIF, or PNG format. Once the Tracing Image has been placed in your page, it is viewable only in Dreamweaver — it will never appear in a browser. A placed Tracing Image hides any background color or background graphic in your Web page. Preview your page in a browser, or hide the tracing layer, to view your page without the Tracing Image.

Adding the Tracing Image to your page

To add a Tracing Image to your Dreamweaver page, select View ➪ Tracing Image ➪ Load. This brings up a Select Image Source dialog box that enables you to select the graphic you would like to use as a Tracing Image. Clicking Select brings up the Page Properties dialog box, shown in Figure 15-14, where you may specify the opacity of the Tracing Image, from Transparent (0%) to Opaque (100%). You can change the Tracing Image or its transparency at any point by selecting Modify ➪ Page Properties to bring up the Page Properties dialog box. You can toggle between hiding and showing the Tracing Image by selecting View ➪ Tracing Image ➪ Show. The Tracing Image can also be inserted directly in the Page Properties dialog box by entering its path in the Tracing Image text box or selecting the Browse button to locate the image.

Moving the Tracing Image

The Tracing Image cannot be selected and moved the same way as other objects on your page. Instead, you must move the Tracing Image using menu commands. You have several options for adjusting the Tracing Image's position to better fit your design. First, you can align the Tracing Image with any object on your page by first selecting the object and then choosing View ➪ Tracing Image ➪ Align with Selection. This lines up the upper-left corner of the Tracing Image with the upper-left corner of the bounding box of the object you've selected.

To precisely or visually move the Tracing Image to a specific location, select View ➪ Tracing Image ➪ Adjust Position. Then enter the *x* and *y* coordinates into the boxes in the Adjust Tracing Image Position dialog box, shown in Figure 15-15. For more hands-on positioning, use the arrow keys to nudge the tracing layer up, down, left, or right one pixel at a time. Holding down the Shift key while pressing the arrow keys moves the Tracing Image in five-pixel increments. Finally, you can return the Tracing Image to its default location of 9 pixels down from the top and 11 pixels in from the left by selecting View ➪ Tracing Image ➪ Reset Position.

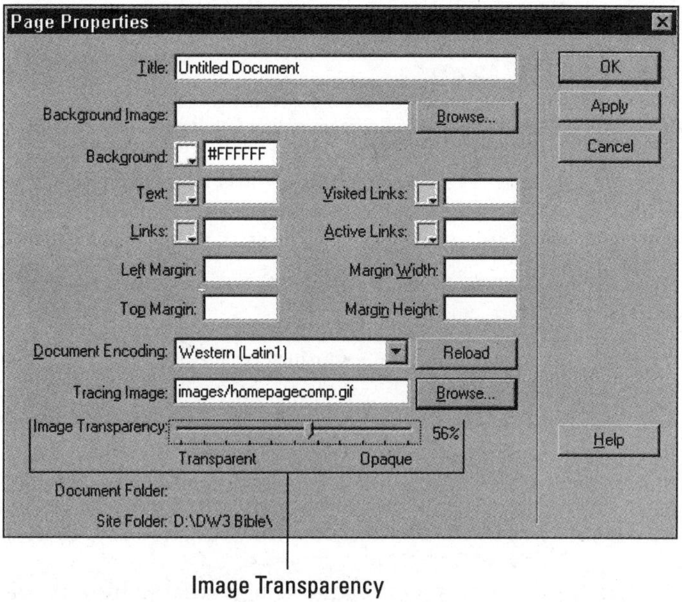

Figure 15-14: Setting the transparency of the Tracing Image to a setting such as 51 percent can help you differentiate between it and the content layers you are positioning.

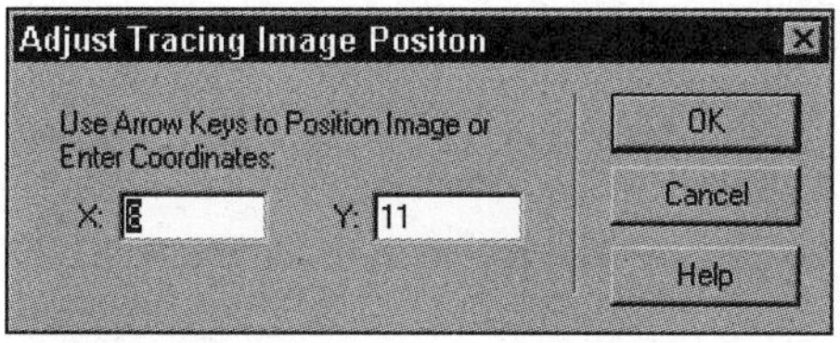

Figure 15-15: Use the Adjust Tracing Image Position dialog box to precisely place your graphic template.

Preventing overlaps

In order to place layers on your page that can later be converted to a table, the layers must not overlap. Before you begin drawing out your layers, open the Layers panel — either by selecting Windows ⇨ Layers or pressing F2 — and put a checkmark in the Prevent Overlap box at the top of the Inspector window. You can also select Modify ⇨ Arrange ⇨ Prevent Layer Overlaps to toggle overlap protection on and off.

Designing precision layouts and converting content to layers

As noted earlier, layers brought pixel-perfect positioning to the Internet. Now, Web designers can enjoy some of the layout capabilities assumed by print designers. Unfortunately, you need a 4.0 browser or better to view any page created with layers, and a portion of the Web audience is still using 3.0 or older browsers. Dreamweaver includes layers-to-tables and back again as part of its round-trip repertoire.

Web designers can freely design their page and then lock it into position for posting. Moreover, if the design needs adjustment — and all designs need adjustment — the posted page can be temporarily converted back to layers for easy repositioning. The Convert Tables to Layers and Convert Layers to Table menu commands work together terrifically and greatly enhance the designer's workflow.

The two commands are described in detail in the following sections, but let's examine a typical Dreamweaver layout session to see how they function together:

1. The Web designer is handed a comp or layout design created by another member of the company or a third-party designer.
2. After creating the graphic and type elements, the Web designer is ready to compose the page in Dreamweaver.
3. Ideally, the comp is converted to an electronic graphic format and brought into Dreamweaver as a Tracing Image.
4. If at all possible, it's best for conversion purposes not to overlap any layers, so the Web designer enables the Prevent Overlap option.
5. Each element is placed in a separate layer and placed in position, following the Tracing Image, if any.
6. With one command (Convert Layers to Table), the layout is restructured from appearing in layers to being in tables for backward browser compatibility.
7. After the client has viewed the page — and made the inevitable changes — the page is converted from tables to layers. Again, in Dreamweaver, this process is triggered by one command (Convert Tables to Layers) and takes seconds to complete.
8. The trip from tables to layers and back again is made as many times as necessary to get the layout pixel-perfect.

Convert Tables to Layers and Convert Layers to Table is a one-two combination that cuts layout time tremendously and frees the designer to create visually instead of programmatically.

Dreamweaver enables you to take any page and enclose all the contents in layers for easy design layout with drag-and-drop ease. Convert Tables to Layers is very flexible and enables the designer to convert pages previously constructed either partially or totally with tables or ones that already have layers in place. You can even quickly convert an all-text page into a layer.

Tip One valuable use for this command is to better prepare a page to use another Dreamweaver feature: Convert to 3.0 Browser Compatible. While you no longer have to have every page element in a layer to use this feature, if you use the Convert Tables to Layers command first, you get better results.

With the page open in Dreamweaver, select Modify ⇨ Convert ⇨ Tables to Layers to view the command's dialog box, shown in Figure 15-16.

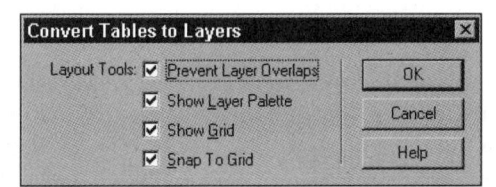

Figure 15-16: Choose the appropriate Layout Tools to help you reposition your content using layers.

By default, each of the following Layout Tools options are enabled:

- **Prevent Layer Overlaps:** You want this option turned on if you plan to convert the layers back to a table.
- **Show Layer Palette:** This automatically opens the Layers panel for you with each layer given a default name by Dreamweaver.
- **Show Grid:** This option reveals the grid overlay that can help with precision layout.
- **Snap to Grid:** With this turned on, layers snap to the nearest gridlines as they are moved onscreen.

You can uncheck any of these options before you convert the page.

Tip Turn off Show Grid and Snap to Grid if you are laying out objects on top of a Tracing Image, as they may interfere with the absolute positions that you are trying to achieve.

Converting layers to tables

To convert a Web page that has been designed with layers into a table for viewing in older browsers, simply select Modify ⇨ Convert ⇨ Layers to Table. This opens the Convert Layers to Table dialog box, shown in Figure 15-17, with the following options:

- **Most Accurate:** This creates as complex a table as is necessary to guarantee that the elements on your Web page appear in the exact locations that you've specified. This is the default setting.

- **Smallest:** Collapse empty cells less than *n* pixels wide: Selecting this option simplifies your table layouts by joining cells that are less than the number of pixels wide that you specify. This may result in a table that takes less time to load; however, it also means that the elements on your page may not appear in the precise locations where you've placed them.

- **Use Transparent GIFs:** When you select this option, Dreamweaver fills all empty cells with a transparent spacer graphic to ensure that the table looks the same across a variety of browsers. When Dreamweaver creates the table layout, it places a file called transparent.gif in the same folder as your Web page. You must make sure to include this file when you upload your page to your server in order for it to display correctly.

- **Center on Page:** Selecting this option puts `<div align=center>` tags around your table so that it displays in the middle of a browser window. Deselecting this option leaves out those tags so that the table starts from its default position in the upper-left corner of a browser.

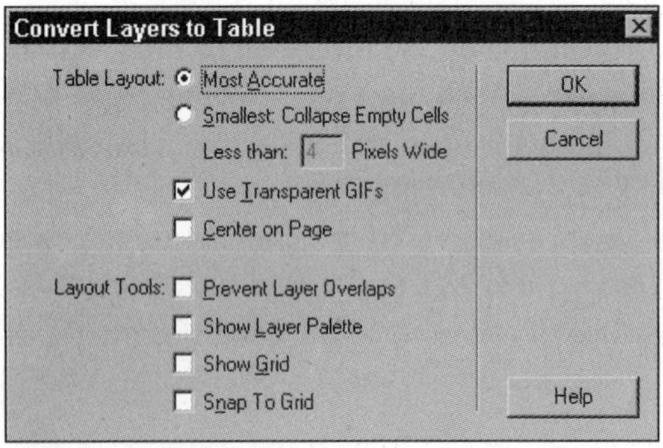

Figure 15-17: Check off the right Layout Tools options to help reposition your content as a table.

Once you have converted your layout into a table, as shown in Figure 15-18, you should preview it in your browser. If you aren't happy with the way your layout looks, or if you wish to do further modifications, you can convert the table back into layers by selecting Modify ⇨ Convert ⇨ Tables to Layers as described previously, selecting the layers to drag and drop the contents into new positions. Finally, transform your layout back into a table and preview it again.

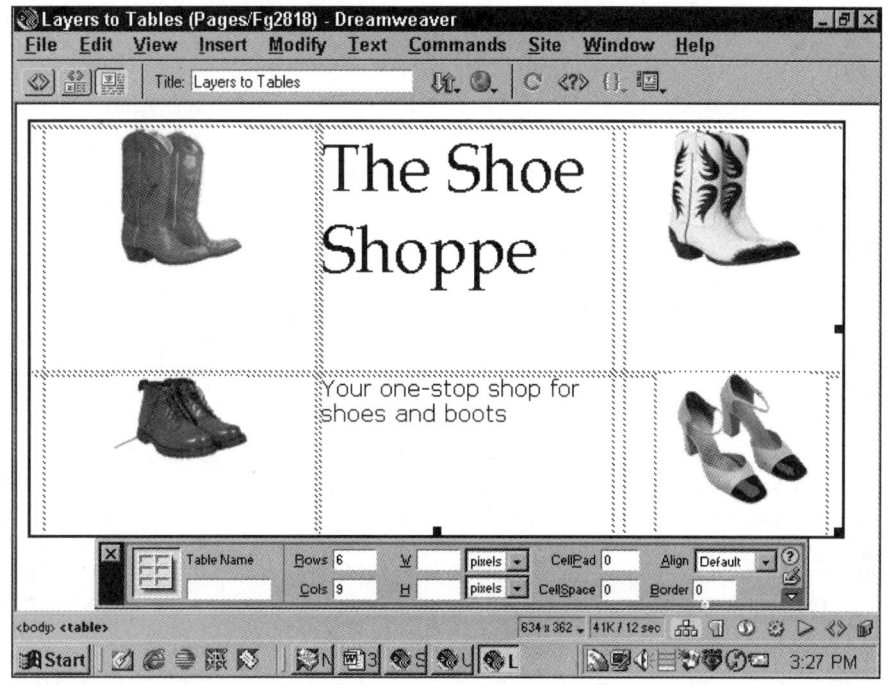

Figure 15-18: The results of transforming layers into a table, using the default settings.

> **Tip** It's worth pointing out that the two Modify ⇨ Convert commands can be easily reversed by choosing Edit ⇨ Undo, whereas the effectively similar File ⇨ Convert ⇨ 3.0 Browser Compatible command cannot.

Activating Layers with Behaviors

While absolute positioning is a major reason to use layers, you may have other motives for using this capability. All the properties of a layer — the coordinates, size and shape, depth, visibility, and clipping — can be altered dynamically and interactively as well. Normally, dynamically resetting a layer's properties entails some fairly daunting JavaScript programming. Now, with one of Dreamweaver's hallmarks — those illustrious behaviors — activating layers is possible for nonprogrammers as well.

> **Cross-Reference** In case you missed it, Chapter 11 describes Dreamweaver's rich behaviors feature.

Behaviors consist of two parts, the event and the action. In Dreamweaver, three standard actions are designed specifically for working with layers:

- **Drag Layer:** Enables the user to move the layer and get a response to that movement.
- **Set Text of Layer:** Interactively alter the content of any layer to include any HTML, not just text.
- **Show-Hide Layers:** Controls the visibility of layers, either interactively or through some preprogrammed action on the page.

You can find detailed information about these actions in their respective sections in Chapter 19. The following sections outline how to use these behaviors to activate your layers.

> **Note** Netscape 6 was released just before Dreamweaver 4; consequently some of the layer-oriented behaviors do not work properly with that version of Netscape's browser. As of this writing, there are third-party replacements for the Drag Layer behavior, written by Jaro von Flocken; and the Set Text of Layer and Show-Hide Layers behavior, both contributed by Al Sparber of Project VII. You can find these extensions on the CD-ROM that accompanies this book or on the Macromedia Exchange.

Drag Layer

For the Web designer, positioning a layer is easy: click the selection handle and drag the layer to a new location. For the readers of your pages, moving a layer is next to impossible — unless you incorporate the Drag Layer action into the page's design.

With the Drag Layer action, you can set up interactive pages in which the user can rearrange elements of the design to achieve an effect or make a selection. Drag Layer includes an option that enables you to execute a JavaScript command if the user drops the layer on a specific target. In the example shown in Figure 15-19, each pair of shoes is in its own layer. When the user drops a pair in the bag, a one-line JavaScript command opens the desired catalog page and order form.

After you've created all your layers, you're ready to attach the behavior. Because Drag Layer initializes the script to make the interaction possible, you should always associate this behavior with the `<body>` tag and the `onLoad` event.

Follow these steps to use the Drag Layer action, and to designate the settings for the drag operation:

1. Choose the `<body>` tag from the Tag Selector in the status bar.
2. Choose Window ⇨ Behaviors or select the Show Behaviors button from either Launcher. The Behaviors panel opens.

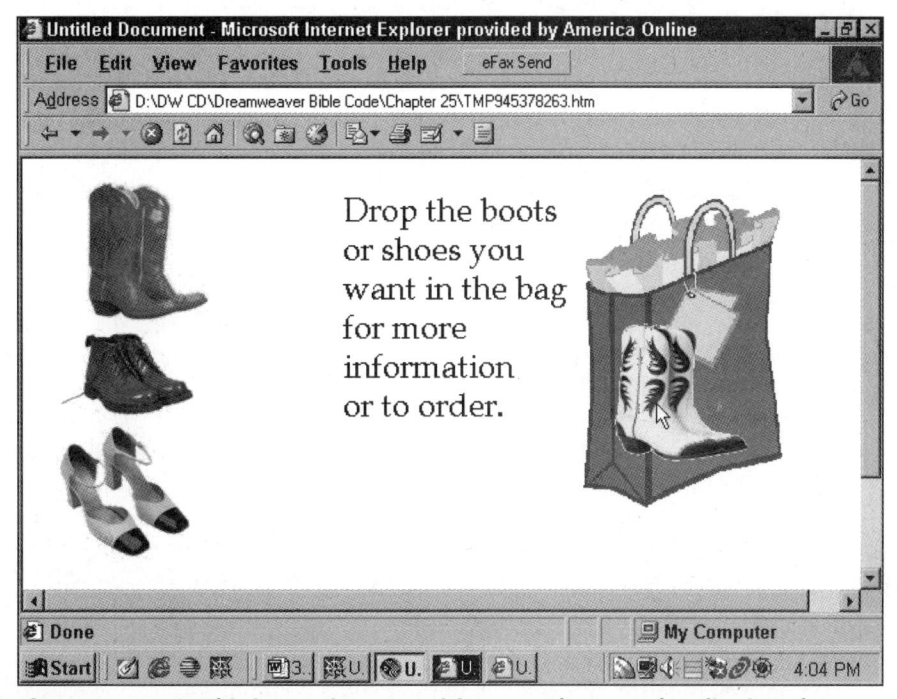

Figure 15-19: On this interactive page, visitors can drop merchandise into the shopping bag; this feature is made possible with the Drag Layer action.

3. In the Behaviors panel, make sure that 4.0 and Later Browsers is displayed in the Show Events For Submenu of the Add Behavior pop-up menu.

4. Click the + (add) action button and choose Drag Layer from the Add Behavior pop-up menu.

5. In the Drag Layer dialog box, select the layer you want to make available for dragging.

6. To limit the movement of the dragged layer, select Constrained from the Movement drop-down list. Then enter the coordinates to specify the direction to which you want to limit the movement in the Up, Down, Left, and/or Right text boxes.

7. To establish a location for a target, enter coordinates in the Drop Target: Left and Top text boxes. You can fill these text boxes with the selected layer's present location by clicking the Get Current Position button.

8. You can also set a snap-to area around the target's coordinates. When released in the target's location, the dragged layer snaps to this area. Enter a pixel value in the Snap if Within text box.

9. Click the Advanced tab.
10. Designate the drag handle:
    - To enable the whole layer to act as a drag handle, select Entire Layer from the drop-down menu.
    - If you want to limit the area to be used as a drag handle, select Area within Layer from the drop-down menu. Enter the Left and Top coordinates as well as the Width and Height dimensions in the appropriate text boxes.
11. If you want to keep the layer in its current depth and not bring it to the front, deselect the checkbox for While Dragging: Bring Layer to the Front. To change the stacking order of the layer when it is released after dragging, select either Leave on Top or Restore z-index from the drop-down list.
12. To execute a JavaScript command when the layer is dropped on the target, enter the code in the Call JavaScript text box. If you want the script to execute every time the layer is dropped, enter the code in the When Dropped: Call JavaScript text box. If the code should execute only when the layer is dropped on the target, make sure there's a check in the Only if Snapped checkbox.
13. Click OK.
14. To change the event that triggers the action (the default is `onLoad`), select an event from the drop-down menu in the Events column.

Set Text of Layer

We've seen how layers can dynamically move, change their visibility, and their depth — but did you know that you could also change a layer's *content* dynamically? With Dreamweaver, you can do it easily. A standard behavior, Set Text of Layer, enables you to swap the entire contents of one layer for whatever you'd like. You're not limited to exchanging just text either. Anything you can put into HTML, you can swap — which, is pretty much everything!

This behavior is extremely useful for putting up context-sensitive help and other information. Rather than construct a series of layers which you show and hide, a single layer is used, and just the contents change. To use Set Text of Layer, follow these steps:

1. Insert and name your layers as desired.
2. Select the graphic, button, or text link you'd like to act as the trigger for your changing the content of the layer.
3. Choose Window ⇨ Behaviors or select the Show Behaviors button from either Launcher to open the Behaviors panel.
4. Choose Set Text ⇨ Set Text of Layer from the + (add) action pop-up menu.

    The dialog box (see Figure 15-20) shows a list of the available layers in the current Web page as well as providing a space for the new content.

Targeted JavaScript Commands

The following simple yet useful JavaScript commands can be entered in the Snap JavaScript text box of the Drag Layer dialog box:

- To display a brief message to the user after the layer is dropped, use the `alert()` function:

    ```
    alert("You hit the target")
    ```

- To send the user to another Web page when the layer is dropped in the right location, use the JavaScript location object:

    ```
    location = "http://www.yourdomain.com/yourpage.html"
    ```

The location object can also be used with relative URLs.

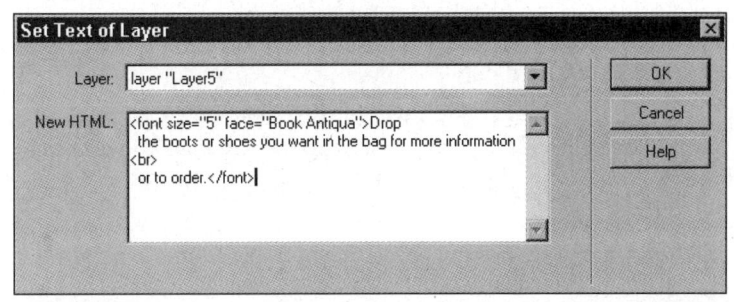

Figure 15-20: Swap out all the contents of a layer using the Set Text of Layer behavior.

5. Select the layer you want to alter from the Layer option list.
6. Enter the text or code in the New HTML text area.

    You can enter either plain text, which is rendered in the default paragraph style, or any amount of HTML code, including <img>, <table>, or other tags.

    Tip: If you're entering a large amount of HTML, don't bother doing so by hand — Dreamweaver can do it for you. On a blank page, create your HTML content and then select and copy it. Then, in the Set Text of Layer dialog box, paste the code using Ctrl+V (Command+V).

7. Click OK when you're done.

If you want several layers to change when a single event is triggered, just add more Set Text of Layer behaviors to the same object.

Note: You may need to change the behavior event from its default; to do so select the down arrow in between the Event and Action columns on the Behaviors panel and choose a new event from the list.

Show-Hide Layers

The capability to implement interactive control of a layer's visibility offers tremendous potential to the Web designer. The Show-Hide Layers action makes this implementation straightforward and simple to set up. With the Show-Hide Layers action, you can simultaneously show one or more layers while hiding as many other layers as necessary. Create your layers and give them a unique name before invoking the Show-Hide Layers action.

To use Show-Hide Layers, follow these steps:

1. Select an image, link, or other HTML tag to which to attach the behavior.

2. Choose Window ⇨ Behaviors or select the Show Behaviors button from either Launcher to open the Behaviors panel.

3. Choose Show-Hide Layers from the + (add) action pop-up menu. The parameters form (see Figure 15-21) shows a list of the available layers in the open Web page.

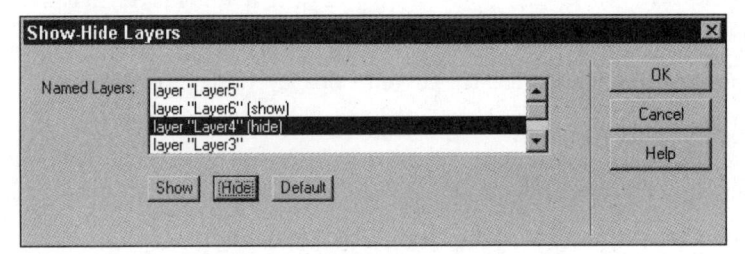

Figure 15-21: With the Show-Hide Layers behavior attached, you can easily program the visibility of all the layers in your Web page.

4. To cause a hidden layer to be revealed when this event is fired, select the layer from the list and click the Show button.

5. To hide a visible layer when this event is fired, select its name from the list and click the Hide button.

6. To restore a layer's default visibility value when this event is fired, select the layer and click the Default button.

7. Click OK when you are done.

8. If the default event is not suitable, use the drop-down menu in the Events column to select a different one.

Dreamweaver Technique: Creating a Loading Layer

As Web creations become more complex, most designers want their layers to zip on and off screen or appear and disappear as quickly as possible for the viewer of the page. A layer can act only when it has finished loading its content — the text and images. Rather than have the user see each layer loading in, some designers use a loading layer to mask the process until everything is downloaded and ready to go.

A loading layer is fairly easy to create. Dreamweaver supplies all the JavaScript necessary in one behavior, Show-Hide Layers. Keep in mind that because this technique uses layers, it's good only for 4.0 browsers and above. Use the following steps to create a loading layer:

1. Create all of your layers with the contents in place and the visibility property set as normal.
2. Create the loading layer. (Choose Insert ⇨ Layer or select the Draw Layer button from the Objects panel.)
3. Enter and position whatever contents you want displayed in the loading layer while all the other layers are loading.
4. Open the Layers panel (F2).
5. Turn off the visibility for all layers except the loading layer. In essence, you're hiding every other layer.
6. Select the `<body>` tag from the Tag Selector.
7. Choose Window ⇨ Behaviors or select Show Behaviors from either Launcher to open the Behaviors panel.
8. Select the + (add) action button and choose Show-Hide Layers from the pop-up menu.
9. In the Show-Hide Layers dialog box, select the loading layer and then click the Hide button.
10. Select all the other layers and set them to Show. Click OK when you are done.
11. Leave `onLoad` (the default) as the event to trigger this action.

Now, when you test your Web page, you should see only your loading layer until everything else is loaded, then the loading layer disappears, and all the other layers are made visible.

Note A loading layer may be the last bastion of the `<blink>` tag. Created by Netscape fairly early in the history of the Web, the `<blink>...</blink>` tag pair was grossly overused and is today generally shunned. However, if you apply it (by switching to Code view, using the Code Inspector or through the Quick Tag Editor) just to the ellipse following the term "Loading..." like this:

```
<h2>Loading<blink>...</blink></h2>
```
you get a small bit of movement on the page, similar to a blinking cursor. Only Netscape Navigator supports the `<blink>` tag. You could also use an animated GIF to create the pulsing image for a cross-browser effect.

Summary

Layers are effective placement tools for developing the layout of a page. Anyone used to designing with desktop publishing tools can quickly learn to work layers effectively. The following points will help guide your way:

- Layers are visible only on fourth-generation and above browsers.
- Layers can be used to place HTML content anywhere on a Web page.
- You can stack layers on top of one another. This depth control is referred to as the *stacking order* or the *z-index*.
- Dreamweaver can convert layers to tables for viewing in earlier browsers, and back again for straightforward repositioning.
- Layers can be constructed so that the end user can display or hide them interactively, or alter their position, size, and depth dynamically.
- Dreamweaver gives you rulers and grids to help with layer placement and alignment.
- Layers can easily be activated by using Dreamweaver's built-in JavaScript behaviors.

In the next chapter, you learn how to develop timelines, which enable layers and their contents to move around the Web page.

✦ ✦ ✦

Working with Timelines

CHAPTER 16

In This Chapter

Adding animation with Dreamweaver timelines

Using the Timelines panel

Incorporating timelines

Automatically starting and looping a timeline

Altering timelines with keyframes

Putting behaviors into timelines

Dreamweaver technique: Creating a multiscreen slideshow

Motion implies time. A static object, such as an ordinary HTML Web page, can exist either in a single moment or over a period of time. Conversely, moving objects (such as Dynamic HTML layers flying across the screen) need a few seconds to complete their path. All of Dreamweaver's Dynamic HTML animation effects use the Timeline feature to manage this conjunction of movement and time.

Timelines can do much more than move a layer across a Web page, however. A timeline can coordinate an entire presentation: starting the background music, scrolling the opening credits, and cueing the voice-over narration on top of a slideshow. These actions are all possible with Dreamweaver because, in addition to controlling a layer's position, timelines can also trigger any of Dreamweaver's JavaScript behaviors on a specific frame.

This chapter explores the full and varied world of timelines. After an introductory section brings you up to speed on the underlying concepts of timelines, you learn how to insert and modify timelines to achieve cutting-edge effects. A Dreamweaver Technique shows you, step by step, how to create a multiscreen slideshow complete with fly-in and fly-out graphics. From complex multilayer animations to slideshow presentations, you can do it all with Dreamweaver timelines.

Cross-Reference Because timelines are so intricately intertwined with behaviors and layers, you need to have a good grasp of these concepts. Before examining the topic of timelines, make sure to read Chapter 11 and Chapter 15.

Entering the Fourth Dimension with Timelines

Web designers in the early days had little control over the fourth dimension and their Web pages. Only animated GIFs, Java, or animation programs such as Macromedia's Flash could create the illusion of motion events. Unfortunately, all of these technologies have some limitations.

The general problem with animated GIF images is related to file size. An animated GIF starts out as an image for every frame. Therefore, if you incorporate a three-second, 15-frames-per-second animation, you are asking the user to download the compressed equivalent of 45 separate images. Even though an animated GIF is an index color file with a limited 256 colors and uses the format's built-in compression, the GIF file is still a relatively large graphic file. Moreover, for all their apparent animated qualities, GIFs enable no true interaction other than as a link to another URL. Animations created with Dynamic HTML and Dreamweaver's timelines, on the other hand, do not significantly increase the overall size of the Web page and are completely interactive. DHTML is not the only low-bandwidth approach to animations with interactive content for the Web. You can create animations, complete with user-driven interactions, with Java — as long as you're a Java programmer. Certainly Java development tools are making the language easier to use, but you still must deal with the rather long load time of any Java applet and the increasing variety of Java versions. As another option, Macromedia Director movies can be compressed or "shocked" to provide animation and interactivity in your pages. As with Java, the Director approach requires a bit of a learning curve. Shockwave movies can also have long load times and require the user to have a plug-in application.

Macromedia's Flash might be the best alternative to GIF images, even though Flash has its own set of caveats to keep in mind. On the plus side, Flash files are small and can be streamed through their own player. This arrangement is tempting, and if you just want animation on a page, Flash is probably a superior choice to any of the approaches previously described. On the minus side, Flash is limited to its own proprietary features and functions, and every user must have the Flash plug-in or ActiveX control installed — although Flash player is rapidly becoming ubiquitous, making this point moot. However, you cannot layer Flash animation on top of other layers on a page. Moreover, once you, or another designer, have created a Flash animation, the animation must be edited with the same animation package.

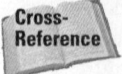

Cross-Reference See Chapter 13 for a discussion of Flash.

Timeline capabilities

Dreamweaver timelines are part of the HTML code. For the movement of one layer straight across a Web page, Dreamweaver generates about 70 lines of code devoted to initializing and playing the timeline. But just what is a timeline? A timeline is composed of a series of frames. A frame is a snapshot of what the Web page, more specifically, the objects on the timeline, look like at a particular moment. You probably know that a movie is made up of a series of still pictures; when viewed quickly, the pictures create the illusion of movement. Each individual picture is a frame; movies show 24 frames per second, and video uses about 30 frames per second. Web animation, on the other hand, generally displays about 15 frames per second (fps). Not surprisingly, Dreamweaver's timeline is similar to the one used in Macromedia's timeline-based, multimedia authoring tool and animation package, Director.

If you have to draw each frame of a 30-second animation, even at 15 fps, you won't have time for other work. Dreamweaver uses the concept of *keyframes* to make a simple layer movement workable. Each keyframe contains a change in the timeline object's properties, such as position. For example, let's say you want your layer to start at the upper left (represented by the coordinates 0,0) and travel to the lower right (at 750,550). To accomplish this task, you need only specify the layer's position for the two keyframes — the start and the finish — and Dreamweaver generates all the frames in between.

Timelines have the following three primary roles:

- ✦ A timeline can alter a layer's position, dimensions, visibility, and depth.
- ✦ Timelines can change the source for any image on a Web page and cause another graphic of the same height and width to appear in the same location.
- ✦ Any of Dreamweaver's JavaScript behaviors can be triggered on any frame of a timeline.

A few ground rules

Keep the following basic guidelines in mind when you're using timelines in the Web pages you create with Dreamweaver:

- ✦ Timelines require a 4.0 or later browser.
- ✦ For a timeline to be able to animate an object, such as text, the object must be within a layer. If you try to create a timeline with an element that is not in a layer, Dreamweaver warns you and prevents you from adding the object to the timeline.
- ✦ Events don't have to start on the beginning of a timeline. If you want to have an action begin five seconds after a page has loaded, you can set the behavior on frame 60 of the timeline, with a frame rate of 15 frames per second.
- ✦ The selected frame rate is a "best-case scenario" because the actual frame rate depends on the user's system. A slower system or one that is simultaneously running numerous other programs can easily degrade the frame rate.

♦ You can include multiple animations on one timeline. The only restriction? You can't have two animations affecting the same layer at the same time. Dreamweaver prevents you from making this error.

♦ You can have multiple timelines that animate different layers simultaneously or the same layer at different times. Although you can set two or more timelines to animate the same layer at the same time, the results are difficult to predict and generally unintended.

Creating Animations with Timelines

Dreamweaver provides an excellent tool for managing timelines — the Timelines panel. Open this tool by choosing Window ⇨ Timelines or using the keyboard shortcut Shift+F9.

The Timelines panel uses VCR-style controls combined with a playback head, which is a visual representation showing which frame is the current one. As shown in Figure 16-1, the Timelines panel gives you full control over any of the timeline functions.

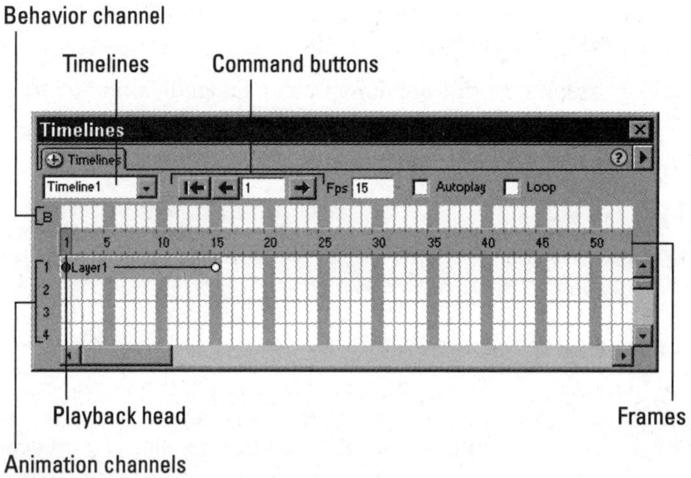

Figure 16-1: Dreamweaver's Timelines panel enables you to quickly and easily master animation control.

The Timelines panel has four major areas:

♦ **Timeline Controls:** Includes the Timeline pop-up menu for selecting the current timeline; the Rewind, Back, and Play buttons; the Fps (frame rate) text box; and the Autoplay and Loop checkboxes.

✦ **Behavior Channel:** Shows the placement of any behaviors attached to specific frames of the timeline.

 ✦ **Frames:** Displays the frame numbers for all timelines and the playback head showing the current frame number.

 ✦ **Animation Channels:** Represents the animations for any included layers and images.

Adding Layers to the Timelines Panel

As with many of Dreamweaver's functions, you can add a layer or an image to the Timelines panel in more than one way. You can either insert a layer into a timeline through the menus (Modify ⇨ Timeline ⇨ Add Object to Timeline), or you can drag and drop an object into a timeline or use the keyboard shortcut, Ctrl+Alt+Shift+T (Command+Option+Shift+T). The default timeline is set at a frame rate of 15 fps. When you add an object to a timeline, Dreamweaver inserts an animation bar of 15 frames in length, labeled with the object's name. The animation bar shows the duration (the number of frames) for the timeline's effect on the object. An animation bar is initially created with two initial keyframes: the start and the end.

To add a layer or image to the Timelines panel through the menus, follow these steps:

1. Choose Window ⇨ Timelines or use the keyboard shortcut, Shift+F9, to open the Timelines panel.

2. In the Document window, select the layer or image you want to add to the timeline.

3. Choose Modify ⇨ Timeline ⇨ Add Object to Timeline. An animation bar appears in the first frame of the timeline, as shown in Figure 16-2.

4. To add another object, repeat Steps 2 and 3. Each additional animation bar is inserted beneath the preceding bar.

Tip The first time you add an image or layer to the Timelines panel, Dreamweaver displays an alert message that details the limitations of timelines. If you don't want to see this alert, turn it off by checking the Don't Show Me This Message Again checkbox.

As previously noted, you can add as many objects to a timeline as you desire. If necessary, increase the size of the Timelines panel by dragging any border of its window.

You have a little more flexibility when you add an object by dragging it into the timeline. Instead of the animation bar always beginning at frame one, you may drop the object in to begin on any frame. This approach is useful, especially if you are putting more than one object into the same animation channel.

498 Part I ✦ **Working with Dreamweaver**

Animation bar

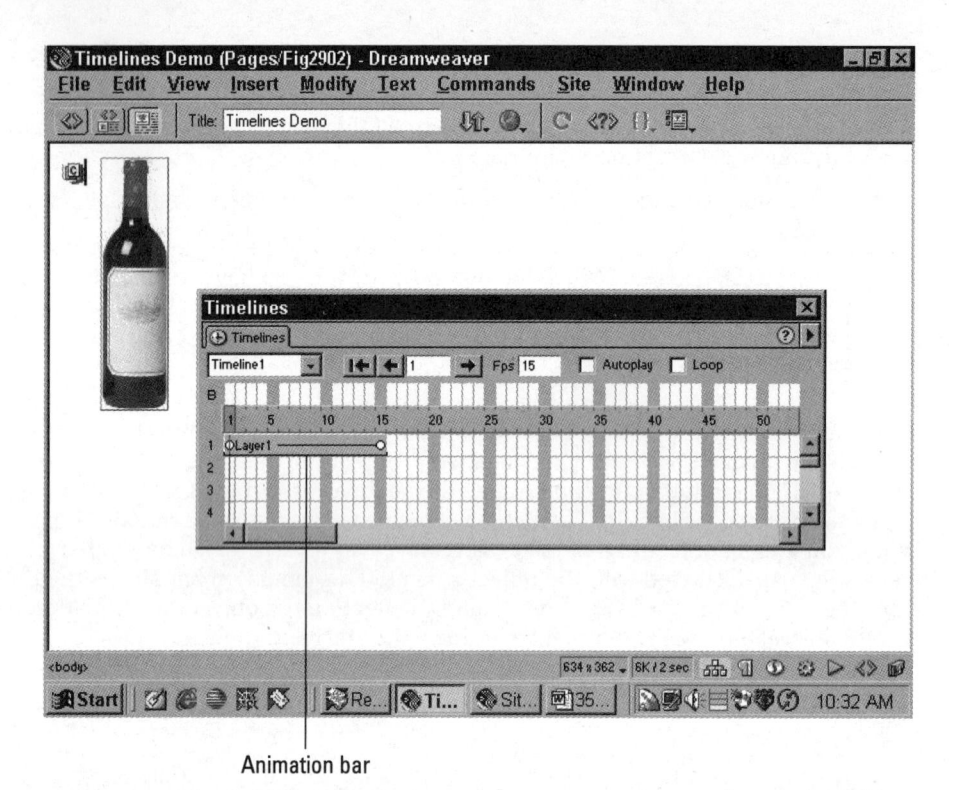

Figure 16-2: The default animation bar is set at 15 frames but can be easily modified.

To place an object in a timeline with the drag-and-drop method, follow these steps:

1. Open the Timelines panel by choosing Window ➪ Timelines or using the keyboard shortcut, Shift+F9.

2. In the Document window, select the object—layer or image—you want to add to the timeline and drag it to the Timelines panel. As soon as the object is over the Timelines panel, a 15-frame animation bar appears.

3. Holding the mouse button down, position the animation bar so that the animation begins in the desired frame. Release the mouse button to drop the object into the timeline.

Note Your placement does not have to be exact; you can modify it later.

Placing a layer or image on a timeline is just the beginning. To begin using your timeline in depth, you have to make changes to the object for the keyframes and customize the timeline.

Modifying a Timeline

When you add an object — either an image or a layer — to a timeline, notice that the animation bar has an open circle at its beginning and end. An open circle marks a keyframe. As previously explained, the designer specifies a change in the state of the timeline object in a keyframe. For example, when you first insert a layer, the two generated keyframes have identical properties — the layer's position, size, visibility, and depth are unchanged. For any animation to occur, you have to change one of the layer's properties for one of the keyframes.

For example, let's move a layer quickly across the screen. Follow these steps:

1. Create a layer. If you like, add an image or a background color so that the layer is more noticeable.
2. Open the Timelines panel.
3. Drag the layer into the Timelines panel and release the mouse button.
4. Select the ending keyframe of the layer's animation bar.

   The playback head moves to the new frame.

5. In the Document window, grab the layer's selection handle and drag the layer to a new location. A thin line connects the starting position of the layer to the ending position, as shown in Figure 16-3. This line is the animation path.
6. To play your animation, first click the Rewind button in the Timelines panel and then click and hold down the Play button.

If you want to change the beginning position of your layer's movement, select the starting keyframe and then move the layer in the Document window. To alter the final position of your layer's movement, select the ending keyframe and then move the layer.

> **Tip** For more precise control of your layer's position in a timeline, select a keyframe and then, in the layer's Property Inspector, change the Left and/or Top values. You can also select the layer and use the arrow keys to move it.

Altering the animation bars

A Web designer can easily stretch or alter the range of frames occupied by a layer or image in an animation bar. You can make an animation longer or smoother, or have it start at an entirely different time. You can also move the layer to a different animation channel so it runs before or after another animation.

Use the mouse to drag an animation bar around the timeline. Click any part of the bar except on the keyframe indicators and move it as needed. To change the length of an animation, select the first or final keyframe and drag it forward or backward to a new frame.

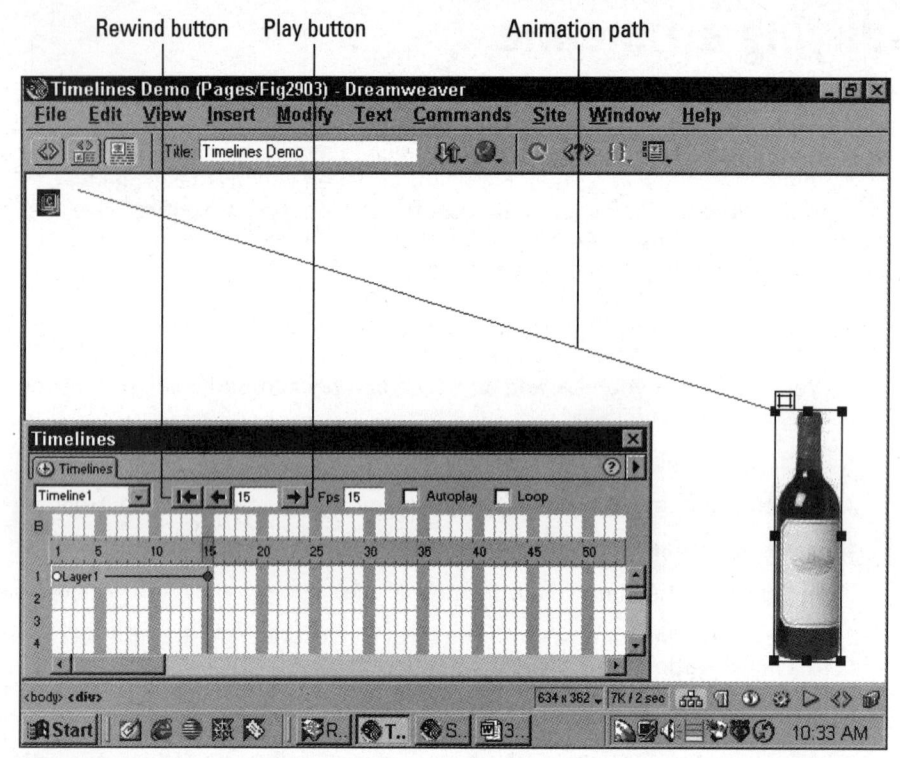

Figure 16-3: When you move a layer on a timeline, Dreamweaver displays an animation path.

You can remove an animation bar in two ways: select it and press Delete, or choose Modify ⇨ Timeline ⇨ Remove Object.

Using the Timeline controls

As you probably noticed if you worked through the example in the preceding section, you don't have to use a browser to preview a timeline. The Timeline controls shown in Figure 16-4 enable you to fine-tune your animations before you view them through a browser.

At the top-left corner is the Timeline pop-up menu, which is used to indicate the current timeline. By default, every new timeline is given the name Timeline*n*, where *n* indicates how many timelines have been created. You can rename the timeline by selecting it and typing in the new name. As you accumulate and use more timelines, you should give them recognizable names.

Tip: If you change the timeline name, you must enter a one-word name using alphanumeric characters that always begin with a letter. Netscape Navigator 4.*x* cannot read spaces or special characters in JavaScript.

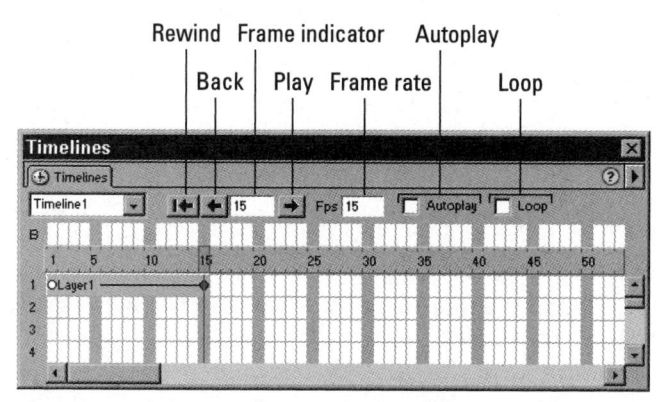

Figure 16-4: The Timeline controls enable you to move back and forth in your timeline, easily and precisely.

The next three buttons in the control bar enable you to move through the frames of a timeline. From left to right:

- ✦ **Rewind:** Moves the playback head to the first frame of the current timeline.
- ✦ **Back:** Moves the playback head to the previous frame. You can hold down the Back button to play the timeline in reverse.
- ✦ **Play:** Moves the timeline forward one frame at a time; hold down the Play button to play the timeline normally. When the last frame is reached, the playback head moves to the first frame of the current timeline and continues playing it.

The field between the Back and Play buttons is the frame indicator text box. To jump to any specific frame, enter the frame number in this box.

The next item in the control bar is the Fps (frames per second) text box. To change the frame rate, enter a new value in the Fps text box and press Tab or Enter (Return). The frame rate you set is an ideal number that a user's browser attempts to reach. The default rate of 15 frames per second is a good balance for both Macintosh and Windows systems.

> **Tip** Because browsers play every frame regardless of the frame rate setting, increasing the frame rate does not necessarily make your animations smoother. A better method for creating smooth animations is to drag the end keyframe farther out and therefore increase the number of frames used by your animation.

The next two checkboxes, Autoplay and Loop, affect how the animation is played.

Autoplay

If you mark the Autoplay checkbox, the current timeline begins playing as soon as the Web page is fully downloaded. Dreamweaver alerts you to this arrangement by telling you that the Play Timeline action is attached to an `onLoad` event. Autoplay is achieved by inserting code into the `<body>` tag that looks similar to the following:

```
<body bgcolor="#FFFFFF" onload="MM_timelinePlay('timeline1')">
```

Caution: If you don't use the Autoplay feature, you must attach the Play Timeline action to another event and tag, such as an `onMouseClick` event and a button graphic. Otherwise, the timeline does not play.

Looping

Mark the Loop checkbox if you want an animation to repeat once it has reached the final frame. When Loop is enabled, the default setting causes the layer to replay itself an infinite numbers of times; however, you can change this setting.

When you first enable the Loop checkbox, Dreamweaver alerts you that it is placing a Go to Frame action after the last frame of your current timeline. To set the number of repetitions for a timeline, follow these steps:

1. In the Timelines panel, check the Loop checkbox.
2. Dreamweaver displays an alert informing you that the Go to Timeline Frame action is being added one frame past your current final frame. To disable these alerts, select the Don't Show Me This Message Again option.
3. In the Behavior channel (above the Frame numbers and playback head), double-click the behavior you just added.

Note: When you first add a behavior to a timeline, Dreamweaver presents a dialog box reminding you how to perform this action. Select the Don't Show Me This Message Again option when you've mastered the technique.

The Behaviors panel opens, with an `onFrame` event in the Events column and a Go To Timeline Frame action showing in the Actions column.

4. Double-click the `onFrame` event. The Go to Timeline Frame dialog box opens (see Figure 16-5).
5. Enter a positive number in the Loop text box to set the number of times you want your timeline to repeat. To keep the animation repeating continuously, leave the Loop text box blank.
6. Click OK when you are finished.

Tip: Your animations don't have to loop back to the beginning each time. By entering a different frame number in the Go to Frame text box of the Go to Timeline Frame dialog box, you can repeat just a segment of the animation.

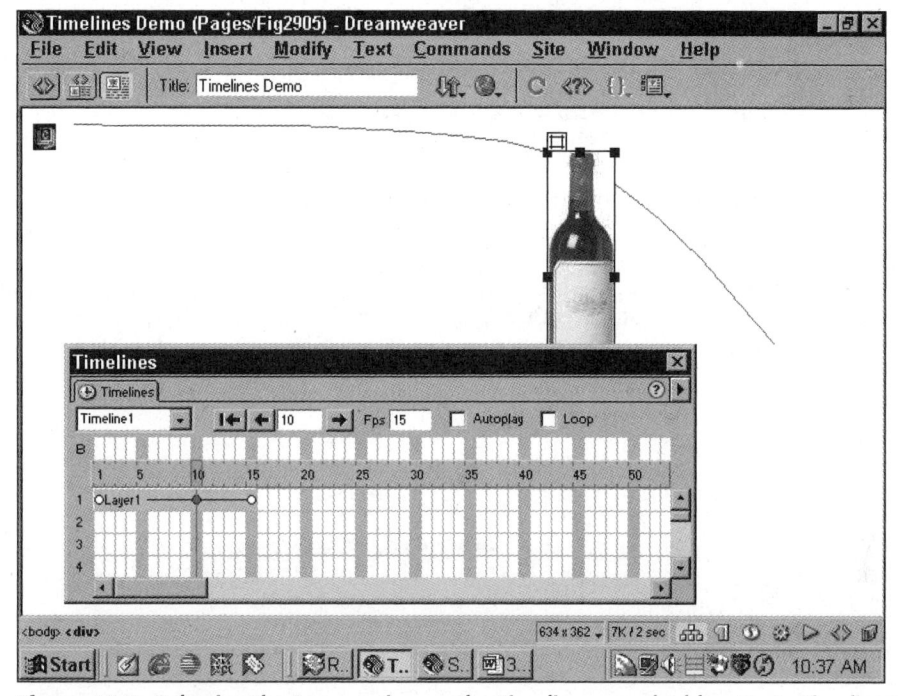

Figure 16-5: Selecting the Loop option on the Timelines panel adds a Go to Timeline Frame action, which you can customize.

Adding keyframes

Animating a timeline can go far beyond moving your layer from point A to point B. Layers (and the content within them) can dip, swirl, zigzag, and generally move in any fashion — all made possible by keyframes in which you have entered some change for the object. Dreamweaver calculates the differences between each keyframe, whether the change is in a layer's position or size. Each timeline starts with two keyframes, the beginning and the end; you have to add other keyframes before you can insert the desired changes.

You can add a keyframe to your established timeline in a couple of different ways. The first method uses the Add Keyframe command, and the second method uses the mouse to click a keyframe into place.

Adding keyframes with the Add Keyframe command

To add a keyframe with the Add Keyframe command, follow these steps:

1. In the Timelines panel, select the animation bar for the object with which you are working.

2. Select the frame in which you want to add a keyframe.

3. Add your keyframe by either of the following methods:

   a. Choose Modify ⇨ Timeline ⇨ Add Keyframe.

   b. Right-click (Control+click) the frame in the animation bar and, from the shortcut menu, choose Add Keyframe.

A new keyframe is added on the selected frame, signified by the open circle in the animation bar.

While your new keyframe is selected, you can alter the layer's position, size, visibility, or depth. For example, if your animation involves moving a layer across the screen, you can drag the layer to a new position while the new keyframe is selected. The animation path is redrawn to incorporate this new position, as illustrated in Figure 16-6.

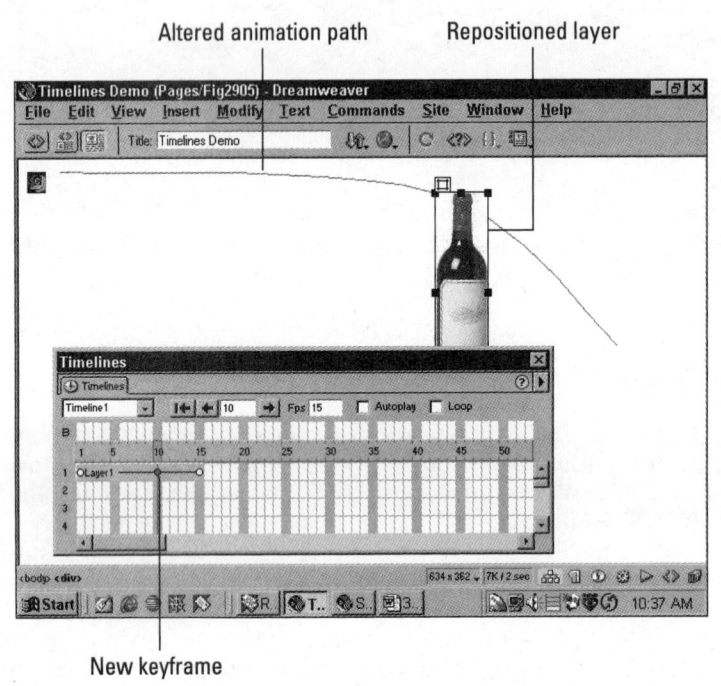

Figure 16-6: Repositioning a layer while a keyframe is selected can redirect your animation path.

Adding a keyframe with the mouse

The second method for adding a keyframe is quicker. To add a keyframe using the mouse, simply hold down the Ctrl (Command) key. Then click anywhere in the animation bar to add a keyframe. Your cursor turns into a small open circle when it is over the Timeline window to show that it is ready to add a new keyframe.

What if you want to move the keyframe? Simply click and drag the keyframe to a new frame, sliding it along the animation bar in the Timelines panel.

> **Tip** If, after plotting out an elaborate animation with a layer, you discover that you need to shift the entire animation — say, six pixels to the right — you don't have to redo all your work. Just select the animation bar in the Timelines panel and then, in the Document window, move the layer in question. Dreamweaver shifts the entire animation to your new location.

Removing timeline elements

The easiest way to remove an object, keyframe, or behavior from the Timelines panel is to select the element and press Delete. You cannot use this technique to delete individual frames or entire timelines, however. For these situations, you must use the menus as follows:

✦ To remove the whole timeline, choose Modify ➪ Timeline ➪ Remove Timeline.

✦ To remove an individual frame, choose Modify ➪ Timeline ➪ Remove Frame.

The Timelines panel's shortcut menu also contains all the removal commands. Right-click (Control+click) the Timelines panel anywhere below the control bar and, in the shortcut menu (see Figure 16-7), choose the removal command you need: Remove Keyframe, Remove Behavior, Remove Object, Remove Frame, or Remove Timeline.

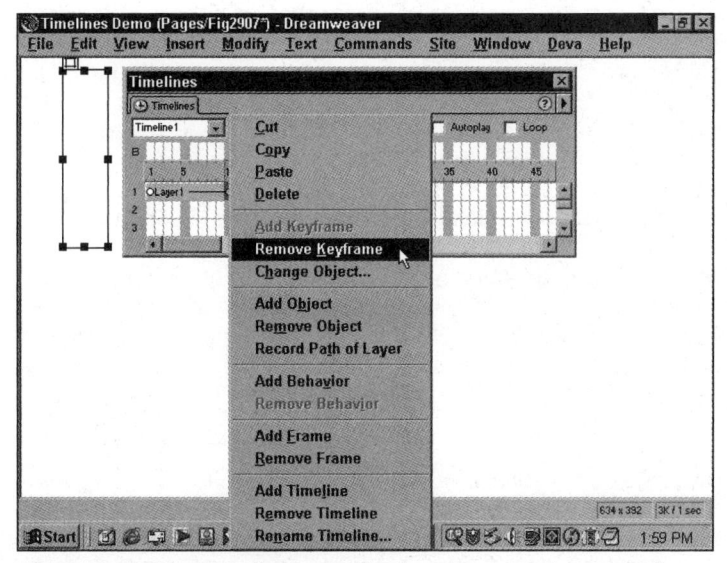

Figure 16-7: The Timelines panel's shortcut menu is extremely handy for doing quick edits.

You can also Cut, Copy and Paste Timelines between documents. The Delete command in the shortcut menu is the same as Remove Timeline.

Changing animation speed

You can alter your Dynamic HTML animation speed with two different methods that can be used separately or together.

- ✦ Drag the final keyframe in the animation bar out to cover additional frames, or back to cover fewer frames. Any keyframes within the animation bar are kept proportional to their original settings. This method works well when altering the speed of an individual animation bar.

- ✦ Change the frames per second value in the Fps text box of the Timelines panel. Increasing the number of frames per second accelerates the animation, and vice versa. Adjusting the Fps value affects every layer contained within the timeline; you cannot use this method for individual layers.

Caution: Browsers play every frame of a Dynamic HTML animation, regardless of the system resources. Some systems, therefore, play the same animation faster or slower than others. Don't depend on every system to have the same timing.

Recording a layer's path

Plotting keyframes and repositioning your layers works well when you need to follow a pixel-precise path, but it can be extremely tedious when you're trying to move a layer more freely on the screen. Luckily, another, easier method exists for defining a movement path for a layer. In Dreamweaver, you can simply drag your layer around the screen to create a path and refine the path or its timing afterward.

The Record Path of Layer command automatically creates the necessary series of keyframes, calculated from your dragging of the layer. To fine-tune your work, you can select any keyframes and reposition the layer or even delete it entirely. This feature is a definite time-saver for quickly inserting your DHTML animation.

Keep in mind that a timeline represents not only positions but also positions over time, and thus, movement. The Record Path of Layer command is very smart when it comes to time; the slower you drag the layer, the more keyframes are plotted. You can vary the positioning of the keyframes by changing the tempo of your dragging. Moreover, the duration of the recorded timeline reflects the length of time spent dragging the layer.

To record a layer's path, do the following:

1. In the Document window, select the layer you are going to move.

Caution: Make sure that you've selected the layer itself and not its contents. If you've correctly selected the layer, it has eight selection boxes around it.

2. Drag the layer to the location in the document where you want it to be at the start of the movement.

3. From the menu bar, select Modify ⇨ Timeline ⇨ Record Path of Layer. You can also right-click (Control+click) the selected layer and choose Record Path from the shortcut menu.

   If it's not already open, the Timelines panel appears.

4. Click the layer and drag it around onscreen to define the movement. As you drag the layer, Dreamweaver draws a gray dotted line that shows you the path it is creating (see Figure 16-8).

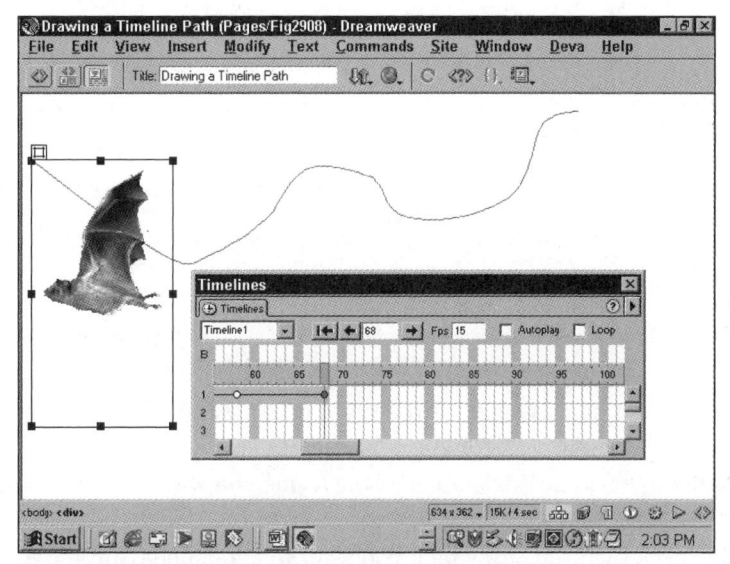

Figure 16-8: To record a layer's path, Select Modify ⇨ Timeline ⇨ Record Path of Layer and then drag your layer in the Document window.

Each dot represents a keyframe. The slower you draw, the closer the keyframes are placed; moving quickly across the Document window causes Dreamweaver to space out the keyframes.

5. Release the mouse. This ends the recording.

   Unless Dreamweaver is instructed not to, Dreamweaver displays an alert reminding you of the capabilities of the Timelines panel. If the alert dialog box does appear, you can select the Don't Show Me This Message Again option to prevent this dialog box from reappearing.

After you've finished recording a layer's movement, you see a new animation bar in the Timelines panel, representing the motion you just recorded. The duration of the new timeline matches the duration of your dragging of the layer. A number of keyframes that define your layer's movement already are inserted in this animation bar. You can use any of the procedures described earlier in this chapter to modify the timeline or its keyframes. If you select the same layer at the end of the generated timeline and perform the Record Path operation again, another animation bar is added at the end of the current timeline.

> **Caution** Any new paths recorded with the same layer are added after the last animation bar. You can't select a keyframe in the middle of a path and then record a path from that point; the starting keyframe of the newly recorded path corresponds to the position of the layer in the last keyframe.

Triggering Behaviors in Timelines

Adding a behavior to a timeline is similar to adding behaviors to any object on a Web page. Because timelines are written in JavaScript, they behave exactly the same as any object enhanced with JavaScript.

Use the Behavior channel section of the Timelines panel to work with behaviors in timelines.

You can attach a behavior to a timeline in four ways:

- ✦ Highlight the frame in which you wish to have the behavior and then right-click (Control+click). Select Add Behavior from the shortcut menu.
- ✦ Highlight the frame in which you want to activate the behavior and choose Modify ⇨ Timeline ⇨ Add Behavior to Timeline.
- ✦ Open the Behaviors panel and click the frame you wish to modify in the Behavior channel.
- ✦ Double-click the frame for which you want to add a behavior in the Behavior channel.

After a behavior is attached to a frame and you open the Behaviors panel, you see that the event inserted in the Events pane is related to a frame number — for example, `onFrame20`. Each frame can trigger multiple actions.

> **Cross-Reference** For more specifics about Dreamweaver behaviors, see Chapter 11.

Behaviors are essential to timelines. Without these elements, you cannot play or stop your timeline-based animations. Even when you select the Autoplay or Loop options in the Timelines panel, you are enabling a behavior. The three behaviors always deployed for timelines are Play Timeline, Stop Timeline, and Go to Timeline Frame.

If you are not using the Autoplay feature for your timeline, you must explicitly attach a Play Timeline behavior to an interactive or another event on your Web page. For example, a timeline is typically set to start playing once a specific picture has loaded, if the user enters a value in a form's text box or — more frequently — when the user selects a Play button. You could use the Stop Timeline behavior to pause an animation temporarily.

> **Caution:** If you find your Behaviors panel locked on the timeline and you're unable to attach a behavior to any other object, you've encountered a known Dreamweaver issue. Click on any other frame in your timeline — besides the one with the attached behavior — to free up the Behaviors panel.

To use the Play Timeline or Stop Timeline behavior, follow these steps:

1. In the Document window, select a tag, link, or image that you want to trigger the event.

2. Choose Window ⇨ Behaviors or select the Show Behavior button from the Launcher to open the Behaviors panel.

3. In the Behaviors panel, click the + (add) Action button, and from the pop-up menu choose either of the following methods:

   a. Timeline ⇨ Play Timeline to start a timeline.

   b. Timeline ⇨ Stop Timeline to end a timeline.

4. In the Play Timeline or Stop Timeline dialog box (see Figure 16-9), choose the timeline that you want to play (or stop) from the appropriate Timeline drop-down list.

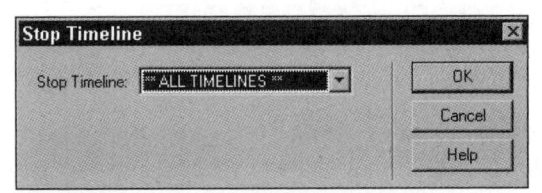

Figure 16-9: You can use the Stop Timeline behavior to stop all timelines or a specific timeline.

5. Click OK when you are finished.

6. Select an event to trigger the behavior from the drop-down menu in the Events column.

When you select the option to loop your timeline, Dreamweaver automatically inserts a Go to Frame behavior — with the first frame set as the target. You can display any frame on your timeline by inserting the Go to Frame behavior manually. To use the Go to Frame behavior, follow these steps:

1. In the Document window, select a tag, link, or image that you want to have trigger the event.
2. Choose Window ⇨ Behaviors or select the Show Behavior button from the Launcher to open the Behaviors panel.
3. In the Behaviors panel, select the + (add) Action button and choose Timeline ⇨ Go to Timeline Frame from the drop-down list.
4. Choose the timeline you want to affect from the Timeline drop-down menu.
5. Enter the frame number in the Go to Frame text box.
6. If you'd like the timeline to loop a set number of times, enter a value in the Loop text box. Click OK when you are finished.

Remember, if you don't enter a value, the timeline loops endlessly.

Tip Depending on the type of effect desired, you may want to use two of the Timeline behaviors together. To ensure that your timeline always starts from the same point, first attach a Go to Timeline Frame behavior to the event and then attach the Play Timeline behavior to the same event.

Dreamweaver Technique: Creating a Multiscreen Slideshow

Moving layers around the screen is pretty cool, but you've probably already figured out that you can do a lot more with timelines. One of the possibilities is a graphics slideshow displaying a rotating series of pictures. To demonstrate the range of potential available to timelines, the following sample project shows you how to construct a slideshow with more than one screen, complete with moving layers and triggered behaviors.

This technique has four steps:

1. **Prepare the graphic elements.** The process is easier if you have most (if not all) of your images for the slideshow — as well as the control interface — ready to go.
2. **Create the slideshow timeline.** In this project, one timeline is devoted to rotating images on four different "screens."

3. **Create the moving layers timeline.** The slideshow begins and ends with a bit of flair, as the screens fly in and fly out.

4. **Add the behaviors.** The slideshow includes controls for playing, pausing, restarting, and ending the slideshow, which then takes the user to another Web page.

This technique is intended to act as a basis for your own creations, not as an end in itself. You can add many variations and refinements; for example, you can preload images, make rollover buttons, and add music to the background. Following is a fundamental structure focused on the use of timelines, which you can expand with additional objects as needed.

> **Note** The end result of this Dreamweaver Technique can be viewed only by 4.0 browsers or later.

Step 1: Preparing the graphic elements

Using a timeline for a slideshow presentation has only one restriction, but this qualification is significant—all the graphics in one "screen" must have the same dimensions. The timeline doesn't actually change the image tag; it only changes the file source for the tag. Thus, the height and width of the last image inserted overrides all the values for the foregoing graphics.

Luckily, all major image-processing software can resize and extend the canvas of a picture with little effort. When creating a slideshow, you may find it useful to do all of the resizing work at one time. Load in your images with the greatest width and height—they may or may not be the same picture—and use these measurements as your common denominators for all graphics.

Go ahead and create your interface buttons earlier rather than later. Experience shows that the more design elements you prepare ahead of time, the less adjusting you have to do later. Also, activating a timeline with a behavior is a straightforward process, and a finished interface enables you to incorporate the buttons quickly.

Finally, you should create and place the layers you want to use. The sample Web page in this technique is built of four screens, all of the same dimensions. The four different layers are uniquely named, but they all have the same size.

> **Tip** If you are making multiple versions of the same layer, consider changing the default layer size to fit your design. Choose Edit ⇨ Preferences and select the Layers category. Once you've customized the height and width values, all the layers incorporated in the Web page with the Insert ⇨ Layer command automatically size correctly. You only have to position those layers once they are created.

To recap, use the following steps to prepare your graphics:

1. Create all the images to be used as slides. All the slides must be the same height and width.
2. Prepare and place your interface buttons.
3. Create the number of layers that you need for the different screens in the slideshow.
4. Position your layers so that each can hold a different slide. The preceding example has four layers, centered on the screen in two rows.
5. Insert your opening slides into each of the layers.

> **Note:** Your opening slide doesn't have to be a graphic image. You could also use a solid-colored GIF or a slide with text.

Try to work backward from a final design whenever layer positioning is involved. At this stage, all of the elements are in their final placement, ready for the slideshow to begin (see Figure 16-10). Next, you can activate the slideshow.

Figure 16-10: Before activating any layers or setting up the slideshow, design the layout.

Step 2: Creating the slideshow timeline

For all the attention that timelines and layers receive, you may be surprised that one of the best features of Dreamweaver timelines has nothing to do with layers. You can use timelines to change images anywhere on your Web page — whether or not they are in layers. As explained in Step 1, the timeline doesn't actually replace one <img> tag with another, but rather alters an image by swapping the src attribute value. The src attribute changes just as changes in a layer's position, shape, or depth must happen at a keyframe.

In planning your slideshow, you need to decide how often a new slide appears, because you need to set keyframes at each of these points. If you are changing your slides every few seconds, you can change the frame rate to 1 fps. This setting helps you easily keep track of how many seconds occur between each slide change (and because no animation is involved with this timeline, a rapid frame rate is irrelevant). Note, however, that on the timeline described previously in this chapter that involved moving layers, the frame rate should be maintained at around 15 fps. Each timeline can have its own frame rate.

The only other choices involve the Autoplay and Loop options. As with frame rate, you can set each timeline to its own options without interfering with another timeline. This example has the slideshow loop but does not start automatically. Use the Play button to enable the user to start the show. But first, let's add the images to the slides.

To put images into a slideshow on a timeline, follow these steps:

1. Choose Window ⇨ Timelines to open the Timelines panel.
2. If desired, rename Timeline1 by selecting the name and typing your own unique name.
3. Select one image from those onscreen in the positioned layers and drag the graphic to the Timelines panel.

Caution: Be sure to grab the image, not the layer.

4. Release the animation bar at the beginning of the timeline.
5. Repeat Steps 3 and 4 for each image until all images are represented on the timeline.
6. Change the frame rate by entering a new value in the Fps text box. This example changes the frame rate to 1.
7. Select the Loop or Autoplay options, if desired.

8. On one of the animation bars representing images, select the frame for a keyframe.

9. Choose Modify ➪ Timeline ➪ Add Keyframe, or right-click (Control+click) the frame on the timeline and choose Add Keyframe from the shortcut menu.

10. In the Image Property Inspector, select the Src folder to locate the graphic file for the next slide image.

11. Repeat Steps 9 and 10 until every animation bar has keyframes for every slide change and each keyframe has a new or different image assigned.

This example changes slides every five seconds, as you can see in Figure 16-11 by looking at the keyframe placement. Although the slideshow has all four images changing simultaneously, you can also stagger the timing of the image changes. Simply drag one or more of the animation bars a few frames forward or backward after the keyframes have been set.

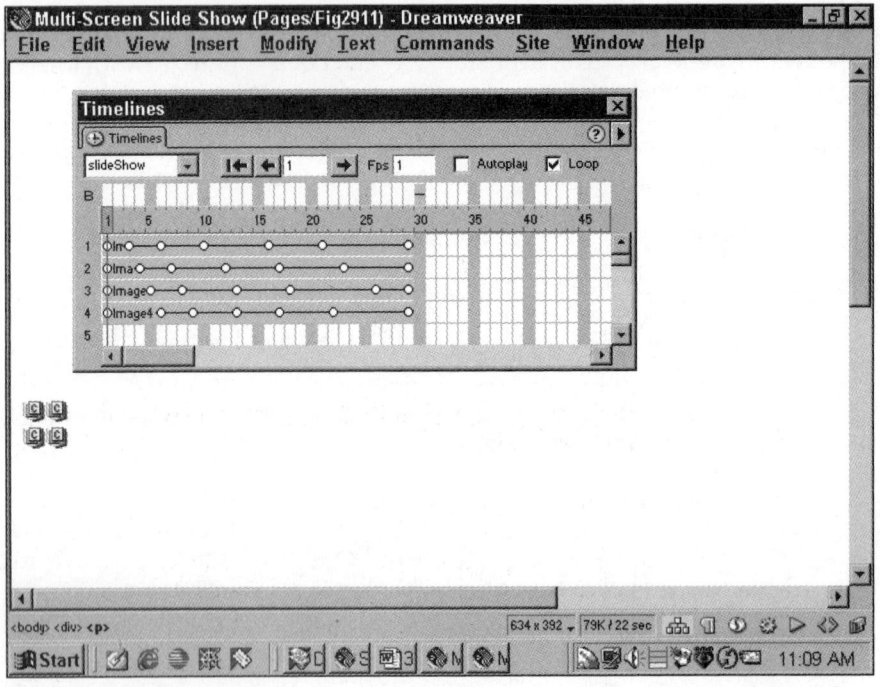

Figure 16-11: Each keyframe on each animation bar signals a change of the slide image.

Tip: To preview your slide changes, you don't have to go outside of Dreamweaver. Just click and hold down the Play button on the Timelines panel.

Step 3: Creating the moving layers timeline

At this stage, the slideshow is functional but a little dull. To add a bit of showmanship, you can "fly in" the layers from different areas of the Web page to their final destination. This task is easy — to complete the effect, the layers "fly out" when the user is ready to leave.

You can achieve these fly-in/fly-out effects in several ways. You can put the opening fly-in on one timeline and the ending fly-out on another. A more concise method combines the fly-in and fly-out for each layer on one timeline — separating them with a Stop Timeline behavior. After the fly-in portion happens when the page has loaded (because the example selects the Autoplay option for this timeline), the fly-out section does not begin to play until signaled to continue with the Play Timeline behavior.

To create the moving layers' opening and closing for the slideshow, follow these steps:

1. Choose Modify ➪ Timeline ➪ Add Timeline, or right-click (Ctrl+click) the Timelines panel and choose Add Timeline from the shortcut menu.

2. Rename your new timeline if desired.

3. Select the Autoplay checkbox so that this timeline begins playing automatically when the Web page is loaded.

4. Select any one of the layers surrounding your images and drag it onto the Timelines panel.

Caution This time, make sure you move the layers — not the images.

5. To set the amount of time for the fly-in section to span, drag the final keyframe of the animation bar to a new frame. The example sets the end at 30 frames, which at 15 fps lasts two seconds.

6. From the Document window, select the same layer again and drag it to the Timelines panel. Place it directly after the first animation bar. This animation bar becomes the fly-out portion.

7. Drag the final keyframe to extend the time, if desired.

8. At this point, all four keyframes — two for each animation bar — have exactly the same information. Now change the positions for two keyframes to enable the layer to move. Select the first keyframe in the opening animation bar.

9. Reposition the layer so that it is offscreen. Although you can complete this task manually to the right or bottom of the screen by dragging the layer to a new location, you can also use the Layer Property Inspector to input new values directly for the Left and Top attributes.

Tip: Use negative numbers to move a layer offscreen to the left or top of the browser window.

  10. From the Timelines panel, select the last keyframe of the closing animation bar.
  11. Reposition the layer offscreen. If you want the layer to return in the same manner as it arrived, enter the same values for the Left and Top attributes as in the first keyframe of the opening animation bar.
  12. Repeat Steps 4 through 11 for every layer.

Now, when you preview this timeline, the layers fly in and immediately fly out again. Figure 16-12 shows the layers in the example in mid-animation. In the final phase of the technique, you add behaviors to put the action under user control.

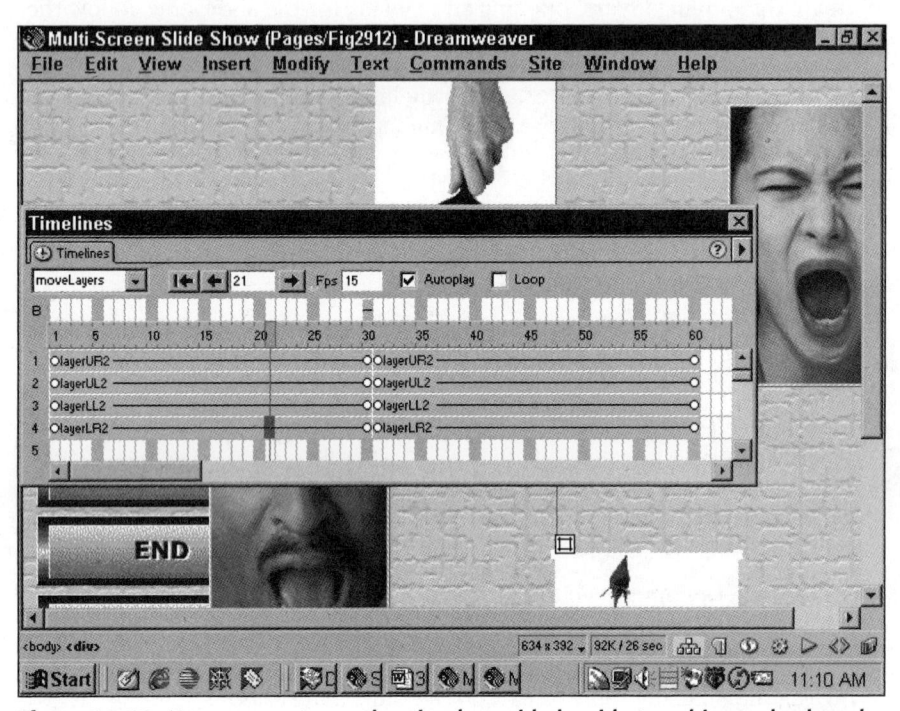

Figure 16-12: You can use two animation bars side by side to achieve a back-and-forth effect.

Step 4: Adding the behaviors

Although it may be fun to watch an unexpected effect take place, giving the user control over aspects of a presentation is much more involving — for the designer as well as the user. The example is ready to incorporate the user-interaction aspect by attaching Dreamweaver behaviors to the user interface and to the Behavior channel of the Timelines panel.

Two timeline behaviors have already been attached to the example. When the Loop option is selected in Step 2 for the slideshow timeline, Dreamweaver automatically includes a Go to Timeline Frame behavior after the final frame that sends the timeline back to the first frame. In the moving layers timeline, enabling the Autostart option causes Dreamweaver to attach a Play Timeline behavior to the onLoad event of the Web page's `<body>` tag. To complete the project, five behaviors need to be added.

First, you need a behavior to stop the moving layers from proceeding after the fly-in portion of the animation:

1. From the Timelines panel, double-click the final frame of the first animation bar in the Behavior channel.
2. In the Behaviors panel, select Timeline ⇨ Stop Timeline from the + (add) Actions pull-down menu.
3. From the Stop Timeline dialog box, select the timeline that contains the moving layers.
4. Click OK. An `onFrame` event is set for the Stop Timeline action by default.

Second, you need a behavior to enable the user to begin playing the slideshow:

1. In the Document window, select the Play button.
2. In the Behaviors panel, select the Timeline ⇨ Play Timeline action from the + (add) Action drop-down list.
3. In the Play Timeline dialog box, choose the timeline representing the slideshow.
4. Click OK. An `onMouseDown` event is set to trigger the action by default.

The next behavior enables the user to stop the slideshow temporarily:

1. In the Document window, select the Pause button.
2. In the Behaviors panel, select Timeline ⇨ Stop Timeline from the + (add) Actions drop-down list.
3. Choose the layer representing the slideshow in the Stop Timeline dialog box.
4. Click OK. An `onMouseDown` event is set to trigger the action by default.

To enable the user to begin the slideshow from the beginning, follow these steps:

1. In the Document window, select the Restart button.
2. In the Behaviors panel, add the Timeline ⇨ Go to Timeline Frame action.
3. In the Go to Timeline Frame dialog box, choose the layer representing the slideshow.
4. Enter a 1 in the Frame text box.
5. Click OK. An onMouseDown event is set to trigger the action by default.
6. Add the next action. In the Behaviors panel, select Timeline ⇨ Play Timeline from the + (add) Action drop-down list.
7. In the Play Timeline dialog box, choose the layer representing the slideshow.
8. Click OK. An onMouseDown event is attached to the action by default.

To end the presentation and move the user on to the next Web page, follow these steps:

1. In the Document window, select the End button.
2. In the Behaviors panel, select the Timeline ⇨ Play Timeline action from the + (add) Action drop-down list.
3. Choose the timeline representing the moving layers in the Play Timeline dialog box and click OK. The timeline begins playing where it last stopped — just before the layers are about to fly out. An onMouseDown event is set to trigger the action by default.
4. Add the next behavior. Select the Go to URL action from the + (add) drop-down list.
5. In the Go to URL dialog box, enter the path to the new page in the URL text box or select the Browse button to locate the file. Click OK when you are finished.

The project is complete and ready to test. Feel free to experiment, trying out different timings to achieve different effects.

Summary

Timelines are effective tools for developing pages in which events need to be triggered at specific points in time.

- ✦ Timelines can affect particular attributes of layers and images, or they can start any Dreamweaver behavior.
- ✦ Use the Timelines panel to set an animation to play automatically, to have it loop indefinitely, and to change the frames-per-second display rate of the timeline.
- ✦ You must use one of the timeline behaviors to activate your timeline if you don't use the Autoplay feature.

✦ ✦ ✦

Using Dreamweaver Templates

CHAPTER 17

◆ ◆ ◆ ◆

In This Chapter

Working with templates

Building your own templates

Working with editable and locked regions

Modifying the default Web page

◆ ◆ ◆ ◆

Let's face it: Web design is a combination of glory and grunt work. Creating the initial design for a Web site can be fun and exciting, but when you have to implement your wonderful new design on 200 or more pages, the excitement fades as you try to figure out the quickest way to finish the work. Enter templates. Properly using templates can be a tremendous time-saver. Moreover, a template ensures that your Web site has a consistent look and feel, which, in turn, generally means that it's easier for users to navigate.

In Dreamweaver, new documents can be produced from a standard design saved as a template, as in a word processing program. Furthermore, you can alter a template and update all the files that were created from it earlier; this capability extends the power of the repeating element Libraries to overall page design. Templates also form the bridge to one of the hottest technologies shaping the Web—XML (Extensible Markup Language).

Dreamweaver makes it easy to access all kinds of templates— everything from your own creations to the default blank page. This chapter demonstrates the mechanism behind Dreamweaver templates and shows you strategies for getting the most out of them.

Understanding Templates

Templates exist in many forms. Furniture makers use master patterns as templates to create the same basic design repeatedly, using new wood stains or upholstery to differentiate the end results. A stencil, in which the inside of a letter, word, or design is cut out, is a type of template as well. With computers, templates form the basic document into which specific details are added to create new, distinct documents.

Dreamweaver templates, in terms of functionality, are a combination of traditional templates and updateable Library elements. Once a new page is created from a template, the new document remains attached to the original template unless specifically separated or detached. Because the new document maintains a connection to previous pages in a site, if the original template is altered, all the documents created from it can be automatically updated. This relationship is also true of Dreamweaver's repeating elements Libraries. In fact, templates can even include Library elements.

> **Cross-Reference** Library items can work hand-in-hand with templates. See Chapter 18 for a detailed discussion of Library items.

Templates are composed of two types of regions: *locked* and *editable*. Every element on the Web page template falls into one category or the other. When a template is first created, all the areas are locked. Part of the process of defining a template is to designate and name the editable regions. Then, when a document is created from that template, the editable regions are the only ones that can be modified.

Naturally, templates can be altered to mark additional editable areas or to relock editable areas. Moreover, you can detach a document created from a template at any point and edit anything in the document — you cannot, however, reattach the document to the template without losing newly inserted content. On the other hand, a document based on one template can be changed to a completely different look but with the same content, if another template with identical editable regions is applied.

Dreamweaver ships with a tutorial that illustrates the power of templates. The tutorial, found in the Dreamweaver/Tutorial folder, is based on an example Web site for a travel company called Compass. Previewing the site in a browser shows that all the sample pages for the different trips in the Destinations section are basically the same — only the destination title, description, and Flash movie vary. The layout, background, and navigation controls are identical on every page. Each of these pages was created from the template page shown in Figure 17-1. Notice the highlighting surrounding certain areas; in a template, the editable regions are highlighted, and the locked areas are not. A tab further identifies each editable region to make it easier to add the right content in the right area.

Creating Your Own Templates

You can use any design that you like for your own template. Perhaps the best course to take is to finalize a single page that has all the elements that you want to include in your template. Then, convert that document to a template and proceed to mark all the changeable areas — whether text or image — as editable regions.

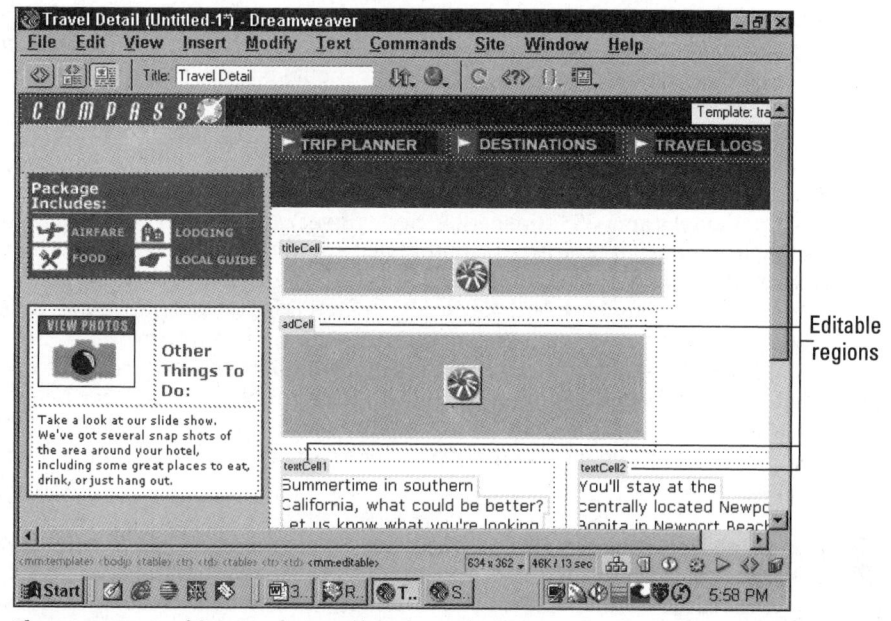

Figure 17-1: In this sample template from the Dreamweaver tutorial, editable regions are highlighted.

Before saving your file as a template, consider these points when designing your basic page:

- **Use placeholders where you can.** Whether it's dummy text or a temporary graphic, placeholders give shape to your page. They also make it easier to remember which elements to include. If you are using an image placeholder, set a temporary height and width through the Property Inspector or by dragging the image placeholder's sizing handles; of course, you can also just insert a sample graphic.

- **Finalize and incorporate as much content as possible in the template.** If you find yourself repeatedly adding the same information or objects to a page, add them to your template. The more structured elements you can include, the faster your pages can be produced.

- **Use sample objects on the template.** Often you have to enter the same basic object, such as a plug-in for a digital movie, on every page, with only the filename changing. Enter your repeating object with all the preset parameters possible on your template page as an editable region, and you only have to select a new filename for each page.

- **Include your `<meta>` information.** Search engines rely on `<meta>` tags to get the overview of a page and then scan the balance of the page to get the details. You can enter a Keyword or Description object from the Head panel of the Objects palette so that all the Web pages in your site have the same basic information for cataloging.

Note: You cannot enter separate `<meta>` tag information into template-derived pages without inserting it directly into the code. Dreamweaver defines one editable area for the title—your hand-entered `<meta>` tags should go in this region. This procedure is described in detail later in this chapter.

+ **Apply all needed behaviors and styles to the template.** When a document is saved as a template, all the code in the `<head>` section is locked. Because most behaviors and CSS (Cascading Style Sheet) styles insert code here, documents created from templates cannot easily apply new behaviors or create new styles.

You can create a template from a Web document with one command: File ⇨ Save As Template. Dreamweaver stores all templates in a Templates folder created for each defined site, with a special file extension, .dwt. After you've created your page and saved it as a template, notice that Dreamweaver inserts `<<Template>>` in the title bar to remind you of the page's status. Now you're ready to begin defining the template's editable regions.

Note: You can also create a template from an entirely blank page if you like. To do so, open the Assets panel and select the Templates category. From the Templates category, select the New Template button. You can find more information on how to use the Assets panel's Templates category later in this chapter.

Using Editable Regions

As noted earlier, when you convert an existing page into a template via the Save As Template command, the entire document is initially locked. If you attempt to create a document from a template at this stage, Dreamweaver alerts you that the template doesn't have any editable regions, and you cannot change anything on the page. Editable regions are essential to any template.

Marking existing content as editable

Two techniques exist for marking editable regions. First, you can designate any existing content as an editable region. Second, you can insert a new editable region anywhere you can place your cursor. In both cases, you must give the region a unique name. Dreamweaver uses the unique name to identify the editable region when entering new content, applying the template, and exporting or importing XML.

Note: As noted, each editable region must have a unique name, but the names need only be different from any other editable region on the same page. The name could be used for objects or JavaScript functions, or for editable regions on a different template.

To mark an existing area as an editable region, follow these steps:

1. Select the text or object that you wish to convert to an editable region.

   Tip: The general rule of thumb with editable regions is that you need to select a complete tag pair, such as `<table>...</table>`. This has several implications. For instance, while you can mark an entire table or a single cell as editable, you can't select multiple cells, a row, or a column to be so marked. You have to select each cell individually (`<td>...</td>`). Also, you can select the content of a layer to be editable and keep the layer itself locked (so that its position and other properties cannot be altered), but if you select the layer to be editable, you can't lock the content.

2. Choose Modify ⇨ Templates ⇨ New Editable Region. You can also use the keyboard shortcut Ctrl+Alt+W (Command+Option+W), or right-click (Control+click) the selection and choose Editable Regions ⇨ New Editable Region from the shortcut menu. Dreamweaver displays the New Editable Region dialog box.

   Tip: If you want the flexibility of adding returns to your editable region, make sure it includes at least one return. The easiest method is to select the <p> tag in the Tag Selector. If just text is selected, Dreamweaver does not allow any returns, although line breaks are accepted.

3. Enter a unique name for the selected area. Click OK when you're done or Cancel to abort the operation.

   Caution: While you can use spaces in editable region names, some characters are not permitted. The illegal characters are the ampersand (&), double quote ("), single quote ('), and left and right angle brackets (< and >).

Dreamweaver outlines the selection with the color picked in Preferences on the Highlighting panel. The name for your newly designated region is displayed on a tab marking the area; the region is also listed in the Modify ⇨ Templates submenu. If still selected, the region name has a checkmark next to it in the Templates submenu. You can jump to any other editable region by selecting its name from this dynamic list.

Tip: Make sure you apply any formatting to your text—either by using HTML codes such as `<font>`, or by using CSS styles—before you select it to be an editable region. Generally, you want to keep the defined look of the content while altering just the text, so make just the text an editable region and exclude the formatting tags. It's helpful to have the HTML Inspector open for this detailed work.

Inserting a new editable region

Sometimes it's helpful to create a new editable region where no content currently exists. In these situations, the editable region name doubles as a label identifying the type of content expected, such as {CatalogPrice}. Dreamweaver always puts new region names in curly braces as just shown and highlights the entry in the template.

To insert a new editable region, follow these steps:

1. Place your cursor anywhere on the template page.
2. Choose Modify ➪ Templates ➪ New Editable Region. You can also use the keyboard shortcut Ctrl+Alt+V (Command+Option+V), or right-click (Control+click) the selection and choose New Editable Region from the shortcut menu.

   Dreamweaver displays the New Editable Region dialog box.
3. Enter a unique name for the new region. Click OK when you're done or Cancel to abort the operation.

Dreamweaver inserts the new region name in the document, surrounded by curly braces, marks it with a named tab and adds the name to the dynamic region list (which you can display by choosing Modify ➪ Templates).

Tip

One editable region, the Web page's title, is automatically created when you save a document as a template. The title is stored in a special editable region called doctitle. To change the title (which initially takes the same title as the template), enter the new text in the Title field of the Toolbar. You can also use the keyboard shortcut Ctrl+J (Command+J) to open the Page Properties dialog box. Finally, you can select View ➪ Head Elements and choose the Title icon to enter the new text in the Property Inspector.

Locking an editable region

Inevitably, you'll mark a region as editable that you'd prefer to keep locked, or you may discover that every page constructed to date has required inputting the same content, so it should be entered on the template and locked. In either event, converting an editable region to a locked one is a simple operation.

To lock an editable region, follow these steps:

1. Place your cursor in the editable region you want to lock.
2. Choose Modify ➪ Templates ➪ Remove Editable Region. The Unmark Editable Region dialog box, shown in Figure 17-2, appears with the selected region highlighted.

Note

You don't have to preselect the editable region to unmark it. If you don't, the Unmark Editable Region dialog box opens but doesn't highlight any selection; you have to choose it by name.

Creating Links in Templates

A common problem that designers encounter with Dreamweaver templates centers on links. People often add a link to their template and discover that it doesn't work when the new page is derived from the template. The main cause of this error stems from linking to a nonexistent page or element by hand — that is, typing in the link rather than using the Select File dialog box to choose it. Designers tend to set the link according to their final site structure without taking into account how templates are stored in Dreamweaver.

For example, when creating a template, let's say that you have links to three pages, products.htm, services.htm, and about.htm, all in the root of your site. Both products.htm and services.htm have been created, so you select the folder icon in the Property Inspector and select those files in turn. Dreamweaver inserts those links like this: `../products.htm` and `../services.htm`. The `../` indicates the directory above the current directory — which makes sense only when you remember that all templates are stored in a subfolder of the site root called Templates. These links are correctly resolved when a document is derived from this template to reflect the stored location of the new file.

Let's assume that the third file, about.htm, has not yet been created, and so that link is entered by hand. The common mistake is to enter it as it should be when it's used: about.htm. However, because the page is saved in the Template folder, Dreamweaver converts that link to /Templates/about.htm for any page derived from the template — and the link will fail. This type of error also applies to dependent files, such as graphics or other media.

The best solution is to always use the folder icon to link to an existing file when building your templates. If the file does not exist, and if you don't want to create a placeholder page for it, link to another existing file in the same folder and modify the link manually.

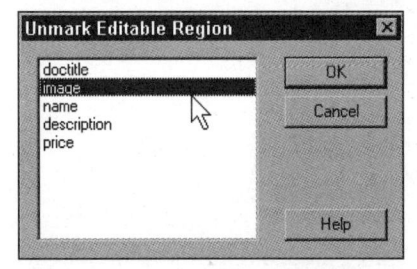

Figure 17-2: Convert an editable region to a locked one with the Unmark Editable Region command.

3. Click OK in the Unmark Editable Region dialog box to confirm your choice.

   The editable region highlight is removed, and the area is now a locked region of the template.

Caution If you are removing a newly inserted editable region that is labeled with the region name in curly braces, then the label is not removed and must be deleted by hand on the template. Otherwise, it appears as part of the document created from a template and won't be accessible.

Adding Content to Template Documents

Constructing a template is only half the job — using it to create new pages is the other half. Because your basic layout is complete and you're only dropping in new images and entering new text, pages based on templates take a fraction of the time needed to create regular Web pages. Dreamweaver makes it easy to enter new content as well — you can even move from one editable region to the next, much like filling out a form (which, of course, is exactly what you're doing).

To create a new document based on a template, follow these steps:

1. In the Template category of the Assets panel, select the desired template and choose the New from Template from the panel's context menu. Alternatively, choose File ⇨ New from Template.

    If you chose the command from the File menu, the Select Template dialog box, shown in Figure 17-3, appears.

Figure 17-3: Create a new document based on any template listed in the Select Template dialog box.

2. If you wish to create a template from a local site other than the current one, select it from the Site drop-down list.
3. Select the desired template from those in the Templates list box.
4. Click OK when you're done.

When your new page opens, the editable regions are again highlighted; furthermore, the cursor is only active when it is over an unlocked region. If you have the Code view open, you also will see that the locked region is highlighted in a different color as shown in Figure 17-4. The highlighting makes it easy to differentiate the two types of regions.

Chapter 17 ✦ **Using Dreamweaver Templates** 529

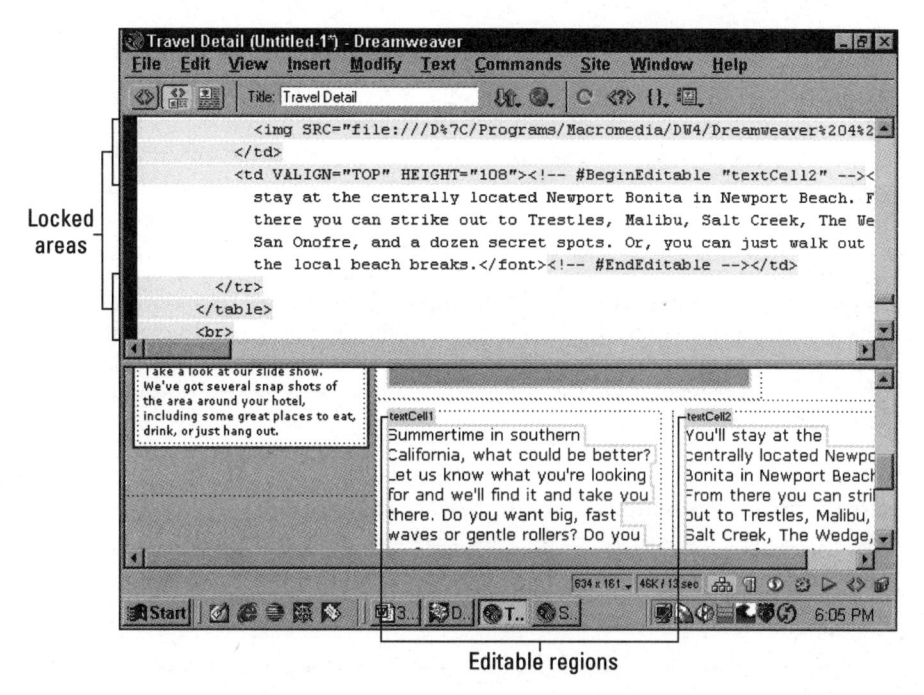

Figure 17-4: In a document based on a template, the editable regions are clearly marked, as are the locked portions in the Code view.

Generally, it is easiest to select the editable region name or placeholder first and then enter the new content. Selecting the editable regions can be handled in several ways:

- ✦ Highlight each editable region name or placeholder with the mouse.
- ✦ Position your cursor inside any editable region and then select the `<mm:editable>` tag in the Tag Selector.
- ✦ Choose Modify ➪ Templates and then select the name of your editable region from the dynamic list.

Note If all your editable regions are separate cells in a table, you can tab forward and Shift+Tab backward through the cells. With each press of the Tab key, all the content in the cell is selected, whether it is an editable region name or a placeholder.

Naturally, you should save your document to retain all the new content that's been added.

Adding behaviors to template-derived documents

The current implementation of Dreamweaver templates does not enable behaviors to be added to any document created from—and still linked to—a template. If you try, Dreamweaver plays a single note, as it does anytime that you try to select a locked region. With behaviors, the `<head>` section—where the code needs to go—is locked in a template.

You have three ways to handle the problem, however. First, if you're just using the template to get the basic layout of the page and don't need to maintain its link for updating, you can detach the Web page from the template by choosing Modify ⇨ Templates ⇨ Detach from Template. Second, if all your pages require the same behavior, as in a Navigation Bar, for example, you can simply add the behavior to the template itself.

The final method is the most involved, but also the most flexible. By adding some code to the original template, new behaviors can be attached, either to the template or to any template-based document. Here are the steps required for the modification:

1. Open the template for editing.
2. Display the HTML Inspector and scroll to the closing `</head>` tag.

   If you select the `<body>` tag from the Tag Selector, the closing `</head>` tag is just above the selected region.

3. Enter this code above the `</head>` tag:

   ```
   <mm:editable>
   <script>
   </script>
   </mm:editable>

   <mm:editable>
   <!-- Dummy comment, to be deleted by Dreamweaver -->
   </mm:editable>
   ```

4. Choose File ⇨ Save and update any documents linked to the template.

When a document is derived from this modified template, Dreamweaver removes the dummy comment but maintains the `<script>...</script>` pair, enabling behaviors to be added.

Inserting meta tags in documents based on templates

With the exception of the `<title>` tag, Dreamweaver locks the entire head section when a template is made. Therefore, a special procedure must be used to add page-specific `<meta>` tags to a document derived from a template. While it is considered a best practice to include as many `<meta>` tags as possible in the general template, often special keyword or description `<meta>` tags must be included on a page-by-page basis. If you try to add any item from the Head category of the Objects panel, Dreamweaver notifies you with a beep that the insertion is not allowed.

To work around the locked `<head>` region, the `<meta>` tag is added within the editable region surrounding the title. Here's the most direct method for accomplishing this task:

1. Choose Show Code and Design Views or Show Code View from the Toolbar.

   You also have the option of selecting the Code Inspector button from the Launcher or pressing the keyboard shortcut F10.

2. In the Code view, scroll up to the top of the document until the `<!-- #BeginEditable -->` ... `<!-- #EndEditable -->` tags surrounding the `<title>` tag are visible.

3. Place the cursor behind the closing `</title>` tag.

4. From the Head category of the Objects panel, choose the desired `<meta>` tag: Insert Meta, Insert Keywords, Insert Description, or Insert Refresh.

   The appropriate dialog box opens.

5. Enter the desired attributes for the `<meta>` tag in the dialog box and select OK when you're done.

   Dreamweaver inserts the completed `<meta>` tag behind the `<title>` tag, but within the editable region.

By using this technique, any updates to the general template will still be reflected in the derived document and you'll have the added advantage of unique `<meta>` tags where necessary.

Working with Templates in the Assets Panel

As a site grows, so does the number of templates it employs. Overall management of your templates is conducted through the Templates category of the Assets panel. You can open the Templates palette by choosing Windows ➪ Templates or by pressing the keyboard shortcut Ctrl+F11 (Command+F11). The Templates category, shown in Figure 17-5, displays a list of the current site's available templates in the lower pane and a preview of the selected template in the upper pane.

The Templates palette has five buttons along the bottom of its window:

- ✦ **Apply** — Creates a document derived from the currently selected template if the current document is blank, or, if the current document is based on a template, changes the locked regions of the document to match the selected template.

- ✦ **Refresh Site List** — Displays the list of all the templates currently in the site.

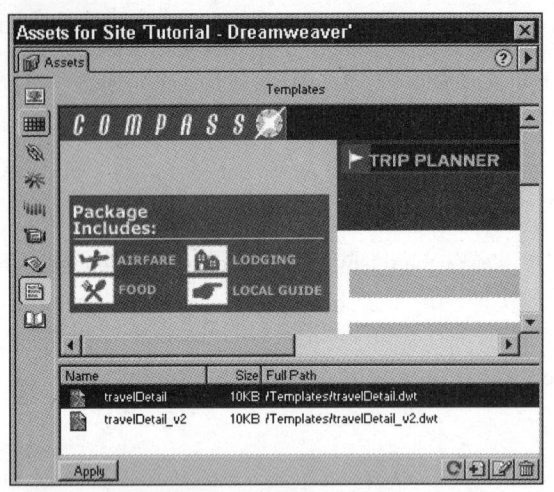

Figure 17-5: Use the Templates category of the Assets panel to preview, delete, open, create, or apply your current site's templates.

- ✦ **New Template**—Creates a new blank template.
- ✦ **Edit**—Loads the selected template for modification.
- ✦ **Delete**—Removes the selected template.

The Assets panel's context menu offers all of these options and more as explained in Table 17-1:

Table 17-1
Template Category Context Menu

Command	Description
Refresh Site List	Displays the list of all the templates currently in the site.
New Template	Starts a new blank template.
New from Template	Creates a new document based on the currently selected template.
Edit	Opens the current template for modifying.
Apply	Creates a document derived from the currently selected template if the current document is blank or, if the current document is based on a template, changes the locked regions of the document to match the selected template. The same effects can also be achieved by dragging the template from the Assets panel to the current document.
Rename	Renames the selected template

Command	Description
Delete	Removes the selected template.
Update Current Page	Applies any changes made in the template to the current page, if the current page is derived from a template.
Update Site	Applies any changes made in any templates to all template-based documents in the site.
Copy to Site	Copies the highlighted template, but none of the dependent files, to the selected site.
Locate in Site	Opens the Site window and highlights the selected template.

Creating a blank template

Not all templates are created from existing documents. Some Web designers prefer to create their templates from scratch. To create a blank template, follow these steps:

1. Open the Templates category of the Assets panel by selecting its symbol or by choosing Window ⇨ Templates.
2. From the Templates category, select New Template. A new, untitled template is created.
3. Enter a title for your new template and press Enter (Return).
4. While the new template is selected, press the Edit button. The blank template opens in a new Dreamweaver window.
5. Insert your page elements.
6. Mark any elements or areas as editable regions using one of the methods previously described.
7. Save your template.

Deleting and opening templates

As with any set of files, there comes a time to clean house and remove files that are no longer in use. To remove a template, first open the Templates category of the Assets panel. Next, select the file you want to remove and choose the Delete button.

Caution

Be forewarned: Dreamweaver does not alert you if files exist that were created from the template that you're about to delete. Deleting the template, in effect, "orphans" those documents, and they can no longer be updated via a template.

You can edit a template — to change the locked or editable regions — in several ways. To use the first method, choose File ⇨ Open and, in the Select File dialog box, change the Files of Type to Template Files (*.dwt) on Window systems and choose Template Files from the Show drop-down list on Macintosh systems. Then, locate the Templates folder in your defined site to select the template to open.

The second method of opening a template for modification uses the Templates category of the Assets panel. Select a template to modify and choose the Edit button. You can also double-click your template to open it for editing.

Finally, if you're working in the Site window, open a template by selecting the Templates folder for your site and open any of the files found there.

Tip After you've made your modifications to the template, you don't have to use the Save As Template command to store the file — you can use the regular File ⇨ Save command or the keyboard shortcut Ctrl+S (Command+S). Likewise, if you want to save your template under another name, use the Save As command.

Applying templates

Dreamweaver makes it easy to try a variety of different looks for your document while maintaining the same content. Once you've created a document from a template, you can apply any other template to it. The only requirement is that the two templates have editable regions with the same names. When might this feature come in handy? In one scenario, you might develop a number of possible Web site designs for a client and create templates for each different approach, which are then applied to the identical content. Or, in an ongoing site, you could completely change the look of a catalog seasonally but retain all the content. Figure 17-6 shows two radically different schemes for a Web site with the same content.

To apply a template to a document, follow these steps:

1. Open the Templates category of the Assets panel.
2. Make sure the Web page you want to apply the style to is the active document.
3. From the Templates category, select the template you want to use and click the Apply button.

Tip You can also drag onto the current page the template you'd like to apply or choose Modify ⇨ Templates ⇨ Apply Template to Page from the menus.

4. If content exists without a matching editable region, Dreamweaver displays the Choose Editable Region for Orphaned Content dialog box. To receive the content, select one of the listed editable regions from the template being applied and click OK.

The new template is applied to the document, and all the new locked areas replace all the old locked areas.

Chapter 17 ✦ Using Dreamweaver Templates   535

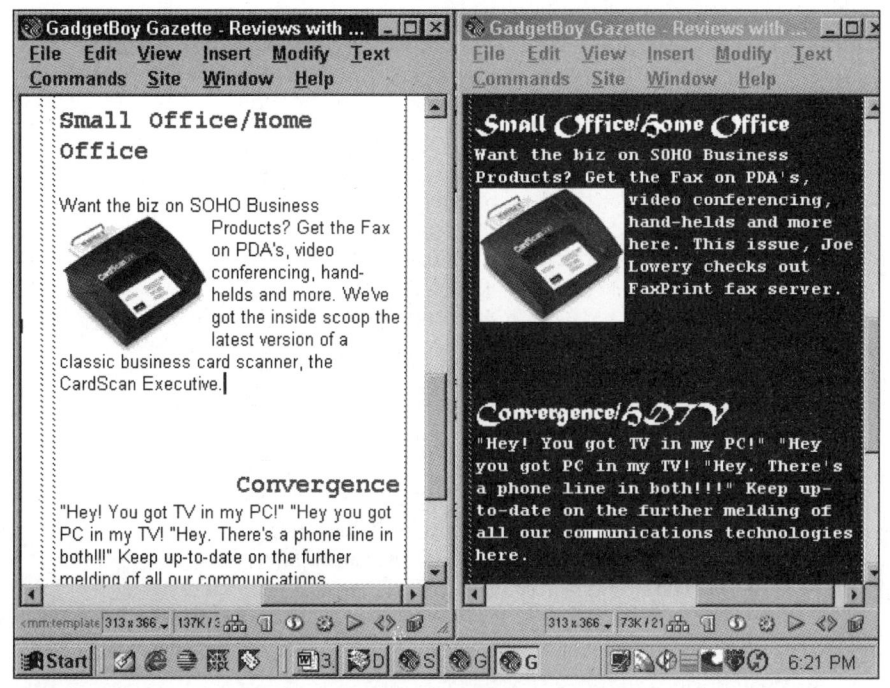

Figure 17-6: You can apply a template to a document created from another template to achieve different designs with identical content.

Updating Templates

Anytime you save a change to an existing template — whether or not any documents have been created from it — Dreamweaver asks if you'd like to update all the documents in the local site attached to the template. As with Library elements, you can also update the current page or the entire site at any time. Updating documents based on a template can save you an enormous amount of time — especially when numerous changes are involved.

To update a single page, open the page and choose Modify ➪ Templates ➪ Update Current Page or select the same command from the context menu of the Assets panel. Either way, the update is instantly applied.

To update a series of pages or an entire site, follow these steps:

1. Choose Modify ➪ Templates ➪ Update Pages.

   The Update Pages dialog box, shown in Figure 17-7, appears.

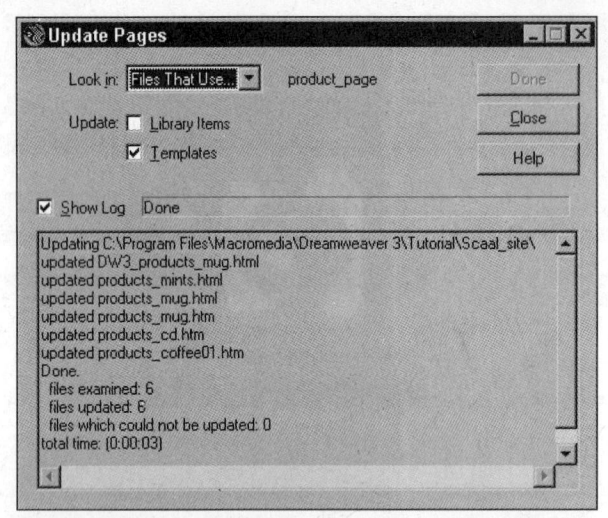

Figure 17-7: Any changes made to a template can be automatically applied to the template's associated files by using the Update Pages command.

2. To update all the documents using all the templates for an entire site, choose Entire Site from the Look In option and then select the name of the site from the accompanying drop-down list.

3. To update pages using a particular template, choose Pages Using from the Look In option and then select the name of the template.

4. To view a report of the progress of the update, make sure that the Show Log option is enabled.

5. Click Start to begin the update process.

The log window displays a list of the files examined and updated, the total number of files that could not be updated, and the elapsed time.

Changing the Default Document

Each time you open a new document in Dreamweaver — or even just start Dreamweaver — a blank page is created. This blank page is based on an HTML file called Default.html that is stored in the Configuration\Templates folder. The default page works in a similar fashion to the templates in that you can create new documents from it, but no editable or locked regions exist — everything in the page can always be altered.

The basic blank-page document is an HTML structure with only a few properties specified: a document type, character set, and white background for the body:

```
<html>
<head>
<title>Untitled Document</title>
<meta http-equiv="Content-Type" content="text/html; charset=iso-8859-1">
</head>

<body bgcolor="#FFFFFF">

</body>
</html>
```

Naturally, you can change any of these elements — and add many, many more — after you've opened a page. But what if you want to have a `<meta>` tag with creator information in every page that comes out of your Web design company? You can do it in Dreamweaver manually, but it's a bother, and chances are that you'll forget. Luckily, Dreamweaver provides a more efficient solution.

In keeping with its overall design philosophy of extensibility, Dreamweaver enables you to modify the Default.htm file as you would any other file. Just choose File ⇨ Open and select the Configuration\Templates\Default.htm file. As you make your changes, save the file as you would normally. Now, to test your modifications, choose File ⇨ New — your modifications should appear in your new document.

Summary

Much of a Web designer's responsibility is related to document production, and Dreamweaver offers a comprehensive template solution to reduce the workload. When planning your strategy for building an entire Web site, remember that templates provide these advantages:

✦ Templates can be created from any Web page.

✦ Dreamweaver templates combine locked and editable regions. Editable regions must be defined individually.

✦ After a template is declared, new documents can be created from it.

✦ If a template is altered, pages built from that template can be automatically updated.

✦ The default template that Dreamweaver uses can be modified so that every time you select File ⇨ New, a new version of your customized template is created.

In the next chapter, you learn how to streamline production and site maintenance with repeating page elements from the Dreamweaver Library.

✦ ✦ ✦

Using the Repeating Elements Library

CHAPTER 18

In This Chapter

Dreamweaver Library basics

Making and inserting Library items

Managing your Dreamweaver Library

Updating your Web sites with Libraries

Using server-side includes

One of the challenges of designing a Web site is ensuring that buttons, copyright notices, and other cross-site features always remain consistent. Fortunately, Dreamweaver offers a useful feature called *Library items* that helps you insert repeating elements, such as a navigation bar or a company logo, into every Web page you create. With one command, you can update and maintain Library items efficiently and productively.

In this chapter, you examine the nature and the importance of repeating elements and learn how to effectively use the Dreamweaver Library feature for all your sites.

Dreamweaver Libraries

Library items within Dreamweaver are another means for you, as a designer, to maintain consistency throughout your site. Suppose you have a navigation bar on every page that contains links to all the other pages on your site. It's highly likely that you'll eventually (and probably more than once) need to make changes to the navigation bar. In a traditional Web development environment, you must modify every single page. This creates lots of opportunities for making mistakes, missing pages, and adding code to the wrong place. Moreover, the whole process is tedious — ask anyone who has had to modify the copyright notice at the bottom of every Web page for a site with over 200 pages.

One traditional method of updating repeating elements is to use *server-side includes*. A server-side include causes the server to place a component, such as a copyright notice, in a specified area of a Web page when it's sent to the user. This arrangement, however, increases the strain on your already overworked Web server and many hosting companies do not permit server-side includes for this reason. To add to the designer's frustrations, you can't lay out a Web page in a WYSIWYG format and simultaneously see the server-side scripts (unless you're using a Dreamweaver translator). So you either take the time to calculate that a server-side script will take up a specific space on the Web page, or you cross your fingers and guess.

A better way in Dreamweaver is to use an important innovation called the *Library*. The Library is designed to make repetitive updating quick, easy, and as error-free as possible. The Library's key features include the following:

- Any item—whether text or graphic—that goes into the body of your Web page can be designated as a Library item.
- Once created, Library items can be placed instantly in any Web page in your site, without your having to retype, reinsert, or reformat text and graphics.
- Library items can be altered at any time. After the editing is complete, Dreamweaver gives you the option to update the Web site immediately or postpone the update until later.
- If you are making a number of alterations to your Library items, you can wait until you're finished with all the updates and then make the changes across the board in one operation.
- You can update one page at a time, or you can update the entire site all at once.
- A Library item can be converted back to a regular non-Library element of a Web page at any time.
- Library items can be copied from one site to another.
- Library items can combine Dreamweaver behaviors—and their underlying JavaScript code—with onscreen elements, so you don't have to rebuild the same navigation bar every time, reapplying the behaviors over and over again.

Using the Library Assets Panel

Dreamweaver's Library control center is located on the Assets panel in the Library category. There you find the tools for creating, modifying, updating, and managing your Library items. Shown in Figure 18-1, the Library category is as flexible and easy to use as all of Dreamweaver's primary panels, with straightforward command buttons, a listing of all available Library items, and a handy Preview pane.

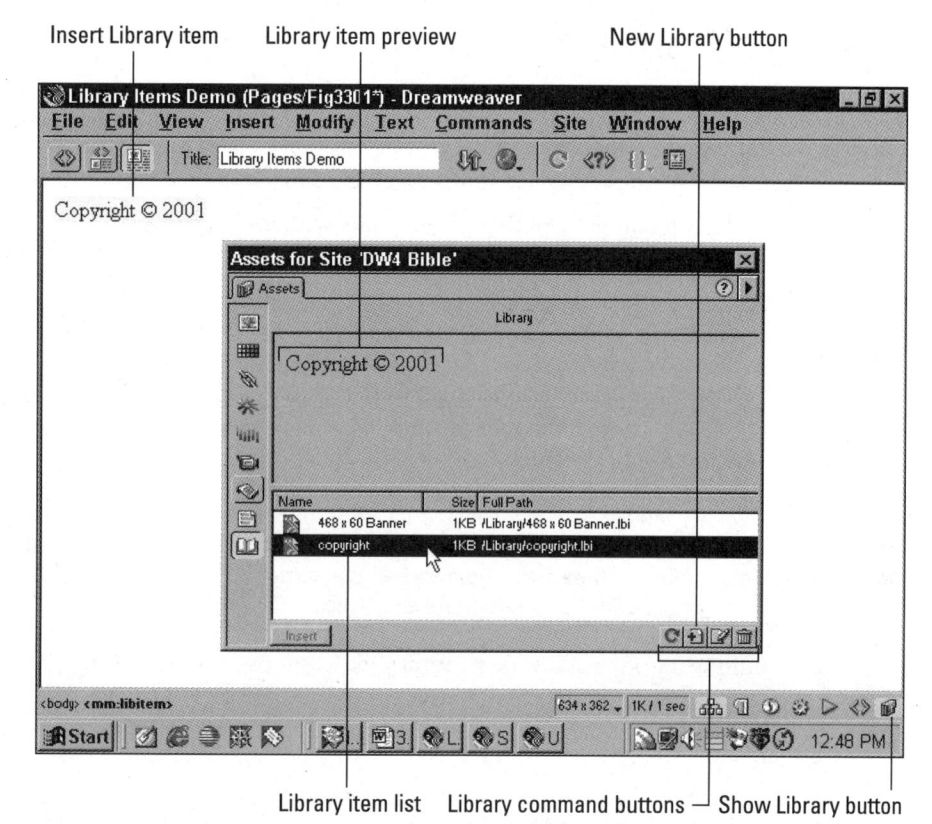

Chapter 18 ✦ Using the Repeating Elements Library 541

Figure 18-1: With the Dreamweaver Library feature, you can easily add and modify consistent objects on an entire Web site.

As usual, you can open the Library panel in several ways:

✦ Choose Window ➪ Library.

✦ Select the Library symbol on the Assets panel.

✦ Select the Library button from the Launcher.

Cross-Reference
To use Library items, you must first create a site root folder for Dreamweaver, as explained in Chapter 2. A separate Library folder is automatically created to hold the individual Library items and is used by Dreamweaver during the updating process.

Ideally, you could save the most time by creating all your Library items before you begin constructing your Web pages, but most Web designers don't work that way. Feel free to include, modify, and update your Library items as much as you need to as your Web site evolves — that's part of the power and flexibility you gain through Dreamweaver's Library.

Adding a Library item

Before you can insert or update a Library item, that item must be designated as such within the Web page. To add an item to your site's Library, follow these steps:

1. Select any part of the Web page that you want to make into a Library item.

2. Open the Library category of the Assets panel with any of the available methods: the Window ⇨ Library command, the Library symbol in the Assets panel or the Library button in the Launcher.

3. From the Library category (see Figure 18-1), select the New Library Item button.

   The selected page element is displayed in the upper pane of the Library category. In the lower pane — the Library item list — a new entry is highlighted with the default name "Untitled."

   Note: If the text you've selected has been styled by a CSS rule, Dreamweaver warns you that the appearance may be different because the style rule is not included in the Library item. To ensure that the appearance is the same, include the Library item only on those pages with the appropriate CSS styles.

4. Enter a unique name for your new Library item and press Enter (Return).

   The Library item list is resorted alphabetically, if necessary, and the new item is included.

When a portion of your Web page has been designated as a Library item, a yellow highlight is displayed over the entire item within the Document window. The highlight helps you to quickly recognize what is a Library item and what is not. If you find the yellow highlight distracting, you can disable it. Go to Edit ⇨ Preferences and, from the Highlighting category of the Preferences dialog box, deselect Show check box for Library Items. Alternatively, deselecting View ⇨ Visual Aids ⇨ Invisible Elements hides Library Item highlighting, along with any other invisible items on your page.

Cross-Reference: Dreamweaver can include Library items only in the `<body>` section of an HTML document. You cannot, for instance, create a series of `<meta>` tags for your pages that must go in the `<head>` section.

Moving Library items to a new site

Although Library items are specific to each site, they can be used in more than one site. When you make your first Library item, Dreamweaver creates a folder called Library in the local root folder for the current site. To use a particular Library item in another site, simply open the Library folder from your system's desktop and copy the item to the new site's Library folder.

Drag-and-Drop Creation of Library Items

A second option for creating Library items is the drag-and-drop method. Simply select an object or several objects on a page and drag them to the Library category (either the top or bottom pane); release the mouse button to drop them in.

You can drag any object into the Library category: text, tables, images, Java applets, plug-ins, and/or ActiveX controls. Essentially anything in the Document window that can be HTML code can be dragged to the Library. And, as you might suspect, the reverse is true: Library items can be placed in your Web page by dragging them from the Library category and dropping them anywhere in the Document window.

Cross-Reference: Be sure to also move any dependent files or other assets such as images and media files associated with the Library items.

Inserting a Library item in your Web page

When you create a Web site, you always need to incorporate certain features, including a standard set of link buttons along the top, a consistent banner on various pages, and a copyright notice along the bottom. Adding these items to a page from the Library can be as easy as dragging and dropping them.

You must first create a Web site and then designate Library items (as explained in the preceding section). Once these items exist, you can add the items to any page created within your site.

To add Library items to a document, use the following steps:

1. Position the cursor where you want the Library item to appear.
2. From the Library category, select the item you wish to use.
3. Select the Insert button. The highlighted Library item appears on the Web page.

Tip: As noted earlier, you can also use the drag-and-drop method to place Library items in the Document window.

When you add a Library item to a page, you notice a number of immediate changes. As mentioned, the added Library item is highlighted. If you click anywhere on the item, the entire Library item is selected.

It's important to understand that Dreamweaver treats the entire Library item entry as an external object being linked to the current page. You cannot modify Library items directly on a page. For information on editing Library entries, see the section "Editing a Library Item," later in this chapter.

While the Library item is highlighted, notice also that the Property Inspector changes. Instead of displaying the properties for the HTML object that is selected, the item is identified as a Library item, as shown in Figure 18-2.

Figure 18-2: The Library Item Property Inspector identifies the source file for any selected Library entry.

You can also see evidence of Library items in the HTML for the current page. Open the Code Inspector, and you see that several lines of code have been added. The following code example indicates one Library item:

```
<!-- #BeginLibraryItem "/Library/title.lbi" -->
<font color="#FF6633" face="Verdana, Arial, Helvetica, sans-serif" ¬
size="-4">
<b>Copyright &copy; 2000</b></font>
<!-- #EndLibraryItem -->
```

In this case, the Library item happens to be a phrase: "Copyright (c) 2000." (The character entity `&copy;` is used to represent the c-in-a-circle copyright mark in HTML.) In addition to the code that specifies the font face, color, and size, notice the text before and after the HTML code. These are commands within the comments that tell Dreamweaver it is looking at a Library item. One line marks the beginning of the Library item:

```
<!-- #BeginLibraryItem "/Library/title.lbi" -->
```

and another marks the end:

```
<!-- #EndLibraryItem -->
```

Two items are of interest here. First, notice how the Library demarcation surrounds not just the text ("Copyright (c) 2000") but all of its formatting attributes. Library items can do far more than just cut and paste raw text. The second thing to note is that the Library markers are placed discreetly within HTML comments. Web browsers ignore the Library markers and render the code in between them.

The value in the opening Library code, `"/Library/title.lbi"`, is the source file for the Library entry. This file is located in the Library folder, inside of the current site root folder. Library source (.lbi) files can be opened with a text editor or in Dreamweaver; they consist of plain HTML code without the `<html>` and `<body>` tags.

The .lbi file for our title example would contain the following:

```
<font color="#FF6633" face="Verdana, Arial, Helvetica, sans-serif" ¬
size="-4">
<b>Copyright &copy; 2000</b></font>
```

The power of repeating elements is that they are simply HTML. There is no need to learn proprietary languages to customize Library items. Anything, except for information found in the header of a Web page, can be included in a Library file.

The importance of the `<!-- #BeginLibraryItem>` and `<!-- #EndLibraryItem>` tags becomes evident when you start to update Library items for a site. You examine how Dreamweaver can be used to automatically update your entire Web site in the section "Updating Your Web Sites with Libraries," later in this chapter.

Deleting an item from the Library

Removing an entry from your site's Library is a two-step process. First, you must delete the item from the Library category. Then, if you want to keep the item on your page, you must make it editable again. Without completing the second step, Dreamweaver maintains the Library highlight and, more importantly, prevents you from modifying the element.

To delete an item from the Library, follow these steps:

1. Open the Web page containing the Library item you want to delete.
2. Open the Library category by choosing Window ⇨ Library or by selecting the Library button from the Launcher.
3. Select the Library item in the list and click the Delete button.
4. Dreamweaver asks if you are sure you want to delete the item. Select Yes, and the entry is removed from the Library item list. (Or select No to cancel.)
5. In the Document window, select the element you are removing from the Library.
6. In the Property Inspector, click Detach from Original.
7. As shown in Figure 18-3, Dreamweaver warns you that if you proceed, the item cannot be automatically updated (as a Library element). Select OK to proceed. The Library highlighting vanishes, and the element can now be modified individually.

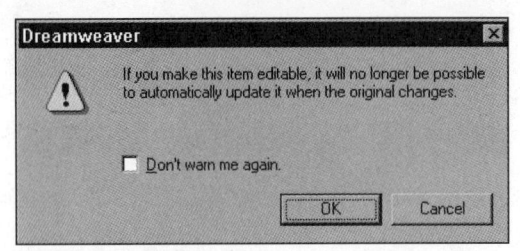

Figure 18-3: When making an item editable from the Library, Dreamweaver alerts you that, if you proceed, you won't be able to update the item automatically using the Library function.

> **Note** Should you unintentionally delete a Library item in the Library category, you can restore it if you still have the entry included in a Web page. Select the element within the page and, in the Property Inspector, choose the Recreate button. Dreamweaver restores the item to the Library item list, with the original Library name.

Renaming a Library item

It's easy to rename a Library item, both in the Assets panel and across your site. Dreamweaver automatically updates the name for any embedded Library item. To give an existing Library entry a new name, open the Library category and click the name of the item twice, slowly—do not double-click. Alternatively, you could choose Rename from the context menu of the Assets panel. The name is highlighted, and a small box appears around it. Enter the new name and press Enter (Return).

Dreamweaver then displays the Update Files dialog box with a list of files in which the renamed Library item is contained. Select Update to rename the Library item across the site. If you select Don't Update, the Library item will be renamed only in the Library category. Furthermore, your embedded Library items will be orphaned—that is, no master Library item will be associated with them and they will not be updateable.

Editing a Library Item

Rarely do you create a Library item that is perfect from the beginning and never needs to be changed. Whether it is due to site redesign or the addition of new sections to a site, you'll find yourself going back to Library items and modifying them, sometimes over and over again. You can use the full power of Dreamweaver's design capabilities to alter your Library items, within the restraints of Library items in general. In other words, you can modify an image, reformat a body of text, add new material to a boilerplate paragraph, and have the resulting changes reflected across your Web site. However, you cannot add anything to a Library item that is not contained in the HTML <body> tags.

To modify Library items, Dreamweaver uses a special editing window identifiable by the double angle brackets surrounding the phrase "Library Item" in the title bar. You access this editing window through the Library category or the Property Inspector. Follow these steps to modify an existing Library item:

1. In the Library category, select the item you wish to modify from the list of available entries.
2. Click the Open Library Item button. The Library editing window opens with the selected entry, as shown in Figure 18-4.
3. Make any necessary modifications to the Library entry.
4. When you are finished with your changes, choose File ⇨ Save or press Ctrl+S (Command+S).

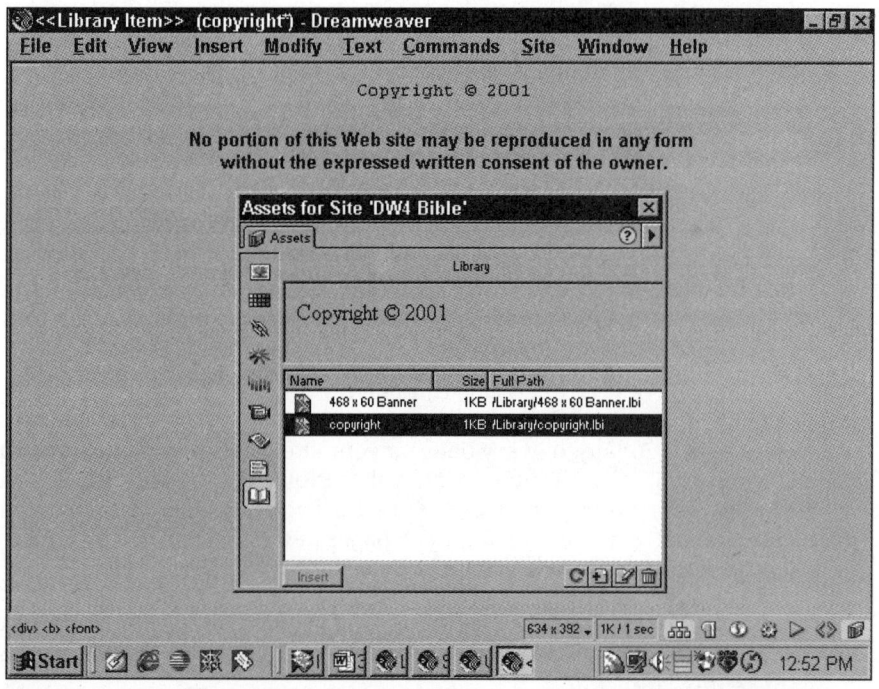

Figure 18-4: Use the Library editing window to modify existing Library items.

5. Dreamweaver notes that your Library item has been modified and asks if you would like to update all of the Web pages in your site that contain the item. Select Yes to update all of the Library items, including the one just modified, or select No to postpone the update. (See the next section, "Updating Your Web Sites with Libraries.")

6. Close the editing window by selecting the Close button or choosing File ⇨ Close.

Once you've completed the editing operation and closed the editing window, you can open any Web page containing the modified Library item to view the changes.

> **Cross-Reference**
> You cannot use some features to their fullest when editing Library items. These include timelines, behaviors, and styles. Each of these modifications requires a JavaScript function to be placed in the `<head>` tags of a page — a task that the Dreamweaver Library function cannot handle. If you add a behavior to a Library item while editing it, the JavaScript function will be copied to your page next to the Library item itself. While this will work in some instances — a pop-up message for example — other behaviors will perform erratically. One workaround is to use a Dreamweaver template to add entire pages with JavaScript functions included, as described in Chapter 17. You could, of course, also add behaviors to a page element before converting it to a Library item.

Updating Your Web Sites with Libraries

The effectiveness of the Dreamweaver Library feature becomes more significant when it comes time to update an entire multipage site. Dreamweaver offers two opportunities for you to update your site:

✦ Immediately after modifying a Library item, as explained in the preceding steps for editing a Library item

✦ At a time of your choosing, through the Modify ⇨ Library command

An immediate update to every page on your site can be accomplished when you edit a Library item. After you save the alterations, Dreamweaver asks if you'd like to apply the update to Web pages in your site. If you click Yes, Dreamweaver not only applies the current modification to all pages in the site, but it also applies any other alterations that you have made previously in this Library.

The second way to modify a Library item is by using the Modify ⇨ Library command, and when you use this method, you can choose to update the current page or the entire site.

To update just the current page, choose Modify ⇨ Library ⇨ Update Current Page. Dreamweaver makes a quick check to see what Library items you are managing on the current page and then compares them to the site's Library items. If any differences exist, Dreamweaver modifies the page accordingly.

To update an entire Web site, follow these steps:

1. Choose Modify ⇨ Library ⇨ Update Pages. The Update Pages dialog box opens (see Figure 18-5).

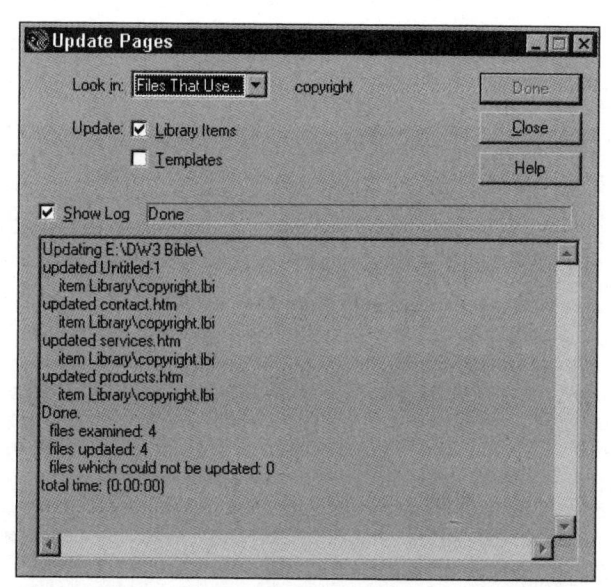

Figure 18-5: The Update Pages dialog box enables you to apply any changes to your Library items across an entire site and informs you of the progress.

2. If you want Dreamweaver to update all of the Library items in all of the Web pages in your site, select Entire Site from the Look In drop-down list and choose the name of your site in the drop-down list on the right. You can also have Dreamweaver update only the pages in your site that contain a specific Library item. Select the Files That Use option from the Look In drop-down list and then select the Library item that you would like to have updated across your site from the drop-down list on the right.

3. If you want to see the results from the update process, leave the Show Log checkbox selected. (Turning off the Log reduces the size of the Site Update dialog box.)

4. Choose the Start button. Dreamweaver processes the entire site for Library updates. Any Library items contained are modified to reflect the changes.

Note Although Dreamweaver does modify Library items on currently open pages during an Update Site operation, you have to save the pages to accept the changes.

The Update Pages log displays any errors encountered in the update operation. A log containing the notation

```
item Library\Untitled2.lbi -- not updated, library item not found
```

indicates that one Web page contains a reference to a Library item that has been removed. Though this is not a critical error, you might want to use Dreamweaver's Find and Replace feature to search your Web site for the code and remove it.

Applying Server-Side Includes

In some ways, the server-side include (SSI) is the predecessor of the Dreamweaver Library item. The difference is that with Library items, Dreamweaver updates the Web pages at design time, whereas with server-side includes, the server handles the updating at runtime (when the files are actually served to the user). Server-side includes can also include server variables, such as the current date and time (both locally and Greenwich mean time) or the date the current file was last saved.

Because server-side includes are integrated in the standard HTML code, a special file extension is used to identify pages using them. Any page with server-side includes is most often saved with either the .shtml or .shtm extension. When a server encounters such a file, the file is read and processed by the server.

Cross-Reference Not all servers support server-side includes. Some Web hosting companies disable the function because of potential security risks and performance issues. Each .shtml page requires additional processing time, and if a site uses many SSI pages, the server can slow down significantly. Be sure to check your Web host's policy before including SSIs in your Web pages.

Server-side includes are often used to insert header or footer items into the <body> of an HTML page. Typically, the server-side include itself is just a file with HTML. To insert a file, the SSI code looks like the following:

```
<!-- #include file="footer.html" -->
```

Note how the HTML comment structure is used to wrap around the SSI directive. This ensures that browsers ignore the code, but servers do not. The file attribute defines the path name of the file to be included, relative to the current page. To include a file relative to the current site root, use the virtual attribute, as follows:

```
<!-- #include virtual="/main/images/spaceman.jpg" -->
```

As evident in this example, you can use SSIs to include more than just HTML files — you can also include graphics.

With Dreamweaver's translator mechanism, server-side includes can be visible in the Document window during the design process. All you need to do is make sure that the Translation preferences are set correctly, as described in the section "Modifying Translators," later in this chapter.

One of the major benefits of SSIs is inserting information from the server itself, such as the current file size or time. One tag, `<!-- #echo -->`, is used to define a custom variable that is returned when the SSI is called, as well as numerous *environmental variables*. An environmental variable is information available to the server, such as the date a file was last modified or its URL.

Table 18-1 details the possible server tags and their attributes.

Table 18-1
Server-Side Include Variables

Tag	Attribute	Description
`<!-- #config -->`	`errmsg`, `sizefmt`, or `timefmt`	Used to customize error messages, file size, or time and date displays
`<!-- #echo -->`	`var` or environmental variables, such as `last_modified`, `document_name`, `document_url`, `date_local`, or `date_gmt`	Returns the specified variable
`<!-- #exec -->`	`cmd` or `cgi`	Executes a system command or CGI program
`<!-- #flastmod -->`	`file` or `virtual`	Displays the last modified date of a file other than the current one
`<!-- #fsize -->`	`file` or `virtual`	Displays the size of a file other than the current one
`<!-- #include -->`	`file` or `virtual`	Inserts the contents of the specified file to the current one

Adding server-side includes

Dreamweaver has made inserting a server-side include in your Web page very straightforward. You can use a Dreamweaver object to easily select and bring in the files to be included. Any other type of SSI, such as declaring a variable, must be entered in by hand, but you can use the Comment object to do so without switching to Code View, or opening the Code Inspector.

To use server-side includes to incorporate a file, follow these steps:

   1. In the Document window, place your cursor in the location where you would like to add the server-side include.

2. Select Insert ⇨ Server-Side Include or choose Insert Server-Side Include from the Common category of the Objects panel.

   The standard Select File dialog box appears.

3. In the Select File dialog box, type in the URL of the HTML page you would like to include in the File Name text box or use the folder icon to locate the file. Click OK when you're done.

   Dreamweaver displays the contents of the HTML file at the desired location in your page. Should the Property Inspector be available, the SSI Property Inspector is displayed (see Figure 18-6).

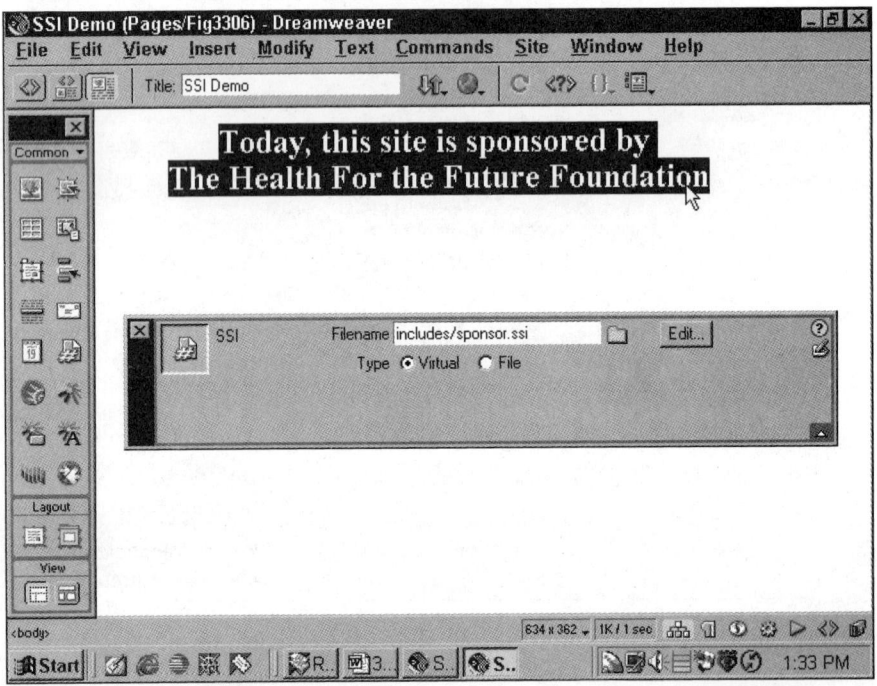

Figure 18-6: The selected text is actually a server-side include automatically translated by Dreamweaver, as is evident from the SSI Property Inspector.

4. In the Property Inspector, if the server-side include calls a file-relative document path, select the Type File option. Or, if the SSI calls a site root-relative file, choose the Type Virtual option.

Tip Because server-side includes can be placed only within the body of a Dreamweaver file, the contents of the HTML page that you wish to include should not have any tags that are not readable within the body section of a document, such as `<head>`, `<title>`, or `<meta>` — or the `<body>` tag itself. You can, however, design your HTML page in Dreamweaver, and then use Code View, or the Code Inspector, to remove any such tags before inserting the page into your document with a server-side include.

Editing server-side includes

As is the case with Library items, it is not possible to directly edit files that have been inserted into a Web page using server-side includes. In fact, should you try, the entire text block highlights as one. The text for a server-side included file is not editable through Dreamweaver's Code View, or Code Inspector, although the SSI code is.

To edit the contents of the server-side included file, follow these steps:

1. Select the server-side include in the Document window.
2. Select the Edit button from the SSI Property Inspector.

   The file opens in a new Dreamweaver window for editing.
3. When you've finished altering the file, select File ⇨ Save or use the keyboard shortcut Ctrl+S (Command+S).
4. Close the file editing window by choosing File ⇨ Close.

Dreamweaver automatically reflects the changes in your currently open document.

Unlike when editing Library items, Dreamweaver does not ask if any other linked files should be updated because all blending of regular HTML and SSIs happens at runtime or when the file is open in Dreamweaver and the SSI translator is engaged.

Extending Dreamweaver with XSSI

Both Dreamweaver Library items and server-side includes are useful for easily updating a range of pages when changing one item. But what if you have to change that one item several times a day — or based on which domain the user is coming from? To handle these tasks automatically, a system must support some form of conditional tags, such as `if-then` statements. Such a system is now available through Apache servers and XSSI, extended server-side includes. Most importantly, a full set of XSSI objects, translators, and Property Inspectors for Dreamweaver have been built by the wonderful programmers at Webmonkey (www.webmonkey.com). You can find the XSSI extensions on the CD-ROM that comes with this book.

In addition to handling standard server-side includes, the XSSI extensions offer a series of conditional statements: `if`, `elif` (else-if), `else`, and `endif`. The beauty of the Webmonkey objects is that you can construct or edit these conditional statements through their graphical user interface. The basic syntax of the conditional statements is as follows:

Continued

Continued

```
<!--#if expr="text_expression" -->
If the above is true, perform this action
<!--#elif expr="text_expression" -->
Else if the above is true, do this
<!--#else -->
Otherwise, do this
<!--#endif -->
```

The XSSI extensions also have the capability of setting an environmental variable so that you can view your page under various conditions. For example, let's say you've written a script that includes a particular file that greets the visitor in a proper way, depending on which browser is being used. Your conditional script would look to the HTTP_USER_AGENT variable to see which message to serve. With the XSSI Set Env Variables command, you could test your script during the design phase without having to visit the server at different times of the day. The following figure displays the Set XSSI Environment Variables dialog box.

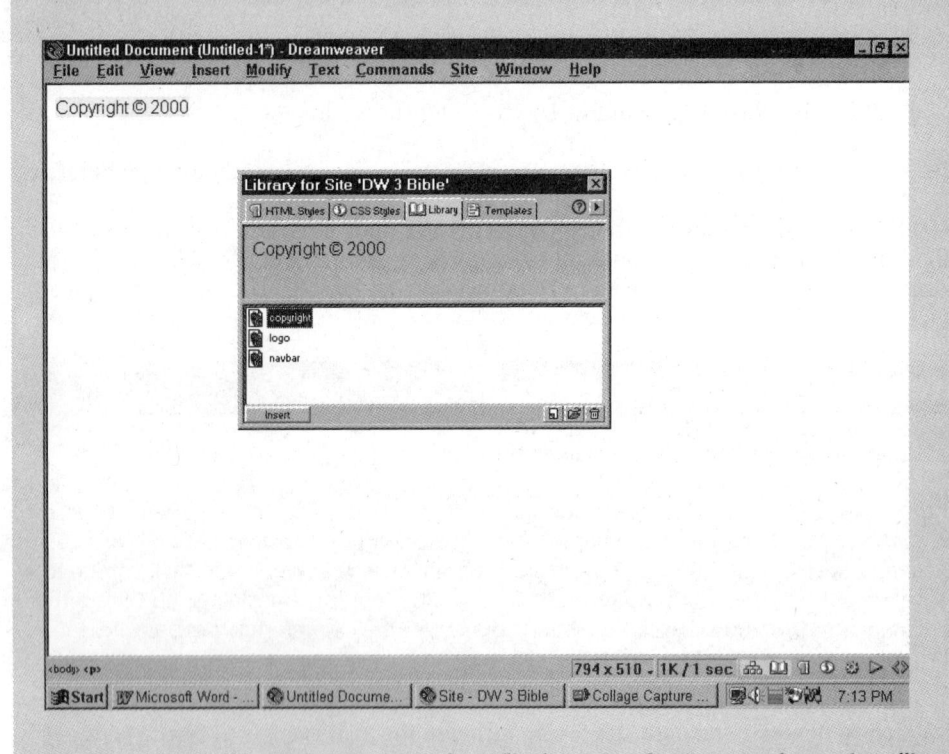

One note of caution: Due to a potential conflict between the two translators, installing the XSSI extensions disables the standard SSI translator. Make sure your system is XSSI compatible (it uses Apache server software) before incorporating the XSSI extensions.

Summary

In this chapter, you learned how you can easily and effectively create Library items that can be repeated throughout an entire site to help maintain consistency.

- Library items can consist of any text, object, or HTML code contained in the `<body>` of a Web page.
- The quickest method to create a Library item is to drag the code from the Dreamweaver Document window into the Library category's list area.
- Editing Library items is also easy: just click the Edit button in the Assets panel or choose Open from the Property Inspector, and you can swiftly make all of your changes in a separate Dreamweaver Library Item window.
- The Modify ⇨ Library ⇨ Update Pages command enables easy maintenance of your Web site.
- Server-side includes enable files to be inserted into the final HTML at runtime by the server. Dreamweaver's translation feature enables you to preview these effects.

✦ ✦ ✦

Working with Fireworks

PART II

In This Part

Chapter 19
Understanding the Interface

Chapter 20
Setting Up Documents

Chapter 21
Creating Vector Objects

Chapter 22
Working with Bitmaps

Chapter 23
Managing Color

Chapter 24
Choosing Strokes

Chapter 25
Structuring Paths

Chapter 26
Composing with Text

Chapter 27
Using Fills and Textures

Chapter 28
Creating Live Effects and Xtras

Chapter 29
Arranging and Compositing Objects

Chapter 30
Exporting and Optimizing

Chapter 31
Working with Fireworks Styles

Chapter 32
Using Symbols and Libraries

Chapter 33
Mastering Image Maps and Slices

Chapter 34
Activating Fireworks with Behaviors

Chapter 35
Applying Animation Techniques

Understanding the Interface

CHAPTER 19

In This Chapter

The Fireworks environment

Working in the document window

Familiarizing yourself with the Tools Panel

Using Windows toolbars

Optimizing the floating panels

Managing the menus

♦ ♦ ♦ ♦

Fireworks was designed to meet a need among Web graphics artists: to simplify the workflow. Before Fireworks, designers typically used different programs for object creation, rasterization, optimization, and HTML and JavaScript creation. Fireworks combines the best features of several key tools — while offering numerous innovative additions of its own — into a sophisticated interface that's easy to use and offers many surprising creative advantages. After you've discovered the power of Fireworks, designing Web graphics any other way is hard.

With Fireworks, the designer has tools for working with both vector objects and bitmap objects. You'll even find ways to combine the two different formats. When your document is ready to make the move to the Web, Fireworks acts as a bridge to the HTML environment by allowing you to create the necessary code in a point-and-click manner.

As with any truly powerful computer graphics program, examining all the tools and options that Fireworks has to offer at one time can be overwhelming. However, that's not how most artists work. You may find it easier to familiarize yourself with a new tool by carrying out a specific task. It's fine to go all the way through this chapter — which covers every element of the Fireworks interface — but you'll probably get the most value from the chapter elements, especially the menu-by-menu description of commands at the end of the chapter, by using them as a reference guide.

Examining the Fireworks Environment

Whether you start your graphics session by creating a new document or loading in an existing one, you'll find yourself working within a complete environment that includes pull-down menus, one or more document windows, and a selection of floating panels, as shown in Figure 19-1. Each document window contains a single Fireworks file; the menus and floating panels affect the file in the active document window.

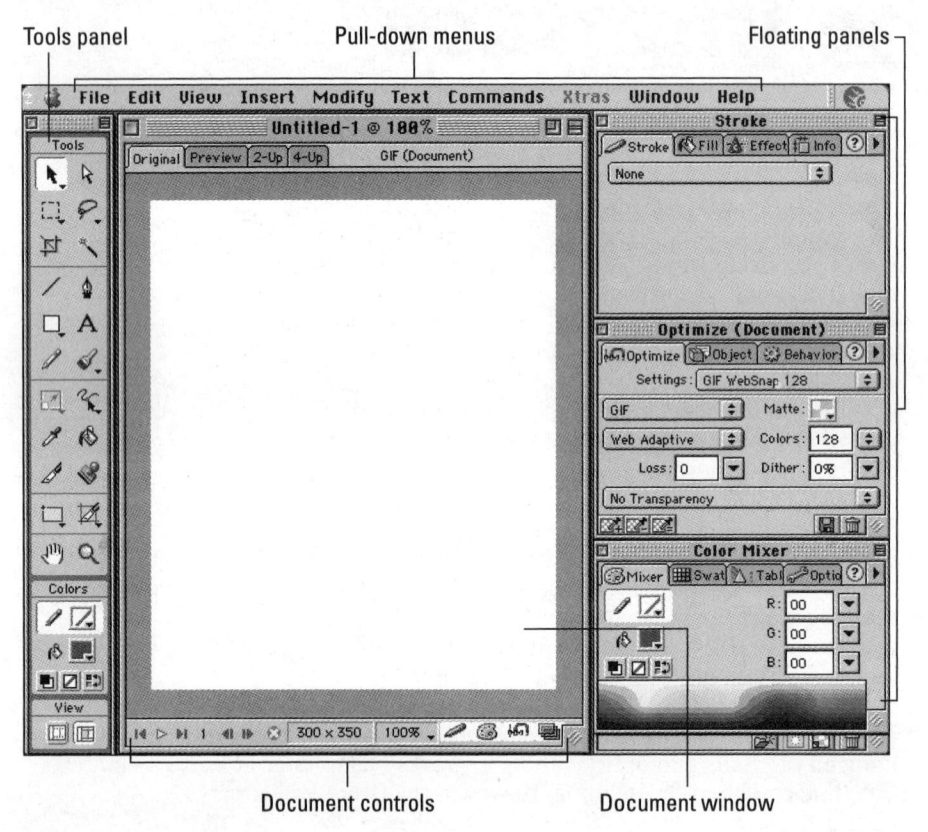

Figure 19-1: The Fireworks environment on both platforms includes menus, a toolbox, one or more document windows, and a complete set of floating panels.

Fireworks for Windows (see Figure 19-2) features the same interface elements as its Macintosh cousin, but also adds two toolbars and a context-sensitive status bar to the mix. The toolbars mimic commonly used functions from the menus, such as opening a document or arranging objects. The Windows version also uses a multiple document interface that contains all the documents and interface elements within a parent Fireworks window. You can dock toolbars to the parent window, or float them as required, by dragging them toward or away from the parent window.

We examine each element of the complete Fireworks environment throughout this chapter. Remember, you can refer to Figures 19-1 or 19-2 at any time if you find yourself losing track of a particular item.

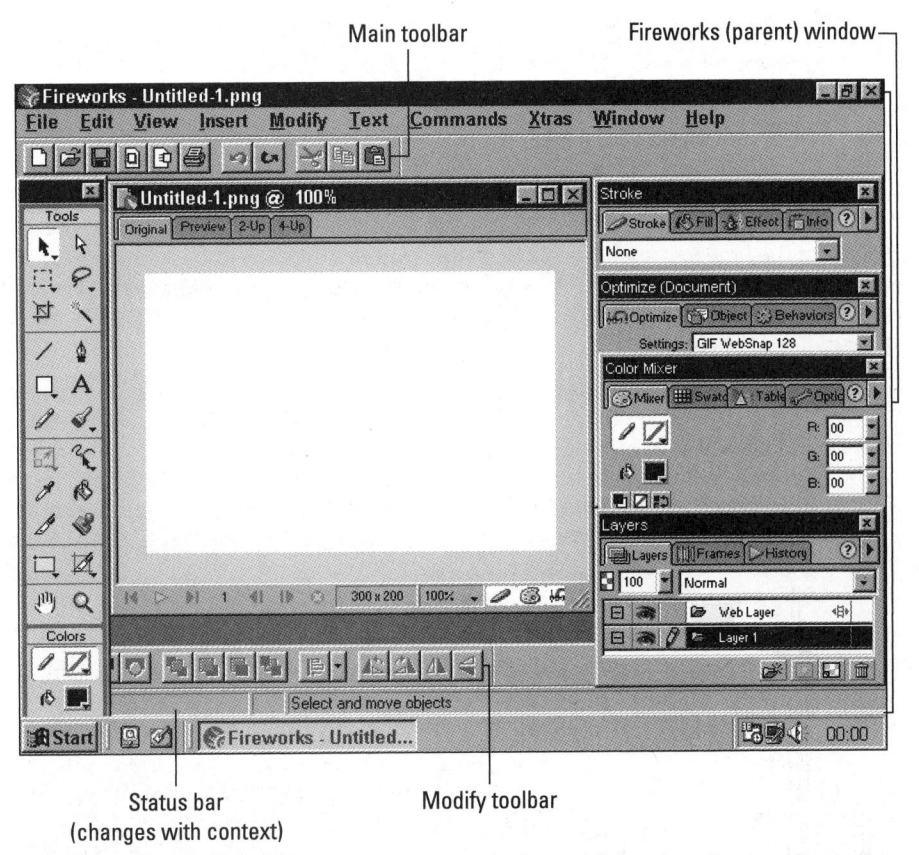

Figure 19-2: The Windows version of Fireworks has additional toolbars and uses a multiple document interface.

Understanding the Document Window

The document window is the central focus of your work in Fireworks. Each Fireworks document you open or create is contained within its own document window, with the filename and zoom setting displayed as the window's title. When your document has unsaved changes, Fireworks places an asterisk next to the filename and zoom setting. This asterisk is sometimes called a "dirty doc" indicator, because it indicates that the document you are looking at has been "dirtied" since it was opened and needs to be saved to disk.

You can open multiple documents and display them simultaneously, as shown in Figure 19-3. The menus, toolbox, and floating panels affect the file in the active document window.

The Macromedia Common User Interface

The Web design workflow often involves more than one application. Many designers are working mainly in a combination of Fireworks and Dreamweaver, or Fireworks and Flash. Unfortunately, previous versions of many of Macromedia's own applications often featured wildly divergent user interface (UI) conventions, such as different key shortcuts and different methods for hiding and showing floating panels. In short, Macromedia was not rewarding users for the time we spent learning one application's user interface. Starting to work in a second Macromedia application was often just like starting over. Moreover, different UI conventions made switching back and forth between two applications during the same session more trouble than it needed to be.

With Fireworks 4, Macromedia has taken the first step to providing some UI conformity across its product line. Some of the common elements you'll notice if you switch between Fireworks and Dreamweaver are icons on floating panel tabs, uniform keyboard shortcuts, customizable keyboard shortcuts, and a mini-launcher for showing and hiding floating panels. Focusing on the "cross-product UI" has also enabled Macromedia to shake out a few longstanding UI quirks and provide the user with a sleeker, more intuitive Fireworks experience.

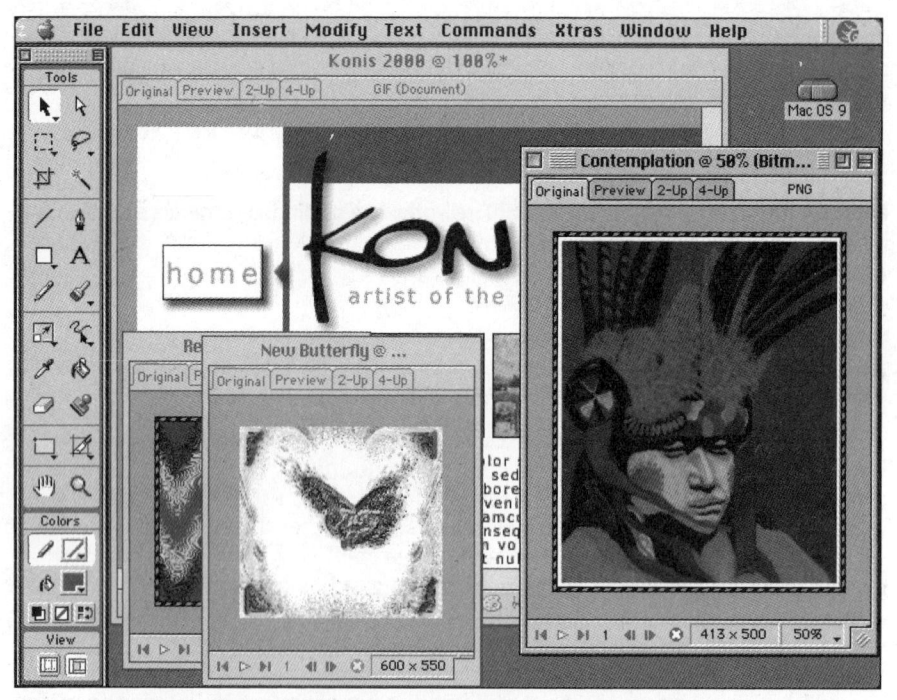

Figure 19-3: Each Fireworks file you open or create is contained within its own document window, and you can open multiple documents simultaneously.

Objects are created and edited on the *canvas* within the document window. The canvas is the active area of your document. To simplify editing at the edges of the canvas, it is surrounded by a gray canvas border. When you zoom in on the edge of a document, the canvas border provides some breathing room so that you can see what you're doing.

New Feature: The canvas border is new in Fireworks 4. Previously, zooming in on a document would cause the canvas to press up against the window border. Now, a border is always available.

If you have multiple documents open and your workspace is getting cluttered, you can organize the document windows in three different ways:

- Choose Window ⇨ Cascade to stack your open documents on top of each other in a diagonal, so that the title bar for each is visible.
- Select Window ⇨ Tile Horizontal to see all open documents evenly distributed from top to bottom in the document window.
- Select Window ⇨ Tile Vertical to view all open documents evenly distributed from left to right in the document window.

You can also hide document windows that you're not currently using. Macintosh users can click the Windowshade button on a document window to hide all but the title bar. Windows users can click the Minimize button on a document window to minimize its title bar to the bottom of the parent window. Windows users can also click Maximize to dock a document window to the parent window, hiding all other windows. Clicking the document window's Restore button undocks it.

In addition to multiple document windows for multiple documents, Fireworks can also display multiple document windows for the same document. To open a new view of a selected document, choose Window ⇨ New Window, or use the keyboard shortcut Ctrl+Alt+N in Windows (Command+Option+N for Macintosh). The new document window opens at the same magnification setting as the original document window but, as Figure 19-4 shows, you can easily zoom in for detail work on one view while displaying the overall effect in another.

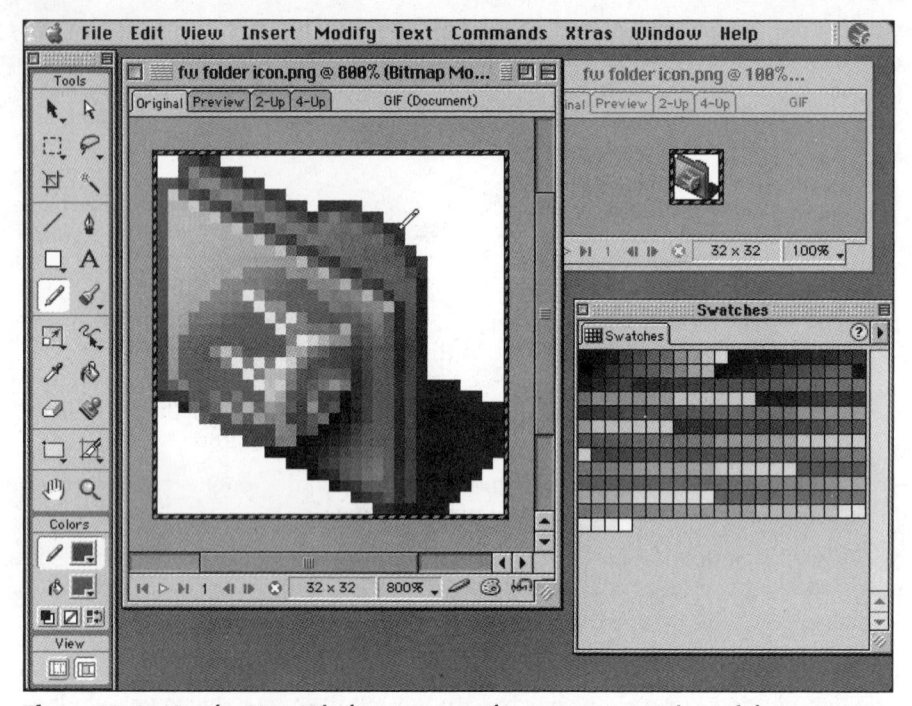

Figure 19-4: Use the New Window command to open a new view of the same document if both pixel-level modifications and the big picture are required, such as when creating small icons.

Document window controls

Fireworks enables you to control what you see in a document window in a number of ways. Tabs along the top of the document window enable you to preview your work in-place; you'll also find zoom and animation controls, and more (see Figure 19-5).

We'll look at each of the document window controls in turn.

New Feature Document window controls are now similarly placed in both versions of Fireworks. Previous users of Fireworks 3 for Windows will notice that the View Controls toolbar is no more. Instead, find those controls along the bottom of your document windows, along with the VCR-style animation controls, and the Exit Bitmap Mode button that used to live in the status bar.

Original/Preview tabs

When you open or create a document in Fireworks, the document window is set on the Original tab, so that you can interact with and edit the objects on the canvas. Choose one of the other tabs and Fireworks will create and display a preview of your work as it will appear in your exported final output.

Chapter 19 ✦ **Understanding the Interface** 565

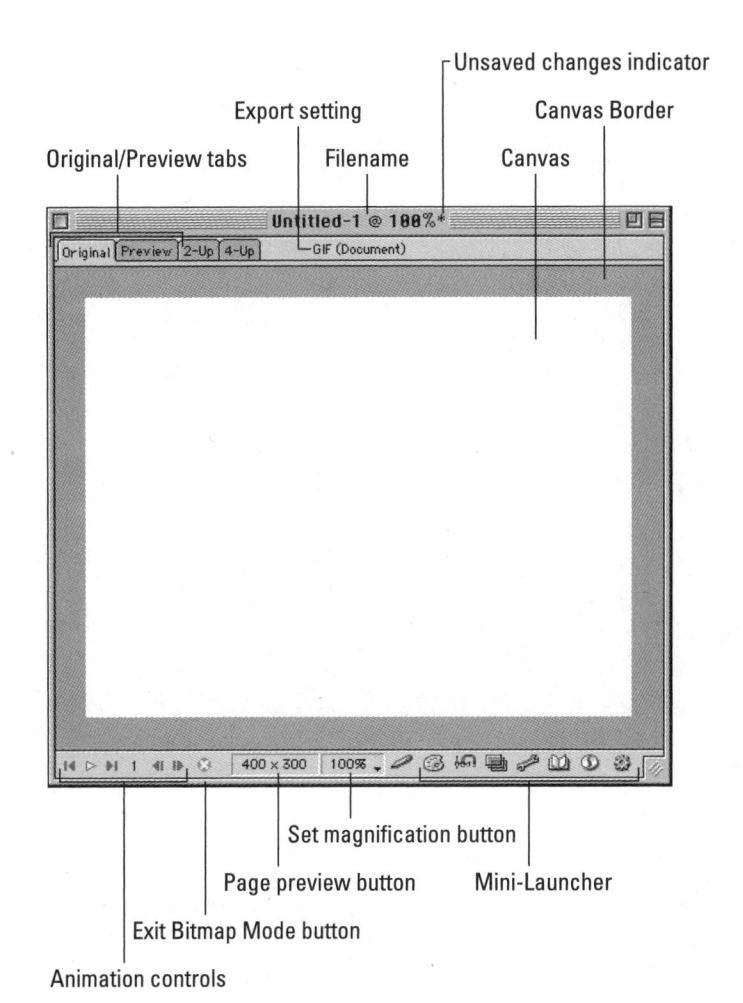

Figure 19-5: Fireworks document window controls enable you to alter how your document is presented in the document window.

You can switch from Original to one of the preview modes at any time. Fireworks generates a preview based on the settings you select in the Optimize panel, as shown in Figure 19-6. Control of the export palette is available in the Color Table panel.

Although the 2-Up preview gives you a side-by-side view of the Original and Preview views of a document, it only shows you half of each unless you manually expand your document window. If you have the screen real estate available, another way to get a side-by-side preview is to open a new document window for the same document (Window ➪ New Window, as described previously) and set it to Preview.

Cross-Reference For more on previewing and exporting, see Chapter 30.

Figure 19-6: A preview of your work is never more than a click away with Fireworks' in-place preview.

Animation controls

With these VCR-like buttons, you can play a frame-based animation straight through, using the timing established in the Frame panel. You'll also find buttons that enable you to move through the animation a frame at a time, or to go to the first or last frame.

Cross-Reference See Chapter 35 for more about animation in Fireworks.

Exit Bitmap Mode button

Click this "Stop" button to quickly exit bitmap mode, and enter vector mode. When you're already in vector mode, the Stop button is grayed out. You can also choose Modify ➪ Exit Bitmap Mode or use the keyboard shortcut Ctrl+Shift+E (Command+Shift+E).

Page Preview

The Page Preview button displays the dimensions of your document in pixels. When you click the Page Preview button, the width, height, and print resolution of your document are displayed in a small pop-up window. Click anywhere outside of the pop-up window to dismiss it.

Magnification settings

Whether you're working with pixels or vectors, a polished, finished graphic often demands close-up, meticulous work. Likewise, the designer often needs to be able to step back from an image in order to compare two or more large images for overall compatibility, or to cut and paste sections of a graphic. Fireworks offers a fast Magnification control with numerous keyboard shortcuts for rapid view changes.

Fireworks uses a series of zoom settings, from 6 percent to 6,400 percent, for its Magnification control. Because Fireworks always works with pixels (even when they're based on vectors), the magnification settings are predefined to offer the best image pixel to screen pixel ratio. When an image is viewed at 100 percent magnification, one screen pixel is used for each image pixel. Should you zoom in to 200 percent, two screen pixels are used for each image pixel. Zooming out reverses the procedure: At 50 percent, each screen pixel represents two image pixels. Fireworks' preset zoom method offers a full range of settings while maintaining an accurate view of your image.

Clicking the arrow button in the Set Magnification option list displays the available settings. Highlight the desired zoom setting and release the mouse button in order to change magnifications. Fireworks also offers a variety of keyboard shortcuts to change the zoom setting, as detailed in Table 19-1. In addition to specifying a magnification setting, you can also have Fireworks fit the image in the current window. With this command, Fireworks zooms in or out to the maximum magnification setting possible — and still displays the entire image.

Table 19-1
Magnification Key Shortcuts

Magnification	Windows	Macintosh
100%	Ctrl+1	Command+1
50%	Ctrl+5	Command+5
200%	Ctrl+2	Command+2
400%	Ctrl+4	Command+4
800%	Ctrl+8	Command+8
3,200%	Ctrl+3	Command+3
6,400%	Ctrl+6	Command+6
Zoom In	Ctrl+Equals (=)	Command+Equals (=)
Zoom Out	Ctrl+Minus (–)	Command+Minus (–)
Fit Selection	Ctrl+Alt+Zero (0)	Command+Option+Zero (0)
Fit All	Ctrl+Zero (0) or double-click Hand tool	Command+Zero (0) or double-click Hand tool
Switch to Zoom tool temporarily	Hold down Ctrl+Spacebar	Hold down Command+Spacebar

Mini-Launcher

The Mini-Launcher enables one-click access to commonly used floating panels. Users of Macromedia Dreamweaver will recognize the Mini-Launcher right away. If your document window is too narrow, you may not be able to see the whole Mini-Launcher. If so, resize your document window until it is wide enough to display the entire Mini-Launcher.

> **New Feature** The Mini-Launcher is part of the Macromedia Common User Interface and is new in Fireworks 4.

Pressing one of the buttons in the Mini-Launcher opens a panel if it is closed, brings a panel to the front if it is behind another panel, or closes a panel if it is open and already up front. To see what a Mini-Launcher button will do before you press it, hover your mouse cursor over it until a descriptive tooltip appears. From left to right, the Mini-Launcher buttons are for the Stroke, Color Mixer, Optimize, Layers, Tool Options, Library, Styles, and Behaviors panels. Unlike Dreamweaver, the Mini-Launcher is not customizable, so you're stuck with the default selection of buttons.

> **Cross-Reference** We cover floating panels in more detail later in this chapter.

Display options

Most of the time, Fireworks designers work in Full Display mode. In fact, this practice is so common that many designers don't realize that another mode is even available. Toggling the View ⇨ Full Display command on and off controls whether the current document is in Full Display or Draft Display mode. Draft Display shows all vector objects with one-pixel-wide outlines and no fill; bitmap objects are shown as rectangles with an "X" in the middle.

> **Note** Selected objects are no longer rendered in Draft Display mode as they were in Fireworks 3.

If you have a complex document with multiple layers that each contain multiple objects (see Figure 19-7), picking out the one object you would like to work on, or getting a feel for the true alignment of objects that have complex strokes or image filters applied, can sometimes be hard.

Figure 19-7: In Full Display mode, picking out individual objects can be hard.

Looking at your document in Draft Display mode (see Figure 19-8) pares the view down to just the barest bones and enables you to pick out objects that are usually obscured by other objects in Full Display mode.

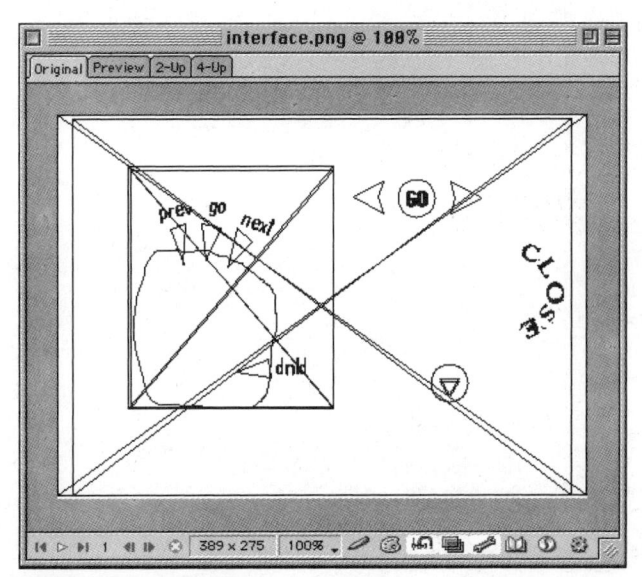

Figure 19-8: While you're in Draft Display mode, only the outlines of your objects are visible.

Exploring the Tools Panel

You can find all the Fireworks drawing and editing tools in the Tools panel. Most tools work with both bitmap and vector objects, although some change their behavior in order to do so. The Eraser, for example, becomes a Knife when you're working with vector objects.

To "pick up" a tool, click its icon in the Tools panel. Your mouse cursor will change to reflect the tool that's currently active. Only one tool can be active at a time. Use the tool by clicking the canvas. Some tools will require that you click and drag, to draw a selection with a Marquee tool, for example. If you want to drag beyond the visible canvas area, the document window will scroll automatically to follow your cursor.

New Feature   Tool scrolling is new in Fireworks 4.

Tools that are similar, such as the Lasso, Polygon Lasso, and Magic Wand, are grouped together into tool groups and accessed through a flyout. A tool group can be recognized by the small triangle in the lower-right corner of the button; clicking and holding the button causes the flyout to appear. After the tool group is visible, you can select any of the tools in the group by moving the pointer over the tool and releasing the mouse. Figure 19-9 shows a dissected Tools panel's anatomy in great detail.

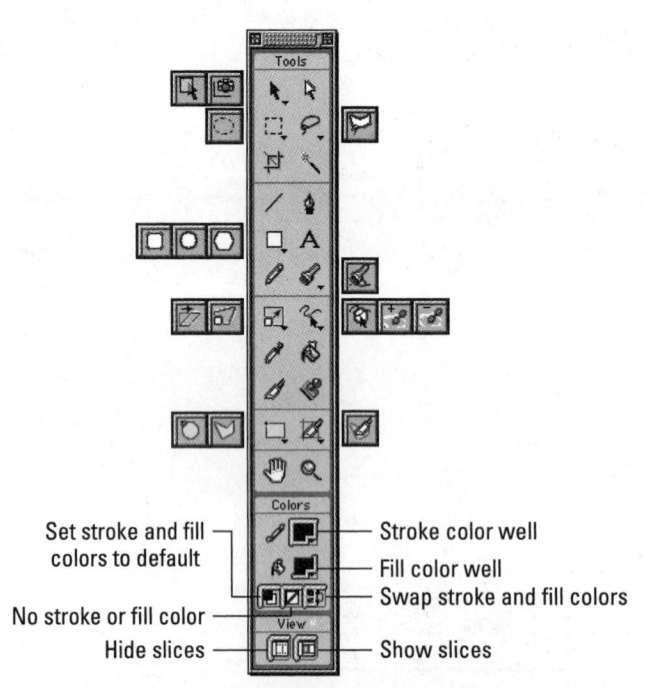

Figure 19-9: The Tools panel contains 38 different creation and editing tools for both graphics and Web objects.

All the tools have keyboard shortcuts. As befits a program that incorporates both bitmap and vector editing tools, these single-key shortcuts parallel the shortcuts for some of the pixel-based tools in Photoshop, and vector-based ones in FreeHand, where possible. If two or more tools share a keyboard shortcut (as with M for Marquee and Oval Marquee), the key acts as a toggle between the tools; the letter R toggles through the shape tools, for example. You can find the button for each tool, as well as its keyboard shortcut and a brief description of the tool, in Table 19-2. More detailed information on each tool is presented throughout this book when the tool is used for various operations.

New Feature The Rounded Rectangle tool is a brand-new addition to the Fireworks tools. Tools that have moved or been modified in some way are displayed in **bold** text in Table 19-2.

Table 19-2
Fireworks Tools

Button	Name	Shortcut	Description
	Pointer	V or Zero	Selects and moves objects
	Select Behind	V or Zero	Selects and moves objects that are behind other objects
	Export Area	J	Exports a selected portion of a document
	Subselection	A or 1	Selects an object within a group or points on a vector path
	Marquee	M	Selects a rectangular portion of a bitmap object
	Oval Marquee	M	Selects an elliptical portion of a bitmap object
	Lasso	L	Selects a freely drawn area of a bitmap object
	Polygon Lasso	L	Selects a polygon-shaped area of a bitmap object
	Crop	C	Increases or decreases canvas size
	Magic Wand	W	Selects similar color areas of a bitmap object
	Line	N	Draws straight lines

Continued

Table 19-2 *(continued)*

Button	Name	Shortcut	Description
	Pen	P	Adds points to vector paths
	Rectangle	R	Draws rectangles, rectangles with rounded corners, and squares
	Rounded Rectangle	R	Draws rectangles with a Roundness setting of 30 percent
	Ellipse	R	Draws ellipses and circles
	Polygon	R	Draws polygons and stars
	Text	T	Inserts text objects
	Pencil	Y	Draws single-pixel freeform strokes
	Brush	B	Draws strokes using the Stroke panel settings
	Redraw Path	B	Redraws portions of a selected vector path
	Scale	Q	Resizes and rotates objects
	Skew	Q	Slants, rotates, and modifies the perspective of objects
	Distort	Q	Reshapes and rotates objects
	Freeform	F	Pulls or pushes a vector path with a variable-size cursor
	Reshape Area	F	Reshapes an object's area with a variable-size cursor
	Path Scrubber (+)	F	Increases the stroke settings that are controlled by cursor speed or pen and tablet pressure

Button	Name	Shortcut	Description
	Path Scrubber (–)	F	Decreases the stroke settings that are controlled by cursor speed or pen and tablet pressure
	Eyedropper	I	Picks up color from anywhere onscreen and applies it to the active color well
	Paint Bucket	K	Fills the selected area with color, gradients, patterns, or textures and enables fills to be adjusted
	Eraser	E	Deletes pixels from bitmap objects in bitmap mode; in vector mode, it is displayed as a knife and cuts the paths of vector objects
	Rubber Stamp	S	Repeats a portion of a bitmap object
	Rectangle Hotspot	U	Draws an image-map hotspot area in a rectangular shape
	Circle Hotspot	U	Draws an image-map hotspot area in an elliptical shape
	Polygon Hotspot	U	Draws an image-map hotspot area in a polygonal shape
	Slice	G	Draws a slice object in a rectangular shape
	Polygon Slice	G	Draws a slice object in a polygonal shape
	Hand	H or press and hold spacebar	Pans the view of a document
	Zoom	Z	Increases or decreases the magnification level of a document by one setting

> **Tip**
>
> Certain tools have keyboard shortcuts that enable you to temporarily replace the active tool. Press and hold Ctrl (Command) in order to switch to the Pointer temporarily, for example. You can also press and hold Ctrl+spacebar (Command+spacebar) in order to access the Zoom tool. Holding down the spacebar by itself temporarily retrieves the Hand tool.

Accessing Toolbars (Windows Only)

Some people hate toolbars, and some people love them. Either way, they're expected in Windows applications and are a welcome part of Fireworks for Windows for many users.

The two toolbars are Main and Modify. The Main toolbar contains common File and Edit menu functions. The Modify toolbar contains Modify menu functions, such as grouping, aligning, or rotating objects.

The toolbars are docked to the parent window by default, but you can position them anywhere within the Fireworks window by undocking them. To detach a docked toolbar, click and drag the toolbar away from the parent window. To dock a detached toolbar, drag the toolbar close to an edge of the Fireworks window until it snaps into position, or double-click its title bar.

Fireworks for Windows also has a context-sensitive Status bar that runs along the bottom of the Fireworks window. We look at that in this section, as well.

Main toolbar

The Main toolbar, shown in Figure 19-10, displays a row of buttons that access the most commonly used menu functions. The Main toolbar enables you to perform several key file operations, such as create a new document, open or save an existing document, and export or import an image, all with just one click. The most often-used editing features — Undo, Redo, Cut, Copy, and Paste — are also located on the Main toolbar. Table 19-3 describes each button on the Main toolbar.

Figure 19-10: The Main toolbar gives Window users one-click access to many commonly used commands.

Table 19-3
Main Toolbar

Button	Name	Description
	New	Creates a new document
	Open	Opens an existing document
	Save	Saves the current document
	Import	Imports a file into the current document
	Export	Exports the current document
	Print	Prints the current document
	Undo	Undoes the last action
	Redo	Redoes the last action that was undone
	Cut	Cuts the selected object to the clipboard
	Copy	Copies the selected object to the clipboard
	Paste	Pastes the clipboard into the current document

Modify toolbar

The Modify toolbar, shown in Figure 19-11, offers single-click access to four primary types of modifications:

✦ **Grouping:** Group or join two or more objects for easier manipulation. Buttons are also available for ungrouping and splitting combined objects.

✦ **Arranging:** Position objects in front of or behind other objects. Objects can also be moved on top of or underneath all other objects.

✦ **Aligning:** Align two or more objects in any of eight different ways, including centered vertically or horizontally.

✦ **Rotating:** Flip selected objects horizontally, vertically, or rotate them 90 degrees, either clockwise or counterclockwise.

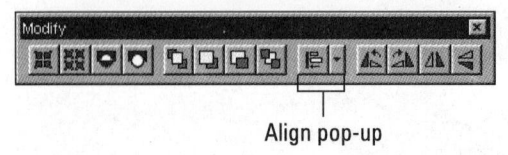

Align pop-up

Figure 19-11: Group, arrange, align, or rotate selected objects with the Modify toolbar.

Instead of directly executing a command—like the other buttons on the Modify toolbar—the Align button opens a pop-up toolbar that contains a range of alignment buttons. In Fireworks, alignment commands—whether they're issued from this pop-up toolbar or from the Modify ⇨ Align submenu—align objects to a theoretical rectangle around the selection, not to the canvas as you might expect. For example, if you select a circle on the left side of the canvas and a bitmap object on the right, clicking the Align Left button causes the bitmap object to align along the left edge of the circle because it is the leftmost object in the selection. Table 19-4 details each button on the Modify toolbar.

Cross-Reference Read more about aligning objects in Fireworks in Chapter 29.

Table 19-4
Modify Toolbar

Button	Name	Description
	Group	Groups selected objects
	Ungroup	Ungroups previously grouped objects
	Join	Joins the paths of two vector objects
	Split	Separates previously joined vector objects
	Bring Front	Positions the selected object on top of all other objects

Button	Name	Description
	Bring Forward	Moves the selected object one step closer to the top
	Send Backward	Moves the selected object one step closer to the bottom
	Send to Back	Positions the selected object underneath all other objects
	Align Left	Aligns the selected objects to the left edge of the selection
	Center Vertical Axis	Centers the selected objects on a vertical line
	Align Right	Aligns the selected objects to the right edge of the selection
	Align Top	Aligns the selected objects along the top edge of the selection
	Center Horizontal Axis	Centers the selected objects on a horizontal line
	Align Bottom	Aligns the selected objects along the bottom edge of the selection
	Distribute Widths	Evenly distributes the selected objects horizontally
	Distribute Heights	Evenly distributes the selected objects vertically
	Rotate 90° CCW	Rotates the selected object 90 degrees counterclockwise
	Rotate 90° CW	Rotates the selected object 90 degrees clockwise
	Flip Horizontal	Flips the selected object horizontally
	Flip Vertical	Flips the selected object vertically

Status bar

The status bar, shown in Figure 19-12, has two sections. The Selection Indicator displays the type of object or objects selected. If you're in bitmap mode, the status bar also displays the object type or selected object here as well. The Description indicator provides tooltips for each of the tools that are selected or moused over.

Description — Press Stop to exit Bitmap mode.
Selection indicator — Select and move objects

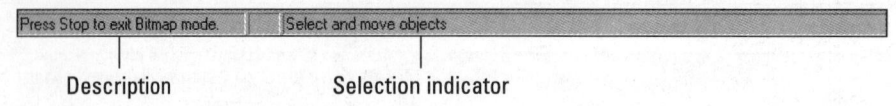

Figure 19-12: The status bar tells you what types of objects you have selected and offers context-sensitive tips.

Note: The Exit Bitmap Mode button and the Animation controls that were on the status bar in Fireworks 3 are now on the document windows in Fireworks 4, and are covered earlier in this chapter.

Managing the Floating Panels

Fireworks maintains a great deal of functionality in its floating panels. In all, the program offers 20 different panels for modifying everything from the stroke color to a JavaScript behavior. Toggling whether a particular panel is shown or hidden is as simple as choosing its name from the Window menu, or pressing its key shortcut. Although an almost dazzling array of panels to choose from exists, the effect is not overwhelming because panels are docked together into groups. When a panel is docked behind another one, click its tab to bring it to the front.

By default, Fireworks combines the floating panels into four different groups, but you can customize the groupings to fit the way you work. If you're working with dual monitors, you might want to display every panel separately, so that all 20 are instantly available. On the other hand, you could conserve maximum screen real estate by grouping all the panels into one supergroup with tabs visible for each individual panel. The middle ground, though, is probably the best for most people: some docked, some not, and commonly used panels always visible.

The more you work in Fireworks, the sooner you'll arrive at a panel configuration that's best for you. I tend to group my floating panels on the right side of the screen and use the left area as my workspace. After you come up with an arrangement you find useful, Fireworks allows you to save that arrangement as a Panel Layout Set and recall it for later use.

Grouping and moving panels

Grouping and ungrouping floating panels is a straightforward process. To separate a floating panel from its current group, click the panel's tab and drag it away from the group. As you drag, you'll see an outline of the panel. Release the mouse button to place the panel onscreen.

Similarly, grouping one panel with another is also a drag-and-drop affair. Drag the panel's tab until the outline appears. When your pointer moves over a different panel, the outline snaps to the outline of the static panel. Release the mouse button and a tab, representing the panel being moved, is added to the right of the existing group.

In addition to the grouping feature, the floating panels also snap to the borders of the document window or another floating panel. This snapping feature enables the designer to move panels out of the way quickly and to align them in a visually pleasing manner. It may seem like a minor detail, but when panels are snapped to an edge, the workspace appears less cluttered and more usable.

The floating panels are easy to position around the screen. Just click the panel's title bar and drag it to a new position. Likewise, you can easily resize and reshape any of the floating panels. In Windows, position your pointer over any border of the panel so that the cursor becomes a two-headed arrow and then drag the border to alter the size or shape of the panel. On the Mac, drag the resize widget on the lower right of the panel in order to alter the panel's size or shape. Each of the panels has a minimum size that you'll "bump" into if you try to make the panel too small.

Panel Layout Sets

After you've discovered a particular arrangement of the floating panels that works for you, Fireworks allows you to save that arrangement as a Panel Layout Set.

To save a panel configuration as a Panel Layout Set, follow these steps:

1. Create an arrangement of floating panels that you would like to save.

2. Choose Commands ➪ Panel Layout. A JavaScript dialog box appears.

> **Cross-Reference**
> This is a JavaScript dialog box because all the items under Fireworks' Commands menu are built with HTML and JavaScript.

3. Enter a name for your new Panel Layout Set. Click OK when you're done.

The arrangement of your floating panels is saved as a new Panel Layout Set and is added to the Commands ➪ Panel Layout Sets submenu.

To access a Panel Layout Set, choose Commands ➪ Panel Layout Sets and then the name of the Panel Layout Set that you want to access.

> **Caution**
> If you want to save your current panel layout, do so before accessing a Panel Layout Set. A restored Panel Layout Set supercedes the current layout and this change cannot simply be undone.

Hiding and revealing panels

The floating panels are extremely helpful for making all manner of alterations to your documents, but they can also get in the way, visually, as well as physically. When working on a large document at 100 percent magnification, I often hide most of the panels, in order to better see and manipulate my work. Hiding — and revealing — all the floating panels is a one-key operation. With just a press of the Tab key, the floating panels all disappear, or, if they are already hidden, reappear.

Although the Tab key is extremely convenient, you can choose a number of other methods to hide and reveal panels:

- Choose View ⇨ Hide Panels to toggle the panels off and on.
- Use the official keyboard shortcut, F4.

Tip Choose Edit ⇨ Keyboard Shortcuts to customize the keyboard shortcuts if there is another key, or key combination, that you prefer.

Windowshade

Windowshading is an alternative to hiding the panels. It is a standard feature in Mac OS 8/9, but is found in the floating panels on both Macintosh and Windows versions of Fireworks. Double-clicking the title bar of a floating panel hides all but the title bar; double-clicking the title bar again reveals the whole panel. Mac users can also click the standard Windowshade button in a panel's title bar.

Examining common features

Although each floating panel does something different, they all share common interface elements. Many of the features, such as sliders and option lists, will be familiar to users of most any computer program. Some, such as color pickers, are more commonly found only in other graphics software. Figure 19-13 displays several different floating panels with different interface features highlighted.

Working with Dual Monitors

Fireworks works with dual monitors on Macintosh and on Windows systems that support the feature. You can set up this arrangement through the Monitors (or Monitors and Sound) Control Panel on Macintosh and through the Display Control Panel on Windows. Traditionally, the best strategy for using two monitors is to keep your documents on one monitor and your floating panels on the other. This setup works especially well if you have one large monitor and one small one, for documents and panels, respectively.

Another advantage of dual monitors is the capability to continuously preview your work at a different screen resolution or color depth than the one that you typically work at. Most designers and graphic artists work at a high resolution and color depth, such as 1,600×1,024 with 319-bit color, whereas most Web surfers are using 800×600, with varying color depths. Work on one monitor, and preview your work in a browser window simultaneously on the other. Adjust the settings of the preview monitor in order to view your work at a wide range of resolution and color depth combinations. Continuously previewing your work as it will ultimately be displayed helps to avoid surprises and the unnecessary revisions.

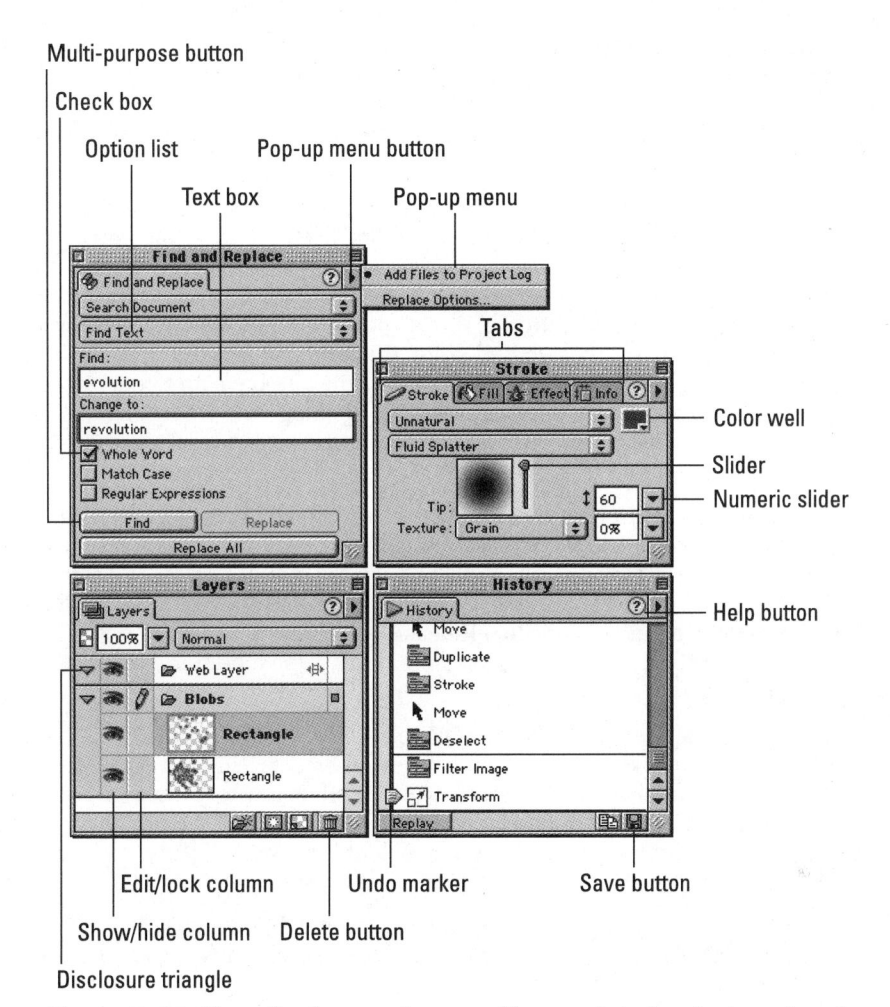

Figure 19-13: These floating panels exemplify many interface features found throughout Fireworks.

Here's an overview of the most common Fireworks interface elements:

- ✦ **Tabs:** As mentioned previously, tabs appear when you dock a panel to one or more panels.

- ✦ **Pop-up menus:** All floating panels except for the Tool Options and Tools panels have a number of different options that you can access by selecting the pop-up menu button (a right-pointing arrow) in the upper right of the panel.

- ✦ **Help button:** All floating panels except for the Tools panel have a context-sensitive Help button that opens Using Fireworks at the appropriate page to help with the current operation.

- **Option lists:** For many selections, Fireworks uses option lists. Click the arrow button of an option list to see the available choices. In some circumstances, as with patterns and textures, the option list displays a visual image, as well as a text listing of the options. This feature makes finding what you're looking for in Fireworks easy.

> **Tip** Windows users can type the first letter of an entry in an options list in order to jump to it. If multiple entries have the same first letter, pressing the letter again cycles through the entries.

- **Color wells:** Any color selection in Fireworks is handled through a color well that displays its currently selected color. Click the color well to pop up the color picker with the active swatch. All color pickers have an Eyedropper tool for choosing colors and a Palette button for opening your operating system's color picker(s). Most Fireworks color pickers also have a No Color button for deselecting any color.

- **Numeric sliders:** Any entry that requires a numeric value — whether it is a percentage, a hexadecimal value, or just a plain number — uses pop-up sliders. Selecting the arrow button next to a variable number, such as a stroke's tip size, pops up a sliding control. Drag the slider and the numbers in the text box increase or decrease in value. Release the mouse button when you've reached the desired value. You can also directly type a numeric value in the adjacent text box.

- **Disclosure triangle:** Several floating panels — Stroke, Fill, and Effect — have an additional preview section that you can reveal by selecting the expander arrow. The expander arrow is a small white triangle in the lower-right corner of a floating panel that acts as a toggle. Select it once, and the floating panel expands to display the preview section; select it again, and the panel returns to its previous size.

- **Text boxes:** Enter values directly into text boxes. All Fireworks sliders have text boxes next to them so that you can quickly enter a number instead of using a mouse to move the slider.

- **Checkboxes:** You can enable an option by clicking the associated checkbox, or disable it by clicking it again in order to remove the checkmark.

Optimize panel

The Optimize panel enables you to specify export settings for the current document. Choose a file type and file type–specific settings, such as Quality for JPEG images, and palette for GIFs. Depending on which file format you choose, the available options change accordingly.

Figure 19-14 shows the Optimize panel set to GIF WebSnap 128.

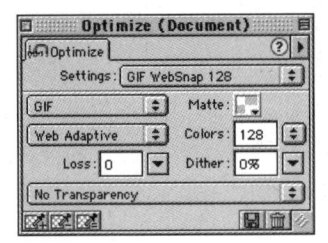

Figure 19-14: The Optimize panel is where you choose export settings for your document.

The Optimize panel's pop-up menu contains commands for fine-tuning your export settings. Table 19-5 details the commands.

Table 19-5
Optimize Panel Pop-up Menu Commands

Option	Description
Save Settings	Saves the current export settings
Delete Settings	Deletes the current saved export setting
Optimize to Size	Optimizes the current document to a particular export file size
Export Wizard	Starts the Export Wizard to assist in exporting a document
Remove Unused Colors	Toggles whether or not Fireworks removes unused colors from the export palette displayed in the Color Table panel
Interlaced	Toggles the interlaced option for formats that support it
Progressive JPEG	Toggles JPEG or Progressive JPEG
Sharpen JPEG Edges	Toggles sharpening of edges in exported JPEGs

Cross-Reference: Find more information about the Optimize panel in Chapter 30.

Object panel

The Object panel displays a number of different interfaces, depending upon what is selected. Each interface has options that are appropriate to the current selection, such as the Roundness setting for rectangle corners that appears only when rectangles are selected. Figure 19-15 shows four examples of the Object panel.

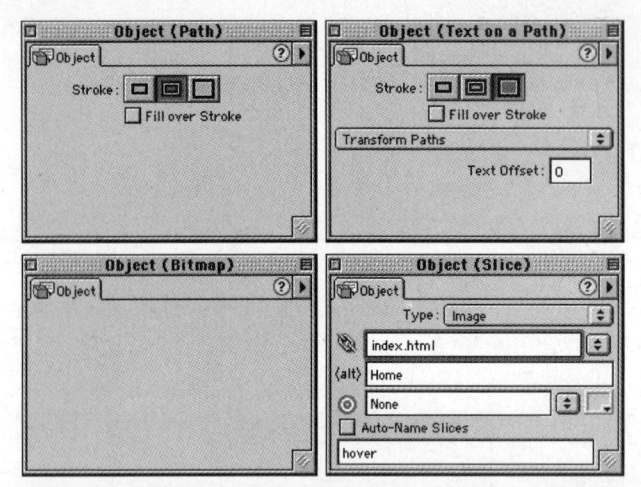

Figure 19-15: The Object panel offers a variety of options, depending upon the type of object selected.

The type of object selected is identified at the top of the Object panel. Following are the possible selections:

- **No Selection:** No object is selected.

- **Path:** When a vector object is selected, the term *Path* is displayed in the Object panel, along with two additional stroke options. One is Stroke Placement, which determines whether the stroke is drawn outside, inside, or centered in the Path; the other is the aptly named Draw Fill Over Stroke option, which tells Fireworks to draw the fill on top of the stroke.

- **Rectangle:** When a rectangle is selected, the Rectangle Object panel is displayed, which is identical to the Path Object panel, except for the addition of the Roundness setting for rectangle corners.

- **Bitmap:** If a bitmap object is selected, the Object panel lets you know it is a bitmap object.

- **Text:** In addition to Stroke options, the Object panel for text enables you to change the Transformation method from Transform as Paths to Transform as Pixels. Chapter 26 explores text objects.

- **Text on a Path:** The Object panel for Text on a Path is the same as that for Text with one addition: You can set the number of pixels by which the text is offset from the Path.

- **Bitmap Mask and Vector Mask:** When you select an object with a bitmap mask, you can choose whether to apply the mask using its alpha channel or its actual appearance converted to grayscale. Vector masks have further options. You learn more about masks in Chapter 29.

- ✦ **Graphic Symbol, Animation Symbol, and Button Symbol:** Choose whether a symbol's pixels or paths are transformed when it's tweened. Button Symbols have further options, such as Button Text. The Object panel for animation symbols contains a range of specific options for fine-tuning the animation. Chapter 32 covers symbols.

- ✦ **Hotspot:** Much of the information necessary for a selected hotspot to function as a Web object is entered through the Object panel: the URL, the `<alt>` tag, and the target. You can also set the color of the overlay and the hotspot's basic shape (Rectangle, Oval, or Polygon) here. Find out how to use hotspots in Chapter 33.

- ✦ **Slice:** In addition to the Web-specific information (URL, `<alt>` tag, and target), the selected Slice object can also choose export settings, the overlay color, and naming conventions.

Most any selected object can be affected by the pop-up menu commands outlined in Table 19-6; you can even convert a Hotspot object to a Slice object and vice versa.

Table 19-6
Object Panel Pop-up Menu Commands

Option	Description
Copy to Hotspot	Copies the object to the Web Layer as a hotspot
Copy to Slice	Copies the object to the Web Layer as a slice

Stroke panel

Any object created using one of the vector drawing tools — Pen, Brush, Rectangle, Ellipse, Line, or Text tool — is initially constructed with a path, the outline of the object. When a path is visible, it is said to be *stroked*. In Fireworks, strokes can be as basic as the one-pixel Pencil outline, or as complex as the multicolored Confetti. The Stroke panel controls all the possible path settings and is a key tool in a graphic artist's palette.

Fireworks comes with a number of built-in stroke settings accessible through the Stroke panel, shown in Figure 19-16. You can also modify existing settings and save them as new strokes. Seven major options can affect the stroke:

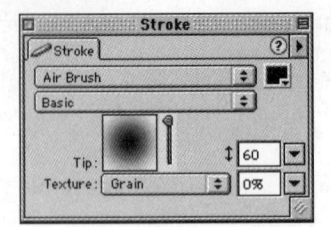

Figure 19-16: The Stroke panel controls the appearance of an object's outline or path.

+ **Stroke category:** Fireworks provides 11 stroke categories from which to choose: Pencil, Basic, Airbrush, Calligraphy, Charcoal, Crayon, Felt Tip, Oil, Watercolor, Random, and Unnatural. To hide the path entirely, choose None.

+ **Specific stroke:** After you've chosen a stroke category, a set of specific strokes, different for each category, is available. When you edit, rename, or save new strokes, the changes are reflected in the specific stroke option list.

+ **Stroke color:** Selecting the arrow button next to the stroke color well displays the pop-up color picker and activates the Eyedropper, which you can use to select a color from one of the swatches or from anywhere on the screen. Click the Palette button to open your operating system's color picker(s).

+ **Stroke edge:** Use the stroke edge slider to soften or harden the stroke. The higher the slider, the softer the stroke; when the slider is all the way to the bottom, the stroke has no softness.

+ **Stroke size:** The stroke size slider determines the stroke size in pixels. You can increase the size by moving the slider up; you can also enter the value (from 1 to 100) directly in the stroke size text box. The size of the brush is previewed dynamically in the Stroke panel.

+ **Stroke texture:** In addition to color, size, and softness, you can also apply a texture to the stroke. Fireworks comes with 26 different textures, and you can also add your own.

+ **Degree of stroke texture:** After a texture has been selected, you must specify how intensely you want the texture applied by using the stroke texture slider, or by entering a percentage value in the appropriate text box. The degree of stroke texture basically controls the opacity of the texture as it overlays the stroke.

If an object is selected, any changes made on the Stroke panel are immediately applied to the object.

You can manage current strokes and create new ones with the commands available in the Stroke panel pop-up menu, detailed in Table 19-7.

Table 19-7
Stroke Panel Pop-up Menu Commands

Option	Description
Save Stroke As	Saves the current stroke settings under a new name
Edit Stroke	Opens the Edit Stroke dialog box
Rename Stroke	Relabels the current stroke settings
Delete Stroke	Removes the current stroke from the menu

Cross-Reference: Chapter 24 covers strokes in detail.

Fill panel

Just as the Stroke panel controls the outline of a drawn shape, the Fill panel controls the inside. Fills can be a solid color, a gradient, a pattern, or a Web dither. All fills can have textures applied with a sliding scale of intensity; moreover, textured fills can even appear transparent.

Once you've chosen the type of fill from the Fill panel, shown in Figure 19-17, you can go on to pick a specific color, pattern, edge, or texture. Following are the key options on the Fill panel:

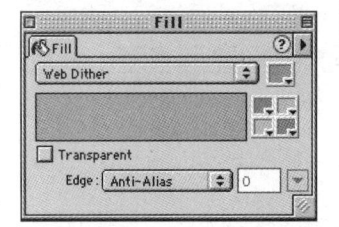

Figure 19-17: The Fill panel offers many options to modify the interior of a drawn shape.

- **Fill category:** Select a fill category from these options: Solid (single color fill), Web dither (two-color pattern), Pattern, or Gradient. The available standard gradients are Linear, Radial, Ellipse, Rectangle, Cone, Starburst, Bars, Ripples, Waves, Satin, and Folds.

- **Specific pattern or gradient color scheme:** If you choose Pattern or one of the gradient options, a second option list appears with choices for each type of fill.

- **Fill edge:** The fill itself can have a hard edge, an antialiased edge, or a feathered edge.
- **Degree of feathering:** If the fill is given a feathered edge, you can specify the degree of feathering (the number of pixels affected) with this slider control, or by entering a value into the text box.
- **Fill texture:** The same textures available to the Stroke panel are available to a fill.
- **Degree of texture:** To make a texture visible, you must increase the degree of the texture's intensity by using the appropriate slider or text box. The higher the value, the more visible the texture.
- **Transparency of texture:** If the Transparency checkbox is selected, the lighter parts of the texture can be seen through.

The gradient fill type offers a number of options for creating and modifying your own gradient patterns. Table 19-8 details the commands available from the Fill panel's pop-up menu.

Table 19-8
Fill Panel Pop-up Menu Commands

Option	Description
Save Gradient As	Saves the current gradient settings under a new name
Edit Gradient	Opens the Edit Gradient dialog box
Rename Gradient	Relabels the current gradient settings
Delete Gradient	Removes the current gradient from the menu

Cross-Reference: To delve deeper into fills, see Chapter 27.

Effect panel

In the early days of the Web, special graphics effects, such as drop shadows and beveled buttons, required many tedious steps in programs such as Photoshop. These days, Fireworks enables you to apply wondrous effects in a single step through the Effect panel. More importantly, like everything else in Fireworks, the effects are "live" and adapt to any change in the object. And you can easily alter them by adjusting values in the Effect panel.

The Effect panel options list contains the actual effects, split into two groups. The top group are Fireworks built-in effects. The bottom group are Photoshop-compatible image filters from your Fireworks Xtras folder and from another folder if you specified one in Fireworks Preferences.

Choosing an effect from the Effect panel option list applies it to the current selection and adds it to the active list in the Effect panel. After an effect is in the active list, you can check or uncheck the box next to it in order to enable or disable it.

Selecting the *i* button next to an applied effect's name enables you to modify its settings. Photoshop-compatible filters each has its own unique dialog box. Many of Fireworks' built-in Live Effects open a small, pop-up edit window with their settings. Clicking anywhere outside the pop-up edit window dismisses it. Raised Emboss is an example of an effect with a pop-up edit window, shown in Figure 19-18.

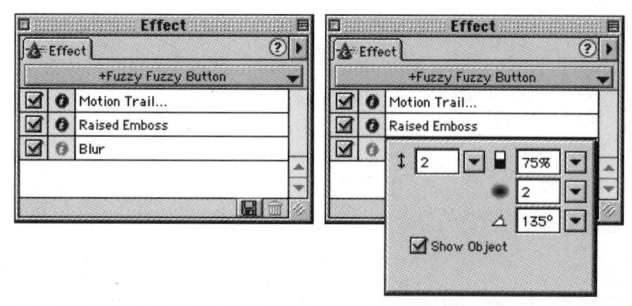

Figure 19-18: The settings for some Live Effects are displayed in an unusual pop-up edit window, such as this one for Raised Emboss.

As you develop specific effects, you can save them for later use with the pop-up menu commands listed in Table 19-9.

Table 19-9
Effect Panel Pop-up Menu Commands

Option	Description
Save defaults	Saves the current setup as the default for new effects
Save Effect As	Saves the current effect settings under a new name
Rename Effect	Relabels the current effect settings
Delete Effect	Removes the current effect from the menu
All on	Turns on all the effects currently active in the Effect panel
All off	Turns off all the effects currently active in the Effect panel
Locate Plug-ins	Shows a dialog box that allows you to select a folder of Photoshop plug-ins

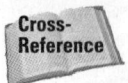

Cross-Reference: Effects can add serious pizzazz to your graphics in a hurry. Find out more about them — with details on how to get the most from each Effects panel — in Chapter 28.

Color Table panel

The Color Table panel, shown in Figure 19-19, displays the current export palette when working with 8-bit images, such as GIFs. The Color Table panel provides feedback that allows you to minimize the file size of exported GIF images by reducing the number of colors in their palette.

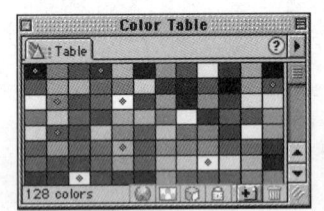

Figure 19-19: The Color Table panel contains a document's current export palette.

The Color Table panel sports an extensive pop-up menu, detailed in Table 19-10.

Table 19-10
Color Table Panel Pop-up Menu Commands

Option	Description
Rebuild Color Table	Updates colors to reflect changes in the document
Add Color	Opens your operating system's color picker(s) so that you can manually add a color to the palette
Edit Color	Opens your operating system's color picker(s) so that you can change the selected color to a different color
Delete Color	Removes the selected color(s) from the palette
Replace Palette Entry	Opens your operating system's color picker(s) so that you can replace the selected palette entry with a different color
Snap to Web Safe	Snaps the selected color(s) to Web-safe
Transparent	Makes the selected color transparent
Lock Color	Locks the selected color so that it cannot be edited
Unlock All Colors	Unlocks all locked colors

Option	Description
Sort by Luminance	Selects sorting by luminance values
Sort by Popularity	Selects sorting by most-used color
Unsorted	Selects no sorting
Show Swatch Feedback	Toggles viewing icons that indicate a color is locked, transparent, or another attribute
Remove Edit	Restores selected color to what it was before editing
Remove All Edits	Restores all colors to what they were before editing
Load Palette	Loads a previously saved palette
Save Palette	Saves the current palette

Swatches panel

Whereas the Color Mixer defines the color universe, the Swatches panel identifies a more precise palette of colors. As the name implies, the Swatches panel contains a series of color samples, as you can see in Figure 19-20. You select a color by clicking on a swatch.

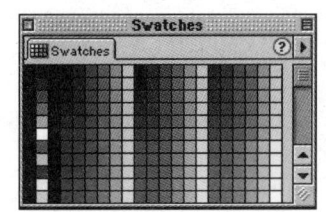

Figure 19-20: Palette management is coordinated through the Swatches panel.

Tip To reset a swatch palette after you've modified it or sorted it by color, select the palette again from the Swatches panel's pop-up menu.

A major feature of the Swatches panel is tucked away in its pop-up menu: palette management. With the commands in the pop-up menu, you can switch to standard palettes (such as the Windows or Macintosh system palettes), save and recall custom palettes, or access the current export palette. The Add Swatches command is especially useful; it can load palettes previously stored in the Photoshop color table file format, or pull the color information from a GIF file. Table 19-11 outlines all the pop-up menu commands.

Table 19-11
Swatches Panel Pop-up Menu Commands

Option	Description
Add Swatches	Imports previously saved palettes from .aco or GIF files
Replace Swatches	Exchanges the current palette set for a previously saved one
Save Swatches	Stores the current palette set
Clear Swatches	Removes all palettes from the panel
Macintosh System	Switches to the Macintosh system palette
Windows System	Switches to the Windows system palette
Grayscale	Switches to a grayscale palette
Current Export Palette	Switches to the current export palette
Sort by Color	Sorts the swatches by color

Color Mixer panel

Web designers come from a variety of backgrounds: Some are well-rooted in computer graphics, others are more familiar with print publishing, whereas an increasing number know only Web imagery. The Color Mixer lets you opt for the color model that you're most familiar with and that is best suited to your work.

The Color Mixer, shown in Figure 19-21, displays three different ways to choose colors:

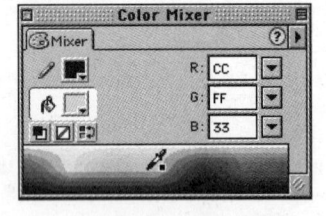

Figure 19-21: Select your stroke and fill colors from the color wells, the color ramp, or the color component sliders in the Color Mixer panel.

- ✦ **Stroke and Fill color wells:** Select a color well to open the pop-up color picker and gain access to the system color picker(s) through the Palette button.
- ✦ **Color ramp:** The full-spectrum preview of the chosen color model is known as the color ramp. You can select any color by clicking it.

✦ **Color component sliders:** Like the color ramp, the color component sliders change according to the chosen color model. Four of the five color models — RGB, Hexadecimal, CMY, and HSB — display three different sliders, whereas Grayscale shows only one, K (black).

Like the Tools panel, the Color Mixer also features a Default Colors button for restoring the preset stroke and fill colors, and a Swap button for reversing the colors. Choose a color model by selecting it from the pop-up menu, detailed in Table 19-12.

Table 19-12
Color Mixer Panel Pop-up Menu Commands

Option	Description
RGB	Changes the color mixer display to Red, Green, and Blue
Hexadecimal	Changes the color mixer display to Hexadecimal Red, Green, and Blue, the standard way to specify colors in HTML
CMY	Changes the color mixer display to Cyan, Magenta, and Yellow
HSB	Changes the color mixer display to Hue, Saturation, and Balance
Grayscale	Changes the color mixer display to Grayscale, which is 256 shades of gray

Cross-Reference
A full understanding of the color possibilities and pitfalls is a must for any Web designer. Learn more about using the color mixer in Chapter 23.

Tool Options panel

Many tools from the Fireworks Tools panel have configurable settings accessible through the Tool Options panel. You have two basic ways to expose the Tool Options panel for a specific tool:

✦ Display the panel by choosing its tab, or by choosing Window ➪ Tool Options, and then select the tool from the Tools panel.

✦ Double-click the tool in the Tools panel.

Like the Object panel, the Tools panel's options vary according to what is selected. Some tools, such as the Eraser shown in Figure 19-22, provide numerous choices. Several tools — including the Hand, Zoom, Line, Pen, Ellipse, Brush, and the Web tools — have no options. Each tool's options are covered in the section devoted to that tool.

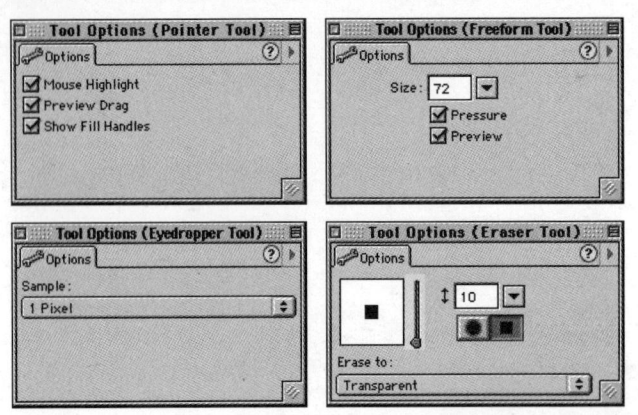

Figure 19-22: When the Eraser tool is double-clicked, several options become available through the Tool Options panel.

> **Note:** The Tool Options panel is the only panel that doesn't have a pop-up menu.

Layers panel

Layers in Fireworks enable the creation of extremely complicated graphics, as well as compatibility with files stored in Photoshop format. Fireworks layers are like folders that can contain multiple objects, each with its own stacking order. Layers, in turn, have their own stacking order, and can be placed on top of, or beneath, other layers. Moreover, each layer can be hidden from view for easier editing of complex documents, and can be locked to prevent accidental editing. Layers can be shared across frames, allowing you to instantly add a static element to every frame of an animation.

All Web objects, such as slices and hotspots, are stored in the Web Layer, which can be hidden or locked, or have its stacking order changed, but which cannot be deleted. The Web Layer is always shared across all frames.

The Layers panel, shown in Figure 19-23, is the central control center for layers. The layer list contains each layer's name, a thumbnail of its contents, as well as Expand/Collapse, Show/Hide, and Lock/Unlock columns. Create or delete layers with the New/Duplicate Layer and Delete Selection buttons. The Add Mask button adds a mask to the selected object or layer. The New Bitmap Image button creates an empty bitmap object as the next object on a layer.

A good portion of Fireworks' layer management is coordinated through the Layers panel's pop-up menu commands, as described in Table 19-13.

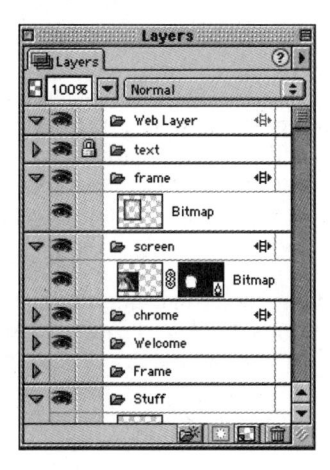

Figure 19-23: Objects on a layer can be hidden or locked with a single click on the Layers panel.

Table 19-13
Layers Panel Pop-up Menu Commands

Option	Description
New Image	Creates a new, empty bitmap object
New Layer	Adds a new layer on top of all current layers
Duplicate Layer	Clones the current layer
Share this Layer	Enables all objects on the selected layer to be shared across all frames
Single Layer Editing	Restricts edits to the current layer
Delete Layer	Removes the current layer
Hide All	Conceals all layers in the document
Show All	Reveals all layers in the document
Lock All	Prevents editing in the selected layer
Unlock All	Enables a locked layer to be edited
Add Mask	Adds a mask to the selected object
Edit Mask	Puts Fireworks in mask edit mode, so only the mask of the currently selected object can be modified in the document window
Disable Mask	Disables the currently selected object's mask
Delete Mask	Removes the currently selected object's mask
Thumbnail Options	Opens the Thumbnail Options dialog box, which offers a range of thumbnail sizes to choose from

Frames panel

Frames have two primary uses in Fireworks: rollovers and animations. When used to create rollovers, each frame represents a different state of the user's mouse with up to four frames being used. To create an animated GIF, each frame in Fireworks corresponds to one frame of the animation. You can use as many frames for your animation as necessary (although file size often dictates that the fewest frames possible is best).

By default, frame timing is set to 7 milliseconds. Double-click the frame timing setting to edit it in the pop-up dialog box, similar to the ones displayed by the Effect panel. Double-click a frame's name to edit it in another pop-up dialog box.

The Frames panel, shown in Figure 19-24, is laid out like the Layers panel, with a list of Frames featured prominently.

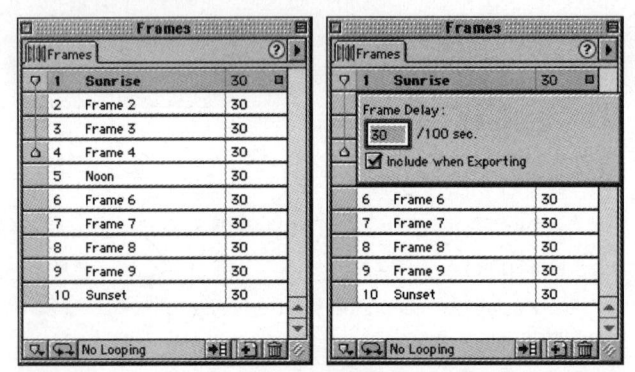

Figure 19-24: The Frames panel is Fireworks' center stage for creating rollovers and animated GIF images.

The Frames panel's pop-up menu, detailed in Table 19-14, enables you to further control your interaction with frames.

Table 19-14
Frames Panel Pop-up Menu Commands

Option	Description
Add Frames	Opens the Add Frames dialog box
Duplicate Frame	Duplicates the current frame
Delete Frames	Deletes the current frame
Copy to Frames	Copies the selected object to a frame or a range of frames

Option	Description
Distribute to Frames	Distributes each selected object to a different frame, as determined by the stacking order of the objects
Auto Crop	Sets the frame disposal method to Auto Crop
Auto Difference	Sets the frame disposal method to Auto Difference
Properties	Opens the pop-up edit window for the current frame

History panel

The History panel, shown in Figure 19-25, allows precise control over Fireworks' multiple level Undo command. The Undo Marker points to your preceding step. To roll back to even earlier steps, slide the Undo Marker up one or more notches. The number of steps the History panel keeps track of is the number of Undo steps you have specified in Fireworks preferences.

Caution The maximum number of Undo steps you can specify in Fireworks is 1,009.

Figure 19-25: The History panel contains a record of your actions that you can undo, repeat, or save as a command.

The capability to save or replay your steps makes the History panel more than just an enhanced Undo. Saving your previous steps as a command enables you to automate almost anything you do in Fireworks. If you have a project that requires you to tediously edit a number of objects in the same way, do it once and save the steps as a command that you can run on all the other objects.

The History panel's pop-up menu contains the commands detailed in Table 19-15.

Table 19-15
History Panel Pop-up Menu Commands

Option	Description
Replay Selected Steps	Replays the selected steps
Copy Steps	Copies the selected steps to the clipboard
Save as Command	Saves the selected steps as a Command
Clear History	Deletes all steps

Info panel

Often, checking an object's size or position when you're creating an overall graphic is necessary. The Info panel not only provides you with that feedback, but it also enables you to modify those values numerically for precise adjustments. The Info panel, shown in Figure 19-26, also lists the current pointer coordinates and the color values of the pixel found under the pointer, updated in real time. When you use a Transform tool, the Info panel keeps you advised of things such as rotation angle, enabling more accurate free transforms.

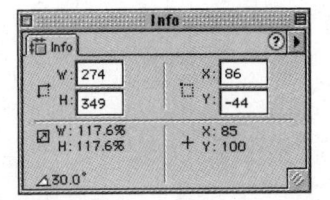

Figure 19-26: You can find any object's dimensions and position in the Info panel.

Caution Be sure to press Enter (Return) after changing a value in the Info panel. You can press the Tab key to move from one value to another within the Info panel, but the values you enter won't take effect until you press Enter (Return).

You can alter the color model and measurement system shown in the Info panel by choosing another from the Info panel's pop-up menu, detailed in Table 19-16.

Table 19-16
Info Panel Pop-up Menu Commands

Option	Description
Hexadecimal	Changes the color settings display to Hexadecimal Red, Green, and Blue
RGB	Changes the color settings display to Red, Green, and Blue
CMY	Changes the color settings display to Cyan, Magenta, and Yellow
HSB	Changes the color settings display to Hue, Saturation, and Balance
Pixels	Changes the measurement display to pixels
Inches	Changes the measurement display to inches
Centimeters	Changes the measurement display to centimeters
Scale Attributes	Enables attributes to be scaled with the object

Behaviors panel

One of the key features of Fireworks that separates it from other graphics programs is its capability to output HTML and JavaScript code along with images. The code activates an image and makes it capable of an action, such as changing color or shape when the user passes the mouse over it. The code is known in Fireworks as a *Behavior*. A Behavior is actually composed of two parts: an action that specifies what is to occur, and an event that triggers the action.

Behaviors require a Web object, such as a slice or a hotspot, to function. After you've selected the desired Web object, you assign a Behavior by choosing the Add Action button (the plus sign) from the Behaviors panel. Fireworks comes with five main groups of Behaviors from which to choose: Simple Rollover, Swap Image, Set Nav Bar Image, Set Pop-Up Menu, and Set Text of Status Bar.

All assigned Behaviors for a given Web object are listed in the Behaviors panel, as shown in Figure 19-27. The events, such as OnMouseOver or OnClick, are listed in the first column and the actions in the second. The third column, Info, offers specifics that identify the Behavior. To remove a Behavior, select it and then choose the Remove Action button (the minus sign). You can also delete a Behavior — or all the Behaviors for a Web object — through the pop-up menu commands listed in Table 19-17.

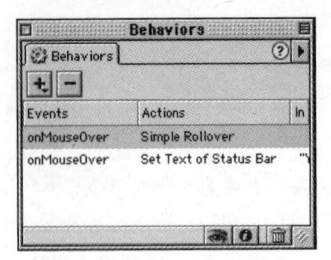

Figure 19-27: Use the Behaviors panel to generate HTML and JavaScript code at the click of a mouse.

Table 19-17
Behaviors Panel Pop-up Menu Commands

Option	Description
Edit	Opens the dialog box for the selected Behavior
Delete	Removes the currently selected Behavior from its attached object
Delete All	Removes all Behaviors attached to the current object
Show All	Shows all Behaviors in a group
Ungroup	Ungroups a group of Behaviors

> **Cross-Reference:** Behaviors are a rich feature of Fireworks. To find out more about them, see Chapter 34.

URL panel

URLs are the life-blood of the Web. When a URL (Uniform Resource Locator, also known as a *link*) is attached to an image on a Web page, the user need only click once to jump to another section of the document, another page on the Web site, or another computer halfway around the world. For all their power, URLs can be difficult to manage; one typo in the often-complex string of letters and symbols can break a link.

The URL panel, shown in Figure 19-28, greatly eases the work required for managing URLs by listing all the Internet addresses inserted in the current session or loaded from an external file. You can easily assign URLs with a click of a listed item; more importantly, you can maintain a list of links for a particular Web site so that you don't have to re-enter them each time. To add the current URL to the Library, select the Add button (the plus sign).

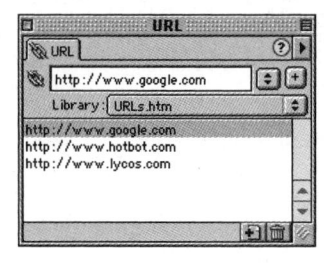

Figure 19-28: Adding links to your Web objects is easy with the URL panel.

You can access most of Fireworks' URL management utilities through the URL panel's pop-up menu, detailed in Table 19-18.

Table 19-18
URL Panel Pop-up Menu Commands

Option	Description
Add Used URLs to Library	Adds the list of current URLs to the URL Library
Clear Unused URLs	Removes all URLs from the current listing
Add URL	Adds a new URL to the URL Library
Edit URL	Opens the Edit URL dialog box
Delete URL	Removes the selected URL from the URL Library
New URL Library	Creates a new URL Library
Import URLs	Loads a new set of URLs from a previously stored URL Library, a bookmark file, or an HTML page
Export URLs	Stores the current URL Library

Styles panel

If you've ever spent hours getting just the right combination of stroke, fill, and effects for an object — and then find you need to apply the same combination to all the navigation buttons throughout a Web site — you'll greatly appreciate the Fireworks Styles feature.

In Fireworks, a *style* is a collection of attributes that you can apply to any object. The Styles panel is preset with a number of such designs, which appear as graphical buttons and text, with many more available on the Fireworks CD-ROM. To apply a style, select the object and then select the style; you can even select multiple objects (such as a row of navigation buttons) and apply the same style to them all with one click. Styles are a terrific time-saver and a great way to maintain a consistent look and feel.

The Styles panel, shown in Figure 19-29, is composed of a series of icons, each representing a different style. A style can have the following attributes: fill type, fill color, stroke type, stroke color, effect, text font, text size, and text color. In addition to the preset styles, you can also save your own combinations. Just highlight the object with the desired attributes and select the New Style button on the Styles panel. You can also accomplish this by choosing New Style from the pop-up menu. A full list of the Styles panel's pop-up menu commands appears in Table 19-19.

Figure 19-29: Automate applying a consistent look and feel to your objects by using the Styles panel.

Table 19-19
Styles Panel Pop-up Menu Commands

Option	Description
New Style	Creates a new style based on the current object
Edit Style	Opens the Edit Style dialog box
Delete Styles	Removes a selected style or styles
Import Styles	Loads a new set of styles after the currently selected style
Export Styles	Stores the currently selected style or styles
Reset Styles	Reloads the default configuration of styles
Large Icons	Displays the available styles with icons twice as large as normal

Cross-Reference: Find out more about creating and applying styles in Chapter 31.

Library panel

The Library panel contains Fireworks Libraries: collections of symbols that you can save and reopen as required. Symbols are edited right in the Library. Dragging a symbol from the Library panel and dropping it into a document creates an *instance* of that symbol. Instances are copies of symbols that remain linked to the symbol and inherit changes to the symbol. Instances are similar to a Windows file shortcut or Mac alias — right down to the arrow badge — and can be animated, tweened, and edited as a group. You can save symbols in Symbol Libraries and use them again and again in multiple documents.

Figure 19-30 shows the Library panel, and the commands detailed in Table 19-20 are located in the Library panel's pop-up menu.

Figure 19-30: The Library panel enables you to store libraries of symbols.

Table 19-20
Library Panel Pop-up Menu Commands

Option	Description
New Symbol	Creates a new symbol
Duplicate	Duplicates the current symbol
Delete	Removes the current symbol from the Library
Edit Symbol	Opens the selected symbol in its own window for editing
Properties	Displays the Symbol Properties dialog box for the current symbol
Select Unused Items	Selects unused symbols in the Library
Update	Updates symbols that were imported from other Libraries
Play	Consecutively displays all frames of a button
Import Symbols	Imports symbols from a saved Library
Export Symbols	Exports symbols to a saved Library

Find and Replace panel

Let's suppose you've just finished the graphics for a major Web site, chock-full of corporate logos, and you receive *the call*. You know, the one from the client who informs you that the company has just been acquired and instead of NewCo, Inc., it's now New2Co, Inc. Could you please redo all the graphics — by tomorrow?

Because Fireworks objects are always editable, the Find and Replace panel, shown in Figure 19-31, makes updating a series of Web graphics a snap. You can change all the graphics in a selection, a file, a frame, or a series of files. Moreover, Find and Replace can handle more than just text; you can also alter fonts, colors, and URLs, or even snap all the colors to their nearest Web-safe neighbor.

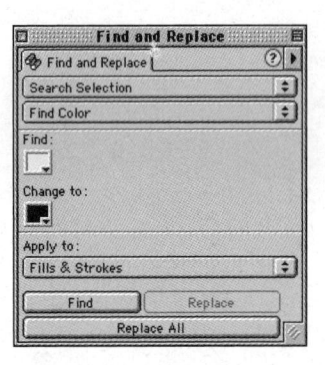

Figure 19-31: Need to make global changes in text, font, color, or URLs? Pull up the Find and Replace panel and get the job done fast.

The Find and Replace feature works with the Project Log panel, which tracks changes made to your documents. You can enable Project Log tracking through the pop-up menu commands listed in Table 19-21, as well as specify replacement options for multiple file operations.

Table 19-21
Find and Replace Panel Pop-up Menu Commands

Option	Description
Add Files to Project Log	Tracks changes made in a Find and Replace operation in the Project Log
Replace Options	Displays options for multiple-file Find and Replace operations

Cross-Reference: You can really ramp up your production level of Web graphics if you master the Find and Replace feature.

Project Log panel

With the power inherent in Fireworks automation tools, such as Find and Replace and Batch Processing, you need a way to keep track of the many changes that may have occurred. The Project Log panel, shown in Figure 19-32, details each change that has taken place and enables you to not only receive confirmation of the change, but also easily open any file that was affected.

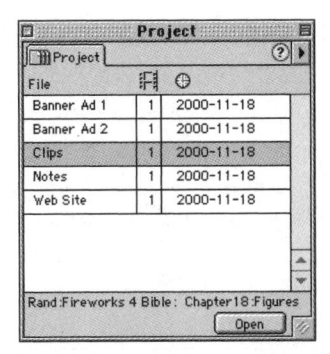

Figure 19-32: Use the Project Log to manage your Find and Replace and Batch Process operations.

In addition to listing documents altered during an automated process, you can use the Project Log to keep a number of files close at hand, ready to be opened at will. Through the Add Files to Log command, in the pop-up menu detailed in Table 19-22, files can be made accessible, but not immediately opened. The pop-up menu also enables you to quickly make changes to files in the Project Log and to re-export them using their previous settings.

Table 19-22
Project Log Pop-up Menu Commands

Option	Description
Export Again	Exports selected files in the Project Log using their previous settings
Add Files to Log	Includes additional graphic files in the Project Log without initially opening them
Clear Selection	Removes the selected files from the Project Log
Clear All	Removes all files from the Project Log

Using the Menus

You can also find many of the commands and options available in the various Fireworks panels in the menus. You'll also find, however, many features that are unavailable anywhere else. This section provides a reference to every menu item in Fireworks, along with its corresponding default keyboard shortcut, if available. Windows users won't see all of Fireworks' menus unless a document window is open.

> **Note:** In the tables in this section, commands in **bold** text are new or have changed menu locations in Fireworks 4.

File menu

Placing basic computer operations — creating, saving, and printing files — in the File menu is standard practice. Fireworks follows this practice and also includes commands for importing and exporting. All File menu commands are listed in Table 19-23.

Table 19-23
File Menu Commands

Command	Description	Windows	Macintosh
New	Displays the New Document dialog box before creating a new document	Ctrl+N	Command+N
Open	Displays the Open dialog before opening existing box documents	Ctrl+O	Command+O
Scan ⇨ Twain Acquire	Displays the interface dialog box for a Twain source, such as a scanner, if one is available and has been selected, before acquiring an image	n/a	n/a
Scan ⇨ Twain Select	Displays the Select Source dialog box before allowing you to select a Twain source to acquire an image from	n/a	n/a
Scan ⇨ Your Photoshop Acquire Plug-Ins (Macintosh only)	Lists currently installed Photoshop Acquire plug-ins. Typically, each plug-in enables you to acquire an image from a corresponding device.	—	n/a

Command	Description	Windows	Macintosh
Close	Closes the current document	Ctrl+W	Command+W
Save	Saves a document, or displays the Save As dialog box for an unnamed document	Ctrl+S	Command+S
Save As	Displays the Save As dialog box before saving a document	Ctrl+Shift+S	Command+Shift+S
Save a Copy	Displays the Save Copy As dialog box before saving a copy of a document	n/a	n/a
Update HTML	Places or updates Fireworks HTML code in another HTML file on the same computer	n/a	n/a
Revert	Replaces the current document with the previously saved version of the same document	n/a	n/a
Import	Displays the Import dialog box before importing a file into any open document	Ctrl+R	Command+R
Export	Displays the Export dialog box before exporting a document in the format specified in the Optimize panel	Ctrl+Shift+R	Command+Shift+R
Export Preview	Displays the Export Preview dialog box before exporting a document	Ctrl+Shift+X	Command+Shift+X
Export Wizard	Displays the Export Wizard before exporting a document	n/a	n/a
Batch Process	Displays the Batch Process dialog box before processing multiple image files	n/a	n/a
Run Script	Displays the Open dialog box before running a script	n/a	n/a
Preview in Browser ⇨ Preview in Primary Browser	Previews a document in your primary browser	F12	F12
Preview in Browser ⇨ Preview in Secondary Browser	Previews a document in your secondary browser	Shift+F12	Shift+F12

Continued

Table 19-23 *(continued)*

Command	Description	Windows	Macintosh
Preview in Browser ⇨ Set Primary Browser	Displays the Locate Browser dialog box before selecting a browser as your primary browser	n/a	n/a
Preview in Browser ⇨ Set Secondary Browser	Displays the Locate Browser dialog box before selecting a browser as your secondary browser	n/a	n/a
Page Setup	Displays the Page Setup) dialog box (for printing	n/a	n/a
Print	Displays the Print dialog box before printing a document	Ctrl+P	Command+P
HTML Setup	Displays the HTML Setup dialog box	n/a	n/a
Recent Files (Windows Only)	Displays the last four opened files; select any filename to reopen the file	n/a	—
Exit (Quit)	Quits Fireworks	Ctrl+Q	Command+Q

Edit menu

As evidenced by its name, the Edit menu holds the standard editing commands, such as Undo, Cut, Copy, and Paste, as well as numerous commands specific to Fireworks graphics, such as Paste Inside and Crop Document. The Edit menu is detailed in Table 19-24.

Table 19-24
Edit Menu Commands

Command	Description	Windows	Macintosh
Undo	Reverses the last action. The number of Undo steps is set in Preferences.	Ctrl+Z	Command+Z
Redo	Redoes the last edit that was undone by Undo	Ctrl+Y	Command+Y
Cut	Moves the current selection to the system clipboard	Ctrl+X	Command+X
Copy	Copies the current selection to the system clipboard	Ctrl+C	Command+C
Copy as Vectors	Copies a Fireworks vector object from the current selection to the system clipboard as vector information	n/a	n/a
Copy HTML Code	Displays the Copy HTML Code wizard that guides you through the process of exporting images and copying HTML code to the system clipboard for pasting into an HTML editor, such as Macromedia Dreamweaver	Ctrl+Alt+C	Command+Option+C
Paste	Copies the contents of the system clipboard to the current cursor position	Ctrl+V	Command+V
Clear	Removes the current selection from the document	Backspace	Delete
Paste as Mask	Copies the content of the clipboard as a mask	n/a	n/a
Paste Inside	Copies the contents of the system clipboard into a selected, closed path	Ctrl+Shift+V	Command+Shift+V
Paste Attributes	Copies the Fireworks-specific attributes of the contents of the system clipboard to a selected object	Ctrl+Alt+Shift+V	Command+Option+Shift+V

Continued

Table 19-24 *(continued)*

Command	Description	Windows	Macintosh
Select All	Selects all objects in a document in vector mode, or all pixels in a bitmap object in bitmap mode	Ctrl+A	Command+A
Select Similar	Selects pixels that are similarly colored to the selection while in bitmap mode	n/a	n/a
Superselect	Selects the entire group to which the current (sub)selection belongs	n/a	n/a
Subselect	Selects an individual object within a group	n/a	n/a
Deselect	Deselects all objects or pixels	Ctrl+D	Command+D
Duplicate	Creates a copy of the selected object, offset slightly from the original	Ctrl+Alt+D	Command+Option+D
Clone	Creates a copy of the selected object, directly on top of the original	Ctrl+Shift+D	Command+Shift+D
Find and Replace	Displays the Find and Replace dialog box	Ctrl+F	Command+F
Crop Selected Bitmap	Displays crop handles around the selected bitmap object	Ctrl+Alt+C	Command+Option+C
Crop Document	Selects the crop tool	n/a	n/a
Preferences	Displays the Preferences dialog box	Ctrl+U	Command+U
Keyboard Shortcuts	Displays the Keyboard Shortcuts dialog box before modifying keyboard shortcuts	n/a	n/a

View menu

The View menu commands, listed in Table 19-25, control a Web artist's views during the creation phase. In addition to numerous magnification commands, the View menu also contains helpful layout aids, such as Rulers, Grids, and Guides. You'll also find several features to help you see just the graphic when you need to have a clear, uncluttered perspective.

Table 19-25
View Menu Commands

Command	Description	Windows	Macintosh
Zoom In	Increases the magnification level of a document by one setting	Ctrl+Equals (=)	Command+ Equals (=)
Zoom Out	Decreases the magnification level of a document by one setting	Ctrl+Minus (–)	Command+ Minus (–)
Magnification ⇨ 6%	Sets the magnification level of a document to 6 percent	n/a	n/a
Magnification ⇨ 12%	Sets the magnification level of a document to 12 percent	n/a	n/a
Magnification ⇨ 25%	Sets the magnification level of a document to 25 percent	n/a	n/a
Magnification ⇨ 50%	Sets the magnification level of a document to 50 percent	Ctrl+5	Command+5
Magnification ⇨ 100%	Sets the magnification level of a document to 100 percent	Ctrl+1	Command+1
Magnification ⇨ 200%	Sets the magnification level of a document to 200 percent	Ctrl+2	Command+2
Magnification ⇨ 400%	Sets the magnification level of a document to 400 percent	Ctrl+4	Command+4
Magnification ⇨ 800%	Sets the magnification level of a document to 800 percent	Ctrl+8	Command+8
Magnification ⇨ 1600%	Sets the magnification level of a document to 1,600 percent	n/a	n/a
Magnification ⇨ 3200%	Sets the magnification level of a document to 3,200 percent	Ctrl+3	Command+3
Magnification ⇨ 6400%	Sets the magnification level of a document to 6,400 percent	Ctrl+6	Command+6
Fit Selection	Sets the magnification level of a document so that all selected objects are visible	Ctrl+Alt+ Zero (0)	Command+ Option+Zero (0)
Fit All	Sets the magnification level of a document so that all objects are visible	Ctrl+Zero (0)	Command+ Zero (0)

Continued

Table 19-25 *(continued)*

Command	Description	Windows	Macintosh
Full Display	Toggles Full Display	Ctrl+K	Command+K
Macintosh Gamma (Windows only)	Toggles the document display to simulate a typical Macintosh Gamma setting	n/a	—
Windows Gamma (Macintosh only)	Toggles the document display to simulate a typical Windows Gamma setting	—	n/a
Hide Selection	Hides selected objects	Ctrl+L	Command+L
Show All	Shows all hidden objects	Ctrl+Shift+L	Command+Shift+L
Rulers	Toggles display of rulers	Ctrl+Alt+R	Command+Option+R
Grid ⇨ Show Grid	Toggles display of the grid	Ctrl+Alt+G	Command+Option+G
Grid ⇨ Snap To Grid	Toggles whether objects snap to the grid or not	Ctrl+Alt+Shift+G	Command+Option+Shift+G
Grid ⇨ Edit Grid	Displays the Edit Grid dialog box	n/a	n/a
Guides ⇨ Show Guides	Toggles display of guides	Ctrl+Semicolon (;)	Command+Semicolon (;)
Guides ⇨ Lock Guides	Toggles whether or not guides can be edited and moved	Ctrl+Alt+Semicolon (;)	Command+Option+Semicolon (;)
Guides ⇨ Snap to Guides	Toggles whether objects snap to Guides or not	Ctrl+Shift+Semicolon (;)	Command+Shift+Semicolon (;)
Guides ⇨ Edit Guides	Displays the Edit Guides dialog box	n/a	n/a
Slice Guides	Toggles display of Slice Guides	Ctrl+Alt+Shift+Semicolon (;)	Command+Option+Shift+Semicolon (;)
Slice Overlay	Toggles display of the Slice Overlay	n/a	n/a

Command	Description	Windows	Macintosh
Hide Edges	Toggles display of selection borders	F9	F9
Hide Panels	Toggles display of all open panels	F4	F4
Status Bar (Windows only)	Toggles display of the status bar	n/a	—

Insert menu

The Insert menu, detailed in Table 19-26, contains commands for inserting buttons, symbols, hotspots, layers, frames, and more.

Table 19-26
Insert Menu Commands

Command	Description	Windows	Macintosh
New Button	Displays the Button Editor before creating a new button	n/a	n/a
New Symbol	Displays the Symbol Properties dialog box before creating a new symbol	Ctrl+F8	Command+F8
Convert to Symbol	Displays the Symbol Properties dialog box before converting an object to a symbol	F8	F8
Libraries ⇨ Libraries	Your Lists Libraries contained in the Libraries folder. Choose a Library to display the Import Symbols dialog box before importing a symbol from the Library.	n/a	n/a
Animations	Sample animations included with Fireworks	n/a	n/a
Bullets	Sample bullets included with Fireworks	n/a	n/a
Buttons	Sample buttons included with Fireworks	n/a	n/a

Continued

Table 19-26 (continued)

Command	Description	Windows	Macintosh
Themes	Sample themes included with Fireworks	n/a	n/a
Libraries ⇨ Other	Displays the Open dialog box before importing a Library	n/a	n/a
Hotspot	Inserts a hotspot object	Ctrl+Shift+U	Command+Shift+U
Slice	Inserts a slice object	Alt+Shift+U	Option+Shift+U
Pop-up Menu	Displays the Set Pop-up Menu dialog box	n/a	n/a
Image	Displays the Import dialog box before importing an image into the document	n/a	n/a
Empty Bitmap	Inserts an empty bitmap object	n/a	n/a
Layer	Creates a new layer	n/a	n/a
Frame	Creates a new frame	n/a	n/a

Modify menu

After you've created your basic objects, you'll undoubtedly spend as much, if not more time, tweaking and modifying them in order to get them just right. The Modify menu commands, detailed in Table 19-27, are quite numerous and specific.

Table 19-27
Modify Menu Commands

Command	Description	Windows	Macintosh
Image Size	Displays the Image Size dialog box before changing the size of a bitmap	n/a	n/a
Canvas Size	Displays the Change Canvas Size dialog box before changing the size of the canvas	n/a	n/a

Command	Description	Windows	Macintosh
Canvas Color	Displays the Canvas Color dialog box before changing the color of the canvas	n/a	n/a
Trim Canvas	Shrinks the canvas to fit snugly around all objects	Ctrl+Alt+T	Command+Option+T
Fit Canvas	Shrinks or expands the canvas to fit snugly around all objects	Ctrl+Alt+F	Command+Option+F
Rotate Canvas ➪ Rotate 180°	Rotates the canvas 180 degrees	n/a	n/a
Rotate Canvas ➪ Rotate 90° CW	Rotates the canvas 90 degrees clockwise	n/a	n/a
Rotate Canvas ➪ Rotate 90° CCW	Rotates the canvas 90 degrees counterclockwise	n/a	n/a
Animate ➪ Animate Selection	Displays the Animate dialog box before creating an animation symbol	Alt+Shift+F8	Option+Shift+F8
Animate ➪ Settings	Displays the Animate dialog box for the selected animation symbol	n/a	n/a
Animate ➪ Remove Animation	Changes an animation symbol into a graphic symbol, removing the animation	n/a	n/a
Symbol ➪ Edit Symbol	Displays the selected symbol in its own canvas for editing	n/a	n/a
Symbol ➪ Tween Instances	Displays the Tween Instances dialog box before creating intermediate steps between two selected symbol instances	Ctrl+Alt+Shift+T	Command+Option+Shift+T
Symbol ➪ Break Apart	Breaks the link between the selected symbol and its instances	n/a	n/a
Edit Bitmap	Switches to bitmap mode	Ctrl+E	Command+E
Exit Bitmap Mode	Exits bitmap mode	Ctrl+Shift+E	Command+Shift+E

Continued

Table 19-27 *(continued)*

Command	Description	Windows	Macintosh
Marquee ⇨ Select Similar	Selects pixels that are similarly colored to the current selection	n/a	n/a
Marquee ⇨ Select Inverse	Selects all deselected pixels and deselects all selected pixels in bitmap mode	Ctrl+Shift+I	Command+Shift+I
Marquee ⇨ Feather	Displays the Feather Selection dialog box before feathering the edges of a pixel selection in bitmap mode	n/a	n/a
Marquee ⇨ Expand	Displays the Expand Selection dialog box before expanding the current selection in bitmap mode	n/a	n/a
Marquee ⇨ Contract	Displays the Contract Selection dialog box before contracting the current selection in bitmap mode	n/a	n/a
Marquee ⇨ Border	Displays the Select Border dialog box before selecting a border around the current selection in bitmap mode	n/a	n/a
Marquee ⇨ Smooth	Displays the Smooth Selection dialog box before smoothing the edges of the current selection in bitmap mode	n/a	n/a
Marquee ⇨ Save Selection	Stores the current marquee selection for later recall	n/a	n/a
Marquee ⇨ Restore Selection	Recalls a stored marquee selection	n/a	n/a
Mask ⇨ Reveal All	Shows an object and its mask when editing a mask	n/a	n/a
Mask ⇨ Hide All	Shows only the mask when editing a mask	n/a	n/a
Mask ⇨ Paste as Mask	Copies the contents of the clipboard as a mask	n/a	n/a
Mask ⇨ Group as Mask	Groups one or more selected objects with the top object used as an alpha mask	n/a	n/a

Command	Description	Windows	Macintosh
Mask ⇨ Reveal Selection	Shows the area defined by a pixel selection	n/a	n/a
Mask ⇨ Hide Selection	Hides the area defined by a pixel selection	n/a	n/a
Mask ⇨ Disable Mask	Disables the selected object's mask	n/a	n/a
Mask ⇨ Delete Mask	Deletes the selected object's mask	n/a	n/a
Selective JPEG ⇨ Save Selection as JPEG Mask	Saves a selection as a selective JPEG mask	n/a	n/a
Selective JPEG ⇨ Settings	Displays the Selective JPEG Settings dialog box	n/a	n/a
Selective JPEG ⇨ Restore JPEG Mask as Selection	Creates a selection that matches a selective JPEG mask	n/a	n/a
Selective JPEG ⇨ Remove JPEG Mask	Removes a selective JPEG mask	n/a	n/a
Convert to Bitmap	Converts one or more selected objects into a single bitmap object	Ctrl+Alt+Shift+Z	Command+Option+Shift+Z
Flatten Layers	Flattens visible layers into one layer, discarding hidden layers	n/a	n/a
Transform ⇨ Free Transform	Toggles the display of an object's transformation handles	n/a	n/a
Transform ⇨ Scale	Sets transformation handles to resize and rotate objects	n/a	n/a
Transform ⇨ Skew	Sets transformation handles to slant, change perspective, and rotate objects	n/a	n/a
Transform ⇨ Distort	Sets transformation handles to distort and rotate objects	n/a	n/a
Transform ⇨ Numeric Transform	Displays the Numeric Transform dialog box	Ctrl+Shift+T	Command+Shift+T
Transform ⇨ Rotate 180°	Rotates an object 180 degrees	n/a	n/a

Continued

Table 19-27 *(continued)*

Command	Description	Windows	Macintosh
Transform ▷ Rotate 90° CW	Rotates an object 90 degrees clockwise	Ctrl+9	Command+9
Transform ▷ Rotate 90° CCW	Rotates an object 90 degrees counterclockwise	Ctrl+7	Command+7
Transform ▷ Flip Horizontal	Flips an object horizontally	n/a	n/a
Transform ▷ Flip Vertical	Flips an object vertically	n/a	n/a
Transform ▷ Remove Transformations	Removes all transformations from an object	n/a	n/a
Arrange ▷ Bring to Front	Moves an object to the front of a layer	Ctrl+Shift+Up	Command+Shift+Up
Arrange ▷ Bring Forward	Moves an object in front of the object just in front of it	Ctrl+Up	Command+Up
Arrange ▷ Send Backward	Moves an object in back of the object just behind it	Ctrl+Down	Command+Down
Arrange ▷ Send to Back	Moves an object to the back of a layer	Ctrl+Shift+Down	Command+Shift+Down
Align ▷ Left	Aligns selected objects to the left edge of the selection	Ctrl+Alt+1	Command+Option+1
Align ▷ Center Vertical	Aligns selected objects to the vertical center of the selection	Ctrl+Alt+2	Command+Option+2
Align ▷ Right	Aligns selected objects to the right edge of the selection	Ctrl+Alt+3	Command+Option+3
Align ▷ Top	Aligns selected objects to the top edge of the selection	Ctrl+Alt+4	Command+Option+4
Align ▷ Center Horizontal	Aligns selected objects to the horizontal center of the selection	Ctrl+Alt+5	Command+Option+5
Align ▷ Bottom	Aligns selected objects to the bottom of the selection	Ctrl+Alt+6	Command+Option+6
Align ▷ Distribute Widths	Distribute selected objects horizontally throughout the selection	Ctrl+Alt+7	Command+Option+7
Align ▷ Distribute Heights	Distribute selected objects vertically throughout the selection	Ctrl+Alt+9	Command+Option+9

Command	Description	Windows	Macintosh
Join	Joins two or more selected paths or endpoints	Ctrl+J	Command+J
Split	Splits an object into component paths	Ctrl+Shift+J	Command+Shift+J
Combine ⇨ Union	Combines two or more selected closed paths into a single object	n/a	n/a
Combine ⇨ Intersect	Combines overlapping parts of two or more selected closed paths	n/a	n/a
Combine ⇨ Punch	Combines two or more selected closed paths by punching holes in the back object with the front object(s)	n/a	n/a
Combine ⇨ Crop	Crops the back object of a selection with the front object of a selection of two or more closed paths	n/a	n/a
Alter Path ⇨ Simplify	Displays the Simplify dialog box before removing points from a path while keeping its overall shape	n/a	n/a
Alter Path ⇨ Expand Stroke	Displays the Expand dialog box	n/a	n/a
Alter Path ⇨ Inset Path	Displays the Inset dialog box before expanding or contracting one or more closed paths	n/a	n/a
Alter Path ⇨ Hard Fill	Removes antialiasing or feathering from the edges of a selection	n/a	n/a
Alter Path ⇨ Anti-Alias Fill	Antialiases the edges of a selection	n/a	n/a
Alter Path ⇨ Feather Fill	Feathers the edges of a selection	n/a	n/a
Group	Groups one or more selected objects	Ctrl+G	Command+G
Ungroup	Ungroups a Group or Mask Group	Ctrl+Shift+G	Command+Shift+G

Text menu

Text in a traditional graphics program plays a relatively small, but key role. In a Web graphics program such as Fireworks, text becomes more important because graphics are the only way to incorporate heavily styled text into Web pages. The Text menu commands, described in Table 19-28, offer many shortcuts that enable you to manipulate text objects without opening the Text Editor.

Table 19-28
Text Menu Commands

Command	Description	Windows	Macintosh
Font ⇨ Your Font List	Changes the selected text object's typeface or the default typeface if no text object is selected	n/a	n/a
Size ⇨ Other	Displays the Text Size dialog box	n/a	n/a
Size ⇨ 8 to 120	Changes the selected text object's type size or the default type size if no text object is selected	n/a	n/a
Style ⇨ Plain	Removes bold, italic, and underline formatting from the selected text	n/a	n/a
Style ⇨ Bold	Makes the selected text bold	Ctrl+B	Command+B
Style ⇨ Italic	Italicizes the selected text	Ctrl+I	Command+I
Style ⇨ Underline	Underlines the selected text	n/a	n/a
Align ⇨ Left	Left-aligns the selected text	Ctrl+Alt+Shift+L	Command+Option+Shift+L
Align ⇨ Center Horizontally	Centers the selected text	Ctrl+Alt+Shift+C	Command+Option+Shift+C
Align ⇨ Right	Right-aligns the selected text	Ctrl+Alt+Shift+R	Command+Option+Shift+R
Align ⇨ Justified	Justifies the selected text	Ctrl+Alt+Shift+J	Command+Option+Shift+J
Align ⇨ Stretched	Force-justifies the selected text	Ctrl+Alt+Shift+S	Command+Option+Shift+S

Command	Description	Windows	Macintosh
Align ⇨ Top	Aligns vertically flowing text to the top of the text block	n/a	n/a
Align ⇨ Center Vertically	Aligns vertically flowing text to the vertical center of the text block	n/a	n/a
Align ⇨ Bottom	Aligns vertically flowing text to the bottom of the text block	n/a	n/a
Align ⇨ Justified Vertically	Justifies vertically flowing text to the top and bottom of the text block	n/a	n/a
Align ⇨ Stretched Vertically	Force-justifies vertically flowing text to the top and bottom of the text block	n/a	n/a
Editor	Displays the Text Editor dialog box	n/a	n/a
Attach to Path	Attaches the selected text block to a selected path	Ctrl+Shift+Y	Command+Shift+Y
Detach from Path	Detaches the selected text block from a path if it's attached to one	n/a	n/a
Orientation ⇨ Rotate Around Path	Orients attached text so that the bottom of each letter is closest to the path	n/a	n/a
Orientation ⇨ Vertical	Orients attached text so that the side of each letter is closest to the path	n/a	n/a
Orientation ⇨ Skew Vertical	Skews attached text vertically	n/a	n/a
Orientation ⇨ Skew Horizontal	Skews attached text horizontally	n/a	n/a
Reverse Direction	Reverses the direction of text attached to a path	n/a	n/a
Convert to Paths	Converts text objects into vector objects	Ctrl+Shift+P	Command+Shift+P

Commands menu

Commands are a way for the Fireworks user to extend the basic feature set and are relatively easy to create because they're written in JavaScript. Table 19-29 details the commands that are included with Fireworks.

Table 19-29
Commands Menu Commands

Command	Description	Windows	Macintosh
Edit Command List	Displays the Edit Command List dialog box	n/a	n/a
Creative ⇨ Convert to Grayscale	Converts the selection to grayscale	n/a	n/a
Creative ⇨ Convert to Sepia Tone	Converts the selection to a sepia tint	n/a	n/a
Creative ⇨ Create Picture Frame	Creates a faux-wood picture frame around the current document	n/a	n/a
Document ⇨ Center in Document	Centers the selection in the middle of the document	n/a	n/a
Document ⇨ Distribute to Layers	Distributes the selected objects in your document so that each one is on its own layer	n/a	n/a
Document ⇨ Hide Other Layers	Hides all layers except the current layer	n/a	n/a
Document ⇨ Lock Other Layers	Locks all layers except the current layer	n/a	n/a
Document ⇨ Reverse All Frames	Reverses the order of the frames in a document	n/a	n/a
Document ⇨ Reverse Frame Range	Reverses the order of a range of frames in a document	n/a	n/a
Panel Layout Sets ⇨ 1024×768/ 1280×1024/ 800×600/Your Panel Layout Sets	Panel Layout Set are examples that arrange the floating windows to the right of the screen, sized for optimal viewing at various display resolutions, and lists panel layout sets created with Commands ⇨ Panel Layout	n/a	n/a

Command	Description	Windows	Macintosh
Panel Layout	Displays a dialog box where you can name the current panel layout and save it so that it appears under Commands ⇨ Panel Layout Sets	n/a	n/a
Reset Warning Dialogs	Resets all Warning dialog boxes that have a "Don't show this again" back to their default of appearing	n/a	n/a
Web ⇨ Create Shared Palette	Creates a shared palette from multiple files	n/a	n/a
Web ⇨ Select Blank ALT Tags	Selects all hotspots or slices that do not have alt text specified	n/a	n/a
Web ⇨ Set ALT Tags	Displays a dialog box where you can specify alt text for a document's hotspots and slices	n/a	n/a

Xtras

In Macromedia parlance, an Xtra is a plug-in that extends the capabilities of a program. With Fireworks, Xtras are primarily image filters. As you can see in Table 19-30, Fireworks comes with four groups of filters, plus three Eye Candy 4000 filters, referred to as Eye Candy 4000 LE. Because Fireworks can read most Photoshop filters and plug-ins, you can greatly extend the available Xtras by assigning an additional Photoshop plug-ins folder in Fireworks Preferences.

Caution Because all Fireworks Xtras are pixel-based image filters, any Xtra applied to a vector object first converts it into a bitmap object. Many Xtras are also available in the Effect panel as Live Effects, which work on both bitmap and vector objects without reducing editability.

Table 19-30
Xtras Menu Commands

Command	Description	Windows	Macintosh
Repeat Xtra	Repeats the most recently used Xtra	Ctrl+Alt+Shift+X	Command+Option+Shift+X
Adjust Color ⇨ Auto Levels	Auto corrects the selection's levels	n/a	n/a
Adjust Color ⇨ Brightness/Contrast	Displays the Brightness/Contrast dialog box before adjusting the selection's brightness and/or contrast levels	n/a	n/a
Adjust Color ⇨ Curves	Displays the Curves dialog box before adjusting the selection's color curves	n/a	n/a
Adjust Color ⇨ Hue/Saturation	Displays the Hue/Saturation dialog box before adjusting the selection's hue and saturation levels	n/a	n/a
Adjust Color ⇨ Invert	Changes each color in the selection to its mathematical inverse	Ctrl+Alt+Shift+I	Command+Option+Shift+I
Adjust Color ⇨ Levels	Displays the Levels dialog box before adjusting the selection's levels	n/a	n/a
Blur ⇨ Blur	Blurs the selection	n/a	n/a
Blur ⇨ Blur More	Blurs the selection across a larger radius than Blur	n/a	n/a
Blur ⇨ Gaussian Blur	Displays the Gaussian Blur dialog box before blurring the selection	n/a	n/a
Other ⇨ Convert to Alpha	Converts the selection into an alpha mask	n/a	n/a
Other ⇨ Find Edges	Identifies edges in the selection	n/a	n/a
Sharpen ⇨ Sharpen	Sharpens the selection	n/a	n/a
Sharpen ⇨ Sharpen More	Sharpens the selection more than Sharpen	n/a	n/a

Command	Description	Windows	Macintosh
Sharpen ⇨ Unsharp Mask	Displays the Unsharp Mask dialog box before sharpening the selection	n/a	n/a
Eye Candy 4000 LE ⇨ Bevel Boss	Displays the Eye Candy 4000 Bevel Boss dialog box	n/a	n/a
Eye Candy 4000 LE ⇨ Marble	Displays the Eye Candy 4000 Marble dialog box	n/a	n/a
Eye Candy 4000 LE ⇨ Motion Trail	Displays the Eye Candy 4000 Motion Trail dialog box	n/a	n/a

Window menu

The Window menu commands, listed in Table 19-31, give you access to all of Fireworks' floating panels and toolbars. In addition, several commands help you work with multiple documents or multiple views of the same document.

Table 19-31
Window Menu Commands

Command	Description	Windows	Macintosh
New Window	Creates a duplicate of the current document window	Ctrl+Alt+N	Command+ Option+N
Toolbars ⇨ Main (Windows only)	Toggles display of the Main toolbar	n/a	—
Toolbars ⇨ Modify (Windows only)	Toggles display of the Modify toolbar	n/a	—
Tools	Toggles display of the Tools panel	n/a	n/a
Stroke	Toggles display of the Stroke panel	Ctrl+Alt+F4	Command+ Option+F4
Fill	Toggles display of the Fill panel	Shift+F7	Shift+F7
Effect	Toggles display of the Effect panel	Alt+F7	Option+F7
Info	Toggles display of the Info panel	Alt+Shift+F12	Option+ Shift+F12

Continued

Table 19-31 *(continued)*

Command	Description	Windows	Macintosh
Optimize	Toggles display of the Optimize panel	n/a	n/a
Object	Toggles display of the Object panel	Alt+F2	Option+F2
Behaviors	Toggles display of the Behaviors panel	Shift+F3	Shift+F3
Color Mixer	Toggles display of the Color Mixer	Shift+F9	Shift+F9
Swatches	Toggles display of the Swatches panel	Ctrl+F9	Command+F9
Color Table	Toggles display of the Color Table panel	n/a	n/a
Tool Options	Toggles display of the Tool Options panel	Ctrl+Alt+O	Command+Option+O
Layers	Toggles display of the Layers panel	F2	F2
Frames	Toggles display of the Frames panel	Shift+F2	Shift+F2
History	Toggles display of the History panel	Shift+F10	Shift+F10
Styles	Toggles display of the Styles panel	Shift+F11	Shift+F11
Library	Toggles display of the Library panel	F11	F11
URL	Toggles display of the URL panel	Alt+Shift+F10	Option+Shift+F10
Find and Replace	Toggles display of the Find and Replace panel	Ctrl+F	Command+F
Project Log	Toggles display of the Project Log panel	n/a	n/a
Cascade	Cascades the document windows	n/a	n/a
Tile Horizontal	Tiles the document windows horizontally	n/a	n/a
Tile Vertical	Tiles the document windows vertically	n/a	n/a
Your Open Documents List	Lists the currently open document windows	n/a	n/a

Help menu

Everyone needs help now and then, especially when working with a program as rich and deep as Fireworks. The Help menu provides quick access to Using Fireworks, various online resources, and a number of key tutorials that explain the basics of the program.

The Macromedia and Fireworks Web sites offer a tremendous range of support options. If you're troubleshooting a problem, you should start with the searchable TechNotes, which cover virtually every aspect of working with Fireworks. You'll also find links to useful tutorials, articles on Web graphics design, and interviews with industry leaders in Fireworks' main Support section.

One of the most important resources is the Fireworks newsgroup, hosted by Macromedia. This discussion group, located at `<news://forums.macromedia.com/macromedia.fireworks>`, is an essential source for contacting other users of Fireworks. Fireworks support staff, as well as expert and novice users alike, frequent the newsgroup. Need a quick answer to a perplexing graphics problem? Can't figure out the final step in a procedure? Looking to have users with different systems and browsers check your site for compatibility? The Fireworks newsgroup can help in all of these areas and more.

The Help menu commands are detailed in Table 19-32.

Table 19-32
Help Menu Commands

Command	Description	Windows	Macintosh
About Balloon Help (Macintosh only)	Describes Balloon Help	—	n/a
Show Balloons (Macintosh only)	Toggles Balloon Help on or off	—	n/a
Welcome	Opens a dialog box allowing you to choose the What's New file, the Tutorial, and the Lessons	n/a	n/a
Using Fireworks	Opens the Fireworks online manual in your browser	F1	help/ Command+/
Lessons	Opens example lesson files	n/a	n/a
Fireworks Support Center	Connects to the Internet to view the Fireworks Support Center Web site	n/a	n/a

Continued

Table 19-32 *(continued)*

Command	Description	Windows	Macintosh
Register Fireworks	Connects to the Internet to register your copy of Fireworks with Macromedia	n/a	n/a
About Fireworks (Windows only)	Displays the About Fireworks dialog box	n/a	—

> **Tip:** Mac OS 8/9 users can display the About Fireworks dialog box by choosing Apple Menu ⇨ About Fireworks.

Summary

With a program as feature-laden as Fireworks, having an overview of what's possible is helpful. The Fireworks user interface is very flexible and customizable. The more familiar you become with the layout of the program, the smoother your workflow will become. When you're looking at the Fireworks interface, keep these points in mind:

✦ In some ways, Fireworks combines tools from several different types of applications: a bitmap graphic program, a vector drawing program, an image optimizer, and an HTML editor.

✦ The Macromedia Common UI streamlines the Fireworks interface and simplifies moving between multiple Macromedia apps.

✦ All the tools found in Fireworks' Tools panel have one-key shortcuts, such as V for the Select Behind tool and Z for the Zoom tool.

✦ Customize your workspace in Fireworks by grouping, referred to as *docking*, the floating panels however you want, and then save that grouping as a Panel Layout Set.

✦ Many tools have special options you can access by double-clicking their Tools panel buttons, or by choosing the tool and then opening the Tool Options panel.

✦ ✦ ✦

Setting Up Documents

CHAPTER 20

In This Chapter

Prepping a new canvas

Opening existing images

Bringing in multiple files

Saving your work

Adjusting canvas size and color

Oil painters must complete a fairly involved set of preparation rituals even before they can begin to paint. Although Web artists don't have to stretch or prime their canvases, choosing certain options prior to undertaking a new work can save time down the line. Of course, one of the major benefits of electronic illustration in general, and Fireworks in particular, is that you can modify virtually anything at any stage.

This chapter covers all you need to know about "prepping your canvas" in Fireworks. How big should it be, and what kinds of things are you going to put on it? In addition, you discover how to open, save, and close Fireworks documents. We also look at how you can modify a canvas at any stage of the creative process.

Creating New Documents

Before you actually begin work, it's best to consider what you are aiming to create. The better you can visualize the final result, the fewer modifications you'll have to make along the way. This is not to say that trial and error is out of the question, but a little planning can save a lot of time and trouble later.

Exploring two approaches

A fundamental question that you have to answer before you even choose File ➪ New, is what approach you're going to take in creating the multiple image files that typically make up Web pages. The two basic approaches are as follows:

 ✦ Create multiple small images in multiple Fireworks documents and assemble them into a Web page later in another application, such as Macromedia Dreamweaver.

✦ Populate one Fireworks canvas with a complete Web page design, including all the navigation elements, text, and images.

Before I started using Fireworks, I created Web page designs in Macromedia FreeHand, and then copied individual elements into separate Adobe Photoshop documents for touching up and final rendering. Later, I found myself replicating this workflow, but substituting Fireworks for Photoshop. Each of the images for the Web site lived in its own Fireworks document, as shown in Figure 20-1.

Figure 20-1: In a traditional workflow, each graphic is a separate document.

For many projects, though, your best option may be to create one large canvas, as shown in Figure 20-2, and populate it with your entire page design, either created from scratch or a mixture of from-scratch and imported elements. Fireworks allows you to happily draw, filter, effect, slice, specify hyperlinks, leave space for HTML text and finally, export the whole lot as HTML and JavaScript, along with GIF and JPEG images. And if, at any time, you want to export a single layer or slice all on its own, Fireworks enables you to do that, too.

Cross-Reference: Turn to the color insert to see an example of a complete Web design in a single Fireworks document.

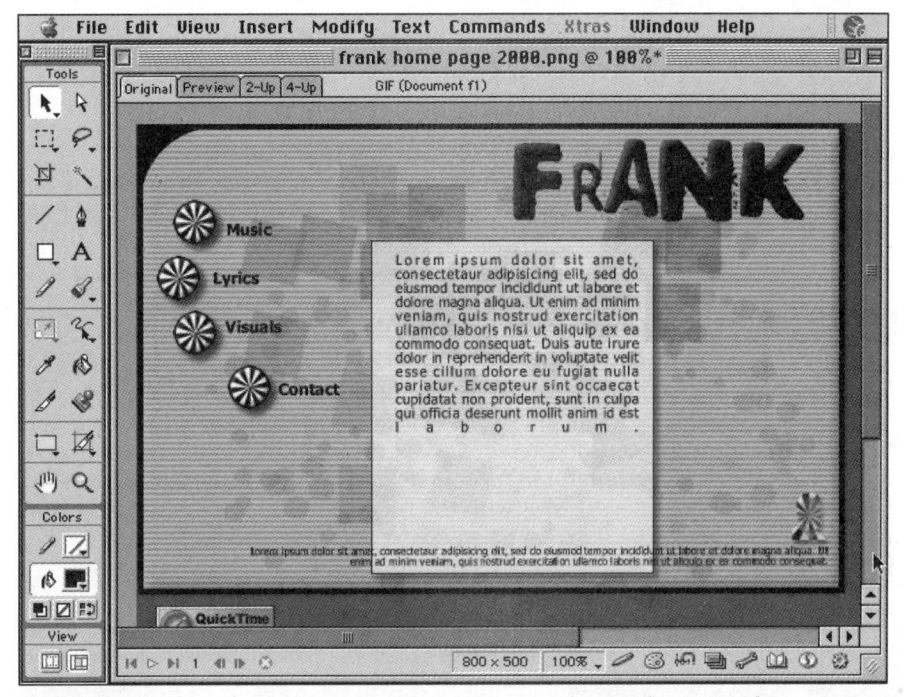

Figure 20-2: You can design and implement a complete Web page within one Fireworks document.

Whichever method you choose is a matter of personal preference, of course. I'll go on record as recommending the one-canvas approach. Fireworks excels at one-stop Web graphics, and an integrated approach takes full advantage of the variety of tools Fireworks places at your disposal.

Understanding the canvas options

The "canvas" in Fireworks is a background for the visible area of a document. Fireworks gives you control over the following four basic elements of the canvas:

- ✦ **Width:** The horizontal dimension of a document, available in pixels, inches, or centimeters.

- ✦ **Height:** The vertical dimension of a document, also available in pixels, inches, or centimeters.

- ✦ **Resolution:** A print-style dots-per-inch (or centimeter) setting that Fireworks uses to translate inches or centimeters into pixels, if you don't want to specify dimensions in pixels.

- ✦ **Canvas color:** The color of the underlying layer for your work. A transparent option is also considered a valid "color."

Discerning width and height

Although it may appear otherwise, all Web graphic files are ultimately rectangular. A document's width and height determine not only a document's size, but also its shape. Although the size of an image is theoretically unlimited, the Web designer must always consider file size as a vital factor and, everything else being equal, the larger the image, the bigger the file size. Typically, image dimensions are given in pixels, short for picture elements. Pixels are the red, green, and blue dots that make up a computer color monitor's screen. From time to time, it's helpful to switch to non-screen-based measurement systems, like inches or centimeters, and Fireworks gives you that option. But Web design is a pixel-oriented world, and you'll find yourself primarily using them for measuring.

If you are building an entire page design in one Fireworks document, a typical size would be 600 pixels wide and 800 pixels tall for a page that is easily viewable at any display resolution and calls for an acceptable amount of scrolling at smaller resolutions (about two screen lengths). Another option is to make a page that's suitable for viewing on an 800×600 display with the browser filling the screen. If you start with a canvas that's 760×400 pixels (leaving space for browser toolbars), users won't have to scroll at all after they size their browser window correctly.

> **Tip** Don't be afraid to make your canvas a little bigger than you actually require. I find that a little elbow room is nice while drawing, especially when using a pen and tablet . . . you can experiment with strokes in the extra space before marking up your actual work. When you're done, delete the test strokes and choose Modify ➪ Trim Canvas to quickly get rid of the extra space and get your document ready for export.

Examining resolution

Even if you sized your canvas in inches or centimeters, the canvas itself is an online (onscreen) item, made up of pixels, and it has to have a pixel measurement, too. The (print) Resolution setting allows you to specify how Fireworks should make the translation from dots to inches. If you sized your canvas to 8.5 by 11 inches in order to print a standard letter-sized page at 150 dots per inch (dpi), then put 150 in the Resolution box, and you'll be able to print your document correctly when you're done.

If you're only using Fireworks to create online images — like most of us — the good news is that you can leave the Resolution setting at its default of 72 and continue to size your canvas and all of your objects in pixel measurements. As long as you leave the default at 72 for all the documents you make and work with, you can completely ignore it.

Why 72?

The screen image on the original Macintosh computer was 512×342 pixels and 7.1×4.5 inches. This works out to 72 dots per inch (dpi) for every Mac of that time period, because they all had the exact same display. If you wanted something to be exactly an inch wide on the screen (an inch on an on-screen ruler, for example) you would make it 72 pixels wide and it would work on all Macs. The number 72 is also convenient because there are 72 points (a standard typographical measure) in an inch, so one pixel could easily represent one point as well. Today, far too much variety exists in computer display resolutions and dimensions for there to be an actual, real-world common measurement, so 72 remains an arbitrary standard dpi setting. Although Windows and some Windows applications use 96, Fireworks on both platforms uses the standard 72.

Determining your display's actual dpi involves measuring its visible height and width and then dividing those measurements by your display resolution. A display with a visible area of 12×9 inches, running at 1024×768, has a resolution of 85 dpi. An 85×85 pixel object on that display would be one inch square.

Using canvas color

Canvas color is not only very important in Fireworks, but it's also very flexible. When you're creating Web graphics, the canvas color often needs to match the background color of a Web page. You don't have to match the colors when creating your new page, but if you can, you should in order to save a step or two in the near future. You can modify the canvas color at any point in Fireworks by choosing Modify ⇨ Canvas Color.

Initially, you have three basic choices for a canvas color: white, transparent, or custom. Although white is not the default color for all browsers, it's a common default background in Web authoring tools and a popular choice on the Web in general. Naturally, transparent is not really a color — it's the absence of color. However, as many Web pages use an image or pattern for a background, designers often choose the transparent option to enable part of the background to be visible through their graphics. This enables graphics — which are always saved in a rectangular format — to appear nonrectangular. Fireworks includes many techniques for outputting a graphic with a transparent background, but many artists like to work with a transparent canvas regardless.

The third choice, marked custom color, is really all the colors. Selecting the Custom Color radio button enables you to choose a color from the 216 Web-safe colors that display the same way in the major browsers on Macintosh and Windows computers running at eight-bit color. You can also choose a color from your operating system's color picker(s), or use the eyedropper to sample a color from anywhere on your display. The Custom Color option is great when you're trying to match a Web-page background.

Cross-Reference: An understanding of color on the Internet is crucial for the Web graphics designer. See Chapter 23 for more information on using color in Fireworks.

Discovering the steps to create a new document

To create a new document, follow these steps:

1. Choose File ➪ New or use the key shortcut Ctrl+N (Command+N). Windows users can also click the New button on the Main toolbar. The New Document dialog box, shown in Figure 20-3, opens.

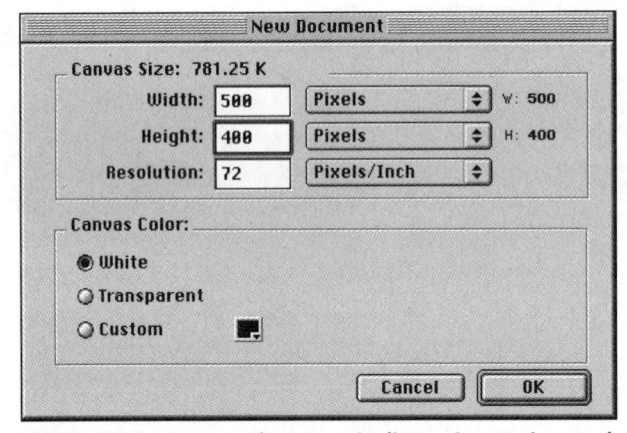

Figure 20-3: Set your document's dimensions, print resolution, and canvas color in the New Document dialog box.

2. To change the horizontal measurement of the canvas, enter a new value in the Width text box.

Tip: Press Tab when you're done to move on to the Height text box.

3. To change the vertical measurement of the canvas, enter a new value in the Height text box.

4. To enter a new resolution for the canvas, enter a value in the Resolution text box. The default resolution in Fireworks is 72 pixels per inch. Unless you have a specific reason to change it, leave it at 72.

5. To change the measurement systems used for Width, Height, or Resolution, select the arrow button next to the corresponding list box. You can choose Pixels, Inches, or Centimeters for both Width and Height; with Resolution, you can select either Pixels/Inch or Pixels/cm (centimeter).

Note: Whenever you switch Width or Height measurement systems, Fireworks automatically converts the existing values to the new scale. For example, if the new canvas was originally 144 pixels wide at 72 pixels per inch resolution, and the Width measurement system was changed to inches, Fireworks converts the 144 pixels to 2 inches. No matter which system you choose, Fireworks always displays the dimensions in pixels on the right side of the dialog box as W (width) and H (height).

6. Select a Canvas Color: White, Transparent, or Custom Color.

7. To choose a Custom Color, select the arrow button next to the color swatch and pick the desired color from the pop-up color palette.

8. For a more extensive color choice (beyond the 216 Web-safe colors in the pop-up display), either select the Palette button on the pop-up display or double-click the swatches to reveal the system color picker(s).

9. Click OK when you're done.

Tip: The New Document dialog box remembers your last settings the next time you create a new file, with one exception. If you've cut or copied a graphic to your system's clipboard and you select File ⇨ New, the dialog box contains the dimensions of the image on the clipboard. This feature makes pasting an existing image into a new file easy.

Opening Existing Images

Your Fireworks documents will fall into two distinct categories. Sometimes you'll start from scratch in Fireworks, and sometimes you'll import work from another application just to prepare it for the Web. Because Fireworks is terrific at optimizing images for the Web, you're just as likely to find yourself opening an existing file as creating a new one.

Tip: Use a lossless file format such as PNG or TIFF to move images between applications. The GIF and JPEG formats are unsuitable for use as master copies because information — and quality — is thrown away when you create them in order to achieve a smaller file size.

Opening a regular PNG file is just like opening a Fireworks document. Opening a file of another type creates a new Fireworks document that will need to be saved as a Fireworks PNG-format document under a new name. Export GIF, JPEG, or other files from your Fireworks document as required.

Examining file formats

As probably anyone who's ever touched a computer graphic is aware, different computer programs, as well as platforms, store files in their own file format. Fireworks opens a wide range of these formats. With formats from advanced graphic applications, such as Photoshop, Fireworks retains as much of the special components of the image — like layers and editable text — as possible. You can even open ASCII or RTF (Rich Text Format) files to import text into Fireworks.

> **Cross-Reference** Opening the native file formats of Macromedia FreeHand, Adobe Illustrator, or CorelDRAW causes Fireworks to display a dialog box for setting special options.

Table 20-1 details formats supported by Fireworks.

Table 20-1
Supported File Formats

Format	Filename Extension	Macintosh Type Code	Notes
Fireworks File Format	.png	PNGf	A PNG file with Fireworks-only information such as vectors added. The default file format for Fireworks 3 and 4.
Fireworks 2.0	.png	PNGf	Updated automatically when opened. Cannot be saved and then opened again in Fireworks 2.0.
Fireworks 1.0	.png	PNGf	Updated automatically when opened. Cannot be saved and then opened again in Fireworks 1.0. The Background is placed on its own layer.
Portable Network Graphic	.png	PNGf	Standard PNG documents that don't have extra Fireworks information.
Photoshop Document	.psd	8BPS	Version 3.0 or later only. Layers, editable text, and Layer Effects are preserved.
FreeHand Document	.fh7 or .fh8	AGD3	The vector-based format of FreeHand 7 or 8.
Illustrator 7 Document	.ai	UMsk	Adobe Illustrator 7's vector-based default format.
CorelDRAW 8 Document	.cdr	CDR8	CorelDRAW's vector-based format must have been saved without CorelDRAW's built-in bitmap or object compression to be openable in Fireworks.

Format	Filename Extension	Macintosh Type Code	Notes
GIF	.gif	GIFf	Graphics Interchange File Format. Static or animated. Each frame of an animated GIF is placed on its own frame in Fireworks.
JPEG	.jpg or .jpeg or .jpe	JPEG	Avoid importing JPEG images due to their lossy compression scheme and low quality.
Targa	.tga	TPIC	Common UNIX image format.
WBMP	.wbm	WBMP	Wireless bitmap format. Used in wireless devices.
EPS	.eps	UMsk	Encapsulated PostScript format. Vectors are rasterized.
TIFF	.tif or .tiff	TIFF	Tag Image File Format. High-quality lossless compression similar to PNG.
ASCII Text	.txt or .text	TEXT	Plain text.
Rich Text Format	.rtf	RTF	Microsoft's styled text format, easily exported from Word and many other word processors.
Microsoft Bitmap	.bmp	BMP	Default image format for Windows 3+.
PICT (Macintosh only)	.pct or .pict or .p	PICT	Default image format for Mac OS 1–9. Combination vector/bitmap format. Fireworks renders any vectors as bitmaps.

To open an existing file in Fireworks, follow these steps:

1. Choose File ⇨ Open or use the keyboard shortcut, Ctrl+O (Command+O). Windows users can also select the Open button from the Main toolbar. The Open dialog box appears, as shown in Figure 20-4.

2. Select the desired file in the Open dialog box. Fireworks identifies the file and displays a thumbnail of the image for certain file types in the Preview section of the dialog box.

Tip   Windows users: To limit your view to a specific file format, click the arrow button next to the Files of Type drop-down list and select a format. To choose from every file type, select All Files (*.*) from the Files of Type drop-down list, or type an asterisk in the File Name text field. To choose from Fireworks-compatible files, select All Readable Files from the Files of Type drop-down list.

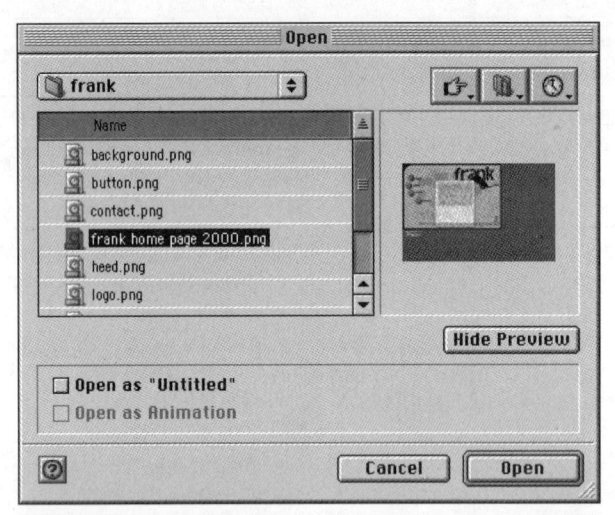

Figure 20-4: Preview files before opening them with the Fireworks Open dialog box.

3. To open a copy of the graphic, choose the Open as "Untitled" option.
4. Click OK when you're done. Fireworks opens the file, reducing the magnification, if necessary, so that the full image is displayed.

> **Tip**
> You can also open files in Fireworks with the drag-and-drop method. In Windows, drop compatible image files on the Fireworks application icon, onto a shortcut to it, directly into the Fireworks window, or into an open document. On the Mac, you can drop image files on the Fireworks application, onto an alias of it, or onto the Fireworks icon in the floating Application Switcher (Mac OS 8 or 9), or the Dock (Mac OS X).

Opening Photoshop Files

Fireworks makes opening and working with Photoshop images relatively easy. When you open or import a Photoshop file, Fireworks displays a dialog box to allow you to adjust how the file will be converted. By default, Fireworks maintains Photoshop's layers and editable text, but you can also choose to flatten the file if you don't need to edit it in Fireworks. Photoshop masks created from grouped layers are converted to Mask Groups and Photoshop's Layer Effects are converted to editable Fireworks Live Effects.

Opening multiple images

It's the rare Web page that has but a single image on it. Most Web pages contain multiple graphics and, occasionally, a designer needs to work on several of them simultaneously. With the Open command, you can select as many files as you want to load into Fireworks, all at the same time. Hold down the Ctrl (Shift) key as you click on each file in turn in the Open dialog box. When you're ready, click Open and Fireworks opens and displays all the files in a series of cascading windows.

> **Tip** Macintosh users can also open multiple Fireworks documents by selecting a group of them in the Finder and either double-clicking them or choosing File ➪ Open (or Command+O). Multiple image files that don't have a Fireworks Creator code can be selected as a group in the Finder and dropped on the Fireworks icon.

One significant advantage to being able to open multiple images is that you can create an animation by combining all the documents. When you choose the Open as Animation option in the Open dialog box, Fireworks inserts each chosen file in a single graphic, but on an individual frame. Then, preview the animation using Fireworks VCR controls, or adjust the timing in the Export dialog box.

To open several files in one operation, follow these steps:

1. Choose File ➪ Open or use the keyboard shortcut Ctrl+O (Command+O). The Open dialog box appears, as shown in Figure 20-5.

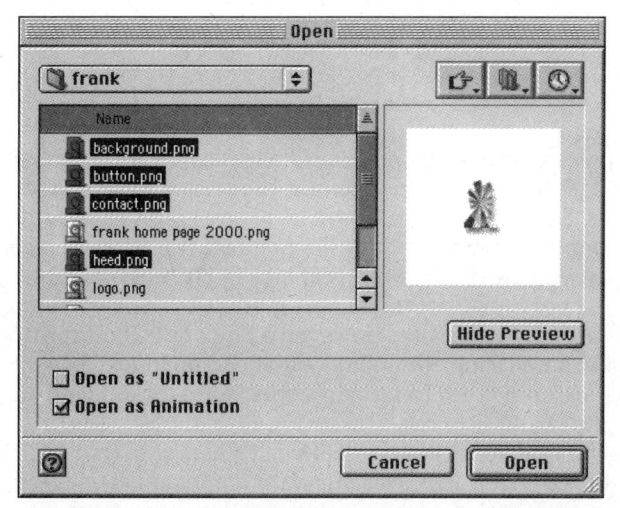

Figure 20-5: Select multiple files in the Open dialog box by holding down the Ctrl (Command) key as you click them.

2. Navigate to the folder containing the images to open.

3. To add a continuous range of files, select the first file, press and hold the Shift key, and then select the last file in the range.

4. To select a number of files that are not in a continuous range, press and hold the Ctrl (Command) key and click the files you want to open, one by one.

5. To open all the files in the current folder, press Ctrl+A (Command+A).

Tip

You can also open an entire folder of images by dragging and dropping the folder on the Fireworks icon. Fireworks will open all images in the selected folder and any existing subfolders.

Caution

On the Macintosh, dropping a folder of files on the Fireworks icon opens them all in Fireworks as expected, but Fireworks will always finish the process with an error. Although the error seems to be harmless, a workaround is to open the folder, select all the files with Command+A, and drag the files themselves onto the Fireworks icon (or just double-click them if they have a Fireworks Creator code).

6. To place the selected images in a series of frames, choose the Open as Animation option. Each image is placed in a separate frame of a single graphic, in the order listed.

7. To deselect a selected file, press and hold the Ctrl (Command) key and click the file.

8. Click the Open button to open your images.

Storing Files

Every computer graphics professional has one — a nightmare story about the system crash that erased all the intense, meticulous, time-consuming effort that went into an unsaved image. Saving your files is crucial in any graphics program, but it becomes even more important in Fireworks. To maintain the "everything's editable, all the time" capability, you must save your graphics in Fireworks' native format, PNG. Fireworks offers a very full-featured Export module to convert your graphics into whichever Web format you choose. However, a Fireworks file exported as a GIF or JPEG loses its all-encompassing editability — text can no longer be edited as text, vector-based objects are converted to bitmaps, effects are locked, and so on.

To keep the full range of Fireworks features active, it's essential that each file be saved, as well as exported. Fireworks uses standard commands to save: File ⇨ Save, the keyboard shortcut Ctrl+S (Command+S), and, for Windows users, a Save button on the Main toolbar. When you select any of these methods to store your file the first time, the Save dialog box (see Figure 20-6) automatically opens.

Cross-Reference

To get all the details on exporting from Fireworks, see Chapter 30.

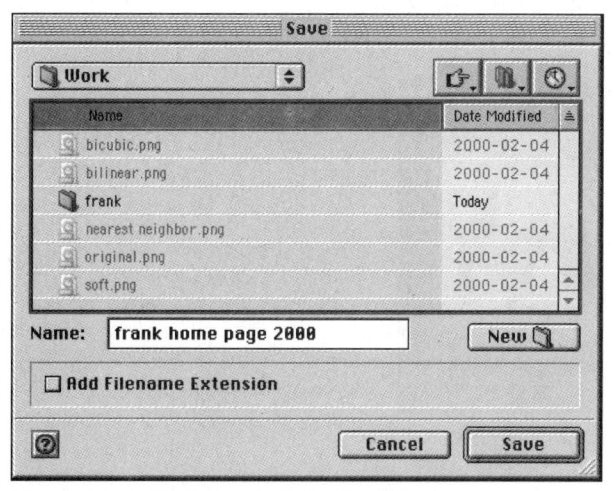

Figure 20-6: To maintain full editability, be sure to save every working graphic as a master Fireworks file, in addition to exporting it as a GIF, JPEG, or other format.

Saving a file after the initial save overwrites the existing file. If you would like to store multiple versions of the same file, Fireworks gives you two options: Save As and Save a Copy. Save As enables you to rename the file, and Save a Copy enables you to store a backup file in another folder (without saving the current document under its own name as well). Both are accessed in an identical manner. Choose File ⇨ Save As or File ⇨ Save a Copy to open the Save dialog box. Enter the new filename or navigate to a new folder in which to store the file (or both) and press the Save button.

Closing a file

When you're finished with a document, but want to continue working in Fireworks, you can close the file in one of several ways:

- ✦ Choose File ⇨ Close.
- ✦ Use one of the keyboard shortcuts, Ctrl+W (Command+W) or Ctrl+F4 (Windows only).
- ✦ Click the document window's Close button.

If the document has not been saved since the last modification, Fireworks asks whether you want to save the file before proceeding. You can identify documents that have not been saved (said to be "dirty") by the "dirty-dot" asterisk (see Figure 20-7) that Fireworks places in the title bar of document windows with unsaved changes. Document windows that don't have the asterisk in the title bar are exactly the same as the file saved on disk.

Figure 20-7: The "dirty-dot" asterisk enables you to identify documents with unsaved changes at a glance.

> **New Feature:** Fireworks displays a "dirty-dot" asterisk in the title bar of documents that have unsaved changes. Macromedia's Dreamweaver also has this feature.

Reverting to a saved file

Part of the joy of computer graphics is the capability to try different approaches without fear of losing your earlier work. I'm a big fan of the Revert command, which enables you to completely alter a graphic, and then restore it to its last-saved condition with one command. Among Revert, Undo, Save a Copy, and the History panel, you have a lot of options for safe creative experimentation.

The Revert command is very straightforward to use. After you've made some changes to your graphic and want to return to the original, choose File ➪ Revert. Fireworks asks for confirmation to revert to the last saved version of the file, and, when confirmed, replaces the onscreen image with the stored version.

Modifying Canvases

What do you mean, you want to change the size of your canvas? And its color, too? Are you saying you're not perfect and didn't predict needing these alterations? Don't worry, you're certainly not alone. In fact, most of my images undergo some degree of document surgery before they're done. It's the nature and the glory of computer graphics in general, and Fireworks in particular, to be very forgiving about changes.

In Fireworks, you can easily change the size of a complete image and its canvas, just the canvas dimensions, or the canvas color. It's very easy to expand the canvas in a particular direction, making it wider on the right, for example, either visually with the Crop tool, or numerically with the command Modify ⇨ Canvas Size.

Altering the canvas size

Sometimes, the canvas is perfectly sized for all the objects it contains, but you may want to add another object, or apply a Glow or similar effect around an existing object, and there's no room. On the other hand, very often you'll start out with a canvas larger than necessary and you'll need to trim the canvas to fit the image. Whatever the situation, Fireworks has you covered.

Fireworks offers three different methods for enlarging or reducing the canvas: numerically, using a menu command; visually, using the Crop tool; or actually, according to the image, by trimming the canvas.

Specifying a new canvas size numerically

Quite often, I find myself needing to add a drop shadow and realize that I have to expand the canvas just a few pixels to the right and down for the effect to fit. With Fireworks, you can expand the canvas from the center out, or in any of eight specific directions. Naturally, only the size of the canvas is modified; the objects it contains don't change at all, except for their placement on the canvas.

The key concept to understand when you're resizing the canvas numerically is the anchor. The placement of the anchor (handled through the Canvas Size dialog box) determines how the canvas changes to meet the newly input dimensions. By default, the anchor is placed in the center of the canvas. If, for example, the canvas dimensions were increased by 100 pixels horizontally and 100 pixels vertically with a center anchor, the canvas edge would increase by 50 on all four sides. However, if the upper-left anchor was chosen and the same increase in dimensions entered, the canvas would increase by 100 pixels on the right and bottom border; because the upper-left is the anchor, the canvas in that corner does not change. You can think of the anchor as specifying where on the new canvas the old canvas should be.

To resize the canvas numerically, follow these steps:

1. Choose Modify ⇨ Canvas Size. The Canvas Size dialog box opens, as shown in Figure 20-8.

2. To alter the dimensions of the canvas horizontally, enter a new value in the width (the horizontal double-headed arrow) text box.

3. To alter the dimensions of the canvas vertically, enter a new value in the height (the vertical double-headed arrow) text box.

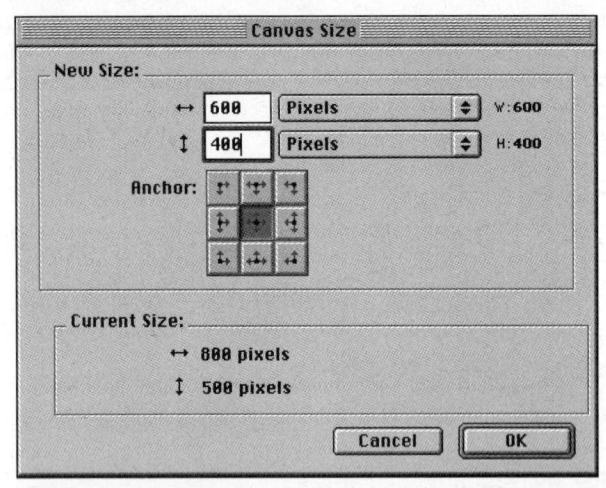

Figure 20-8: Enter new dimensions and select an anchor point in the Canvas Size dialog box to alter the canvas size.

Note Fireworks always displays the original canvas size in pixels in the Current Size section of the dialog box.

4. To alter the canvas size by inches or centimeters rather than the default pixels, select the arrow button next to the width and height drop-down lists and choose the desired alternative. The dimensions in pixels appear to the right of the height and width text boxes.

5. Choose one of the buttons inside the Anchor grid to determine how the canvas will expand or contract.

Tip When one of the elements in the Anchor grid is selected, by tabbing through the dialog box, you can use the arrow keys to select a different anchor.

6. Click OK when you're done.

Using the Crop tool

Resizing the canvas numerically is great when you have to match a specific width or height for your image. Unfortunately, it can also take a lot of trial and error to get the tightest fit for an effect, like a glow or a drop shadow. The Crop tool provides a much faster method. Cropping is a familiar concept to anyone who has ever worked with photographs and needs to eliminate extraneous imagery. To *crop* means to cut off the excess. In addition to making the image smaller by cutting away the canvas, the Crop tool can expand the canvas as well.

The Crop tool works by enabling you to draw a rectangle with numerous sizing handles around an image. You then use these sizing handles to adjust the dimensions and shape of the cropped area. When the cropped region looks right, a double-click in the defined area completes the operation. The cropping border can stretch out past the edge of the canvas and, when double-clicked, the canvas is extended to the new cropped area.

Find the Crop tool in the Fireworks Tools panel, third down on the left. You can also use the keyboard shortcut by pressing C.

New Feature The Crop tool now has its own place in the Fireworks Tools panel, third down on the left. For those keeping score: In Fireworks 3, the Crop tool was on the Marquee tool flyout; in Fireworks 2, it was on the Pointer tool flyout.

Using the Crop tool to extend the canvas, as shown in Figure 20-9, requires an additional step. When you first use the Crop tool and try to draw on the outside of the current canvas, you'll find that Fireworks snaps the cropping border to the edge of the canvas. As most designers are familiar with using the Crop tool to remove excess canvas, this starting point is convenient for most operations. To extend the cropping border, you then need to drag any of the sizing handles to a new position outside the canvas.

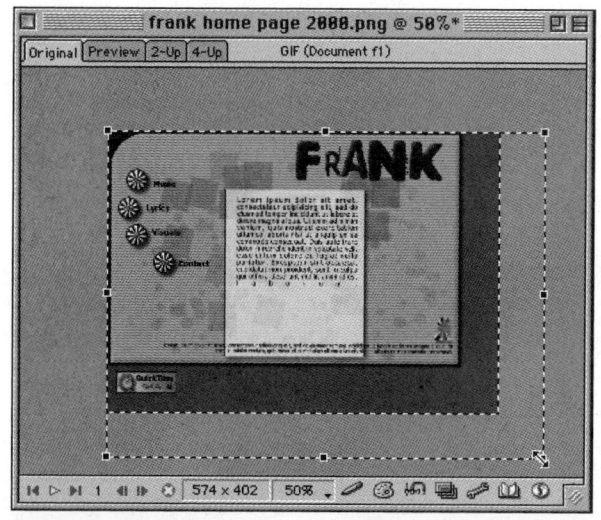

Figure 20-9: Adding some more canvas to the right and bottom of this Fireworks document is easy with the Crop tool.

Changing canvas size for a single image

If your document contains only a single bitmap image, many times you'll want to adjust the size of an entire completed image either up or down to make it fit properly in a Web page. Fireworks allows you to make your adjustments either through specifying absolute pixel values or relative percentages with the Image Size command and automatically sizes the canvas appropriately, allowing you to work with single images as you would in Photoshop.

You can maintain the original proportions of your graphic or stretch it in one direction or another. The Image Size command enables you to resample your image, as well as resize it. *Resampling* refers to the process of adding or subtracting pixels when the image is resized. Resizing always works better with object-oriented (or vector-based) graphics than with bitmap graphics, especially when you're scaling to a larger size. However, Fireworks offers you a choice of interpolation methods to help create a scaled image that looks great.

Fireworks enables you to independently alter the onscreen pixel dimensions and the print size, by changing the print resolution of the image. With this capability, you can print a higher or lower resolution of the image, at the original image size. It does, however, proportionately alter the pixel dimensions of the image for onscreen presentation. In Figure 20-10, for example, the original image on the top is 1440×657 pixels — although it's been zoomed to a 25% view in Fireworks — with a print size of roughly 20×9 inches at 72 pixels per inch. The image on the bottom has been resized by setting the resolution to 18 pixels per inch (one-quarter of the original resolution) and is now only 360×164 pixels. The two images will print at the same size, though, with the resized one lacking one-quarter of the detail.

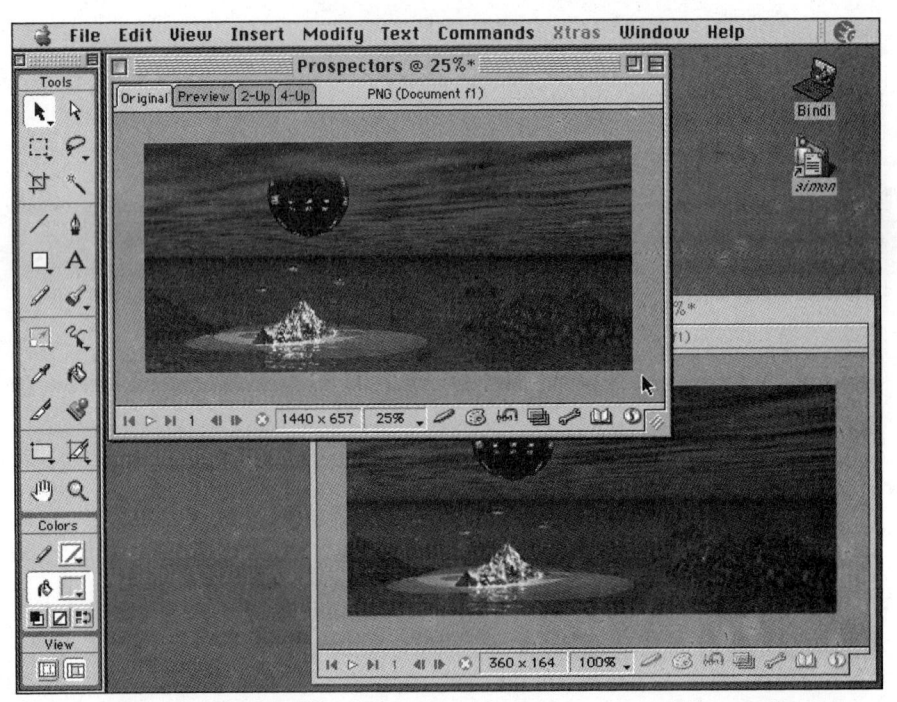

Figure 20-10: The bottom image, shown at 100%, was resampled at one-quarter the size of the original image, shown at 25%.

Note: Once again, if you're using Fireworks exclusively to create online images — as most of us — stay entirely away from the Print Size settings and resize your images using the Pixel Dimensions settings in the Image Size dialog.

To alter the image size, follow these steps:

1. Choose Modify ⇨ Image Size. The Image Size dialog box opens, as shown in Figure 20-11.

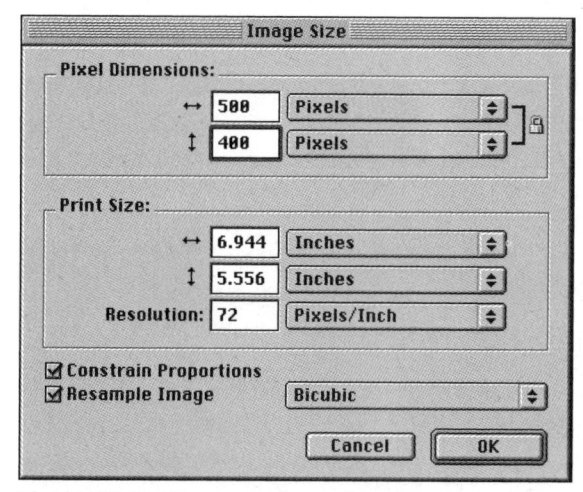

Figure 20-11: To proportionately enlarge or reduce your entire graphic, use the Image Size command.

2. To alter the dimensions of the image proportionately, enter a new value in width (the horizontal double-headed arrow) or height (the vertical double-headed arrow) text boxes.

Tip: If the default option, Constrain Proportions, is selected, changing one value causes the other to change as well.

Caution: It's better to select the entire value in the text boxes first and then enter in your new number. If you try to backspace through each digit, you'll encounter an alert when you delete the final number. Fireworks warns you that you're entering an invalid number, because it interprets this as trying to reduce the dimensions below one.

3. To alter the dimensions by percentage rather than by pixel measurement, select the arrow button next to the width or height drop-down lists and choose Percent.

4. To use the print size as a guide for adjusting the image size, enter a value in the Print Size width and height text boxes.

5. To alter the print size by percentage or centimeters rather than the default inches, select the arrow button next to the Print Size width and height drop-down lists and choose the desired alternative.

6. To change the number of pixels per inch, enter a new value in the Resolution text box.

7. To disable the proportional sizing, deselect the Constrain Proportions option.

8. To change the print size, but not the onscreen image, deselect the Resample Image option and choose new values for the Print Size width and height text boxes. When Resample Image is deselected, the Pixel Dimensions section becomes unavailable.

9. Choose an interpolation method from the interpolation method option list. Bicubic is the default and works well for most images.

> **Cross-Reference**
> A complete description of the various interpolation methods Fireworks offers is available in Chapter 22.

10. Click OK when you're done.

Trimming the canvas

What's the fastest, most accurate way to reduce the canvas to just the essential objects? Trim it, of course. If you've ever trimmed a real canvas with a razor-sharp matte knife, you know it's a very dramatic, fast operation. However, the Trim Canvas command is even faster — it handles four edges at once and there's no need to keep a supply of bandages.

The beauty of the Trim Canvas command is that it's all automatic — you don't even have to select any objects for Fireworks to trim to. Moreover, this feature even takes into account soft edges like glows or drop shadows, so you can't accidentally truncate your effect. In fact, it's a great command to use in combination with other canvas expanders, like the Crop tool or Canvas Size. Just open up the canvas more than you think necessary, make the alterations, and then choose Modify ⇨ Trim Canvas. Presto! All the canvas edges are hugging the graphics as tightly as possible.

> **Note**
> As the name indicates, Trim Canvas can only make your overall document size smaller; it can't expand it even if part of the image is moved off the canvas.

Picking a new canvas color

Although you set the canvas color when you create the document, you're by no means stuck with it. You can adjust the color at any point by choosing Modify ⇨ Canvas Color. Invoking this command opens the Canvas Color dialog box (see Figure 20-12), which replicates the Canvas Color section of the New Document dialog box. Again, you have three choices: White, Transparent, and Custom Color. Of course, selecting the arrow button next to Custom Color opens the pop-up color picker with the palette of 216 Web-safe choices. For a wider color selection, click the Palette button on the pop-up color picker to display your operating system's color picker(s).

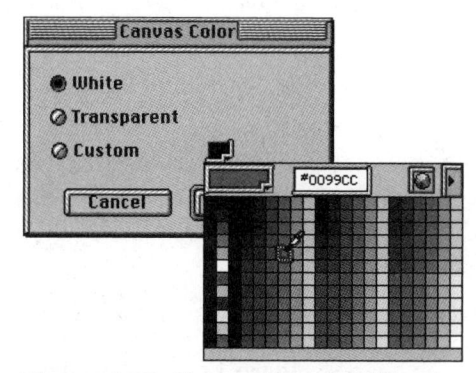

Figure 20-12: The pop-up color picker is useful for quickly picking a Web-safe color for the canvas.

Tip If you open a Photoshop or Fireworks 1.0 document, you may find that a solid-color Background layer is created. Hide this layer by clicking the Show/Hide Layer icon next to it in the Layers panel in order to see your document's actual canvas color.

Rotating the canvas

Although you can rotate objects with the Transform tools, the canvas itself always stays in the same place. If your canvas is not square, rotating a group of objects 90 degrees will often leave them hanging off the canvas. Instead of rotating objects, rotate the entire canvas. Choose Modify ⇨ Rotate Canvas and then one of the options: Rotate 180 degrees, Rotate 90 degrees CW (clockwise), or Rotate 90 degrees CCW (counterclockwise).

Summary

Setting up your document is the basis for all the work you do in Fireworks. Whether you're starting with the fresh slate of a new document, or opening an existing file, Fireworks gives you all the tools you need to build a solid foundation and modify it when necessary. When working with your objects from an overall document perspective, keep the following points in mind:

- The more you can visualize your graphics and thus design the canvas, the less time you'll spend making modifications.
- When you're creating a new document, Fireworks enables you to set the height, width, print resolution, and color of the canvas.
- Fireworks can open more than a dozen different file formats, including common ones such as TIFF, FreeHand, and Photoshop.
- You can open multiple files simultaneously.
- To get the most out of Fireworks, always save at least one version of your graphic in the native PNG format.
- You can alter the canvas size using any one of three different methods: Canvas Size, the Crop tool, or Trim Canvas.
- You can modify the canvas color or rotate the canvas at any time.

In the next chapter, you begin exploring the heart of Fireworks graphics: objects.

✦ ✦ ✦

Creating Vector Objects

CHAPTER 21

In This Chapter

Mastering basic vector concepts

Forming geometric shapes

Drawing freely with the Pencil and Brush

Shaping Bézier curves

Vector objects are the foundation of Fireworks. Don't get me wrong: All the other elements — bitmap objects, Web objects, Live Effects, and more — are vital, but vector objects are what give Fireworks its flexibility, precise control, and pervasive editability. They're what separate Fireworks from its contemporaries, such as Adobe Photoshop or ImageReady.

As you might suspect, a great number of Fireworks tools and features focus on vector objects. This chapter covers the basic vector operations — creation of the simple, geometric shapes and freeform lines and drawings — that draw special attention to one of the most difficult to master, but most rewarding concepts: Bézier curves.

Understanding Vector Objects in Fireworks

A Fireworks vector object is a free-floating vector-based graphic. Vector graphics are also called path-based, or simply *drawings*. Unlike bitmap objects that use rows of pixels to form mosaic-like images, vector objects use lines, or more accurately, the description of a line. Instead of plotting a series of pixels on the screen, a vector-based graphic basically says, "Start a line at position X, Y and draw it to position A, B." Or, "Draw a circle with a midpoint at C, D and make it 1.5 inches in diameter." Of course, you don't see all these instructions on the screen — it's all under the hood of the graphics engine — but it's what enables drawing programs, such as FreeHand and Adobe Illustrator, to maintain a smooth line, regardless of how the image is scaled.

Whereas Fireworks vector objects maintain the underlying path structure, their surfaces are composed of pixels. Although this may seem to be a contradiction, it's really at the heart of Fireworks' brilliance as a graphics tool. Whenever you modify a vector object — slanting a rectangle, for example — Fireworks first applies the modification to the path structure, and then reapplies the pixel surface. It is as if an image of a ballerina in a magazine suddenly became alive, leaped across the stage, and then became an image again.

Examining Paths

Vector objects begin as *paths*. Paths are lines with at least two points. Whether you draw a squiggly line with the Pencil tool, or a multipoint star with the Polygon tool, the outline of your drawing is what is referred to as the path. Although Fireworks highlights selected paths for editing, by themselves, paths are invisible and won't appear in your exported images at all (see Figure 21-1).

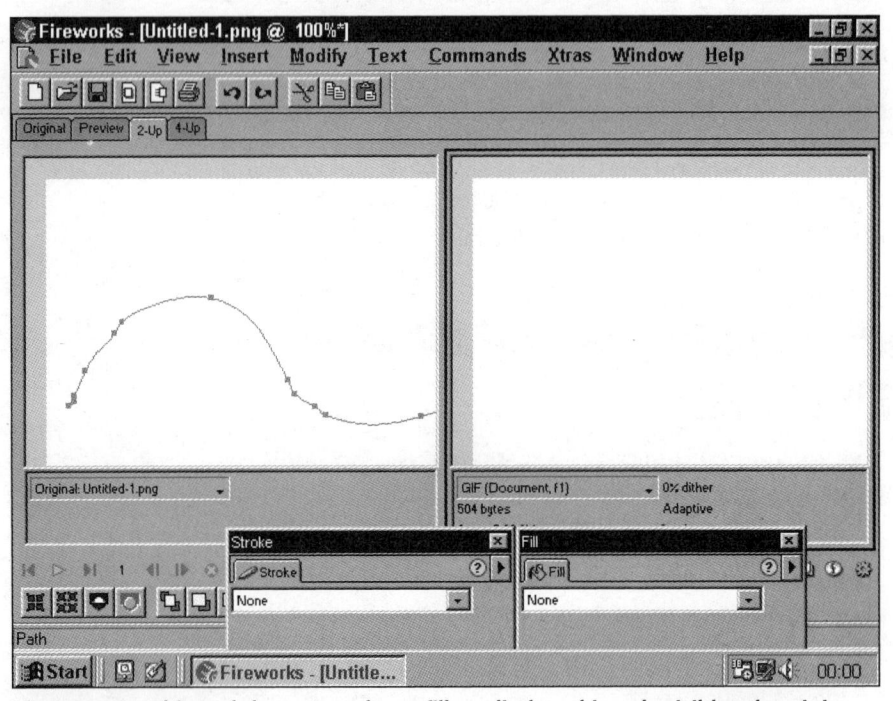

Figure 21-1: This path has no stroke or fill applied, and is only visible when it is selected for editing. The preview on the right shows that the path itself is invisible in Fireworks output.

Applying a stroke

To make a path visible, you have to apply a *stroke* to see the outline. You can quickly apply a stroke to a selected object by choosing a color from the Stroke color well, located on the Tools panel, or on the Color Mixer. This action applies a 1-pixel Pencil stroke with a soft or *antialiased* edge. Strokes can vary in category, color, width, softness, and texture, to name a few characteristics; several examples of different strokes are shown in Figure 21-2. You'll notice in the figure how, regardless of their different attributes, strokes always follow the path of the vector object.

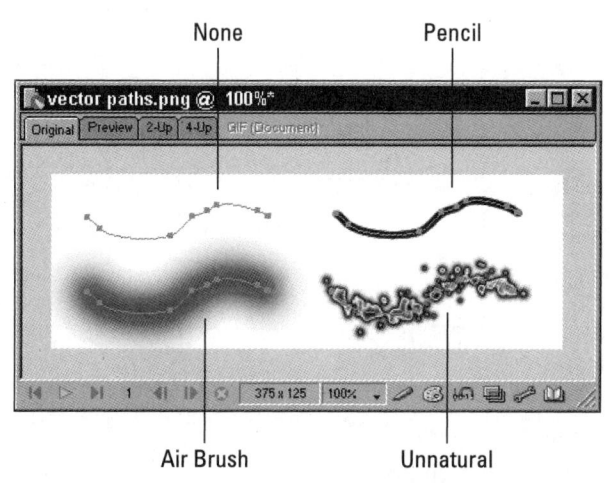

None   Pencil

Air Brush   Unnatural

Figure 21-2: You can see the same path in each of these different strokes.

> **Cross-Reference:** Part of Fireworks' power is derived from the wide range of strokes possible. To find out more about strokes, see Chapter 24.

Looking at open and closed paths

The two types of paths are *open* and *closed*. The difference between the two is simple: A closed path connects its two endpoints (the start and finish of the line), and an open path doesn't. Closed paths define different shapes, whether standard, such as a circle or polygon, or custom, such as a freeform drawing. Just as a stroke gives the outline of a path substance, a *fill* makes the interior of a path visible. Like strokes, fills come in different categories, colors, and textures. In addition, a *pattern*, created from a PNG file, can be used as a fill. You can even change the softness of a fill's edge. As Figure 21-3 shows, regardless of what the interior fill is, it always follows the established path.

> **Tip:** Even though fills are most often applied to closed path vector objects, it's perfectly legal to apply a fill to an open path vector object — although the results are not as predictable. But then, that's one of the beauties of computer graphics — try it and if you don't like it, undo it.

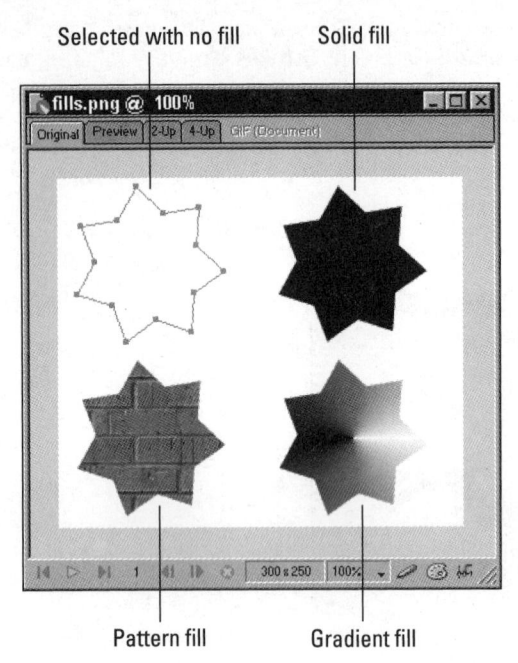

Figure 21-3: A vector object can be filled with a solid color, a gradient, or a pattern.

Grasping the center point

One common feature that all objects in Fireworks share is a *center point*. With vector objects, the center point is an invisible point in the middle of any path; if the path is open, the center point is on the line. If the path is closed, it's inside the object. Center points are useful when you need to rotate an object. You can also adjust the center point of an object when its transform handles are visible in order to rotate it around a different axis, or control how its center aligns to other objects.

> **Cross-Reference**
> You find out how to work with rotation in Chapter 25.

Examining direction

The final point to keep in mind about vector objects is that their paths all have *direction*. Though it's more obvious with an object like a line that you start drawing at one point and finish at another, it's true even with rectangles and ellipses. Generally, Fireworks draws vector objects in a clockwise direction, starting at the upper-left corner of rectangles or squares and the left center of an ellipse or circle, as shown in Figure 21-4. Path direction becomes important when you begin attaching text to a path — wrapping a slogan around a circle, for example. Fireworks includes several tools for adjusting the path's direction.

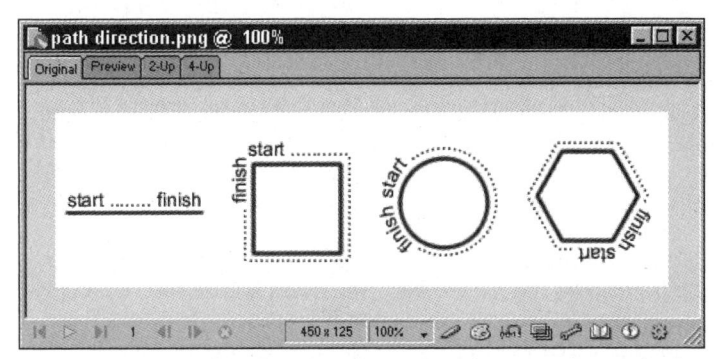

Figure 21-4: A path's direction determines how text is attached.

Starting from Shapes

Most Fireworks documents include many vector objects of different shapes, sizes, colors, and attributes. Drawing shapes sounds easy, but you must understand how to create each of the basic elements to get the greatest effect in the shortest amount of time.

Fireworks provides tools for creating a series of basic geometric shapes — rectangles, ellipses, and polygons — as well as those for drawing structured and freeform lines. All of these tools will be familiar to anyone who has worked with a vector drawing program in the last few years. In fact, many of the key shortcuts are industry-standard. This chapter, though, is written for a complete novice. Even if you've never used a computer to draw before, you'll have a full understanding of the basic tools in Fireworks after working your way through this chapter.

Tip: If you have access to a graphics tablet, don't be afraid to use it here. Drawing is always easier with a pen and tablet than with a mouse.

The quickest way to create a Web page design, particularly the often-required navigational buttons, is to use one of Fireworks' shape-building tools. Although at first glance there only seem to be four such tools — the Rectangle, Rounded Rectangle, Ellipse, and Polygon — these tools each have options that allow them to produce a wide range of objects.

Tip: Consider making the Info panel visible while you draw or edit vector objects. The Info panel displays the pixel width and height of new objects as they are drawn, making it easy to create a 50×50-pixel square, for example. It also informs you of the canvas position of objects as you work with them.

Examining rectangles and squares

My dictionary defines a rectangle as "any four-sided figure with four right angles." A Web designer generally sees a rectangle as a basic building block for designs that are, after all, going to be viewed within the rectangular confines of a browser window. The Rectangle and Rounded Rectangle tools are very straightforward to use and offer a number of very useful options.

The two Rectangle tools are functionally the same. Anything you can do with one, you can do with the other. The difference between them is that the rectangles you draw with the Rounded Rectangle tool have rounded corners, whereas the Rectangle tool creates rectangles with perfectly square corners.

Creating rectangles

Like almost every other computer drawing tool on the planet, Fireworks creates rectangles using the familiar click-and-drag method. To draw a rectangle in Fireworks, follow these steps:

1. Select the Rectangle tool or use the keyboard shortcut, R.

2. Click once to select your originating corner and drag to the opposite corner to form the rectangle, as shown in Figure 21-5. As you drag your pointer, Fireworks draws a preview outline of the form.

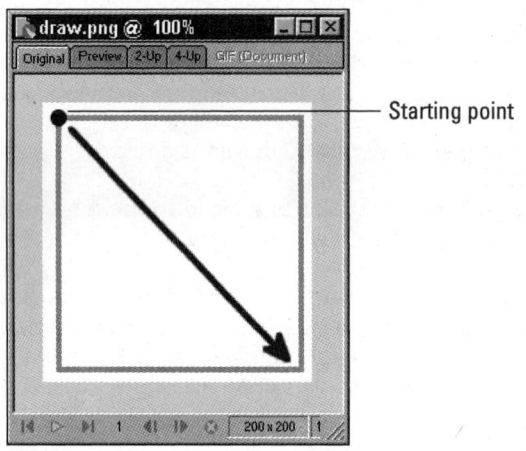

Figure 21-5: Once you've selected your originating corner with the Rectangle tool, you can drag out a box shape in any direction, as indicated by the arrow.

3. Release the mouse button when the rectangle is the desired size and shape. If any stroke or fill has been previously set, these attributes are drawn when you release the mouse button.

Using keyboard modifiers

You can use two keyboard modifiers with the Rectangle or Rounded Rectangle tool, Shift and Alt (Option), in order to apply two very commonly required behaviors.

✦ **To create a square:** You can easily make your rectangle into a square by pressing Shift while you drag out your shape. Unlike some other graphics programs, you don't have to press Shift before you begin drawing; pressing Shift at any time while you're drawing causes Fireworks to increase the shorter sides to match the longer sides of the rectangle to form a square.

✦ **To draw from the center:** To draw your rectangle from the center instead of from the corner, press Alt (Option) when dragging out the shape. While Alt (Option) is held down, Fireworks uses the distance from your originating point to the current pointer position as the radius, rather than the diameter of the shape. As with Shift, you can press Alt (Option) at any time when drawing to change to a center origin, as shown in Figure 21-6.

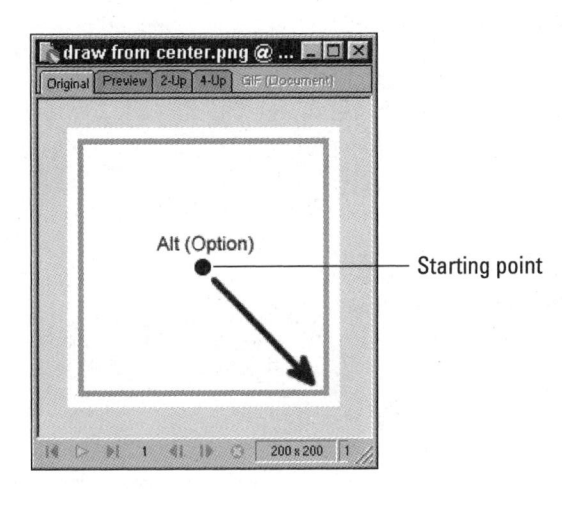

Figure 21-6: Holding down Alt (Option) while drawing a shape centers the shape around your starting point.

> **Tip** Of course, you can use Shift and Alt (Option) together to draw a square from the center.

You can use the Info panel to check the pixel placement of your rectangle as you are drawing. One section displays the Width and Height (marked with a W and H) dynamically, while another displays the upper-left point of the rectangle, even if it is being drawn from the center.

Working with rounded corners

The square and the circle are the most basic shapes, and are obviously useful for the Web designer in a number of ways. Fireworks also offers you a pleasant and useful shape that's somewhere in between: the Rounded Rectangle. Whereas rectangles that are created with the Rectangle tool have perfectly square corners, the Rounded Rectangle tool creates rectangles with rounded corners. The most obvious use for rounded rectangles is more aesthetically pleasing square buttons. Rounding squares and rectangles used as design elements can also quickly lead to a better-looking graphic.

New Feature The Rounded Rectangle tool is new in Fireworks 4, providing even easier access to this pleasant and useful shape.

Although you can't specify the degree of roundness that the Rounded Rectangle tool creates, you can alter the setting for any rectangle you've already created by changing the Roundness setting that's available on the Object panel when a Rectangle is selected. You can display the Object panel by choosing Window ⇨ Object, or using the keyboard shortcut, Alt+F2 (Option+F2).

After the Object panel is available, select a rectangle to choose how rounded you want the corners to appear, by entering a value in the Roundness text box or by using the Roundness slider. The Roundness scale is percentage-based: 0 represents a standard rectangle with perfectly square corners, and 100 creates a fully rounded rectangle — also known as a circle. As Figure 21-7 shows, the higher the Roundness value, the more rounded the rectangle's corners become.

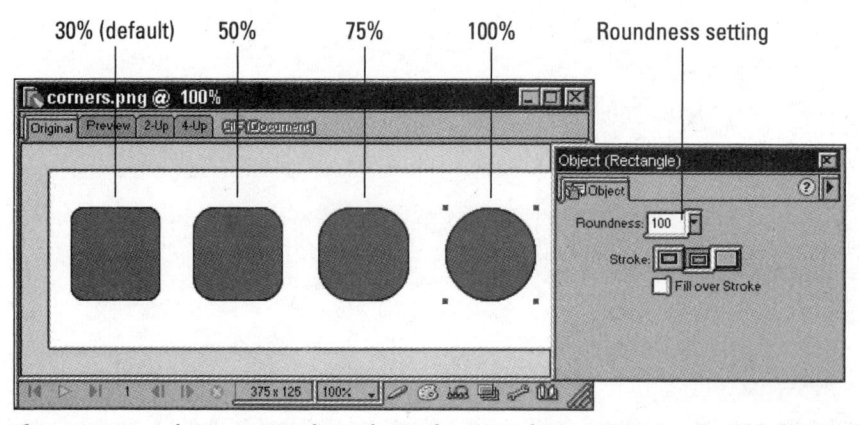

Figure 21-7: Select a rectangle and use the Roundness setting on its Object panel to determine the degree of roundness for your rectangle or square's corners.

Exactly how Fireworks applies the Roundness percentage is most easily explained with an example. Let's say you draw a rectangle 100 pixels wide by 50 pixels tall, and then give it a Roundness value of 50 percent. As shown in Figure 21-8, Fireworks plots the points of the corner 50 pixels along the top edge (50% of 100 pixels = 50 pixels) and 25 pixels along the side edge (50% of 50 pixels = 25 pixels). The resulting arc makes the corner. If you created an ellipse with a horizontal diameter of 50 pixels and a vertical one of 25, it would fit right into the newly rounded corner.

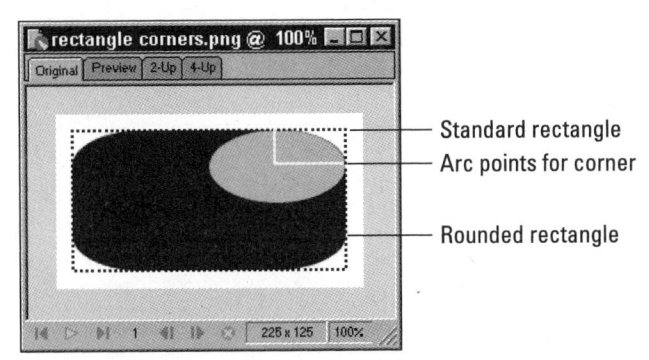

Figure 21-8: Fireworks draws the rounded corner of a rectangle according to a percentage formula.

Using ellipses and circles

In Fireworks, ellipses and circles are created in exactly the same manner as rectangles and squares. Clicking the mouse once sets the origin point, and then the shape is drawn out as you drag the pointer. Even the Shift and Alt (Option) keyboard modifiers function in the same way as they do with rectangles. In fact, only two differences exist between the Rectangle tools and the Ellipse tool. First, it's pretty obvious that no need exists for an ellipse function equivalent to the Roundness option for rectangles; ellipses are already rounded. Second — less apparent, but notable nonetheless — is the fact that the origin point of an ellipse or a circle never appears on its path. This fact is particularly important for novice designers who are trying to place an ellipse correctly.

Using an imaginary bounding box

When Fireworks draws an ellipse, an imaginary bounding box is used, as shown in Figure 21-9. The origin point of the bounding box acts as one corner, while the end point becomes the opposite corner. As with rectangles, if Alt (Option) is pressed, the center point is used as the origin. In either case, neither the origin nor the end point are located on the path of the ellipse. It's as though you're drawing a rectangle, and Fireworks fits an ellipse inside it when you're done.

> **Tip** It's particularly helpful to keep the concept of the imaginary bounding box in mind when you are trying to align ellipses of different sizes. The Align commands and snapping to the grid work by using an ellipse's bounding box rather than the drawn path of the shape.

Drawing an ellipse or circle

To draw an ellipse or a circle, follow these steps:

1. Select the Ellipse tool. If the Ellipse tool is not visible, click and hold the Rectangle, Rounded Rectangle, or Polygon tool until the flyout appears, and then choose the Ellipse tool.

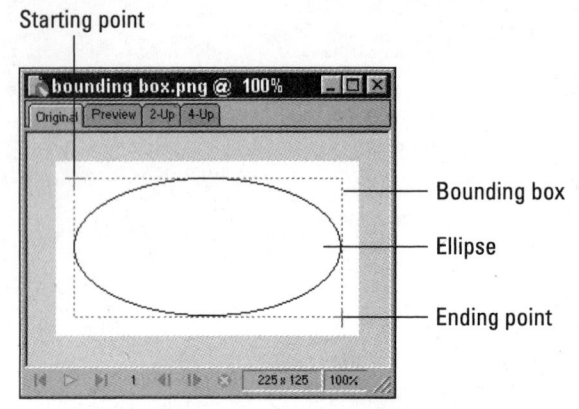

Figure 21-9: When you drag out a circle or oval using the Ellipse tool, Fireworks draws the shape using an imaginary bounding box, indicated by the dashed rectangle.

> **Tip** You can also press R until the Ellipse tool is selected. The R key shortcut cycles through the shape tools.

2. Click once to select the origin point and drag to the opposite corner to create the ellipse. As you drag your pointer, Fireworks draws a preview outline of the form.

3. Release the mouse button when the ellipse is the desired size and shape. If any stroke or fill has been set, these attributes are drawn when you release the mouse button.

4. To draw a circle, press the Shift key while you are drawing the ellipse.

5. To draw an ellipse or circle that uses the center point of the shape as the origin, press the Alt (Option) key while you are drawing.

> **Tip** Combine the Alt (Option) key with the Shift modifier key to draw perfect circles and squares from the center.

Exploring polygons and stars

In Fireworks, the Polygon tool creates many-sided objects where all the sides — and all the angles connecting the sides — are the same. The technical term for this type of geometric shape is an *equilateral polygon*. Fireworks permits the graphic designer to specify the number of sides, from 3 to 25. You can also use the Polygon tool to create a special type of polygon, a star. Star shapes can be drawn with anywhere from 3 to 25 points (and thus, 6 to 50 sides). Moreover, Fireworks gives you the option of either specifying the angles for the star points, or having the program assign them automatically.

Looking at a drag-and-draw affair

As with rectangles and ellipses, making polygons is a drag-and-draw affair. Click once to set the origin point and then drag out the shape. However, that's where the similarities end. With polygons, there's only one possible origin point: the center; there is no keyboard modifier to switch to an outside edge. You'll also immediately notice as you draw your first polygon that you can quickly set both the size and the rotation. Dragging the pointer straight out from the origin increases the dimensions of the polygon; moving the pointer side to side rotates it around its midpoint.

Drawing a polygon

To draw a polygon, follow these steps:

1. Select the Polygon tool by clicking and holding the Rectangle, Rounded Rectangle, or Ellipse tool until the flyout appears, and then choosing the Polygon button. Alternatively, press the keyboard shortcut, R, until the Polygon tool is visible.

2. To set the number of sides for a polygon:

    • First, choose Window ⇨ Tool Options or double-click the Polygon tool to open the Tool Options panel shown in Figure 21-10.

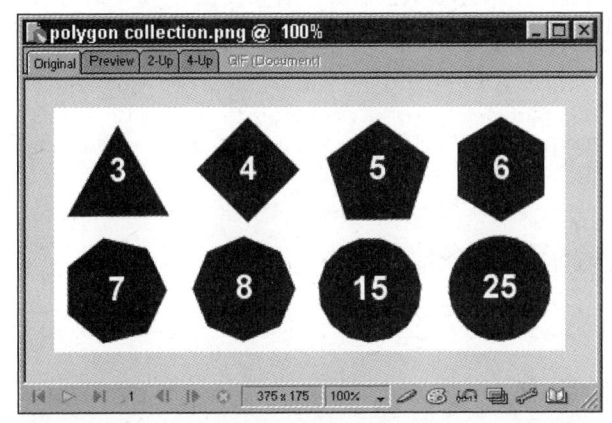

Figure 21-10: Polygons in Fireworks can have up to 25 sides — although anything above 15 tends to start looking like a circle.

   • In the Tool Options panel, make sure the shape type is set to Polygon (instead of Star).

   • Next, enter a value in the Sides text box, or use the Sides slider.

3. Click and hold down the mouse button where you want the center of the polygon to appear and drag out the polygon shape. Fireworks displays a preview of the polygon as you draw.

4. Rotate the polygon to the desired position by moving your pointer from side to side.

5. Release the mouse button when you're done. Fireworks draws the polygon with the current stroke and fill settings.

Fireworks interprets the distance from the origin point to the release point as the radius to each of the points on the polygon. As you can see in Figure 21-10, just changing the number of sides results in a wide range of basic shapes.

Pressing the Shift key while drawing a polygon constrains a side's angle to a multiple of 45 degrees. Because, however, each shape as it is initially drawn is equilateral — with identical sides and angles — you'll only notice a couple of variations for each type of polygon. When drawing a hexagon and constraining the angle with the Shift key, you'll only notice three differently angled shapes, although you can actually draw eight (eight increments of 45 degrees are in a full 360-degree circle).

Tip For most polygons, you can draw it so that the bottom of the shape is parallel to the bottom of your canvas, by either dragging straight up or straight to one side while holding down the Shift key.

Examining automatic angles

Although you can specify up to 25 sides for a polygon, polygons with more than 10 or 15 sides look very much like a circle. Not so with Fireworks stars, which, with the proper angle setting, can create very distinctive graphics with any number of sides. Fireworks offers both automatic and customizable angle options. When Automatic Angles is selected (the default), Fireworks draws stars so that the opposite arms are automatically aligned. With a five-pointed star, such as the one shown in Figure 21-11, the tops of the left and right arms are aligned.

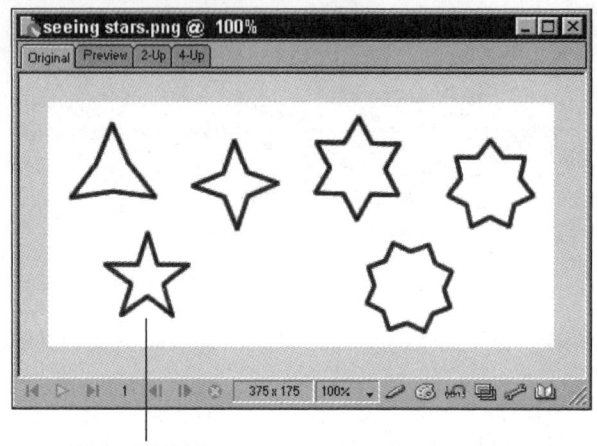

Figure 21-11: With the Automatic Angle option enabled, a star's opposing arms are aligned.

As is readily apparent in Figure 21-11, the automatic angles on stars with a higher number of sides tend to flatten out the sharpness of the points. These types of angles are known as *obtuse* angles. An obtuse angle is one over 90 degrees. The opposite of an obtuse angle is an *acute* angle. Acute angles create much sharper points on stars, as shown in Figure 21-12. To create an acute star in Fireworks, you need to enter a custom value in the Angle text box.

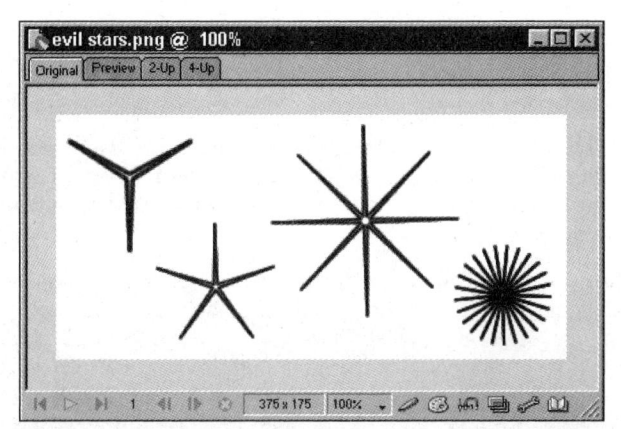

Figure 21-12: Create acute stars by lowering the Angle value in the Tool Options panel and drawing with Star selected for the Polygon tool type.

Creating a star

To create a star in Fireworks, follow these steps:

1. As with drawing a regular polygon, select the Polygon tool. If it is not visible, click and hold the Rectangle, Rounded Rectangle, or Ellipse tool until the fly-out appears, and then choose the Polygon button. Alternatively, you can repeatedly press the keyboard shortcut, R, until the Polygon tool is visible.

2. Choose Window ⇨ Tool Options or double-click the Polygon tool to open the Tool Options panel.

3. In the Tool Options panel, change the shape type by selecting the option arrow and choosing Star.

4. To change the number of points, enter a value in the Sides text box, or use the Sides slider.

5. To change the angle of the star arms, enter a value in the Angle text box, or use the Angle slider.

Tip Use lower numbers for sharper points and higher numbers for blunter ones.

6. If you want to use the Fireworks predetermined angle for your star, choose the Automatic checkbox.

7. Click on the canvas to set the origin point for the center of the star and drag out to the desired size and rotation.

8. Release the mouse when you're done. As with any other shape, Fireworks applies the current stroke, fill, or effect setting, if any.

Precisely Adjusting a Shape's Dimensions and Position

Like any graphic design, Web graphics are a blend of visual flair and precise placement. To many artists, an image isn't right until it's aligned just so. Whereas much of Fireworks' interface enables very intuitive drawing with a mouse or graphics pad, you can also position and size objects numerically through the Info panel.

Typically, I use the Info panel to get a general sense of the dimensions of an object or its X, Y coordinates. However, I occasionally need to render an exact rectangle, one that's exactly 205 pixels wide by 166 high, say, and starts at 20 pixels in from the left and 35 pixels down. With Fireworks, you can rough out your shape and placement, and then numerically resize and reposition the object. You can enter values into each of the four text boxes on the Info panel representing the dimensions and the position of the bounding box surrounding the object. If the object were a circle or a triangle, for example, the height and width displayed would be that of the invisible rectangle encompassing them.

To specify a new dimension or placement of an object, follow these steps:

1. Select the object you want to alter.

2. Double-click the value in the Info panel that you want to change. The four possibilities are

   - W (width)
   - H (height)
   - X (horizontal origin)
   - Y (vertical origin)

3. Enter a new value.

4. Confirm your entry by pressing Enter (Return) — not Tab. Fireworks changes the selected object.

5. To change another value, repeat Steps 2–4.

Note that numerous other alignment and transformation tools are in Fireworks, in addition to those available through the Info panel.

Drawing Lines and Freeform Paths

The path drawing tools in Fireworks primarily vary according to how structured they are. At one end of the spectrum is the Line tool, which only draws single straight lines; at the other end are the Pencil and Brush tools, both of which are completely freeform. In the middle (leaning more toward the Line tool) is the Pen tool, which draws mathematically accurate curves.

Like a geometric shape, a path is invisible unless a particular stroke or fill is applied to it. If the two endpoints that define a line are joined, the path is said to be closed. When you're drawing paths and two endpoints are about to be joined, Fireworks displays a special square cursor badge. If the two endpoints of a line are not joined, the path is said to be open. Unlike most vector drawing tools, Fireworks allows you to apply fills to open paths, as well as closed.

Making straight lines

The Line tool is perhaps the simplest member of the Fireworks Tools panel. Click once to set the beginning of the line, drag in any direction, and release to set the end of the line. Two endpoints and a straight line in between; that's it and there's not a whole lot more to the tool. Straight lines are, by definition, open paths and thus can only display the stroke and not the fill settings. You can apply effects and Styles to Line-created paths, as shown in Figure 21-13.

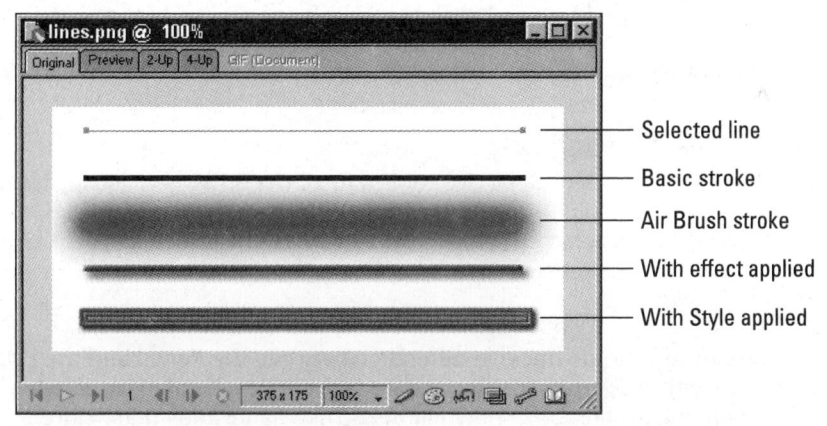

Figure 21-13: The Line tool draws straight-as-a-ruler lines that can take on a stroke setting and even an effect.

To use the Line tool, follow these steps:

1. Select the Line tool or use the keyboard shortcut, N.
2. Position the pointer where you would like the line to begin and click and hold the mouse button.

Tip: Holding down the Shift key while drawing with the Line tool draws perfectly horizontal or vertical lines only. Many drawing tools take advantage of the Shift modifier to make drawing common shapes more convenient.

3. When the line is at the desired size and angle, release the mouse button.

Drawing with the Freeform Pencil and Brush

The Pencil and Brush are also drag-and-draw tools, but without any of the restraints imposed on all the other tools. Anything you can draw with a mouse or graphics tablet, you can draw with the Pencil or Brush. As you move your pointer on the screen, Fireworks tracks the movements and plots points to replicate your drawing. Remember, these are vector objects, not bitmap objects; to draw a perfectly straight line, Fireworks only needs two points to depict the line. All the points that make up a line can be edited — moved, deleted, or increased — and the line changes accordingly.

Cross-Reference: Fireworks not only tracks your pointer's movement across the screen, it also follows the speed with which you draw your lines. With certain strokes, such as Watercolor and Charcoal, the velocity is translated visually when the stroke is rendered. For more details on varying your strokes, see Chapter 24.

Freehand drawing with the mouse is particularly difficult, and many artists avoid it whenever possible. I prefer a graphics tablet and highly recommend them to others whenever I get the chance. For some images that require an unrestrained look — like the fellow in Figure 21-14 — the Brush is ideal. Choosing one of the Fireworks strokes that are pressure sensitive allows you to emulate the look of a calligraphy pen, a pencil, or other drawing implement.

Applying strokes automatically

The major difference between these two tools and all the other geometric shape tools (including Line), is that both Pencil and Brush automatically apply a particular stroke, even if none is selected. This feature enables you to see all paths completed with these tools instantly — instead of having to wait until a stroke is selected and applied.

The stroke setting also holds the sole difference between the Pencil and the Brush. Any path drawn with the Pencil tool is rendered with a Pencil-category, single-pixel-width stroke with a hard edge, as shown in the Stroke panel shown in Figure 21-15 — even if a different stroke has been predetermined.

Note: The only exception to the Pencil's adherence to these basic parameters is color. If you alter the stroke color, the Pencil tool draws with the new color.

Chapter 21 ✦ **Creating Vector Objects** 667

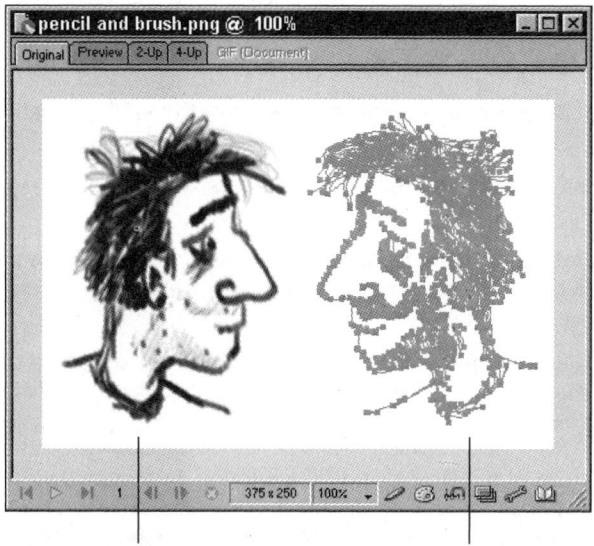

Paths with Calligraphy Quill stroke — Selected paths only

Figure 21-14: Freehand drawing is best done with a graphics tablet using the Brush tool set a pressure sensitive stroke.

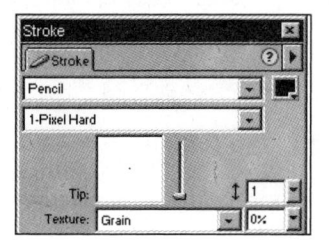

Figure 21-15: The Pencil enables you to draw freeform shapes that always use the same Pencil stroke that's shown here in the Stroke panel.

The Brush tool also uses the same single-pixel Pencil type stroke, but only as a default, when no other stroke has been established. After you select a different setting from the Stroke panel, the Brush tool uses that setting until you change it.

As noted previously, both the Pencil and the Brush are capable of creating either open or closed paths. Remember, a closed path is one in which the beginning and final endpoints meet. With many graphic tools, this simple procedure becomes quite difficult, because positioning one pixel directly on top of another is often hard. Fireworks makes closing a path very straightforward. When you draw a path over the initial endpoint, a small black square appears on the lower right of the Pencil cursor. Releasing the mouse button when this cursor is displayed forces Fireworks to close the path.

Using the Pencil or Brush

To use the Pencil or Brush, follow these steps:

1. To draw with the Pencil, select the Pencil tool, or press the keyboard shortcut, Y.
2. To draw with the Brush, select the Brush tool, or press the keyboard shortcut, B.
3. Click and drag the pointer on the canvas. Fireworks renders the drawn path for a Pencil with a one-pixel width stroke, and the Brush with the current settings of the Stroke panel.
4. To draw a perpendicular line, press the Shift key while you're dragging the pointer. If your movement is primarily left to right, a horizontal line is drawn; if it is up and down, a vertical line is drawn.

Here's a rather peculiar feature of the Brush and Pencil tools: If you use the Shift key to constrain your Brush path to a perpendicular line and then release the mouse button — but not the Shift key — a small plus sign appears next to the Brush cursor. Draw another Brush stroke (still holding down the Shift key), and Fireworks connects the final point of your previous stroke with the beginning point of your new stroke.

Cross-Reference The Pencil tool has one other use. If you are in bitmap mode, modifying a pixel-based graphic, the Pencil changes any pixels it touches to the current Stroke color. You can find out more about editing pixel-based images in Chapter 22.

Constructing Bézier Curves

Remember those plastic stencils you used in school to trace different-size circles, stars, and other shapes? One of those "other shapes" was probably an asymmetrical, smoothly curving line that was referred to as a French curve. The Frenchman who invented this type of curve was a mathematician named Pierre Bézier. His theoretical work, collectively known as *Bézier curves,* forms the foundation for much of vector computer graphics, both in print through PostScript and on the screen through programs such as FreeHand, Illustrator, and, of course, Fireworks. The learning curve — pun definitely intended — for Bézier curves is a steep one, but it's one that every graphic designer using vectors must master. Bézier curves are amazingly flexible, often graceful to behold, and worth every bit of effort it takes to understand them fully. So let's get started.

New Feature Bézier curve handling has been enhanced and simplified in Fireworks 4. If you previously used another version of Fireworks, a range of small enhancements should lead to an improved feel when working with control and anchor points.

Pierre Bézier's breakthrough was the realization that every line — whether it was straight or curved — could be mathematically described in the same way. Imagine a rainbow. The shape appears to start in one place, arch to the sky, and then land some distance away. The beginning and ending points of the rainbow are easily described; if we were plotting them on a piece of graph paper, we could set down their location as X and Y coordinates. But what about the arc itself? Consider an imaginary element in the sky that attracts the rainbow, almost magnetically, which causes the center of the rainbow to arch up, anchored by the beginning and ending points. Bézier postulated that every anchor point on a curve had two such magnetic elements, called *control points* — one that affects the curve going into the anchor point and one that affects it coming out of the anchor point, as shown in Figure 21-16. In the Bézier vernacular, an anchor point with curves on either side is called, naturally enough, a *curve anchor point.* An anchor point with a curve on just one side is known as a *corner anchor point.*

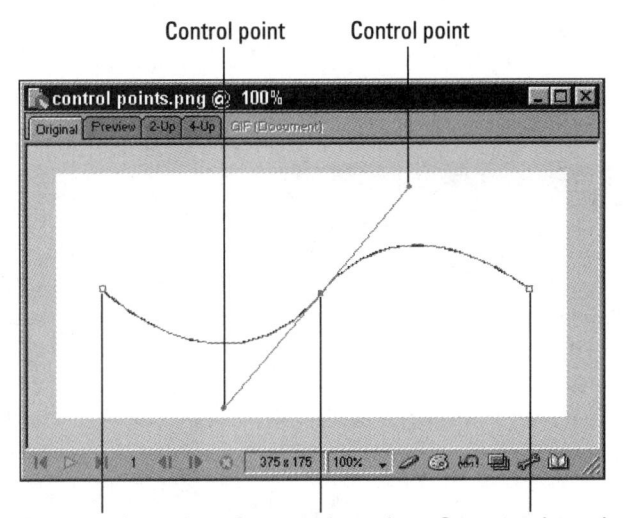

Figure 21-16: Use control points to alter the shape of a Bézier curve, as defined by the placement of the curve and corner anchor points.

Drawing lines with the Pen

Fireworks' primary tool for creating Bézier curves is the Pen, although all path objects use Bézier curves. But how could a Bézier curve describe a straight line? When the control points are in the same location as the anchor points, the line is not pulled one way or the other; it remains straight. In fact, the Pen is terrific for creating connected straight lines. Unlike the Line tool, which draws a single straight line by clicking and dragging, the Pen draws a series of straight lines by plotting each point and letting Fireworks draw the connecting lines.

To draw a straight line with the Pen, follow these steps:

1. Select the Pen, or use its keyboard shortcut, P.
2. Click once where you want the line to start.
3. Move your pointer to where you want the line to end, and click once. Fireworks draws a path from your starting point to the second point.

To draw a continuing series of straight lines with the Pen, follow these steps:

1. Select the Pen, or use its keyboard shortcut, P.
2. Click once where you want the line to start.
3. Move your pointer to where you want the next point on the line to be, and either double-click to finish your line, or click once to add another point and continue drawing. Fireworks draws paths between the points as you work, as shown in Figure 21-17.

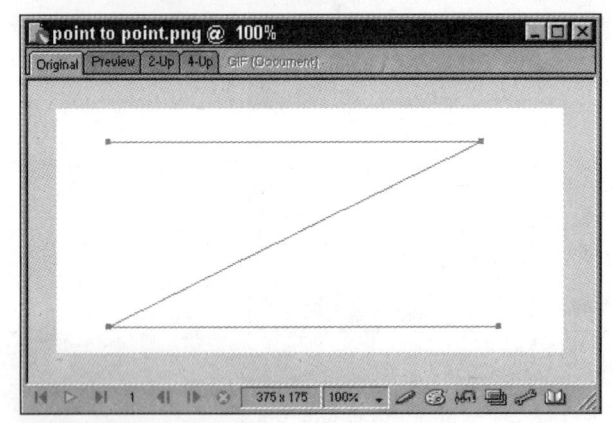

Figure 21-17: Create a Z with the Pen tool much like Zorro carves one with his sword, moving and clicking from point to point.

4. Repeat Step 3 as many times as is necessary to draw your series of lines.

As with the Brush and Pencil tools, you can close an open path created by the Pen by moving the pointer over the beginning point.

Creating smooth curves with the Pen

Laying out a series of straight lines is a fine feature, but the Pen tool really shines when it comes to drawing curves. The key difference between Pen-drawn lines and curves is that, with curves, you drag the pointer after you've set the anchor's position to drag out the control handles and start a curve, whereas with lines, there is no dragging whatsoever; you are just plotting corner points.

Follow these steps to create a smooth curve:

1. With the Pen tool, click and drag out control points where you want your curve to start. This creates an anchor point with control handles that will be the start of your line.

2. Choose the location of your next anchor point, click to add it, and then drag to pull out the control handles. Fireworks joins the two points with a path. While keeping the mouse button held down, you can move your cursor to adjust the control points to set the angle of your curve. Let go of the mouse button when you're done (see Figure 21-18).

Click and drag out handles

Click and drag out handles or double-click to finish

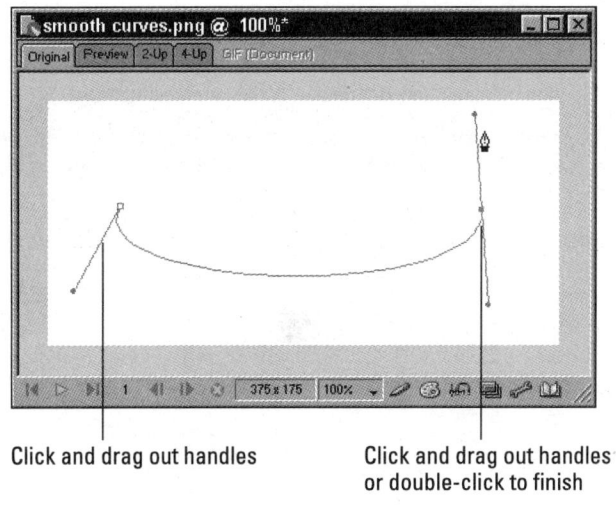

Figure 21-18: When you drag out one Bézier curve, you begin to create this curve.

3. Select the Subselection tool and fine-tune your curve by manipulating the control points.

Tip

Hold down the Ctrl (Command) key while using the Pen tool to switch temporarily to the Subselection tool, which is suitable for manipulating control points. When you let go of the Ctrl (Command) key, the Pen tool is automatically selected again.

Mixing lines and curves

You can, of course, combine the straight and curved line techniques with the Pen by alternating just clicking with both clicking and dragging. However, because dragging a control point affects curves on either side of the curve point, placing a straight line directly next to a curve is often difficult. Fireworks uses the Alt (Option) key to constrain the control point that affects the previous curve, while permitting you to manipulate the current curve. As an example of this option, follow these steps to create a shape like the one shown in Figure 21-19.

1. Use the straight-line capability of the Pen to draw the outer edge of the arch by clicking once for each of the outside points, starting at the inside left corner and moving in a clockwise direction. After you've drawn all the straight lines, you'll have the outer shell of the arch, minus the inner arc, completed.

2. Move your pointer back over the beginning point. The closed path cursor is displayed.

3. Click and hold the mouse button as if you are going to drag it. Press the Alt (Option) key while continuing to hold down the mouse button.

4. Drag the control point away from the arch. If Alt (Option) was not pressed, the connecting line (on the left side of the arch) would be affected by the control-point drag.

5. Release the mouse button when the arch is in the desired shape.

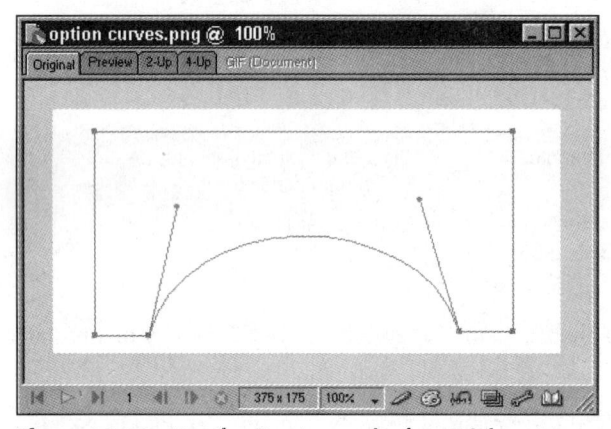

Figure 21-19: Use the Pen to manipulate Bézier curves and create objects with combinations of straight and curved lines.

You can also use this constraining property to draw uneven curves, where you drag a little bit before pressing Alt (Option) and effectively lock the previous curve.

Adjusting curves

The alternative name for the two control points in Bézier curves is *control handles*. As the name implies, you can grab and manipulate control handles. By changing the position of the control handle, you can adjust the shape of the curve. Here are a few guidelines for moving control handles:

- The closer the control handle is to its associated curve point, the flatter the curve.
- Alternatively, the further away the control handle is from its curve point, the steeper the curve.
- If a control handle is on top of its curve point, the curve becomes a straight line, and the curve point becomes a corner point.
- You can convert straight lines into curves by pulling the control handle away from the corner point.
- After you've drawn a curve point, you can retract one of the control handles so that the next segment can be either a curve or a straight line.

All the manipulations involving control handles can be accomplished after the fact using the Subselection tool; you can find a discussion of how to use this point adjustment device in Chapter 25. However, you can perform a few of these operations while drawing with the Pen. The two key operations involve adding and removing a control handle.

Adding a control handle to a corner point

To add a control handle to a corner point, follow these steps:

1. Use the Pen to draw a path with a curve point. Two control points are visible.
2. Move the pointer over the last curve point set.
3. Click once. The curve point is converted into a corner point, and one control handle is retracted.
4. To draw a straight line from the corner point, move your pointer away and click once.
5. To draw a curve, move your pointer away and click and drag out the control handles.

This technique is very handy for drawing a series of scallop or wave shapes where the curves all go in the same direction (see Figure 21-20).

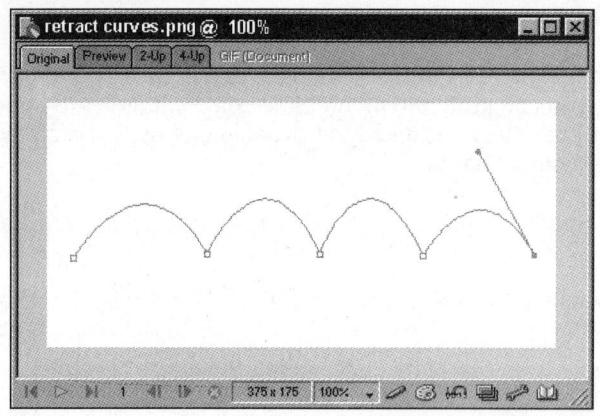

Figure 21-20: By retracting one control handle, you can continue the curve in the same direction.

Extending a control handle from a corner point

The opposite of retracting a control handle is extending one. To extend a control handle from a corner point, you need to enlist the aid of a couple of keyboard modifiers: Ctrl+Alt (Command+Option) to be specific. When you extend a control handle while drawing, you are, in effect, changing your mind. Instead of proceeding with the straight line that you first indicated you wanted with the corner point, you can now draw a curve.

To extend a control handle from a corner point while drawing, follow these steps:

1. Draw a straight line segment with the Pen.
2. Move the pointer over the last point set.
3. Press Ctrl+Alt (Command+Option) and then click and drag a control handle out from the point. When you press the keyboard modifiers, the pointer changes to a white arrowhead.
4. Release the mouse button when you've positioned the control handle where desired.
5. Move the pointer to the position for the curve to end.
6. Continue drawing or double-click the final point to complete the shape.

In this technique, it's important that you press the keyboard modifiers before you drag the control handle. If you begin dragging before pressing the special keys, you'll move the anchor point instead of extending a control handle. This is actually a feature and enables you to move a previously set point by starting the drag and then pressing the Ctrl (Command) key; the Alt (Option) key has no effect on this sequence.

Using the keyboard modifiers

Bézier curves in Fireworks use a fair number of keyboard modifiers to achieve various effects. While I've explained the use of these special keys throughout this section in context, I thought it would be useful to put them all in one place (see Table 21-1) for easy reference.

Cross-Reference: There's a lot more to manipulating Bézier curves and other Fireworks objects, as you find out in Chapter 25.

Table 21-1
Bézier Curves Keyboard Modifiers

Windows Keys	Macintosh Keys	Description
Shift	Shift	Constrains the straight line or control handle to a 45-degree angle
Ctrl	Command	Moves a set curve or corner point or a control handle to a new position
Ctrl and double-click	Command and double-click	Completes an open path without adding another point
Ctrl+Alt	Command+Option	Extends a control handle from a corner point

Summary

I once had to indoctrinate a corporate design team into "The Fireworks Way" in a two-day training session. When it came to vector objects, I described them as being the "skeleton" of Fireworks graphics. After the vector object is completed—and the body of fills and clothing of strokes have been applied—you won't be able to see its underlying structure, but it is the basis of the image. As you begin to build vector objects, keep these points in mind:

✦ Paths are the most basic element of Fireworks' vector objects. A path must be stroked and/or filled before it becomes visible in your image.

✦ The geometric shape tools—Rectangle, Rounded Rectangle, Ellipse, and Polygon—can also create squares, circles, and stars.

✦ The Line tool creates one straight line at a time.

- Two freeform tools, Pencil and Brush, enable you to draw on the Fireworks canvas without restriction. The Pencil tool always defaults to a 1-pixel-wide stroke.

- The Pen draws Bézier curves, which use a series of corner and curve points in conjunction with control points and handles to make smooth curves and connected straight lines.

In the next chapter, you find out about the other side of Fireworks graphics: bitmap objects.

✦ ✦ ✦

Working with Bitmaps

CHAPTER 22

In This Chapter

Getting to know bitmaps

Examining bitmap mode

Opening bitmaps in Fireworks

Resizing bitmaps

Selecting bitmap elements

Defining a drawing area

Working with bitmap tools

Vector objects are the backbone of Fireworks, and are perfectly suited for the bulk of the work a Web artist does: building navigation bars, drawing shapes and lines, and inserting editable text. These design elements benefit from the precision that vector drawing provides, and are the kinds of things you're likely to draw right from scratch in Fireworks.

Some kinds of images couldn't possibly benefit from a vector-based substructure, though. Photographic images that started out life in a digital camera or scanner are pure bitmap, through and through. Think of product photographs for an online store, or digitized paintings for an online art gallery; incorporating them into a Web page won't involve drawing. Instead you'll cut and paste pixel selections and manipulate alpha masks and blending modes.

Almost all work with images takes place in Fireworks' bitmap mode. Fireworks leaves vector mode and enters bitmap mode whenever you use a bitmap tool, such as the Magic Wand. It will seem like a subtle transition, but it's an important one. You're telling Fireworks to stop moving pixels around in convenient vector containers; to shift gears and focus instead on the pure pixels themselves.

This chapter begins with a discussion of how Fireworks generally handles bitmaps. We delve into an exploration of the various tools available for bitmap editing: those dedicated to bitmap mode, as well as the vector mode tools that function slightly differently when applied to bitmap graphics. Finally, we cover how to change a vector object into a bitmap object and the benefits you might realize by doing so.

Understanding Bitmaps in Fireworks

Here's a quick refresher course on bitmap images — just in case you're coming from the world of vector graphics and can't tell a pixel from a pig in a poke. The word *pixel* is derived from the term *picture element* (*pix* for picture and *el* for element). A pixel is the smallest component part of a bitmap image. In the early days of computer graphics, the color of each pixel was stored in 1 bit of memory; which was either on for white or off for black. Map these bits along an *x* and *y* axis and you can create an image out of them. Editing a bitmap basically involves adding or removing pixels, or changing their colors. Even when you erase part of an image, you're just setting the color of those excess pixels to whatever your background color is (or to "transparent" so that they show another image underneath) so that they appear to have been erased.

The best way I can think to describe the difference between a bitmap image (also called a *raster graphic*) and a vector object, is to ask you to think of a line, 100 pixels long and 1 pixel wide. With vector graphics, all you need to make this line visible is two points and a stroke in between. With a bitmap, you need exactly 100 pixels. To move one end of the vector version of this line up a notch, you just need to move one of the endpoints. With pixel-based images, however, you have to erase all the pixels in the line and redraw them in another location.

Examining bitmap mode

As you can see, manipulating vector objects and bitmap objects are two completely different operations. For that reason, Fireworks has two different modes: a vector mode for vector objects (discussed in Chapter 21) and a bitmap mode for bitmap images. Some tools work in one mode but not the other, whereas some tools seem to work the same, but actually return different results. It's not that one mode is better than the other; they are just used for different purposes.

You can ask Fireworks to change over to bitmap mode, but you don't have to. Mode changes are tool-driven: Start to use an image-editing tool and you automatically enter bitmap mode. Pick a vector-editing tool, start to work, and you're back in vector mode. Sometimes the transition is accompanied by a helpful message from Fireworks explaining that the change is necessary. For example, if you try to use the Freeform tool in bitmap mode, Fireworks warns you that it's only good for vectors.

Tip The mode-shifting warnings all include a "don't show again" checkbox, so you can switch them off when you feel comfortable enough to do so. To switch the warnings back on, choose Commands ⇨ Reset Warning Dialogs.

All the objects you work on in Fireworks start out in one camp or the other — either they're all bitmap, or all vector. However, eventually the lines begin to blur (pun intended, maybe), and you find yourself moving back and forth between the two modes effortlessly and with no real conscious thought.

Starting bitmap mode

In addition to automatically invoking bitmap mode by choosing a particular tool, you can also enter it explicitly in several ways:

- Double-click a bitmap object with the Pointer or Subselection tool. This technique is probably my most commonly used for accessing bitmap mode.

> **Tip:** After you're in bitmap mode, double-click to go back to vector mode.

- Choose Modify ➪ Edit Bitmap, or use the keyboard shortcut, Ctrl+E (Command+E).
- Choose Insert ➪ Empty Bitmap. This creates a new bitmap object, which you can paint with pixel-based tools.

It's easy to tell when you're in bitmap mode; in fact, Fireworks offers several different visual cues, as shown in Figure 22-1. First, a striped border surrounds the canvas, unless you uncheck the "Expand to Fill Document" preference, in which case the striped border only surrounds the bitmap object itself. Second, you'll notice the phrase "(Bitmap Mode)" in the title bar of the graphic you're working on, and also in the title bar of the Object panel. Finally, the Exit Image Edit "Stop" button on the bottom of the document window is active instead of grayed-out.

> **Tip:** Windows users will also see the helpful hint "Press Stop to exit Bitmap mode" right next to the Stop button itself.

Leaving bitmap mode

When you leave bitmap mode, any bitmap image, if selected normally, has a bounding box around it. In Fireworks, bitmaps can also be manipulated—moved, resized, aligned, distorted—as bitmap objects. In vector mode, bitmap objects act like rectangular vector objects filled with a bitmap image. You can even apply an effect, such as a drop shadow, to a selected bitmap object.

The most obvious way to leave bitmap mode and go to vector mode is to select the Stop button. However, the Fireworks team created a number of other exits, as well. Here's a list of all the methods for leaving bitmap mode:

- Press the Stop button on the document window, as mentioned.
- Choose Modify ➪ Exit Bitmap Mode, or use the keyboard shortcut, Ctrl+Shift+E (Command+Shift+E).
- If the bitmap mode border surrounds just the bitmap object and not the canvas, then the cursor changes into a Stop button when it's not over the object itself. Click once when you see the Stop button cursor.
- If the bitmap mode border surrounds the entire document, choose a selection tool (Marquee, Oval Marquee, Lasso, Polygon Lasso, or Magic Wand) and double-click any open area.

Figure 22-1: Fireworks tells you that you're in bitmap mode in a number of ways. Note the tooltip describing the function of the Stop button.

To specify whether the bitmap mode border surrounds just the bitmap object or the whole canvas:

1. Choose Edit ➪ Preferences.
2. Select the Editing tab in the Preferences dialog box.
3. Check or uncheck Expand to Fill Document under When Editing Bitmaps.
4. Choose OK.

The change takes place immediately.

Why would you want to have the bitmap mode border surround more than just the bitmap? Quite often, you need to expand the area of a bitmap while you're editing — to blur the edges or make the shape nonrectangular, for example.

If the bitmap mode border tightly hugs the bitmap graphic, there's no room for expansion. By enabling the Expand to Fill Document option, you have plenty of canvas in which to maneuver. You're still just editing the one bitmap object.

Examining other bitmap mode functions

The other three When Editing Bitmaps options under the Editing panel in Preferences can also prove useful. The following preferences are all checked by default:

+ **Open in Bitmap Mode:** Tells Fireworks to automatically go into bitmap mode when you open a document that contains only a single bitmap. If you prefer, you can uncheck this option and always start out in vector mode. This option takes effect the next time you start Fireworks.

+ **Turn Off Hide Edges:** Turns off the View ⇨ Hide Edges command when you change between vector and bitmap modes. This is convenient to make your selection easy to find, but if you really think edges are a visual nuisance, uncheck this preference. Turn Off Hide Edges takes effect immediately.

+ **Display Striped Border:** Tells Fireworks to draw a striped "barber-pole" border around the canvas when in bitmap mode. It takes effect immediately.

Opening existing bitmaps

I'm sure you've heard the expression, "Success is 1 percent inspiration and 99 percent perspiration." In the Internet graphics field, the formula is a bit different: "Web design is 20 percent creation and 80 percent modification." Of course, this is just my rough estimate — but it definitely feels like I spend most of my day revising an image already created by myself or someone else.

Fireworks offers multiple ways to open existing bitmaps — and it supports a wide range of file formats as well. Increasingly, more of your work will be stored in Fireworks' PNG-based format, which enables both vector and bitmap editing. However, many times you'll find yourself working with a bitmap file created in another application such as Photoshop.

As with many computer programs, Fireworks loads images and other files through the File ⇨ Open command. This command displays the Open dialog box (see Figure 22-2), which can preview various file types: PNG, TIFF, Photoshop, FreeHand, GIF, JPEG, and others. You can select multiple files by pressing Shift or Ctrl (Command) as you click on filenames. The Open dialog box also has a very useful option, Open as Animation, which creates an animation from multiple files by distributing them across the frames of one document. Make sure you select more than one file in order to enable the Open as Animation checkbox.

Figure 22-2: Opening an image sequence as an animation using Fireworks Open as Animation option

Scaling bitmaps

Changing the size of a pixel-based bitmap image is something we probably take for granted, but it's actually a pretty complex task, requiring Fireworks to literally create a new image — with the newly specified dimensions — by analyzing the old image. Fireworks looks at groups of pixels and basically makes a best guess about how to represent them, with either more or fewer pixels. Coming up with intermediate values based on analysis of known values is called interpolation.

Fireworks offers you four interpolation methods (see Figure 22-3):

- **Bicubic:** With bicubic interpolation, Fireworks averages every pixel with all eight pixels surrounding it — above, below, left, right, and all four corners. This scaling option gives the sharpest results under the most conditions and is recommended for most graphics.

- **Bilinear:** Bilinear interpolation is similar to bicubic, but only uses four neighboring pixels (above, below, left, and right), instead of eight.

- **Nearest Neighbor:** The Nearest Neighbor algorithm causes Fireworks to copy neighboring pixels whenever a new pixel must be interpolated. Consequently, the Nearest Neighbor scaling option creates very pixelated, stairstep-like images.

- **Soft:** Soft interpolation was the original scaling option used in Fireworks 1, and it offers a smoothing blur to the scaled-down images. The Soft Interpolation scaling option is a good choice if your images are producing unwanted artifacts using the other scaling options.

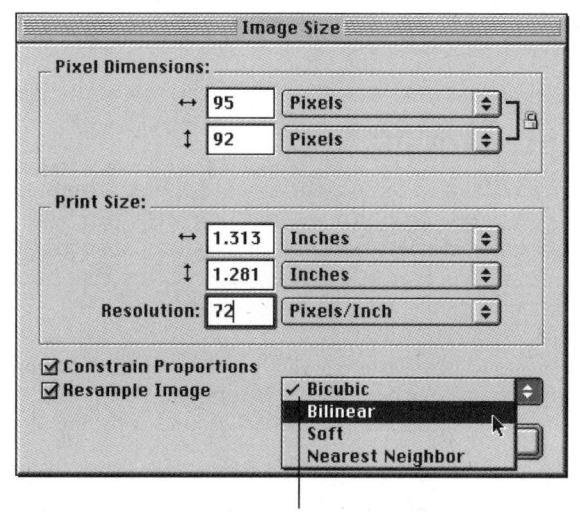

Interpolation methods option list

Figure 22-3: Fireworks offers four scaling options to suit different kinds of images.

I've found that although I tend to use Bicubic Interpolation most of the time, I do turn to Bilinear and Soft Interpolation in some cases, usually when small text is involved. I haven't found much use for the blockiness produced by the Nearest Neighbor scaling option. Experimenting with the different interpolation methods is the best way to become familiar with their results.

Inserting a bitmap into a document

Collage — the mixing of various images and other graphics — is a very important design tool, on or off the Web. Whether you're overlapping bitmaps or just laying them side-by-side, Fireworks' Insert ➪ Image command enables you to include an existing graphic wherever necessary in an open document.

To include a bitmap in a document, follow these steps:

1. Choose Insert ➪ Image, or use the keyboard shortcut, Ctrl+R (Command+R). Fireworks displays the Import dialog box.

2. Select your image and choose Open when you're done. The cursor changes to the Import cursor: a corner bracket.

3. Position the Import cursor wherever you would like the upper-left corner of the image to be initially located, and click once. The chosen image is inserted into the document as a new bitmap object and selected.

If you need to adjust the position of the newly inserted bitmap object, select the Pointer tool, and click and drag it to a new place. For more precise placement, use the cursor keys to move the selected bitmap object any direction, one pixel at a time.

Tip When pressing Shift, the arrow keys move the selected bitmap object in 10-pixel increments.

Inserting an empty bitmap

So far you've seen how Fireworks can open a wide range of file formats for bitmap editing. But what if you want to create a bitmap image directly from within Fireworks? Whereas vectors are far more editable than bitmaps, occasionally only a bitmap will do. For those times, you can use a Fireworks feature that creates an editable bitmap area by choosing Insert ⇨ Empty Bitmap.

Tip The Empty Bitmap command is extremely helpful when you need to paint a fairly large background with a brush, such as the Air Brush, and don't want to use the Fill tool. You can then modify the Air Brushed background with any of the pixel-based tools, such as the Eraser.

When you insert an empty bitmap, Fireworks immediately goes into bitmap mode and selects the Marquee tool. If you want to limit your drawing area, use the Marquee tool to draw out a rectangle. Any drawing will now be clipped to the selected region. Otherwise, use any of the available tools to draw straight to the bitmap. When you leave bitmap mode, the bitmap object just created is sized to be only as large as necessary to encompass all the applied pixels. This automatically trimmed bitmap object can naturally be repositioned or manipulated like any other bitmap object.

Using bitmap mode tools

The scoreboard shows a fairly equal number of Fireworks tools dedicated to working with bitmaps (six), as opposed to those that work only with vectors (seven). The vast majority of tools work in both modes, some in a different manner and others exactly the same. Naturally, the better you understand what a tool is intended for and how it is best used, the more fluid your workflow becomes. This section discusses tools that are intended for use in the bitmap mode only.

The bitmap mode-specific tools are primarily concerned with *selection,* and there's a very good reason for this emphasis. Selecting pixels is much harder than selecting vectors. The most complicated vector possible can be selected with just one click. Pixels are chosen either by their position with a tool, such as the Marquee, or by their color with the Magic Wand. Quite often you need to use a combination of tools and methods to get the desired results.

Luckily, Fireworks offers a full range of selection tools: Pointer, Marquee, Oval Marquee, Lasso, Polygon Lasso, and Magic Wand. Each has its own way of working, as well as a variety of user-definable options.

Examining the Pointer

Although technically the Pointer should be listed as one of the tools capable of being used in both modes, I included it here for a simple reason. Double-clicking the Pointer on a bitmap is one of the fastest and most intuitive methods of entering bitmap mode. You can also use the Pointer to reposition the bitmap after you're in bitmap mode by clicking and dragging anywhere within the bitmap object, as shown in Figure 22-4. Just make sure that there are no active pixel selections.

Figure 22-4: Even in bitmap mode, you can use the Pointer to move whole bitmap objects around the canvas.

Tip
It's not obvious, but you can also use the Pointer to resize a bitmap object, whether you're in bitmap or vector mode. You can drag the border surrounding the image to a new position, resizing the graphic much like the Distort tool. You can even obtain proportional resizing by pressing Shift while dragging a corner or border. The bitmap object, however, is a tad easier to use, because the sizing handles are apparent.

Using the Marquee tools

The Marquee tool is one of the most frequently used selection tools, and not only because it's the default tool after entering bitmap mode. The Marquee selection tool is quite similar to the Rectangle drawing tool. Both are generally used by selecting a point for one corner of the rectangular shape and dragging diagonally to the opposite corner. However, the Marquee tool doesn't draw a shape on the bitmap; it temporarily surrounds and selects an area of pixels for another operation to take place, such as a copy or a fill.

Examining the Rectangular and Oval Marquee tools

There are actually two different Marquee tools. The first is the default rectangular Marquee, which you select through its button on the toolbar, or by pressing the keyboard shortcut, M. The second parallels the Ellipse drawing tool: The Oval Marquee selects an oval or circular area. Pressing and holding down the Shift key while using the Marquee and Oval Marquee tools constrains the shapes you draw to perfect squares and circles, as it would when using the Rectangle or Circle drawing tools.

> **Tip** If you find yourself making a lot of perfect square and circle marquee selections, double-click the Marquee or Oval Marquee tool to open its Options panel, and choose Fixed Ratio from the Style box. Set the ratio at 1 to 1, and you'll be easily drawing perfect square and circle selections instead of rectangles and ovals, with no need to press the Shift key.

To use the Marquee or Oval Marquee tool, follow these steps:

1. To select a rectangular or square region, select the Marquee tool from the Tools panel or through its keyboard shortcut, M.

2. To select an elliptical or circular region, select the Oval Marquee tool from the Tools panel by clicking and holding the Marquee tool and choosing the button from the flyout menu. Alternatively, you can press the keyboard shortcut, M, twice.

3. Click where you want one corner of your selection to begin, and drag to the opposite corner. Fireworks displays a moving dashed line, called a marquee or, more familiarly, "marching ants" (see Figure 22-5).

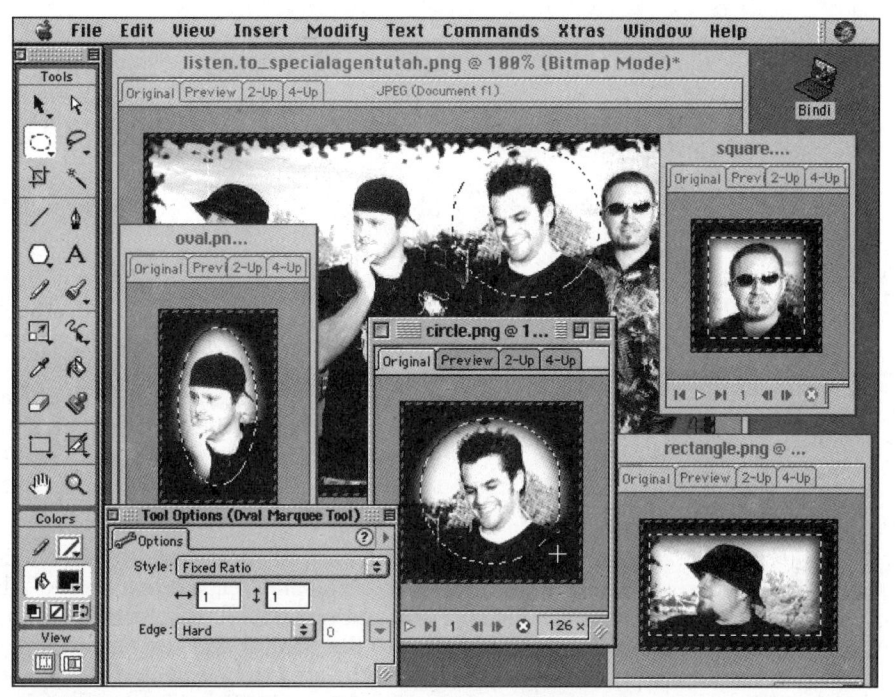

Figure 22-5: The Marquee tools are used for marking rectangular, square, oval, or circular areas for selection.

Exploring the Tool Options panel

The two Marquee tools also share a set of options available from the Tool Options panel. You can display the Tool Options panel, as shown in Figure 22-6, by double-clicking either the Marquee or Oval Marquee tool, or by choosing one of the tools, and then selecting Window ⇨ Tool Options. The Marquee Tool Options affect two separate areas: Style and Edge.

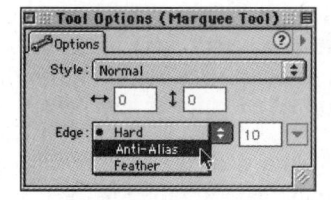

Figure 22-6: Use the Tool Options panel to set the Marquee to a predetermined size or ratio; you can also choose a type of edge for the selection: Hard, Anti-Alias, or Feather.

Discovering the Style portion

Generally, the Marquee tools are unrestrained, meaning the selection can be any size or shape drawn out. However, sometimes being able to specify the needed selection dimensions is helpful. The Style portion of the Marquee Tool Options panel has three possibilities:

+ **Normal:** This default state enables you to drag out your rectangular or elliptical selections freely.

+ **Fixed Ratio:** Sets the horizontal-to-vertical ratio for the Marquee selection tools. Enter horizontal values in the first text box (marked with the side-to-side double-headed arrow) and vertical values in the second (marked with the up-and-down double-headed arrow). This option is useful when you know that the selection must be a particular proportion. If, for example, you knew that the selection should be twice as wide as high, you would enter a 2 in the horizontal text box and a 1 in the vertical text box. To get a perfect square selection, specify 1 to 1. When you use either Marquee tool with a Set Ratio option enabled, the selection size varies, but not the proportion.

+ **Fixed Size:** Sets the dimensions to a particular pixel width and height. Enter the desired pixel values in the horizontal and vertical text boxes. When either Marquee tool is selected with this option enabled, a selection outlining the specified dimensions is attached to the pointer and can be easily repositioned on the screen. After you've located the area to be selected, clicking once drops the selection outline on the bitmap. The Fixed Size option works especially well when you need to create a number of same-sized selections.

Tip If you enter a value in one of the Fixed Size text boxes, but leave the other blank, Fireworks creates a selection outline the width or height specified that spans the entire bitmap. It's a great way to grab a slice of an image, one or two pixels wide or tall, and ensures that you get the full image without having to draw it. For this technique, using the Marquee tool rather than the Oval Marquee tool is best.

Learning the types of edges

The Tool Options panel also controls the type of edge that the selection uses. The default edge-type is a hard-edged line — what you select is what you get. The other two types, Anti-Alias and Feather, act to soften the selection. Anti-Alias is the more subtle of the two options. When you choose the Anti-Alias option for your selection, any jagged edges caused by an elliptical or circular selection are blended into the background, much like bitmap type is antialiased to make it appear less jagged.

Tip You can get a very smooth bitmap crescent by making a circular selection using the Oval Marquee tool on a solid color. Set the Edge type on the Marquee Tool Options panel to Anti-Alias, and make your selection. Then, use the arrow keys to move the selection one or two pixels vertically and the same distance horizontally. You'll be left with a crescent shape that blends smoothly into its points.

Feathering a selection is much more noticeable. Basically, think of feathering as blending. After selecting the Feather option, the value box becomes active with a default of 10 pixels. Any feathered selection blends equally on either side of the selection outline. If, for example, you choose a small Feather value of 2 pixels for a rectangular selection, four rows of pixels will be altered — two inside the selection and two outside. If you delete a feathered selection, you'll be left with a hole in the image, blending smoothly into the canvas, because both the selection and the surrounding image are feathered. If you move a feather selection and the pixels it contains, the selection will have a blended edge, as shown in Figure 22-7.

Figure 22-7: Moving a feathered selection blends both the selection and the remaining image to create a gentle transition.

Tip   Remember to press Ctrl (Command) while you move a Marquee selection in order to move both the selection and the pixels it contains.

Using the Lasso and Polygon Lasso tools

Not all regions to be selected are rectangular or elliptical. The Lasso tools select irregularly shaped areas of an image. As the name implies, the Lasso tools surround or *lasso* the desired pixels to select them. The standard Lasso tool is a click-and-drag type instrument that enables freeform selection, much like the Pencil or Brush is used for freeform drawing. The Polygon Lasso tool, on the other hand, is more like the Pen in its straight-line mode, and makes selections through a series of connected straight lines.

All Lasso selections are by their very nature closed paths. As with the drawing tools, when you drag the pointer near the beginning of a Lasso selection, Fireworks displays a closed-path cursor with a black square, as shown in Figure 22-8. You can also close a Lasso tool selection by releasing the mouse button; Fireworks draws a line from the beginning point to the ending point, closing the shape. With the Polygon Lasso, double-click the last point to close the shape automatically in the same manner.

If you're selecting an area that has more curves than straight lines, use the Lasso. If your selection has some long straight lines, you may find the Polygon Lasso is more suitable, even if you also have some curves to deal with, because the straight lines will be quick and accurate. Lots of short lines with the Polygon Lasso will allow you to draw around curves.

Closed path Polygon Lasso cursor

Figure 22-8: Drawing with the Polygon Lasso. The little block on the Polygon Lasso cursor means that one more click will close the path and create the selection.

To make a freeform selection, follow these steps:

1. To use the Lasso, select it from the Tools panel, or use the keyboard shortcut, L.

2. With the Lasso, click at the starting point for your selection, and drag the mouse around the desired area, releasing the mouse when you're done.

3. To use the Polygon Lasso, select and hold the Lasso tool until the flyout appears, and then choose the Polygon Lasso, or press the keyboard shortcut, L, twice.

4. With the Polygon Lasso, click at the starting point for your selection, and then move the mouse to the next point on the outline, surrounding the desired area and click again. Fireworks connects each point that you set down with a straight line.

5. Repeat Step 4 until you've outlined the entire area, and then close the selection by moving your pointer over the starting point and clicking once or double-clicking to permit Fireworks to connect the first and final points.

As a matter of personal preference, I get a lot more use out of the Polygon Lasso than I do the regular drawing Lasso. Selecting an area of pixels is often a painstaking chore, and I find the Polygon Lasso to be far more precise. Generally, I use the Lasso to outline some stray pixels for deletion only when there's little chance that I'll select part of the main image.

You can determine the type of edge the Lasso tools use through the Tool Options panel. As with the Marquee tools, the three options are Hard Edge, Anti-Alias, and Feather, and they work in exactly the same manner as described in the previous Marquee section.

Working with the Magic Wand

The Magic Wand is a completely different type of selection tool from those already discussed. Instead of encompassing an area of pixels, the Magic Wand selects adjacent pixels of similar color. This type of tool enables you to select single-color backgrounds or other regions quickly.

Using the Magic Wand is very straightforward. Choose the Magic Wand tool from the flyout that appears by clicking and holding the Lasso tool, or use the keyboard shortcut, W. Now select any pixel in the bitmap — it, and all pixels of a similar color next to it, are selected.

Tip With both the Magic Wand and the Lasso, I find that the representational pointers sometimes get in the way. It's hard to see exactly which pixel you're pinpointing if there is a sparkly wand cursor obscuring the area. You can toggle Precise Cursors — a crosshair pointer — whenever you like, by pressing the Caps Lock key.

The key phrase in the description of the Magic Wand is "pixels of a similar color." Many bitmap images, especially photographic JPEGs, tend to use a range of colors, even when depicting a seemingly monochromatic area. You control what Fireworks defines as a "similar color" through the Tolerance setting on the Tool Options panel. The Tolerance scale goes from 0 to 255; lower tolerance values select fewer colors and higher values select more.

Here's how the Magic Wand and the Tolerance work. By default, the initial Tolerance is set to 32. The Tolerance value is applied to the RGB values of the selected pixel — the exact one selected by the Magic Wand. If the Tolerance value is 50 and the selected pixel's RGB values are 200, 200, and 200, Fireworks judges any adjacent pixel with an RGB from 150, 150, 150 to 250, 250, 250 as being similar enough to select. Pixels within that color range, but not in some way touching the originally selected pixel, will not be chosen.

In addition to varying the Tolerance, you can also determine the type of edge for a Magic Wand selection. Edge options, like those for Marquee and Lasso tools, are Hard Edge, Anti-Alias (the default), or Feather. For a detailed explanation of how these tools work, see the "Using the Marquee tools" section earlier in this chapter.

Increasing or Reducing the Selection Area

Fireworks' selection tools are very full-featured, but, for complex selections, you need more flexibility. Adding several selections together, or using one selection tool to eliminate part of an existing selection, opens up a whole range of possibilities.

The key to adding or removing pixels is to use the keyboard modifiers as you draw your selections: Press Shift to add selections and Alt (Option) to remove them. You'll notice that the pointer indicates the operation; a plus sign (+) appears when Shift is pressed and a minus sign (–) appears when Alt (Option) is pressed.

For example, I often use Shift in combination with the Magic Wand to select additional areas of an image, rather than alter the Tolerance. Your first Magic Wand selection may have a couple of small gaps that need filling. Holding down Shift and clicking in those gaps is usually the quickest way to fill out the selection, as shown in the accompanying figure.

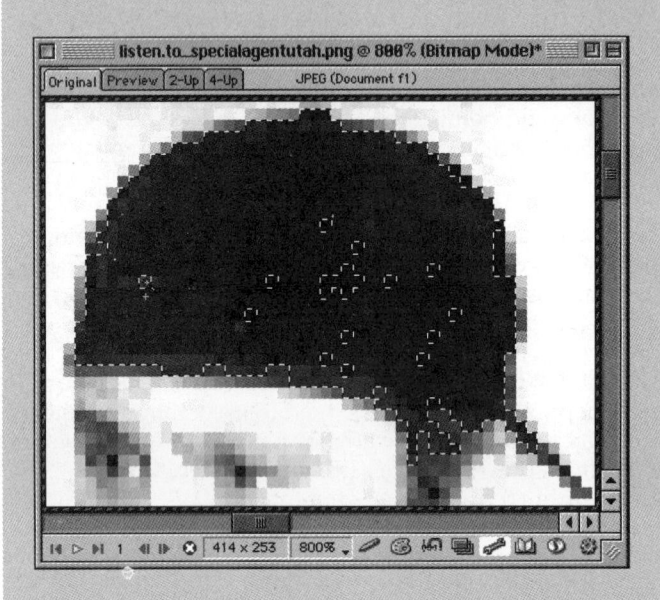

Just as you can add onto selections, you can take away from them, too. Use the Alt (Option) key when applying any of the selection tools to reduce an existing selection. The basic technique is to "carve out" the undesired selection; in the following figure, the donut shape was created by first drawing a circular selection, and then pressing Alt (Option) while drawing a smaller circular selection inside. An Xtra was then applied to the donut-shaped selection to create a frame around the subject's face. Obviously, the selection reduction feature enables you to create some very unusual shapes.

Rubber Stamping

If you're looking for a unique tool, look no further than the Rubber Stamp. One of the few pixel-based drawing tools, Rubber Stamp acts like a real rubber stamp: picking up a section of your document and stamping it out somewhere else. The Rubber Stamp tool makes picking up portions of an image and blending them into other areas of the graphic easy.

The Rubber Stamp is a two-part tool, with both source and destination pointers. The source, or origin, pointer is initially placed on the area of the document that you want to duplicate. The destination pointer draws the duplicated section in a different location on the image. While you are drawing, the two pointers maintain the same relationship to each other; if you move the destination pointer to the left, the source pointer moves to the left as well. Because the "ink" that the Rubber Stamp tool uses is always changing while you move it (because the source pointer is also moving), you can achieve a smooth blend, as in Figure 22-9. Getting a handle on this tool is a little tricky, but well worth the time you spend mastering it.

To use the Rubber Stamp tool, follow these steps:

1. Select the Rubber Stamp tool from the Tools panel, or use the keyboard shortcut, S.
2. Set the source pointer by clicking once on the bitmap. If you attempt to set the source pointer on a vector object, Fireworks tells you that the Rubber Stamp tool can only be used on floating bitmap objects.

3. Move the destination pointer to where you want the copied image to appear, and draw by clicking and dragging. As the source pointer moves over the image, following the movement of the mouse, the image is copied under the destination pointer.

Figure 22-9: Using the Rubber Stamp tool to create an extra head that practically draws itself

Understanding Aligned Source and Fixed Source modes

You can use the Rubber Stamp in two basic modes, selectable from the Source options list found on the Rubber Stamp Tool Options panel. First, with the Aligned Source mode (default), you can always keep the relationship between the source and destination pointers constant, not just when you're drawing. This is useful if you want to copy different portions of the image to a remote area, but keep them proportionally spaced. For example, if I wanted to position two eyes as if they were floating in space above my model's head, I would copy one eye using the Rubber Stamp tool, release the mouse button, and position the source pointer over the second eye and then begin dragging and drawing again until the second eye was completed.

The other Rubber Stamp mode is Fixed Source. In Fixed Source mode, whenever the mouse button is released, the source pointer snaps back to its original starting place. This mode enables you to copy the same image in several locations. If, for example, I wanted to place a series of floating eyes around my model's head, I would use Fixed Source mode.

> **Tip** Press Alt (Option) to reset the origin for the Rubber Stamp.

Learning about other options

Although the Rubber Stamp only draws pixels, you can use it to copy any part of your document, whether bitmap or vector object. In the Sample option list, choose Image to copy only from the image and Document to copy from anywhere in the document. There is one small trick to using the Sample Document option, however. Because the Rubber Stamp tool is intended as a pixel-based tool, you can't start by clicking outside of the image; Fireworks won't permit it. You can, however, click once on the image to set the source pointer, and then immediately move it by pressing Alt (Option) and resetting it on an area outside of the image. Then you can set the destination pointer normally, and begin copying the image.

Two other controls are available on the Rubber Stamp Tool Options panel. The Edge Softness slider affects the hardness of the duplicated image's edge; the higher the slider, the softer the edge. To blend a copied image more, use a softer edge. You can also change the size of the source and destination pointers with the Stamp Size slider. The range of the Stamp Size slider is from 0 to 72, and the default is 16 pixels. The selected Stamp Size includes any feathering that may be required by the Edge Softness setting.

Exploring the Eraser

As you might suspect, the Eraser removes pixels from an image, just like the trusty gum-based version erases pencil drawings. What you might not guess, however, is that the Eraser tool has numerous options and can achieve a variety of effects. The Eraser, which works only on pixel-based images, shares a spot in the Tools panel with its vector-oriented counterpart, the Knife. To see the Eraser button appear on the Tools panel, double-click a bitmap image to enter bitmap mode.

To use the Eraser, follow these steps:

1. Select the Eraser (or the Knife) from the Tools panel; alternatively, you can use the keyboard shortcut, E.
2. If necessary, select the image you want to work on.
3. Click and drag over the pixels you want to remove. Fireworks deletes the pixels according to the preferences selected in the Tool Options panel, as shown in Figure 22-10.

Figure 22-10: The Eraser tool removes pixels from your image according to the settings established on the Tool Options panel.

In addition to being able to set the Edge Softness and Size of the Eraser on the Tool Options panel, as you can with the Rubber Stamp tool, you can also select its basic shape. By default, the Eraser is circular, but you can change it to a square by choosing the Square Eraser button.

The final set of choices on the Tool Options panel gives the Eraser a fair degree of power. With some graphics programs, you're always erasing to whatever the current background is or, in Fireworks jargon, the canvas color. In Fireworks, you can select what will replace the area erased from four different choices:

- ✦ Transparent
- ✦ Fill color
- ✦ Stroke color
- ✦ Canvas color

Note If the image is floating over the canvas and you choose the Erase To Transparent option, it will look like you're erasing to the canvas color. However, if you move the image over another object, you'll see that the area erased is indeed transparent.

Fireworks Technique: Limiting Your Drawing Area

Not only can the selection tools modify your images after they're created, but they can also help to structure them while they're being made. When you place a selection on an image canvas — whether it's an existing image or an inserted Empty Image — any subsequent drawing is limited to that selected area. The selected area can be any shape possible, with any or all the selection tools: Marquee, Oval Marquee, Lasso, Polygon Lasso, and Magic Wand. In Figure 22-11, a feathered selection around the subjects' faces was inverted so that everything in the document, except the faces, was selected. The entire document was then painted over with the Paintbrush tool. Note that the Paintbrush could only paint in the selected area.

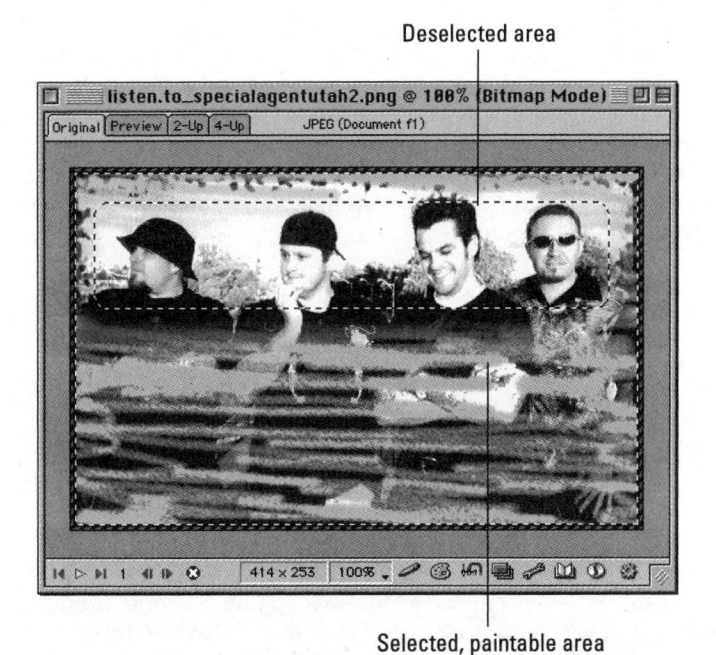

Figure 22-11: The subjects' faces aren't selected, so they don't get painted.

Tip If you have a pixel selection in your document, an Xtra will only apply to the selected area as well. A Film Look Xtra was also applied to Figure 22-11 after painting, to dirty the background a little and cause the faces to stand out even more.

The only prerequisite for using this technique is to make sure that the selection is active — it has a marquee border — before you begin drawing.

Making Pixel Selections

The Tools panel's selection tools are handy, but they aren't the only selection options in Fireworks. The Edit menu contains several commands pertinent to making selections, and the Modify ⇨ Marquee submenu contains a host of useful options for fine-tuning and even saving and restoring your pixel selections.

New Feature The commands for modifying marquee selections have moved from the Edit ⇨ Modify Marquee submenu to a new submenu under Modify ⇨ Marquee, which also includes commands for making similar and inverse selections, and new commands for saving and restoring pixel selections.

After you've made a pixel selection, the "marquee" or "marching ants" border acts almost like a new object. You can drag the marquee selection around, or modify its properties, without affecting the underlying pixels of your image. When you want to move pixels along with a marquee selection, hold down the Ctrl (Command) key while you drag your marquee. Fireworks adds a small scissors icon to your cursor when Ctrl (Command) is pressed, indicating that you're about to edit the selected pixels.

New Feature Dragging a marquee selection moves the selection without modifying the pixels of your image. Create marquees and fine-tune their placement before choosing to alter your image. Hold down Ctrl (Command) while dragging a selection to move the pixels as well.

Selecting all

When you need to select all the objects — both bitmap and vector — in the current document, choose Edit ⇨ Select All. I often find myself using the keyboard shortcut for this command, Ctrl+A (Command+A), in combination with the Delete key when I want to erase all the work in a document and start over. Of course, any operation that needs to be applied universally to every portion of a document benefits from the Select All command.

If you are in bitmap mode and issue the Select All command, just the image is selected, because — by nature — bitmap mode focuses you on just one bitmap image. If, on the other hand, you're in vector mode, all the vector and bitmap objects are selected. Keep in mind, however, that the bitmap objects are selected as free-floating objects, and bitmap mode tools, such as the Rubber Stamp, that work only with individual pixels, will not function.

Selecting similar

The Select Similar command is an extension of the Magic Wand selection tool. Whereas the Magic Wand selects pixels within a particular color range adjacent to the one initially chosen, Select Similar selects *all* the pixels in a document within that color range, whether they are adjacent to the original pixel or not. To use this command, choose Edit ➪ Select Similar, or Modify ➪ Marquee ➪ Select Similar, after setting the Tolerance level on the Magic Wand Tool Options panel.

Caution This very powerful command is one that you should use with care. It's often extremely difficult to predict all the areas of an image that will be affected. You may find yourself using this command in concert with Undo or the History panel, until you get a feel for what it does.

Cross-Reference The Edit menu Superselect and Subselect commands are concerned with groups and are therefore covered in Chapter 29.

Selecting none

The opposite of Select All is Deselect. I use this command so frequently, it goes on my Top 10 Keyboard Shortcuts to Memorize list: Ctrl+D (Command+D). It's a very straightforward and extremely useful command. Choose Edit ➪ Deselect to remove all selections in the current document for any bitmap, vector, or text object.

Selecting inverse

Sometimes I think I select inverse more than I select the pixels I want directly. Often, the background in an image contains fewer or flatter colors than the foreground, making it easier to select with the Magic Wand tool. After the background is selected, use the Select Inverse command to invert the selection, and select the foreground elements. On the other hand, if you want to select a background full of irregular colors and shapes, selecting the foreground elements and then inverting the selection to select the background may be easier. This command can be a time-saver over and over again.

1. First, select your foreground object through whatever tool or combination of tools is required.
2. Choose Modify ➪ Marquee ➪ Select Inverse, or use the keyboard shortcut, Ctrl+Shift+I (Command+Shift+I). Fireworks inverts the marquee selection so that the background is now selected (see Figure 22-12).

Figure 22-12: Selecting the foreground element and inverting the selection quickly isolated this complex, blended background.

Feathering an existing selection

You've seen the Feather option for all the selection tools, but you may have noticed that in each case, feathering has to be established prior to the selection being made, whether through the Marquee or the Magic Wand. But what do you do when you want to feather an existing selection? Make your selection and choose Modify ⇨ Marquee ⇨ Feather to open the Feather Selection dialog box, as shown in Figure 22-13. Whatever value you enter into the Radius text box is then applied to the current selection.

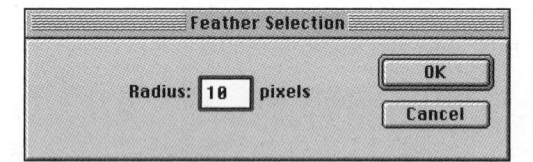

Figure 22-13: The Feather Selection dialog box permits you to feather the edges of the current selection.

Remember that the Feather command does not blur the selection's edges, but rather alters the selection's alpha channel, which controls transparency. To see the effect of a feathered selection, moving or cutting and pasting the selection is often necessary. As with all the other feathering options, both the selection and the area adjacent to the selection are affected.

Cross-Reference: If you do just want to blur all or part of an image, you'll want to use one of the Blur commands found under the Xtras menu. Find out more about these commands in Chapter 28.

Expanding or contracting a marquee

Sometimes a hand-drawn marquee selection is just a few pixels too large or small. Make a selection, and then choose Modify ➪ Marquee ➪ Expand to open the Expand Selection dialog box and specify the number of pixels by which you want to expand the selection. Conversely, if you want to contract the selection, choose Modify ➪ Marquee ➪ Contract, and enter the number of pixels to contract the selection in the Contract Selection dialog box. Click OK when you're done in either case.

Adding a border

To create an additional marquee around a current marquee, choose Modify ➪ Marquee ➪ Border, enter the width of the border you want to create in the Select Border dialog box, and click OK when you're done. Instead of your previous selection, what is now selected is a border around the previous selection.

Using the Smooth command

The Smooth command smooths the outline of a selection to turn a jagged, complicated marquee into a simpler one. This command is especially useful for the jagged marquees that are easily created with the Magic Wand tool. Create a selection, and then choose Modify ➪ Marquee ➪ Smooth. Enter a sample radius in the Smooth Selection dialog box; a higher number means a greater smoothing effect. Click OK when you're done.

Saving and restoring selections

The Modify ➪ Marquee submenu has two final commands that you haven't yet looked at. Choose Modify ➪ Marquee ➪ Save Selection to save the current pixel selection to a sort of selection clipboard within Fireworks. This selection is stored until you choose Modify ➪ Marquee ➪ Save again, and overwrite it with another selection. Choose Modify ➪ Marquee ➪ Restore Selection to restore a saved selection at any time.

New Feature The capability to save and restore a pixel selection is a welcome addition to the feature list of Fireworks.

Applying Vector Tools to Bitmaps

Whether you're creating a bitmap image from scratch, or touching up an existing graphic, you'll need additional tools. In Fireworks, all the geometric shapes — Rectangle, Oval, and Polygon — and most of the drawing tools — such as the Pencil and Brush — are applied in exactly the same way in bitmap mode as in vector mode. The primary difference is that what's drawn is easily editable when it's a vector object, and not when it's a bitmap object. Sometimes, however, you don't have a choice, and you have to work in bitmap mode because that's the way your image started out. Table 22-1 explains how the vector tools are used in bitmap mode.

Table 22-1
Tools in Bitmap Mode

Tool	Effect
Rectangle and Rounded Rectangle	Works the same way in bitmap mode as with vectors and uses the current Stroke and Fill settings.
Ellipse and Circle	Works the same way in bitmap mode as with vectors and uses the current Stroke and Fill settings.
Polygon and Star	Works the same way in bitmap mode as with vectors and uses the current Stroke and Fill settings.
Line	Works the same way in bitmap mode as with vectors and uses the current Stroke settings.
Pencil	Works the same way in bitmap mode as with vectors and uses the basic 1-pixel Stroke setting.
Brush	Works the same way in bitmap mode as with vectors and uses the current Stroke settings.
Pen	Ends bitmap mode; tool must be selected again to use in vector mode.
Text	Ends bitmap mode and opens Text Editor.
Transform, Skew, and Distort	No effect in bitmap mode. You can, however, use these tools to modify a selected bitmap object.
Freeform, Reshape Area, and Path Scrubber	No effect in bitmap mode; Fireworks will warn that these tools can be used only with vectors.

Converting a Vector into a Bitmap

Keeping parts of your document in vector form for easy modification is best, but occasionally you may want to convert a vector object into a bitmap object. To accomplish this, select one or more vector or bitmap objects, and then choose Modify ⇨ Convert to Bitmap, or use the keyboard shortcut Ctrl+Shift+Alt+Z (Command+Shift+Option+Z). Fireworks converts the vector outline to a rectangular bounding box, surrounding all the pixels from the vector object's fill, stroke, and effect settings.

If you have selected multiple objects, you can convert them all at one time with this command. However, you lose the capability to reposition them individually, as they all become part of one image; as the command's name implies, you are merging the images.

Caution After you've converted a vector to a bitmap, you can't go back without using the Undo command or the History panel to actually reverse your work. New bitmap objects in documents that have been saved and reloaded cannot return to their vector state under any circumstances. Fireworks throws away the vector information when you convert a vector object into a bitmap object.

Summary

Bitmap images are used throughout the Web, and Fireworks offers a robust set of tools for creating and manipulating them. Whereas bitmaps don't have the flexibility of vectors, editing them is an important part of the Web designer's job. When the time comes to begin modifying an existing image in Fireworks, keep these points in mind:

- ✦ Images are composed of pixels, and each pixel is assigned a particular color. At the most basic level, editing images involves changing the colors of pixels.

- ✦ In Fireworks, images are modified primarily in bitmap mode, which you can enter by double-clicking a bitmap object with the Pointer, or working with any image-based tool, such as the Marquee. You can also exit bitmap mode by double-clicking the bitmap again.

- ✦ All the image selection tools in Fireworks — Marquee, Oval Marquee, Lasso, Polygon Lasso, and Magic Wand — have numerous options available through the Tool Options panel.

- ✦ Marquee — or "marching ants" — selections can be moved, modified, and even saved without affecting the underlying image pixels.

- ✦ By selecting an area of the image prior to drawing, you can limit your drawing area.

- ✦ Most of the primary drawing tools, such as the Rectangle, Pen, and Brush, work in bitmap mode as well, with some restrictions.

In the next chapter, you find out how to handle color in Fireworks.

✦ ✦ ✦

CHAPTER 23

Managing Color

In This Chapter

Understanding Web color fundamentals

Blending new colors

Picking palettes

Fireworks technique: converting print colors

For any graphic designer, the importance of color is a given. Not only can color attract the eye and convey emotions, but it's also an important commercial consideration. On the Web, as with any mass medium, color also becomes a key factor in branding. After all, if you're working on a logo for the Coca-Cola Web site, you had better make sure you're using genuine Coca-Cola red.

Fireworks outputs graphics for a screen-based medium. You won't find complex color separation, halftone, or calibration tools in Fireworks; those instruments are for the world of print. Moreover, Fireworks is not just screen-based, it's Internet-based — a distinction that signifies an important balance of freedoms and restrictions.

This chapter covers color on the Web — both its basic theory with the various standards, and its actual practice with Fireworks. If you're familiar with how computers handle color in general, feel free to skip the initial part of the chapter, and dive right into the more hands-on Fireworks sections. If, on the other hand, you think RGB is a one-hit wonder band from the '80s and hexadecimal is a library catalog system, the first section should be pixel-perfect for you.

Working with Color on the Web

Color in the natural world comes at us full force, without any impediments. Color on the Web, however, passes through many filters. At the most basic level, the computer dictates how color is generated. Rather than using a system of blending inks as with print, the computer blends light — red, green, and blue light, to be precise. Next, the color settings and capability of a viewer's specific system determine the range of colors to be used. The final filter for Web-based color is the browser, in all of its varied configurations and versions.

To get the most out of your Web graphics, you need a basic understanding of how computers create color. The smallest component of a computer screen that you can see is the pixel, which, you'll remember, is short for *picture element*. Pixels are displayed by showing three colors in combination: red, green, and blue, often referred to by the initials, RGB. The blend of red, green, and blue at full intensity creates white.

> **Tip** If you're coming from a print background, you'll probably be more familiar with the CMYK (cyan, magenta, yellow, and black) color model than the RGB model. It's generally not too difficult to make the transition; Fireworks offers ways to convert a color in one system to its equivalent in the other, as explained in the section, "Using the Color Mixer," later in this chapter.

If RGB blended at full intensity creates white, and if a pixel that's turned off displays black, how are other colors created? The intensity of each of the key colors in a pixel — red, green, and blue — and their combinations can be varied. For example, if you have red set all the way up and both blue and green off, you get pure red; if you add a full dose of blue to the red, you create a deep purple. However, having only the capability to turn a color on or off greatly limits the number of color combinations possible. What's needed is an increase in the number of steps or levels between on and off.

Examining bit depth

The number of accessible RGB levels is called the *bit depth*. A bit is the smallest element of computer memory, and each bit is basically an on-off switch. A computer display with a bit depth of one is capable of showing two colors — one color in the on position and another in the off position. Now, if the bit depth is doubled, twice as many colors can be defined.

Each time you increase the bit depth, the number of colors increases exponentially. Table 23-1 takes a look at how bit depth affects color range.

Table 23-1
Bit Depth and Color Range

Bit Depth	Number of Colors	Description
1	2	Black and white, corresponding to the "on" or "off" possible with one bit.
2	4	Typically, computers with two-bit color depth (usually handhelds or portables) display four shades of gray.
4	16	The minimum color depth of VGA (Video Graphics Adapter) displays, the most common computer display technology.

Bit Depth	Number of Colors	Description
8	256	Most computers manufactured after 1995 can display 8-bit color or better.
16	65,536	Often called "Thousands of Colors" or "HiColor."
24	16,777,216	Referred to as "Millions of Colors" or "True Color."
32	16,777,216	True Color with an additional 8-bit alpha mask.

In Table 23-1, I skipped some bit depths because they're not commonly used on computer displays. Note that 32-bit color has the same number of colors as 24-bit. Although with 32-bits you could potentially describe more than four billion colors, the human eye can't differentiate that many. Thirty-two-bit color is therefore a combination of 24-bit color, with its 16.7 million colors, and an 8-bit grayscale overlay (known as a *mask*) that primarily specifies transparency and how graphics should be composited. For example, a mask can be used to make a graphic appear round or have holes in it, by showing parts of the graphic beneath it. This grayscale mask is known as an alpha mask, or the *alpha channel*.

Because bit depth is directly related to computer memory (remember that a bit is a chunk of memory), the higher the color range, the more memory required. And not just any memory, but video memory. Until recently, video memory was fairly limited, and most computer systems were shipped displaying only 256 colors (8-bit). Therefore, when designing for the Web, artists have been forced to work with the lowest common denominator and create work in 256 colors.

Note Increasingly, the average computer used for surfing the Web has an increased bit depth and can display more colors. A recent poll showed that out of 7 million Web visitors, less than 15 percent were using 256 color systems. However, this doesn't mean that all graphics can now be in millions of colors. The more colors used in a GIF image, the larger the file size, and download speed over the Internet is a major consideration in Web design.

Cross-Reference You can find examples of the appearance of various bit depths in the color insert.

Understanding hexadecimal colors

In HTML, the language of the Web, RGB color values are given in *hexadecimal*. Hexadecimal (or *hex*, as it is more commonly called), is a base-16 number system, which means that instead of the numbers running from 0 to 9 and then repeating, there is an initial series of 16 number values:

```
0, 1, 2, 3, 4, 5, 6, 7, 8, 9, A, B, C, D, E, F
```

The single letters represent values that would normally take two digits in the decimal system: A equals 10, B equals 11, C equals 12, and so on. When you want to count beyond single hex digits — in other words, go higher than F — you place a one in front of the numbers and continue, just as you do in decimals when you want to go beyond single digits. Although this looks strange to our decimal-trained eyes, continuing the above hex series looks like this (keep in mind that "10" is actually 16):

    10, 11, 12, 13, 14, 15, 16, 17, 18, 19, 1A, 1B, 1C, 1D, 1E,
    1F, 20

In the decimal number system, two digits can be used to express any number up to 99; but in the hexadecimal number system, the highest two-digit number is FF. Although they're both two-digit numbers, in hex, you have to count 255 things to fill up two digits.

> **Tip** Don't cheat and convert FF to 1515 and think of it as one thousand, five hundred and fifteen. When you look at the decimal number 99, you assume that the first 9 is really 90, or 9 multiplied by (base) 10. When you look at the hexadecimal number FF, remember that the first F is really 15 multiplied by (base) 16, which is equal to 240 in decimal. Add the other F, and you can see how FF is equal to 255.

RGB values are expressed in hex with a set of three two-digit numbers, with each of the three values corresponding to 256 levels of red, green, and blue, respectively. For example, white in RGB values would be represented as 255, 255, 255 — each color being its most intense. The equivalent in hex is FF, FF, FF, which in HTML is written all together, like this: FFFFFF. Black is 0, 0, 0 in RGB and 000000 in hex, whereas a pure red would be 255, 0, 0 in RGB, and FF0000 in hex.

Though it may seem completely foreign to you initially, hexadecimal colors quickly become recognizable. You'll even start to notice patterns; for example, any color where the hex triplets are all the same represents a shade of gray — 111111 is the darkest gray, and EEEEEE is the lightest.

Exploring Web-safe colors

As noted previously, the generally accepted lowest-common denominator in monitor displays is 8-bit, or 256 colors. Unfortunately, yet one more restriction exists on Web colors: the browser. Each of the major browsers from Microsoft and Netscape uses a fixed palette of 256 colors to render 8-bit images on both Windows and Macintosh operating systems. After the 40 unique colors used for system displays in both Macintosh and Windows platforms are subtracted — because you generally would like your Web graphics to look the same on both Windows and Macintosh platforms — a common palette of 216 colors remains. Because any system can safely use any of these colors without dithering — faking the color with a combination of two others — they are collectively referred to as the *browser-safe* or *Web-safe* palette.

> **Tip** Interestingly enough — and thankfully — Web-safe colors are easy to spot when given in hexadecimal. Any hex color that contains some combination of 00, 33, 66, 99, CC, or FF — such as 0000FF, 336699, or FFCC00 — is Web-safe.

It's important to realize that the Web-safe palette is for use with flat-color images, such as illustrations, logos, and headline text — the kinds of images that are drawn or created right on a computer and exported in the GIF format. Using Web-safe colors in these images keeps flat areas of color flat. Photographic images are still exported with a 24-bit palette — usually in the JPEG format — and dithered by the browser if necessary.

Because of its importance in Web design, Fireworks makes extensive use of the Web-safe palette, and includes a number of features for efficiently working with it:

- By default, the pop-up color picker that is accessible from every color well in the program is set to the Web-safe palette.

- Holding down the Shift key when you use the Eyedropper tool causes the tool to convert any color that it samples to Web-safe.

- The Find and Replace panel can search for colors that fall outside the Web-safe palette and snap them to their nearest neighbor, in one document or a range of documents, all in one step.

- The Fill panel has a Web Dither category that can convert any color into a pattern of Web-safe colors that closely approximates the color.

As you continue to work with Fireworks and in Web design in general, you'll become more and more familiar with the Web-safe palette.

Looking at platform differences

Not only does the Web designer have to contend with a limited palette and a host of issues with the wide variety of browsers in the market, but also many differences worth noting exist between the Windows and Macintosh platforms. Chief among these is the *gamma* setting.

The gamma setting, or more properly, the *gamma correction* setting, is designed to avoid having midtones onscreen appear too dark. The problem is that different gamma settings exist for different systems. The Macintosh typically defaults to a setting of 1.8, whereas Windows uses 2.2, which is also the standard for television. The lower gamma setting on the Mac works well to emulate print output, but the display seems brighter when compared to Windows. Consequently, the same graphic appears darker on a Windows machine than on a Macintosh.

Tip Mac users who want to set their system to 2.2 for Web or television work can do so if they have ColorSync enabled. Open the Monitors or Monitors and Sound Control Panel, click the Color button, and then follow the instructions to calibrate your display. Choose 2.2 as a gamma setting. You can also choose to use the "native" gamma setting of your display, which may be 2.2.

It's also worth noting that Windows machines are typically paired with much more diverse varieties of display hardware, while most Macs typically use very similar graphics adapters and a matching, or even built-in, display. Actual testing might lead us to find that typical Windows gamma varies more than typical Mac gamma; after all, we're talking about many different manufacturers instead of one. Aiming squarely at 2.2 in your work won't necessarily guarantee that your work is viewed properly by all Windows users.

One solution to this problem — still, unfortunately, at the "coming soon" stage — you can find in Fireworks' native format, PNG. Images saved in a PNG format have built-in gamma correction, so that they will be displayed correctly, regardless of the user's system. Although displaying a PNG image in a browser is old hat these days, support for the gamma correction elements of the format is still unavailable anywhere except in Internet Explorer for Windows.

In the future, the influence of television on the Internet, and the Internet on computing, may result in a 2.2 gamma correction setting becoming standard on the Macintosh (I already run my Mac at this setting). For now, the best solution is to view your work under both settings and compromise a little when necessary, in order to achieve acceptable results on both platforms. To aid in this, Fireworks provides a shortcut for viewing the "other" gamma setting: the Macintosh Gamma and Windows Gamma commands.

Choose View ⇨ Macintosh Gamma in Fireworks for Windows in order to see a representation of how your work will appear on most Macs. Similarly, choose View ⇨ Windows Gamma in Fireworks for Macintosh in order to view the way your work will look on most Windows machines.

> **Tip**
> Mac users: If you're using a gamma setting of 1.8 while preparing an image for television, remember that Windows gamma is the same as TV gamma, so the Windows Gamma command doubles as a TV gamma preview.

> **Cross-Reference**
> See the effects of Fireworks' cross-platform gamma view in the color insert.

Working with color management

ColorSync (Macintosh only) and Kodak color management systems work with Photoshop and certain other applications to achieve accurate color representations across monitors, scanners, and printers. If you import an image from one of these applications into Fireworks, you may find that the color values are shifted slightly, because Fireworks does not work with color management systems.

The easiest way to prevent this color shifting is to disable color management in the source application before exporting or saving an image. Alternatively, you can import the image into Fireworks and use the Hue slider on the Hue/Saturation Xtra to adjust all the colors slightly, moving them all back to Web-safe values, for example.

Mixing Colors

The general color mechanism in Fireworks is the Color Mixer. With the Color Mixer, you can select your Fill and Stroke colors from the entire spectrum available to you in any of five different color models. You can also directly determine a color by entering the appropriate values through the sliders or text boxes.

Using the Color Mixer

To open the Color Mixer, choose Window ⇨ Color Mixer. The Color Mixer, shown in Figure 23-1, is divided into three main areas:

- **Color wells:** The Stroke and Fill color wells display the active color for the selected object stroke and fill, respectively. The color defaults can also be applied and swapped through buttons in this section.
- **Color sliders:** Use the color sliders to choose a color by altering its components.
- **Color ramp:** The color ramp displays all colors of a particular color model and enables you to select them with an Eyedropper tool.

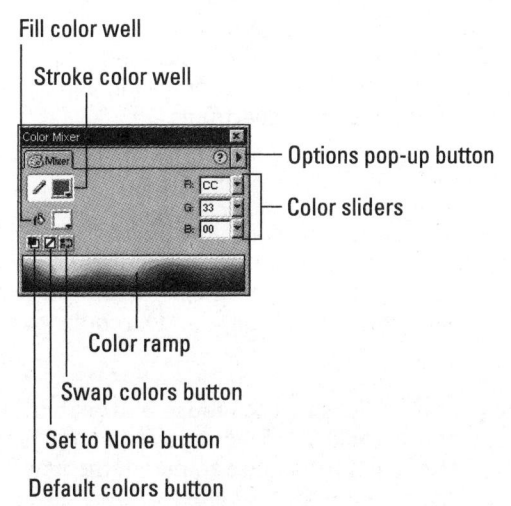

Figure 23-1: Open the Color Mixer to select your Stroke and Fill colors from the color ramp, or set them with the color sliders.

Choosing a color

The Web artist alternates between creating new graphics fresh from the mind's eye and matching or adapting existing imagery. Both methods are valid ways of working, and Fireworks enables you to select the colors you need accordingly. Should you want to create visually, selecting your colors direct from the palette, you can sample colors either from a full-spectrum color ramp, the more limited showing of the active swatches, or directly off the screen from another image. If you would prefer to work more formulaically, the color sliders enable you to enter a precise value in five different color models.

Using the color ramp

To select a color from the color ramp, follow these steps:

1. Open the Color Mixer by choosing Window ⇨ Color Mixer.

2. Select either the Stroke or Fill color well. The selected color well is highlighted with a border around it.

3. Move your pointer over the color ramp. The pointer changes into one of two Eyedropper tools. The Eyedropper tool with a wavy line indicates that a Stroke color is to be selected, whereas the Eyedropper tool with the solid block indicates that you're choosing a Fill color.

> **Tip** Initially, the color ramp display matches the chosen color model, such as RGB, Hexadecimal, or Grayscale. You can change the color ramp, however, by Shift+clicking it. With each Shift+click, the color ramp cycles through one of three displays: the Web-safe, full-color, and grayscale spectrums.

4. Choose any desired color in the color ramp by clicking it once.

> **Tip** If you click and drag your pointer across the color ramp, the wells and the slider settings update dynamically. This gives you a better idea of the actual color you're selecting — the swatch in the color well is large and the color values are easy to follow. If the color chosen is unsatisfactory, select Edit ⇨ Undo in order to return to your previous setting.

5. After you've selected the color by releasing the mouse button, both the color well and sliders display the new color. If an object was selected when the new color was chosen, its Fill or Stroke color changes to match the new one.

Using Color Mixer sliders

Another method of selecting a color uses the Color Mixer sliders. As with other Fireworks sliders, you can enter the values either directly in the text boxes, or by dragging the slider handle up or down. The availability of sliders depends upon the color model chosen. Sliders for RGB, CMY, and HSB all match their respective initials. Choosing the Hexadecimal model displays the R, G, and B color sliders. Selecting Grayscale shows just one slider, K, which represents the percentage of black.

If you're not trying to match a specific RGB or other value, you can visually — as opposed to numerically — mix your colors by moving the slider and watching the selected color well. If you have an object selected, its stroke or fill settings will update when you release the mouse button.

Accessing the color models

Aside from the previously described RGB and Hexadecimal models, Fireworks offers three other possible color models. The capability to switch between different color models is important in Web design. Quite often the Web artist is asked to convert graphics from another medium, be it another computer-based medium or print. You can also switch from one system to another in order to take advantage of its special features. For example, switching the HSB enables you to select a tint of a particular color by reducing the saturation.

All color models are chosen by selecting the pop-up menu button in the upper-right corner of the Color Mixer. Choose a color model from the list that appears, as shown in Figure 23-2.

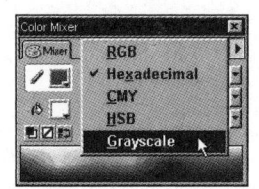

Figure 23-2: Choose from five different color models in the Color Mixer's pop-up menu.

RGB

Choosing the RGB color model enables you to select any one of 16.7 million colors that are available in the 24-bit color spectrum. Whereas not all the colors are represented on the RGB color ramp (at a resolution of 72 pixels per inch, displaying all pixels would require over 19,000 square feet — that's a mighty big monitor), you can enter any required value in the color sliders shown in Figure 23-3. The color sliders use values from 0 to 255.

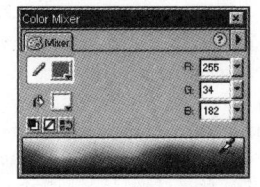

Figure 23-3: Work with the RGB color model to specify any one of 16.7 million colors.

Caution: If your computer display is not capable of showing as many colors as are viewable in the color model—for example, if your system is set on 256 colors and you choose RGB—you'll see some dithering in the color ramp. *Dithering* is the combination of two or more colors to simulate another color, and it appears as noticeable dots. Although the display may dither, the colors that the Eyedropper tool chooses are accurate RGB values.

Hexadecimal

When you select the Hexadecimal color model, two things happen. The Color Mixer sliders translate their displayed values to hexadecimal values, and the color ramp depicts a Web-safe spectrum, as shown in Figure 23-4. With a Web-safe color ramp (which is the default when Fireworks first starts up after installation), you'll notice what's referred to as *banding*. Banding occurs when the range of colors is not large enough to make a smooth gradation.

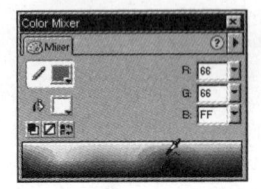

Figure 23-4: Although you can enter any valid hexadecimal RGB value in the color sliders with the Hexadecimal color model, only Web-safe colors are selectable in the default color ramp.

Caution: All values entered manually in the slider text boxes must be in the proper hexadecimal pair format. If you try to enter a numeric value outside of hexadecimal range, such as 225, Fireworks just drops the first number without properly converting the value.

CMY

As mentioned previously in the section "Working with Color on the Web," most designers coming from a print background are used to expressing color as a mixture of cyan, magenta, yellow, and black: CMYK, also known as the four-color process. In theory, the color range should be representable with just the first three colors, but in printing practice, the fourth color, black, is necessary to produce the darker colors.

Fireworks presents CMY colors as a range of numbers from 0 to 255. In some ways, CMY can be considered the opposite of RGB. RGB is referred to as an *additive* process, because you add the colors together to reach white. CMY is a *subtractive* process, because you take colors away to make white. When you choose CMY from the pop-up menu, the Color Mixer panel displays a slider for C (Cyan), one for M (Magenta), and one for Y (Yellow), as shown in Figure 23-5.

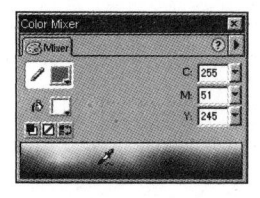

Figure 23-5: Print designers new to the Web will find the CMY color model familiar.

Fireworks isn't concerned with output to a print medium, so it can express the color spectrum with just cyan, magenta, and yellow, without resorting to the addition of black. This, however, does make translating a CMYK color to a CMY color difficult. The best workaround I've found is to use a common third model, such as RGB, or a specific Pantone color.

HSB

HSB is short for Hue, Saturation, and Brightness. It is a color model available on numerous graphics programs, including Photoshop. Hue represents the color family, as seen on a color wheel. Because of the circular model, Hue values are presented in degrees from 0 to 360. Saturation determines the purity of the color, in terms of a percentage. Saturation of 100 percent is equal to the purest version of any hue. The Brightness value, also expressed as a percentage, is the amount of light or dark in a color — 0 percent is black, and 100 percent is the brightest that a color can appear. If the brightness is reduced to zero, the Hue and Saturation values are automatically reduced to zero, as well. After choosing HSB from the pop-up menu on the Color Mixer panel, the three sliders change to H, S, and B (see Figure 23-6).

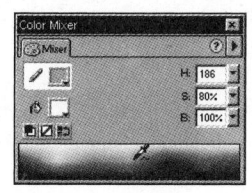

Figure 23-6: Use the HSB color model to easily lighten or darken a particular hue.

Caution: Don't attempt to directly translate HSB values from the similarly named HLS color model. HLS (Hue, Luminosity, and Saturation), a color model used in FreeHand and other drawing programs, also available in the Mac OS color picker, uses Luminosity rather than Brightness as its "light" component. The key difference between Luminosity and Brightness lies in how a color is affected at the higher end of the scale. In HSB, when full Brightness is combined with full Saturation, colors are at their most vivid. In HLS, full Luminosity, regardless of Saturation level, makes colors white.

Grayscale

Despite the richness of the realm of color — or maybe because of it — grayscale images have an undeniable power. Whether you're constructing graphics as homage to black-and-white movies, or blending black-and-white photographs in a full-color site, access to a grayscale palette is essential. The Fireworks grayscale palette is a full range of 256 tones, ranging from absolute white to absolute black.

When you select Grayscale from the Color Mixer's pop-up menu, the three sliders of the other palette are reduced to one slider and marked K, for black. As Figure 23-7 shows, the black value is expressed as a percentage, where 100 percent is black and 0 percent is white.

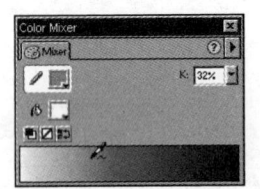

Figure 23-7: To access any one of 256 shades of gray, select the Grayscale color model.

Selecting Swatches of Color

Quite often the graphics for a Web site are designed with a particular palette in mind. The most common palette contains the 216 Web-safe colors, which people use to keep images from shifting colors on different platforms. Palettes are also devised to match a particular color scheme — either for an entire Web site or for one particular area. Each palette can be saved as a separate swatch file.

Fireworks provides very full palette support through its Swatches panel. You can modify, store, load, or completely scrap swatches to start fresh. You can even grab the palette from a sample image.

Choosing from the color wells

The standard Fireworks pop-up color picker is quite powerful. When it's "popped up," your cursor changes into an Eyedropper tool that enables you to select a color from any onscreen image — whether it's in the pop-up color picker, in another part of Fireworks, or even anywhere else on your computer display. You can quickly set a stroke or fill to None by using the No Color button, without opening the respective panels. Finally, the Palette button gives you instant access to your operating system's color picker(s).

New Feature

In Fireworks 3, the Eyedropper tool wasn't active until you pushed a button on the pop-up color picker. Now, the Eyedropper tool is instantly available as soon as you open the pop-up color picker.

To access the colors in the current swatch set, select the arrow button next to any color well. When the pop-up color picker appears, as shown in Figure 23-8, move your pointer over any of the color swatches. As you move your pointer, notice that the color chip in the upper-right corner dynamically updates to show the color underneath the pointer; the color name in hexadecimal is also displayed. Click once to choose a color.

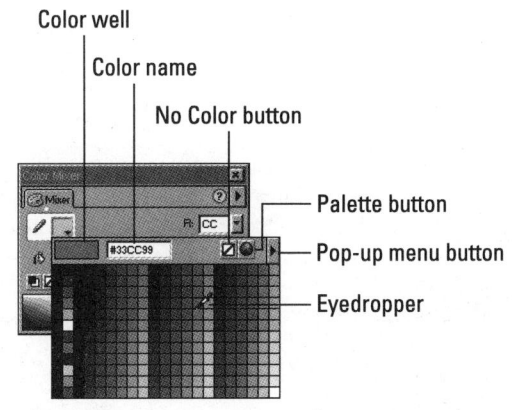

Figure 23-8: You can open the pop-up color picker from any color well in Fireworks.

Tip

If you've selected a color for a stroke or fill where previously none existed, Fireworks automatically enables the setting, turning the Stroke type to Pencil and the Fill type to Solid for the selected color.

Even though the pop-up color picker is handy, you might want to switch between different swatch sets quite regularly. For example, if you decide to focus your work on an object that's composed entirely of grayscale colors, changing the pop-up color picker to the grayscale swatch set will simplify your work. A pop-up menu on the pop-up color picker enables you to quickly choose another swatch set (see Figure 23-9).

New Feature

You'll find a pop-up menu on the pop-up color picker, enabling you to quickly choose another set of swatches.

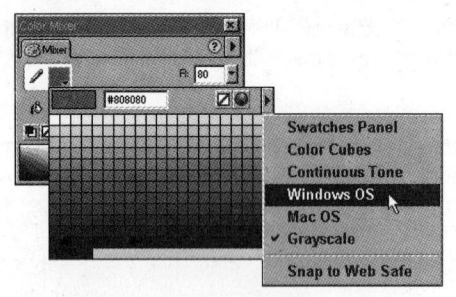

Figure 23-9: A pop-up menu on the pop-up color picker enables you to quickly choose another set of swatches.

Using the Eyedropper

The Eyedropper is a great tool for ensuring color fidelity across images. Need to match a particular shade of purple in the background graphic for the outline of the navigation bar you're building? Click once with the Eyedropper to grab that color, and the selected color well fills with the chosen color.

The Eyedropper tool is straightforward to use. Once you've displayed the pop-up color picker, the Eyedropper is already "in your hand," and your cursor changes into its namesake shape. Now you can easily select a color from anywhere within Fireworks.

Moreover, the Eyedropper tool is not limited to sampling colors from Fireworks. You can pick up a color from any application or graphic displayed on your computer. However, a slight difference exists in the way this feature works on each computing platform:

✦ With Macintosh systems, the Eyedropper works the same way outside of Fireworks as it does within Fireworks. Any color anywhere on your display is fair game, at all times.

✦ With Windows systems, click within the Fireworks window and hold down the mouse button, then drag the mouse cursor outside of the Fireworks window. Release the mouse button when the cursor is over the color you want to sample.

> **Tip**
> It's possible — even likely — that the color you sample with the Eyedropper won't be Web-safe. To snap the sampled color to the closest Web-safe value, press Shift when you select your color.

Accessing the system color picker(s)

If you work with a number of graphics applications, you may find working with your operating system's color picker(s) rather than with those in Fireworks more convenient. To open the system color picker(s), click the Palette button on the Fireworks color picker. Closing the system color picker(s) automatically assigns the last selected color to the Fireworks color well.

The Macintosh system color picker dialog box has several color pickers from which to choose. Table 23-2 details these different schemes.

Table 23-2
Color Models in the Macintosh Color Picker Dialog Box

Color Model	Description
CMYK	Standard model for color printing.
Crayon	A box of crayons with names such as Banana and Cool Marble. Click a crayon to select that color.
HLS	Hue, Luminosity, and Saturation.
HSV	Hue, Saturation, and Value model with a color wheel.
HTML	RGB expressed in hexadecimal numbers, with an optional Web-safe snap.
RGB	Standard model for computer displays, with an optional Web-safe snap.

Choose a color model from the left part of the color picker dialog box, as shown in Figure 23-10, and specify settings on the right. The color that the Fireworks color picker is set to is shown in the upper right of the window as the "original" color, for comparison with the color you're currently choosing.

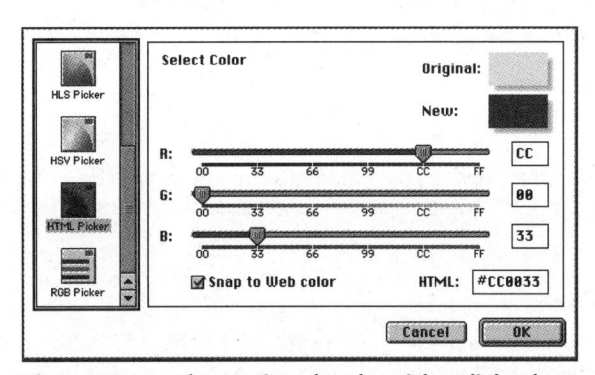

Figure 23-10: The Macintosh color picker dialog box offers numerous color models from which to choose.

> **Tip**
> If you hold down Option while you're in the Macintosh color picker dialog box, the cursor changes into an Eyedropper tool that works just like the one in Fireworks. Use it to sample colors from anywhere on the screen.

In addition to these seven default color pickers, the Macintosh color picker system is extensible, so you may have other color pickers, depending on the hardware and software you have installed. Color pickers are installed by Apple Display Software, for example, or you may have installed a third-party color picker yourself. My favorite — no pun intended — is FVPicker, available from http://www.at-soft.net, which enables you to store your favorite colors for easy recall.

The Windows system color picker is split into two parts, as shown in Figure 23-11. On the left, you'll find 48 color chips from the Windows system palette. Located on the right is a full-color spectrum with a value bar for mixing colors. Both RGB and Hue, Saturation, and Luminance text boxes are available below the spectrum. To choose a color beyond the basic 48, you must create it by choosing a color from both the main spectrum and the value bar on the right, and then adding it to one of the 16 custom color wells on the left.

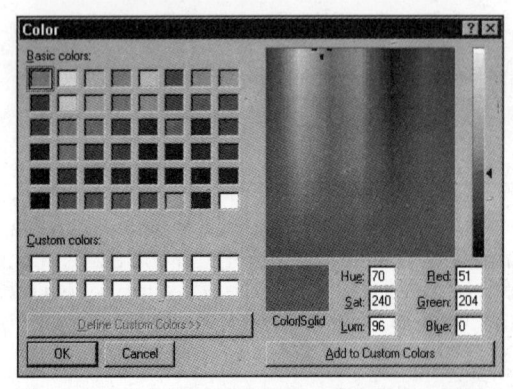

Figure 23-11: The Windows color picker offers easy access to colors from the Windows system palette, or create 16 of your own colors from the full spectrum.

Tip In order to avoid overwriting a previously created custom color, select an empty custom color well in the Windows color picker before creating a new custom color.

Opting for no color

When it comes to stroke and fill colors, remember that "no color" is as valid an option as any color. To disable a fill or a stroke, just choose the No Color button from the Fireworks color picker. When you select the No Color button, the color chip displays the checkerboard pattern used to depict transparency in Fireworks.

Note The No Color button is available in the pop-up color pickers that are called from the Stroke and Fill color wells found on the Tools panel, but not on the other pop-up color pickers. In Windows, the No Color button you can also find in the color picker in the Color Mixer panel.

Using the Swatches panel

The Swatches panel is deceptively simple in appearance. Consisting of just colors (with the exception of the pop-up menu button), the Swatches panel enables you to choose a stroke, fill, or effect color from the active palette. As with all other Fireworks floating panels, the Swatches panel can be moved and resized — the latter feature is especially important if you want to show a larger palette.

Caution Remember that the Swatches panel displays the current Fireworks palette, not the palette of the current document.

The most basic use of the Swatches panel is similar to that of the Color Mixer and the pop-up color picker. Select the color well you want to alter, and then choose a color by clicking any of the color chips in the Swatches panel, as shown in Figure 23-12. There's no real feedback in the Swatches panel to identify the color other than visually; you would need to have the Info panel visible to see the RGB or other components.

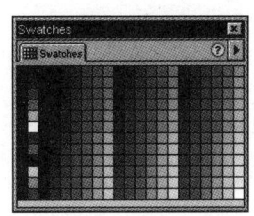

Figure 23-12: Pick a color, any color, from the Swatches panel.

As you find out in the next section, you can choose from a number of preset color palettes. However, you can also add any custom mixed color — or color selected with the Eyedropper — to a swatch. The custom color then becomes available from anywhere in the program where you can click a color well or access the Swatch panel. You can add new colors, extending an existing palette or replacing a color on the palette. You can also delete standard or custom colors from a palette.

To add, replace, or remove a color in the Swatches panel, follow these steps:

1. Mix or sample the color you want to add, so that it appears in the active color well.

2. Display the Swatches panel by choosing Window ⇨ Swatches, or by clicking the Swatches tab if the panel is behind other panels in a group.

3. Position your pointer over an open area in the Swatches panel and click once to add a new color to the current palette. When over an open area, the Eyedropper pointer becomes a paint bucket.

4. Press Shift while you position your pointer over the color to be replaced, and click once to replace an existing color in the current palette. If you press Shift when the pointer is positioned over an existing color, the pointer becomes a paint bucket.

5. Hold down Ctrl (Command), position the pointer over the color to be deleted, and click once to remove a color from the current palette. When you press Ctrl (Command), the pointer becomes a pair of scissors. For best results, position the scissors so that the crossing of the blades — the middle of the X — is placed directly over the color you want to delete.

To reset any standard palette that has been modified, select that palette from the pop-up menu.

Picking preset swatches

Fireworks has four standard palettes that you can select at any time:

- **Web 216 Palette:** Colors common between both major browsers, Netscape Navigator and Internet Explorer, on Macintosh and Windows
- **Windows System:** The color palette used by Windows to display its system elements
- **Macintosh System:** The color palette used by the Macintosh operating system
- **Grayscale:** A monochrome palette ranging from white to black

All palettes, with the exception of Web 216, are composed of 256 colors.

To switch palettes, select a different one from the Swatches panel's pop-up menu, as shown in Figure 23-13.

Figure 23-13: The Swatches panel's pop-up menu enables you to select different standard palettes, or to load your own.

One additional palette is available from the pop-up menu: the Current Export palette. Choosing this option loads the current document's export palette from the Color Table panel — detailed later in this chapter — into the Swatches panel.

Managing swatches

The real power of Fireworks swatches is in the capability to load and store custom palettes. The remaining five commands on the pop-up menu are dedicated to managing swatches. Fireworks can load and save palettes in a format known as Active Color Table (ACT). Adobe Photoshop can also read and write ACT files, so loading Photoshop palettes in Fireworks is easy.

However, you don't have to save your palettes as ACT files in order to work with them in the Swatch panel. Fireworks can also glean the palette from any GIF or other 8-bit indexed color file. Moreover, you have two different ways to access a previously stored palette. You can either append the saved palette to the current swatch, or you can use just the saved palette.

To load palettes into the Swatches panel, follow these steps:

1. Click the pop-up menu button in the Swatches panel.
2. Choose Add Swatches if you want to extend the existing palette with a new palette.
3. Choose Replace Swatches if you want to use the just saved palette.

   In either case, the Open dialog box appears for you to select a palette.
4. Choose the type of palette you want to load:
   - Color table (filename typically ends in .act)

Note: On the Mac, a color table file may not have (and doesn't require) the .act filename extension. Color table files have a File Type code of 8BCT. Although Fireworks doesn't provide an icon for its color table files, color table files saved by Photoshop have an icon with color wells and the description CLUT on them.

   - GIF files (filename ends in .gif)
5. Locate the file and click Open when you're ready.

If you chose Add Swatches, the new palette is appended to the end of the existing swatch. If Replace Swatches is used, the existing swatch is removed, and the new palette is displayed in its place.

Tip: Although the feature is a bit hidden, you can also load Adobe Swatches in addition to Adobe Color Tables. Adobe Swatches have a file extension of .aco, rather than the Color Tables extension of .act. Fireworks for Windows does not offer the .aco file type in its Open dialog boxes; enter ***.aco** in the File Name text box, and press Return in order to force the dialog box to list files with the filename extension .aco.

In Fireworks, all palettes are saved in Active Color Table format. To save a current swatch, simply choose Save Swatches from the pop-up menu, and name the file in the standard Save As dialog box.

You can erase the entire palette from the Swatches panel by choosing Clear Swatches from the pop-up menu. This removes any palette displayed in the Swatches panel, but it doesn't affect the default palettes at all. If you do issue the Clear Swatches command, the color wells revert to using the default Web-safe palette in the pop-up color pickers.

The final pop-up menu command in the Swatches panel is Sort by Color. As the name implies, Sort by Color displays the active palette by color value, rather than by the default mathematical order. If new colors have been added — or a completely new palette loaded — those colors are sorted, as well. Please note that no way exists to undo a Sort by Color command; to restore a standard palette to its previous configuration, choose the particular palette from the pop-up menu.

Accessing the Color Table

If you've specified a reduced export palette in the Optimize panel — generally by specifying to export as a GIF — then the current document's export palette will be reduced accordingly and won't match any standard palette. The Color Table panel offers easy access to the export palette.

To display the Color Table panel, shown in Figure 23-14, choose Window ⇨ Color Table, or click the Color Table tab if the Color Table panel is docked behind another panel.

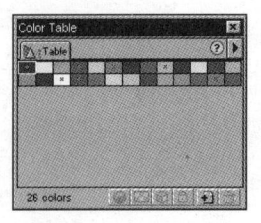

Figure 23-14: The Color Table panel enables you to access the current document's export palette.

If you've carefully reduced the export palette for your document to 16 or 32 colors, you probably don't need or want access to colors outside that range while you're still working with the document. Accidentally adding a new color at this point may simply undo optimization work you've already done. In the later stages of working with a GIF image, I'll often use the Swatches panel to load the export palette, and then choose my colors there.

If the Color Table displays the message "(Rebuild)" in its title bar, the colors it's displaying are "out of date," because you've made some modification to the export palette in the Optimize panel. Choose Rebuild Color Table from the pop-up menu. Menu items on the pop-up menu — as well as the buttons along the bottom of the Color Table panel — enable you to add, remove, edit, and lock colors as required.

Cross-Reference For more about working with the Color Table panel, see Chapter 30.

Fireworks Technique: Converting Pantone Colors to Web-Safe Colors

Many Web designers have clients with specific concerns regarding the use of their logos, trademarks, and other brand identifiers. Many larger companies have spent large amounts of money to develop a distinct look in their print, television, and other media advertising and marketing — and they want to ensure that their look continues over the Internet. Most designers work with a set series of colors — Pantone colors are among the most popular — that can be specified for print work. It should come as no surprise to discover that many of these colors fall outside of the Web-safe palette of 216 colors.

A way exists, however, to bring the two seemingly divergent worlds together. In fact, several ways exist. Pantone makes a product called ColorWeb Pro that converts its colors so they are usable in computer graphics. ColorWeb Pro is a small utility that enables you to look up a Pantone color by number and then displays a color chip with the equivalent RGB and/or HTML color values.

ColorWeb Pro runs in two modes: the Pantone Matching System, which allows you to choose from all 1,012 Pantone colors; and the Pantone Internet Color System, which converts your choice to a Web-safe color before sending it to Fireworks. If you're satisfied with a simple conversion from Pantone to Web-safe, use the Internet Color System to choose a Pantone color and convert it to Web-safe.

To get a more accurate representation of a Pantone color, you can combine the Pantone Matching System with Fireworks' Web Dither fill, sampling a Pantone color and allowing Fireworks to create a Web Dither equivalent. This option opens many of the Pantone colors for use on the Internet where it counts the most — in the fill areas. Though this system is not perfect — I occasionally find Pantone colors that do not have a good duplicate in the Web Dither mode — it's quite close.

In Windows, ColorWeb Pro runs as an application that is basically a floating color chip. Double-clicking this chip opens the Pantone color pickers. Right-clicking the chip displays a context menu that enables you to specify options.

On the Mac, ColorWeb Pro simply installs its color pickers into the Mac's extensible color picker dialog box. Access these new color pickers as you would access any other system-level color picker: Choose the Palette button from the Fireworks color picker or choose Add Color from the Color Table panel.

> **Caution**
>
> Mac users may find that they already have Pantone color pickers because they were installed by ColorSync or Apple Display Software. In this case, installing the ColorWeb Pro demo overwrites your Pantone color pickers, necessitating a reinstall of ColorSync or Apple Display Software if you don't purchase ColorWeb Pro after the demo times out.

Using ColorWeb Pro for Windows

To convert a Pantone color to a Web Dither color in Fireworks for Windows, follow these steps:

1. Start ColorWeb Pro.

2. If the Pantone color chip doesn't stay on top of Fireworks, right-click (Control+click) the color chip and enable Stay on Top from the shortcut menu. Because you'll be working with both Fireworks and ColorWeb Pro, you need to see both programs simultaneously.

3. Double-click the Pantone color chip in order to display the Pantone Color Picker, as shown in Figure 23-15.

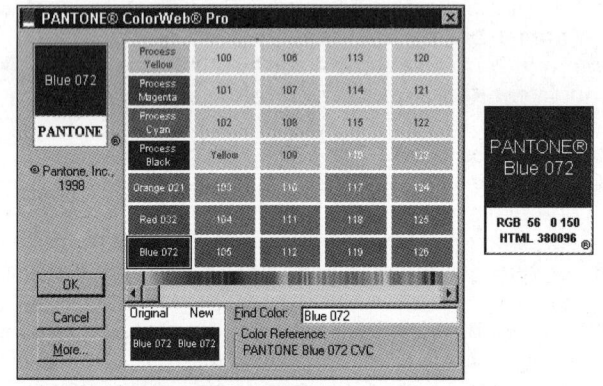

Figure 23-15: ColorWeb Pro offers you an extensive palette of Pantone colors.

4. Locate the desired color either by entering its number in the Find Color text box, or by selecting it. Click OK when you're done in order to return to the color chip.

5. Select the object you want to fill with a Pantone color.

6. Display the Fill panel by choosing Window ⇨ Fill, or use the keyboard shortcut Shift+F7.

7. Select the Fill color well arrow in order to open the pop-up color picker and enable the Eyedropper tool.

Caution: Be sure to pick the main color well (the top one) and not either of the two dither color wells.

8. Use the Eyedropper to sample the Pantone color chip. Windows users must click the Eyedropper while it's over Fireworks, drag it to the Pantone color chip, and then release to sample the color.

Fireworks calculates the closest match using the Web Dither technique. If the Pantone color is Web-safe, both dither color wells hold the same color.

Using ColorWeb Pro for Macintosh

To convert a Pantone color to a Web Dither color in Fireworks for Macintosh, follow these steps:

1. Select the object you want to fill with a Pantone color.
2. Display the Fill panel by choosing Window ⇨ Fill, or use the keyboard shortcut, Shift+F7.
3. Choose the Web Dither category from the Fill panel.
4. Open the Fill panel color picker, and choose the Palette button in order to display the Macintosh color picker dialog box.

Caution: Make sure to choose the Fill panel color picker from the upper color well, not the lower Web dither color wells.

5. Select the Pantone DC (Pantone Digital Color) color picker from the left part of the Macintosh color picker dialog box, as shown in Figure 23-16. Choose the desired color on the right by entering its number in the text box, or by selecting it. Click Done.

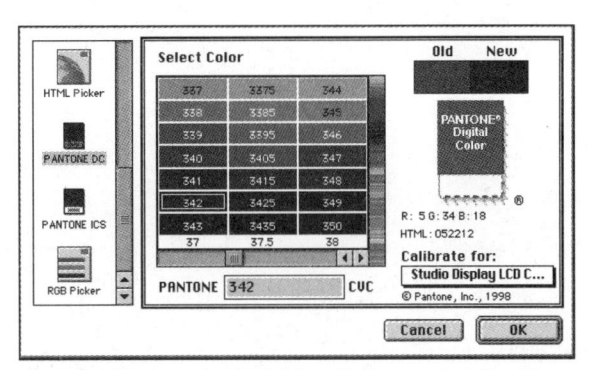

Figure 23-16: ColorWeb Pro offers you an extensive palette of Pantone colors within the Macintosh color picker dialog box.

Fireworks calculates the closest match using the Web Dither technique. If the Pantone color is Web-safe, both dither color wells hold the same color.

Summary

Fireworks offers brisk color control, enabling the designer to select from the overall color model and specific palette that best serves. As you begin to delve deeper into color with your Fireworks graphics, considers these points:

- RGB is the language of color for the screen. Pixels depend on a mixture of red, green, and blue in order to achieve their color variations. HTML uses hexadecimal notation to designate RGB colors.

- Fireworks enables you to switch between several color models, such as Hexadecimal, RGB, CMY, and grayscale.

- To ensure that your colors appear the same regardless of which browser you use to view them, work with Web-safe colors. Fireworks allows you to choose a Web-safe palette to pick colors from, and it enables you to snap selected colors to their nearest Web-safe equivalent.

- Fireworks uses three floating panels for color control: the Color Mixer, the Swatches panel, and the Color Table panel. The Color Mixer enables the designer to specify a new custom color or to modify an existing one. The Swatches panel displays a series of color chips that can come from a standard palette, such as Web 216, or from a custom palette. The Color Table panel displays the current document's export palette.

- The Eyedropper tool in the pop-up color picker can sample colors from any onscreen image, whether the image is in Fireworks or another application.

In the next chapter, you explore working with the fine lines of Fireworks graphics — strokes.

✦ ✦ ✦

Chapter 24

Choosing Strokes

In This Chapter

Applying strokes

Mastering the Stroke panel

Working with graphics tablets

Investigating with the standard strokes

Creating custom strokes

Fireworks technique: building a dotted stroke

Stroke orientation

Strokes are one of the three key features of a Fireworks document. Along with fills and effects, strokes can give each element its own unique character. The stroke is what makes a path visible. It's far more than just "visibility," however; you can vary a stroke's width, color, softness, and shape, as well as control how it reacts to the speed, pressure, and direction of your drawing. Moreover, you can modify strokes already applied to any selected path and instantly see the results.

In addition to 48 built-in, standard strokes in Fireworks, you can customize your strokes with an almost infinite set of variations. Numerous options, such as color, stroke width, and edge softness, exist right on the Strokes panel for easy experimentation. Additionally, Fireworks enables you to custom build your own stroke from the ground up. You can find explanations for all the controls in this chapter, as well as step-by-step instructions for developing special strokes, such as dotted lines.

Using the Stroke Panel

The Stroke panel is your control center for all stroke settings. Though you can set the stroke color in two other places, the Toolbox and the Color Mixer, the Stroke panel is the only place to select all the options.

Here's the typical process for setting up or modifying an existing stroke that uses all the options available on the Stroke panel:

1. Choose Window ⇨ Stroke to open the Stroke panel (see Figure 24-1). Alternatively, you can use the keyboard shortcut, Ctrl+Alt+F4 (Command+Option+F4), or choose the Stroke tab, if it's onscreen.

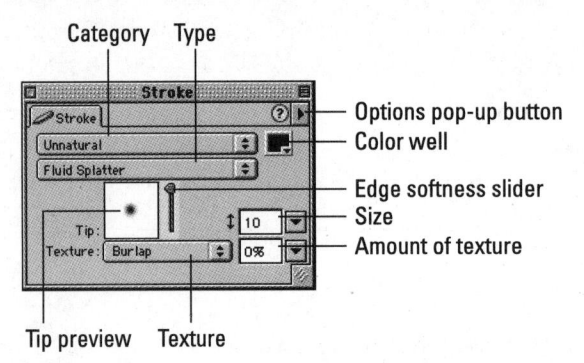

Figure 24-1: Use the Stroke panel controls to modify the stroke for an existing path or to establish a stroke before you draw with the Brush.

2. Select one of the 11 categories from the Category option list. To turn off the stroke, select None from the Category option list.

3. Choose any of the available types listed for each category from the Type option list. When you choose a type, the default settings for that type's size, edge softness, and texture are also selected.

4. If desired, select a new color from the stroke color well.

5. To change how the stroke blends, use the Edge Softness slider.

6. Alter the size of the stroke by using the Size slider, or by entering a value directly in the Size text box.

7. Add a texture by choosing one from the Texture option list and setting its opacity through the Amount of texture slider.

As noted previously, you can either modify the stroke for an existing, selected path, or you can set up the stroke before you draw. To select a path, with or without a stroke already applied, first move the Pointer tool over the desired path and then click the highlighted path once. The path displays a red highlight if it is capable of being selected and, by default, a light-blue highlight after it has been selected.

Tip If your work uses the same or similar color that Fireworks uses for highlighting a chosen path, you can change the color. Choose Edit ⇨ Preferences, and on the General tab (options list on Macintosh) select the Highlight color well in order to pick a different hue or shade.

Sometimes selecting the path for stroke modification by using the marquee feature of the Pointer tool is easier. If you click and drag the Pointer, a temporary rectangle is drawn out. Any paths touched by this rectangle are selected. The Pointer marquee is a great way to select multiple paths if you want to simultaneously change the stroke settings for several paths. Alternatively, pressing Shift enables you to select multiple paths, one at a time, with the Pointer tool.

> **Tip**
> You can quickly switch to the Pointer tool from any other tool by pressing and holding Ctrl (Command). When you release the key, the previously selected tool returns.

When you're setting up your next stroke, be sure that no path or object is selected — otherwise, that selected object will be modified. Use the Pointer to click an empty canvas area, or choose Edit ➪ Deselect — or its keyboard equivalent, Ctrl+D (Command+D) — to clear any previous selections.

Stroke categories and types

With the None option, Fireworks offers a dozen stroke categories. From the simplest, Pencil and Basic, to the most outrageous, Random and Unnatural, the stroke categories run the gamut, as evident in Figure 24-2. When you select a category, that category's types become available, with the first one in an alphabetical list chosen.

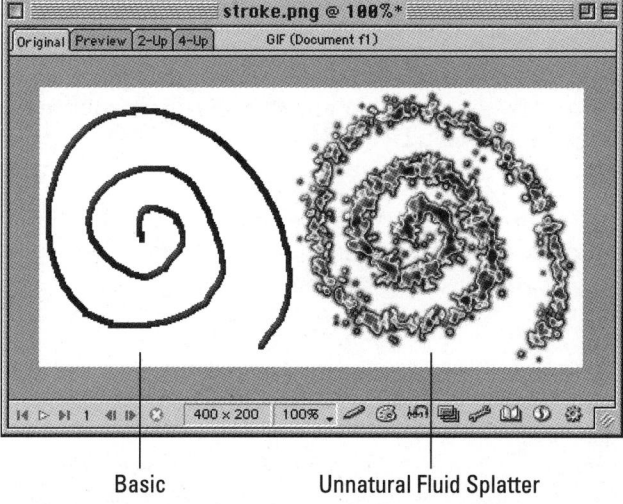

Figure 24-2: Choose any of the preset stroke types — from the Basic to the farthest out Unnatural Fluid Splatter.

The standard strokes are covered in detail later in this chapter, but two primary factors apply to all the basic strokes. First, when a particular stroke category and type are selected, the default settings for that stroke are selected — even if you just modified it seconds ago and are returning from trying out another stroke. Second, you can modify, alter, and adjust every facet of all the standard strokes.

> **Cross-Reference**
> Later in this chapter, in the section "Creating New Strokes," you discover how to store and reuse a modified stroke.

Stroke edge and size

If you're reading this book in sequence, you've already discovered the concept of feathering as it relates to bitmap images in Chapter 6. As you'll remember, a feathered edge is one that blends into the background. You can "feather" strokes through the Edge Softness slider found in the Stroke panel. Moving the slider all the way to the bottom creates the hardest edge, with no blending, whereas sliding it to the top creates the softest edge, with maximum blending for the current stroke size.

As in feathering, edge softness is actually an application of the alpha channel, which controls transparency. There are 256 degrees of transparency in the alpha channel and only 100 degrees of edge softness, but the overall control is similar. Although you can select any degree of softness from the full range for any stroke, you won't see much of a difference if the stroke is thin. The thicker the stroke, the more softness variations are apparent. At the softest setting, Fireworks maintains roughly two-thirds of the stroke size. The object's opacity and the other one-third are blended into transparency equally on either side of the stroke.

You can change the thickness of a stroke either by entering a value in the Size box, or by using the Size slider to select from the range of possible values: 1 to 72 pixels wide. The Tip preview is not big enough to show the full stroke width. On the Mac, the Tip preview stops being useful at about 50 pixels and just goes black; on Windows you'll notice "2x" or "4x" appears after about 50 pixels to indicate the actual width of large strokes, as shown in Figure 24-3.

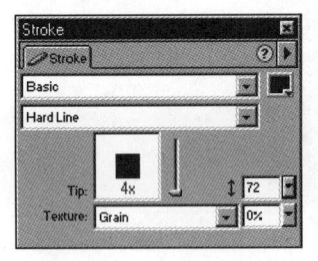

Figure 24-3: When you select a larger than the Tip preview can display, the Windows version of Fireworks compensates numerically.

Stroke texture

Applying texture to a stroke can give a line true character and depth. Fireworks comes with a number of standard textures built in and an additional library of them on the product's CD-ROM. You can apply each of these textures to any stroke with a variable degree of intensity. Some of the preset strokes, such as the Textured Air Brush or the Basic Crayon, use a texture to create their distinctive look.

To apply a texture to a stroke, follow these steps:

1. On the Stroke panel, select the category and type of stroke to which you want to apply the texture.
2. If necessary, set the size, color, and edge softness for the stroke. Note: Many textures will not be apparent if the stroke width is too small.
3. Choose a texture from the Texture option list.
4. Set a degree of intensity for the Texture from the Amount of texture slider. You can also enter a percentage value (with or without the percent sign) into the Amount of texture text box.

Note: You must enter a percentage value greater than 0 percent, or no texture will be visible.

Textures, in effect, are image patterns that are overlaid on top of the stroke. The Amount of texture slider controls how transparent or opaque those textures become. At 0 percent, the texture is transparent and, for all intents and purposes, nonexistent. At 100 percent, the texture is as visible as possible. Figure 24-4 displays the same stroke with several variations of a single texture. As a general rule, textures containing highly contrasting elements show up better, whereas those with less contrast are more subtle and probably only useful on extremely thick strokes.

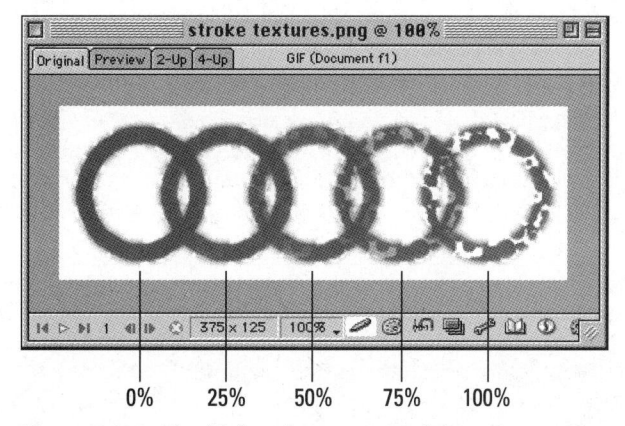

Figure 24-4: The higher the amount of the texture value, the more visible the texture becomes.

On the CD-ROM: Can't get enough of those fabulous textures? You'll find another 50, courtesy of Massimo Foti, in the Extensions folder of the CD-ROM.

Using a Graphics Tablet

Using a mouse to create objects is often derided as being like "drawing with a bar of soap," and for good reason. In the past, graphics tablets—flat panels that you draw on with a pen-like stylus—were often expensive, insensitive, and unwieldy. But, like most technologies, graphics tablets have steadily become cheaper and better. These days, a range of sizes and specifications are available for any Macintosh or Windows computer. For beginners or casual use, Wacom's Graphire is a 4×5-inch tablet that hardly costs more than a mouse. Wacom's professional range of Intuos tablets extends from 4×5 inches to 12×18 inches with features and options to satisfy any artist. However, a 4×5-inch tablet can be quite acceptable for the typically small canvases used for Web graphics.

There's really almost no learning curve to using a graphics tablet with Fireworks. Everything works as with the mouse, except that you have far more control. The first advantage is the accuracy provided by the tablet's one-to-one relationship with areas on the screen. The classic test is a signature—try signing your name with a mouse and then with a pen and tablet—there's a world of difference because similar horizontal and vertical movements of the mouse don't correspond to similar movements of the mouse pointer.

The more obvious advantage is that you're drawing with a pen, and the pressure that you apply directly affects the appearance of the strokes that you create. Press down harder and you'll get a heavier line, or use a lighter touch for a softer line. This feature often leads to a slightly more imperfect, or "human" look to the graphics that you create, and the imperfect appearance can be quite pleasing. Many standard Fireworks strokes are sensitive to pressure, including all the Air Brush, Calligraphy, Charcoal, Oil, and Watercolor presets. How strokes respond to pressure is also adjustable, as you discover later in this chapter when you look at how to create strokes.

Even if you're not much of an artist, I find that selecting tools and drawing rectangles and ovals is easier with a graphics tablet. After a short while, you'll find yourself "reaching" for objects on your canvas without having to look at them or track them down with a mouse, because they're always in the same place on your tablet. It's an intuitive and creative way to assemble computer graphics.

If you don't have a tablet, you can simulate increased or decreased pressure with your keyboard. Press 1 to decrease the pressure and 2 to increase it. Be aware, however, that unlike a graphics tablet, the pressure doesn't even out when you stop drawing. If you press 1 three times to decrease the pressure, the pressure will continue to be light until you press 2 three times to restore it to its default state, or until you relaunch Fireworks.

Working with the Built-in Strokes

One of the key advantages of Fireworks' preset strokes is speed—just pick one and go. The other main advantage is consistency. You can use the Textured Air Brush time and again, and you'll always get the same effect. Even if you prefer to work only with custom strokes, you generally begin the creation process with one of the standard ones.

This section explores each of the stroke categories and the different presets each one offers. Fireworks starts the stroke categories with two of the simplest, Pencil and Basic. After these, the list proceeds alphabetically from Air Brush to Unnatural. The overall impression, however, is that the more often-used standard strokes are at the top of the list, and the more elaborate decorative strokes at the end.

Pencil

When you start to draw with the Pencil tool, the path is rendered in the Pencil 1-Pixel Hard stroke, regardless of any previous stroke settings for other tools. If you use the Brush, and no stroke settings have been established, you get the same Pencil 1-Pixel Hard stroke. You might say that the Pencil is one of the real workhorses of the preset strokes.

The Pencil is a fairly generic stroke, intended to give a simple representation to any path without any embellishments. You can see the differences between its four presets, listed in Table 24-1, and depicted in Figure 24-5. The 1-Pixel Soft Pencil stroke antialiases the path to avoid the jaggies that may be apparent with the 1-Pixel Hard setting. The Colored Pencil, at four pixels, is slightly wider and is designed to be affected by pressure and speed in the same way that a real colored pencil would be affected. The final preset, Graphite, is also affected by the pressure and speed at which the paths are drawn; in addition, a high degree of texture is added to further break up the stroke.

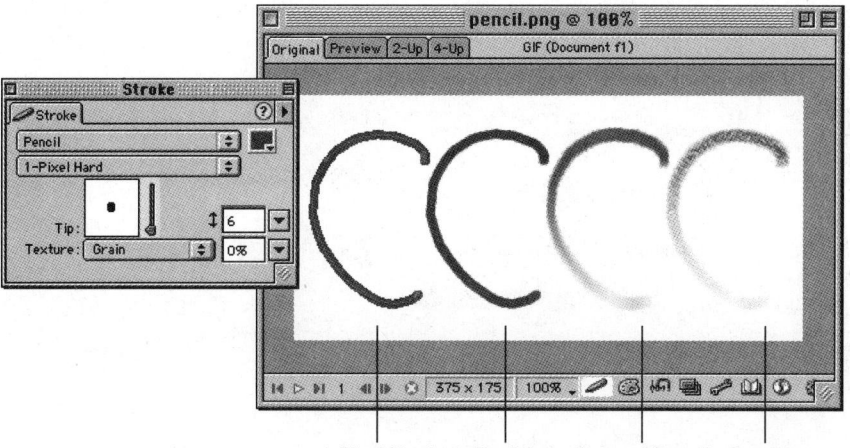

Figure 24-5: The 1-Pixel Hard and 1-Pixel Soft strokes remain constant when drawn, but the Colored Pencil and Graphite strokes are affected by pressure and speed.

Table 24-1
Pencil Type Attributes

Name	Size	Edge Softness	Texture	Amount of Texture
1-Pixel Hard	1	0 percent	None	n/a
1-Pixel Soft	1	0 percent	None	n/a
Colored Pencil	4	0 percent	None	n/a
Graphite	4	0 percent	Grain	80 percent

Basic

Another, slightly heavier variation of the simple path is the appropriately named Basic stroke. All the Basic presets, detailed in Table 24-2, are 4 pixels wide and vary only with the basic shape of the line (square or round) and its antialias setting. Hard Line and Hard Line Rounded are not antialiased, whereas both Soft Line and Soft Line Rounded are. The variations, shown in Figure 24-6, are subtle, but can make quite a difference on some objects.

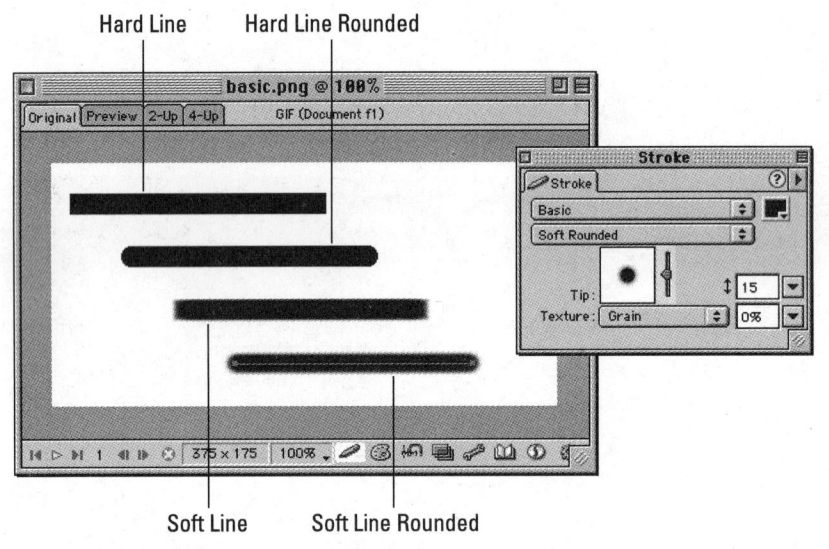

Figure 24-6: You can see the differences between the four Basic stroke types when you look closely at them.

Table 24-2
Basic Type Attributes

Name	Size	Edge Softness	Texture	Amount of Texture
Hard Line	4	0 percent	None	n/a
Hard Line Rounded	4	0 percent	None	n/a
Soft Line	4	0 percent	None	n/a
Soft Line Rounded	4	0 percent	None	n/a

Air Brush

I'll 'fess up — I'm an airbrush addict. I can't get enough of the variations that the Fireworks Air Brush stroke offers. Both presets (see Table 24-3) are very sensitive to changes in speed and pressure; plus — like a real airbrush — the ink builds up if you stay in one spot, as shown in Figure 24-7. The Textured Air Brush is significantly different from the Basic Air Brush and offers a good example of what's possible when applying a texture to a stroke.

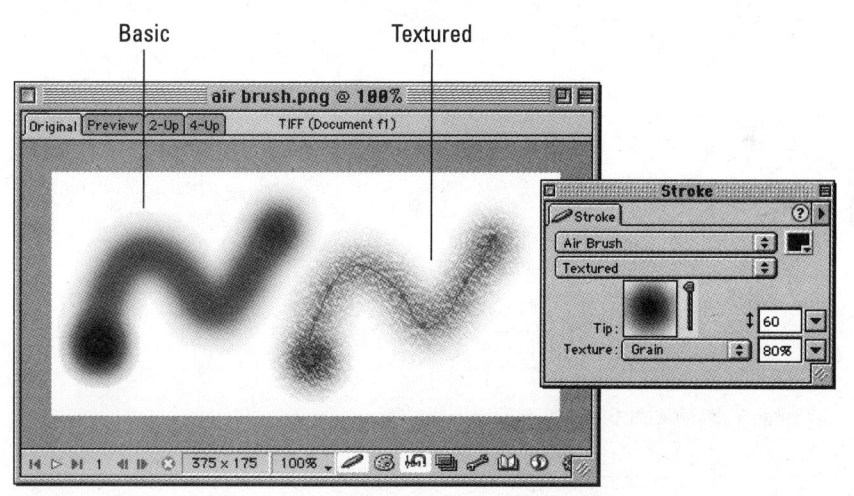

Figure 24-7: The difference between the two Air Brush presets is quite noticeable, as is the build-up on each at the end of the two strokes.

Table 24-3
Air Brush Type Attributes

Name	Size	Edge Softness	Texture	Amount of Texture
Basic	60	100 percent	None	n/a
Textured	50	100 percent	Grain	80 percent

Calligraphy

Calligraphy is an elegant handwriting art in which the thickness of a stroke varies as a line curves. The Calligraphy stroke in Fireworks offers five variations on this theme, as detailed in Table 24-4 and shown in Figure 24-8. Only the Bamboo preset does not create distinct thick-and-thin curved lines — that's because all the others use a slanted brush, whereas Bamboo's brush is circular, like a bamboo stalk. The Quill preset is pressure- and speed-sensitive and, along with the Ribbon and Wet presets, builds up ink as it rounds a curve, emphasizing the angles.

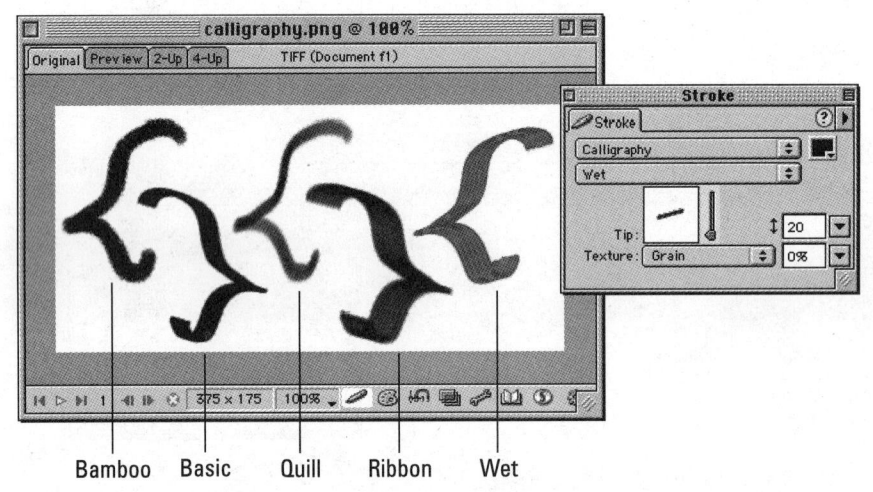

Figure 24-8: Great lettering possibilities are the hallmark of the Calligraphy stroke.

Table 24-4
Calligraphy Type Attributes

Name	Size	Edge Softness	Texture	Amount of Texture
Bamboo	20	0 percent	Grain	50 percent
Basic	14	0 percent	None	n/a
Quill	20	20 percent	Grain	25 percent
Ribbon	25	0 percent	None	n/a
Wet	20	0 percent	None	n/a

Charcoal

The Charcoal strokes are notable for their textures, both within the strokes themselves and on their edges. As you can see in Table 24-5, each preset uses some degree of Grain texture. The Creamy and Pastel presets vary according to a stroke's pressure and speed — Creamy more so than Pastel. The key difference between the Soft preset and the other preset strokes is that with the Soft preset the size of the brush changes randomly as you draw — the width fluctuates from a maximum of 20 pixels to a minimum of 5 pixels. Figure 24-9 shows a side-by-side comparison of the Charcoal presets.

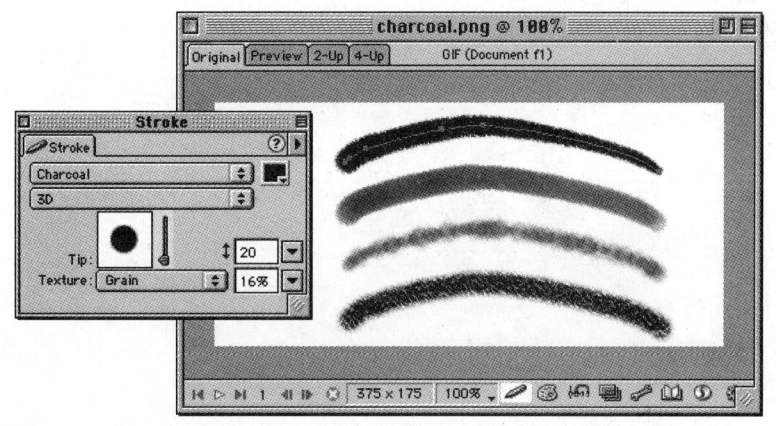

Figure 24-9: The Charcoal strokes offer a range of rough textures.

**Table 24-5
Charcoal Type Attributes**

Name	Size	Edge Softness	Texture	Amount of Texture
Creamy	20	0 percent	Grain	16 percent
Pastel	20	0 percent	Grain	24 percent
Soft	20	20 percent	Grain	30 percent
Textured	20	60 percent	Grain	85 percent

Crayon

Kids can never understand why their parents like to draw with crayons as much as they do. The Crayon stroke in Fireworks captures that broken edge that gives real-world crayons character. The three Crayon presets are interesting to compare; if you look at the samples in Figure 24-10 and their details in Table 24-6, you'll see an obvious anomaly. The Rake preset has the smallest stroke size, but actually appears slightly thicker than both the Basic and Thick preset. This difference is because the Rake preset uses four tips; it's as if you were simultaneously drawing with four crayons. Because there are four tips, the lines overlap, and one tip can extend farther than the other three.

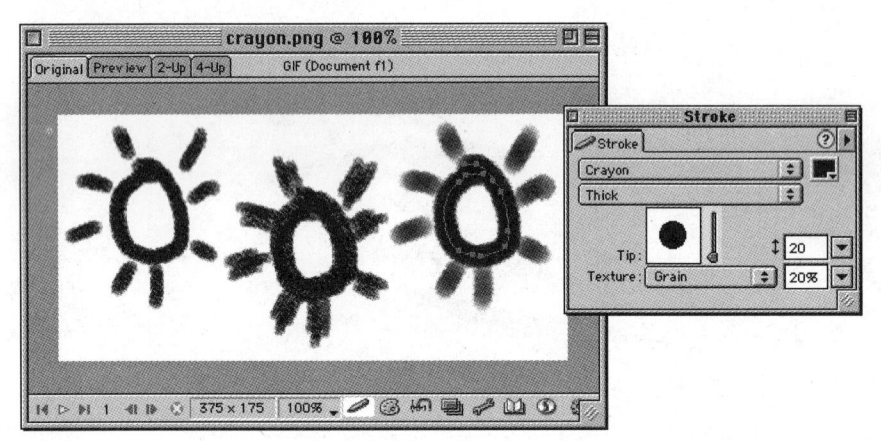

Figure 24-10: Return to your childhood—this time with scientific precision—through the Crayon strokes.

Table 24-6
Crayon Type Attributes

Name	Size	Edge Softness	Texture	Amount of Texture
Basic	12	0 percent	Grain	65 percent
Rake	8	0 percent	Grain	65 percent
Thick	20	0 percent	Grain	20 percent

Felt Tip

The four presets for the Felt Tip stroke, shown in Figure 24-11, offer different degrees of transparency that mimic the real-world drawing implements they're named after. The Highlighter and the Light Marker presets are largely transparent, in fact. The Light Marker also uses a slightly softer edge than the other presets, as noted in Table 24-7.

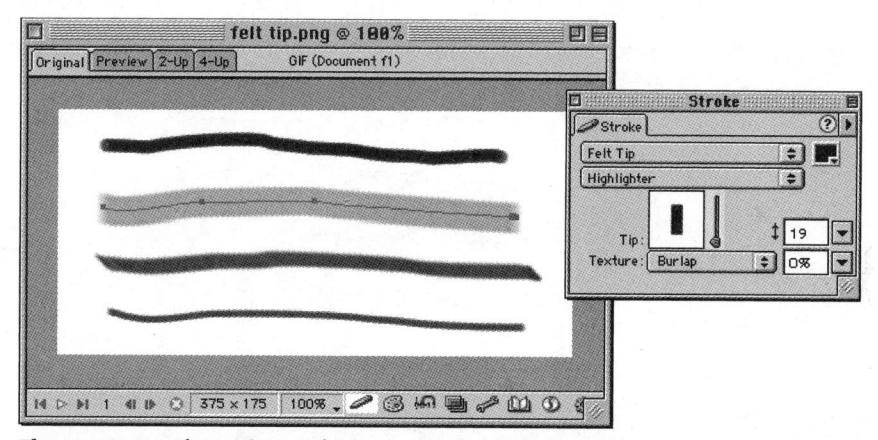

Figure 24-11: The various Felt Tip strokes achieve transparent and opaque effects when used over graphics or images.

Table 24-7
Felt Tip Type Attributes

Name	Size	Edge Softness	Texture	Amount of Texture
Dark Marker	8	0 percent	None	n/a
Highlighter	16	0 percent	None	n/a
Light Marker	12	5 percent	None	n/a
Thin	4	0 percent	None	n/a

Oil

When you look at the five Oil stroke presets in Figure 24-12, it's hard to believe that the second stroke from the left, Broad Splatter, is a single stroke. Although the size for Broad Splatter is only 10 pixels — the same as for the Bristle and Splatter presets, all shown in Table 24-8 — the larger width is because it uses two tips instead of one, and they're spaced 500 percent apart. In other words, the Broad Splatter preset can be five times the width of its pixel size. All but the Splatter preset use multiple tips, as well, but because they're set to be less than 100 percent apart, the strokes appear as single lines.

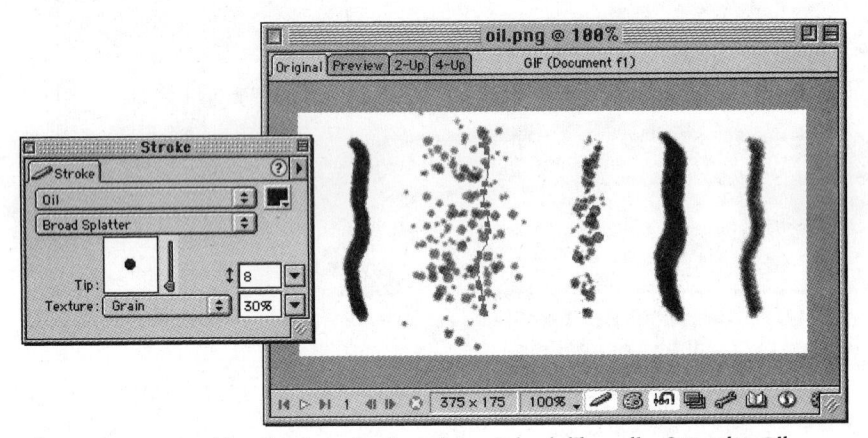

Figure 24-12: Looking for a stroke that doesn't look like a line? Try the Oil Splatter and Oil Broad Splatter presets.

Table 24-8
Oil Type Attributes

Name	Size	Edge Softness	Texture	Amount of Texture
Bristle	10	0 percent	Grain	20 percent
Broad Splatter	10	0 percent	Grain	30 percent
Splatter	10	0 percent	Grain	30 percent
Strands	8	43 percent	None	n/a
Textured Bristles	7	0 percent	Grain	50 percent

Watercolor

Like any of the pressure- and speed-sensitive strokes, you can't get a true Watercolor feel if you draw using one of the geometric shapes; you have to use a freeform tool, such as the Brush, to achieve the more realistic look apparent in Figure 24-13. The Thin preset especially appears to run out of ink when completing a stroke. Both the Heavy and Thick presets are quite transparent and blend well when applied over an image because of their relatively soft edges (see Table 24-9).

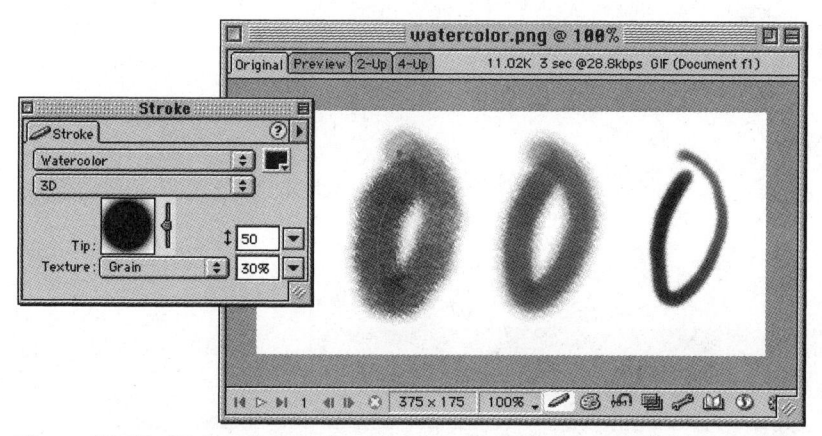

Figure 24-13: Watercolor strokes blend well and fade naturally due to their pressure and speed sensitivity.

Table 24-9
Watercolor Type Attributes

Name	Size	Edge Softness	Texture	Amount of Texture
Heavy	50	50 percent	Grain	30 percent
Thick	40	70 percent	Grain	5 percent
Thin	15	25 percent	None	n/a

Random

So much for natural media — it's time to create strokes that only a computer can create. In addition to the varying sizes, edge softness, and textures shown in Table 24-10, Random strokes also change the shape and color of the resulting stroke. The basic brush shape is evident both by the Random preset names — Dots, Fur, Squares, and Yarn — and in the sample strokes shown in Figure 24-14, but you'll have to turn to the color insert to really see the color variations. The Confetti preset is the most colorful and Dots the least colorful, but all the Random strokes exhibit some changing hues.

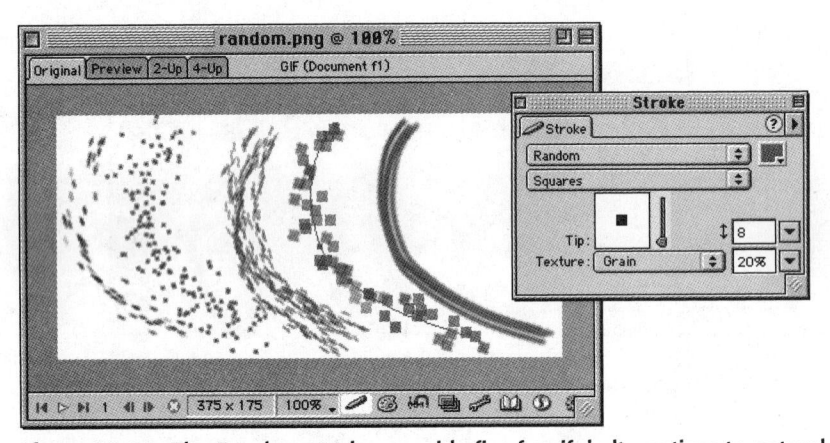

Figure 24-14: The Random strokes provide five fanciful alternatives to natural media strokes.

Table 24-10
Random Type Attributes

Name	Size	Edge Softness	Texture	Amount of Texture
Confetti	6	25 percent	None	n/a
Dots	3	20 percent	None	n/a
Fur	10	0 percent	None	n/a
Squares	5	0 percent	Grain	20 percent
Yarn	8	0 percent	None	n/a

Unnatural

I think it's a pretty safe bet that the Unnatural strokes were developed in a, shall we say, party-like atmosphere. How else do you explain the messiness of Fluid Splatter, or the glow-in-the-dark feel of Toxic Waste — not to mention the otherworldliness of Viscous Alien Paint? No matter how they were developed, I find myself returning to them time and again when I need a unique and distinctive look for my graphics. Experiment by applying them to almost any object when you're up against a creative wall; the results are often surprising and useful. As you can see in Table 24-11, all the presets are roughly the same size, with the exception of Chameleon. Several of the strokes have a transparent area: 3D Glow, Fluid Splatter, Outline, Paint Splatter, and Toxic Waste. Although you can get a sense of the preset variations from Figure 24-15, you'll have to turn to the color insert to see the Unnatural strokes in all their glory.

Table 24-11
Unnatural Type Attributes

Name	Size	Edge Softness	Texture	Amount of Texture
3D	20	12 percent	None	n/a
3D Glow	19	100 percent	None	n/a
Chameleon	6	0 percent	Grain	31 percent
Fluid Splatter	12	100 percent	None	n/a
Outline	19	100 percent	None	n/a
Paint Splatter	12	100 percent	None	n/a
Toothpaste	18	50 percent	None	n/a
Toxic Waste	18	100 percent	None	n/a
Viscous Alien Paint	12	30 percent	None	n/a

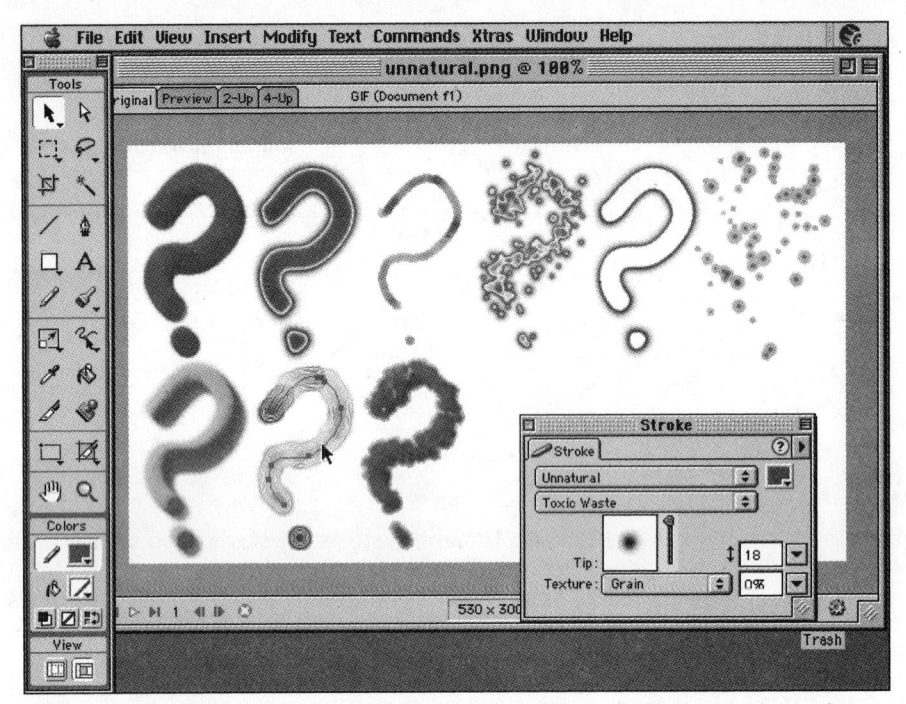

Figure 24-15: The Unnatural strokes provide an offbeat alternative to Fireworks' natural media strokes.

Creating New Strokes

What, the standard 48 strokes aren't enough? You need a slightly smaller Air Brush or a Calligraphy stroke with more texture? What about a dashed or dotted line instead of a solid one? Fear not; in Fireworks, custom strokes are just a click or two away. Not only can you store your minor adjustments as new strokes, but you can completely alter existing strokes and save them, either within the document or as a Fireworks Style that you can use in any document, or export and share with a colleague or workgroup.

This section is divided into two parts. The first section explains how to manage your strokes so that the ones you need are always available. The second part delves into the somewhat complex—but altogether addictive—option of editing your strokes.

Managing your strokes

Stroke management is handled through the Stroke panel pop-up menu, which is shown in Figure 24-16.

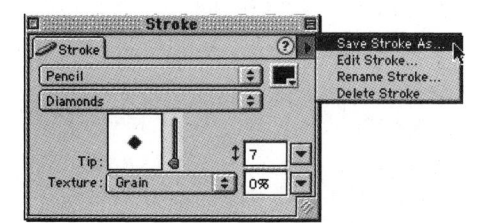

Figure 24-16: Manage your strokes through the Strokes panel pop-up menu.

The pop-up menu contains four menu commands:

+ **Save Stroke As:** Stores the current stroke under a new name within the active document

+ **Edit Stroke:** Displays the Edit Stroke dialog box, covered in detail later in this chapter

+ **Delete Stroke:** Removes the current stroke, custom or standard, from the Stroke panel

Caution Use the Delete Stroke command carefully — although Fireworks asks for confirmation, you can't undo removing a stroke.

+ **Rename Stroke:** Relabels the current stroke

To store a modified stroke, follow these steps:

1. Modify any existing stroke by changing the Edge Softness, Size, Texture, and/or Amount of texture. The stroke color is not stored as part of the stroke.

2. Choose Save Stroke As from the pop-up menu. The Save Brush As dialog box appears. Fireworks 1 users will remember that strokes were previously known as brushes.

3. Enter a unique name for the stroke. If you choose a name already in use, Fireworks asks whether you want to replace the existing brush.

4. After entering a new name, choose Save. The new stroke name is displayed alphabetically in the Type list options of the active Stroke category.

It's important to understand that any new or modified strokes are stored within the document in which they're used. The newly defined stroke will always be available for use in the document in which it was stored, even if no paths currently employ it. To use the stroke in another document, follow these steps:

1. Open the document containing the stroke you want to use.
2. Select a path using the new stroke. If no path currently uses the stroke, draw a temporary one and select it.
3. Open the new document in which you want to use the new stroke.
4. Copy the selected path to the new document, either by using Edit ⇨ Copy and Edit ⇨ Paste, or by dragging and dropping the path from one document to the other. The new stroke setting is added to the Stroke panel when the path containing the stroke is pasted into the document.
5. If desired, delete the copied path from the new document; the stroke will still be available for later use in the document.

You can achieve the same effect of transferring strokes from one document to another in several other ways:

- Import a document containing one or more custom strokes. After you've clicked once to place the document, choose Undo. The graphics will vanish, but all custom strokes will be incorporated into the Strokes panel. With this technique, only custom strokes actually applied to paths in the source document are transferred.
- Copy the path with the custom stroke in one document, and just paste the attributes to a path in the new document by selecting that path and choosing Edit ⇨ Paste Attributes.

Perhaps the best way to always be sure your custom strokes are available is to use the Styles feature. To create a new style using a custom stroke, follow these steps:

1. Select a path that uses the custom stroke.
2. If necessary, choose Window ⇨ Styles, use the keyboard shortcut Shift+F11, or click the Style tab, if visible, to display the Styles panel.
3. On the Styles panel, select the New Style button. The New Style dialog box appears, as shown in Figure 24-17.
4. In the Edit Style dialog box, enter a descriptive name for your stroke in the Name text box and deselect all checkboxes except Stroke Type.
5. Click OK when you're done. A new style is entered in the Styles panel.

Any style added in the fashion just described is always available for any Fireworks document. To apply the stroke, just highlight any Fireworks path object and select the new style. Your custom stroke is then added to the Stroke panel.

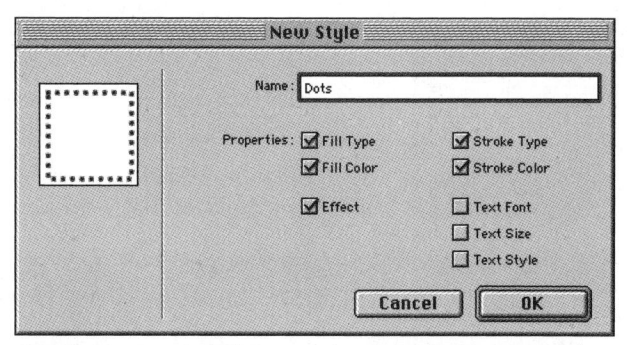

Figure 24-17: Declaring a stroke through the New Style dialog box stores the stroke definition for easy access from all Fireworks documents.

> **Cross-Reference:** To find out more about the powerful Styles feature, see Chapter 31.

Editing the stroke

Whereas you can make certain modifications through the Strokes panel, if you really want to customize your strokes, you have to use the Edit Stroke dialog box. Although the array of choices the dialog box offers can be a bit overwhelming, after you understand how to achieve certain effects, creating new strokes becomes easy, fun, and compelling.

You can access the Edit Stroke dialog box in one of two ways:

- ✦ Choose Edit Stroke from the Strokes panel pop-up menu.
- ✦ Double-click the Strokes panel Tip preview where the stroke shape is displayed.

The Edit Stroke dialog box is divided into three tabs: Options, Shape, and Sensitivity. Each of the tabs contains a preview panel that updates after every change is made. If you have selected a stroke prior to opening the Edit Stroke dialog box, you can also see the effect by using the Apply button.

> **Caution:** In my explorations of the Edit Stroke dialog box, I uncovered one technique that worked differently than I expected. First, if you make a change to a stroke without selecting a path, the change does not register. Always select a path, even a temporary one, before you create a custom stroke.

The Options tab

The Options tab hosts a number of general, but important, attributes. In addition to providing controls for familiar parameters, such as a stroke's degree of texture and opacity, the Options tab, as shown in Figure 24-18, also holds the key to affecting the tightness of the stroke, how it reacts over time, and what, if any, edge effect is employed.

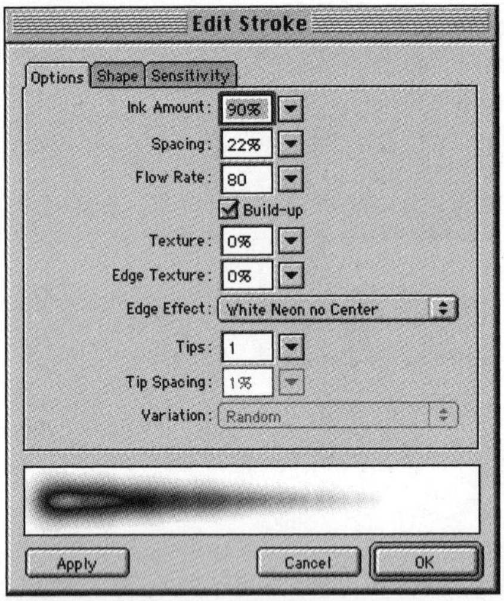

Figure 24-18: The Options tab of the Edit Stroke dialog box contains many key controls.

Ink Amount

The first stroke attribute on the Option tab is Ink Amount. Generally, this parameter is set at 100 percent, but lowering it is a possibility for any stroke. The Ink Amount value is responsible for a stroke's opacity: 100 percent is completely opaque, and 0 percent is completely transparent. The bottom of the two "CLICK" buttons in Figure 24-19 shows how a stroke is affected when the Ink Amount is reduced to 60 percent.

You can also alter an object's overall opacity through the Object panel, but changing just the Ink Amount value alters just the stroke. Combine the two and the effect is additive; if, for example, you see a stroke's Ink Amount at 50 percent and you reduce the opacity of the path object to 50 percent, the stroke would appear to be 25 percent opaque (because half of 50 percent is 25 percent). The Felt Tip Highlighter preset is a good example of a stroke that uses a reduced Ink Amount in order to obtain transparency.

Spacing

Technically, each stroke consists of a long series of stroke *stamps*. A stamp is the smallest unit of a stroke; you can see it by selecting a stroke and the Brush tool, and then clicking the mouse once, without moving. As you draw with the Brush or another tool, one stamp after another is laid down. How close those stamps are to each other is determined by the Spacing attribute. As detailed later in this chapter, you can create dotted lines by changing the Spacing value.

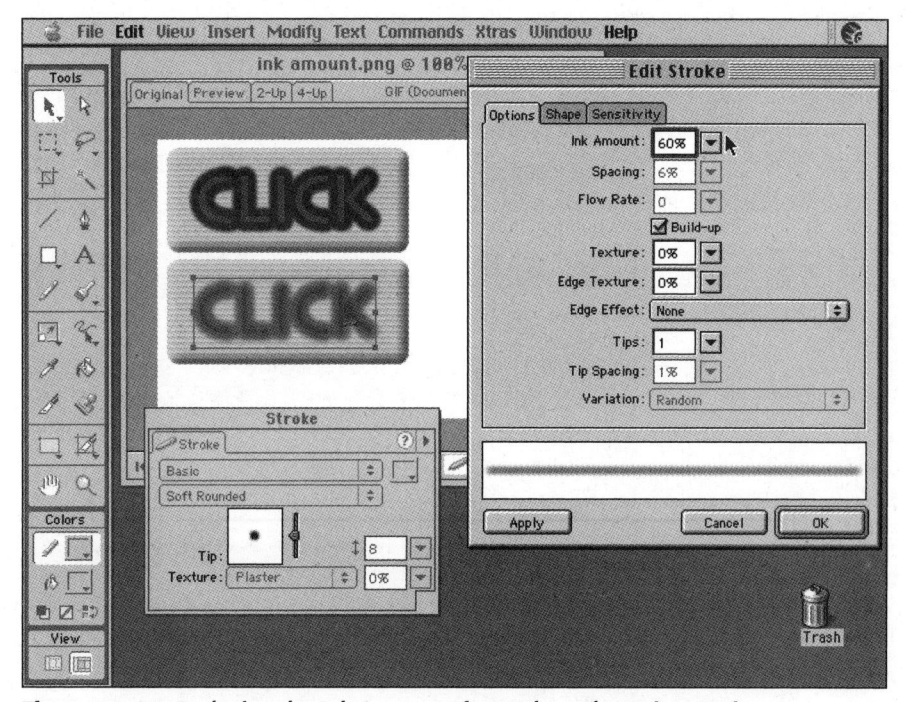

Figure 24-19: Reducing the Ink Amount of a stroke reduces its opacity.

> **Note**
> If you try to modify the Pencil 1-Pixel strokes or any of the Basic strokes, you'll find that no matter what you do, you won't be able to enable the Spacing or Flow Rate options. These strokes actually use a different rendering engine than all the other strokes, which sacrifices spacing and flow control to gain pinpoint pixel accuracy. To see the effects of changing either the Spacing or Flow Rate options, edit any other stroke.

The Spacing value ranges from 0 percent to 1,000 percent. If the Spacing attribute is set at 100 percent, stroke stamps in a straight line are positioned directly next to each other. If the Spacing is less than 100 percent, the stamps are overlaid on top of one another. If the Spacing is greater than 100 percent, the stamps are separated from one another. Strokes with a soft edge, such as the Air Brush, appear to be separated even when the Spacing is set to less than 100 percent, but this is only because the soft edge is incorporated into the stroke stamp. The effect in Figure 24-20 is achieved by increasing the spacing of a Felt Tip stroke to more than 200 percent.

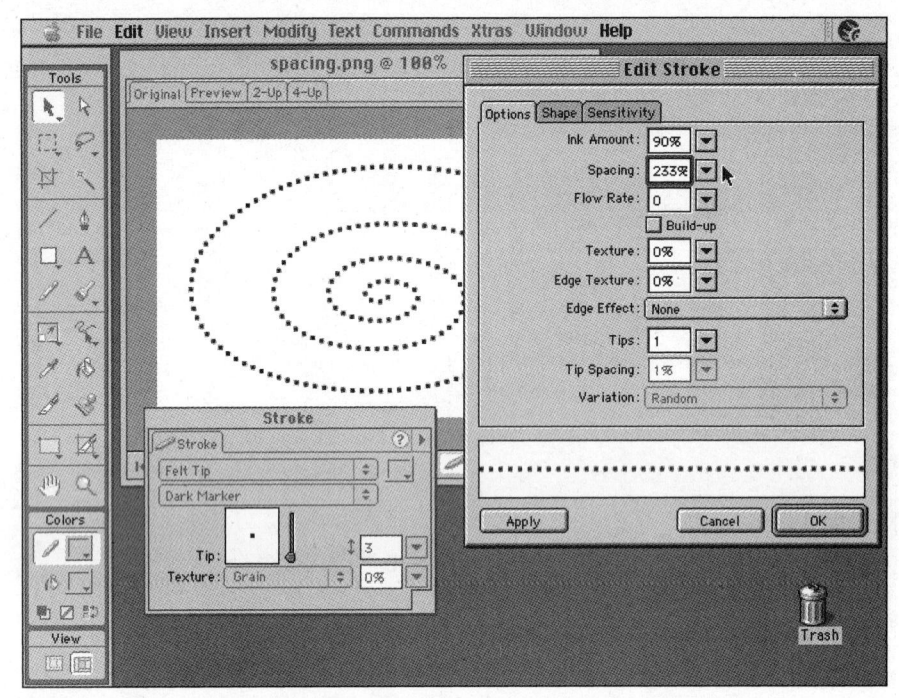

Figure 24-20: Create dotted line patterns by increasing the Spacing value.

Flow Rate and Build-up

Most stroke settings alter how a stroke changes as it's drawn across a screen. However, the Flow Rate percentage value represents how fast ink flows; the higher the number, the faster it flows. The Air Brush category is the best example of the use of Flow Rate. Both preset Air Brushes, Basic and Textured, use a fairly high value of 80 percent.

The Build-up option is another way of affecting a stroke's opacity. If Build-up is enabled, for example, as with the Air Brush preset, and the stroke crosses itself as in Figure 24-21, you'll notice a darker area at the overlap of the stroke. If you disable the Build-up option, the stroke has a much flatter, monochrome appearance.

Texture, Edge Texture, and Edge Effect

The Texture setting in the Edit Stroke dialog box is reflected on the Stroke panel as the Amount of Texture value. Increase the Texture value to make the chosen texture more visible on the opaque portion of the stroke; a value of 0 percent effectively turns off the texture.

Figure 24-21: With the Build-up option enabled, the Air Brush stroke acts like a real airbrush, building up where it crosses itself.

Caution
You cannot specify the type of texture from within the Edit Stroke dialog box; you must set it through the Stroke panel. Whereas the texture type is saved with the stroke when you select the Save Stroke As command, if another texture type is chosen temporarily, the original texture does not reappear when you reselect the custom stroke. Reload the document with the saved stroke in order to again establish the custom texture settings.

Just as the Texture value causes the chosen texture to appear over the opaque portion of the stroke, the Edge Texture setting causes the texture to appear over the transparent portion. Remember that in Fireworks, you create edge softness by affecting the stroke's alpha channels or transparency. By increasing the Edge Texture and lowering the Texture value, the soft edge of the stroke is textured more noticeably than the center.

Note
Edge Texture values, no matter how high, will be, in effect, invisible if the Edge Softness is at 0 percent.

In addition to altering an edge's texture, you can also create an Edge Effect. Technically speaking, the five Edge Effects are created by applying an algorithm affecting the alpha channel for both the stroke and its edge. In this case, descriptions are a poor second to a visual representation of the intriguingly named Edge Effects, shown in Figure 24-22. Because Edge Effects rely on the transparency of the stroke's edge, you can't apply an Edge Effect to a stroke with a 0 percent Edge Softness value.

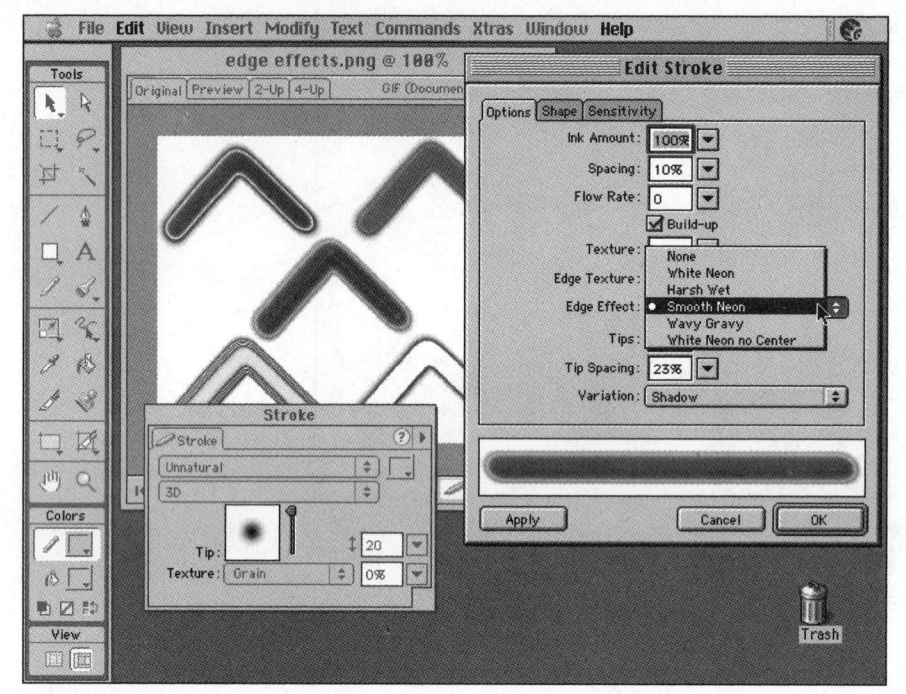

Figure 24-22: The five preset Edge Effects combine both stroke and edge transparency.

Tips, Tip Spacing, and Variations

Have you ever drawn with a fistful of colored pencils or noticed, too late, that your paint brush has dried with the bristles separated? In each case, the result is a series of separate strokes that curve and move together. In Fireworks jargon, each pencil or separate bristle is referred to as a *tip* and is determined by the Tips attribute. Every stroke must have at least one and can have as many as ten tips.

> **Note** For either the Tip Spacing or Variations attribute to become active, you must have more than one tip.

Whether the number of tips is apparent or not is determined primarily by the Tip Spacing attribute. Similar to the Spacing parameter, Tip Spacing is set in a range from 0 percent (where each tip is drawn on top of one another) to 1,000 percent (where each tip is as far apart as possible). You can see the results of an extreme experiment in Figure 24-23, where the Unnatural 3D stroke is set to use one, five, and ten tips with a Tip Spacing of 1,000 percent. A single star was drawn for each graphic.

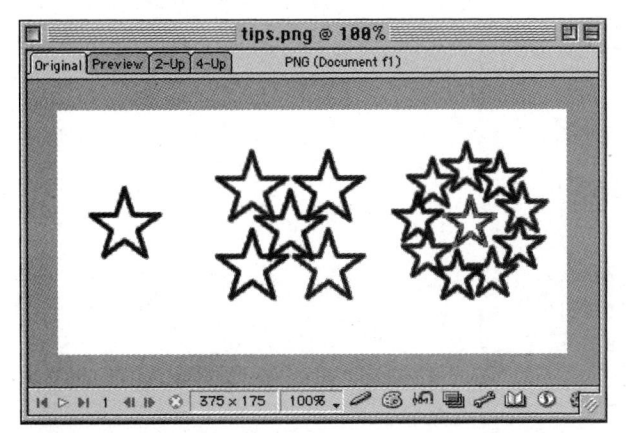

Figure 24-23: Although it looks like the stars in the two groups were cloned, only a single star was drawn in each group; multiple tips and wide Tip Spacing are the key to drawing many identical images with one stroke.

Variations are the final elements on the Options tab. When multiple tips are used, how the different tips are depicted is determined by which of the Variations are selected. Each of the Variations alter the color of the additional tips. The five Variations are as follows:

- **Random:** A new color is selected at random for each tip with each new stroke.
- **Uniform:** All tips use the base color selected in the Stroke color well.
- **Complementary:** If the stroke uses two tips, one tip is displayed in the complementary color (on the opposite side of an HLS (Hue, Lightness, Saturation) color wheel) of the base color. If more than two tips are specified, the additional tips are selected from evenly spaced hues that are located between the initial complementary colors.
- **Hue:** Multiple tips are presented in hues similar (plus or minus 5 percent on an HLS color wheel) to the stroke color.
- **Shadow:** Additional tips are shown in alternating lighter and darker shades of the stroke color (the Lightness).

The Shape tab

Compared to the Object tab, the Shape tab of the Edit Stroke dialog box (see Figure 24-24) is almost self-explanatory. The upper pane shows the stroke stamp, and the lower pane shows a representation of the stroke over distance.

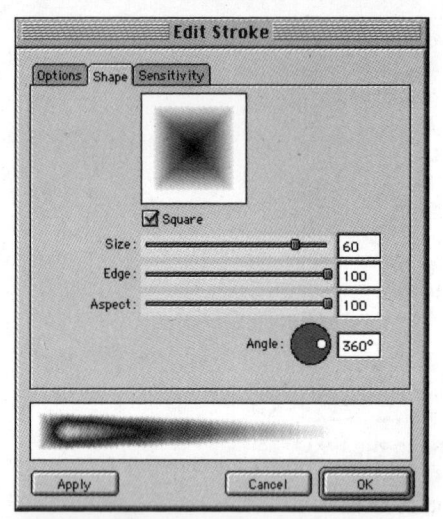

Figure 24-24: The look of the stroke stamp, and ultimately the stroke itself, is influenced by the attributes of the Shape tab.

The Shape tab offers the following five parameters:

- **Square:** When enabled, the Square option makes the stroke stamp square or rectangular, according to the Aspect setting. If Square is disabled, the stroke stamp is circular or elliptical.

- **Size:** Sets the initial stroke width, in pixels, from 1 to 100. The value is displayed in Stroke panel.

- **Edge:** Determines the softness of the stroke's edge. This value is also reflected in the Stroke panel.

- **Aspect:** Sets the height to width aspect ratio. Values 0 and 100 make circles or squares — any other value creates rectangles or ellipses.

- **Angle:** Determines the angle of the stroke stamp. You can enter values directly, or drag the dial in a circle.

You can achieve a wide range of different shapes by combining different parameters from the Shape tab. I've found the Aspect and Angle controls to be especially useful. For example, I used them to create a diamond dotted stroke, as detailed later in this chapter.

The Sensitivity tab

The Sensitivity tab of the Edit Stroke dialog box, shown in Figure 24-25, permits you to establish somewhat interactive controls for custom strokes. By altering your drawing pressure, speed, or direction, your strokes can assume different sizes, angles, opacities, or colors. You can even set up the stroke to alter any of its properties randomly.

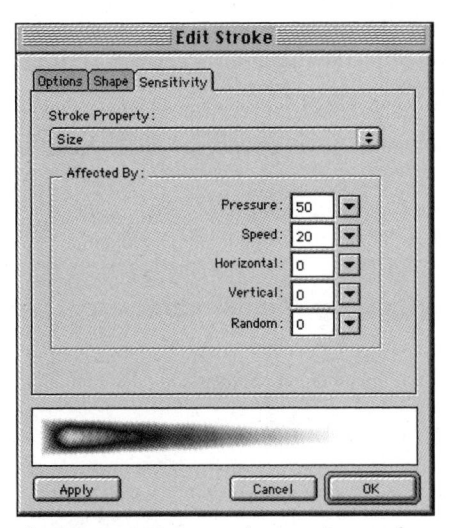

Figure 24-25: Create interactive strokes through the Sensitivity tab of the Edit Stroke dialog box.

The basic procedure for working in the Sensitivity tab is to select one of the stroke attributes from the Brush Properties option list, and then set the desired control found in the Affected By area. For example, if you wanted your stroke to shift colors when it is drawn across the document but not down it, you would choose Hue from the Brush Properties option list and set the Affected By Horizontal value to a high percentage value. The higher the value, the more impact the condition (Pressure, Speed, and so on) will have.

The seven stroke attributes are as follows:

- **Size:** When the Size property is affected, the stroke always gets smaller than the initial width, never larger. If the setting is at 50 percent, the stroke loses, at most, one-half of its size.
- **Angle:** The angle of the stroke stamp can be affected by as much as 90 degrees if Angle property is selected and an Affected By value is set to its maximum, 100 percent.
- **Ink Amount:** As on the Options tab, Ink Amount refers to opacity. At the highest setting, the affecting condition can make the stroke transparent.
- **Scatter:** The amount of variance with which stroke stamps are drawn away from the path. Scatter is really only effective with the Random condition.
- **Hue:** The color of the stroke. Multicolored strokes, such as those in the Random category, make great use of this property.
- **Lightness:** The amount of white in a color. To make a stroke fade more as you draw faster, choose the Lightness property and increase the Speed condition.

- **Saturation:** The intensity of the color. The higher the value set in the condition, the more the Saturation lessens. A stroke with a high Speed setting for Saturation becomes grayer as the path is drawn faster.

The conditions that affect these properties each have a separate slider and text box for entering values directly:

- **Pressure:** The degree of pressure applied by a stylus used with a pressure-sensitive graphics tablet.
- **Speed:** The amount of speed used when a path is drawn either with a graphics tablet or a mouse.
- **Horizontal:** Drawing paths from left to right, or vice versa.
- **Vertical:** Drawing paths from top to bottom, or vice versa.
- **Random:** The selected property is affected without any additional input from the user.

The Affected By conditions can be used together. For example, setting Angle to be equally affected by both the Horizontal and Vertical conditions causes a stroke, such as Random Fur, to change direction as the path is drawn.

Generally, the Sensitivity tab settings tend to react more predictably with hand-drawn paths, such as those created with the Brush tool, than paths constructed with one of the geometric shapes, such as the Rectangle or Ellipse. However, experimentation is the key to uncovering unique effects with almost all the Edit Stroke parameters, and you have nothing to lose by trying a particular setting.

Fireworks Technique: Making Dotted Lines

All the strokes in Fireworks' standard arsenal are more or less solid lines with nothing that you can use as a dotted line. Although a few exceptions exist, such as most of the Random presets, these tend to be too unconventional to use for a basic dotted line. As discussed in the previous section, however, Fireworks offers you a tremendous degree of control in customizing your own strokes. The procedure for creating a dotted line is fairly straightforward and a good introduction to the world of custom stroke creation.

The key to creating a dotted line is in the Spacing control found on the Options tab of the Edit Stroke dialog box. When the Spacing value is 100 percent, each stroke stamp (the smallest component of a stroke) is right next to the one following it. If the value is less than 100 percent, the stroke stamps overlap and — here's the heart of the dotted line — when the value is greater than 100 percent, the stroke stamps are separated.

When creating any custom stroke, you want to start with the built-in stroke that's closest to your goal. Although either of the Basic or Pencil 1-Pixel strokes would be ideal, the key attribute for creating a dotted line, Spacing, is not available for these strokes. As explained earlier in this chapter, these strokes are rendered with an eye toward pixel precision that is incompatible with the Spacing and Flow attributes. However, one of the other Pencil presets, Colored Pencil, works quite well as a stroke on which to build a custom dotted line, with a minimum of adjustments required.

To create a simple dotted line, follow these steps:

1. Display the Stroke panel by choosing Window ➪ Stroke or selecting its tab, if it is visible.
2. Choose Pencil from the Category option list.
3. Choose Colored Pencil from the Type option list.
4. Open the Edit Stroke dialog box by choosing Edit Stroke from the Strokes panel pop-up menu, or by double-clicking the Tip preview pane.
5. On the Options tab of the Edit Stroke dialog box, change the Spacing value from 15 percent to 200 percent.

    You'll notice in the preview pane that you now have a dotted line, as shown in Figure 24-26.

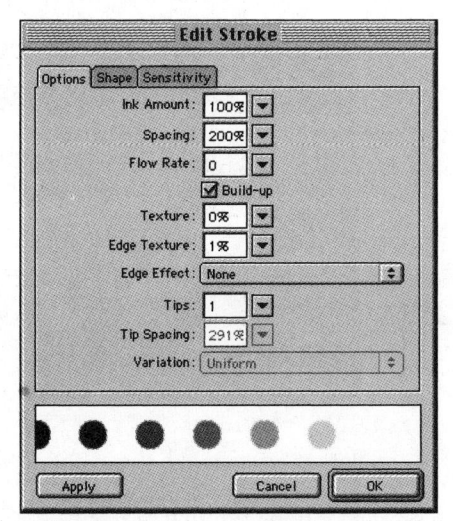

Figure 24-26: You can easily create a dotted line by modifying the Edit Stroke settings.

6. Click OK when you're done.

7. From the pop-up menu, choose Save Stroke As.

8. In the Save Stroke As dialog box, enter a unique name for the custom stroke.

Test out your new dotted line by using almost any of the path drawing tools — the Rectangle, Ellipse, Polygon, Brush, or Pen.

Now that you've seen how easy customizing a brush stroke is, try a few variations, such as the ones shown in Figure 24-27. Each set of instructions assumes that you're working in the Edit Stroke dialog box.

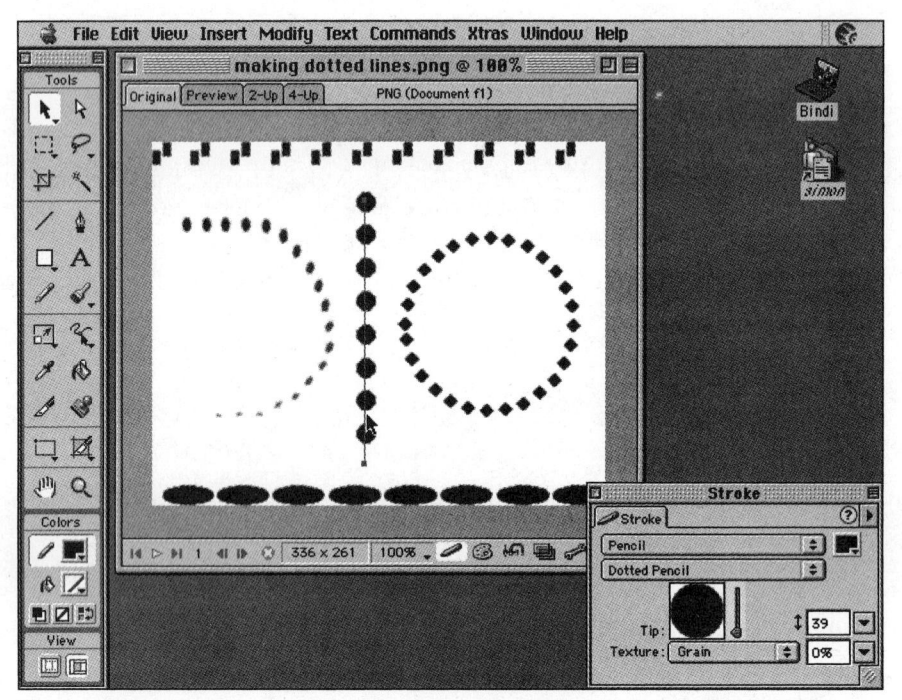

Figure 24-27: You can create a wide variety of dotted lines by modifying the Edit Stroke settings.

To give the dotted line a harder, more consistent edge, make these changes:

✦ Change the Edge Texture value on the Options tab to 0 percent.

✦ On the Shape tab, change the Edge value to 0 percent.

✦ On the Sensitivity tab, change the Size Speed setting to 0, the Ink Amount Pressure and Speed settings to 0, and the Lightness Pressure and Speed settings to 0.

Make these changes in order to create a dotted line with circles instead of squares:

- ✦ On the Shape tab, deselect the Square option.
- ✦ Also on the Shape tab, change the Aspect value to 100.

To create a horizontal line with dashes, change these values:

- ✦ From the Shape tab, change the Aspect value to 50.
- ✦ Also on the Shape tab, change the Angle to 0.

To create a vertical line with dashes, change these values:

- ✦ From the Shape tab, change the Aspect value to 50.
- ✦ Also on the Shape tab, change the Angle to 270.

Change the following values in order to create a dotted line with diamonds:

- ✦ From the Shape tab, make sure the Square option is selected.
- ✦ Also on the Shape tab, change the Aspect value to 100.
- ✦ Change the Angle to 45.

Orienting the Stroke

Strokes are useful, whether they are intended for an open path, such as a line, or a closed path, such as a circle or rectangle. When a stroke is applied to a closed path, however, Fireworks offers an additional set of options. By default, when strokes are rendered they are centered on a path. Select any closed path object and you'll see the stroke rendered on either side of the actual path. The orientation of a stroke to a path can be changed: the stroke can also be drawn completely inside the path or outside the path. As you can see from Figure 24-28, wildly different effects are possible with this option.

The controls for orienting a stroke to a path are in the Object panel. The three buttons, respectively from left to right, place the stroke inside the path, centered on the path, or outside the path. A fourth option, Draw Fill over Stroke, is located below the stroke orientation controls. By default, the stroke always appears on top of the fill color, Pattern, or gradient. However, by enabling the Draw Fill over Stroke option, you can reverse this preference.

Tip By combining the Draw Fill over Stroke option with a stroke rendered on the center of the path and a fill with a feathered edge, the stroke appears to blend into the fill while retaining a hard outer edge.

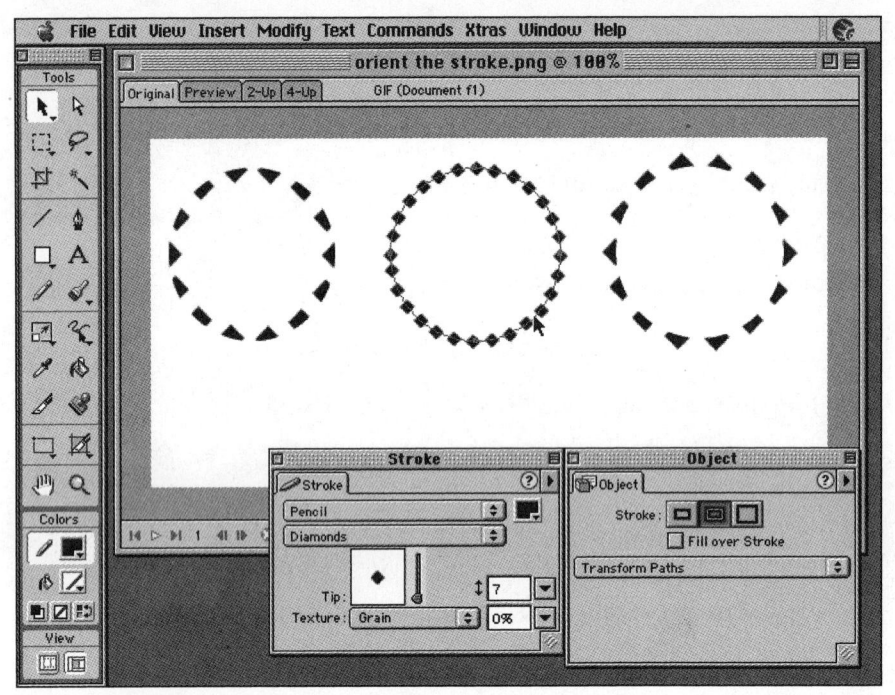

Figure 24-28: The same stroke is rendered outside the path, centered on the path, and inside the path.

One of my favorite applications of the stroke orientation controls is to use inside strokes as a sort of auxiliary fill, creating the effect of a more complex fill, as shown in Figure 24-29. Hard to believe Fireworks allows you to do this kind of thing completely with paths!

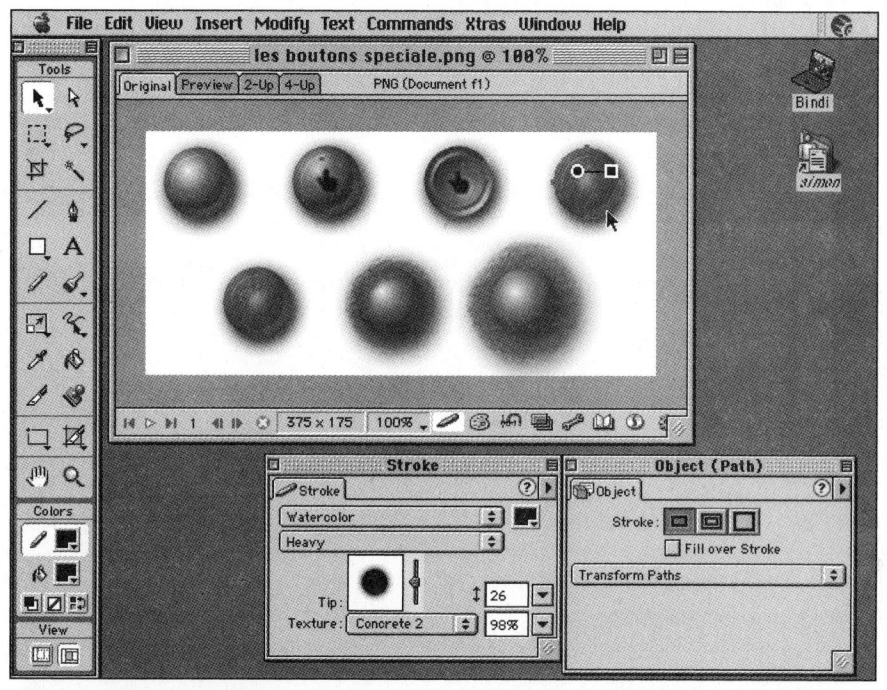

Figure 24-29: Inside strokes figure prominently in this set of buttons. The bottom row is the selected button shown again, this time after each of the three stroke orientation options has been applied.

Summary

In many ways, the stroke is the defining surface of a graphic. Fireworks offers a superb catalog of standard strokes and even more flexibility to create your own. As you begin to work with strokes, use these guidelines:

- ✦ Strokes make paths visible. An unstroked line cannot be seen unless the path is closed and a fill added.

- ✦ The Stroke panel offers immediate control over a stroke's color, size, edge, and texture. Tip preview shows the tip of the stroke.

- ✦ Fireworks includes 48 different preset strokes spread over 11 categories. Many of the stroke presets are interactive and vary according to the speed and pressure with which you draw.

- ✦ You can customize Fireworks strokes with a great number of variations through the Edit Stroke dialog box.

✦ After you've customized your stroke, you can save it with the document by using the Stroke panel pop-up menu commands. You can also store your custom strokes within a Fireworks Style.

✦ Although Fireworks doesn't come with a preset dotted-line pattern, creating one is easy.

✦ Fireworks works well with graphics tablets and takes great advantage of their pressure sensitivity.

In the next chapter, you find out how you can employ advanced path techniques in Fireworks.

✦ ✦ ✦

Structuring Paths

CHAPTER 25

In This Chapter

Transforming vectors

Fireworks technique: creating perspective

Working at the point level on a vector path

Editing existing vectors

Using vector power tools

Even with the coolest stroke, the snazziest fill, and the wildest effect, you rarely get exactly the graphic you need the first time you draw an object. Maybe it needs to be a little bigger, smaller, taller, or wider, or maybe it's perfect — but it's facing the wrong way, and it's upside down. Whatever the problem, Fireworks has the tools to fix it and, because Fireworks blends pixel surfaces with vector skeletons, you'll get amazingly sharp results.

Fireworks has the kinds of tools you would normally expect to find in a full-fledged vector drawing application. You can combine several vector objects in any number of ways with evocatively named tools, such as Union, Intersect, Punch, and Crop. Naturally, what you have joined together you can split apart and regroup as needed. Vector objects can be simplified, expanded, or inset with Fireworks commands.

This chapter covers all the tools and techniques you'll find in Fireworks for transforming and combining objects. You'll also find a section that describes how you can use Fireworks to create perspectives in your imagery.

You really begin to appreciate the power of Fireworks' vector/bitmap combination when you start transforming your objects. In a pure bitmap graphics application, if you increase the size of a bitmap, you have to add pixels, whereas shrinking a bitmap causes the program to throw away pixels — you rarely achieve ideal results in either situation. However, in Fireworks, when you rescale a vector object, the vector path is altered (a snap for vector graphics), and the pixels are reapplied to the new path, just as if you had drawn it that way to begin with.

Transforming Objects Visually

Fireworks includes methods for transforming objects, both visually and numerically. The visual method relies on three key tools found in the Tools panel: Scale, Skew, and Distort.

Note: Although I primarily use vector objects as examples in this section, all the transformation tools work with bitmap objects, as well.

Using scaling

In Web design, the size of an object frequently needs adjustment. Sometimes a button is too large for the current navigation bar, or the client wants the "On Sale" notice to be much bigger. Other times a graphic just looks better at a particular size. Regardless of the reason, Fireworks gives you a quick way to resize an object — either up or down — through the Scale tool.

The Scale tool is the first of three transformation tools in the Tools panel that become active when an object is selected. Choose the Scale tool (or use the keyboard shortcut, Q) and the standard selection highlight is replaced with a transforming highlight, as shown in Figure 25-1. There are eight sizing handles — one on each corner and one in the middle of each side — and a centerpoint on the transforming highlight. You can drag any of the sizing handles to a new position in order to resize the selected object. Dragging any corner handle scales the object proportionately.

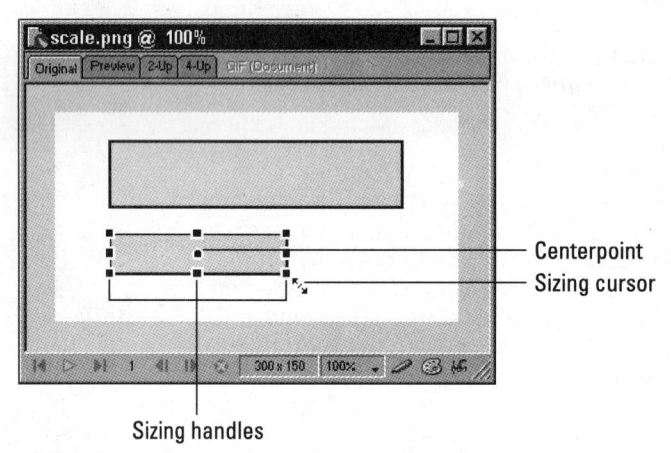

Figure 25-1: Choose the Scale tool and sizing handles, and a centerpoint appears on the selected object.

To resize an object using the Scale tool, follow these steps:

1. Select the object you want to resize.
2. Choose the Scale tool from the Tools panel, or use the keyboard shortcut, Q. Alternatively, you can use the menu command, Modify ➪ Transform ➪ Scale. Sizing handles and a centerpoint appear on the selected object.
3. Position your pointer over any sizing handle until it changes into a two-headed arrow.
4. Click and drag the sizing handle in the direction you want the object to grow or shrink. To scale an object while maintaining the current proportions, click and drag a corner sizing handle.
5. To cancel a resizing operation and return the object to its original dimensions, press Esc.
6. To accept a rescaled object, double-click anywhere on the document. You can also complete the resizing by selecting the Transform button in the Options panel, if it's visible.

You can also move or rotate an object when any of the transform tools are selected. When the pointer is positioned within the selected object and it becomes a four-headed arrow, click and drag the object to a new position. If the pointer is outside of the selected object's bounding box, the pointer turns into a rotate symbol; clicking and dragging when this occurs rotates the object around its centerpoint.

The transform tools all have two options available through the Options panel. By default, when you resize an object, the stroke, fill, and effect settings are resized, as well. If you disable the Scale Attributes option, these settings are reapplied without being recalculated. Why might you want to do this? Although the results can be unpredictable, interesting variations can occur, such as the variations in Figure 25-2.

Tip In my experiments with the Scale Attributes option, the most interesting effects occurred when my object was filled with a gradient and the Scale Attributes option was turned off.

The other option in the transform tools Options panel is Auto-crop Images. When you enable this option, Fireworks automatically removes transparent pixels around bitmap objects before resizing them.

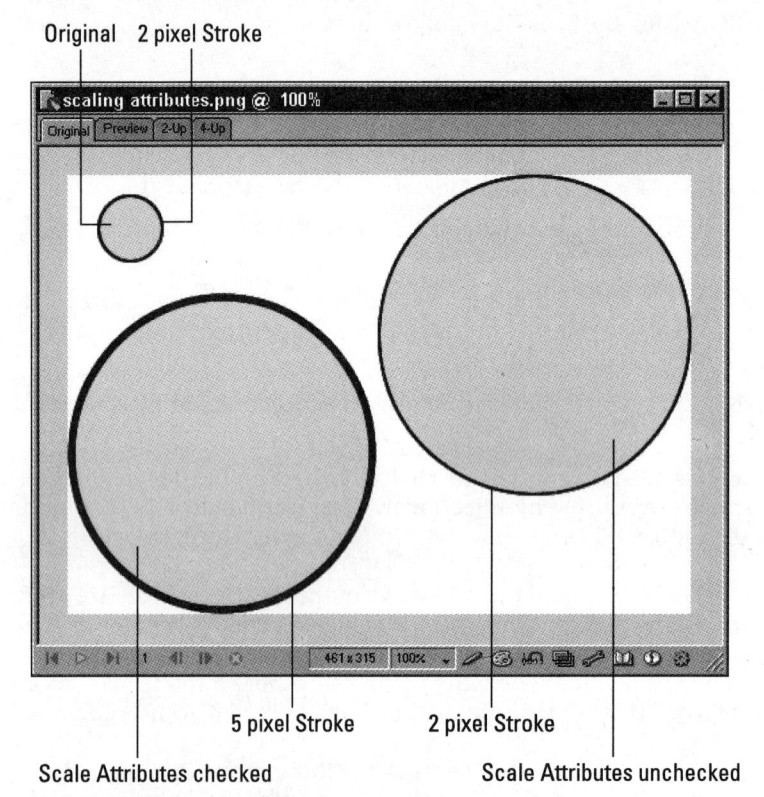

Figure 25-2: Most of the time you want your stroke, fill, and effects to rescale along with your object, but turning off the Scale Attributes option can lead to some interesting effects.

Examining skewing

You use the Skew tool to move one side of an object, while the opposing side remains stationary. Select the Skew tool by clicking and holding the Scale tool until you can choose the Skew tool from the flyout menu, or by pressing the keyboard shortcut, Q, twice. Selecting the Skew tool causes transform handles to appear on the selected object, just like selecting the Scale tool. The Skew handles work somewhat differently, though:

✦ Drag any middle Skew handle in order to slant that side of the object.

✦ Drag any corner Skew handle in order to slant that side and the opposing side in the opposite direction.

Skewing a corner is a useful technique for giving an object a dynamic appearance, as shown in Figure 25-3.

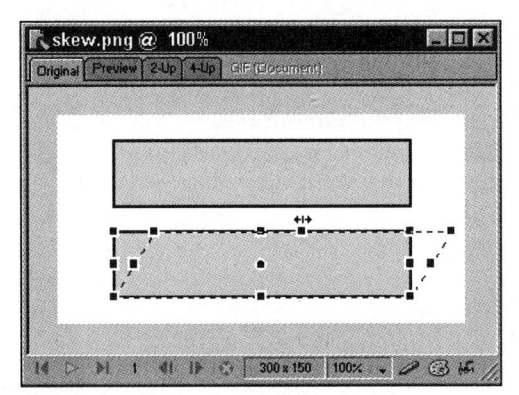

Figure 25-3: Skew an object along one side by dragging the middle handle.

Completing a Skew operation is handled the same as completing a scaling operation: Press Esc to cancel, or double-click anywhere to accept the new shape.

Discovering distorting

With both the Scale and Skew tools, entire sides move when you adjust one of the transform handles. The Distort tool (the third tool on the transform flyout) removes this restriction. When the Distort tool is selected, you can adjust the bounding box surrounding the selected object by dragging the handles in any direction. The object is then redrawn to fit within the confines of the new bounding box shape, as in Figure 25-4.

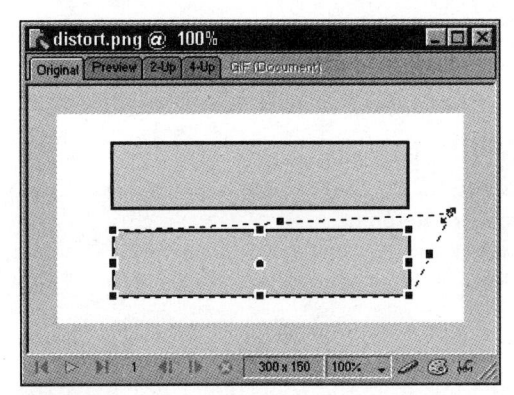

Figure 25-4: Use the Distort tool to reshape a bitmap or vector object by altering its bounding box.

The Distort tool is useful for warping flat objects—especially bitmaps—into novel shapes, or for fitting an object into the shape of another object.

Tip Use the Distort tool to flip a bitmap horizontally or vertically by dragging a middle handle across the opposite side. This technique won't automatically size the bitmap to match the original size, as do the Flip Horizontal or Flip Vertical commands, but you can control the sizing.

Understanding rotating

Rotating is available with any of the transform tools: Scale, Skew, or Distort. Moving your mouse cursor just outside of the bounding box causes the Rotate cursor to appear. As you can see in Figure 25-5, an object rotates around its centerpoint and can rotate a full 360 degrees.

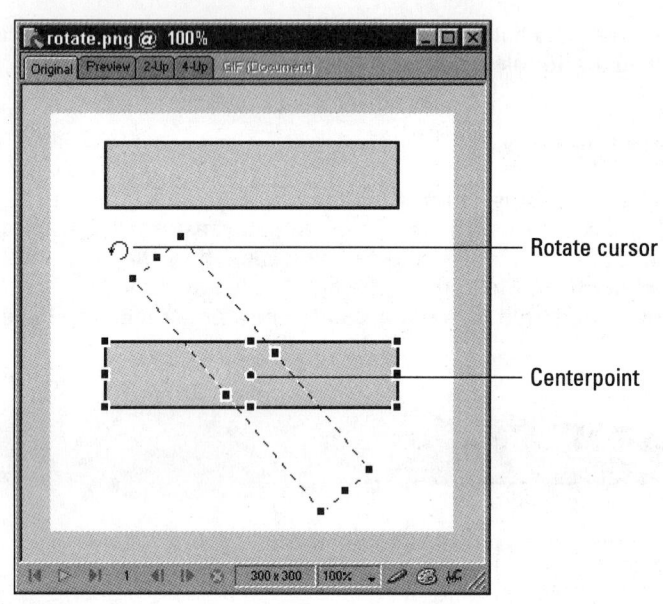

Figure 25-5: An object rotates around its centerpoint when the Rotate cursor drags the object.

To rotate any object, follow these steps:

1. Select any one of the transform tools from the Tools panel, or choose the equivalent tool from the Modify ⇨ Transform menu.

2. Move your pointer outside of the bounding box. The pointer turns into a Rotator cursor.

3. Click and drag in any direction to rotate the object.
4. To cancel the rotation and return to the original object, press Esc.
5. To accept the transformation, double-click anywhere, or click the Transform button in the Options panel.

An object's centerpoint is placed in the middle of the transform bounding box by default. To change the rotation axis, click and drag the centerpoint to a new location — the centerpoint can remain within the object's bounding box or be placed outside of it. If the centerpoint is placed outside of the object, the radius used connects the centerpoint and the nearest corner handle, as shown in Figure 25-6.

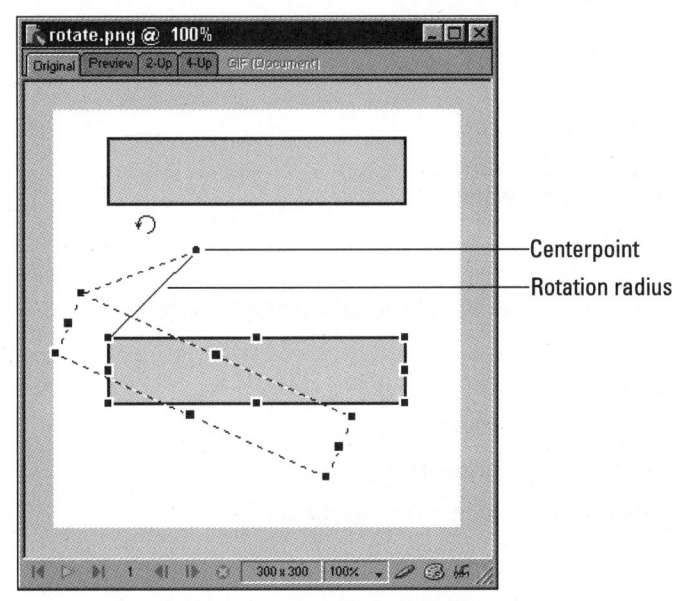

Figure 25-6: Rotate an object around a different axis by dragging the centerpoint to a new location, even outside of the object's bounding box.

> **Tip:** Pressing Shift while you rotate an object constrains the rotation to 15-degree increments.

Transforming Objects Numerically

Transforming an object interactively by clicking and dragging works well for many situations, but sometimes specifying your new measurement or rotation precisely is preferable. For those exacting occasions, turn to Fireworks' Numeric Transform feature. With Numeric Transform, you can scale any object up or down by a percentage, set a specific pixel size, or rotate to an exact degree.

To use Numeric Transform, follow these steps:

1. Select the object you want to change.
2. Choose Modify ⇨ Transform ⇨ Numeric Transform, or use the keyboard shortcut, Ctrl+Shift+T (Command+Shift+T). The Numeric Transform dialog box, shown in Figure 25-7, appears.

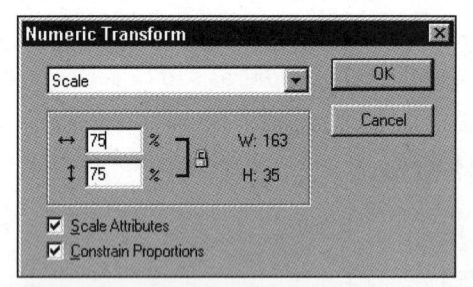

Figure 25-7: The Numeric Transform dialog box gives you exacting control when scaling or rotating an object.

3. Check Scale Attributes to reapply the object's attributes after the transformation.
4. Check Constrain Proportions to preserve the object's aspect ratio.
5. To scale an object proportionately:
   a. Choose Scale from the Option list.
   b. Enter a new percentage value in either the height or width text boxes.

> **Tip** If the height and width boxes are "locked" and you want to unlock them, uncheck Constrain Proportions.

6. To resize an object to a specific pixel size:
   a. Choose Resize from the Option list.
   b. Enter the pixel dimensions in either the width or height text boxes.
7. To rotate an object by a specific number of degrees:
   a. Choose Rotate from the Option list.
   b. Enter a degree value in the text box, or drag the knob to select a rotation degree.
8. Click OK when you're done.

Fireworks Technique: Creating Perspective

Though Fireworks is hardly a 3D modeling program, you can quickly generate perspective views using several of its transform and other tools. If you've ever taken Drawing 101, you understand the basic principles of perspective: The particular view you're illustrating has a vanishing point where the imaginary lines of the drawing meet on the horizon. The vanishing point concept is most simply applied by using a special property of the Skew tool.

To give an object the illusion of perspective, follow these steps:

1. Select the object you want to modify.
2. Choose the Skew tool from the Tools panel, or press the keyboard shortcut, Q, twice.
3. Choose the direction of perspective:
    - To make the object appear as if it is along a left wall, vertically drag the top- or bottom-left corner away from the object.
    - To make the object appear as if it is along a right wall, vertically drag the top- or bottom-right corner away from the object.
    - To make the object appear as if it is on the floor, horizontally drag the bottom-left or -right corner away from the object.
    - To make the object appear as if it is on the ceiling, horizontally drag the top-left or -right corner away from the object.
4. To intensify the perspective, repeat Step 3 with the opposite corner, dragging in the opposite direction. For example, in Figure 25-8, I dragged the bottom-right corner away from the object and the bottom-left corner into the object to exaggerate the effect.

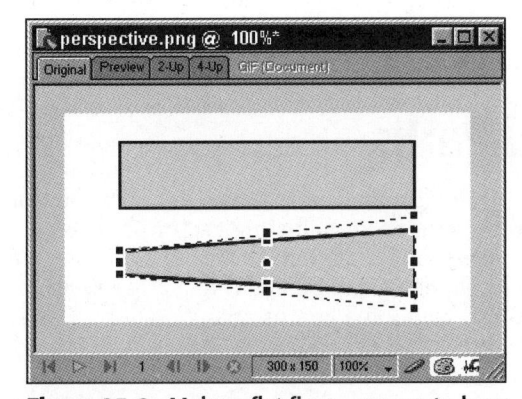

Figure 25-8: Make a flat figure appear to have perspective by using the Skew tool.

Applying textures to a rectangle fill is a good way to start building a perspective background. I've found that breaking up the textures into small rectangles, rather than use one large rectangle is better. The room depicted in Figure 25-9 uses a series of rectangles with a Wood-Light Pattern fill, which are then grouped and skewed together to gain the perspective feel. By duplicating and flipping this skewed group, I'm able to quickly build the other sides of the room.

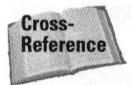

Cross-Reference I discuss texture fills at length in Chapter 27.

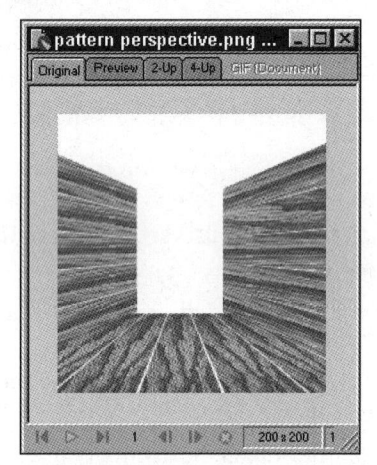

Figure 25-9: When using a pattern for perspective, try smaller rectangles of the same pattern, grouped and skewed together.

Tip Dragging a corner with the Skew tool always moves the top opposite sides equally. This operation makes an object's vanishing point appear to be evenly spaced between the sides of an object, which is not always the case. You can also use the Distort tool to drag one corner unevenly. But use the Distort tool with caution — or perhaps with the Grid visible; there's no way to snap a dragged corner when using the Distort tool, and straight lines are often difficult to maintain.

Managing Points and Paths

Sometimes transforming an object in its entirety is more than you really want or need to do. Fireworks offers numerous options for adjusting vector paths on a point-by-point basis. You can easily move, add, or delete points. In addition, paths can be joined, either to themselves — changing an open path to a closed path — or to another path. Naturally, you can also split joined paths at any point.

Moving points with the Subselection tool

Much path work on the point level is handled through the Subselection tool. Similar to the Pointer tool in that you use it for selecting and dragging, the Subselection tool works on the components of the path, rather than on the path itself.

The Subselection tool is located directly to the right of the Pointer in the Tools panel; you can also choose it through its keyboard shortcut, A. When you select a path with the Subselection tool, all the points that create the path appear, not just the path that becomes visible when you use the Pointer. Each point on a path initially resembles a small filled-in square. When you approach a point with the Subselection tool, the white pointer changes into a single white arrowhead, indicating that a point is available for selection, as shown in Figure 25-10. Clicking that point selects it and changes the solid square to a hollow square.

Tip If no Bézier control handles are visible from a point on a path, you can use the Subselection tool in combination with the Alt (Option) key in order to drag them out.

Clicking and dragging any point causes the path to move with it. You can completely reshape any path by using the Subselection tool.

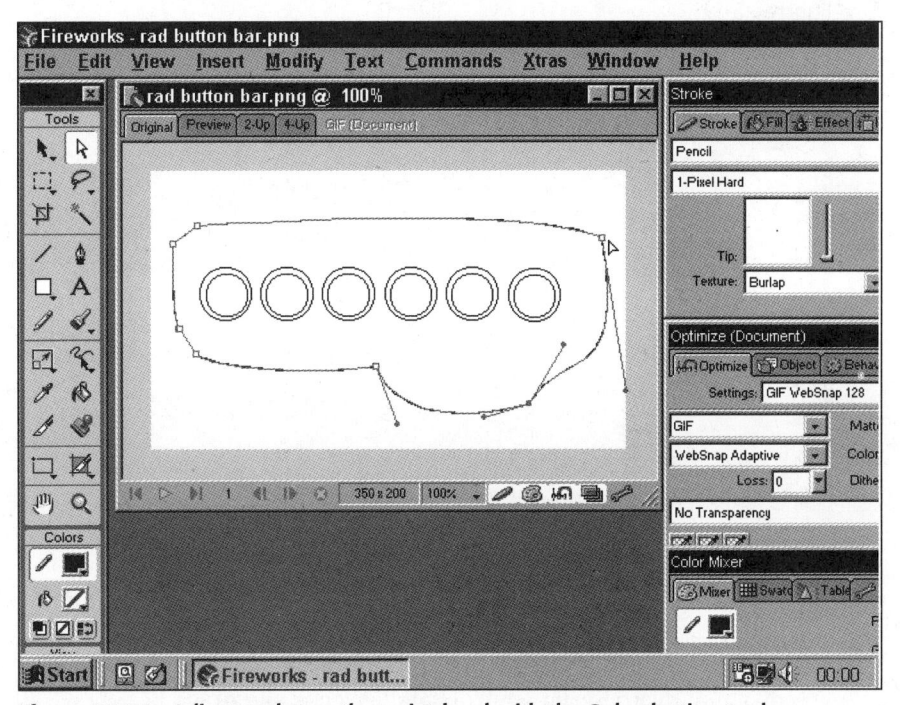

Figure 25-10: Adjust paths on the point level with the Subselection tool.

Adding and removing points

Adding or deleting points on a path is easy. Why would you want to increase the number of points? Most commonly, the object you're working on has a line that you need to extend in a different direction, and the Bézier curves create too smooth a transition. The reasoning behind removing points is just the reverse: You have a sharp break where you would prefer a smooth curve. You'll also find that drawing any path with a freeform tool, such as the Brush or Pencil, creates many points. Not that there is really any increased overhead, such as file size, associated with additional points; working with an object that has fewer points is just easier.

To add a point on a path, follow these steps:

1. Choose the Pen tool from the Tools panel, or use its keyboard shortcut, P.
2. Press and hold Ctrl (Command) to temporarily switch to the Subselection tool.
3. Select the path that you want to work on.
4. Release Ctrl (Command).
5. Position your pointer over the area on the path where you want to add a point. A small plus sign is added to the Pen tool pointer, as shown in Figure 25-11.

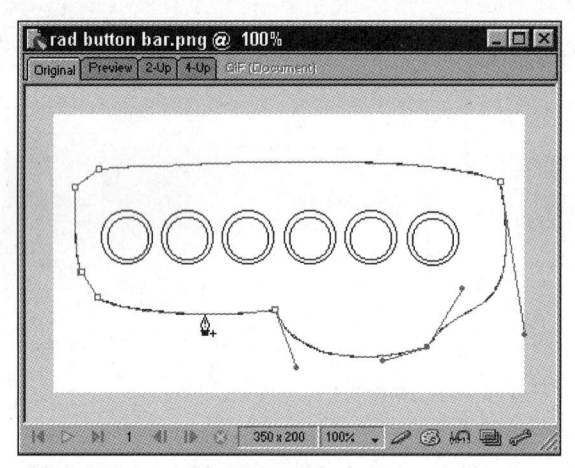

Figure 25-11: Add points with the Pen tool by clicking a selected line.

6. To add a single point, click once.
7. To add a point with Bézier control handles, click and drag.
8. Continue adding points by repeating Steps 5 through 7.
9. When you're finished adding points, select another tool.

To delete points from a path, follow these steps:

1. Choose the Subselection tool from the Tools panel.
2. Select the path from which you want to delete points.
3. Move the pointer over the point you want to delete. A small X is added to the pointer when you are over a point on the path.
4. Click once to select the point.
5. Press Backspace (Delete) to remove the point.

> **Tip** To delete multiple points, press Ctrl (Command) to temporarily use the Pointer tool and drag a selection rectangle around the points that you want to remove. Alternatively, hold down Shift while selecting points to keep adding to your selection. Press Backspace (Delete) to remove the points.

Closing an open path

Whether by accident ("Drat, I thought I closed that path") or design ("I like the simpleness of the open path"), sometimes you need to convert an open path to a closed path. The Pen tool makes this a simple operation.

> **Tip** If your path is almost closed — the end points are right next to each other — you can also select both points with the Subselection tool and choose Modify ⇨ Join, or you can use the keyboard shortcut Ctrl+J (Command+J) to close your path.

To close an open path, follow these steps:

1. Select the path you want to close.
2. Choose the Pen tool from the Tools panel.
3. Position your pointer over one endpoint of the path. An X is added to the lower right of the Pen cursor when it is over an existing endpoint.
4. Click once on the endpoint. A small square replaces the X at the lower right of the Pen cursor, as shown in Figure 25-12.
5. Continue the path with the Pen. With each plotted point, any stroke or effects attributes are applied to the extended path.
6. To close the path, position the Pen over the remaining endpoint. A solid square appears on the lower right of the Pen cursor.
7. Click once to close the path.

> **Tip** If your stroke varies its thickness or opacity by speed or pressure, the section of the path that was completed with the Pen may look odd. This is because the Pen recognizes neither speed nor pressure. However, you can use the Path Scrubber tools, discussed later in this chapter, to increase or reduce these types of effects.

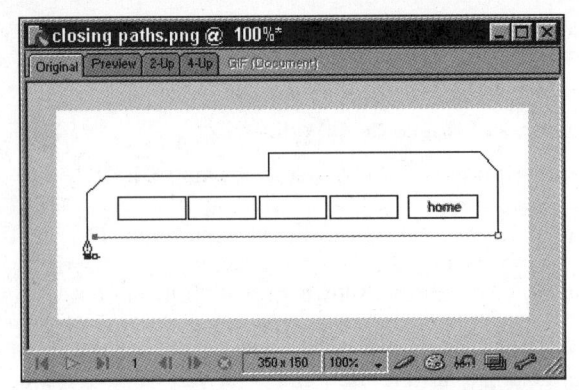

Figure 25-12: Use the Pen tool to close any open path.

Working with multiple paths

You can join any path with another path with a simple command. Initially, this capability may appear to fall into the "Yeah, so what?" category; but after you realize that paths don't have to overlap, touch, or even be near each other, the design possibilities open considerably. Joining a number of simple shapes is an easy way to make one complex shape. For example, joining empty circles with an object effectively cuts holes in the object, as shown in Figure 25-13. Note that the joined object has the attributes — stroke, fill, effect, and so on — of the original object that was lowest in the stacking order (in other words, closest to the canvas).

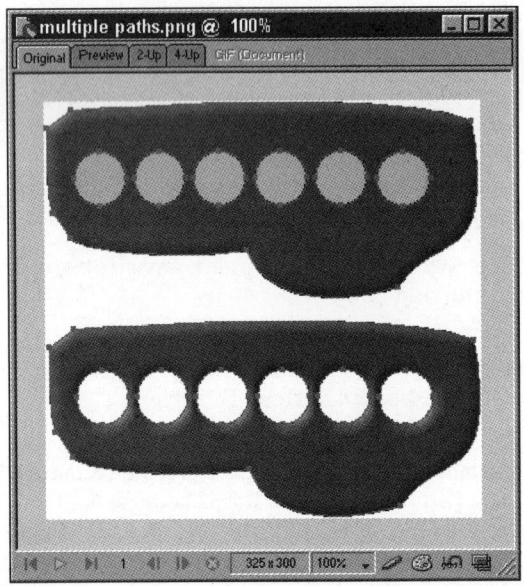

Figure 25-13: Joining paths is an easy way to create complex objects.

To join two or more paths, follow these steps:

1. Select each path you would like to join with the Pointer tool.
2. Choose Modify ➪ Join, or Ctrl+J (Command+J).

    Windows users can also select the Join button on the Modify toolbar.

After you've joined paths, they will stay that way until you split them. To split joined paths, choose Modify ➪ Split, or use the keyboard shortcut, Ctrl+Shift+J (Command+Shift+J). In Windows, you can also select the Split button on the Modify toolbar.

Editing Paths

So far in this chapter, most of the path editing tools have been fairly extreme; delete, distort, rescale, rotate — these terms don't promise much degree of subtlety. Fireworks does offer several other tools, however, that can redraw portions of a path or reshape an area with a varying amount of pressure. And for those times that require a precise, almost surgical removal of path segments, Fireworks offers a Knife tool that performs as sharply as any real blade.

Redrawing a path

If you've ever drawn a shape that was perfect except for one little area of it, you'll greatly appreciate the Redraw Path tool. As the name implies, this tool enables you to redraw any portion of a completed path, in effect throwing away the portion of the original path that you're replacing.

The Redraw Path tool, found in the flyout under the Brush, is a freehand drawing tool. When you're redoing a segment of a path, you initially select any part of the path to start redrawing and then reconnect to the original path. Fireworks erases the portion of the original path that is between the beginning and the ending points of your redrawn section and connects your new path to the old path.

To redraw a portion of a path, follow these steps:

1. Select the path you want to redraw.
2. Choose the Redraw Path tool from the flyout under the Brush tool. Alternatively, you can press the keyboard shortcut, B, twice.
3. Move the pointer over the area of the path where you want to start redrawing. Fireworks displays a small caret (^) in the lower right of the pointer when you are in position over the path.

4. Click and drag out your new path.

5. Position your pointer over the original path in the spot where you want to connect the new and old paths, and then release the mouse button. Fireworks removes the old path segment and connects the new path segment.

The Redraw Path tool isn't just for correcting mistakes, though. Figure 25-14 shows how you can use the Redraw Path tool to make a portion of a geometric shape more organic-looking.

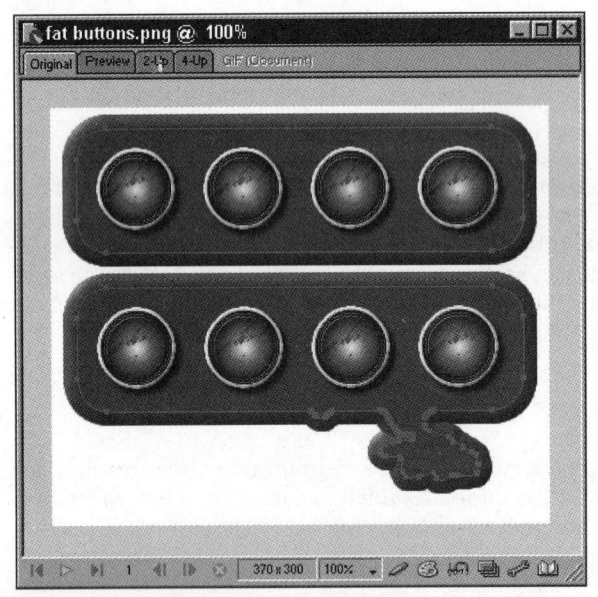

Figure 25-14: The Redraw Path tool can easily alter a standard shape into something unique.

Tip Pressing Shift while using the Redraw Path tool constrains your replacement path to lines in increments of 45 degrees.

Examining the Freeform and Reshape Area

Looking for a cool tool to give your objects that unique twist? Look no further than Freeform and Reshape Area. Rather than add or delete points like other tools, these reshaping features let you sculpt a path, pulling and pushing a line like so much stretchable clay.

Although similar, a couple of key differences exist between the two tools:

- **Freeform:** Both pushes and pulls a segment of a selected path.
- **Reshape Area:** Only pushes a path, but controls the degree it pushes through the strength field in the Tool Options. Moreover, this tool can reshape an entire object, as well as just a segment.

Pushing a path into a new shape

To push a path into a new shape with the Freeform tool, follow these steps:

1. Select the path you want to alter.
2. Choose the Freeform tool from the Tools panel, or use its keyboard shortcut, F.
3. Position your cursor slightly off the path that you want to push. This could be to either side of an open path, or inside or outside of a closed path.

Note: Positioning your cursor slightly off a path enables the Freeform push cursor. Positioning your cursor directly on a path enables the Freeform pull cursor, covered later in this chapter.

The cursor changes into a circle, as shown in Figure 25-15. Think of the circle as an object that you will use to push against the stroke.

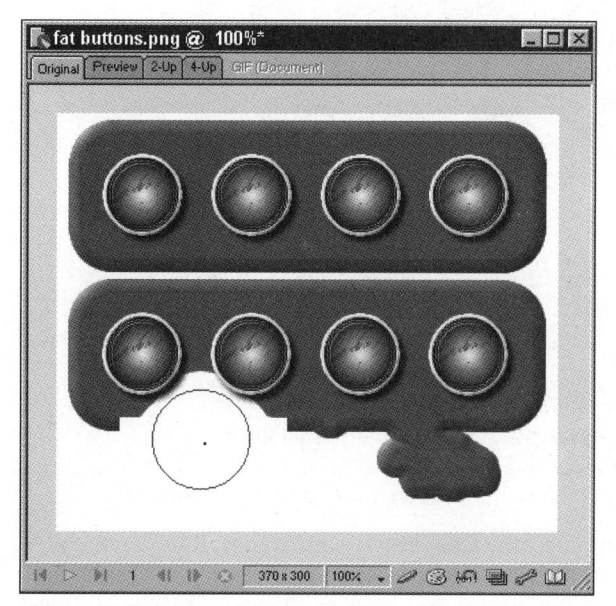

Figure 25-15: Round out your paths with the Freeform tool's push mode.

4. Click and drag the ball cursor into the path, pushing it into a new shape.

> **Caution** Pushing a closed path too fast or too far results in an overlapping path line with unpredictable results.

5. Release the mouse button when you're satisfied with the shape.

Pulling a path segment into a new shape

To pull a segment of a path into a new shape, follow these steps:

1. Select the path you want to alter.
2. Choose the Freeform tool from the Tools panel, or use its keyboard shortcut, F.
3. Position your cursor directly over the segment of the path that you want to pull. An S-curve is added to the lower right of the Freeform cursor, as shown in Figure 25-16.

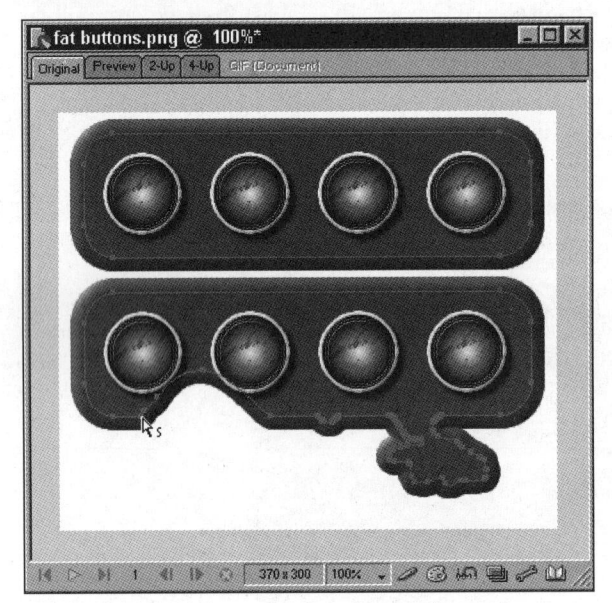

Figure 25-16: The Freeform tool is used to pull out a segment of a path.

4. Click and drag in the direction that you want to pull the segment. You can pull the path away from or into the object.
5. Release the mouse button in order to complete the pull.

Fireworks adds as few pixels as possible when you are pulling with the Freeform tool. Pulling is like pinching just the one point of the path and dragging it away from the rest of the shape. By contrast, the push mode of the Freeform tool is more like using a ball to reshape the path. The size of the ball with which you push is determined through the Freeform Tool Options panel.

Learning about the Freeform Tool Options panel

To alter the size of the ball used with Freeform push mode, double-click the Freeform tool to view its Tool Options panel, shown in Figure 25-17, and enter a new value in the Size text box, or use the slider to choose a new pixel size. The Size option ranges from 1 to 500 pixels.

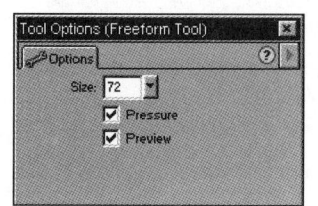

Figure 25-17: The Freeform tool's Tool Options panel allows you to set options, such as the size of the push cursor.

The Options panel offers two other options for the Freeform tool. The Preview option draws the stroke and fill, if any, while you use the Freeform tool. Although this can be a bit processor-intensive, I enable it whenever I'm using Freeform on an object with a wide stroke, such as an Airbrush, because the final effect can be so different from just the path. When the Preview option is not on, you'll see both the old outline and the new one while you are using the tool; when you stop drawing, the old outline vanishes.

The other option, Pressure, is generally useful only if you're using a pressure-sensitive graphics tablet. When enabled, a medium amount of pressure specifies a push cursor to the size set in the Tool Options panel; lighter amounts of pressure reduce the size, and greater amounts increase it.

Altering a vector object with one operation

Though the Reshape Area tool, when set to a small size, achieves similar effects to the Freeform tool, that's not what makes it special. The Reshape Area tool is best when used to warp or to reshape an entire object. Take Figure 25-18, for example. I start with a star created with the Polygon tool and then apply the Reshape Area tool, set to a size on the Options panel larger than the star. By dragging the Reshape Area tool over the star, I transform the entire standard shape — not just one segment — into something unique.

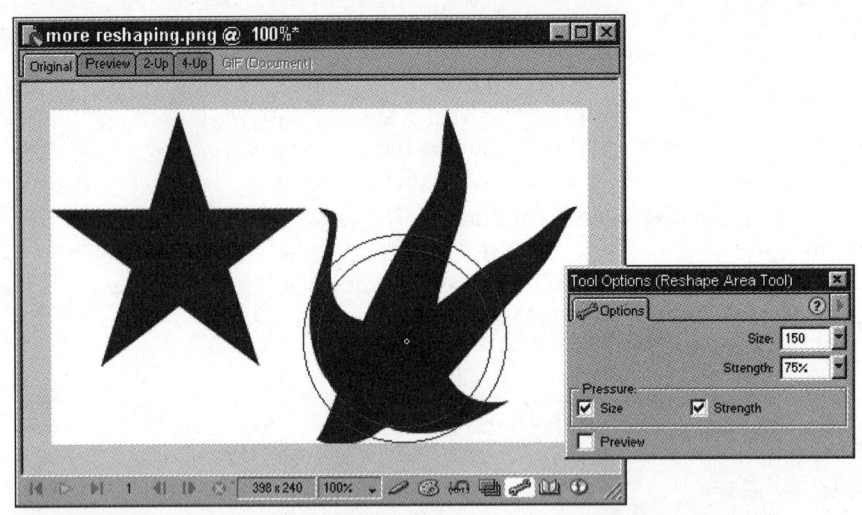

Figure 25-18: The Reshape Area tool can alter an entire vector object with one operation.

To use the Reshape Area tool, follow these steps:

1. Select the path you want to alter.
2. Choose the Reshape Area tool from the flyout underneath the Freeform tool, or press the keyboard shortcut, F, twice.

> **Tip:** Each time you press F, you toggle between the Freeform and Reshape Area tools.

3. Position your pointer over the object that you want to reshape.
4. Click and drag in the desired direction.
5. Release the mouse button when you're satisfied with the resulting object.

Like the Freeform tool, the Size is set on the Tool Options panel; you'll also find Pressure and Preview options that function in the same manner as those for the Freeform tool. In addition, the Reshape Area tool has a Strength option. The Strength value determines the strength of the Reshape Area tool's gravitational-like pull. Strength is percentage based; at 100 percent, you'll get the maximum effect from the tool. If you're using a pressure-sensitive graphics tablet, you can alter both the size and the strength of the Reshape Area tool while drawing with your stylus.

> **Tip:** Don't have a graphics tablet yet? To simulate a lighter stylus touch, use either 1 or the left arrow key; pressing 2 or the right arrow key simulates increasing the pressure on a graphics pad.

Discovering the Path Scrubber

The Path Scrubber tools are fairly subtle compared to the other tools covered in this chapter. If you've experimented with strokes such as Airbrush, you've noticed how the stroke can change according to how fast or, with a graphics tablet, how much pressure you use when you draw. The Path Scrubber tools alter these variables, after you've completed the path. One Path Scrubber tool increases the interactive effect, and one lessens it, as shown in Figure 25-19.

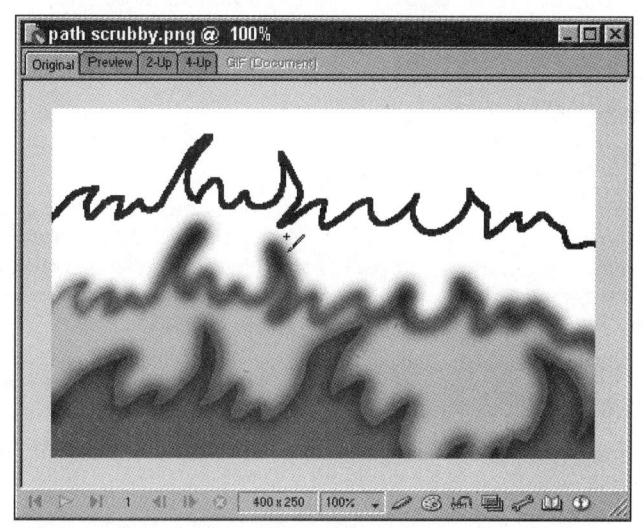

Figure 25-19: The Path Scrubber tools can turn a simple path into one that looks like it was created with a pressure-sensitive pen and tablet.

To use the Path Scrubber tools, follow these steps:

1. Apply a stroke to your path that uses speed- or pressure-sensitive effects, such as Air Brush.

2. If you want to increase the pressure effect, choose the Path Scrubber Plus tool; if you want to decrease the pressure effect, choose the Path Scrubber Minus tool. Both are in the flyout underneath the Freeform tool. You can also select them by pressing the keyboard shortcut, U, twice.

3. Trace over the portion of the path where you want to adjust the speed or pressure effect.

Using the Options panel

When Fireworks draws a path, both speed and pressure data are gathered. The Path Scrubber tools can work with either the speed or pressure information, or both; moreover, they can do it at a variable rate. The Options panel for these tools has all the controls you'll need:

- **Rate:** The relative strength of the tool. Pick a value from 10 (the most effect) to 1 (the least effect).
- **Pressure:** Enabling this option directs the Path Scrubber tools to adjust the path, according to the simulated pressure of the stroke.
- **Speed:** Enabling this option directs the Path Scrubber tools to adjust the path according to the simulated speed of the stroke.

Understanding the Knife

One of my favorite — and most useful — design tools is my X-acto knife. The capability to finely trim the tightest curves has saved me many times. The computer equivalent of this excellent implement is the Knife tool. The Knife tool is used only with paths, just as its counterpart, the Eraser, is only used with bitmap objects. Basically, the Knife tool divides one path into two separate paths.

The Knife cuts paths by drawing a line where you want the separation to take place. You can use the Knife tool on open or closed paths, or on any path-based object. With an open path, you need only intersect the path once in order to make the cut once; with a closed path, you have to draw a line all the way across the object with the Knife, as shown in Figure 25-20.

Figure 25-20: The Knife stroke on the left cut the object into two pieces, which can then be pulled apart, as shown on the right.

To use the Knife, follow these steps:

1. Select the path you plan to divide.
2. Choose the Knife tool from the Tools panel, or use the keyboard shortcut, E.
3. Draw a line through the path with the Knife tool. Fireworks separates the path, although this is not always immediately obvious because both new paths are still selected.
4. To move one of the newly divided paths, choose the Pointer tool and click once on the canvas away from any object. The split paths are deselected.
5. Select either portion of the original path. Only one part is now selected and can be deleted, moved, or otherwise modified.

The Knife tool is also great for making specific shapes, such as arcs. Just draw a standard circle and then use the Knife to slice off a portion of it. Like many tools, pressing Shift constrains the Knife to angles with increments of 45 degrees.

Caution Although the Tool Options panel shows various selections for the Eraser tool, all the parameters are only useful for the bitmap mode Eraser tool. Changing the options does not affect the Eraser tool in vector mode (when it looks like a knife).

Discerning Path Operations

The more you work in vector-based drawing programs such as Fireworks, the sooner you begin to look for new and novel shapes. Face it, no matter how many points you put on that star, it's still a star. Whereas you can warp and reshape any existing object using the various tools described elsewhere in this chapter, creating a compound shape composed of two or more basic shapes is often far easier.

You can find all the commands that merge paths — Union, Intersect, Punch, and Crop — under the Modify ⇨ Combine menu option. You can find the stroke commands — Simplify, Expand Stroke, and Inset Path — under Modify ⇨ Alter Path.

When you combine multiple paths, the stroke, fill, and effects settings of the bottom object in the stacking order — the one closest to the canvas — are applied to the new combined object.

Understanding the Union command

The Union command enables you to combine two or more objects into one merged object. One technique that helps me decide whether Union is the proper command to use is that time-honored artist's tool, squinting. After I've positioned objects with which to form my new shape, I lean back from the monitor and squint so that I can see just the outline of the new shape. That's precisely what Union does — it combines the shapes into an overall outline and removes any overlapping areas.

The technique for using Union, like all the Combine commands, is straightforward. Just position your objects, select them all, and then choose Modify ⇨ Combine ⇨ Union. Occasionally, you'll have to adjust the individual paths to get them just right. For example, when I created the martini glass in Figure 25-21, I united three objects: a triangle, a rectangle, and a custom Pen-drawn shape for the base. After my first attempt, I realized that the rectangle and the base didn't quite match, so I chose Edit ⇨ Undo — okay, I actually used the shortcut, Ctrl+Z (Command+Z) — and adjusted the base. Then, after reselecting them and reissuing the command, I was ready to pour.

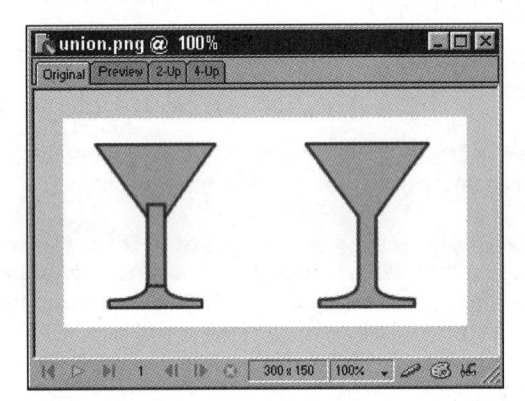

Figure 25-21: I combined the three objects on the left with the Union command to form the new object on the right.

Examining the Intersect command

Whereas Union throws away the overlapping parts of combined paths, Intersect keeps only the overlapping areas from all selected paths. Believe it or not, the key word in the previous sentence is *all* — if even one object doesn't overlap at least some part of all the other selected objects, the Intersect operation erases all of your objects. That caveat out of the way, you'll find Intersect to be a useful command. I mean, how else could you create the perfect pizza slice, as I did in Figure 25-22? After the two objects on the left were selected, I chose Modify ⇨ Combine ⇨ Intersect. Pizza's ready!

Using the Punch command

Remember the paper punch you had in school? That little handheld device that took a round bite out of whatever you could get between its jaws? The Punch command uses the same concept, except you define the punch shape to be anything you want. When two vector objects overlap, the shape on top is punched out of the shape on the bottom. You can see the Punch command illustrated in Figure 25-23, as I continue the food metaphors with the creation of a doughnut, of sorts. After making sure that my two circles were centered on each other, I selected them both and chose Modify ⇨ Combine ⇨ Punch.

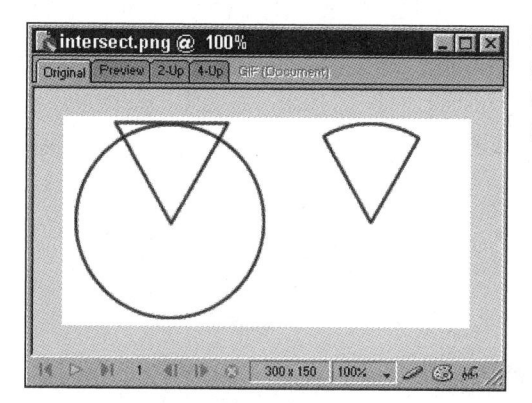

Figure 25-22: Combining a circle and a triangle with the Intersect command creates the perfect pizza slice.

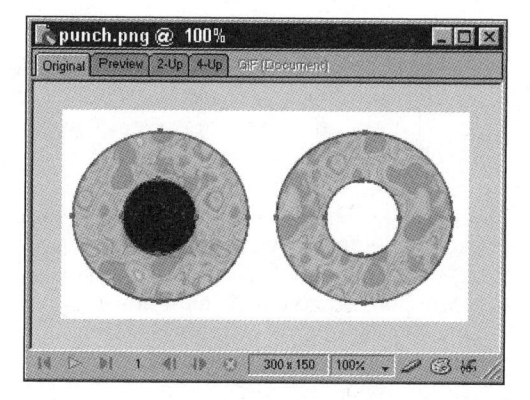

Figure 25-23: The Punch command removes the shape of the top object from the bottom object.

Tip: What happens when you apply the Punch command to more than two selected objects? The top object is still used as the punch pattern—and all the objects are affected, but not joined.

Exploring the Crop command

Plainly put, Crop is the opposite of Punch. With Punch, the top object is cut out of any other selected object. With Crop, the bottom object forms the clipping path for the top object. To round out our food-like illustrations of the Combine commands, Figure 25-24 disposes of all but the last bite of a cookie. I created the shapes of the remains, joined the shapes into a single object, selected that object and the cookie, and then chose Modify ⇨ Combine ⇨ Crop. Almost all gone in one bite.

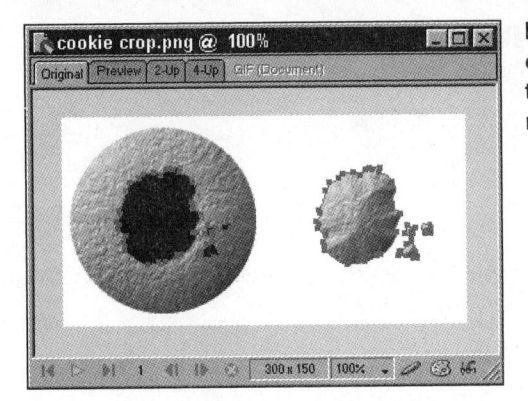

Figure 25-24: With the Crop command, the shape of the original top object provides the shape of the resulting object.

Looking at the Simplify command

Freeform drawing tools are terrific for quickly sketching out a specific shape. But, quite often, the computer representation of your flowing strokes turns out pretty blocky. The Simplify command is designed to reduce the number of points used in a path while maintaining the overall shape of the object.

If you choose Modify ⇨ Alter Path ⇨ Simplify, the Simplify dialog box opens and enables you to specify the number of pixels affected. The range is from 1 to 100; a relatively low value of 12 was used to dramatic effect in Figure 25-25. The original hand-drawn fellow on the left has too many points; trimming them down by hand would be arduous. After I applied the Simplify command, a smoother, simpler object resulted. That's not necessarily the last step, though. Usually, you'll find yourself tweaking a simplified object's Bézier handles in order to get things just right.

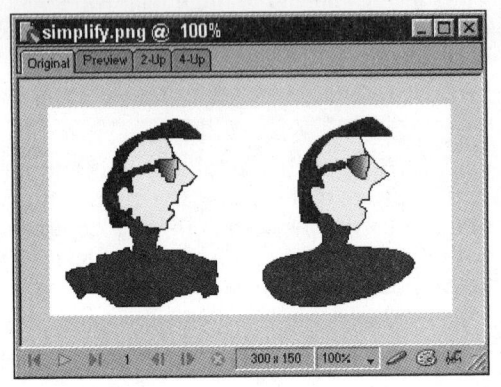

Figure 25-25: After the Simplify command is applied to the original hand-drawn paths, the result is the smoother and simpler gentleman on the right.

Applying the Expand Stroke command

Though you can accomplish much with an open path through the Stroke panel, sometimes you need a Fill, as well. The Expand Stroke command offers an easy way to convert any path — open or closed — into a larger closed path by enclosing the existing path, and then deleting it.

When you apply this command by choosing Modify ⇨ Alter Path ⇨ Expand Stroke, the Expand Stroke dialog box appears, as shown in Figure 25-26. As you can see, it offers quite a few options that enable you to control exactly what kind of path to use to expand the stroke. The options include the following:

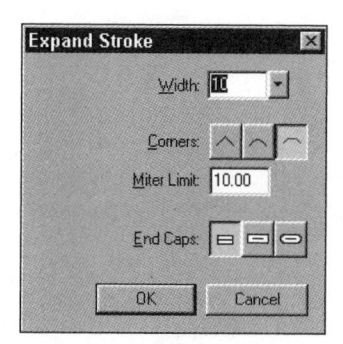

Figure 25-26: Choose your options in the Expand Stroke dialog box in order to make a wide range of Expanded strokes.

+ **Width:** Determines the final width of the expanded stroke. The range is from 1 to 99 pixels.

+ **Corners:** Choose from three types of corners. From left to right, the buttons represent:

    • **Miter:** With a miter corner, the outside edges of the path extend until they touch in a sharp corner. Because miter corners can become quite long, you can limit their length with the Miter Limit option, which is explained in this list.

    • **Round:** The corner is rounded equally from both sides of the path approaching the corner. Round corners and round end caps are often used together.

    • **Bevel:** The corner is cut off at the center of the meeting paths, rather than on the outside edge, as with the miter corner. This results in a truncated corner.

+ **Miter Limit:** The number of pixels the miter corner can extend before being cut off. The Miter Limit works only with miter corners.

♦ **End Caps:** Choose among the following three End Cap types for closing off the expanded path:
- **Butt Cap:** The Butt Cap creates a right-angle End Cap where the end is perpendicular to the last point of the stroke.
- **Square Cap:** Similar to the Round Cap, the Square Cap attaches a square to the end of the path, extending it the same radius as half the set width.
- **Round Cap:** A Round Cap attaches a semicircle to the end of the path, extending it the same radius as half the set width.

Figure 25-27 shows the three different End Cap types, as well as an example of what it looks like to change an object that consists of strokes and fills into an object made up entirely of fills. After you've expanded the strokes, set the stroke to None, and apply a fill to the whole object. Note that the third and fourth face use the hair from the first face.

Discovering the Inset Path command

Whereas Expand Stroke applies strokes on both sides of a selected path, Inset Path only applies strokes on one side. The Inset dialog box is identical to the Expand Stroke dialog box, except for the addition of Inside and Outside options. You'll get the most predictable results with Inset Path if you apply it to closed paths, but you can use it with any kind of path, except straight lines.

Figure 25-27: The Expand Stroke command can change strokes to fills.

Often, a plain and boring object can be replaced with an interesting variation just by applying the Inset Path command, as shown in Figure 25-28.

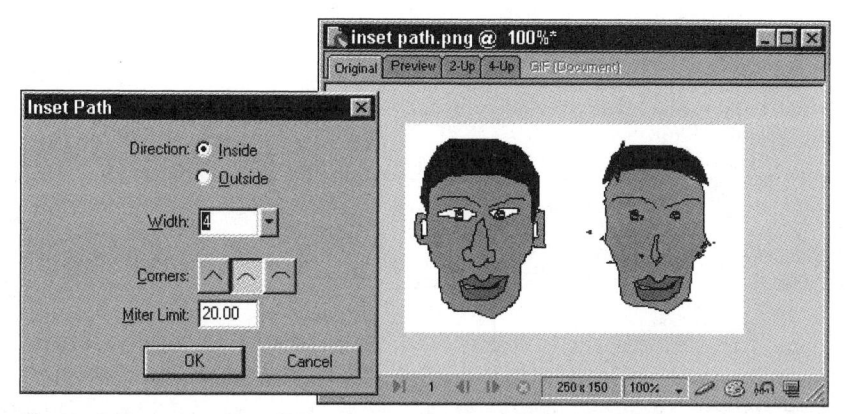

Figure 25-28: Create variations of an object with the Inset Path command.

One of my favorite applications of the Inset Path command is to create concentric shapes, each one within the next.

To use the Inset Path command to create concentric shapes, follow these steps:

1. Select the closed path to which you want to add concentric shapes.
2. Choose Edit ⇨ Clone. Because Inset Path erases the original path, you must apply the command to a clone of the original path.
3. Choose Modify ⇨ Alter Path ⇨ Inset Path. The Inset dialog box appears.
4. Choose the Direction, Width, and Corner option. If you choose the Miter Corner, you can enter a Miter Limit. Click OK when you're done. The new path is drawn and the old path is deleted.
5. Repeat Steps 2 through 4 for as many concentric shapes as desired, keeping the same values in the Inset dialog box in order to create equidistant shapes.

After you've created your basic shapes, you can go in and vary the stroke width or other settings in order to create interesting effects.

Summary

Mastering the manipulation of paths is essential in order to achieve the most that's possible with Fireworks. You can distort, resize, rotate, and adjust vector objects in many subtle ways in order to create the basic shapes you need for unique Web graphics. When altering Fireworks objects, keep these points in mind:

- You can manipulate objects as a whole by using the transform tools: Scale, Skew, and Distort.
- You can rotate an object using any one of the transform tools.
- For precise sizing or rotation, use the Numeric Transform feature.
- The Skew tool is great for simulating perspective views — especially of bitmap objects. You can enhance the illusion by adding simulated light and shadow effects.
- Whereas the Pointer is used to move an entire path, the Subselection tool is used to maneuver individual points — and their Bézier control handles.
- After you draw a path, you can edit it in numerous ways by using tools such as Freeform, Redraw Path, Redraw Area, and Path Scrubber.
- The Union, Intersect, Punch, Crop, Simplify, Expand Path, and Inset Path commands are extraordinary power tools for working with paths in Fireworks.

In the next chapter, you find out how to add text to your Web graphics in Fireworks.

✦ ✦ ✦

Composing with Text

CHAPTER 26

In This Chapter

Composing with the Text Editor

Inserting text files

Applying strokes and fills to text

Changing from text to paths

Flowing text on a path

Masking images with text

Text has a special place in Web graphics. Although the vast majority of text — paragraphs, lists, and tables of information — is a product of the HTML page viewed through a browser, graphic-based text is generally used to create logos, fancy headings, and other decorative elements that aren't possible with basic HTML. In addition, text is an integral part of a key Web element: navigation. Many navigation buttons use text, either alone or in combination with symbols, to quickly convey meaning.

Before Fireworks, a recurring nightmare for Web designers involved modifying a text graphic. Whether it was a typo or a client change-of-mind that forced the revision, the designer was stuck having to redo an entire graphic because any text, once applied, was just another bunch of pixels. Fireworks changed all that with the introduction of editable text. Now, if a client's logo changes because of a $7-billion merger, or you just forgot to put the period at the end of *Inc.*, text modifications are just a double-click away.

A few programs have since followed Macromedia's lead, but Fireworks still leads the way. In this chapter, I show you basic things like choosing fonts and aligning text, as well as more advanced features, such as attaching text to a path. I also show you a technique that enables you to combine images with text using Fireworks Mask Groups.

Using the Text Editor

In Fireworks, all text creation, and most modification, takes place in the Text Editor. The Text Editor, shown in Figure 26-1, is a separate window with a full range of text controls and its own preview pane. After you create the text, a *text object* appears in the current Fireworks document, surrounded by a bounding box. The text object has many, but not all, of the properties of a path object—you can, for example, use the transform tools such as Skew, but you can't use Reshape Area to warp the text as you can a path. On the other hand, text objects have features unlike any other object, such as the capability to be aligned to a path; for example, a circle. If necessary, converting a text object to a path object or an image object is possible, but you can no longer edit the text.

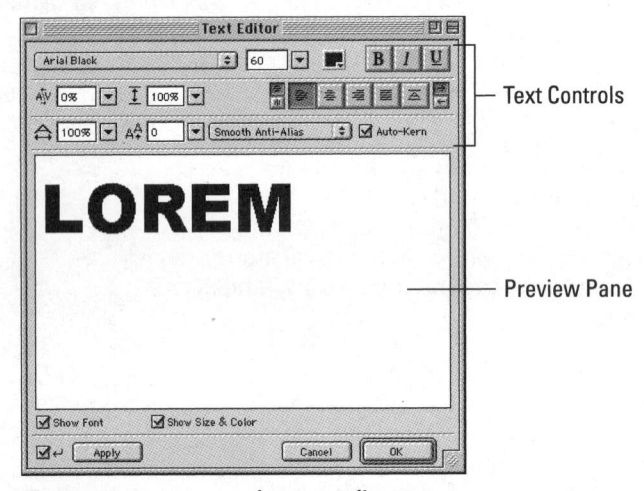

Figure 26-1: You use the Text Editor to compose and edit text in Fireworks.

The Text tool is your initial gateway into the Text Editor. You can use the Text tool two ways:

✦ Click once on the canvas with the Text tool to set a starting point for your text. If necessary, the text flows to the edge of the current document and expands downward toward the bottom of the document.

✦ Drag out a rectangular text region with the Text tool. The text created in the Text Editor wraps on the horizontal boundaries of the established region and, if necessary, expands downward.

The general steps for inserting text into a Fireworks document are

1. Select the Text tool from the Tools panel, or use the keyboard shortcut, T.
2. Set the text area by
   - Clicking once on the document where you want the text to start
   - Dragging out a text area for the text to fit into

   Either method opens the Text Editor.

3. From the Text Editor, choose the text characteristic, such as font, size, color, and alignment.

4. Click in the Preview pane and input the text. If Auto-Apply is enabled, Fireworks updates the text object in the document after each keystroke.

5. Click OK when you're done.

Tip

Pressing Enter (Return) when your cursor is in the Preview pane adds a line break, as you might expect. Unfortunately, the OK button in the Text Editor is highlighted, which may tempt you to press Enter (Return) to dismiss the Text Editor dialog box. Press the other Enter on the numeric keypad to dismiss the Text Editor.

After the text object is onscreen, you move it as you would any other Fireworks object, by clicking and dragging with the Pointer tool. To adjust the shape of the text object, drag any of the six handles that become available when you select the object.

Note

Dragging a text object's handles doesn't resize the text itself, but instead changes the outside boundaries of the text object, after which, the text reflows through its new boundaries. A text object can only be vertically resized to fit the current text it contains. If you want your text object to take up more vertical room, select it and choose a larger font size from the Text ⇨ Size menu.

When you need to edit an existing text object, you have several ways to open the Text Editor. You can select the text object as you would any other Fireworks object, and then choose Text ⇨ Editor. You can also choose the Text tool and hover it over an existing text object; when the I-beam cursor gains a small, right-pointing triangle, click once to open the Text Editor. Finally, the most efficient method (and certainly my most often-used one) is to double-click the text object with the Pointer or Subselection tool.

Previewing on the fly

Fireworks features real-time text updating in the document for each change made in the Text Editor. Any edit — either to the text itself in the Preview pane, or through the text controls — is instantly reflected in the text object, as shown in Figure 26-2.

You can also move text objects around the canvas, even with the Text Editor open. This simplifies both the creation phase, when you're trying to find the right overall look, and the tweaking phase, as you make incremental adjustments.

New Feature

You can move text objects around the canvas with the Text Editor open. Previously, Fireworks required you to close the Text Editor in order to adjust the position of a text object.

Figure 26-2: Updates in the Text Editor are instantly applied to the text object in the document in Fireworks. A space added between the E and the M in the Text Editor shows up immediately on the canvas.

Choosing basic font characteristics

Within the Text Editor, you have full control over the look and style of your text. The Text Editor offers two methods of working, just like a word-processing program. To set your options, use either one of the following techniques:

- ✦ Set the font attributes prior to entering text into the Preview pane.
- ✦ Select the text you want to modify in the Preview pane — all or a portion — and then alter the attributes.

You can find all the core characteristics at the top of the Text Editor, as shown in Figure 26-3.

The basic attributes are very straightforward to establish:

- ✦ **Font:** To choose a typeface, select a name from the Font list. The Font list displays all the available TrueType or Type 1 fonts on your system.

Tip Windows users can also select the Font list itself and either use the cursor keys to move up or down the list one font at a time, or type the first letter of a font's name to jump to that part of the list.

Figure 26-3: Select your font typeface, size, color, and style from the top of the Text Editor.

- ✦ **Size:** Choose the text size using the Text Size slider, or by entering a value directly in the Text Size box. Size is the height of a font in points. Fireworks accepts sizes from 4 to 1,000 points, although the slider only goes from 8 to 128.

   Caution: You can also adjust text size by using the Scale tool on your text object, just as you would resize any other object. Although the text remains editable, its point size in the Text Editor doesn't change as you resize it. This can become confusing when you attempt to edit a huge text object and find that it says it's 10pt in the Text Editor.

- ✦ **Color:** Initially, the Text Editor applies the color specified in the Fill color well. However, you can easily choose a new text fill color by selecting the option arrow next to the color well in the Text Editor. The standard pop-up color picker is displayed with the current swatch set. Each character in your text object can have its own color.

   New Feature: The Text Editor now remembers its color setting independent from the Stroke and Fill color wells, so that your new text objects are more likely to be initially visible on top of other objects.

✦ **Style:** Choose from Bold, Italic, and Underline styles for your text; each style button is a toggle, and you can apply any or all to one text object.

> **Tip** The Underline style is useful for mimicking hyperlinks in design mock-ups you might create for client approval, before actually making any HTML.

All the basic attributes are applicable on a letter-by-letter basis. You can — although it's inadvisable for aesthetic reasons — change every letter's font, size, color, or style. Ransom notes were never easier.

Adjusting text spacing

All adjustments to how text is located within the text object occurs in the Text Editor only. Fireworks includes five text-spacing controls, as shown in Figure 26-4.

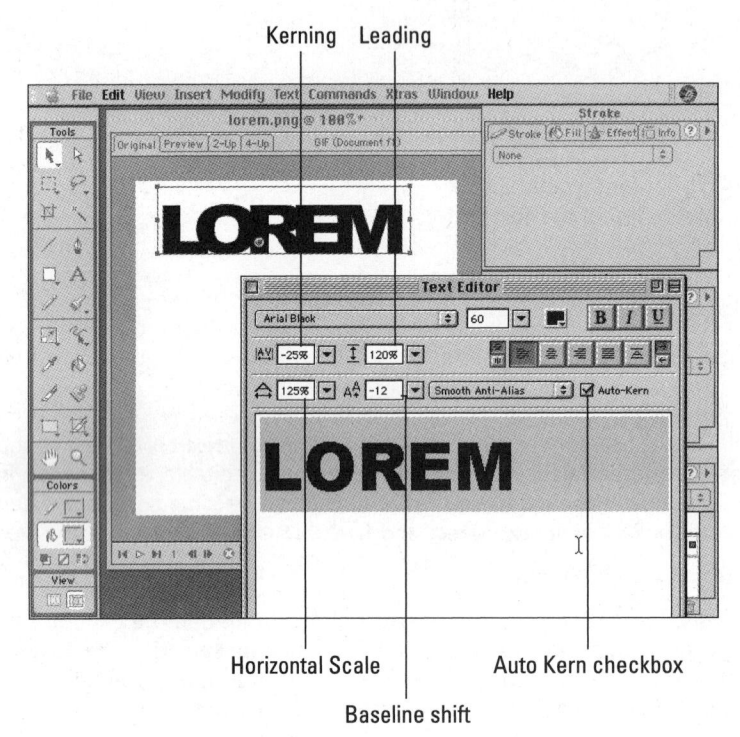

Figure 26-4: Control your text character and line positioning through Fireworks' text-spacing controls.

Kerning

Kerning determines how close letters appear to each other. The default value of 0 percent uses the standard font spacing. Increasing the Kerning slider (1 percent to 100 percent) moves letters further apart, whereas decreasing it (–1 percent to –100 percent) moves letters closer together, or overlaps them. Alter the kerning between two letters by placing the cursor between the letters in the Preview pane of the Text Editor and moving the Kerning slider, or entering a new value. To change the kerning for a range of letters, or the entire text in the Preview pane, select the letters before changing the kerning value.

Note: The Preview pane does not show changes in the kerning. However, if you have the Auto-Apply option checked, you can see the effect of kerning on your text object in the document itself after each change.

Auto Kern

Many fonts define the spacing for *kerning pairs,* like the letters "WA" or "ov," which fit together, to make text more legible. Some fonts come with as many as 500 kerning pairs defined. Fireworks applies the kerning pair information whenever the Auto Kern option is enabled. The Auto Kern option affects the entire text object.

The effect of kerning pairs is most noticeable in the larger font sizes. The top text object in Figure 26-5 has Auto Kern enabled, which is the default. The bottom object is identical, except that the Auto Kern option has been unchecked. Note the differences in the overall length of the word, as well as how the first *A* fits between the *W* and the *V*. Leave Auto Kern checked unless you have a specific reason not to do so.

Figure 26-5: The Auto Kern option uses a font's built-in spacing for better kerning, as shown in the top text object.

Leading

Leading (pronounced *ledding*) is the printer's term for line spacing. In Fireworks, leading is expressed as a percentage of the font size and only affects text with multiple lines. Single-spaced lines use the default 100 percent; a value of 200 percent would give you a double-spaced paragraph. Leading values less than 90 percent or so will cause lines to touch or overlap (see Figure 26-6). Unless you're creating a special effect, you'll probably want to keep your leading at 90 percent or higher.

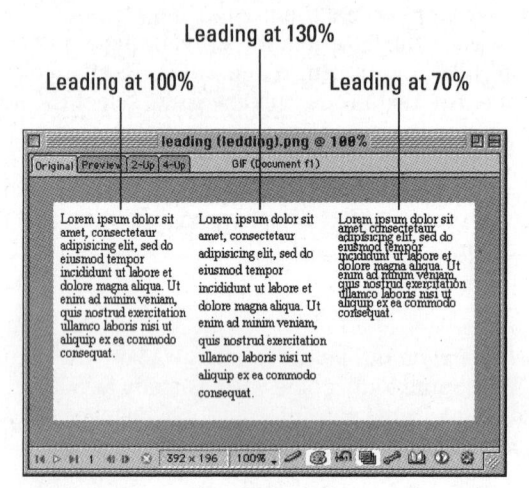

Figure 26-6: The Leading value controls the space between multiple lines of text.

Horizontal Scale

You can alter the relative width of any text through the Horizontal Scale control. The range of the Horizontal Scale slider is from 50 percent to 300 percent, but you can specify another value through the text box. You can see the effect of the Horizontal Scale in Figure 26-7, where the same text is presented at 200 percent, 100 percent, 50 percent, and 25 percent. Horizontal Scale does not display in the Preview pane.

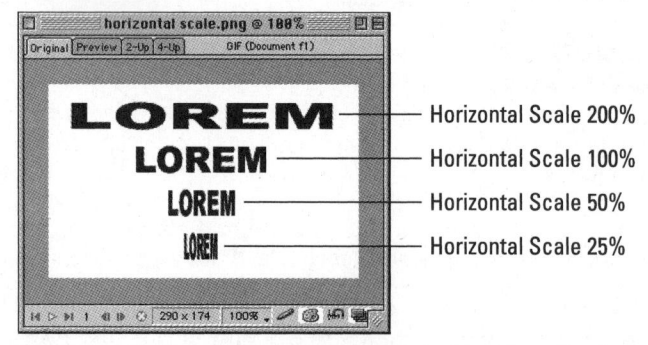

Figure 26-7: Change the width of a text object by adjusting the Horizontal Scale slider in the Text Editor.

Note: Don't confuse kerning and Horizontal Scale. Kerning is the space between individual characters; Horizontal Scale affects the size of the whole text object as one.

Baseline Shift

If you're building a Web site on which chemical formulas are a key element, you'll be happy to discover the Baseline Shift control. Normally, all text is rendered along the same baseline so that the bottoms of most letters are aligned. The Baseline Shift control enables you to place letters or words above or below the normal baseline. Fireworks specifies the Baseline Shift value in points: Negative values go below the baseline, and positive values go above. For a standard subscript letter, such as the 2 in H_2O, use a negative value about half the size of the current font (see Figure 26-8). Likewise, for a superscript, choose a positive value; again, about half the current font size.

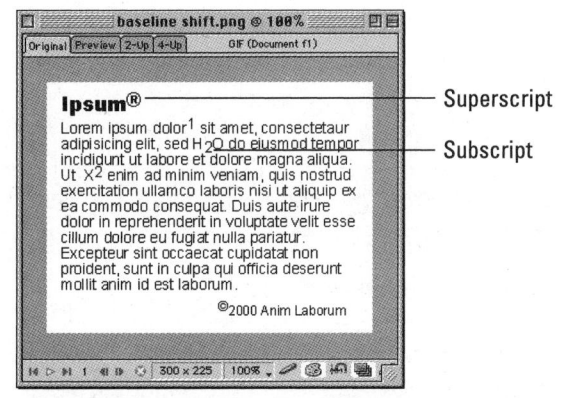

Figure 26-8: Specify a new Baseline Shift value for subscript characters like the 2 in H_2O, and superscript characters such as the (r) and the (c).

Aligning text

All text objects, when selected in the Fireworks document, are surrounded by a bounding box. The bounding box sets the position of the text through its upper-left corner coordinates, but it also determines the limits for the text block. Most importantly, all alignment for the text is relative to the bounding box.

You can apply different alignment options to different text in the same text object, as long as each piece of text is on its own line. Figure 26-9 illustrates this capability with each of the five horizontal alignment options in one paragraph, as well as showing whole paragraphs of each option.

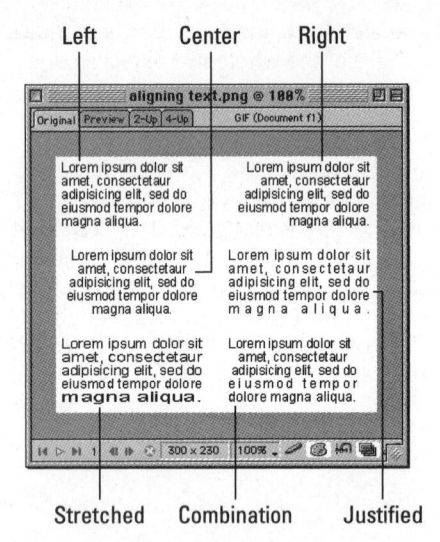

Figure 26-9: Fireworks offers many text alignment options.

The Text Editor contains controls for specifying text alignment (see Figure 26-10). Text can be either Horizontal (the default) or Vertical, and run left to right (the default) or right to left. Depending on whether you choose Horizontal or Vertical, the remaining alignment buttons change.

When Horizontal is selected, the alignment choices are

- **Left Alignment:** Text is aligned to the left edge of the bounding box.
- **Right Alignment:** Text is aligned to the right edge of the bounding box.
- **Center Alignment:** Text is centered between the left and right edges of the bounding box.
- **Justified Alignment:** Text is evenly spaced so that the letters of each line touch both the left and right edges of the bounding box; the letters, however, remain the size specified in the Font size.
- **Stretched Alignment:** Text is expanded horizontally so that the letters of each line touch both the left and right edges of the bounding box.
- **Text Flows Left to Right:** Text is rendered across the screen, from left to right.
- **Text Flows Right to Left:** Text is rendered across the screen, from right to left.

Tip: The middle sizing handles on a text object's bounding box are always adjustable. This feature is very useful, because you can quickly center text in a document by dragging the middle sizing handles to either edge of the canvas and choosing the Center alignment option in the Text Editor.

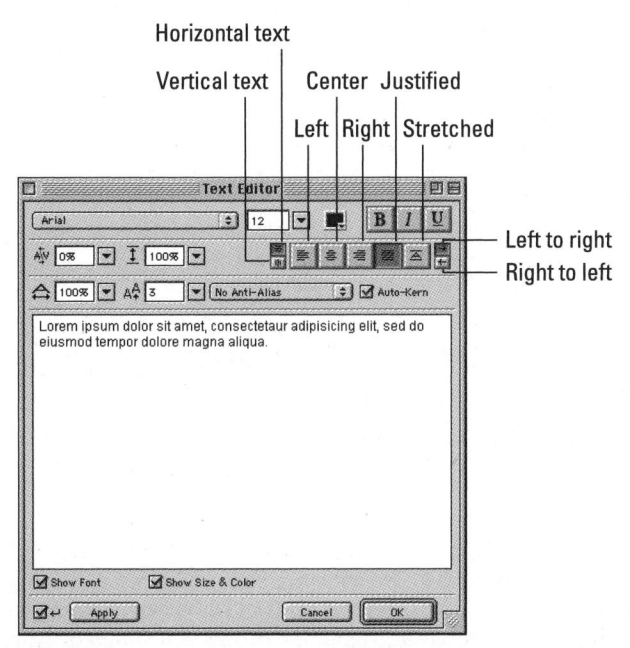

Figure 26-10: Use the Horizontal Alignment controls to align text left, center, right, justified, or stretched.

When Vertical Text is chosen, the alignment options change to

- **Top Alignment:** Text is aligned to the top of the bounding box.
- **Center Alignment:** Text is centered between the top and bottom of the bounding box.
- **Bottom Alignment:** Text is aligned to the bottom of the bounding box.
- **Justified Alignment:** Text is evenly spaced so that the letters of each line touch both the top and bottom edges of the bounding box, however, the letters remain the size specified in the Font size.
- **Stretched Alignment:** Text is expanded vertically so that the letters of each line touch both the top and bottom edges of the bounding box.
- **Text Flows Down and Up:** Text is rendered down the screen, starting from the top of the bounding box.
- **Text Flows Up and Down:** Text is rendered up the screen, starting from the bottom of the bounding box.

Enabling Text Editor options

The final element found in the Text Editor are the options: two for the Text Editor itself and three for the final product. To get the closest approximation possible in the Preview pane, enable both the Show Font and Show Size & Color options. The Show Font option displays the text in the current selected typeface; when the Show Font option is turned off, the Preview pane shows text in a sans serif font, such as Arial or Helvetica. The Size & Color option — no surprises here — let you see your text in the current size and color. Without this option enabled, you'll see text at approximately 24 points and black.

The three other options, Anti-Alias, Auto Kern, and Apply, are applicable to the text object. The Anti-Alias option smoothes the text by providing an antialiased edge to the fill for the text object. Auto Kern, as discussed in the previous section "Adjusting text spacing," uses a font's kerning pairs. Apply enables any changes made in the Text Editor to be automatically updated and viewed in the document's text object.

In my way of working, only occasionally do these features actually become optional. If I have a large block of text in the Preview pane, I might disable the Size & Color option, but I almost never turn off the Font option. Only when I'm trying to achieve a special effect would I even consider disabling either Anti-Alias or Auto Kern. And I've noticed that I'm totally dependent on the Apply function for constant feedback as I work.

Re-Editing Text

The Text Editor is perhaps the most commonly used method for editing text in Fireworks, but it's not the only one. To make a global change to a text object, such as altering the typeface or size, you can use a menu command. Although you do sacrifice the full range of features, menus can be much faster than using the Text Editor, especially if you take advantage of the keyboard shortcuts.

In all, you can apply four menu items under the Text heading to a selected text object:

- **Font:** Lists the fonts available on your system, in alphabetical order.
- **Size:** To quickly change your selected text object to a set size, choose Text ⇨ Size, and then one of the dozen point sizes: 8, 9, 10, 12, 14, 18, 24, 36, 48, 72, 96, and 120. Choose Other to enter a different size than those available.
- **Style:** In addition to the options available through the Text Editor (Bold, Italic, and Underline), the Text ⇨ Style menu enables you to remove all styles with one command, Text ⇨ Style ⇨ Plain.

✦ **Align:** The Text ⇨ Align menu is broken up into two groups, one for horizontal text and one for vertical text. Choosing an alignment from one group automatically alters the orientation of the text, if necessary. For example, if you apply Text ⇨ Align ⇨ Bottom to a horizontal text object, the text object converts to a vertical text object and aligns the text to the bottom, simultaneously.

To be completely thorough, one other command in the Text menu could be listed in this category: Text ⇨ Editor, which opens the Text Editor for the selected text object.

Importing Text

Almost all the text that's used in Web graphics is relatively short; longer paragraphs are generally part of the HTML file rendered by the browser. There are numerous reasons why text on the Web is generally not in graphic form, although first and foremost — as with many aspects of the Web — is file size. Download times for a page of graphic text is considerably longer than for that of HTML text.

However, in the for-every-rule-there's-an-exception category, occasionally blocks of text have to be rendered as a graphic. Some clients insist on an absolute fidelity to their traditional printed material across all platforms. The only way to keep these types of clients happy — even at the expense of a longer download — is to render the text as a graphic. In these cases, you'll have the potential for taking advantage of one of Fireworks' least-known features: text import.

In addition to the numerous graphic file types supported by Fireworks, you can also open ASCII and Rich Text Format (RTF) files. ASCII (American Standard Code for Information Interchange) files are the lowest common denominator of all text files and contain no formatting whatsoever. RTF files, on the other hand, convey a good deal of basic formatting, such as typeface, size, styles (bold, italic, and underline), and alignment.

Although you can copy short passages of text from another program and paste them into Fireworks' Text Editor, for a large block of text, you're better off importing it.

To import a text file, follow these steps:

1. Be sure the file you want to import is saved in either ASCII or RTF format.
2. Choose File ⇨ Import, or use the keyboard shortcut, Ctrl+R (Command+R).
   The Import dialog box appears.
3. If you're working in Windows, choose either ASCII Text (*.txt) or RTF Text (*.rtf) from the Files of Type option list.

4. Navigate to your ASCII or RTF file, select it, and click Open.

After the Import dialog box closes, the Insert cursor appears.

5. Place the imported text in your document in one of two ways:
   - Position the cursor where you want the upper-left corner of the text object to start and click once.
   - Click and drag out the bounding box for the text file.

The text flows into the new text object.

Caution The click-and-drag method for creating a text object is currently somewhat limited. Rather than have the full freedom to draw whatever shape you desire, the rectangle is constrained to a 4:1 ratio of vertical to horizontal space. In other words, the initial text object will always be four times as wide as it is tall. More importantly, Fireworks renders the text to fit within this bounding box, regardless of its previous font size.

Transforming Text

You really start to feel the power of Fireworks after you begin adding strokes, textured gradient fills, and multiple effects to a block of text — and you're still able to edit it. You can even use any of the transform tools — Scale, Skew, or Distort — to warp the text completely, and it's still editable.

No real shortcut exists to mastering text in your images. You really can only get a sense of what's possible by working, experimenting, trying — in essence, playing. In the following sections, you'll find some avenues to begin your text explorations.

Adding strokes

When you first create a text object, only the basic fill color is applied. However, this doesn't mean you can't add a stroke to your text — any combination of stroke settings is fair game. You do have to be a bit careful, though. Some of the preset strokes, such as Basic Airbrush, are quite hefty and can completely obscure all but text in the larger font sizes. However, modifying a stroke size (or color, softness, or texture) is quite easy, and you can generally adjust the presets to find a workable setting.

One use for text with an added stroke is to create outlined text. Almost all fonts are presented with solid, filled-in letters. In Fireworks, however, you can make almost any font an outline font, with a fairly straightforward procedure:

1. Select a text object.
2. Open the Stroke panel by choosing Window ⇨ Stroke, or clicking the Stroke panel's tab if it's docked behind another.

3. Change the stroke category from None to any of those available in the Category option list.

Tip Try Basic or Pencil strokes for simple outlines; experiment with Airbrush or Random strokes for more unusual results.

4. Select any desired preset from the Type option list, and modify its settings as needed.
5. Open the Fill panel by choosing Window ⇨ Fill, or clicking the Fill tab.
6. Set the fill category to None in the Category option list. The solid fill disappears, and the remaining stroke outlines the text.

The results of these steps are shown in Figure 26-11.

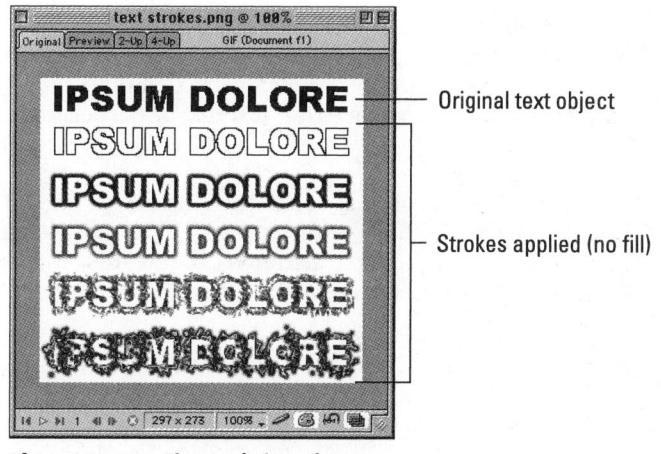

Figure 26-11: Fireworks' strokes can turn almost any font into an outline version.

Another technique for adjusting the look of a stroke on text is to alter the stroke's orientation. With most path objects, an applied stroke is centered on the path. With text objects, however, the default is to place the stroke on the outside of the path. Change the orientation of the stroke on the Object panel with the text object selected. By altering the stroke orientation, you can get three completely different graphic looks, as shown in Figure 26-12.

Cross-Reference To find out more about strokes, turn to Chapter 24.

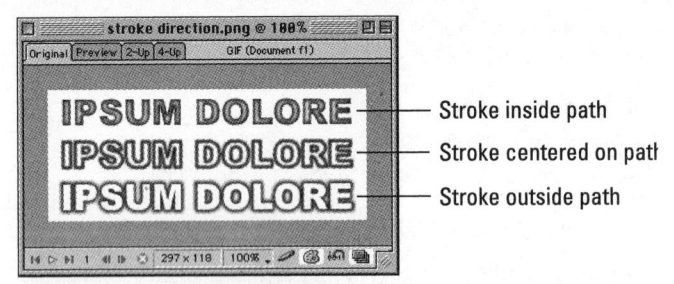

Figure 26-12: The only difference between these three variations is the orientation of the stroke.

Enhancing fills

Although the default method of displaying text already uses a colored fill, it's just the tip of what's possible with Fireworks text. Any type of fill that you can devise — solid color, Web dither, gradient, or textured — is applicable to text objects. Moreover, you can alter the edges of a fill to give either a softer or harder textual appearance.

Applying a fill to text is very straightforward. Just select the text object, and choose your fill from the Fill panel. Fireworks treats the entire text object as a single unit, so gradients and Patterns flow across all the separate letters and words. You can, however, adjust the way the fill is distributed by adjusting the gradient and Pattern controls, as described in these steps:

1. Select your text object.
2. Choose Window ⇨ Fill, or click the Fill tab, if visible.

    The Fill panel opens.
3. Choose a gradient or Pattern fill.
4. If Auto-Apply is not enabled, select Apply.

    The gradient or Pattern fill is applied to the text object.
5. Select the Paint Bucket tool.

    The gradient editing handles appear on the filled text object, as shown in Figure 26-13.
6. To adjust the centerpoint of the gradient, click and drag the round starting handle.
7. To adjust the direction of the gradient, click and drag the square ending handle.

Gradient ending handle

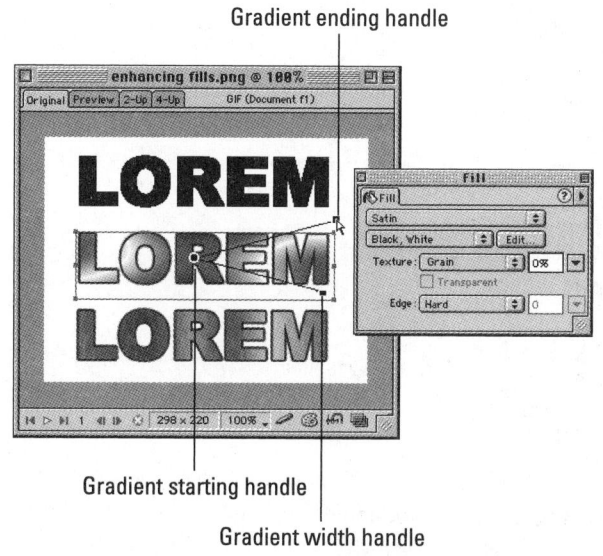

Figure 26-13: Alter the way a gradient moves across your text by moving the Gradient Fill handles.

Gradient starting handle
Gradient width handle

Some gradients, such as Ellipse, Rectangle, and Starburst, have a third handle, which you can move to adjust the width and skew of the gradient.

8. Click any tool, other than the Paint Bucket, to leave the Edit Gradient mode.

Cross-Reference
Want to know more about fills? Turn to Chapter 27.

Using the transform tools

You can apply each of the three transform tools — Scale, Skew, and Distort — to any text object. This means that you can be resize, rotate, slant, and even pull text out of shape and you can still edited it in the Text Editor. In this regard, text objects act just like path objects: The same sizing handles appear, and you can even use the Flip Horizontal/Vertical or Numeric Transform commands, as in Figure 26-14.

Keep a few points in mind about transforming text:

✦ Before using the Skew tool on a text object, narrow the bounding box on either side of the text object as much as possible. Skew affects all portions of a text object, and excess area will probably give you an undesirable effect.

✦ As with a regular path object, both Skew and Distort are useful for providing perspective effects with text. Adding an effect to text, such as inner bevel or drop shadow, also helps the effect.

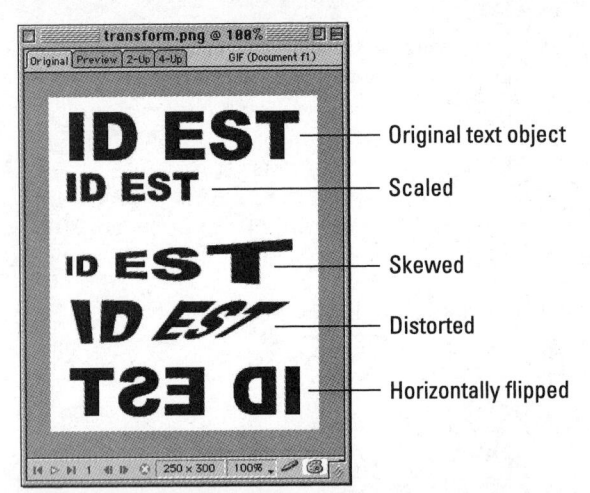

Figure 26-14: Text objects are fair game for Fireworks transform tools. Text, as always, remains editable.

- You can transform text in one of two ways: as a path object, or as a pixel image. These options are available on the Object panel when the text object is selected. The Transform as Path option (the default) results in smoother, less jagged text than the Transform as Pixels option; however, in some instances, you may prefer the more ragged look.

Converting text to paths

So if editability of text is such a big deal, why would you ever want to give it up? After you convert text to a path, you can combine it with other path objects by using commands on the Modify ⇨ Combine submenu. You might also want to alter a letter's shape, but to do that, you need to convert it to a path in order to gain access to its underlying points. You might find an interesting graphic hiding in a dingbats font and want to use it as a clipart foundation for a new drawing. In any case, select your text and choose Text ⇨ Convert to Paths, or use the keyboard shortcut Ctrl+Shift+P (Command+Shift+P).

Tip Before I convert a text object to a path object, I always, always, always make a copy of it and keep the copy on a hidden layer or unused frame. It's a good backup for when things go wrong, and an additional design element for an unforeseen creative moment 10 or 20 steps down the line.

Converting text to an image

Not only can you convert text to paths, you can also convert it to a bitmap image. Just select the text object and choose Modify ⇨ Convert to Bitmap, or use the keyboard shortcut Ctrl+Alt+Shift+Z (Command+Option+Shift+Z). As with the path conversion, text converted to pixels is no longer editable through the Text Editor.

Fireworks Technique: Cookie-Cutter Text

One of my favorite things to do with text is to convert it to a path and punch it through other path objects. The resulting objects make great guinea pigs for experimentation with Xtras or Live Effects. Buttons created this way are easy to turn into rollovers, because the text — or rather, the hole that the text punches out — is transparent. You can make these buttons glow different colors by placing them over different backgrounds, or place them over an image so the image shows through.

In any case, to use a former text object as a cookie cutter on other path objects, follow these steps, which are illustrated in Figure 26-15:

1. Create a text object.
2. Choose Text ➪ Convert to Paths, or use the keyboard shortcut, Ctrl+Shift+P (Command+Shift+P). Each letter in the text object is converted to a path, and then grouped.
3. Select your text path object and choose Modify ➪ Ungroup, and then Modify ➪ Join, or use the keyboard shortcuts Ctrl+Shift+G (Command+Shift+G) and Ctrl+J (Command+J), respectively.

   This ungroups the individual letters, and then joins them all into one composite path.
4. Create a path object — such as a rectangle — to punch your text through. Make sure that it has a fill of some sort.
5. Place the text path object on top of your path object, aligning the text path object carefully where you want it to punch through.

Tip You may have to select your text paths and choose Modify ➪ Arrange ➪ Bring to Front to bring it higher in the stacking order than your path object. Alternatively, you could send the path object to the back.

6. Select both objects, and choose Modify ➪ Combine ➪ Punch.

Your two objects are combined into a new path object with the same fill, stroke and other properties of the bottom object. Experiment with different fills, strokes, and effects, or place your new object on top of other objects that will show through.

Fireworks Technique: A Font Safety Net

Ideally, source files such as Fireworks documents would never go anywhere without the fonts that were used to create them. Of course, this is not always the case. You may archive a document, find a need for it a year later and then upon opening it, discover that you no longer have one or more of the fonts you originally used. You might send a document to someone and forget to send the fonts, or need to open a Fireworks document on another platform where your fonts won't work without conversion. Suddenly, a careful design is thrown into disarray because the substituted fonts don't have the same spacing or characteristics.

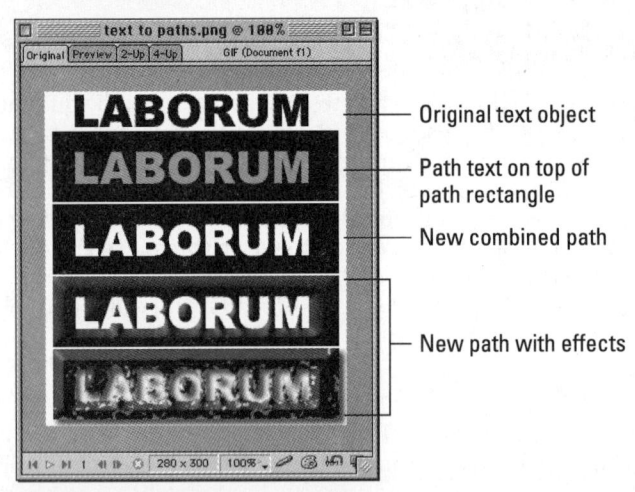

Figure 26-15: Text is converted to a path and then punched through another path object, cookie-cutter style.

One simple way to provide a little insurance against the preceding situations is to make backup image layers of all the text in a Fireworks document before you archive it. Then, if you open the document later without the correct fonts, you can hide the editable text layer(s) and show the image text layer(s). At the very least, the design is preserved and can be re-created. If all you wanted to do was modify a graphic element slightly and then publish it, you might save a significant amount of time because your safety-net text was in place.

> **Note:** This technique assumes you've followed the common practice of giving text objects their own layers — with names like Logo, Headline, Body Text, and so on. If not, then you can select all of your text objects manually, and copy them to a separate layer and then see the following instructions from Step 4 on. Be careful to preserve the correct stacking order, if necessary. Combining objects on one layer may bring them in front of other objects they were previously behind.

To create backup image layers of the editable text in a Fireworks document, follow these steps:

1. Select a text layer in the Layers panel, and drag it to the New Layer button (it looks like a "new folder").

   Fireworks makes a copy of the layer and appends a 1 to the new layer's name.

> **Caution:** Leave the copied layer where it is in the stacking order. You want it to shadow the original layer as closely as possible.

2. Repeat Step 1 until you have copies of all of your text layers.

3. Choose Single Layer Editing from the Layers panel pop-up menu so that you can work on one layer at a time.

   With Single Layer Editing checked, choosing a layer from the Layers panel effectively locks all other layers.

4. Select a copied text layer from the Layers panel and choose Edit ➪ Select All to select all the text objects on that layer.

5. Choose Modify ➪ Convert to Bitmap to convert the text objects into a bitmap image.

6. Repeat Steps 4 and 5 until you have converted all of your copied text layers to images.

7. Hide your copied text layers by clicking the eye icon next to each layer in the Layers panel.

Your document is now ready to travel font-free, while still leaving the graphic elements editable.

Using the Text on a Path Command

For the most part, text is either strictly horizontal or vertical. The Text on a Path command, however, enables you to flow text in the shape of any path — whether the path is a circle, rectangle, or freeform shape.

The basic procedure is pretty simple: First, create each part — a text object and a path — and then combine them. Because paths can come in so many shapes, Fireworks offers a number of different controls and options to help you get what you want. Amazingly enough, text remains editable even after it's been attached to a path.

To align text on a path, follow these steps:

1. Draw or create any path object.
2. If necessary, create a text object.
3. Select both the path and the text object.
4. Choose Text ➪ Attach to Path, or use the keyboard shortcut, Ctrl+Shift+Y (Command+Shift+Y).

   The text flows along the path and the attributes of the path (stroke, fill, and effect) disappear, as shown in Figure 26-16.

5. To edit the text, double-click it to open the Text Editor.
6. To separate the text from the path, choose Text ➪ Detach from Path.

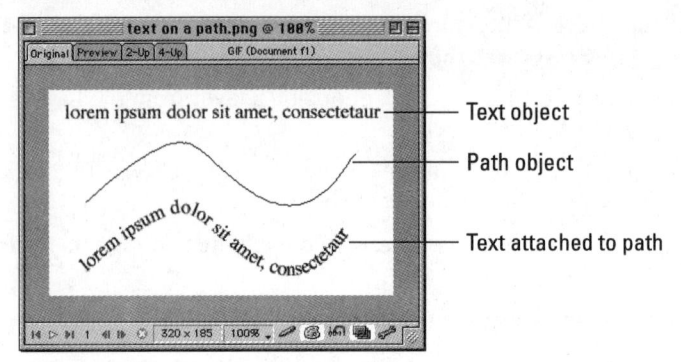

Figure 26-16: The two separate objects — text and path — are combined in one with the Attach to Path command.

Several variables affect exactly how the text flows along the path. First, the alignment of the text itself can have an effect:

+ **Left Aligned:** The text starts at the beginning of the path.
+ **Centered:** The text is centered between the beginning and end of the path.
+ **Right Aligned:** The text ends at the end of the path.
+ **Justified:** All the characters are evenly spaced along the path with additional spacing, if necessary.
+ **Stretched:** All the characters are stretched to fit along the path with standard spacing.

It's pretty easy to guess where a linear path starts and ends, but how about a circle? If you remember the discussion on using the Ellipse tool in Chapter 21, you might recall I mentioned that circle paths generally start at about 9 o'clock and travel in a clockwise direction, around the outside of the circle. To cause the text to begin its flow in a different area, you have three options:

+ Rotate the text attached to the path using one of the transform tools.
+ Choose Modify ⇨ Transform ⇨ Numeric Transform, and select Rotate from the option list before choosing the angle of rotation.
+ Enter an Offset value in the Objects panel.

The Offset value moves the text the specified number of pixels in the direction of the path. Because circle diameters vary, trial and error is the best method for using the Offset value. The Offset option also accepts negative numbers to move the text in the opposite direction of the path.

To flow the text along the inside of the circle, choose Text ⇨ Reverse Direction (see Figure 26-17). With an Offset value at 0, the text will begin at 6 o'clock and flow counterclockwise.

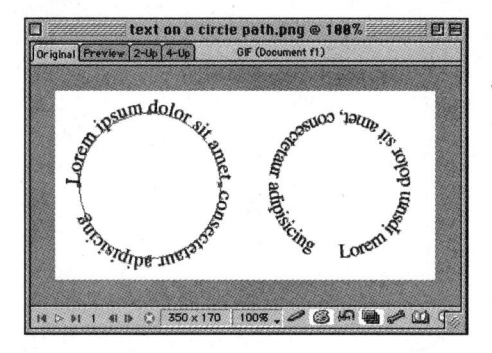

Figure 26-17: Use the Reverse Direction command in combination with Offset to properly place your text in a circle.

The final aspect that you can control with regard to attaching text to a path is the text's orientation to the path. You can find the options, shown in Figure 26-18, under Text ➪ Orientation:

- ✦ **Rotate Around Path:** Each letter in the text object is positioned perpendicularly to its place on the path (the default).
- ✦ **Vertical:** Each letter of the text object remains straight relative to the document, as the letters travel along the path.
- ✦ **Skew Vertical:** Rotates the letters along the path, but slants them vertically.
- ✦ **Skew Horizontal:** Keeps the letters straight on the path, and slants them horizontally according to the angle of the curve.

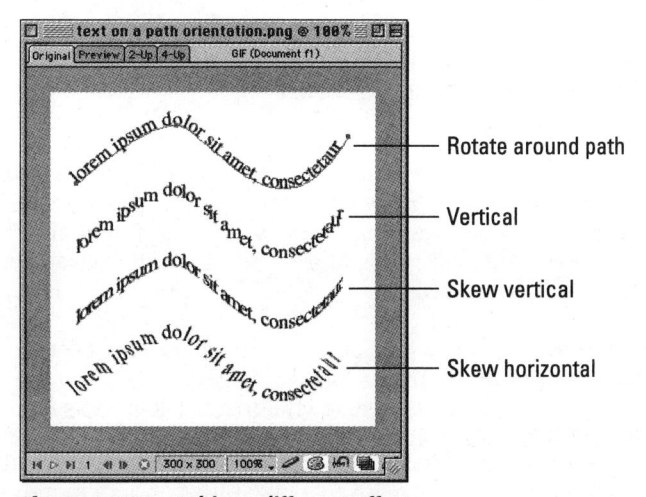

Figure 26-18: Achieve different effects by changing the orientation of the text to its attached path.

After looking at the Skew Horizontal example in Figure 26-18, you might be wondering why this option was included. One of the reasons why it looks so unappealing is that the skew changes when the underlying path changes its angles. When Skew Horizontal is applied to a path with no or fewer curves, you can achieve a more pleasing effect, as shown in Figure 26-19.

Figure 26-19: The horizontal skew orientation looks best when it's applied to a path with few or no curves.

Fireworks Technique: Masking Images with Text

What do you get when you combine images and text so that the text becomes the image? A graphic worth a thousand and one words? Actually, I think the technique of masking images is often worth far more. Moreover, its relative ease of creation in Fireworks makes it especially valuable.

A mask group is two or more objects grouped together where the bottom object is visible only through the top object. Take a look at Figure 26-20, and you'll see immediately what I mean. Because color is often so vital to a mask group's effect — and because I think it's cool — I've also included the image in the color insert.

Figure 26-20: Combine imagery and text through a mask group. Note the bevel Live Effect on the text, which remains after grouping.

To mask an image with text, follow these steps:

1. Create an image and a text object, or move existing image and text objects into the same document.
2. Position the text object over the image in its approximate final place.
3. Select both objects.
4. Choose Modify ➪ Mask ➪ Group as Mask.

   The image is now only visible through the text.
5. Use the Subselection tool to select and modify the placement of the image, if necessary.

Tip You can still edit the text used in a Mask Group—you just have to ungroup it and select it by itself. When you're finished with your edits, apply the Group as Mask command again.

The basic technique for masking an image with text is the same as using any other object as a mask. I've found, however, that manipulating the text into the proper shape beforehand creates a more successful mask. I try to start with a fairly wide font so that much of the image comes through, and then apply the Horizontal Scale and/or Kerning controls in the Text Editor to get the largest possible type. For example, the font used in Figure 26-20 is the very thick Arial Black, with a –12 percent Kerning value, so that the characters touch and don't break up the image.

Summary

Text and images are codependents on the Web. It's nearly impossible to have one without the other, but the text-handling features of Fireworks make for a smooth integration. Gaining a complete understanding of creating and editing Fireworks' text objects is essential for strong Web design. Keep these considerations in mind as you work with text in Fireworks:

- ✦ Text is always editable for files saved in Fireworks' native format. You can apply a stroke, fill, or effect, and you can transform text repeatedly — and you'll still be able to edit all the text, all the time.

- ✦ Text in Fireworks is represented in the document as a text object. You create text objects through the Text Editor or import them from ASCII or RTF files.

- ✦ The Text Editor is the major text interface and contains all the controls necessary for assigning attributes, such as typeface, size, color, spacing, and alignment to text.

- ✦ Alterations made in the Text Editor are instantly visible in the document.

- ✦ You can reposition text objects on the canvas while the Text Editor is open.

- ✦ Text can accept the full range of strokes, fills, and effects available in Fireworks. The transform tools — Scale, Skew, and Distort — also work with text objects.

- ✦ Converting a text object into a series of paths allows you to combine those paths with other path objects for interesting effects.

- ✦ Fireworks has a very full-featured Align Text with Path command that enables you to flow text around a circle, down a curving slope, or tracing any path you desire. Moreover, you can adjust the spacing of the text through the Alignment and Offset features.

- ✦ You can easily combine text and images by using the Fireworks Group as Mask command.

In the next chapter, you get into the center of Fireworks objects, as I explain fills and textures.

✦ ✦ ✦

Using Fills and Textures

CHAPTER 27

In This Chapter

Understanding fills

Choosing a fill type

Extending color range with Web Dither

Modifying a Gradient fill

Fireworks technique: Making transparent gradients

Enhancing your graphics with Patterns

Fireworks technique: Developing seamless Patterns

Texturizing your Web graphics

Filling parts of an image with the Paint Bucket

Fills and strokes are fairly equal partners in Fireworks graphics. A fill gives substance to the inside of an object, just as a stroke does the outside. Fills in Fireworks come in many flavors — solid colors, gradations of color, and image patterns — and, as with strokes, they are astoundingly flexible and almost infinitely variable. Moreover, fills in objects are always editable, which means changing from a flat color to a repeating pattern takes only a click or two.

After touring the standard fills included with Fireworks, this chapter begins to explore the many ways you can customize and enhance fills. In addition to the techniques for editing gradients, Patterns, and the many variations obtainable through textures, you'll see how you can add custom gradients, Patterns, and textures.

Using Built-in Fills

As with strokes and the Stroke panel, you generally apply and modify fills from the Fill panel, shown in Figure 27-1. You can display the Fill panel by choosing Window ➪ Fill, clicking the Fill tab if visible, or using the keyboard shortcut, Shift+F7.

The five primary fill categories are

- **None:** No fill.
- **Solid:** Specifies a flat color fill, selectable with the Eyedropper in the pop-up color picker.
- **Web Dither:** Extends the Web-safe color range by using a repeating pattern of two Web-safe colors that simulates an unsafe color.

✦ **Pattern:** Applies a full-color image as a repeating pattern.

✦ **Gradient:** Inserts one of 11 gradient patterns blending two or more colors. The Gradient category is not separately listed, but implied through the listing of the gradient patterns.

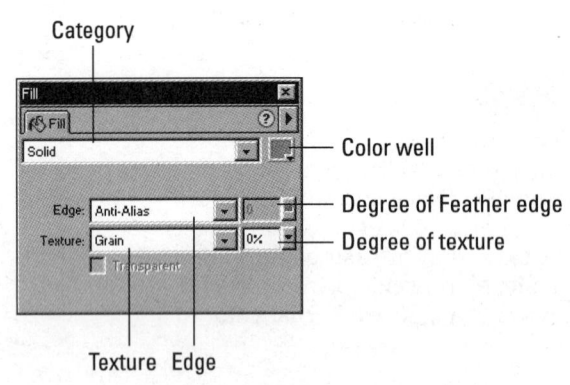

Figure 27-1: The Fill panel is your command center for applying and modifying any type of fill.

Each of the different categories offers a slightly different Fill panel. If you choose Solid, for example, no additional presets are presented; if you select Pattern, an option list with all the available Patterns appears. All fill types (except for None) have some similarities: The standard color well is present in all categories, as is the Edge option list.

The Edge option acts exactly as the one found in the Stroke panel, with three choices: Hard Edge, Anti-Alias, and Feather. Choosing a Hard Edge fill uses only the fill specified with no enhancements; Anti-Alias blends the edge a bit, softening away the jaggies, if any; and Feather blends the edge the number of pixels specified through the Amount of Feather slider.

Textures work with fills in the same fashion as they do with strokes, but because they're so much more visible, you'll find a special section later in this chapter that delves deeper into their use.

Turning off an object's fill

Knowing how to remove the fill is just as important as adding a fill. In Fireworks, two methods exist for removing a fill. One is to choose None from the Category option list on the Fill panel. The other is to choose the No Color button from the pop-up color picker in the Tools panel, shown in Figure 27-2. Selecting the No Color button eliminates any type of fill, regardless of whether it's a solid, gradient, or pattern.

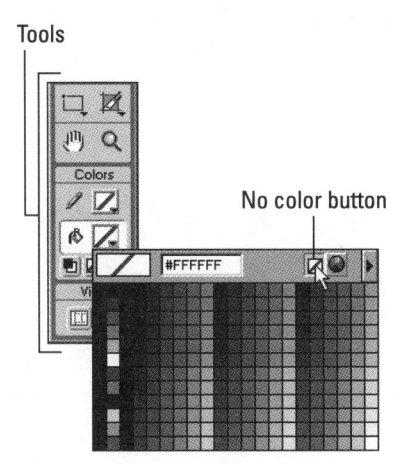

Figure 27-2: The color picker in the Tools panel is unique in that it has a No Color button for completely removing a fill.

Using a Solid fill

A Solid fill is a basic, monochrome fill, sometimes called a *flat fill*. The color used in the Solid fill type is selected from the Fill color well — whether it's the one on the Fill panel, the Tools panel, or the Mixer. The Fill color well uses the standard Fireworks pop-up color picker, shown in Figure 27-3. The color picker displays the swatches active in the Swatches panel, which, by default, is the Web-safe, 216-color palette.

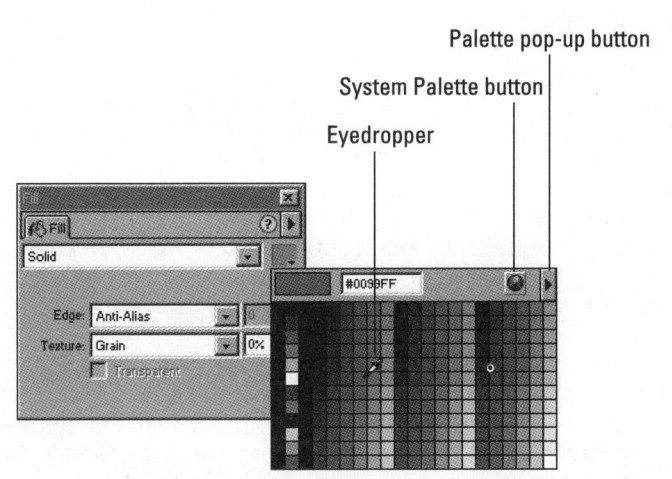

Figure 27-3: Assign a solid color fill through the Fill color well.

To apply a solid color to an object, follow these steps:

1. Select the object.
2. Access the Fill color well in one of these three ways:
   - Choose Window ⇨ Fill to open the Fill panel, and select the color well.
   - Select the Fill color well, as marked by the Paint Bucket, in the Tools panel (refer to Figure 27-2).
   - Choose Window ⇨ Color Mixer to display the Color Mixer panel and select the Fill color well, as marked by the Paint Bucket.

   Any one of these methods displays the pop-up color picker.
3. Use the Eyedropper to choose a color from the current swatch set, or select any color that's currently visible on your screen.
4. To access the operating system color picker(s), select the Palette button and select one of the colors in that dialog box.

You can adjust solid fills in several ways. You can select different edge options (Hard, Anti-Aliased, or Feather) from the Edge option list on the Fill panel; if you choose Feather, the Amount of Feather slider becomes available. In addition, a texture chosen from the Texture option list on the Fill panel may be applied. Remember, though, for a texture to be visible, you have to increase the Amount of texture past zero percent.

Using the Web Dither fill

Color is one of the most frustrating elements of Web design. Most Web designers use a palette of 216 Web-safe colors that the major browsers display correctly on both Macintosh and Windows computers set to 256 colors (8-bit color). The most obvious limitation is the relatively small number of colors: 216 out of a visible palette of millions of colors. Another limitation is the distance between colors; each Web-safe color is a large jump from its nearest Web-safe neighbor. These limitations become particularly acute when a client's logo contains colors that aren't available in the Web-safe palette. Luckily, Fireworks offers you a way to increase the Web-safe color variations to over 45,000: the Web Dither fill.

To understand how to use the Web Dither fill, you'll need a little more background in computer color. *Dithering* refers to the process where two or more pixels of different colors are positioned to create a pattern which, to the human eye, appears to be a third color. This technique works because a small pattern of pixels tends to blend visually; the eye can't separate the individual pixels. Dithering was originally used to overcome the 256-color restriction of early computer monitors. If you convert a photograph with millions of colors to a GIF with only 256 colors, you'll notice dithered areas where the computer graphics program is attempting to simulate the unavailable colors. For flat-color graphics, though, relying on dithering forces the designer to give up a lot of control. You don't know what you're going to get until you export.

Hybrid-Safe Colors were developed initially by Don Barnett and Bruce Heavin and later popularized by Web designer Lynda Weinman. A Hybrid-Safe color consists of two Web-safe colors in an alternating 2×2 pattern. Fireworks has adopted this technique and renamed it Web Dither. Not only does this feature now give you a total of 46,656 (216×216) Web-safe colors, but it also enables you to make any solid fill semitransparent, opening up a whole new area of graphic design.

When you choose the Web Dither category from the Fill panel, you'll notice a new set of options becomes available, as shown in Figure 27-4. Instead of one color well, there are now three. The top color well represents the current Fill color, whereas the other two color wells are used to create the dither pattern. If the current Fill color is already Web-safe, both dither colors will be identical. If the Fill color is not Web-safe, Fireworks creates the closest match possible by dithering two Web-safe colors.

To apply a Web Dither fill, follow these steps:

1. Select your object.

2. Open the Fill panel by choosing Window ⇨ Fill, clicking the Fill tab (if visible), or using the keyboard shortcut, Shift+F7.

3. Select the arrow button next to the topmost color well to display the pop-up color picker.

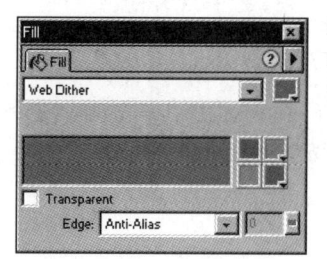

Figure 27-4: The Web Dither fill greatly expands the range of possible Web-safe colors that you can use.

4. Pick a color that is not Web-safe in one of these ways:

   - To select a color from the swatch in your active palette, choose the color from the pop-up color picker. The active color must not be from the Web 216 Palette for this method.

   - To select a color from an image onscreen, sample the desired color with the Eyedropper in the pop-up color picker.

   - To select a color using your system's color picker, choose the Palette button from the pop-up color picker.

Tip If you can't find an unsafe color, go outside of Fireworks with the Eyedropper and sample one elsewhere on your display. Windows users should hold down the mouse button while still over Fireworks, and keep the mouse button down as you hover the mouse over the color you want to sample, and release the mouse button to sample it.

Fireworks creates the closest color match possible by dithering your original color, as shown in Figure 27-5.

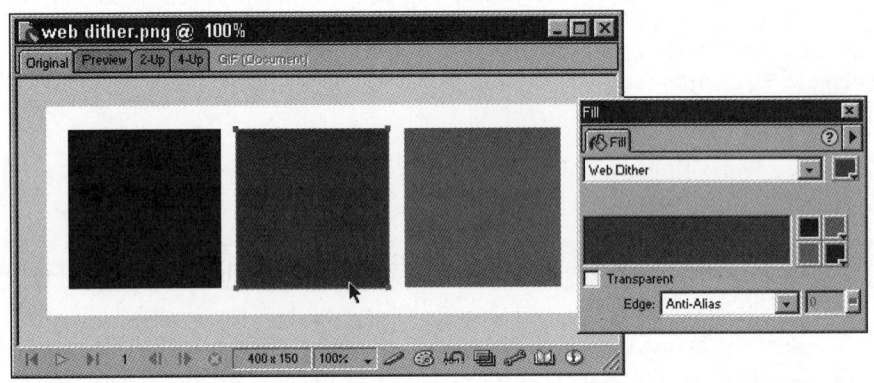

Figure 27-5: The middle square has a Web Dither fill applied. The squares on the left and right are the Web-safe colors used in the Web Dither, shown for example.

The Web Dither fill is terrific for finding absolutely must-have colors, such as those used for a logo, in a Web environment. When working from print materials, you can sample the color for the Web Dither fill.

Tip Though the Web Dither does give you a huge range of colors to choose from, that doesn't mean all the color combinations are useful. If you choose two highly contrasting colors for the dither color wells, the dithered pattern appears to be dotted. It's usually better to select the desired color for the Fill color well by using the Eyedropper or any other method, and let Fireworks create the dither pattern for you.

Fireworks takes the Web Dither fill further by including a Transparent option. When you enable the Transparent option, Fireworks sets the first dither color well to None, while snapping the second dither color well to the nearest Web-safe color. The dither pattern now alternates a transparent pixel with a Web-safe colored pixel, and the resulting fill pattern is semitransparent.

Tip When you export a figure using a Transparent Web Dither fill, be sure to select either the Index or Alpha Transparency option.

Managing Gradients

A *gradient* is a blend of two or more colors. Gradients are used to add a touch of 3D or to provide a unique coloration to a graphic. A gradient is composed of two parts: a *color ramp,* which defines the colors used and their relative positioning, and a *gradient pattern,* which describes the shape of the gradient.

Fireworks includes 11 different types of gradient patterns and 13 preset color combinations. As you might have guessed, that just scratches the surface of what's possible with gradients because, as with many features in Fireworks, gradients are completely editable.

Applying a Gradient fill

A Gradient fill is applied in a slightly different manner than a Solid or Pattern fill. To apply a Gradient fill, follow these steps:

1. Select your object.
2. Choose Window ➪ Fill, or click the Fill tab to bring the Fill panel to the front.
3. From the Category option list, choose one of the gradient options below the divider. When the selected gradient is initially applied, the current Stroke and the Fill colors are used to create the blend, and a Preset option list appears in the Fill panel, as shown in Figure 27-6.

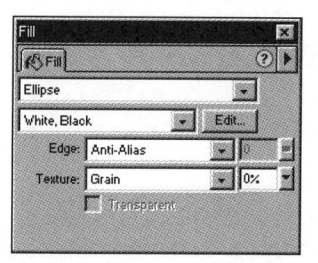

Figure 27-6: Select a gradient pattern and preset color combination from the Fill panel.

4. Choose a color combination from the Preset option list.
5. Change the fill edge or add a texture, if desired.

Rather than describe the standard gradients in words, grasping the differences visually is much easier, as demonstrated in Figure 27-7.

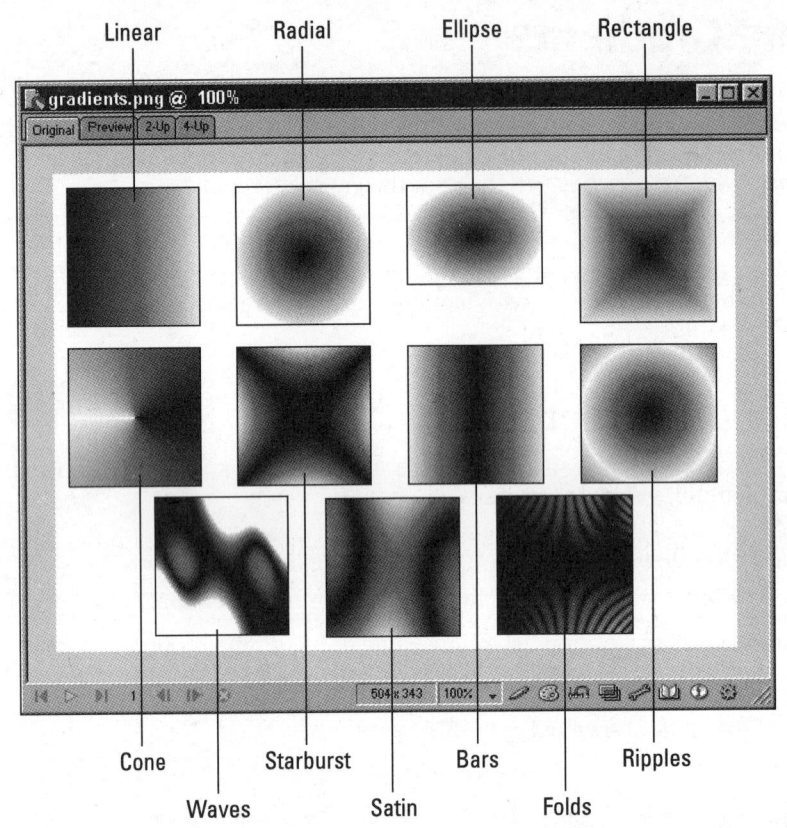

Figure 27-7: Fireworks provides 11 different gradient patterns.

Altering gradients

Fireworks' built-in gradient patterns and preset colors offer a good number of possibilities, but the real power of gradients comes in their customizability. You can modify gradients in two major ways:

✦ Every gradient pattern's center, width, and skew (if any) are all adjustable. With this facility, you can reshape the gradient's appearance with any object.

✦ The color ramp used to create the progression of colors in a gradient is completely flexible. Existing colors can be changed, deleted, or moved, and new colors can be added anywhere in the gradation.

You can save the custom color ramp information as a new preset, much like a custom stroke. However, a modified gradient pattern cannot be saved, either as a gradient or style. Unfortunately, no way exists to transfer a modified gradient pattern, other than copying and pasting the actual object.

Modifying the gradient pattern

Each gradient object has handles. Handles are the keys to unlocking — and customizing — the gradient patterns. Selecting an object that has a Gradient or Pattern fill with the Pointer tool causes the gradient controls to appear. All gradients have a starting point and an ending point, and four (Ellipse, Rectangle, Starburst, and Ripples) use two controls to adjust the size and skew of the pattern. The gradient controls are placed differently for each gradient pattern, as is evident in Figure 27-8.

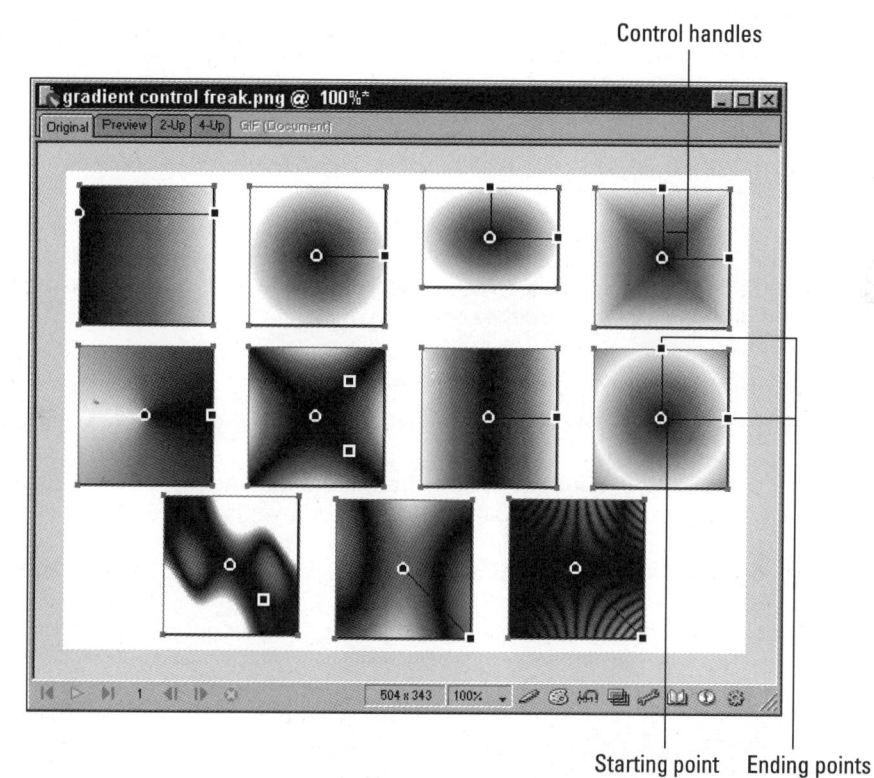

Figure 27-8: Each of the 11 standard gradients has individual control handles.

New Feature Gradient handles can now be activated by clicking a gradient-filled object with the Pointer tool, as well as the Paint Brush. This makes selecting and modifying gradients quite a bit easier.

To modify a gradient pattern, follow these steps:

1. Select the object with the Gradient fill. The gradient controls appear.
2. To move the starting point for the gradient, drag the circular handle to another position.

3. To rotate the direction of the gradient, move the cursor over the length of any control handle until the Rotate cursor appears, and then drag the handles to a new location. As you rotate the gradient, Fireworks uses the gradient's starting point as a center axis.

4. To change the size of any gradient, drag the square handle straight to another position.

5. To alter the skew of an Ellipse, Rectangle, Starburst, or Ripples gradient, drag either square handle in the desired direction.

You're not limited to keeping the gradient controls within the selected object. You can move any gradient control — beginning, ending, or sizing/skewing handle — away from the object. In fact, many of my nicest gradient patterns resulted from placing the controls completely outside of the object. Experiment and think "outside the box."

Caution

Remember, no way exists to copy a modified gradient pattern from one object to another — much less one image to another — outside of copying and pasting the object itself. To mimic an effect on two widely different objects, you have to duplicate the placement of the gradient controls by hand.

Editing gradient colors

If you cycle through the preset gradient color combinations, you'll notice that some presets have as few as two colors and others have as many as six. To see how the color preset is structured, choose the Edit Gradient command from the Fill panel pop-up menu. The Edit Gradient pop-up dialog box, shown in Figure 27-9, is divided into three main areas: the color ramp, the color wells, and the preview pane. You can dismiss pop-up dialog boxes in Fireworks by clicking anywhere outside of them.

New Feature   The Edit Gradient dialog box is now a pop-up dialog box for quicker, easier access.

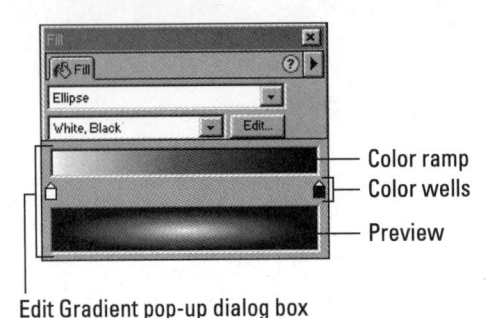

Figure 27-9: Modify the colors used in a gradient through the Edit Gradient pop-up dialog box.

The color ramp shows the current color combination as it blends from one key color to another. The key colors are displayed in the color wells, located beneath the color ramp. The preview pane shows how the color combination would be applied to the active gradient pattern. You can either modify a preset gradient, or adjust a gradient created from the Fill and Stroke colors.

To edit a gradient, follow these steps:

1. Choose Window ⇨ Fill, or use the keyboard shortcut, Shift+F7 to display the Fill panel.
2. Choose Edit Gradient from the Fill panel pop-up menu. The Edit Gradient pop-up dialog box appears.
3. To adjust the rate of change between colors, drag the color wells into new positions. One color well can be dragged on the far side of another color well.
4. To remove a color well completely, drag the color well and drop it outside of the Edit Gradient pop-up dialog box.
5. To add a new color well, click anywhere directly below the color ramp. The added color well displays the color directly above it in the color ramp.

Tip You'll notice a little plus sign added to your cursor where clicking will add another color well.

6. To select a new color for a color well, click the color well. The standard pop-up color picker appears. Select any of the available swatches, or use the Eyedropper tool to sample an onscreen color, including one from another color well. You can use the Palette button on the pop-up color picker to access the system color picker(s).
7. Click OK when you're done.

Although no real limit exists as to the number of colors you can add to an edited gradient, adding more than two dozen or so is not practical. With so many colors, the color wells begin to overlap, and selecting the correct one to modify becomes increasingly difficult.

Saving and renaming

After you've modified an existing gradient, you need to save it in order to recall it. In Fireworks, you can store an altered gradient two ways:

✦ Use the Save Gradient command, found on the Fill panel pop-up menu, to store the gradient color combination in the current document.

✦ Create a new style and save just the Fill type.

Examining Fill panel options

The Fill panel pop-up menu offers several gradient management options:

- **Save Gradient As:** Stores the current gradient under a new name within the active document.
- **Edit Gradient:** Displays the Edit Gradient dialog box.
- **Rename Gradient:** Relabels the current gradient.
- **Delete Gradient:** Removes the current gradient, custom or standard, from the Gradient panel.

Storing a modified gradient

To store a modified gradient, follow these steps:

1. Choose Save Gradient As from the Fill panel pop-up menu. The Save Gradient As dialog box appears.
2. Enter a unique name for the gradient. If you choose a name already in use, Fireworks asks whether you want to replace the existing gradient.
3. After entering a new name, choose Save. The new gradient name is displayed alphabetically in the Preset option list of any gradient.

Using the gradient in another document

It's important to understand that new or modified gradients are stored only within the document in which they're used. To use the gradient in another document, follow these steps:

1. Open the document containing the gradient you want to use.
2. Select an object using the new gradient.
3. Open the new document in which you want to use the new gradient.
4. Copy the selected object to the new document either by using Edit ⇨ Copy and Edit ⇨ Paste, or by dragging and dropping the object from one document to the other. The new gradient setting is added to the Fill panel when the object containing the gradient arrives in the new document.
5. If desired, delete the copied object from the new document.

Several other ways exist to achieve the same effect of transferring gradients from one document to another:

- Use Insert ⇨ Image to insert a document containing one or more custom gradients. After you've clicked once to place the document, choose Undo. The graphics will vanish, but all custom gradients will be incorporated into the Gradients panel.

✦ Copy the object with the custom gradient to the clipboard, then select a vector object in another document, and choose Edit ➪ Paste Attributes to apply the gradient fill from the first object.

Using the Styles feature

Perhaps the best way to ensure that your custom gradients are available is to save them as styles and store them in the Styles panel. To create a new style using a custom gradient, follow these steps:

1. Select an object that uses the custom gradient.
2. If necessary, choose Window ➪ Styles, use the keyboard shortcut, Shift+F11, or click the Style tab, if visible. The Style panel appears.
3. On the Style panel, select the New Style button.
4. In the Edit Style dialog box, enter a descriptive name for your gradient in the Name text box and deselect all checkboxes except Fill Type.
5. Click OK when you're done. A new style is entered in the Style panel.

Any style added in the previously described fashion is always available for any Fireworks document. To apply the gradient, simply highlight any Fireworks object and select the new style. Your custom gradient is then added to the Fill panel.

Cross-Reference: To find out more about using styles, see Chapter 31.

Fireworks Technique: Making Transparent Gradients

Although you can pick any available color in the spectrum for a gradient color well, you can't select "no color." In other words, you can't create a gradient that uses transparency in the Edit Gradient dialog box. However, a fairly straightforward and flexible technique exists that you can apply to get the desired effect of having any Fireworks object—vector or bitmap—fade away.

Almost all of Fireworks' transparency effects take advantage of the Mask Group feature—and the transparent gradient is no exception. A Mask Group combines two or more objects, and uses the topmost object as an alpha mask. Where the mask is black, the underlying objects are transparent; where the mask is white, the underlying objects are opaque. Shades of gray in between are semi-transparent. Because there is a gradual blend from black to white in a gradient, using a gradient as a mask enables you to create a smooth transition from transparent to opaque.

To create a transparent gradient, follow these steps:

1. Create or insert an object or image that you want to make partially transparent.
2. Draw a second masking object that completely encompasses the original object. If you are masking a vector object, rather than a bitmap object, you can clone the original.
3. Open the Fill panel.
4. With the masking object selected, choose a gradient pattern, such as Linear or Radial.
5. From the Preset option list, choose Black, White.
6. If necessary, reposition the masking object over the original object, ensuring that the masking object is in front of the original object.
7. Select both objects by drawing a selection around them with the Pointer tool.
8. Choose Modify ⇨ Mask ⇨ Group as Mask.

As you can see in Figure 27-10, where I combined the top two objects to make the mask group below them, the transparent background shows through quite well. In fact, it may show through a bit too well. I often find that I need to adjust the standard Black and White gradient preset so that there is more black than white. I do this by choosing Edit Gradient in the Fill panel pop-up menu and sliding the black color well closer to the white one. To edit the gradient in this fashion, it's better to first select the Mask Group, and then choose the Paint Bucket tool to expose the gradient control handles. When the gradient controls are active, you can use the Edit Gradient feature and immediately apply it — otherwise, you must first ungroup the Mask Group and reselect just the Gradient fill.

Using Patterns

Simply put, a Pattern fill uses a repeating image to fill an object. Patterns are often used to provide a real-world surface, such as denim or water, to a computer-generated drawing. More abstract Patterns are also used to vary the look of a graphic. Fireworks includes an extensive collection of standard Patterns with even more available in the Goodies/Patterns folder of the Fireworks CD-ROM. Not surprisingly, you can also add your own images to be used as a Pattern.

Cross-Reference Fireworks' built-in patterns are detailed in the color insert.

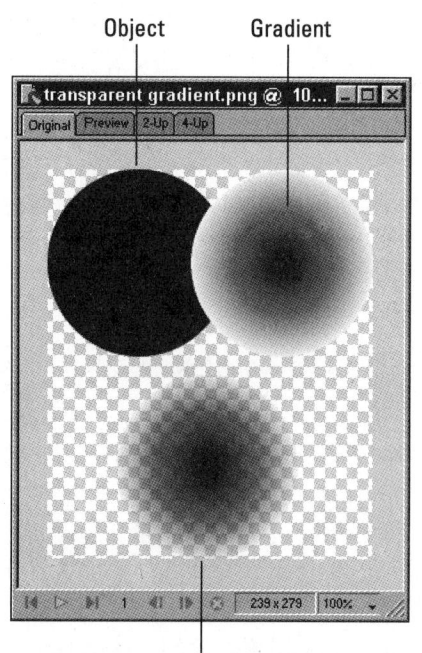

Figure 27-10: A gradient-filled object is combined with another object to make a Mask Group that enables a fade to transparency.

The Pattern fill is one of the primary categories found on the Fill panel. When you select the Pattern option, a second option list, Fill Name, appears with all the available Patterns. As you move down the Fill Name option list, a small preview of the Pattern is displayed next to each highlighted file, as shown in Figure 27-11.

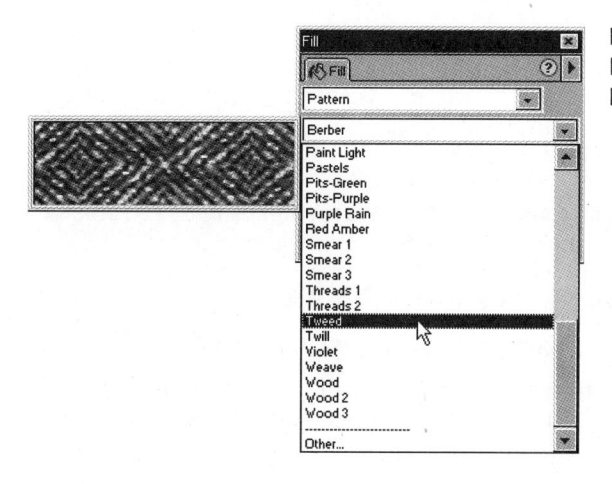

Figure 27-11: Choose your Pattern fill from the Pattern Fill Name option list.

The only Fireworks requirement for a Pattern fill image is that the image be in PNG format. However, not all images are well-suited to making Patterns; the best Patterns are those that repeat seamlessly so that the boundaries of the original file cannot be detected. All the standard Fireworks files fill this requirement, as is clearly visible in the color insert.

As with any other fill, you can apply Pattern fills to any shape object. The other fill attributes — edge and texture — are also applicable.

Adding new Patterns

The two ways to add Patterns to the Pattern Name option list so that they are available every time you use Fireworks are

- Save or export a file in PNG format to the Configuration/Patterns folder within the Fireworks program folder.

Tip

The Fireworks program folder is typically found at C:\Program Files\Macromedia\Fireworks 4 on Windows-based computers, and at `Macintosh HD: Applications:Macromedia Fireworks 4:` on the Mac.

- Through the Fireworks Preferences dialog box, assign an additional folder for Patterns.

PNG is a native format of Fireworks, so storing any file as a Pattern just by saving it is quite easy. Pattern images are usually full-color (whereas textures are displayed in grayscale), but that's not a hard-and-fast rule. Likewise, Patterns are generally 128 pixels square, but that's just a convention, not a requirement; one of the Patterns found on the Fireworks CD, Light Panel, is 12 pixels wide by 334 pixels high.

After you've saved a file in your Patterns folder and restarted Fireworks, the new Pattern is listed along with the other Patterns. As shown with my new Patterns in Figure 27-12, they even preview in the same way.

Assigning an external Patterns folder is a very easy way to add a whole group of folders at one time, as well as a good way to share resources in a networked environment. To assign an additional Patterns folder, follow these steps:

1. Choose Edit ⇨ Preferences. The Preferences dialog box opens.
2. Select the Folders tab (choose Folders from the option list on the Macintosh).
3. Choose the Browse button in the Additional Materials section, next to the Patterns option. A navigation dialog box appears.

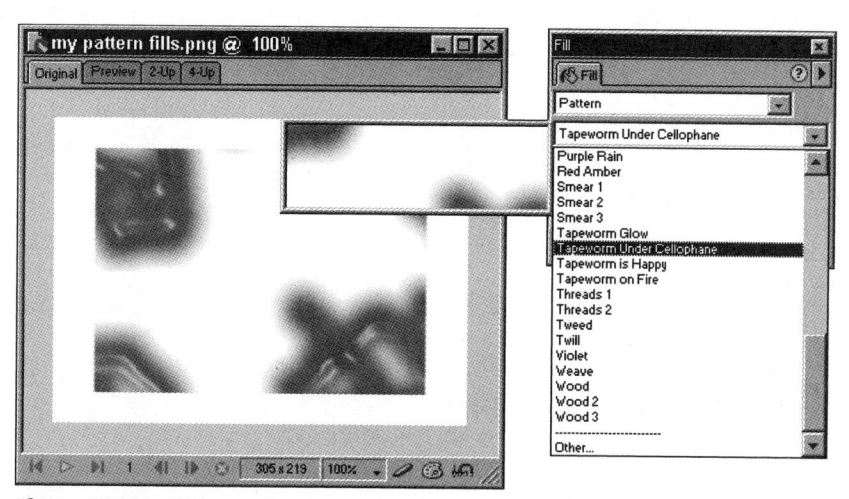

Figure 27-12: My own Tapeworm Patterns are available from the Pattern Name option list after saving them in the Configuration/Patterns folder and restarting Fireworks.

   4. Locate the external folder that contains the PNG files you want to access as Patterns. Click OK when you've selected the folder. The Patterns checkbox is now enabled on the Preferences dialog box.
   5. Click OK to accept the changes and close Preferences.
   6. Relaunch Fireworks to make the additional Patterns available for use.

> **Tip** Want quick access to the Patterns on the Fireworks CD? Assign your external Patterns folder in Preferences to the Goodies/Patterns folder and restart Fireworks. When Fireworks opens, if the CD is present, the additional Patterns are integrated into the Fill panel list — and you can remove the CD after Fireworks has finished loading, and the Patterns will still be available. If the CD is not available, Fireworks loads normally, but the additional Patterns are not incorporated.

Adding Patterns to a document

Adding commonly used Patterns to your default list in Fireworks is great, but what if you want to quickly grab an image file and use it as a Pattern without the hassle of moving it into the Fireworks Patterns folder first? On such an occasion, Fireworks enables you to work with Patterns on a document-by-document basis.

To access an external PNG image as a Pattern in the current document, follow these steps:

1. Select the object you would like to apply the Pattern to.
2. Choose Window ➪ Fill, or click the Fill tab to view the Fill Panel.
3. Choose Pattern from the Fill panel category list.
4. From the Pattern Name option list, choose Other to display an Open dialog box.
5. Navigate to the PNG file you would like to use as a Pattern and select it. Click OK when you're done.

Fireworks adds your new Pattern to the Pattern Name option list and applies it to your selected object. The Pattern will be accessible from the Pattern Name option list only within the current document. When you save the document, the Pattern is saved within the document.

> **Tip**
> The fact that the Pattern is saved within the document makes it portable. If you share work with someone at another location, adding the custom Patterns you use to your document automatically makes them available to that coworker when he or she receives the document.

Altering Patterns

You can adjust Patterns in the same manner as gradients. After a Pattern fill has been applied to an object, selecting the Paint Bucket tool causes the control handles to appear, as shown in Figure 27-13. The same types of vector controls are available:

+ Adjust the center of the Pattern fill by dragging the round starting point.
+ Rotate the Pattern fill by moving the cursor over the length of any control handle until the Rotate cursor appears, then drag the handles to a new angle.
+ Change the size of any Pattern by dragging either square handle straight to another position.
+ Alter the skew of any Pattern by dragging either square handle in the desired direction.

Unlike gradients, all Patterns have two control handles in addition to the starting point of the fill. The handles are always perpendicular to one another and presented in the same ratio as the height to the width.

> **Caution**
> When rotating an object, the Pattern or gradient fill does not rotate with it. Instead, you'll need to use the Pattern or gradient control handles to change the angle of the fill.

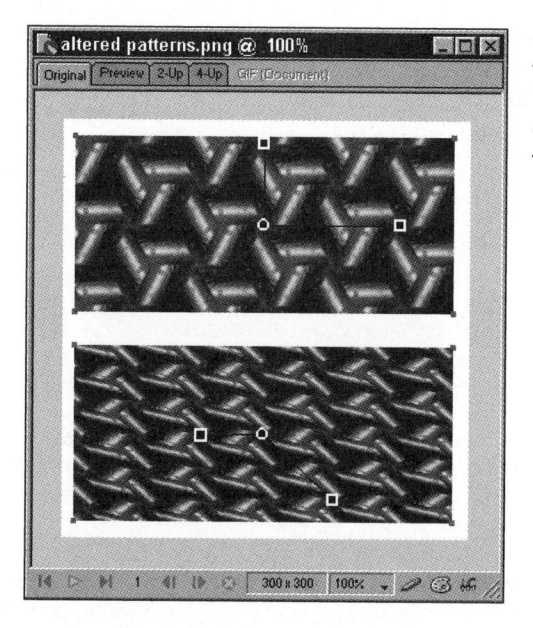

Figure 27-13: Both rectangles were filled with the standard Illusion2 Pattern and then the control handles of the bottom rectangle were rotated to change the Pattern direction.

Fireworks Technique: Creating Seamless Patterns

The biggest problem with creating new Pattern fills is making them appear seamless. When Fireworks tries to fill an object larger than the size of the Pattern file, it repeats or tiles the image until the object is completely filled. If an image is used with even the smallest border, the repeating pattern is immediately noticeable; in most cases, this is not the desired effect. Several methods eliminate the appearance of seams.

The first, and simplest, technique is to avoid placing graphic elements near the edge of your Pattern image. This enables the canvas — or background color — to blend smoothly from one instance of a Pattern into another. For example, the image shown in Figure 27-14 could be made into a Pattern without showing any seams.

Many images, of course, rely on a visually full background where the canvas color is completely covered. To convert this type of graphic into a Pattern, a fair amount of image editing is necessary to make the edges disappear. Luckily, Fireworks contains enough graphic editing power to make this procedure feasible.

Figure 27-14: An image that has the same color all around its outside border can easily be made into a Pattern, because areas of identical color will appear seamless when they touch.

A tiled Pattern places images next to every side of the original image. To remove any indication of a boundary, you need to simulate a tiled Pattern and then blend the images so that no edges show. The following steps detail the procedure I use to smooth Pattern edges in Fireworks.

> **Note:** Throughout this technique, I refer to the menu syntax for the command, such as Edit ⇨ Copy. Naturally, feel free to use whatever keyboard shortcuts you're familiar with.

1. Open the image you want to convert to a Pattern.
2. Select a portion of the image to use as the basis for your Pattern.

   Using a portion of a scanned image or other graphic as a Pattern is quite common. The best technique I've found for this is to determine how large you want your Pattern to be (128×128 pixels is a good size), and then use the Fixed Size feature of the Marquee tool available through the Options panel to set those dimensions. This lets you work with a preset Marquee and move it into position more easily.

3. Choose Edit ⇨ Copy to copy the selected area.
4. Choose File ⇨ New to create a new document. The document should be at least three times the size of your selected image. Because mine is 128 pixels square, 384×384 pixels would be my minimum size.
5. To guide placement, choose View ⇨ Grid ⇨ Edit Grid to set the size of the grid the same as your image, and enable the Show Grid and Snap to Grid options.
6. Choose Edit ⇨ Paste to paste the copied area in the upper-left corner of the document, as shown in Figure 27-15.

Figure 27-15: After setting the grid to help with alignment, the first image is pasted down.

7. Copy the image with the Alt+drag (Option+drag) method. Place the copy of the image to the right of the original.
8. Repeat Step 7 twice more, but place the two new image copies below the two already in place, as shown in Figure 27-16.

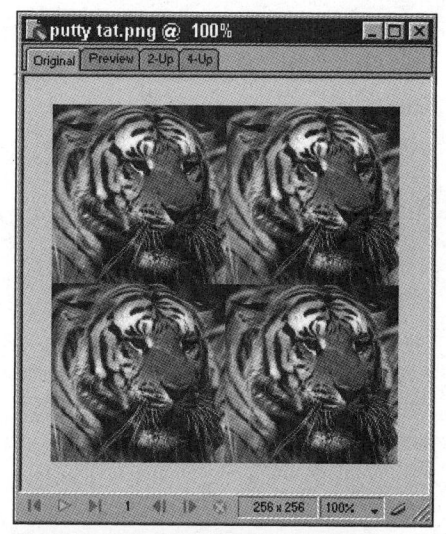

Figure 27-16: With all four copies in place, the edges are plainly visible.

9. Turn off both the grid (toggle View ⇨ Grid ⇨ Show Grid) and the Snap to Grid options (toggle View ⇨ Grid ⇨ Snap to Grid).

10. Select all four copies of the image and choose Modify ⇨ Convert to Bitmap. This step is necessary because the core of this technique uses the Rubber Stamp tool, which only works with bitmap objects. By selecting all copies, the four separate bitmap objects have been merged into one.

11. Select the Rubber Stamp tool from the Tools panel.

    The next step is the core of this procedure and, as such, requires a bit of finesse and trial-and-error to get it right. You might want to save the document at this stage so you can restart the process without having to start completely over.

12. Working on the vertical seam between the copies on the left and the right, click the Rubber Stamp origin point down one side a few pixels to the side, near the edge. Drag over the edge in a left-to-right motion (or from right to left, depending on which side the Rubber Stamp origin is located), extending the side of one image into the side of another.

    Follow this procedure down the vertical seam. Occasionally, you might need to switch directions and origin point to vary the blurring. Press Alt to reset the origin point of the Rubber Stamp tool. If necessary, set the Rubber Stamp options to the softest possible edge on the Options panel.

13. After you've blurred the vertical seam, repeat the process for the horizontal seam, changing the direction of the Rubber Stamp as needed.

    When you're done blurring both the vertical and horizontal edges, the resulting image should appear to be a seamless Pattern, as shown in Figure 27-17. After this step, it's time to copy the portion of the image used to make the Pattern.

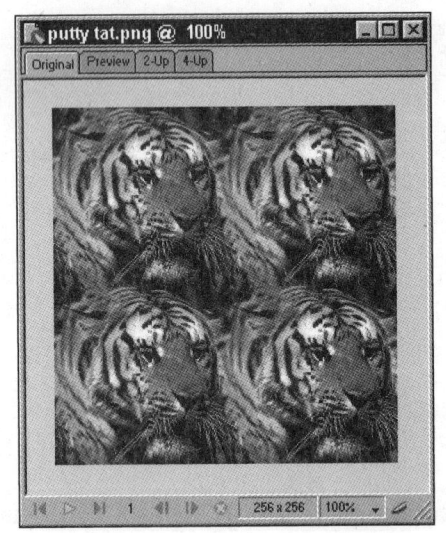

Figure 27-17: After the edges are blurred, it's hard to tell where one image stops and the other starts.

14. Choose View ⇨ Grid ⇨ Edit Grid, and reset the grid to half of its former size, enabling both the view and the snap options as well. Using a half-sized grid allows you to easily grab the center of the current image. My original grid was 128×128 pixels, so my new one for this step is 64×64.

15. Choose the Marquee tool from the Tools panel. The Marquee's Options should still be set to the Fixed Size option, using your original dimensions.

16. Use the Marquee tool to select the central portion of the overall image, as shown in Figure 27-18. Notice that the selection takes a part of all four images, previously separate.

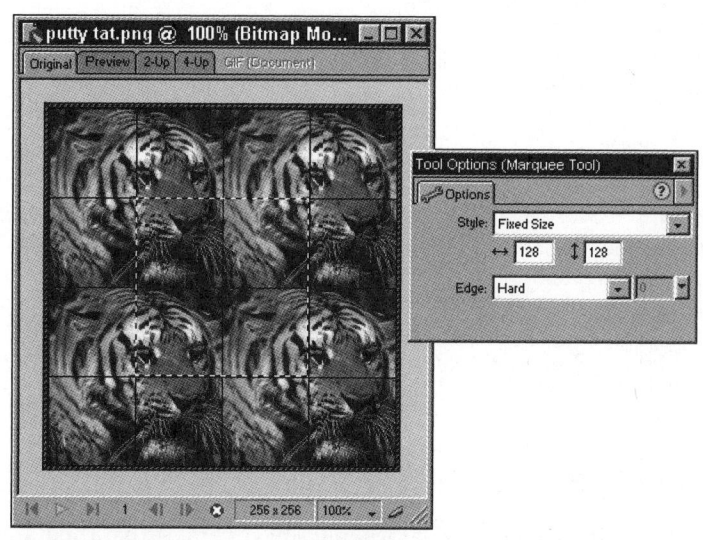

Figure 27-18: The combination of the grid and the Fixed Size marquee selection make selecting part of all four original images easy.

17. Choose Edit ⇨ Copy to copy the selection.

18. Choose File ⇨ New to create a new document. Fireworks automatically sizes the new document to match the graphic on the clipboard.

19. Choose Edit ⇨ Paste to paste the selection. This is your finished Pattern file (see Figure 27-19).

20. Choose File ⇨ Save, and store the image in the Configuration/Patterns folder, within your Fireworks program folder.

21. Restart Fireworks.

Tip

If you don't want to restart Fireworks, you don't have to, but you'll have to use the Other option from the Pattern Name option list to select your Pattern file for use.

Figure 27-19: The final Pattern uses the center of four adjacent images so that its edges will meet seamlessly when patterned.

22. Test your Pattern by drawing out a closed path and filling it with your new Pattern.

23. If necessary, open the just-saved Pattern file and edit to remove any noticeable edges.

There are numerous other ways to blur the line between your edges, but the Rubber Stamp tool works in many situations. Although it does take a bit of practice to get the hang of the tool and this technique, the results are definitely worth it.

Cross-Reference: For more information on the Rubber Stamp tool and its options, see Chapter 22.

Adding Texture to Your Fills

A common complaint about computer graphics in general is that their appearance is too artificial. If you take a quick look around the real world, very few surfaces are a flat color — most have some degree of texture. Fireworks simulates this reality by enabling any fill (or stroke, for that matter) to combine with a texture. In Fireworks, a texture is a repeating image that you can apply on a percentage basis.

As with Fireworks patterns, textures are PNG images designed to be repeated, and are stored in a specific folder. But that's where the similarity with patterns ends. Whereas a pattern replaces any other fill, a texture is used in addition to the chosen fill. A texture is, in effect, another object, which is blended on top of the original object. As you increase the degree of a texture through the Fill panel slider, you are actually increasing the opacity of the texture. When the amount of texture is at 100 percent, the texture is totally opaque and the textured effect is at its maximum.

Another difference between pattern and texture is color: Patterns can be any range of color, whereas textures are displayed in grayscale. The reason for this is purely functional: If textures included color, the color of the original fill or stroke would be altered. One consequence of the grayscale property is that flat white fills are almost totally unaffected by textures.

Extending Textures to Strokes and Images

Textures aren't limited to enhancing fills. You can just as easily apply them to strokes and, with a little more work, images as well. Sometimes a stroke is used to define a filled object, and it's best not to extend the texture onto the stroke. Certain images, however, benefit from a continuation of the texture from fill to stroke.

Take, for example, the following figure. I created a very simple texture of alternating lines that is applied to the stroke (a big Air Brush) in the top example. Because the same set of textures are available from both the Fill and Stroke panel, it's easy to duplicate settings from one panel to the other, so in the middle example, a fill has been added and the same lines texture applied to it. The bottom example has had some Live Effects added, but the lines still show through and bring the stroke and fill together.

Applying a texture to an image requires an additional step. Strokes and fills cannot be applied directly to an image. The technique then is to create a vector object that completely covers the image and apply the texture to that vector object. Blend it into the image either by altering the opacity of the vector object, and/or its blending mode (both of these controls are in the Layers panel), or by using the vector object as a mask for the image. As is often the case with Fireworks, a little experimentation can lead to some very interesting results.

Tip Generally, textures work better with darker colors, which permit more range of contrast.

Fireworks includes a wide range of textures, and provides even more on the Fireworks CD-ROM. Each texture is chosen from an option list on the Fill panel and, as with patterns, a preview is displayed for each texture. Next to the Texture option list is a slider that controls the chosen texture's degree of intensity. The higher the amount of texture, the more pronounced the texture's effect on the fill, as shown in Figure 27-20.

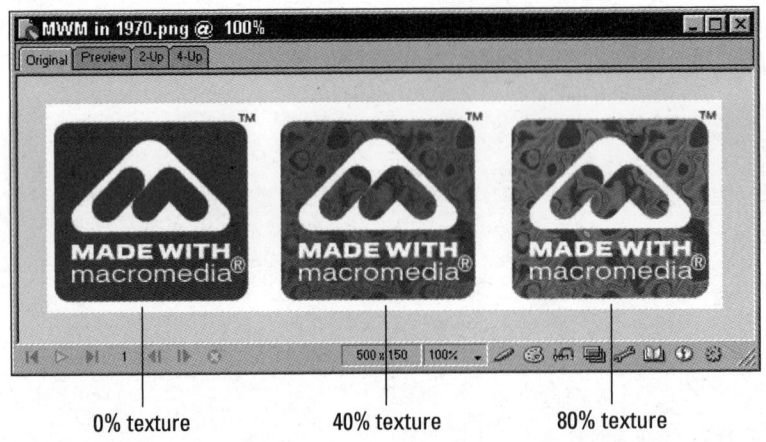

0% texture   40% texture   80% texture

Figure 27-20: Increasing the amount of texture on the Fill panel makes the texture more visible.

An additional property of textures is transparency. If your textured object is on top of other objects, enabling the Transparent option lets the background objects show through the light portions of the texture. The higher the degree of texture, the more transparent an object becomes.

Adding new textures

New textures are added exactly the same way that new patterns are added:

✦ Save or export a file in PNG format to the Configuration/Textures folder within your Fireworks program folder.

✦ Through the Preferences dialog box, assign an additional folder for textures.

Textures files work best when they enable a repeating pattern without visible edges and, as mentioned previously, all textures are shown in grayscale.

Converting a color image to grayscale

Although you don't have to convert images to grayscale before saving them as textures—Fireworks simply displays color textures as grayscale, anyway—converting them allows you to get a better sense of how the texture will ultimately look, and also gives you a chance to alter the overall brightness and contrast to achieve the best-looking texture.

To convert a color vector or bitmap object to grayscale using the Convert to Grayscale Command, follow these steps:

1. Select the object you want to convert.
2. Choose Commands ⇨ Creative ⇨ Convert to Grayscale. Fireworks converts your object to grayscale.

Assigning an additional textures folder

If you have an entire group of textures you want to add at one time, you can assign an additional folder for Fireworks to include in the texture list. To assign an additional Textures folder, follow these steps:

1. Choose Edit ⇨ Preferences. The Preferences dialog box opens.
2. Select the Folders tab (choose Folders from the option list on a Macintosh).
3. In the Additional Materials section, choose the Browse button next to the Textures option. A navigation dialog box appears.
4. Locate the external folder that contains the PNG files you want to access as textures. Click OK when you've selected the folder. The Textures checkbox is now enabled on the Preferences dialog box.
5. Click OK to accept the changes and close Preferences.
6. Restart Fireworks to make the additional textures available.

On the CD-ROM: Can't get enough textures? You'll find more in any of the Textures folders listed under particular authors in the Additional Extensions folder on the CD-ROM accompanying this book.

Adding textures to a document

As with patterns, you can open textures one at a time and use them with your current document, allowing easy access to textures stored anywhere on your computer. Textures opened in this way are saved within the current document.

To access an external PNG image as a texture in the current document, follow these steps:

1. Choose Window ⇨ Fill, or click the Fill tab to view the Fill Panel.

2. Choose Solid, Pattern, or a gradient from the Fill panel category list in order to view the Texture Name option list.

3. From the Texture Name option list, choose Other to display an Open dialog box.

4. Navigate to and select the PNG file you want to use as a texture. It can be a color or a grayscale image, but the result will always be a grayscale texture. Click OK when you're done.

Fireworks adds your new texture to the Texture option list.

Filling with the Paint Bucket Tool

The Paint Bucket tool is used to fill a selected area with the current Fill panel settings — whether those settings involve a solid color, a gradient, or a pattern. The Paint Bucket can be used to fill both vector objects and bitmap objects. However, the Paint Bucket fills all of a vector object completely, whereas it only fills the selected portion of a bitmap object, or a range of like, adjacent colors if there is no selection, as shown in Figure 27-21.

With vector objects, nothing is simpler than using the Paint Bucket. Simply choose the Paint Bucket tool (or use the keyboard shortcut, K), and then click the object once to apply the current Fill panel settings. If the Fill panel is set to None, the current fill color — shown on the Tools panel and Mixer — is used to give the object a Solid fill.

Caution Fireworks doesn't distinguish between open and closed paths when the Paint Bucket is used. If the Paint Bucket is used on an open path, such as an S-curve, an invisible line is drawn from the beginning to the ending point and the fill is applied.

Bitmap objects are a different story with regard to the Paint Bucket. If you click a bitmap object with the Paint Bucket without selecting an area using one of the selection tools (Marquee, Ellipse Marquee, Lasso, Polygon Lasso, or Magic Wand), one of three things will happen:

✦ The current Fill settings will be applied to the selected pixel and the neighboring pixels that fall within the Tolerance range set in the Options panel.

✦ The entire bitmap object will be filled with the current Fill settings, if the Fill Selection Only object is selected from the Options panel and the Expand to Fill Document option from Preferences is not enabled.

✦ The entire document will be filled with the current Fill settings, if the Fill Selection Only object is selected from the Options panel and the Expand to Fill Document option from Preferences is enabled.

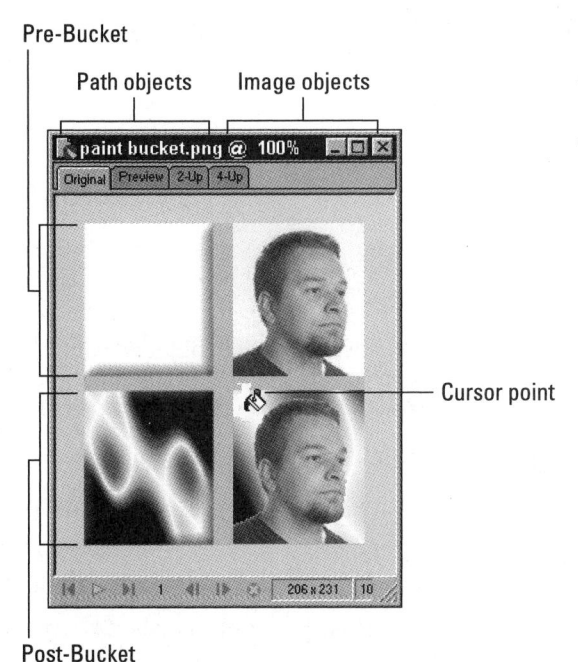

Figure 27-21: The vector object on the bottom left is filled completely by the Paint Bucket. Applying the same fill to the bitmap object on the bottom right only affects pixels colored similarly to those under the cursor.

Pre-Bucket
Path objects
Image objects
Cursor point
Post-Bucket

As you can see, the Options panel, shown in Figure 27-22, becomes very important when you apply the Paint Bucket tool to bitmap objects.

The available options are as follows:

- **Mouse Highlight:** Highlights a selectable area when passed over with the pointer.

- **Fill Selection Only:** Disregards color tolerance settings and fills a selected area, or if no area is selected, either the bitmap object or document according to the Expand to Fill Document setting.

- **Preserve Transparency:** Only colors existing pixels, so that transparent pixels stay transparent.

- **Tolerance:** Sets the range of colors to be filled when Fill Selection Only is not enabled. The Tolerance slider accepts values from 0 (where no additional colors are filled) to 255 (where all additional colors are filled).

- **Edge:** Determines the type of edge on the fill — Hard, Anti-Aliased, or Feather. If Feather is selected, the Amount of Feather slider becomes available, which sets the degree to which the fill is blended into surrounding pixels.

Tip After you've made a selection in a bitmap object, you don't have to click in the selected area with the Paint Bucket to change it. Clicking anywhere in the document automatically fills the selected area.

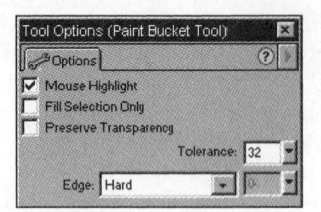

Figure 27-22: The Options panel for the Paint Bucket tool has a major effect on how bitmap objects are filled.

Summary

Fills are one of Fireworks' basic building blocks. Without fills, objects would appear to have outlines only and arranging objects on top of one another would be difficult, if not impossible. As you begin to work with fills, keep these points in mind:

- ✦ You can apply Fills to any Fireworks object: vector or bitmap.
- ✦ Access all the fill settings through the Fill panel. You can also find the Fill color well on the Tools panel and the Mixer.
- ✦ The five options for fills are None, Solid, Web Dither, Pattern, and Gradient.
- ✦ The Web Dither fill visually blends two Web-safe colors to make a third color outside the limited Web-safe palette.
- ✦ You can modify a Gradient or Pattern fill by selecting the filled object with the Pointer or Paint Bucket tool and adjusting the control handles.
- ✦ New gradient color combinations can be saved in each document and reused, or stored in a style.
- ✦ A Pattern fill can be made from any repeating image, stored in PNG format, or can be stored within a document.
- ✦ Textures can bring a touch of realism to an otherwise flat graphic, and can also be stored within a document.
- ✦ The Paint Bucket options control whether the entire bitmap object is filled, or just a selection is filled.

In the next chapter, you find out about the razzle-dazzle side of Fireworks: Live Effects and Xtras.

✦ ✦ ✦

Creating Live Effects and Xtras

CHAPTER 28

♦ ♦ ♦ ♦

In This Chapter

Understanding Fireworks effects

Using the Effect panel

Working with Live Effects

Fireworks technique: creating perspective shadows

Managing Live Effects

Applying Xtras

Using Photoshop-compatible plug-in filters

Third-party filters

♦ ♦ ♦ ♦

Many Fireworks graphics are based on three separate but interlocking features: strokes, fills, and effects. Not everyone would put effects — the capability to quickly add a drop shadow or bevel a button — on the same level as strokes and fills, but most Web designers would. Effects are pretty close to essential on the Internet. Not only are the look and feel of many Web sites dependent on various effects, but much of their functionality, especially when techniques like button rollovers are concerned, demands it.

Live Effects are a Fireworks innovation. For the first time, designers can edit common effects without having to rebuild the graphic from the ground up. But what makes Live Effects truly "Live" is Fireworks' capability to automatically reapply the effects to any altered graphic — whether the image is reshaped, resized, or whatever. You can even use many standard Photoshop-compatible filters as Live Effects, and apply, edit, or remove them as easily as Fireworks' own classic bevels and glows.

Later in the chapter, we look at how you can apply Xtras and what you can apply them to. You work with the Xtras that are included with Fireworks and examine some of the techniques that you can use to apply them creatively. You also see how you can add more Xtras to Fireworks, including ones that you may already have as part of another application. Finally, this chapter reviews two very popular third-party image filter packages: Eye Candy and Kai's Power Tools.

Understanding Fireworks Effects

Although the Xtras menu contains the definitive list of the image filters to which Fireworks has access, many image filters are also available in "live" versions from the Effect panel.

You can treat Photoshop-compatible filters in the Effect panel just like any other Live Effect: Add and remove them as you please, reorder them, or adjust their settings at any time.

New kinds of creative experimentation are made possible with many of the same image filters that you may have used for years in Photoshop. Rearranging the order that filters are applied without having to start from scratch, or easily saving favorite combinations of filters, is truly liberating. Exciting new combinations of effects are made possible, just because they're so easy to mix, match, and experiment with.

Using the Effect panel

The Effect panel, shown in Figure 28-1, is a powerful tool that centralizes almost all the effects in Fireworks, with the exception of some third-party image filters, which remain only accessible from the Xtras menu. The Effect panel fundamentally offers you access to two lists: the Effect Category option list, which contains all the Live Effects to which you have access; and the Effects list, which contains only the Live Effects that are currently applied to a selection.

The Effect Category option list is divided into five distinct parts:

- **None:** Choosing this option removes all the effects from the selection.
- **Use Defaults:** Loads the classic Inner Bevel, Outer Bevel, Drop Shadow, and Glow Live Effects into the Effects list. Check them to enable them for your selection.
- **Effects combinations that you save:** This section is not visible until you save your first combination.
- **Included Live Effects:** Such as bevels, blurs, and glows.
- **Third-party Photoshop-compatible image filters.**

Not all third-party image filters can be used as Live Effects. Those that can't simply don't show up in the Effect Category option list and can only be accessed in the Xtras menu.

Applying Live Effects

You can only apply Live Effects to objects selected in vector mode. If you want to apply a Live Effect to a pixel selection, you have two choices:

- Select an area with the pixel selection tools and copy it to the clipboard. Choose Modify ➪ Exit bitmap mode. Next, paste the selection as a new bitmap object. The new bitmap object is placed exactly where your pixel selection was located. Apply the Live Effect to your new bitmap object. If you like, you can then group the new bitmap object and the original bitmap object from which the pixel selection was taken.

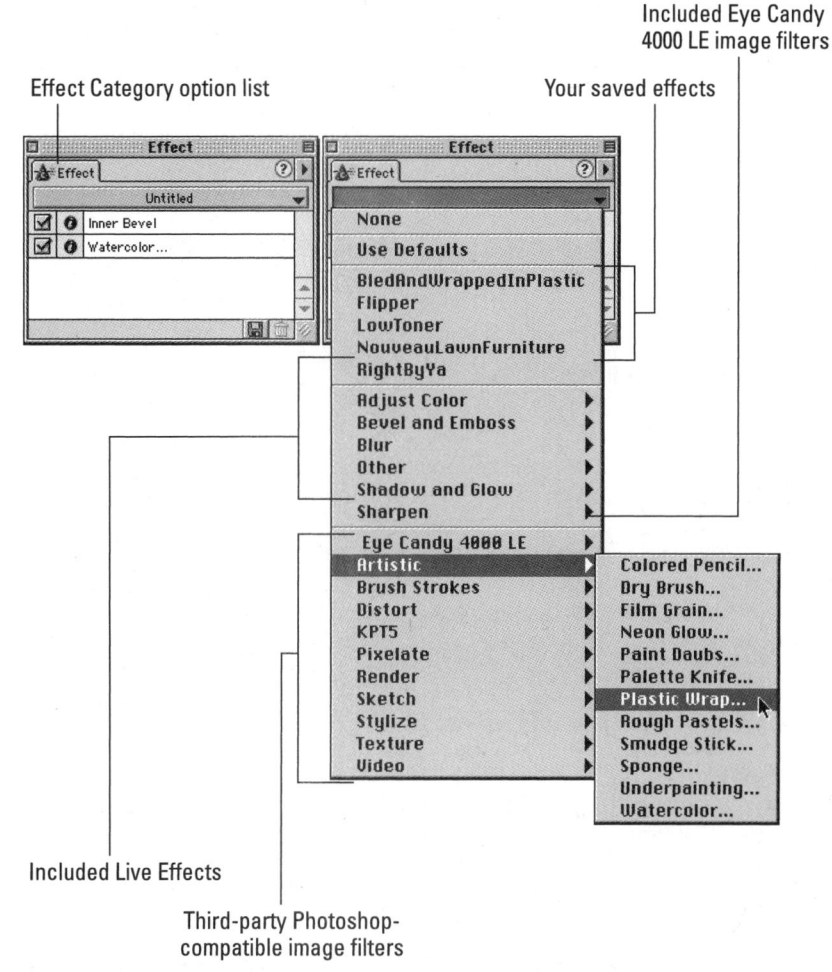

Figure 28-1: The Effect panel with its Effect Category option list is a central access point for almost all the effects available in Fireworks.

- ✦ Some Live Effects are also available from the Xtras menu and can be applied to a pixel selection from there, although this doesn't maintain editability.

Although each effect has its own unique settings, you apply them all in basically the same fashion:

1. Select an object or objects. Fireworks can simultaneously apply the same effect to multiple objects.

Tip If you are currently in bitmap mode, click the "Stop" button on the bottom of the document window to enter vector mode.

2. Choose Window ⇨ Effect to open the Effect panel. Alternatively, you could use the keyboard shortcut, Alt+F7 in Windows (Option+F7 on a Macintosh), or click the Effect tab, if it is visible.

3. Select your effect from the Effect Category option list. If the effect has editable settings — most do — Fireworks displays either a pop-up dialog box (see Figure 28-2) or a regular dialog box, depending on the effect.

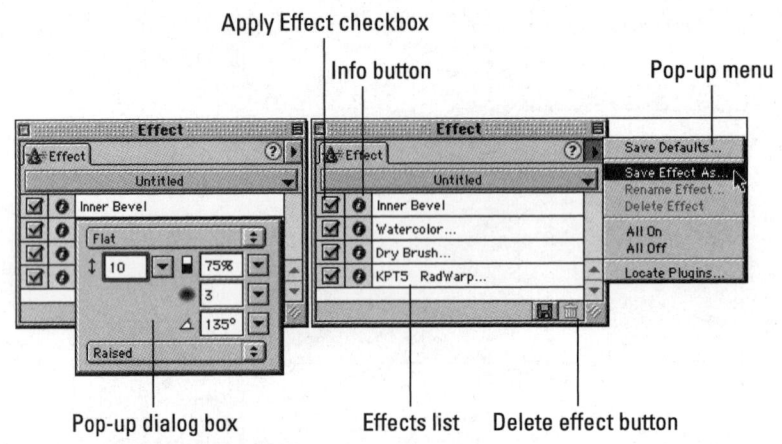

Figure 28-2: The Effect panel offers a high level of control over the way effects are applied, edited, and removed.

4. Modify the settings in the dialog box to achieve the desired effect. After you're done, click anywhere outside a pop-up dialog box, or click OK in a regular dialog box, or press Enter (Return) in either.

The effect is applied to all selected objects.

After an effect is applied, it is added to the Effects list in the Effect panel, and Fireworks keeps it alive throughout any other changes that the object may undergo. Fireworks actually recalculates the required pixel effects and reapplies the effect after a change is made for vector, bitmap, or text objects. To my mind, the capability to make completely editable vector artwork (see Figure 28-3) look like bitmaps that have undergone numerous image filter modifications is a superb addition to the Web designer's toolbox.

Cross-Reference: For another look at Figure 28-3, turn to the color insert.

To edit the parameters for an applied effect, select the object, and click the Info button next to the effect that you want to modify in the Effects list. Fireworks displays the effect's dialog box. Edit the parameters and dismiss the dialog box by clicking OK, or by clicking anywhere outside it if it is a pop-up dialog box.

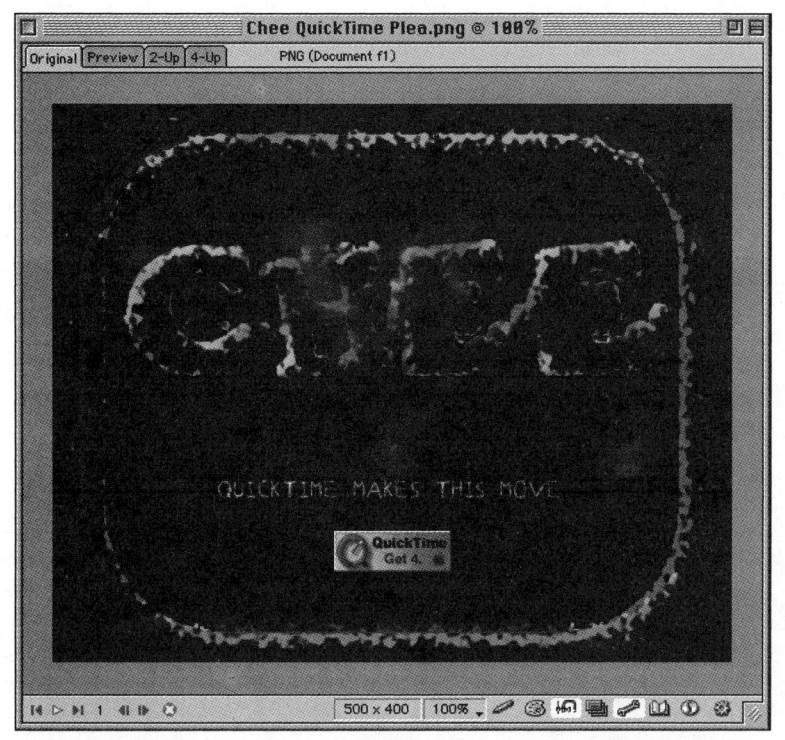

Figure 28-3: Fireworks' always-editable Live Effects make these vector objects look like bitmaps that have been extensively modified with image filters.

As good as Fireworks effects look, sometimes objects look better with no effects. To remove all effects from an object, select the object and then, from the Effect panel, choose None from the Effect Category option list. To temporarily disable a single effect, deselect the checkbox next to that effect in the Effects list. To temporarily disable all effects, choose All Off from the Effect panel pop-up menu. Of course, choosing All On from the pop-up menu enables all applied effects. To remove a single effect permanently, select the effect in the Effects list and click the Delete Effect button, which looks like a trash can and is located at the bottom of the Effect panel.

Examining the Xtras menu

Many bitmap-editing applications offer you a dedicated menu that contains Photoshop-compatible plug-in image filters. Fireworks is no exception, and the Xtras menu, shown in Figure 28-4, is it. When you launch Fireworks, it populates the Xtras menu with all the image filters it has access to. Generally, these are installed in Fireworks' Xtras folder (more on that later), or in the Photoshop plug-ins folder specified in your Fireworks preferences.

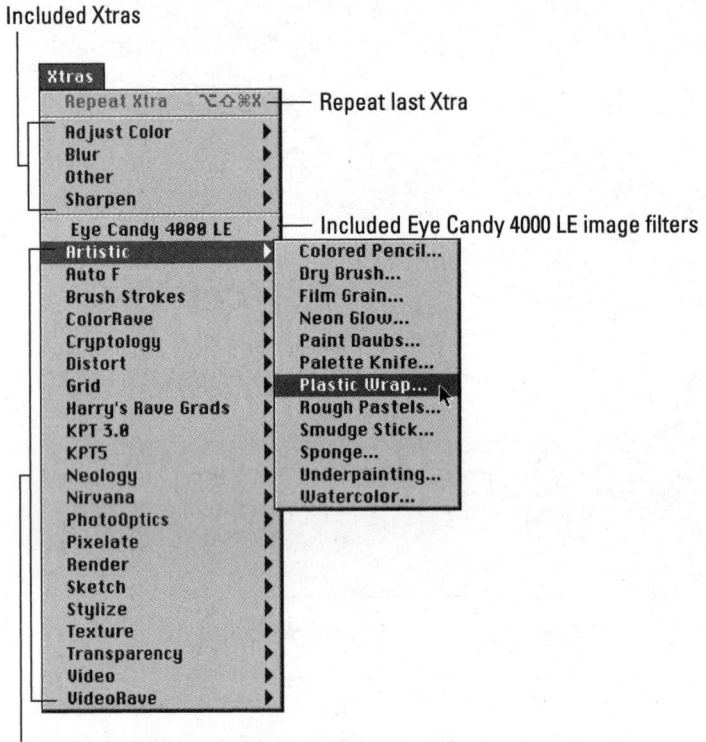

Figure 28-4: The Xtras menu contains built-in Fireworks image filters, as well as any third-party, Photoshop-compatible image filters you've added.

Labels in figure: Included Xtras; Repeat last Xtra; Included Eye Candy 4000 LE image filters; Third-party Photoshop-compatible image filters.

Menu items shown: Xtras, Repeat Xtra; Adjust Color, Blur, Other, Sharpen; Eye Candy 4000 LE; Artistic, Auto F, Brush Strokes, ColorRave, Cryptology, Distort, Grid, Harry's Rave Grads, KPT 3.0, KPT5, Neology, Nirvana, PhotoOptics, Pixelate, Render, Sketch, Stylize, Texture, Transparency, Video, VideoRave. Submenu: Colored Pencil..., Dry Brush..., Film Grain..., Neon Glow..., Paint Daubs..., Palette Knife..., Plastic Wrap..., Rough Pastels..., Smudge Stick..., Sponge..., Underpainting..., Watercolor...

> **Tip:** Image filters are called "filters" because every pixel in the image is evaluated — filtered — and either modified or not according to the settings and the effect that's being applied. I use the terms Xtras and filters interchangeably throughout this chapter.

In a nutshell, the difference between the effects contained in the Xtras menu and the ones in the Effect panel are that the ones in the Xtras menu are not live. You can only apply Xtras to bitmap objects; applying them to a text or vector object flattens the object into a bitmap object. After an Xtra is applied, there is no way to remove the effect except with the Undo command or the History panel.

The Xtras menu is divided into three sections. From top to bottom, they are the following:

✦ A single menu command that identifies and repeats the last-used filter

✦ Image filters that are included with Fireworks itself

Caution: One exception is the DitherBox filter that's included with Photoshop 5. It finds its way onto the Other menu if you make it available to Fireworks.

✦ Third-party, Photoshop-compatible image filters

Plug-in image filters automatically organize themselves into submenus that are specified by the developer of the plug-in.

Working with Included Live Effects

Fireworks is shipped with a range of useful Live Effects built-in, contained in the following submenus of the Effect panel's Effect Category option list:

- ✦ **Adjust Color:** Auto Levels, Brightness/Contrast, Curves, Hue/Saturation, Invert, and Levels
- ✦ **Bevel and Emboss:** Inner Bevel, Inset Emboss, Outer Bevel, and Raised Emboss
- ✦ **Blur:** Including Blur, Blur More, and Gaussian Blur
- ✦ **Other:** The unclassifiable Convert to Alpha and Find Edges
- ✦ **Shadow and Glow:** Drop Shadow, Glow, Inner Glow, and Inner Shadow
- ✦ **Sharpen:** Including Sharpen, Sharpen More, and Unsharp Mask

Table 28-1 details the Live Effects that are included with Fireworks, and what each one does.

Table 28-1
Included Live Effects

Live Effect	Description
Auto Levels	Automatically produces an image with the maximum tonal range.
Brightness/Contrast	Adjusts the brightness and/or contrast of all the pixels in an image.
Curves	Enables you to adjust the level of a particular color in an image, without affecting other colors.
Hue/Saturation	Adjusts the color in an image.
Invert	Changes the color of each pixel to its mathematical inverse. Creates a photo-negative-type effect.

Continued

Table 28-1 *(continued)*

Live Effect	Description
Levels	Enables you to adjust the tonal range of all the pixels in an image.
Inner Bevel	Adds a three-dimensional look to an object by beveling its inside edge.
Inset Emboss	Simulates an object in relief against its background.
Outer Bevel	Frames the selected object with a three-dimensional, rounded rectangle.
Raised Emboss	Simulates an object raised from its background.
Blur	Blurs pixels together to create an unfocused effect.
Blur More	Same as Blur but across a slightly larger radius, for a more pronounced blur.
Gaussian Blur	Same as Blur More but with a Gaussian bell curve and a dialog box that enables you to specify the blur radius.
Convert to Alpha	Converts an image into a grayscale image that's suitable for use as an alpha mask. White pixels are colored transparent.
Find Edges	Detects the outlines of forms and converts them to solid lines.
Drop Shadow	Shadows the object against the background to make it stand out more effectively.
Glow	Puts a halo or soft glow around an object.
Inner Glow	Puts a glow within the inner edge of an object.
Inner Shadow	Puts a shadow within the inner edge of an object.
Sharpen	Sharpens by finding edges and increasing the contrast between adjacent pixels.
Sharpen More	Same as Sharpen but across a larger radius.
Unsharp Mask	Same as Sharpen More, but with control over which pixels are sharpened (and which are left "unsharp") according to the image's grayscale mask.

Cross-Reference For more about mask groups, see Chapter 29.

Adjusting color

The Adjust Color submenu of the Effect Category option list contains powerful tools for adjusting the tonal range and color correcting, or for adding special effects to objects. Traditionally, these tools have only been available in a destructive form:

You adjust an image's tonal range, and if you find out later you went a little too dark or light, you had to start with an earlier iteration of a document and redo your work. Introducing these tools to Fireworks users as Live Effects provides a dramatic increase in workflow flexibility.

Adjusting tonal range

Ideally, a photographic image would have a fairly even ratio of dark tones, midtones, and light tones. Too many dark pixels hides detail; too many light pixels and your image appears washed out. Too many midtones — darks aren't dark enough and lights aren't light enough — and your image appears bland, like the Before image in Figure 28-5. Fireworks offers you a few different methods for adjusting the tonal range of images. Which one you choose to use depends on how bad the damage is.

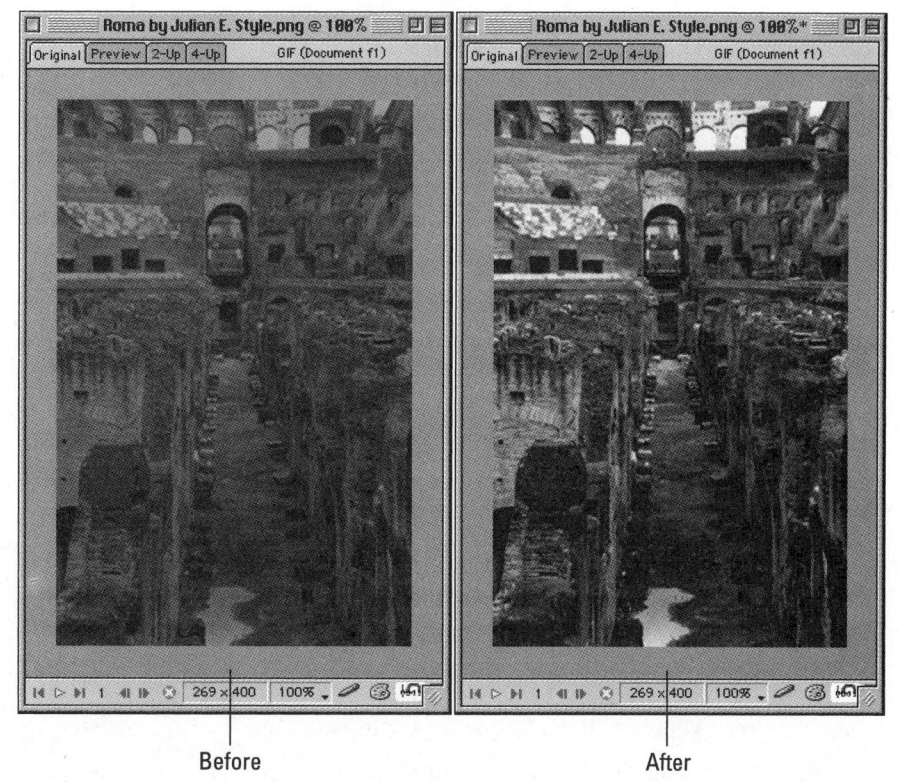

Before   After

Figure 28-5: Before and after increasing an image's tonal range to add contrast. Dark pixels are darkened and light pixels are lightened.

Dissecting Brightness/Contrast

For images that are only a little too dark or light, or lacking slightly in contrast, slight adjustments made with the Brightness/Contrast effect may be all you need. Fireworks can provide visual feedback by previewing your adjustments in the document window.

To use the Brightness/Contrast filter, follow these steps:

1. Select the object that you want to apply the effect to.
2. If the Effect panel is not currently visible, choose Window ➪ Effect to display it, or use the keyboard shortcut, Alt+F7 (Option+F7).
3. Choose Adjust Color ➪ Brightness/Contrast. Fireworks displays the Brightness/Contrast dialog box, as shown in Figure 28-6.

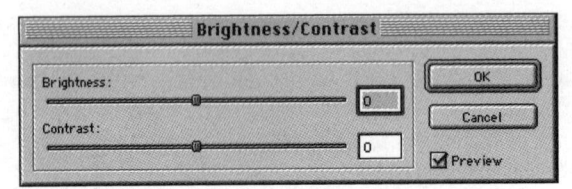

Figure 28-6: Adjust an image's brightness or contrast with the controls in the Brightness/Contrast dialog box.

4. Check Preview to view your changes as you make them in the document window.
5. Use the Brightness and/or Contrast sliders to adjust the settings. Values for the sliders range from –100 to 100. Click OK when you're done.

Coloring with Color Fill

The Color Fill Live Effect enables you to color the pixels of an object without permanently altering them.

New Feature: The Color Fill Live Effect is new in Fireworks 4.

To use the Color Fill Live Effect, follow these steps:

1. Select the object that you want to modify.
2. If the Effect panel is not currently visible, choose Window ➪ Effect to display it, or use the keyboard shortcut, Alt+F7 (Option+F7).
3. Choose Adjust Color ➪ Color Fill from the Effect Category option list. Fireworks displays the Color Fill dialog box.

4. Select the desired fill color from the pop-up color picker.
5. Alter the opacity setting with the Opacity slider.
6. Choose a blending mode from the Blending Mode option list.

Cross-Reference: See Chapter 29 for more about opacity and blending modes.

7. Click anywhere outside the pop-up dialog box to dismiss it, or press Enter (Return).

Fireworks applies the effect to your selected object.

Getting to know Levels and Auto Levels

For images that need more adjustment than is possible with Brightness/Contrast, Fireworks offers the Levels and Auto Levels filters. Auto Levels works just like Levels, except that you skip the Levels dialog box entirely, and Fireworks maps the darkest pixels in your image to black and the lightest ones to white. For many images, you may find that Auto Levels does the trick in record time. If not, you can take matters into your own hands with Levels.

Cross-Reference: See the Auto Levels filter demonstrated in the color insert.

The Levels dialog box introduces a special set of three eyedropper tools, shown in Figure 28-7, that are also available in the Curves dialog box, which I discuss in the next section. The trio of eyedroppers, one for highlights, one for midtones, and one for shadows, enable you to remap the highlights, midtones, or shadows of an image to new levels by pointing to a pixel with the desired level. For example, if your image is too dark, use the Shadow eyedropper and select a pixel that is a little lighter than the darkest pixels. Fireworks substitutes the tones of the newly selected "shadow" pixels for the darkest pixels in your image, lightening the image. The highlights and midtones eyedroppers work in a similar fashion, providing target levels for highlights and midtones, respectively.

Tip: Clicking Auto in the Levels dialog box is just like using the Auto Levels filter.

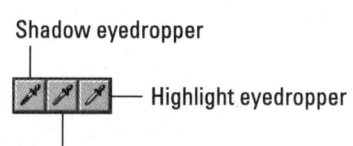

Shadow eyedropper
Highlight eyedropper
Midtone eyedropper

Figure 28-7: These special Eyedropper tools enable you to specify a new highlight, midtone, or shadow level by pointing to pixels.

Part II ✦ Working with Fireworks

> **Note** Identify the three eyedroppers by the ink they seem to contain. The highlight eyedropper has white ink, whereas the midtone eyedropper has gray ink, and the shadow eyedropper has black ink.

The Levels dialog box also includes a Histogram — essentially a chart — that reports the levels of dark, middle, and light tones in your image, giving you a quick graphical representation of what might need to be fixed. The horizontal axis is dark to light, from left to right. The vertical axis is a level from 0 to 255.

To apply the Levels filter and modify the tonal range of an image, follow these steps:

1. Select the object that you want to modify.
2. If the Effect panel is not currently visible, choose Window ➪ Effect to display it, or use the keyboard shortcut, Alt+F7 (Option+F7).
3. Choose Adjust Color ➪ Levels from the Effect Category option list. Fireworks displays the Levels dialog box, as shown in Figure 28-8.

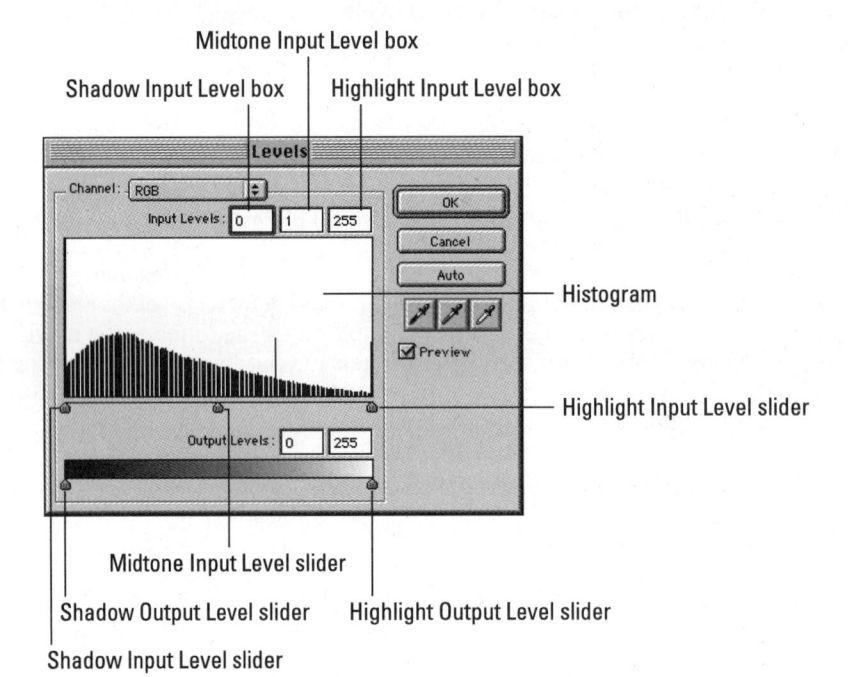

Figure 28-8: The Levels dialog box displays a Histogram of the light, midtone, and dark tones in your image.

4. Check the Preview checkbox to view your changes as you make them in the document window.

5. Select which channels you want to modify from the Channels option list: just Red, just Green, just Blue, or RGB to modify all three.

Tip: Modifying just the Red channel in an RGB image is similar to adjusting a color by increasing or decreasing the R value in the Color Mixer panel when it's set to RGB or Hexadecimal.

6. Modify the highlights and shadows in your image with the Highlight, Midtone, and Shadow Input Levels sliders, or enter new values directly in the Highlight and Shadow Input Levels boxes. Highlights and shadows are specified from 0 to 255, whereas midtones are specified with 1.0 being neutral, or 50 percent gray.

Note: The Shadow value can't be higher than the Highlight value, and the Highlight value can't be lower than the shadow Value.

7. Use the Highlights and Shadows Output Levels sliders to adjust your image's overall contrast.

8. If desired, use the Highlight, Midtone, or Shadow eyedropper to select a target level for highlights, midtones, or shadows, respectively, from your image.

9. Click OK when you're satisfied with the changes you've made.

The changes you've made are applied to the selected object.

Cross-Reference: Turn to the color insert to see a demonstration of the Levels filter.

Evaluating Curves

The Curves filter essentially serves the same purpose as the Levels filter, but it presents the information to you in a different way. Whereas the Levels filter enables you to adjust the individual levels of light, mid, and dark tones in an image, the Curves filter focuses on the levels of individual colors. You can adjust the level of red, for example, without affecting the balance of light to dark in an image.

The Curves dialog box contains a grid. The horizontal axis is the original brightness values, which are also shown in the Input box. The vertical axis displays the new brightness values, which are also shown in the Output box. The values that are represented are 0 to 255, with 0 being complete shadow. The line plotted on the grid always starts out as a perfect diagonal, indicating that no changes have been made (the Input and Output values are the same).

As mentioned previously, the Curves dialog box also contains a trio of eyedropper tools just like the Levels dialog box. The Curves dialog box also contains an Auto button, which yields the same result here as it does in the Levels box: The darkest pixels in your image are mapped to black and the lightest to white, just as if you had used the Auto Levels filter.

To use the Curves filter, follow these steps:

1. Select the object that you want to modify.
2. Choose Window ➪ Effect, or use the keyboard shortcut, Alt+F7 (Option+F7) to display the Effect panel, if it's not already visible.
3. Choose Adjust Color ➪ Curves from the Effect Category option list. Fireworks displays the Curves dialog box, as shown in Figure 28-9.

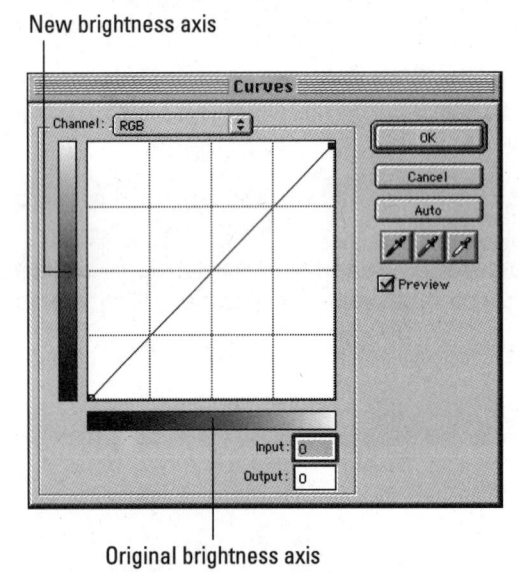

Figure 28-9: The Curves dialog box enables you to graphically alter a color curve.

4. Check the Preview checkbox to view your changes as you make them in the document window.
5. Select which channels you would like to modify from the Channels option list: just Red, just Green, just Blue, or RGB to modify all three.
6. Click a point on the grid's diagonal line, and drag it to a new position to adjust the curve. Changing the curve changes the Input and Output values.
7. To delete a point from the curve, select it and drag it out of the grid.

Caution You can't delete the curve's endpoints.

8. If desired, use the Highlight, Midtone, or Shadow eyedropper to select a target level for highlights, midtones, or shadows, respectively, from your image.
9. Click OK when you're satisfied with the changes you've made.

Fireworks applies the changes you've made to the selected object.

> **Cross-Reference**
> See the color insert to compare the effects of the Curves filter.

Looking into Hue/Saturation

The Hue/Saturation filter is similar to specifying colors using the HSL (Hue, Saturation, and Lightness) color model. If you're familiar with the concept of a color wheel, adjusting the hue is like moving around the color wheel, selecting a new color. Adjusting the saturation is like moving across the radius of the color wheel, selecting a more or less pure version of the same color.

> **Tip**
> Find examples of color wheels in your operating system's color picker(s), accessed by clicking the Palette button on the Fireworks pop-up color picker. Mac users can choose to view different color methods, including an HLS picker.

To adjust the hue or saturation of an image with the Hue/Saturation filter, follow these steps:

1. Select the object that you want to modify.
2. Choose Window ⇨ Effect, or use the keyboard shortcut, Alt+F7 (Option+F7) to display the Effect panel, if it's not already visible.
3. Choose Adjust Color ⇨ Hue/Saturation from the Effect Category option list. Fireworks displays the Hue/Saturation dialog box, as shown in Figure 28-10.

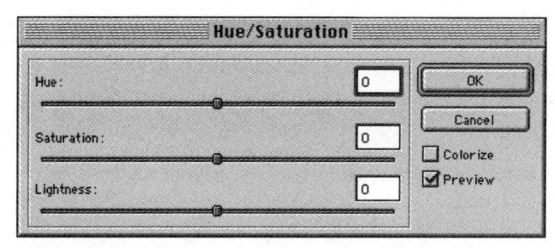

Figure 28-10: The Hue/Saturation dialog box offers Hue, Saturation, and Lightness sliders.

4. Check the Preview checkbox to view your changes in the document window as you make them.
5. Choose Colorize to add color to a grayscale image, or change an RGB image into a two-tone image.

> **Note**
> If you choose Colorize, the range of the Hue slider changes from −180 through 180, to 0 through 360; the range of the Saturation slider changes from −100 through 100, to 0 through 100.

6. Adjust the purity of the colors with the Saturation slider.

7. Adjust the color of the image with the Hue slider.

8. Adjust the lightness of the colors with the Lightness slider.

9. When you're satisfied with the changes you've made, click OK.

The changes you've made are applied to the selected object.

Cross-Reference: See the Hue/Saturation filter in action in the color insert.

Using three dimensions with Bevel and Emboss

The Bevel and Emboss effects are Fireworks' key to 3D. Both types of effects simulate light coming from a specific direction, illuminating an object that seems to be raised out of, or sunken into, the background.

Identifying Bevel effects

The Bevel effects are similar in terms of user interface, available attributes, and preset options. In fact, they only differ in two key areas:

- As the names imply, the Inner Bevel creates its edges inside the selected object, whereas the Outer Bevel makes its edges around the outside of the selected object.

- The Outer Bevel effect has one attribute that the Inner Bevel does not: color. The Inner Bevel uses the object's color to convert the inside of the graphic to a bevel, whereas the Outer Bevel applies the chosen color to the new outside edge.

When you select either Inner Bevel or Outer Bevel from the Effect Category option list, Fireworks displays their pop-up dialog boxes so that you can adjust their parameters, as shown in Figure 28-11.

Table 28-2 explains how to control aspects of bevel effects.

Table 28-2
Bevel Effects

Bevel effect	Description
Effect name	Seven different types of bevel effects are accessible through the Effect name option list. Each type of effect alters the number, shape, or degree of the bevel.
Width	Sets the thickness of the beveled side. The Width slider has a range from 0 to 10 pixels, although you can enter a higher number directly in the text box.

Bevel effect	Description
Contrast	Determines the difference in relative brightness of the lit and shadowed sides, where 100 percent provides the greatest contrast and 0 percent provides no contrast.
Softness	Sets the sharpness of the edges used to create the bevel, where 0 is the sharpest and 10 is the softest. Values above 10 have no effect.
Angle	Provides the angle for the simulated light on the beveled surface. Drag the knob control to a new angle or enter it directly in the text box.
Button Preset	Offers four preset configurations, primarily used for creating rollover buttons.
Color	Available for Outer Bevel, this standard color well is used to determine the color of the surrounding border.

Caution Although you can apply the bevel effects to any object, if the object's edge is feathered too much, you won't be able to see the effect. To combine a feathered edge with a bevel, set the Amount of Feather to less than the width of the bevel.

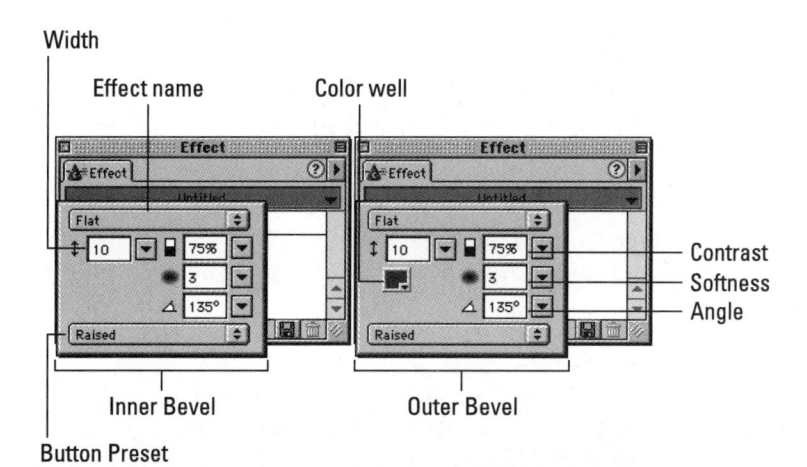

Figure 28-11: The Outer Bevel's pop-up dialog box is the same as the one for Inner Bevel, except for the addition of a color well.

Each of the bevel effects has the same types of edges. Compare the Inner Bevel and Outer Bevel effects in Figure 28-12, and you'll see the similarities among the seven types for both effects. Found under the Effect name option list, these types vary primarily in the shape of the bevel itself. Looking at each of the bevel shapes from the side makes differentiating between the possible shapes easier.

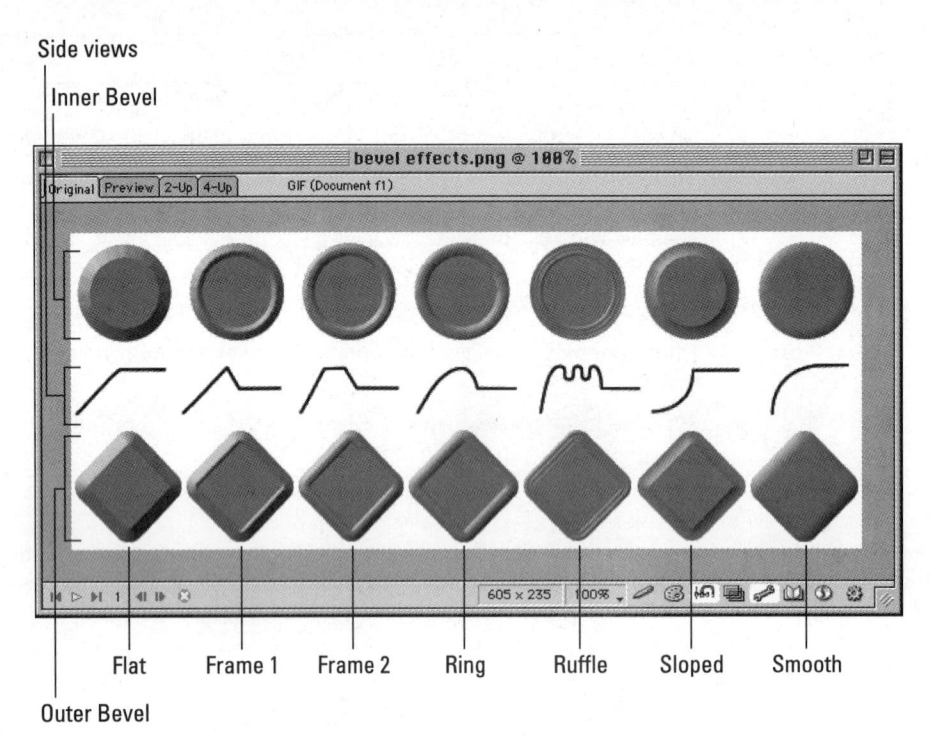

Figure 28-12: Inner Bevel effects are all contained within the original vector of the object, whereas Outer Bevel effects create edges outside the original vector. The side views make telling the types of effects apart easier.

Mastering Bevel effects Button presets

Bevel effects are terrific for creating buttons for all purposes: navigation, forms, links, and so on. One of the most common applications of such buttons involves *rollovers*. Rollover is the commonly used name (another is *mouseover*) for the effect when a user moves the pointer over a button and it changes in some way. Both bevel effects provide four presets under the Button preset option list — Raised, Highlight, Inset, and Inverted — that you can employ for rollovers.

Unlike Stroke or Fill panel presets, the bevel Button presets do not actually change the panel attributes, but rather internally change the lighting angle and lighten the object (see Figure 28-13). The Raised and Highlight presets use the same lighting angle, derived from the Angle value, but Highlight is about 25 percent lighter. The Inset and Inverted presets, on the other hand, reverse the angle of the lighting — and, of this pair, Inverted is the lighter one.

Chapter 28 ✦ **Creating Live Effects and Xtras** 869

> **Tip** To take the fullest advantage of the bevel effect Button presets in creating rollovers, set your lighting angle first with the Effect panel Angle knob. Then duplicate the object and apply the different Button presets to each copy.

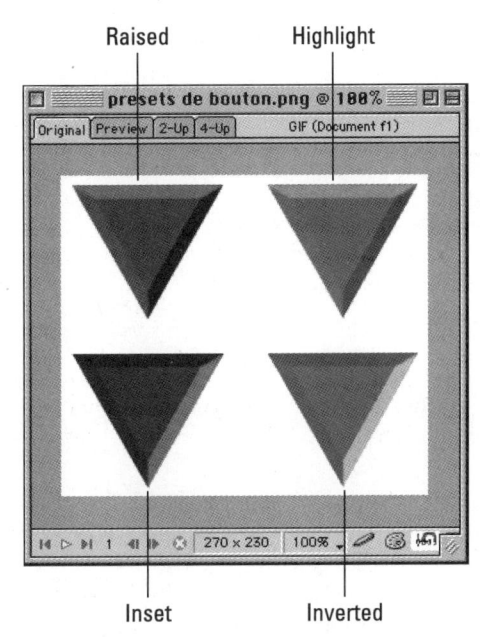

Figure 28-13: Both the bevel effects offer four Button presets: Raised, Highlight, Inset, and Inverted.

Outlining embossing

If you've ever seen a company's Articles of Incorporation or other official papers, you've probably encountered embossing. An embossing seal is used to press the company name right into the paper — so that it can be both read and felt. Fireworks' emboss effects provide a similar service, with a great deal more flexibility, of course.

Both emboss effects replace an object's fill with the canvas color or the color of background objects, and then add highlights and shadows. Inset Emboss and Raised Emboss each reverse the placement of these highlights and effects in order to make the embossed object appear to be pushed into or out of the background, respectively, as shown in Figure 28-14.

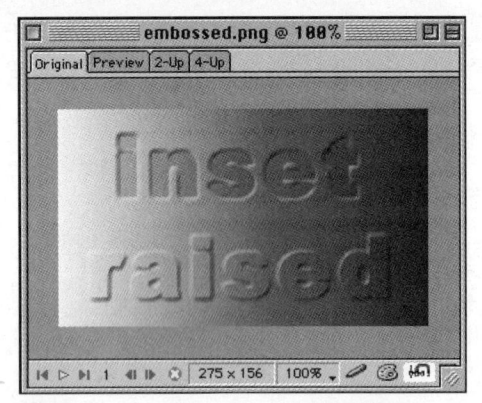

Figure 28-14: The two emboss effects make an object appear to be part of the background—either pushed into or out of it.

The Emboss effects are applied like any other Live Effect, with the options presented in a pop-up dialog box, shown in Figure 28-15.

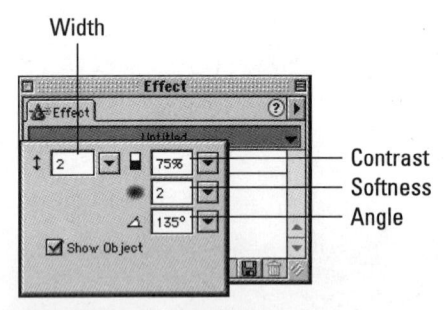

Figure 28-15: Adjust the parameters of either the Inset Emboss or Raised Emboss effects through their identical pop-up dialog boxes.

Following are the adjustable emboss parameters:

- ✦ **Width:** Determines the thickness of the embossed edges. As with other effects, the slider's range is from 0 to 30, but you can enter higher values directly into the associated text box.
- ✦ **Contrast:** Contrast controls the relative lightness of the highlights to the darkness of the shadows.
- ✦ **Softness:** Sets the sharpness of the embossed edges; higher numbers make the edges fuzzier.
- ✦ **Angle:** Establishes the direction of the embossed edges.

✦ **Show Object:** Shows or hides the embossed object. The emboss itself is always visible.

New Feature: The Emboss Live Effect's Show Object option is new in Fireworks 4.

Adding depth with blurring

Sometimes, what should be the focal point of your image can get lost among other elements of the composition. This is especially true when you're compositing multiple objects, or really laying the filters on thick. Adding a little blur to the background area of an image can cause the foreground to stand out, immediately drawing the viewer's eye to it.

To add depth to the background area of an image, follow these steps:

1. Use one of the marquee selection tools to create a pixel selection around the part of your bitmap object that you want to remain in the foreground. You might create a circle to focus attention within that circle, or use the Magic Wand to create a complex selection, such as around a person's head or face.

Note: Fireworks automatically enters bitmap mode when you use one of the marquee selection tools.

2. Choose Modify ➪ Marquee ➪ Invert Selection to invert your selection and select the background of your image.

3. Choose Window ➪ Effect, or click the Effect tab, if it is visible. The Effect panel opens.

4. From the Effect Category option list, choose Blur ➪ Gaussian Blur.

   Fireworks displays the Gaussian Blur dialog box.

Note: Some Live Effects have an ellipsis after their menu command, which indicates that choosing that command will open a dialog box in which you can specify settings. Xtras without the ellipsis either don't have any parameters for you to change, or display their parameters in a pop-up dialog box.

5. Adjust the Blur Radius slider to specify the intensity of the effect. The more blur you add, the more depth you add to your image. Generally, a blur radius of between 1 and 2 creates a depth effect without destroying the edges of the elements in the image. Click OK when you're done.

The area that was within your original pixel selection now seems to stand out and draws the eye at first glance (see Figure 28-16), because it is clear and sharp and appears to be closer to your eyes. In addition, an overall feeling of depth has been created by the blurred background, because background elements seem to be a little further away.

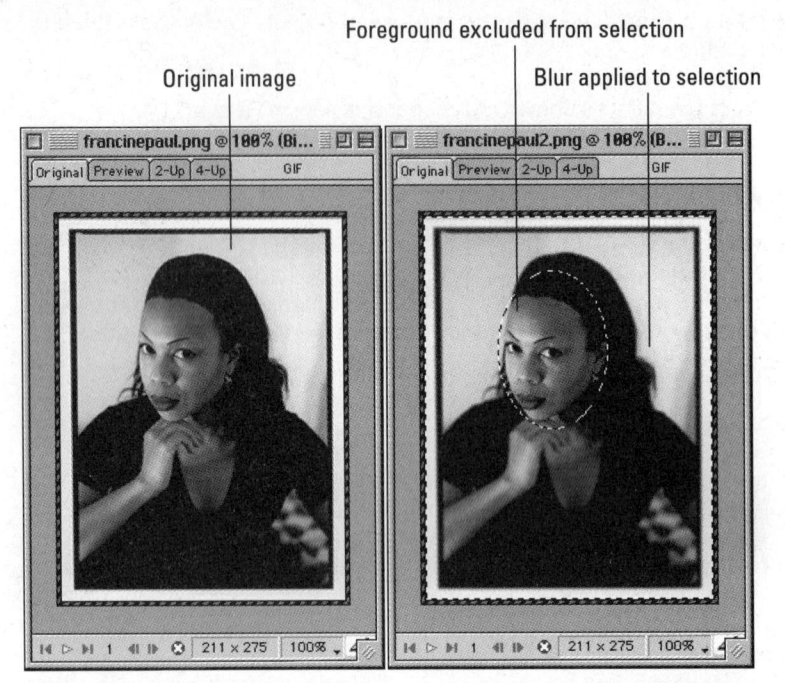

Figure 28-16: Blurring the background seems to give an image extra depth and makes the foreground stand out. Notice how your eye is immediately drawn to the subject's face.

The Blur and Blur More effects work similarly to the Gaussian Blur effect, except that they don't have parameters. Blur provides a slight blurring effect, and Blur More — well, you get the idea.

Learning holdover effects

The two effects on the Other submenu of the Effect panels Effect Category option list are holdovers all the way from Fireworks 1. The Convert to Alpha filter is unnecessary now that Fireworks has mask groups, but you may find creative uses for it. Applying it converts the selection to grayscale and sets white to transparent. The Find Edges filter detects the outlines of forms and converts them to solid lines. This feature can be useful for special effects, or for creating masks.

Examining Shadow and Glow

The shadow and glow effects help to create depth and softness in your Fireworks documents.

Understanding drop and inner shadows

I remember the overwhelming sense of pride I felt after I made my first drop shadow in an early version of Photoshop. Of course, it had taken me all afternoon to follow two different sets of instructions and involved masking layers, Gaussian blurs, nudged layers, and who remembers what else. My pride was quickly deflated when I tried out my new drop-shadowed image against a color background — and found a completely undesired halo of white pixels around my graphic.

All of that effort and anxiety is out the window with Fireworks. Applying a drop shadow to an object can be a simple, two-step process: Select the object and then choose Drop Shadow from the Effect panel. Best of all, you can position the drop shadow against any colored background; Fireworks adjusts the blending of shadow to background, eliminating the unwanted halo effect.

> **Note** I'm not trying to defame Photoshop, which is a fine application. It's only fair to acknowledge that newer versions also have a Drop Shadow effect that's easily applied and also easily imported into Fireworks, with editability intact.

A drop shadow is a monochrome copy of an image, offset so that it appears behind the image to one side. Drop shadows are usually presented in a shade of gray (although they can be any color) and can be either faded on the edge or hard edged. Drop shadows are used extensively on the Web — some would say that they're overused. However, the effect of giving flat images dimension by adding a shadow behind it is so compelling and downright useful that I think drop shadows will be around for a long time.

In addition to Drop Shadow, Fireworks also offers an Inner Shadow effect. Both effects are essentially the same — and even use the same pop-up dialog box for setting parameters — except for the location of the shadow. Inner Shadow places the shadow within your object, as though it is recessed and the shadow is being cast by the edges of whatever it's recessed into.

To apply a Drop Shadow or Inner Shadow to any object in Fireworks, follow these steps:

1. Select the object you want to apply the effect to. Drop shadows work well on most any object: open or closed vectors, geometric shapes, bitmap objects, text objects, and more.

2. Choose Window ⇨ Effect, or click the Effect tab, if it is visible. The Effect panel opens.

3. Choose either Drop Shadow or Inner Shadow from the Effect Category option list. The initial parameters — which are the same for both effects — are displayed in a pop-up dialog box, as shown in Figure 28-17.

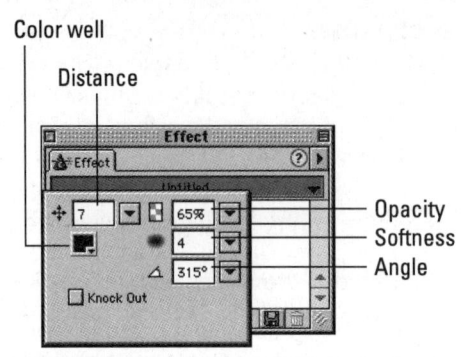

Figure 28-17: The default Drop Shadow effect offers a classic soft shadow, slightly cast to the right, but you can modify it in the pop-up dialog box.

4. To make the shadow appear farther away or closer, change the Distance slider, or enter a value directly in the associated text box.

> **Tip:** The Distance slider has a range from 0 to 100 pixels, but you can enter a higher number in the text box to make the shadow appear even farther away. The text box also accepts negative numbers, which cause the shadow to be cast in the opposite direction of the Angle setting.

5. To change the shadow color from the default black, pick a color from the color well.

6. To change the transparency of the shadow, alter the Opacity slider or text box. Opacity is given in a percentage value; 100 percent is completely opaque and 0 percent is completely transparent (and therefore invisible).

7. To make the edge of the shadow softer or harder, move the Softness slider, or enter a value in its text box. The Softness slider goes from 0 to 30, but you can enter a higher value directly in the text box.

8. To change the direction of the shadow, drag the Angle knob to a new location, or enter a degree (0 to 360) directly in the text box.

9. To display just the shadow and make the object disappear, choose the Knock Out option.

I find myself using a hard-edged shadow almost as much as I do the soft-edge versions, particularly in graphics, where file size is paramount. Any image with a blended edge is larger than the same image with a solid edge, because more pixels are necessary to create the faded look — typically half again as many. When file size is key — and you like the look of a solid drop shadow — bring the Softness slider all the way down to zero.

I do find softer shadows particularly effective, however, when one shadow overlaps another. A good way to enhance the three dimensionality of your Web graphics is to place one object with a shadow over another object, also with a shadow.

Using the Knock Out option

The Knock Out option offered in the shadow effects deserves special mention. The phrase knock out is an old printer's term referring to the practice of dropping the color out of certain type to let background show through. Obviously if you eliminated the color from an ordinary bit of type — without an outline or other surrounding element — the type would seem to disappear. A shadow is perfect for surrounding knocked out type because of the way the mind has of filling in the details that are missing from the actual image. Selecting the Knock Out option removes both the fill and stroke color of the object and leaves just the shadow, as shown in Figure 28-18.

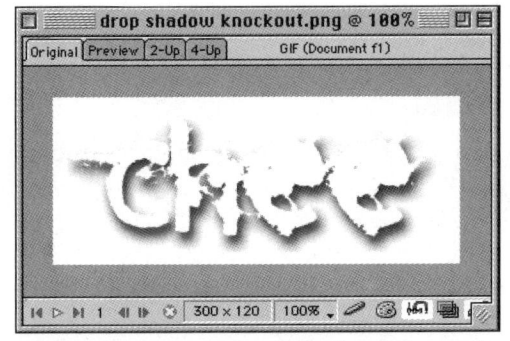

Figure 28-18: Use a Drop Shadow effect with Knock Out checked to highlight text or other objects with just the shadow.

> **Tip**
> In the introduction to this section, I noted how it's easy in Fireworks to avoid the so-called halo effect that occurs when you move a drop shadow built against one background to another. In Fireworks, there are really two ways to do this. If you don't need the object or its shadow to be transparent, change the canvas color to the background color of your Web page and export the image normally. To avoid the halo effect, but maintain a transparent image, make the background color transparent during export.

Exploring Glow

Whereas a shadow is only visible on one or two sides of an object, the glow effects — Glow and Inner Glow — create a border all around the object. The glow's color is user selectable, as is its width, opacity, and softness.

To apply a glow, follow these steps:

1. Select the object you want to apply the effect to.
2. Choose Window ➪ Effect, or click the Effect tab, if it is visible. The Effect panel opens.
3. Choose either Glow or Inner Glow from the Shadow and Glow submenu on the Effect Category option list. Fireworks displays the glow parameters in a pop-up dialog box, which is identical to the drop-shadow dialog box, shown previously in Figure 28-17, except for the lack of a Knock Out option.
4. Set the other options — Width, Color, Opacity, and Softness — as desired.

All the Glow effect parameters are the same as those found on the shadow effects.

Tip   One effect you can create with Glow that's not immediately obvious is a border. Apply the Glow effect to an object and set the Softness to 0 and the Opacity to 100 percent. *Voilà,* a border.

Sharpening to bring out detail

Sharpening an image can bring out depth that's not there, by finding the edges of objects and creating more contrast between pixels on either side of that edge. It can especially help to fix a bad scan, or bring out detail after you go overboard with special effects Xtras.

To sharpen an image a little bit, select it and choose Sharpen ➪ Sharpen, or Sharpen ➪ Sharpen More from the Effect Category option list in the Effect panel.

To sharpen an image with control over individual settings, follow these steps:

1. Select an object.
2. Choose Window ➪ Effect, or click the Effect tab, if it is visible. Alternatively, use the keyboard shortcut, Alt+F7 (Option+F7). The Effect panel opens.
3. From the Effect Category option list, choose Sharpen ➪ Unsharp Mask.

   Fireworks displays the Unsharp Mask dialog box, as shown in Figure 28-19.

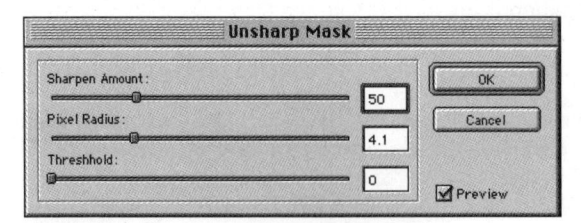

Figure 28-19: Specify the parameters for Unsharp Mask in the Unsharp Mask dialog box.

4. Moving the Sharpen Amount slider specifies the intensity of the effect. You might start with this slider at about midway and increase or decrease it later, after setting other options.

5. Move the Pixel Radius slider to control how many pixels are evaluated simultaneously. A larger radius value results in a more pronounced effect, because the differences among a larger group of pixels typically are greater.

6. Move the Threshold slider to determine which pixels are affected. Only pixels that have a grayscale value higher than the threshold value are affected. A lower threshold affects more pixels. Click OK when you're done.

Your image should now have a crisper, sharper look (see Figure 28-20).

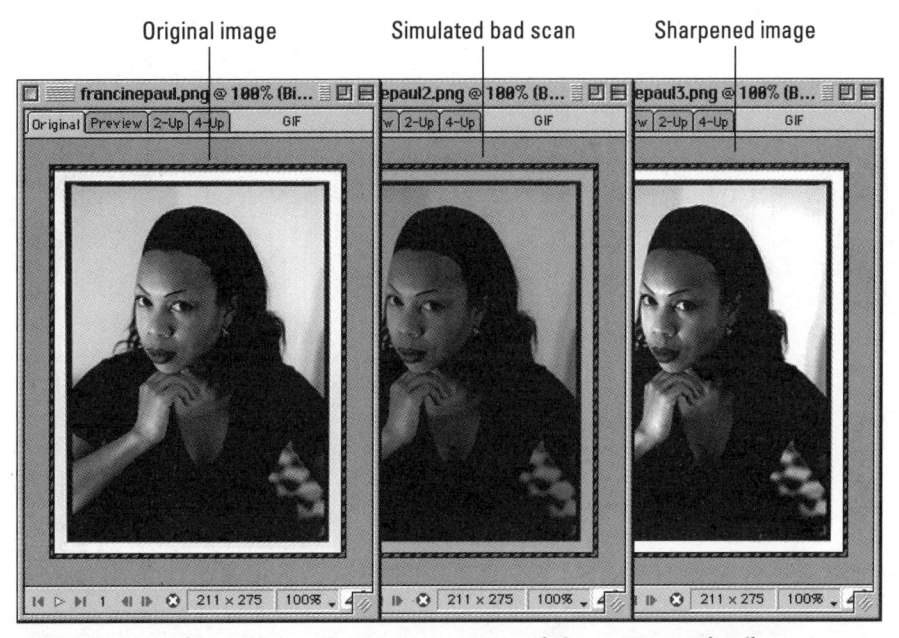

Figure 28-20: Sharpening an image may seem to bring out extra detail.

Tip Sometimes, a sharpened image will seem too harsh. Adding a touch of blur with the Blur Live Effect, or applying the Auto Levels filter may help to remedy this.

Fireworks Technique: Making Perspective Shadows

Fireworks is flexible enough to enable you to extend its Live Effects to create many of your own effects. One such possibility is perspective shadows. Unlike drop shadows, perspective shadows are not flat carbon copies of the selected object, but rather shadows that appear to exist in a three-dimensional world. In addition, perspective shadows can appear in front, behind, or to the side of the object.

> **Cross-Reference:** Alien Skin's Eye Candy filters, covered later in this chapter, include a perspective shadow effect that's worth investigating, if you have the Eye Candy package.

This perspective shadow technique takes advantage of Fireworks' facility with vector objects and its capability to adjust gradients and edges. With this technique, you can add perspective shadows to text, bitmap, or vector objects. A bitmap object that received this treatment is shown in Figure 28-21.

Figure 28-21: Create perspective shadows in Fireworks, by combining gradient fills to distorted copies of an object.

To create a perspective shadow, follow these steps:

1. Duplicate the outline of the original object to create a new shadow object. Depending on the type of object, this first step is either very simple, very time-consuming, or something in-between. Here are techniques for working with the three basic types of objects:

   - **Vector objects:** By far the easiest of the three, simply choose Edit ➪ Clone to copy any vector object. Cloning is a better choice than Duplicating, because aligning the shadow and its source later is easier.

   - **Text objects:** Although it's not absolutely necessary, I've found it sometimes easier to work with text as a vector for my shadow object than with regular text. In my experience, distorting vector objects gets more predictable results than distorting text. Therefore, I first Clone the text and then choose Text ➪ Convert to Paths. Finally, to reduce the gradients of the separate letters to one, choose Modify ➪ Combine ➪ Union.

   - **Bitmap objects:** Bitmap objects can be simple rectangles, or irregular shapes. If your object is rectangular or another geometric shape, use the Rectangle, Ellipse, or Polygon to create a same-size copy of the object. Otherwise, the best tool I found for this particular job is the Pen. For outlining an image, I use the Pen primarily in its straight-line mode, clicking from one point to the next, although occasionally when I need to copy a curve, I can with the Pen's Bézier curve feature. The outline doesn't have to be exact, although the more details you include, the more realistic your shadow will be.

2. If necessary, flip the shadow object. Depending on your hypothetical light source, you'll want to flip the shadow object vertically so that the perspective shadow falls in front of the original object.

3. If necessary, move the shadow object into position.

   You won't need to move the shadow object if the perspective shadow falls behind the original object. However, for perspective shadows in front, you do need to move the shadow object so that the bases of each object meet. Although using the mouse to drag the shadow object into position is entirely possible, I often find myself using the cursor keys to move the selected shadow object in one direction. Pressing Shift+Arrow keys moves the object in ten-pixel increments and the regular arrow keys, one pixel.

4. Send the shadow object behind the original object.

   Whether you choose Modify ➪ Arrange ➪ Send Backward, or Modify ➪ Arrange ➪ Send to Back depends on what other objects are in the document and how you want the shadow to relate to them. But even if the perspective shadow falls in front of the source object, you'll want to put it behind to mask the meeting point.

5. Distort the shadow object.

   Here's where the real artistry — and numerous attempts — enter the picture. Select the shadow object, and choose the Skew tool from the Tools panel to slant the shadow in one direction; again, the direction depends on where the apparent "light" for the shadow is coming from. Next, while the Skew tool is still active, switch to the Scale tool. (By pressing the keyboard shortcut, Q, twice, you don't have to move the mouse.) You can now easily resize the same bounding box. Choose the middle horizontal sizing handle on the edge farthest away from the original object. Now you can drag that handle to either shorten or lengthen the shadow.

6. Optionally, fill the shadow object with a gradient.

   You may be satisfied with the shadow as it stands now, but adding and adjusting a gradient will add more depth and realism to the image. From the Fill panel, choose the Linear gradient with a Black, White preset color combination.

7. Adjust the gradient of the shadow object.

   As applied, the Linear gradient just goes left to right. If you need it to flow at a different angle (and you probably will), choose the Paint Bucket tool while the shadow object is selected to activate the gradient controls. Reposition and angle the gradient, so that the starting point is at the juncture of the source and shadow object, and the ending point is just beyond the end of the shadow. This enables the shadow to gently fade away.

8. If desired, slightly feather the edge of the shadow object.

   To my eye, shadows look a bit more realistic if they're not so hard-edged. I like to set my Fill panel Edge option list to Feather and set the Amount of Feather relatively low, about three or four pixels. You may have to adjust the shadow object a bit to hide the feathered edge where it touches the original object.

You can add many enhancements to this technique. For example, you could add an object for the shadow to fall over, by bending or pulling the shadow object with the Freeform or Reshape Area tools, or the shadow itself could be not so realistic to make a point. Computer graphics make turning anyone's shadow into a horned devil or winged angel oh-so-tempting. Play with perspective — you'll be glad you did.

Managing Live Effects

Like strokes and fills, you can save custom configurations of Live Effects with each document. You can then later apply these custom effects to other objects in the same document or, if the object is copied to another document, other graphics. As with strokes and fills, management of custom effects is easily handled through the pop-up menu.

The Effect panel pop-up menu commands are as follows:

- **Save Defaults:** Stores the effects settings of the currently selected object as defaults for those effects.
- **Save Effect As:** Stores the current effect settings under a unique name in the Effect name option list.
- **Rename Effect:** Renames any custom or standard effect.
- **Delete Effect:** Removes any custom or standard effect. If you remove a standard effect, it will be restored when you restart Fireworks, or when you access another document.
- **All On** and **All Off:** Turns all applied effects on or off, respectively. This is the same as checking or unchecking all the checkboxes in the Effects list.
- **Locate Plugins:** A shortcut to specifying a folder of Photoshop-compatible plug-ins for Fireworks to use. This is the same as modifying the Photoshop Plug-Ins option in the Folders area of Fireworks preferences. Fireworks must be restarted for this option to take effect.

Storing a customized effect

Creating your own effects is a tremendous time-saver and an enjoyable creative exercise, as well. You can apply even complex effects with one action. The effects shown in Figure 28-22 combine Fireworks default effects with some that are borrowed from Photoshop 5.5.

Figure 28-22: A range of effects like these can be created and stored under sometimes goofy names for instant recall.

To store a customized effect, follow these steps:

1. Apply effects to an object until you create a combination that you would like to save.
2. Choose Save Effect As from the Effect panel pop-up menu. The Save Effect As dialog box appears.
3. Enter a unique name for the effect. If you choose a name already in use, Fireworks asks whether you want to replace the existing effect.
4. After entering a new name, click Save. The new effect name is displayed alphabetically in the user area of the Effect Category option list.

Cross-Reference: See some saved effects in greater detail in the color insert.

Grasping missing effects

As great as it is to include all kinds of third-party filters in your saved effects, the downside is that documents that use those effects depend upon them being available. If you try to open a document from a colleague, for example, who used effects that you don't have on your system, Fireworks displays the Missing Effects dialog box (see Figure 28-23), warning you that certain effects are unavailable. Obviously, the remedy is to install the correct effects, but you can edit the document in the meantime.

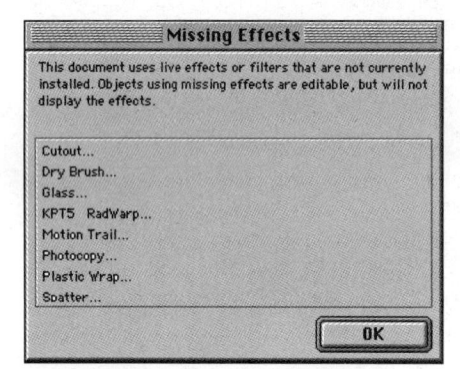

Figure 28-23: Fireworks displays the Missing Effects dialog box when you open a document that uses filters that are not available.

Saving effects in Styles

Another way to save and recall custom effects is to save them as styles. As well as saving fills, strokes, and text properties, styles remember Live Effects settings, even image filters used as Live Effects. If you save only the effect setting, you can apply that effect setting with one click. This also provides a graphical thumbnail of the effect, visible in the Styles panel, as shown in Figure 28-24.

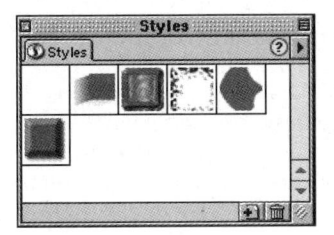

Figure 28-24: The saved effects from Figure 28-22, saved as Styles, display a thumbnail of what the effect looks like.

To create a new style using a custom effect, follow these steps:

1. Select an object that uses the custom effect.
2. If necessary, choose Window ⇨ Styles, use the keyboard shortcut, Shift+F11 (Shift+F11), or click the Style tab, if it is visible. The Styles panel appears.
3. On the Styles panel, click the New Style button.
4. In the Edit Style dialog box, enter a descriptive name for your effect in the Name text box and deselect all checkboxes except Effect.
5. Click OK when you're done. A new style is entered in the Styles panel.

Any style added in the just-described fashion is always available for any Fireworks document. To apply the effect, just highlight any Fireworks object and select the new style.

> **Caution:** If you export your new style, it won't work properly on another machine that doesn't have the same effects installed. If you only use Fireworks' default Live Effects, you can avoid this problem, of course.

As well as being useful for complex combinations of effects, saving simple effects can save you much time, as well. I often find myself choosing the same simple drop shadow, or using the same 4-pixel flat Inner Bevel on almost every standard 88×31 pixel microbutton that I create. An effects-only style for each of the preceding shaves a small amount of time and trouble out of my day, over and over again.

> **Cross-Reference:** To find out more about the powerful Styles feature, see Chapter 31.

Reading All About Xtras

Although many of the items in the Xtras menu are also available in the Effect panel, choosing them from the Xtras menu has a few key differences:

- ✦ You can apply a filter in the Xtras menu to any kind of selection in Fireworks, in either bitmap mode or vector mode, whereas you can apply items from the Effect panel only in vector mode.

- ✦ Unlike the Effect panel, applying a filter from the Xtras menu flattens text and vector objects into bitmap objects, reducing their editability.

Before you choose a filter from the Xtras menu, you have to decide what you want to modify with that Xtra and select it in the appropriate way. All the Xtras that are included with Fireworks will work on any type of selection, but some third-party Xtras work better on pixel selections within bitmap objects, or even require such a selection to run.

Using vector objects

As mentioned previously, applying an Xtra to a vector object, or vector object group flattens it into a bitmap object. The vector information is thrown away and you lose the advantages, such as scalability and editability, that vector objects provide. Try using Live Effects on your vector objects to achieve the look that you want before you apply Xtras. After your vector object becomes a bitmap object, there's no going back, except by using the Undo command, or the History panel.

> **Tip** Sometimes, though, you can get the best of both worlds. If you're using an Xtra that draws outside the selection (for example, the Eye Candy Fire filter, which draws flames around your image), you can apply the Xtra to a copy of your object and then place the resulting, filtered image behind your original object and group them. Later, you can still color and use Live Effects on your vector object. If you resize it, you should throw away the filtered image and reapply the saved settings of the filter to a new copy of your object. If you're applying an Xtra that alters within the selection, try applying the Xtra to a copy of your object, and then using the copy as an alpha mask for your original. You can create some interesting effects this way, without being stuck in bitmap mode.

When you do apply an Xtra to a vector object, Fireworks warns you that doing so will convert it to a bitmap object. You can disable this warning by checking the "Don't show again" checkbox. I recommend that you leave it unchecked for a little while, until you get used to this conversion. If you accidentally convert a vector object to a bitmap object and then save your file, your vector information may be gone for good.

To apply an Xtra to a vector object, select it with the mouse and then choose the Xtra's command from the Xtras menu.

Examining bitmap objects

Applying an Xtra to a bitmap object couldn't be easier. The only thing to keep in mind is that some Xtras draw outside the selection, to create effects such as motion trails and drop shadows. If your bitmap object is the same size as the canvas, the effect will either be invisible, because it's off the canvas, or, with some Xtras, won't even be drawn. Before applying one of these filters, resize the canvas to give them a little room.

To apply an Xtra to a bitmap object, select it and then choose the Xtra from the Xtras menu.

Identifying pixel selections in a bitmap object

Many filters work best when applied to a pixel selection within a bitmap object, because they create a difference between the area inside the selection and the area outside the selection. Often, complex pixel selections, such as those made with the Magic Wand or the Polygon Lasso, work better than simple rectangular or circular selections. The extra complexity creates areas where some filters create things, such as bevels, shadows, or textures.

Note: Creating a pixel selection doesn't necessarily mean that you've limited an Xtra to drawing only inside the selection. Although most will stay inside, some draw outside the selection to create their effect. Your selection marks a focal point for whatever filter you're applying.

To apply an Xtra to a pixel selection within a bitmap object, use one of the marquee selection tools from the Tools panel to draw your selection in bitmap mode, and then choose an Xtra from the Xtras menu.

Cross-Reference: For more on creating selections within bitmap objects, see Chapter 22.

Checking out false pixel selections

Some filters will ignore your pixel selections and apply their effect to an entire bitmap object. If you find that a particular filter exhibits this behavior, you can work around it by creating a "false pixel selection," by copying your pixel selection to the Clipboard and pasting it as a new bitmap object.

Tip: All the filters in Kai's Power Tools 5, detailed later in this chapter, apply their effects to your entire bitmap object and require that you use a false pixel selection to limit them to a portion of your image.

To create a false pixel selection, follow these steps:

1. Choose Modify ➪ Edit Bitmap, or use the keyboard shortcut, Ctrl+E (Command+E), to enter bitmap mode.
2. Create a selection around the area to which you want to apply the Xtra, by using one of the marquee selection tools from the Tools panel.
3. Copy the selection to the Clipboard by choosing either Edit ➪ Copy, or the keyboard shortcut, Ctrl+C (Command+C).
4. Paste the selection back into the document by choosing either Edit ➪ Paste, or the keyboard shortcut, Ctrl+V (Command+V).

   The selection is pasted as a new bitmap object, on top of the area it was copied from. Even though it now has a square marquee selection, the bitmap object is, in fact, the same size and shape as what you originally copied to the clipboard.

5. Apply an Xtra to the new bitmap object by choosing the Xtra from the Xtras menu.

   The filter affects only the new bitmap object.

6. Either choose Modify ➪ Exit bitmap mode, use the keyboard shortcut, Ctrl+Shift+E (Command+Shift+E), or press the Stop button on the bottom of the document window to return to vector mode.

The original bitmap object and the new one that you created and then filtered are merged into one. The net result is that only the area of your original pixel selection is modified.

Evaluating multiple objects

In addition to individual objects, you can apply Xtras to a selection or group of multiple objects. If your selection or group contains any vector objects, they will be converted to bitmap objects, just as they would be if you were applying the Xtra to them individually. When applying Xtras to multiple objects, keep the following in mind:

✦ If you apply an Xtra to a selection of objects in vector mode, the Xtra runs multiple times, applying to each object in turn. If you select three objects, for example, the Xtra runs three times in a row, once on each object. If you select Cancel in any of the filter's dialog boxes, it cancels the entire operation, and none of your objects will be altered.

✦ If you apply an Xtra to a group of objects, they will act as if they are one object. After you apply the Xtra, the objects actually are one bitmap object, and you can't separate them. To make a selection of objects into a group, select multiple objects and choose Modify ➪ Group, or use the keyboard shortcut, Ctrl+G (Command+G).

Caution: The exceptions to the preceding list are the Adjust Color, Blur, Other, and Sharpen Xtras that come with Fireworks (all of those above the line in the Xtras menu). They act on a selection of objects as if they are already grouped.

The differences in the way groups and selections are handled by Xtras is actually quite handy. Imagine that you have created five objects that are going to be five buttons in a navigation interface. If you want to apply an Xtra with the exact same settings to all of them, group them and apply the Xtra. If, however, you want to apply the same Xtra to all of them, but tweak the settings for each — to add a slightly different texture to each one, for example — just select them and apply the Xtra.

Tip: Many Xtras start with the same settings as when you last used them. When applying an extra to a selection of objects, the second time the Xtra starts, it will have the same settings that you used on the first object, making it easier to apply a similar effect across a selection of objects. You can also save settings in some Xtras.

Using Third-Party, Photoshop-Compatible Filters

So far, you've seen what you can do with the Live Effects and Xtras that are included with Fireworks, but that's just the tip of the iceberg. Many third-party, Photoshop-compatible, plug-in filters are available.

Caution: Fireworks supports Photoshop-compatible filters, but some developers target their filters directly at Photoshop itself, creating filters that don't work in other applications. Check the Disabled plugins file in your Fireworks Xtras folder for a list of filters that are known to be incompatible. Just because a filter is not on that list doesn't mean that it's guaranteed to work with Fireworks, though. Whenever possible, ask the software publisher about Fireworks compatibility before purchasing filters.

Installing third-party filter packages

Most filter packages come with installers that are just like the installers provided with full applications, such as Fireworks. Before you install a package, close Fireworks. You have to restart Fireworks before you use the filters, anyway. When the installer's instructions ask you to locate your Photoshop Plug-Ins folder, specify Fireworks' Xtras folder, which is inside the Configuration folder in your Fireworks program folder. If the package did not come with an installer, you have to copy the filters to your Xtras folder yourself.

Tip The Fireworks program folder is typically found at C:\Program Files\Macromedia\Fireworks 4 on Windows-based computers, and at Macintosh HD:Applications: Macromedia Fireworks 4: on the Mac.

After the installation is complete, start Fireworks. You should see a new option under the Xtras menu, and — if Fireworks can use the filters as Live Effects — on the Effect Category option list in the Effect panel. This will be a whole new submenu, which often has multiple filters available. Sometimes, new effects will hide themselves on menus you already have. If you have a Distort submenu, for example (some of Photoshop 5's filters create this), and you install a filter that also wants to live in a Distort submenu, it may not be apparent that you've gained a filter until you open the Distort submenu.

Tip Where can you get more filters? A good place to start is The Plugin Site, at www.thepluginsite.com, where you'll find lots of free filters and filter-related links. Some great individual developers: Alien Skin, at www.alienskin.com; Furbo Filters, at www.furbo-filters.com; and VanDerLee at www.v-d-l.com. Of course, Adobe also sells Photoshop-compatible filters at www.adobe.com.

Using filters with multiple applications

If you use another image-editing application in addition to Fireworks, you may have a whole host of filters on your computer that you can also use in Fireworks. Sharing filters among numerous applications can instantly add many features to all of them and can also speed up your workflow, because you don't have to leave an application to apply a particular effect.

Aside from Fireworks, here are some other applications that use Photoshop-compatible filters:

- Adobe Photoshop and Illustrator
- Macromedia FreeHand and Director
- Corel Photo-Paint and CorelDRAW

I have about six or seven applications that use filters, so I keep all of my filters in one folder, independent of all the applications, and then I have all the applications use that folder as their plug-ins folder. The alternative would be to install filters numerous times into the plug-ins folder of each and every application. If you have multiple applications that use standard filters, you might want to do the same thing.

You may have only one other application that uses standard filters, perhaps Photoshop itself. If this is the case, you can tell Fireworks to use that application's plug-ins folder in addition to using Fireworks' own Xtras folder.

To specify an additional filters folder, follow these steps:

1. Choose Edit ➪ Preferences.

   Fireworks displays the Preferences dialog box.

2. Choose the Folders tab (Folders option on Macintosh), as shown in Figure 28-25.

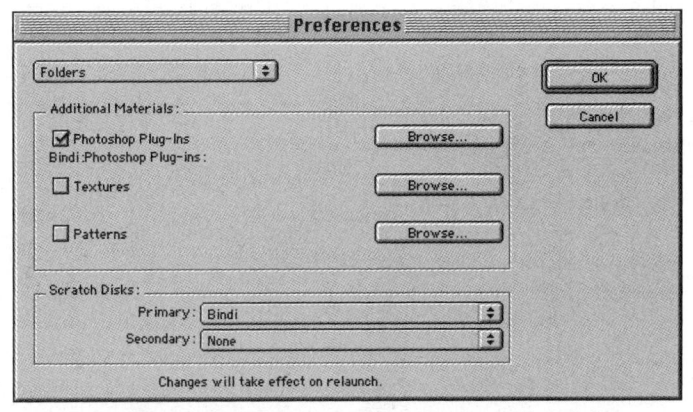

Figure 28-25: Fireworks can use filters from another folder on your computer, such as Photoshop's Plug-Ins folder.

3. Check the Photoshop Plug-Ins checkbox.
4. Click the Browse button to the right of the Photoshop Plug-Ins checkbox.

   Fireworks displays the Browse for Folder dialog box.

5. Select the folder that contains the filters you want to use. Click OK when you're done.
6. Restart Fireworks to see the changes to the Xtras menu and to use your newly available filters.

Using shortcuts (aliases) to plug-in folders

Another method for specifying an additional plug-in folder or folders is to place shortcuts (aliases) to those folders into Fireworks' Xtras folder. As well as being an intuitive way to specify where filters are located, this also has the advantage of enabling you to specify more than one additional folder (see Figure 28-26).

To create a shortcut to a folder of filters on Windows, select the folder, right-click it, and then drag it into your Fireworks Xtras folder. When you drop it, choose Make Shortcut from the contextual menu that appears. On the Mac, hold down Command+Option while you drag the folder into your Fireworks Xtras folder, and an alias to the plug-ins folder will be created.

Central folder of filters   Alias in Photoshop's Plug-ins folder

Alias in Fireworks' Xtras folder   Alias in FreeHand's Xtras folder

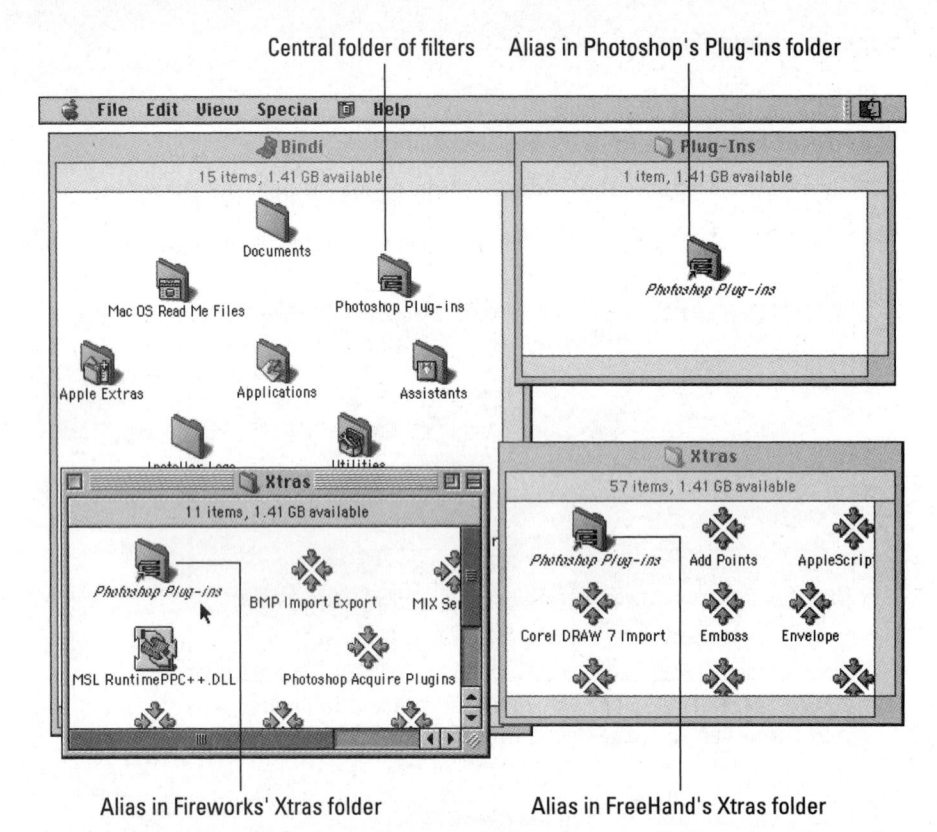

Figure 28-26: Place shortcuts (aliases) to folders that contain filters into Fireworks Xtras folder to enable Fireworks to access the filters.

Exploring Alien Skin Eye Candy

Eye Candy is a popular filter collection that you can purchase and install as Xtras in Fireworks. Fireworks even includes three of the Eye Candy filters as Eye Candy 4000 LE. Even if you don't (yet) have the full Eye Candy 4000 package, this section introduces you to the kinds of things that are possible with filters in general, and may also help you evaluate other, similar packages for their quality and creative potential.

Tip   Alien Skin has optimized Eye Candy 4000 for use as Live Effects in Fireworks, and has also made an updater patch available that enables better Fireworks operation for the previous release, Eye Candy 3.1. Visit Alien Skin on the Web at www.alienskin.com, or go directly to Eye Candy at www.eyecandy.com.

The theme here is classic effects done right: beveling, drop shadows, smoke, motion trails, distortion. The Eye Candy filters are a great foundation for any filter collection, because they're the kind of blue-collar, hard-working, tried-and-true effects that are used again and again in the kinds of tasks that the working Web artist does every day.

Following are some of the features you'll find in Eye Candy:

+ Many presets for each filter enable you to start using them quickly. In addition, you can save your own settings to the preset list for later recall.
+ A dynamic preview capability enables you to zoom in or out on your image for precise, detailed modifications.
+ All Eye Candy filters share common interface features, which cuts down the learning curve (see Figure 28-27).

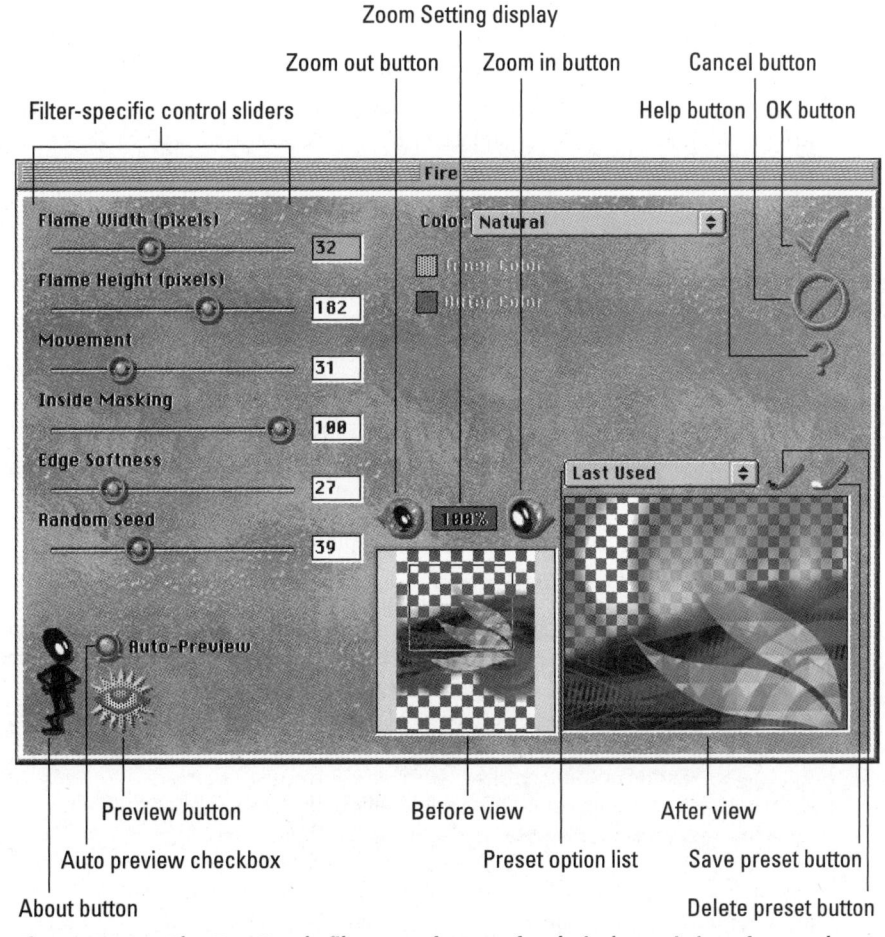

Figure 28-27: The Eye Candy filters are famous for their dynamic interface and easy-to-use presets. This figure shows the Fire filter igniting the Fireworks logo.

Table 28-3 details each of the filters that make up Eye Candy and explains what they do. Many of the filters are the same whether you have Eye Candy 4000, or the previous Version, 3.1; however, the Eye Candy 4000 filters have been updated with a host of new features.

Caution: Many Eye Candy filters draw outside the selection and, therefore, rely heavily on having a pixel selection within a bitmap object, or having space around a bitmap object against the canvas.

Table 28-3
Alien Skin Eye Candy 4000

Filter	Description
Antimatter	Inverts brightness without affecting hue and saturation values. For example, dark red becomes light red, but is still red.
Bevel Boss (Carve, Inner Bevel, and Outer Bevel in 3.1)	Makes a pixel selection appear to be beveled or carved out of an object. Eye Candy 4000 also has a sophisticated bevel editor for advanced bevels.
Chrome	Applies a metallic effect that you can use to simulate chrome, silver, gold, and other metals.
Corona (4000 only)	Creates astronomical effects such as gaseous clouds and solar flares.
Cutout	Makes a pixel selection appear as a hole in the image, including a shadow, so that it appears recessed.
Drip (4000 only)	A sophisticated version of the classic wet paint effect.
Fire	Creates a realistic flame effect rising from a pixel selection or object.
Fur	Applies randomly placed clumps of fur.
Glass	Superimposes a sheet of colored glass.
Gradient Glow (Glow in 3.1)	Adds a semitransparent glow around the outside edge of a pixel selection or object. Eye Candy 4000 also includes a gradient editor for more advanced glow effects.
HSB Noise	Adds noise by varying hue, saturation, brightness, and transparency.
Jiggle	Creates a bubbling, gelatinous, or shattered effect.
Marble (4000 only)	Creates marble textures.

Filter	Description
Melt (4000 only)	Makes objects look like they are melting.
Motion Trail	Creates the illusion of motion by smearing a pixel selection or object outward in one direction.
Shadowlab (Drop Shadow and Perspective Shadow in 3.1)	Adds a drop shadow or a realistic perspective shadow to a pixel selection or an object.
Smoke	Creates smoke coming from a pixel selection or object.
Squint	Unfocuses a pixel selection or object in a way similar to bad eyesight.
Star	Creates stars and other polygon shapes.
Swirl	Adds randomly placed whirlpools.
Water Drops	Adds randomly placed water drops.
Weave	Applies a woven effect.
Wood (4000 only)	Creates wood textures.

Using Jiggle

Jiggle produces a unique distortion based on randomly placed bubbling. The patterns that it produces seem more random and organic — less computerized — than many distortion filters. A selection can seem like it's bubbling, gelatinous, or shattered.

To use Jiggle, select an image and follow these steps:

1. Choose Xtras ➪ Eye Candy 4000 (or 3.1) ➪ Jiggle.

   The Jiggle dialog box appears (see Figure 28-28).

2. Adjust these controls to achieve the effect you desire:

   - **Bubble Size slider:** Controls the frequency of the distortion. The lower the value, the more closely spaced the distortion.
   - **Warp Amount:** Controls how much your selection is stretched.
   - **Twist:** Controls the amount of twisting that occurs, measured in degrees.
   - **Movement Type drop-down list:** Use to select the way you want the image jiggled. The three types of jiggling are Bubbles, which is a smooth, even distortion; Brownian Motion, which is a more ragged effect; and Turbulence, which creates sharper breaks in the image.

3. If you like, you can save your settings by using the Save Preset button. Click OK (the checkmark) when you're done.

The effect is applied to your image.

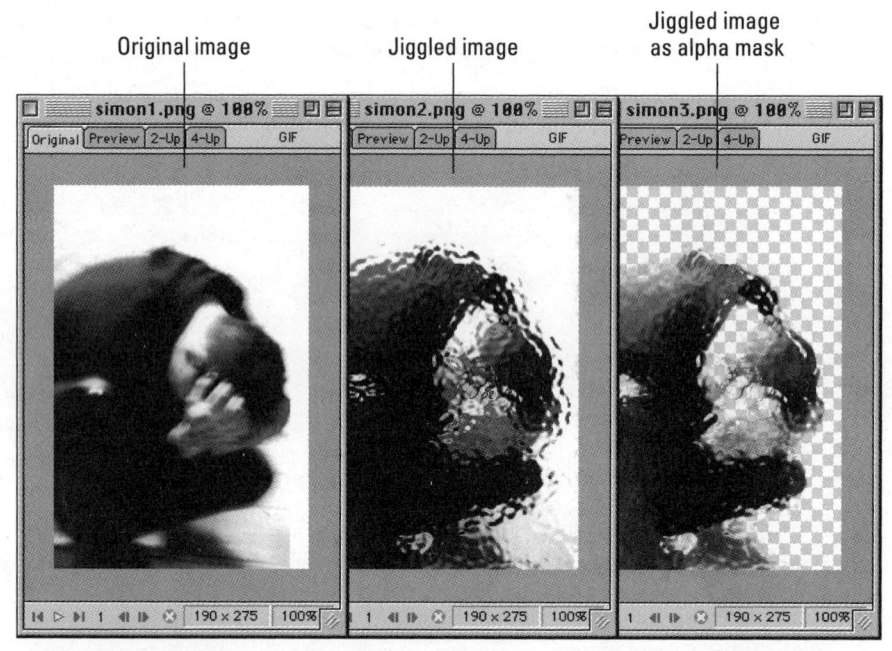

Figure 28-28: Jiggle is organic distortion in action, using the Bubbles type of movement. The third image (right) is the original image with the jiggled image as its alpha mask, and the canvas color changed to show through.

Understanding Shadowlab (Perspective Shadow in 3.1)

The ubiquitous drop shadow has its place, but a more realistic shadow that mimics the effects of the sun can be applied with Eye Candy 4000's Shadowlab, or 3.1's Perspective Shadow. The effect makes your selection appear to be standing up as the light comes from above and in front. The shadow is attached to the object rather than floating, which creates the three-dimensional perspective.

To use Shadowlab or Perspective Shadow, select an object and follow these steps:

1. Choose Xtras ⇨ Eye Candy 4000 ⇨ Shadowlab, or Xtras ⇨ Eye Candy 3.1 ⇨ Perspective Shadow.

The Shadowlab or Perspective Shadow dialog box appears.

2. Select any of these preset effects and/or adjust the controls, if necessary, to achieve the effect you desire:

   - **Vanishing Point Direction:** Controls the direction in which the shadow falls behind your selection. The shadow always falls behind your selection.
   - **Vanishing Point Distance:** Controls how far the vanishing point on the horizon is from your selection. Lower values are closer.
   - **Shadow Length:** Controls the length of the shadow without affecting the tapering much. Lower values produce a shorter shadow.
   - **Blur:** Controls how blurred the edges of the shadow will be. Higher values make the shadow blurrier and create the effect of a faraway light source.
   - **Opacity:** Adjusts the overall transparency of the shadow.
   - **Color:** Changes the color of the shadow.

3. If you like, you can save your settings, using the Save Preset button. Click OK (the checkmark) when you're done.

The effect is applied to your image, as shown in Figure 28-29.

Figure 28-29: Eye Candy 4000's Shadowlab and Eye Candy 3.1's Perspective Shadow put a realistic 3D shadow at your disposal. The original is a vector object. The other is a bitmap object with the Perspective Shadow filter applied to it.

Investigating Kai's Power Tools 5

Kai's Power Tools 5 (KPT 5) stands out from the crowd with the extremity of the modifications you can make to your images. Ending up with a completely unrecognizable image after applying just one Xtra is easy. In fact, making sure your image stays recognizable takes some work.

> **Tip** The Kai in Kai's Power Tools is Kai Krause, who became a legend among graphic artists when he introduced the original Kai's Power Tools.

Some highlights of KPT 5 include the following:

- Complex masking and transparency options
- Complex three-dimensional lighting and environment options
- Interactive Preview windows
- Presets with thumbnail views
- Common interface elements shared by the entire set of filters (see Figure 28-30)

> **Cross-Reference** The color insert shows what you can do with FraxPlorer.

Table 28-4 details KPT 5 filters.

> **Tip** The KPT 5 package also includes Kai's Power Tools 3, with 19 completely separate and useful plug-ins, making the KPT 5 package an excellent value.

Table 28-4
Kai's Power Tools 5

Filter	Description
Blurrrr	All the blur effects you could ever need, including spins, zooms, spirals, and motion blurs.
Noize	Typical and unusual noise effects, including transparent noise.
RadWarp	Creates or corrects a fish-eye lens effect. Sort of like a fun-house mirror on steroids.
Smoothie	Multiple ways to clean up dirty, jagged edges, quickly and easily.
Frax4D	Creates 3D or "4D" fractal sculptures. The "4D" ones look like really chewed-up versions of the 3D ones.
FraxFlame	Fractal effects that look like fire. Reminiscent of long-exposure photographs of fireworks.
FraxPlorer	An incredible Fractal Explorer with real-time fly-throughs, which are like fractal movies. Create amazing textures or backgrounds, or just have fun playing.

Chapter 28 ✦ **Creating Live Effects and Xtras** 897

Filter	Description
FiberOptix	Adds true three-dimensional fibers onto images, including masks. You can make something hairy and then composite it easily.
Orb-It	Creates very detailed three-dimensional spheres. Make bubbles, raindrops, lenses, and distortions.
ShapeShifter	Makes three-dimensional shapes from masks, including environment maps and textures.

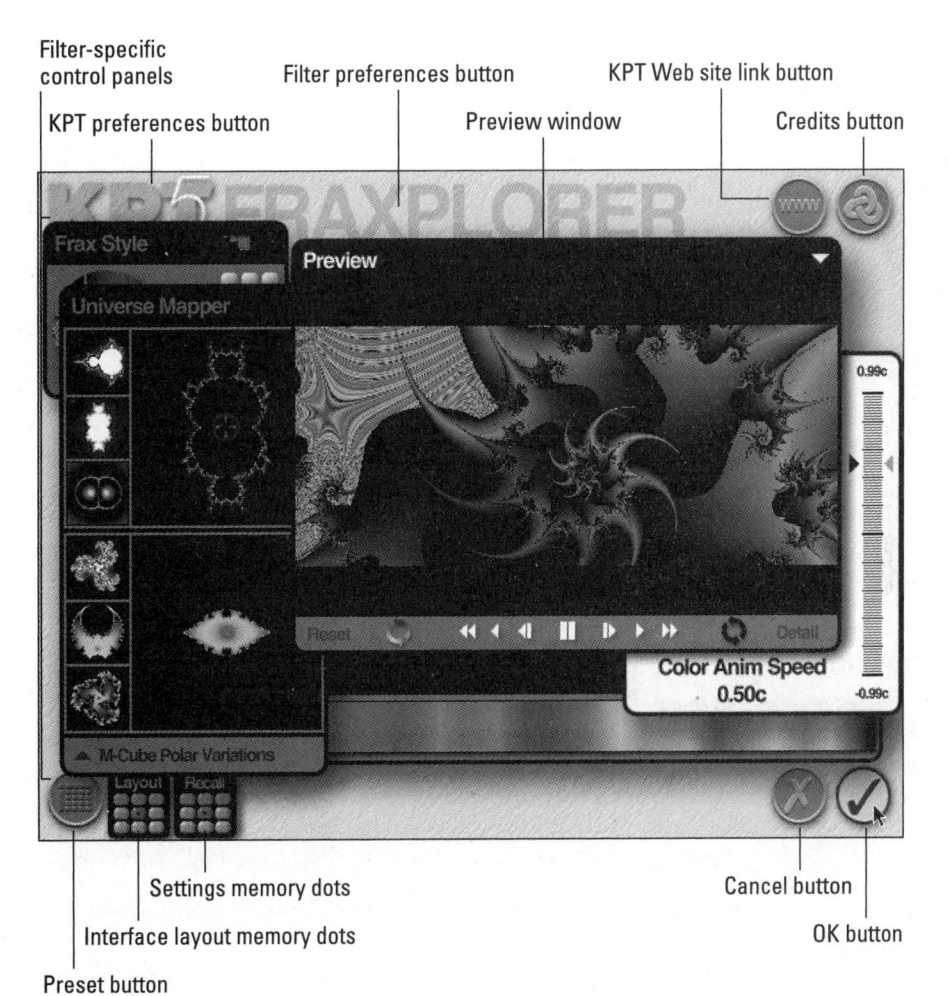

Figure 28-30: The KPT 5 interface is a bit tricky at first, but it contains much functionality. This is FraxPlorer.

Using RadWarp

KPT RadWarp simulates a photographic effect called barrel roll. You can either add the fish-eye effect to create fantastic variations on an image, or use the filter to "unfish-eye" an image with a slight, unwanted barrel roll.

Caution All KPT 5 filters will affect your entire bitmap object, even if you have created a selection. If you want to affect just a portion of a bitmap object, see the workaround in the section "Checking out false pixel selections," earlier in this chapter.

To use RadWarp, select a bitmap object and follow these steps:

1. Choose Xtras ⇨ KPT 5 ⇨ RadWarp.

   The RadWarp dialog box appears (see Figure 28-31).

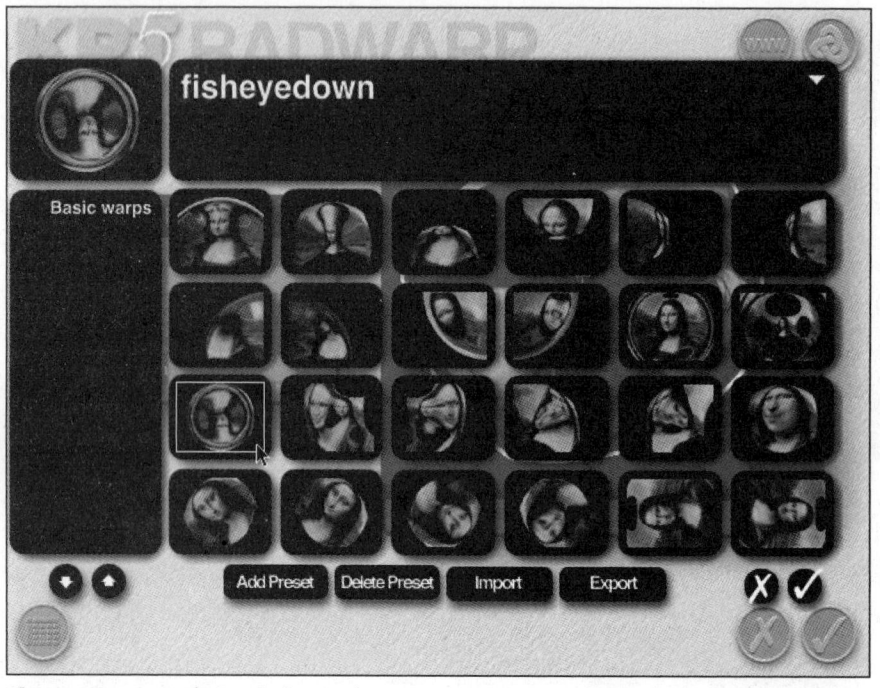

Figure 28-31: RadWarp is fun and can create extreme effects, including especially strange-looking faces.

> **Tip**
>
> By default, KPT 5 dialog boxes open up full-screen, but you can snap the dialog boxes to a number of pixel sizes, if you prefer. Hold down Ctrl (Command) and press 1 for 640×480, 2 for 800×600, 3 for 1024×768, 4 for 1152×870, 5 for 1280×1024, and 0 for full-screen. The panels are also set to Panel Auto Popup by default, which I found distracting. Click the name of the filter at the top of its dialog box to select the panel options. If your display has a low resolution, Panel Solo mode will save the day.

2. Adjust these controls to achieve the effect you desire:
   - **Alpha slider:** Controls how much of a rounded distortion is added
   - **Beta slider:** Controls how much of another type of slightly squarer distortion is added
   - **X Center:** Controls where the horizontal center of the warping effect is located
   - **Y Center:** Controls where the vertical center of the warping effect is located

> **Tip**
>
> You can also modify *X* and *Y* Center by dragging your mouse in the real-time Preview window.

   Rotation rotates the image.

3. Click OK (the checkmark) to apply the effect.

   The effect is applied to your image.

Understanding ShapeShifter

When you're working with vector objects in Fireworks, you can use Live Effects to apply amazing three-dimensional effects. If you've ever tried to get the same effect with a bitmap object using Live Effects, you were probably quite disappointed. KPT 5's ShapeShifter filter enables you to make those bitmap objects compete with your vector objects.

To use ShapeShifter, select an object and follow these steps:

1. Choose Xtras ➪ KPT 5 ➪ ShapeShifter.

   The ShapeShifter dialog box appears (see Figure 28-32).

2. In the Main Shape panel, click the thumbnail preview to import a mask. The mask specifies how the three-dimensional shape is added to your image. Adjust the Bevel Scale and Height to determine how much of a three-dimensional effect you're going to create. Select from the three bevel modes.

Note Unfortunately, Portable Network Graphics (PNG) images are not among the types that KPT 5 can use as masks. When you create a mask for KPT 5, export it from Fireworks as a Tag Image File Format (TIFF) image.

3. In the 3D Lighting panel, add light sources by clicking the plus (+) button. Drag light sources to different locations to affect the highlights and shadows on your image.

Figure 28-32: Using ShapeShifter gives your bitmap objects that three-dimensional look so that they can compete with Live Effects on vector objects.

4. In the Bump Map panel, add a three-dimensional texture to your image and set the scale and height. Scale zooms in on the texture. Height specifies how three-dimensional the bump map will be.

5. In the Glow panel, add a colored glow to your image, if you want to. You can choose to offset it from the image and also vary the transparency.

Tip Click the eye icon on the Glow panel to show or hide the glow, just like the eye icons in the Fireworks Layers panel.

6. In the Shadow panel, add a shadow to your image, if you want to. Just like glow, you can offset the shadow by varying degrees, choose colors, and specify transparency.

7. In the Top Mask panel, you can import another mask to create an emboss effect on top of your three-dimensional object, as if you had stamped out a shape in the top.

8. In the Environment Map panel, load an image to be used as an environment map. This image will be reflected by your three-dimensional shape as if it were the sky being reflected on a quiet lake. This adds much depth and character to your image.

> **Tip**
> You can also alter the settings by dragging your mouse across the Preview window.

9. Click OK (the checkmark) to apply the effect.

Summary

Effects may be the icing on the cake, but then what's cake without icing? Seriously, effects play an important role in Web graphics, particularly when it comes to creating buttons with variations that can be used for rollovers. Fireworks makes the hardest effect easy by providing five standard effects and numerous preset looks. When you first begin applying effects to your graphics, consider these points:

- Filters and effects applied from the Effect panel remain editable. Filters applied from the Xtras menu flatten text and vector objects.

- Fireworks applies Live Effects, which are recalculated every time a graphic is altered.

- All Fireworks effects are specified through the Effect panel, which changes to offer different attributes according to the effect chosen.

- The Inner Bevel and Outer Bevel effects are similar, but result in completely different looks. The Inner Bevel effect uses the object's color to create an edge within the object itself, whereas the Outer Bevel effect uses a separate color chosen by the designer to make a border around the outside of the object.

- The Drop Shadow sets off any vector, text, or bitmap object with a shadow behind the figure — large or small, subtle or bold, your choice.

- Emboss removes the fill and stroke from any selected object and builds edges from the underlying canvas or objects to make it appear as if the object is emerging from the background, or sinking into it.

✦ Fireworks Glow effect creates a soft glow around an object.

✦ Using a combination of other Fireworks tools and commands, any object can have a perspective shadow.

✦ In Fireworks, you can easily apply multiple effects.

✦ Custom effects combinations can be saved and quickly recalled, or saved as part of a Fireworks style.

✦ You can share filters among multiple, compatible applications, to have access to them wherever you're working.

In the next chapter, you discover how to use Fireworks to arrange and composite different objects.

✦ ✦ ✦

Arranging and Compositing Objects

CHAPTER 29

In This Chapter

Using layers

Aligning and distributing objects

Getting layout assistance

Grouping objects

Masking and transparency

Using opacity and blending

Simulating a light source with blending modes

Feathering selections

Applied compositing

Fireworks differs dramatically from other bitmap-editing applications in that the component parts of your document are independent objects — often with vector information — and are always editable. Individual objects float above the canvas and can easily be arranged and aligned with each other. One of the best aspects of this creative power is that it enables you to easily composite, layer, and blend objects and then return to them later and undo or change any aspect of your work. Even advanced operations, such as alpha masking, leave the masked image — and the mask itself — intact and editable.

Tip *Compositing* is the process of combining multiple images into one image, usually by feathering, blending, masking, and altering the transparency of the images.

This chapter looks at the various ways to combine, group, arrange, align, blend, and generally lay out multiple objects within Fireworks.

Using Layers

Layers are a powerful Fireworks feature that enable you to organize your document into separate divisions that you can work with individually or hide from view when convenient. Think of an artist drawing on separate transparencies instead of one sheet of paper. He or she could take one transparency out of the stack and draw only the background elements of the drawing and then take another transparency and put related foreground elements on that. Another could have text elements, and another a signature. Restacking the transparencies produces a finished drawing.

The Layers panel (see Figure 29-1) is the central control center for using layers. To show or hide the Layers panel, choose Window ⇨ Layers, or use the keyboard shortcut, F2. The Layers panel enables you to see at a glance how many layers you have in your document, which ones are locked or hidden, and even whether a selection exists on the current layer. As with most other Fireworks panels, the Layers panel also has a pop-up menu that provides easy access to commands related to the functions of the panel.

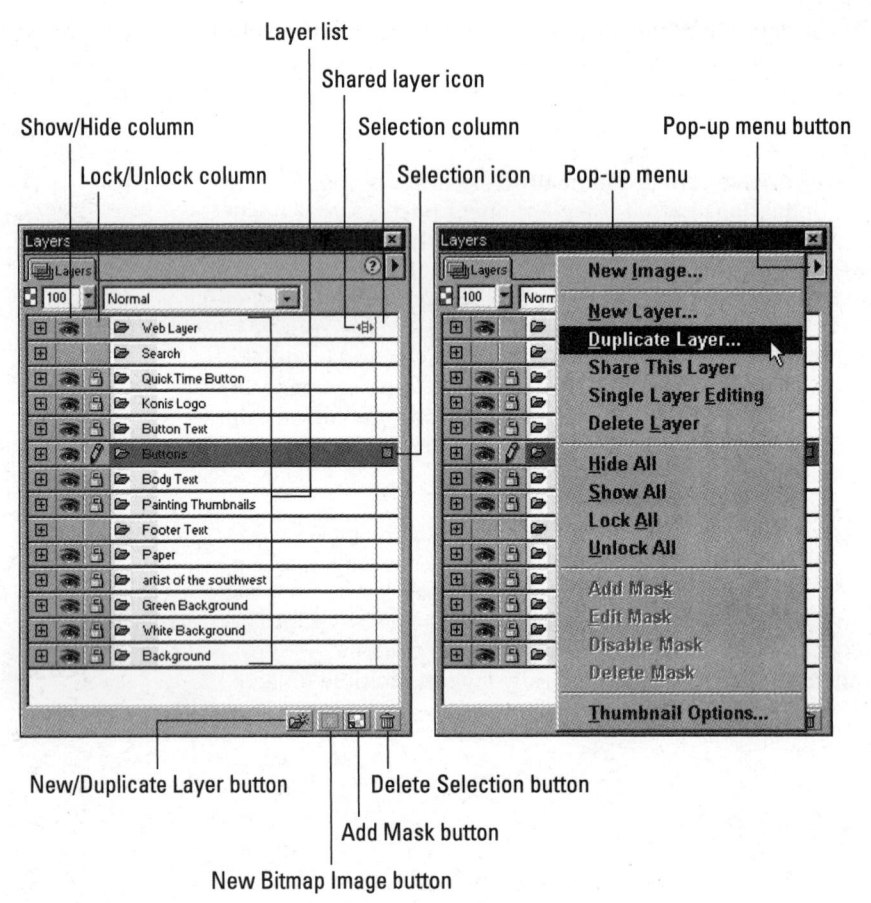

Figure 29-1: The Layers panel packs many layer-manipulation options into a small, convenient space.

You may find it helpful to refer to the Layers panel features in Figure 29-1 as you explore their functions throughout this chapter.

When you create a new document in Fireworks, it initially has two layers:

✦ **Web Layer:** A special layer just for hotspots and slices
✦ **Layer 1:** A regular layer on which all the objects you create will reside until you create another layer

Adding a layer

Each new layer that you add to your document is placed above the current layer in the layers list. The stacking order in the Layers panel reflects the stacking order on the canvas, so objects on the bottom layer in the Layers panel are also the closest to the canvas.

To add a new, blank layer to your document, do one of the following:

✦ Click the New/Duplicate Layer button on the Layers panel.

Tip
Hold down the Alt (Option) key while you press the New/Duplicate Layer button, and Fireworks displays the New Layer dialog box, enabling you to give your layer a custom name before creating it.

✦ Choose New Layer from the Layers panel pop-up menu.
✦ Choose Insert ⇨ Layer.

Naming a layer

To change the name of a layer, double-click its name in the layer list and type a new name in the pop-up dialog box that appears. Press Enter (Return), or click anywhere outside the pop-up dialog box to dismiss it.

Duplicating a layer

You can also add a layer to your document by duplicating one that already exists. When you duplicate a layer, all the objects on that layer are also duplicated. Working with layers in this fashion is reminiscent of working with folders and files in Windows Explorer or the Macintosh Finder, where duplicating a file duplicates the file, and duplicating a folder duplicates the folder and all of its contents.

To duplicate an existing layer and all of its contents, do one of the following:

✦ Drag the layer from the layers list and drop it onto the New/Duplicate Layer button on the Layers panel.

- ✦ Hold down the Alt (Option) key, and drag and drop the layer within the layers list.
- ✦ Choose Duplicate Layer from the Layers panel pop-up menu.

Duplicating a layer and then hiding the duplicate is a quick way to make a backup of all the objects on a layer before you perform extensive edits. If the edits don't go well, you can always delete them and show the "backup" layer again, taking you back to square one. Even better, I find that making "backup" layers every once in a while builds up a library of objects that often become creatively useful at a later stage. For example, you may find yourself wrapping text around the same circle that you used earlier to mask a bitmap object. Reusing such objects automatically makes your designs more consistent.

Deleting a layer

When you delete a layer, all the objects on that layer are also deleted. If you delete a layer accidentally, choose Edit ⇨ Undo right away to get it back.

To delete a layer, do one of the following:

- ✦ Drag a layer from the layer list in the Layers panel to the Delete Selection button (Trash) on the Layers panel.
- ✦ Select a layer from the layer list in the Layers panel and click the Delete Selection button.
- ✦ Select a layer from the layer list in the Layers panel and choose Delete Layer from the Layers panel pop-up menu.

Changing stacking order

After you have more than one layer in your document, you may want to change the stacking order at some point. To change the stacking order of layers in your document, simply click and drag a layer higher or lower in the layer list in the Layers panel. Layers that are higher up the layer list are higher up in the stacking order in relation to the canvas.

Editing layer by layer

By default, all objects, no matter which layer they reside on, are fair game for editing on the canvas. To protect the contents of a layer from editing, you can lock or hide the individual layer. Objects on locked or hidden layers are not editable on the canvas.

To lock or unlock a layer, click within the Lock/Unlock column of the Layers panel, next to the layer you want to lock or unlock. After a layer is locked, a padlock icon appears in the Lock/Unlock column next to the layer's name, and none of the objects on that layer can be selected or edited in the document window. When a layer is unlocked, the Lock/Unlock column next to its name is empty.

To show or hide a layer, click within the Show/Hide column of the Layers panel, next to the layer that you want to show or hide. When the eye icon is visible, the layer is visible. When the eye icon is not showing, the layer is hidden, and all the objects on that layer are invisible in the document window.

Tip When a layer is hidden, it is also locked. When you hide a layer, you don't need to lock it as well.

The Layers panel pop-up menu features commands for hiding or showing all layers simultaneously, or locking or unlocking all layers simultaneously. Alternatively, you can hold down Alt (Option) and click in the Show/Hide or Lock/Unlock column to affect all layers at once.

An alternative method of layer-by-layer editing is to enter Single Layer Editing mode, by choosing Single Layer Editing from the Layers panel pop-up menu. When you're in Single Layer Editing mode, you can select or edit only the objects on the current layer, although you can still see objects on other layers. As you select each layer from the layers list in the Layers panel, the other layers automatically act as if they are locked. When working with a complex document, this is an easy way to limit the scope of your edits.

Giving your layers descriptive names before using Single Layer Editing really speeds up things. If your layers are named Background, Text, and so forth, you can quickly select a layer based on which objects you want to edit, without worrying about accidentally altering objects on other layers.

Tip Two of the commands in the Command menu also enable you to quickly work on a single layer without using Single Layer Editing mode. Choose Commands ⇨ Document ⇨ Hide Other Layers to hide all but the current layer. Choose Commands ⇨ Document ⇨ Lock Other Layers to lock all but the current layer.

Using the Selection column

When you want to move objects from one layer to another, you might be inclined to cut them to the clipboard, change to another layer in the Layers panel, and then paste the objects into the new layer. That works fine, but the Layers panel provides you with another method. Whenever you select an object or objects on the canvas or in the Layers panel, a small blue box appears in the Selection column next to the layer that the selected objects are located on. Drag this box up or down and drop it next to another layer, and the objects are moved there. Hold down the Alt (Option) key as you drag and drop to copy the selection instead of moving it.

Opening layers

The Layers panel uses a folder icon for layers, and for good reason. Just as your overall document is divided into discrete layers, each layer is itself divided into objects, which appear in the Layers panel as an object sublayer, complete with thumbnail images. To open a particular layer and display its contents, click the plus/minus box (disclosure triangle on the Mac) in the Expand/Collapse column next to the layer's name, as shown in Figure 29-2. To hide the contents of the layer, click the square (disclosure triangle) again. Hold down the Alt (Option) key as you click in the Expand/Collapse column to open or close all the layers in your document at once. I often find myself Alt- (Option-) clicking to quickly close all layers when I don't want to work with individual objects.

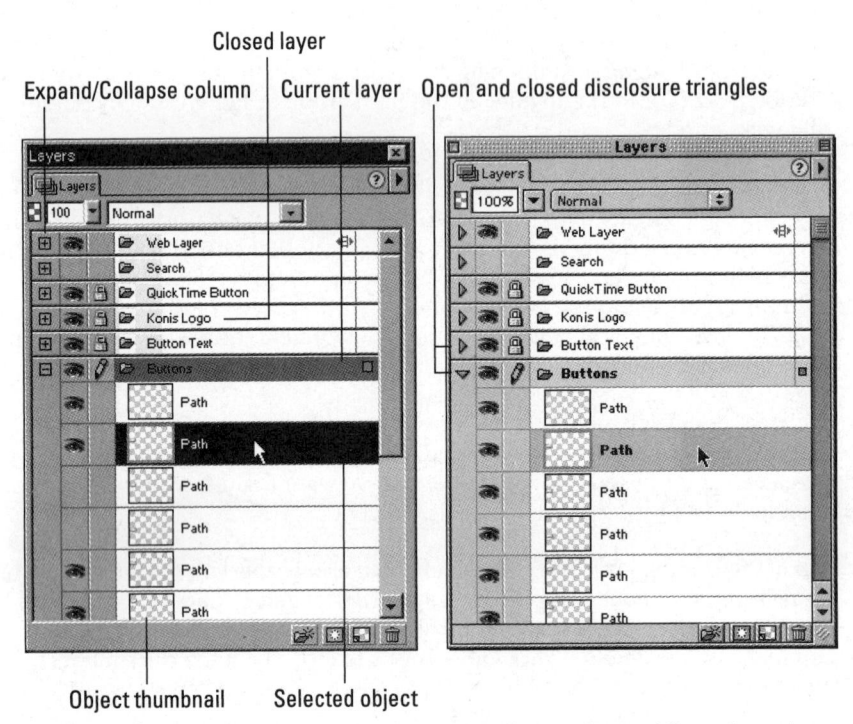

Figure 29-2: Each layer is a container for the objects that reside on it. Each object on the layer is displayed as its own sublayer.

New Feature The Layers panel has been almost completely redesigned for Fireworks 4 and resembles Photoshop 6's layers and layer sets more than Fireworks 3's layers. You can now select individual objects as though they were layers, as well as change the stacking order of objects simply by moving them up or down the layer list.

Many of the same techniques you use to work with layers in the Layers panel also apply to working with object sublayers. Keep the following points in mind:

+ **To add a new object sublayer:** Simply create a new object on the canvas with any of the usual methods, such as importing, drawing, copying and pasting, and so on. As each new object is added to your document, Fireworks adds new object sublayers to the current layer, complete with a thumbnail image. You can also click the New Bitmap Image button on the Layers panel to create a new, empty bitmap object directly above the currently selected object.

+ **To name an object:** Double-click its generic name, such as "rectangle" in the layer list, and type a new name. Press Enter (Return) when you're done.

+ **To change the stacking order of objects:** Drag their object sublayers up or down the layers list in the Layers panel. Note that you can move objects up or down within their layers, or further up or down into other layers (see Figure 29-3). Dragging and dropping between layers is physically easier if you open both the source and target layer, exposing the objects inside each. This also enables you to choose where your dropped object resides within the stacking order of the target layer.

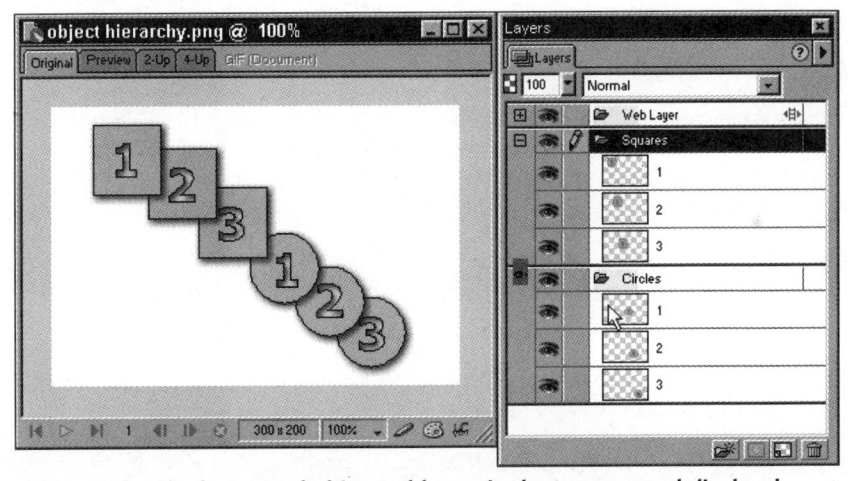

Figure 29-3: The layers and object sublayers in the Layers panel display the complete hierarchy of the stacking order in your document.

Tip: Dragging and dropping between layers is physically easier if you open both the source and target layer, exposing the objects inside each. This also enables you to choose where your dropped object resides within the stacking order of the target layer.

✦ **To duplicate an object sublayer:** Hold down the Alt (Option) key and drag and drop the object sublayer up or down the layer list. A copy is created, and your original object is unaffected. You can even drop the copy in another layer.

Tip Use the Shift modifier key to make multiple selections of object sublayers, just as you would with objects on the canvas.

✦ **To hide an object:** Click the eye icon in the Show/Hide column next to the object's sublayer in the Layers panel. You can also hide a selection of objects by choosing View ➪ Hide Selection. To show the objects again, choose View ➪ Show All.

✦ **To delete an object:** Select it — on the canvas or in the Layers panel — and click the Delete Selection button on the Layers panel.

Tip Old-school Fireworks users — like myself — may find it a little annoying that the Layers panel defaults to fully expanded when you initially open a Fireworks document. Derren Whiteman has created a scriptlet that sets a hidden Fireworks preference so that the Layers panel defaults to fully collapsed. Find it — and a companion script that sets the preference back to its default — on Derren's Fireworks Web site at www.derren.com/geek/fireworks.

Examining the Web Layer

All Fireworks documents have a Web Layer on which you can draw "Web objects," such as hotspots and slice guides. You can move the Web Layer in the stacking order by dragging it up or down the layer list in the Layers panel, but you can't delete the Web Layer. The Web Layer is always shared across all frames.

Cross-Reference For more information about using the Web Layer, see Chapters 33 and 34. For more details about sharing layers across frames, and about frames in general, see Chapter 35.

In addition to creating hotspots with one of the hotspot tools, you can create hotspots out of regular bitmap and vector objects by using the Layers panel. This is a handy way to quickly add hotspots to objects if you want the hotspots to be the same size as the objects.

To create hotspots out of objects, follow these steps:

1. Select the object or objects that you want to make into hotspots.

    Fireworks displays a selection icon (a blue box) in the Selection column of the Layers panel, next to the layer that the selected objects are located in.

2. Drag the selection icon and drop it in the same column on the Web Layer.

    If you have multiple objects selected, Fireworks asks whether you want to create one hotspot or multiple hotspots. Choosing to create one hotspot combines the shapes into one.

The hotspots are created on the Web Layer, and your original objects are unaffected.

Aligning and Distributing Objects

One of the most basic layout techniques is aligning and distributing objects. If you've ever used any kind of drawing or publishing application, then you're familiar with the concept. When you're in vector mode in Fireworks, every object on the canvas "floats" and can be easily aligned with another.

Using a theoretical rectangle

When you're aligning a selection of objects, imagine a rectangle around your selection (see Figure 29-4) described by the objects themselves. The top of the rectangle is the topmost point on the topmost object, the left side of the rectangle is the far-left point on the farthest-left object in the selection, and so on. This theoretical rectangle is what you align objects to, and what you distribute them across. For consistent results, imagine this theoretical rectangle each time you prepare to use an Align command.

Figure 29-4: Imagine a theoretical rectangle around your selection. This is what the selected objects align to when you choose one of the commands from the Modify ⇨ Align submenu.

When you left-align a selection of objects, all the objects move left until they bump into the left border of the theoretical rectangle. Similarly, if you align to the bottom, all the objects move down until they hit the bottom border of the rectangle. It's very important to understand that alignment in Fireworks has nothing to do with a page or the canvas, as in some applications. In Fireworks, objects are aligned to other selected objects. If you try to align only one object, the alignment commands are unavailable.

> **Cross-Reference**
> I show you a workaround for aligning a single object to the canvas later in this chapter.

To align a selection of objects to the selection's left, right, top, or bottom, select the objects that you want to align and choose the appropriate alignment command:

- **Left alignment:** To align all objects to the far-left point of the farthest-left object (see Figure 29-5), choose either Modify ➪ Align ➪ Left, or the keyboard shortcut, Ctrl+Alt+1 (Command+Option+1).

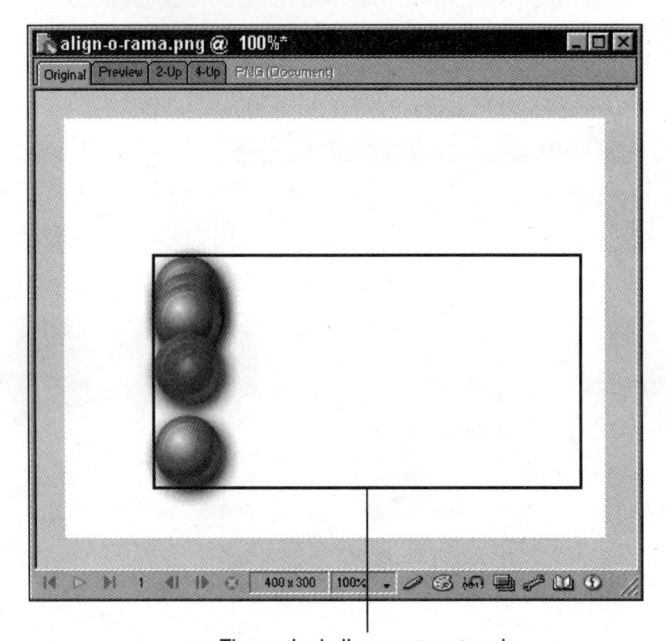

Figure 29-5: The selection of objects shown in Figure 29-4 moves to the left side of the theoretical alignment rectangle when you use the Modify ➪ Align ➪ Left command.

♦ **Right alignment:** To align all objects to the far-right point of the farthest-right object, choose either Modify ⇨ Align ⇨ Right, or the keyboard shortcut Ctrl+Alt+3 (Command+Option+3).

♦ **Top alignment:** To align all objects to the topmost point of the topmost object (see Figure 29-6), choose either Modify ⇨ Align ⇨ Top, or the keyboard shortcut, Ctrl+Alt+4 (Command+Option+4).

♦ **Bottom alignment:** To align all objects to the bottommost point of the bottommost object, choose either Modify ⇨ Align ⇨ Bottom, or the keyboard shortcut, Ctrl+Alt+6 (Command+Option+6).

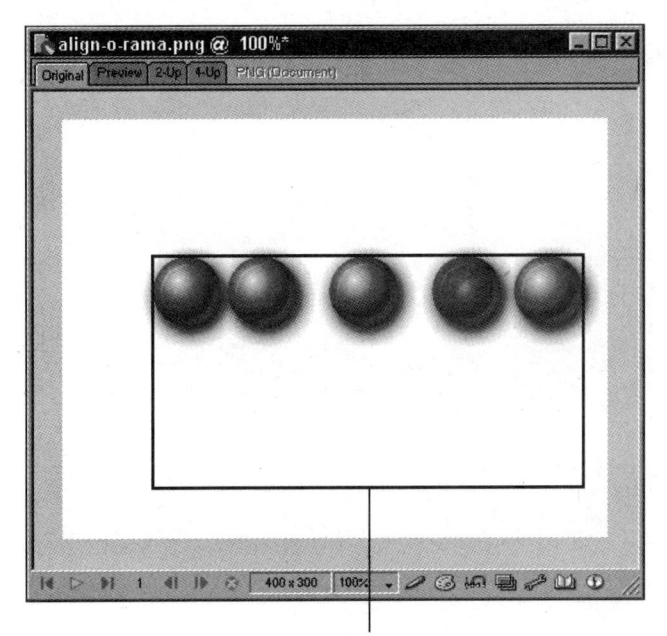

Theoretical alignment rectangle

Figure 29-6: The selection of objects shown in Figure 29-4 moves to the top of the theoretical alignment rectangle when you use the Modify ⇨ Align ⇨ Top command.

Fireworks also has two alignment commands that deal with centering objects. Again, rather than centering objects on the canvas, Fireworks centers them to a theoretical horizontal or vertical line drawn through the selection. In order to understand what to expect from these commands, imagine a cross drawn over the theoretical alignment rectangle shown previously in Figure 29-4. This cross demonstrates the vertical and horizontal center lines that objects can be aligned to.

✦ **Center Vertical alignment:** To align all objects to a theoretical vertical center line, choose either Modify ➪ Align ➪ Center Vertical, or the keyboard shortcut, Ctrl+Alt+2 (Command+Option+2).

Caution Remember that the center in question is not the center of the canvas, but the center of the selection.

✦ **Center Horizontal alignment:** To align all objects to a theoretical horizontal center line (see Figure 29-7), choose either Modify ➪ Align ➪ Center Horizontal, or the keyboard shortcut, Ctrl+Alt+5 (Command+Option+5).

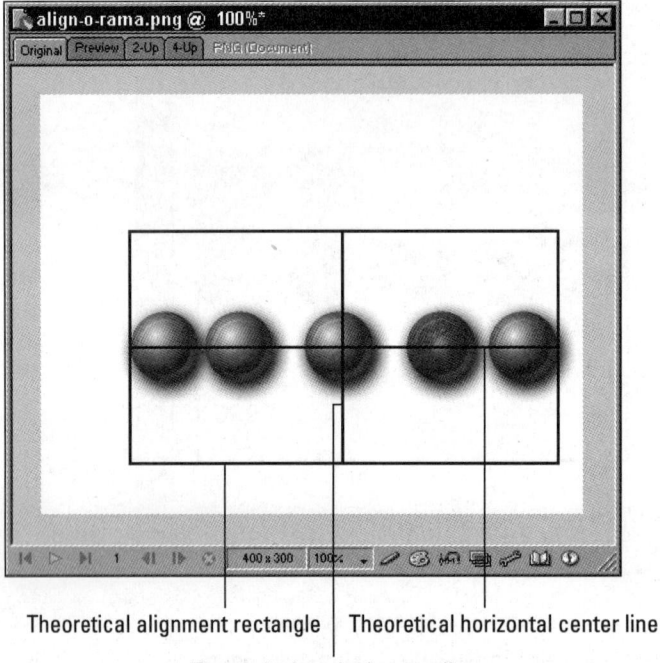

Figure 29-7: The selection of objects from Figure 29-4 snaps to a theoretical horizontal line when you use the Modify ➪ Align ➪ Center Horizontal command.

You can also distribute objects across a selection, which is handy when you have a few objects, such as a row of buttons, that you want to space evenly. To distribute a selection of objects across the width of the selection, select the objects that you want to distribute and choose the appropriate command:

✦ **Even horizontal distribution:** To space your objects evenly from left to right (see Figure 29-8), choose either Modify ➪ Align ➪ Distribute Widths, or the keyboard shortcut, Ctrl+Alt+7 (Command+Option+7).

✦ **Even vertical distribution:** To space your objects evenly from top to bottom, choose either Modify ➪ Align ➪ Distribute Heights, or the keyboard shortcut, Ctrl+Alt+9 (Command+Option+9).

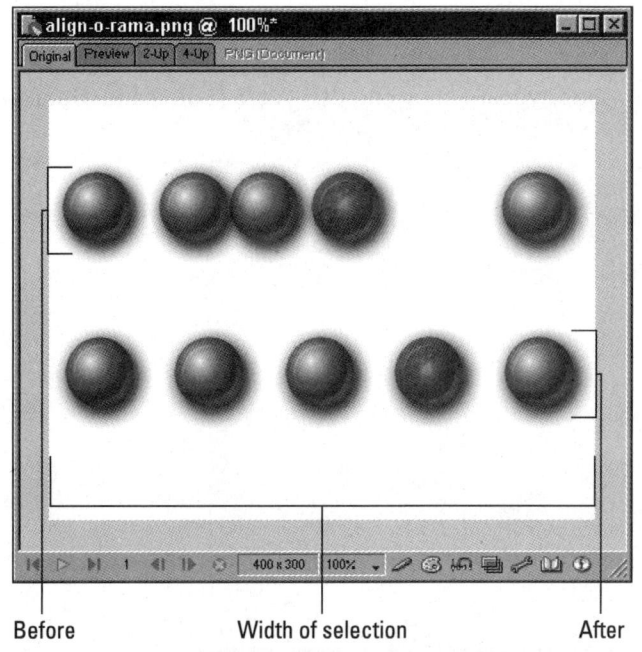

Before   Width of selection   After

Figure 29-8: A selection of objects can be distributed across the width of the selection with the Distribute Widths ommand. Note that the leftmost and rightmost object do not move at all. They define the width of the selection.

Aligning to the canvas

Although Fireworks' alignment tools are very powerful, the commands in the Modify ➪ Align submenu have no knowledge of the canvas at all. What do you do when you just want to snap an object to the center of the canvas, or align it to the left edge of the canvas? Fortunately, a command and a simple technique enable you to meet almost any kind of alignment challenge.

For those times when all you want to do is take a selection and center it on the canvas, choose Commands ➪ Document ➪ Center in Document. Your selected object or objects snap to the absolute (horizontal and vertical) center of the canvas. This handy shortcut demonstrates the power of Fireworks' built-in extensibility.

For more sophisticated canvas alignment, such as aligning a selection to the left side of the canvas, draw a rectangle the size and shape of the canvas and then align other objects to the rectangle. Visually, the effect is exactly the same as aligning to the canvas, with the added feature that you can easily create a border around your document, just by reducing the alignment rectangle in size by a small amount, as shown in Figure 29-9. You may want to keep your alignment rectangle on its own layer, so that it is very easy to hide, show, lock, or delete.

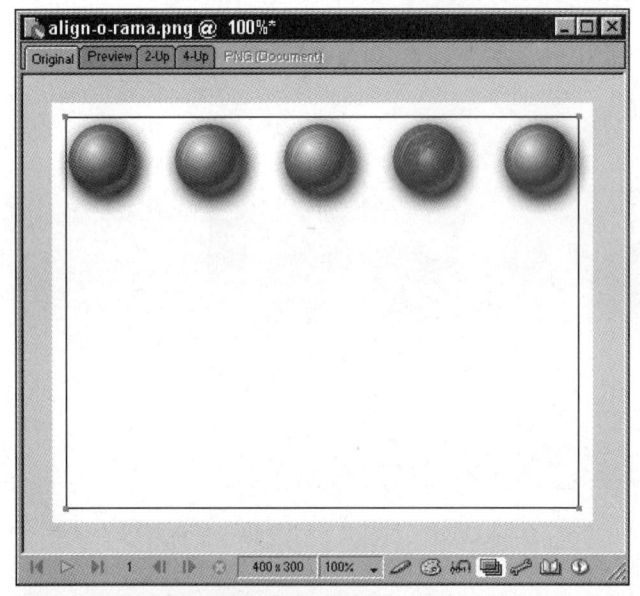

Figure 29-9: Although you can't align objects to the canvas, you can create a rectangle that's roughly the size of the canvas and align objects to the rectangle for the same effect.

Tip Fireworks considers the edges of the canvas to be guides. Enabling View ⇨ Guides ⇨ Snap to Guides causes a dragged selection to snap to the edge of the canvas. Align objects to each other, and then select them all and drag them near a canvas edge to create the same effect as an alignment to the canvas.

Looking at Layout Assistance

Fireworks provides a variety of ways to precisely lay out objects on the canvas. Rulers enable you to place guides at precise locations and snap objects to those guides as you move them around. Or, you can choose to lay a grid over your document to help you align things correctly.

Using rulers

Rulers are a standard feature of pretty much every drawing or graphics application. In fact, rulers (the kind that you hold in your hand) are a standard feature of traditional, paper-based layouts, as well. Rulers enable you to keep track of the size of your objects and their placement on the canvas with much more precision than the naked eye alone.

To toggle the visibility of the rulers, choose either View ⇨ Rulers, or the keyboard shortcut, Ctrl+Alt+R (Command+Option+R). The rulers appear within your document, running along the top and left borders (see Figure 29-10).

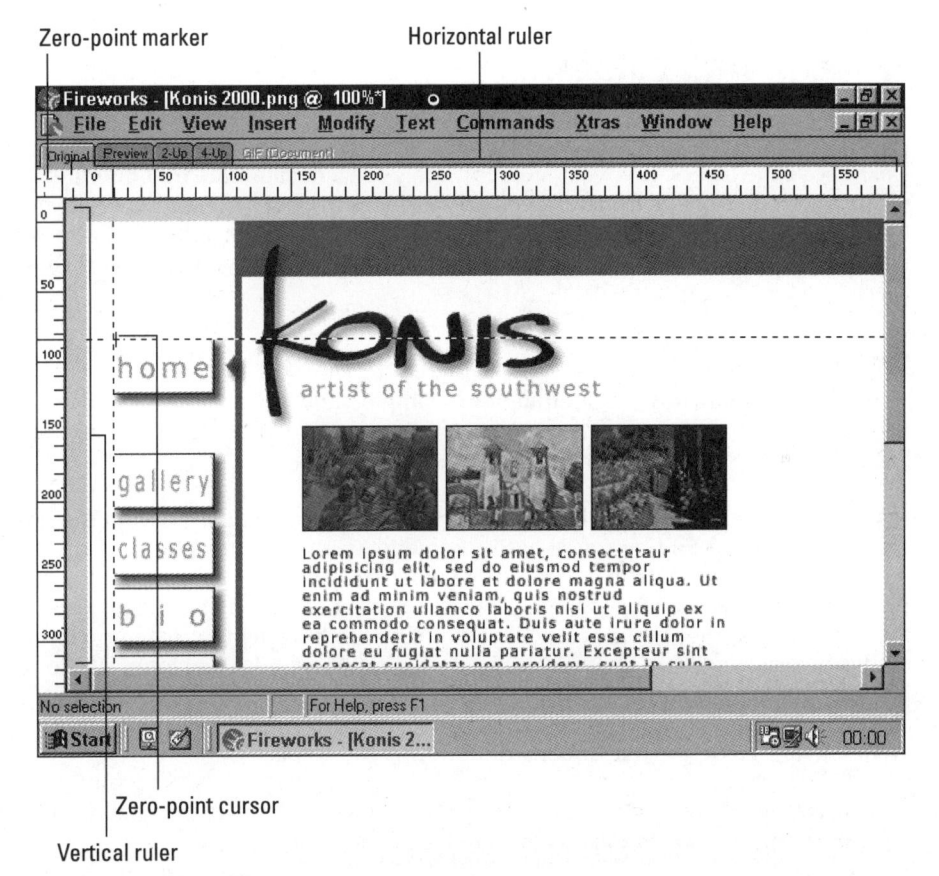

Figure 29-10: Dropping the zero-point cursor next to the top-left object you're aligning simplifies the math involved in aligning objects.

Tip You can see your mouse pointer's position on the canvas in the rulers as they track your mouse. This is helpful when you want to draw a new object at a precise position on the canvas.

By default, the ruler's *zero-point*—the point where the horizontal and vertical rulers meet—is set to 0 pixels, but you can set it to another location in your document by dragging the zero-point marker to a new location and releasing it. The zero-point marker is in the upper-left corner of the document window when the rulers are visible. If all objects in your document are going to be at least 20 pixels from the top and 20 pixels from the left, moving the zero-point to 20×20 pixels simplifies the math that you have to do later as you align objects. To set the zero-point back to zero again, double-click the zero-point marker.

Working with guides

Guides are simply lines that you can position to mark important points in your documents, such as a margin or center point. Guides don't print or export, and they exist above the layers of your document. They are a design-time tool intended to make laying out objects easier. For example, if your layout calls for many objects to be placed at 20 pixels from the top, then creating a horizontal guide at that position enables you easily to see where that point is located so that you can place objects there.

Creating guides

Adding a new guide to your document is a simple, mouse-only affair. Simply clicking and dragging the horizontal ruler into your document creates a new horizontal guide that you can drop anywhere.

A horizontal guide runs parallel to the horizontal ruler, so you drag from the horizontal ruler to make a horizontal guide. Sometimes, this can be a bit confusing because you'll tend to drop a horizontal guide after checking its position on the vertical ruler. In other words, you might place a horizontal guide at 20 pixels from the top according to the vertical ruler. If you find yourself trying to create horizontal guides by dragging from the vertical ruler, think of the guides as clones of the rulers from which you drag them—horizontal for horizontal, vertical for vertical.

To add a new guide to your document, follow these steps:

1. If the rulers aren't visible, choose either View ⇨ Rulers, or the keyboard shortcut, Ctrl+Alt+R (Command+Option+R), to show them.
2. Drag from the horizontal ruler to create a new horizontal guide. Drag from the vertical ruler to create a new vertical guide (see Figure 29-11). When you reach the position where you want to place your guide, simply drop it in place by releasing the mouse button.

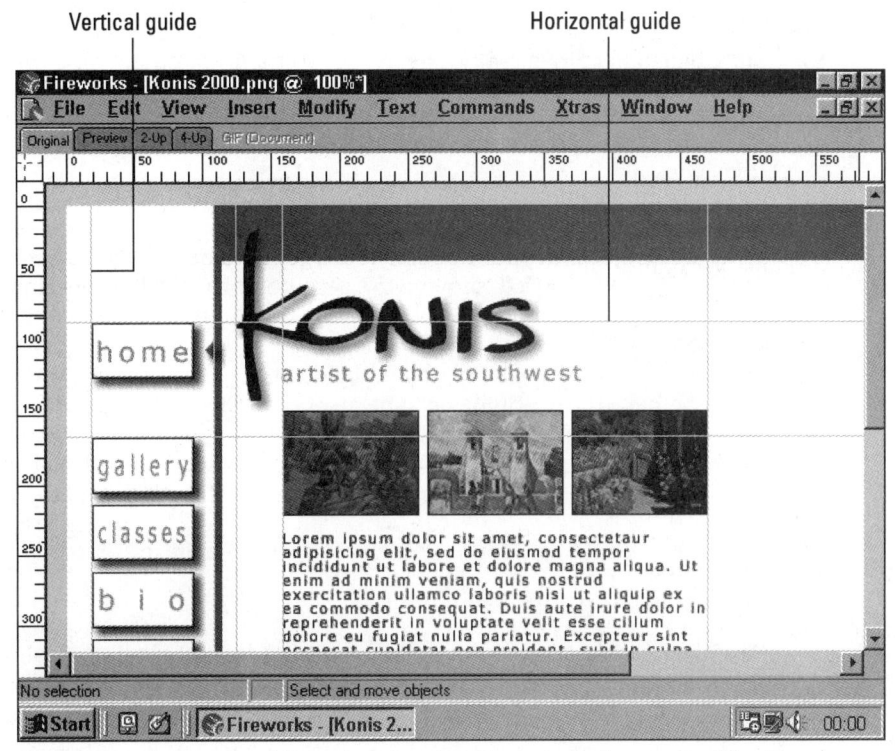

Figure 29-11: Create guides at key locations in your design to simplify object alignment.

Locking or hiding guides

After you create quite a few guides, you may find that they get in the way. Because they aren't on a layer, you can't just lock or hide their layer to make them invisible or not editable. Carefully placing a guide in the correct spot and then dragging it somewhere else accidentally goes a long way toward negating the primary time-saving aspect of using guides.

To show or hide guides, choose either View ⇨ Guides ⇨ Show Guides, or use the keyboard shortcut, Ctrl+Semicolon (Command+Semicolon). Hiding guides periodically gives you a better sense of what your final image will look like.

To lock all of your guides so that they can't be moved, choose either View ⇨ Guides ⇨ Lock Guides, or the keyboard shortcut, Ctrl+Alt+Semicolon (Command+Option+Semicolon).

Snapping to guides

Snapping objects to guides really uses guides to their full potential. With a little planning, you can create guides at important points in your document so that your layout comes together almost automatically as you move objects around the canvas.

To toggle whether objects snap to the nearest guide, choose either View ➪ Guides ➪ Snap to Guides, or the keyboard shortcut, Ctrl+Shift+Semicolon (Command+Shift+Semicolon).

Using guide colors

If your document contains a lot of green objects, the default green color of the guides may be hard to see. Guides can be any color. Choosing a color that contrasts sharply with the color scheme of your document makes guides easier to see and also has the effect of separating them from your document, so that you can see your layout through the guides without having to hide the guides all the time.

To change the color that guides are displayed in, follow these steps:

1. Choose View ➪ Guides ➪ Edit Guides.

    Fireworks displays the Guides (Grids and Guides) dialog box, as shown in Figure 29-12.

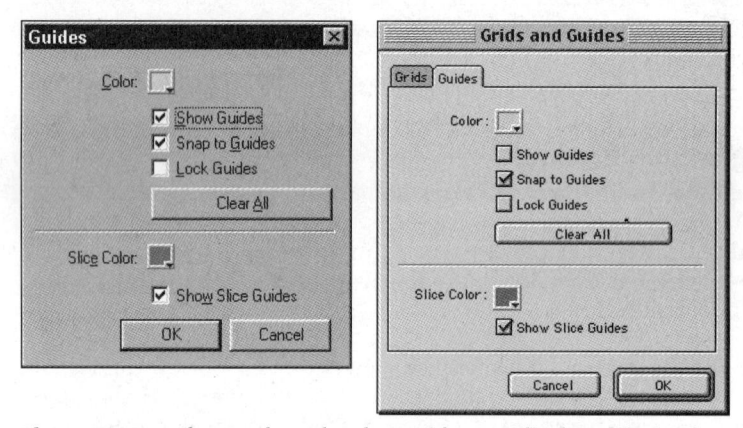

Figure 29-12: Change the color that guides are displayed in (and other options) by using the Guides (Grids and Guides) dialog box.

Note: On the Macintosh, instead of a Guides dialog box and a Grids dialog box, the single Grids and Guides dialog box offers a Grids tab and a Guides tab that selects between Grids and Guides views.

2. Use the guides color picker to specify the color you want the guides to be displayed in, and then click OK.

For convenience, all the guide options have been collected into the Guides (Grids and Guides) dialog box. You can check or uncheck Show Guides to toggle the visibility of the guides; check Snap to Guides to cause objects to snap to the guides; or check Lock Guides to lock them. Options for slice guides are also available here.

Clearing guides

Removing a single guide from your document is a drag-and-drop affair, just like adding one. Simply grab the guide with your mouse and drag it out of your document. You can drag it out to the left, right, top, or bottom, and it will disappear from your document.

You can also clear all the guides out of your document simultaneously, by using the Guides (Grids and Guides) dialog box. To clear all guides, follow these steps:

   1. Choose View ⇨ Guides ⇨ Edit Guides.

      Fireworks displays the Guides (Grids and Guides) dialog box (refer to Figure 29-12).

   2. Click the Clear All button to remove all the guides from your document. Click OK when you're done.

Note: The Clear All button removes ruler guides, but not slice guides.

Exploring the grid

The *grid* is a quick way to achieve more precise layouts. Usually, you'll want objects to align in a fairly regular pattern. The grid makes it easy to see the relationship between the elements of your layout by splitting the document into smaller, more manageable sections. Grid lines don't export or print, and they aren't on a layer. They're simply a visual aid at design time.

To show or hide the grid, choose either View ⇨ Grid ⇨ Show Grid, or the keyboard shortcut, Ctrl+Alt+G (Command+Option+G).

Snapping to the grid

You can choose to have objects snap to the grid automatically, just like you did earlier with guides. When this feature is enabled, you'll notice that objects are attracted to the grid lines like magnets. Because all of your objects are snapping to the same grid, you can get more precise layouts without any extra effort.

To make objects snap to the grid, choose either View ⇨ Grid ⇨ Snap to Grid, or the keyboard shortcut, Ctrl+Alt+Shift+G (Command+Option+Shift+G).

Changing grid color and frequency

Again, just like guides, you can change the color of the grid to make it stand out from your document. The default color for each new document is black.

If you're creating a navigation bar with numerous buttons that are 100 pixels wide and 50 pixels tall, set the grid so that it also is 100 pixels wide and 50 pixels tall, so that you can easily see where each button should sit. Enable Snap to Grid, and your layout will come together automatically. The default grid frequency for new documents is 36×36 pixels.

To modify the grid, follow these steps:

1. Choose View ⇨ Grid ⇨ Edit Grid.

    Fireworks displays the Edit Grid (Grids and Guides) dialog box, as shown in Figure 29-13.

2. Use the grid color picker to specify the color in which you want the grid to be displayed.

    For convenience, you can also toggle the visibility of the grid, or enable Snap to Grid while you're in the Edit Grid (Grids and Guides) dialog box.

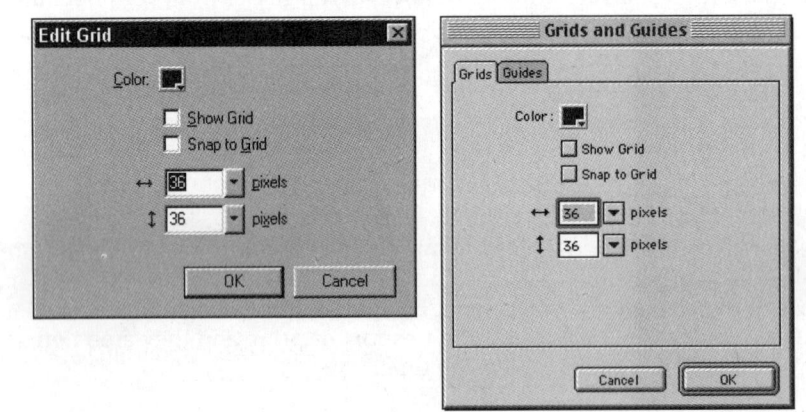

Figure 29-13: Set grid options in the Edit Grid (Grids and Guides) dialog box.

3. In the horizontal spacing box, enter the horizontal spacing that you want the grid to have. This is the space, in pixels, between vertical grid lines.

4. Enter in the vertical spacing box the vertical spacing that you want the grid to have. This is the space, in pixels, between horizontal grid lines.

5. Click Apply to see the results of your modifications without exiting the Edit Grid (Grids and Guides) dialog box. Click OK when you're done.

Grouping Objects

When you group objects, you basically create a new object that is made up entirely of other objects. You can treat a group as if it's a single object, apply Live Effects, alter blending modes, and more.

Objects in a group maintain their positions and stacking order relative to each other. They retain their effects settings until you modify the whole group. If half the objects in a group have a drop shadow, and you apply a drop shadow to the whole group, then all the objects will have a drop shadow. Fireworks is smart enough to apply that drop shadow to the whole group, as if all members were one object. You can also select and modify the component objects of a group individually, without ungrouping them.

Grouping objects is a good way to keep a complex drawing under control. For example, you might build a logo out of vector and text objects and then group those objects together so that you can easily manipulate the whole logo. Grouping together any objects that you don't need to manipulate individually essentially reduces the number of discrete objects that you have to manipulate as you work.

To group two or more objects, select them and choose either Modify ➪ Group, or the keyboard shortcut, Ctrl+G (Command+G). Your grouped objects now behave as if they are one object. A Live Effect or opacity setting applied to a group affects the whole group, as if it were one object (see Figure 29-14).

After you make a group, you can ungroup it at any time. To ungroup a group, select it and choose either Modify ➪ Ungroup, or the keyboard shortcut, Ctrl+Shift+G (Command+Shift+G).

Caution If you have applied Live Effects, opacity settings, or blending modes to a group, they are lost when you ungroup it.

To modify individual objects within a group, you can either ungroup them, or use the Subselection tool to subselect only the objects you want to work with. If you move a subselected object to another layer, it is removed from the group. To select all the component objects within a group, choose Edit ➪ Subselect. To select the parent group of an object, choose Edit ➪ Superselect.

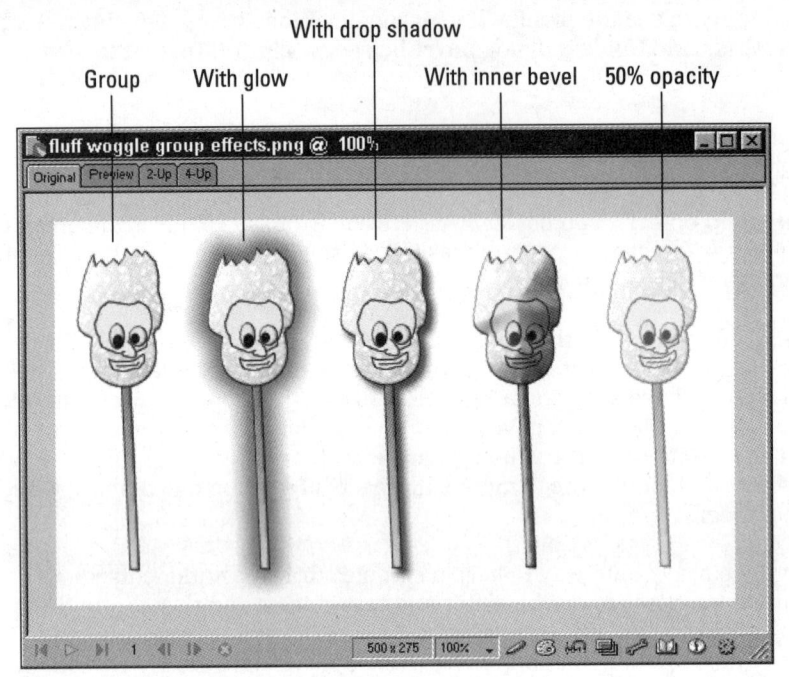

Figure 29-14: Applying a Live Effect or opacity setting to a group shows how it acts like one object.

Working with Alpha Masks

In a nutshell, an *alpha mask* is an 8-bit grayscale image that is used to describe the transparency of another image. Areas of the alpha mask that are solid black represent areas of the resulting masked image that are completely opaque, whereas areas of solid white represent areas that are completely transparent. The 254 grays between black and white each represent a different level of translucency: Dark gray is almost opaque, and light gray is almost transparent.

If you've ever created a transparent Graphics Interchange Format (GIF) with a light-colored background and then placed that GIF in a Web page with a dark background, you've seen a graphic (no pun intended) example of the challenges of compositing transparent images. The edges of your image, where they meet the transparent color, are antialiased to either a light color or a dark color. Artifacts are visible when the image is placed over the opposite-colored background.

The 8-bit alpha mask used in Fireworks and the PNG image format solves this problem, enabling you to composite transparent objects without worrying about the color of the objects on which you're placing them because transparency is specified for each and every pixel (see Figure 29-15).

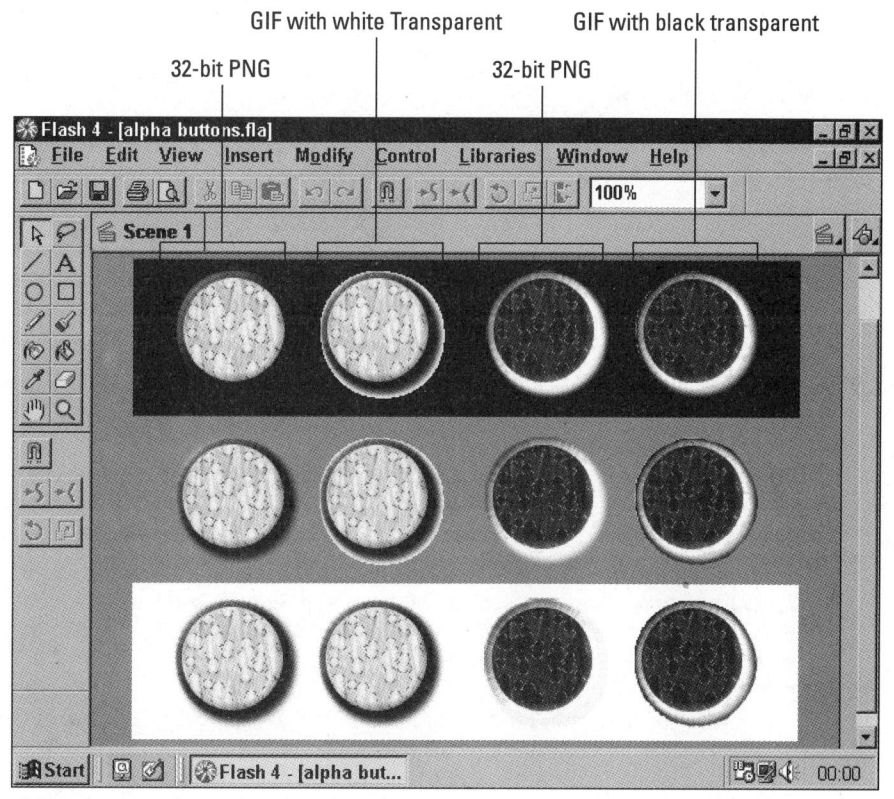

Figure 29-15: Shown here in Macromedia Flash, 32-bit PNG images created with Fireworks can be attractively placed on any background color while maintaining their transparency. GIF images, on the other hand, show artifacts when they are placed on a background color that's much darker or lighter than the one they were created for.

Typically, your Fireworks images have three 8-bit channels — one for red, one for green, and one for blue — resulting in a 24-bit RGB image that accurately describes every color that the human eye can see. When you add one more 8-bit grayscale channel to describe the levels of transparency — the so-called "alpha channel" — you get a 32-bit image (see Table 29-1) that describes exactly the same colors as the 24-bit image, but also knows where its transparent and translucent edges are.

Table 29-1
Channels and Bit Depth

Image	Channels	Bit Depth
Grayscale	1 grayscale	8-bit
True Color	1 red, 1 green, 1 blue	24-bit
True Color with Alpha Mask	1 red, 1 green, 1 blue, 1 grayscale (as mask)	32-bit

Each pixel of the alpha mask has a value between 0 and 255 to indicate the amount of transparency, which ranges from completely opaque (black, or 0) to completely transparent (white, or 255). The grays in between can be thought of as shades of transparency. Fireworks uses the value of each pixel of the mask to determine the transparency level for the underlying pixel of the masked object, which in turn determines how to blend that pixel with the background pixel it sits on.

If you haven't worked with 32-bit PNG images yet and are used to the limited transparency options inherent in the GIF format, the ease with which alpha transparency allows you to composite transparent objects will thrill you.

Caution Currently, no Web browsers are available that support the PNG alpha channel. Alpha transparency is still useful for working within Fireworks and exporting transparency to other applications, such as Macromedia Director and Flash. Incidentally, both Director and Flash can import your Fireworks PNG files — no need to export as a regular, non-Fireworks-specific PNG.

In brief, working with masks in Fireworks is centered around the Layers and Object panels. The Layers panel contains controls and commands related to masks, and displays a thumbnail of an object's mask next to the thumbnail of the object itself. Click the thumbnail of the mask to edit it, and the Object panel displays mask-related options. In vector mode, masked objects have a Move Handle in their centers, which you can click and drag to reposition the masked object without moving the mask.

I show you the various masking controls in greater detail throughout this section.

Creating vector masks

Whenever possible, I try to use vector masks for the same reason I always try to use vector objects: editability. Vector masks enable you to radically alter the look of a masked object using all the standard techniques you use to edit vector objects, such as fills, strokes, and Live Effects. Vector masks can also be easily scaled, skewed, and distorted with the transformation tools. Text objects can also be used as vector masks, creating exciting text effects.

Cross-Reference   See Chapter 26 for more about text masking effects.

To create and apply a vector mask, follow these steps:

1. Choose an object to mask, as shown in Figure 29-16.

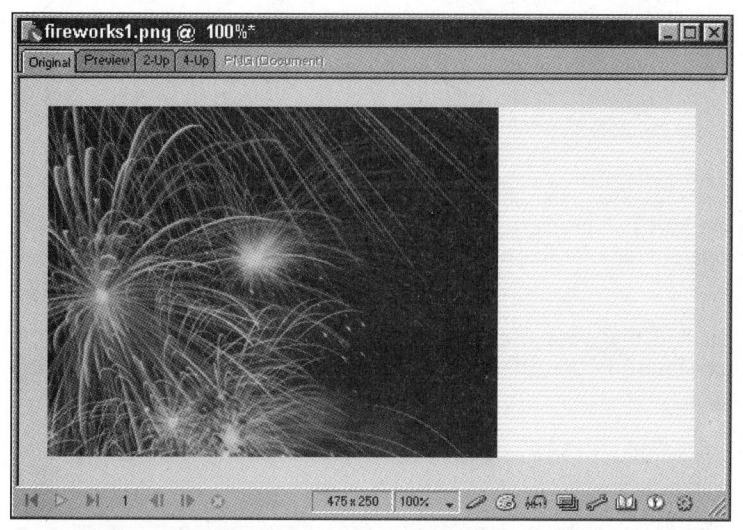

Figure 29-16: The image of the fireworks display doesn't blend into the striped background.

2. Create an object to act as a mask for your original object, as shown in Figure 29-17. The size of the mask will specify the size of the resulting masked object. Where the mask is white, the resulting masked object will be transparent; where the mask is black, the masked object is opaque. Shades of gray in the mask vary the transparency of the group, according to how light or dark they are.

3. Position the mask in relation to the object you are masking.

4. Select the mask and choose Edit ⇨ Cut, or use the keyboard shortcut, Ctrl+X (Command+X), to cut the mask to the clipboard.

5. Select the object you want to apply the mask to and choose Modify ⇨ Mask ⇨ Paste as Mask.

6. Choose Window ⇨ Object to display the Object panel. Select Grayscale Appearance.

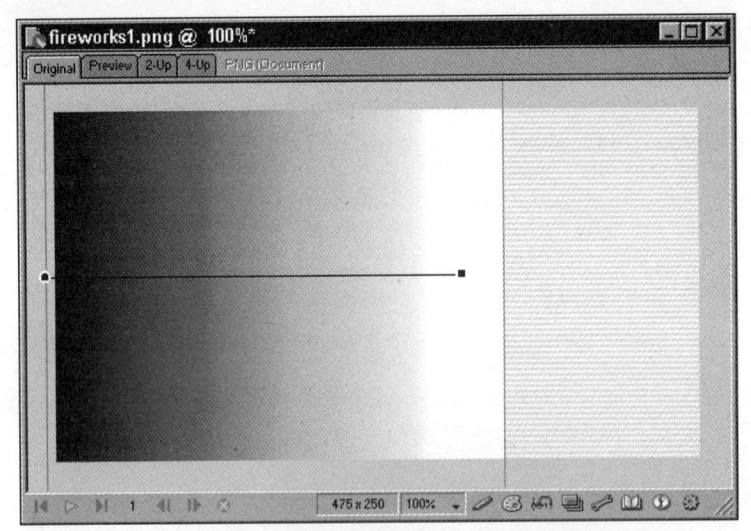

Figure 29-17: A gradient fill for the mask provides a smooth transparent fade for the masked object.

Tip If you find that your mask is the inverse of what you wanted, the Invert Live Effect — found in the Effect panel — can quickly invert your mask and set things straight.

The mask is applied to the original object, as shown in Figure 29-18.

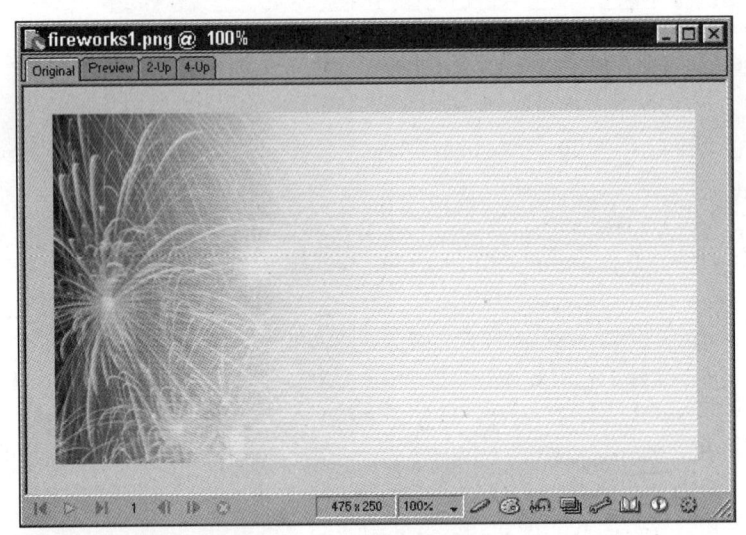

Figure 29-18: The masked object blends into the background because the mask's fade from black to white is translated into a transparency fade from opaque to transparent.

Applying bitmap masks

There are almost as many ways to create a bitmap mask in Fireworks as there are ways to create a bitmap. Whatever method you choose, however, you are ultimately creating a simple 8-bit grayscale image that will mask another object. As with any alpha mask, black areas of the mask will become completely opaque in the final, masked object, whereas white areas will be completely transparent, and varying shades of gray describe varying levels of transparency.

Adding a bitmap mask

The Layers panel provides a number of masking controls, including a simple Add Mask button that creates a new, empty bitmap mask and selects it for editing. If the mask you're after is so simple that you can draw it with Fireworks tools, then adding a mask is a good way to get started.

To add a bitmap mask to an object, follow these steps:

1. Select the object that you want to apply a mask to.
2. Choose Window ⇨ Layers to display the Layers panel, or use the keyboard shortcut, F2.
3. If necessary, click in the Expand/Collapse column in the Layers panel to open the current layer so that you can see the currently selected object.
4. Click the Add Mask button on the Layers panel.

Fireworks creates an empty bitmap mask and applies it to the currently selected object. The mask is also selected for editing.

Cross-Reference Find out about editing masks later in this chapter.

Using Reveal All and Hide All

Fireworks provides a quick method for getting masks started with the Reveal All and Hide All commands.

To use the Reveal All or Hide All command, follow these steps:

1. Select the object that you want to mask.
2. To apply a completely white mask to the object, choose Modify ⇨ Mask ⇨ Reveal All. Alternatively, you can apply a completely black mask to the object by choosing Modify ⇨ Mask ⇨ Hide All.

Fireworks creates the mask and selects it for editing.

Using Reveal Selection and Hide Selection

The Reveal Selection and Hide Selection commands basically change marquee selections into bitmap masks, which makes applying simple bitmap masks a breeze.

To create a bitmap mask with the Reveal Selection or Hide Selection command, follow these steps:

1. Make a pixel selection with one of the pixel selection tools, such as the Marquee.
2. To show just the pixels inside the selection, choose Modify ⇨ Mask ⇨ Reveal Selection. Alternatively, you can hide the pixels inside of the selection by choosing Modify ⇨ Mask ⇨ Hide Selection.

Fireworks creates the appropriate mask and selects it for editing.

Fireworks technique: The contrast method

One common reason for creating a bitmap mask is to remove the background from an image, isolating the foreground figure or object. Duplicating an image and then increasing the overall contrast of the duplicate can often isolate foreground and background areas, helping to create a suitable mask.

To create a mask using the contrast method, follow these steps:

1. Duplicate the bitmap object that you want to mask, as shown in Figure 29-19. The mask will be created from the duplicate.

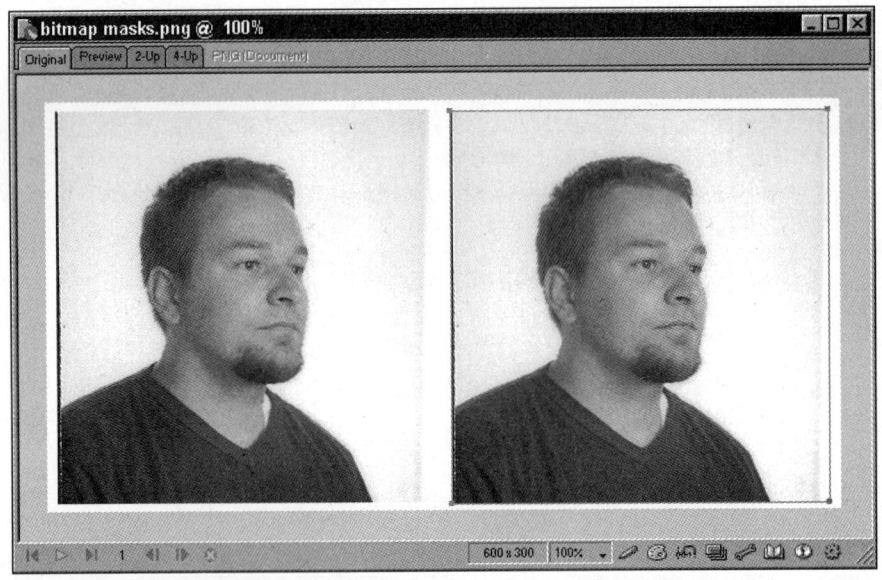

Figure 29-19: A duplicate of your original object is a good starting point for creating a mask.

2. Select the duplicate and choose Commands ➪ Creative ➪ Convert to Grayscale to convert it into a grayscale image.

3. Choose Window ➪ Effect to display the Effect panel.

4. From the Effect Category option list in the Effect panel, choose Adjust Color ➪ Brightness/Contrast.

   Fireworks displays the Brightness/Contrast dialog box.

5. Set the Contrast slider to 100%.

6. Adjust the Brightness slider until your object looks as much like the desired mask as possible, with sharply delineated foreground and background areas (see Figure 29-20). Depending on the image you use, you may need to make a large adjustment, or none at all.

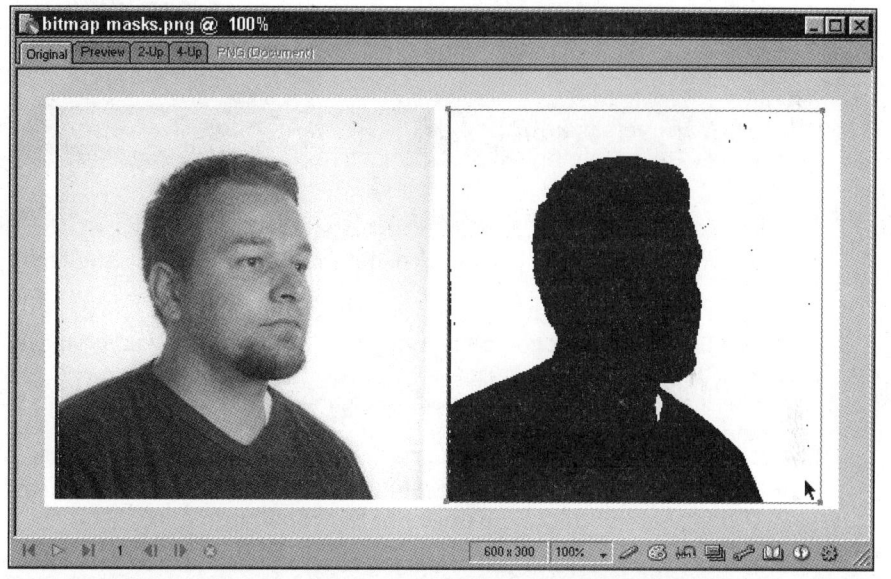

Figure 29-20: Increase the contrast to maximum, and then adjust the brightness in order to isolate foreground and background elements.

Tip For some images, you may find that using the Levels Live Effect provides better control than the Brightness/Contrast Live Effect.

7. Choose Modify ➪ Convert to Bitmap to convert your object and its Live Effects to a bitmap object.

Caution Your nascent bitmap mask will no longer be editable after it is converted into a bitmap.

8. Use the Paint Bucket tool and/or the Eraser tool to clean up your mask, filling in and erasing pixels as required, until your mask is complete (see Figure 29-21).

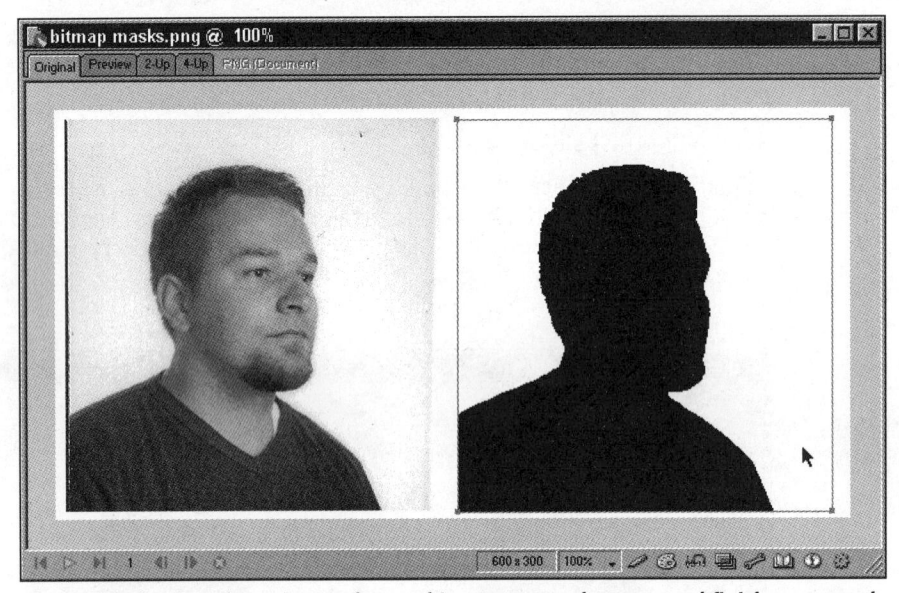

Figure 29-21: Use the Paint Bucket and/or Eraser to clean up and finish your mask.

9. Position your mask correctly in relation to the object you are masking.

Tip Use the commands in the Modify ⇨ Align submenu to precisely align your mask and object, if required.

10. Select the mask and choose Edit ⇨ Cut, or use the keyboard shortcut, Ctrl+X (Command+X), to cut the object to the clipboard.

11. Select the object that you are going to apply the mask to, and choose Edit ⇨ Paste as Mask to apply the mask from the clipboard, as shown in Figure 29-22.

Editing masks

After you've created a masked object — whether you used a vector or bitmap mask — the Layers panel makes it easy to select and edit it.

To edit a mask, follow these steps:

1. Choose Window ⇨ Layers to display the Layers panel, and Window ⇨ Object to display the Object panel. Keep both in view while editing masks in order to have all the necessary controls "at your fingertips."

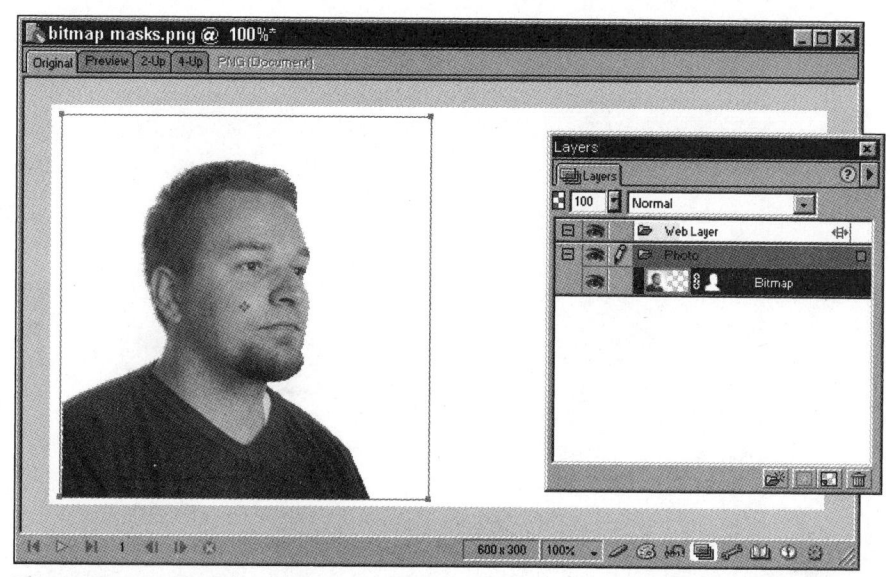

Figure 29-22: After the mask is applied, the background area is no longer visible.

2. Click the mask's thumbnail in the Layers panel. Alternatively, you can select the masked object, either on the canvas or from the Layers panel, and choose Edit Mask from the Layers panel pop-up menu.

> **Tip** You can also double-click the Move Handle that appears in the center of a masked object to edit its mask.

Fireworks selects the mask for editing on the canvas.

If you're editing a bitmap mask, the Object panel says Bitmap Mask; Fireworks enters bitmap mode and displays the Mask Edit Border around the canvas, as shown in Figure 29-23.

If you are editing a vector mask, the Object panel says Vector Mask.

3. Edit the mask with any of the pixel-editing tools in the Tools panel, just as you would edit the pixels of a bitmap image. Although the mask itself is not shown on the canvas, the results of edits that you apply to the mask are shown.

4. Apply Live Effects or Xtras to the mask, if desired.

5. If desired, convert a vector mask into a bitmap mask by choosing Modify ⇨ Convert to Bitmap.

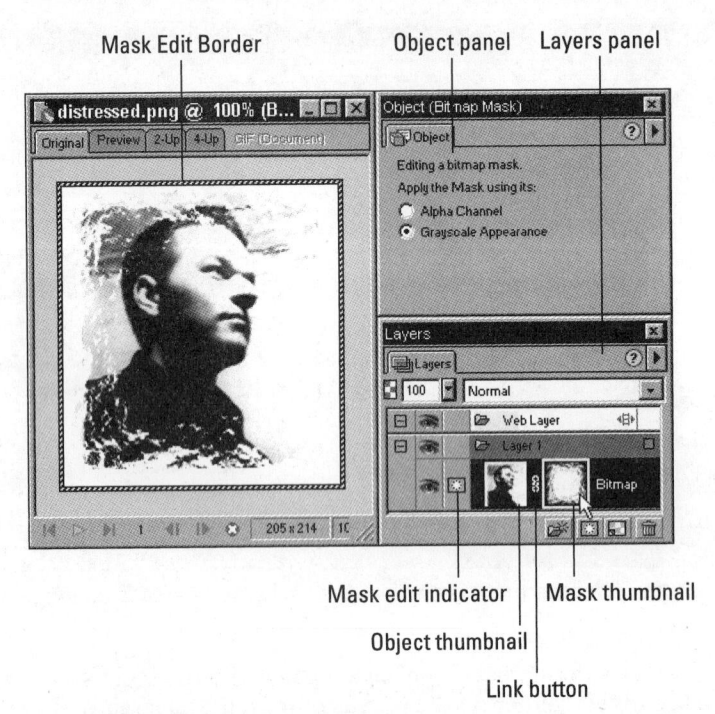

Figure 29-23: Fireworks masking controls include the Layers and Object panels, and the Mask Edit Border, which appears on the canvas when you're editing a bitmap mask.

6. If desired, change the way the mask is applied, using the controls in the Object panel:

    - If you're editing a vector mask, choose whether to apply the mask using the vector outlines — optionally with the fill and stroke shown — or using the object's grayscale appearance. The grayscale appearance option effectively treats the vector mask like a bitmap mask.

    - For bitmap masks, choose whether to use the bitmap's alpha channel or grayscale appearance.

7. Deselect the masked object when you're done, either by choosing Edit ➪ Deselect, or by using the keyboard shortcut, Ctrl+D (Command+D).

Tip

If you're editing a bitmap mask, you can exit bitmap mode to stop editing a mask. With a vector mask, you can click an empty part of the canvas to stop editing.

Your mask-editing options don't stop at directly editing the mask itself. Keep these points in mind as you edit masks:

✦ Just as you can edit a mask by selecting its thumbnail in the Layers panel, selecting the object's thumbnail enables you to edit the object independently from the mask.

✦ Click the Link button in between an object and mask thumbnail (refer to Figure 29-23) to unlink a mask from an object, enabling you to position them independently. Click again in the empty space between two unlinked thumbnails to relink them.

✦ Click and drag the Move Handle (see Figure 29-24) that appears in the center of masked objects in vector mode to position the underlying object without moving the mask. This is especially useful when cropping a bitmap with a vector mask, because it enables you to reposition the bitmap within its vector "frame."

Figure 29-24: Drag the Move Handle to move the underlying image without moving the mask.

✦ To temporarily disable a mask, select the mask thumbnail or the masked object and choose Modify ➪ Mask ➪ Disable Mask, or choose Disable Mask from the Layers panel pop-up menu. Fireworks displays a red X through the mask's thumbnail in the Layers panel to alert you that the mask is disabled. To restore the mask, choose Modify ➪ Mask ➪ Enable Mask, or choose Enable Mask from the Layers panel pop-up menu.

- To remove a mask permanently — aside from the Undo command, of course — select the mask thumbnail or masked object and choose Modify ➪ Mask ➪ Delete Mask. Or, you can choose Delete Mask from the Layers panel pop-up menu.

Masking suggestions

Masked objects are a creative and powerful tool that you can experiment with again and again. Here are some suggestions to try:

- Apply Live Effects or styles to vector objects, and then use them as masks.
- Alter the Stroke or Fill settings of a vector mask.
- Use a text object as a vector mask.
- Apply texture fills to vector masks.
- Apply Xtras to bitmap masks.

Fireworks technique: Quick photo edges

Often, when you are working with a bitmap object in Fireworks, you'll want to crop the image to a smaller size. Although you could use the Crop tool to crop out a section or make a pixel selection and copy out that area, those techniques are destructive. You alter the bitmap object permanently. For example, if later you want to add back 100 pixels, or add 10 pixels all around the image so that you can feather the edges, you're out of luck. That information has been thrown away.

Masked objects provide a way around this, however, enabling you not only to crop an image nondestructively, but also to use Live Effects and other methods to create some nice border effects. Modifying a vector object and using it as an alpha mask for an image gives you fine control over your image's shape and transparency. To create an image border, open an image in Fireworks and follow these steps:

1. If you're in bitmap mode, choose Modify ➪ Exit Bitmap Mode, or use the keyboard shortcut Ctrl+Shift+E (Command+Shift+E).
2. Use the drawing tools to draw a rectangle on top of your image, but make the rectangle a bit smaller than the image itself (see Figure 29-25). The area outside the rectangle will be invisible after masking.
3. Convert the rectangle into a regular vector object by choosing Modify ➪ Ungroup.

Tip You can also use a circle or polygon as a mask, if you prefer. Circles and polygons don't require ungrouping in Step 3, however.

Figure 29-25: Use a rectangle to block out the area of your photograph that you want to keep.

4. Color the rectangle black by selecting it and choosing black from the fill color well at the bottom of the Tools panel.

   You may want to experiment at this point, giving your shape various gradient fills or textures. Remember, any black area will be completely visible in your final image, whereas any white area will be invisible. The darker the areas in between these extremes, the more transparent they become.

5. Select the rectangle and feather its edges by choosing Modify ➪ Alter Path ➪ Feather Fill.

   Stop at this point, if you like, and experiment with applying Live Effects, styles, Xtras, or various strokes to your shape, instead of feathering it. If you have Photoshop 5's filters installed, the Distort, Brush Strokes, Sketch, and Stylize filters are good choices. If you use Alien Skin's Eye Candy, the Jiggle feature is a great choice, too.

6. Position the mask correctly in relation to the object you're masking.

7. Select the mask and choose Edit ➪ Cut, or use the keyboard shortcut, Ctrl+X (Command+X), to cut it to the clipboard.

8. Select the object that you're masking and choose Edit ➪ Paste as Mask to apply your mask to it.

> **Tip**
>
> The Paste as Mask command is also available in another menu location: Modify ➪ Mask ➪ Paste as Mask.

The masked object is now the same size and shape as the black-colored shape that you drew on top of it, as shown in Figure 29-26.

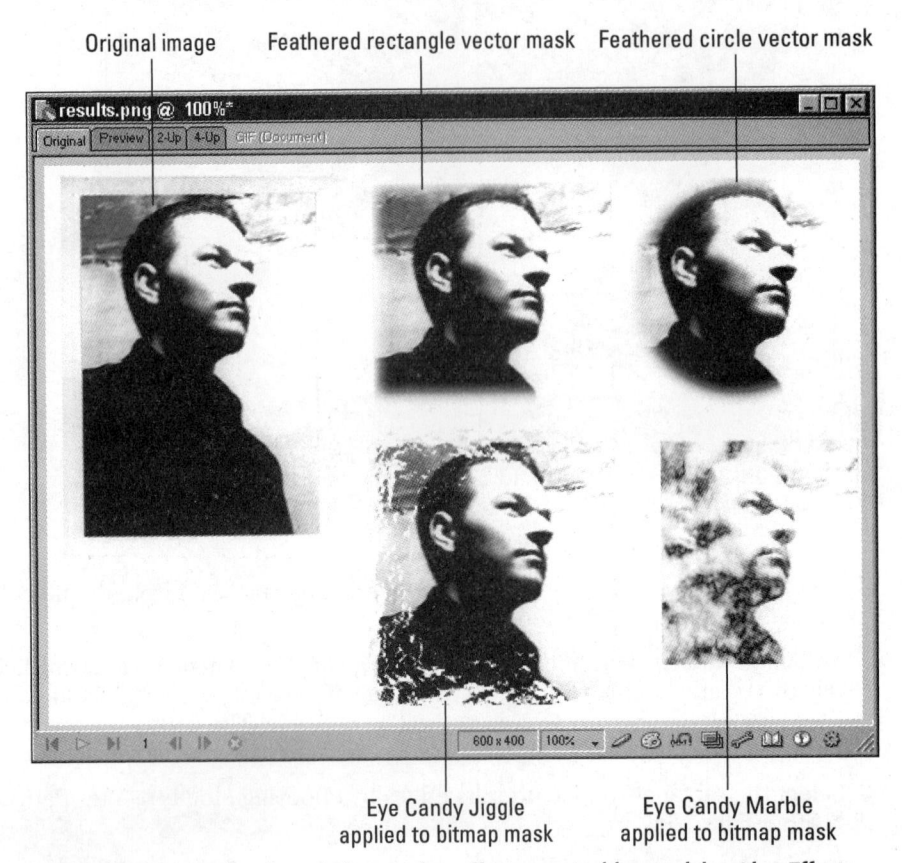

Figure 29-26: A selection of photo edge effects created by applying Live Effects to a vector object and using it as an alpha mask for an image.

Examining Opacity and Blending

The primary tools in compositing images are opacity and blending. Altering these properties can literally merge two images together. You can make one image show through the other by giving the top image a lower opacity setting, or you can use a blending mode to make them steal colors from each other. A bitmap object or pixel selection that appears to float above a background can be seamlessly integrated in just a few short steps.

Tip Feathering objects before compositing them often provides good results. With a softer edge, removing the borderline between the two images is easier. Experiment with blending Fireworks strokes, texture fills, and effects.

After you select an object in Fireworks, you can use the Layers panel to control its opacity and blending (see Figure 29-27).

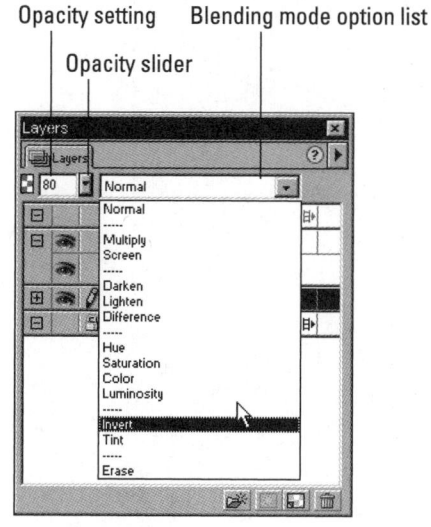

Figure 29-27: The Layers panel's opacity and blending controls affect the selected object(s).

Controlling opacity

As you make an object more transparent, more of the background shows through. This can go a long way toward integrating two images.

Controlling opacity in Fireworks is easy. Select an object, open the Layers panel by choosing either Window ⇨ Layers, or the keyboard shortcut, F2, and then slide the opacity slider. A setting of 100 equals no transparency, completely opaque. A setting of 1, with the slider all the way down, brings an object as close to invisible as possible in Fireworks (see Figure 29-28). If you do want to make an image completely invisible, you can type a zero (0) in the opacity box and press Enter (Return).

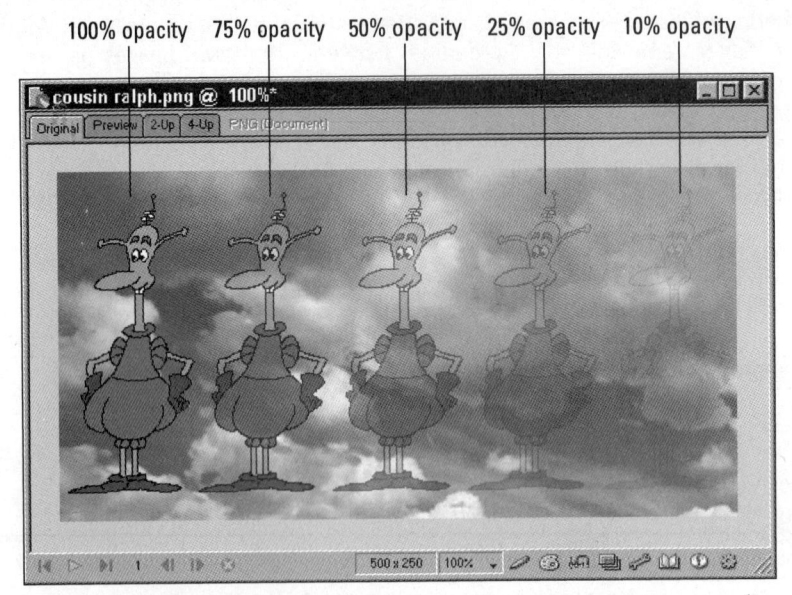

Figure 29-28: Vary the opacity level of an object with the Layers panel's opacity slider. The fellow on the left is 100 percent opaque. On the extreme right, he's 10 percent opaque.

Caution If you specify an opacity setting without an object selected, you will set a default opacity for objects that you create from that point on. If you accidentally set it to 10 percent or less, you might not even be able to see some of the objects that you draw. If this happens, you'll know where to go to change it back. Deselect all objects with Edit ⇨ Deselect and move the opacity slider in the Layers panel back to 100.

Using blending modes

Blending modes manipulate the color of pixels in a foreground image and the color of pixels beneath them in the background image in a variety of ways to blend the two together. Before you start using blending modes, here's the terminology that you need to know:

+ **Blend color:** The color of the selected object, typically a foreground object
+ **Base color:** The color beneath the selected object, typically a background object
+ **Result color:** The color resulting from the blend of the blend color and base color

For the sake of simplicity, this discussion primarily uses foreground, background, and result.

As you've seen earlier, Fireworks enables you to alter the opacity of an object at any time with the Opacity slider in the Layers panel. The opacity of an object also effects the way it blends.

A blending mode applies to an individual object or to an entire group. If you give an object a certain blending mode and then group it, the blending mode disappears because the object is given the group's blending mode instead (although ungrouping will restore the individual object's blending mode). If you're working extensively with blending modes, instead of grouping your objects, you might want to use layers to separate and organize your objects. This also enables you to stack blending modes for interesting effects, as objects on each layer blend into objects on the layer below.

Depending on what kind of object you have selected, the blending modes work in one of the following ways:

- **Vector mode:** The blending mode affects the selected object.
- **Bitmap mode:** If you have a marquee selection drawn, the blending mode affects the selection of pixels. If you don't have a marquee selection drawn, the blending mode affects the strokes and fills that you draw from then on.

Select an object and modify its blending mode setting in the Layers panel. If no object is selected, modifying the blending mode creates a new default blending mode for objects that you create from that point on.

Investigating blending modes

Blending modes can be confusing and strangely mathematical. The best way to start understanding them is to compare their results, which is what Figure 29-29 does.

> **Cross-Reference:** You can see the dogs in Figure 29-29 in full color in the color insert.

Twelve mysterious blending modes can seem like much at first, but most modes have an opposite partner or other related modes. After you understand one mode of a group, you're well on your way to understanding them all.

References to the foreground or background color refer to the color at the pixel level, not at the object level. Individual pixels of the foreground and background objects are compared.

Multiply and Screen

Multiply mode multiplies the foreground color with the background color. It can give your blended image a deeper, richer tone. The result color is always darker. If the foreground or background color is black, the result will be black; if one of them is white, Multiply has no effect.

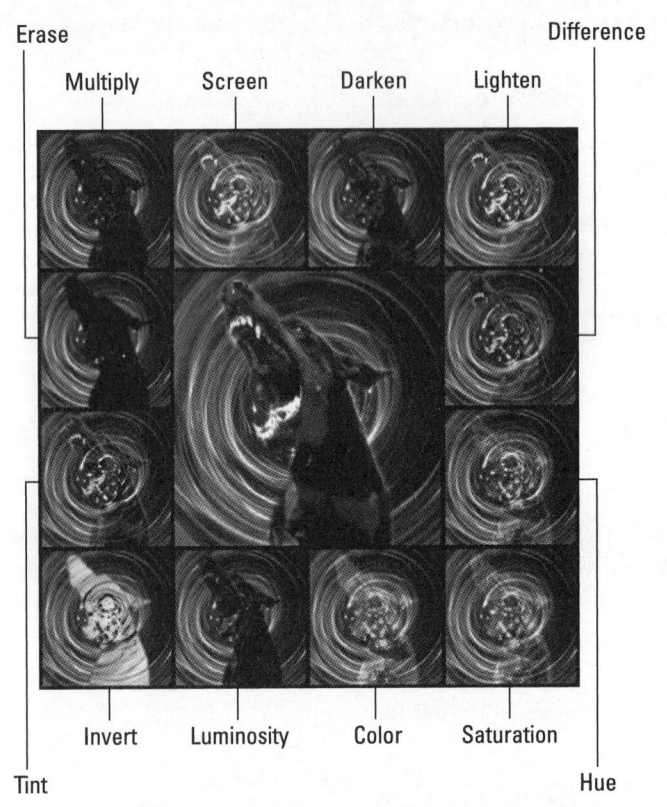

Figure 29-29: Comparing the 12 blending modes that Fireworks offers, with the unaltered image in the center

Screen mode is basically the opposite of Multiply. The result color is a ghostly, faded blend. It works by inverting the foreground color and then multiplying it with the background color. Whereas Multiply always results in a darker color, Screen always results in a lighter one. If either the foreground or background is white, the result color will be white. If either is black, Screen has no effect.

Darken, Lighten, and Difference

Darken compares the foreground and background colors and keeps the darkest one, whereas *Lighten* does the opposite; the foreground and background color is compared and only the lightest is kept.

Difference compares the foreground color and the background color, and it subtracts the darker color from the lighter color. It can result in some surprising color choices.

Hue, Saturation, Color, and Luminosity

Hue combines the hue value of the foreground color with the luminance and saturation of the background color. Essentially, you get the foreground color, but as dark or light as the background.

Saturation combines the saturation of the foreground color with the luminance and hue of the background color.

Color combines the hue and saturation of the foreground color with the luminance of the background color. Grays are preserved, so this is a good way to add color to a black-and-white photograph, or to tint color photographs.

Luminosity combines the luminance of the foreground color with the hue and saturation of the background color.

Invert and Tint

Invert and Tint don't bother with the foreground color at all. With Invert, the foreground object's colors are replaced with inverted background colors. With Tint, gray is added to the background color to create the result.

Erase

Erase removes all background color pixels, leaving the canvas color.

Fireworks technique: Simulating a light source with blending modes

One key to creating a good three-dimensional look is providing a simulated light source. Blending an object that uses a black-and-white gradient fill into another object mimics the interplay of light and shadows. In other words, the image has a controllable light to dark range added. This enables you to adjust the "lighting" so that it looks appropriate with your particular graphic.

To use blending modes to simulate light and shadow and create objects like those shown in Figure 29-30, follow these steps:

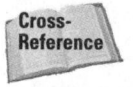

Cross-Reference The color insert provides another look at light source effects.

1. Create a new, empty layer by clicking the New Layer button on the Layers panel. Double-click the new layer in the layers list and name it **Object1**.

2. Using one of the geometric drawing tools (Rectangle, Ellipse, or Polygon), draw an object on the Object1 layer. This object will be your base object (not the light source).

Figure 29-30: Get the lights: Blend a gradient-filled object and adjust the gradient to simulate a light source.

3. In the Fill panel, give your object a Solid fill and add a texture, such as Parchment, to it. Set the texture to 100 percent.

Tip Alternatively, you might also use a Pattern fill, instead of a Solid fill with a texture.

4. Choose Edit ⇨ Clone to create a copy of your object directly on top of the original.

5. From the Fill panel, choose a Radial gradient fill for the new object with the White, Black color preset. Remove the texture (if any) by sliding the Amount of texture slider to 0 percent.

6. Choose Window ⇨ Layers to display the Layers panel. Change the blending mode to Multiply and alter the Opacity setting to taste, depending on the color of your original object.

7. Note the Fill modification handles that appear on your object. Drag the round starting handle of the gradient fill to reposition the gradient so that the center of the white portion is located where you want the brightest "light" to fall. Slightly up and to the left is a good choice. If desired, drag the square-ending handle to adjust the angle of the gradient. In a sense, you are adjusting the light source.

Tip: You may want to use the Select Behind tool to select your original object — the one with the texture or Pattern fill — and apply one of the bevel Live Effects. Adjusting the bevel height can make a big difference to how realistically 3D your object looks.

8. Select both objects and position them, if necessary. Lock the Object1 layer and don't put other objects on it. Both of the objects it contains must be moved together, but they cannot be grouped, or they will share the same blending mode and the lighting effect will be lost. Keeping them on their own layer makes it easy to use Single Layer Mode to isolate them during later editing.

I used the Radial gradient in the previous example, but you can get some really great effects (such as a starburst of light) by applying different gradient types. Moreover, you can adjust the subtlety of the lighting by editing the gradient and toning down the pure white to a more muted gray. Feel free to experiment with different blending modes, as well.

Cross-Reference: For more about gradients, see Chapter 27.

Fireworks Technique: Feathering Selections

A common image-editing task is to remove a subject from one image and place that subject in another document against another background. Feathering your selection can make this process much more forgiving, hiding ragged edges and stray background pixels that come along for the ride.

To copy a foreground image from one document and place it into another, follow these steps:

1. Open your source and target documents in Fireworks. The source document should have a foreground element. The target document should contain a suitable background.

2. In the source document, use the Lasso or Polygon Lasso tools to make a pixel selection (see Figure 29-31). Select your foreground element as accurately as possible.

3. Choose Modify ⇨ Marquee ⇨ Feather, enter **10** in the Feather Selection dialog box, and then click OK. This feathers your selection, which will hide any rough edges.

4. Choose either Edit ⇨ Copy, or the keyboard shortcut, Ctrl+C (Command+C), to copy the pixel selection to the Clipboard.

Figure 29-31: Copying a feathered pixel selection into another document

5. Switch to your target document. To enter vector mode (if you aren't there already) choose Modify ➪ Exit Bitmap Mode, use the keyboard shortcut, Ctrl+Shift+E (Command+Shift+E), or click the Stop button on the bottom border of the document window.

6. Choose either Edit ➪ Paste, or the keyboard shortcut, Ctrl+V (Command+V), to paste the pixel selection from the clipboard into your document as a new bitmap object.

7. Move the subject around until it's placed where you want it.

Fireworks Technique: Applied Compositing

Presenting separate elements as an integrated image often means applying a few different compositing techniques. In the following example, you'll use masked objects, opacity, blending modes, and layering, along with texture fills and drop shadows to unify seven or eight separate objects into one final, composited image.

> **Cross-Reference**
> If you want to take a look at the final result of the techniques in this section before you start, turn to the color insert.

Starting from the bottom of the stacking order, the first step is a canvas color; in this case, it's black, as shown in Figure 29-32. Only a small portion of the canvas will show along the bottom of the final image. The background object has a mesh texture fill, which will show through other elements later and provide a feeling of depth. It also has a red drop shadow effect that softens the transition between it and the canvas. Avoiding straight lines and obvious borders — or hiding them — helps to make separate objects appear to be one.

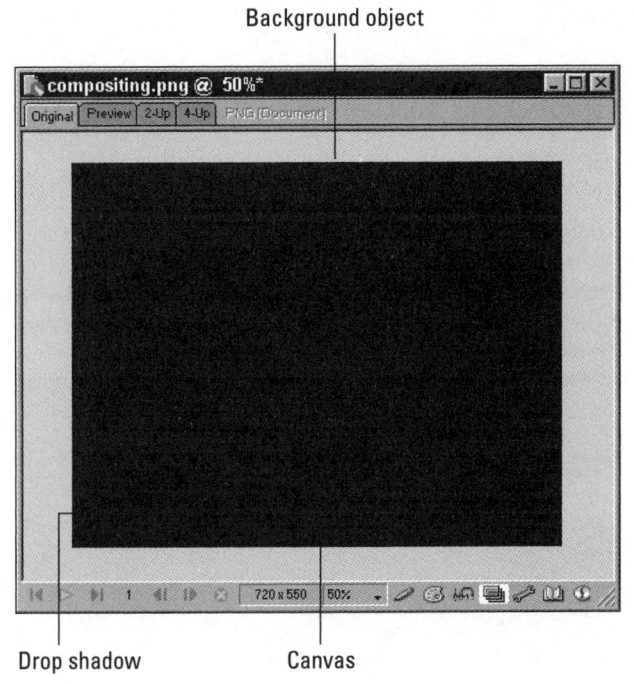

Figure 29-32: This textured background will show through translucent objects that are placed on it, whereas a drop shadow blends it into the black-colored canvas.

The next layer up contains a red and black pattern. In order to blend it with the background object, I want to use an alpha mask to make the red and black pattern fade from opaque at the top to fully transparent at the bottom. This can be achieved by combining it into a masked object, with the mask shown in Figure 29-33. Where the mask is black, the underlying object will be opaque; where it's white, the object will be completely transparent. Shades of gray provide varying degrees of transparency.

Combining the mask and object into the masked object shown in Figure 29-34 is as simple as selecting them both and choosing Modify ⇨ Mask ⇨ Paste as Mask. The background object is now showing through the mask. All the objects appear to be part of the same image, rather than distinct objects. Of course, the vector mask is still editable.

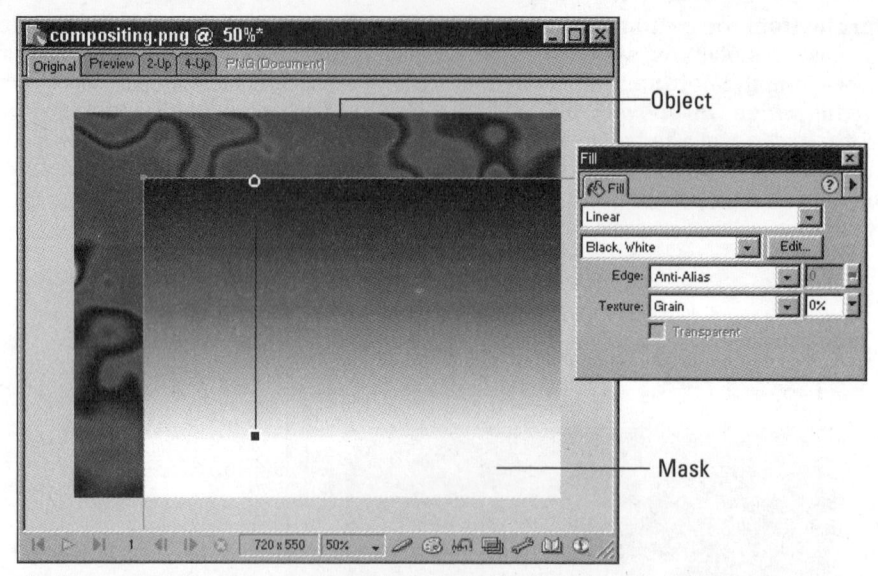

Figure 29-33: When used as a mask, this gradient-filled vector object will make the red and black pattern appear to fade away from top to bottom.

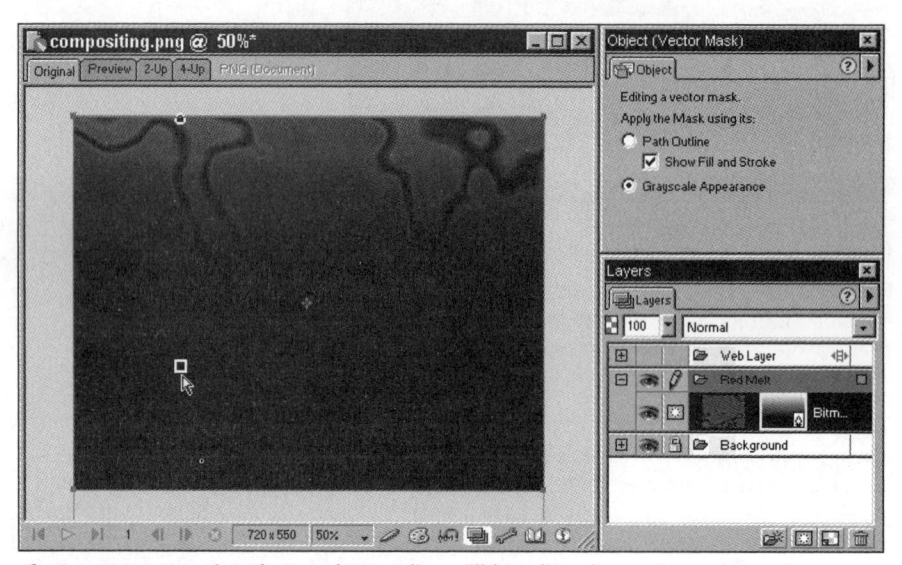

Figure 29-34: Moving the mask's gradient fill handle adjusts the opacity of the underlying object.

Chapter 29 ✦ **Arranging and Compositing Objects** 949

The three separate variations on the Fireworks logo in Figure 29-35 are on separate layers. The Big Crinkley Logo has holes in it where the background shows through, and its Bevel effect raises it off the canvas and provides a feeling of depth. The Real Logo — quickly purloined from the Fireworks Web site or somewhere similar — looks a little ragged, but will be mostly covered by the Hand-Drawn Logo, so that only its colors show through. The drop shadow and inner bevel applied to the Hand-Drawn Logo adds more depth and provides a nice transition between it and the Real Logo beneath it.

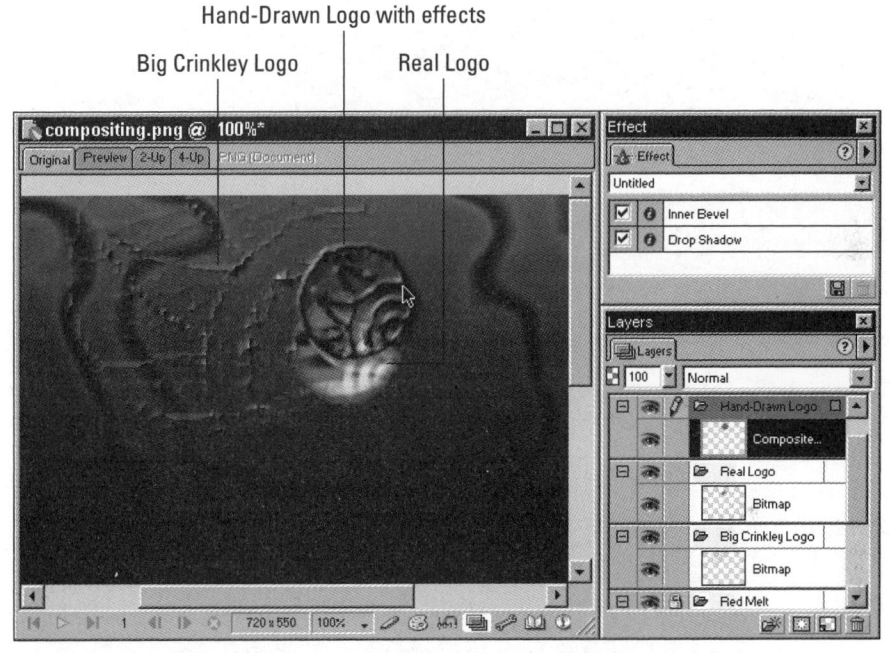

Figure 29-35: These foreground elements stack nicely because of their transparent holes and the depth provided by drop shadows and bevel effects.

The leathery look of the bottom half of the document seems like a good place to put some text. In Figure 29-36, you can see that my chosen typeface — Heavy Rotation — is structured to look as if it's been pressed into something. A 50 percent opacity setting for the text object allows some of the underlying texture to show through and adds to the inset look of the text. Changing the text object's blending mode to Screen completes the illusion; inverting the foreground color and multiplying it with the background color to blend them.

The final product — completed using masked objects, opacity settings, blending modes, and layers along with texture fills and effects, such as drop shadows — is shown in Figure 29-37.

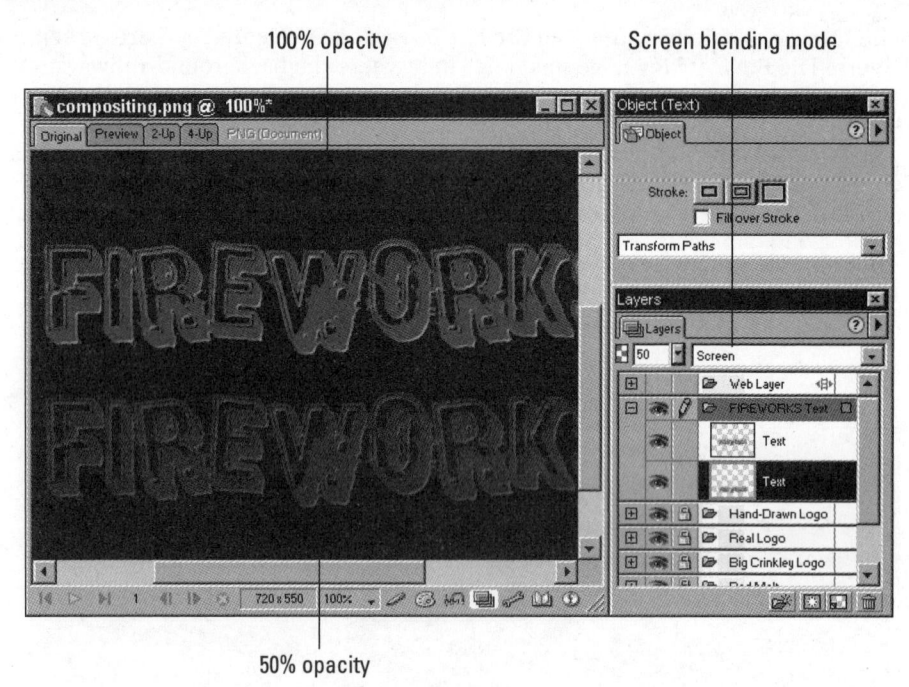

Figure 29-36: The opacity setting and blending modes in the Layers panel help to sink the basic text object (top) into the underlying texture of the background (bottom).

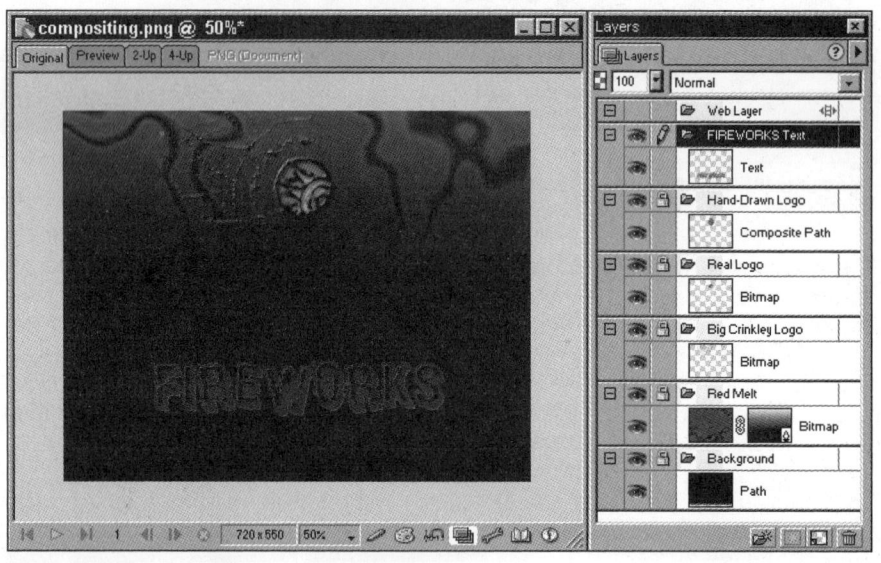

Figure 29-37: A number of compositing techniques were used to combine multiple objects into this integrated, multilayer image.

Summary

Fireworks gives you lots of options for combining many types of objects to create more complex objects or special effects. When you're arranging or compositing objects in Fireworks, keep these points in mind:

- You can use layers to organize your document, enabling easier selection and editing of similar objects.
- The Layers panel is your control center for working with layers.
- You can choose to work with individual layers in a variety of ways, including hiding, showing, and locking layers.
- Layers are also containers for object sublayers. Show, hide, move, copy, and delete sublayers using the same techniques you use with layers.
- The ruler, grid, and guides are all available to help you precisely position objects on the canvas.
- Objects can be grouped, and a group behaves as if it's one object.
- Masks give you amazing control over alpha transparency.
- Blending modes enable you to blend objects quickly and easily.
- Multiple compositing techniques can be utilized together to integrate many objects into a seamless image.

✦ ✦ ✦

Exporting and Optimizing

CHAPTER 30

In This Chapter

Introducing export fundamentals

Optimizing indexed color

Working with photographic images

Using Export Preview

Summoning Export wizards

Examining other export features

The cross-platform, almost universal access of the Web is achieved with limitations. Although many different image file formats exist, browsers are currently limited to displaying only three of them: GIF, JPEG, and PNG. What's more, only GIF and JPEG enjoy truly wide acceptance. Bandwidth is severely limited for the mass market. Although an increasing number of Web surfers enjoy the speed of a DSL or cable modem, the vast majority still view the Internet through a 56K dial-up modem.

These limitations make optimizing and exporting graphics a necessity, and not just a nicety. Your work in Fireworks has to be exported in the correct format and with the smallest file size possible. Macromedia realized the importance of export features when it created Fireworks; much of the program centers around making the best-looking graphic, with the smallest file size, in an accepted format. The features covered in this chapter rank among the best available with advanced controls, such as lossy GIF, selective JPEG, and color locking. Fireworks takes the limitations imposed by the Web and turns them into an art form.

Cross-Reference This chapter covers the fundamentals of exporting and optimizing your graphics. You can find details on exporting animations in Chapter 35.

Exploring Optimization Features

Although using a graphic stored in Fireworks' native format, PNG, in a Web page is possible, it really isn't practical, nor is it the intention of the program for you to do so. The PNG images that you create with the Save command in Fireworks contain extra Fireworks-specific information beyond the simple PNG bitmap image. Although this makes them great for opening and editing in Fireworks, the file size is too heavy to place in a Web page. Publishing your work requires the use of the Export command, which enables you to create a number of image file types, covering both bitmap and vector formats. Although some of these formats, such as GIF and JPEG, are suitable for publishing on the Web, others, such as BMP and Photoshop, are more suited to moving your work between different graphics applications, or sharing with colleagues (see Figure 30-1).

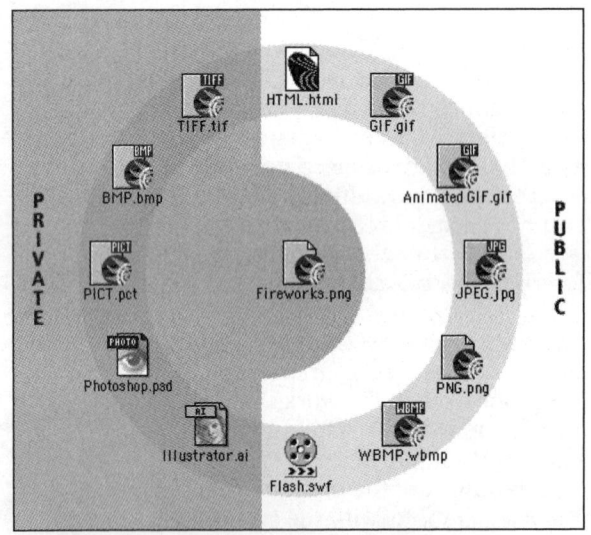

Figure 30-1: Create a Fireworks PNG document (center) with the Save command, and the entire surrounding family of image file formats can be created from it with the Export command. The "private" formats enable you to move your work to other applications, whereas the "public" formats are ready to publish as-is on the Web — or wireless Web in the case of WBMP (Wireless BitMaP).

Working hand-in-hand with selecting an appropriate file type is the other main goal of exporting, referred to as *optimization*. Optimization is the process of producing the best-looking, smallest possible file. An optimized image loads faster, without sacrificing perceived quality. Because data is thrown away in the optimization process, avoid opening and editing the so-called public file types, shown in Figure 30-1, whenever possible. Store your work and move it between applications using the private file types. Think of the private file types as originals, and the public file types as photocopies made for sharing.

Optimizing and exporting in Fireworks is focused around the preview tabs of the document window, the Optimize and Color Table panels, and the Frames panel for animations. Adjusting settings in these panels is a necessary precursor to choosing File ➪ Export to create your exported image file. After you've made these settings, they are saved with your Fireworks PNG file for next time. Export settings are as much a part of a document as the kinds of fills or strokes you used.

The hardest part of optimizing is finding a balance between image quality and file size. Fireworks takes a lot of the guesswork out of this task by providing up to four comparison views of different formats at various color resolutions or compressions. Optimizing every image that goes out on your Web page is important, because the smaller your files, the shorter the loading time of your Web pages — and the quicker visitors can view your work.

You'll explore individual export features in much greater depth throughout this chapter, but for now, here's an overview of the typical procedure to use when optimizing a file:

1. Create your image with optimization in the back of your mind at all times; scale and crop images as small as possible, and create large areas of flat color or horizontal stripes of color to make the smallest GIFs.
2. Select a file format in the Optimize panel, based on the type of image you're working on. Choose an indexed color format, such as GIF, for illustrations and flat-color artwork, or a continuous-tone, True Color format, such as JPEG for photographic images.
3. For indexed color images, reduce the number of colors as much as possible, using the setting in the Optimize panel in concert with the Color Table panel. Reducing the number of colors is the primary method of reducing the file size of indexed color images. The fewer colors used, the smaller the file.
4. For the JPEG format, use the Quality slider in the Optimize panel to choose the lowest acceptable quality in order to achieve the smallest file size.
5. Select any additional format-specific options in the Optimize panel, such as Interlaced GIF or JPEG Smoothing.
6. Choose File ➪ Export to export your document and create the optimized file.

Optimize panel

The Optimize panel is the main control center for your image optimization efforts in Fireworks, containing nearly all the controls you use to set export options. Choose an export file format and modify settings unique to that format. The Optimize panel's settings affect your entire Fireworks document, except when you have an individual slice object selected, in which case the settings are for that slice only.

If the Optimize panel (see Figure 30-2) is not visible, choose Window ➪ Optimize to view it. Many factors contribute to image optimization, but the format of an image plays perhaps the most important role. In Fireworks, all format selections are made in the Optimize panel's Export File Format option list. Selecting a particular format displays the available options, such as Bit Depth or Quality, for that format. Choosing GIF, for example, makes the transparency controls available, whereas choosing JPEG removes the transparency controls and displays the Quality slider.

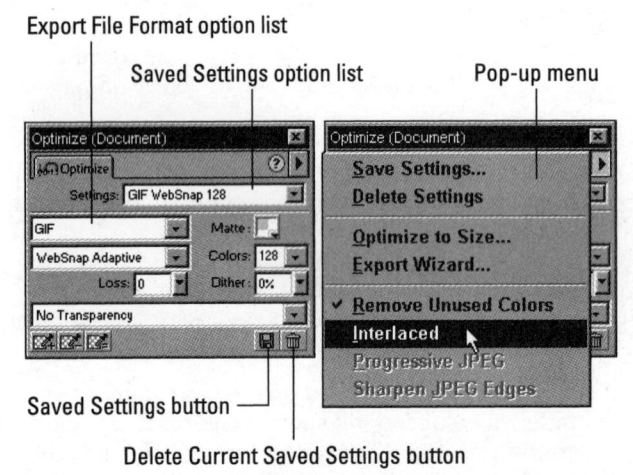

Figure 30-2: Virtually all export options are set in the Optimize panel.

The Optimize panel also allows you to save its settings as a preset at any time. Your preset is added to the default presets on the Saved Settings option list. Choosing a preset and then adjusting any setting (except Matte) creates a custom setting. To save a custom export setting, click the Save Settings button (the disk icon) on the bottom of the Optimize panel. A simple Preset Name dialog box appears for you to enter a unique name for the setting. After you enter the name and click OK, the setting is added to the preset list and is always available. To delete the current saved setting, click the Delete Current Saved Settings button (the Trash icon).

Note: We look more closely at the features of the Optimize panel as we work with specific export formats later in this chapter.

Color Table panel

The Color Table panel comes alive when you optimize an indexed color image, such as a GIF or 8-bit PNG. These formats carry their own limited palette of colors with them, and limiting the size of this palette is the primary way to limit the file size of indexed color images. The Color Table provides easy access to this palette, and enables you to add, remove, and lock specific colors and more.

If it's not already visible, view the Color Table panel, shown in Figure 30-3, by choosing Window ⇨ Color Table. Choosing the Rebuild Color Table command from the Color Table's pop-up menu displays swatches of the current document's export palette. The number of colors in your document is displayed at the bottom of the Color Table.

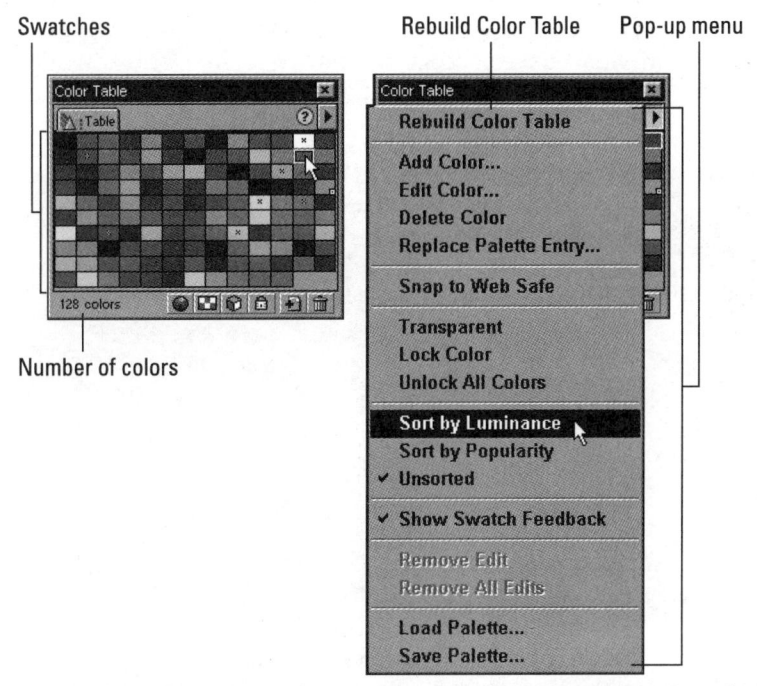

Figure 30-3: The Color Table panel displays the export palette for 8-bit indexed color images.

Workspace preview

The Preview tab of the document window, shown in Figure 30-4, offers you an optimized view of your document according to the settings in the Optimize panel. The Preview tab provides a view so similar to the working Original view, that I sometimes find myself grabbing a tool and getting back to work without switching away from Preview.

Previewing Cross-Platform Gamma

As well as seeing what your work will look like after it's exported, Fireworks can also give you an idea of what your work will look like on both the Windows and Macintosh platforms. Windows machines use a gamma correction setting of 2.2, whereas most Macs use 1.8 by default. The difference in gamma correction settings — which regulate how dark or light the display looks — means that the same image will look brighter on a Mac than on Windows.

At any time during a Fireworks session — not just when you're looking at one of the preview tabs of the document window — a Windows user can choose View ➪ Macintosh Gamma, or a Mac user can choose View ➪ Windows Gamma, to toggle the document window to simulate the other platform. Viewing your images at both gamma settings enables you to avoid a surprise when seeing your work on the opposite platform.

Figure 30-4: An optimized preview of your work is never more than a click away, thanks to the document window's in-place previews.

Multiple previews

Fireworks' ability to offer side-by-side comparisons of the effects of different export settings on an image is often crucial to optimizing a graphic. This chapter has noted several times that an optimized graphic is one that strikes a balance between the best appearance and the smallest file size. That balance can be directly judged through Fireworks' multiple previews.

The 2-Up and 4-Up tabs show you both sides of the export equation: how the image looks, and the file size. The file size is given in both kilobytes and its approximate download time with a 28.8 Kbps modem. Although the visual representation of your document is an obvious benefit, the file size information that accompanies a preview is just as important. Every adjustment you make in the Optimize panel is reflected in a recalculated and updated file size estimate. The file size is shown in both kilobytes and the approximate length of time the exported image will take to download.

> **Note** If your image contains multiple frames, the file size shown is for the current frame only, unless the chosen format is Animated GIF. Images with rollovers, for example, use multiple frames, and each frame is exported as a separate image. To find the total "weight" of a multiple-framed image, you must add all the frames together.

Each of the document window's three preview tabs offers its own kind of multiple preview.

Preview tab

You can access a somewhat hidden multiple preview by choosing Window ⇨ New Window to create a second document window for your current document. Then select the Preview tab in the new window, as shown in Figure 30-5. With one document window set to Original and one set to Preview, your work in the Original window is immediately reflected in the Preview window.

2-Up tab

The 2-Up tab splits the document window vertically and provides two views of your image (see Figure 30-6). By default, the left pane displays your original image, while the right displays the optimized version, according to the settings in the Optimize panel. An option list at the bottom of each pane enables you to choose whether to display an original view (your work as it looks in Fireworks), or an export preview. Setting a second preview in the left pane enables you to closely compare two sets of export settings without looking at the original image. When you select a pane with the mouse, Fireworks draws a border around it. The Optimize panel affects only the settings for the selected pane.

> **Tip** When viewing the 2-Up preview, you can stretch the document window to get a complete side-by-side view.

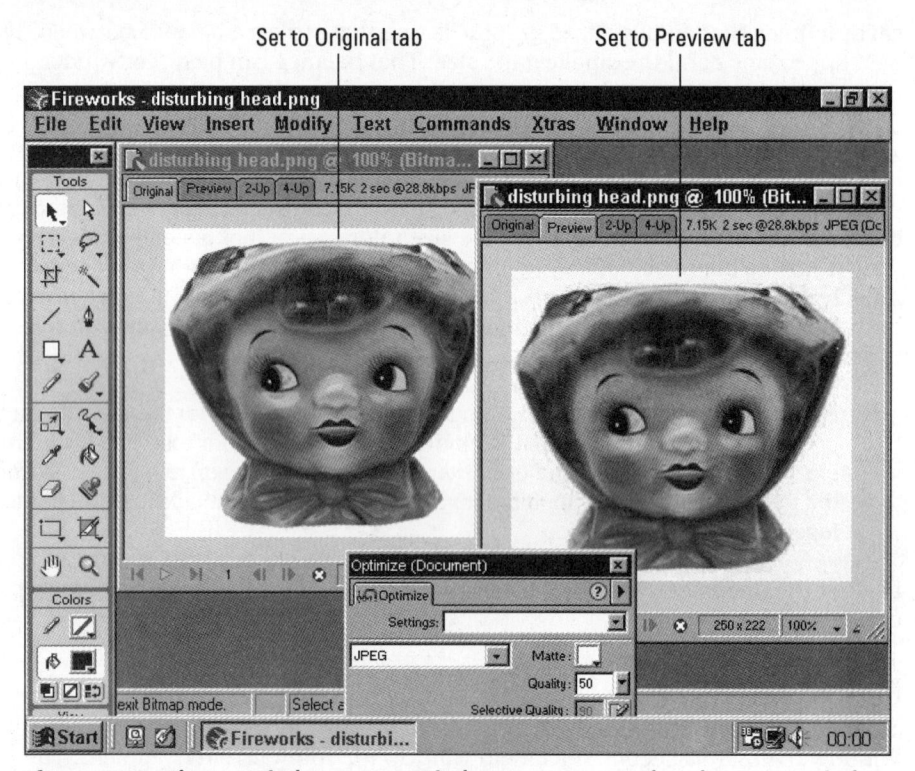

Figure 30-5: Choose Window ⇨ New Window to create another document window and set one to Original and one to Preview.

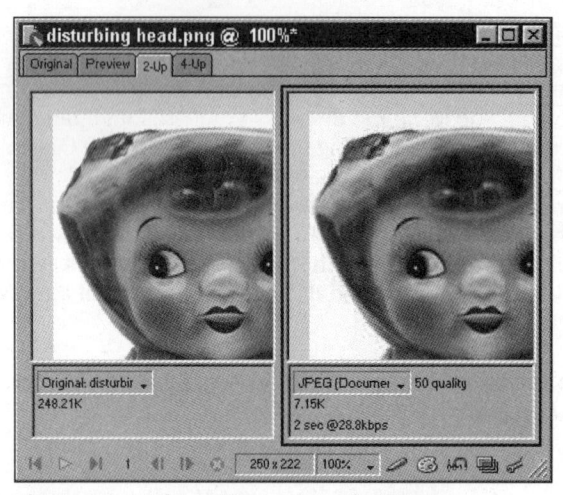

Figure 30-6: The 2-Up preview shows you one original and one optimized view of your document by default.

4-Up tab

The 4-Up tab (see Figure 30-7) offers four views, each approximately one quarter of the document window, arranged in a square. The upper-left view is initially your original document, while the other three panes display optimized views. 4-Up works just like 2-Up in other respects.

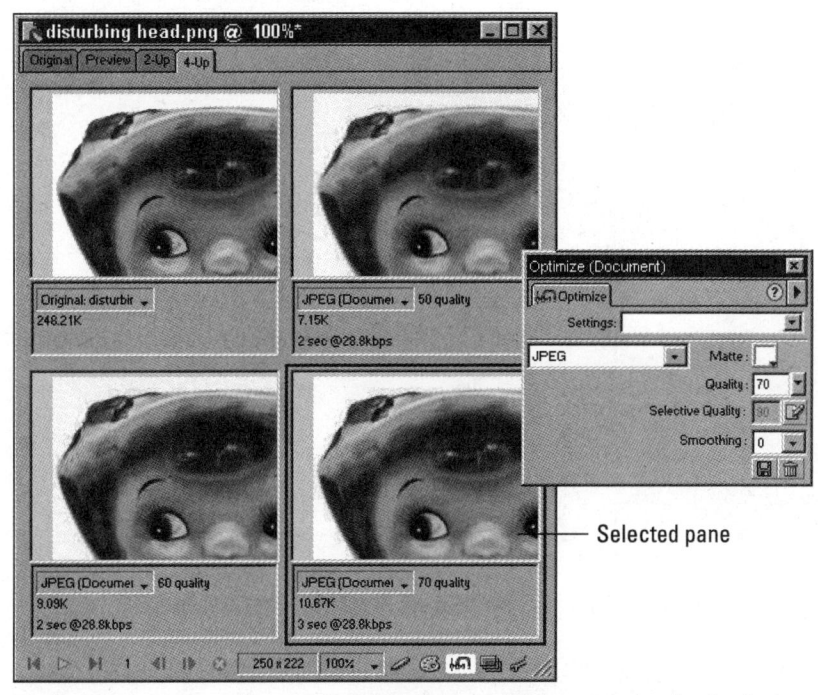

Figure 30-7: In the 4-Up preview, you have to select a pane to be the focus of your work in the Optimize panel. Here, the lower-right pane is selected.

I find that the 4-Up view is especially useful when optimizing an image for JPEG export. The JPEG format is finicky; reducing the quality to 70 percent might make one image look terrible, whereas another might still look great with the quality dialed all the way down to 50 percent. Achieving the perfect JPEG quality setting for a particular image is often best accomplished by viewing it at three different settings at once.

> **Tip** You may have to resize the document window to get a good look at your document, especially if your document is on the small size. A portion of each preview pane is given over to the file size report, which can be most of the window for a 200×200 or smaller document.

Panning

If the image is too big to view all at once in the preview area, you can use the Hand tool to pan the image. When you select an image in a preview area with the Hand tool, the cursor becomes a hand, and you can drag the other parts of the image into view. The panning capability of the Hand tool is especially valuable when viewing multiple settings. Panning one of the multiple views causes all the other views to pan as well, as shown in Figure 30-8. This feature makes direct comparison very straightforward.

Figure 30-8: With multiple views, if you pan in one view, the other view pans, too.

Zooming

One of the export features in Fireworks is *color locking;* you can lock the color of any pixel in the preview by selecting it and then clicking the Lock Color button on the Color Table. How do you identify just the right pixel? You zoom in, naturally. The Zoom tool and the document window view controls work exactly the same way in the preview views as they do in the original view of the document window. To magnify a view, either select the Zoom tool and click the image, or choose a magnification from the magnification option list on the bottom of the document window. To reduce the magnification of the view, press Alt (Option) while clicking with the Zoom tool — or choose a lower magnification.

> **Tip**
>
> Keep in mind that your Web graphics will almost *always* be viewed at 100 percent. Although you might be tempted to make a decision on which file format to use based on a magnified view, the magnified view is largely irrelevant to how the graphics are ultimately viewed.

If you have two or four multiple views enabled, changing the magnification of one view changes the magnification for all of them, as shown in Figure 30-9.

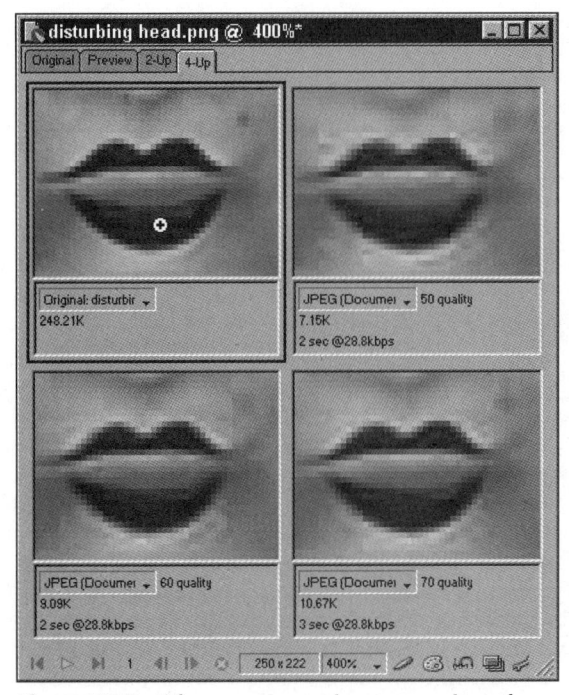

Figure 30-9: When you zoom in on one view, the accompanying views also zoom in.

> **Tip**
>
> To pan in for a close-up view without having to switch away from the Zoom tool, press and hold down the spacebar to temporarily switch to the Hand tool.

Frame controls

You can use the VCR-like animation controls on the document window no matter which document window Original/Preview tab you are currently viewing. When optimizing in one of the preview tabs, you can use the frame controls to quickly call up a specific frame for optimization, or to play the frames in sequence.

The controls, from left to right, are as follows:

- **First Frame:** Displays the first frame of the image.
- **Play/Stop:** Plays all the frames in sequence. When the frames are playing, the button image changes to a square and, if pressed, stops the playback.
- **Last Frame:** Displays the last frame of the image.
- **Current Frame:** Displays the current frame number of the image.
- **Previous Frame:** Displays the frame before the current one.
- **Next Frame:** Displays the frame after the current one.

In addition to being useful for viewing the separate frames of an animation, I often use the VCR controls to step through the frames of a rollover. Remember that each frame in your document is exported as a separate file, and thus can be optimized individually.

Exporting Indexed Color

Images that have large areas of flat color (typically illustrations, as opposed to photographic images) and that can get by with only a limited number of colors are exported in an indexed color format. Indexed color formats have a maximum of 256 different colors, also known as 8-bit color. A particular image file contains which 256 colors it uses and is maintained in a color index inside the file, hence the name *indexed color*.

A key feature of indexed color files is that their index can be reduced to only the specific colors actually used in the image. Reducing the number of colors has a major impact on file size. In fact, this method is the primary one for optimizing indexed color files. Fireworks' Color Table panel provides a comprehensive access point to this index.

When an indexed color graphic needs to create the impression of more than 256 colors, dithering can be used. A dithered color is made from a pattern of two or more colored pixels that, because the eye cannot differentiate the individual pixels, blend into the new color.

The indexed color formats that Fireworks exports are detailed in Table 30-1.

Table 30-1
Indexed Color Export Formats

Format	Description
GIF	Graphics Interchange Format. The overwhelmingly most popular indexed color format for the Web. Excellent Web browser support; small file sizes; 1-bit transparency.
Animated GIF	Same as GIF, except that it contains multiple images that are shown one after the other, usually rapidly, as in a film or flipbook.
PNG 8	Portable Network Graphic. Offers similar features to GIF, but transparency is not supported by Web browsers.
WBMP	A 1-bit (black/white) file format specifically for Wireless Application Protocol (WAP) pages, which are displayed on mobile devices with small screens and limited color depth.
TIFF 8	Tag Image File Format. Not suitable for the Web, but common for print work.
BMP 8	Microsoft Bitmap image. The native graphics format of Microsoft Windows. Not suitable for the Web, but a good way to share images between Windows applications.
PICT 8 (Macintosh only)	Macintosh Picture. The native graphics format of Mac OS. Vectors are not supported by Fireworks. Not suitable for the Web, but a good way to share image files between Mac applications.

Of all the indexed color formats, only GIF and PNG 8 can be used on the Web. GIF is the most popular and the most suitable on today's Web, because an overwhelming number of browsers support it. Although PNG is a superior format in many ways, its transparency features have yet to find support in a wide range of browsers.

Both GIF and PNG support transparency, but again, PNG suffers from lack of browser support. This feature is extremely valuable on the Web, because it enables you to create graphics that appear nonrectangular, or create the illusion that one image is in front of another. Both GIF and PNG files can be optionally interlaced. An interlaced image appears to be developing on the page as it downloads.

The WBMP format is notable for its color support, or lack thereof. This 1-bit format stores each pixel as either on or off, yielding a color palette that's essentially one dark gray and one light gray, once the WBMP image is ultimately viewed on the limited gray display of a mobile device. Unfortunately, a bug in Fireworks 4 causes exported WBMP files to have blank icons, but you can identify them by their standard filename extension of ".wbmp".

New Feature: Support for the export — and import — of the Wireless Bitmap (WBMP) format is new in Fireworks 4, opening up a whole new range of target devices for your Fireworks imagery in the form of Wireless Application Protocol (WAP) devices.

The process of exporting any indexed color image is very similar, no matter which format you choose. The GIF format has more options, and is the most popular, so we'll focus mainly on the GIF format throughout this section. After you can export a GIF, applying that knowledge to exporting any of the other indexed color formats is easy, because when you switch from GIF to another format in the Optimize panel, Fireworks removes the controls that are no longer applicable, while those that are left function in the same way.

Color palette

A *palette* is the group of colors actually used in the image. Fireworks offers nine preset palettes in the Optimize panel's Indexed Palette option list, plus the Custom setting that refers to a deviation from one of the preset palettes. After you customize a palette, you can store it as a preset and add it to the Indexed Palette option list.

Each of the nine different palettes (available to all indexed formats, not only GIF) accesses a different group of colors. The WebSnap Adaptive and Web 216 palettes are the choices generally made for Internet graphics, although other palettes are appropriate in some situations. The following are the nine preset palettes:

✦ **Adaptive:** Examines all the colors in the image and finds a maximum of the most suitable 256 colors; it's called an *adaptive* palette because the best 256 colors are adapted to the image, instead of a fixed set of colors. If possible, Fireworks assigns Web-safe colors initially and then assigns any remaining non-Web-safe colors. The Adaptive palette can contain a mixture of Web-safe and non-Web-safe colors.

✦ **WebSnap Adaptive:** This palette is similar to the Adaptive palette insofar as both are custom palettes in which colors are chosen to match the originals as closely as possible. After selecting the initial matching Web-safe colors, all remaining colors are examined according to their hexadecimal values. Any colors close to a Web-safe color (plus or minus seven values from a Web-safe color) are "snapped to" that color. Although this palette does not ensure that all colors are Web-safe, a greater percentage of colors will be Web-safe.

Note: Exactly how does Fireworks decide which colors are within range for the use of WebSnap Adaptive? The plus or minus seven value range is calculated by using the RGB model. For example, suppose that one of the colors is R-100, G-100, B-105 — a medium gray. With the WebSnap Adaptive palette, that color snaps to R-102, G-102, B-102, because the difference between the two colors is seven or less (R-2, G-2, B-3 = 7). If, however, the color was slightly different, say R-99, G-100, B-105, the difference would be outside the snap range and the actual color would be used.

- **Web 216:** All colors in the image are converted to their nearest equivalent in the Web-safe range.
- **Exact:** Uses colors that match the exact original RGB values. Useful only for images with less than 256 colors; for images with more colors, Fireworks alerts you to use the Adaptive palette.
- **Macintosh:** Matches the system palette used by the Macintosh operating system when the display is set to 256 colors.
- **Windows:** Matches the system palette used by the Windows operating system when the display is set to 256 colors.
- **Grayscale:** Converts the image to a grayscale graphic with a maximum of 256 shades of gray.
- **Black & White:** Reduces the image to a two-tone image; the Dither option is automatically set to 100 percent when you choose this palette, but you can modify this setting.
- **Uniform:** A mathematical progression of colors across the spectrum are chosen. This palette has little application on the Web, although I have been able to get the occasional posterization effect out of it by severely reducing the number of colors and by reducing the 100 percent Dither setting that is automatically applied.
- **Custom:** Whenever a stored palette is loaded or a modification is made to one of the standard palettes, Fireworks labels the palette Custom. Such changes are made through the pop-up menu found on the Options panel.

Given these options, what's the recommended path to take? Probably the best course is to build your graphic in Fireworks by using the Web-Safe palette, and then exporting them by using the WebSnap Adaptive palette. This approach ensures that your image remains the truest to its original colors, while looking the best for Web viewers whose color depth is set to 24-bit or higher, and still looking good on lower-end systems that are capable of showing only 256 colors.

Keep in mind that even if you use all Web-safe colors in your graphic, the final result won't necessarily be within that complete palette. Fireworks generates other colors to antialias, to create drop shadows, and to produce glows, and the colors generated may not be Web-safe. For this reason, either the Adaptive palette or WebSnap Adaptive palette often offers the truest representation of your image across browsers.

Number of colors

One of the quickest ways to decrease an image's file size is to reduce the number of colors. Recall that GIF is referred to as an *8-bit format;* this means that the maximum number of available colors is 256, or 8-bit planes of information — math aficionados will remember that 256 is equal to 2^8 (two raised to the eighth power). Each bit plane used permits exponentially more colors and reserves a certain amount of memory (but also increases the file size). For this reason, the Number of Colors option list contains powers of 2, 4, 8, 16, 32, 64, 128, and 256.

Color Table panel

For complete control of individual colors, the controls on the Color Table panel enable you to add, edit, and delete individual colors, as well as store and load palettes. Fireworks enables you to select a color from the swatches and then lock it, snap it to its closest Web-safe neighbor, or convert it to transparent by clicking one of the Color Table panel's buttons, or choosing a command from its pop-up menu.

Locking one or more colors in your graphic ensures that the most important colors — whether they're important for branding, a visual design, or both — can be maintained. After a color is locked, it does not change, regardless of the palette chosen. For example, you could preview your image by using the Web 216 palette, lock all the colors, and then switch to an Adaptive palette to broaden the color range, but keep the basic colors Web-safe. Web-safe colors are displayed in the swatches with a diamond symbol in them, and locked colors are identified by a square in the lower-right corner of the swatch, as shown in Figure 30-10.

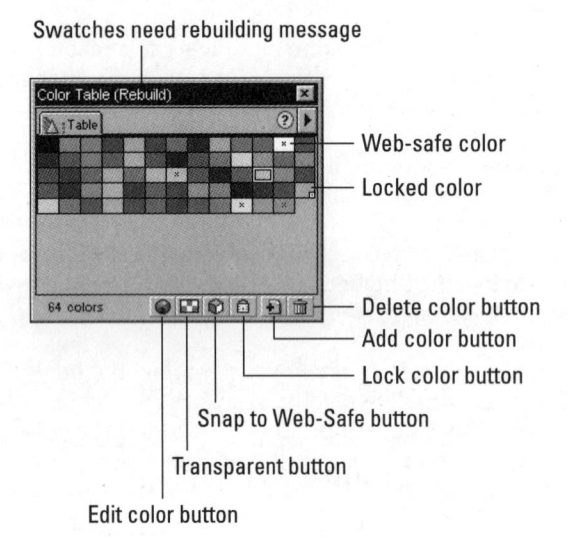

Figure 30-10: The Color Table panel is your window into an image's color index.

Tip Clicking a pixel in the preview with the Pointer tool selects its color in the Color Table panel.

The Color Table panel's pop-up menu commands are detailed in Table 30-2, along with whether they are also represented by a button.

Table 30-2
Color Table Panel Pop-Up Commands

Command	Button	Description
Rebuild Color Table	No	Rebuilds the color table swatches according to the settings in the Optimize panel.
Add Color	Yes	Allows you to insert an additional color into the current palette by choosing it from the system color picker(s).
Edit Color	Yes	Opens the system color picker(s) to permit a new color to be chosen to replace the selected color.
Delete Color	Yes	Removes the selected color(s).
Replace Palette Entry	No	Swaps the selected color for the color chosen through the system color picker(s).
Snap to Web-Safe	Yes	Converts the selected color(s) to the closest color in the Web-safe palette.
Transparent	Yes	Makes the selected color(s) transparent.
Lock Color	Yes	Maintains the current color during any overall palette transformations, such as bit-depth reduction or palette changes. The color, however, can still be edited directly.
Unlock All Colors	No	Allows all colors to be changed.
Sort by Luminance	No	Sorts the current palette swatch set from brightest to darkest.
Sort by Popularity	No	Sorts the current palette swatch set from most pixels used to least pixels used.
Unsorted	No	Restores the default swatch arrangement.
Remove Edit	No	Reverts the swatch to its original color.
Remove All Edits	No	Restores the current palette to its original state.
Load Palette	No	Allows a palette to be loaded from Adobe Color Table (ACT) files or from GIF.
Save Palette	No	Stores the current palette as a Color Table file.

Tip All of these commands are also available from the shortcut menu that appears when you right-click (Control+click) an individual swatch.

Sort by popularity

The Sort by Popularity command is available from the Color Table's pop-up menu, and is very helpful when it's time to trim file size down by cutting colors. By default, the swatches are displayed in an unsorted order. After you choose Sort by Popularity from the pop-up menu, the most-used color is displayed first, in the upper-left corner, and the least-used color is shown last, in the lower-right corner. This makes it easy to select and delete the colors that are least likely to be missed. You can Shift+click two colors to select them and the range between them, or Ctrl+click (Command+click) to select multiple swatches that are not adjacent to each other.

Matte

When a photograph is framed, the framer often mounts the image on a matte, which provides a different, contrasting background to make the photograph stand out. Fireworks uses the matte idea to allow the Web designer to export images with varying canvas colors — without changing the canvas. One of the biggest problems with GIF transparency is the unwanted "halos" that result from creating a drop shadow or other gradation against a different background. The traditional method of handling this problem is to change your canvas color in the graphics program to match the background color on the Web page. This solution works well for graphics you're only going to use once, but many Web designers find that they need to use the same graphic in many different situations, against many different backgrounds. The Matte feature enables you to keep one master graphic and export as many specific instances — against as many different mattes or canvases — as necessary, as shown in Figure 30-11.

Choosing a matte color is very straightforward: Simply click the Matte arrow button to display the standard pop-up color picker. From there, choose one of the swatches or a color from elsewhere onscreen using the Eyedropper tool. To return a matte color to transparent, click the No Color button in the pop-up color picker.

Lossy GIF compression

Recall that the GIF format uses lossless compression; so what's this Loss option in the Optimize panel all about? The so-called Lossy GIF is not a separate format at all, but rather a method for optimizing an image so that when it's actually saved as a GIF it will have a smaller file size. When it comes to determining the ideal Loss setting, Fireworks multiple previews are invaluable, as shown in Figure 30-12. I usually start with an extreme setting, such as 60 or 70 percent, and then gradually reduce it until the image looks acceptable.

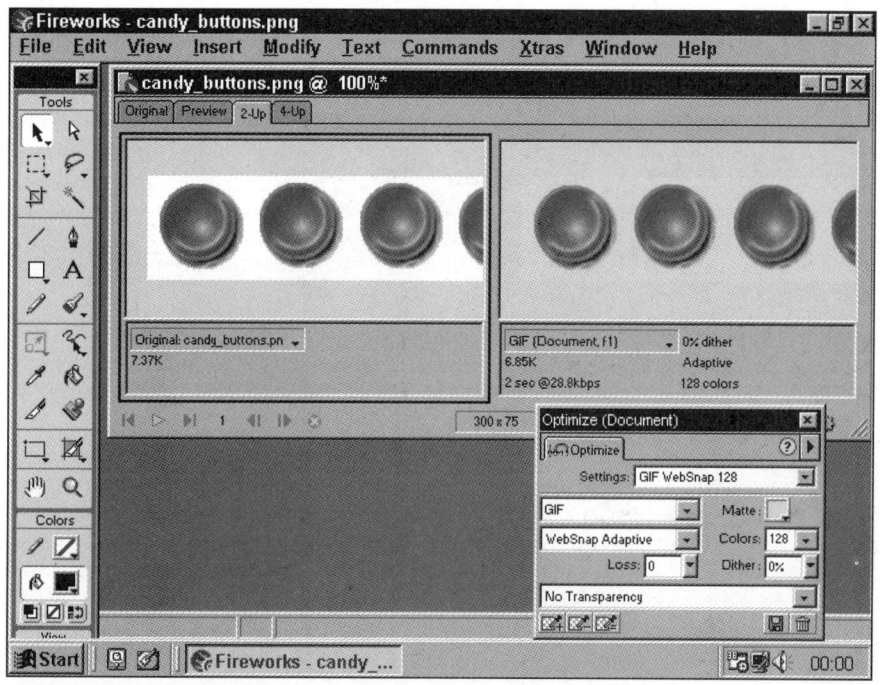

Figure 30-11: The Matte feature enables you to export your image against different canvas colors, without having to modify the original image.

I find that the Loss option works for some images and not for others. Sometimes it will actually increase the resulting file size until you really get into a high Loss setting. For those times when it trims a particular image down to a much lower weight, you'll be happy to have this tool in your export toolkit.

Dither

One way — although not necessarily the best way — to break up areas of flat color caused by the lower color capabilities of GIF is to use the Dither option. When the Dither option is enabled, Fireworks simulates new colors by using a pattern of existing colors — exactly how the Web Dither fill is created. However, because dithering is not restricted to a single area, but instead is spread throughout the graphic, the dithering can be significantly more noticeable — dithering makes the image appear "dotty," as shown in Figure 30-13, and usually increases your file size. The degree of dithering is set by changing the Dither Amount slider, or by entering the amount directly in the text box.

Figure 30-12: In the lower-left pane, the lossy compression at 30 percent is starting to become visible. In the lower-right pane, at 60 percent, it's unacceptably so.

Transparency

One of the main reasons GIF is often selected as a format over JPEG is GIF's ability to specify any one color — and thus certain apparent areas — of the graphic transparent. As mentioned previously, transparency is the key to making nonrectangular-shaped graphics, and the Fireworks transparency controls (see Figure 30-14) are the key to making transparency.

The transparency controls in detail are as follows:

✦ **Type of Transparency option list:** Choose either No Transparency, Index Transparency, or Alpha Transparency to specify the transparency type. By default, the canvas color is initially made transparent.

Figure 30-13: The image on the right was produced with dithering at 100 percent, causing the solid color to be heavily dotted.

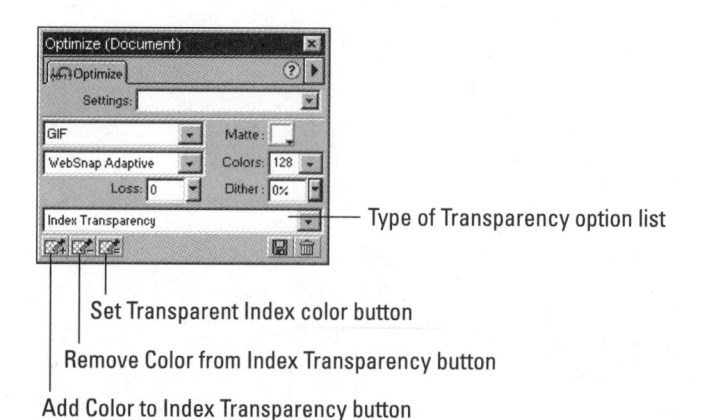

Figure 30-14: The Optimize panel contains transparency controls for file formats that support it, such as GIF.

- ✦ **Add Color to Index Transparency button:** Enables you to choose additional colors to make transparent, either from the swatch set or sampled directly from the previewed image.
- ✦ **Remove Color from Index Transparency button:** Converts transparent colors to their original color, either from the swatch set, or sampled directly from the previewed image.
- ✦ **Set Transparent Index Color button:** Select to choose a single color to be transparent, either from the swatch set, or sampled directly from the previewed image.

When a color is made transparent, its swatch and pixels in the Preview image are replaced with a gray-and-white checkerboard pattern, as shown in Figure 30-15. You can choose as many colors as you would like to make transparent.

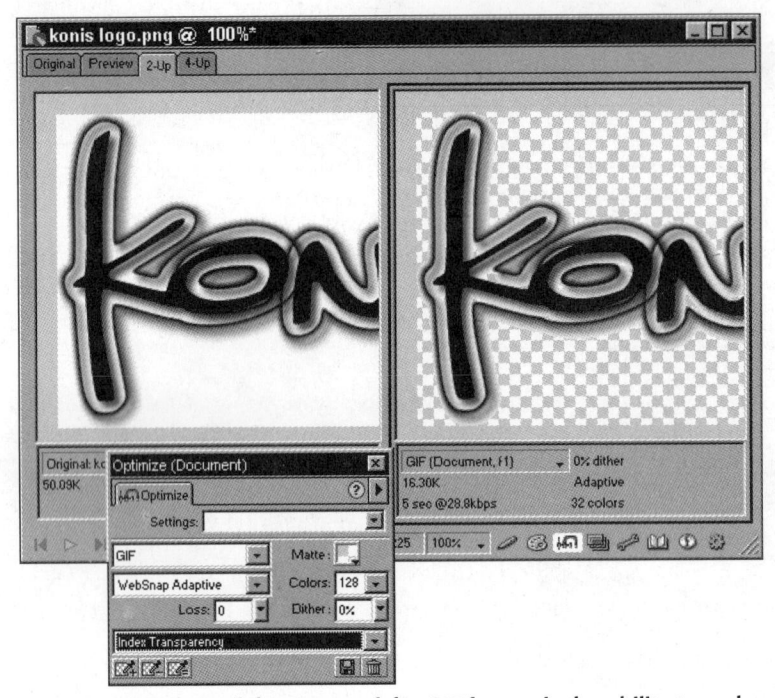

Figure 30-15: Part of the power of the GIF format is the ability to make any color transparent, so that the GIF image can be seamlessly composited into a Web page.

To make portions of your GIF image transparent, follow these steps:

1. Select a document window preview tab to view a preview of your document.
2. If the Optimize panel is not visible, choose Window ➪ Optimize to view it.

3. If necessary, select GIF from the Optimize panel's Export Format option list.

4. To make the canvas color transparent, select Index Transparency from the Type of Transparency option list.

5. To make a color other than the canvas transparent, click the Set Transparent Index Color button and sample a color either from a swatch or from the preview image.

Tip

If you want to select a small area in your image for transparency, use the Zoom tool to magnify that selection before choosing the color.

6. To make more colors transparent, click the Add Color to Index Transparency button and sample the colors, either from the swatch or from the Preview image.

7. To restore a transparent color to its original color, click the Remove Color from Index Transparency button and select the color either from a swatch or from the Preview image.

8. For even greater control, select a color or colors from the Color Table panel and click the Transparent button.

As noted in the Transparency option list description, two different types are available: Index and Alpha Transparency. Index Transparency enables you to make any color totally transparent — think of it as an On/Off switch; the color is either transparent or it isn't. Alpha Transparency, on the other hand, enables you to create degrees of transparency, such as tints and shades of a color. You can discover more details about Alpha Transparency in the PNG section, later in this chapter.

Index Transparency is generally used for the GIF format, because, technically, only the PNG format truly supports Alpha Transparency. However, the Fireworks engineers have left Alpha Transparency enabled for GIFs, to achieve a slightly different effect. When Alpha Transparency is chosen, a new color register is created for the canvas and then made transparent. How is this different from converting the canvas color to transparent, as occurs with Index Transparency? If you've ever created an image where part of the graphic is the same color as the background — the white of a person's eyes is also the white of a canvas — you'll quickly understand and appreciate this feature. Basically, Alpha Transparency, as applied in Fireworks' GIF format, leaves your palette alone and only makes the canvas transparent, as shown in Figure 30-16.

Note

If you don't notice a new color register being added when you select Alpha Transparency, check to see whether the Optimized option is enabled. If it is, Fireworks may combine other colors to keep the same number of colors.

Figure 30-16: The Alpha Transparency feature enabled me to make the white background of this image transparent without also making the white areas within the subject transparent.

Remove unused colors

The Remove Unused Colors option — which is enabled by default — is a Fireworks-only feature that causes the program to discard duplicate and unused colors from a palette. This can seriously reduce your file size, particularly when choosing one of the fixed palettes, such as Web 216, or either of the operating system palettes. Find the Remove Unused Colors option on the Optimize panel's pop-up menu.

Interlaced

The Interlaced option on the Optimize panel's pop-up menu enables a GIF property that displays a file as it downloads. The file is shown in progressively finer detail as more information is transferred from the server to the browser. Although a graphic exported with the Interlaced option won't download any faster, it provides a visual cue to Web page visitors that something is happening. Interlacing graphics is a matter of taste; some Web designers would never design a page without them; others are vehemently opposed to their use.

Saved settings

Four of the six presets in the Saved Settings option list in the Optimize panel relate to the GIF format:

- **GIF Web 216:** Sets the GIF format using the Web 216 palette.
- **GIF WebSnap 256:** Sets the GIF format using the WebSnap Adaptive palette and a maximum of 256 colors.
- **GIF WebSnap 128:** Sets the GIF format using the WebSnap Adaptive palette and a maximum of 128 colors.
- **GIF Adaptive 256:** Sets the GIF format using the Adaptive palette and a maximum of 256 colors.

Use these presettings when exporting GIFs, or use them as a starting point for your own optimizations.

Fireworks technique: Creating GIF-friendly images

Before you even get to the Optimize panel, you can make an image more GIF-friendly by paying attention to the patterns of pixels that make up the image, and understanding how the GIF format compresses pixels. Taking a little time to create more GIF-friendly images can be an even more effective means of reducing export file size than the obvious methods offered by Fireworks' export tools.

The easiest way to create a GIF-friendly document is to include large areas of flat color. Any changes from pixel to pixel are less compressible than large similar areas. A small experiment shows just how much the GIF format loves flat color. Create a new document, 400×400 pixels, and choose a canvas color. Click the Preview tab of the document window and note the tiny export file size of about 600 bytes, or 0.6K (you may have to stretch the document window to see the file size). Switch back to the Original tab and use the Pencil tool to draw a large *X* through your document, touching each corner. Go back to Preview and note that your file size has increased to about 1.74K — or almost triple — all for that skinny, penciled X.

The next best thing to large areas of flat color in the GIF format is horizontal lines. GIF compresses pixels from left to right, so a horizontal line of identically colored pixels is very compressible. Without compression, a line of red pixels might be expressed as "red pixel, red pixel, red pixel, red pixel, red pixel." You can see that expressing only five pixels takes a lot of explaining. With GIF compression, that same line might be "red pixel×5." That's an enormous savings in and of itself, but "red pixel×300" is an even more dramatic savings when compared to spelling out each pixel in turn. It's obvious that paying a little attention to using horizontal lines in your designs can minimize GIF file size.

The simplest way to put more horizontal lines into your images is to replace complex, chaotic texture fills such as Fiber with a simpler, horizontal lines texture, as shown in Figure 30-17. The two documents are identical except that the one on the left uses a 50 percent Fiber texture fill in the circle, and the one on the right uses a 50 percent Line-Horiz texture fill. Other export settings are the same, but the one with the horizontal lines texture is one third of the weight.

Figure 30-17: Replacing a Fiber fill with an alternating lines texture reduced the export file size from 19K to less than 6K (note the export file sizes next to the preview tabs) because of the compressibility of long horizontal lines of similar pixels in the GIF format.

Another way to make an image more GIF-friendly is to reduce areas of stray pixels. Sometimes an area of otherwise flat color will have some randomly placed pixels of colors one or two shades away. When viewed at 100 percent, these pixels may not be obvious, but their random nature is reducing the GIF-compressibility of your image. Zooming in and cleaning up those stray pixels is optimization-time well spent.

Tip One way to end up with lots of stray pixels is to work from a JPEG original. Sometimes an image goes through a few hands before it ends up in yours. I've had clients submit flat-color artwork such as illustrations or logos — obvious candidates for GIF export — as JPEGs, in spite of my protestations. What's worse, they've lost the original PNG or TIFF files. As good as the JPEG format can be for photographic images, it mangles areas of flat color, creating lots of unsightly and uncompressible stray pixels. Use this technique to reduce or eliminate stray pixels and reclaim the image for the GIF format.

You can use the Pencil tool to clean up areas of stray pixels, as shown in Figure 30-18. Drawing the predominant flat color over the strays creates more areas of flat horizontal lines, often dramatically reducing export file size.

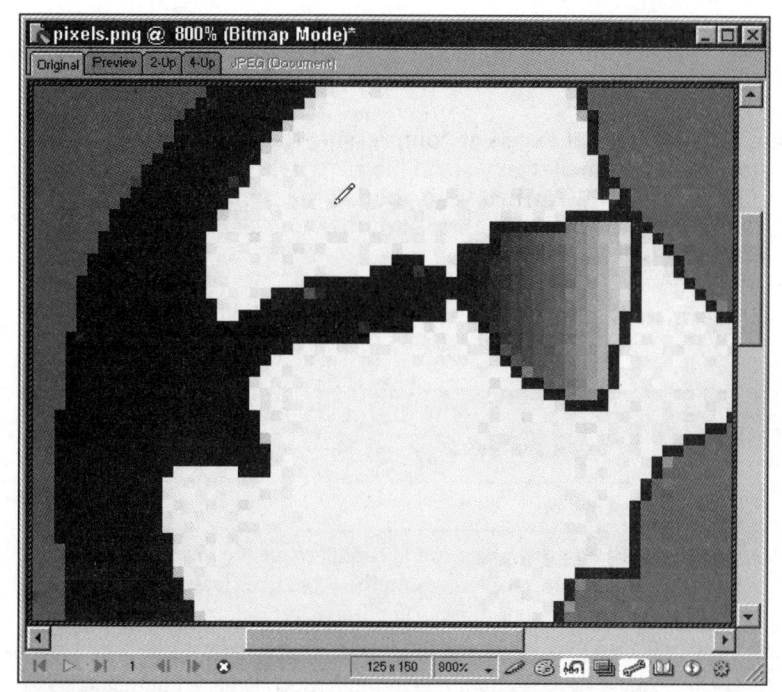

Figure 30-18: Zoom in on an image and eliminate stray pixels to create bigger areas of flat color that compress better upon GIF export.

To zap stray pixels, follow these steps:

1. Choose the Pencil tool from the Tools panel.
2. Use the Stroke color well on the Tools panel to sample a predominant flat color from your image.
3. Use the Pencil tool to color over stray pixels that are adjacent to that flat color, converting them to the flat color.
4. Repeat Steps 2 and 3 until you have flattened as many stray pixel areas as possible.

Tip

While you're zoomed in on your image, Choose Window ⇨ New Window to create a new, 100% window to monitor how your changes are affecting your image at its true size.

Exporting Photographic Images

Photographic images are most often displayed in 24-bit True Color, in a format such as JPEG, rather than the limited palette of an indexed color image, such as a GIF. Photographic images contain subtle gradations that are not easily reproduced in fewer colors, and yet are dithered quite serviceably by the browser if the client machine is running in a 256-color video mode.

What's more, the JPEG format excels at compressing the smooth tones of photographic images down to unbelievably small file sizes, without an appreciable loss of quality. The fact that the JPEG format is so good at the things the GIF format fails miserably at is part of the reason for their enduring, successful partnership as the king and queen of Web graphics formats.

The True Color formats that Fireworks exports are detailed in Table 30-3.

Table 30-3
True Color Export Formats

Format	Description
JPEG	Joint Photographic Experts Group image file format. Used for almost all the true color images on the Web. Uses lossy compression to achieve maximum reduction in file size.
PNG 24, PNG 32	Portable Network Graphic. Offers lossless compression that results in larger file sizes than JPEG — often much larger — but maintains pristine quality.
TIFF 24, TIFF 32	Tag Image File Format. Print artists commonly use 24- and 32-bit TIFFs, although they are not suitable for the Web.
BMP 24	Microsoft Bitmap image. The native graphics format of Microsoft Windows. Not suitable for the Web, but a good way to share images between Windows applications.
PICT 24 (Macintosh only)	Macintosh Picture. The native graphics format of Mac OS. Vectors are not supported by Fireworks. Not suitable for the Web, but a good way to share image files between Mac applications.

Cross-Reference: The Photoshop file format can also contain photographic images, as well as layers and other extended attributes. Exporting a Photoshop document from Fireworks is covered later in this chapter.

Of all the formats in Table 30-3, only JPEG and PNG 24 can be used on the Web. PNG 32's alpha mask is ignored by browsers, rendering it the same as PNG 24. If you want to display an image with the highest quality, regardless of file size, then PNG

24 is a good choice. If bandwidth is an issue at all — and it's very rare that it isn't — then JPEG is the better choice, providing excellent quality photographic images in a much smaller file size than PNG.

To alter the bit depth for an exported image, choose a lower bit-depth export format from the Optimize panel's Export Format option list. Instead of PNG 32, for example, choose PNG 24. Although a change from 24-bit to 8-bit means lowering the maximum number of colors supported, a change from 32-bit to 24-bit supports the same colors, but removes the alpha mask. The upper 8 bits of a 32-bit image are always an alpha channel — an 8-bit grayscale image that defines the image's transparency.

Cross-Reference For more about alpha masks, see Chapter 29.

JPEG

Whereas GIFs generally are made smaller by lowering the number of colors used, JPEGs use a sliding scale that creates smaller file sizes by eliminating pixels. This sliding scale is built on a *lossy* algorithm, so-called because the lower the scale, the more pixels are lost. The JPEG algorithm is a very good one, and you can significantly reduce the file size by lowering the JPEG Quality setting.

Other characteristics of the JPEG format include the following:

✦ JPEG images are capable of displaying over 16 million colors. This wide color range, also referred to as *24-bit,* enables the subtle shades of a photograph to be depicted easily.

✦ Although JPEG images can display almost any color, none of the colors can be made transparent. Consequently, any image that requires transparency in a Web browser must be stored as a GIF.

✦ For JPEG images to be viewed as they are downloaded, they must be stored as Progressive JPEGs, which appear to develop onscreen, like an interlaced GIF. Progressive JPEGs have a slightly better compression engine and can produce smaller file sizes.

Note Internet Explorer doesn't fully support Progressive JPEGs. They are displayed just as if they were not Progressive, though, so there's no harm in using them.

Quality

The major method for altering a JPEG's file size is by changing the Quality value. In Fireworks, the Quality value is gauged as a percentage, and the slider goes from 0 percent to 100 percent. Higher values mean less compression, and lower values mean that more pixels are discarded. Trying to reduce a JPEG's file size by lowering the Quality slider is always worthwhile; you can also enter a value directly in the text box. The JPEG compression algorithm is so good that almost every continuous-tone image can be reduced in file size without significant loss of quality, as shown in Figure 30-19. On the other hand, increasing a JPEG's Quality value from its initial setting is never helpful. Whereas JPEG is very good at losing pixels to reduce file size, adding pixels to increase quality never works — you'll only increase the file's size and download time.

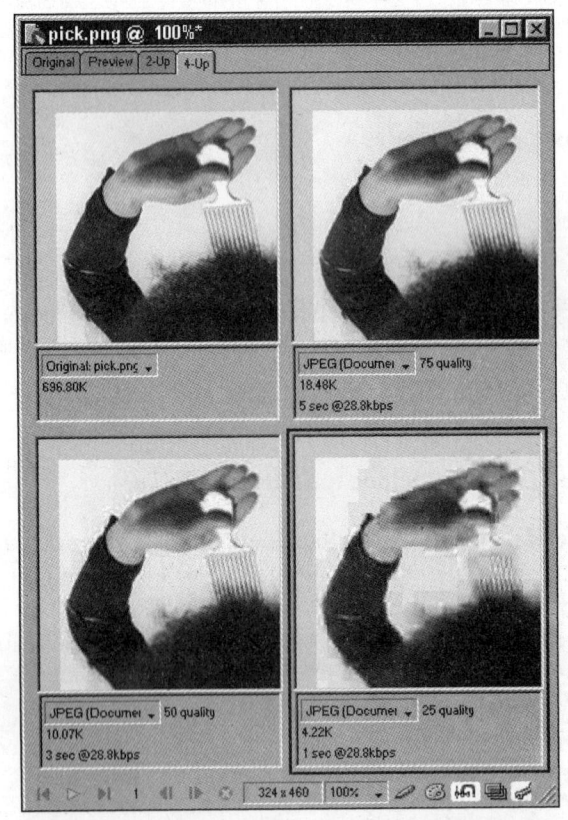

Figure 30-19: Each of these four previews uses a different JPEG quality value; only when the quality is lowered significantly (bottom right) does the image become unacceptable.

Tip With the JPEG image-compression algorithm, the initial elements of an image that are "compressed away" are least noticeable. Subtle variations in brightness and hue are the first to disappear. With additional compression, the image grows darker and less varied in its color range.

A good technique for comparing JPEG images in Fireworks is to use the 4-Up preview option. The upper-left pane shows your original document, so that you always have an image on which to base your comparisons. In another view, reduce the Quality to about 75 percent or so. If that image is acceptable, reduce the Quality setting to 50 percent in another view. By then, you'll probably start to get some unwanted artifacts, so use the fourth window to try a setting midway between the last acceptable and the unacceptable Quality settings, such as 65 percent. Be sure to view your images at 100 percent magnification. That's how your Web audience will see them, so you should, too.

> **Tip** Don't forget that you can stretch the document window to a larger size to increase the size of the multiple preview panes.

Selective Quality

The Selective Quality setting works just like the Quality setting, except that its value only applies to areas of your document that are covered by a JPEG mask. This enables you to isolate foreground areas and apply a high Selective Quality setting to them while applying a very low quality setting to the rest of your image. Basically, you trade some of the quality of the least important areas of an image for better quality where it matters most.

> **New Feature** Fireworks 4 enables you to create even smaller JPEG images in many cases with the combination of two separate quality settings: Selective Quality for text, buttons, and specific areas you specify with a JPEG mask, and Quality for the rest of the image.

You can create JPEG masks from Marquee selections by choosing Modify ➪ Selective JPEG ➪ Save Selection as JPEG Mask. Fireworks displays JPEG masks as a translucent pink overlay by default, as shown in Figure 30-20.

If you've ever created a JPEG image that contains text or flat color graphics such as buttons, you know that the JPEG compression process is murder on GIF-like images. Text and flat color areas turn into an unsightly, blocky patchwork. You can choose to have your Selective Quality setting also apply to the text objects and Button Symbols in your document, without having to cover each element individually with a JPEG mask. To do so, choose Modify ➪ Selective JPEG ➪ Settings to display the Selective JPEG Settings dialog box (see Figure 30-21), and check the Preserve Text Quality and/or Preserve Button Quality checkboxes. You can also enable or disable the Selective Quality setting in the same dialog box.

Figure 30-20: Convert a marquee selection into a JPEG mask and Fireworks colors it pink.

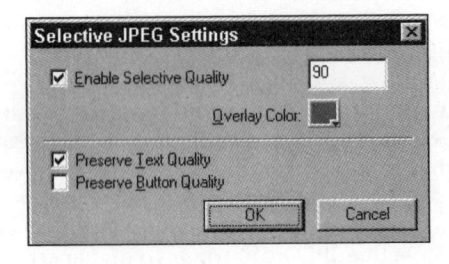

Figure 30-21: Choose whether the Selective Quality setting also applies to text and buttons in the Selective JPEG Settings dialog box.

> **Tip** You can also click the Edit Selective Quality Options button that appears on the Optimize panel when it's set to JPEG to display the Selective JPEG Settings dialog box.

Figure 30-22 shows the Quality and Selective Quality settings in action, using the image and JPEG mask from Figure 30-20.

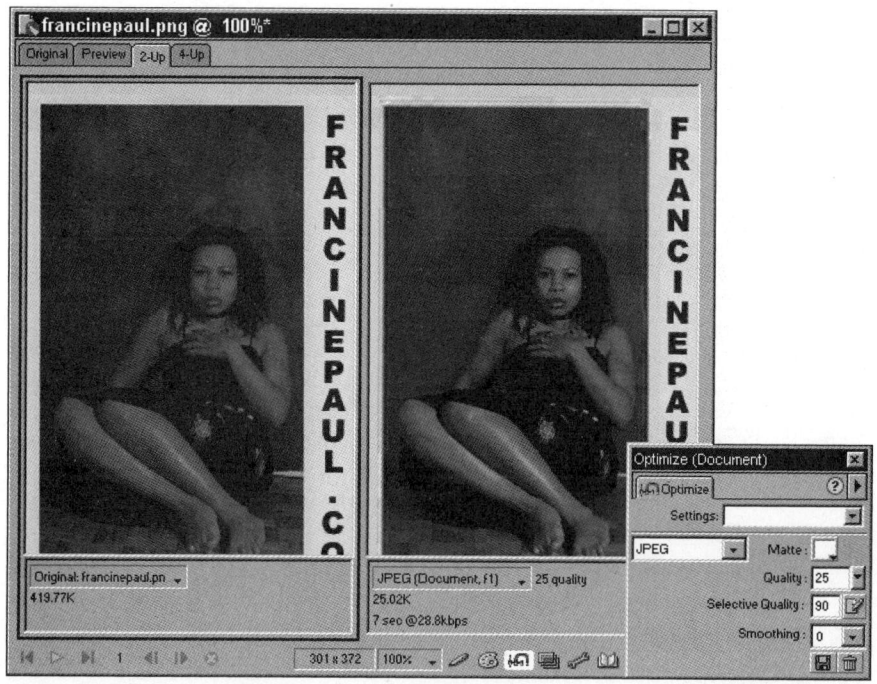

Figure 30-22: The text and the area under the JPEG mask are clear and sharp because they have a high Selective Quality setting of 90. The rest of the image, however, is all but obscured by JPEG artifacting, due to its low Quality setting of 25.

Sharpening edges

Graphics on the Web are often a montage of photographs, illustrations, and text. Although JPEG is the right choice for a continuous tone image, such as a photograph, it can make text that overlays a photograph appear fuzzy, because JPEG is far better at compressing gradations than it is at compressing images with hard edges and abrupt color changes. To overcome these obstacles, use Fireworks' Sharpen JPEG Edges option, which is on the Optimize panel's pop-up menu.

As the name implies, Sharpen JPEG Edges restores some of the hard-edge transitions that are lost during JPEG compression. This is especially noticeable on text and simple graphics, such as rectangles superimposed on photographs (see Figure 30-23). Keep an eye on the balance between image quality and file size, though, because Sharpen JPEG Edges can sometimes increase file size to the point where you may be better off simply increasing the Quality setting for your whole image.

Figure 30-23: When a photographic image includes sharp edges such as text, keep them from getting too blurry by enabling the Sharpen JPEG Edges option in the Optimize panel's pop-up menu.

Smoothing

The more that a JPEG file is compressed, the "blockier" it becomes. As the compression increases, the JPEG algorithm throws out more and more similar pixels — after a certain point, the transitions and gradations are lost and areas become flat color blocks.

Fireworks' Smoothing feature slightly blurs the overall image so that stray pixels resulting from the compression are less noticeable. The Smoothing scale in the Optimize panel runs from zero to eight. Smoothing offers two benefits: It reduces the blockiness that is sometimes evident with JPEG compression, and it also slightly decreases file size.

Just as images with lots of straight lines or text benefit from the Sharpen JPEG Edges setting, Smoothing works best for images with lots of curves and generally smooth shapes.

Progressive

To most, Progressive JPEG is seen only as an incremental display option for JPEGs, similar to Interlaced for the GIF format. The Progressive JPEG option on the Optimize panel's pop-up menu is more than that though: It actually enables a different compression algorithm—a second generation one—that often offers lower file sizes at the equivalent quality of the original JPEG compression. The Progressive JPEG format was developed by Netscape, but has won the support of recent browser versions from Microsoft, as well.

Note Although Internet Explorer displays Progressive JPEG images, it displays them without the progressive look of developing as they download. They appear to the user to be regular JPEG images.

In practice, I find that enabling the Progressive JPEG option often (but not always) gives me a smaller file size. For me, choosing this option generally depends on whether the client prefers to see the images slowly develop as they download or prefers them to download completely and appear as a finished image.

PNG 32 and 24

As a Web format, PNG is still in its infancy—well, maybe early childhood—as far as general browser acceptance is concerned. The PNG format holds great promise for Web graphics. Combining the best of both worlds, PNG has lossless compression, like GIF, and is capable of millions of colors, like JPEG. Moreover, PNG offers an interlace scheme that appears much more quickly than either GIF or JPEG, as well as transparency support that is far superior to both other formats.

One valuable aspect of the PNG format makes the display of PNG pictures appear more uniform across various computer platforms. Generally, graphics made on a PC look brighter on a Macintosh, and Mac-made images seem darker on a PC. PNG includes *gamma correction* capabilities that alter the image, depending on the computer used by the viewer.

Until recently, the various browsers supported PNG only through plug-ins. After PNG was endorsed as a new Web graphic format by the World Wide Web Consortium (W3C), both Netscape and Microsoft 4.0 browser versions added native, inline support of the new format. Perhaps most importantly, however, Macromedia's Dreamweaver was among the first Web-authoring tools to offer native PNG support. Inserted PNG images preview in the document window as GIFs and JPEGs do. Then, Fireworks was introduced, which not only allows you to export PNG image, but uses PNG as its own format.

Although support for PNG is growing steadily, browser support currently is not widespread enough to warrant a total switchover to the PNG format. PNG is capable of many more features, such as Alpha Transparency, that are not fully in use by any major browser. Interestingly enough, Fireworks is way ahead of most other graphic programs in its support of PNG. Greg Roelofs, one of the developers of the PNG format, calls Fireworks, "the best PNG-supporting image editor available."

Unlike an Index Transparency color, which is either completely transparent or completely opaque, an Alpha Transparent color can be partially transparent — in fact, the transparency can use as many as 256 gradations. This allows a 32-bit image to be easily composited with other images, meaning that although PNG is not yet the best choice for the browser, it is an excellent choice for creating graphics for use in multimedia presentations, such as Shockwave or Flash movies, where animated objects are often stacked on top of each other, or composited with different backgrounds. Director and Flash are also both happy to import your actual Fireworks PNG files, Fireworks header and all.

Caution The Fireworks native PNG format is considered an extended PNG format, because of the additional effects, text, and other data included in the header of each file. Other programs capable of generally displaying PNG files may show the basic Fireworks image, but won't be able to edit it in the same way. To display a file in PNG format on a Web page, specifying PNG as the format when you export is best, so that your PNG image lacks extra Fireworks information and is as small as possible.

Other formats

The issues that are involved in exporting a PNG 24 or PNG 32 image are the same as those for exporting a TIFF, BMP, or PICT (Macintosh only) image from Fireworks. Generally, this export is straightforward, involving only the Matte setting.

Working in the Export Preview

As convenient as optimizing and previewing images in Fireworks' workspace is, you may sometimes find that you want to access all the export features in one centralized location. Fireworks' Export Preview dialog box (see Figure 30-24) is just the place, and offers some extra export options that are unavailable in the workspace, to boot.

The three tabbed panels in the Export Preview dialog box are as follows:

- **Options:** The primary panel for optimizing your image. The file format, bit-depth, compression, transparency, and other preferences are selected here. All color control — such as locking, editing, and deleting colors — is handled here, as well. The controls here are analogous to those found in the Optimize and Color Table panels.

- **File:** Controls two aspects of an exported file — scale and numeric cropping. The exported image can be resized either by a percentage or to a precise pixel measurement. The image can be cropped by entering X and Y coordinates for the upper-left corner, and width and height dimensions of the new area. In Fireworks, the exported image can also be cropped visually in the Preview area.

Chapter 30 ✦ **Exporting and Optimizing** 989

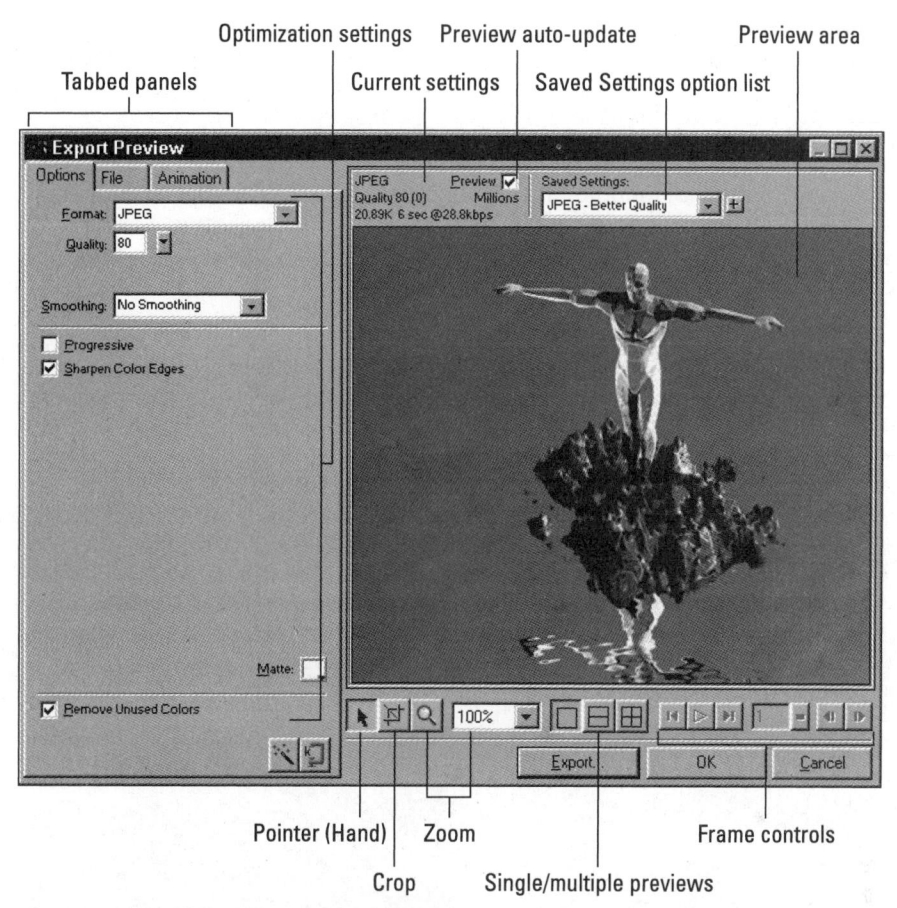

[Figure 30-24 screenshot of the Export Preview dialog box with labeled callouts: Tabbed panels, Optimization settings, Preview auto-update, Preview area, Current settings, Saved Settings option list, Pointer (Hand), Crop, Zoom, Single/multiple previews, Frame controls]

Figure 30-24: The Export Preview dialog box centralizes Fireworks' export features, and offers a few special features of its own.

✦ **Animation:** Contains all the settings for running an animated GIF, including the frame delay, disposal method, and looping preferences. Many of these options are also available in the Frames panel when you're optimizing in the workspace.

The always-visible Preview area provides a visual reference to compare different settings, and also allows you to visually crop the image. Also included are a panning tool (the Pointer), a Zoom tool (the magnifying glass), and a VCR-like control for playing an animation or other multiframe file. You may experience some *déjà vu* as you look around the Export Preview dialog box. Many of the controls are the same or very similar to those you use when optimizing in the workspace, and with good reason. There's no need to learn the Export Preview dialog box from scratch.

As previously mentioned, the Export Preview dialog box does contain some additional, unique export features, such as cropping and scaling exported images.

Cropping

The Export Area tool found on the Tools panel might seem a logical place to define an export area within the document window, but using the Export Area tool is only a first step to exporting an image with the Export Preview dialog box. In other words, although the Export Area tool is used in the document window, it's not part of the document window's in-place preview or export.

You can export a cropped version of a document by outlining an area with the Export Area tool and double-clicking that area to open the Export Preview dialog box, or you can simply open the Export Preview dialog box directly and then crop your image in its preview. When you initiate a cropping session in the Export Preview dialog box by clicking the Export Area button in the Preview area, the familiar dashed cropping outline surrounds the image, as shown in Figure 30-25. The eight handles are used to narrow the exported area. The original image is not permanently cropped or altered in any way.

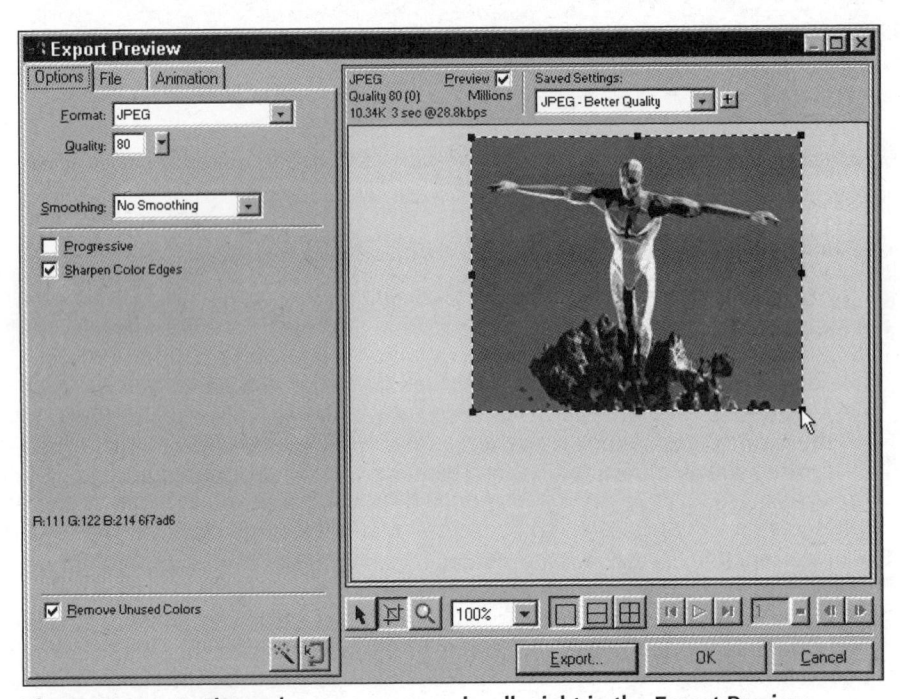

Figure 30-25: In Fireworks, you can crop visually right in the Export Preview dialog box.

Note: Unlike the regular Crop tool in the document window, you can't use the Export Area tool to expand the boundaries of the canvas.

If the File tab is displayed in the Export Preview while you're cropping, the X and Y coordinates of the upper-left corner of your exported area, as well as the width and height dimensions, are visible. The numeric cropping information is updated each time after a cropping handle is dragged to a new position. Alternatively, you can adjust the visual cropping precisely by entering values in the appropriate Export Area text boxes.

Tip: You can also crop an image by selecting an area in the document window with the Export Area tool (the camera on the flyout under the Pointer tool) and double-clicking the area. The Export Preview opens, and you can export your cropped image without affecting the original.

To crop an image visually, follow these steps:

1. Choose either the Export Area tool beneath the Preview window(s), or the Export Area option on the File tab. An outline with cropping handles appears around the image.
2. Drag the handles to a new position so that only the area you want to export is displayed.
3. Choose any other tool (Pointer or Zoom), or click either the Set Defaults or the Next button to accept the new cropped area.

To crop an image numerically, follow these steps:

1. From the File tab, select the Export Area option.
2. Select a new upper-left coordinate by entering new values in the X and/or Y text boxes, and press Tab to accept the changed value.
3. Select a new image size by entering new values in the W (Width) and H (Height) text boxes, and press Tab to accept the changed value.

Both cropping methods — visual and numeric — work together as well as separately. While viewing the File panel, select the Export Area tool and crop the image visually. When you release the mouse button, the numeric values automatically update. Similarly, change the numeric values, and the visual display is redrawn.

Scaling exported images

It might seem redundant to note that "Web graphics come in all shapes and sizes" — except it's also true to say that the *same* Web graphic often comes in different shapes and sizes. Reusing graphic elements is a very key design strategy in product branding in most media, and the technique is especially useful on the Web. Fireworks makes it very easy to export resized or cropped graphics from a master file, through the Export Preview dialog box.

Scaling controls are under the File tab in the Export Preview dialog box. You can resize a graphic by specifying either a percentage or an exact pixel size. By default, all rescaling is constrained to the original height-to-width ratio — however, you can disable the Constrain option to alter one dimension separately from the other.

To resize an image, follow these steps:

1. From the Export Preview dialog box, select the File tab.
2. To rescale an image by percentage, use the % slider, or enter a value directly into the % text box.

    The % slider's range is from 1 percent to 200 percent, but you can enter any value in the text box.

3. To resize an image to an exact dimension, enter a figure in the W (Width) and/or H (Height) text box.

    If the Constrain option is selected, enter a value in only one of the dimension text boxes and press Tab. The other dimension will be calculated for you according to the image's original height-to-width ratio.

4. To alter the height-to-width ratio, deselect Constrain and perform Step 3.

Tip

One of my favorite image optimization techniques is to scale an image to 50 percent of its size upon export and then place it in an HTML page at double size; doubling the width and height attributes of the `img` tag. The effects of this are usually noticeable, but often not objectionable, especially for flat color images. One thing's for sure: no faster way exists to halve the weight of an exported document. Experiment with this technique and see whether it works for you.

Using the Export Wizards

Fireworks' export options are very full-featured and can certainly be overwhelming if you're new to Web graphics. If you're not even sure how best to begin optimizing your image, let one of Fireworks' Export Wizards guide you. In addition to the original Export Wizard, which is very helpful for selecting the appropriate file format, Fireworks introduces the Export to Size Wizard, to meet those absolute file-size limits.

If you are ready to export, but don't know where to start, bring up Fireworks' Export Wizard, which not only helps you to determine the correct file format best suited to the graphic's purpose, but it also provides you with an alternative in certain cases. For this reason, seasoned Web designers can also use the Export Wizard to get quickly to a jumping-off place for further optimization.

Regardless of the selection that the Export Wizard makes for you, it always presents you with a visual display through the Export Preview dialog box, covered extensively earlier in this chapter. Feel free to either accept the recommendations of the Export Wizard as is — and click the Next button to complete the operation — or tweak the settings first before you proceed.

The Export Wizard has three primary uses:

- To help you select an export format
- To offer suggestions to optimize your image after you select an export format
- To recommend export modes that will reduce a graphic to a specified file size

To use the Export Wizard to select an export format, follow these steps:

1. Choose File ⇨ Export Wizard.

    The initial screen of the Export Wizard appears, as shown in Figure 30-26.

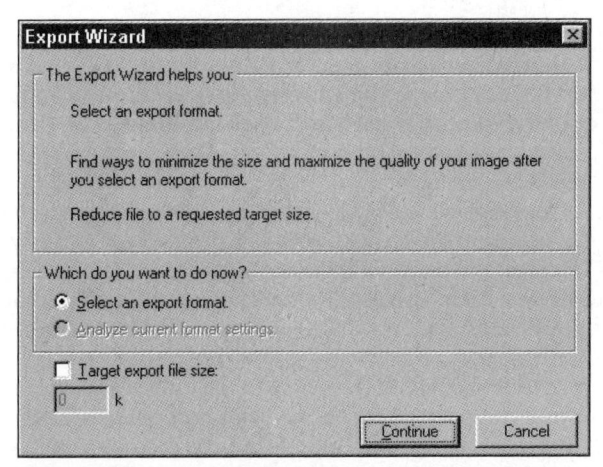

Figure 30-26: The Export Wizard provides a good launchpad for export selections.

2. With the "Select an export format" option selected, click Continue.

3. The next screen of the Export Wizard appears and offers four choices for the graphic's ultimate destination:

    - **The Web:** Restricts the export options to the most popular Web formats, GIF and JPEG.

    - **An image-editing application:** Selects the best format for continuing to edit the image in another program, such as Photoshop. Generally, Fireworks selects the TIFF format.

- **Desktop publishing application:** Selects the best print format, typically TIFF.

- **Dreamweaver:** The same as The Web option, restricts the export options to the most popular Web formats—GIF and JPEG.

Note: If your graphic uses frames, the Export Wizard asks instead whether your file is to be exported as an Animated GIF, a JavaScript button rollover, or a single image file.

4. Click Continue after you make your choice.

    Fireworks presents its analysis of your image, with suggestions on how to narrow the selection further, if more than one export choice is recommended.

Caution: If you select Animated GIF as your destination for your multiframe image, you must select the resulting Preview window to display the details in the Options panel.

5. Click Exit to open the Export Preview dialog box and complete the export operation.

If you choose either The Web or Dreamweaver for your graphic's export destination, Fireworks presents you with two options for comparison: a GIF and a JPEG. The file in the upper Preview window is the smallest file size. Fireworks is fairly conservative in this aspect of the Export Wizard and does not attempt to seriously reduce the file size at the cost of image quality.

If you would like to limit the file size while selecting an export format, select the "Target export file size" option on the Export Wizard's first screen. After you enable this option, you need to enter a file size value in the adjacent text box. File size is always measured in kilobytes. After you enter a file size, click Continue for Fireworks to calculate the results.

When Fireworks attempts to fit a graphic into a particular file size, it exports the image up to 12 times to find the best size with the least compression. Although it's usually very fast, this process can take several minutes to complete with a large graphic. Again, for graphics intended for the Web, Fireworks presents two choices—both at, or under, your specified target size.

In addition to specifying a file size through the Export Wizard, you can choose the Optimize to Size Wizard by clicking the button on the Options tab of the Export Preview dialog box. The Optimize to Size Wizard opens a simple dialog box that asks for the specified file size. The major difference between this wizard and the Target export file size option on the Export Wizard is that the Optimize to Size Wizard works only with the current format—no alternative choices are offered. Consequently, the Optimize to Size Wizard is faster, but it's intended more for the intermediate-to-advanced user who understands the differences between file formats.

Examining Additional Export Options

The vast majority of the time graphics are exported from Fireworks as single images, or as an HTML document with separate image slices, or as a Dreamweaver Library item. However, Fireworks also offers several other export options. You can export the following:

- Fireworks layers, frames, or slices as Cascading Style Sheet (CSS) layers in an HTML document for use in Dynamic-HTML-capable Web browsers
- Fireworks layers or slices as an HTML document for easy import into Macromedia Director
- The layers of a Fireworks document as separate image files
- Fireworks frames as separate image files
- The four frames of a rollover button as an Image Well format image used by Lotus Domino Designer
- Vector artwork as a Flash movie
- Vector artwork in Adobe Illustrator format
- Your complete Fireworks document as a multi-layer Photoshop document, suitable for further editing in Photoshop

All of these additional export methods are grouped in the Save as type (Save As on the Mac) option list in the Export dialog box, as shown in Figure 30-27. To display the Export dialog box, choose File ⇨ Export.

Tip Regardless of which type of export operation you undertake, the current settings in the Optimize panel determine the image file format and other settings where applicable.

Cross-Reference The items HTML and Images and Dreamweaver Library on the Export dialog box's Save as Type option list are covered in Chapter 34.

Exporting as CSS layers

The term *layers* is used quite often in the Web graphics field. To the Photoshop user, a "layer" is a division capable of holding a single graphic element. In Fireworks, a "layer" is a useful organizational tool that can hold any number of objects. In Dynamic HTML and in Web-authoring tools such as Dreamweaver, a "layer" is a type of container that can be precisely positioned, hidden, or displayed — or flown across the screen with JavaScript-driven animation. You can create these layers by using a standard known as Cascading Style Sheets (CSS). Fireworks enables you to save the contents of Fireworks layers, frames, or slices along with the CSS-based HTML. This facility enables you to achieve effects, such as the "flying" buttons in Figure 30-28.

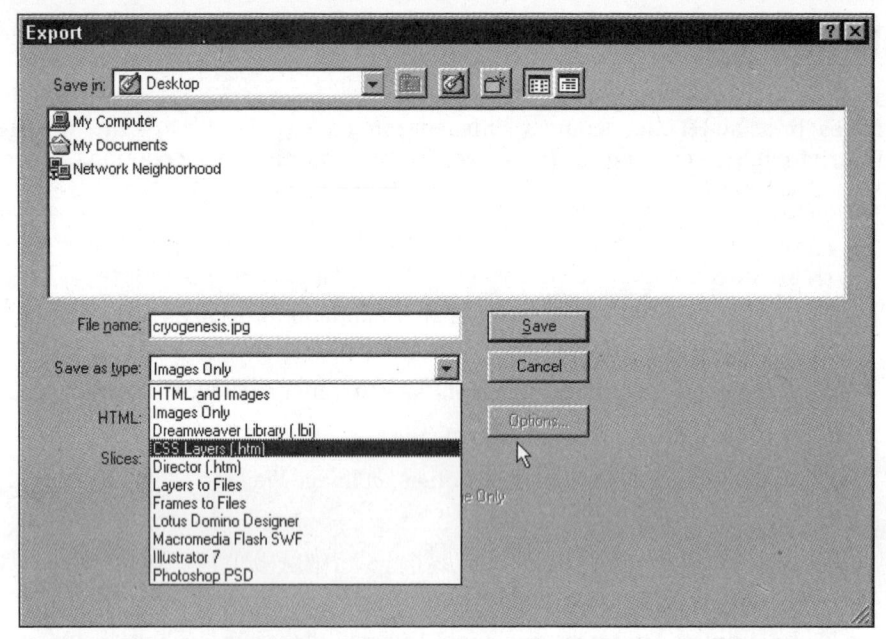

Figure 30-27: The Save as type (Save As) option list in the Export dialog box handles a variety of individual export situations.

To export Fireworks components as CSS layers, follow these steps:

1. Specify format and optimization settings in the Optimize panel.
2. Choose File ⇨ Export.

   The Export dialog box appears.

3. Choose CSS Layers from the Save as type (Save As) option list.

   Fireworks displays further options relating to exporting CSS Layers.

4. From the Source option list, select the Fireworks component to export as CSS Layers. The options are Fireworks Layers, Fireworks Frames, or Fireworks Slices.

5. Check the Trim Images checkbox to export the individual components on the smallest-sized canvas necessary.

   If Trim images is not selected, each exported file will be the same dimensions as the original image.

6. If you're exporting from Fireworks Frames, check the Current Frame Only checkbox to limit the export to the current frame only.

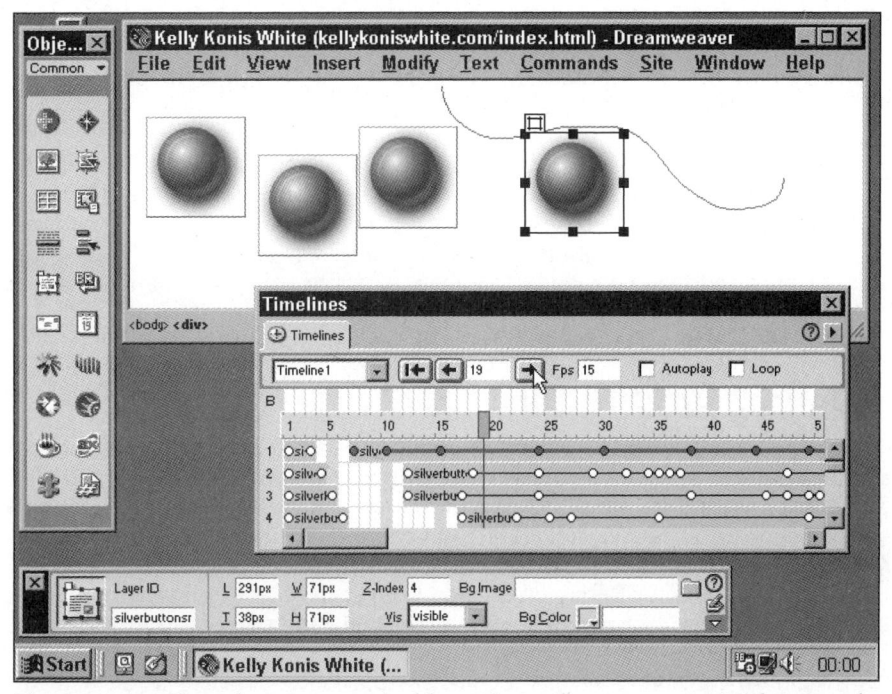

Figure 30-28: These buttons, exported from Fireworks as separate CSS layers and then animated in Dreamweaver, fly into place.

7. Check the Put Images in Subfolder checkbox to have Fireworks place the image files in their own folder.

   Click the Browse button to select a particular folder.

8. Click Save when you're done.

After you complete the export process, you'll have both the separate images and the HTML necessary to place each image in its own CSS layer. To use the layers on your Web page, you need to incorporate the generated code into your own Web page. You can accomplish this with any Web-authoring tool that allows you to access the HTML directly. Initially, the code appears overwhelming, but only the plain-English phrases that bracket it are important. In your favorite HTML or text editor, select the code from the line

```
<! ---------- BEGIN COPYING THE CODE HERE ---------->
```

and end your selection with the line

```
<! ---------- STOP COPYING THE CODE HERE ---------->
```

After you select the code, copy it to the clipboard and then open your working HTML page and paste the clipboard contents anywhere in the `<body>` section. Now, you can continue to manipulate the layers in any manner that you prefer in your Web-authoring program.

> **Note:** Dreamweaver users don't have to use the HTML Source window or any other text tool to copy and paste the Fireworks code. In Dreamweaver, simply find the Invisible Element symbols that enclose the layer code — you'll see a Dreamweaver HTML comment symbol on either side of the layer symbols. Select all of these symbols and then copy and paste them into your working document. You must have Invisible Elements enabled for this technique to work.

Exporting for Director

Fireworks is a key component of Macromedia's Director Shockwave Internet Studio, and as such, has developed some extra features that simplify creating and editing bitmaps for use in Director. Buttons and rollovers that you've created in Fireworks can be exported as images and HTML that can then be imported into Macromedia Director. Director does its part by converting the JavaScript-based Fireworks Behaviors into Director Behaviors. In addition, each object or layer from Fireworks becomes a Director cast member, with antialiasing and correct alpha transparency.

> **New Feature:** Although Fireworks' Director export was previously available as an add-on for Fireworks 3, it is included by default in Fireworks 4.

To export a Fireworks document for use in Director, follow these steps:

1. Choose File ⇨ Export.

   The Export dialog box appears.

2. Select Director (.htm) from the Save as type (Save As) option list.

3. Select either Fireworks Frames or Fireworks Layers from the Source option list.

4. Select the Trim images option to export the individual components on the smallest-sized canvas necessary.

5. Click Save when you're ready.

> **Caution:** Director 7 or above is required in order to import the Fireworks-generated HTML. A Director Xtra may also be required to enable this feature. Consult your Director documentation and/or Macromedia's Web site.

Exporting files

Occasionally, you may want to break up the component layers or frames of your Fireworks document into separate files. Perhaps you need to reuse some of these elements in another part of the Web site, or maybe you want to process the files in another application before reintegrating them in Fireworks. Whatever the reason, Fireworks provides a fairly straightforward method for generating separate graphic files for almost any situation.

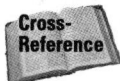

Cross-Reference: Chapter 33 discusses exporting a single slice as an image file.

To export a Fireworks element as a separate file, follow these steps:

1. Specify format and optimization settings in the Optimize panel.
2. Choose File ⇨ Export.

   The Export dialog box appears.

3. To export frames as files, select Frames to Files from the Save as type (Save As) option list. Alternatively, to export layers as files, select Layers to Files.
4. Select the Trim images option to export the individual components on the smallest-sized canvas necessary.

   If Trim images is not selected, each exported file will be the same dimensions as the original image.

5. Click Save when you're ready.

Tip: You can control which frames or layers are exported by turning off their visibility in their respective panels. The visibility is controlled by the Eye symbol next to each item name. The frame or layer will not be exported if it is not visible when you choose the Export command.

Exporting as Image Wells

Image Wells are used by Lotus Domino Designer to create rollover effects. Just as Fireworks uses frames to separate the different rollover states — up, over, down, and overdown — Domino Designer uses Image Wells. An Image Well is a single graphic with each rollover state side by side, separated by a single pixel vertical line, as the example in Figure 30-29 shows.

Note: Image Wells are similar to the four state rollovers in Fireworks, but not exactly the same. The last two states — over and overdown — are reversed. Fireworks, however, understands this difference and exports your Image Well so that it will work correctly in Lotus Domino Designer.

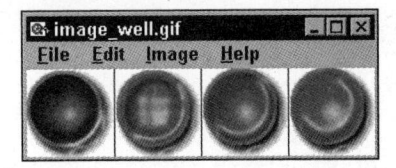

Figure 30-29: The final output of an Image Well export is used by Lotus Domino Designer to create rollover button effects.

This feature is best used to convert your existing multiframe images to Image Wells for use as rollovers. To export a graphic as an Image Well, follow these steps:

1. Specify format and optimization settings in the Optimize panel.
2. Choose File ➪ Export.

   The Export dialog box appears.
3. Select Lotus Domino Designer from the Save as type (Save As) option list.
4. Select Fireworks Frames, Fireworks Layers, or Fireworks slices from the Source option list to create an Image Well from frames, layers, or slices, respectively.
5. Select the Trim images option to export the individual components on the smallest-sized canvas necessary.

   If Trim images is not selected, each exported file will be the same dimensions as the original image.
6. Click Save when you're ready.

Fireworks saves your document as an Image Well, in the image format specified in the Optimize panel.

Exporting vectors

You can choose to export the vector shapes in your document as either a Flash SWF movie or an Adobe Illustrator document. The Flash format can be viewed in the majority of Web browsers as-is, and the Illustrator format can be imported into the majority of vector drawing applications, such as Adobe Illustrator and Macromedia FreeHand.

It's important to keep in mind that although Fireworks works with vector lines, it uses vector lines only as a substructure or "skeleton" for bitmaps and bitmap-based effects, such as bevels and drop shadows. Exporting this vector skeleton is a useful feature, but keep in mind that the exported objects will often bear only a passing resemblance to their Fireworks-native counterparts, as shown in Figure 30-30.

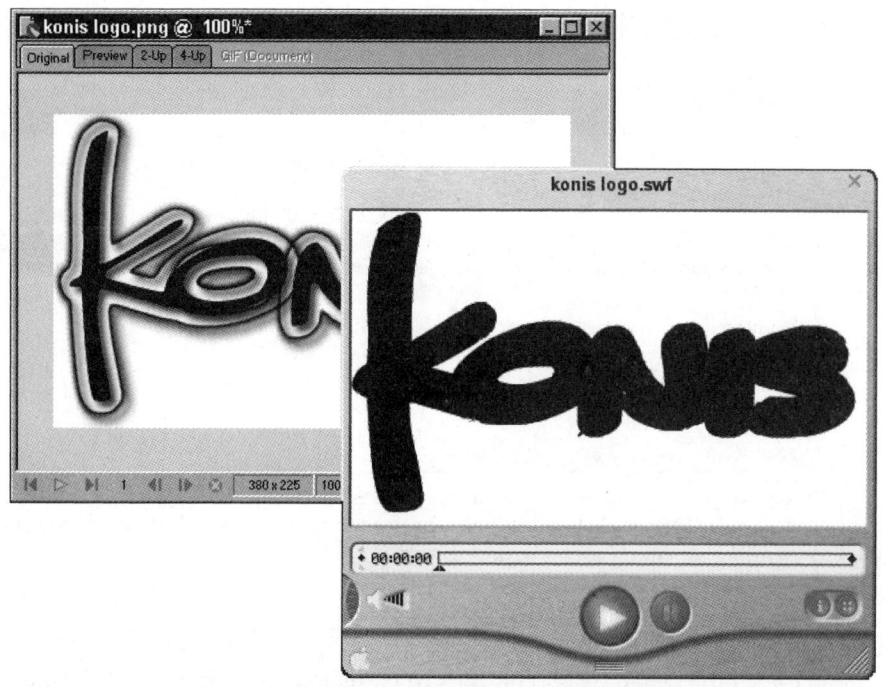

Figure 30-30: The object in Fireworks (top left) is a vector shape, but much of its look comes from Fireworks' stroke settings and Live Effects. After exporting as a Flash movie, shown bottom right, the object is expressed only in vector lines and its appearance changes dramatically.

To export vector shapes from Fireworks, follow these steps:

1. Choose File ➪ Export.

   Fireworks displays the Export dialog box.

2. To export as Flash, choose Macromedia Flash SWF from the Save as type (Save As) option list. Alternatively, to export in Illustrator format, choose Illustrator 7.

   Caution Fireworks Illustrator export is Adobe Illustrator 7 compatible, and may not import correctly into applications that expect a previous or later version of the Illustrator format.

3. Click the Options button to specify format-specific options.

   Fireworks displays the options dialog box for the vector type you are exporting, as shown in Figure 30-31.

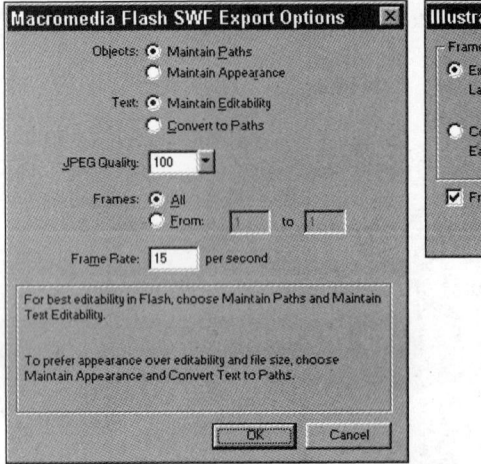

Figure 30-31: Specify export options for a vector format in the Macromedia Flash SWF Export Options dialog box (left), or the Illustrator Export Options dialog box, depending on which vector export format you choose.

4. If you are exporting as Macromedia Flash SWF, set the appropriate options:
    - Set the Objects radio buttons to Paths to export paths, or to Maintain Appearance to export as JPEG bitmaps. If you choose Maintain Appearance, set the JPEG Quality slider to specify the quality of the JPEGs.
    - Choose to maintain text, or convert text to paths with the Text radio buttons.
    - Export all frames, or a range of frames with the Frames option.
    - If necessary, change the target frame rate in the Frame Rate box. Otherwise, leave it at its default of 15.

    Click OK when you're done.

5. If you are exporting Illustrator 7, set the appropriate options:
    - Choose to export the current frame only, or to export Fireworks frames as Illustrator layers.
    - If you are going to import your file into Macromedia FreeHand, make sure the FreeHand 8 Compatible checkbox is checked.

    Click OK when you're done.

6. Click Save in the Export dialog box when you're done.

Your document's vector shapes are exported.

If you have the standalone Flash Player, double-clicking your Flash SWF file will open it for viewing. If not, you can also view Flash movies in a Web browser that's equipped with the Flash Player plug-in, or in the QuickTime Player.

If you exported as an Illustrator 7 document, open this document with Illustrator, FreeHand, Flash, or another vector art application.

Exporting Photoshop documents

Exporting your Fireworks document in the Photoshop format enables you to open and edit your Fireworks work in Photoshop, while maintaining the editability of individual objects, text objects, and Live Effects. You can later import the Photoshop document into Fireworks again for further editing and optimization. This feature is invaluable if you use both applications, or if your workgroup is made up of a mix of Fireworks and Photoshop users.

New Feature Photoshop format export is new in Fireworks 4.

To export a Fireworks document as a Photoshop document, follow these steps:

1. Choose File ⇨ Export.

   The Export dialog box appears.

2. Select Photoshop PSD from the Save as type (Save As) option list.

Tip PSD refers to PhotoShop Document, and also to the typical filename extension for Photoshop documents: ".psd".

3. From the Settings option list, choose one of the following:

   - Maintain Editability over Appearance strictly converts Fireworks elements to their corresponding Photoshop elements, but may result in your work looking slightly different after it's opened in Photoshop. This option is the default, and the best one for most situations.

   Caution Keeping at least a backup of your original Fireworks document is always a good idea, even after exporting to Photoshop format. If you choose any option other than Maintain Editability over Appearance, though, be absolutely certain to keep your original Fireworks document. The other export options all result in editable information being flattened or thrown away.

   - Maintain Fireworks Appearance keeps your Fireworks objects as Photoshop layers, but renders Live Effects and text objects as bitmap images, sacrificing editability for the cause of strictly maintaining the look of your work.

- Smaller Photoshop File converts Fireworks layers to Photoshop layers, flattening all the objects on each Fireworks layer.
- Custom enables you to choose specifically whether to maintain or flatten layers, and whether to maintain or render text and effects.

4. Click Save when you're ready.

Fireworks exports a Photoshop document, ready to be opened in Photoshop.

Caution Importing files with more than 100 layers requires Photoshop 6 or above. Flatten or remove some objects or layers from your Fireworks document before export if you are using Photoshop 5.5 or earlier.

Summary

Every graphic created or edited in Fireworks is eventually exported for use on the Web or in another application. Reducing file size is a key facet of making Web graphics, so Fireworks offers a wide variety of export options. Keep the following points in mind as you optimize and export images:

✦ Maintaining at least two versions of any file is considered the best practice: one version in the Fireworks PNG format as a master copy, and a second version in whatever format you've exported for use on the Web.

✦ The primary goal of an export operation for the Web is to create the best-looking image with the smallest file size. This is called optimizing a graphic.

✦ Fireworks provides access to optimization and export options directly in the workspace, through the Optimize, Color Table, and Frames panels, and with the multiple tabs of the document window. Alternately, you can choose to use the Export Preview dialog box, which you open by choosing File ➪ Export Preview.

✦ Fireworks offers up to four comparison views of an image being exported, so that you can quickly judge appearance alongside the displayed file size and approximate download time.

✦ The two major formats for the Web — GIF and JPEG — are each best used for different types of images. The GIF format is good for graphics with flat color, for which transparency is important, such as logos. The JPEG format works best with continuous-tone images, such as photographs.

✦ Another format, PNG, is considered the heir apparent to GIF, but still doesn't have enough support to warrant widespread usage. The PNG format has many advantages, such as full alpha transparency and gamma correction, which ameliorate image differences on different platforms. These are currently poorly supported by common Web browsers, however.

✦ Images can be easily — and precisely — scaled and cropped during the export operation, by using the Export Preview dialog box.

✦ Fireworks' advanced color control allows you to lock or replace any color in an indexed palette.

✦ Fireworks offers expert export guidance in the form of the Export Wizard.

✦ In addition to the standard image export, Fireworks can also export components of an image, such as layers, frames, or slice objects, in several different ways. Fireworks can even export just the vector shapes of your Fireworks objects as Macromedia Flash SWF or Illustrator documents.

✦ Fireworks can export to the Adobe Photoshop format, while maintaining the editability of individual elements.

In the next chapter, you find out how to maintain a consistent look and feel for your Web graphics through Fireworks Styles.

✦ ✦ ✦

Working with Fireworks Styles

In This Chapter

Introducing styles

Working with the Styles panel

Making your own styles

Maintaining a styles library

Fireworks technique: Isolating patterns or textures from styles

Although not obvious to the beginning designer, Web graphics is as much about repetition as it is creation. After you establish a particular look and feel, that theme — the palette, fonts, effects, and more — are often carried through Web page after Web page. Several reasons exist for this repetition:

- Consistency of approach is one of the fundamental tenets of design work.
- For commercial sites, a consistent look and feel often ties in with the particular marketing message or branding that is being pursued.
- With regard to the Internet, repetition of graphic elements aids visitors in the navigation of a Web site: If navigation buttons look the same from page to page, users can quickly learn how to move around the site — even on their first visit.

However, no matter how many reasons exist declaring that repetition is good, it can also be mind-numbing drudgery. Fireworks rescues Web designers from repetitive drudgery by offering a marvelous time- and work-saver known as *styles*. By using styles, you can easily apply the overall look and feel to any selected object. A single style can contain a variety of user-definable settings, and styles are always available as you move from document to document. Moreover, Macromedia designed styles to be very portable — you can import and export them as a group. This facility enables you, as a working Web designer, to keep different style files for different clients. Styles are, without a doubt, a major boost in Web productivity.

Understanding Styles

A Fireworks object is potentially composed of several separate formatting choices: a path, a stroke, a fill, and one or more Live Effects. Each of these elements can be broken down further; for example, a stroke consists of a particular stroke type set to a specific color. Duplicating all the individual settings, one by one, that are necessary to establish a custom look would be extremely time-intensive and error-prone. Although you can copy an object to the clipboard and then paste its formatting onto another object, this requires that you first have a suitable object available to copy. Rather than keep example objects around just in case you want to recreate their look, Fireworks allows you to separate the appearance of an object from the object itself, and save that appearance as a style.

Fireworks provides a very novel, graphical method of maintaining and presenting styles: the Styles panel, shown in Figure 31-1. Acting as if a formatting library, the Styles panel enables you to create, import, export, delete, and otherwise manage styles.

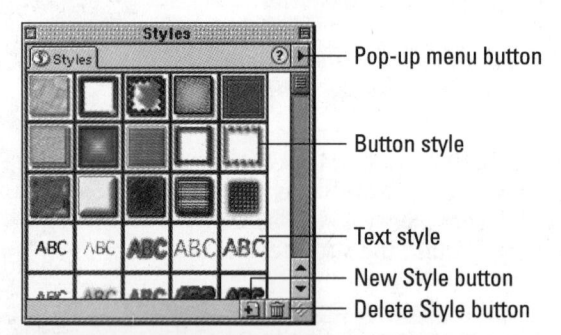

Figure 31-1: Fireworks includes a default palette of styles, available through the Styles panel.

Styles are visually divided in the Styles panel with two different types of icons: button styles and text styles. The only difference between the two is that a text style contains additional information: a typeface, size, and style, or any combination of the three. Button styles are depicted as squares and text styles are displayed as the letters ABC, but both preview the appearance that their style contains. Fireworks comes with 20 button styles and 10 text styles in its built-in default collection (which can be restored at any time) and over 300 more styles are available on the Fireworks CD-ROM, or on the Web at www.macromedia.com/software/fireworks/download/styles. If you think the default styles are a little bland for your taste, be sure to check out the wide variety of additional styles.

On the CD-ROM: You'll find even more styles to add to your collection.

Even though the Styles panel is divided between the button and text style types, you can apply both to any Fireworks object. In other words, you can apply button styles to text objects, and text styles to path objects. Any unusable style information (such as font color for a path object) is disregarded. You might think of button styles as styles, and text styles as "styles-plus;" the extra information they contain doesn't stop them from being a perfectly good choice for a button or other graphic.

> **Caution** The term *styles* is commonly used in computer programs. Unlike the styles you typically find in word processing, Fireworks styles do not maintain a link between the original style and the applied objects. If you edit a style, any objects that the style was previously applied to remain unaffected.

Applying Styles

To apply a style, you must first access the Styles panel, which you can open in any one of several ways:

- ✦ Choose Window ⇨ Styles.
- ✦ Use the keyboard shortcut, Shift+F11 (Shift+F11).
- ✦ Click the Styles tab, if the Styles panel is docked behind another, visible panel.

After the Styles panel is available, actually applying the style is very straightforward: simply select the object you want to apply the style to and then click a style from the Styles panel. If you don't like the results, you can select another style. You can even duplicate the object and apply several styles, to select the best option, as shown in Figure 31-2.

> **Caution** Applying one style overrides another style only if both styles affect the same settings. Styles that contain every possible setting can be mixed and matched freely because they will always override the previously applied style. However, applying multiple styles that contain only a few of the possible settings — just a fill and stroke color, or just an effect, for example — will lead to your object having a mix of those styles. Suppose that you apply a style that only contains a green fill and then apply another style that only contains a drop shadow effect. Your object will now have a green fill and a drop shadow.

After you apply a style, the object remains completely independent of the style, and you can adjust all the settings on the various panels — Stroke, Fill, Effects, and Text — to customize the object. Regardless of what changes you make to a styled object, the style itself is unaltered.

Figure 31-2: Applying different styles to the same object gives you a wide range of choices.

Creating New Styles

Although using the standard styles — or any of those included on the Fireworks CD-ROM — is a quick way to establish a consistent look and feel, you may not be able to find the exact style that you want. The real power in Fireworks styles comes from the ability to create, save, and use your own styles. The look of any object — the stroke, fill, effect, or text settings — can be converted to a style and easily used over and over again, by you or a colleague.

Imagine you've created an object — a button, say — with a finely tuned stroke setting, a perfect fill color, and five complex effects modifications with a mix of Fireworks' built-in drop shadows and bevels and third-party Photoshop plug-ins such as Kai Power Tools or Alien Skin's Eye Candy. The entire process might take five minutes to recreate, but instead of doing so, select your object and create a style from it. Image or path objects can look incredibly textured and fussed-over in the time it takes to apply a style. It's worth noting again that these effects remain completely editable on each new object they're applied to.

Cross-Reference

For more about Live Effects and Xtras, see Chapter 28.

To create a new style, follow these steps:

1. Select the object upon which you want to base the style.

Tip

If you want to base your new style on a style you already have, apply the style to your object, modify the object's formatting accordingly, and then continue with Step 2.

2. If the Styles panel is hidden, choose Window ⇨ Styles to view it, or use the key shortcut Shift+F11 (Shift+F11), or click the Styles panel's tab if it is docked behind another, visible window.

3. Click the New Styles button at the bottom of the Styles panel. The New Style dialog box appears, as shown in Figure 31-3.

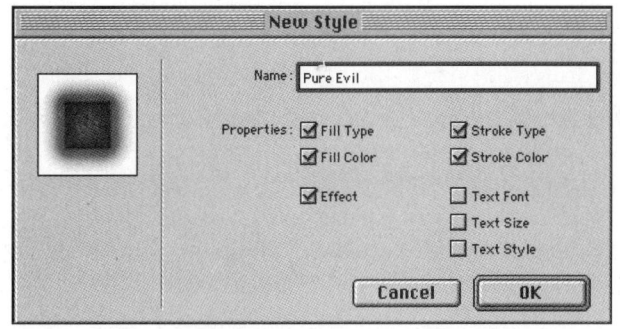

Figure 31-3: Create a new style by selecting available options in the New Style dialog box.

4. Enter a unique name for your new style in the Name text box.

Caution

Fireworks automatically names new styles Style 1, Style 2, Style 3, and so on, which it considers to be different than the Style 01, Style 02, Style 03, and so on with which its built-in styles are named. You can rename your new style by deleting the suggested name and entering your own choice. Be aware, however, that Fireworks does not check for conflicting names, so you can easily end up with two or more styles with the same name. I find it's best to make very descriptive names for the styles I create, so that they're easy to recall later, and harder to duplicate accidentally. If you hover your mouse over a style's icon in the Styles panel, Fireworks will show you the style's name at the bottom of the panel.

5. Select which of the available style settings you want to save with your style. Available settings are the following:

- **Fill Type:** Stores the Fill category (Solid, Gradient, Web Dither, or Pattern), the name of the gradient or Pattern, the edge settings (including the Amount of Feather, if applicable), and all the texture settings (name, degree, and transparency).

- **Fill Color:** Stores the Fill colors for Solid fills. For Gradient, Web Dither, and Pattern fills, the colors are stored with the Fill Type option.

- **Stroke Type:** Stores the category, name of stroke, all stroke stamp information (even if customized through the Edit Stroke command), the edge softness, the stroke size, and the texture settings (name and amount of texture).

- **Stroke Color:** Stores the selection in the current object's Stroke color well.

- **Effect:** Stores all the settings for an object's Live Effect, whether single (Inner Bevel, Outer Bevel, Drop Shadow, Glow, or Emboss) or multiple.

- **Text Font:** Stores the name of the current font for a text object.

- **Text Size:** Stores the size of the current font for a text object.

- **Text Style:** Stores the style (bold, italic, and/or underline) for a text object.

6. Click OK when you're done.

For all the information that styles are capable of retaining, you should note that the following few items are *not* stored (although you might expect them to be):

✦ Although a style remembers gradients, Fireworks styles do not retain any gradient settings pertaining to modified Gradient Control handles, accessed through the Paint Bucket tool.

✦ None of the Text Style settings store any information on text spacing (kerning, leading, horizontal scale, or baseline shift), text alignment (horizontal, vertical, left, center, right, stretched, or direction), or antialias.

You should remember two points when you are creating and applying new styles. First, if a style does not affect a particular setting, that setting is left as is on the selected object. Second, a Stroke, Fill, or Effect set to None is as valid a setting as any other. For example, if the object on which you base your new style does not include a fill, but you've selected Fill Type on the Edit Style dialog box, any object to which this style is applied — whether it has a fill or not — will have the fill removed.

Managing Styles

Every time that you add a style, it stays available for every document opened in Fireworks. If you really become adept at using styles, you'll quickly begin to have a massive collection of styles — truly too much of a good thing. Fireworks offers several commands, mostly grouped under the Styles panel's pop-up menu, for managing your styles.

> **Tip** Before you start selecting styles in order to delete or modify them, make sure that you don't have any objects in your document selected, or selecting a style will apply that style to the object. Click the mouse in an empty area of the canvas, or choose Edit ⇨ Deselect, or use the keyboard shortcut Ctrl+D (Command+D).

You've seen how you can create a style by selecting the New Style button from the bottom of the Styles panel. Its obvious companion is the Delete Style button (the trash can) right next to it. To remove any unwanted style, select its icon in the Styles panel and choose the Delete Style button.

> **Tip** You can select multiple styles at the same time. Hold down Ctrl (Command) while you select Styles to add one at a time. Hold down Shift to select a range of adjacent styles; Fireworks will select the two styles you click on and every style along the shortest route between them. This selection method is more similar to a spreadsheet than a word processor. To select a row of styles, hold down Shift and click the first and last in the row. To add another row to your selection, keep holding Shift and click the last style in the second row. To add part of a row to your selection, switch to holding down Ctrl (Command) and add the final styles one by one. The same technique applies to selecting columns.

A total of seven commands are available in the Styles panel's pop-up menu, shown in Figure 31-4:

- **New Style:** Creates a new style based on the selected object. This command is identical to the New Style button.

- **Edit Style:** Opens the Edit Style dialog box, enabling you to select or deselect the setting options.

> **Tip** You can also access the Edit Style dialog box by double-clicking a style's icon in the Styles panel.

- **Delete Styles:** Removes a selected style or styles.

- **Import Styles:** Loads a new set of styles after the currently selected one. You must store styles in the Fireworks Styles format, and you can't import them from a Fireworks document, for example.

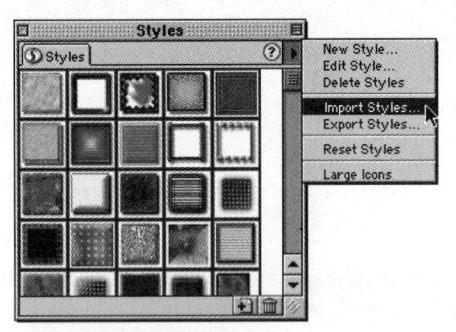

Figure 31-4: Manage your styles through the commands in the Styles panel's pop-up menu.

- ✦ **Export Styles:** Stores the currently selected style or styles in the Fireworks Styles format.
- ✦ **Resets Styles:** Removes any styles you have added to the Styles panel and reloads the default configuration of styles.
- ✦ **Large Icons:** Toggles between regular and large-sized icons. When checked, icons are displayed twice their normal size.

Earlier in this chapter, I showed you how to create and delete styles; the New Style and Delete Styles commands work in the same way as their respective buttons. Editing an existing style is also a familiar process. Choose Edit Style, and you are presented with the same options in the Edit Styles dialog box as when you create a new one. Just make any changes, click OK, and your revised style is ready to use.

> **Tip** The Edit Style command is also a good way to check what formatting options a particular style affects before applying it. Double-click the style or select it and choose Edit Style from the pop-up menu to see which formatting options are checked.

The Export Styles command opens a dialog box, shown in Figure 31-5. Fireworks offers to save your new file in its Styles folder under the name "Custom Styles.stl," ("Custom Styles" on the Macintosh) but you can change the name to anything else and store the file wherever you want (as long as you can find it later). If you use a Macintosh, the .stl filename extension is not necessary, but leaving it on keeps your style files cross-platform-ready, and will enable you to share your styles with Windows users or use them yourself on a Windows machine.

The Import Styles command opens a standard Open dialog box. Choose a style file and click Open to import it.

> **Tip** Mac users: If you receive a Fireworks style file from a Windows-using friend or download it unarchived from the Internet, it may not have a Mac OS Creator or Type and will appear with a blank icon. As long as it still has its .stl filename extension, though, Fireworks will recognize it and allow you to import and use it. If you want, you can use the File Exchange Control Panel or a utility such as File Buddy or FinderPop to give the file the proper creator of *MKBY* (Fireworks, of course) and type of *STYf*, which will restore its icon.

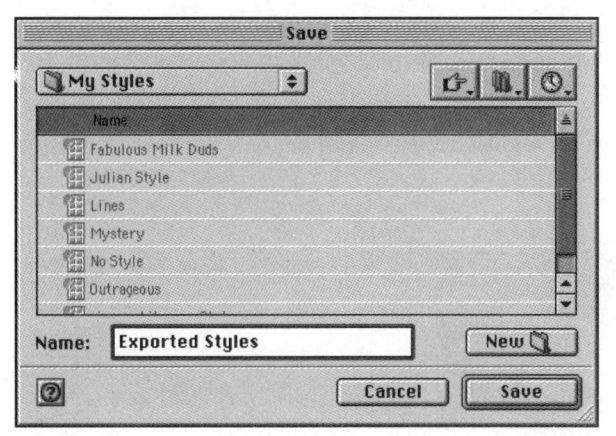

Figure 31-5: Export a collection of styles and save them as a Fireworks style file with the filename extension .stl.

As noted previously, when you import a set of Fireworks styles, all styles are inserted after the currently selected style. For this reason, I typically find it best to select the last currently loaded style before importing. You also can create a spacer or two — create a style from a plain object with no fill, stroke, or effects. The style icon will appear blank and acts to separate your imported styles from the standard ones.

> **On the CD-ROM**
>
> You'll find a style file called No Style.stl in the Configuration/Styles folder that contains only one style that applies a Fill, Stroke, and Effect of none. This makes a handy spacer and a quick, easy way to unformat an object before applying another style. You could also save this as the first or last style in your exported Style files to provide an easy-to-see start or finish.

The final two Styles panel commands, Reset Styles and Large Icons, are fairly self-explanatory. Reset Styles removes all styles currently in the Styles panel and reloads the standard set of styles in their place. Because this measure is fairly drastic, Fireworks asks for confirmation before proceeding. Selecting Large Icons displays the style icons at twice their standard size — they enlarge from 36 pixels square to 72. This feature is sometimes useful when trying to differentiate between two similar styles.

Fireworks Technique: Isolating Patterns and Textures from Styles

A close look at some of the styles that come with Fireworks — both the defaults and the extras found on the Fireworks CD-ROM — reveals several exciting Patterns and textures. On the CD you'll find a style — quite innocently named Style 37, and contained within text1-201.stl — that has an intriguing spotted Pattern, shown in

Figure 31-6. A quick check of the Fill panel reveals that a texture, called (appropriately) cow, is in use as part of the style. However, no such file exists in the Textures folder; so, where did it come from? The texture is actually embedded in the style.

> **Tip** Find text1-201.stl on the Fireworks CD-ROM at Goodies/Styles/Styles/text/text1-201.stl.

Figure 31-6: Examine the cow texture from Style 37. It works fine on a plain circle and also specifies 170pt Arial Black when applied to text.

Donna Casey, a Web designer whose work you can see at `www.n8vision.com`, uncovered a technique for extracting the embedded textures and Patterns that you may find in a style. Why would you do this? You might find that the Pattern and/or texture is, to your eye, better when combined with a different stroke or effects setting — or you might want to incorporate only the Pattern or texture in an image. This problem has two approaches. First, you could edit the style, removing all the options except for Fill Type. This is, at best, a partial solution. The Pattern/texture is still encased in the other pertinent settings; textures, for example, could be part of a Solid, Pattern, or Gradient Fill. To completely separate the texture or Pattern and then save it, follow these steps:

1. Draw a fairly large rectangle or square, approximately 500×500 pixels.

   The goal is to make the object large enough so that the pattern clearly repeats.

2. From the Styles panel, select the style whose texture or fill you want to isolate.

   The style is applied to the object.

3. From the Stroke panel, choose None in the Stroke category.

4. In the Effect panel, select None in the Effect category.

5. To retrieve a texture, make the following changes to the Fill panel:
   - Set the Fill category to Solid.
   - Set the Fill color to black.
   - Set the Amount of texture to 100%.

6. To retrieve a Pattern, set the Amount of texture to 0%.

7. Choose the Crop tool from the Toolbox.

8. Crop the object to encompass the repeating pattern.

   This is, by far, the hardest part; it might take several attempts to get it just right. It is a good idea is to save the file before you begin to crop the object. With most textures, the repeating pattern will actually be smaller than it might first appear.

9. When you finish cropping, save the file in either the Patterns or Textures folders in the Configuration folder within your Fireworks program folder.

Tip The Fireworks program folder is typically found at C:\Program Files\Macromedia\Fireworks 4 on Windows-based computers, and at Macintosh HD:Applications:Macromedia Fireworks 4: on the Mac.

10. Restart Fireworks to refresh the Pattern and texture lists.

Tip You can also use your new Pattern or texture without restarting Fireworks by choosing Other from the Pattern or texture list in the Fill panel and selecting your newly saved file.

Your new extricated Pattern or texture should now be available to you in the Stroke and Fill panels.

Summary

Styles are a major production boost, allowing you to easily build up a library of formatting choices and add a consistent look and feel to all of your graphics on a client-by-client or site-by-site basis. Styles are also a significant work-saver — rather than having to add individually all the characteristics that compose a particular look, you can add them all with one click of the Styles panel. The main points with regard to styles are:

- Styles are accessible through the Styles panel.
- A style may contain almost all the information for reproducing a graphic's stroke, fill, effect, and text settings.
- Unlike some other programs, such as Macromedia FreeHand, Fireworks styles do not retain a link to objects that use them.
- Any newly created style is available to all documents until the style is removed from the Styles panel.
- Styles can be edited, imported, exported, and otherwise managed through the commands found in the Styles panel's pop-up menu.
- A style can be "reverse engineered" to isolate the Pattern or texture that it contains.

In the next chapter, you find out how to use Symbols and Libraries to cut down on even more repetitive work.

✦ ✦ ✦

Using Symbols and Libraries

In This Chapter

Understanding symbols

Creating and modifying symbols

Modifying Instances

Working with buttons

Managing Libraries

Many Fireworks features are specifically designed to prevent duplication of effort on the part of the busy Web artist. Perhaps none more so than the symbols. In a nutshell, a *symbol* is an object that's been designated as a master copy and stored in a Symbol Library. Copies of a symbol, called *Instances*, retain a link to their symbol so that they can be modified as a group. Editing the symbol causes its Instances to inherit the changes.

This chapter begins with a discussion of the basics of using symbols, Instances, and Libraries in Fireworks. Later, you'll discover how to make, modify, and manage symbols, Instances, and Libraries.

Understanding Symbols and Instances

Symbols in Fireworks are like templates for single objects. The symbol itself is like a rubber stamp that you dip in ink. You can "stamp out" virtually unlimited copies of any symbol, called *Instances*. Instances are copies of symbols that retain a link to their parent symbol. Editing the symbol causes its Instances to inherit many of the changes, such as fill and stroke settings. On the other hand, Instances have some independent properties of their own: You can apply the Transform tools to them, add Live Effects, or alter opacity settings on an individual basis, as shown in Figure 32-1. From a design perspective, symbols and Instances enable you to maintain a common look without losing a feeling of variety.

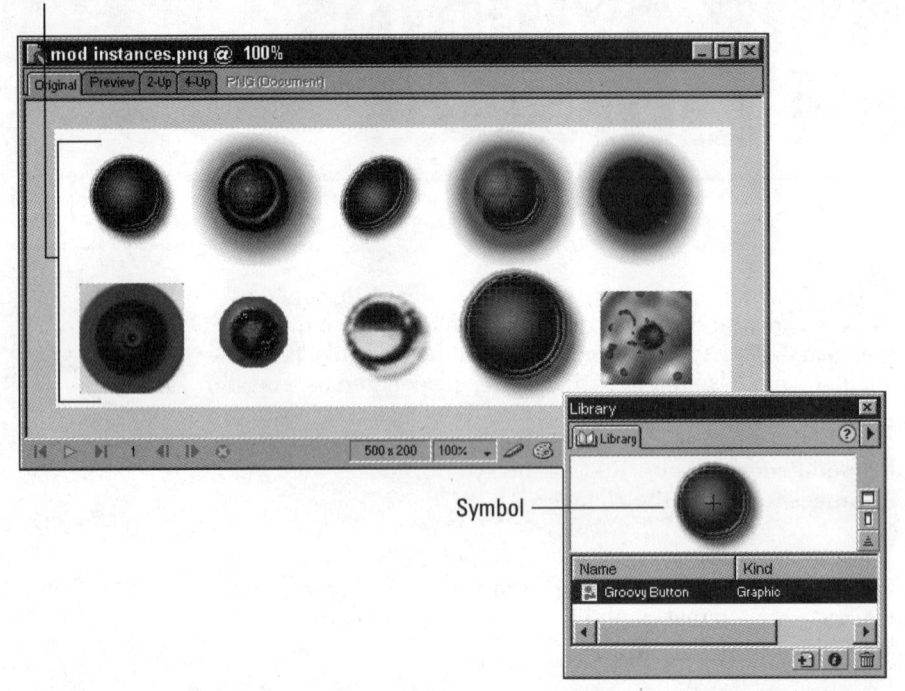

Figure 32-1: These are all Instances of the same symbol, with modifications made to scale, skew, opacity, and with Live Effects. The Instance at top left is unmodified and looks exactly like the parent symbol.

When you edit a symbol in the Symbol Editor, the link that its Instances have with the parent symbol causes them to inherit the changes, as shown in Figure 32-2. Fireworks automatically updates Instances to match their parent symbol as soon as you close the Symbol Editor. Note that any modifications that were made to the individual Instances — such as applying a Live Effect, Photoshop filter, or Transform tool — are unaffected.

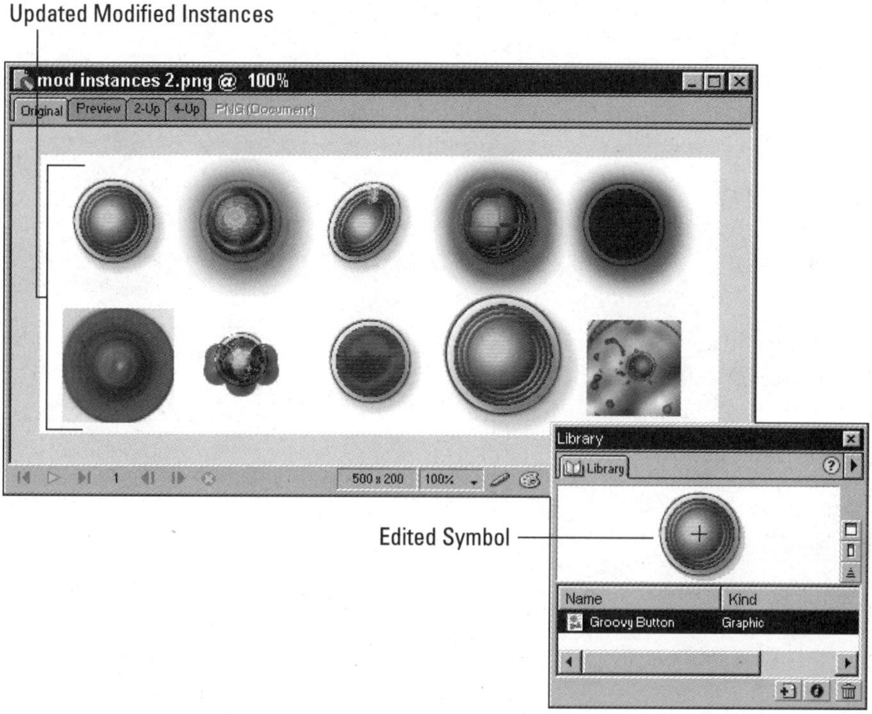

Figure 32-2: The Instances from Figure 32-1 are automatically updated by Fireworks after their parent symbol is modified. Even though most of the Instances have been heavily modified themselves, the change to the basic Instance (top left) shows through.

Symbols themselves are always stored in a *Library*, accessible through the Library panel, shown in Figure 32-3. Converting an object to a symbol places it in the Library and leaves a copy behind — an Instance — in the document window. The Library panel provides a range of functions for managing and modifying symbols and Libraries, but its most basic function is as a way to make Instances. Dragging a symbol from the Library and dropping it in the document window makes a new Instance, much like making a shortcut to a file in Windows, or a file alias on the Mac. In fact, Instances even have the little arrow badge that Windows shortcuts and Mac aliases share.

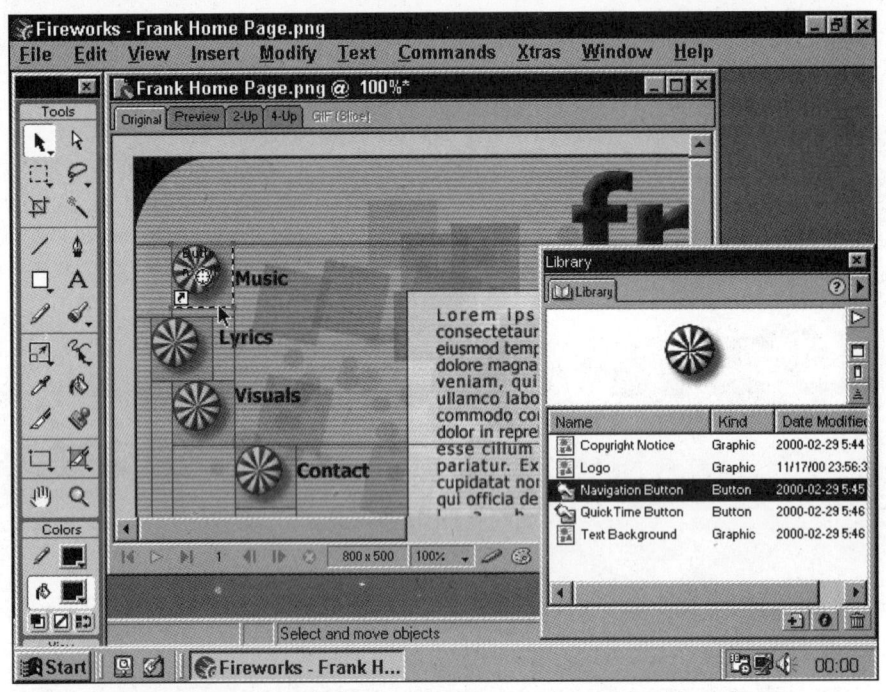

Figure 32-3: Symbols are stored in the Library panel. Dragging them into a document creates an Instance, identified by the arrow badge in its bounding box.

An advantage of Instances that's not so obvious is that they are simplified renderings of their parent symbol. Where a symbol might be a complex vector object with an intricate stroke and gradient fill, an Instance of it is just a simple bitmap object. Using many Instances rather than using independent objects, as shown in Figure 32-4, improves your computer's performance because Fireworks draws bitmap objects instead of the more-complex vector objects over and over again.

Fireworks has these two types of symbols:

- ✦ **Graphic Symbols:** You might think of a Graphic Symbol as a basic, vanilla symbol. Generally, when you refer to a symbol, you're talking about a Graphic Symbol. An Instance of a Graphic Symbol acts much the same way as any Fireworks object. You can place it anywhere on the canvas, move it to another layer, and modify many of its properties.

- ✦ **Button Symbols:** Button Symbols are *Symbols-Plus*. A Button Symbol has multiple frames that contain the different states of the button, such as Up, Over, and Down. Instances of Button Symbols carry their own slice object with them, which can have a URL or Behavior attached. In a sense, a Button Symbol is a combination of all the separate Fireworks objects you would need to use to make a button, wrapped up into a tidy package that's easy to edit and reuse.

Original vector drawing

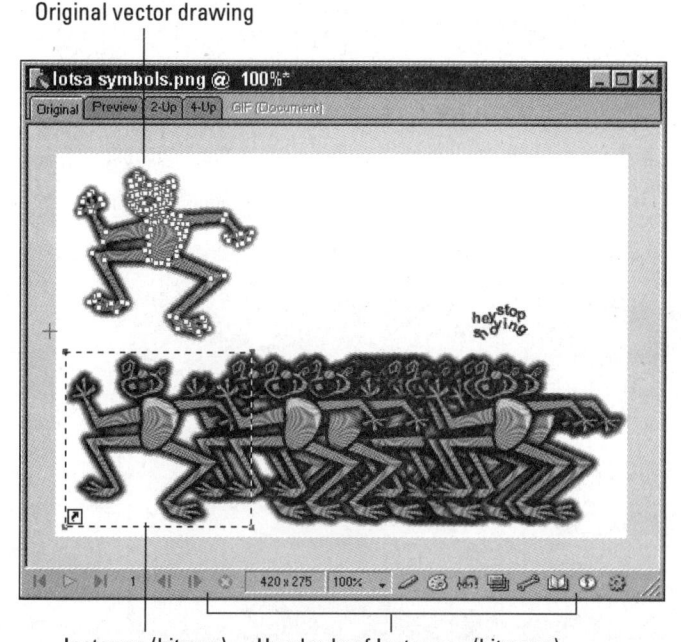

Instance (bitmap)   Hundreds of Instances (bitmaps)

Figure 32-4: Instances are simplified, bitmap versions of their parent symbols. You can use numerous Instances without adversely affecting Fireworks' performance.

The steps you take to create and modify the two types of symbols are slightly different, as each type of symbol has its own editor, but they are also similar in many ways. Button Instances share the same properties with their parent symbols as Graphic Instances.

Instances also enable advanced animation building because Fireworks can tween two or more of them and automatically create intermediate steps, simplifying and speeding up the animation process. Tweening a scaled-down Instance with a scaled-up one, for example, causes Fireworks to connect them with stair steps of new Instances, which are then easily distributed to frames to create an animation of a single object growing or shrinking.

Cross-Reference   Find out more about tweening Instances in Chapter 35.

Introducing the Library Panel

The *Library panel*, shown in Figure 32-5, is a central place to access and manage a Symbol Library. Every symbol in the current document is displayed in the symbol list in the Library panel, and they are identified as either a Graphic Symbol or

Button Symbol by a distinctive icon. Like most other Fireworks panels, the Library panel has a pop-up menu and can be docked with other panels. To display the Library panel, choose Window ⇨ Library, or use the keyboard shortcut, F11.

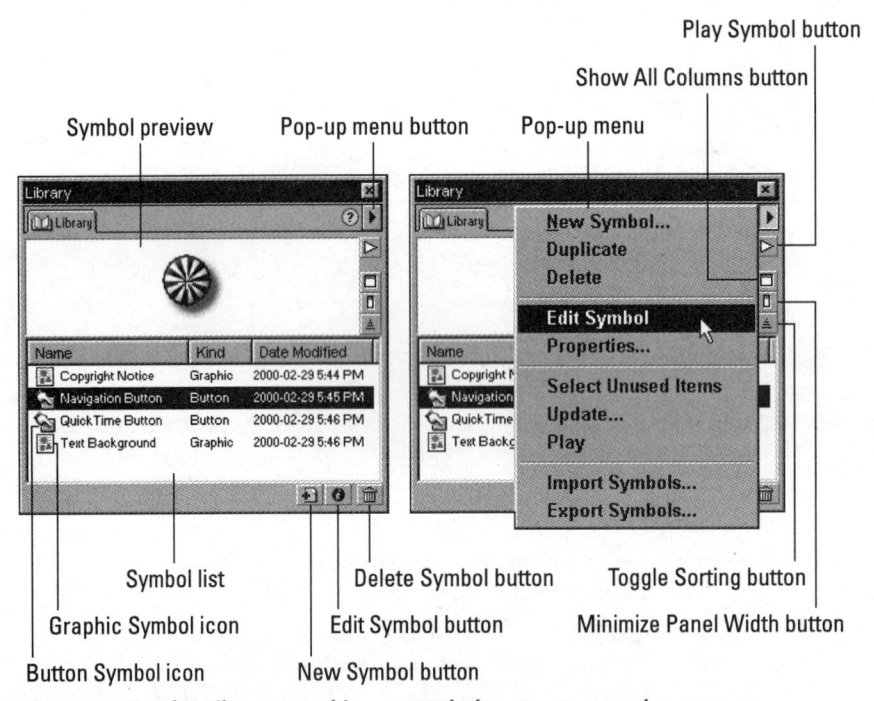

Figure 32-5: The Library panel is a central place to store and manage Symbol Libraries.

Following are the main features of the Library panel to keep in mind:

✦ **Symbol list:** As you create or import symbols, they are added to the symbol list automatically. Initially, when you create a new document, the Library panel is completely empty. The symbol list is divided into columns that detail different properties of the symbols it contains, similar to the columns you see in a Windows or Macintosh folder that is set to List view. Double-clicking a symbol's entry in the symbol list opens the Symbol Properties dialog box for that symbol, enabling you to rename the symbol, or convert it from a Button to a Graphic Symbol, or vice versa.

✦ **Symbol preview:** Selecting a symbol from the symbol list displays a preview of the symbol. Dragging the symbol's preview into a document creates an Instance of the symbol in the document. Double-clicking the symbol preview opens the symbol for editing.

✦ **Pop-up menu:** The Pop-up menu contains commands for creating and managing symbols.

You'll look more closely at the Library panel as you use it throughout this chapter to create, edit, and manage symbols.

Making and Modifying Symbols

Most of the time, you create and manage symbols using the commands in the Insert menu, although similar commands are also available through the pop-up menu on the Library panel, which you'll look at in detail later in this chapter.

Creating a symbol

Obviously, the first step in using symbols is to actually make one. Fireworks provides three routes to a new symbol: convert an existing object into a symbol, create a symbol from scratch, or duplicate an existing symbol. Converting an existing object is probably the most common method of creating a new symbol. Fireworks even betrays this bias for converting existing objects in the key shortcuts it uses: plain F8 to convert an object into a symbol, and the slightly less convenient Ctrl+F8 (Command+F8) to create a symbol from scratch.

> **Caution:** Mac users: If you have mapped the keyboard's function keys in the Mac OS Keyboard Control Panel to start programs or perform other tasks, function key shortcuts in Fireworks are superceded by those mappings. Use the menu commands in Fireworks instead, or disable the mappings in the Keyboard Control Panel.

Converting an object

You can convert almost any object into a symbol, whether it is a vector object or a bitmap object, or even a group.

> **Note:** Although you can convert an Instance into a symbol, doing so breaks the link to its original parent symbol.

To convert an object into a symbol, follow these steps:

1. Select the object you want to convert to a symbol.
2. Choose Insert ⇨ Convert to Symbol, or use the keyboard shortcut, F8. Fireworks displays the Symbol Properties dialog box (see Figure 32-6).

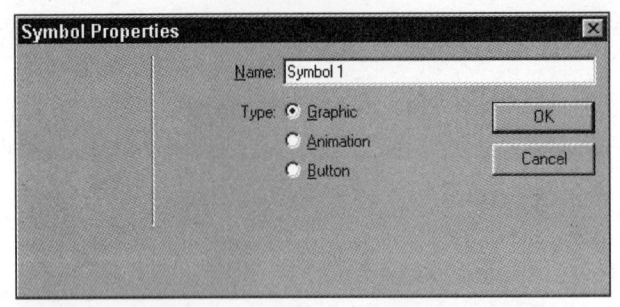

Figure 32-6: Give a symbol a name in the Symbol Properties dialog box and decide whether it will be a Graphic or a Button Symbol.

3. In the Name box, change "Symbol" to a unique name for your symbol.

4. By default, Fireworks offers to create a Graphic Symbol. Leave the Type radio buttons set to Graphic. Click OK when you're done.

> **Cross-Reference:** I cover Button Symbols later in this chapter, and Animation Symbols in Chapter 35.

Fireworks places your original object into the Library panel and leaves an Instance behind in its place in the document. You can identify the Instance by its arrow badge.

Creating a symbol from scratch

When you have the presence of mind to know that an object should be a symbol right from the start, you can make one entirely from scratch. You may also want to create a symbol that's a combination of different objects. In this case, you can create a new symbol and then copy and paste different elements from the document window into your new symbol.

To create a brand-new symbol, follow these steps:

1. Choose Insert ⇨ New Symbol, or use the keyboard shortcut, Ctrl+F8 (Command+F8). Alternatively, you can choose New Symbol from the pop-up menu on the Library panel. Fireworks displays the Symbol Properties dialog box.

2. Change the generic "Symbol" name in the Name box to a unique name for your symbol.

3. Leave the Type radio buttons set to Graphic to create a Graphic Symbol. Click OK when you're done.

4. Fireworks displays the Symbol Editor (see Figure 32-7).

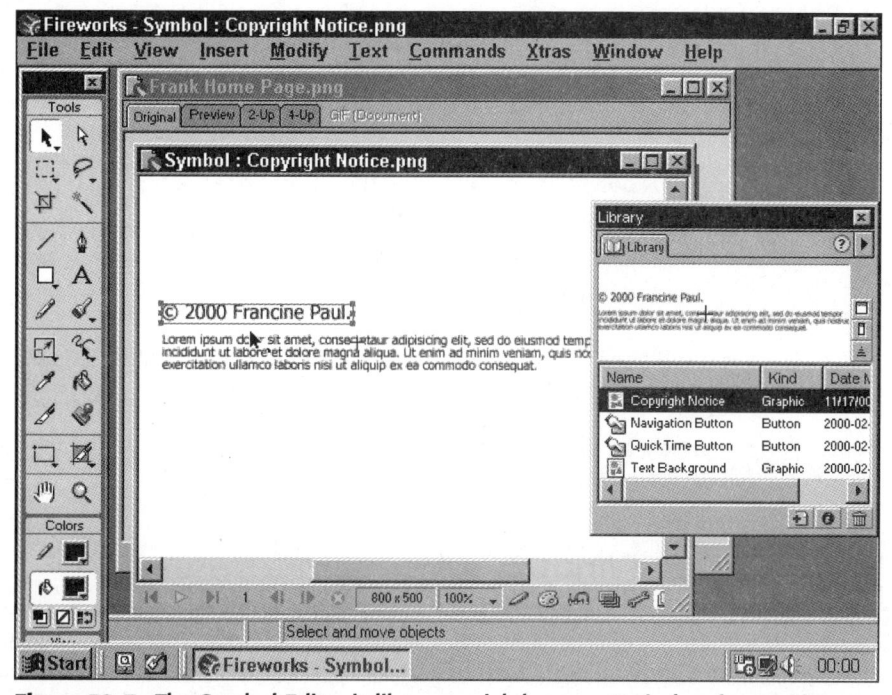

Figure 32-7: The Symbol Editor is like a special document window for creating or editing Graphic Symbols.

5. Create your new symbol in the Symbol Editor, just as you would in the document window, using any combination of Fireworks tools and floating panels, such as Live Effects. You can copy and paste between the Symbol Editor and the document window, as well.

> **Tip**
> You can easily edit and modify your new symbol later, so don't worry about making it absolutely perfect.

6. Close the Symbol Editor when you're done by clicking its close box, located on the upper-right corner of the box in Windows and on the upper-left corner on a Mac.

Your new symbol appears in the Library panel, and an Instance is placed in the document window.

> **Caution**
> A bug in Fireworks 4 disables the Save command when the Symbol Editor is open. Pressing Ctrl+S (Command+S) while in the Symbol Editor does not save your current document. The workaround is to save your document before opening the Symbol Editor.

Duplicating an existing symbol

The final way to create a new symbol is to duplicate an existing one.

To duplicate a symbol, follow these steps:

1. Choose Windows ⇨ Library, or use the keyboard shortcut, F11, to view the Library panel, if it is not already visible.
2. Select a symbol to duplicate from the symbol list.
3. Choose Duplicate from the Library panel pop-up menu.

Fireworks duplicates the selected symbol, adding a number after its name to distinguish it from the original.

> **Tip** To rename a symbol, double-click its name in the symbol list and change its name in the Symbol Properties dialog box.

Modifying symbols

You can easily edit symbols in the Symbol Editor. When you're done editing a symbol and have closed the Symbol Editor, the changes that you've made are applied to the symbol and to all of its Instances. Editing a symbol, then, is also editing all of its Instances.

To modify an existing symbol, follow these steps:

1. Choose Window ⇨ Library, or use the keyboard shortcut, F11, to view the Library panel, if it isn't already visible.
2. Select the symbol you want to edit from the symbol list.
3. Double-click the symbol preview to open the symbol in the Symbol Editor. Alternatively, you can choose Edit Symbol from the Library panel's pop-up menu.
4. Modify the symbol in the Symbol Editor. When you're done, close the Symbol Editor by clicking its close box, located on the upper-right corner in Windows and on the upper-left corner on a Mac.

Your edits are applied to the symbol and to all of its Instances.

Using symbol-editing shortcuts

Fireworks also provides these two shortcuts for editing symbols:

✦ If you have an Instance selected in the document window and you just want to edit its parent symbol, choose Modify ⇨ Symbol ⇨ Edit Symbol to view the Instance's parent symbol in the Symbol Editor.

✦ If you are editing a symbol's properties in the Symbol Properties dialog box (detailed in the next section), you can click the Edit button to open the symbol in the Symbol Editor.

When using either of these shortcuts, closing the Symbol Editor applies your changes to all the symbol's Instances.

> **Tip**
> If you take a wrong turn with your edits in the Symbol Editor, you can close the Symbol Editor — which applies your changes — and then choose Edit ⇨ Undo to undo those changes.

Modifying symbol properties

In addition to modifying the symbol itself, you can also modify a symbol's properties, changing its name, or converting it from a Graphic Symbol to a Button Symbol, or vice versa.

To edit a symbol's properties, follow these steps:

1. Choose Window ⇨ Library, or use the keyboard shortcut, F11, to view the Library panel, if it isn't already visible.

2. Open the Symbol Properties dialog box by doing one of the following:

    • Double-click a symbol's name in the symbol list.

    • Select the symbol in the symbol list and choose Properties from the pop-up menu.

    Fireworks displays the Symbol Properties dialog box, shown in Figure 32-8.

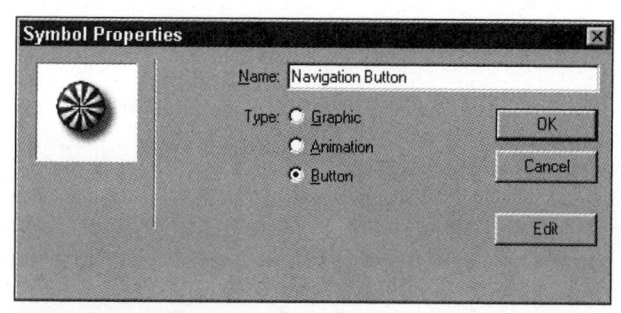

Figure 32-8: The Symbol Properties dialog box displays a thumbnail of an existing symbol and enables you to rename a symbol, or convert its Type.

3. Modify the symbol's properties in the Symbol Properties dialog box and click OK when you're done.

Fireworks applies your changes to the symbol. If you converted the symbol's Type, all of its Instances also take on that change. For example, if you converted a symbol from a Graphic Symbol to a Button Symbol, all of its Instances become buttons.

Deleting a symbol

Deleting a symbol is an easy affair, but keep in mind that if the symbol has Instances, they will be deleted, too.

To delete a symbol, follow these steps:

1. If the Library panel is not visible, choose Window ⇨ Library, or use the keyboard shortcut, F11, to display it.
2. Select the symbol you want to delete in the symbol list.
3. Choose Delete from the Library panel pop-up menu. If the symbol doesn't have any Instances, it is deleted immediately without confirmation. If the symbol does have Instances, Fireworks displays the Delete Symbol dialog box, shown in Figure 32-9.

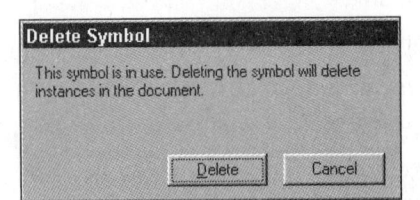

Figure 32-9: The Delete Symbol dialog box confirms that you really want to delete a symbol.

4. Click the Delete button in the Delete Symbol dialog box to delete the symbol.

The symbol and its Instances are removed from your document.

Creating Instances

Creating an Instance is a common task that you can accomplish with one of two simple methods:

- Drag and drop a symbol from the Library panel onto the canvas. You can drag it from either the symbol preview, or from the symbol list.

Tip: You can create Instances of multiple symbols in one step by selecting a group of symbols from the symbol list and dragging them all onto the canvas.

✦ **Duplicate an Instance in the document window.** A copy of an Instance is also an Instance. Any of the methods that you're used to using to duplicate objects in Fireworks also work to duplicate Instances:

- Select the Instance and choose Edit ➪ Duplicate or Edit ➪ Clone.
- Copy the Instance to the Clipboard and Paste back a copy.
- Hold down the Alt (Option) key, and drag an Instance to create a copy.

You can identify the new Instance as another Instance by the arrow icon in the lower-left corner of its bounding box.

Modifying Instances

Although modifying a symbol passes changes on to all of its Instances, you can also make modifications to individual Instances. Fireworks treats Instances like groups, enabling you to apply similar transformations. The relationship between transformations applied to a symbol and transformations applied to an Instance is the same as making transformations to individual objects, and then grouping them and applying a transformation to the group. In fact, you can observe the group-like behavior of an Instance by breaking the link with its symbol. What you're left with is a group.

Caution: Although you can apply an Xtra to an Instance, doing so breaks the link and turns it into a bitmap object.

Applying modifications to an Instance has no effect on any other Instance, or on the parent symbol. Scale one Instance, for example, and its parent symbol and other Instances of that symbol are unaffected. In other words, the link goes one way, only from symbol to Instance.

You can apply these transformations to Instances:

✦ **Shape transformations:** Adjust the width, height, skew, distortion, and rotation, or flip the Instance vertically or horizontally. Anything on the Modify ➪ Transform submenu is fair game.

✦ **Opacity:** Alter the opacity setting in the Object panel.

✦ **Blending mode:** Alter the blending mode in the Object panel.

Cross-Reference: For more about opacity and blending modes, see Chapter 29.

✦ **Live Effects:** Apply Live Effects from the Effect panel. The effects that are applied to the symbol are flattened in the Instance, so even though an Instance may appear to have Live Effects, there are actually no Live Effects applied until you add them to an individual Instance.

Cross-Reference: For more about Live Effects, see Chapter 28.

Breaking links

If you want to break the link between an Instance and its parent symbol, select the Instance and choose Modify ⇒ Symbol ⇒ Break Apart. The link is broken and your Instance is now a regular group, even if the symbol only contained one object. To separate the group, choose Modify ⇒ Ungroup.

Deleting Instances

Deleting an Instance works just like deleting any Fireworks object and has no effect on the parent symbol or any other Instance. To delete an Instance, select it and press Delete.

Working with Buttons

Button Symbols enable you to encapsulate up to four button states, such as Up, Over, and Down, along with a slice object containing a URL or a Behavior into a single object that you can think of as a button.

New Feature: Button Instances no longer appear on shared layers. Instead, they appear on their own layer on Frame 1 of the document.

You can place button Instances onto the canvas again and again, and change the link and Button Text independently for each one. In addition, Behaviors are applied to the Button Symbol itself, meaning that you only have to build one rollover for an entire Web site of rollover buttons.

Cross-Reference: I cover Behaviors in Chapter 34.

Making and modifying Button Symbols

The Fireworks Button Editor is a special Symbol Editor window with tabs for each state of a button that makes it easy to make or modify a Button Symbol.

To create a Button Symbol, follow these steps:

1. Choose Insert ⇒ New Button.

   Fireworks displays the Button Editor, as shown in Figure 32-10.

2. Create the Up state of your button in the Up tab of the Button Editor.

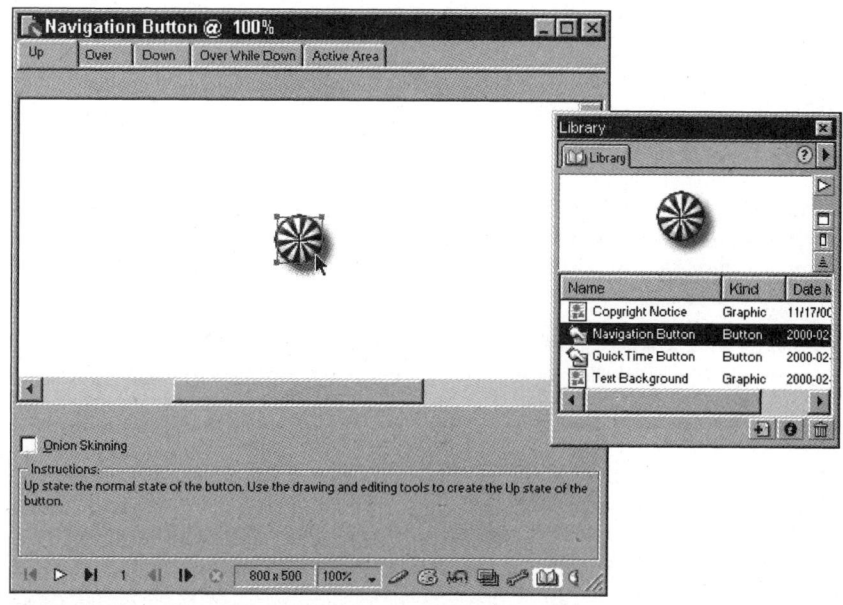

Figure 32-10: The Button Editor has individual tabs for each state of a button.

3. Select the Button Editor's Over tab and create the Over state of your button. To start with the Up state and modify it to be an Over state, click Copy Up Graphic. Fireworks copies the Up state to the Over tab, ready for editing.

   Tip: At any time, you can view all the tabs in the Button Editor at once, by checking the Onion Skinning box.

4. If you want to include a Down state in your button, select the Down tab and create the Down state of your button. Fireworks automatically checks Include Down State when you start building a down button. Again, you can click Copy Over Graphic to copy the previous state to this tab for modification.

5. Check Show Down State Upon Load to display the Down state when a page loads, when your button is exported as a Nav Bar.

6. To add an Over While Down state to your button, switch to the Over While Down tab and either create a new state, or copy the previous one — click Copy Down Graphic — and modify it to create the Over While Down state.

7. Switch to the Active Area tab. Fireworks automatically creates a slice in the Active Area tab that encompasses the area of your button. Adjust the size of the slice if necessary.

8. Click the Link Wizard button to access the Link Wizard. Move from tab to tab in the Link Wizard dialog box and set defaults for each Button Instance that will later be created from this Button Symbol.

Cross-Reference: I talk about the Link Wizard later in this chapter.

9. Close the Button Editor when you're done.

   Your new Button Symbol is added to the Library panel, and an Instance is placed in the document window.

To modify a Button Symbol, double-click its symbol preview in the Library panel, double-click one of its Instances in the document window, or select it in the symbol list and choose Edit Symbol from the Library panel's pop-up menu.

Converting existing objects into Button Symbols

Converting an existing object into a Button Symbol is a quick way to get a button started. Because each state of a multistate button is usually a variation on the first state, converting an existing object into a Button Symbol, and then modifying it slightly in the Button Editor to create Over, Down, and Over While Down states is an excellent strategy.

To convert an object into a button, select it and choose Insert ⇨ Convert to Symbol, or use the keyboard shortcut, F8. Choose Button from the Type setting in the Symbol Properties dialog box, give your button a unique name in the Name box, and click OK. Fireworks converts your object into a Button Symbol, creating a slice object on top of it in the document window, as shown in Figure 32-11.

Figure 32-11: Converting an object into a Button Symbol also covers it with a slice object.

Add more states to your button by editing it in the Library panel.

Converting Button Symbols into Graphic Symbols

If you convert a Button Symbol into a Graphic Symbol by editing its properties in the Symbol Properties dialog box, the slice object that makes up the Active Area of the button remains with the symbol. To remove it, edit your symbol in the Symbol Editor and manually delete the slice object.

Using Button Instances

In addition to the standard, modifiable Instance properties, such as opacity and Live Effects, Button Instances have two additional editable properties: their Button Text and the links that are applied to their slice objects (see Figure 32-12). Selecting the Button Instance and viewing the Object panel modifies both of these, enabling you to assign each Button Instance a separate URL and some unique text.

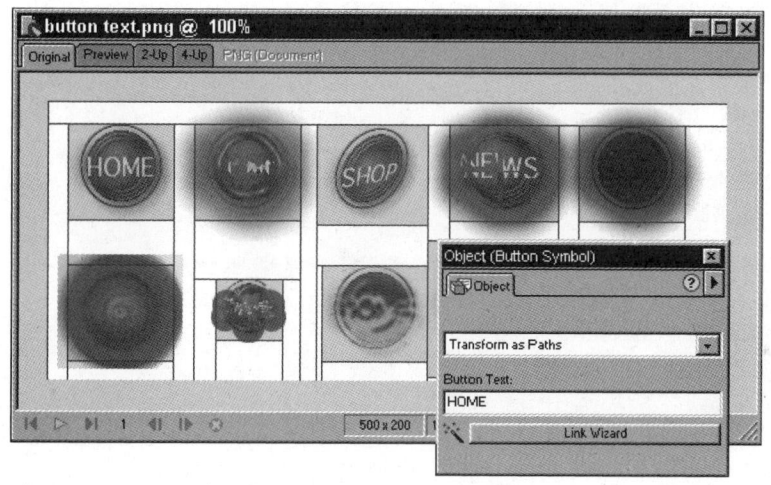

Figure 32-12: Modify the Button Text and the URL for each Button Instance in the Object panel to truly turn each Instance into a separate button.

To modify the Button Text, type new text into the Button Text box in the Object panel and press Enter (Return). Fireworks prompts you with a dialog box asking whether you would like to apply the edited text to just the current button, or to all the buttons in the document. The Text in your Button Instance is modified to reflect the new text, but retains its original formatting.

Note You can only modify Button Text if your Button Symbol contains a text object. If it doesn't, the Button Text area of the Object panel is grayed out.

To modify a button's link, click the Link Wizard button to access the Link Wizard, detailed next.

Examining the Link Wizard

The Link Wizard enables you to modify the properties of a Button Instance that would normally be applied to a regular slice object. The tabbed dialog box, accessed from the Button Instance Object panel, walks you through the steps required to edit all the link properties of the selected Button Instance.

The Link Wizard offers these four tabs:

- **Export Settings:** Export settings for the button, such as GIF WebSnap 128. An Edit button also enables you to create additional export settings.
- **Link:** A URL, alternate text, and a Status Bar message — displayed when the user hovers their mouse — for the button (see Figure 32-13).

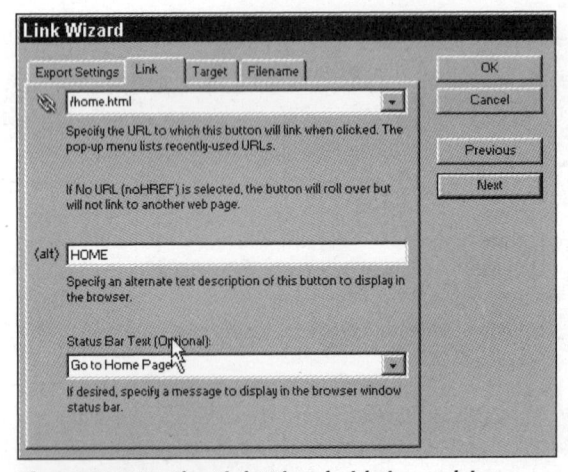

Figure 32-13: The Link Wizard aids in applying a URL to a Button Instance.

- **Target:** A target window or frame for the hyperlink to open in.
- **Filename:** A filename for this button's slice, or leave Auto-Name Slices checked to have Fireworks name the slice.

After you select a Button Instance in your document, you can access the Link Wizard for that button and apply the appropriate settings.

> **Tip** You can also access the Link Wizard from the Active Area tab of the Button Editor, enabling you to set defaults for the symbol and, consequently, for each new Button Instance.

Managing Libraries

Making and managing buttons is a common task for the Web artist, and having a central place to store buttons and an easy way to reuse them — drag and drop from the Library panel to a document — saves time and work, again and again.

Libraries exist in one of two places: within a document by default, or as a stand-alone PNG file that you create by exporting a Library.

Importing a Library

You can import Libraries from other Fireworks documents, or from Library-only PNG files that are created by exporting a Library from Fireworks.

To import a Library into the current document, follow these steps:

1. Choose Window ⇨ Library, or use the keyboard shortcut, F11, to view the Library panel, if it's not visible.
2. From the Library panel pop-up menu, choose Import Symbols.

    Fireworks displays an Open File dialog box.

3. Navigate to the Fireworks PNG file that contains the Library you want to import, and choose Open when you're done.

    Fireworks displays the Import Symbols dialog box, as shown in Figure 32-14.

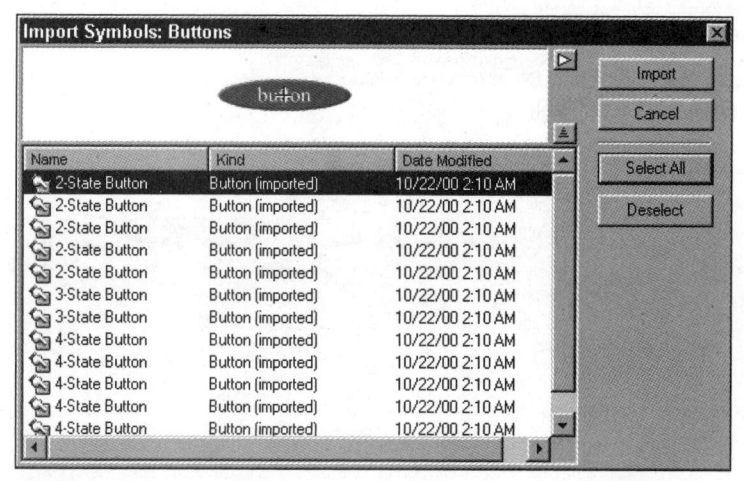

Figure 32-14: Fireworks displays the Import Symbols dialog box when you import a Library.

4. Choose symbols to import in one of the following ways:
   - To import all the symbols, click the Select All button.
   - To import a contiguous list of symbols, hold down Shift and click the first and last symbol in the contiguous list.
   - To pick and choose symbols from the list, hold down Ctrl (Command) and, in turn, click each symbol you want to import.

Tip To quickly import a single symbol, double-click its name in the Import Symbols dialog box.

5. After you make your selection, click Import to import the symbols into the current document.

Fireworks imports the symbols and makes them available in the Symbol list.

Accessing often-used Libraries

Choose a library from the Insert ⇨ Libraries submenu to begin importing it. This submenu reflects the contents of Fireworks' Libraries folder, shown in Figure 32-15. The Libraries folder is inside the Configuration folder, inside your Fireworks program folder. Placing a Fireworks PNG file into this folder and restarting Fireworks makes it available as a Library on the Insert ⇨ Libraries submenu. If you frequently access the same sets of Libraries, this can be a real timesaver.

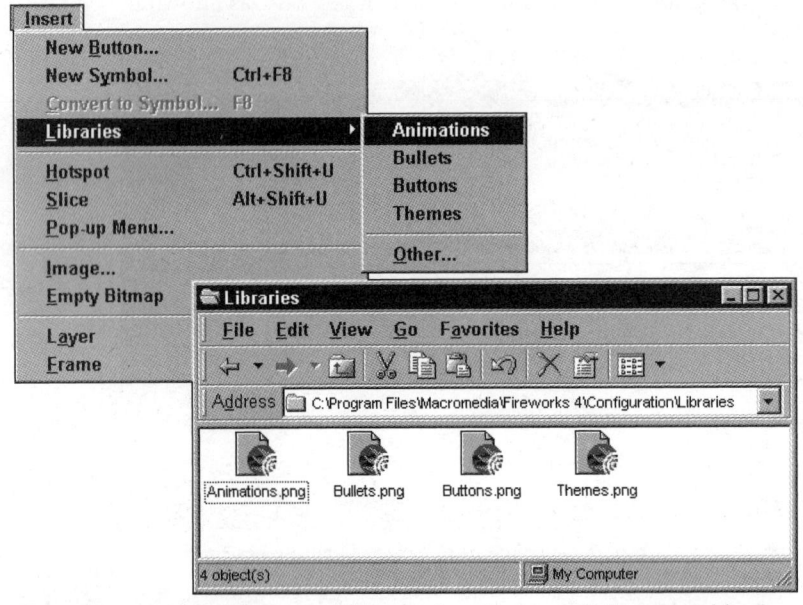

Figure 32-15: Place often-used Libraries into Fireworks' Libraries folder for easy import.

Tip The Fireworks program folder is typically found at C:\Program Files\Macromedia\Fireworks 4 on Windows-based computers, and at Macintosh HD:Applications:Macromedia Fireworks 4 on the Mac.

You can also import a Library from the Insert ⇨ Libraries submenu without restarting Fireworks by choosing Insert ⇨ Libraries ⇨ Other and navigating to the Library PNG file anywhere on your computer. Fireworks imports the Library into the current document.

Updating imported Libraries

Fireworks remembers where it originally acquired an imported symbol and can update imported symbols from that original source. This enables you, for example, to maintain a single Library of buttons for a Web site and to import that Library into multiple documents. If you need to modify a button later, modify it in the Library, and then click Update in each of the documents that uses that Library. In one step for each document, any number of documents can be updated from a single edit of the master Library.

To update imported symbols from their original sources, choose Update from the Library panel pop-up menu.

Caution If you try to edit an imported symbol, Fireworks notifies you that doing so breaks the link to the original symbol. In effect, you are creating a new symbol based on that symbol by editing it.

Exporting and sharing Libraries

Although you can import Libraries directly from any Fireworks document that contains symbols, exporting a group of symbols as a standalone Library — which is still a standard Fireworks PNG file — is a good way to share symbols with colleagues or to create archives of symbols for later use.

To export symbols as a standalone Library, follow these steps:

1. Choose Window ⇨ Library, or use the keyboard shortcut, F11, to view the Library panel, if it is not visible.
2. Choose Export Symbols from the Library panel pop-up menu.

   Fireworks displays the Export Symbols dialog box, as shown in Figure 32-16.
3. Choose symbols to export in one of the following ways:
   - To export all the symbols in your document, click Select All.
   - To export a contiguous list of symbols, hold down Shift and click the first and last symbol in the contiguous list.
   - To pick and choose symbols from the list, hold down Ctrl (Command) and click each symbol you want to export.

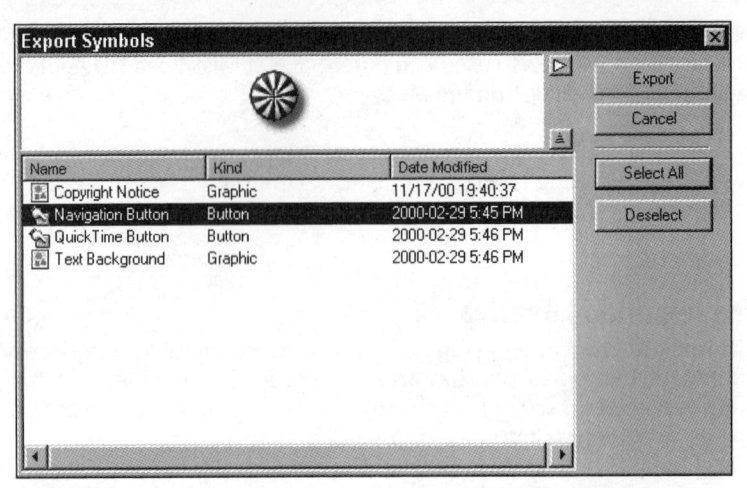

Figure 32-16: Fireworks displays the Export Symbols dialog box, enabling you to choose which symbols you'd like to export.

4. After you make your selection, click Export.

    Fireworks displays the Export Symbols As dialog box.

5. Navigate to a folder where you want to save your symbols file and provide a filename. Click Save when you're done.

The exported file contains your exported symbols, and you can import it into another document or share it with others.

Summary

Symbols and Libraries can greatly simplify many of the most common tasks of the Web artist. Keep these things in mind:

+ Fireworks has three kinds of symbols: Graphic, Animation, and Button.
+ Symbols are kept in the Library panel. Dragging a symbol from the Library panel onto the canvas creates an Instance of the symbol.
+ Symbols can contain any object, except Instances.
+ Every copy that you make of an Instance is another Instance.

✦ Some properties of Instances, such as Live Effects, and some transformations, such as scale and skew, can be modified independently of the parent symbol or other Instances. Some properties, such as fill and stroke, can be modified only on the symbol and are then inherited by its Instances.

✦ Symbols are stored in Libraries, which you can export from and import into the current document using the Library panel.

✦ ✦ ✦

Mastering Image Maps and Slices

CHAPTER
33

In This Chapter

Working with Web objects

Assigning hotspots in image maps

Inserting exported code into a Web page

Dividing an image with slices

Exporting slices to HTML

Animating a slice

Have you ever encountered a Web page in which all the image links are broken? All you see amidst the text is a bunch of rectangles with the browser's icon for "No graphic found." That's what a Web page really is to a browser: text and rectangles. You can use GIF transparency to disguise the box-like shape of an image file, but that won't limit the image link to just the visible area. For that, you need to use image maps or slices, which also enable you to create the effect of intertwined, irregularly shaped image links, such as a yin yang symbol.

Fireworks excels in its support of image maps and slices. Collectively known as *Web objects* in Fireworks, both slices and image maps (or their individual parts, referred to as *hotspots*), serve several functions. In addition to helping designers break out of the rectangularity of the Web, Web objects add interactivity through links and a bit of flair through rollovers and other Behaviors. Although you could design a site full of Web graphics without ever coming near hotspots or slices, fully understanding their uses and limitations significantly increases your Web design repertoire.

Cross-Reference This chapter covers the basics of setting up hotspots and slices, and includes some techniques for incorporating them into your Web pages. For detailed information on building rollovers and using other Fireworks Behaviors, see Chapter 34.

Understanding Image Maps and Hotspots

To understand how an image map works, you need look no further than an actual map of almost any country in the world. Divisions between regions, territories, or states are usually geographic and rarely rectangular. To best translate any such map to the Web, you would make each region (territory or state) a separate clickable area (see Figure 33-1). This is exactly the type of job for which an image map is intended.

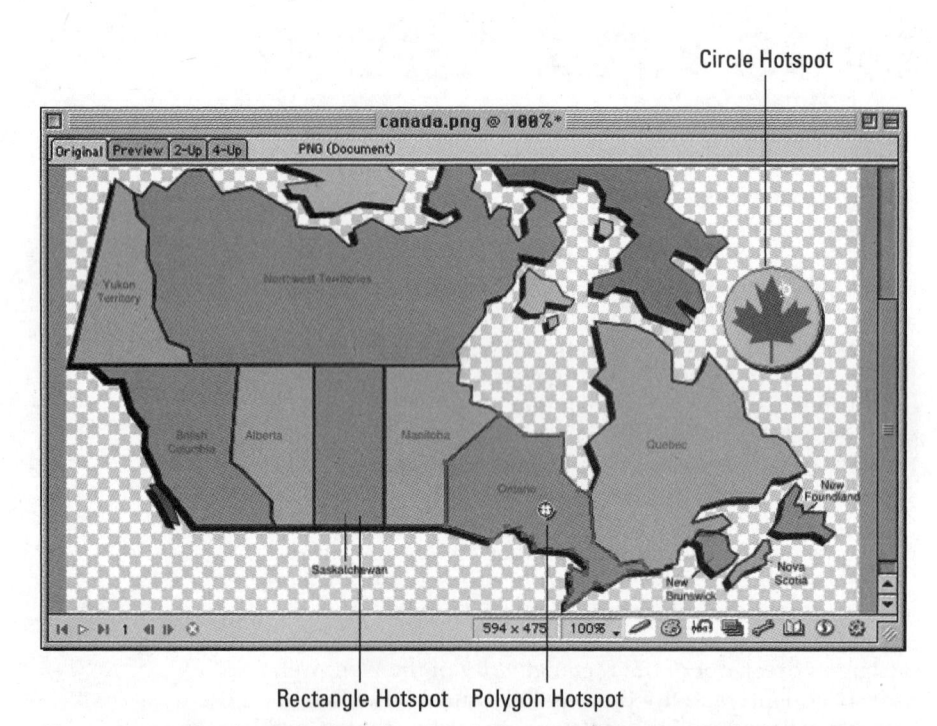

Figure 33-1: The simplest example of an image map is one made from a real map.

Each separately defined area of an image map is referred to as a *hotspot*. Hotspots come in three basic shapes: rectangles, circles, and polygons. Rectangles can be rectangles or squares, and circles can be circles or ovals; every other shape is a polygon. After you define an area of an image map, you can name it and assign a URL to it. Hotspots can also be used to trigger other events, such as rollovers or the display of messages. Hotspots are not visible on the graphic when viewed through the browser. Hotspots themselves are not actually part of the final image; to be used, the hotspot information is translated into HTML code, which is embedded in the Web page.

Because image maps and hotspots are HTML constructs and not data embedded in your graphics file, you need to export both the image and the code from Fireworks — and insert them both in your Web page. As you find out later in this chapter, Fireworks handles this dual export quite effortlessly and gives you many options for incorporating graphics and code however you like.

Using the Hotspot Tools

In Fireworks, the Hotspot tools are immediately accessible in the bottom-left area of the Tools panel. The following are the three basic Hotspot tools, corresponding to the three basic hotspot shapes:

- **Rectangle:** Use to draw rectangular or square hotspots. You can't round the corner of a rectangle, as you can with the standard Rectangle tool, although the keyboard modifiers work the same.
- **Circle:** Use to draw elliptical or circular hotspots. Again, the keyboard modifiers, Shift and Alt (Option), function the same as they do with the regular Ellipse tool.
- **Polygon:** Use to draw irregular-shaped hotspots. It functions similarly to the Polygon Lasso and uses a series of points, plotted one at a time, to make the hotspot shape.

When drawn, the hotspot appears as a shape overlaying the other graphics, as shown in Figure 33-2. Fireworks keeps all hotspots — and slices, for that matter — on the *Web Layer*, which is always shared across all frames and can be both hidden and locked and moved up or down in the stacking order like other layers. Hotspots are displayed initially with the same color, but you can assign each hotspot its own color, if desired, through the Object panel.

Examining the rectangle hotspot

As noted previously, all the Hotspot tools work in a similar fashion to corresponding standard tools. However, a few key differences exist. To create a rectangle hotspot, follow these steps:

1. Select the Rectangle Hotspot tool from the Tools panel.
2. Click once to select your originating corner and drag to the opposite corner to form the rectangle. As you drag your pointer, Fireworks draws a preview outline of the hotspot.

> **Tip** To create a square hotspot, press Shift while you drag out your shape. To draw your hotspot from the center instead of from the corner, press Alt (Option) when dragging out the shape. You can also combine the two modifier keys to create a square drawn from the center.

3. Release the mouse button when the rectangle is the desired size and shape.

Fireworks creates the hotspot with a colored fill, as shown in Figure 33-3.

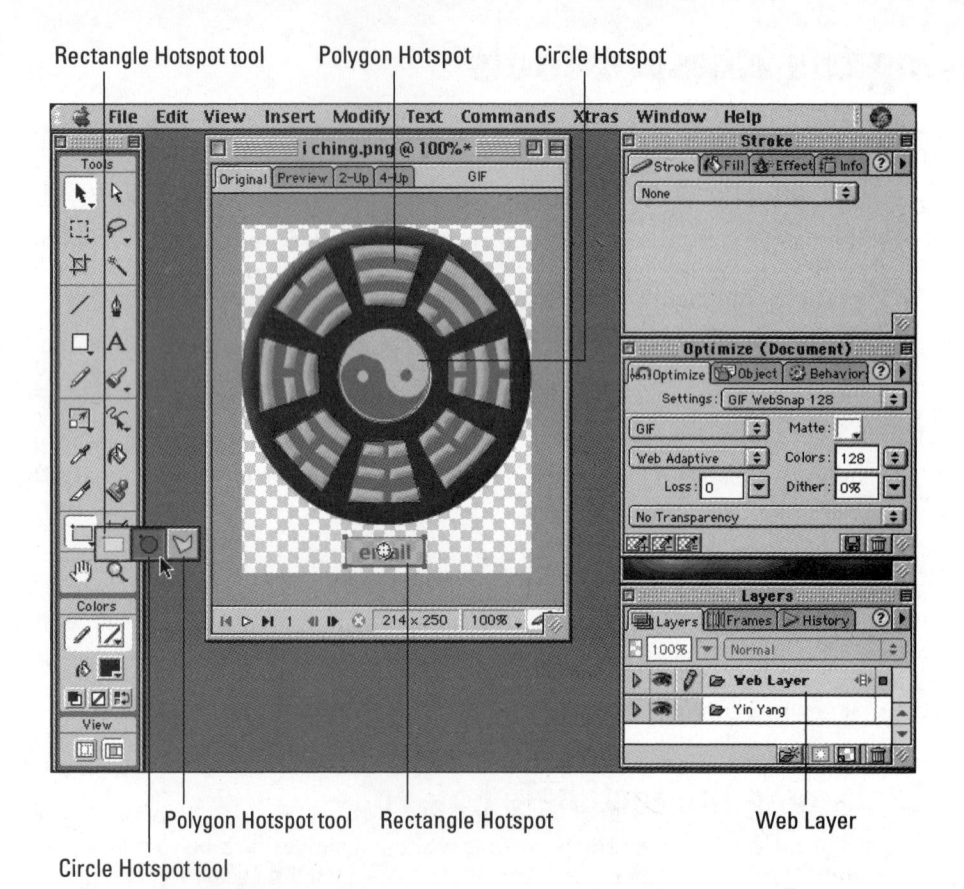

Figure 33-2: Use the three Hotspot tools to draw Hotspots on the Web Layer.

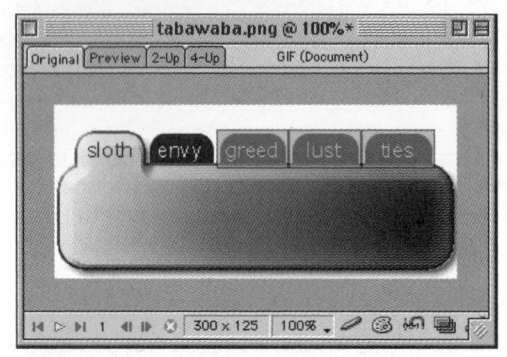

Figure 33-3: Use the Rectangle Hotspot tool to create square or rectangular hotspots.

Examining the circle hotspot

To draw an elliptical or circular hotspot, follow these steps:

1. Select the Circle Hotspot tool from the Tools panel. If it's not visible, click and hold the visible Hotspot tool until the flyout appears, and then click the Circle Hotspot button.

2. Click once to select the origin point, and then drag to the opposite corner to create the circle or ellipse. As you drag your pointer, Fireworks draws a preview outline of the form.

Tip Hold down Shift while drawing to create a perfect circle, and/or hold down Alt (Option) to draw from the center.

3. Release the mouse button when the circle or ellipse is the desired size and shape.

   Fireworks creates the hotspot, as shown in Figure 33-4.

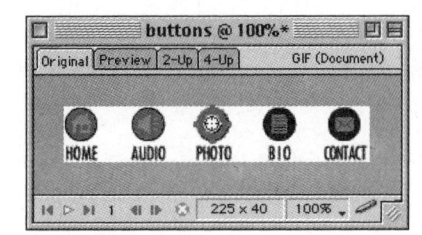

Figure 33-4: Use the Circle Hotspot tool to create circular and elliptical hotspots.

Tip Precisely matching the size and shape of an elliptical object with a corresponding hotspot is fairly difficult. After you create hotspot objects, however, you can move them with the pointer, resize them with the transform tools, or adjust them numerically through the Info panel. If the oval you're creating a hotspot for is a separate object — as opposed to a region of a larger object — the easiest method by far is to select the object and choose Insert ⇨ Hotspot, which tells Fireworks to make the hotspot for you.

Examining the polygon hotspot

To draw a polygon hotspot, follow these steps:

1. Select the Polygon Hotspot tool from the Tools panel. If it's not visible, click and hold whichever Hotspot tool is visible until the flyout appears, and then click the Polygon Hotspot button.

2. Click the starting point for your hotspot and move the mouse to the next point on the outline surrounding the desired area, and then click again.

   Fireworks connects each point that you set down with a straight line, as shown in Figure 33-5.

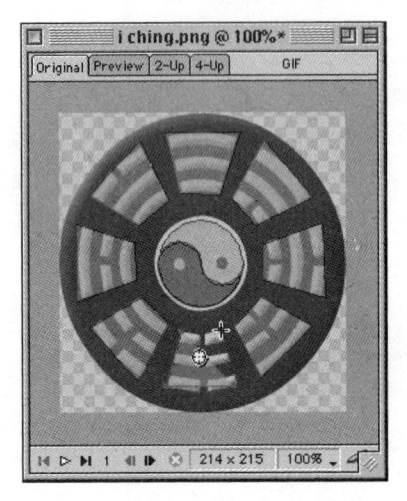

Figure 33-5: Fireworks fills in the polygon hotspot as you select each point.

3. Repeat Step 2 until you've outlined the entire area.

   As you create more points, Fireworks fills in the polygon with the default hotspot color.

4. To finish creating the hotspot, click your original starting point to close the polygon.

   Fireworks creates the hotspot with a colored fill.

Assigning links to hotspots

The Object panel does much more for hotspots than choose their color. In fact, the Object panel (see Figure 33-6) could easily be regarded as the fourth Hotspot tool. To be truly useful, you must assign hotspots a link and other HTML options — all of which you handle in Fireworks through the Object panel.

The Object panel options for a hotspot include:

- **Current URL:** Use this text box to both assign and display the link associated with the selected hotspot. You can either enter a new link by typing directly into the text field, or choose an existing link by selecting one from the option drop-down list. The option list can be divided into as many as three parts: the No URL (noHREF) choice; the URL History list for the current document; and the current URL Library.

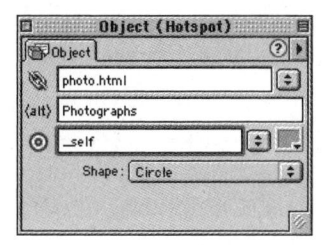

Figure 33-6: Use the Object panel for a selected hotspot to enter essential Web data, such as the linked URL.

- **Alt tag:** Alternate image text entered here is shown when either the server can't find the image, or the user's mouse is hovering over the image. In the latter case, the text appears in a tooltip attached to the pointer. Fireworks includes both the standard alt attribute and the title attribute required by Internet Explorer in the generated HTML.
- **Link Target:** The target defines where the Web page requested by a link appears. Targets are commonly used with HTML framesets. You can enter a named frame directly in the Target text box, or choose one of the following target keywords:
    - **_blank** opens the link into a new browser window and keeps the current window available.
    - **_parent** opens the link into the parent frameset of the current frame, if any.
    - **_self** opens the link into the current frame, replacing its contents (this keyword is the default).
    - **_top** opens the link into the outermost frameset of the current Web page, replacing all frames.
- **Color:** When created, all hotspots are filled with the same semitransparent color. You can, however, alter an individual hotspot's color by selecting a new one from the pop-up color picker.
- **Shape:** Displays the current hotspot shape. This shape is initially derived from the tool used to create the hotspot, and is used to determine a portion of the HTML code. You can change the shape by selecting a different one from the option drop-down list, although doing so can radically alter your hotspot.

Converting an object to a hotspot

As one who has played connect-the-dots one too many times while trying to create a star-shaped hotspot, I heartily embrace Fireworks' object-to-hotspot converter. Instead of attempting to outline an object with any of the hotspot drawing tools, select the object and choose Insert ⇨ Hotspot. A hotspot precisely matching the shape of the object is created on the Web Layer, ready for linking. This command works for rectangular, elliptical, and irregular shapes, whether they are path, image, or text objects.

> **Note** If you select multiple objects before using the Insert ⇨ Hotspot command, Fireworks asks whether you want to create one hotspot or multiple hotspots. Choosing to create one hotspot combines the Web Layer shapes into one rectangular hotspot encompassing all the selections.

Exporting Image Map Code

When an image map is translated into HTML, it appears in two key parts. The first part is the image tag, `<img>`, which holds the information for the overall graphic. The `<img>` attributes include `src` (the filename of the graphic), the dimensions of the image, and a connection to the map data, `usemap`. The `usemap` attribute is set to the name of the second image map element, the `<map>` tag. For every hotspot in the image map, a corresponding `<area>` tag exists within the `<map>`...`</map>` tag pair. The following code is for an image map with five hotspots:

```
<img name="sloth" src="sloth.gif" width="300" height="125"ù
 border="0" usemap="#m_sloth">
<map name="m_sloth">
<area shape="rect" coords="14,18,68,46" href="sloth.html">
<area shape="rect" coords="68,18,122,46" href="envy.html">
<area shape="rect" coords="122,18,176,46" href="greed.html">
<area shape="rect" coords="176,18,230,46" href="lust.html">
<area shape="rect" coords="230,18,284,46" href="ties.html">
</map>
```

Fireworks handles outputting all of this code for you — and in several different styles for various authoring tools, as well. All that you're responsible for is incorporating the code in your Web page.

Choosing an HTML style

Fireworks generates the HTML code for an image map when you export your image. The style of the HTML code that Fireworks exports depends on the HTML Style setting in the HTML Setup dialog box, as shown in Figure 33-7. Choosing an HTML style that matches your Web-authoring program makes incorporating the Fireworks-generated code easier.

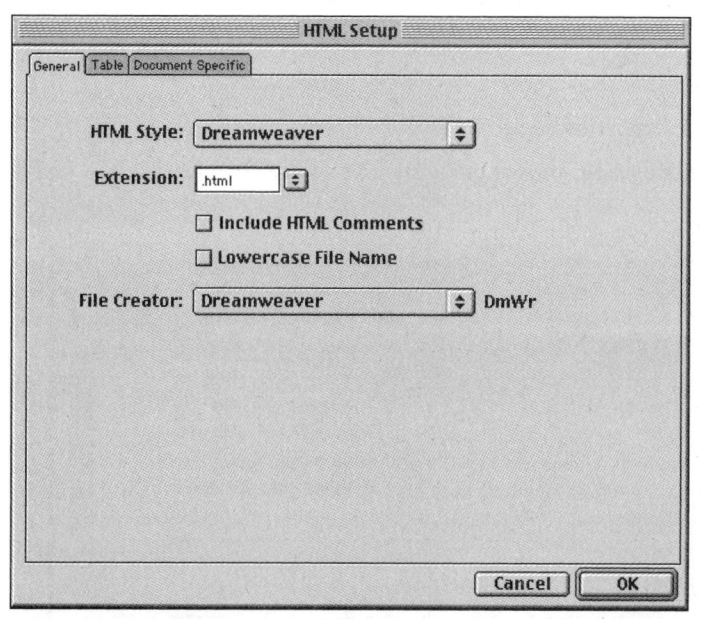

Figure 33-7: Select an HTML style and more through the HTML Setup dialog box.

The standard HTML styles included in Fireworks are:

- **Generic:** The basic code, useful in hand-coded Web pages and the majority of Web-authoring tools that work with standard HTML.
- **Dreamweaver:** Code styled for Macromedia Dreamweaver. For image maps, no real difference exists between the Generic and the Dreamweaver code.

> **Cross-Reference:** Fireworks can also export HTML code as a Dreamweaver Library Item. Details later in this chapter.

- **GoLive:** Code optimized for use with Adobe's GoLive HTML editor.
- **FrontPage:** FrontPage uses a series of *webbots* to format its code; Fireworks includes the code necessary for an image map webbot, as well as instructional code that displays when the document is opened in FrontPage.

To export an image map, follow these steps:

1. Optimize your image as needed in the Optimize panel.
2. Choose File ➪ Export to begin the exporting process.

   The Export dialog box, shown in Figure 33-8 appears.

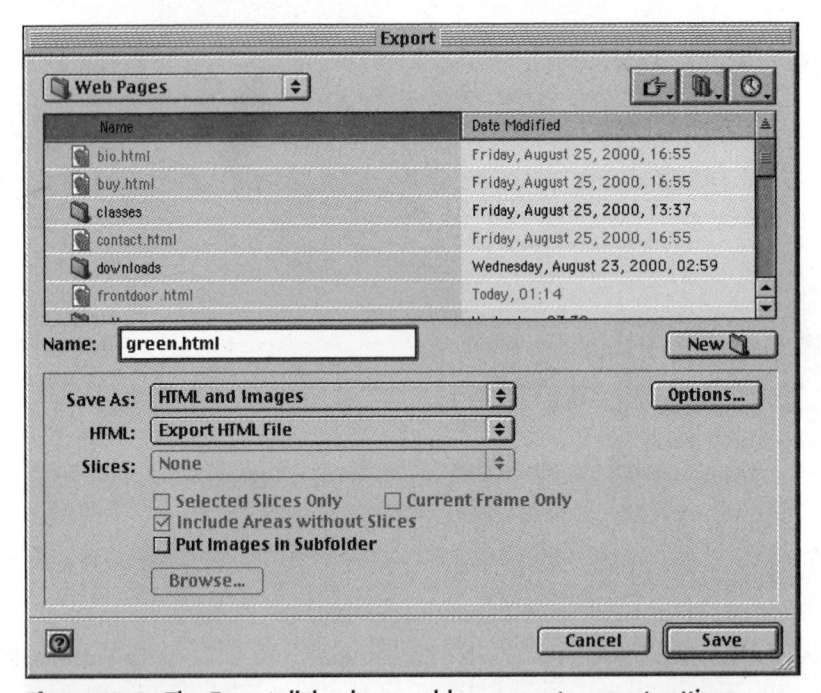

Figure 33-8: The Export dialog box enables access to export settings.

3. Choose a folder and provide a filename to save your exported file under.
4. Select HTML and Images from the Save as type (Save As) option list.
5. From the HTML option list, select whether you want to export the HTML file, or copy the code to the clipboard.
6. Select None from the Slices option list.
7. If desired, check the Put Images in Subfoler checkbox, and click Browse to choose the desired location for the image files only.
8. To alter any of the settings in the HTML Setup dialog box, click the Options button to open the HTML Setup dialog box and adjust your settings.

9. After you make your selections, click Save to complete the export.

10. If you copied the HTML code to the clipboard, paste it into an HTML editor.

Inserting image map code in a Web page

After you create the graphic, link the hotspots, and generate the code, how do you integrate all of that material within an existing Web page? Although the thought of touching code may be just this side of horrifying for many graphic designers, for most situations it's really not that bad — and for some, it's an absolute breeze. Bottom line? If you can cut and paste in a word processor, you can insert an image map in your Web page.

Although the process is much the same for most of the different style outputs, some variations exist in the procedure. The following sections detail how to integrate the Fireworks-generated code for each of the standard HTML styles.

Examining Generic code style

The Generic HTML code style is, as the name implies, used in most general situations. If you're building Web pages by hand — using a text editor, such as Notepad in Windows or SimpleText on the Macintosh — the Generic HTML style is for you. Likewise, if you're using a Web-authoring program, but not one for which Fireworks has a specific template, such as Dreamweaver or GoLive, you should use Generic HTML.

The general procedure for incorporating a Generic image map is fairly straightforward:

1. Open the Generic code in a text editor or in the text editor portion of your Web-authoring tool.

2. Select and copy to the clipboard the section in the `<body>` tag that starts with

   `<!---------- BEGIN COPYING THE HTML ---------->`

   and ends with

   `<!---------- STOP COPYING THE HTML HERE ---------->`

3. Open your existing Web page in a text editor or in the text editor portion of your Web-authoring tool.

4. In the `<body>` section of your Web page, insert the code where you want the image to appear.

Caution Be sure that you insert the code between the `<body>` and `</body>` tags, and not between the `<head>` and `</head>` tags.

5. Preview the page in a browser and adjust the placement of the `<img>` tag, if necessary.

It's not essential that the `<img>` part of the image map code and the `<map>` section appear side by side, as long as they are in the same document.

Note If the image map is to form the basis of your document — and you don't have another existing page to use — you don't have to delete or move any code whatsoever. Just add HTML elements around the image map as you build your new page. If you want, you can remove the HTML comments, but, frankly, they don't add much weight to a page, so removing them really isn't necessary.

Incorporating Dreamweaver code

You can incorporate the standard Dreamweaver HTML code into a Web page in two ways. The first is similar to the procedure used for including Generic code: Cut the code from the Fireworks-generated page and paste it into the Dreamweaver page in Dreamweaver's Code Inspector, or in Dreamweaver's Code View. As long as you make sure to insert the code in the `<body>` section of the document, and not the `<head>` section, you won't have any problems.

The other method takes advantage of Dreamweaver's Invisible Elements to completely avoid opening the Code Inspector or switching to Code View. To incorporate Dreamweaver-style HTML visually, follow these steps:

1. In Dreamweaver, open the Fireworks-generated HTML page, which was created with the Dreamweaver HTML style option.

2. Make sure that View ⇨ Visual Aids ⇨ Invisible Elements is enabled.

   Notice an HTML Comment symbol beside your image, followed by a Map symbol, shown selected in Figure 33-9.

3. Select the image, press Shift, and click the Map symbol on the right of the image.

Note If you want to transfer all the comments as well, click the first Comment symbol, press Shift, and then click the last Comment symbol.

4. Choose either Edit ⇨ Copy, or use the keyboard shortcut, Ctrl+C (Command+C).

5. Open the existing Web page to which you want to add the image map.

6. Place the cursor where you want the image map to appear.

7. Choose either Edit ⇨ Paste, or use the keyboard shortcut, Ctrl+V (Command+V).

The image map—and its code—is inserted into the Dreamweaver document.

> **Note**
> If for some reason you don't see either the Comment symbols or the Map symbol in Dreamweaver's document window, choose Edit ⇨ Preferences in Dreamweaver and, from the Invisible Elements panel, make sure that the Comments and Client-side Image Map options are selected. If you still don't see the Comment or Map symbols, choose File ⇨ HTML Setup in Fireworks and make sure that Include HTML Comments is checked.

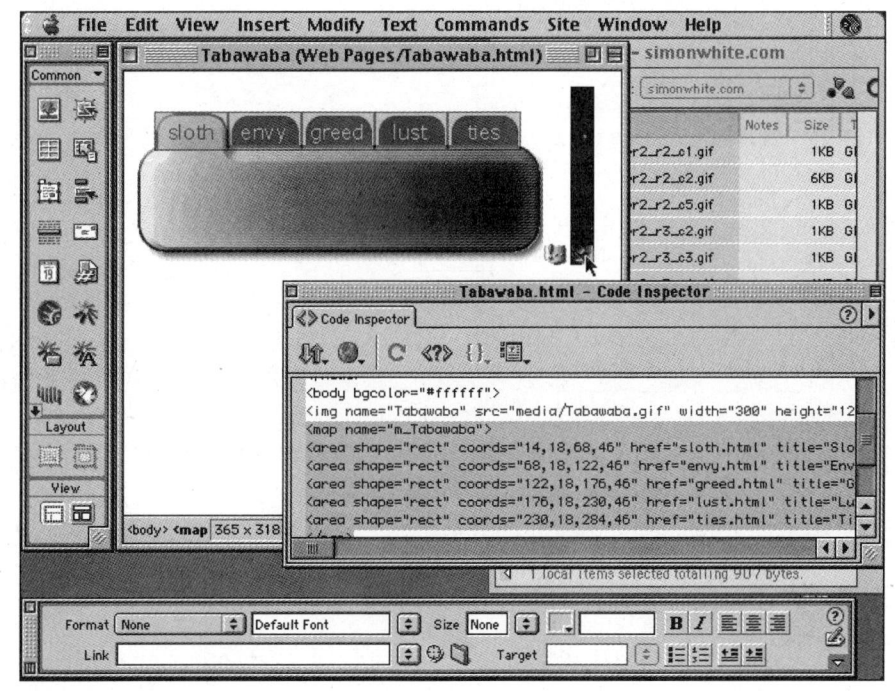

Figure 33-9: With Dreamweaver's Invisible Elements feature, you can copy and paste or drag and drop visual icons in the document window instead of moving blocks of code in the Code Inspector or in Code View.

Using GoLive

You can easily select and then copy and paste HTML code in GoLive's HTML Source Editor, or drag and drop it between HTML Outline windows (see Figure 33-10). The HTML Outline windows make it easy to move individual tags between documents, because the `<img>` or `<map>` tag can be easily collapsed to a single line. As well as the `<img>` and `<map>` tags, code exported with the GoLive style contains a `cssscriptdict` tag that tells GoLive how to edit the image map. Make sure to copy all three tags to the new document, placing the `<img>` and `<map>` tags into the body tag and the `cssscriptdict` tag into the head tag. HTML code exported with the GoLive option is very plain, with just a single "exported by Fireworks" comment.

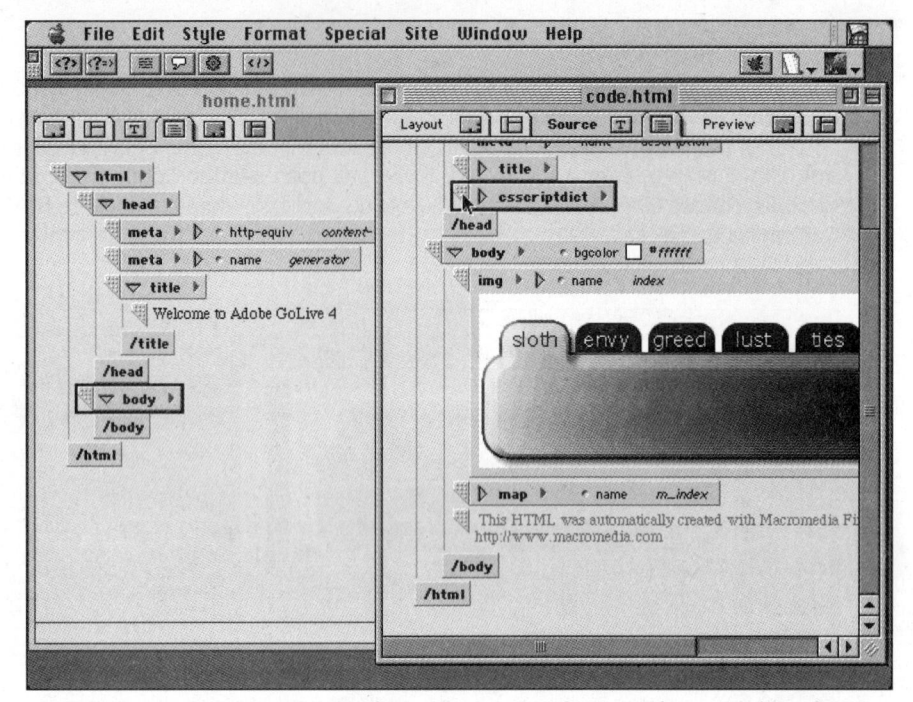

Figure 33-10: GoLive's HTML Outline view is a good way to drag and drop the `<img>`, `<map>`, and `cssscriptdict` tags from your exported code to another document.

To insert an image map from Fireworks into a GoLive document, follow these steps:

1. In GoLive, open the Fireworks-generated HTML page, which was created with the GoLive style option.
2. Switch to the HTML Outline view for both your source and target documents.
3. Select the `<img>` tag in the exported Fireworks code and drag it into place in your target document. Do the same for the `<map>` tag, placing both tags within the body tag in your target document.
4. Select the `cssscriptdict` tag from the head of your source document and drag it into the head of your target document.

Note: If you want to transfer the "created by Fireworks" comments as well, select it in the source document and drag it to the target document.

Using FrontPage

Microsoft's FrontPage is an introductory Web-authoring tool that uses proprietary code for many of its special effects, including image maps. Fireworks outputs code to match the FrontPage format when you select FrontPage from the HTML Style option list during export. The exported image map is inserted into an HTML page that instructs the FrontPage user how to incorporate the code.

To insert an image map from Fireworks into a FrontPage document, follow these steps:

1. Open the Fireworks-generated page in FrontPage.

Caution: Both the FrontPage document and the Fireworks-generated document must be in the same folder.

2. Select the HTML View.
3. Select the code starting with

   ```
   <!---------- BEGIN COPYING THE HTML ---------->
   ```

   and ending with

   ```
   <!---------- STOP COPYING THE HTML HERE ---------->
   ```

4. Choose Edit ⇨ Copy.
5. Open the document into which the image map is to be inserted.
6. While still in HTML View, choose Edit ⇨ Paste to insert the code into the document.

Understanding Slices

If image maps enable you to target areas of a graphic for links, why not use them for everything? The primary drawback to an image map is also one of its key characteristics: An image map is a single file. As such, image maps of any size — and they tend to be sizable, to take advantage of multiple hotspots — take a long time to download and can be frustrating for the Web page visitor. Moreover, with one file, you're locked into one graphic format with a single panel. What if your image map contains a photographic image in one color with lots of flat color in the rest of the graphic? You would be forced to export the entire file as a JPEG, to make the photo look good, and the file size would be much higher than if you exported the image as a GIF. And forget about including animations or special effects, such as rollovers — duplicating frames of a large graphic would make the file huge.

An alternative approach to image maps is a technique known as slicing. Slicing takes a large image and literally carves it into multiple smaller graphics, which are reassembled in an HTML table for viewing. Each separate image is referred to as a slice and the whole process is often just called *slices*. Here are some of the key features of slices:

✦ **Incremental download:** On most servers, each slice appears as it's downloaded, which makes the whole image appear to be loading faster.

✦ **Linking without image maps:** Each slice can have its own link, although all such links are rectangular.

✦ **Mixed file formats:** Each slice can be optimized separately, reducing the overall file size of the image while enhancing the quality. This technique means that you not only can have a JPEG and GIF side by side, but can also export one slice as a JPEG at 100 percent and another slice as a JPEG at 30 percent.

✦ **Update image areas:** If your graphic includes an area that must be updated frequently, such as a headline or a date, you can simply alter the single image in the slice and leave the rest of the image untouched.

✦ **Embedded rollovers:** One of the chief uses of slices, especially in Fireworks, is to create rollovers (also known as *mouseovers*). With slices, you can have a series of rollovers, as with a navigation bar, all tied together in one graphic. You can also use one slice to trigger a rollover in another part of the image.

✦ **Embedded animation:** With a GIF animation in one slice, you can achieve special effects, such as a flashing neon sign in a large graphic, without doubling or tripling your file size.

The key, fact-of-life, limitation to slices is their shape: All slices are rectangular. Not only are images that make up each individual slice always rectangular, but the table cells into which the slices must fit are, too. To create any illusion of nonrectangular shapes, you must use GIF or PNG files with transparency. An additional restriction is that slices cannot overlap.

When deciding whether or not to slice an image, keep in mind that slices depend on HTML tables to hold them together in the browser. Tables, in turn, have some of their own limitations. For example, you can't place two tables side by side on a Web page; the code won't allow it. However, you can nest one table inside another to achieve a similar effect.

Because slices are tied to HTML tables, you must take special care to ensure that all browsers treat the tables identically. Under some situations, tables viewed in some browsers can "collapse" and lose all their width and height information that is necessary to appear as a single graphic. The workaround for this problem is to use very small (one pixel) transparent images called *spacer images*. Fireworks automatically generates the spacer images if you like, or outputs the code for the sliced image without them. Spacer images are covered in detail later in this chapter.

Cross-Reference: This chapter covers the basics of creating slices. For information on how to use slices to build rollovers, see Chapter 34.

Slicing Images in Fireworks

Slices and hotspots are created in a similar manner — generally, you draw a slice area on top of an image. However, although hotspots can be any shape, including circular, slices are ultimately rectangular, although Fireworks aids in creating complex slices by enabling you to use the Polygon Slice tool to draw complex polygon-shaped slices, which Fireworks then converts into multiple rectangular slices upon export.

The two Slice tools are located on the lower right of the Tools panel, on a flyout similar to the one used for the Hotspot tools.

As you draw slices with the Slice tools, Fireworks creates *slice guides*, which help you to keep the number of files exported to a minimum, by aligning the slices. The fewer images you ultimately use, the faster your work displays in a browser and the less taxing the page will be for the browser to display. When slices overlap, Fireworks considers slices that are higher in the stacking order to be more important.

New Feature Fireworks now uses the stacking order of slices to determine how overlapping slice objects will be exported. This reduces the number of slices Fireworks exports in most cases.

Looking at rectangle slices

To slice an image with the Slice tool in Fireworks, follow these steps:

1. Select the Slice tool from the Tools panel.
2. Click the image and draw out a rectangle the size and shape of the desired slice, as shown in Figure 33-11.

Figure 33-11: The Slice tool divides a Fireworks document into straightforward rectangular slices that are exported as individual image files.

> **Tip**
>
> As with the regular Rectangle tool, the Alt (Option) key causes the Slice tool to draw from the center rather than from a corner, and the Shift key constrains the slice to a square.

   3. Release the mouse when you're satisfied with the shape.

Fireworks creates the slice object and fills in the rectangle with the default, semi-transparent slice color. If enabled, the slice guides appear.

After you draw the slice object, you can manipulate it as with any other object in Fireworks. You can use the four handles on the slice object to resize it — just drag one corner in the desired direction. Rectangular slices are constrained to rectangles, so moving just one point moves the entire side. In fact, you don't have to select the corner; it's just as effective to click and drag a slice object's side.

You can also use the transform tools, such as Scale, although any resulting nonrectangular shape is converted back into an encompassing rectangle. To move the slice object one pixel at a time, use the arrow keys.

An alternative to the Slice tool is to use the standard guides. In this technique, guides are dragged from the horizontal and vertical rulers to form the slicing grid. Then, during export, choose the Slice Along Guides option. This technique works well when your goal in slicing an image is to enable smaller portions of the image to appear quicker than a single large image could load. If you want to add a URL or a Behavior to a slice, you have to create slice objects.

Looking at polygon slices

As previously mentioned, polygon slices exist only within Fireworks. When you export your document, Fireworks uses your polygon slices as a guide in creating more-complex rectangular slices. Polygon slices can be any shape — just like Polygon hotspots — as shown in Figure 33-12.

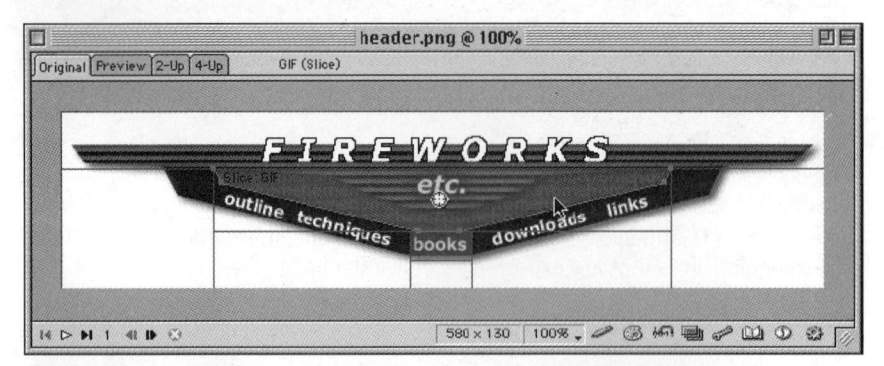

Figure 33-12: Outline nonrectangular areas with the Polygon Slice tool.

A side effect of this conversion is that polygon slices can often result in a large number of individual image files. This adds to the overhead of displaying the page in a browser. Each image file must be asked for by the browser and sent by the server, and each image must be rendered by the browser separately. When you incorporate 10 or 15 images, the user may start to notice the difference in the perceived speed of the download.

To draw a polygon slice, follow these steps:

1. Select the Polygon Slice tool from the Tools panel. If it's not visible, click and hold the Slice tool until the flyout appears, and then click the Polygon Slice button.

2. Click at the starting point for your slice and move the mouse to the next point on the outline surrounding the desired area, and then click again.

   Fireworks connects each point that you set down with a straight line.

3. Repeat Step 2 until you've outlined the entire area.

   As you create more points, Fireworks fills in the polygon with the default slice color.

4. To finish creating the slice, click your original starting point to close the polygon.

   Fireworks creates the slice with a colored fill.

Working with slice guides

Before Fireworks, creating a sliced image by hand was very meticulous, eye-straining work. Each slice had to be measured and cut precisely to the pixel—if you were off even one pixel, the resulting image would either have gaps or over-lapping areas. You can approximate this level of frustration by disabling the slice guide features in Fireworks.

Unlike regular guides, you don't position slice guides by hand; they are automatically created as you draw out your slices. The slice guides effectively show you the table layout that would result from the existing slices. More importantly, the slice guides take advantage of the Snap to Guide feature and help you to avoid overlapping slices or sliced images with gaps.

Personally speaking, I find the slice guides very useful, and I highly recommend using them. Choose View ➪ Slice Guides to show or hide slice guides. Slices automatically snap to the edge of a document, but to snap to the guides themselves, choose View ➪ Guides ➪ Snap to Guides.

The standard guides and the slice guides are drawn in two different colors. Occasionally, the slice guide color is too similar to that of the current image and you can't see where the guides are. To change the color of the slice guides, select View ➪ Guides ➪ Edit Guides to see the Guides (Grids and Guides) dialog box, shown in Figure 33-13. Select a new color from the Slice Color pop-up menu.

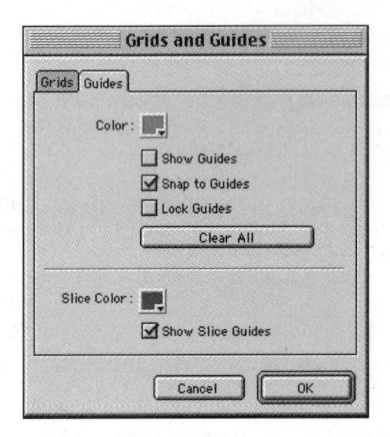

Figure 33-13: Choose a new slice guide color from the Guides (Grids and Guides) dialog box.

Note On Windows, the grid and guide options are displayed in separate Grids and Guides dialog boxes. On the Mac, a single Grids and Guides dialog box contains both sets of options, separated by tabs.

You can also enable the slice guide feature from the Guides (Grids and Guides) dialog box by choosing Show Slice Guides, or turn on the Snap feature by selecting Snap to Guides.

Note Unlike the regular guides, the slice guides can't be dragged to a new location; their position is controlled by the slices themselves. Therefore, the Lock Guides option on the Guides (Grids and Guides) dialog box applies only to standard guides.

Copying an image to a slice

Sometimes, making sure that you have all of a particular object can be very tricky — especially if that object has a drop shadow or glow effect. Incorrect placement of a slice could cut off part of the image. To avoid these problems, you can have Fireworks do all the work for you. Just as Fireworks can convert any object to a hotspot, any object can also be made into a slice.

To make an object into a slice, select the object and choose Insert ➪ Slice. Fireworks draws the slice completely encompassing the selected object — special effects and all. If you select multiple objects, Fireworks asks whether you want to create slices for all the items together or separately.

Setting URLs in slices

To use a slice as a link, the slice must be assigned a URL. You can assign URLs to slices in two different locations: the Object panel or the URL panel. Slices have the same options on both panels as those covered earlier in this chapter for Hotspots.

To assign a link to a slice by using the Object panel, follow these steps:

1. Select the slice to which you want to assign a link.
2. Choose Window ⇨ Object, or use the keyboard shortcut, Alt+F2 (Option+F2), to display the Object panel, as shown in Figure 33-14.

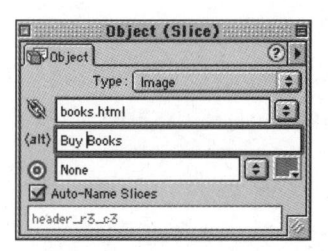

Figure 33-14: The Object panel enables you to assign a link and alternate text to a slice.

3. Enter a link directly in the Current URL text box, or select one from the option list. The option list shows both the URL History and the URL Library.
4. If desired, enter any alternative text in the Alt text field.
5. To set the target for the linked page to load into, choose one of the presets from the Target option list, or enter a frame name.
6. To change the color of the selected slice object, pick a new one from the pop-up color picker.
7. To assign a custom name for the slice, deselect the Auto-Name Slices option and enter a new name in the Custom Base Name text box.

You can also set a different pattern for the Auto-Naming scheme in the HTML Setup dialog box, as described later in this chapter.

Using Text Slices

One little known, but useful feature of slices is the ability to create a Text Slice. A Text Slice displays HTML text in your image instead of part of the image, as shown in Figure 33-15.

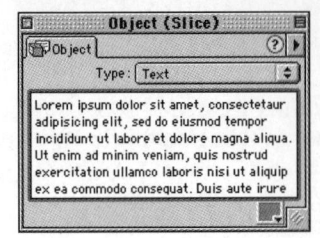

Figure 33-15: Setting a slice's type to Text enables you to incorporate HTML text inside a sliced graphic.

To make a Text Slice, follow these steps:

1. Select the slice and display the Object panel.
2. From the Type option list, choose Text.

   The Object panel displays a text area.
3. Enter the desired text and/or HTML directly in the text area of the Object panel.
4. Select any other tool or object when you're done.

   Fireworks displays your entered text within its slice's overlay.

New Feature Fireworks 4 makes text slices obvious by showing the text itself within a text slice's overlay.

5. To edit the text, select the slice object and make your changes in the Object panel.

Tip HTML tables used for slices typically have no borders or additional cell spacing or padding, so that all the images fit snugly next to each other. However, if you are using a Text Slice, this can be a problem, because the text fits too snugly to the image, with no surrounding margin. You can work around this problem by creating a slightly larger, but empty, Text Slice in front of the Text Slice with the content.

Using slice options

Even with only two slices explicitly defined — depending on their placement — you can generate many slices for an image. For the slices to be inserted into a table, each slice has to have a unique filename. To save you the work of entering in name after name each time you export a sliced image, Fireworks enables you to create a slice-naming policy in the HTML Setup dialog box (File ⇨ HTML Setup). If desired, you can override the automatic naming on a slice-by-slice basis by unchecking the Auto-Name Slices option on the Object panel and entering a unique name in the associated text box. Although I like to name slices individually in a navigation bar so that I can easily find the image reference in the HTML code, I tend to let Fireworks automatically name most of my slices.

Fireworks can create some extremely complex tables as a result of slicing; multiple column and row spans are quite normal. In some ways, such complex tables are like a house of cards — and certain browsers are a big wind, ready to knock them down. In some circumstances, the table cells appear to lose their carefully calculated widths and heights, and the table literally breaks apart to display the separate images.

To support such tables, Fireworks uses a series of *spacer images*. A spacer image is a very small (one pixel by one pixel) transparent GIF image placed in cells along the top and right of the HTML table. Fireworks takes advantage of how HTML works, to use just one image, spacer.gif, which weighs just 43 bytes — or, in other words, .04K. The same image is used in all the spacer cells and sized appropriately in the code. HTML enables you to specify a different height and width for an image, and then enables the browsers to handle the scale. Although this is generally a bad idea for most images — browsers don't use very sophisticated scaling algorithms — it works well for spacer images. The spacer images are almost invisible: Those along the top row remain one pixel in height, and those on the side remain one pixel in width. But, most importantly, spacer images do the job for which they were intended — a sliced table with spacer images maintains its shape and integrity, regardless of the browser.

Despite all their intended good, transparent spacer images are not for every situation. Therefore, Fireworks offers a degree of user control over spacer image creation, through the Table tab of the HTML Setup dialog box. You can choose to space with a One-Pixel Transparent Spacer, Single Table - No Spacers, or Nested Table - No Spacers. If you select Single Table - No Spacers, be sure to test the results in a variety of browsers to make sure your spacing is acceptable in each one.

Exporting Slices

When exporting an image map, you end up with an image and a snippet of HTML code. When exporting slices, you could get a whole lot of images and a bit more HTML. You need to realize that each sliced image ultimately means numerous files that must all be stored together. Fireworks offers two different slicing techniques and a variety of HTML styles from which to choose. The options you select are determined by how your slices were created and which Web-authoring tool you are using.

Exporting slices as different image types

Another advantage of slices over hotspots is that each slice can be a different image format, because each slice is an individual image file. This enables you to export one slice as a JPEG, one as a GIF, and another as a PNG, if you so desire.

Specifying the export format for a slice is easy: Simply select the slice object in the document window and choose Window ⇨ Optimize to view the Optimize panel. While a slice object is selected, the Optimize panel displays its individual export settings. Choose a format and optimization options. Then select another slice and modify its options, or deselect all slices to modify the export options for the whole document.

Setting the Export options

After deciding on a path and filename for your images, you must select which slicing technique to use. In the Export dialog box, the options under Slicing are

- **None:** When this option is chosen, the image is exported in one piece, regardless of the number of slice objects.
- **Export Slices:** The exported slices are created from the slice objects on the image.
- **Slice Along Guides:** The standard guides are used to determine the slices.

For most situations, Export Slices is the best choice. Slice objects are required for rollovers or any other Behavior, and they are very easy to create. The only reason to choose Slice Along Guides is to carve a large image into numerous smaller ones, without any attached Behaviors. To use Slice Along Guides, you must have set the standard guides into place, as detailed earlier in this chapter.

To export an image in slices, follow these steps:

1. Choose File ⇨ Export.

    The Export dialog box appears.

2. Set the filename and path of the Export in the upper part of the dialog box.
3. Select HTML and Images from the Save as type (Save As) option list.
4. Choose Export HTML File, or Copy to Clipboard from the HTML option list.
5. Choose either Export Slices, or Slice Along Guides from the Slicing option list.
6. To save the image files in a different folder, check the Put Images in Subfolder checkbox, click Browse, and choose the desired folder for your images.
7. To alter any of the slice settings previously set, click Options to open the HTML Setup dialog box and adjust your settings.
8. After you make your selections, click Save to complete the export.
9. If you copied the code to the clipboard, paste it into a document in your HTML editor.

Inserting slices in a Web page

As with image maps, four HTML styles — Generic, Dreamweaver, GoLive, and FrontPage — dictate some aspects of the HTML code that Fireworks generates. Inserting code from a simple sliced image is straightforward. From an HTML perspective, all the code is contained within one tag, `<table>`. Remember, in HTML, tags containing data use both a starting and ending tag; in the case of the tags for an HTML table, the starting tag is `<table>`, and the ending tag is `</table>`. So, all the necessary code is between `<table>` and `</table>`, inclusive. Fireworks plainly marks this code with HTML comments, showing where to begin copying and where to stop.

> **Cross-Reference**
> The techniques provided in this chapter for integrating slices in your Web pages are for simple sliced images, without rollovers or other Behaviors. To learn how to export slices with Behaviors, see Chapter 34.

Using the Generic template

Use the Generic template when you are hand-coding your pages in a text editor or using a Web-authoring tool without a specific template.

Follow these steps to incorporate a Generic sliced image:

1. Open the Generic code in a text editor, or in the text editor portion of your Web-authoring tool.

2. Select and copy to the clipboard the section in the `<body>` tag that starts with

   `<!---------- BEGIN COPYING THE HTML ---------->`

   and ends with

   `<!---------- STOP COPYING THE HTML HERE ---------->`

3. Open your existing Web page in a text editor, or in the text editor portion of your Web-authoring tool.

4. In the `<body>` section of your Web page, insert the code where you want the image to appear.

5. Preview the page in a browser and adjust the placement of the `<img>` tag, if necessary.

Using Dreamweaver

Although you can use Dreamweaver's Code Inspector or Code View to integrate the Fireworks-generated code, you can also stay in Design View and do it visually, thanks to Dreamweaver's Tag Selector.

To insert Fireworks-generated code for a sliced image into Dreamweaver, follow these steps:

1. In Dreamweaver, open the HTML page generated in Fireworks.
2. Click the exported image once.

   Because the image is now sliced into different sections, the entire image is not selected, just one slice.

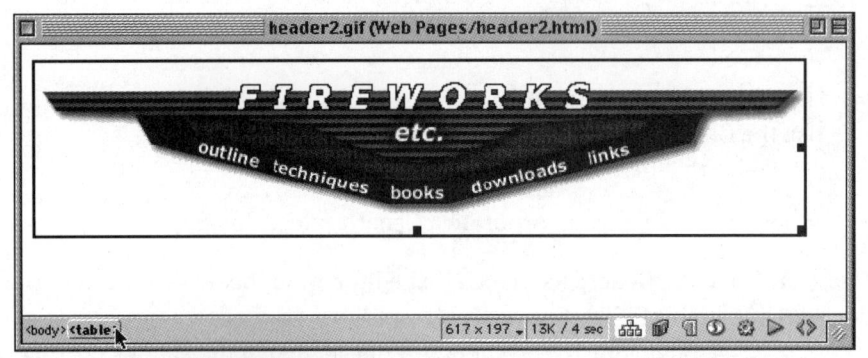

3. On the bottom left of the document window, select the <table> tag from the Tag Selector, as shown in Figure 33-16.

   The entire sliced image and all the code is selected.

Figure 33-16: Use Dreamweaver's Tag Selector to easily select the entire sliced image for cutting and pasting.

4. Choose either Edit ⇨ Copy, or the keyboard shortcut, Ctrl+C (Command+C).
5. Open the existing Web page to which you want to add the sliced image.
6. Place the cursor where you want the sliced image to appear.
7. Choose either Edit ⇨ Paste, or the keyboard shortcut, Ctrl+V (Command+V).

The sliced image and corresponding code are inserted into the document.

Using GoLive

GoLive's HTML Outline view is an easy way to drag and drop HTML code between two documents. Code exported with the GoLive style also contains a `csscript-dict` tag that tells GoLive how to edit the code. Make sure to copy the `csscript-dict` tag, as well as your plain HTML code.

To insert Fireworks-generated code for a sliced image into GoLive, follow these steps:

1. In GoLive, open the HTML page generated in Fireworks.
2. Switch to the HTML Outline view for both your source and target documents.
3. In the source document, select the `<table>` tag. This table contains all of your sliced images.
4. Drag and drop the table tag into place in your target document.
5. Select the `cssscriptdict` tag from the head of your source document and drag it into the head of your target document.

Using FrontPage

Microsoft's FrontPage stores external code — including any JavaScript — in a structure (or webbot in FrontPage jargon) called HTML markup. Fireworks produces the proper structure through the FrontPage template, so that the code can be seamlessly integrated.

To insert an image map from Fireworks into a FrontPage document, follow these steps:

1. Open the Fireworks-generated page in FrontPage.

Caution: Both the FrontPage document and the Fireworks-generated document must be in the same folder.

2. Select the HTML View.
3. Select the code starting with

   `<!---------- BEGIN COPYING THE HTML ---------->`

   and ends with

   `<!---------- STOP COPYING THE HTML HERE ---------->`
4. Choose Edit ⇨ Copy.
5. Open the document in which the sliced image is to be inserted.
6. While still in HTML View, choose Edit ⇨ Paste to insert the code into the document.

Exporting single slices

Sometimes I find myself wanting to quickly export a small area of the Fireworks canvas as a single image file. Rather than copying a section of the overall image and placing it into a new document and then exporting that, a quick way to define the area for an exported image file is to place a slice object on top of it, and then export that single slice. You can even separately optimize that single slice before export.

To export a single slice, follow these steps:

1. Select the slice that you want to export.
2. Choose Window ➪ Optimize to view the Optimize panel if it is not already visible.
3. Specify export settings in the Optimize panel.

   These settings affect only the selected slice.
4. Choose File ➪ Export.

   The Export dialog box appears.
5. Navigate to a folder to export your slice into, and specify a filename.
6. Choose Images Only from the Save As option list.
7. Choose Export Slices from the Slices option list.
8. Check the Selected Slices Only checkbox.
9. Click Save when you're done.

Your selected slice is exported as an individual image file.

Fireworks Technique: Exporting Dreamweaver Library Items

Library Items are a powerful Dreamweaver feature that enable a section of a Web page to be updated once, after which Dreamweaver automatically updates all pages on which the section appears. Originally intended to replace page elements that are often repeated, such as a copyright line or logo, Dreamweaver Library items also enable you to regard a section of code as a single, easy-to-manage unit. If, as a designer, you're familiar with Encapsulated PostScript, think of Dreamweaver Libraries as Encapsulated HTML.

For a Library item to be recognized as such, it must be stored in a special folder for each local site. When you choose the Dreamweaver Library (.lbi) option from the Save as type (Save As) option list in the Export dialog box, Fireworks prompts you to locate your site's Library folder. If you've never created a Library item for the current site before, you need to make a new folder. You must place the folder in the local site root and must name it, appropriately enough, Library. For example, if your local site root is located in a folder called Web Pages, you must create the Library folder at Web Pages/Library.

Tip Most Web sites use a lowercase-only naming convention. You can name your Library folder "library" if that suits you, and Dreamweaver will use it without complaint.

The Dreamweaver Library (.lbi) export option exports your image map or slices within the same table as the Dreamweaver HTML style template, but it also marks the table as a Dreamweaver Library item that can be inserted over and over again. You can export using the Dreamweaver Library (.lbi) option at any time, no matter what your HTML style setting in the HTML Setup dialog box.

To export HTML and images from Fireworks as a Dreamweaver Library Item, follow these steps:

1. Choose File ➪ Export.

   Fireworks displays the Export dialog box.

2. Navigate to your Dreamweaver site root folder, and then into the site's Library subfolder. If your site does not yet have a Library folder, create one and then navigate into it.

3. Specify a filename for your library item, if necessary.

4. Select Dreamweaver Library (.lbi) from the Save as type (Save As) option list.

Note

If you have not previously navigated to a Library folder, Fireworks warns you at this point that a Library folder is required. Then, Fireworks asks you to choose one. Navigating to the Library folder before selecting the Dreamweaver Library (.lbi) option avoids this warning — as you did in Step 2, earlier — enabling you to choose the Library folder in a larger dialog box, and having Fireworks return to that folder the next time you export from the same document.

5. Check the Put Images in Subfolder checkbox, and click Browse to choose your site's images folder.

6. Click Save when you're done.

Now that you've exported your Library Item from Fireworks, follow these steps to incorporate the Library Item into your work in Dreamweaver:

1. In Dreamweaver, choose Window ➪ Assets, or use the keyboard shortcut, F11, to display the Assets panel.

   The current site's Assets panel appears.

Caution

Mac users: If you have mapped the keyboard's function keys in the Keyboard Control Panel to start programs or perform other tasks, function key shortcuts in Fireworks are superceded by those mappings. Use the menu commands instead, or disable the mappings in the Keyboard Control Panel.

2. Select the Library category of the Assets panel, as shown in Figure 33-17.

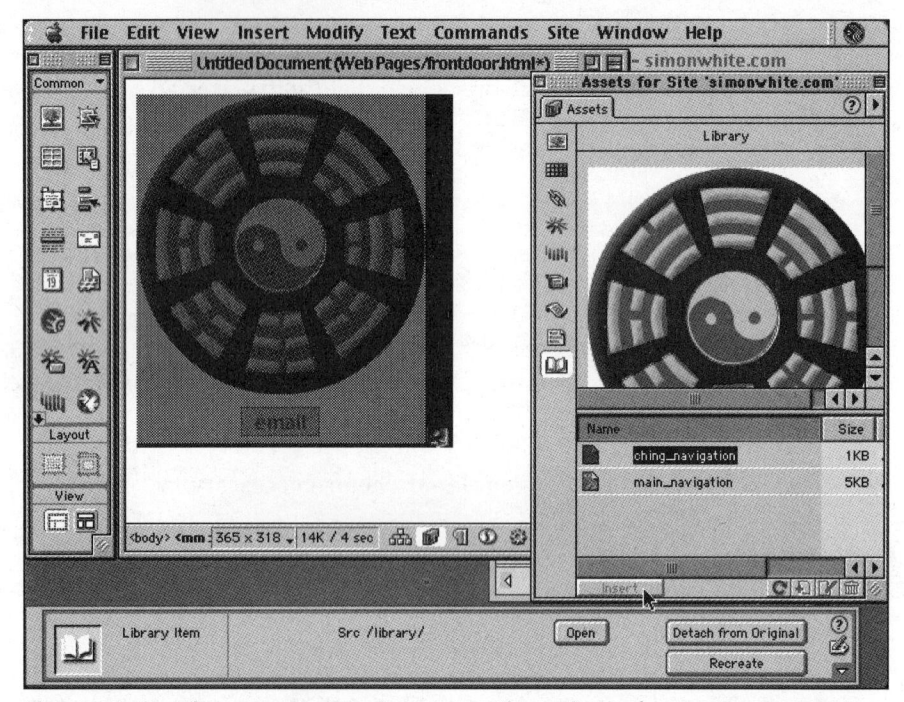

Figure 33-17: After you export an image map from Fireworks as a Dreamweaver Library item, it is available from the Library category of Dreamweaver's Assets panel.

3. Place your cursor in the document window where you want the image map to appear.
4. In the Assets panel, select your exported image map from the list window.

   The preview pane of the Assets panel displays the selected Library item.
5. Click the Insert button or, alternatively, drag the item from either the preview pane or the list window and drop it in the document window.

The image map and all the necessary code are inserted into the Dreamweaver page.

If you ever need to edit the image map, you first need to select it and then click Open from Dreamweaver's Property inspector. A document window appears with just the Library item in it. From there, you can choose the image and select either Edit from the Property Inspector, or Optimize Image in Fireworks from the Commands menu. After you edit the image, closing the Library document window prompts Dreamweaver to ask whether you would like to update the Library. Click Yes to update the Library items; click No to postpone the update.

Fireworks Technique: Animating a Slice

Fireworks can build terrific animations — and with just a little technique, you can integrate any animation into a larger image through slices. Animations can be fairly heavy in terms of file size. If only a small section of an overall image is moving — such as a radar screen on a control panel — converting the entire image to an animation is prohibitive, due to the file size that would result. However, with slices, you can animate just the area that you need to animate, and keep the rest of the image static, thus dropping the size of the file dramatically.

To include an animation in Fireworks, follow these steps:

1. Build your animation in Fireworks as you would normally.
2. If the animation is not already part of a larger image, go to Frame 1 in the Frame panel, choose Modify ⇨ Canvas Size, and enlarge the canvas as desired.
3. Complete the graphics surrounding the animation.
4. Make a slice object from the animation either by choosing the animation and selecting Insert ⇨ Slice, or by using the Slice tool to draw a rectangle around the entire animation.
5. If it's not already visible, display the Object panel.
6. In the Object panel, set the link and any other desired options.
7. If it's not already visible, display the Optimize panel.
8. From the Export File Format option list, choose Animated GIF.
9. Specify other image optimization options as necessary.

Cross-Reference: Chapter 30 details Fireworks' image optimization options.

10. Repeat Steps 4–9 for the static slices in your document, but choose formats other than animated GIF in the Optimize panel. Alternatively, deselect all slices and set an overall document export format in the Optimize panel. This format is used for any slices that are not explicitly set to another format.
11. When your document is ready for export, choose File ⇨ Export.

    The Export dialog box opens.
12. Set your path and filename in the upper portion of the dialog box.
13. Choose HTML and Images from the Save as type (Save As) option list.
14. Choose whether to export an HTML file, or copy the code to the clipboard from the HTML option list.

15. Select Export Slices from the Slices option list.
16. To modify HTML Setup options, click the Options button to display the HTML Setup dialog box.
17. Click Save when you're ready to complete the export.

Your animation is exported as part of the overall image, as shown in the example in Figure 33-18.

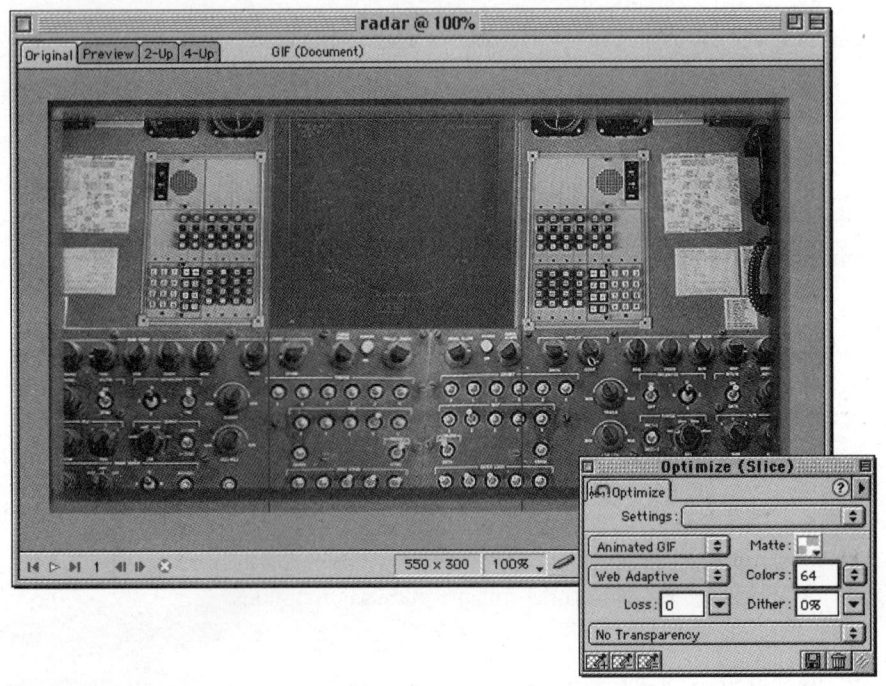

Figure 33-18: In this image, the radar screen is animated, and the rest of the graphic is static.

Summary

Fireworks Web objects — hotspots and slices — provide a gateway from graphic imagery to the Internet. By integrating Web objects with other graphic elements, the Web designer can seamlessly migrate from one medium to another, all the while maintaining editability. When working with Web objects, keep these points in mind:

- ✦ Fireworks supports two types of Web objects: hotspots and slices. A hotspot marks part of a larger graphic through code, whereas slices actually divide the larger image into smaller files.

- ✦ Hotspots come in three basic shapes: rectangle, circle, and polygon. Fireworks has a different tool for each type of hotspot. The term *hotspot* denotes an area of the overall image, called an image map.

- ✦ You can easily convert any Fireworks object into a hotspot by selecting the image and choosing Insert ➪ Hotspot.

- ✦ When exporting image maps, be sure to work with both parts of the code: the `<img>` tag containing the link to the source image, and the `<map>` tag that contains the hotspot data.

- ✦ Fireworks makes slices in three ways: with the Rectangle or Polygon Slice tool, with the Insert ➪ Slice command, and with the standard guides.

- ✦ Enabling the View ➪ Slice Guides option helps you to reduce the number of slices to a minimum.

- ✦ You can export individual slices as different image types, even as animated GIFs, enabling you to mix animated and static slices.

In the next chapter, you learn how to assign Behaviors for interactive effects.

✦ ✦ ✦

Activating Fireworks with Behaviors

CHAPTER 34

In This Chapter

Using Behaviors

Creating rollover buttons

Using the URL panel

Exporting rollovers for the Web

Working with the Button Editor

Making disjointed rollovers

Creating external rollovers

Incorporating rollovers in slices

From a user's perspective, the Web includes two types of images: graphics that you look at and graphics that you interact with. You can create the "look, but don't touch" variety of graphics with most any graphics program — Fireworks is among the few graphics programs that can output interactive graphics.

Although the result may be a complex combination of images and code, Fireworks uses *Behaviors* to simplify the process. With Fireworks Behaviors, you can create everything from simple rollovers — exchanging one image for another — to more complicated interactions, in which selecting a hotspot in one area may trigger a rollover in another, while simultaneously displaying a message in the status bar. And you can do it all in Fireworks without writing a line of code.

This chapter covers all the intricacies of using Behaviors and demonstrates some techniques that combine several Behaviors. You may never use each and every one of the Fireworks Behaviors, but after you start to use them, your Web pages will never be the same.

Understanding Behaviors

Before Fireworks, making your Web pages responsive to Web page visitors required in-depth programming skills or a Web-authoring program (such as Macromedia's Dreamweaver) that automated the process for you. The basic Web page, scripted in HTML, is fairly static; only forms allow any degree of user interaction. To activate your page, you have to use a more advanced language. Because of its integration into both major browsers, JavaScript is the language of choice for this task for most Web programmers. Although JavaScript is not as difficult to use as, say, C++, the majority of Web designers don't have the time or the inclination to master it. Because Fireworks permits Behaviors to be integrated into graphics, Web designers don't have to master a programming language.

A Behavior consists of two parts: an *event* and an *action*. An event is a trigger that starts an action, the way pushing Play on a VCR starts a videotape. Events on the Web are either user driven, such as moving a pointer over an image; or automatic, such as when a page finishes loading. Generally speaking, actions range from displaying a message to launching a whole new browser window.

Behaviors are said to be "attached" to a specific element on the Web page, such as a text or image link; Behaviors in Fireworks are always attached to slices or hotspots. Several other products in the Macromedia family, including Dreamweaver and Director, use Behaviors in much the same way as Fireworks.

In one sense, you can think of Behaviors as Encapsulated JavaScript. As a designer, you need only make a few key decisions, such as which two images to swap, and Fireworks handles the rest. Then, the code is written for you, in the HTML style of your choice. With Fireworks, you can output code that's tweaked for various Web-authoring programs, including Dreamweaver. Before you can export your images and associated Behavior code, however, you must assign the Behavior through the Behaviors panel.

Using the Behaviors Panel

The Behaviors panel is used to add and remove Behaviors. Although each Behavior has its own dialog box for selecting options and entering parameters, the Behaviors panel lists basic information for every Behavior assigned. You can assign multiple Behaviors — either the same Behavior or different ones — to any slice or hotspot; the number of Behaviors that you can attach to a single Web object has no practical limit.

Fireworks includes five main groups of Behaviors:

- ✦ **Simple Rollover:** Automatically swaps the image on Frame 1 with the image from Frame 2 when the user's mouse cursor rolls over the image. Optionally, the third and fourth frames can be swapped, as well.
- ✦ **Swap Image (Swap Image Restore):** Displays one image in place of another. The swapped image can be located on a different frame, in a different slice, or both. An external image can also be exchanged for the current or any other slice in the document. The Swap Image Restore Behavior is automatically applied to restore the swap to its original state.

✦ **Set Nav Bar Image (Nav Bar Over, Nav Bar Down, Nav Bar Restore):** This group of Behaviors specifies in which state of a navigation bar the selected slice should be.

✦ **Set Pop-up Menu:** This Behavior creates a pop-up menu in a Web page.

✦ **Set Text of Status Bar:** This Behavior shows a message in the browser's status bar.

The Behaviors panel (see Figure 34-1) is the central control center for Behaviors. To show or hide the Behaviors panel, choose Window ➪ Behaviors, use the keyboard shortcut Shift+F3, or click the Behaviors tab, if it is visible. The Behaviors panel enables you to select a hotspot or slice object and to add or to remove Behaviors. It also shows any Behaviors that have been previously added to the selected object. After you add a Behavior to a hotspot or slice object, selecting it again enables you to remove the Behavior or change its settings.

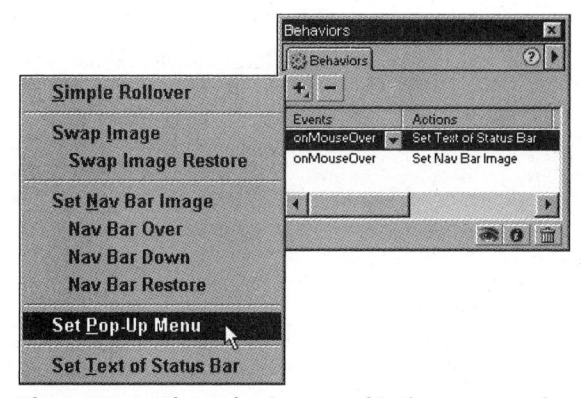

Figure 34-1: The Behaviors panel is the command center for attaching and removing Behaviors from hotspots and slices.

Attaching Behaviors

As noted previously, Behaviors are attached to Fireworks Web objects, either hotspots or slices. It's important to understand that hotspots are only capable of triggering events and are incapable of performing actions. Slices, on the other hand, can both trigger and receive events.

Practically, this means that hotspots by themselves can be used only in conjunction with the Set Text of Status Bar Behavior; all other Behaviors require slices in order to work. However, you can use hotspots to trigger an action that occurs in a slice, as explained later in the section "Working with hotspot rollovers."

Following is the general procedure for adding a Behavior to a Web object:

1. Select the hotspot or slice that you want to attach the Behavior to.
2. Choose either Window ⇨ Behaviors, or use the keyboard shortcut, Shift+F3 to open the Behaviors panel. Alternatively, if it is docked behind another panel, click the Behaviors panel's tab to bring it forward.

Note: If you have anything other than a Web object selected, Fireworks alerts you to this fact and gives you the option to create a Web object from the selected object. If nothing is selected when you try to add a Behavior, Fireworks asks you to choose a hotspot or slice first.

3. Click the Add Action button (the plus sign), and choose a Behavior from the drop-down list.

    A dialog box, which is specific to the chosen Behavior, opens.

4. Enter the desired options for the Behavior, and click OK when you're done.

    The Behaviors panel displays the newly attached Behavior in the list window.

Modifying a Behavior

To modify a Behavior that you've already added to a hotspot or slice object, select a hotspot or slice object and double-click the Behavior's entry on the Behaviors list in the Behaviors panel. Fireworks displays the Behavior's dialog box, in which you can adjust the settings that you made when you added the Behavior.

In addition to modifying the Behavior's settings, you can select another event to trigger the Behavior. By default, Fireworks initially assigns the onMouseOver event for all events. Following is a list of available events:

✦ **onMouseOver:** A user's mouse cursor hovers over an image and triggers the Behavior.

✦ **onMouseOut:** When a user's mouse cursor moves away from an image, the Behavior is triggered.

✦ **onClick:** A user clicks an image and the Behavior is triggered.

✦ **onLoad:** When the Web page has finished loading, the Behavior is triggered.

When a Behavior is selected in the Behaviors list, the Event pop-up menu button (a down-pointing arrow) appears just to the right of the event. Click this button to choose a new event from the Event pop-up menu, as shown in Figure 34-2.

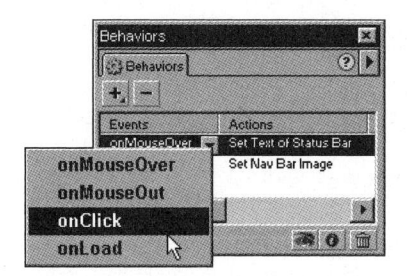

Figure 34-2: Click the Event pop-up button to choose another trigger for any selected Behavior.

Deleting a Behavior

When you delete a Behavior, all the settings that you have created are lost.

To delete a Behavior, follow these steps:

1. Select the hotspot or slice object from which you want to remove the Behavior.
2. Choose the Behavior that you want to remove from the Behaviors list in the Behaviors panel.

   The Behavior's event, action, and information are highlighted.
3. Click the Remove Action button (the minus sign) on the Behaviors panel.

The Behavior is removed from your hotspot or slice object, and its entry disappears from the Behaviors list.

Creating Rollovers

Perhaps the most common use of JavaScript on the Web is the rollover. *Rollovers* are images in a Web page that change appearance when a user rolls a mouse cursor over them.

Rollovers are popular because they're fairly simple to implement, are supported by many browsers, and are an effective way to heighten the feeling of interaction for Web site visitors.

Examining how rollovers work

To understand how a rollover works, you need to grasp a fundamental HTML concept. Web pages do not contain images in themselves — they only contain links to images. With an image, the link is referred to its source and is specified in the `<img>` tag in HTML as the `src` attribute. When a user's mouse pointer hovers over an image — or in some cases, clicks an image — the `src` attribute is changed to another image file. Because this happens quickly, it appears as if the image itself is changing.

Before the rollover effect, a typical `<img>` tag might read like the following:

```
<a href="home.html"><img src="button_regular.gif" height="100" width="50" alt="home"></a>
```

After the rollover effect is applied, the effect is as if the code was the following code:

```
<a href="home.html"><img src="button_over.gif" height="100" width="50" alt="home"></a>
```

As this code shows, the height, width, and alt text for the image doesn't change, nor does the link that the hyperlink is pointing to (in this example, `home.html`), as specified in the `<a>` tag. All that changes — and this can't be overemphasized — is the actual GIF (Graphics Interchange Format), JPEG (Joint Photographic Experts Group), or PNG (Portable Network Graphics) image file that's being used; the file referenced by the `src` attribute.

Caution Because only the `src` attribute changes with a rollover, the original image and any swapped images must have the same dimensions. You can't swap a smaller image with a larger one, or vice versa. If you do, the browser applies the height and width dimensions of the original image, leading to a distorted image.

Note that any `<img>` tag can be modified, not just the `<img>` tag that is rolled over. This is the foundation for disjointed rollovers, as discussed later in this chapter.

Learning rollover states

Although a rollover actually switches one image for another, the illusion that most Web designers want is of a button changing into different states. Before the user triggers the rollover effect, the image is in the Up state. When the rollover is triggered, the image changes to an Over state, because the cursor of the user's mouse is over the image. In Fireworks, the easiest and most typical method of creating the different states for a rollover is with frames.

A basic rollover uses just two states (and, thus, two Fireworks frames): Up and Over. Rollovers, though, can have up to four states, in which case they would be built across four Fireworks frames. Table 34-1 details the rollover states and their typical associated frames.

Table 34-1
Rollover States

Frame	State	Description
1	Up	The way the button looks when the user is not interacting with it; how it looks when the page first loads into the browser.
2	Over	The button's appearance when the user's mouse cursor is hovering over it.
3	Down	The button's appearance after it's pressed. The Down state of a rollover button depicts the button's state on the destination Web page. For example, the Down state is commonly used to show which button was clicked to view the current Web page.
4	Over Down	The way a button that's in its Down state looks when the user's mouse cursor hovers over it.

Creating rollover images

The first step in building a rollover is to create the separate rollover images that reside on the separate frames of a Fireworks document. I use either of two basic techniques to create images. Which technique I choose depends upon whether the rollovers are to be independently used, each in their own unique Fireworks document, or if they're part of a complete design in a larger document. Both techniques involve creating an initial button object, which is then duplicated and modified.

If your rollover buttons exist independently, use the following technique to create its images:

1. Create the initial button in Frame 1, as it should appear before being clicked by the user.

2. Click the button and choose Edit ➪ Clone to create a duplicate directly on top of the button.

3. If you are going to create a Down state for this button, repeat Step 2. If you are also going to create an Over Down state, repeat Step 2, so that you have a total of four objects stacked on top of each other in Frame 1.

4. Select all of your button states by drawing a selection around them with the mouse. Click the Distribute to Frames button (which resembles the small movie strip) in the Layers panel.

   Your objects are distributed to separate frames, so that each button state is now in its own frame.

5. Frame 1 already contains a suitable Up state for your button. Go to Frame 2 and modify your button object slightly in order to create an interesting Over state for the button. You might add a Glow Live Effect to the Over state, or change the Fill or Stroke settings.

6. If you have Down and Over Down states, as well, modify them slightly on Frame 3 and Frame 4 so that each frame now contains a unique — but similar — button.

Tip   If the Over state of your button has a Live Effect bevel on it to give it a three-dimensional appearance, a good way to modify subsequent states is to click the button object and then modify the Button Preset settings of the bevel Live Effect (the bottom option list on the pop-up edit window) in order to create the impression of a three-dimensional button moving up and down. For example, the Up state could be set to Raised, the Over state to Highlighted, the Down state to Inset, and the Over Down state to Inverted.

If your rollovers are part of a larger document that contains many buttons or objects that you want to create rollovers for, use the following technique to create the images:

1. Create all the initial objects in Frame 1 of your document.

2. From the options pop-up menu on the Frames panel, select Duplicate Frames.

   The Duplicate Frames dialog box appears.

3. In the Duplicate Frames dialog box, enter the number of frames that you want to add. In the Number text box, add one frame for each additional state used.

   For a simple rollover with just an Up and Over state, add one frame. For a rollover that also uses the Down and Over Down states, add three frames.

4. Make sure that the Insert New Frame After the Current Frame option is selected and click OK when you're done.

   The duplicate frames are inserted.

Tip   Another way to duplicate a frame is to drag its name to the New/Duplicate Frame button in the Frames panel. Each time you do this, another duplicate frame is added after the one you dragged. Layers can also be duplicated in this fashion in the Layers panel.

5. In each new frame, modify the rollover objects slightly in order to create a different look in each frame.

Tip   You can modify many objects simultaneously — to make them all glow, for example — by selecting all of them at once and applying the changes through the Stroke, Fill, or Effects panel.

No matter which technique you use to create the separate rollover images, the best effect usually results from applying a degree of subtlety. If one button is too drastically different from another of its states, the underlying image swap becomes overt and the illusion of a single button being clicked or highlighted is lost. Instead, the user sees one image simply change into another. Small shifts in position, or an incremental change in an effect seem to work best, as shown by the examples in Figure 34-3.

Figure 34-3: Subtle modifications to your original button image create convincing state changes. Here, three buttons are exploded in order to view (from left to right) their Up, Over, Over Down, and Down states.

> **Tip** You can preview your soon-to-be rollover by clicking Play on the animation controls; the frames of your image are then shown one after the other.

After you create your separate button images, they are ready to have Behaviors applied to them and to be used as true buttons.

Applying the Simple Rollover Behavior

Fireworks takes the *simple* in simple rollover very seriously: The Behavior creates a classic Up-and-Over rollover effect, while offering exactly zero user settings. When you just want a classic rollover, Fireworks makes creating one a snap.

The only difference between the simple rollover and Swap Image Behaviors is the interface and the number of options. The code you generate is the same compatible JavaScript you always expect from Fireworks.

To apply the Simple Rollover Behavior, follow these steps:

1. Select a slice on the Web Layer of your document.
2. From the Behaviors panel, choose Simple Rollover from the Add Action pop-up menu in the Behaviors panel.

To preview your rollover, select the document window's Preview tab and roll the mouse over your button. You can also preview your rollover in your primary browser by pressing F12.

The Simple Rollover Behavior doesn't have any options that need to be specified. In fact, if you double-click the Behavior in the Behaviors list, Fireworks just explains the Behavior, as shown in Figure 34-4.

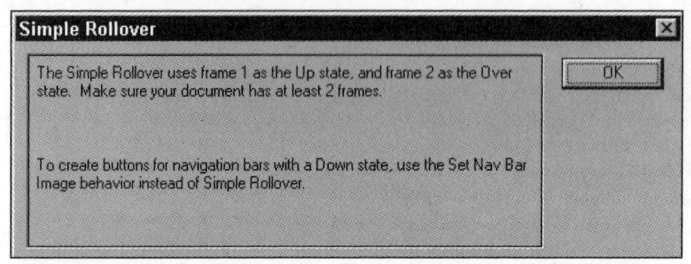

Figure 34-4: The "options dialog" for a simple rollover simply explains what a simple rollover is without offering any options; it's that simple.

Of course — as with any Behavior — you can still choose a different kind of event, such as onClick or onLoad, from the Behaviors panel Event list.

Cross-Reference: If you plan to use the rollover as a link, you first need to assign it a URL. For detailed information on how to add a link to a Web object, see Chapter 33.

Exporting Rollovers for the Web

Obviously, you can export images from Fireworks. When you create rollovers, the JavaScript code that controls the behavior of your images is exported within an HTML file. The JavaScript itself is compatible with Netscape Navigator 3 and above, and Microsoft Internet Explorer 4 and above. The Macintosh version of Internet Explorer 3 will also display your rollover effects, but in Internet Explorer 3 for Windows, your rollover effects will not be visible, although hyperlinks still work.

Macromedia has continually improved the HTML editor compatibility of Fireworks' exported JavaScript. In the first version of Fireworks, only one type of rollover code was generated; it worked in browsers, sure, but you had to edit it by hand if you opened it in a visual editor. In Fireworks 4, you can pick the style of code that's best for your workflow, or even create a template of your own to fine-tune the settings even further.

Before exporting your first rollovers, it pays to make a quick stop in the HTML Setup dialog box, if only to choose an HTML style that suits your workflow. For the most part, this choice is governed by the Web-authoring tool that you are using to lay out the Web page onto which the rollover will be placed. The standard HTML styles included in Fireworks are the following:

- **Dreamweaver:** Code styled for Dreamweaver. Dreamweaver-style rollover code generated by Fireworks appears as native Dreamweaver Behaviors when opened in Dreamweaver.

- **GoLive:** Code styled for Adobe's GoLive, including special tags that make editing the code in GoLive easier.

- **FrontPage:** FrontPage uses a series of *webbots* — FrontPage-only code snippets — to create Web elements; Fireworks includes the code necessary for an image map webbot, so that it displays correctly when the document is opened in FrontPage.

- **Generic:** The basic functional code, useful in hand-coded Web pages and the majority of Web authoring tools that work with standard HTML. If you're not sure which HTML style to choose, go with this one.

While you're in the HTML Setup dialog box, you may also want to change the default filename extension for HTML files from the non-standard .htm, to the standard .html. You can also choose whether Fireworks inserts its own comments in your HTML output and force Fireworks to lowercase the exported filenames for better compatibility with different kinds of servers. Mac users can also choose the Creator code that exported HTML files should have, so that double-clicking them opens them in your HTML editor.

Integrating a Fireworks-generated rollover into your Web page is a three-stage process.

- **Stage 1:** Create and test your rollover in Fireworks.

- **Stage 2:** Export the images and code from Fireworks. You can export code as an HTML file, or copy it to the clipboard.

- **Stage 3:** Insert the code into your Web page, using whatever HTML editor you prefer (even a plain text editor, such as NotePad or SimpleText, will work). Either open the HTML file in your editor, or if you copied the code to the clipboard, simply paste it into your editor.

Exporting the code from Fireworks

To export a rollover — and its code — from Fireworks, follow these steps:

1. Specify your image export settings in the Optimize panel.
2. Choose File ➪ Export.

   The Export dialog box, shown in Figure 34-5, appears.

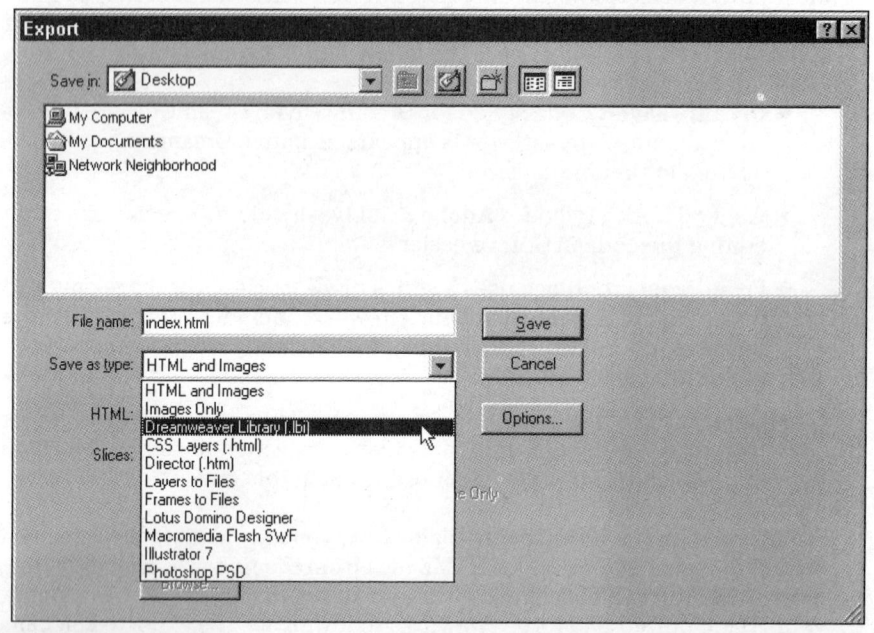

Figure 34-5: You can choose an alternative to HTML and Images from the Save as Type (Save As) option list in the Export dialog box.

3. Choose a target folder for your exported image file(s) and specify a filename for the HTML file.
4. From the Save as Type (Save As) option list, select HTML and Images to export HTML, or choose Dreamweaver Library (.lbi) to export the HTML as a Dreamweaver Library.

   If you chose the Dreamweaver Library HTML style, the Locate Site Library Directory opens so that you can identify your site's Library folder.
5. Choose either HTML File, or Copy to Clipboard from the HTML option list.

6. Choose from among the following options in the Slices option list:

    • **None:** Disables slicing altogether.

    • **Export Slices:** Causes your image to be sliced according to the placement of Slice objects.

> **Tip** Export Slices is the option you'll probably use most of the time.

    • **Slice Along Guides:** Slices your image along guides (not slice guides).

7. Check Selected Slices Only to export the selected slice(s) only.
8. Check Current Frame to export images from the current frame only.
9. Check Include Areas without Slices to export images that don't have a slice specified.
10. To save the image files in a different folder, check the Put Images in Subfolder checkbox, click Browse, and choose the desired folder for your images.
11. To alter any of the slice settings previously set, click Options to reopen the HTML Setup dialog box and adjust your settings accordingly.

> **Cross-Reference** To review the possible slice settings, see Chapter 33.

12. When you're ready to complete the export, click Save.

Inserting rollover code in your Web page

After you select your HTML style, Fireworks automatically outputs the requested type of code, either to an HTML file or to the clipboard, according to which option you selected. If you chose to output the HTML code to the clipboard, open your target HTML file in your HTML editor and paste the code into place. If you chose to output to a file, you'll have to open that file and your target HTML file in a text or HTML editor and then copy and paste between them.

The process for transferring rollover code to a Web page is essentially the same as that for transferring image maps or sliced images, with one important exception; the code generated for rollovers — and all Behaviors — generally comes in these two parts:

✦ The event portion of a code, which contains the <img> tags and their triggers, is stored in the <body> section of a Web page.

✦ The action portion of a code — with all the JavaScript functions — is kept in the <head> section.

You must transfer both parts of the code in order for the rollover to function properly.

With Dreamweaver, Generic, and GoLive code, the process is similar. Cut or copy the code from both the `<body>` and the `<head>` sections of the Fireworks-generated document and paste it into your existing Web page. FrontPage does not separate the `<head>` and the `<body>` sections for rollovers in its code, so simply copy the one section of code from the source to the target page. When you export as a Dreamweaver Library, the process is even simpler: Include the Library item and its code in your Web page, using the Library category of the Assets panel, just as you would any Library item.

For Dreamweaver, FrontPage, Generic, and GoLive styles of code, follow these steps to insert Fireworks code into your Web page:

1. Open the Fireworks-generated source HTML file in a text or HTML editor.
2. Select and copy to the clipboard the section in the `<body>` tag that starts with

   `<!---------- BEGIN COPYING THE HTML HERE ---------->`

   and ends with

   `<!---------- STOP COPYING THE HTML HERE ---------->`

   Tip: If you're using Dreamweaver, you don't have to open the HTML Source window or an external text editor in order to copy the code. Just make sure that View ⇨ Invisible Elements is enabled and copy the icons that represent the code.

3. Open your existing target Web page in a text or HTML editor.
4. In the `<body>` section of your Web page, insert the code where you want the image to appear.

   If you're using the FrontPage template, your code transfer is complete; skip the rest of the steps. You can now view your rollover.

5. Return to the source HTML file and locate the `<head>` section.
6. Select and copy to the clipboard the section in the `<body>` tag that starts with

   `<!------ BEGIN COPYING THE JAVASCRIPT SECTION HERE ------>`

Preloading Rollover Images

When the HTML document that contains your rollovers is first displayed, the Up state of your rollovers is visible, along with the other image files on the Web page. Ideally, as the user interacts with your document, the other states of the rollovers will be instantly available from the browser cache, instead of slowly available from the Web. Instantaneous reactions reinforce the illusion that an object is being modified — a button pushed, for example — instead of one image being replaced with another. To make sure that the other states are available from the browser cache, Fireworks includes JavaScript with its HTML output that "preloads" the Over, Over Down, and Down image files.

and ends with

```
<!------ STOP COPYING THE JAVASCRIPT HERE ------>
```

7. Switch to your existing Web page.

8. Paste the copied code in the `<head>` section of the document.

> **Tip** Placing the JavaScript code after the `<title>` and any `<meta>` tags makes your page friendlier to the spider programs that add pages to Web search engines.

After you insert both sections of the rollover code, you can view your rollovers in any supported browser.

Dreamweaver's Library feature enables a single repeating element to be inserted in multiple Web pages, which can then all be updated simultaneously, after you modify the original item. The only stipulation is that the rollover code must be stored in a special folder, called Library, within each local site, during export. If you've never created a Library item for the current site, you need to make a new Library folder in the local site folder.

After you export the HTML file as a Dreamweaver Library item, follow these steps to incorporate the rollover images and code:

1. In Dreamweaver, choose Window ➪ Assets.

Dreamweaver displays the Assets panel.

2. Select the Library category of the Assets panel.

The Assets panel displays the site's current Library items.

3. Place your cursor in the document window where you want the rollover to appear.

4. Select your exported rollover's Library item from the list in the Assets panel.

A preview of the Library item appears in the Assets panel.

5. Click the Insert button to insert your Library item in the page. Alternatively, you can drag the item from either the preview pane or the list window of the Assets panel, and drop it in your page.

The sliced image, and all the necessary code, is inserted into your Dreamweaver page.

Looking at Nav Bar Behavior

A *Nav Bar* is a way to turn a series of rollover buttons into a set of radio buttons. Each button is linked to the others, so that clicking one button and setting it to a Down state sets the other buttons to an Up state. Fireworks creates Nav Bars by using JavaScript cookies. In JavaScript, a *cookie* is a small bit of information written to the user's computer. Cookies generally are used by Web sites to record visitors' selections as they travel from one Web page to another, as with a shopping cart on an e-commerce site. Fireworks uses this same technology to keep track of which button in a group has been selected.

Nav Bars and cookies might seem like advanced topics, but if you've implemented a three- or four-frame Simple Rollover Behavior, you've already used them. Fireworks automatically creates a Nav Bar (named FwNavBar) for each simple rollover that uses a Down and/or Over Down state. You don't need to do anything else to get the toggle effect. However, if you use Swap Image to create your rollover, or want to toggle just the two Up and Over states of a simple rollover, you need to apply the Nav Bar Behavior explicitly.

Creating a Nav Bar

To create a Nav Bar, follow these steps:

1. Create your rollover buttons, with appropriate states (Up, Over, Down, and Over Down) on the appropriate frames, 1 through 4.
2. In Frame 1, draw a slice object over each rollover button.
3. Select each slice object, in turn, and turn it into a rollover by choosing Simple Rollover from the Add Action pop-up menu in the Behaviors panel.

   Your rollovers are now ready to be turned into a Nav Bar.
4. Select all the slice objects to be included in the Nav Bar.
5. Choose Set Nav Bar Image from the Add Action pop-up menu in the Behaviors panel.

   Fireworks displays the Set Nav Bar Image dialog box (see Figure 34-6).
6. If you have included the Over Down state in your rollovers, check the Include Over While Down State box. Click OK when you're done.
7. If you want one of the buttons to appear in its Down state by default, first deselect all the slices and then select the individual slice. Next, double-click the Set Nav Bar Image Behavior in the Behaviors panel, and then check Show Down Image Upon Load. Click OK when you're done.

Tip The term *radio buttons* comes from tuning buttons on AM/FM radios. Only one station can be tuned in at a time, so only one button can be down at a time. Clicking a button causes all other buttons to pop up.

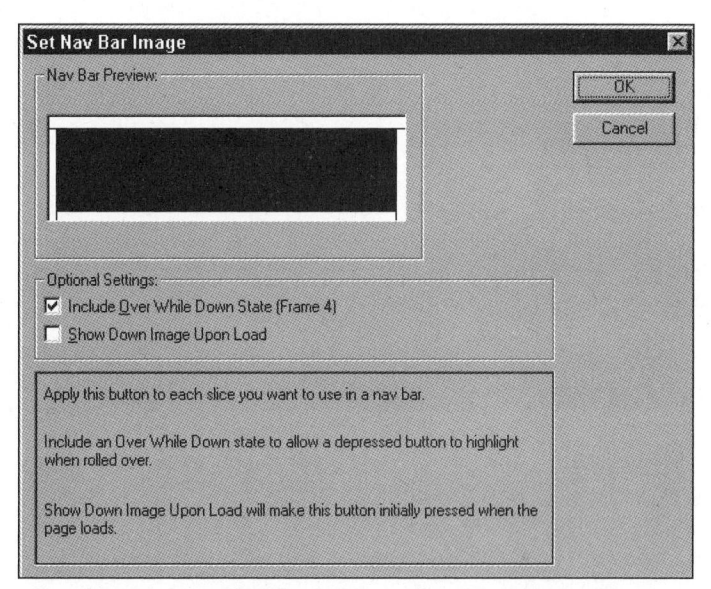

Figure 34-6: The Nav Bar Behavior makes any set of rollovers mutually exclusive; therefore, only one button can be selected at any time.

When you view your Nav Bar on the Preview tab of the document window or in a Web browser (see Figure 34-7), the buttons change depending upon which one is clicked.

Figure 34-7: The second button in this Nav Bar is in the Down state. Only one button in a Nav Bar can be down at a time, creating the impression of a group of radio buttons.

Building buttons in the Button Editor

The Fireworks Button Editor enables you to create or assemble a button Symbol that includes a two-, three- or four-state rollover. A special tabbed window — similar to the document window — walks you step by step through the process.

To create a rollover button with the Button Editor, follow these steps:

1. Choose Insert ➪ New Button.

    Fireworks displays the Button Editor (see Figure 34-8).

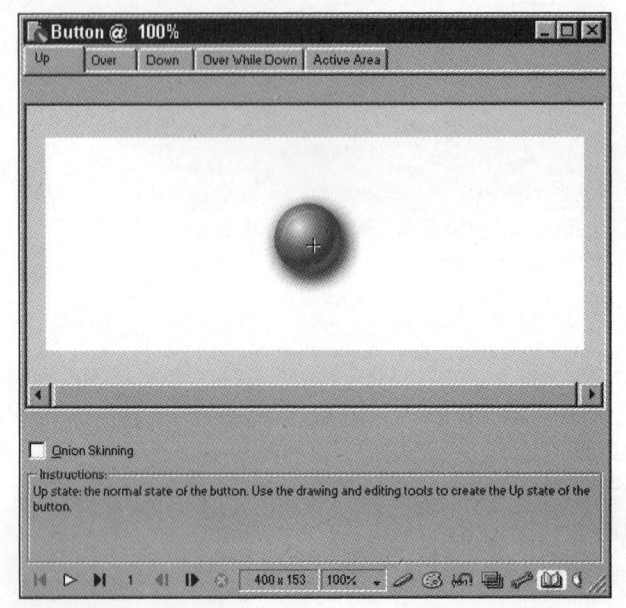

Figure 34-8: The Button Editor can display four button states — four Fireworks frames — plus a slice object on its five tabbed canvases.

2. Create the Up state of your button in the initial Up tab of the Button Editor.

3. Select the Button Editor's Over tab and create the Over state of your button. Alternatively, to start with the Up state and modify it to be an Over state, click Copy Up Graphic. Fireworks copies the Up state to the Over tab, ready for editing.

Tip At any time, you can check the Onion Skinning box to simultaneously view all the tabs in the Button Editor, helping you to align your buttons correctly. You can also use the view controls to zoom in or out on your button, and you can choose a display option to view the buttons in Full or Draft display. Click the Play button at the bottom left of the Button Editor to cycle through the states of your button.

4. If you want to include a Down state in your button, select the Down tab and create the Down state of your button. Again, you have the option to click a button and copy the previous state to this tab for modification. Click Copy Over Graphic to do this.

5. If your button is exported as a Nav Bar, check Show Down State Upon Load to display the Down state when a page loads.

6. To add an Over While Down state to your button, switch to the Over While Down tab and either create a new state or copy the previous one — click Copy Down Graphic — and modify it to create the Over While Down state.

7. Switch to the Active Area tab. Fireworks automatically creates a slice in the Active Area tab that encompasses the area of your button, but you can adjust its size if necessary.

Tip The slice on the Active Area tab is similar to the Hit area in Flash buttons.

8. To have Fireworks help with the process of adding a link to your button, click the Link Wizard button and move from tab to tab in the Link Wizard dialog box.

9. Close the Button Editor when you're done.

Your new Button Symbol is added to the Library panel, and a copy of it — an Instance — is placed in the document window, as shown in Figure 34-9. Switch to the Preview tab of the document window to preview your new button's rollover actions in the document window.

Figure 34-9: The Button Editor creates a new Button Symbol, which is added to the Library. An Instance of that symbol is placed on the canvas.

Cross-Reference: For more about symbols and Libraries, see Chapter 32.

Examining Advanced Rollover Techniques

The simple rollover is quick and easy, and I use it quite often. However, sometimes a Web page needs more than just a simple rollover. You can extend traditional rollovers with advanced techniques in order to create interesting effects, or even more navigation help for your users. The underlying engine for the simple rollover, the Swap Image Behavior, is key to these advanced techniques.

Making disjointed rollovers

A *disjointed rollover* is one in which the user hovers his or her mouse cursor over one part of an image (the event area), and another part of the image (the target area) does the actual rollover. A typical use for a disjointed rollover is to display details of each button in a navigation bar in a common area. Creating a disjointed rollover generally involves outlining the event and target areas with slice objects, although it is possible to trigger a disjointed rollover from a hotspot.

To create a disjointed rollover, follow these steps:

1. Create a slice object over the event area (the part of your image that the mouse cursor needs to hover over in order to trigger the rollover).

2. Create a slice object over the target area (the part of the image that will seem to change).

3. Select the event area slice and choose Swap Image from the Add Action pop-up menu in the Behaviors panel.

   Fireworks displays the Swap Image dialog box (see Figure 34-10).

4. Choose the slice for the target area by choosing it from either the Target list of slice names or the Slice preview to the right of the Target list. Whichever you choose, the other is updated to reflect your choice.

5. Choose the Source for the swap by selecting a frame number from the Frame list.

   The area below the target slice on that frame will be used as the source for the image swap.

6. Check Restore Image onMouseOut to undo the swap again when the user moves his mouse cursor away from the event area. Click OK when you're done.

7. Repeat this process until all of your slices have been assigned the Swap Image Behavior.

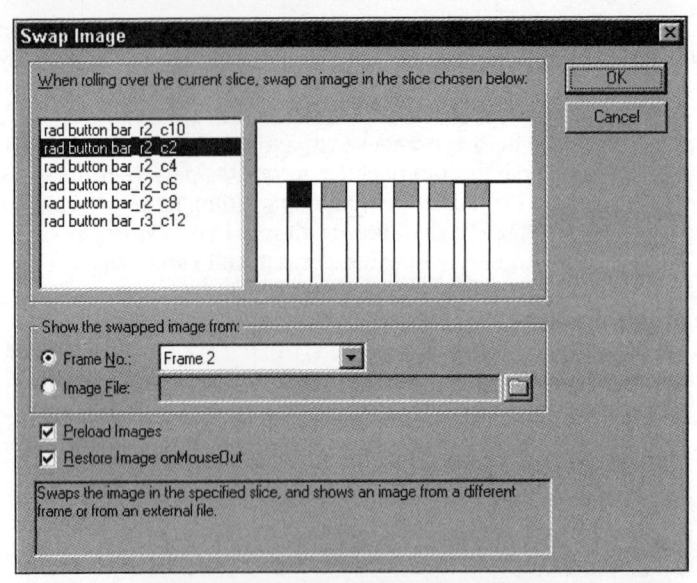

Figure 34-10: The Swap Image dialog box contains options that enable you to swap any slice in your document after any other slice is selected by the user.

To swap more than one slice simultaneously, repeat the preceding steps to apply multiple Swap Image Behaviors to the same Web Layer object. Through this technique, your navigation button can roll over itself and display a disjointed rollover at the same time.

Creating external rollovers

Instead of using an object in another frame as the Over state for a rollover, Fireworks can also use external GIF images (regular or animated), JPEG images, or PNG images. When the rollover is viewed in a Web browser, the external file is used as the source file for a rollover, instead of using an area of a frame within your Fireworks document. External rollovers enable you to easily include animated GIF images into an existing image.

Caution You can't swap one image file format for another because of Web browser limitations. If you're going to export a slice as a GIF, make sure to use an external GIF or animated GIF only as the Over state. Similarly, if you're exporting a slice as a JPEG or a PNG, include only external JPEG images and PNG images, respectively, as the Over state.

Keep in mind that only the image source is changed (the `src` attribute of the `img` tag), so the browser will resize your external image to fit the size of the initial slice object it's being swapped for.

> **Tip** If you need to make a slice object the same size as an external image so that you can swap that sliced area of your image for an external file, select the slice object; choose either Modify ⇨ Transform ⇨ Numeric Transform, or the keyboard shortcut, Ctrl+Shift+T (Command+Shift+T); choose Resize from the list in the Numeric Transform dialog box; and then enter the desired width and height.

To create an external rollover, follow these steps:

1. Select the slice to trigger the external rollover.
2. Choose Swap Image from the Add Action pop-up menu in the Behaviors panel.

   Fireworks displays the Swap Image dialog box.
3. Select the slice where the external image will be swapped into.
4. To locate the external file through the standard Open dialog box, choose the Source for the swap by clicking the Folder icon.
5. Check Restore Image onMouseOut to undo the swap again when the user moves his mouse cursor away from the event area.
6. Click OK when you're done.

Working with hotspot rollovers

Hotspot rollovers enable you to create the effect of irregularly shaped rollovers. All images are rectangular boxes, so all image swaps involve swapping a rectangular area or slice. However, the image triggering the rollover does not have to be rectangular — you can use any hotspot. The key to the illusion of the hotspot rollover is Fireworks' ability to swap entire slices from different frames.

Figure 34-11 shows an image with slices that are far from rectangular, but the design requires that each area highlight independently when rolled over and link to different pages on the Web site. Hotspot rollovers swap the entire image, though, so each highlight can be any shape.

One limitation applies, though: Because each hotspot swaps the entire image, the hotspots can't overlap, or the illusion of separate highlighted areas is lost. It's also a good idea to keep the overall image small, because each added hotspot requires another copy of the whole image. A larger image could lead to a significant download time for the user.

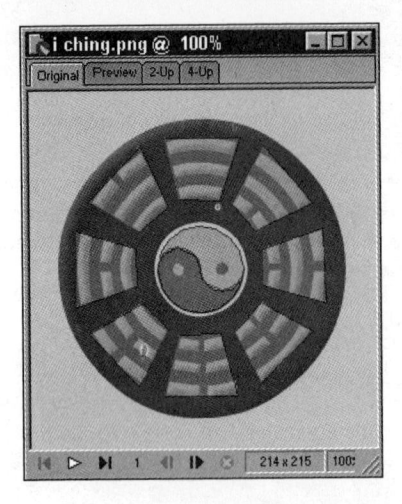

Figure 34-11: This navigation system uses hotspots to trigger a rollover of the whole image in order to create the impression of irregularly shaped rollover buttons.

To create hotspot rollovers, follow these steps:

1. Create a hotspot for each active area with the Rectangle, Circle, or Polygon Hotspot tool.
2. Create a single slice that covers your whole image.
3. Select the slice and choose Modify ⇨ Arrange ⇨ Send to Back to send it behind your hotspots so that you can easily access the individual hotspots in order to apply Behaviors to them.
4. Duplicate your current frame until you have a separate frame for each active area. If you have made ten hotspots, make ten frames.
5. In each frame, modify a different active area so that it appears highlighted in some way. This will be the "Over" state for that area. The other areas in each frame are left in their default state.

Tip Hiding the Web Layer — and your hotspots — makes it easier to see what you're doing when modifying your active areas. Hide the Web Layer by clicking the eye icon next to its name in the Layers panel.

6. Select a hotspot and fill in a URL for the hotspot in the Object panel.
7. With your hotspot still selected, open the Behaviors panel and apply a Swap Image Behavior to it. In the Swap Image dialog box, make sure you follow these steps:
   - Select the lone slice in the slice list.
   - Under "Show the swapped image from," set the Frame number to the corresponding highlighted frame for the selected hotspot. If the highlight for a hotspot is in Frame 3, set the hotspot to swap to Frame 3.

8. Repeat Steps 6 and 7 for each hotspot until all of your hotspots have a URL and a Behavior attached.

9. Export your image along with the HTML code. In the Export dialog box, choose Export Slices from the Slices option list.

Fireworks will export an HTML document along with an image file for each frame of your document. When displayed in a browser, the overall impression that's created is that of a single image with eccentrically shaped, individual rollovers.

Displaying a status bar message

You can provide the user with additional navigational assistance by supplying a message in the status bar. Status bar messages are often used with hotspots and image maps. They are limited by the width of the status bar area in the viewer's browser, which in the case of Internet Explorer 4 for Windows (but not 5) is very, very small. Even in other browsers, because browser window sizes can vary tremendously, lengthy messages are not recommended.

To add a status bar message to your document, follow these steps:

1. Select a slice object or hotspot, and choose Set Text of Status Bar from the Add Action pop-up menu in the Behaviors panel.

   Fireworks displays the Set Text of Status Bar dialog box (see Figure 34-12).

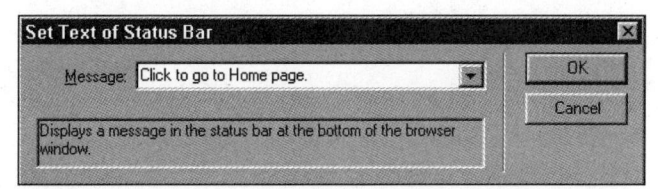

Figure 34-12: The Set Text of Status Bar dialog box enables you to add a status bar message to a slice or hotspot, which assists your users in navigating your site.

2. Type in the Message box the message that you want to display when the user activates this slice. Click OK when you're done.

3. Change the event from onMouseOver to onMouseOut, onClick or onLoad, if desired, by choosing that event from the event list.

Working with Pop-Up Menus

Web sites are becoming increasingly complex and now routinely offer their visitors a choice of hundreds, or even thousands of pages of information. The traditional Web button bar with a handful of options can be strained to the seams by the bulk of topics and subtopics such complex sites contain. Luckily, the Set Pop-Up Menu Behavior aids in the quick creation of powerful hierarchical navigation systems that are easy for the Web user to grasp at first glance (see Figure 34-13).

Figure 34-13: Pop-up menus are easy to create in Fireworks, and easy for the Web user to navigate when viewed in the browser.

New Feature The Set Pop-Up Menu Behavior, with a few simple steps you do right in Fireworks itself, replaces the code-jockeying that was previously required to incorporate pop-up menus in a Web page.

To add pop-up menus to your Fireworks document, follow these steps:

1. Select a slice or hotspot, and choose Set Pop-Up Menu from the Add Action pop-up menu in the Behaviors panel, or choose Insert ⇨ Pop-Up Menu.

   Fireworks displays the Set Pop-Up Menu dialog box (see Figure 34-14).

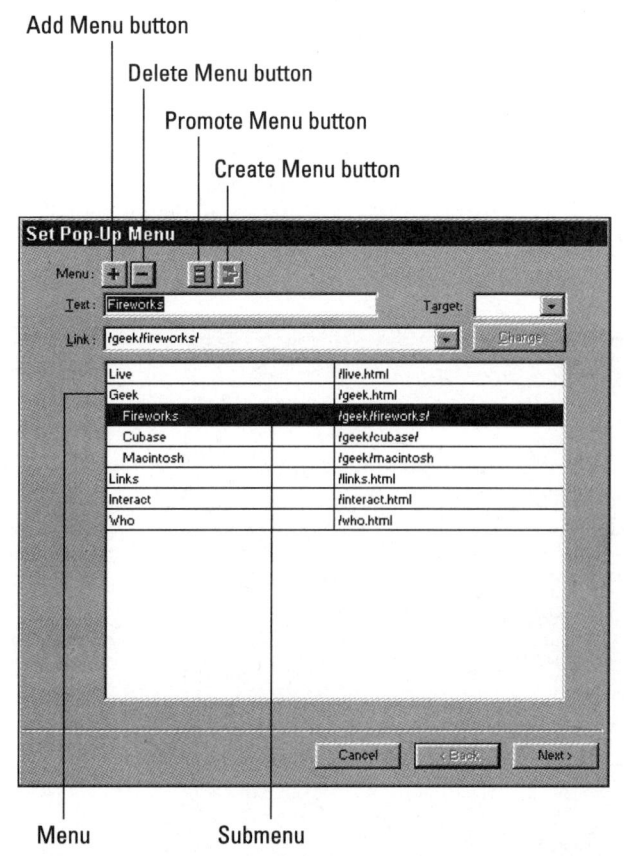

Figure 34-14: The Set Pop-Up Menu dialog box asks for the specifications for your pop-up menu in fairly plain terms.

2. To create a new menu item, specify a name in the Text box, a URL in the Link box, and a URL target in the Target box (if desired), and click the Add Item button or press Enter (Return).

3. To change the properties of a menu item, select the menu item and change the contents of the Text, Link, or Target boxes, and click the Change button. The Link box is also an option list, enabling access to all the URLs in your document.

4. To convert a menu item into a submenu, select the menu item, and click the Create Menu button. To covert a submenu into a menu, click the Promote Menu button.

5. To move a menu item up or down the list, select it and drag it up or down.

6. Click Next when you're done with the available options.

Tip After clicking Next, you can click Back at any time to return to the previous state of the Set Pop-Up Menu dialog box.

Fireworks displays a second state of the Set Pop-Up Menu dialog box.

7. Specify a menu style, either HTML (see Figure 34-15) or Image (see Figure 34-16).

   HTML menus are composed of plain HTML text and tables after export. Image menus use images formatted with Fireworks styles.

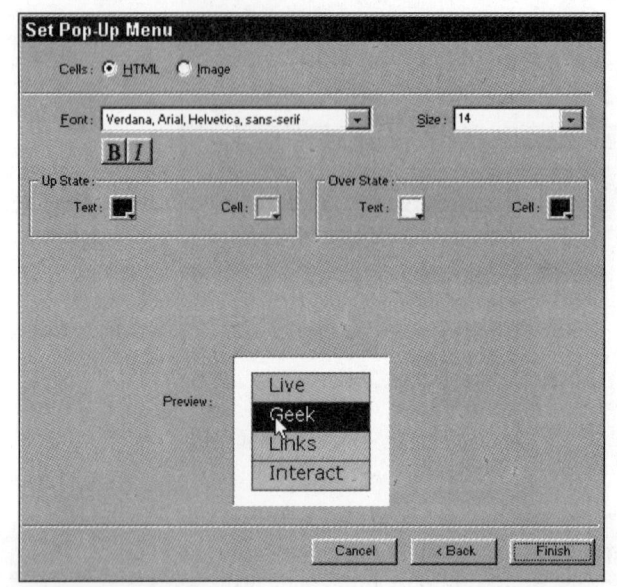

Figure 34-15: HTML Pop-Up Menu formatting options include text and table cell colors. A preview of the look of your eventual pop-up menu system is always available.

8. Specify a font, size, and bold and/or italic style for the text in your menu system.

9. Select Text and Cell colors for the Up State of your menu.

   This is how the menu will look initially.

10. Select Text and Cell colors for the Over State of your menu.

    This is the way the menu will look under the user's mouse cursor.

> **Tip:** As you adjust settings, keep an eye on the preview of the finished product that Fireworks provides.

   11. If you are creating an Image Pop-Up Menu (see Figure 34-16), choose an Up Style and an Over Style for the images that make up the menu.

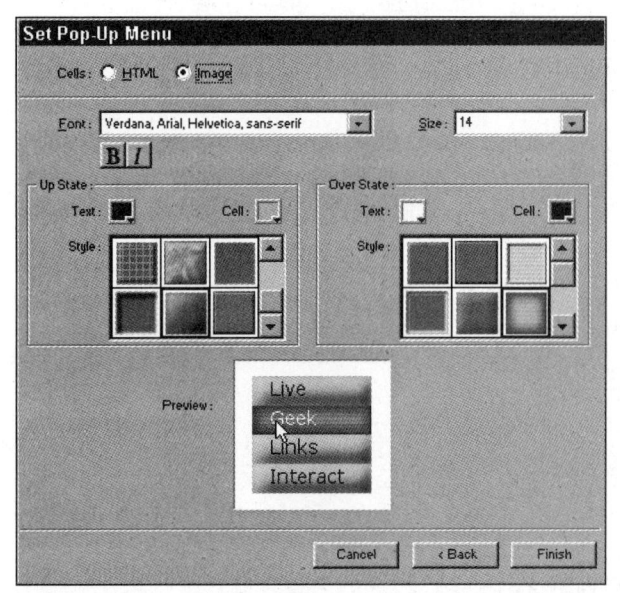

Figure 34-16: The formatting options for Image Pop-Up Menus use Fireworks' styles feature to dress up otherwise drab menus.

   12. Click Finish when you're done.

After you add a Pop-Up Menu Behavior to your document, you can edit its settings at any time by double-clicking its name in the Behavior panel, or by double-clicking the pop-up menu outline in your document.

> **Note:** You can't preview Pop-Up Menus in the workspace. Press F12 to preview your work in your primary browser and see your pop-up menus in action.

Pop-up menu styles are stored in a folder called Nav Menu, in the Configuration folder in your Fireworks application folder. These styles are the same styles that we know and love from the Styles panel, so adding your own styles to the Set Pop-Up Menu dialog box and making them available for use in a Pop-Up menu is as simple as exporting the styles from the Styles panel to the Nav Menu folder.

Tip The Fireworks program folder is typically found at C:\Program Files\Macromedia\Fireworks 4 on Windows-based computers, and at Macintosh HD:Applications: Macromedia Fireworks 4: on the Mac.

To add your own styles to the Set Pop Up Menu Behavior, follow these steps:

1. Create an object with the fill, stroke, and effect properties that you would like your pop-up menu to have.
2. Choose Window ⇨ Styles to display the Styles panel.
3. Select your object and click the New Style button on the Styles panel.

    The properties of your object are saved as a new style.

4. Select the new style in the Styles panel and choose Export Styles from the Styles panel's pop-up menu.

    Fireworks displays a Save dialog box.

5. Navigate to your Fireworks application folder, then into the Configuration folder, and then the Nav Bar folder. Click Save to export your selected style as a Fireworks .stl file.

Next time you use the Set Pop-Up Menu Behavior, your added styles will be available for use.

Using Drag-and-Drop Behaviors

Drag-and-drop Behaviors enable you to quickly create rollovers using simple drag-and-drop methods. Instead of selecting a slice or hotspot and then interacting with the Behaviors panel, drag-and-drop Behaviors enable you to directly interact with the trigger Web object — over the area where the user hovers or clicks to trigger the Behavior — and the target Web object — where the rollover itself happens. Join the two areas with a drag-and-drop, and you have created a rollover.

New Feature Drag-and-drop Behaviors now provide an additional way to work with Behaviors in Fireworks.

When selected, each hotspot and slice object displays a drag-and-drop handle, as shown in Figure 34-17. Drag the drag-and-drop Behavior handle from a triggering slice or hotspot onto a target slice to create a rollover. You can create a simple rollover by dragging the drag-and-drop Behavior handle and dropping it on the same slice, whereas you can create a disjoint rollover by dragging the drag-and-drop Behavior handle and dropping the Behavior handle on a different slice.

It's important to realize that you must prepare the slices and frames before dragging and dropping. Fireworks won't add frames to your document just because you attach a rollover Behavior to a slice.

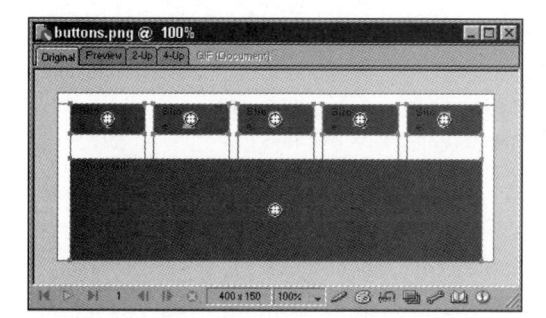

Figure 34-17: Each hotspot or slice has a drag-and-drop handle that displays when the hotspot or slice is selected.

Creating a simple rollover with drag and drop

To create a simple rollover where the trigger and target areas are the same, follow these steps:

1. Make sure that you have created a second frame in your document, which contains the image that will be shown when the user rolls his mouse over the trigger area.
2. Select the trigger slice, which covers the area of the image that will trigger the Behavior.
3. Click and hold on the drag-and-drop Behavior handle in the center of the slice.

    The mouse cursor changes into a fist.

4. Drag the cursor slightly and drop over the same slice.

    A blue drag-and-drop Behavior line displays from the center to the top-left corner of the hotspot or slice (see Figure 34-18).

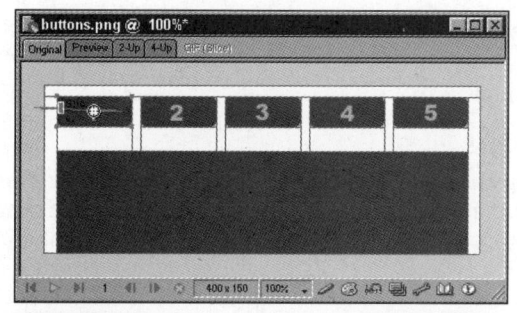

Figure 34-18: When you drag and drop within one hotspot or slice, a drag-and-drop Behavior line displays from the center to the top-left corner of the hotspot or slice.

Fireworks displays the Swap Image dialog box (see Figure 34-19).

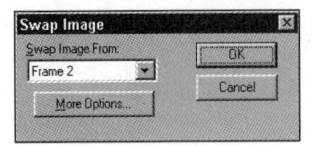

Figure 34-19: A special Swap Image dialog box displays after you drag and drop.

5. Choose a frame to swap for the current frame, from the Swap Image From options list.
6. To access the full Swap Image Behavior dialog box, click More Options.

> **Cross-Reference**
>
> The full Swap Image dialog box is covered earlier in this chapter.

7. Click OK when you're done.

Fireworks attaches the Behavior to the slice.

Creating disjoint rollovers with drag and drop

To create a disjoint rollover — where the trigger and target Web objects are not the same — join the trigger and target Web objects with a drag-and-drop Behavior line.

To create a disjoint rollover with drag and drop, follow these steps:

1. Make sure that you have created a second frame in your document, which contains the image that will be shown when the user rolls his mouse over the trigger area.
2. Make sure that you have both a trigger and target hotspot or slice.
3. Select the Web object over the trigger area.
4. Click and hold on the drag-and-drop Behavior handle in the center of the hotspot or slice.

   The mouse cursor changes into a fist.
5. Drag the cursor and drop it on the target slice.

   The blue drag-and-drop Behavior line is displayed from the center of the trigger Web object to the top-left corner of the target slice, as shown in Figure 34-20.

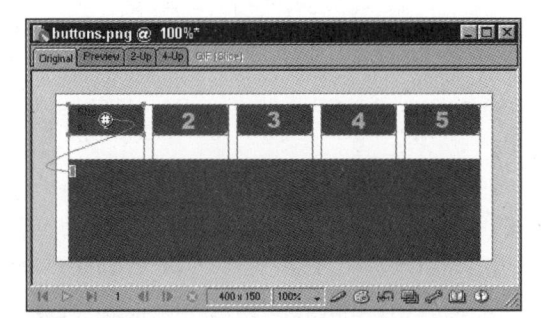

Figure 34-20: A blue drag-and-drop Behavior line shows the relationship between the trigger and target slice after a drag and drop. Here, a click on the button by the user will swap the larger slice at the bottom.

Fireworks displays the Swap Image dialog box.

6. Select the frame to swap from in the Swap Image From options list.
7. To access the full Swap Image Behavior dialog box, click More Options.
8. Click OK when you're done.

Fireworks attaches the Behavior to the selected Web object.

Removing drag-and-drop Behaviors

To remove a drag-and-drop Behavior attached to a hotspot or slice, follow these steps:

1. Select the hotspot or slice.

    The drag-and-drop Behavior relationships for the Web object are shown as blue lines.

2. Click on the blue line you want to delete.

    Fireworks displays a dialog box, confirming that you want to remove the Behavior.

3. Click OK to remove the Behavior.

Summary

Fireworks enables you to add dynamic JavaScript effects to your images, even if you don't know JavaScript, through the use of Fireworks Behaviors. When using Behaviors, keep these points in mind:

- ✦ The Behaviors panel is your control center for working with Behaviors.
- ✦ Behaviors are attached only to Web Layer objects (either hotspots or slices) and not to regular vector or bitmap objects on other layers.
- ✦ Rollovers can be rollover buttons, or they can be disjointed rollovers, in which the image that changes is not the same as the one that triggered the event.
- ✦ Fireworks includes a Button Editor that simplifies the process of building a Button Symbol.
- ✦ You can preview rollovers in the document window by selecting the Preview tab.
- ✦ Fireworks can also show text in the browser's status bar through Set Text of Status Bar Behavior.
- ✦ The Set Pop-Up Menu Behavior option enables you to create powerful, complex navigation systems with a minimum of time and effort.
- ✦ Drag-and-drop Behaviors provide a quick and easy method for creating rollover Behaviors.

✦ ✦ ✦

Applying Animation Techniques

CHAPTER 35

In This Chapter

Understanding Web animation

Managing frames

Animating objects

Using Onion Skinning

Using the VCR controls

Exporting your animated GIF

Tweening graphic symbols

Working with animation symbols

Animation has become a prominent feature of the Web, and very few Web sites get by without at least a little of it. Animated GIF banner ads have proliferated from common to ubiquitous. Animated logos and buttons are an easy way to add spice to a site. Short, animated cartoons are increasingly popular as Web bandwidth increases.

This chapter looks briefly at some animation basics and then focuses on the Fireworks features that enable you to create animations. We'll work with Fireworks frames and animated GIF export features, such as timing and looping. Next, we look at specific issues that you might confront when making animated banner ads, and then go through the process from start to finish.

Understanding Web Animation

Animation is a trick. Show me a rapid succession of similar images with slight changes in an element's location or properties, and I'll think that I see something moving. This movement can be very complex or very simple. The 24 frames per second of a motion picture aren't even required; in as little as three frames, an object can actually appear to be moving (loop two frames and an object just appears to flash).

Because Fireworks creates animated GIF images, this chapter focuses on that format. You'll find, though, that many of the ideas that go into creating good animated GIF images also apply when creating images in other Web animation formats.

Getting a handle on bandwidth

Remember first and foremost that bandwidth is always an issue. Then, remember that bandwidth is always an issue. I'll end up harping on that again and again, because bandwidth affects everything. You must analyze each and every bold, creative move for its eventual effect on the overall *weight* of the resulting animated GIF file (the total file size). Throughout the entire process of creating an animation for display on the Web, you need to balance variables carefully, such as the number of colors you use, the number of frames, the timing of those frames, and how much area of your image is actually animated. If you want more colors, you may have to take out a few frames and settle for a less fluid animation. If you're animating complex shapes that don't compress well, you may have to get by with fewer colors.

The dial-up connection is the great equalizer. The Web is slow and generally static, and almost everybody knows it. If you can give your audience a quick, dynamic presentation, you'll score two times. Keep in mind the nature of GIF compression as you create your designs. Big blocks of cartoonish color and horizontal stripes compress much better than photographic images, vertical stripes, or gradients and dithers.

Making a statement

So, maybe you're not going to win an Oscar with your animation; that doesn't mean you shouldn't give it a reason for existing. Every part of your animation needs to be focused and necessary, because each little movement that you add you also purchase with a corresponding amount of bandwidth. A short, tight, and concise animation will be much more popular with your audience. This applies whether you're creating a complex cartoon with an intricate story line, a flashy, abstract design, or even an animated logo. If you decide before you start what you want to accomplish creatively, you increase your chances of ending up with a tight, presentable result.

Animated GIF images are good at some things, but not so good at others. Consider those limitations carefully, and focus on creating a good animated GIF — not just a good animation that happens to be forced into the framework of an animated GIF. Logos, buttons, and simple frame-by-frame animations work best. You might find that thinking of an animated GIF image as a slideshow rather than a movie is helpful. Typically, you work with fewer frames than a movie uses, and with slow, simple, animated elements. I find that thinking of animated GIFs as little PowerPoint-style presentations reminds me of the limitations of the format. You can make a little movement go a long way. You can show that something's moving either by smoothly animating it frame by frame across the entire width of the image, or you can place it once on the left side of the canvas, followed by a blurred version in the center, and then display it again at the right side.

Tip Don't forget everything that you learned by watching Saturday morning cartoons or reading comic books. Techniques such as word balloons and lines that illustrate movement or action in still comics can help you get your message across without adding significantly to the frame count (and the file size). Instead of moving an element off the canvas in ten smooth frames, replace it with a puff of smoke and some lines that point to which way the element went. Study animations for tricks like that and make lean, mean animations that really make an impression and get your message across.

As usual on the Web, you're at the mercy of your users' browsers — and you don't even know which browsers they'll be using. However, generally, animated GIF images play back a little faster in Internet Explorer than in Navigator (and, naturally, play back faster on faster computers). Don't try to be too precise, attempting to measure the time between frames and worrying about it. Instead, embrace a little of the Web's anarchy and just try to find a good middle ground. Trust the timing settings in Fireworks and hope for the best.

Examining why to animate a GIF

Fireworks is the perfect place to create animated GIF images. Creating the illusion of animation means changing the objects on the canvas over time, and an always-editable object in Fireworks is easy to move, scale, or modify with effects. And when your animation is complete, Fireworks' unmatched image optimization enables you to create the lightest-weight animated GIF possible. (There's that bandwidth issue again.)

Tip Although you usually create GIF animations directly in Fireworks, you also can export an animation as a series of files by choosing File ⇨ Export and then selecting either Frames to Files or Layers to Files from the Save As option list. These files — which can be other image formats, such as PNG or JPEG — can then be modified in another application, or used in another animation format, such as an SMIL presentation in RealPlayer, or an interactive Dynamic HTML (DHTML) slideshow.

The animated GIF has its share of limitations and gets its share of disrespect, especially when sized up feature for feature against some of the more "serious" animation formats used on the Web. Table 35-1 makes just such a comparison.

Table 35-1
Comparing Web Animation Formats

Format	Sound	Interactivity	Streaming	Transparency	Colors
Animated GIF	No	No	No	Yes	256
Dynamic HTML	No	Yes	Yes	Yes	Millions
Java	Yes	Yes	Yes	No	Millions
Flash	Yes	Yes	Yes	Sometimes	Millions
Shockwave	Yes	Yes	Yes	No	Millions
QuickTime	Yes	Yes	Yes	No	Millions
RealPlayer	Yes	Yes	Yes	No	Millions

Note: Transparency refers to a transparent background when the animation is placed in a browser, not support within the editing environment or the animation format itself.

Based on this table, the animated GIF seems like a fairly poor choice. Other formats feature high levels of interactivity and automatically stream or simulate streaming with multiple component files. Some have video and many have sound. What's more, Flash gets a lot more done in a much smaller file size.

So, why is the animated GIF used so often? Why haven't designers dropped it in favor of one or more of these other, seemingly superior methods? Find the answers to these questions and more in Table 35-2, which details browser support for each format.

Table 35-2
Browser Support for Web Animation Formats

Format	Navigator 2/3 and IE 3	Navigator 4/6 and IE 4 and 5	Most Other Browsers
Animated GIF	Yes	Yes	Yes
Dynamic HTML	No	Yes	No
Java	Yes; user can disable	Yes; user can disable	No
Flash	With plug-in	With plug-in	No
Shockwave	With plug-in	With plug-in	No
QuickTime	With plug-in	With plug-in	No
RealPlayer	With plug-in	With plug-in	No

When you consider who can actually view your animation, the animated GIF doesn't look so bad after all. Other formats may be flashier, but the animated GIF is "old reliable." No matter which platform or browser, the animated GIF is always available.

Using the Fireworks Animation Toolkit

Animation in Fireworks focuses on these major tools:

+ **Frames panel:** The heart of Fireworks' animation features, where you manipulate individual frames — like a director editing the frames of a film — adding, removing, reordering, and specifying timing for individual frames.

> **Tip:** The Export Preview dialog box also duplicates some of the Frames panel controls, such as animation timing.

+ **Layers panel:** Where you manage each frame's layers. Organize your animation by keeping objects on the same layer from frame to frame, or share a layer across every frame, so that backgrounds or static objects can be created once for the entire animation.

+ **VCR-style controls:** Where you flip through frames, or play your entire animation right in the document window.

+ **Graphic symbols:** Fireworks can create intermediate steps between two instances of the same symbol, quickly generating a complete animation.

+ **Animation symbols:** A multi-frame symbol that is a self-contained animation.

Managing frames

What separates an animation from a regular Fireworks document is that the animation has multiple frames. The relationship between layers and frames can be hard to understand when you first start animating in Fireworks. However, understanding how they work — and work together — is essential.

Frames are like the frames of a traditional filmstrip (see Figure 35-1) that you might run through a movie projector. When you play your animation, only one frame is visible at a time. Frame 1 is shown first, and then Frame 2, Frame 3, and so on. When you add a frame to your document, you're extending the length of the filmstrip and making a longer movie. When you change the order of frames in the Frames panel, imagine that you're cutting a frame out of your filmstrip and splicing it back in at another point on the strip. If you move Frame 5 to the beginning of your movie, before Frame 1, all the frames are renumbered, so that what used to be Frame 5 is now Frame 1, what used to be Frame 1 becomes Frame 2, and so on.

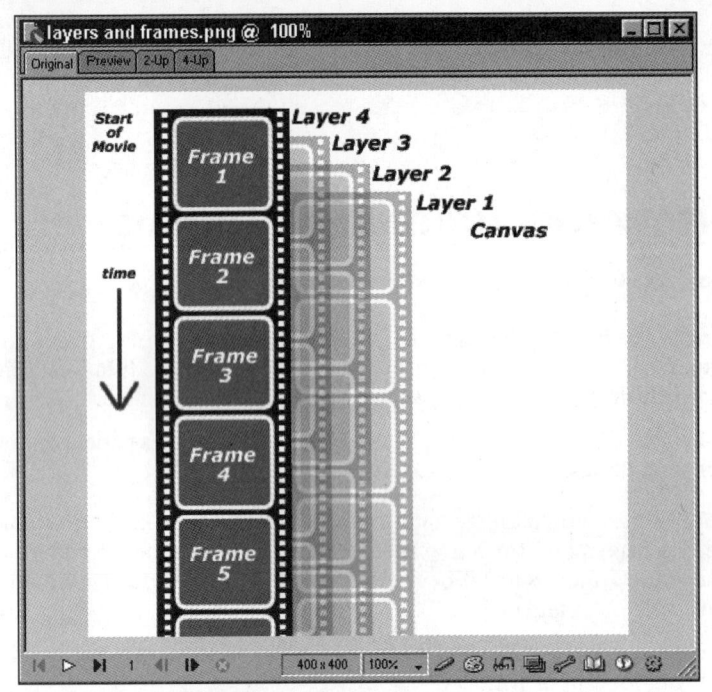

Figure 35-1: Think of frames as the frames of a filmstrip, and layers as a stack of filmstrips stuck together.

The layers in an animation are like separate filmstrips stacked together. When you play your animation, all the layers of Frame 1 are shown together, and then all the layers of Frame 2 are shown, and then Frame 3, and so on. Just like when you use layers in a static Fireworks document, layers provide a way to organize the order of objects and keep dissimilar objects separate from each other, for easier editing. When you add a layer to your document, you add a whole new filmstrip to the stack. Changing the order of layers in the Layers panel is like changing the order of that filmstrip in the stack of filmstrips.

Note When you add a frame to your movie, it automatically has the same layers as all the other frames. To continue the filmstrip metaphor, adding a frame to one filmstrip in the stack adds it to all the filmstrips. When you add a layer to your movie, it is added to every frame. Adding a layer adds a whole new filmstrip the same length as the others.

One very useful interaction between layers and frames is the ability to share a layer. When a layer is shared, its content is the same on every frame, and no matter which frame you are viewing when you edit the objects in that layer, the changes appear on every frame. This is handy for static elements, such as backgrounds. We take a closer look at this later.

You do the bulk of your animation work in the Frames panel (see Figure 35-2), so you need to have it open all the time while creating an animation. From there, you can add, delete, reorder, or duplicate frames. You can view and edit a single frame, a group of frames, or all of your frames simultaneously. You can copy or move objects from frame to frame. You can specify the timing each frame will have in your animated GIF. As with the Layers panel, when a Frame contains a selection, a selection icon appears next to its name in the Frames panel.

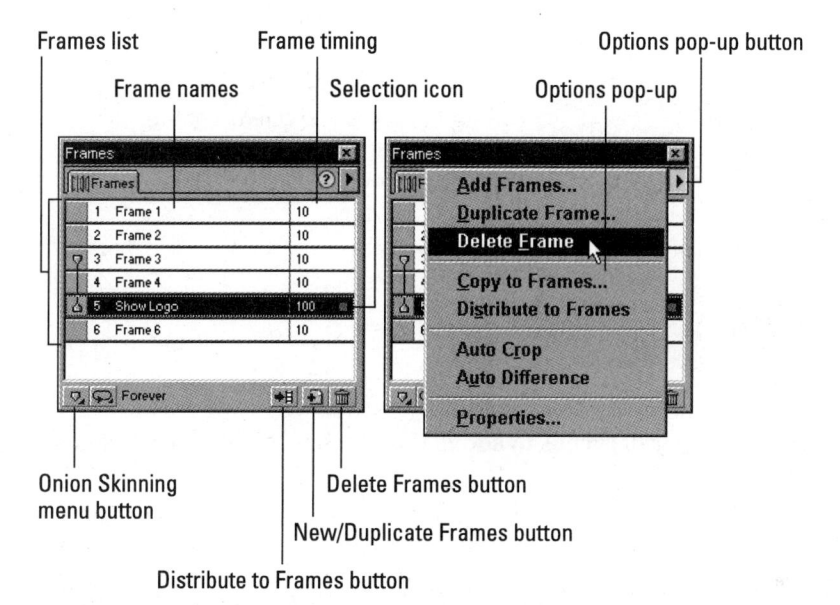

Figure 35-2: Manage frames with the Frames panel and its handy options pop-up.

Tip

When working on animation, you might want to dock your Layers panel with your Frames panel, if it isn't already, so that you can easily move between the panels. If you're not short on screen real estate, you could even keep them side by side. Location doesn't matter, as long as they're both close at hand.

Adding frames

When you start creating an animation in Fireworks, your document has exactly one frame. Obviously, this has to change before you can simulate any kind of movement. At first, you might make a rough guess at how many frames your animation should contain, and then add that number of frames to your document. Later, you can add or remove frames as the need arises. Another approach is to start with just two frames: the first and the last. After you establish where your animation starts and finishes, filling in the intervening frames is often easier.

To add a frame to the end of the Frame list, click the Add Frames button (blank sheet of paper with a plus sign on it) at the bottom of the Frames panel, or choose Insert ➪ Frame.

To add one or more frames at a specific point in the Frame list, follow these steps:

1. Choose Add Frames from the Frames panel options pop-up.

    Fireworks displays the Add Frames dialog box (see Figure 35-3).

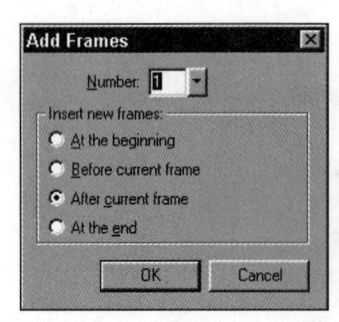

Figure 35-3: The Add Frames dialog box gives you careful control over how many frames you add and where you add them.

2. Enter the number of frames to add in the Number box, or use the slider to add up to ten frames.

3. Choose where to insert the new frames. The options are At the beginning, Before current frame, After current frame, and At the end. Click OK when you're done.

The new frames are created and added to the Frame list at the point you specified.

Naming frames

By default, Fireworks names each frame with a very generic "Frame 1" or "Frame 2." When you're animating, moving objects back and forth from frame to frame, these generic names can be very confusing. To name a frame with a descriptive name, double-click its name in the Frames panel. Fireworks displays a small pop-up dialog box that enables you to type any name you please, as shown in Figure 35-4. After you've entered a new name, dismiss the pop-up dialog box by clicking anywhere outside it, or by pressing Enter (Return).

New Feature Fireworks 4 enables you to name the frames in the Frames panel with descriptive names.

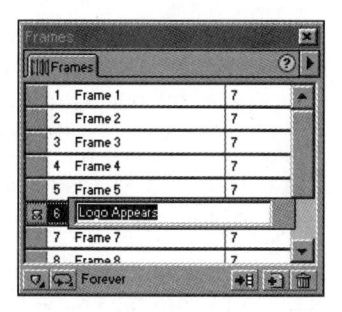

Figure 35-4: Name your frames just as you please, by double-clicking them in the Frames panel.

Deleting a frame

The most important thing to remember when you delete a frame is that you also delete all the objects that it contains, except for those that are on a shared layer. Take care to identify and delete the correct frame.

> **Tip** If you delete a frame accidentally and want to restore it to the Frame list, choose either Edit ➪ Undo, or the keyboard shortcut, Ctrl+Z (Command+Z).

To delete a frame, select it on the Frame list and do one of the following:

✦ Click the Delete Frames button (a Trash icon) at the bottom of the Frames panel.

✦ Drag the frame to the Delete Frames button at the bottom of the Frames panel.

✦ Choose Delete Frame from the Frames panel options pop-up.

Reordering frames

As you continue to work on your animation, you might want to change the order of your frames, by moving them earlier or later in the animation.

To reorder a frame, click and drag it up or down the Frame list in the Frames panel.

> **Note** From working with layers in the Layers panel, you may be accustomed to seeing the layer retain its name as you change its stacking order by dragging it up or down the layers list. When you reorder a frame, though, all frames are renumbered to reflect their new positions. The first frame in your animation will always be Frame 1.

Duplicating frames

One way to save a significant amount of time and effort is to copy a sequence of frames that you've already created and then modify the copies further. If you have created an animation sequence of a sunrise, you can copy those frames and then reverse their order to get an automatic sunset. This not only saves you the time and effort of creating the sunset animation from scratch, but also has the added advantage that the sun will set in the same place from which it rose.

To duplicate a single frame, drag it from the Frame list onto the Add Frames button at the bottom of the Frames panel. Fireworks inserts the copy into the Frame list right after the original.

To duplicate one or more frames and place the copies in a specific place in the Frame list, follow these steps:

1. Choose Duplicate Frame from the Frames panel options pop-up.

   Fireworks displays the Duplicate Frames dialog box.

> **Note** The Duplicate Frames dialog box is very similar to the Add Frames dialog box, shown previously in Figure 35-3.

2. Enter the number of frames to duplicate in the Number box, or use the slider to duplicate up to ten frames.

3. Choose where to insert the copies. The options are At the beginning, Before current frame, After current frame, and At the end. Click OK when you're done.

The frames are duplicated and the copies are added to the Frame list at the point you specified.

Animating objects

A significant part of creating animation is managing how objects in your document change over time. If you are creating a simple, animated sunrise, the sun starts out at a low point on the canvas and, over time (through later frames), moves to a higher point on the canvas. At the same time, a cloud might move from left to right, while the ground and sky stay the same.

You certainly don't want to draw each of these objects numerous times. Aside from being a lot of extra effort, you would probably end up with objects that are not exactly the same dimensions or properties from frame to frame. If the sun were to change size slightly in each frame, it would detract from the illusion that the animation contains just one moving sun.

Instead, when you create an animation, draw objects once and then copy or distribute them from frame to frame, where the copies can be moved or modified slightly to give the appearance of the same object moving or changing over time.

Keeping similar objects on their own layers makes working with just those objects easier as you copy objects to frames. In the animated sunrise example, you might keep the sun on its own layer, the clouds on another layer, and the unchanging background objects on another.

Copying objects to frames

Most of the time, you'll be adding objects to other frames by copying them. To copy an object or objects to another frame, follow these steps:

1. Select the object(s).
2. Choose Copy to Frames from the Frames panel options pop-up.

   Fireworks displays the Copy to Frames dialog box (see Figure 35-5).

3. Choose where the selection will be copied. The available options are All frames, Previous frame, Next frame, or Range, which is used to specify a specific range of frames. Click OK when you're done.

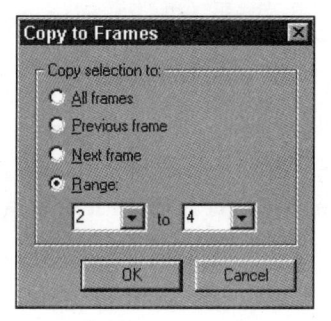

Figure 35-5: Use the Copy to Frames dialog box to copy objects to all of your frames, or just a specific range of frames.

Distributing objects to frames

When you choose to distribute a group of objects to frames, the objects are distributed after the current frame, according to their stacking order. The bottom object in the group stays on the current frame, the next one up goes to the next frame, the next one above that goes to the frame after that, and so forth. If you start with a blank canvas and create three objects, such as a square, circle, and star, the star will be on top, because it was created last. If you select those objects and distribute them to frames, the star — which was created last — will now be in the last frame of your animation. New frames are added to contain all the objects, if necessary. For example, if you distribute ten objects to five frames, five more frames will be added to contain all the objects.

You can quickly turn a static document into an animation in this way. Objects that were created first on the canvas end up first in the animation.

To distribute a selection of objects across multiple frames, select the objects and then do one of the following:

- Click the Distribute to Frames button (a filmstrip icon) at the bottom of the Frames panel.
- Choose Distribute to Frames from the Frames panel options popup.
- Drag the blue selection knob on the object's bounding box to the Distribute to Frames button.

Managing static objects

Fireworks simplifies management of the objects in your animation that aren't animated, because any layer can be shared across every frame of your animation. For example, if you create a background in Frame 1, you can share the layer that contains the background, and that background will appear in every frame. After the layer is shared, you can modify the objects it contains in any frame, and the modifications will show up everywhere. Any static element in your animation needs to be created or edited only once.

To share a layer across all the frames of your animation, follow these steps:

1. In the Layers panel, double-click the layer that you want to share.

   Fireworks displays the Layer Options dialog box.

2. Check Share Across Frames, and then click OK.

   Fireworks warns you that any objects on this layer in other frames will be deleted. Click OK to delete those objects and share the layer.

To stop sharing a layer across all frames of your animation, follow these steps:

1. In the Layers panel, double-click the layer that you want to stop sharing.

   Fireworks displays the Layer Options dialog box.

2. Uncheck Share Across Frames, and then click OK.

   Fireworks asks whether you want to leave the contents of the layer in all frames, or just in the current frame. Choose Current to leave the contents of the layer just in the current frame. Choose All to leave the contents of the layer in all frames.

Note Another way to modify whether or not a layer is shared is to select the layer in the Layers panel and check or uncheck Share Layer on the Layers panel options pop-up.

Using the VCR controls

While building your animations in Fireworks, you'll no doubt want to play them to get a feel for the motion between frames. Fireworks offers VCR-style controls available along the bottom of each document window, so that you can preview your animations (see Figure 35-6).

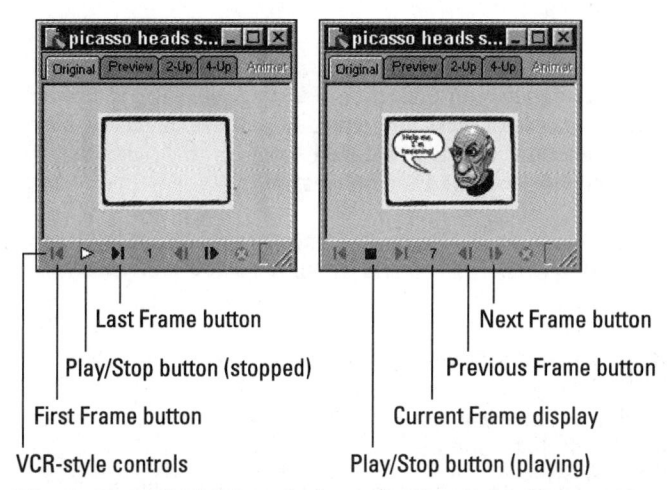

Figure 35-6: The VCR controls on the Fireworks document window enable you to control your multiframe Fireworks document like a movie.

When you click the Play button, Fireworks plays your animation, using the timing that is specified in the Frames panel or on the Animation tab of the Export Preview dialog box. If you don't set the timing yourself, your animation plays at the default of $7/100$ of a second between frames. We'll look at frame delay in the next section.

While the animation is playing, the Play button turns into a Stop button. Fireworks also displays the current frame, and has buttons available to jump quickly to the previous or next frame, or to the first or last frame of your animation.

Tip You can also stop a running animation by clicking your mouse inside the document window.

When you play your animation in the document window, it always loops, whether you have looping enabled in the Frames panel or not. The setting in the Frames panel controls looping only in the animated GIF file your animation eventually becomes.

Setting frame delay timing

The first thing to remember about controlling animation speed is that the settings you specify are ultimately approximate. Although Fireworks is perfectly happy to follow your directions, after your animation becomes an animated GIF, timing is in the virtual hands of the playback software, usually a browser. Internet Explorer tends to play animations faster than Navigator, and both browsers play animated GIFs faster on faster computers.

Tip As if approximated GIF timing isn't enough, an animation that is currently being downloaded staggers along with no attention to timing, because each frame is displayed as it arrives. A couple of tricks for getting around the staggering playback of a downloading animated GIF are detailed later in this chapter, under "Examining Web Design with Animated GIF Images."

The default frame delay setting for new frames is 7, specified in hundredths of a second. For example, a setting of 25 is a quarter second, 50 is a half second, and 200 is two seconds.

To change a frame's delay setting, follow these steps:

1. If the Frames panel is not already open, choose Window ⇨ Frames, or use the keyboard shortcut, Shift+F2 to open it.
2. Double-click the frame timing for the frame you want to modify in the frame list. Fireworks displays a pop-up edit window with the frame's delay settings (see Figure 35-7).

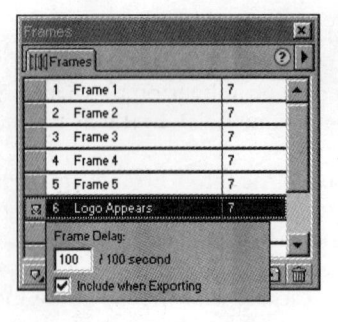

Figure 35-7: Double-click the frame timing for a particular frame in the Frames panel to view a pop-up edit window with the frame's delay settings.

3. Type a new setting in the Frame Delay field.
4. Uncheck Include when Exporting if you want this frame delay setting to affect the way the animation is viewed in Fireworks, without being included in the animated GIF you export.
5. Click anywhere outside the pop-up edit window, or press Enter (Return) to dismiss it.

Alternatively, if you're using the Export Preview dialog box to export your animated GIF, you can alter frame delay by choosing the frame from the list on the Animation tab and changing the value in the Frame Delay field.

Using Onion Skinning

Most of the time, your document window displays the contents of a single frame. By flipping back and forth from frame to frame, you can get a feel for how the animation is flowing, but this is just a rough guide. To get a more precise view of the changes from one frame to the next, turn on Onion Skinning to view, and even edit, multiple frames simultaneously.

Note *Onion skinning* is the traditional animation technique of drawing on translucent tracing paper — like an onion skin — to view a series of drawings simultaneously.

The Onion Skinning button in the lower-left corner of the Frames panel enables you to access the Onion Skinning menu (see Figure 35-8) and select which frames you want to view. You can choose to view any range of frames within your animation, or all of them.

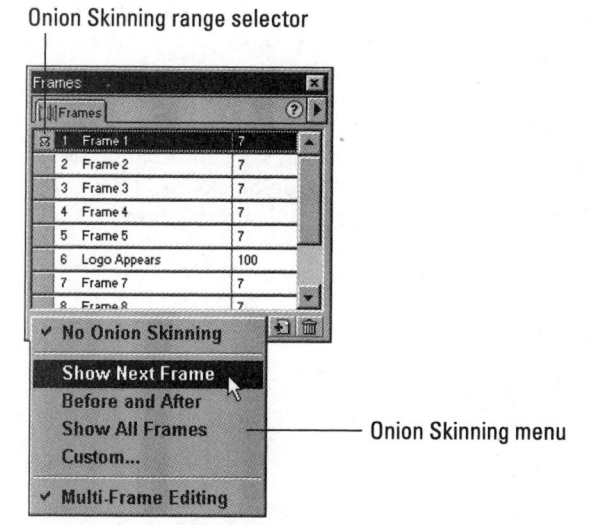

Figure 35-8: The Onion Skinning menu on the Frames panel provides various ways to select which frames you want to view, and even edit, simultaneously.

When Onion Skinning is turned on, objects on the current frame are displayed normally, while objects on other frames are shown slightly dimmed. When playing an animation by using the Frame controls at the bottom of the document window, Onion Skinning is switched off temporarily.

Setting the range of frames to onion skin

You can turn on Onion Skinning and choose a range of frames to display in any one of three ways:

+ Specify a range of frames by using the Onion Skinning range selector, located in the Frame list's left margin in the Frames panel (refer to Figure 35-2). This is the quickest way to specify a range of frames, especially for shorter animations. To expand the range to include earlier frames, click inside an empty box above the selector. To expand the range to include later frames, click inside an empty box below the selector. To contract the range, click inside the selector itself. To turn off Onion Skinning, click the bottom end of the selector.

+ Choose predefined ranges from the Onion Skinning menu on the Frames panel. To show the current frame and the next frame, choose Show Next Frame. To show the previous frame, the current frame, and the next frame, choose Before and After. To show all frames, choose Show All.

+ Choose Custom from the Onion Skinning menu to display the Onion Skinning dialog box (see Figure 35-9), which gives you precise control over the frames that you view, all the way down to the opacity of other frames. Fill in the number of frames Before Current Frame and After Current Frame that you want to view, and specify an Opacity setting for those frames. A setting of 0 makes frame contents invisible, whereas a setting of 100 makes objects on other frames appear as though they're on the current frame.

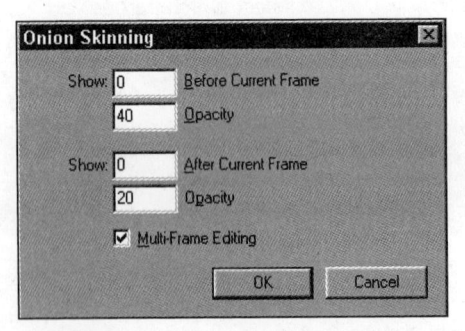

Figure 35-9: Select a specific range of frames to onion skin, and control the opacity of the onion-skinned frames with the Onion Skinning dialog box.

Exploring Multi-Frame Editing

When Multi-Frame Editing is enabled, you can select and edit objects in the document window that are on different frames. Whether an object is on the current frame and displayed regularly or on another frame and dimmed makes no difference. You can easily select all versions of a particular object across multiple frames and move or scale them as one.

To enable multi-frame editing, check Multi-Frame Editing on the Onion Skinning dialog box or the Onion Skinning menu. To switch off multi-frame editing, uncheck Multi-Frame Editing. on the Onion Skinning dialog box.

Examining export settings and options

The animated GIF format contains support for frame delay timing, looping, and various frame disposal methods. These options are built right into the Frame panel itself, or the Animation tab of the Export Preview dialog box.

The first export setting that you must specify is the animated GIF format itself. Choose Window ➪ Optimize to view the Optimize panel, if it isn't already visible, and choose Animated GIF from the format options pop-up, as shown in Figure 35-10.

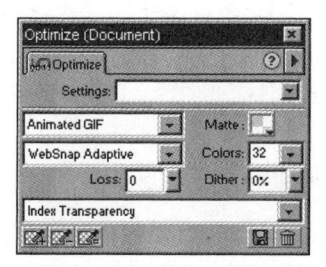

Figure 35-10: Choose Animated GIF as your export format in the Optimize panel.

As usual, the last step before publishing Web media is to put that media on a "diet." All the same rules for exporting a regular, static GIF also apply to animated GIFs. Limiting the number of colors reduces file size, and specifying a transparent background makes for easier compositing with the browser's background when your animated GIF becomes part of a Web page.

Cross-Reference: For more on specifying GIF export options, such as number of colors and transparency, see Chapter 30.

Using frame disposal

In addition to regular GIF options, the animated GIF format has a special trick up its sleeve for reducing file size: frame disposal. For the most part, you can use Fireworks' default frame disposal settings to produce very lightweight animated GIF images. Learning to tweak the Export settings might save you some valuable kilobytes here and there, though, depending on the type of animation you've created.

The frame disposal options are only available from the Frame Disposal menu on the Animation tab of the Export Preview dialog box. Access the Export Preview dialog box by choosing File ⇨ Export Preview. Choose from one of these options:

- **Unspecified:** Fireworks automatically selects the disposal method for each frame. This option is the default and generally creates the lightest animated GIF images.

- **None:** Overlays each frame on top of the previous frame. The first frame is shown, and then the next frame is added on top of it, and the following frame is added on top of that, and so forth. This option is suitable for adding a small object to a larger background, if the object doesn't move throughout the animation. For example, this technique works well with an animation that features parts of a logo that steadily appear until the animation is complete.

- **Restore to Background:** Shows the contents of each new frame over the background color. For example, to move an object in a transparent animated GIF.

- **Restore to Previous:** Shows the contents of each new frame over the contents of the previous frame; for example, to move an object across a background image.

In addition to the Frame Disposal menu, two related options greatly affect the export file size:

- **Auto Crop:** Causes Fireworks to compare each frame of the animation with the previous frame, and then crop to the area that changes. This reduces file sizes by saving information in each animated GIF only once, and avoids a situation in which, for example, a patch of blue in a certain position is saved repeatedly in each frame.

> **Tip:** If you are exporting your animated GIF for editing in another application, turning off Auto Crop is recommended. Some applications don't handle this type of optimization very well, and you may end up with artifacts. Macromedia's Director 7 is one such application.

- **Auto Difference:** Converts unchanged pixels within the Auto Crop area to transparent, which sometimes reduces file size further.

Auto Crop and Auto Difference can be checked or unchecked on the Frames panel options pop-up, or from the Animation tab of the Export Preview dialog box.

Looping

Looping is fairly straightforward. An animated GIF can loop any number of times, or it can be set to loop "forever," which means it never stops. If the last frame of your animation is a final resting point that looks good all on its own, setting your animation to loop a finite number of times is a good option.

If you're creating an animated rollover button, set looping to Forever for best results. Roll over to an animated GIF that plays once, and you may find that it doesn't play at all, or you may catch it in mid-play. Different browsers treat preloaded animated GIF images in different ways.

To change the looping setting for your animated GIF, do one of the following:

✦ Choose No Looping, a specific number, or Forever from the Looping menu in the Frames panel (shown in Figure 35-11).

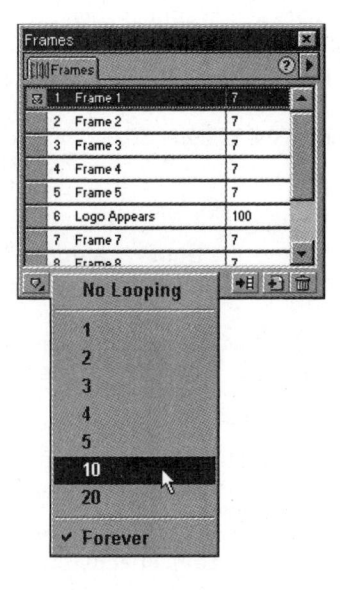

Figure 35-11: Choose your looping option from the Frames panel's Looping menu.

✦ Select the Play Once button or the Loop button from the Animation tab of the Export Preview dialog box, while exporting your animation. If you choose the Loop button, choose Forever, or a number from the Number of Loops options list, or type your own number directly into the box.

Exporting with the Export Preview dialog box

Although you can specify most of the options for your exported animated GIF within the Optimize and Frames panel, the Export Preview dialog box centralizes animation options and also provides a more realistic preview than Fireworks provides in the document window.

To export your animation with the Export Preview dialog box, follow these steps:

1. Choose File ⇨ Export.

   Fireworks displays the Export Preview dialog box, as shown in Figure 35-12.

2. On the Options tab, choose Animated GIF from the format options list.

3. On the Options and File tabs, specify settings, such as Bit Depth and Transparency, just as you would for a regular, static GIF image.

4. On the Animation tab, choose each frame from the list, in turn, and enter a number (in hundredths of a second) in the Frame Delay field. Set the Frame Delay to 0 to make frames display as quickly as possible. Preview the results of your timing settings by using the VCR controls, located below the Preview window in the bottom-right area of the Export Preview dialog box.

Cross-Reference: For more about optimizing GIF Export settings, see Chapter 30.

5. If necessary, click the Frame View/Hide buttons (the eye icons) at the left of each frame on the list to show or hide a frame. If a frame is hidden, it isn't exported, and thus isn't shown when the animation is played in Fireworks.

Note: The Frame Delay settings are saved with your file after you export. Fireworks will continue to use these settings when you play your animation in the document window using the VCR controls.

6. Specify a method for frame disposal by clicking the Frame Disposal menu button (the Trash icon next to the Frame Delay field) and choosing an option.

7. Choose whether or not your animation will loop by clicking either the Play Once or the Loop button. If you click the Loop button, specify the number of times to loop in the Number of Loops options list. You can either choose a number from the list, type another number, or choose Forever to loop continuously. Click the Next button when you're done.

   Fireworks displays the Export dialog box.

8. Choose the target folder and filename for your animated GIF, and then click Save.

Your animation is exported as an animated GIF image.

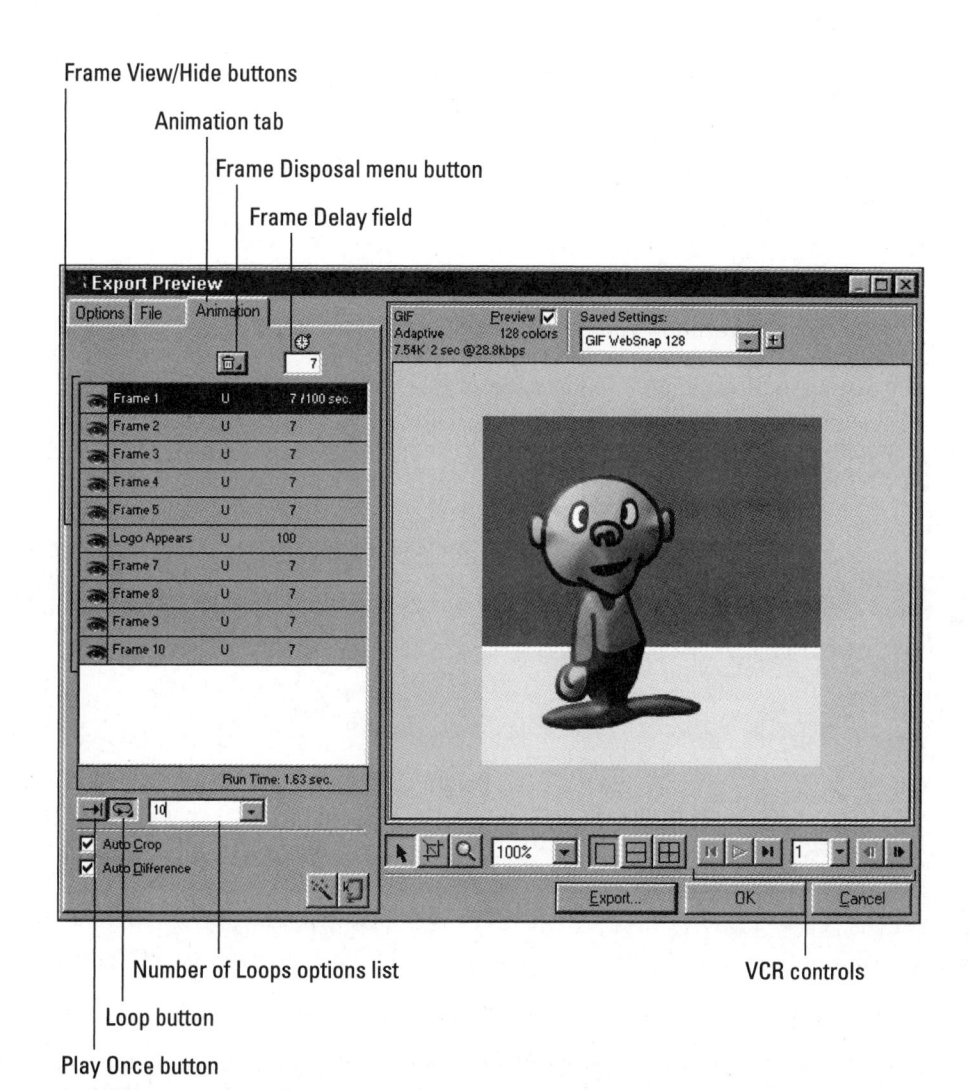

Figure 35-12: The Export Preview dialog box's Animation tab centralizes animation export settings.

Examining Web Design with Animated GIF Images

One of the nicest things about animated GIF images is that you can place them in a Web page just as easily as you can place regular GIF images. This section describes some ways you can incorporate animated GIF images into your Web pages to create a complete presentation.

Animating background images

Version 4 and up browsers can display an animated GIF as a background image. A small animated GIF will be tiled across the whole page, creating a very dynamic presentation with a very low weight.

Reusing animations

A viewer has to download your animated GIF only once. If you use it again on the same page or on another page, it will play from their browser's cache. This is especially useful for an animated logo, or for animated buttons.

Scaling an animation

Use the `height` and `width` attributes of the `img` tag to present an animation at a larger size without increasing its weight. The slight reduction in quality that comes from scaling a bitmap image to double its size — in effect, you're halving its resolution — is a very small price to pay for the impact of a large animation. For example, if you create an animation that is 200×200 pixels, you can put it in a page at 400×400 pixels with the following `img` tag:

```
<img src="example.gif" width="400" height="400">
```

You can also use a percentage width or height to make an animation fit a page. This works better for some animations than others, but again, it can create quite an impact. Set the `width` and `height` to 100% and fill the entire browser window. The `img` tag would look like this:

```
<img src="example.gif" width="100%" height="100%">
```

Using the browser's background image

One of the limitations of animated GIF images is the small number of colors that the GIF format can contain — and the high price you pay in weight for each extra color. However, you can give your animation a colorful background by making it transparent, and then placing it in a Web page with a JPEG background. The weight of the whole presentation remains low because you combine the strengths of the GIF format — animation and transparency — with the strengths of the JPEG format — lots of colors with a low weight.

Preloading an animation

Two ways exist to preload an animated GIF, to avoid the staggering playback that you see when an animation plays while it's downloading:

- **Use the `lowsrc` attribute of the `img` tag.** The browser will show the `lowsrc` image until the regular image finishes downloading. The following line of code tells the browser "Show `spacer.gif` until `animated.gif` has downloaded, and then replace `spacer.gif` with `animated.gif`":

  ```
  <img src="animated.gif" lowsrc="spacer.gif" width="200"
  height="200">
  ```

  The file `spacer.gif` is the transparent 1×1-inch image that Fireworks uses to space tables. You've seen it and have a few copies of it on your hard drive if you've ever exported a sliced image from Fireworks. If you haven't, you can make your own by creating a 1×1-inch image with a transparent canvas and exporting it. Because it's lightweight, it doesn't affect the weight of your page too much. Because it's transparent, the background color shows through until the animation starts.

  > **Note** Internet Explorer does not support the `img` tag's `lowsrc` attribute.

- **Use a Fireworks Swap Image behavior to swap a static image or `spacer.gif` with your animated image.** Modify the Event that triggers the Swap Image behavior to `onLoad`. When the entire page's content has loaded, the `onLoad` event fires and the static image is replaced with your fully downloaded animated GIF.

  > **Cross-Reference** For more about using Fireworks behaviors, see Chapter 34.

Using animated rollovers

Replacing the Over state of a rollover button with an animation of the same size can create an exciting effect. When the viewer's mouse hovers over your button, the animation begins. When it stops hovering over your button, the animation stops.

> **Caution** Some browsers have problems with complex animated GIF images in rollovers. A small, simple animation that loops forever will likely work best.

To create a simple animated rollover, follow these steps:

1. Create a rollover button with at least three states (Up, Over, and Down), and export it as a GIF in the usual way. (A rollover with two states appears to flash rather than move.) Note the filename that Fireworks gives the Over state of your button; it will be something like button_r2_c2_f2, where f2 stands for frame 2, where you created the Over state.

> **Cross-Reference** For detailed instructions about creating rollover buttons, see Chapter 34.

After you export your file once as a rollover, you need to export it again as an animated GIF. The individual frames that served as each state of the rollover button will now serve as the frames of an animation.

2. To export your file again as an animated GIF, choose File ➪ Export Preview.

   Fireworks displays the Export Preview dialog box.

3. On the Options tab, choose Animated GIF from the format options list.

4. On the Animation tab, click the Loop button, choose Forever, and then click Next.

   Fireworks displays the Export dialog box.

5. Under Slicing, select No Slicing.

6. Under HTML Style, select None.

7. Choose the filename of the Over state of your rollover button, and click Save to save your animated GIF with that name.

   Fireworks asks whether you want to replace the original file. Click Yes.

When you open the HTML file that Fireworks created, you'll find that hovering your mouse over the button makes the button start cycling through its Up, Over, and Down states.

Tip

You can also make an animated rollover button that stops animating when the user places his mouse over it. Instead of replacing the f2 image with an animation, as before, replace the f1 image. The animation plays as the page loads, but stops with a hover of the mouse over the button.

Slicing animations

Don't be afraid to unleash Fireworks' formidable slicing tools on your animations.

Caution

In the Object panel, set static slices to GIF, JPEG, PNG, or whatever format you desire. Set animated slices to export as Export Defaults and then choose Animated GIF as the format when you export the whole document.

Some ideas for things you might do with slicing and animation:

✦ **Add extra colors:** Slice colorful, static areas and set the slice to export as a JPEG or PNG, and your animation will appear to have sections of 24-bit color.

✦ **Add interactivity:** Replace a blank slice of your animated GIF with an HTML form element, such as an options list, or a set of radio buttons.

Cross-Reference

For more information about slicing images in Fireworks, see Chapter 33.

Chapter 35 ✦ **Applying Animation Techniques** 1135

Tweening Graphic Symbols

You can really unleash your animations in Fireworks by incorporating graphic symbols. Symbols are reusable objects that have been placed in a Fireworks Library. Copies of symbols placed onto the canvas are called Instances. Instances maintain a link to their symbols, so that changing certain properties of a symbol also updates all of its Instances.

> **Cross-Reference**: A basic knowledge of symbols will serve you well for the rest of this chapter. Read more about graphic symbols in Chapter 32.

Two or more Instances of the same symbol can be "tweened" automatically by Fireworks. Tweening is a traditional animation term that refers to generating intermediate frames be*tween* two images to create the effect of the first image changing smoothly into the second image. In Fireworks, you provide the starting point for an animation with one Instance, and the ending point of the animation with another, and Fireworks creates the intermediate steps between them. Each new Instance is slightly changed from the one before it, so that the first Instance seems to evolve into the last. You can also tween more than two Instances (Figure 35-13), in which case it might be helpful to think of each Instance as a resting point, or a keyframe.

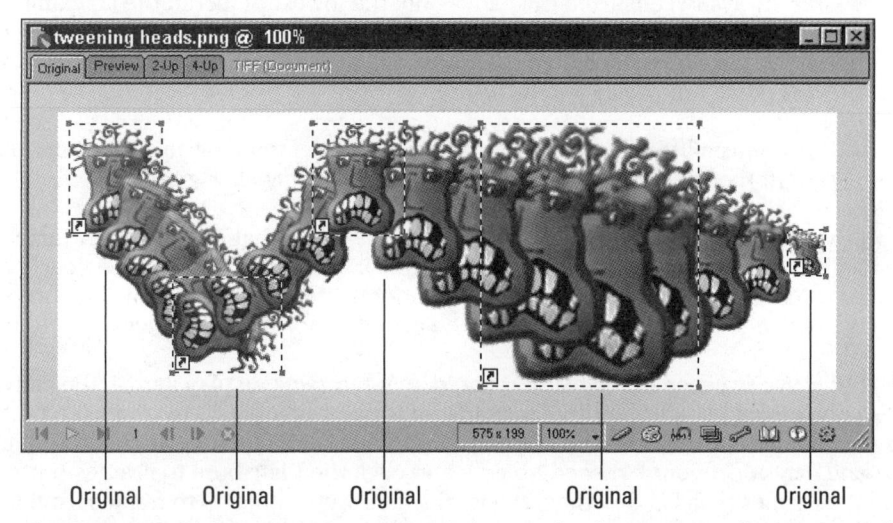

Figure 35-13: Each Instance is a resting point, or a keyframe. Fireworks automatically creates the rest of the objects with tweening.

You can obviously use tweening to simulate motion, but by tweening object properties, you can also make an object appear to change over time. If you scale an Instance to a larger size and then tween it with another that's not scaled, the tweened Instances will be sized to create a smooth transition, as was the case in Figure 35-12. Any property of an Instance that can be independently modified can be tweened. These include:

- Transformations such as width, height, and skew made with the Transform tool, or with the Modify ⇨ Transform submenu.

> **Note:** Fireworks always tweens two or more Instances of the same symbol, and as such, can't tween shapes (morphing) because the shapes of the Instances are always the same. If you want to tween shapes, you can do a blend in Macromedia FreeHand and then import the file into Fireworks and distribute the shapes to frames. You can also do a shape tween in Macromedia Flash, save the result as an Adobe Illustrator document, and then import that document into Fireworks in order to retain the vector information.

- Opacity and/or Blending modes adjusted in the Object panel.
- Live Effects. As long as all the Instances have the same Live Effect applied, you can tween the properties of that Live Effect. If you want to make an object appear to go from not having an effect to having one, set the effect's settings to 0 on one of the Instances and a higher value on another.

Fireworks always tweens from the canvas up; the lowest object in the stacking order is first, and the highest object last, as shown in Figure 35-14. If you're tweening more than two objects, adjust their stacking order to make sure that they tween in the order that you want them to.

> **Tip:** Don't be confused into thinking that objects tween from left to right across the canvas. The stacking order is always the guideline for tweening order.

After you set the stacking order to determine the order that objects get tweened, you also have to decide how many steps Fireworks should fill in between each object. Refer again to Figure 35-13. The number of steps in that tween was three, so Fireworks filled in three objects between each of the original Instances.

So far, we've tweened objects and created an interesting display across the canvas. Usually, though, you'll want to distribute your tweened objects to frames to create a real animation. You have the option to do this at the same time as the tweening, or you can select your tweened objects and click the Distribute to Frames button on the Frames panel at any time. Fireworks distributes objects to frames from bottom to top, the same way that it tweens, so that your objects stay in the correct order.

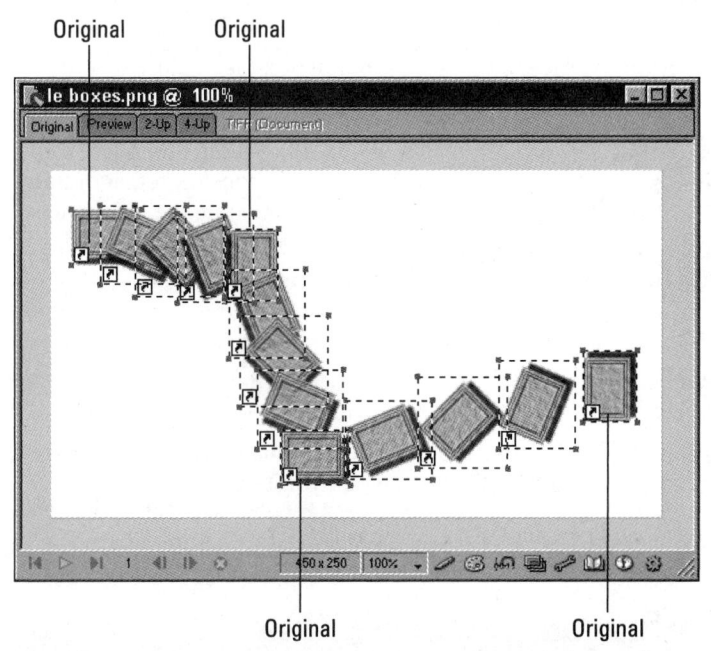

Figure 35-14: Four Instances become an entire animation after tweening. Note that Fireworks tweened according to the stacking order. The start of the tween is the object closest to the canvas, and the highest object in the stacking order is the end.

To tween Instances, follow these steps:

1. Create an object or a group of objects, and convert it to a symbol. Select the object and choose Insert ⇨ Convert to Symbol. Name your symbol in the Symbol Properties dialog box, and click OK when you're done. Your object is converted into a symbol and stored in the Library. An Instance is left in its place on the canvas.

2. Choose Edit ⇨ Duplicate, or use the keyboard shortcut, Ctrl+Alt+D (Command+Option+D) to create a copy of the Instance. A copy of an Instance is also an Instance. Keep in mind that the duplicate will be one higher in the stacking order.

3. Position the duplicate Instance to a spot on the canvas where you want the tween to stop.

4. Select both Instances either by dragging a selection box around them with your mouse, or by holding down the Shift key and clicking each one in turn.

5. Choose Modify ➪ Symbol ➪ Tween Instances.

   Fireworks displays the Tween Instances dialog box (see Figure 35-15).

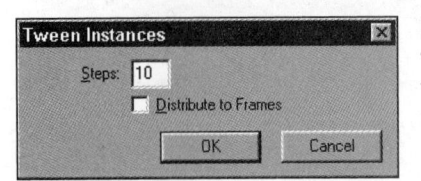

   Figure 35-15: Set the number of steps to tween, and choose whether or not you want to distribute the objects to frames in the Tween Instances dialog box.

6. Enter the number of steps to tween. A setting of 3 makes Fireworks create three new objects between each of your original Instances.

7. Check Distribute to Frames to distribute the tweened objects to frames and make them into an animation. Click OK when you're done.

Fireworks creates the new objects, and you have an instant animation.

Fireworks technique: Tweening Xtras

Unlike Live Effects, you can't really tween Xtras, because they're applied directly to bitmap objects only. Applying them to linked objects also breaks the link and leaves you with regular bitmap objects. You can use tweening, though, to create an animation quickly, in which the only changes are the settings of the Xtra as it's applied to each frame.

> **Cross-Reference**
> This example uses an Xtra called Fire, which is part of a third-party package called Eye Candy, from Alien Skin. Fire is available in both Eye Candy 3.1 and Eye Candy 4000. If you don't have the full version of Eye Candy, use one of the Eye Candy 4000 LE filters included with Fireworks 4, or another third-party Xtra — many are available free on the Web. For more information about Xtras and about Eye Candy 4000, see Chapter 28.

To animate Xtras in Fireworks, follow these steps:

1. Create the basic object or group to which you're going to apply the Xtra, and then make the group or object into a symbol using Insert ➪ Convert to Symbol. Name your symbol in the Symbol Properties dialog and click OK when you're done. The symbol is placed in the Library and an Instance is left in its place.

2. Select your Instance and create another Instance directly on top of it by choosing either Edit ➪ Clone, or by using the keyboard shortcut, Ctrl+Shift+D (Command+Shift+D).

3. Select both Instances by dragging a selection box around them. Alternatively, if they are the only objects in your document, you can select them both by choosing either Edit ⇨ Select All, or Ctrl+A (Command+A).

4. Create tweened Instances between your two Instances by choosing Modify ⇨ Symbol ⇨ Tween Instances.

   Fireworks displays the Tween Instances dialog box.

5. Set the number of steps to a small number, such as 5.

6. Uncheck the Distribute to Frames checkbox, and then click OK.

   Now we have a stack of identical objects, to which we're going to apply an Xtra, changing the settings slightly each time so that each object looks slightly different.

7. Select all the Instances by dragging a selection around them with the mouse.

8. Choose Xtras ⇨ Eye Candy 4000 ⇨ Fire.

   Fireworks displays the Fire dialog box for the first Instance.

9. Specify the settings that you want, and then click OK.

   Fireworks displays the Fire dialog box for the second Instance.

10. The controls are set the same way you left them after the first Instance. Modify the controls slightly to create a difference between this Instance and the previous one. Click OK when you're done.

    Fireworks displays the Fire dialog box for the third Instance.

11. Continue to change control settings slightly in each box as it appears, until you have modified all the Instances.

> **Tip** Clicking Cancel at any time in the Xtra's dialog box cancels the operation for all the Instances.

12. With your Instances still selected, click the Distribute to Frames button (the filmstrip icon) on the Frames panel.

All Instances are distributed over frames to create an animation, such as the one in Figure 35-16. Preview your animation with the VCR controls on the bottom of the document window. Alternatively, you can choose File ⇨ Export Preview and preview your animation in the Export Preview dialog box, or choose a browser from the File ⇨ Preview in Browser submenu to see your work in a browser.

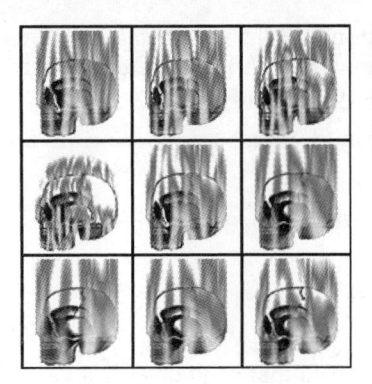

Figure 35-16: This animation depends entirely on the slight changes in the Fire effect applied to each Instance to make our subject's skull appear to be vigorously aflame.

Fireworks technique: Tweening depth

A quick and useful effect that you can create with tweened Instances is 3D depth, wherein your object appears to fly out from the canvas.

To create a depth effect with tweened Instances, follow these steps:

1. Create the basic object or group that you're going to work with, and then convert it into a symbol using Insert ⇨ Convert to Symbol. Name your symbol in the Symbol Properties dialog box, and click OK when you're done. The symbol is placed in the Library and an Instance is left in its place.

2. Move the Instance near the top of the canvas.

3. Choose Edit ⇨ Clone, or use the keyboard shortcut, Ctrl+Shift+D (Command+Shift+D), to create another Instance directly on top of the first.

4. Hold down the Shift key and, at the same time, use the arrow down key to move the new Instance down the canvas, without moving it left or right. A few hundred pixels is usually all you can get away with while still keeping the depth effect looking like depth.

5. With the Instance still selected, choose Modify ⇨ Transform ⇨ Numeric Transform.

   Fireworks displays the Numeric Transform dialog box.

6. Scale the Instance to 30 percent of its size, by selecting Scale from the options list, checking Scale Attributes, checking Constrain Proportions, and entering 30 in one of the fields. Click OK when you're done.

7. Set the Instance's opacity to 10 percent by double-clicking it and entering 10 in the Opacity field of the Object panel.

8. With the Instance still selected, choose Modify ⇨ Arrange ⇨ Send to Back, or press Ctrl+Shift+down arrow (Command+Shift+down arrow).

9. Hold down Shift and click each Instance to select all of them. If they are the only objects in your document, you can choose Edit ⇨ Select All, or press Ctrl+A (Command+A).

10. Choose Modify ⇨ Symbol ⇨ Tween Instances.

    Fireworks displays the Tween Instances dialog box.

11. Set the number of steps you want in between the two Instances, uncheck Distribute to Frames, and then click OK.

    Fireworks tweens the Instances.

> **Tip** You can choose Edit ⇨ Undo and then do Steps 10 and 11 again if you find that you want to change the number of steps.

12. If you like, you can select the original Instance and make it stand out by adding a Live Effect such as glow or inner bevel to it.

Your object now appears to fly out from the canvas (see Figure 35-17).

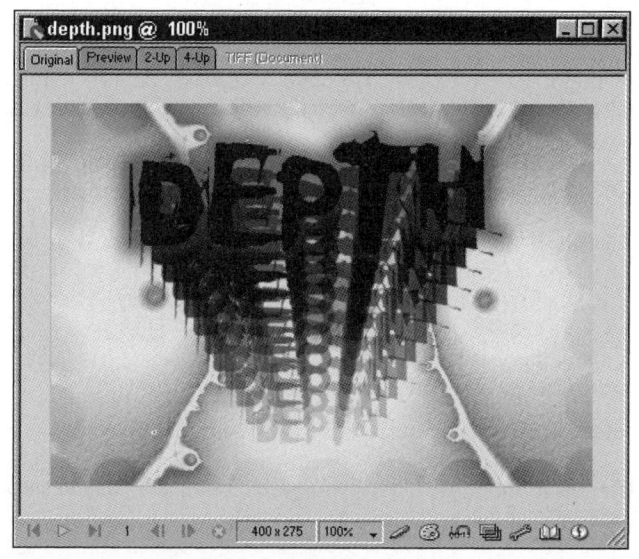

Figure 35-17: Fireworks created the steps between the front and back Instances with tweening. A little of the Glow Live Effect was then added to the front object to make it stand out.

> **Tip** To change this depth effect into an animation, select all the Instances by drawing a selection around them with the mouse (or, if they are the only objects in your document, choose Edit ⇨ Select All), and then click the Distribute to Frames button on the Frames panel. Your object animates its way toward you.

Fireworks technique: Fading in and out

Fading an object in and out is a common effect that's easy to create in Fireworks. Tweening two Instances that are positioned in the same place on the canvas, one with an Opacity setting of 0 percent, and one with an opacity of 100 percent, produces a fade. Which Instance is higher in the stacking order determines whether it's a fade-in or a fade-out. In this section, we create an animation in which the object fades in, then fades back out, and then loops, so that it seems to fade in and out continuously.

To fade an object in and out, follow these steps:

1. Create the basic object or group to which you're going to apply the fade, and then convert the object or group into a symbol. Select it and choose Insert ⇨ Convert to Symbol. Name your symbol in the Symbol Properties dialog box, and click OK when you're done. Your new symbol is stored in the Library and an Instance is left in its place.

2. Select the Instance and choose Edit ⇨ Clone, or press Ctrl+Shift+D (Command+Shift+D), to create another Instance directly on top of it.

3. Open the Object panel and set the Opacity of the new Instance to 0 percent.

Note The Opacity setting might not seem to have any effect, because you will be able to see the original Instance through the newer Instance, which is now transparent.

4. Choose Modify ⇨ Arrange ⇨ Send to Back to send the transparent Instance directly behind the original Instance.

5. Select both Instances by dragging a selection box around them. If they are the only objects in your document, you can select them by choosing either Edit ⇨ Select All, or by using the keyboard shortcut, Ctrl+A (Command+A).

6. Choose Modify ⇨ Symbol ⇨ Tween Instances.

   Fireworks displays the Tween Instances dialog box.

7. Set the number of steps to 5.

Note You can choose a different number of steps, if you prefer, but during this example, I'll count steps and frames as if you've chosen 5.

8. Check the Distribute to Frames checkbox, and then click OK.

   Play your animation. Your object should appear to fade in. You should have seven frames. In the first frame, the Instance is completely transparent (opacity of 0); in the second frame, the Instance is slightly more opaque, making it appear to fade in; and so on until the seventh frame, in which the Instance is fully opaque.

Chapter 35 ✦ Applying Animation Techniques 1143

Note: At this point, you can choose to either leave your animation as is, or continue and make your animation appear to fade out as well.

9. Open the Frames panel and select the final frame in your animation to display it in the document window. This frame contains your fully opaque Instance.

10. Select the Instance and choose either Edit ➪ Clone, or use the keyboard shortcut, Ctrl+Shift+D (Command+Shift+D), to create another Instance directly on top of the first.

11. Open the Object panel and set the Opacity of the Instance to 0 percent.

12. Select both Instances by dragging a selection box around them. If they are the only objects in this frame, you can select them by choosing either Edit ➪ Select All, or by using the keyboard shortcut, Ctrl+A (Command+A).

13. Choose Modify ➪ Symbol ➪ Tween Instances.

    Fireworks displays the Tween Instances dialog box.

14. Set the number of steps to the same number you used when fading the object in (in this case, 5).

15. Check the Distribute to Frames checkbox, and then click OK.

16. Select the final frame of your animation in the Frames panel and remove it by clicking the Delete Frame button (the Trash icon). This final frame is redundant, because the first frame is also a fully transparent object. Your animation will loop more smoothly without it.

Click Play to preview your animation. The object appears to fade in and then fade out (see Figure 35-18). If you like, you can double-click the fully opaque frame in the middle of your animation (Frame 7 in the example), and specify a longer frame delay so that the pause between the fade-in and fade-out is longer. Choose File ➪ Export Preview to preview your animation in the Export Preview dialog box, where it will often run more smoothly than in the document window.

Figure 35-18: Fading an object in and out is easy with tweening.

Using Animation Symbols

Animation symbols are self-contained, multi-frame symbols with their own animation properties, such as number of frames, rotation, and scaling. You can create an animation symbol from any object, and it can even contain other symbols. Like graphic and button symbols, animation symbols are stored in the Library and can be reused.

New Feature: Animation symbols are new in Fireworks 4.

You can graphically edit an animation symbol in the Symbol Editor, and its properties in the Object panel, or with the Modify ⇨ Animate ⇨ Settings command. You can edit its motion path directly in the document window.

Creating animation symbols

You can create a new animation symbol from scratch, or convert an existing object into an animation symbol.

To create an animation symbol, follow these steps:

1. Choose Insert ⇨ New Symbol.

   Fireworks displays the Symbol Properties dialog box, as shown in Figure 35-19.

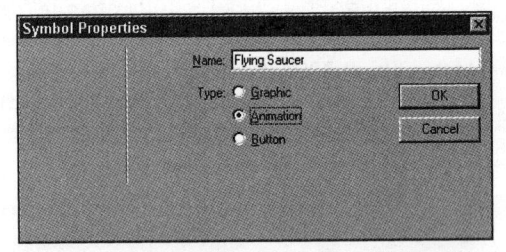

   Figure 35-19: Name your new symbol and specify animation in the Symbol Properties dialog box.

2. Enter a name for the new symbol.
3. Select the Animation radio button under Type. Click OK when you're done.

   Fireworks displays the Symbol Editor.
4. Use the drawing tools to create a new graphic.

5. Close the Symbol Editor window when you're done.

   Fireworks places the new animation symbol in the Library, and places a copy of it in your document.

6. To add new frames to the new animation symbol, select it on the canvas and adjust the Frames slider in the Object panel.

7. To edit the symbols animation properties, select it and choose Modify ⇨ Animate to display the Animate dialog box.

To convert an existing object into an animation symbol, follow these steps:

1. Select the object that you want to convert into an animation symbol.

2. Choose Modify ⇨ Animate ⇨ Animate Selection, or use the keyboard shortcut, Alt+Shift+F8 (Option+Shift+F8).

   Fireworks displays the Animate dialog box, as shown in Figure 35-20.

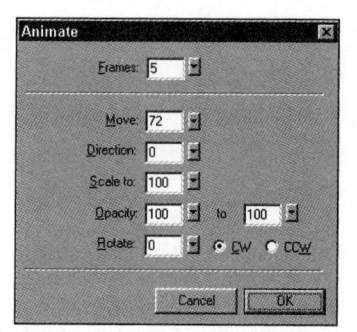

Figure 35-20: Modify animation settings in the Animate dialog box.

3. Modify the settings in the Animate dialog box:

   - **Frames:** The number of frames you want to include in the animation.

   > **Tip:** The Frames slider only goes to 250, but you can type a higher number in the text field. Fireworks automatically adds the required number of frames to your document.

   - **Movement:** The distance that you want each object to move. Possible values range from 0 to 250 pixels. The default is 72.

   - **Direction:** The direction in which you want the object to move. Possible values range from 0 to 360 degrees.

   - **Scaling:** The percent change in size from start to finish. The default is 100 percent. You can specify a number from 0 to 250.

- **Opacity:** Specifies how much to fade in or out from start to finish. Possible values range from 0, which is completely transparent, to 100 (the default), which is completely opaque.
- **Rotation:** The amount that the symbol rotates from start to finish, specified in degrees. The default is 0 degrees, which is no rotation. Specify 90 degrees for a quarter-turn, 180 for a half-turn, and 360 for a complete rotation. Enter a number higher than 360 to start a second rotation.
- **CW and CCW:** Clockwise and counterclockwise, respectively; determine the object's rotation direction.

4. Click OK when you're done.

Your new symbol is added to the Library, and a copy is placed on the canvas.

Editing an animation symbol

There may be a handful of skilled animators who can create the perfect animation symbol the first time through, but for most of us, the settings of our animation symbols will require careful adjustment in order to achieve the effect that we desire.

You can use a number of methods to alter the settings of an animation symbol. We'll explore each of them.

Adjusting animation settings

Select an animation symbol and choose Modify ⇨ Animate ⇨ Settings to display the Animate dialog box. Alter any of the settings as desired.

Cross-Reference   I covered the settings in the Animate dialog box earlier in this chapter, in the section "Creating animation symbols."

Using the Object panel

When an animation symbol is selected, the Object panel changes to display animation symbol options that are similar to the Animate dialog box, as shown in Figure 35-21. Modify any of these options to adjust the corresponding setting.

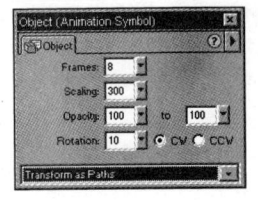

Figure 35-21: Use the Object panel to modify animation symbol options.

Adjusting the motion path

When selected, Animation symbols display a motion path that describes their frame-by-frame movement across the canvas, as shown in Figure 35-22. The green dot on the motion path indicates the start of the animation's path, and the red dot shows the end point. The blue points on the path represent each frame of the animation. The object itself is shown on the current frame.

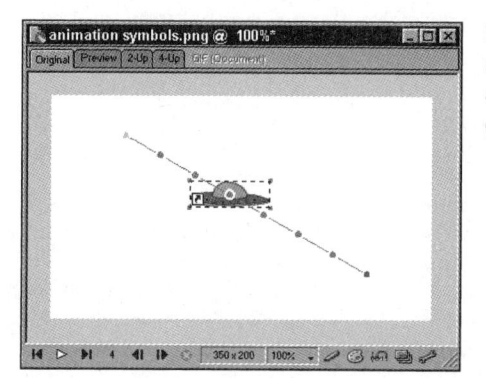

Figure 35-22: The motion path describes the movement of the animation symbol. The visible object is on the current frame, frame 4.

You can change the direction of the animation symbol's motion by changing the angle of the motion path. Drag one of the animation handles to a new location:

Tip: Hold down the Shift key while dragging to constrain the movement to perfectly horizontal or vertical.

- Move the green point to move the starting point of the animation.
- Move the red point to move the ending point of the animation.
- Move any blue point to move the object on the corresponding frame. Click a blue point to switch to that frame.

Converting into a graphic symbol

Choose Modify ⇨ Animate ⇨ Remove Animation to convert the animation symbol into a graphic symbol. Although your symbol is no longer animated, Fireworks retains the animation settings, in case you convert the symbol back into an animation symbol.

Removing the symbol

To remove an animation symbol from the Library, follow these steps:

1. Choose Window ➪ Library to display the Library panel.
2. In the Library panel, select the animation symbol you want to remove.
3. Click the Delete Symbol button (the trash can) on the Library panel.

    Fireworks displays a dialog box, asking you to confirm that you want to remove the symbol.

4. Click Delete to remove the symbol.

Editing symbol graphics

Just like button and graphic symbols, animation symbols are based on a graphic that you can edit in the Symbol Editor. When you modify the graphic that your animation symbol is based on, all of its instances — the copies on the canvas — inherit those changes, as well.

To edit the graphic in an animation symbol, follow these steps:

1. Select the animation symbol you want to edit.
2. Choose Modify ➪ Symbol ➪ Edit Symbol to open the Symbol Editor. Alternatively, you can choose Window ➪ Library and double-click your symbol in the Library panel.
3. Perform your graphical edits in the Symbol Editor.
4. Close the Symbol Editor window when you're done.

Cross-Reference: See Chapter 32 for more on the Symbol Editor.

Summary

Fireworks enables you to create and edit animation by using a variety of techniques, most of which revolve around the Frames panel. When working with animation in Fireworks, keep these points in mind:

+ The overall weight of your animated GIF is always a consideration. Every creative decision must be examined for its effect on file size.
+ The Frames panel is the heart of Fireworks' animation tools, but the Layers panel is also important.

✦ Each frame in your Fireworks document is like a frame of a filmstrip. Copy objects to other frames by using the Frames panel, and then change the objects' locations on the canvas or their properties to create animation.

✦ Layers can be shared across multiple frames, to manage static objects better in an animation.

✦ Onion Skinning enables you to view and edit multiple frames simultaneously.

✦ The Web design opportunities for animated GIF images are numerous, such as animated rollover buttons, sliced animations, and animated browser backgrounds.

✦ Tweening is a great time- and work-saver, because Fireworks fills in the middle elements of an animation automatically. Any selection of two or more instances of the same symbol can be tweened.

✦ Fireworks tweens objects starting at the bottom of the stacking order, nearest the canvas, and moving up.

✦ Distribute a tweened sequence to frames to create an instant animation.

✦ You can use tweening to create advanced effects, such as objects fading in and out, or flying out from the canvas.

✦ Animation symbols provide an intuitive way to work with animations.

✦ ✦ ✦

APPENDIX

What's on the CD-ROM?

Here's what you'll find on the CD-ROM that accompanies the *Dreamweaver and Fireworks Bible*:

✦ Trial versions of Dreamweaver, Fireworks, Dreamweaver UltraDev, Flash, and FreeHand

✦ An Eye Candy demo of special effects for Fireworks from Alien Skin Software, the leading manufacturer of such tools

✦ A time-limited demo of Pantone's ColorWeb Pro

✦ Code examples used in the book

Also included are hundreds of Dreamweaver and Fireworks extensions from the leaders in the Dreamweaver community, designed to make you more productive:

✦ Behaviors

✦ Objects

✦ Commands for both Dreamweaver and Fireworks

✦ Browser profiles

✦ Inspectors

✦ Floaters

Using the Accompanying CD-ROM

The CD-ROM is what is known as a *hybrid CD-ROM*, which means it contains files that run on more than one computer platform — in this case, both Windows and Macintosh computers.

Several files, primarily the Macromedia trial programs and the other external programs, are compressed. Double-click these files to begin the installation procedure. Most other files on the CD-ROM are uncompressed, and you can simply copy them to your system by using your file manager.

A few of the Dreamweaver extensions include files that must be placed in different folders and are also compressed. In the Configuration folder, the file structure replicates the structure that Dreamweaver sets up when it's installed. For example, objects found in the Dreamweaver\Configuration\Objects folder should be in that location for both the CD-ROM and the installed program. *One slight variation:* In the Additional Extensions folder, you'll find the various behaviors, objects, and so on, filed under the author's name.

Likewise, where possible, the file structure of the CD-ROM replicates the structure that Fireworks sets up when it's installed.

See the installation instructions at the very back of the book, just before the bound-in disc, for more detailed directions about installing the programs provided on the CD-ROM.

Files and Programs on the CD-ROM

The *Dreamweaver and Fireworks Bible* contains a host of programs and auxiliary files to assist your exploration of Dreamweaver and Fireworks, as well as your Web page design work in general. The following is a description of the files and programs on the CD-ROM that comes with this book.

Macromedia trial versions

If you haven't had a chance to work with Dreamweaver or Fireworks, the CD-ROM offers trial versions of these and other key Macromedia programs for both Macintosh and Windows systems. Each of the trials run for 30 days; you can't reinstall them in order to gain additional time. The CD-ROM offers these trial programs:

- Dreamweaver
- Dreamweaver UltraDev
- Fireworks
- Flash
- FreeHand

To install any of these programs, just double-click the program icon in the main folder of the CD-ROM where the program is located and follow the installation instructions on your screen.

Caution: The trial versions of Macromedia programs are very sensitive to system date changes. If you alter your computer's date, the programs will time-out and no longer function. It's a good idea to check your system's date and time before installing these programs. Moreover, if you've previously run the trial version of the same program from another source (such as downloading it from the Internet), you won't be able to run the trial version again.

Dreamweaver extensions

Dreamweaver is fully extensible, and the Dreamweaver community has built some amazing extensions. In the Additional Extensions folder of the CD-ROM, you can find hundreds of behaviors, objects, commands, inspectors, and more. The extensions are grouped according to author, and within each author's folder they are organized by function. Almost all of these extensions were written prior to the availability of the Extension Manager, so they don't require that program for installation.

Note: Within the Additional Extensions folder, all behaviors are stored in the Behaviors folder to make it easy to access them. When installing, be sure to put the behaviors in the Configuration\Behaviors\Action folder on your system and not simply in the Behaviors folder.

You'll find a `ReadMe.htm` file in each author's folder, with links to the author's Web site and more information about the author's creations.

Following is a partial list of extension authors featured on the CD-ROM (alphabetized by the first name or word to match how you'll see them on the disc):

- Andrew Wooldridge
- Brendan Dawes
- Eddie Traversa
- Hal Pawluk
- Jaro von Flocken
- Lucas Lopatin
- Machak FX

- Massimo Foti
- Olle Karneman
- Project VII
- Robert Sherman — SnR Graphics
- Simon White — MediaFear
- Webmonkey

Author-created Dreamweaver extensions

The majority of the following extensions were built specifically for *Dreamweaver Bible* by the author. You can find these extensions in the Configuration folder on the CD-ROM.

> **Note** Where available, extensions are packaged in an MXP file that you can install easily by using the Extension Manager. To run the Extension Manager from Dreamweaver, choose Commands ⇨ Manage Extensions. Then choose File ⇨ Install Extension and browse to the location of the extension's MXP file. Other extensions need to be installed by copying the required files to your Dreamweaver\Configuration folder as described in the following sections.

Behaviors

Dreamweaver behaviors automate many functions that previously required extensive JavaScript programming. The behaviors included on the CD-ROM are in addition to the standard set of behaviors included with Dreamweaver and discussed in Chapter 11. The behaviors on the CD-ROM are stored in the Configuration\Behaviors\Actions folder. Copy the behaviors to the similarly named folder in your system installation of Dreamweaver, and restart Dreamweaver to access the new behaviors.

Objects

Much of Dreamweaver's power is derived from its extensibility. Each of the standard Dreamweaver objects is based on an HTML file. The CD-ROM contains various Dreamweaver objects designed to help you create your Web pages faster and more efficiently.

Each Dreamweaver object consists of two files, an HTML file and a GIF file with the same name that is used to create the button on the Objects Palette. For example, the Character Entities object comprises the files `char_entities.htm` and `char_entities.gif`.

To install the Dreamweaver objects, go to Additional Extensions\Dreamweaver Extensions\Configuration\Objects and copy any pair of files from the subfolders Common, Forms, Invisibles, Media, and New to similarly named folders in your system installation of Dreamweaver. (The Media and New folders are not included in the standard release of Dreamweaver and must be created on your system.) Restart Dreamweaver to access the new objects.

Commands

Commands are proving to be the real workhorses of Dreamweaver extensibility. Not only can they do pretty much everything that behaviors and objects do, but they also have their own capabilities as well. Command files come in many shapes and sizes — from a single file to five or more files split across multiple folders. The commands found in the Configuration\Commands folder on the CD-ROM go into the equivalent Dreamweaver folder on your system. The commands are as follows:

- **Repeat History:** Repeats any selected actions in the History palette any number of times. This command requires the Extension Manager to install.
- **Replicator:** Duplicates any selected object, any number of times. Be sure to copy both Replicator.htm and Replicator.js into the Commands folder.
- **Insert Shockwave HTML:** Reads an HTML file generated by Director to insert a Shockwave object, complete with proper dimensions and other needed parameters.
- **Change Case:** Converts the case of the selected text to uppercase or lowercase.

Browser profiles

Dreamweaver recognizes the proliferation of browsers on the market today and makes it easy for you to check your Web page creations against specific browser types. In addition to the standard profiles that come with Dreamweaver, the CD-ROM contains several browser profiles for checking various implementations of HTML, including the following:

- HTML 2.0
- HTML 3.2
- HTML 4.0
- Opera 3.0
- Pocket Internet Explorer 1.0 (for Windows CE 1.0)
- Pocket Internet Explorer 1.1 (for Windows CE 1.0)
- Pocket Internet Explorer 2.0 (for Windows CE 2.0)

Each additional browser profile is contained in the Dreamweaver\Configuration\BrowserProfiles folder of the CD-ROM. To install the browser profiles, the files must be copied to a similarly named folder in your system installation of Dreamweaver. Restart Dreamweaver to access the new browser profiles.

Dreamweaver examples

You can find the code examples used in the Dreamweaver chapters by opening the Dreamweaver\Code and Examples folder on the CD-ROM and then opening the appropriate chapter folder.

Dreamweaver Web page examples

One of the best ways to begin working in Web design is to customize another's designs. The CD-ROM includes several Web page examples aimed at giving you a running start in creating your own pages. You'll find these web page examples scattered throughout the individual chapter subfolders under Code and Examples. You can use these examples from within Dreamweaver by opening them directly from the CD-ROM by choosing File ⇨ Open, or you can transfer the files to your system and open them from there.

Web resource directory

The World Wide Web is a vital resource for any Web designer, whether a seasoned professional or a beginner. The CD-ROM contains an HTML page with a series of links to resources on the Web; the series contains general as well as Dreamweaver-specific references.

Fireworks extensions

Fireworks is blessed with a robust community that not only creates great artwork and utilities but also shares what it creates. Included on the CD-ROM are numerous extensions — commands, styles, and textures — from the Fireworks community. Not only can these tools ease your workflow, but they can also vary and enhance your designs.

On the CD-ROM, in addition to the extensions that I created, you'll find contributions from the following Fireworks designers:

- ✦ Kleanthis Economou
- ✦ Massimo Foti

- Linda Rathgeber
- Eddie Traversa
- Simon White

Commands

With the availability of the Fireworks graphics engine through its JavaScript API and Document Object Model, Fireworks commands are really taking off. Commands are undeniably powerful, whether they are used to automate tedious production or produce fun effects. You can access a Fireworks command from anywhere by choosing File ⇨ Run Script. If you prefer to centralize your commands, copy the ones you want from the CD-ROM to the Fireworks/Settings/Commands folder. The next time you run Fireworks, you'll find your new tools under the Commands menu.

Styles and textures

Part of the power of Fireworks is that it gives you the ability to extend both its image-creating capabilities and its HTML output. Making a set of textures available is as simple as copying a folder from one location to another. For the textures included with this CD-ROM, you simply need to copy the images in any of the Textures folders found under the various contributors' names to the equivalent Fireworks folder and then relaunch Fireworks. The CD-ROM includes over 50 new textures.

Tip You can also use an individual texture without having to copy it to your Textures folder by selecting Other from the Textures list in Fireworks and then choosing the texture from another folder on your computer.

Gradients, strokes, and image libraries

Fireworks lets you add many other components to an image, such as a stroke or gradient fill. For your graphics-creation pleasure, the CD-ROM includes a useful compendium of various gradient fills, strokes, and image libraries, each in its own self-named folder. Although these are fairly simple to create in Fireworks, why reinvent the wheel when you have so much other work to do? Included in this collection is a wide variety of dotted and dashed strokes as well as an arrowhead library.

Fireworks examples

You can find the code examples used in the Fireworks chapters by opening the Code and Examples folder on the CD-ROM and then opening the appropriate chapter folder.

Fireworks image examples

You can find the example images used in the Fireworks chapters in the Code and Examples folder of the CD-ROM, organized by the chapter in which they appear in the book. You'll find examples of everything from alpha transparency to a pseudo banner ad that conforms to industry-wide specifications.

Web resource directory

The Web is a vital resource for any Web designer, whether you're a seasoned professional or a beginner. The CD-ROM contains an HTML page with a series of links to resources on the Web; the series contains general as well as Fireworks-specific references.

Additional Fireworks related programs

Fireworks 4 is definitely one program that "plays well with others." Virtually any Photoshop-compatible plug-in can be used as a Fireworks Effect—good news if you're a Photoshop user or have Photoshop-compatible filters from another application. Alien Skin Software, the leading filter and effects manufacturer has kindly loaned its Eye Candy program for inclusion on this CD-ROM. In addition to these effects, the world-renowned color specialist, Pantone, has contributed a program, ColorWeb Pro, to help ease the transition for designers from the world of print to the Web.

Eye Candy 4000 from Alien Skin

Alien Skin Software has contributed a demo version of Eye Candy 4000, which is a terrific collection of effects applicable to any Fireworks image.

ColorWeb Pro from Pantone

Many new Web designers are not new to design at all and bring a rich history—as well as a client list—from their print backgrounds. One constant in print color reproduction is the Pantone Color System. Many clients require that all of their graphics, whether intended for print or for the Internet, conform to a specific selection of Pantone colors. The ColorWeb Pro application translates Pantone colors into their RGB equivalents.

Dreamweaver 4 Bible and *Fireworks 4 Bible* in PDF format

Need to quickly find out how to do something that you know you read before and can't quite remember? Search for it in the *Dreamweaver 4 Bible* or *Fireworks 4 Bible* files in PDF format located on the CD-ROM. The full versions of both titles are included for your convenience. You'll need Adobe Acrobat Reader to view the PDF files; if you don't already have it installed on your system, you can find it on the CD-ROM.

✦ ✦ ✦

Index

Numerics
8BCT files, 723

A
<a> and </a> tags, 195–196, 202
accessing
 Libraries, 1038–1039
 text styles, 135
 toolbars, 574
ACT files, 723
ActionScript, 375
Active Color Tables, 723
Add External Editor dialog box, 357
<address> and </address> tags, 137–138
Adjust Tracing Image Position dialog box, 480–481
adjusting
 colors, 858–863
 curves, 673–674
 tonal ranges, 858–860
Adobe color swatches, 723
Adobe GoLive
 image maps, 1055–1056
 slices, 1068–1069
Adobe Web site, 888
Advanced Validate Form dialog box, 411
advertising (banner ads), 182–184
alerts
 Popup Message behavior, 331–332
 timelines, 497
aliases, 889–890
Alien Skin Eye Candy filters, 890–895, 1158
Alien Skin Web site, 888
alignment
 canvas, 915–916
 layers (Dreamweaver), 475–477
 objects (Fireworks), 911–916
 tables, 222–224, 232–233
 text, 152–153
 text objects, 803–805, 807
 Tracing Image, 480–481
 Web graphics, 173–175
alpha masks, 924–926
alt text, 172
America Online browser, 17
anchor tags, 195–196, 202
animation
 animated GIFs, 161, 181–182, 494, 1112–1115, 1131–1132
 animation symbols, 1144–1148

 effects, 852–854
 fills, 848–850
 filters, 856
 HTML styles, 139–140
 Live Effects, 852–854
 server-side includes, 550–551
 strokes, 652–653, 666–667
 style sheets, 428–430
 styles, 1009–1010
 templates (Dreamweaver), 531, 534–535
 Xtras, 856, 884–887
Assets panel (Dreamweaver), 166–168, 197–199
attaching
 behaviors, 306–310, 1079–1080
 style sheets, 428–429
audience considerations
 animations, 1112
 Web sites, 20
audio
 Flash, 387
 Play Sound behavior, 330–331

B
<b> tag, 86, 137
background colors
 Cascading Style Sheets (CSS), 439–440
 layers, 459, 472
 tables, 229, 235
 Web pages, 8, 73
background images
 animation, 1132
 Cascading Style Sheets (CSS), 438–440
 frames, 290
 layers, 459, 472
 Web pages, 8, 177–178
bandwidth considerations
 animation, 1112
 entire Web site, 21
 interactivity, 494
banner ads
 download times, 183
 inserting, 183
 placeholders, 183–184
 standard sizes, 182–183
<base> tag, 84
baseline shift (text objects), 803
BBEdit HTML editor, 87

behaviors (Dreamweaver)
    actions, 305–306, 313, 316
    attaching, 306–310
    behaviors available on CD-ROM, 1154
    browsers, 306, 310–315
    Call JavaScript, 316–317
    Change Property, 317–319
    Check Browser, 319–320
    Check Plugin, 320–322
    Control Shockwave or Flash, 322–323
    deleting, 349
    Drag Layer, 323–326, 486–488
    event files, 313
    event handlers, 311–312
    events, 305, 310–311, 313–315
    Go to Frame, 510
    Go to Timeline Frame, 343–345
    Go to URL, 326–327
    HTML tags, 306
    Jump Menu, 270–271, 327–329
    Jump Menu Go, 327–329
    layers, 485–491
    managing, 347
    modifying, 348
    Open Browser Window, 329–330
    parameter forms, 306
    Play Sound, 330–331
    Play Timeline, 343–345, 509
    Popup Message, 331–332
    Preload Images, 333–334
    sequencing, 349
    Set Nav Bar Image, 334–335
    Set Text of Frame, 336–337
    Set Text of Layer, 337–338, 488–489
    Set Text of Status Bar, 338–339
    Set Text of Text Field, 339–340
    Show-Hide Layers, 340–341, 490–491
    Simple Rollover, 362–363
    Stop Timeline, 343–345, 509
    structure, 306
    Swap Image, 14, 341–343
    Swap Image Restore, 341–343
    templates, 530
    timelines, 497, 502, 508–510, 517–518
    triggering from Flash movies, 402–405
    uses, 13–14
    Validate Form, 345–347
behaviors (Fireworks)
    actions, 1078
    attaching, 1079–1080
    deleting, 1081
    drag-and-drop behaviors, 1106–1109
    editing, 1080
    events, 1078, 1080–1081
    modifying, 1080
    Nav Bar Down, 1079
    Nav Bar Over, 1079
    Nav Bar Restore, 1079
    Set Nav Bar Image, 1079
    Set Pop-up Menu, 1102–1106
    Set Text of Status Bar, 1079, 1101
    Simple Rollover, 1078, 1085–1086
    Swap Image, 1078, 1096
    Swap Image Restore, 1078
behaviors (Flash)
    Alphanumeric Validation, 412
    Credit Card Validation, 412
    Date Validation, 412
    E-mail Validation, 412
    Entry Length Validation, 412
    Fast Forward Flash, 406, 408
    Flash Dispatcher, 417–418
    Floating Point Validation, 412
    Go To Flash Frame, 406, 408
    Go To Flash Frame Based on Cookie, 406, 409
    Integer Validation, 412
    International Phone Validation, 412
    Like Entry Validation, 412
    Load Flash Movie, 407, 409
    Mask Validation, 413
    Nonblank Validation, 413
    Pan Flash, 407, 409
    Play Flash, 407–408
    Radio Button Validation, 413
    Rewind Flash, 407–408
    Selection Made in List Validation, 413
    Set Flash by List, 407, 409
    Social Security Validation, 413
    Stop Flash, 407–408
    Time Validation, 413
    URL Validation, 413
    US Phone Validation, 413
    Zip Code Validation, 413
    Zoom Flash, 407, 409
Behaviors panel (Dreamweaver), 307–308
Behaviors panel (Fireworks), 599–600, 1078–1079
bevel effects, 866–869
Bézier curves, 668–675
<big> tag, 86
bit depth (colors), 706–707
bitmap masks, 929–932
bitmaps
    anti-alias edges, 688
    bitmap mode, 678–681
    borders for selections, 701
    bounding boxes, 679–680

converting vector objects to bitmaps, 702–703
creating, 684
decreasing selections, 692, 701
Dreamweaver, 377
editing, 678–681
empty bitmaps, 684
erasing pixels, 695–696
feathering edges, 688–689, 700
feathering selections, 700
increasing selections, 692, 701
inserting, 683
instances (symbols), 1022
Live Effects, 852
modifying, 679–681
opening, 681–682
Paint Bucket tool, 848–850
perspective shadows, 879
pixels, 677–678
resizing, 685
restoring selections, 701
saving selections, 701
scaling, 682–683
selecting pixels, 684–695, 698–700
selecting selections, 697
shapes, 701–702
smoothing selections, 701
versus vector objects, 678
Xtras, 885–886
blending, 940–945
<blockquote> tag, 153–154
blur effects, 871–872
<body> and </body> tags, 72, 85
boldfacing text, 137
borders
    canvas, 563
    Cascading Style Sheets (CSS), 443–444
    forms, 256
    frames, 279–280, 287–288, 292–293
    graphics, 172
    layers, 465
    masks, 936–938
    selections (bitmaps), 701
    tables, 212, 228–229, 235

 tag, 128–129, 175–176
breaks
    line breaks, 128–129
    word breaks, 130
Brightness/Contrast dialog box, 860
Browser Scripts for Flash, 415–417
browser-safe colors, 708–709, 725–727, 825–826

browsers
    animation, 506, 1113–1115
    AOL, 17
    behaviors, 306, 310–315
    Cascading Style Sheets (CSS), 426
    Check Browser behavior, 319–320
    frames, 299–300
    head section, 73
    HTML, 72
    layers, 459, 473, 478
    Open Browser Window behavior, 329–330
    previewing Web pages, 35–36
    profiles, 1155
    supported graphics formats, 159, 163
    text styles, 136
    timelines, 501
Brush tool, 572, 666–668, 702
brushes. *See* strokes
budgets for Web sites, 21
BulletBuilder extension, 369
bullets
    Cascading Style Sheets (CSS), 444–445
    converting to graphics, 369
Button Editor, 362, 1032–1034, 1094–1096
Button Property Inspector, 273
buttons
    bevel effects, 868–869
    Button editor, 362
    Button Instances, 1035
    button styles, 1008–1009
    Button Symbols, 1022–1023, 1032–1034
    converting objects into buttons, 1034
    creating, 1094–1096
    Flash Buttons, 15, 388–391
    forms, 272–274
    Go buttons (jump menus), 271–272
    graphics, 274
    Link Wizard, 1036
    radio buttons, 261, 263–264, 1092
    rollovers, 358–360

C

Call JavaScript behavior, 316–317
Call JavaScript dialog box, 316–317
canvas
    alignment, 915–916
    borders, 563
    colors, 631, 633, 649
    cropping, 644–645
    dimensions, 631–632
    editing, 642–648
    expanding, 645
    matte colors, 970

Continued

canvas *(continued)*
- modifying, 642–648
- resizing, 643–644, 646–648
- resolution, 631–633
- rotating, 649
- sizing, 643–644, 646–648
- trimming, 648

Canvas Size dialog box, 643–644
cascading documents (Fireworks), 563
Cascading Style Sheets (CSS)
- applying, 424, 428–430
- attaching, 428–429
- background colors, 439–440
- background images, 438–440
- blocks of text, 440–441
- borders, 443–444
- boxes, 442–443
- browsers, 426
- bulleted lists, 444–445
- capabilities, 422
- cascading characteristics, 423–424
- changing, 430–431
- class definitions, 424, 432–433
- converting styles into an external style sheet, 436
- custom styles, 432–433
- deleting, 431–432
- Dreamweaver, 421
- editing, 434–435
- embedded style rules, 425–426
- exporting CSS layers, 995–998
- extensions, 446–447
- external style sheets, 424–425, 429
- filters, 448, 450, 477, 479
- grouping properties, 422
- how they work, 422
- importing, 435–436
- inheritance of properties, 423
- internal style sheets, 425
- layers, 460–461
- lists, 444–445
- logical style tags, 85–86
- modifying, 434–435
- physical style tags, 86–87
- positioning, 445–446
- precedence of rules, 423
- previewing, 437
- pseudo-classes, 433
- pseudo-elements, 433–434
- style definitions, 432–433, 436
- support for, 421
- switching, 430–431
- tables, 423
- text, 437–438
- type, 437–438

Cascading Style Sheets-Positioning (CSS-P), 453–454
CASIE (Coalition for Advertising Supported Information and Entertainment), 182–183
CD-ROM
- behaviors, 1154
- browser profiles, 1155
- code examples, 1156
- ColorWeb Pro (Pantone), 1158
- commands, 1155, 1157
- compressed files, 1152
- Dreamweaver extensions, 1153–1154
- Eye Candy 4000 (Alien Skin), 1158
- Fireworks examples, 1158
- Fireworks extensions, 1156–1157
- gradients, 1157
- image libaries, 1157
- Macintosh, 1151
- Macromedia trial versions, 1152
- objects, 1154
- PDF files of this book, 1159
- styles, 1157
- textures, 1157
- Windows, 1151

cells (tables), 210–212, 229–230
center point (vector objects), 654
CGI scripts (forms), 254
Change Property behavior, 317–319
Change Property dialog box, 318
Check Box Property Inspector, 262
Check Browser behavior, 319–320
Check Plugin behavior, 320–322
Check Spelling dialog box, 111–112
checkboxes (forms), 261–262
checking
- hyperlinks, 57–58, 200
- spelling, 111–113

checking in/out files, 45, 53–55
Choose Local Directory dialog box, 27
Circle Hotspot tool, 573, 1045, 1047
Circle tool, 702
circles
- drawing, 659–660
- hotspots, 1045–1047

<cite> tag, 86, 137
clipping layers, 469–471
closing
- documents (Fireworks), 641
- layers (Fireworks), 908
- paths, 777–778
- Web pages, 34

Coalition for Advertising Supported Information and Entertainment (CASIE), 182–183

code
  braces, 91
  color coding, 90
  commenting, 156–157
  copying, 109–110
  editing, 87–98
  examples, 1156
  finding, 117–127
  graphics, 361–363
  image maps, 1050, 1053–1056
  indenting, 90
  line numbers, 90
  pasting, 109–110
  replacing, 117–127
  rollovers, 361, 1086–1091
  searching, 117–127
  selecting, 90
  word wrap, 90
Code Inspector, 87–91
<code> tag, 86, 137
Code view, 87–91
collaborative teams
  checking in/out files, 45, 53–55
  Design Notes, 45–46
  file view columns, 48–49
  synchronizing files, 55–57
color coding HTML, 90
Color dialog box, 148–149
Color Fill dialog box, 860
Color Mixer panel (Fireworks), 592–593
Color Mixer tool, 711–716
Color Table panel (Fireworks), 590–591, 724, 956–957, 968–970
colors
  Active Color Tables, 723
  Adaptive palette, 966
  adjusting, 858–863
  Adobe color swatches, 723
  alpha channel, 707
  background colors, 73
  bit depth, 706–707
  Black & White palette, 967
  branding, 705
  brightness, 715
  canvas, 631, 633, 649
  CMY model, 714–715
  CMYK model, 706
  color correction, 858
  color palettes, 75–77
  color pickers, 147, 718–720
  color range, 706–707
  color schemes, 8
  converting color images to grayscale images, 847
  converting Pantone colors to Web-safe colors, 725–726
  curves, 863–865
  Custom palette, 967
  deleting palettes, 724
  dithering, 714, 824–825, 971–972
  Exact palette, 967
  export palettes, 724
  fills, 823–824, 860–861
  Flash Buttons, 389
  fonts, 147–150
  gamma settings, 709–710
  GIFs, 160
  gradients, 827–835
  graphics, 160–163
  grayscale model, 716
  Grayscale palette, 967
  grids, 477, 922
  guides, 920–921
  hexadecimal colors, 707–708, 714
  highlighting, 730
  HLS model, 715
  HSB model, 715
  HSL model, 865–866
  hue, 715, 865–866
  Hybrid-Safe colors, 825
  hyperlinks, 8, 197
  indexed color, 964–966
  JPEGs, 161
  layers, 459, 472
  limitations of color on the Web, 707
  loading palettes, 723
  locking, 962
  luminosity, 715
  Macintosh palette, 967
  managing, 710, 723
  matte colors, 970
  mixing, 711–715
  no color option, 720
  optimized graphics, 956–957
  palettes, 722
  Pantone colors, 725–727
  pixels, 705–706
  PNGs, 162–163
  reducing number of colors, 967–976
  RGB model, 706–707, 713
  sampling, 76, 718
  saturation, 715, 865–866
  selecting, 712–715, 721–722
  sorting palettes, 724
  swatches, 716–718, 722–724
  Swatches panel, 721–722

Continued

colors *(continued)*
    switching palettes, 722
    system color pickers, 718–720
    tables, 229, 234–235
    text, 8, 147–150
    text objects, 799
    textures, 846
    tonal ranges, 858–860
    Uniform palette, 967
    Web 216 palette, 967
    Web page backgrounds, 8
    Web page text, 8
    Web pages, 73
    Web-safe colors, 708–709, 725–727, 825–826
    WebSnap Adaptive palette, 966
ColorSync color-management system, 710
ColorWeb Pro (Pantone), 725–727, 1158
Column Properties dialog box, 234
columns
    framesets, 278, 286–287
    tables, 210, 212, 226–227
combining
    paths, 787–788
    vector objects, 787–788
commands. *See* commands by menu
Commands menu commands (Dreamweaver)
    Create Web Photo Album, 367
    Manage Extensions, 1154
    Optimize Image in Fireworks, 355
    Set Color Scheme, 77
    Sort Table, 238
Commands menu commands (Fireworks)
    Creative, Convert to Grayscale, 622
    Creative, Convert to Sepia Tone, 622
    Creative, Create Picture Frame, 622
    Document, Center in Document, 622
    Document, Distribute to Layers, 622
    Document, Hide Other Layers, 622
    Document, Lock Other Layers, 622
    Document, Reverse All Frames, 622
    Document, Reverse Frame Range, 622
    Edit Command List, 622
    Panel Layout, 579, 623
    Panel Layout Sets, 579, 622
    Reset Warning Dialogs, 623
    Web, Create Shared Palette, 623
    Web, Select Blank ALT Tags, 623
    Web, Set ALT Tags, 623
commenting code, 156–157
compositing, 903, 946–950
configuring MIME types, 394
Contract Selection dialog box, 701
Control Shockwave or Flash behavior, 322–323

Control Shockwave or Flash dialog box, 323, 399
Convert Layers to Table dialog box, 484
Convert Tables to Layers dialog box, 483
converting
    animation symbols to graphic symbols, 1147
    bullets to graphics, 369
    Button Symbols into Graphic Symbols, 1035
    color images to grayscale images, 847
    images into slices, 1062
    layers to tables, 482–485
    objects into buttons, 1034
    objects to hotspots, 1049–1050
    objects to symbols, 1025–1026
    open paths to closed paths, 777–778
    Pantone colors to Web-safe colors, 725–727
    site maps to graphics, 68
    styles into an external style sheet, 436
    tables to layers, 482–483
    text object to paths, 812
    text objects to images, 812
    text to graphics, 369
    vector objects to bitmaps, 702–703
cookies, 1091–1092
Copy to Frames dialog box, 1121
copying
    code, 109–110
    HTML, 109–110
    objects to animation frames, 1121
    tables, 219–220
    templates (Dreamweaver), 533
    text in Web pages, 108–109
Create Web Photo Album dialog box, 367
Crop tool, 571, 644–645
cropping
    canvas, 644–645
    paths, 789–790
    photographs, 990
    vector objects, 789–790
CSS (Cascading Style Sheets)
    applying, 424, 428–430
    attaching, 428–429
    background colors, 439–440
    background images, 438–440
    blocks of text, 440–441
    borders, 443–444
    boxes, 442–443
    browsers, 426
    bulleted lists, 444–445
    capabilities, 422
    cascading characteristics, 423–424
    changing, 430–431
    class definitions, 424, 432–433
    converting styles into an external style sheet, 436

custom styles, 432–433
deleting, 431–432
Dreamweaver, 421
editing, 434–435
embedded style rules, 425–426
exporting CSS layers, 995–998
extensions, 446–447
external style sheets, 424–425, 429
filters, 448, 450, 477, 479
grouping properties, 422
how they work, 422
importing, 435–436
inheritance of properties, 423
internal style sheets, 425
layers, 460–461
lists, 444–445
logical style tags, 85–86
modifying, 434–435
physical style tags, 86–87
positioning, 445–446
precedence of rules, 423
previewing, 437
pseudo-classes, 433
pseudo-elements, 433–434
style definitions, 432–433, 436
support for, 421
switching, 430–431
tables, 423
text, 437–438
type, 437–438
CSS Styles panel (Dreamweaver), 426, 428
CSS-P, 453–454
current date/time, 154–155
curves
adjusting, 673–674
Bézier curves, 668–675
mixing lines and curves, 672
Curves dialog box, 863–864
customizing strokes, 729
cutting
paths, 786–787
slices, 1061–1062
tables, 219–220
text in Web pages, 108–109

D

databases (SourceSafe), 29–30
dates
formatting, 154–156
inserting, 154–155
Define HTML Style dialog box, 142
Define Sites dialog box, 4

defining
HTML styles, 141–143
Web sites, 24–25
definition text, 137
deleting
animation symbols, 1148
behaviors (Dreamweaver), 349
behaviors (Fireworks), 1081
effects, 855, 881
fills, 822–823
frames, 295
frames (animations), 1119
gradients (colors), 832
guides, 921
highlighting, 542
HTML styles, 140–141
hyperlinks, 65
instances (symbols), 1032
keyframes (timelines), 505
layers (Dreamweaver), 475
layers (Fireworks), 906
Library items, 545–546
Live Effects, 855, 881
masks, 936
objects from timelines, 505
points (paths), 776–777
strokes, 747
style sheets, 431–432
styles, 1013
swatches (colors), 724
symbols, 1030
table rows/columns, 227
templates (Dreamweaver), 532–533
text in Web pages, 109
timelines, 505–506
underlines from links, 197, 427–428
dependent files (site maps), 67
Dependent Files dialog box, 52
deselecting paths, 731
Design Notes, 45–46
design of Web sites, 6, 19–24, 479–480
Design view, 88
<dfn> tag, 86, 137
dictionaries (spell checker), 113
disabling
effects, 855
Live Effects, 855
underlining of links, 427–428
Distort tool, 572, 702, 769–770, 774
distorting vector objects, 769–770
dithering colors, 714, 824–826, 971–972
<div> tag, 454, 467

docking toolbars, 574
documents (Fireworks)
    animation controls, 566
    canvas, 563
    cascading, 563
    closing, 641
    creating, 629–631, 634–635
    dirty-dot asterisk, 642
    display options, 568–569
    document window, 561–562, 564–566
    exporting to Director, 998
    hiding, 563
    magnification settings, 567
    opening, 561–562
    organizing, 563
    previewing, 564–566
    reverting to last saved version, 642
    saving, 640–641
    storing, 640–641
    tiling, 563
    viewing, 563–564
    zooming in/out, 567
domain names, 194
dotted lines, 758–761
download statistics, 16
Drag Layer behavior, 323–326, 486–488
Drag Layer dialog box, 487, 489
drag-and-drop behaviors, 1106–1109
drawing
    Bézier curves, 670–675
    circles, 659–660
    ellipses, 659–660
    freehand drawing, 666
    graphics tablets, 734
    layers, 456
    limiting drawing areas, 697
    lines, 665–668
    polygons, 660–662
    rectangles, 656–657
    rounded rectangles, 656–659
    rounded squares, 656–659
    squares, 656–657
    stars, 660, 662–664
    tables, 242–244
drawings. *See* vector objects
Dreamweaver
    Cascading Style Sheets (CSS), 421
    exiting, 34
    image maps, 1054–1055
    integration with Fireworks, 351, 370–371
    opening Fireworks windows, 352
    slices, 1067–1068
    starting, 31–32
    trial version (CD-ROM), 1152
    tutorials, 522
Dreamweaver 4 Bible PDF format, 1159
Dreamweaver UltraDev trial version (CD-ROM), 1152
drop shadows, 873–875
drop-down lists in forms, 264–266
drop-down menus in forms, 264–266
dual monitors, 580
Duplicate Frames dialog box, 1084
duplicating
    frames (animations), 1120
    layers (Fireworks), 905–906
    symbols, 1028

E

echoing, 260
Edit Date Format dialog box, 156
Edit Font List dialog box, 151–152
Edit Gradient dialog box, 830–831
Edit Grid dialog box, 922
Edit menu commands (Dreamweaver)
    Balance Braces, 91
    Clear, 109
    Cut, 109
    Find, 113
    Find Next (Find Again), 116
    Paste, 109
    Preferences, 214
    Redo, 111
    Replace, 113
    Select All, 108
    Undo, 111
Edit menu commands (Fireworks)
    Clear, 609
    Clone, 610
    Copy, 609
    Copy as Vectors, 609
    Copy HTML Code, 609
    Crop Document, 610
    Crop Selected Bitmap, 610
    Cut, 609
    Deselect, 610
    Duplicate, 610
    Find and Replace, 610
    Keyboard Shortcuts, 610
    Paste, 609
    Paste as Mask, 609
    Paste Attributes, 609
    Paste Inside, 609
    Preferences, 610
    Redo, 609

Select All, 610
Select Similar, 610
Subselect, 610
Superselect, 610
Undo, 609
Edit Stroke dialog box, 747, 749–750
Edit Style dialog box, 1013
Edit Style Sheet dialog box, 426, 434–436
editing
    animation, 1126–1127
    animation symbols, 1146
    behaviors (Fireworks), 1080
    bitmaps, 678–681
    canvas, 642–648
    code, 87–98
    effects, 854
    Flash Buttons, 390
    Flash Text, 394
    frames, 289
    gradients (colors), 828–832
    grids, 477
    HTML, 87–98
    hyperlinks, 64–65
    images in Dreamweaver, 168–170
    images in Fireworks, 356–357
    instances (symbols), 1020–1021, 1023, 1031
    jump menus, 270
    layers, 463, 465–466
    layers (Fireworks), 907
    Library items, 546–548
    Live Effects, 854
    masks, 932–935
    navigation bars, 189–190
    patterns, 838–839
    photographs, 678, 680–681
    redoing actions, 110–111
    server-side includes, 553
    slices, 364–365
    strokes, 729–730, 747, 749–750
    style sheets, 434–435
    styles, 1013–1014
    symbols, 1020–1021, 1023, 1028–1030
    tables, 214–215, 218, 220–221
    templates (Dreamweaver), 532, 534
    text in Web pages, 107
    text objects, 797, 806
    timelines, 499–501
    titles (Web pages), 65
    undoing actions, 110–111
    Web pages, 66
editors
    Button Editor, 362, 1032–1034, 1094–1096
    launching, 59
    opening, 59

    Symbol Editor, 1026–1029
    Text Editor, 795–797, 806–807
Effect panel (Fireworks), 588–590, 851–853
effects. *See also* filters; Live Effects
    applying, 852–854
    Auto Levels, 857, 861–863
    Blur, 858, 872
    Blur More, 858, 872
    Brightness/Contrast, 857, 860
    built-in effects, 857
    Color Fill, 860–861
    Convert to Alpha, 858, 872
    Curves, 857, 863–865
    deleting, 855, 881
    disabling, 855
    Drop Shadow, 858, 873–874
    editing, 854
    Effect panel, 851–852
    Find Edges, 858, 872
    Gaussian Blur, 858, 871–872
    Glow, 858, 875–876
    Hue/Saturation, 857, 865–866
    Inner Bevel, 858, 866–868
    Inner Glow, 858, 875–876
    Inner Shadow, 858, 873–874
    Inset Emboss, 858, 869–871
    Invert, 857
    Levels, 858, 861–863
    missing effects, 882
    modifying, 854
    naming, 881
    Outer Bevel, 858, 866–868
    Raised Emboss, 858, 869–871
    renaming, 881
    saving, 881
    Sharpen, 858, 876–877
    Sharpen More, 858, 876–877
    storing, 881–882
    styles, 883
    turning on/off, 881
    Unsharp Mask, 858, 876–877
Ellipse tool, 572, 659, 702
ellipses
    drawing, 659–660
    hotspots, 1047
<em> tag, 86, 137
e-mail links, 195, 201–202
emboss effects, 869–871
emphasis text, 137
encoding form results, 257
Eraser tool, 573, 695–696
erasing bitmap pixels, 695–696

Index ✦ E–F

event files, 312–313
Expand Selection dialog box, 701
Expand Stroke dialog box, 791
expanding canvas, 645
Export Area tool, 571
Export dialog box, 359, 1052
export files, 355
Export module (Fireworks), 353
Export Preview dialog box, 988–990, 1129
Export Previewing dialog box, 1130–1131
Export Wizard, 992–994
exporting
    animation, 1113, 1129–1131
    CSS layers, 995–998
    Fireworks documents to Director, 998
    Fireworks files, 999
    image maps, 1050, 1052
    image wells, 999–1000
    indexed color, 964–966
    Libraries, 1039–1040
    Library items, 1070–1072
    photographs, 980–988
    Photoshop files, 1003–1004
    preview options, 988–990
    rollovers, 1086–1089
    slices, 1065–1066, 1069–1070
    styles, 1014
    symbols, 1039–1040
    vector objects, 1000–1003
Extensible Markup Language (XML), 521
Extension Manager, 1154
extensions
    BulletBuilder, 369
    Cascading Style Sheets (CSS), 446–447
    Extension Manager, 1154
    extensions available on CD-ROM, 1153–1154
    Fireworks extensions, 1156–1157
    FWLaunch, 370–372
    InstaGraphics Extensions, 369
    installing, 1154
    Repeat History, 111
    StyleBuilder, 369
    XSSI, 553–554
external style sheets, 424–425, 429, 435–436
Eye Candy filters, 625, 890–895, 1158
Eyedropper tool (Dreamweaver), 76
Eyedropper tool (Fireworks), 573, 717–718

F

fading in/out objects, 1142–1143
Feather Selection dialog box, 700
feathering
    bitmap edges, 688–689, 700

    selections, 945–946
    strokes, 732
fields
    forms, 257–261, 275
    Set Text of Text Field behavior, 339–340
file management, 4–5, 25–29
File menu commands (Dreamweaver)
    Check Links, 57
    Close, 34
    Exit, 34
    Import, Import Tabular Data, 239
    Import, Import Word HTML, 131
    New from Template, 528
    Open, 32
    Open Selection, 66
    Preview in Browser, BrowserName, 35
    Preview in Browser, Edit Browser List, 35
    Quit, 34
    Save, 34
    Save As Template, 524
File menu commands (Fireworks)
    Batch Process, 607
    Close, 607
    Exit (Quit), 608
    Export, 359, 607
    Export Preview, 607
    Export Wizard, 607
    HTML Setup, 608
    Import, 607
    New, 606
    Open, 606
    Page Setup, 608
    Preview in Browser, Preview in Primary Browser, 607
    Preview in Browser, Preview in Secondary Browser, 607
    Preview in Browser, Set Primary Browser, 608
    Preview in Browser, Set Secondary Browser, 608
    Print, 608
    Recent Files, 608
    Revert, 607
    Run Script, 607
    Save, 607
    Save a Copy, 607
    Save As, 607
    Scan, Twain Acquire, 606
    Scan, Twain Select, 606
    Scan, Your Photoshop Acquire Plug-ins, 606
    Update HTML, 607
file size
    animation, 1127–1128
    GIF animations, 1112
    image maps, 1057

Index ✦ F

JPEGs, 981–985
    lossy GIF compression, 970–971
    matte colors, 970
    reducing number of colors, 967–976
    slices, 1057
File Transfer Protocol (FTP)
    ending sessions, 51
    FTP host, 44
    Passive FTP, 44
    starting sessions, 51
    Web server connections, 29
file view columns, 48–49
files. *See also* documents (Fireworks)
    8BCT files, 723
    ACT files, 723
    checking in/out, 45, 53–55
    dependent files, 52, 67
    event files, 312–313
    export files, 355
    exporting Fireworks files, 999
    exporting Photoshop files, 1003–1004
    finding, 32
    hidden files, 67
    HTML syntax checking, 33
    opening, 32–33
    pointing to files, 199–200
    source files, 354–355
    synchronizing, 55–57
    transferring, 37, 51–52
Fill panel (Fireworks), 587–588
fills
    applying, 848–850
    built-in fills, 821–822
    Color Fill Live Effect, 860–861
    colors, 823–824, 860–861
    deleting, 822–823
    flat fills, 823
    Gradient fill, 822, 827–828
    None fill, 821–823
    Pattern fill, 822, 834, 836–844
    Solid fill, 821, 823
    text objects, 810–811
    textures, 844, 846–848
    turning on/off, 822–823
    vector objects, 653–654
    Web Dither fill, 821, 824–826
filters
    aliases, 889–890
    Alien Skin, 888
    Alpha filter, 448
    applying, 856
    BlendTrans filter, 448

    Blur filter, 448
    Cascading Style Sheets (CSS), 448, 450, 477, 479
    Chroma filter, 448
    DitherBox filter, 857
    DropShadow filter, 448, 479
    Effect panel, 852
    Eye Candy filters, 890–895
    Find and Replace filters, 119–121
    FlipH filter, 479
    FlipV filter, 479
    Furbo Filters, 888
    Glow filter, 479
    Gray filter, 479
    installing, 887–888
    Invert filter, 479
    Kai's Power Tools 5, 896–901
    Light filter, 479
    Mask filter, 479
    Photoshop filters, 887–888
    plug-in filters, 857
    Plugin Site, 888
    RevealTrans filter, 479
    Shadow filter, 450, 479
    shortcuts, 889–890
    using with multiple applications, 888–889
    VanDerLee, 888
    viewing available filters, 855–857
    Wave filter, 450
    Xray filter, 450
    Xtras, 623–624
Find and Replace dialog box, 114–116
Find and Replace panel (Fireworks), 604
Find Source dialog box, 354
finding
    code, 117–127
    files (Dreamweaver), 32
    HTML, 117–127
    misspelled words, 111–113
    text in Web pages, 113–117
firewalls, 44–45
Fireworks
    animation controls, 566
    bitmap mode, 566, 678–681
    canvas, 563
    capabilities, 559
    display options, 568–569
    document window, 561, 564–566
    dual monitors, 580
    environment, 559–561
    examples available on CD-ROM, 1158
    Export module, 353
    integration with Dreamweaver, 351, 370–371

Continued

Fireworks *(continued)*
    interface, 559–561
    launching, 568
    menus, 606
    Mini-Launcher, 568
    mode-shifting warnings, 678
    opening Fireworks window in Dreamweaver, 352
    panels, 578
    status bar, 577–578
    toolbars, 574–578
    Tools panel, 570–573
    trial version (CD-ROM), 1152
    vector mode, 566, 678
Fireworks 4 Bible PDF format, 1159
Fireworks extensions, 1156–1157
Flash
    ActionScript, 375
    animations, 181–182, 377, 494
    Browser Scripts, 415–417
    Browser Scripts for Flash, 415
    capabilities, 375
    Control Shockwave or Flash behavior, 322–323
    JavaScript Integration Kit (JIK), 405–408
    MIME types, 394
    versus Shockwave, 376–378
    sound, 387
    supported graphics formats, 376
    trial version (CD-ROM), 1152
Flash Buttons, 15, 388–391
Flash Dispatcher, 417–418
Flash movies
    controls, 398–399, 406–410
    form validation, 410–415
    FSCommands, 387
    inserting, 378–380
    links, 396–397
    loading, 387
    looping, 385
    parameters, 383–386
    playing, 385
    scaling, 385–387
    triggering behaviors, 402–405
    user interaction, 398–399, 406–410
Flash Player, 387
Flash Text, 392–394
floating panels. *See* panels (Dreamweaver); panels (Fireworks)
<font> tag, 87
fonts
    colors, 147–150
    copyright issues, 392
    faces, 87
    Flash Text, 392

    selecting, 150–152
    sizes, 87
    sizing, 144–146
    text objects, 798–799, 806, 813–815
    typefaces, 150–151
foreign language spell checking, 112
<form> and </form> tags, 254
Form Property Inspector, 255–256
Format Table dialog box, 235
formats
    Web graphics (Dreamweaver), 159
    Web graphics (Fireworks), 636–637
formatting
    dates, 154–156
    tables, 235–237
    text, 12, 144–146
    time, 155
forms
    borders, 256
    CGI scripts, 254
    checkboxes, 261–262
    Command buttons, 272–273
    drop-down lists, 264–266
    drop-down menus, 264–266
    echoing, 260
    encoding results, 257
    file fields, 275
    <form> and </form> tags, 254
    graphical buttons, 274
    hidden fields, 275
    input devices, 254
    inserting, 254–256
    layers, 256, 478–479
    layout, 259
    multiline text areas, 260–261
    naming, 255
    parsing, 255
    password fields, 260
    radio buttons, 261, 263–264
    Reset buttons, 272–273
    resizing, 256
    scrolling lists, 266–268
    submission methods, 255
    Submit buttons, 272–273
    submitting, 255
    tables, 256
    text fields, 257–261
    uses, 253
    Validate Form behavior, 345–347
    validating, 410–415
Frame Property Inspector, 291
<frame> tags, 278

frames
    background images, 290
    borders, 279–280, 287–288, 292–293
    browser support, 299–300
    creating, 279–285
    deleting, 295
    editing, 289
    editing content, 295
    evolution, 277
    frameless browsers, 299–300
    Frames Objects, 283–285
    framesets, 278–281, 283–289
    iframes, 301–302
    inline frames, 301–302
    margins, 295
    modifying, 289
    modifying content, 295
    movies, 399–401
    naming, 292
    no resize option, 294
    opening Web pages into frames, 292
    optimized graphics, 963–964
    previewing, 295
    properties, 289, 291
    recursive frames, 297
    resizing, 284, 286–287, 294
    saving, 288–289
    scroll bars, 293–294
    selecting, 291
    Set Text of Frame behavior, 336–337
    Shockwave movies, 399–401
    sizing, 278–279
    splitting, 280–283
    targets, 296–297
    titles, 291
    updating, 298–299
frames (animations)
    copying objects to frames, 1121
    deleting, 1119
    distributing objects to frames, 1121–1122
    duplicating, 1120
    frame delay settings, 1124–1125
    frame disposal, 1127–1128
    inserting, 1117–1118
    managing, 1115–1117
    multi-frame editing, 1126–1127
    naming, 1118–1119
    onion skinning, 1125–1126
    reordering, 1119
Frames panel (Fireworks), 596–597, 1117
Frameset Property Inspector, 280–281, 286–287
<frameset> tag, 278

Freeform tool, 572, 702, 780–783
freehand drawing, 666
FreeHand trial version (CD-ROM), 1152
FrontPage (Microsoft)
    image maps, 1056–1057
    slices, 1069
FTP
    ending sessions, 51
    FTP host, 44
    Passive FTP, 44
    starting sessions, 51
    URLs, 194
    Web server connections, 29
Furbo Filters Web site, 888
FutureSplash movies, 394
FWLaunch extension, 370–372

G

gamma settings, 709–710
Gaussian Blur dialog box, 871
Generator
    capabilities, 375
    cost, 376
    graphics, 394–395
    templates, 390–391, 395
GIFs
    animated GIFs, 161, 181–182, 494, 1112–1115, 1131–1132
    animation, 161
    browser support, 159
    colors, 160
    download times, 160
    GIF87a, 160
    GIF89a, 160–161
    indexed color, 965
    interlacing, 160
    interlacing GIFs, 976
    lossless compression, 161
    lossy GIF compression, 970–971
    optimizing, 976–979
    transparency, 160–161, 972–975
glow effects, 872, 875–876
Go buttons (jump menus), 271–272
Go to Frame behavior, 510
Go to Timeline Frame behavior, 343–345
Go to Timeline Frame dialog box, 502
Go To URL dialog box, 298, 326–327
GoLive (Adobe)
    image maps, 1055–1056
    slices, 1068–1069
Gopher, 194

gradients (colors)
  color ramp, 827
  deleting, 832
  editing, 828–832
  fills, 822, 827–828
  gradient pattern, 827
  gradients available on CD-ROM, 1157
  modifying, 828–832
  naming, 831–832
  saving, 831–832
  storing, 832
  styles, 833
  transferring between documents, 832–833
  transparency, 833–835
graphics
  alignment, 173–175
  alt text, 172
  animated GIFs, 494
  animation, 181–182
  background graphics, 177–178, 290
  banner ads, 182–184
  bitmap graphics versus vector graphics, 377
  borders, 172
  bullets, 369
  buttons, 274
  code, 361–363
  colors, 160–163
  compression, 161–162
  converting bullets to graphics, 369
  converting color graphics to grayscale graphics, 847
  converting graphics into slices, 1062
  converting text objects to graphics, 812
  converting text to graphics, 369
  dimensions, 647–648
  download times, 160, 172–173
  editing in Dreamweaver, 168–170
  editing in Fireworks, 356–357
  export files, 355
  exporting in indexed color format, 964–966
  Flash, 376–377
  formats, 159, 636–637
  Generator, 394–395
  GIFs, 159–161
  Graphic Symbols, 1022–1023
  grayscale, 716
  height attribute, 170–171
  horizontal rules, 178–181
  hotspots, 361–362
  hspace attribute, 171
  inline graphics, 163–164, 166–168
  inline images, 165
  interlacing, 160, 162, 976
  JPEGs, 159, 161
  layers, 459, 472
  lossless compression, 161
  lossy compression, 161
  lowsrc attribute, 172–173
  magnification settings, 567
  margins, 171
  modifying, 168–170
  naming, 172
  navigation bars, 186–190
  opening in Fireworks, 635, 637–640
  optimizing, 352–355, 953–963, 966–967, 973–979
  PNGs, 159
  Preload Images behavior, 333–334
  Progressive JPEGs, 162
  refreshing, 354
  replacing, 169
  resampling, 646
  resizing, 170–171, 647
  rollovers, 184–186
  Set Nav Bar Image behavior, 334–335
  sharpening, 876–877
  Shockwave, 376–377
  site maps, 69
  sizing, 647–648
  slices, 361–362, 364–365, 1057–1058, 1060–1070
  source files, 354–355
  spacer images, 1058
  Swap Image behavior, 341–343
  Swap Image Restore behavior, 341–343
  symbols, 1022–1023
  textures, 845
  thumbnails, 167, 366–368, 370
  tiling, 179
  titles, 172
  Tracing Image, 480–481
  vspace attribute, 171
  Web photo albums, 366–368, 370
  white space, 171
  width attribute, 170–171
  wrapping around jump menus, 270–271
  wrapping text around graphics, 175–176
Graphics Interchange Format (GIF)
  animated GIFs, 161, 181–182, 494, 1112–1115, 1131–1132
  animation, 161
  browser support, 159
  colors, 160
  download times, 160
  GIF87a, 160
  GIF89a, 160–161
  indexed color, 965

interlacing, 160
interlacing GIFs, 976
lossless compression, 161
lossy GIF compression, 970–971
optimizing, 976–979
transparency, 160–161, 972–975
graphics tablets, 734
Graphire (Wacom), 734
grayscale images, 716, 847
Grid Settings dialog box, 477
grids
    colors, 922
    hiding, 921
    layers, 477
    snapping to, 921
    spacing grid lines, 922
    tables, 245
Grids and Guides dialog box, 920, 922
grouping
    objects (Fireworks), 923–924
    panels (Fireworks), 578
    regular expressions, 127–128
    style sheet properties, 422
guides
    clearing, 921
    colors, 920–921
    deleting, 921
    hiding, 919
    horizontal guides, 918–919
    inserting, 918
    locking, 919
    slice guides, 1059–1062
    snapping to, 920
    vertical guides, 918–919
Guides dialog box, 920

H

<h1> to <h6> tags, 103–105
Hand tool, 573
<head> and </head> tags, 72–73
head section, 6–7, 72–85
head tag objects
    Base, 78, 83–84
    Description, 78, 80–81
    Keywords, 78, 80–81
    Link, 78, 84–85
    Meta, 78–80
    Refresh, 78, 82–83
headers (tables), 233
headings
    Flash Text, 392
    tables, 211
    Web pages, 103–105

Help menu commands (Fireworks)
    About Balloon Help, 627
    About Fireworks, 628
    Fireworks Support Center, 627
    Lessons, 627
    Register Fireworks, 628
    Show Balloons, 627
    Using Fireworks, 627
    Welcome, 627
hexadecimal colors, 707–708, 714
hidden fields (forms), 275
hidden files (site maps), 67
hiding
    documents (Fireworks), 563
    floating panels, 579–580
    grids, 921
    guides, 919
    layers, 475
    layers (Fireworks), 906–907
    panels (Fireworks), 579–580
highlighting
    color options, 730
    deleting, 542
    invalid HTML tags, 90
    Library items, 542
hint list (Quick Tag Editor), 94
History panel (Dreamweaver), 111
History panel (Fireworks), 597–598
home page
    design considerations, 6
    site maps, 66
Homesite HTML editor, 87
Horizontal Rule Property Inspector, 178
horizontal rules, 178–181
Hotspot tools, 1045
hotspots
    attaching behaviors, 1079–1080
    converting objects to hotspots, 1049–1050
    creating, 910–911
    deleting behaviors, 1081
    drag-and-drop behaviors, 1109
    explanation of, 361
    inserting, 362
    links, 1048–1049
    modifying behaviors, 1080
    rollovers, 1099–1101
    shapes, 1044–1048
    Web Layer, 910–911
<hr> tag, 178
HTML
    attributes, 72–73
    body section, 72, 85–86

Continued

HTML *(continued)*
  browsers, 72
  color coding, 90
  comments, 156–157
  copying, 109–110
  editing, 87–98
  elements, 71
  event files, 312–313
  finding, 117–127
  Fireworks HTML, 364
  head section, 6, 72–85
  head tag objects, 78–85
  highlighting invalid tags, 90
  indenting, 90
  layers, 454
  logical style tags, 85–86
  markup elements, 71
  pasting, 109–110
  physical style tags, 86–87
  Quick Tag Editor, 91–98
  replacing, 117–127
  searching, 117–127
  Shockwave, 381–382
  special characters, 98–101
  structure of HTML pages, 71–72
  styles, 1050–1051
  symbols, 98–101
  syntax checking, 33
  tables, 209–211
  tag pairs, 72
  Tag Selector, 107
  tags, 71
<html> and </html> tags, 72
HTML editors, 87
HTML forms
  borders, 256
  CGI scripts, 254
  checkboxes, 261–262
  Command buttons, 272–273
  drop-down lists, 264–266
  drop-down menus, 264–266
  echoing, 260
  encoding results, 257
  file fields, 275
  <form> and </form> tags, 254
  graphical buttons, 274
  hidden fields, 275
  input devices, 254
  inserting, 255–256
  layers, 256, 478–479
  layout, 259
  multiline text areas, 260–261
  naming, 255
  parsing, 255
  password fields, 260
  radio buttons, 261, 263–264
  Reset buttons, 272–273
  resizing, 256
  scrolling lists, 266–268
  submission methods, 255
  Submit buttons, 272–273
  submitting, 255
  tables, 256
  text fields, 257–261
  uses, 253
  Validate Form behavior, 345–347
  validating, 410–415
HTML Parser Results dialog box, 33
HTML Setup dialog box, 1052
HTML styles
  applying, 139–140
  versus CSS, 138
  defining, 141–143
  deleting, 140–141
  transferring from site to site, 141
HTML Styles panel (Dreamweaver), 139
HTML tags
  <a> and </a> tags, 195–196, 202
  <address> and </address> tags, 137–138
  anchor tags, 195–196, 202
  <b> tag, 86, 137
  <base> tag, 84
  behaviors, 306
  <big> tag, 86
  <blockquote> tag, 153–154
  <body> and </body> tags, 72, 85

 tag, 128–129, 175–176
  <cite> tag, 86, 137
  <code> tag, 86, 137
  <dfn> tag, 86, 137
  <div> tag, 454, 467
  <em> tag, 86, 137
  <font> tag, 87
  <form> and </form> tags, 254
  <frame> tag, 278
  <frameset> tag, 278
  <h1> to <h6> tags, 103–105
  <head> and </head> tags, 72–73
  <hr> tag, 178
  <html> and </html> tags, 72
  <i> tag, 86, 137
  <iframe> tag, 301
  <ilayer> tag, 455, 467
  <img> tag, 168, 1050
  <kbd> tag, 86, 137
  <layer> tag, 455, 467

Index ✦ H–I

<link> tag, 84–85
<map> and </map> tags, 1050
<meta> tag, 77–81, 129, 530–531
<nobr> tag, 129
<noframes> and </noframes> tags, 299–300
<option> and </option> tags, 264
<p> and </p> tags, 105–106
<pre> tag, 134–135
redefining, 433
<s> tag, 86, 137
<samp> tag, 86, 137
<select> and </select> tags, 264
selecting, 107
<small> tag, 86
<span> tag, 430–431, 454, 467
<strong> tag, 86, 137
<sub> tag, 86
<sup> tag, 86
<table> and </table> tags, 210
Tag Selector, 107
<td> and </td> tags, 211
<th> tag, 211
<tr> tag, 211
<tt> tag, 86, 137
<u> tag, 86, 137
<var> tag, 86, 137
<wbr> tag, 130
HTTP, 194
Hybrid-Safe colors, 825
hyperlinks
    base URLs, 83–84
    checking, 57–58, 200
    colors, 8, 197
    creating, 62–64, 195–196
    deleting, 65
    editing, 64–65
    Flash movies, 396–397
    hotspots, 1048–1049
    images, 196–197
    Link Checker, 42
    Link Wizard, 1036
    mailto: hyperlinks, 195, 201–202
    named anchors, 202–205
    pointing to files, 199–200
    removing underlining, 197, 427–428
    site maps, 61
    slices, 1057, 1063
    special characters, 196
    symbols, 196
    targets, 205–206
    templates, 527
    testing, 17, 57–58

    text, 196–197
    validating, 17
    verifying, 200
HyperText Markup Language. *See* HTML
HyperText Transport Protocol (HTTP), 194

I

<i> tag, 86, 137
IAB (Internet Advertising Bureau), 182–183
<iframe> tag, 301
iframes, 301–302
<ilayer> tag, 455, 467
image editors, 170
image filters. *See* filters
image libraries (CD-ROM), 1157
image maps
    code, 1050, 1053–1056
    Dreamweaver, 1054–1055
    exporting, 1050, 1052
    file size, 1057
    FrontPage (Microsoft), 1056–1057
    GoLive (Adobe), 1055–1056
    hotspots, 1044–1050
    how they work, 1043–1044
    <img> tag, 1050
    inserting, 1053–1056
    <map> and </map> tags, 1050
Image Property Inspector, 169
Image Size dialog box, 647
image wells, 999–1000
images
    alignment, 173–175
    alt text, 172
    animated GIFs, 494
    animation, 181–182
    background images, 177–178, 290
    banner ads, 182–184
    bitmap images versus vector images, 377
    borders, 172
    bullets, 369
    buttons, 274
    code, 361–363
    colors, 160–163
    compression, 161–162
    converting bullets to images, 369
    converting color images to grayscale images, 847
    converting text objects to images, 812
    converting text to images, 369
    cropping, 990–991
    dimensions, 647–648
    download times, 160, 172–173
    editing in Dreamweaver, 168–170

Continued

images *(continued)*
    editing in Fireworks, 356–357
    export files, 355
    exporting in indexed color format, 964–966
    Flash, 377
    formats, 159, 636–637
    Graphic Symbols, 1022–1023
    grayscale images, 716
    height attribute, 170–171
    horizontal rules, 178–181
    hotspots, 361–362
    hspace attribute, 171
    hyperlinks, 196–197
    inline images, 163–168
    interlacing, 160, 976
    layers, 459, 472
    lowsrc attribute, 172–173
    magnification settings, 567
    margins, 171
    modifying, 168–170
    naming, 172
    navigation bars, 186–190
    opening in Fireworks, 635, 637–640
    optimizing, 352–355, 953–963, 966–967, 973–979
    Preload Images behavior, 333–334
    refreshing, 354
    replacing, 169
    resampling, 646
    resizing, 170–171, 647–648
    rollovers, 184–186
    scaling, 991–992
    Set Nav Bar Image behavior, 334–335
    sharpening, 876–877
    Shockwave, 376–377
    sizing, 647–648
    slices, 361–362, 364–365, 1057–1058, 1060–1070
    source files, 354–355
    spacer images, 1058
    Swap Image behavior, 341–343
    Swap Image Restore behavior, 341–343
    symbols, 1022–1023
    textures, 845
    thumbnails, 167, 366–368, 370
    tiling, 179
    titles, 172
    Tracing Image, 480–481
    vspace attribute, 171
    Web page backgrounds, 8
    Web photo albums, 366–368, 370
    white space, 171
    width attribute, 170–171
    wrapping around jump menus, 270–271
    wrapping text around images, 175–176

<img> tag, 168, 1050
Import Symbols dialog box, 1037
Import Table Data dialog box, 239–240
Import Word HTML dialog box, 131
importing
    Libraries, 1037–1039
    style sheets, 435–436
    styles, 1013–1015
    symbols, 1037–1039
    tables, 239–241
    text, 12, 807–808
    text to Web pages, 108
    Word documents, 12
    Word HTML documents, 130–134
Include Dependent Files dialog box, 17
indenting
    code, 90
    paragraphs, 153–154
    text, 107, 153–154
indexed color, 964–966
Info panel (Fireworks), 598–599
inline frames, 301–302
inline images, 163–168
Insert Base dialog box, 83
Insert Comment dialog box, 156
Insert Date dialog box, 155
Insert E-mail Link dialog box, 201
Insert Fireworks HTML dialog box, 364
Insert Flash Button dialog box, 388–389
Insert Flash Text dialog box, 392–393
Insert Generator dialog box, 395
Insert Jump Menu dialog box, 268
Insert Link dialog box, 84–85
Insert menu commands (Dreamweaver)
    Date, 154
    Form, 255
    Head Tags, Base, 83
    Head Tags, Description, 80
    Head Tags, Keywords, 80
    Head Tags, Link, 84
    Head Tags, Meta, 79
    Head Tags, Refresh, 82
    Horizontal Rule, 178
    Interactive Media, Fireworks HTML, 364
    Layer, 456, 458
    Media, Flash, 380
    Media, Shockwave, 380
    Named Anchor, 202
    Rollover Image, 185
    Server-Side Include, 552
    Table, 211

Insert menu commands (Fireworks)
    Animations, 613
    Bullets, 613
    Buttons, 613
    Convert to Symbol, 613
    Empty Bitmap, 614
    Frame, 614
    Hotspot, 362, 614
    Image, 614
    Layer, 614
    Libraries, Libraries, 613
    Libraries, Other, 614
    New Button, 359, 362, 613
    New Symbol, 613
    Pop-up Menu, 614
    Slice, 362, 614
    Themes, 614
Insert Meta dialog box, 79
Insert Navigation Bar dialog box, 187
Insert Refresh dialog box, 82
Insert Rollover Image dialog box, 185, 360
Insert Rows or Columns dialog box, 227
Insert Table dialog box, 212–213
inserting
    banner ads, 183
    bitmaps, 683
    dates, 154–155
    Fireworks HTML, 364
    Flash Buttons, 388–389
    Flash movies, 378
    Flash Text, 392–393
    forms, 255–256
    frames (animations), 1117–1118
    Generator graphics, 394–395
    guides, 918
    hotspots, 362
    image maps, 1053–1056
    inline images, 163–168
    jump menus, 268–270
    keyframes (timelines), 503–504
    layers (Dreamweaver), 456, 458, 460–461
    layers (Fireworks), 905
    Library items, 542–545
    movies, 378–380
    named anchors, 202
    navigation bars, 186–187, 189
    objects in layers, 477–478
    objects in timelines, 497–498
    photographs, 683
    points (paths), 776
    rollovers, 185–186, 358–361, 1086–1091
    server-side includes, 551–552
    slices, 362, 1067–1069

    table rows/columns, 226–227
    tables, 211–212
    text, 11–12
    text in Web pages, 107–108
    text objects, 796–797
    time, 155
    URLs, 197–199
InstaGraphics Extensions, 369
installing
    CD-ROM programs, 1153
    extensions, 1154
    filters, 887–888
    objects, 1154–1155
instances (symbols)
    bitmaps, 1022
    breaking links between symbol and instance, 1032
    Button Instances, 1035
    deleting, 1032
    editing, 1020–1021, 1023, 1031
    making, 1021, 1030–1031
    modifying, 1020–1021, 1023, 1031
    overview, 1019
    tweening, 1023, 1135–1138, 1140–1141
interactive forms. *See* forms
interfaces in Macromedia applications, 562
interlacing graphics, 160, 162, 976
internal style sheets, 425
international Web sites, 155
Internet Advertising Bureau (IAB), 182–183
intersecting paths/vector objects, 788
IP addresses, 194
italicizing text, 137

J

JavaScript
    Call JavaScript behavior, 316–317
    URLs, 195
JavaScript Integration Kit (JIK)
    Advanced Form Validations, 410–415
    Browser Scripts, 415–417
    contents, 405–406
    Flash Dispatcher, 417–418
    Macromedia Flash Player Controls, 406, 408–410
joining paths, 778–779
Joint Photographic Experts Group (JPEG), 161
JPEGs
    browser support, 159
    colors, 161
    compression, 161–162
    file size, 981–985
    indexed color, 965
    interlacing, 162

Continued

JPEGs *(continued)*
    lossy compression, 161
    Progressive JPEGs, 162, 986–987
    quality, 981–985
Jump Menu behavior, 270–271, 327, 329
Jump Menu dialog box, 271, 327–328
Jump Menu Go behavior, 327–329
Jump Menu Go dialog box, 328
jump menus, 268–272

K

Kai's Power Tools 5, 896–901
<kbd> tag, 86, 137
kerning text objects, 801, 803
keyboard modifiers
    Bézier curves, 674–675
    Rectangle tool, 657
    Rounded Rectangle tool, 657
keyboard shortcuts for tools, 571
keyboard text, 137
keyframes (timelines)
    deleting, 505
    how they work, 495
    inserting, 503–504
    moving, 505
Knife tool, 786–787
knock outs (shadow effects), 875
Kodak color-management system, 710

L

Lasso tool, 571, 689–691
launching
    editors, 59
    Fireworks, 568
Layer Property Inspector, 465–467
<layer> tag, 455, 467
layers (Dreamweaver)
    alignment, 475–477
    attributes, 458–459
    background colors, 459, 472
    background images, 459, 472
    behaviors, 485–491
    borders, 465
    browsers, 459, 473, 478
    capabilities, 453
    clipping, 469–471
    colors, 459, 472
    converting to tables, 482–485
    creating, 455–458, 460–461
    CSS, 460–461
    deleting, 475
    design, 479–480
    Drag Layer behavior, 323–326, 486–488
    drawing out as objects, 456
    editing, 463, 465–466
    forms, 256, 478–479
    height, 459
    hiding, 475
    HTML, 454
    HTML tags, 467
    <ilayer> tag, 455, 467
    inserting, 456, 458, 460–461
    inserting objects in layers, 477–478
    Layer icon, 458
    <layer> tag, 455, 467
    layout, 479
    loading layers, 491–492
    managing, 473–474
    modifying, 463, 465–466
    moving, 457, 465
    naming, 467, 474
    nesting, 459, 463, 474–475
    order, 470–472, 474
    outlines, 465
    overflow, 468–469
    overlaps, 481
    positioning, 455, 458, 461–463, 482
    preferences, 458–459
    preventing overlaps, 481
    recording paths, 506–508
    resizing, 465
    selecting, 463–465
    Set Text of Layer behavior, 337–338, 488–489
    Show-Hide Layers behavior, 340–341, 490–491
    sizing, 465
    style sheets, 460–461
    timelines, 497–498, 506–508, 515–516
    Tracing Image, 480
    visibility, 458, 468, 474
    width, 459
    z-index, 470–472, 474
layers (Fireworks)
    capabilities, 903
    closing, 908
    deleting, 906
    duplicating, 905–906
    editing, 907
    hiding, 906–907
    inserting, 905
    Layer 1, 905
    locking, 906–907
    modifying, 907
    moving objects between layers, 907, 909
    naming, 905
    opening, 908
    stacking order, 906, 909

Index ✦ L

sublayers, 909–910
unlocking, 907
viewing, 904
Web Layer, 905, 910–911
Layers panel (Dreamweaver), 473–474
Layers panel (Fireworks), 594–595, 904
layout
   creating, 9–10
   evolution of layout techniques on Web, 454
   forms, 259
   grids, 477, 921–922
   guides, 918–921
   layers, 479–480
   Layout View, 9–10
   rulers, 475–476, 917–918
   tables, 11, 209, 241–250
leading text objects, 801–802
Levels dialog box, 861–862
Library (Dreamweaver)
   Assets panel, 540–541
   editing window, 547–548
   features, 540
   opening, 541
Library (Fireworks)
   accessing, 1038–1039
   exporting, 1039–1040
   importing, 1037–1039
   symbols, 1021–1022
   updating, 1039
Library Item Property Inspector, 544
Library items
   capabilities, 539
   creating, 15
   deleting, 545–546
   editing, 546–548
   exporting, 1070–1072
   highlighting, 542
   inserting, 542–545
   modifying, 546, 548
   moving, 542–543
   naming, 546
   previewing, 541
   renaming, 546
   restoring, 546
   templates, 522
   updating Web sites, 548–550
   using, 541
Library panel (Fireworks), 603, 1021–1025
light source simulation, 943–945
line breaks, 128–129
line spacing
   text, 130
   text objects, 801–802

Line tool, 571, 665, 702
lines
   dotted lines, 758–761
   drawing, 665–668
   effects, 665
   mixing lines and curves, 672
   straight lines, 665–666
   styles, 665
Link Checker, 42, 57–58
Link Checker dialog box, 58
Link External Style Sheet dialog box, 435
<link> tag, 84–85
Link to New File dialog box, 61–62
Link Wizard, 1036
linking
   external style sheets, 435–436
   named anchors, 204–205
   symbols and instances, 1032
links
   base URLs, 83–84
   checking, 57–58, 200
   colors, 8, 197
   creating, 62–64, 195–196
   deleting, 65
   disabling underlining of links, 427–428
   editing, 64–65
   Flash movies, 396–397
   hotspots, 1048–1049
   images, 196–197
   Link Checker, 42
   Link Wizard, 1036
   mailto: links, 195, 201–202
   named anchors, 202–205
   pointing to files, 199–200
   removing underlining, 197
   site maps, 61
   slices, 1057, 1063
   special characters, 196
   symbols, 196
   targets, 205–206
   templates, 527
   testing, 17, 57–58
   text, 196–197
   validating, 17
   verifying, 200
List Values dialog box, 265–266
List/Menu Property Inspector, 265, 267, 270
listing
   symbols, 1024
   templates (Dreamweaver), 531
Live Effects
   applying, 852–854
   Auto Levels, 857, 861–863

Continued

Live Effects *(continued)*
    Blur, 858, 872
    Blur More, 858, 872
    Brightness/Contrast, 857, 860
    built-in Live Effects, 857
    Color Fill, 860–861
    Convert to Alpha, 858, 872
    Curves, 857, 863–865
    deleting, 855, 881
    disabling, 855
    Drop Shadow, 858, 873–874
    editing, 854
    Find Edges, 858, 872
    Gaussian Blur, 858, 871–872
    Glow, 858, 876
    Hue/Saturation, 857, 865–866
    Inner Bevel, 858, 866–868
    Inner Glow, 858, 875–876
    Inner Shadow, 858, 873–874
    Inset Emboss, 858, 869–871
    Invert, 857
    Levels, 858, 861–863
    missing effects, 882
    modifying, 854
    naming, 881
    Outer Bevel, 858, 866–868
    Raised Emboss, 858, 869–871
    renaming, 881
    saving, 881
    Sharpen, 858, 876–877
    Sharpen More, 858, 876–877
    storing, 881–882
    styles, 883
    turning on/off, 881
    Unsharp Mask, 858, 876–877
loading
    color palettes, 723
    Flash movies, 387
    styles, 1013, 1015
loading layers, 491–492
local site root, 25–27, 42
locking
    colors, 962
    guides, 919
    layers (Fireworks), 906–907
logical style tags, 85–86
looping
    animations, 502–503, 510, 1123, 1128–1129
    Flash movies, 385
Lotus Domino Designer, 999–1000

M

Macromedia
    Dreamweaver Object Exchange, 112
    trial programs (CD-ROM), 1152–1153
Macromedia Dreamweaver. *See* Dreamweaver
Macromedia Fireworks. *See* Fireworks
Macromedia Flash. *See* Flash
Macromedia Shockwave. *See* Shockwave
Magic Wand tool, 571, 691–692
mailto: links, 195, 201–202
Main toolbar, 574–575
managing
    behaviors, 347–348
    color, 723, 710
    floating panels, 578
    frames (animations), 1115–1117
    layers, 473–474
    panels (Fireworks), 578
    strokes, 747
    styles, 1013–1015
    swatches (colors), 723
    timelines, 496–497
<map> and </map> tags, 1050
margins
    frames, 295
    graphics, 171
    Web pages, 8
Marquee tool, 571, 686–689
masks
    alpha masks, 707, 924–926
    bitmap masks, 929–932
    borders, 936–938
    deleting, 936
    editing, 932–935
    modifying, 932–935
    photo edges, 936–938
    text objects, 818–819
    transparency effects, 833–835
    vector masks, 926–928
menus
    drop-down menus, 264–266
    jump menus, 268–272
merging table cells, 229
messages
    Popup Message behavior, 331–332
    status bars, 1101
<meta>tag, 77–81, 530–531
Microsoft FrontPage
    image maps, 1056–1057
    slices, 1069
Microsoft Word
    importing Word documents, 12
    importing Word HTML documents, 130–134

Index ✦ M

MIME types, 394
Mini-Launcher (Fireworks), 568
Missing Effects dialog box, 882
Mixing colors, 711–715
Modify menu commands (Dreamweaver)
    Arrange, Prevent Overlaps, 481
    Convert, Layers to Tables, 484
    Convert, Tables to Layers, 483
    Frameset, Edit NoFrames Content, 299
    Library, 548
    Library, Update Current Page, 548
    Library, Update Pages, 549
    Page Properties, 8, 73
    Quick Tag Editor, 91
    Table, Insert Column, 226
    Table, Insert Row, 226
    Table, Select Table, 215
    Templates, Apply Template to Page, 534
    Templates, Detach from Template, 530
    Templates, New Editable Region, 525
    Templates, Remove Editable Region, 526
    Templates, Update Pages, 535
    Timeline, Add Keyframe, 504
    Timeline, Add Object to Timeline, 497
    Timeline, Record Path of Layer, 507
    Timeline, Remove Frame, 505
    Timeline, Remove Object, 500
    Timeline, Remove Timeline, 505
Modify menu commands (Fireworks)
    Align, Bottom, 618
    Align, Center Horizontal, 618
    Align, Center Vertical, 618
    Align, Distribute Heights, 618
    Align, Distribute Widths, 618
    Align, Left, 618
    Align, Right, 618
    Align, Top, 618
    Alter Path, Anti-Alias Fill, 619
    Alter Path, Expand Stroke, 619
    Alter Path, Feather Fill, 619
    Alter Path, Hard Fill, 619
    Alter Path, Inset Path, 619
    Alter Path, Simplify, 619
    Animate, Animate Selection, 615
    Animate, Remove Animation, 615
    Animate, Settings, 615
    Arrange, Bring Forward, 618
    Arrange, Bring to Front, 618
    Arrange, Send Backward, 618
    Arrange, Send to Back, 618
    Canvas Color, 615
    Canvas Size, 614
    Combine, Crop, 619
    Combine, Intersect, 619
    Combine, Punch, 619
    Combine, Union, 619
    Convert to Bitmap, 617
    Edit Bitmap, 615
    Exit Bitmap Mode, 566, 615
    Fit Canvas, 615
    Flatten Layers, 617
    Group, 619
    Image Size, 614
    Join, 619
    Marquee, Border, 616
    Marquee, Contract, 616
    Marquee, Expand, 616
    Marquee, Feather, 616
    Marquee, Restore Selection, 616
    Marquee, Save Selection, 616
    Marquee, Select Inverse, 616
    Marquee, Select Similar, 616
    Marquee, Smooth, 616
    Mask, Delete Mask, 617
    Mask, Disable Mask, 617
    Mask, Group as Mask, 616
    Mask, Hide All, 616
    Mask, Hide Selection, 617
    Mask, Paste as Mask, 616
    Mask, Reveal All, 616
    Mask, Reveal Selection, 617
    Rotate Canvas, 615
    Selective JPEG, Remove JPEG Mask, 617
    Selective JPEG, Restore JPEG Mask as Selection, 617
    Selective JPEG, Save Selection as JPEG Mask, 617
    Selective JPEG, Settings, 617
    Split, 619
    Symbol, Break Apart, 615
    Symbol, Edit Symbol, 615
    Symbol, Tween Instances, 615
    Transform, Distort, 617
    Transform, Flip Horizontal, 618
    Transform, Flip Vertical, 618
    Transform, Free Transform, 617
    Transform, Numeric Transform, 617
    Transform, Remove Transformations, 618
    Transform, Rotate 180°, 617
    Transform, Rotate 90° CCW, 618
    Transform, Rotate 90° CW, 618
    Transform, Scale, 617
    Transform, Skew, 617
    Trim Canvas, 615
    Ungroup, 619
Modify Navigation Bar dialog box, 189–190
Modify toolbar, 574–577

modifying
- animation, 1126–1127
- animation symbols, 1146
- behaviors (Dreamweaver), 348
- behaviors (Fireworks), 1080
- bitmaps, 679–681
- canvas, 642–648
- effects, 854
- Flash Buttons, 390
- Flash Text, 394
- frames, 289
- gradients (colors), 828–832
- graphics, 168–170
- instances (symbols), 1020–1021, 1023, 1031
- jump menus, 270
- layers, 463, 465–466
- layers (Fireworks), 907
- Library items, 546–548
- Live Effects, 854
- masks, 932–935
- navigation bars, 189–190
- patterns, 838–839
- photographs, 679–681
- server-side includes, 553
- site maps, 47
- slices, 364–365
- strokes, 729–730, 747, 749–750
- style sheets, 434–435
- styles, 1013–1014
- symbols, 1020–1021, 1023, 1028–1030
- tables, 214–215
- templates (Dreamweaver), 532, 534
- text objects, 797, 806
- timelines, 499–501
- Web pages, 66

monitors
- dual monitors, 580
- gamma settings, 709–710

monospaced text, 137
mouseovers. *See* rollovers
Movie Properties dialog box, 379
movies
- controls, 398–399, 406–410
- dimensions, 379
- frames, 399–401
- FutureSplash movies, 394
- height, 379
- inserting, 378–380
- links, 396–397
- loading, 387
- looping, 385
- parameters, 383–386
- playing, 380, 385, 399–401
- previewing, 380
- properties, 381–382
- scaling, 385–387
- stopping, 380
- triggering behaviors, 402–405
- user interaction, 397–399, 406–410
- width, 379

moving
- floating panels, 578–579
- keyframes (timelines), 505
- layers, 457, 465
- Library items, 542–543
- objects between layers (Fireworks), 907, 909
- panels (Fireworks), 578–579
- paths, 775
- text in Web pages, 108–109
- text objects, 797
- Tracing Image, 480
- vector objects, 767

N

Named Anchor dialog box, 202
Named Anchor Property Inspector, 203
named anchors, 202–205
naming
- effects, 881
- forms, 255
- frames, 292
- frames (animations), 1118–1119
- gradients (colors), 831–832
- graphics, 172
- layers, 467, 474
- layers (Fireworks), 905
- Library items, 546
- Live Effects, 881
- strokes, 747
- styles, 1011
- timelines, 500
- Web pages, 34
- Web sites, 5, 42

Nav Bar Down behavior, 1079
Nav Bar Over behavior, 1079
Nav Bar Restore behavior, 1079
Nav Bars. *See* navigation bars
Navigation Bar object, 186–187
navigation bars
- buttons, 186–188, 1094–1096
- cookies, 1091–1092
- creating, 187–189, 1092–1093
- editing, 189–190
- inserting, 186–187, 189
- modifying, 189–190
- Nav Bar Down behavior, 1079

Index ✦ N–P

Nav Bar Over behavior, 1079
Nav Bar Restore behavior, 1079
  rollovers, 187
  Set Nav Bar Image behavior, 334–335, 1079
  Swap Image behavior, 1096
navigation tools
  frames, 296–297
  jump menus, 268–272
  pop-up menus, 1102–1105
navigational models
  full web navigational model, 23
  hierarchical navigational model, 22
  importance of, 21
  linear navigational model, 22
  spoke-and-hub model, 22–24
nesting
  layers, 459, 463, 474–475
  tables, 244
New Document dialog box, 634–635
New Editable Region dialog box, 525
New Home Page dialog box, 66
New Style dialog box, 460, 748–749, 1011
no break tags, 129
<nobr> tag, 129
<noframes> and </noframes> tags, 299–300
Numeric Transform dialog box, 772

O

Object panel (Fireworks), 583–585
objects (Dreamweaver)
  deleting from timelines, 505
  inserting in layers, 477–478
  inserting in timelines, 497–498
  installing, 1154–1155
  objects available on CD-ROM, 1154
objects (Fireworks)
  alignment, 911–916
  animation, 1120–1122
  blending, 940–945
  compositing, 903, 946–950
  converting to buttons, 1034
  converting to hotspots, 1049–1050
  converting to symbols, 1025–1026
  fading in/out, 1142–1143
  feathering, 945–946
  grouping, 923–924
  light source simulation, 943–945
  objects available on CD-ROM, 1154
  opacity, 938–940
  spacing, 914–915
Onion Skinning dialog box, 1126–1127
opacity, 938–940
Open Browser Window behavior, 329–330

Open dialog box (Fireworks), 637, 639, 681–682
Open File dialog box (Dreamweaver), 32
Open SourceSafe Database dialog box, 29
opening
  bitmaps, 681–682
  documents (Fireworks), 561–562
  editors, 59
  files (Dreamweaver), 32–33
  Fireworks window in Dreamweaver, 352
  images in Fireworks, 635, 637–640
  layers (Fireworks), 908
  Library, 541
  photographs, 681–682
  Photoshop files, 638
  site maps, 60
  Site window, 50
  templates (Dreamweaver), 533–534
  Web pages, 33–34
  windows (Dreamweaver), 33
operating systems, 36
Optimize Images dialog box, 355
Optimize panel (Fireworks), 582–583, 955–956
optimizing graphics
  balance of image quality and file size, 955
  color palettes, 966–967
  colors, 956–957
  Dreamweaver, 352–355
  file types, 953–954
  frames, 963–964
  GIFs, 976–979
  importance of, 953
  interlacing, 976
  lossy GIF compression, 970–971
  platforms, 958
  preview options, 957–963
  procedure, 955
  reducing number of colors, 967–976
  slices, 1058
<option> and </option> tags, 264
organizing documents (Fireworks), 563
orienting strokes, 761–763
Oval Marquee tool, 571, 686–689

P

<p> and </p> tags, 105–106
Page Properties dialog box, 8, 11, 73–75
pages
  activating, 13–15
  background colors, 8, 73
  background images, 8, 177–178
  behaviors, 306–310
  closing, 34

Continued

pages *(continued)*
  color palettes, 75–77
  colors, 8
  design, 479–480
  Design Notes, 45–46
  detaching from templates, 530
  download statistics, 16
  editing, 66
  find and replace, 113
  finding text, 113–117
  frames, 292
  headings, 103–105
  horizontal rules, 178–180
  hyperlink colors, 8
  hyperlinks, 195–196
  importing text, 108
  interactivity, 13–15
  jump menus, 268
  layout, 9–11, 209, 241–250, 454, 479–480
  Library items, 543–544
  links, 84–85
  margins, 8
  modifying, 66
  navigation bars, 186–190
  opening, 33–34
  paragraphs, 105–106
  photographs, 683
  placeholder pages, 31
  previewing, 15–16, 35–36
  properties, 73–75
  publishing, 36–37
  redirecting users, 83
  refreshing, 82–83
  reloading, 82–83
  replacing text, 113–117
  rollovers, 184–186, 358–361
  saving, 33–34
  server-side includes, 551–553
  spell checking, 111–113
  tables, 241–250
  templates, 32
  testing, 15–16
  text colors, 8
  text deletion, 109
  text edits, 107
  text indentation, 107
  text insertion, 107–108
  text manipulation, 108–109
  text selection, 108
  title bars, 33
  titles, 7, 65, 73
  transferring, 37
  uploading, 17
Paint Bucket tool, 573, 848–850
panels (Dreamweaver)
  Assets panel, 166–168, 197–199
  Behaviors panel, 307–308
  CSS Styles panel, 426, 428
  History panel, 111
  HTML Styles panel, 139
  Layers panel, 473–474
  Templates panel, 531–533
  Timelines panel, 496–498
panels (Fireworks)
  Behaviors panel, 599–600, 1078–1079
  Color Mixer panel, 592–593
  Color Table panel, 590–591, 724, 956–957, 968–970
  common features, 580–582
  Effect panel, 588–590, 851–853
  Fill panel, 587–588
  Find and Replace panel, 604
  Frames panel, 596–597, 1117
  grouping, 578
  hiding, 579–580
  History panel, 597–598
  Info panel, 598–599
  Layers panel, 594–595, 904
  layout sets, 579
  Library panel, 603, 1021, 1023–1025
  managing, 578
  moving, 578–579
  Object panel, 583–585
  Optimize panel, 582–583, 955–956
  Project Log panel, 605
  showing, 579
  snapping, 579
  Stroke panel, 585–587, 729–730
  Styles panel, 601–602, 1008
  Swatches panel, 591–592, 721–722
  Tool Options panel, 593–594
  Tools panel, 570–573
  URL panel, 600–601
  windowshading, 580
Pantone colors, converting to Web-safe colors, 725–727
Pantone ColorWeb Pro, 725–727, 1158
paragraphs
  indenting, 153–154
  Web pages, 105–106
Parameters dialog box, 383, 386
parsing forms, 255
passwords for forms, 260
pasting
  code, 109–110
  HTML, 109–110
  tables, 219–221
  text in Web pages, 108–109

Path Scrubber tool, 572–573, 702, 785–786
paths
    applying strokes, 652–653
    closed paths, 653
    closing open paths, 777–778
    combining, 787–788
    converting text object to paths, 812
    corners, 791
    cropping, 789–790
    cutting, 786–787
    deleting points, 776–777
    deselecting, 731
    direction, 654–655
    end caps, 792
    expanded strokes, 791–792
    inserting points, 776
    inset paths, 792–793
    intersecting, 788
    joining, 778–779
    moving, 775
    open paths, 653
    overview, 651
    pressure-sensitive effects, 785–786
    pulling into shapes, 782–783
    punching out, 788–789
    pushing into shapes, 781–782
    redrawing, 779–780
    selecting, 730
    selecting points, 775
    shapes, 781–783
    smoothing, 790
    speed-sensitive effects, 785–786
    splitting, 779
    text objects, 815–818
patterns
    editing, 838–839
    fills, 834, 836–844
    modifying, 838–839
    seamless patterns, 839–844
    styles, 1015–1017
    vector objects, 653–654
PDF Files
    Dreamweaver 4 Bible, 1159
    Fireworks 4 Bible, 1159
Pen tool, 572, 669–672, 702
Pencil tool, 572, 666–668, 702
Perl, 254
perspective shadows, 878–880, 893–895
photo albums. *See* Web photo albums
photographs
    anti-alias edges, 688
    borders for selections, 701
    bounding boxes, 679–680
    cropping, 990–991
    decreasing selections, 692, 701
    editing, 678, 680–681
    erasing pixels, 695–696
    exporting, 980–988
    feathering edges, 688–689, 700
    increasing selections, 692, 701
    inserting, 683
    Live Effects, 852
    modifying, 679–681
    opening, 681–682
    pixels, 677–678
    resizing, 685
    restoring selections, 701
    saving selections, 701
    scaling, 682–683, 991–992
    selecting pixels, 684–695, 698–700
    selecting selections, 697
    sharpening, 876–877
    sharpening edges, 985–986
    smoothing edges, 986
    smoothing selections, 701
    tonal ranges, 858–860
Photoshop files
    exporting, 1003–1004
    opening, 638
Photoshop filters, 887–888
physical style tags, 86–87
placeholder pages, 31
planning Web sites, 19–21
platforms
    gamma settings, 709–710
    optimizing graphics, 958
    previewing Web pages, 36
Play Sound behavior, 330–331
Play Timeline behavior, 343–345, 509
Play Timeline dialog box, 509
playing
    animations, 502, 509, 1123
    Flash movies, 385
    movies, 380, 399–401
Plugin Site Web site, 888
plug-ins
    Check Plugin behavior, 320–322
    filters, 857
    MIME types, 394
    Xtras, 623–624
PNGs
    browser support, 159, 163
    colors, 162–163
    gamma correction, 987
    indexed color, 965

Continued

PNGs *(continued)*
  lossless compression, 162
  PNG 24, 987–988
  PNG 32, 987–988
Pointer tool, 571, 685, 730
pointing to files, 199–200
points (paths)
  deleting, 776–777
  inserting, 776
  selecting, 775
Polygon Hotspot tool, 573, 1045, 1047–1048
Polygon Lasso tool, 571, 689–691
Polygon Slice tool, 573, 1060–1061
Polygon tool, 572, 660–662, 702
polygons
  drawing, 660–662
  hotspots, 1045–1048
  slices, 1060–1061
pop-up menus
  creating, 1102–1105
  Set Pop-up Menu behavior, 1079, 1102–1106
  styles, 1105–1106
Popup Message behavior, 331–332
Portable Network Graphics (PNGs)
  browser support, 159, 163
  colors, 162–163
  gamma correction, 987
  indexed color, 965
  lossless compression, 162
  PNG 24, 987–988
  PNG 32, 987–988
positioning
  Cascading Style Sheets (CSS), 445–446
  Cascading Style Sheets-Positioning (CSS-P), 453–454
  layers, 455, 458, 461–463, 482
  shapes, 664
  Tracing Image, 480–481
  vector objects, 664
<pre> tag, 134–135
preformatted text, 134–135
Preload Images behavior, 333–334
preloading animation, 1132–1133
presentations, 510–518
previewing
  animation, 1123, 1129–1131
  documents (Fireworks), 564–566
  Flash Buttons, 391
  frames, 295
  inline images, 164
  Library items, 541
  movies, 380
  optimized graphics, 957–963
  rollovers, 1085

style sheets, 437
symbols, 1024
text object edits, 797–798
Web pages, 15–16, 35–36
Progressive JPEGs, 162, 986–987
Project Log panel, 605
Property Inspector
  Button Property Inspector, 273
  Check Box Property Inspector, 262
  Form Property Inspector, 255–256
  Frame Property Inspector, 291
  Frameset Property Inspector, 280–281, 286–287
  Horizontal Rule Property Inspector, 178
  Image Property Inspector, 169
  Layer Property Inspector, 465–467
  Library Item Property Inspector, 544
  List/Menu Property Inspector, 265, 267, 270
  Shockwave Property Inspector, 381
  SSI Property Inspector, 553
  Table Property Inspector, 214
  Text Field Property Inspector, 260
  Text Property Inspector, 144
publishing Web pages, 36–37
punching out
  paths, 788–789
  vector objects, 788–789

Q

queries, find and replace, 118
Quick Tag Editor, 91–98
quitting
  Dreamweaver, 34
  FTP sessions, 51

R

radio buttons, 261, 263–264, 1092
raster graphics. *See* bitmaps
Recording layers' paths, 506–508
Rectangle Hotspot tool, 573, 1045–1046
Rectangle tool, 572, 656–657, 702
rectangles
  drawing, 656–657
  hotspots, 1045–1046
  slices, 1058–1059
  stroke stamps, 756
redirecting users to another Web page, 83
redoing actions, 110–111
Redraw Path tool, 572, 779–780
redrawing paths, 779–780
refreshing
  graphics, 354
  templates (Dreamweaver), 533
  Web pages, 82–83

regular expressions, 124–128
reloading Web pages, 82–83
remote site root, 25, 27–29, 43–44
removing. *See* deleting
renaming
    effects, 881
    Library items, 546
    Live Effects, 881
Repeat History extension, 111
repeating elements
    Library items, 539
    server-side includes, 540, 550–553
    styles, 1007
    symbols, 1019
    updating, 539–540
replacing
    code, 117–127
    graphics, 169
    HTML, 117–127
    swatches (colors), 723
    text in Web pages, 113–117
    tools, 574
resampling images, 646
Reshape Area tool, 572, 702, 780–781, 783–784
resizing
    bitmaps, 685
    canvas, 643–644, 646–648
    Flash Buttons, 390
    Flash Text, 394
    forms, 256
    frames, 284, 286–287, 294
    graphics, 170–171
    images, 647–648
    layers, 465
    photographs, 685
    slices, 1060
    tables, 224–226, 234
    text objects, 797
    vector objects, 766–768, 772
resolution of canvas, 631–633
restoring
    Library items, 546
    selections (bitmaps), 701
reverting to last saved document (Fireworks), 642
Rollover Image object, 185
rollovers
    animation, 1133–1134
    bevel effects, 868–869
    code, 361, 1086–1091
    creating, 184–185, 1081–1085
    disjointed rollovers, 1097–1098, 1108–1109
    drag-and-drop behaviors, 1106–1109
    exporting, 1086–1089
    external rollovers, 1098–1099
    frame states, 358
    frames, 359–361, 1083–1085
    hotspot rollovers, 1099–1101
    how they work, 1082
    image wells, 999–1000
    inserting, 185–186, 358–361, 1086–1091
    navigation bars, 187
    preloading rollover images, 1090
    previewing, 1085
    Simple Rollover behavior, 362–363, 1078, 1085–1086
    slices, 1058
    states, 1082–1083
    Swap Image behavior, 1096
rotating
    canvas, 649
    vector objects, 767, 770–772
Rounded Rectangle tool, 572, 658, 702
rounded rectangles, drawing, 656–659
rounded squares, drawing, 656–659
rows
    framesets, 278, 286–287
    tables, 210–212, 226–227
Rubber Stamp tool, 573, 693–695
rulers
    Dreamweaver, 475–476
    Fireworks, 917–918

S

<s> tag, 86, 137
<samp> tag, 137
sampling colors, 76, 718
Save Brush As dialog box, 747
Save Copy As dialog box, 165
Save dialog box, 34
Save Effect As dialog box, 882
Save Gradient As dialog box, 832
saving
    documents (Fireworks), 640–641
    effects, 881
    frames, 288–289
    gradients (colors), 831–832
    Live Effects, 881
    selections (bitmaps), 701
    strokes, 747
    swatches (colors), 723
    templates (Dreamweaver), 524, 534
    Web pages, 33–34
Scale tool, 572, 766–767
scaling
    animations, 1132
    bitmaps, 682–683

Continued

scaling *(continued)*
    Flash movies, 385–387
    photographs, 682–683, 991–992
    vector objects, 766–768, 772
scripting languages
    JavaScript Integration Kit (JIK), 405–415
    Perl, 254
scroll bars (frames), 293–294
scrolling lists (forms), 266–268
search engines
    head section, 73
    <meta> tags, 80–81
searching
    code, 117–127
    Flash Text, 392
    HTML, 117–127
    regular expressions, 124–128
    text, 113–117
    wildcard characters, 124–125
<select> and </select> tags, 264
Select Behind tool, 571
Select Border dialog box, 701
Select File dialog box, 64, 380
Select Image Source dialog box, 164, 166, 480
Select Template dialog box, 528
selecting
    bitmap pixels, 684–695, 698–700
    code, 90
    colors, 712–715, 721–722
    fonts, 150–152
    frames, 291
    HTML tags, 107
    layers, 463–465
    paths, 730
    photographs (pixels), 684–695, 698–700
    points (paths), 775–776
    selections (bitmaps), 697
    styles, 1013
    swatches (colors), 716–718
    table elements, 214–217
    tables, 215–216
    templates (Dreamweaver), 528
    text in Web pages, 108
    tools, 570
    Xtras, 884
selections (bitmaps)
    borders, 701
    decreasing, 692, 701
    feathering, 700
    increasing, 692, 701
    restoring, 701
    saving, 701
    selecting, 697
    smoothing, 701

sequencing behaviors, 349
server-side includes, 540, 550–553
servers
    FTP, 29
    models, 19
    staging server, 27
    WebDav servers, 29–30
Set Color Scheme dialog box, 77
Set Nav Bar Image behavior (Dreamweaver), 334–335
Set Nav Bar Image behavior (Fireworks), 1079
Set Nav Bar Image dialog box, 334–335, 1092
Set Pop-up Menu behavior, 1102–1106, 1079
Set Pop-up Menu dialog box, 1102–1103
Set Text of Frame behavior, 336–337
Set Text of Frame dialog box, 336
Set Text of Layer behavior, 337, 488–489
Set Text of Layer dialog box, 337–338, 488–489
Set Text of Status Bar behavior (Dreamweaver), 338–339
Set Text of Status Bar behavior (Fireworks), 1101, 1079
Set Text of Status Bar dialog box, 1101
Set Text of Text Field behavior, 339–340
Set Text of Text Field dialog box, 340
shadows
    drop shadows, 873–875
    DropShadow filter, 448–449
    perspective shadows, 878–880, 893–895
    shadow effects, 872–875
    Shadow filters, 450, 479
    Shadowlab Eye Candy filters, 893–895
shapes
    bitmaps, 701–702
    circles, 659–660
    dimensions, 664
    ellipses, 659–660
    hotspots, 1044–1048
    paths, 781–783
    polygons, 660–662
    positioning, 664
    rectangles, 656–657
    rounded rectangles, 656–659
    rounded squares, 656–659
    slices, 1058–1061
    squares, 656–657
    stars, 660, 662–664
    strokes, 755–756
    vector objects, 655–656, 783–784
sharpening
    photographs, 985–986
    sharpening images, 876–877, 985–986
Shockwave
    capabilities, 375
    CD-ROM look and feel, 375

Control Shockwave or Flash behavior, 322–323
versus Flash, 376–378
HTML, 381–382
MIME types, 394
supported graphics formats, 376
Shockwave movies
controls, 398–399
frames, 399–401
inserting, 378–380
parameters, 383–384
playing, 399–401
properties, 381–383
user interaction, 397–399
Shockwave Property Inspector, 381
shortcuts
filters, 889–890
tools, 571
Show-Hide Layers behavior, 340–341, 490–491
Show-Hide Layers dialog box, 341, 490–491
Simple Rollover behavior, 362–363, 1078, 1085–1086
Simplify dialog box, 790
simulating light sources, 943–945
Site Definition dialog box, 5, 24, 26, 28, 41–43
Site Information dialog box, 30
site management
local site root, 42
overview, 39–40
remote site root, 43–44
Site window, 40, 50–53
site maps
columns, 47
converting to graphics, 68
creating hyperlinks, 62–64
deleting hyperlinks, 65
dependent files, 67
editing hyperlinks, 64–65
file display, 61
hidden files, 67
home page, 47, 66
hyperlinks, 61
icon labels, 48
modifying, 47
modifying pages, 66
opening, 60
Point to File feature, 62
storyboarding, 61–63
titles, 65
uses, 59
viewing, 67–68
zooming in/out, 68
Site menu commands (Dreamweaver)
Change Link, 64
Link to a New File, 61
Link to Existing File, 63
New Home Page, 66
New Site, 26, 41
Open Source of Link, 66
Synchronize, 55
Site window
Check In/Check Out buttons, 53
commands, 40
Connect button, 51
Disconnect button, 51
features, 40
Get button, 51–52
Link Checker, 42, 57–58
local root directory, 51
opening, 50
Put button, 51–52
Refresh button, 53
remote site, 51
Stop Current Task button, 53
uses, 50
sizing
canvas, 643–644, 646–648
Flash Buttons, 390
fonts, 144–146
frames, 278–279
images, 647–648
layers, 465
tables, 212–213
text objects, 797
vector objects, 766–768
Skew tool, 572, 702, 768, 773–774, 811
skewing vector objects, 768–769
Slice tool, 573, 1059–1060
slices
animation, 1058, 1073–1074, 1134
attaching behaviors, 1079–1080
converting images into slices, 1062–1063
creating, 1058–1060
cutting, 1061–1062
deleting behaviors, 1081
download times, 1057
drag-and-drop behaviors, 1109
Dreamweaver, 1067–1068
editing, 364–365
explanation of, 361
exporting, 1065–1066, 1069–1070
features, 1057
file formats, 1065
FrontPage (Microsoft), 1069
GoLive (Adobe), 1068–1069
guides, 1059–1062
HTML tables, 1058, 1064–1065

Continued

slices *(continued)*
  inserting, 362, 1067–1069
  links, 1057, 1063
  modifying, 364–365
  modifying behaviors, 1080
  optimizing, 1058
  resizing, 1060
  rollovers, 1058
  shapes, 1058–1061
  spacer images, 1058
  stacking order, 1059
  text objects, 1063–1064
slideshows, 510–518
<small> tag, 86
Smooth Selection dialog box, 701
Sort Table dialog box, 238
sorting
  swatches (colors), 724
  tables, 237–239
sound
  Flash, 387
  Play Sound behavior, 330–331
source files, 354–355
SourceSafe databases, 29
spacer images, 1058
spacing
  grid lines, 922
  grids, 477
  line spacing, 130, 801–802
  objects (Fireworks), 914–915
  strokes, 750–752
  text objects, 800
<span> tag, 430–431, 454, 467
special characters
  HTML, 98–101
  hyperlinks, 196
spell checking, 111–113
Split Cell dialog box, 230
splitting
  frames, 280–283
  paths, 779
  table cells, 229–231
squares
  drawing, 656–657
  hotspots, 1045–1046
  stroke stamps, 756
SSI Property Inspector, 553
SSIs. *See* server-side includes
staging server, 27
Star tool, 702
stars, drawing, 660, 662–664

starting
  Dreamweaver, 31–32
  FTP sessions, 51
statistics for downloads, 16
status bars, 338–339, 577–578, 1079, 1101
Stop Timeline behavior, 343–345, 509
Stop Timeline dialog box, 509
stopping
  animations, 509, 1123
  movies, 380
storing
  documents (Fireworks), 640–641
  effects, 881–882
  gradients (colors), 832
  Live Effects, 881–882
  strokes, 747–748
storyboarding Web sites, 21, 61–63
strikethrough text, 137
Stroke panel (Fireworks), 585–587, 729–730
strokes
  Airbrush stroke, 737–738
  applying, 652–653, 666–667
  attributes, 749–750
  Basic stroke, 736–737
  build-up, 752–753
  built-in strokes, 734–746
  Calligraphy stroke, 738–739
  categories, 731
  Charcoal stroke, 739–740
  Crayon stroke, 740–741
  creating, 729–730, 746
  customizing, 729
  default settings, 731
  deleting, 747
  dotted lines, 758–761
  edge effects, 753–754
  edges, 732
  editing, 729–730, 747, 749–758
  expanded strokes, 791–792
  feathering, 732
  Felt Tip stroke, 741–742
  flow rate, 752
  ink amount, 750–751
  managing, 747
  modifying, 729–730, 747, 749–758
  naming, 747
  Oil stroke, 742–743
  orienting, 761–763
  Pencil stroke, 735–736
  pressure sensitivity, 734, 756–758
  Random stroke, 744–745
  saving, 747

shapes, 755–756
sizes, 732
spacing, 750–752
stamps, 750–751
storing, 747–748
strokes available on CD-ROM, 1157
styles, 748–749
text objects, 808–810
textures, 732–733, 752–753, 845
thicknesses, 732
tips, 754–755
transferring to other documents, 748
types, 731
Unnatural stroke, 745–746
using, 748
velocity (speed), 666, 758
Watercolor stroke, 743–744
strong emphasis text, 137
`<strong>` tag, 86, 137
Style Definition dialog box, 426, 436
style sheets
    applying, 424, 428–430
    attaching, 428–429
    background colors, 439–440
    background images, 438–440
    blocks of text, 440–441
    borders, 443–444
    boxes, 442–443
    browsers, 426
    bulleted lists, 444–445
    capabilities, 422
    cascading characteristics, 423–424
    changing, 430–431
    class definitions, 424, 432–433
    converting styles into an external style sheet, 436
    custom styles, 432–433
    deleting, 431–432
    Dreamweaver, 421
    editing, 434–435
    embedded style rules, 425–426
    extensions, 446–447
    external style sheets, 424–425, 429
    filters, 448, 450, 477, 479
    grouping properties, 422
    how they work, 422
    importing, 435–436
    inheritance of properties, 423
    internal style sheets, 425
    layers, 460–461
    lists, 444–445
    logical style tags, 85–86
    modifying, 434–435
    physical style tags, 86–87
    positioning, 445–446
    precedence of rules, 423
    previewing, 437
    pseudo-classes, 433
    pseudo-elements, 433–434
    style definitions, 432, 436
    support for, 421
    switching, 430–431
    tables, 423
    text, 437–438
    type, 437–438
StyleBuilder extension, 369
styles
    applying, 1009–1010
    button styles, 1008–1009
    creating, 1010–1013
    default styles, 1014
    deleting, 1013
    editing, 1013–1014
    effects, 883
    exporting, 1014
    Flash Buttons, 389
    gradients (colors), 833
    HTML styles, 138–143, 1050–1051
    importing, 1013–1015
    line styles, 665
    Live Effects, 883
    loading, 1013, 1015
    managing, 1013–1015
    modifying, 1013–1014
    naming, 1011
    patterns, 1015–1017
    pop-up menus, 1105–1106
    repeating elements, 1007
    selecting, 1013
    settings, 1012
    stroke styles, 748–749
    styles available on CD-ROM, 1157
    text styles (Dreamweaver), 85–87, 134–137
    text styles (Fireworks), 800, 806, 1008–1009
    textures, 1015–1017
Styles panel (Fireworks), 601–602, 1008
`<sub>` tag, 86
submitting forms, 255
Subselection tool, 571, 775
`<sup>` tag, 86
Swap Image behavior (Dreamweaver), 14, 341–343
Swap Image behavior (Fireworks), 1078, 1096
Swap Image Restore behavior (Dreamweaver), 341–343
Swap Image Restore behavior (Fireworks), 1078

swatches (colors)
    Adobe color swatches, 723
    deleting, 724
    loading, 723
    managing, 723
    replacing, 723
    saving, 723
    selecting, 716–718
    sorting, 724
    switching, 722
Swatches panel (Fireworks), 591–592, 721–722
switching
    color palettes, 722
    style sheets, 430–431
    tools, 731
    views, 88
    windows (Dreamweaver), 33
Symbol Editor, 1026–1029
Symbol Properties dialog box, 1024–1026, 1029
symbols
    animation symbols, 1144–1148
    animations, 1135–1138
    breaking links between symbol and instance, 1032
    Button Instances, 1035
    Button Symbols, 1022–1023, 1032–1034
    converting animation symbols to graphic symbols, 1147
    converting Button Symbols into Graphic Symbols, 1035
    converting objects to symbols, 1025–1026
    creating, 1025–1027
    deleting, 1030
    deleting instances, 1032
    duplicating, 1028
    editing, 1020–1021, 1023, 1028–1030
    exporting, 1039–1040
    Graphic Symbols, 1022–1023
    HTML, 98–101
    hyperlinks, 196
    importing, 1037–1039
    instances, 1019
    Library, 1021–1022
    listing, 1024
    making instances, 1030–1031
    modifying, 1020–1021, 1023, 1028–1030
    modifying instances, 1031
    previewing, 1024
    tweening instances, 1023, 1135–1138, 1140–1141
    updating, 1039
Synchronize Files dialog box, 55
synchronizing files, 55–57
system color pickers, 718–720

T

<table> and </table> tags, 210
Table Format dialog box, 236–237
Table Property Inspector, 214
tables
    alignment, 222–224, 232–233
    background colors, 229, 235
    borders, 212, 228–229, 235
    cell padding, 212, 229–230
    cell spacing, 212, 229–230
    cell wrap, 233
    cells, 210–212, 229–230
    colors, 229, 234–235
    columns, 210, 212, 226–227
    converting to layers, 482–485
    copying, 219–220
    cutting, 219–220
    deleting rows/columns, 227
    drawing, 242–244
    editing, 214–215, 218, 220–221
    Faster Table Editing, 214
    formatting, 235–237
    forms, 256
    grids, 245
    headers, 233
    headings, 211
    importing tabular data, 239–241
    inserting, 211–212
    inserting rows/columns, 226–227
    layout, 11
    Layout view, 209, 241–250
    merging cells, 229
    modifying, 214–215
    moving through, 219
    navigating, 219
    nesting, 244
    pasting, 219–221
    preferences, 214
    properties, 231–235
    resizing, 224–226, 234
    rows, 210–212, 226–227
    selecting entire tables, 215–216
    selecting table elements, 214–217
    sizing, 212–213
    slices, 1058, 1064–1065
    sorting, 237–239
    spacer image, 250–251
    splitting cells, 229–231
    style sheets, 423
    <table> and </table> tags, 210
    <td> and </td> tags, 211
    <th> tag, 211
    <tr> tag, 211

tablets, 734
Tag Selector, 107
tags
    <a> and </a> tags, 195–196, 202
    <address> and </address> tags, 137–138
    anchor tags, 195–196, 202
    <b> tag, 86, 137
    <base> tag, 84
    behaviors, 306
    <big> tag, 86
    <blockquote> tag, 153–154
    <body> and </body> tags, 72, 85

 tag, 128–129, 175–176
    <cite> tag, 86, 137
    <code> tag, 86, 137
    <dfn> tag, 86, 137
    <div> tag, 454, 467
    <em> tag, 86, 137
    <font> tag, 87
    <form> and </form> tags, 254
    <frame> tag, 278
    <frameset> tag, 278
    <h1> to <h6> tags, 103–105
    <head> and </head> tags, 72–73
    <hr> tag, 178
    <html> and </html> tags, 72
    <i> tag, 86, 137
    <iframe> tag, 301
    <ilayer> tag, 455, 467
    <img> tag, 168, 1050
    <kbd> tag, 86, 137
    <layer> tag, 455, 467
    layers, 467
    <link> tag, 84–85
    <map> and </map> tags, 1050
    <meta> tag, 77–81, 129, 530–531
    <nobr> tag, 129
    <noframes> and </noframes> tags, 299–300
    <option> and </option> tags, 264
    <p> and </p> tags, 105–106
    <pre> tag, 134–135
    redefining, 433
    <s> tag, 86, 137
    <samp> tag, 86, 137
    <select> and </select> tags, 264
    selecting, 107
    <small> tag, 86
    <span> tag, 430–431, 454, 467
    <strong> tag, 86, 137
    <sub> tag, 86
    <sup> tag, 86
    <table> and </table> tags, 210
    Tag Selector, 107
    <td> and </td> tags, 211
    <th> tag, 211
    <tr> tag, 211
    <tt> tag, 86, 137
    <u> tag, 86, 137
    <var> tag, 86, 137
    <wbr> tag, 130
targets
    frames, 296–297
    hyperlinks, 205–206
<td> and </td> tags, 211
team collaboration
    checking in/out files, 45, 53–55
    Design Notes, 45–46
    file view columns, 48–49
    synchronizing files, 55–57
Teletype text, 137
Telnet, 195
templates
    Flash Buttons, 388, 390–391
    Generator templates, 390–391, 395
templates (Dreamweaver)
    applying, 531, 534–535
    behaviors, 530
    content, 528–529
    copying, 533
    creating, 32, 522–524, 532–533
    default document option, 536–537
    deleting, 532–533
    detaching from Web pages, 530
    editable regions, 522, 524–526, 528
    editing, 532, 534
    formatted text, 525
    hyperlinks, 527
    Library items, 522
    links, 527
    listing, 531
    locked regions, 522, 526–527
    meta tags, 530–531
    modifying, 532, 534
    opening, 533–534
    overview, 521–522
    placeholders, 523
    refreshing, 533
    regions, 522, 524–528
    saving, 524, 534
    selecting, 528
    Templates panel, 531–533
    tutorial, 522
    updating, 533, 535–536
    uses, 521–522
    using, 528–529
    XML, 521

Templates panel (Dreamweaver), 531–533
testing
    hyperlinks, 17, 57–58
    Web pages, 15–16
text
    alignment, 152–153
    boldface, 137
    Cascading Style Sheets (CSS), 437–438, 440–441
    citation text, 137
    colors, 8, 147–150
    converting to graphics, 369
    definition text, 137
    emphasis text, 137
    Flash Buttons, 389
    Flash Text, 392–394
    font sizes, 144–146
    formatting, 12, 144–146
    HTML styles, 138–143
    hyperlinks, 196–197
    importing, 12, 807–808
    indenting, 153–154
    inserting, 11–12
    italics, 137
    keyboard text, 137
    line breaks, 128–129
    line spacing, 130
    monospaced, 137
    non-breaking text, 129
    preformatted text, 134–135
    searching, 113–117
    sizes, 87
    strikethrough, 137
    strong emphasis text, 137
    styles, 85–87
    Teletype, 137
    typefaces, 150–151
    typography, 11
    underlined, 137
    word breaks, 130
Text Editor, 795–797, 806–807
Text Field Property Inspector, 260
text fields
    forms, 257–261
    Set Text of Text Field behavior, 339–340
text in Web pages
    copying, 108–109
    cutting, 108–109
    deleting, 109
    drag-and-drop, 109
    editing, 107
    find and replace, 113
    headings, 103–105
    importing, 108
    indenting, 107
    inserting, 107–108
    moving, 108–109
    paragraphs, 105–106
    pasting, 108–109
    selecting, 108
    spell checking, 111–113
    Text Property Inspector, 104
Text menu commands (Dreamweaver)
    Alignment, 153
    Check Spelling, 111
    Color, 148
    Font, 151
    Font, Edit Font List, 151
    Indent, 154
    Outdent, 154
    Paragraph Format, Preformatted, 134
    Size, 87
    Style, 87, 135
Text menu commands (Fireworks)
    Align, Bottom, 621
    Align, Center Horizontally, 620
    Align, Center Vertically, 621
    Align, Justified, 620
    Align, Justified Vertically, 621
    Align, Left, 620
    Align, Right, 620
    Align, Stretched, 620
    Align, Stretched Vertically, 621
    Align, Top, 621
    Attach to Path, 621
    Convert to Paths, 621
    Detach from Path, 621
    Font, 620
    Orientation, Rotate Around Path, 621
    Orientation, Skew Horizontal, 621
    Orientation, Skew Vertical, 621
    Orientation, Vertical, 621
    Reverse Direction, 621
    Size, 8 to 120, 620
    Size, Other, 620
    Style, Bold, 620
    Style, Italic, 620
    Style, Plain, 620
    Style, Underline, 620
text objects
    alignment, 803–805, 807
    backup image layers, 814–815
    baseline shift, 803
    colors, 799
    converting to images, 812
    converting to paths, 812

cookie-cutter text, 813–814
creating, 795–796, 808
editing, 797, 806
fills, 810–811
fonts, 798–799, 806, 813–815
horizontal scale, 802–803
inserting, 796–797
kerning, 801, 803
leading, 801–802
line spacing, 801–802
masks, 818–819
modifying, 797, 806
moving, 797
outlined text, 808–810
paths, 815–818
perspective, 811
perspective shadows, 879
point size, 799, 806
previewing edits, 797–798
resizing, 797
sizing, 797
skewing, 811
slices, 1062–1064
spacing, 800
strokes, 808–810
styles, 806
subscript, 803
superscript, 803
text styles, 800, 1008–1009
transforming as paths, 812
transforming as pixels, 812
vanishing point, 811
Text Property Inspector, 104, 144
text styles
accessing, 135
browsers, 136
preformatted text styles, 134–135
style tags, 137
Text tool, 572, 702, 796–797
textures
colors, 846
fills, 844, 846–848
images, 845
strokes, 732–733, 752–753, 845
styles, 1015–1017
textures available on CD-ROM, 1157
<th> tag, 211
third-party filters. *See* filters
thumbnails (graphics), 366–368, 370
tiling
documents (Fireworks), 563
images, 179
time, 155

timelines
alerts, 497
animation bar, 497–500
animation speed, 506
animations, 496–497, 502–503
behaviors, 497, 502, 508–510, 517–518
browsers, 501
capabilities, 494–496
controls, 496, 500–501
deleting, 506
deleting objects, 505
editing, 499–501
frames, 495, 497
frames per second (fps), 501
Go to Frame behavior, 510
Go to Timeline Frame behavior, 343–345
inserting objects, 497–498
keyframes, 495, 503–505
layers, 497–498, 506–508, 515–516
looping animations, 502–503, 510
managing, 496–497
modifying, 499–501
naming, 500
Play Timeline behavior, 343–345, 509
playing animations, 502
presentations, 510–518
recording layers' paths, 506–508
slideshows, 510–518
Stop Timeline behavior, 343–345, 509
Timelines panel (Dreamweaver), 496–498
titles
editing, 65
frames, 291
graphics, 172
site maps, 65
Web pages, 7, 33, 65, 73
Tool Options panel (Fireworks), 593–594
toolbars
accessing, 574
docking, 574
Main toolbar, 574–575
Modify toolbar, 574–577
undocking, 574
tools
Brush tool, 572, 666–668, 702
Circle Hotspot tool, 573, 1045, 1047
Circle tool, 702
Color Mixer tool, 711–716
Crop tool, 571, 644–645
Distort tool, 572, 702, 769–770, 774
Ellipse tool, 572, 659–660, 702
Eraser tool, 573, 695–696

Continued

tools *(continued)*
    Export Area tool, 571
    Eyedropper tool, 76, 573, 717–718
    Freeform tool, 572, 702, 780–783
    Hand tool, 573
    Hotspot tools, 1045
    keyboard shortcuts, 571
    Knife tool, 786–787
    Lasso tool, 571, 689–691
    Line tool, 571, 665, 702
    Magic Wand tool, 571, 691–692
    Marquee tool, 571, 686–689
    Oval Marquee tool, 571, 686–689
    Paint Bucket tool, 573, 848–850
    Path Scrubber tool, 572–573, 702, 785–786
    Pen tool, 572, 669–672, 702
    Pencil tool, 572, 666–668, 702
    Pointer tool, 571, 685, 730
    Polygon Hotspot tool, 573, 1045, 1047–1048
    Polygon Lasso tool, 571, 689–691
    Polygon Slice tool, 573, 1060–1061
    Polygon tool, 572, 660–662, 702
    Rectangle Hotspot tool, 573, 1045–1046
    Rectangle tool, 572, 656–657, 702
    Redraw Path tool, 572, 779–780
    replacing, 574
    Reshape Area tool, 572, 702, 780–781, 783–784
    Rounded Rectangle tool, 572, 658, 702
    Rubber Stamp tool, 573, 693–695
    Scale tool, 572, 766–767
    scrolling, 570
    Select Behind tool, 571
    selecting, 570
    Skew tool, 572, 702, 768, 773–774, 811
    Slice tool, 573, 1059–1060
    Star tool, 702
    Subselection tool, 571, 775
    switching, 731
    Text tool, 572, 702, 796–797
    Transform tool, 702
    Zoom tool, 573
Tools panel (Fireworks), 570–573
<tr> tag, 211
Tracing Image, 480–481
transferring
    files, 37, 51–52
    gradients (colors) between documents, 832–833
    HTML styles from site to site, 141
    strokes to other documents, 748
    Web pages, 37
Transform tool, 702

transparency
    alpha masks, 924–926
    animation, 1114
    Eraser tool, 696
    GIFs, 972–975
    gradients (colors), 833–835
    masks, 833–835
    no color option, 720
    shadow effects, 874
    Tracing Image, 480–481
trimming the canvas, 648
<tt> tag, 86, 137
turning on/off
    effects, 881
    fills, 822–823
    Live Effects, 881
tweening
    instances (symbols), 1023, 1135–1138, 1140–1141
    Xtras, 1138–1140
typefaces, 150–151
typography, 11

U

<u> tag, 86, 137
underlining text, 137
undocking toolbars, 574
undoing actions, 110–111
Uniform Resource Locators. *See* URLs
unlocking layers (Fireworks), 907
Unmark Editable Region dialog box, 526–527
Unsharp Mask dialog box, 876
Update Files dialog box, 64, 546
Update Pages dialog box, 535–536, 549
updating
    frames, 298–299
    Libraries, 1039
    repeating elements, 539–540
    symbols, 1039
    templates (Dreamweaver), 533, 535–536
    Web sites with Library items, 548–550
uploading Web sites, 17
URL panel (Fireworks), 600–601
URLs
    addresses, 200
    base URLs for hyprlinks, 83–84
    directory paths, 194
    domain names, 194
    filenames, 194
    Flash Buttons, 389
    Flash Text, 393
    FTP, 194
    function, 193

Go to URL behavior, 326–327
Gopher, 194
hotspots, 1048–1049
HTTP, 194
inserting, 197–199
IP addresses, 194
JavaScript, 195
jump menus, 271
Mailto, 195
named anchors, 194, 202–205
parts, 193–194
port numbers, 194
slices, 1063
Telnet, 195
Usenet newsgroups, 195
user interfaces in Macromedia applications, 562

V

Validate Form behavior, 345–347
Validate Form dialog box, 345
validating
    forms, 410–415
    hyperlinks, 17
VanDerLee Web site, 888
<var> tag, 86, 137
vector masks, 926–928
vector objects
    Bézier curves, 668–675
    versus bitmaps, 678
    center point, 654
    combining, 787–788
    converting to bitmaps, 702–703
    cropping, 789–790
    dimensions, 664
    distorting, 769–770
    exporting, 1000–1003
    fills, 653–654
    intersecting, 788
    lines, 665–668
    mixing lines and curves, 672
    moving, 767
    numeric transformations, 771–772
    overview, 651
    Paint Bucket tool, 848–849
    path direction, 654–655
    paths, 651–653
    patterns, 653–654
    perspective, 773–774
    perspective shadows, 879
    pixels, 651–652
    positioning, 664
    punching out, 788–789
    resizing, 767–768, 772
    rotating, 767, 770–772
    scaling, 766–768, 772
    shapes, 655–664, 783–784
    sizing, 766–768
    skewing, 768–769
    smoothing, 790
    strokes, 652–653
    transforming into new shapes, 783–784
    vanishing point, 773–774
    Xtras, 884
verifying hyperlinks, 200
video. *See* movies
View menu commands (Dreamweaver)
    Code, 88
    Code and Design, 88
    Code View Options, 90
    Grid, Edit Grid, 477
    Grid, Show Grid, 245, 477
    Grid, Snap To Grid, 245, 477
    Head Content, 7, 80
    Invisible Elements, 157
    Plugins, Play, 380
    Plugins, Stop, 380
    Rulers, 476
    Rulers, Reset Origin, 476
    Rulers, Show, 475
    Show Page Titles, 65
    Table Borders, 228
    Table View, Layout View, 241
    Tool Tips, 67
    Tracing Image, Adjust Position, 480
    Tracing Image, Align with Selection, 480
    Tracing Image, Load, 480
    Tracing Image, Reset Position, 480
    Tracing Image, Show, 480
    Visual Aids, Frame Borders, 279
    Visual Aids, Invisible Elements, 542
    Visual Aids, Layer Borders, 465
View menu commands (Fireworks)
    Fit All, 611
    Fit Selection, 611
    Full Display, 568, 612
    Grid, Edit Grid, 612
    Grid, Show Grid, 612
    Grid, Snap To Grid, 612
    Guides, Edit Guides, 612
    Guides, Lock Guides, 612
    Guides, Show Guides, 612
    Guides, Snap to Guides, 612
    Hide Edges, 613
    Hide Panels, 613

Continued

View menu commands (Fireworks) *(continued)*
  Hide Selection, 612
  Macintosh Gamma, 612
  Magnification, 611
  Rulers, 612
  Show All, 612
  Slice Guides, 612
  Slice Overlay, 612
  Status Bar, 613
  Windows Gamma, 612
  Zoom In, 611
  Zoom Out, 611
viewing
  documents (Fireworks), 563–564
  layers (Fireworks), 904
  site maps, 67–68
views
  Layout View, 9–10
  switching, 88

W

Wacom Graphire, 734
<wbr> tag, 130
Web graphics
  alignment, 173–175
  alt text, 172
  animated GIFs, 494
  animation, 181–182
  background graphics, 177–178, 290
  banner ads, 182–184
  bitmap graphics versus vector graphics, 377
  borders, 172
  bullets, 369
  buttons, 274
  code, 361–363
  colors, 160–163
  compression, 161–162
  converting bullets to graphics, 369
  converting color graphics to grayscale graphics, 847
  converting graphics into slices, 1062
  converting text objects to graphics, 812
  converting text to graphics, 369
  dimensions, 647–648
  download times, 160, 172–173
  editing in Dreamweaver, 168–170
  editing in Fireworks, 356–357
  export files, 355
  exporting in indexed color format, 964–966
  Flash, 376–377
  formats, 159, 636–637
  Generator, 394–395
  GIFs, 159–161
  Graphic Symbols, 1022–1023
  grayscale, 716
  height attribute, 170–171
  horizontal rules, 178–181
  hotspots, 361–362
  hspace attribute, 171
  inline graphics, 163–164, 166–168
  inline images, 165
  interlacing, 160, 162, 976
  JPEGs, 159, 161
  layers, 459, 472
  lossless compression, 161
  lossy compression, 161
  lowsrc attribute, 172–173
  magnification settings, 567
  margins, 171
  modifying, 168–170
  naming, 172
  navigation bars, 186–190
  opening in Fireworks, 635, 637–640
  optimizing, 352–355, 953–963, 966–967, 973–979
  PNGs, 159
  Preload Images behavior, 333–334
  Progressive JPEGs, 162
  refreshing, 354
  replacing, 169
  resampling, 646
  resizing, 170–171, 647
  rollovers, 184–186
  Set Nav Bar Image behavior, 334–335
  sharpening, 876–877
  Shockwave, 376–377
  site maps, 68
  sizing, 647–648
  slices, 361–362, 364–365, 1057–1058, 1060–1070
  source files, 354–355
  spacer images, 1058
  Swap Image behavior, 341–343
  Swap Image Restore behavior, 341–343
  symbols, 1022–1023
  textures, 845
  thumbnails, 167, 366–368, 370
  tiling, 179
  titles, 172
  Tracing Image, 480–481
  vspace attribute, 171
  Web photo albums, 366–368, 370
  white space, 171
  width attribute, 170–171
  wrapping around jump menus, 270–271
  wrapping text around graphics, 175–176
Web Layer, 905, 910–911
Web objects. *See* hotspots; slices

Web pages
    activating, 13–15
    background colors, 8, 73
    background images, 8, 177–178
    behaviors, 306–310
    closing, 34
    color palettes, 75–77
    colors, 8
    design, 479–480
    Design Notes, 45–46
    detaching from templates, 530
    download statistics, 16
    editing, 66
    find and replace, 113
    finding text, 113–117
    frames, 292
    headings, 103–105
    horizontal rules, 178–180
    hyperlink colors, 8
    hyperlinks, 195–196
    importing text, 108
    interactivity, 13–15
    jump menus, 268
    layout, 9–11, 209, 241–250, 454, 479–480
    Library items, 543–544
    links, 84–85
    margins, 8
    modifying, 66
    navigation bars, 186–190
    opening, 33–34
    paragraphs, 105–106
    photographs, 683
    placeholder pages, 31
    previewing, 15–16, 35–36
    properties, 73–75
    publishing, 36–37
    redirecting users, 83
    refreshing, 82–83
    reloading, 82–83
    replacing text, 113–117
    rollovers, 184–186, 358–361
    saving, 33–34
    server-side includes, 551–553
    spell checking, 111–113
    tables, 241–250
    templates, 32
    testing, 15–16
    text colors, 8
    text deletion, 109
    text edits, 107
    text indentation, 107
    text insertion, 107–108
    text manipulation, 108–109
    text selection, 108
    title bars, 33
    titles, 7, 65, 73
    transferring, 37
    uploading, 17
Web photo albums, 366–368, 370
Web servers
    FTP, 29
    models, 19
    staging server, 27
Web sites
    activating, 13–15
    audience, 20
    bandwidth, 21
    budgets, 21
    colors, 8
    concepting, 20
    creating, 41
    defining, 24–25
    design, 6, 19–24
    file management, 4–5, 25–29
    file view columns, 48–49
    head section, 6–7
    home page, 6
    interactivity, 13–15
    layout, 9–11
    Library items, 15
    Link Checker, 42, 57–58
    local site root, 25–27, 42
    Macromedia Dreamweaver Object Exchange, 112
    naming, 5, 42
    navigational models, 21–24
    planning, 19–21
    previewing, 15–16
    remote site root, 25, 27–29, 43–44
    server models, 19
    site information, 30
    site management, 39–40, 42–44, 50–53
    site maps, 5, 47–48, 59–68
    storyboarding, 21, 61–63
    structure, 4–5
    testing, 15–16
    text formatting, 12
    text insertion, 11–12
    typography, 11
    updating with Library items, 548–550
    uploading, 17
WebDav servers, 29–30
Web-safe colors, 708–709, 725–727, 825–826

whitespace
    graphics, 171
    line breaks, 128–129
    no breaks, 129
    word breaks, 130
wildcard characters (searches), 124–125
Window menu commands (Dreamweaver)
    Assets, 198
    Behaviors, 307
    Code Inspector, 88
    CSS Styles, 460
    Layers, 473
    Library, 541
    Site Files, 4
    Site Map, 61
    Timelines, 497
Window menu commands (Fireworks)
    Behaviors, 626
    Cascade, 563, 626
    Color Mixer, 626
    Color Table, 626
    Effect, 625
    Fill, 625
    Find and Replace, 626
    Frames, 626
    History, 626
    Info, 625
    Layers, 626
    Library, 626
    New Window, 563, 625
    Object, 626
    Optimize, 626
    Project Log, 626
    Stroke, 625
    Styles, 626
    Swatches, 626
    Tile Horizontal, 563, 626
    Tile Vertical, 563, 626
    Tool Options, 626
    Toolbars, Main, 625
    Toolbars, Modify, 625
    Tools, 625
    URL, 626
    Your Open Documents List, 626
windowshading, 580
wizards
    Export Wizard, 992–994
    Link Wizard, 1036

Word
    importing Word documents, 12
    importing Word HTML documents, 130–134
word break tags, 130
wrapping
    graphics around jump menus, 270–271
    text and images in table cells, 233
    text around graphics, 175–176

X

XML, 521
XSSI extensions, 553–554
Xtras
    applying, 856, 884–887
    bitmaps, 885–886
    Fireworks, 623–624
    selecting, 884
    tweening, 1138–1140
    vector objects, 884
Xtras menu commands (Fireworks)
    Adjust Color, Auto Levels, 624
    Adjust Color, Brightness/Contrast, 624
    Adjust Color, Curves, 624
    Adjust Color, Hue/Saturation, 624
    Adjust Color, Invert, 624
    Adjust Color, Levels, 624
    Blur, Blur, 624
    Blur, Blur More, 624
    Blur, Gaussian Blur, 624
    Eye Candy 4000 LE, Bevel Boss, 625
    Eye Candy 4000 LE, Marble, 625
    Eye Candy 4000 LE, Motion Trail, 625
    Other, Convert to Alpha, 624
    Other, Find Edges, 624
    Repeat Xtra, 624
    Sharpen, Sharpen, 624
    Sharpen, Sharpen More, 624
    Sharpen, Unsharp Mask, 625

Z

Zoom tool, 573
zooming in/out
    documents (Fireworks), 567
    optimized graphics, 962
    site maps, 68

Hungry Minds, Inc.
End-User License Agreement

READ THIS. You should carefully read these terms and conditions before opening the software packet(s) included with this book ("Book"). This is a license agreement ("Agreement") between you and Hungry Minds, Inc. ("HMI"). By opening the accompanying software packet(s), you acknowledge that you have read and accept the following terms and conditions. If you do not agree and do not want to be bound by such terms and conditions, promptly return the Book and the unopened software packet(s) to the place you obtained them for a full refund.

1. **License Grant.** HMI grants to you (either an individual or entity) a nonexclusive license to use one copy of the enclosed software program(s) (collectively, the "Software") solely for your own personal or business purposes on a single computer (whether a standard computer or a workstation component of a multi-user network). The Software is in use on a computer when it is loaded into temporary memory (RAM) or installed into permanent memory (hard disk, CD-ROM, or other storage device). HMI reserves all rights not expressly granted herein.

2. **Ownership.** HMI is the owner of all right, title, and interest, including copyright, in and to the compilation of the Software recorded on the disk(s) or CD-ROM ("Software Media"). Copyright to the individual programs recorded on the Software Media is owned by the author or other authorized copyright owner of each program. Ownership of the Software and all proprietary rights relating thereto remain with HMI and its licensers.

3. **Restrictions On Use and Transfer.**

    (a) You may only (i) make one copy of the Software for backup or archival purposes, or (ii) transfer the Software to a single hard disk, provided that you keep the original for backup or archival purposes. You may not (i) rent or lease the Software, (ii) copy or reproduce the Software through a LAN or other network system or through any computer subscriber system or bulletin-board system, or (iii) modify, adapt, or create derivative works based on the Software.

    (b) You may not reverse engineer, decompile, or disassemble the Software. You may transfer the Software and user documentation on a permanent basis, provided that the transferee agrees to accept the terms and conditions of this Agreement and you retain no copies. If the Software is an update or has been updated, any transfer must include the most recent update and all prior versions.

4. **Restrictions on Use of Individual Programs.** You must follow the individual requirements and restrictions detailed for each individual program in the "What's on the CD-ROM?" appendix of this Book. These limitations are also

contained in the individual license agreements recorded on the Software Media. These limitations may include a requirement that after using the program for a specified period of time, the user must pay a registration fee or discontinue use. By opening the Software packet(s), you will be agreeing to abide by the licenses and restrictions for these individual programs that are detailed in the Appendix and on the Software Media. None of the material on this Software Media or listed in this Book may ever be redistributed, in original or modified form, for commercial purposes.

5. Limited Warranty.

   (a) HMI warrants that the Software and Software Media are free from defects in materials and workmanship under normal use for a period of sixty (60) days from the date of purchase of this Book. If HMI receives notification within the warranty period of defects in materials or workmanship, HMI will replace the defective Software Media.

   (b) HMI AND THE AUTHOR OF THE BOOK DISCLAIM ALL OTHER WARRANTIES, EXPRESS OR IMPLIED, INCLUDING WITHOUT LIMITATION IMPLIED WARRANTIES OF MERCHANTABILITY AND FITNESS FOR A PARTICULAR PURPOSE, WITH RESPECT TO THE SOFTWARE, THE PROGRAMS, THE SOURCE CODE CONTAINED THEREIN, AND/OR THE TECHNIQUES DESCRIBED IN THIS BOOK. HMI DOES NOT WARRANT THAT THE FUNCTIONS CONTAINED IN THE SOFTWARE WILL MEET YOUR REQUIREMENTS OR THAT THE OPERATION OF THE SOFTWARE WILL BE ERROR FREE.

   (c) This limited warranty gives you specific legal rights, and you may have other rights that vary from jurisdiction to jurisdiction.

6. Remedies.

   (a) HMI's entire liability and your exclusive remedy for defects in materials and workmanship shall be limited to replacement of the Software Media, which may be returned to HMI with a copy of your receipt at the following address: Software Media Fulfillment Department, Attn.: *Dreamweaver and Fireworks Bible*, Hungry Minds, Inc., 10475 Crosspoint Blvd., Indianapolis, IN 46256, or call 1-800-762-2974. Please allow four to six weeks for delivery. This Limited Warranty is void if failure of the Software Media has resulted from accident, abuse, or misapplication. Any replacement Software Media will be warranted for the remainder of the original warranty period or thirty (30) days, whichever is longer.

   (b) In no event shall HMI or the author be liable for any damages whatsoever (including without limitation damages for loss of business profits, business interruption, loss of business information, or any other pecuniary loss) arising from the use of or inability to use the Book or the Software, even if HMI has been advised of the possibility of such damages.

(c) Because some jurisdictions do not allow the exclusion or limitation of liability for consequential or incidental damages, the above limitation or exclusion may not apply to you.

7. **U.S. Government Restricted Rights.** Use, duplication, or disclosure of the Software for or on behalf of the United States of America, its agencies and/or instrumentalities (the "U.S. Government") is subject to restrictions as stated in paragraph (c)(1)(ii) of the Rights in Technical Data and Computer Software clause of DFARS 252.227-7013, or subparagraphs (c) (1) and (2) of the Commercial Computer Software - Restricted Rights clause at FAR 52.227-19, and in similar clauses in the NASA FAR supplement, as applicable.

8. **General.** This Agreement constitutes the entire understanding of the parties and revokes and supersedes all prior agreements, oral or written, between them and may not be modified or amended except in a writing signed by both parties hereto that specifically refers to this Agreement. This Agreement shall take precedence over any other documents that may be in conflict herewith. If any one or more provisions contained in this Agreement are held by any court or tribunal to be invalid, illegal, or otherwise unenforceable, each and every other provision shall remain in full force and effect.

CD-ROM Installation Instructions

The *Dreamweaver and Fireworks Bible* CD-ROM contains trial versions of Dreamweaver, Fireworks, Dreamweaver UltraDev, Flash, and Freehand, in addition to a host of extensions, objects, commands, and code from this book.

Accessing the Programs on the CD-ROM

The CD-ROM is what is known as a *hybrid CD-ROM*, which means that it contains files that run on more than one computer platform — in this case, both Windows and Macintosh computers.

Several files, primarily the Macromedia trial programs and the other external programs, are compressed. Double-click these files to begin the installation procedure. Most other files on the CD-ROM are uncompressed and you can simply copy them to your system by using your file manager.

For a detailed synopsis of the contents of the CD, see the "What's on the CD-ROM?" appendix.

Installing Dreamweaver and Fireworks

To install Dreamweaver and/or Fireworks on your Windows system, follow these steps:

1. Insert the *Dreamweaver and Fireworks Bible* CD-ROM into your CD-ROM drive.
2. Open the Dreamweaver or Fireworks folder located inside the Macromedia Programs folder.
3. Double-click the .exe file located in the folder to unpack it and begin the installation process.
4. Follow the on-screen instructions. Accept the default options for program location.

To install Dreamweaver and/or Fireworks on your Macintosh system, follow these steps:

1. Insert the Dreamweaver and Fireworks Bible CD-ROM into your CD-ROM drive and double-click the CD icon to display the CD's contents.
2. Open the Dreamweaver or Fireworks folder located inside the Macromedia Programs folder and double-click the Installer.
3. Follow the onscreen instructions.

Changing the Windows read-only attribute

You may not be able to access files on the CD-ROM after you copy the files to your computer. After you copy or move the entire contents of the CD-ROMs to your hard disk or another storage medium (such as a Zip disk), you may get the following error message when you attempt to open a file with its associated application:

```
[Application] is unable to open the [file]. Please make sure
the drive and file are writable.
```

Windows sees all files on a CD-ROM drive as read-only. This normally makes sense because a CD-ROM is a read-only medium—that is, you can't write data back to the CD-ROM. However, when you copy a file from a CD-ROM to your hard disk or to a Zip disk, Windows doesn't automatically change the file attribute from read-only to writable.

Installation software normally takes care of this chore for you; but in this case, because the files are intended to be manually copied to your disk, you have to change the file attribute yourself. Luckily, it's easy—just follow these steps:

1. Click the Start menu button.
2. Select Programs.
3. Choose Windows Explorer.
4. Highlight the file name(s) on the hard disk or Zip disk.
5. Right-click the highlighted file name(s) to display a pop-up menu.
6. Select Properties to display the Properties dialog box.
7. Click the Read-only option so that it is no longer checked.
8. Click the OK button.

You should now be able to use the file(s) with the specific application without getting the annoying error message.